Southwest
USA

Becca Blond

Sara Benson, Lisa Dunford, Andrea Schulte-Peevers

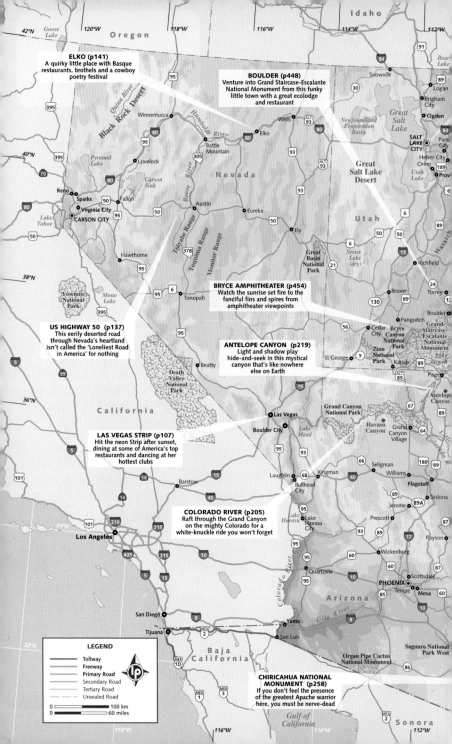

ELKO (p141)
A quirky little place with Basque restaurants, brothels and a cowboy poetry festival

BOULDER (p448)
Venture into Grand Staircase-Escalante National Monument from this funky little town with a great ecolodge and restaurant

BRYCE AMPHITHEATER (p454)
Watch the sunrise set fire to the fanciful fins and spires from amphitheater viewpoints

US HIGHWAY 50 (p137)
This eerily deserted road through Nevada's heartland isn't called the 'Loneliest Road in America' for nothing

ANTELOPE CANYON (p219)
Light and shadow play hide-and-seek in this mystical canyon that's like nowhere else on Earth

LAS VEGAS STRIP (p107)
Hit the neon Strip after sunset, dining at some of America's top restaurants and dancing at her hottest clubs

COLORADO RIVER (p205)
Raft through the Grand Canyon on the mighty Colorado for a white-knuckle ride you won't forget

CHIRICAHUA NATIONAL MONUMENT (p258)
If you don't feel the presence of the greatest Apache warrior here, you must be nerve-dead

LEGEND
Tollway
Freeway
Primary Road
Secondary Road
Tertiary Road
Unsealed Road

0 _____ 100 km
0 _____ 60 miles

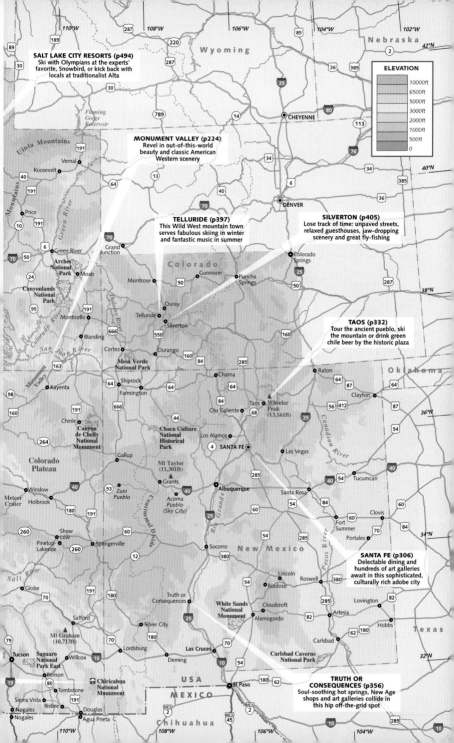

ELEVATION

	10000ft
	6500ft
	5000ft
	3000ft
	2000ft
	1000ft
	500ft
	0

SALT LAKE CITY RESORTS (p494)
Ski with Olympians at the experts' favorite, Snowbird, or kick back with locals at traditionalist Alta

MONUMENT VALLEY (p224)
Revel in out-of-this-world beauty and classic American Western scenery

TELLURIDE (p397)
This Wild West mountain town serves fabulous skiing in winter and fantastic music in summer

SILVERTON (p405)
Lose track of time: unpaved streets, relaxed guesthouses, jaw-dropping scenery and great fly-fishing

TAOS (p332)
Tour the ancient pueblo, ski the mountain or drink green chile beer by the historic plaza

SANTA FE (p306)
Delectable dining and hundreds of art galleries await in this sophisticated, culturally rich adobe city

TRUTH OR CONSEQUENCES (p356)
Soul-soothing hot springs, New Age shops and art galleries collide in this hip off-the-grid spot

On the Road

BECCA BLOND Coordinating Author
My bulldog Duke and I are diligently researching Silverton, CO, here. We've detoured to this spot by the river to check out the stupendous views and sage scents. Duke ranks Silverton as his favorite town for its liberal attitude towards his canine kinfolk.

LISA DUNFORD Dangling from a rope above a 50ft drop is something I've always wanted to do. Canyoneering rappels, down-climbing and squeezing through narrow slot canyons north of Zion National Park proved easy to learn from my apt guide. What I had trouble with was climbing up to start!

SARA BENSON Ah, the joys of being a guidebook writer. When it's blusteringly bad weather outside, all you can do is hole up in your hotel room, or if you're lucky enough to be researching Nevada, the nearest casino to play some poker or blackjack until the storm rolls by.

ANDREA SCHULTE-PEEVERS There's something intensely spiritual about the Southwest. The haunting beauty of rock formations. Silent desert where only the unseen wind moves. Cliff villages built by peoples who vanished long ago. Forests where the Apaches hid and hunted. It's a land of ancient murmurings, and if you sit very still, they will speak to you.

For full author biographies, see p545.

BEST OF THE SOUTHWEST

Welcome to epic America, the luscious backdrop of Hollywood blockbusters and red-rock land of limitless road-tripping. Where Native American ruins and Wild West legends hark back to distant eras, and quirky art communities sit next to saguaro cacti on lonely rural routes. From ghost towns to spa towns, mysterious space aliens to Route 66 Americana, so many themes invite exploration here. And whether you're rafting the Grand Canyon, partying in Las Vegas, gallery- and spa-hopping in Santa Fe or hiking past psychedelic sandstone in Zion National Park, the pursuit of pleasure is paramount.

Legendary Drives

Pump up the tunes and hit the highway, because road trips were invented for regions like the Southwest. Whether you're looking for iconic America on the Mother Road or soul-soothing beauty on the Million Dollar Hwy, the Southwest has some of the most inspiring and memorable drives in the USA.

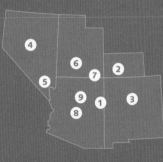

❶ Route 66

Cruise America's 'main street,' Route 66, across the belly of Arizona (p255) and New Mexico (p270), passing tumbleweeds, 1950s billboards, greasy-spoon diners and half a century's worth of nostalgia in the small towns along the way.

❷ Million Dollar Hwy, Colorado

US 550 between Silverton and Ouray (p404), Colorado, is one of the region's most scenic stretches of pavement. The road gets its 'Million Dollar' name from the valuable ore lining the roadbed, but the jagged peak and narrow canyon views are worth just as much.

❸ Turquoise Trail, New Mexico

Passing stunning Bandelier National Monument and quirky art communities like Madrid, New Mexico's Rte 14 (Turquoise Trail; p303) is the back road between Santa Fe and Albuquerque. Did you know it's served as a major trade route since at least 2000 BC?

❹ Loneliest Road in America

Follow eerily deserted US Hwy 50 (p137) through the shifting, surreal landscape of the Great Basin, Nevada's heartland; make sure to stop for a picture by one of the lonely signs.

❺ Las Vegas Strip, Nevada

It's only 4.5 miles long, but the Strip (p107) is one of America's most legendary drives. For the ultimate cruise, rent a convertible, dress up as Elvis and drive (slowly) after dark, when Sin City really starts to sizzle.

❻ Hwy 12 from Capitol Reef to Bryce Canyon National Park, Utah

Drive Utah's spectacular Hwy 12 (p448) scenic byway from Capitol Reef to Bryce Canyon National Park and take advantage of the pull-offs to see how dramatically the landscape changes from slickrock desert to red-rock canyon to wooded high plateau.

❼ Hwy 163 through Monument Valley, Arizona

Hwy 163 through Monument Valley Navajo Tribal Park (p224) is a superlative sensory experience. Straddling the Utah–Arizona border, this fantasyland of sandstone towers, sheer-walled mesas and soaring fiery-red spindles is made all the more surreal by the drab middle-of-nowhere scenery surrounding it.

❽ Red Rock Loop Rd, Arizona

Drive the high-desert Red Rock Loop Rd (p182) off Hwy 89A outside Sedona, Arizona, in the late afternoon. You'll want to stop and record the dramatic sunset over iconic Cathedral Rock, a sacred vortex; the intensity of light and blend of colors is mindblowing.

❾ Hwy 180 from Flagstaff to the Grand Canyon, Arizona

The most popular way to get between Flagstaff and the Grand Canyon's South Rim is via Hwy 180 (p197), a super-scenic Arizona route that winds through the San Francisco mountains and lots of forested land.

Geological Wonders

When it comes to natural attractions, the Southwest hits the jackpot. Nowhere else in the country can compete with the sheer number of geological works of art as those found amid the soaring peaks, yawning canyons, rainbow deserts and white dunes of this blessed region.

❶ Antelope Canyon, Arizona

Wind and water have carved the small Antelope Canyon (p219) into an astonishingly sensuous sandstone temple of nature, where light and shadow play hide-and-seek amid a symphony of shapes and textures.

❷ Chiricahua National Monument, Arizona

In remote southern Arizona desert, Chiricahua National Monument (p258) is a wonderfully rugged, whimsical wonderland where rain, thunder and wind have chiseled volcanic rock into fluted pinnacles, natural bridges, gravity-defying balancing boulders and soaring spires reaching skyward like totem poles.

❸ Grand Canyon, Arizona

One of the world's Seven Natural Wonders, the Grand Canyon (p198) is most intense at sunrise or sunset, when the multihued wedding-cake layers of the canyon appear glazed with an ethereal golden icing against a pink-and-purple sky.

❹ Zion National Park, Utah

Red-and-white cliffs rise over the deep crimson gash that is Zion Canyon. One of southern Utah's most dramatic natural wonders, it was carved eons ago by the Virgin River, which still flows through Zion National Park (p463) today.

❺ Bryce Canyon National Park, Utah

Graceful spires of pink, yellow, white and orange hoodoos stand like sentinels at the eroding edges of the vast plateau that is Bryce Canyon National Park (p453) – the most visually stunning of the southern Utah parks.

❻ Arches National Park, Utah

Sweeping arcs of chunky sandstone create windows on the snowy peaks and desert landscapes at the amazing Arches National Park (p436) – a park of more than 2500 rock arches. Some arches are tiny, at just 2in high; others are gigantic, soaring upwards 200ft or spanning 300ft!

❼ White Sands National Monument, New Mexico

The captivating windswept, white chalky dunes of White Sands National Monument (p369) are one of New Mexico's most unusual attractions. Try to time a visit to the ethereal park with sunrise or sunset (or both), when the towering waves of sand appear even more magical than normal.

❽ Great Basin National Park, Nevada

Wheeler Peak rises mirage-like out of the barren desert to an impressive height of 13,063ft in the remote Great Basin National Park (p140), also home to glacial lakes, groves of ancient bristlecone pines (some over 5000 years old) and a permanent ice field.

Native American Southwest

From Mesa Verde's ancient mysteries to the realities of modern-day life in the Navajo Nation, the Native American story is rich, and told in many mediums. See it in art-work in Santa Fe galleries; in the movement of Hopi performing a traditional dance; or in the elegant adobe of the Taos Pueblo.

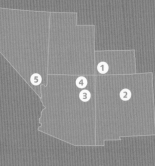

Author Tip

Each village decides whether to allow non-Hopis at ceremonial dances – many of the Kachina dances are closed affairs. It's much easier to attend Social dances and Butterfly dances, held late August through November.

❶ Mesa Verde National Park, Colorado

In the ruins of Mesa Verde National Park (p391) there's a mystery without conclusion: the tale of Ancestral Puebloans who built an entire civilization of sophisticated dwellings right into the sandstone cliffs before vanishing in 1300.

❷ Santa Fe, New Mexico

No city in the Southwest can compete with Santa Fe (p314) when it comes to buying Native American art. Browse the turquoise and silver for sale under the plaza's portal, or purchase an original RC Gorman from a chic Canyon Rd gallery.

❸ Village of Walpi on First Hopi Mesa, Arizona

The most dramatic of the Hopi enclaves, Walpi (p228) dates back to AD 1200 and clings like an aerie onto the mesa's narrow end – the mostly empty sandstone-colored stone houses seem to sprout from the cliffs organically.

❹ Navajo Nation, Arizona

Navajo Nation is renowned for its handicrafts such as woven rugs, silver jewelry and sandpainting. Vast areas of barren desert are punctuated with stunning sights like Monument Valley (p224), Canyon de Chelly (p224) and Navajo National Monument (p223).

❺ Springs Preserve, Las Vegas, Nevada

The brand-new Springs Preserve (p114) is a Native American educational complex with a natural- and cultural-history museum, a sustainable architecture center, interpretive trails and gardens, and an ecocafé by Wolfgang Puck.

The Great Outdoors

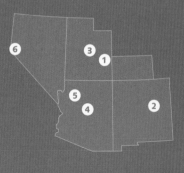

When it comes to the great outdoors, the Southwest is one giant playground. Not only is this place easy on the eye, it serves an all-you-can-take buffet of adrenaline-pumping adventures – from epic white-water rafting down the Grand Canyon to scuba diving in a New Mexico dam.

1 Mountain Biking in Moab, Utah

The single-track trails around Moab (p428), the granddaddy of the Southwest cycling scene, are still the place for mountain-bike junkies to come and spin their fat tires on sick, slick red-rock.

2 Dam Diving in Santa Rosa, New Mexico

One of the USA's top 10 scuba-diving spots is, oddly, in Santa Rosa (p279). How could that be? You can thank the natural spring-fed Blue Hole dam, a crystal-clear 81ft-deep lake with diving platforms suspended 25ft below the surface.

3 Skiing the Wasatch Mountains, Utah

Because of the Great Salt Lake effect, up to 500in of snow a year falls on the 10,000-plus-ft peaks of the Wasatch Mountains (p492). There are seven world-class ski resorts within 45 miles of Salt Lake City!

4 Hiking Vortices in Sedona, Arizona

New Age Sedona (p181) has a number of vortices – sites where the earth's energy is believed to be highly concentrated – you can hike to. Climb Cathedral Rock at sunset and channel your inner goddess as the sky blazes orange, pink and purple.

5 Rafting the Grand Canyon, Arizona

For an epic river adventure, raft the Colorado River through the Grand Canyon (p205). The 160-plus white-water rapids along this famous multiday stretch are the wildest in America – so gnarly they merit their own rating system.

6 Snowboarding at Lake Tahoe, Nevada

Straddling the Nevada–California line, the sun-soaked Lake Tahoe (p147) area is home to nearly a dozen ski resorts offering fresh powder and fantastic 360-degree views of the emerald lake sparkling below.

5

Old West & Silver Screen Towns

Hollywood has long had a love affair with America's Wild West of yesteryear, choosing to feature Southwestern towns such as Bisbee, AZ, and Kanab, UT, in hundreds of movies set against the region's stunning scenery – Monument Valley is an A-list backdrop star on the silver screen.

4

1 Kanab, Utah

Four hundred John Wayne–era movies have been filmed amid the rugged desert surrounding remote Kanab (p472). Tour this little outpost's old sets, stay where John Wayne did and chat with grandmas about their stunt-double golden days.

2 Tombstone, Arizona

Home of the infamous 1881 shoot-out at the OK Corral, Tombstone (p250) is the Wild West. Yes it's a tourist trap, but a delightful one. The entire downtown has been a National Historic Landmark since the 1960s.

3 Bisbee, Arizona

Squeezed between the narrow walls of Tombstone Canyon, Bisbee (p252) oozes old-fashioned ambience. Fine Victorian buildings line skinny streets housing classy galleries and charming hotels. A darling of Hollywood filmmakers, Bisbee has played itself, New York and even Greece on the silver screen.

4 Jerome, Arizona

Wedged into steep Cleopatra Hill and clinging to a cliff, Jerome (p178) enjoys the most spectacular setting of any Arizona town. During its copper heyday it was the wickedest town in the West, teeming with brothels, saloons and opium dens.

5 Telluride, Colorado

It's been a Ute hunting ground, a rough-and-ready silver-mining camp and a ghost town, but nowadays folks flock to the over-easy (both on the eyes and attitude) mountain village of Telluride (p397) for the fabulous bluegrass and film festivals and endless outdoor adventures.

6 Silver City, New Mexico

Billy the Kid's childhood stomping ground, Silver City (p358) retains its Wild West feel but has become an art and adventure hot spot with quirky galleries and gelato shops, plus 15 mountains, four rivers and a kick-ass forest just outside its door.

7 Ely, Nevada

On the loneliest road in America, miles from anywhere, little Ely (p139) is an 1860s mining town deserving of an overnight stop. Its old downtown has beautiful regional history murals and fabulous vintage neon signs.

Fantasy Resorts

When it comes to fantasy resorts, the Southwest serves you everything but an ocean. But what Santa Fe and Phoenix lack in beachfront property, they make up for with world-class shopping, dining, art and golf. Plus, Las Vegas offers the chance to go around the world in one neon-drenched, couture-spiked evening.

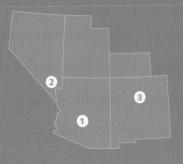

❶ Boulders Resort, Scottsdale, Arizona

After a session on the massage table or a treatment in the posh Golden Door Spa at Boulders Resort (p165) you'll understand bliss. For romance, book an individual casita; for sport, play the 18-hole Jay Morris–designed championship golf course at this Phoenix-area resort.

❷ Palms, Las Vegas, Nevada

We love the sleazy sex appeal of the Palms (p114). A favorite with A-list celebrity party stars like Paris Hilton and Hef's girlfriends (the Playboy Club has been reborn here), its ultraglam restaurants, rooms and nightclubs are the hottest in Sin City.

❸ Bishop's Lodge Resort & Spa, Santa Fe, New Mexico

Play cowgirl at the posh, family-friendly Bishop's Lodge Resort & Spa (p321) on 450 acres of piñon wilderness just outside Santa Fe. It boasts gorgeous rooms and casitas, and offers guests everything from yoga classes to horseback riding through the mountains.

Contents

Regional Map Contents

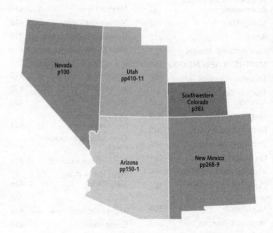

Nevada
p100

Utah
pp410-11

Southwestern
Colorado
p383

Arizona
pp150-1

New Mexico
pp268-9

Destination Southwest USA

The Southwest USA is cool enough to merit two Las Vegases. And both cities represent this triculturally diverse, historically rich, always artistic, sometimes outrageous and naturally gorgeous region with equal accuracy.

Home to UFO fanatics, vortex junkies, Native American casino owners, pious Mormons, pot-smoking hippies, New Age artists and environmental warriors, the region is like nowhere else in the USA. The howl of a coyote, the smack of a golf club, the clank of a slot machine – all these images are the Southwest. A place that embraces adventure head-on and somehow manages to maintain a balance between Las Vegas' sex appeal and Salt Lake City's virgin saintliness.

Mother Nature's beauty remains relatively untouched and ripe for exploration in the Southwest. Whatever outdoor pursuit you choose – be it horseback riding past majestic saguaro cacti in the Arizona desert, roaring down the Grand Canyon in a rubber raft or mountain biking slickrock in Utah's rainbow-hued canyon country – you can be sure the scenery will be stunning. This is the land of giant red arches, slickrock walls, humongous canyons, salt flats and vast deserts. A place where crimson rock monuments and crumbling rust buttes meet dazzling blue skies; where the desert landscape seems to have been invented for the backdrop of a John Wayne classic – or a John Denver music video.

Natural scenery isn't the Southwest's only ace. The human-created stuff, be it from 1798 or 2008, is also pretty damn cool. Sinfully delicious Las Vegas is one neon-lit chaotic dream sequence that never wakes up (or goes to sleep, depending on your perspective and how much you've had to drink). You can dine in Paris (France), in a restaurant at the Eiffel Tower, where you just might bump arms with the other Paris (Hilton), in town to host a party at the Palms resort down the Strip. Which just happens to be where Jessica Simpson, Britney Spears and Hugh Hefner and the Girls Next Door also like to hold court. Yes, it's safe to say Las Vegas, NV, is as hot as Los Angeles when it comes to Hollywood star power these days.

Vegas is far from the Southwest's only hot vacation spot. Also in Nevada is one of our favorite drives in the region, the 'Loneliest Road in America.' Running across the Great Basin, this is one solitary drive past barren brown hills and tumbleweeds, through stubborn old towns where the vintage neon signs are as authentic as the legal prostitutes and you can stop literally in the middle of nowhere at an oh-so-American family-run restaurant for fried eggs, a smoke and a spin on the poker slot machine. Or head to Lake Tahoe for sunbathing on sandy shores come summer and skiing fresh powder on the surrounding mountains in winter. In New Mexico, spunky Santa Fe is not just the USA's oldest capital, it's also its top art destination. Home to an eclectic lot of retired filmmakers and world-class artists, and all adobe architecture, it's the heart and soul of the 'Land of Enchantment.' Santa Fe's little sister, Taos, is almost as hot in the art department, and offers fantastic skiing, green chile beer, delicious food and the most famous Native American pueblo in the state. In Arizona, Phoenix and Tucson boast swank resorts, awesome golfing, big cacti and warm, sunny weather year-round. Places like New Mexico's Truth or Consequences, Arizona's Jerome and Utah's Torrey and Boulder, all filled with New Age crystal

FAST FACTS

Population of AZ, NM, UT, NV & Southwestern CO: 12.5 million

Inflation: 5%

Regional unemployment rate: 4.5%

Miles of lighted neon tubing in Las Vegas: 17

Sprinting speed of a roadrunner: 15mph

Grand Canyon's widest chasm: 18 miles

Annual reported UFO sightings in New Mexico: 400-650

Number of pueblos in New Mexico: 19

Percentage of land that is public in Utah: 65%

Miles of railway track on the Durango to Silverton line: 45

shops, quirky galleries and historic inns, are becoming increasingly popular off-the-grid retreats.

The past is alive in the Southwest, which is as traditional as it is trendy, as rural as it is cosmopolitan and as cultural as it is political. As it's home to a large portion of the USA's Native American population, the story of the American Southwest is not always pretty. But it is as haunting, surreal and mysterious, as beautiful, wild and magical, as the land on which it plays out. The legend of the Wild West has always been America's grandest tale, capturing the fascination and igniting the imagination of writers, photographers, singers, filmmakers and travelers the world around. It's taken on mythical proportions and enticed millions to visit.

Overall, Southwesterners are a friendly lot – people say hello on the streets. They're also low-key – cowboy boots and ties suffice for dress attire here. But don't mistake their easy-going approach to life as a lack of interest in world affairs. Whether they're talking politics over coffee in a neon-lit diner in a dusty Route 66 town or chattering about the area's rapid growth, its lack of water, the ongoing drought and the emasculation of subsistence farming in a Durango wine bar, Southwesterners are an opinionated lot. This is a region, after all, that produced two of the four all-star candidates running in the tightly contested 2008 presidential primaries. New Mexico's Governor Bill Richardson and Utah's Governor Mitch Romney may have dropped out of the race early after losing key states to Hillary, Obama and McCain – who by the way hails from Arizona – but they both displayed the fighting charisma the Southwest is famous for while playing.

Getting Started

How do you envisage your trip? As one-part desert pilgrimage and one part high-rolling party, with a dash of Native American mysticism and a pinch of Wild West thrown in for good measure? Do you see yourself dancing on tables at Las Vegas clubs or riding a mule to the base of the Grand Canyon? How you answer these questions will begin to narrow your choices considerably. And in a place as far and wide as the American Southwest, narrower is usually better.

WHEN TO GO

In northern Arizona, New Mexico and Utah, high season equates to summertime – traditionally from Memorial Day (late May) to Labor Day (early September). Expect higher prices and more crowds, except in hot southern Arizona, where luxury resorts cut their prices in half.

Wintertime visitors flock to the highlands for great skiing. Utah has world-class slopes; New Mexico is also pretty darn good. If you don't enjoy hurtling down snow-covered mountains, head to southern Arizona. Hotels in Phoenix, Tucson and other southern Arizona towns consider winter (Christmas to May) their high (and more expensive) season. While the rest of the country is buried under snowdrifts, southern Arizonans enjoy T-shirt weather most days.

Spring and fall are less crowded, but some services may not be available then. Fall is favored in the mountains of northern New Mexico and southwestern Colorado for admiring golden-leaved aspen trees and cottonwoods. In the springtime, the Sonoran Desert near Tucson in Arizona comes alive with tiny wildflowers and blooming cacti.

Be it Robert Redford's cutting-edge Sundance Film Festival in Utah's Park City in January or the country's largest Native American fair, the Navajo Nation Fair, in Arizona's Window Rock each September, the Southwest is filled with festivals throughout the year. For more specifics check out p522.

The Southwest conjures up images of searing desert heat, and this is certainly true in many areas. An excellent rule of thumb is to gauge the climate by the altitude. The lower you are, the hotter and drier it will be. Las Vegas, southwestern and south-central Arizona temperatures exceed 100°F (38°C) for weeks on end and occasionally surpass 120°F (49°C). The humidity is low, however, and evaporation helps to cool the body. Nighttime temperatures drop by 20°F or 30°F. Winter temperatures occasionally drop below freezing, but only for a few hours.

See Climate Charts (p520) for more information.

COSTS & MONEY

If you camp, share a rental car with another person and plan picnics, your daily expenses can be as low as $75 per person. Two people staying in budget motels, eating lunch in fast-food Mexican restaurants and enjoying moderate dinners can expect to spend between $85 and $120 per person per day.

If you spend ample time in cities (like Sedona, Santa Fe, Las Vegas, Taos and Park City) and stay at a preponderance of historic hotels and character-filled B&Bs, costs edge up to about $150 per person per day based on traveling with at least two people – not including extras such as lift tickets or Vegas shows. For those occasions when nothing less than a famous resort or spa will suffice, two people will undoubtedly drop $350 per person per day.

DON'T LEAVE HOME WITHOUT...

- Comfortable footwear with good traction for scrambling over rocky surfaces.
- Strong sunscreen, high-quality sunglasses and a wide-brimmed hat.
- Plenty of layers of clothing – when the sun drops in the mountains, even in summer, it can get cold.
- A great set of road maps (p527) – or better yet a GPS unit in your car.
- Gear for camping and hiking, and reading up on desert survival techniques.
- The sexiest or most outrageous outfit you've ever wanted to wear for anything-goes Vegas.
- Your iPod – fill it with inspiring road-trip songs to pass the time on long drives.
- A bathing suit.
- A travel sleep pillow – preferably down – will make lumpy hotel pillows and nights camping much more comfortable.
- A copy of your passport and driver's license, and phone numbers for your credit cards.
- An open mind and a sense of humor.

Discounts exist, however. To make the most out of your money in this age of rising fuel and food costs try visiting museums on free days and eating at restaurants during happy hour, when many places offer as much as 50% off appetizers – which can be made into a whole dinner – as well as beverages. Families with kids should check for children's menus at restaurants – most dining establishments in this region are kid-friendly and offer discounted meals for children. Many hotels also offer discounts for children – some up to as old as 17, so ask before you shell out extra bucks for your little one's bed. For specifics on booking hotels online, see p517.

Discounts on car rentals and accommodations are also often available to members of the **American Automobile Association** (AAA; ☎ 800-564-6222; www .aaa.com); see p537.

For more on costs, see the Lonely Planet Index on the inside front cover.

HOW MUCH?

National park entry fee $10-20

Ski-lift ticket $50-75

Las Vegas show ticket $75-165

Top-shelf margarita $7-14

Gas-station tamale $1.50

TRAVELING RESPONSIBLY

Since our inception in 1973, Lonely Planet has encouraged travelers to tread lightly, travel responsibly and enjoy the serendipitous magic independent travel affords. International travel is growing at a jaw-dropping rate and we still firmly believe in the benefits it can bring, but, as always, we encourage you to consider the impact your visit will have on both the global environment and the local economies, cultures and ecosystems.

In America, 'going green' has become seriously trendy and businesses of all stripes now slap 'We're green!' stickers on their products and services (though many Americans would agree with *The Simpsons Movie* when it calls global warming an 'irritating truth'). For the traveler, determining how ecofriendly a business actually is can be difficult. Thankfully, many resources are springing up. We have recommended ecofriendly businesses and highlighted local green initiatives throughout this guide; see the GreenDex (p565) for listings.

Please be sensitive to regional cultures and traditions, especially when travelling on Native American land. Always ask before taking photographs and remember that many native dances and ceremonies are not open to the public. For more on Native American customs, see p54.

To Drive or Not to Drive

Where adequate public transportation exists, taking it rather than renting a car will decrease your carbon footprint. But realistically a car is often a necessity in the Southwest, so choose ecofriendly cars when available (ask the majors – they're getting them!). You can drive ecofriendly if you rent in Phoenix, AZ: **EV Rental Cars** (www.evrental.com) at Sky Harbor International Airport specializes in hybrid and electric cars. The auto association **Better World Club** (www.bettterworldclub.com) supports environmental legislation and also offers ecofriendly services. If your car is outfitted to take biodiesel there are more gas stations offering this option each year – at the time of research most of these stations were in the larger metropolitan areas, especially in environmentally proactive New Mexico.

Note that Amtrak runs trains across Arizona and New Mexico and across Nevada, Utah and Colorado (although not north–south between states). See p535 for details.

Responsible Travel Schemes

Sustainable travel is more than making 'green' choices; it's a way of interacting as you walk. It's practicing low-impact hiking and camping. It's perhaps adding volunteering to a vacation. It's also simply learning about your destinations and their cultures and understanding the challenges they face. The following websites provide further advice on traveling sustainably:

Climatecrisis.net (www.climatecrisis.net) Official website for the documentary *An Inconvenient Truth*; offers carbon-offset programs, advice and loads of info.

Go Nomad (www.gonomad.com) Ecotours worldwide, including the Southwest.

Green Hotel Association (www.greenhotels.com) Ecofriendly hotels throughout the Southwest.

Greenprint Denver (www.greenprintdenver.org) Green travel in Colorado.

National Geographic Center for Sustainable Destinations (www.nationalgeographic .com/travel/sustainable) Promotes 'geotourism' with its Geocharter maps; currently three in the US, including Arizona's Sonoran Desert.

Sustainable Arizona (www.sustainablearizona.net) Green travel statewide.

Sustainable New Mexico (www.sustainablenewmexico.org) Ecofriendly travel.

Sustainable Travel International (www.sustainabletravelinternational.org) Ecoguides, tour bookings and carbon-offset schemes.

TRAVEL LITERATURE

Before heading off, pick up some books to help inspire your trip.

Jack Ruby's Kitchen Sink: Offbeat Travels Through America's Southwest by Tom Miller is a quirky read to accompany your own odyssey. *Traveler's Tales: American Southwest*, a collection of regional essays, will infuse your impending adventure with a forthcoming richness.

Barbara Kingsolver's novel *Animal Dreams* yields wonderful insights into a small Hispanic village near the Arizona–New Mexico border and from a Pueblo Indian. *House Made of Dawn*, a Pulitzer Prize winner by Kiowa novelist and poet N Scott Momaday, is about a Pueblo Indian's struggle to return home after fighting in WWII.

For great chick lit that really gives you a feel for the land, adventures, people and even dogs of the Southwest, check out any of Pam Houston's books. We especially like *Waltzing the Cat* and *Cowboys Are my Weakness*. Both are filled with funny, sometimes sad, stories about love lost and found in the great outdoors.

The region doesn't suffer from a drought of inspired writers; for more on Southwestern literature, see p50.

TOP 10

SOUTHWEST USA

FESTIVALS & EVENTS

Southwesterners really know how to throw a party. Whether it involves food or dance (probably both together), or aliens and music (probably not simultaneously), you're bound to find fun. For more comprehensive listings, check the individual towns and p522.

1   Sundance Film Festival (Park City, UT; p503), January

2   Winterfest (Park City, UT; p503), February

3   Green Jell-O Sculpture Competition (Springdale, UT; p469), March

4   World Series of Poker (Las Vegas, NV; p118), June to July

5   Telluride Bluegrass Festival (Telluride, CO; p398), June

6   Solar Music Festival (Taos, NM; p341), June

7   Santa Fe Indian Market (Santa Fe, NM; p318), August

8   Sedona Jazz on the Rocks (Sedona, AZ; p185), September

9   International Balloon Fiesta (Albuquerque, NM; p297), October

10 Helldorado Days (Tombstone, AZ; p251), October

LANDSCAPES & PHOTO OPPORTUNITIES

Upon gazing at a crested butte silhouetted at sunset or dawn breaking over the Grand Canyon, only then will you understand the true meaning of the word 'awesome.' It's no exaggeration to say that jaw-dropping scenery blankets the entire region, but for particularly scenic drives, check out each state's Scenic Routes section. And keep your camera ready.

1   Grand Canyon National Park (AZ; p198)

2   Monument Valley (AZ; p224)

3   Canyon de Chelly National Monument (AZ; p224)

4   Mesa Verde National Park (CO; p391)

5   White Sands National Monument (NM; p369)

6   Chaco Culture National Historical Park (NM; p348)

7   Bryce Canyon National Park (UT; p453)

8   Zion National Park (UT; p463)

9   Arches National Park (UT; p436)

10 Canyonlands National Park (UT; p421)

KILLER MARGARITAS

With the exception of Utah, where a stiff drink is hard to come by, the margarita is a staple on nearly every Southwestern cocktail menu (see p65). They're served frozen, on the rocks or straight up, and flavored versions are also popular.

1   Ore House (Santa Fe, NM; p324)

2   Cowgirl BBQ & Western Grill (Santa Fe, NM; p323)

3   Hyatt Regency Lake Tahoe (Lake Tahoe, NV; p148)

4   El Charro Café (Tucson, AZ; p242)

5   La Roca Restaurant (Nogales, AZ; p249)

6   Coyote Café (Santa Fe, NM; p323)

7   Adobe Bar (Taos, NM; p340)

8   Cowboy Club (Sedona, AZ; p187)

9   Isla Mexican Kitchen (Las Vegas, NV; p123)

10 Pancho McGillicuddy's (Williams, AZ; p262)

INTERNET RESOURCES

American Southwest (www.americansouthwest.net) Arguably the most comprehensive site for national parks and natural landscapes of the Southwest.

Arizona Highways (www.arizonahighways.com) Online version of the glossy magazine with weekend getaways and photography tips; information on local flora and fauna too.

Film New Mexico (www.filmnm.com) Where to get the lowdown on moviemaking in New Mexico, including shoot locations for released feature films, extra casting calls for current productions and a section dedicated to green filmmaking.

Lonely Planet (www.lonelyplanet.com) Succinct summaries, travel news, links and the Thorn Tree bulletin board.

Notes from the Road (www.notesfromtheroad.com) Click on Desert Southwest to enter another world; it'll be hard to return.

Roadtrip America (www.roadtripamerica.com) This site covers the entire USA, but offers a host of classic road trips in the Southwest and includes tips on dining, fuel calculation costs and much more.

Visit Las Vegas (www.visitlasvegas.com) An inclusive site as flashy as the city itself, brought to you by the Las Vegas Convention and Visitors Authority.

Itineraries
CLASSIC ROUTES

VEGAS, GRAND CANYON & SOUTHERN UTAH LOOP   Two Weeks

When you only have enough time for a short loop, this tour offers the chance to get a taste of the Southwest's most famous city, canyon and scenery. Start in **Las Vegas** (p102) and dedicate a few days to going around the world on the Strip. When you've soaked up as much delirious decadence as you can stand, head east to canyon country. **Grand Canyon** (p198) country, that is. You'll want to dedicate a couple of days to exploring America's most famous park. Descend into the South Rim chasm on the back of a mule and spend the night at Phantom Ranch on the canyon floor for a once-in-a-lifetime experience.

From the Grand Canyon head northeast through **Monument Valley** (p224), with scenery straight out of a Hollywood Western, to the national parks in Utah's southeast corner – they're some of the most visually orgasmic in the country. Hike the shape-shifting slot canyons of **Canyonlands National Park** (p421), watch the sunset in **Arches National Park** (p436) or mountain bike sick slickrock outside **Moab** (p428). Drive one of the most spectacular stretches of pavement, **Highway 12** (p448), west until it hooks up with I-15 and takes you back to Las Vegas.

This 1000-mile loop takes you to the Southwest's most iconic landmarks, including Sin City and the Grand Canyon. And with scenery straight out of a John Wayne flick – think crumbling buttes, crimson arches and painted rainbow deserts – it offers enough outdoor diversions to keep you from getting carsick.

GRAND TOUR   Three Weeks to One Month

Throw a pair of cowboy boots, hiking boots and comfy walking shoes into the saddlebag, pardner, and get ready to ride. Suspend judgments and roll the dice on the **Las Vegas Strip** (p107) before receiving some kicks on **Route 66** (p255) between **Kingman** (p257) and **Williams** (p260). Kick back in funky **Flagstaff** (p189), before venturing deep into the **Grand Canyon National Park** (p198). Shine your spirit in **Sedona** (p181) before getting in touch with your shabby-chic side in **Jerome** (p178). Visit the Heard Museum in **Phoenix** (p153), mellow out at **Saguaro National Park** (p238), and hang out in collegiate **Tucson** (p234). Fancy yourself a gunslinger in **Tombstone** (p250) before settling into charming **Bisbee** (p252). Head east for wild camping in remote **White Sands National Monument** (p369), with sprawling dunes as pure as driven snow. Watch bats swoop from caves at **Carlsbad Caverns National Park** (p378). Ponder little green men landing near **Roswell** (p373) before sinking into **Santa Fe** (p306), a foodie haven and magnet for art mavens. Feel tomorrow's science at **Los Alamos** (p304) and yesterday's civilization at **Bandelier National Monument** (p304). Hang with hippies and ski with bums in **Taos** (p332), before driving the luscious **Enchanted Circle** (p344). Chill out in laid-back **Durango** (p386), then explore ancient civilizations at **Mesa Verde National Park** (p391). Scoot through **Monument Valley** (p224), then head to the most stunning collection of national parks in the US. Visit a park a day or spend a few days in two or three parks, including **Canyonlands National Park** (p421) and **Arches National Park** (p436), for which **Moab** (p426) serves as a staging area. From Moab follow **Highway 12** (p448) back to Las Vegas, stopping at **Capitol Reef National Park** (p443), **Grand Staircase-Escalante National Monument** (p450), the spires of **Bryce Canyon National Park** (p453) and the sheer red rock walls at **Zion National Park** (p463) along the way.

Gas up the car, crank up the stereo and get ready for the best road trip in the entire USA. From the wildest national parks and the swankiest art colonies, to the most ancient Native American cultures and woolly Western folklore, it's all here, connected by dozens of scenic byways. Expect to drive about 2750 miles.

FOUR CORNERS/NATIVE AMERICAN JOURNEY   10 Days

Start in **Durango** (p386) and spend a day exploring the historic old mining town. Ride the narrow-gauge railway to **Silverton** (p405) the next day, returning to spend the evening eating and drinking in one of Durango's pleasant microbreweries. Next head to the haunting ruins at **Mesa Verde National Park** (p391), where you can hike and learn about the region's fascinating history. From Mesa Verde head toward Arizona and stop at the **Four Corners Monument** (p226) to snap a picture with your hands and feet in four different states. Head into New Mexico to ogle at **Shiprock** (p353), a stunning, ragged red rock formation. Spend your fourth night here. Begin the dusty and rutted drive to isolated **Chaco Culture National Historical Park** (p348), arguably the most notable architectural sight in the entire region. Sleep near **Window Rock** (p226), the capital of the **Navajo Reservation** (p221), where you can visit the Navajo Nation Museum and its tribal library. Stop at the old-world commercial hub of the region, the **Hubbell Trading Post** (p226), which served as the reservation's lifeline when it was established in the 1870s. Detour (65 miles each way) over to Second Mesa and the heart of the **Hopi Reservation** (p227), where you will find artisans and the Hopi Cultural Center. Make your way into the relatively verdant **Canyon de Chelly National Monument** (p224), an inhabited and cultivated canyon complete with hogans and herds of sheep. Hold onto your hat and lift your jaw off the floor as you approach the out-of-this-world beautiful **Monument Valley** (p224). Continue driving north to **Mexican Hat** (p418) in Utah to drink in the grandeur.

Take a photo of Four Corners then hightail it out to beautiful buttes and majestic mesas, ride narrow-gauge railways, explore ancient Native American ruins, shop for turquoise jewels at trading posts or hike some great trails. This trip is 725 miles.

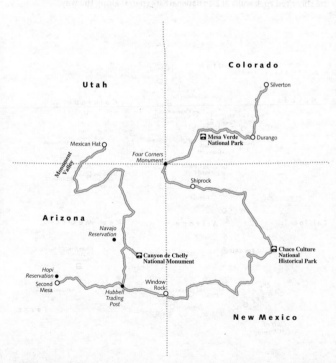

HISTORIC ROUTE 66

One Week

Route 66 aficionados will love driving the Mother Road through Arizona and New Mexico, with long uninterrupted stretches where you can still get a real taste of old-school motoring. Start in little **Topock** (p256) on the California border. Stop and check out the gorge – a dramatic walled canyon and one of the prettiest cut by the Colorado River. The highway runs uninterrupted from Topock to Seligman, which at about 125 miles is the longest remaining stretch in the country. First up is gunslinging **Oatman** (p257), where you can relive wilder days dancing in an old saloon. Cruise through the mining settlement of **Kingman** (p257), the route's main hub. Detour to the little outpost of **Chloride** (p259) for an almost ghost-town experience before heading to **Seligman** (p260), home to 1950s billboards and old motor court hotels. You'll find another vintage 1950s downtown in **Williams** (p260), along with a railroad that goes to **Grand Canyon National Park** (p198) – this makes a great driving break and is an easy way to see the Grand Canyon if you don't have ages of time to drive. From Williams continue down 'America's Main St' to the college town of **Flagstaff** (p189), where the heart of the old west still ticks, and on toward windblown **Winslow** (p263). Pass through **Holbrook** (p263) – there's not much to see – and detour to the **Petrified Forest National Park** (p264), home to 225-million-year-old giant fossilized trees. Next, it's onward to New Mexico. Stop in **Gallup** (p270), the trading epicenter for the Zuni and Navajo Reservations, which also has some sick mountain biking. Then head to feisty **Albuquerque** (p288): the state's largest city and most underrated attraction. Cruise east to **Santa Rosa** (p279), home to the state's best scuba-diving site and the classic Route 66 Auto Museum. The last stop, **Tucumcari** (p280), upholds the mythology of Route 66 with perfection.

A trip along Route 66 – the 'Mother Road' – reveals Americana at its most iconic and nostalgic. And with about 750 miles of pavement between them, Arizona and New Mexico dish up the longest uninterrupted stretches of the country's most famous old east–west highway.

ROADS LESS TRAVELED

WILD WEST TOWNS & OPEN ROADS

Following the outlaw trail from the bottom of Arizona to the heartland of Nevada is one hell of an off-the-grid road trip as long as you don't mind lots of time behind the wheel. Start your journey in **Bisbee** (p252), a perfectly preserved Wild West town. Take a day trip to remote and hauntingly beautiful **Chiricahua National Monument** (p226) for a bit of hiking, before hitting touristy **Tombstone** (p250), home of the famous shoot-out at the OK Corral. From here it's a long haul – although the scenery is mesmerizing for much of the way – northwest on Hwy 10 through **Tucson** (p234) and **Phoenix** (p153) to Hwy 89 north. Follow the scenic byway through ragged mountains to charming **Jerome** (p178), a rough-and-tumble mining town turned artists enclave. Spend the night in a funky B&B, then drive gorgeous Hwy 89A north to New Age **Sedona** (p181) to channel some of the earth's energy and soak up the red rock scenery. When you've had your fill, continue north on Hwy 89 and follow it through Grand Canyon and Navajo country into Utah. Stop at the spectacularly scenic **Grand Staircase-Escalante National Monument** (p450), then continue north until you reach US Hwy 50. Dubbed the 'Loneliest Road in America' for good reason, US Hwy 50 traverses wild, mostly empty, landscape of rolling brown hills and arid valleys – it's the kind of place where the road goes on forever. Stop at **Great Basin National Park** (p140) for awesome hiking before continuing west to **Virginia City** (p146). Once a rip-roaring Wild West boomtown, today it's a charming place of wooden sidewalks and Victorian buildings that makes a great ending point for this epic road trip.

The heart of the Wild West still beats strong along this 960-mile trail that once served as a footpath for the wickedest criminals in the land. Here lonely highways thread through big country, passing a number of charming old mining towns along the way.

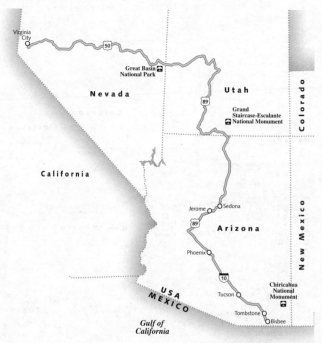

TAILORED TRIPS

PARKS & NATURAL ATTRACTIONS

The crown jewel of all American parks, **Grand Canyon National Park** (p198) simply must not be missed. And anyone with more than a passing interest in Native American history should head to **Mesa Verde National Park** (p391) to explore ancient cliff dwellings and ponder why and how an entire civilization disappeared in AD 1300. For naturalists, **Saguaro National Park** (p238) features classic scenery: majestic, towering cacti and sandy desertscapes as far as the eye can see. For the region's best nightlife, visit **Carlsbad Caverns National Park** (p378) at dusk, when thousands of bats swoop from their bat caves. **Bandelier National Monument** (p304) boasts accessible cliff dwellings and hiking near hip Santa Fe. Pick your method of ascension for **Sandia Crest** (p295), which guards Albuquerque. Southern Utah could occupy hikers and road-trippers for a month all by itself. At **Arches National Park** (p436), sweeping sandstone arches frame million-dollar vistas of sky-punching mountain peaks and vast rugged desert. At **Canyonlands National Park** (p421), Utah's biggest and least-visited national park unfurls in a rugged expanse of serpentine canyons, rock fins and red-and-gray striped spires. At **Capitol Reef National Park** (p443), giant yellow sandstone domes cap the top of Waterpocket Fold, a 100-mile-long buckle in the earth's crust.

SOUTHWEST WITH KIDS

Fly into Phoenix, where you can immediately escape the heat and amuse the little ones at one of the city's numerous water parks. Try **Waterworld Safari** (p163), which boasts a six-story-high waterslide. In Tucson, the educational **Arizona-Sonora Desert Museum** (p237) is home to local desert animals thriving in their natural habitat. Kids also love **Old Tucson Studios** (p238), once an actual film set and now featuring shoot-outs and Wild West events galore. In **Tombstone** (p250), kids delight at OK Corral shoot-outs and outrageous Boothill Graveyard tombstones. Culture reigns in New Mexico, beginning at Santa Fe's festive **Museum of International Folk Art** (p310), where learning and history are fun. And science has never been more interactive or relevant than at **!Explora! Science Center** (p296) in Albuquerque. In Las Vegas, Mandalay Bay's **Shark Reef** (p109) is both exciting and educational for your younger ones, and likely also yourself! Family values are exalted in Mormon culture, which makes Utah a great spot for kids, especially **Salt Lake City** (p485). Or keep them entertained in the great outdoors. Go rafting down the **Colorado River** (p439) or mountain biking around **Moab** (p428). The Olympic town of **Park City** (p500) is attractive for nature walks and horseback rides through meadows of wildflowers, as well as skiing at some of America's best ski resorts.

BOTTOMS UP – BREWPUB TOUR

Beer aficionados on the quest for the perfect microbrew can plan an entire holiday around sampling the best of the Southwest's brewpubs. From Wild West saloons to industrial-style warehouses, this region is packed with home-grown breweries where the stouts, lagers, ales and barley wines – which can be as high as 12% alcohol (watch out!) – are made on the premises.

Start your beer tour in **Durango** (p387), the unofficial microbrew capital of the Four Corners region and home to four breweries. Don't miss an afternoon tasting at **Ska Brewing Company** (p389), known for making big, flavorful dark beers. Colorado is known for its microbrews, and Durango is far from the only mountain beer town in this portion of the state. **Smugglers Brewpub & Grille** (p401) in scenic Telluride is another good option.

In Arizona you'll want to visit the college town of Flagstaff, where there are multiple breweries, including **Flagstaff Brewing Company** (p196), known for handcrafted brews and live music in a rustic ski-lodge atmosphere. The **Mogollon Brewing Company** (p196) is another long-standing favorite.

Northern New Mexico is the state's brew mecca, with the best beers coming out of Santa Fe and Taos. The **Second Street Brewery** (p324) in Santa Fe is our favorite place to drink – head to the patio and sample its beer of the month. Or take the high road to Taos and head to cozy **Eske's Brew Pub & Eatery** (p340) for a bottle of green chile beer – now that's a unique-tasting brew!

SOUTHWEST WITH DOGS

The Southwest is a good place to travel with a four-legged friend. There are many pet-friendly cities and wide open spaces in which to play.

Santa Fe is home to one of the most unexpectedly pet-friendly hotels around, the **Ten Thousand Waves** (p321) spa. Your canine companion can choose from vari-ous-sized doggie beds, treats and bones, and you can choose from Thai or hot stone massages. In Colorado, **Durango** (p386) was our oversized bulldog Duke's top choice for dog-friendly towns – he couldn't believe how many shops let him take a research break in their air-conditioned interiors (some even provided treats!). Also check out the nearby mountain paradise of **Silverton** (p405), where local dogs patrol the unpaved streets and there are plenty of hiking, fly-fishing, swimming and camping opportunities for you and your pet. Speaking of spec-tacular scenery, your furry friend will also appreciate the fabulous views and wide open spaces of **Monument Valley** (p224).

In Arizona, **Kaibab National Forest** (p211) is akin to a giant dog park, with plenty of off-leash trails and good scents to follow. While in the area, check out mystical **Sedona** (p181) – the energy towards pets is as positive as it is towards people, and sev-eral of the top-end resorts vie for your business with outrageous pet pampering packages.

Kanab (p472), in Utah, is possibly the most pet-friendly town in the Southwest. Virtually all the hotels welcome dogs and offer treats upon check-in. The town is home to the Best Friends Animal Sanctuary, which is featured on the TV show *Dogtown*, and also known for adopting Michael Vick's abused pit bulls.

History

It's home to America's oldest state capital (Santa Fe) and the birthplace of the atomic bomb (Los Alamos). It's the region that produced the first Hispanic (New Mexican Bill Richardson) and first Mormon (Mitch Romney) to seek the office of President of the United States. It's home to the Wild West (Tombstone, Jerome and Durango, to start with) and a city built entirely around sinful pleasures (Las Vegas). In fact, the Southwest traces its roots back 25,000 years and is filled with enough history to keep you reading for centuries. We've given you a taste here.

THE FIRST AMERICANS

In the 1920s, workers in Clovis, NM, uncovered a number of 11,000-year-old spear points embedded in bones of extinct mammals that led archaeologists to determine that the region's first inhabitants were initially hunters. The population grew and game became extinct, however, and hunters had to augment their diets with wild berries, seeds, roots and fruits. Hence the hunter-gatherer was born in the United States. After 3000 BC, contacts with farmers in what is now central Mexico led to the beginnings of agriculture in the Southwest. Primitive corn was grown, and by 500 BC beans and squash

For engaging historical information, little else beats Michael S Durham's beautifully illustrated *The Smithsonian Guide to Historic America: The Desert States* (1998).

PETROGLYPHS: WRITTEN ON THE LAND

Anywhere in the Southwest you may encounter it: the crude outlines of human figures and animals, painted handprints, squiggled lines etched into desert varnish. Rock art is mysterious and awesome and always leaves us wondering: who did this, and why? What were they trying to say?

Dating from at least 4000 BC to as late as the 19th century, rock art in the Southwest has been attributed to every known ancestral and modern people. In fact, one way archaeologists track the spread of ancestral cultures is by studying their distinctive rock art styles, which tend to be either abstract or representational and anthropomorphic. Representational rock art is almost always more recent, while abstract designs appear in all ages.

We can only speculate about why rock art was created and what it means. This symbolic writing becomes obscure the moment the cultural context for the symbols is lost. Much of the art was likely the work of shamans or elders communicating with the divine. Some of the earliest, abstract designs may have been created in trance states. Certain figures and motifs seem to reflect a heavenly pantheon, while other rock art may tell stories – real or mythical – of successful hunts or battles.

More prosaic explanations also exist. Some rock art may have marked tribal territory, and some may have been nothing more than idle doodling. Even Ancestral Puebloans must have gotten bored waiting for the rain to pass.

TIMELINE

AD 100	1300	1598
The region's dominant indigenous cultures emerge. The Hohokam settle in the desert, the Mogollon in the mountains and valleys and Ancestral Puebloans (formerly called Anasazi) build cliff dwellings around the Four Corners.	One of history's most enduring unsolved mysteries occurs when the entire civilization of Ancestral Puebloans living in Mesa Verde, CO, vanishes into thin air, leaving behind a sophisticated city of cliff dwellings.	A large force of Spanish explorers, led by Don Juan de Onate, stops near present-day El Paso, TX, and declares the land to the north New Mexico for Spain; Onate becomes governor.

were also cultivated. Between 300 BC and AD 100, distinct groups began to settle in villages in the Southwest.

PRE-AMERICA: THE EARLY YEARS

By about AD 100, three dominant cultures were emerging in the Southwest: the Hohokam of the desert, the Mogollon of the central mountains and valleys, and the Ancestral Puebloans – formerly known as the Anasazi.

The intrepid Hohokam culture existed in the deserts of Arizona from 300 BC to AD 1400, adapting to desert life by creating an incredible river-fed irrigation system. They also developed low earthen pyramids (perhaps serving as temples) and sunken ball courts with earthen walls. Because they cremated their dead, archaeologists have been left with comparatively little information. Nonetheless, a rich heritage of pottery attests to Hohokam artistry.

The Mogollon culture settled near the Mexican border from 200 BC to AD 1400. They lived in small communities, often elevated on isolated mesas or ridge tops, and built simple pit dwellings. Although they farmed, they depended more on hunting and foraging for food. Growing villages featured the kiva – a circular, underground chamber used for ceremonies and other communal purposes.

Around the 13th or 14th century, the Mogollon were likely being peacefully incorporated by the Ancestral Puebloan groups from the north. One indication of this is the beautiful black-on-white Mimbres pottery with its distinctive animal and human figures executed in a geometric style reminiscent of Puebloan ware. Good examples are found in Deming (p361) and Silver City (p359); the Gila Cliff Dwellings (p361) are a late-Mogollon site with Puebloan features.

The Ancestral Puebloans inhabited the Colorado Plateau, also called the Four Corners area (p226), which comprises parts of northeastern Arizona, northwestern New Mexico, southwestern Colorado and southeastern Utah. This culture left the richest archaeological sites and ancient settlements that are still inhabited in the Southwest.

Important Ancestral Puebloan sites can be seen at Mesa Verde National Park (p391), Navajo National Monument (p223), Canyon de Chelly National Monument (p224), Bandelier National Monument (p304), Aztec Ruins National Monument (p353) and Chaco Culture National Historical Park (p348).

Today, descendants of the Ancestral Puebloans live in Pueblo Indian communities along New Mexico's Rio Grande, and in the Acoma (p283), Zuni (p283) and Laguna (p284) Pueblos of New Mexico's northwestern corner. The oldest links with the Ancestral Puebloans are found among the Hopi tribe of northern Arizona (p227). The mesa-top village of Old Oraibi (p228) has been inhabited since the 1100s, making it the oldest continuously inhabited settlement in North America.

The National Park Service's website, www.cr.nps.gov/nr/travel/amsw/intro.htm, covers sites on the National Register of Historic Places and has maps as well as itineraries.

By 1050, the Southwest had many trade routes – and items principally traded were treasures and ornaments in silver, turquoise and copper, seashells and exotic macaws.

1609	1846–48	1847
Santa Fe, America's oldest capital city, is founded. The Palace of Governors is the only remaining 17th-century structure; the rest of Santa Fe was destroyed by a 1914 fire.	The battle for the West is waged with the Mexican-American War. The fight ends with the 1848 signing of the Guadalupe-Hildago treaty that gives most of present-day Arizona and New Mexico to the USA.	Mormons fleeing religious persecution in Illinois start arriving in Salt Lake City by wagon train; over the next 20 years more than 70,000 Mormons will escape to Utah via the Mormon Pioneer Trail.

By about 1400, the Hohokam had mysteriously disappeared, their villages abandoned. There are many theories on this tribe's disappearance, but the most likely involves a combination of factors including drought, overhunting, conflict among groups and disease. The Mogollon people were more or less incorporated into the Ancestral Puebloans, who had also all but disappeared from their ancestral cliff dwellings at Mesa Verde in southwestern Colorado by the 1400s – their mass exodus began in the 1300s.

For more about the Native American peoples of the Southwest, see p54.

Throughout the Southwest's history, Apache, Comanche, Navajo and Hopi tribes were alternately fighting with one another. It was this internal warfare, in fact, that limited further Spanish expansion in the area during the 18th century.

When the Europeans arrived in the Southwest they brought a lifestyle completely foreign to the Native Americans. Mother Earth and Father Sky, bows and arrows, ritual dances and sweat lodges, foot travel, spiritual oneness with the land – all these were challenged by the new concepts of Christ and conquest, gunpowder and sword, European civilization and education, horses and a grasping desire for land.

> Anasazi, a Navajo word meaning 'enemy ancestors,' is a term to which many modern Pueblo Indians object; it's no longer used.

THE SPANIARDS ARRIVE

The initial Spanish incursion into the Southwest occurred after a shipwreck off the coast of Florida in 1528 sent four survivors journeying westward across the US through Texas and up the Rio Grande. Tales of their early sojourns launched the first major expedition, led by Francisco Vasquez de Coronado, in February 1540. It included 300 soldiers, hundreds of Native American guides and herds of livestock. It also marked the first major violence between Spanish explorers and the native people.

The expedition's goal was the fabled, immensely rich Seven Cities of Cibola. For two years, they traveled through what is now Arizona, New Mexico and as far east as Kansas, but instead of gold and precious gems, the expedition found adobe pueblos. During the harsh winters, the expedition expropriated some of the pueblos for their own use, burned one, and killed dozens of Native Americans. This ferocity was the hallmark of many Europeans to come.

> In addition to using stone tools to dig miles and miles of 15ft-wide canals, the Hohokam augmented farming by collecting wild desert foods and living in simple mud shelters over shallow earthen depressions.

Small groups that made forays along the Rio Grande periodically revived persistent fables of rich cities. In 1598, a large force led by Don Juan de Onate stopped near present-day El Paso, TX. Declaring the land to the north New Mexico, he claimed it for Spain and became governor. Then he headed north through the desert, the Jornada del Muerto or 'Journey of the Dead.'

During the Spaniards' first few years in northern New Mexico, they tried to subdue the pueblos, resulting in much bloodshed. The fighting started in Acoma Pueblo (p283) when a Spanish contingent of 30 men led by one of Onate's nephews demanded tax payment in the form of food. The Acoma Indians responded by killing him and about half of his force. Onate retaliated

1849	1859	1864
Regular stagecoach service starts along the Santa Fe Trail. The 900-mile trail will serve as the country's main shipping route for the next 60 years – until the railway finally makes it to town.	The richest vein of silver ever discovered in the USA, the Comstock Lode, is struck in Virginia City, NV, which quickly becomes the most notorious, quick-drawing, hard-drinking mining town in the Wild West.	Kit Carson captures and forces 9000 Navajo to walk 400 miles to a camp near Fort Sumner. Hundreds of Native Americans die from sickness, starvation and gunshot wounds along 'The Long Walk.'

ANCESTRAL PUEBLOAN SETTLEMENT

Why the Ancestral Puebloans entered Mesa Verde is a subject of much speculation. Habitations in Mesa Verde evolved greatly between 450, when the earliest simple structures were constructed, and 1300, when the great cities were mysteriously left behind.

The earliest period of settlement, the so-called Modified Basketmaker phase that extended to about 750, found the Ancestral Puebloans dispersed across the mesa tops in small clusters of permanent pithouse dwellings – semisubterranean structures with posts supporting low-profile roofs.

During the Developmental Pueblo Period, up to 1100, Ancestral Puebloans built surface houses with simple shared walls – like row-house apartments – forming small hamlets surrounded by fields of maize, beans and squash.

The following Classic Pueblo phase, to 1300, saw the Mesa Verde Ancestral Puebloans elaborate on the earlier structures using masonry building materials. Their efforts housed a peak population of perhaps several thousand in pueblo villages, the precursors to cities. Greater clusters of people created opportunities for united accomplishments and perhaps a rudimentary division of labor, social organization, political control and even organized raids on neighboring villages. During this period the Ancestral Puebloans created subsurface round rooms, or kivas – for decades believed by archaeologists to be only for ceremonial use, but more recently seen to also have more basic functions. Hydraulic schemes to irrigate crops and provide villagers with water were developed during this time as well.

There is mounting evidence of regular communication between Mesa Verdeans and Chaco Canyon peoples in northwestern New Mexico during this period. And some researchers suggest the political, economic and social influences extended even farther afield into Mesoamerica (present-day Mexico and Central America).

The Puebloans suddenly moved to the alcoves of the cliff faces around 1200. Community size depended on available cliff space, so while small cavities may have contained only a few compartments, there were many larger communities with more than 200 compartments, including elaborate blocks or rooms, cantilevered balconies, sunken round rooms and even tower structures – many connected with internal passageways.

Ancestral Puebloans inhabited the cliff dwellings for less than a century before disappearing in accord with a regional demographic collapse that is the greatest unexplained event of the era. Death, disease, invasion, internal warfare, resource depletion and climatic change are among the hardships that these peoples faced. Tree-ring chronologies offer proof of a widespread drought from 1276 to 1299, yet this explanation fails to account for the earlier population decline at Chaco Canyon or Mesa Verde's survival of earlier droughts. Population movements did occur and it is probable that many Ancestral Puebloans migrated south to the pueblos of present-day New Mexico and Arizona.

Period	Chronology
I Basketmaker	AD 1-550
II Modified Basketmaker	550-750
III Developmental Pueblo	750-1100
IV Classic Pueblo	1100-1300

1869	1881	1919
Explorer John Wesley Powell leads the first Colorado River descent, a grueling thousand-mile journey that kills half the one-armed Civil War veteran's expedition and takes the rest through the Grand Canyon's rapids.	In 1881, Wyatt Earp, along with his brothers Virgil and Morgan, and Doc Holliday, kill Billy Clanton and the McLaury brothers in a blazing gunfight at the OK Corral in Tombstone, AZ.	The Grand Canyon becomes the USA's 15th national park, and a dirt road to the North Rim is built from Kanab. Only 44,173 people visit the park that year, compared to 4.4 million in 2007.

with greater severity. Relations with the Native Americans, poor harvests, harsh weather and accusations of Onate's cruelty led to many desertions among the colonizers. By 1608, Onate had been recalled to Mexico. A new governor, Pedro de Peralta, was sent north to found a new capital in 1609 – Santa Fe remains the capital of New Mexico today, the oldest capital in what is now the USA.

A particularly destructive Spanish campaign in 1675 was aimed at destroying the Pueblo kivas and powerful ceremonial objects such as prayer sticks and kachina dolls. In 1680, the united northern Pueblos rose up in retaliation in the Pueblo Revolt and succeeded in driving some 2400 Spaniards back down the Rio Grande to El Paso. The Pueblo people took over Santa Fe's Palace of the Governors and held it until 1692. The northern Pueblo people, a mix of many different tribes, languages and beliefs, didn't remain united for long, though. In 1692, the Spaniards again took over Santa Fe and eventually subdued the area's pueblos. During the 18th century, the colony grew and the Spaniards lived uneasily but relatively peacefully alongside the Pueblo peoples.

Less brutal incursions were made into Arizona by the Jesuit priest Eusebio Kino, who garnered nearly mythical status as the one who brought God to southern Arizona. Beginning in 1687, he spent over two decades in the Arizona-Sonora area, establishing missions at Tumacácori (p248) and San Xavier del Bac (p247). After Kino's departure, conditions for the Native Americans deteriorated and led to the short-lived Pima Revolt of 1751 and the Yuma Massacre of 1781.

In an attempt to link Santa Fe with the newly established port of San Francisco and to avoid Native American raids, small groups of explorers pressed into what is now Utah but were turned back by the rugged and arid terrain. The 1776 Dominguez-Escalante expedition was the first to survey Utah, but no attempt was made to settle there until the arrival of the Mormons in the 19th century.

In addition to armed conflict, Europeans introduced smallpox, measles and typhus, to which the Native Americans had no resistance, into the Southwest. Upwards of half of the Pueblo populations were decimated by these diseases, shattering cultures and trade routes and proving a destructive force that far outstripped combat.

THE TERRITORY YEARS

After the Mexican-American War, most of present-day Arizona and New Mexico became the New Mexico Territory; Utah and Nevada became the Utah Territory; Nevada became a separate territory in 1861, Arizona in 1863. Territories, unlike states, could not elect senators and representatives to Congress but were headed by an elected governor, with little power in the nation's capital.

Cochise County in southeastern Arizona has yielded the remains of baskets and stone cooking implements over 10,000 years old.

In 1610, Peralta built Santa Fe's Palace of the Governors (p311), the oldest non–Native American building in the US still in use today.

For a classic Hollywood depiction of Western expansion in the US, look no further than *How the West Was Won* (1962).

1931	**1938**	**1943**
Nevada legalizes gambling and drops the divorce residency requirement to six weeks; this along with legalized prostitution and championship boxing carries the state, particularly Las Vegas, through the Great Depression.	Route 66 becomes the first cross-country highway to be completely paved, including 875 miles across Arizona and New Mexico. After the faster Interstate 40 bypasses it, the Mother Road is officially decommissioned in 1984.	High in the northern New Mexican desert, Los Alamos is chosen as the top-secret headquarters of the Manhattan Project, the code name for the research and development of the atomic bomb.

For decades, US forces pushed west across the continent, killing or forcibly moving whole tribes of Native Americans who were in their way. The most widely known incident is the forceful relocation of many Navajo in 1864. US forces, led by Kit Carson, destroyed Navajo fields, orchards and houses, and forced the people into surrendering or withdrawing into remote parts of Canyon de Chelly (p224). Eventually they were starved out. About 9000 Navajo were rounded up and marched 400 miles east to a camp at Bosque Redondo, near Fort Sumner (p378) in New Mexico. Hundreds of Native Americans died from sickness, starvation or gunshot wounds along the way. The Navajo call this 'The Long Walk,' and it remains an important part of their history.

The last serious conflicts were between US troops and the Apache. This was partly because raiding was the essential path to manhood for the Apache. As US forces and settlers moved into Apache land, they became obvious targets for the raids that were part of the Apache way of life. These continued under the leadership of Mangas Coloradas, Cochise, Victorio and, finally, Geronimo, who surrendered in 1886 after being promised that he and the Apache would be imprisoned for two years and then allowed to return to their homeland. As with many promises made during these years, this one, too, was broken.

Even after the wars were over, Native American people continued to be treated like second-class citizens for many decades. Non–Native Americans used legal loopholes and technicalities to take over reservation land. Many children were removed from reservations and shipped off to boarding schools where they were taught in English and punished for speaking their own languages or behaving 'like Indians' – this practice continued into the 1930s.

Nineteenth-century Southwest history is strongly linked to transportation development. During early territorial days, movement of goods and people from the East to the Southwest was very slow. Horses, mule trains and stagecoaches represented state-of-the-art transportation at the time. Major routes included the Santa Fe Trail and the Old Spanish Trail, which ran from Santa Fe into central Utah and across Nevada to Los Angeles, CA. Regular stagecoach services along the Santa Fe Trail began in 1849; the Mormon Trail reached Salt Lake City in 1847.

The arrival of more people and resources via the railroad led to further land exploration and the frequent discovery of mineral deposits. Many mining towns were founded in the 1870s and 1880s; some are now ghost towns like Santa Rita (see boxed text, p358), while others like Tombstone (p250) and Silver City (p358) remain active.

THE WILD WEST

Romanticized tales of gunslingers, cattle rustlers, outlaws and train robbers fuel Wild West legends. Good and bad guys were designations in flux – a

---

For a comprehensive introduction to the pioneer history, beliefs and secrets of the LDS church, read *Mormon America: The Power and the Promise*, by Richard and Joan Ostling.

Pat F Garrett's *The Authentic Life of Billy, the Kid* (2000) analyzes the myths and falsehoods defining and surrounding one of the greatest Southwestern heroes.

1945

The first atomic bomb is detonated in the ironically named Jornada del Norte (Journey of Death) Valley, a desolate desert area in southern New Mexico that is now part of the White Sands Missile Range.

1946

The opening of the glitzy Flamingo casino in Las Vegas sparks a mob-backed building spree. By the time the fabulous '50s are in full swing Sin City has reached its first golden peak.

1947

In early July, an unidentified object falls in the desert near Roswell. The government first calls it a crashed disk, then a day later calls it a weather balloon and mysteriously closes off the area.

TOP FIVE OLD WEST SITES

- **OK Corral, Tombstone** (AZ; p250) Home of the famous gunfight, where the Earps and Doc Holliday fought the Clantons and McLaurys in 1881.

- **Lincoln** (NM; p372) Historical home of Billy the Kid.

- **Jerome** (AZ; p178) Once known as the 'wickedest town in the old West,' brimming with brothels and gunfights galore.

- **Virginia City** (NV; p146) Where the silver-laden Comstock Lode was struck, a national historic landmark.

- **Silverton** (CO; p405) Old miners' spirit and railroad history with a historical downtown.

---

tough outlaw in one state became a popular sheriff in another. And gunfights were more frequently the result of mundane political struggles in emerging towns than storied blood feuds. New mining towns mushroomed overnight, playing host to rowdy saloons and bordellos where miners would come to brawl, drink, gamble and be fleeced.

Legendary figures Billy the Kid and Sheriff Pat Garrett, both involved in the infamous Lincoln County War (p372), were active in the late 1870s. Billy the Kid reputedly shot and killed more than 20 men in a brief career as a gunslinger – he himself was shot and killed by Garrett at the tender age of 21. In 1881, Wyatt Earp, along with his brothers Virgil and Morgan, and Doc Holliday, shot dead Billy Clanton and the McLaury brothers in a blazing gunfight at the OK Corral (p250) in Tombstone – the showdown took less than a minute. Both sides accused the other of cattle rustling, but the real story will never be known.

Butch Cassidy and the Sundance Kid once roamed much of Utah. Cassidy, a Mormon, robbed banks and trains with his Wild Bunch gang during the 1890s but never killed anyone.

Although it covers everything west of the Mississippi, www .americanwest.com is a treasure trove of popularized information about cowboys, local heroes and pioneers.

DEPRESSION, WAR & RECOVERY

While the first half of the 20th century saw much of the USA in a major depression, the Southwest remained relatively prosperous during the dust-bowl days.

Las Vegas came onto the scene after the completion of a railroad linking Salt Lake City and Los Angeles in 1902, grew during the despair of the '20s and reached its first golden peak (the second came at the end of the 20th century) during the fabulous '50s when mob money ran the city and all that glittered really was gold.

During the Depression, the region benefited from a number of federal employment projects, and WWII rejuvenated a demand for metals mined

1950	1957	1963
A TV game show host wishes out loud that a town somewhere would like his show enough to name themselves after it. The people of Hot Springs, NM, vote and the town officially becomes Truth or Consequences.	Los Alamos opens its doors to ordinary people for the first time after the last restrictions guarding its secrecy are lifted. The city was first exposed to the public after the atomic bomb was dropped on Japan.	The controversial Glen Canyon Dam is finished and Lake Powell begins, eventually covering up ancestral Indian sites and stunning rock formations but creating 1960 miles of shoreline and a boater fantasyland.

in the Southwest. In addition, production facilities were located in New Mexico and Arizona to protect those states from the vulnerability of attack. Migrating defense workers precipitated population booms and urbanization, which was mirrored elsewhere in the Southwest.

The struggle for an adequate supply of water for the growing desert population marked the early years of the 20th century, resulting in federally funded dam projects such as the 1936 Hoover Dam (p132) and, in 1963, the Glen Canyon Dam (p219) and Lake Powell (p219). Water supply continues to be a key challenge to life in this region, with 2001–02 the driest year on record. For more information, see p78.

THE ATOMIC AGE

In 1943, Los Alamos (p304), then a boys school perched on a 7400ft mesa, was chosen as the top-secret headquarters of the Manhattan Project, the code name for the research and development of the atomic bomb. The 772-acre site, accessed by two dirt roads, had no gas or oil lines and only one wire service, and it was surrounded by forest.

Isolation and security marked every aspect of life on 'the hill.' Scientists, their spouses, army members providing security, and locals serving as domestic help and manual laborers lived together in a makeshift community. They were surrounded by guards and barbed wire and unknown even to nearby Santa Fe; the residents' postal address was simply 'Box 1663, Santa Fe.'

Not only was resident movement restricted and mail censored, there was no outside contact by radio or telephone. Perhaps even more unsettling, most residents had no idea why they were living in Los Alamos. Knowledge was on a 'need to know' basis; everyone knew only as much as their job required.

In just under two years, Los Alamos scientists successfully detonated the first atomic bomb at the Trinity site (see boxed text, p365), now White Sands Missile Range.

Latter Days (2003) is a heartfelt story about a gay Mormon boy. (By the way, being gay in Mormonland is *not* OK – though elders apparently look the other way if you absolutely swear you never have sex.)

The political climate is changing in Colorado. In 2006 the historically red state elected its first democratic governor, Bill Ritter, a former Denver district attorney.

IT WAS A FIRST...

There's no question, 2008 was a good year for big-league politics in the Southwest. For the first time in American history a Mormon and a Hispanic had placed serious bids for the presidency of the United States. Governor Bill Richardson, a Hispanic from New Mexico, ran on the Democrat ticket, while Utah's Governor Mitt Romney, a conservative Mormon, placed his name on the Republican primary ballot.

Although neither Romney nor Richardson managed to clinch their party's endorsement for the presidency, both made an impressive early showing that created an electric buzz that has not been seen before in this part of the country but was greatly needed. Just running was an ego booster for regional identity in two states that often struggle for recognition on a national platform.

1973	1981	1996
The debut of the MGM Grand in 1973 signals the dawn of the era of the corporate-owned 'megaresort,' and sparks a building bonanza along the Strip that's still going on today.	Microchip manufacturer Intel Corporation, convinced that Albuquerque's underground aquifer will never be depleted, opens the world's largest chip manufacturing plant in the suburb of Rio Rancho.	President Bill Clinton establishes Utah's Grand Staircase-Escalante National Monument, which is unique in allowing some uses (such as hunting and grazing by permit) usually banned in national parks.

After the US detonated the atomic bomb in Japan, the secret city of Los Alamos was exposed to the public and its residents finally understood why they were there. The city continued to be clothed in secrecy, however, until 1957 when restrictions on visiting were lifted. Today, the lab is still the town's backbone, and a tourist industry embraces the town's atomic history by selling T-shirts featuring exploding bombs and bottles of La Bomba wine.

Some of the original scientists disagreed with the use of the bomb in warfare and signed a petition against it – beginning the love/hate relationship with nuclear development still in evidence in the Southwest today. Ongoing controversies stem from the locations of nuclear power plants and transport, and disposal of nuclear waste, notably at Yucca Mountain, 90 miles from Las Vegas.

THE SOUTHWEST TODAY

Times are changing in the Southwest today. When the centuries flipped less than a decade ago, the Southwest started to flip too, with the entire region diversifying its economy, look and politics. New Mexico dived head first into the film business, and Las Vegas changed its face from sleazy to slick; seemingly overnight, Sin City became the hottest place in America to get your party on.

On the political front, New Mexico and Utah dominated the headlines in 2008. For the first time in US history an African American, a Hispanic, a Mormon and a woman were vying for the leadership of the free world (see boxed text, opposite).

In Arizona and, to a lesser degree, New Mexico, immigration is chilepepper hot. It's estimated that around 1600 people flee Mexico into Arizona each day. In Cochise County alone, on the Arizona–Mexico border, over 230,000 illegal immigrants were arrested in 2005 (one-fifth of the total in the US). Just to give you an idea of how high this number is: Cochise County has a population of just 125,000. Arizona vigilantes took immigration into their own hands in 2005 and founded the Minuteman Project. The patriotic group's goal is to stop Mexicans from crossing the border illegally by patrolling it themselves with posses of armed citizen volunteers. Its ethicality has been questioned, especially by human rights groups and liberal democrats. The Minuteman group also lobbies Congress to build a fence, either solid or virtual (ie using cameras and face-recognition technology to catch people sneaking into the US), along the US–Mexican border. The group is highly controversial and many Americans consider their views more than a little extreme, and even downright racist.

Mormon Utah drew national attention in 2006 with the arrest of Warren Jeffs, the leader of a controversial Mormon fundamentalist polygamist sect called the Fundamentalist Church of Latter-Day Saints (FLDS). Jeffs was arrested in Nevada in August 2006 and charged with multiple counts of

One of the more contentious issues in the Southwest is of ranchers' traditional rights to graze on public land for a small fraction of the current cost of a grazing lease on private land.

From gunslingers and prospectors to Native Americans ancient and contemporary, www .desertusa.com deals the goods on people and places that call (and have called) the Southwestern desert home.

2002	2004	2005
Salt Lake City hosts the Winter Olympics and becomes the most populated place to ever hold the winter games, as well as the first place women competed in bobsled racing.	Sin City is back! Las Vegas enters its second golden heyday when it hosts an amazing 37.5 million visitors, starts work on its latest swank megaresort and becomes the number-one celebrity party destination.	The Minuteman Project, a group of Arizona citizens fed up with the number of illegal immigrants crossing into the United States, is formed and begins citizen patrols on the Arizona–Mexico border.

allegedly arranging marriages between his adult male followers and young teenage girls in Utah, Nevada and Arizona. He was extradited to Utah for trial where a jury found him guilty of two counts of rape as an accomplice in 2007. He was sentenced to 10 years to life in prison and remains inside the Utah State Prison today. In March 2008, more than 400 children (several of them pregnant), were seized by authorities from an FLDS compound in Texas after calls to police alleging child abuse. Children were placed in foster homes around the state, and as this book is going to press many of the children's mothers are fighting the court system to regain custody.

Gordon Hinckley, president of the Church of Jesus Christ of Latter-Day Saints, died at the age of 97 in his hometown of Salt Lake City in January 2008.

From Geronimo to Zane Grey and from historical structures to Native American sites, www .azhistorytraveler.org lives up to its tag line: 'come for the scenery, stay for the stories.'

2006	2007	2008
Warren Jeffs, founder of the Fundamentalist Church of Latter-Day Saints (FLDS), is arrested on charges involving arranged marriages between adults and minors.	Governors Mitt Romney (R-UT) and Bill Richardson (D-NM) become the first Mormon and Hispanic, respectively, to run for president; both drop out of the race after doing poorly in the early primaries.	Gordon Hinckley, president of the Church of Jesus Christ of Latter-Day Saints, dies at the age of 97. Nearly 450 children, whose parents belong to Warren Jeffs' polygamist sect, are seized from a Texas ranch.

The Culture

Individuality is the cultural idiom of the Southwest. The identities of this region, centered on a trio of tribes – Anglo, Hispanic and Native American – are as vast and varied as the land that has shaped them. Whether your personal religion involves aliens, nuclear fission, slot machines, art or peyote, there's plenty of room for you in this harsh and ruggedly beautiful chunk of America.

Although the region's culture as a whole is united by the psychology, mythology and spirituality of its harsh, arid desert landscape, the people here are a sundry assortment of characters not so easily branded. The Southwest has long drawn stout-hearted pioneers pursuing slightly different agendas than those of the average American. Old mining towns like Jerome in Arizona were founded by fierce individualists – gamblers, mining-company executives, storekeepers and prostitutes. When the mining industry went bust in the 20th century, boomtowns went ghost for a while, before a new generation of idealistic entrepreneurs transformed them into New Age art enclaves and Wild West tourist towns. Today these places attract folk similar to the original white pioneers – solitary, red-blooded and self-reliant. Artists are drawn to the Southwest's clear light, cheap housing and wide, open spaces. Collectors, in turn, follow artists and gentrify towns like Santa Fe and Taos in New Mexico, Prescott in Arizona and Durango in Colorado. Then there are the mainstream outcasts who come to the Southwest to 'turn on, tune in and drop out.'

It doesn't matter if you're a yuppie artist drinking wine at a gallery opening in Santa Fe, a drunken celebutante dancing on a table at a Vegas megaclub or a devout Catholic asking God for a miracle while running your fingers through sacred dirt inside a simple New Mexican adobe church. In the Four Corner (plus Nevada) states everyone manages to coexist, and usually even get along, with little strife.

REGIONAL IDENTITY

On the whole, you'll find the people here more laid-back and friendly than their counterparts on the East and West coasts. Even at glitzy restaurants in the biggest cities (with the exception of Las Vegas) you'll see more jeans and cowboy boots than haute couture. Chat with a local at a low-key pub in Arizona or Colorado, and they'll likely tell you they're from somewhere else. They moved out here for the scenery, unpolluted air and slower pace of life. Folks in this region consider themselves environmentally friendly. Recycling is a big deal. So is a healthy lifestyle. They like to hike and mountain bike, ski and ride the rapids. They might have money, but you won't necessarily know it. It's sort of a faux pas to flaunt your wealth. Dogs are bigger assets than Louis Vuitton bags – although the dog is likely to be sporting a Louis Vuitton collar. A good piece of art trumps everything, of course.

Las Vegas is a different story. But everyone knows a place where you can go from Paris to Egypt in less than 10 minutes can't possibly play by the rules. This is a town that's hot and knows it. America's premier party destination has gone from mob to mobbed, and is the celebrity destination du jour – everyone from Paris Hilton to Hugh Hefner and the Girls Next Door party here. Not that everyone in Vegas looks like they just stepped off the set of *Las Vegas*, the glitzy American TV show that advertises the city as its star, but the identity here is a little different. There's an energy to Sin City not found elsewhere in the region. People from Vegas don't say they're from the Southwest, or even from Nevada. They say they're from Las Vegas. Dammit.

Upwards of 30,000 euphoric souls descend upon the Nevada desert each August for the Burning Man 'experiment,' a survivalist camping experience, art festival and rave where freedom of expression, costume and libido are all encouraged; see p148.

For a real-life peek at what it's like to work in a legalized Nevada brothel, read Alexa Albert's highly conflicted *Brothel: Mustang Ranch and its Women*.

Leslie Marmon Silko's novel *Ceremony* describes a young war-stricken Laguna Indian and his return to traditional ways after WWII. Silko, a Laguna Pueblo herself, unfurls the weblike story slowly, interspersing it with fragments of native myths.

WHAT'S IN A NAME?

Though the stereotypes that too often accompany racial labels are largely ignored in the Southwest, it's still a challenge for publishers to figure out the most accurate (and politically correct) term for various ethnic groups. Here's the rundown on our terminology for the region's big three:

■ **Native American** After introducing themselves to one very confused Christopher Columbus, the original Americans were labeled 'Indians.' The name stuck, and 500 years later folks from Mumbai are still trying to explain that, no, they don't speak a word of Tewa. 'Native American' is recommended by every major news organization, but in the Southwest most tribal members remain comfortable with the term 'Indian.' Both terms are used in this book. However, the best term to use is always each tribe's specific name, though this can also get complicated. The name 'Navajo,' for instance, was bestowed by the Spanish; in Athabascan, Navajo refer to themselves as Diné. What to do? Simply try your best, and if corrected, respect each person's preference.

■ **Anglo** Though 'Caucasian' is the preferred moniker (even if their ancestors hailed from nowhere near the Caucuses) and 'White' is the broadest and most useful word for European Americans, in this region the label for non-Iberian Europeans is 'Anglo' ('of England'). Even English speakers of Norwegian-Polish ancestry are Anglo around here, so get used to it.

■ **Hispanic** This is the one that has editors pulling their hair out. Associated Press prefers hyphens: 'Mexican-American,' 'Venezuelan-American' – and are Spanish-speaking US citizens more properly 'American-Americans'? Obviously, it's easier, if less precise, to use 'Latino' to describe people hailing from the Spanish-speaking Americas. Then add to that list 'Chicano,' 'Raza' and 'Hispano,' a de-anglicized term currently gaining popularity, and everyone's confused. But, because this region was part of Spain for 225 years and Mexico for only 25, and many folks can trace an unbroken ancestry back to Spain, 'Hispanic' ('of Spain') is the term used throughout this state and book, sprinkled with 'Spanish' and all the rest.

If Vegas is all about flaunting one's youthful beauty, then Arizona may just be its polar opposite. In the last decade, Arizona has done a great job at competing with Florida for the retiree-paradise award – the warm weather, dry air, abundant sunshine and lots and lots of space draw more seniors with each year. You'll see villages of RV parks surrounding Phoenix and Tucson and early-bird specials are the plat du jour at many restaurants.

Colorado, Arizona and New Mexico all have large Native American and Hispanic populations and these residents take pride in maintaining their cultural identities through preserved traditions and oral history lessons. One such example can be seen in Santa Fe, NM, on Christmas Eve when most residents stroll down Canyon Rd, home to the city's famous galleries, stopping for impromptu caroling sessions at one of the many bonfires along the way. The galleries, and the entire adobe city surrounding the historic downtown square, are lit by the soft glow of hundreds of candles nestled in beds of sand in waxed paper-bag lanterns. The lighting of the *farolitos* and the Canyon Rd Christmas Eve walk are old local Hispanic traditions dating back hundreds of years.

To hear Native American ethnic voices and learn about Mexican-American history, browse www .digitalhistory.uh.edu.

The book *Bringing Down the House* is a fascinating (and true) story of MIT students who broke the bank in Vegas by counting cards in the mid-'90s. The book was then made into the film *21* (2008).

LIFESTYLE

In a region of such diversity and size, it's impossible to describe the 'typical' Southwestern home or family. What lifestyle commonalities, after all, can be seen in the New Age mystics of Sedona, the businesspeople, lounge singers and casino workers of Las Vegas and the Mormon faithful of Salt Lake City? Half the fun of touring the Southwest is comparing and contrasting all these different identities.

Utah's heavily Mormon population stresses traditional family values, and drinking, smoking and premarital sex are frowned upon. You won't see much fast fashion or hear much cursing here, and you'll still need a special card to purchase hard alcohol.

Family and religion are also core values for Native Americans and Hispanics throughout the region. For the Hopi, tribal dances are such sacred events they are mostly closed to outsiders. And although many Native Americans and Hispanics are now living in urban areas, working as professionals, large family gatherings and traditional customs are still important facets of daily life. See p54 for more on contemporary Native American life.

Because of its favorable weather and boundless possibilities for outdoor adventures, much of the Southwest is popular with transplants from the East and West Coasts. In cities like Santa Fe, Telluride, Las Vegas, Tucson and Flagstaff, you'll find a blend of students, artists, wealthy retirees, celebrity wannabes, porn stars and adventure junkies. In urban centers throughout the region (with the exception of Utah) many people consider themselves 'spiritual' rather than religious, and forgo church for Sunday brunch. Women work the same hours as men, and many children attend daycare.

With the exception of Mormon Utah, attitudes towards gays and lesbians in the Southwest are generally open, especially in major cities like Las Vegas, Santa Fe and Phoenix.

POPULATION

The Southwest continues to be one of the fastest-growing regions in the USA. And who can blame the transplants? From young families to retirees, they're drawn by a lower cost of living, a more relaxed quality of life, more sunshine and warmer weather.

From 1990 to 2006, Nevada, Arizona, Colorado and Utah experienced the greatest population growth of all the US states. The metro areas of Las Vegas, Salt Lake City and Phoenix are the fastest-growing and densest cities by far. But despite this influx, the region as a whole is sparsely populated. Arizona's relatively high density is skewed by the greater Phoenix metropolitan area, which accounts for over 60% of the state's inhabitants. Similarly, the Salt Lake City region accounts for three-quarters of Utah's population.

Arizona has 10 times the population it had in the mid-1900s; New Mexico's population has more than tripled since the early 1950s. But Las Vegas, NV, beats them all: it's grown to more than 2.5 million people since it was founded less than 100 years ago.

New Mexico and Arizona have large populations of Native Americans, over half of whom are Navajo. Other tribes include various Apache groups, Havasupai, Hopi, Hualapai, various Pueblo tribes, Tohono O'odham, Ute and a host of smaller groups. Arizona and New Mexico have the third- and fourth-largest Native American populations of the 50 states. Utah is predominantly white. There is a growing, but still small, number of African Americans and Asians in the urban centers throughout the region.

New Mexico (along with Texas and California) has the highest proportion of Hispanics in the US. Southern Arizona also has a lot of Hispanic influence. In the border areas, and the big cities like Phoenix and Tucson, Hispanics are generally of Mexican heritage and proud to call themselves Latino or Chicano.

Hispanics in New Mexico may get offended should you mistake them for Mexican, a term they often use in a derogatory manner. If you call yourself Hispanic in this state, it means you trace your roots straight back to Spain.

> More Hispanics are migrating to Utah today than ever before, with the majority settling in Salt Lake City. In the last decade the number of Hispanic people in Utah grew by 10.6% to more than 250,000.

> You'll know you've entered Nevada – a different place than the rest of the Southwest – by the slot machines in the gas stations. Fill up and maybe you'll get lucky on the way to the bathroom.

> Pulitzer Prize–winner Paul Horgan deftly elucidates the Southwest's three dominant cultures in *The Heroic Triad* with exquisite lyricism.

HOW TO SPEAK SOUTHWESTERN

Sometimes just going out to dinner with Southwestern natives can be beyond confusing – all those Spanish words slipped slickly into cocktail-hour chatter like they're nothing out of the ordinary. If you feel intimidated by all the talk of hanging *ristras* on the *portale*, don't fear: this handy glossary will help.

adobe – building style using straw and mud (traditional) or sand and clay (modern) to make bricks for a home or building

farolitos – Hispanic Christmas tradition; the original *farolito* (still used on Christmas Eve across northern New Mexico) is made by placing a candle inside a waxed bag lined with sand. When the candle is lit, the paper lantern glows. The modern version uses electricity rather than candlelight.

hacienda – old Spanish colonial mansion

kiva – round-fronted adobe fireplace; in the old days it was used for worship, today it's used for warmth and is a fixture in top-end New Mexico and Arizona hotel rooms

latilla – small peeled pole used for creating ceilings (beams) in adobe homes (you'll see these in many New Mexico hotels). Most *latillas* are made from ultrastraight aspen trees, although in Arizona it is not uncommon to see saguaro cactus ribs used instead – these create a more rustic look.

portales – covered porches

ristra – string of dried red chiles, often seen hanging from porches and in kitchens around New Mexico

Sin City – another name for Las Vegas

SPORTS

Professional sports teams are based in Phoenix (p170) and Salt Lake City (p489). The Arizona Diamondbacks of Phoenix play major league baseball from mid-April through September; the only Southwestern major league football team, the Arizona Cardinals, play from September through December. Basketball (played November through April) is more competitive; you can watch hoops with Salt Lake City's Utah Jazz (men), the Phoenix Suns (men) and the Phoenix Mercury (women). Because pro tickets are hard to get, you'll have a better rim shot with college sports. Albuquerque teams (p300) across the board are quite popular. In fact, their minor league baseball team sells more merchandise than most major league pro teams. But it's the University of Arizona Wildcats that consistently place among the best basketball teams in the nation.

Several major league baseball teams (like the Chicago White Sox) migrate from the cold, wintry north every February and March for training seasons in warmer Arizona. They play in what is aptly referred to as the Cactus League.

In *Fire in the Mind,* George Johnson asks: do fact and belief, magic and science differ? This gifted writer juxtaposes groundbreaking scientific theories with Tewa Indian beliefs in northern New Mexico. Prepare to be dazzled.

RELIGION

Inclined towards spirituality rather than religion, New Age practitioners are prevalent in Arizona and New Mexico enclaves. Of the traditional groups, Catholics have the numerical edge in New Mexico, and Mormons are by far the majority in Utah. New Mexico and Utah have very few Jewish people, while Arizona's Jewish population is about 2%, which mirrors the national average.

Native American tribes practice the oldest North American religions. Some, like the Native American church that uses hallucinatory peyote buttons as a sacrament, are partly pan–Native American responses to encroachment by Anglo culture. Generally, though, the Native American ways are beliefs that Native Americans say they feel and know essentially because they are Native Americans: it's not something that non–Native Americans can properly understand or convert to. Different tribes often have particular creation stories, rituals and practices, which means that there are dozens of unique and carefully prescribed spiritual ways of life. Additionally, Native Americans usually maintain a strict sense of privacy about their most important ceremonies and thus books written by even the most respected outsiders, such as anthropologists, usually contain some inaccuracies when describing Native American religion.

POLYGAMY & THE MORMON CHURCH *Lisa Dunford*

Tell someone you live in Chicago and you may hear a gangster joke; say you're from Salt Lake City and likely as not the question of polygamy *will* come up. Throughout its history, Utah has been a predominately Mormon state; more than 60% of the current population has church affiliation. But as late church president Gordon Hinckley was fond of reiterating, the Church of Jesus Christ of Latter-Day Saints (or LDS, as the modern Mormon faith is known) has nothing to do with those practicing polygamy today.

Members of the LDS believe the Bible is the word of God and that the *Book of Mormon* is 'another testament of Jesus Christ,' as revealed to LDS church founder Joseph Smith. It was in the 1820s that the angel Moroni is said to have led Smith to the golden plates containing the story of a family's exodus from Jerusalem in 600 BC, and their subsequent lives, prophesies, trials, wars and visitations by Jesus Christ in the new world (Central America). After the book's publication in 1830, Smith established a new church in New York.

Throughout his life he is said to have received revelations from God, including the 1843 visitation that revealed the righteous path of plural marriage to the prophet. Polygamy was darn controversial even then. Some said Smith got the call as early as 1831 but knew the time had not come to make it public (even though he may have taken several new wives in secret). Problems with neighbors' opposition subsequently drove the Saints to Ohio, then to Missouri, then to Illinois and on to the Utah territory by 1846. Polygamy was formally established as church doctrine in 1852 by the second president, Brigham Young.

For all the impact plural marriage has had, it seems odd that the practice was officially endorsed for less than 40 years. By the 1880s a series of US federal laws had made polygamy a crime and banned Mormon church members from holding office. With the threatened seizure of church assets looming, president Wilford Woodruff received spiritual guidance and abdicated polygamy in 1890. Change took some time; in the ensuing years, some church leaders may have secretly given plural unions the go-ahead and other members left for Mexico. Excommunication of polygamous marriage proponents didn't begin until 1910, but once the Saints went mainstream, the community prospered.

Today the church has more than 12 million members and a missionary outreach that spans the globe. But what happened to polygamy? Well, fundamentalist sects broke off to form their own churches almost immediately; they continue to practice today. The official Mormon church disavows any relationship to these fundamentalists, and shows every evidence of being embarrassed by the past. Some young, international missionaries don't even seem to know of the LDS's historical involvement with plural marriage. Radical elements, on the other hand, believe the LDS church members have gone astray as the worst kind of apostates.

Estimates for the number of people still practicing polygamy range as high as 80,000 in Utah. Some you'd never recognize; they're just large families who wear long sleeves and go about their business in the everyday world. Others belong to isolated, cultlike groups such as the FLDS in Hildale-Colorado City, on the Utah–Arizona border. The secretive nature of polygamous groups has helped conceal heinous crimes (see boxed text, p480).

Though polygamy is illegal, prosecution is rare. Without a confession or videotaped evidence, the case is hard to prove. Men typically marry only their first wife legally (subsequent wives are considered single mothers by the state, and are therefore entitled to more welfare). The larger Utah populace is deeply ambivalent about polygamy. Tens, maybe hundreds, of thousands of them wouldn't exist but for the historic practice. I should know: my great-great-great grandmother, Lucy Bigelow, was the 18th wife of Brigham Young.

ROUND 'EM UP

Those in search of patriotic Wild West America can find it at the rodeo. These events, which mean 'roundup' in Spanish, began in the 1880s. The rodeo's characters – from cowboys and cowgirls to judges and clowns – all play important parts in the passion play that's a distinct show of Southwestern grit. From barrel racing to team roping, steer wrestling and bronc and bull riding, the rodeo is vintage Western Americana at its most raw and, to some, exciting.

Of all the sports practiced at a rodeo, bronc and bull riding are the most popular to watch. Neither is an easy feat. In bronc riding, the rider must stay on a randomly assigned wild horse for eight seconds while it tries its best to land their ass in the dirt, or worse! Bull riding is even scarier and more dangerous. This time you're placed on a mad-as-hell bucking bull.

Below we've listed the most popular rodeos in the region, but we'd also like to issue a word of caution. Some readers may find rodeos disturbing and unethical. According to **People for the Ethical Treatment of Animals** (PETA; www.peta.org), these Wild West macho displays of man trumping animal often come at the expense of the animals and for the profit of big rodeo promoters. At the same time, rodeos are an intrinsic part of Western American culture. Only you can decide whether you'd like to support this type of sportsmanship.

Fiesta de los Vaqueros (p240) Tucson, AZ; late February.

Rodeo de Santa Fe (p318) Santa Fe, NM; late June.

New Mexico State Fair (p297) Albuquerque, NM; September.

Navajo Nation Fair (p227) Window Rock, AZ; early September.

Dixie Roundup (p476) St George, UT; mid-September.

National Finals Rodeo (p119) Las Vegas, NV; December.

ARTS

Art is, and has always been, a major part of Southwest culture, the way in which its people express their heritage and ideologies. The rich history and cultural texture of the Southwest is a fertile source of inspiration for artists, filmmakers, writers, photographers and musicians. The Southwest is loaded with options for observers to enjoy art in all its forms – from gallery-hopping in Santa Fe to browsing for turquoise and hand-woven Navajo rugs in northern Arizona.

New Mexico is exploding as the new spot to shoot TV shows and movies, thanks in large part to the efforts of Governor Bill Richardson to lure big Hollywood producers to film in his state so they can bring energy, and funds, to economically ailing towns.

For more on the rich Native American culture, see p59.

New Mexico's Green Filmmaking Initiative encourages producers to think sustainable when creating movies and TV shows here. Visit www.nmfilm.com for resources on creating ecofriendly shoots, and the opportunity to win grants for creating green films.

Literature

Literature of the Southwest is as varied as the culture is broad. From the classic Western novels of Zane Gray, Louis L'Amour and Larry McMurtry to contemporary writers like eco-savvy Barbara Kingsolver and Native American Louise Erdrich, authors imbue their work with the scenery and sensibility of the Southwest. Drawing from the mystical reality that is so infused in Latin literature, Southwestern style can sometimes be fantastical and absurdist, yet poignantly astute. The beauty, rich texture, tragedy and historical tension have provided inspiration and context for thousands of writers of fiction, poets and playwrights. The following writers are arguably the best known.

DH Lawrence moved to Taos in the 1920s for health reasons, and went on to write the essay 'Indians and Englishmen' and the novel *St Mawr*. Through his association with artists like Georgia O'Keeffe, he found some of the freedoms from puritanical society that he longed for.

Tony Hillerman, an enormously popular author from Albuquerque, wrote *Skinwalkers, People of Darkness, Skeleton Man* and *The Sinister Pig*. His award-winning mystery novels take place on the Navajo, Hopi and Zuni Reservations.

Hunter S Thompson, who committed suicide in early 2005, wrote *Fear and Loathing in Las Vegas*, set in the temple of American excess in the desert; it's the ultimate road-trip novel, in every sense of the word.

Edward Abbey, a complex writer, created the thought-provoking and seminal works of *Desert Solitaire* and *The Journey Home: Some Words in Defense of the American West*. His classic *Monkey Wrench Gang* is a fictional and comical account of real people who plan to blow up Glen Canyon Dam before it floods Glen Canyon.

John Nichols wrote *The Milagro Beanfield War*, part of his New Mexico trilogy. It's a tale of a western town's struggle to take back its fate from the Anglo land barons and developers. It's a telling, brave and sometimes comical look at the region's tensions, hatreds and history; Robert Redford's movie of the novel was filmed in Truchas, NM (p332).

Cinema

The movie business is enjoying a renaissance in the Southwest, with New Mexico the star player. The state, and Governor Bill Richardson in particular, has put a lot of time into wooing big Hollywood to shoot motion pictures on New Mexico's enchanted soil. His effort is paying off in spades. Check out the critically acclaimed – though slightly depressing – American TV series *Breaking Bad*, set and filmed in and around Albuquerque. The 2007 Oscar winner *No Country for Old Men* was filmed almost entirely around Las Vegas, NM (doubling for 1980s west Texas), helping to revitalize the city's lackluster economy, at least for a few months.

New Mexico aside, the rest of the Southwest doesn't fare too poorly either when it comes to box-office hits. Sin City, otherwise known as Las Vegas, sees its fair share of TV shows and movies starring its wonderfully devilish, extravagant self. A few places have doubled as film and TV sets so often, in fact, they have come to define the American West. Aside from Utah's Monument Valley – which has been in so many movies we've lost count – popular Southwestern destinations include Moab (p426) for *Thelma and Louise* (1991), Dead Horse Point State Park (p426) for *Mission Impossible: 2* (2000), Lake Powell (p219) for *Planet of the Apes* (1968) and Tombstone (p250) for the eponymous *Tombstone* (1993).

The region also specializes in specific location shots. Snippets of *Casablanca* (1942) were actually filmed in Flagstaff's Hotel Monte Vista (p194); *Butch Cassidy and the Sundance Kid* (1969) was shot at the Utah ghost town of Grafton (p471); *City Slickers* (1991) was set at Ghost Ranch (p329) in Abiquiú, NM.

Music

The larger cities of the Southwest offer titillating options for classical music. Choose among Phoenix' Symphony Hall (p170), which houses the Arizona Opera and the Phoenix Symphony Orchestra, the famed Santa Fe Opera (p325), the New Mexico Symphony Orchestra (p300) in Albuquerque, and the Arizona Opera Company (p170) in Tucson and Phoenix.

Nearly every major town attracts country, bluegrass and rock groups. A notable major venue is Flagstaff's Museum Club (p196), with a lively roster of talent. Surprisingly, Provo, UT (p510), has a thriving indie rock scene, which offers a stark contrast to the Osmond-family image that Utah

Although the story is set in west Texas, No Country for Old Men was filmed almost entirely around Las Vegas, NM – a few scenes were shot in Texas. The US–Mexico border-crossing bridge depicted in the movie is actually the I-25 freeway overpass in Las Vegas!

Whether you are interested in being an extra in a movie filmed in New Mexico, the latest state industry news or simply want the back story to your favorite film, check out www.nmfilm.com for comprehensive info.

For live broadcasts of Mormon Tabernacle Choir concerts, visit www.mormontabernaclechoir.com.

often conjures. A fabulous festival offering is Colorado's Telluride Bluegrass Festival (p398).

Las Vegas is a mecca for entertainers of every stripe; current headliners include popular icons like Bette Midler and Toni Braxton, but for a little gritty goodness head to the Joint (p126).

Try to catch a mariachi ensemble (they're typically dressed in ornately sequined, body-hugging costumes) at New Mexico's International Mariachi Festival (p363). In Santa Fe, keep an eye out for mariachi bands escorting a grinning bride and groom across the plaza to a reception site following a wedding at the Loretto Chapel. The picture is visually magnificent, and the tradition completely northern New Mexican.

Santa Fe, dating back to at least 1607, is the oldest US capital. Since heritage preservation can be a challenge in such an old state, check out www.nmheritage.org.

Architecture

Not surprisingly, architecture has three major cultural regional influences. First and foremost are the ruins of the Ancestral Puebloans – most majestically their cliff communities and Taos Pueblo (p287). These traditional designs and examples are echoed in the Pueblo Revival style of Santa Fe's Museum of Fine Arts (p311) and are speckled across the region today. Santa Fe overflows with them.

The most traditional structures are adobe – mud mixed with straw, formed into bricks, mortared with mud and smoothed with another layer of mud. This style dominates many New Mexico cityscapes and landscapes.

Acoma Pueblo's new 40,000-sq-ft Sky City Cultural Center and Haak'u Museum (www .skycity.com) showcases vibrant tribal culture ongoing since the 12th century.

You can catch examples of 17th- and 18th-century mission-style architecture, characterized by red tiled roofs, ironwork and stucco walls, in religious and municipal buildings like Santa Fe's State Capitol (p316). The domed roof and intricate designs of Arizona's Mission San Xavier del Bac (p247) embody the Spanish Colonial style.

In the 1800s Anglo settlers brought many new building techniques and developed Territorial-style architecture, which often includes porches, wood-trimmed doorways and other Victorian influences.

Master architect Frank Lloyd Wright was also a presence in the Southwest, most specifically at Taliesin West (p157) in Scottsdale, AZ. More recently, architectural monuments along Route 66 (see p271) include kitschy motels lit by neon signs that have forever transformed the concept of an American road trip.

Painting, Sculpture & Visual Arts

The region's most famous artist is Georgia O'Keeffe (1887–1986; see p330 and p329), whose Southwestern landscapes are seen in museums throughout the world. Also highly regarded is Navajo artist RC Gorman (b 1932), whose sculptures and paintings of Navajo women are becoming increasingly famous worldwide. Gorman has lived in Taos for many years. Both Taos (p332) and Santa Fe (p306), in New Mexico, have large and active artist communities considered seminal to the development of Southwestern art. The area around Arizona's Flagstaff (p189) also has many thriving artist communities.

Freezing February temps are made bearable during Santa Fe's ART Feast (www.artfeast.com). An annual event held the last weekend in February, it focuses on art, food, wine and fashion. Profits go towards art departments at city schools.

The vast landscapes of the region have long appealed to large-format black-and-white photographers like Ansel Adams, whose *Moonrise, Hernandez New Mexico* (near Chimayo) can be seen at the Center for Creative Photography (p237) at the University of Arizona.

For something completely different, pop into art galleries and museums in Las Vegas, specifically the Bellagio (p107).

Jewelry & Crafts

Hispanic and Native American aesthetic influences are evident in the region's pottery, paintings, weavings, jewelry, sculpture, woodcarving and leather-working. See p60 for a discussion of Navajo rugs and the boxed text on p56 for Hopi kachina dolls; for Zuni silverware, see p60. Excellent examples of Southwestern Native American art are displayed in many museums, most notably in Phoenix' Heard Museum (p156) and Santa Fe's Institute of American Indian Arts Museum (p316). Contemporary and traditional Native American art is readily available in hundreds of galleries.

Kitsch & Folk Art

The Southwest is a repository for kitsch and folk art – just look at the preponderance of roadside stands, antique shops and curio stores that fill countless small towns and big cities. In addition to the predictable Native American knock-offs and beaded everything (perhaps made anywhere but there), you'll find invariable UFO humor in Roswell and unexpected nuclear souvenirs at Los Alamos, both in New Mexico. Perhaps you'd like to be the first on your block to own an Atomic City T-shirt, emblazoned with a red and yellow exploding bomb, or a bottle of La Bomba wine.

More serious cultural artifacts fill the Museum of International Folk Art (p310) in Santa Fe.

Dance & Theater

Native Americans have a long tradition of performing sacred dances throughout the year – for more on the history of these extraordinary dances, see p61.

Dance and theater productions are flashy and elaborate in Las Vegas (p102), where they have always been a staple of the city's entertainment platform.

The Indian Pueblo Cultural Center's website, www.indianpueblo.org, features historical information and current events for New Mexico's 19 pueblos.

Native American Southwest
Jeff Campbell

The Southwest is often called 'Indian Country,' but it's something of a misnomer. Enter the Navajo Reservation, the Hopi Reservation or the Zuni Pueblo, and you indeed enter another country – one at times so unlike the United States you feel for your passport – but the people are not themselves homogenous. The Southwest may still be the Indians' country, but they are not the same. Each tribe maintains distinctions of law, language, religion, history and custom that in fact turn the Southwest's incomparable, seemingly borderless painted desert into a kaleidoscopic league of nations.

This chapter, then, is just a brief introduction to this vast cultural wealth. It overviews the Southwest's largest reservations and tribes and the main Native American arts and crafts you'll find today. For more on Native American history, see p35. For some info about appropriate terminology for Native American people, see What's in a Name? (p46).

> North America still has well over 200 native languages, some as different as English and Chinese. Learn more at Native Languages of the Americas (www.native-languages.org), an in-depth, Native American–created resource.

THE PEOPLE

Circled, bright-plumed dancers, chanting, eyes closed, as beaded moccasins stamp the drum's rhythm; a rusted pick-up truck, elbows jutting over the sides, trailing dust down an empty reservation road. Today, as

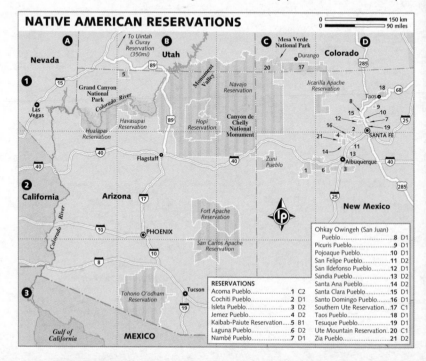

NATIVE AMERICAN RESERVATIONS

RESERVATIONS		
Acoma Pueblo	1	C2
Cochiti Pueblo	2	D1
Isleta Pueblo	3	D2
Jemez Pueblo	4	D2
Kaibab-Paiute Reservation	5	B1
Laguna Pueblo	6	D2
Nambé Pueblo	7	D1
Ohkay Owingeh (San Juan) Pueblo	8	D1
Picuris Pueblo	9	D1
Pojoaque Pueblo	10	D1
San Felipe Pueblo	11	D2
San Ildefonso Pueblo	12	D1
Sandia Pueblo	13	D2
Santa Ana Pueblo	14	D2
Santa Clara Pueblo	15	D1
Santo Domingo Pueblo	16	D1
Southern Ute Reservation	17	C1
Taos Pueblo	18	D1
Tesuque Pueblo	19	D1
Ute Mountain Reservation	20	C1
Zia Pueblo	21	D2

for many decades, these two images encapsulate the common perception of the USA's native peoples: Native Americans seem as rich in culture and heritage as they are impoverished in condition.

This dual image is of course reductive, even a stereotype. Native Americans, and the lives they lead, are incredibly diverse. Yet this dichotomy reflects a widespread reality, as well as a central challenge for Southwest tribes: how do you overcome history and become economically self-sufficient in today's America without losing the ancient culture, society and spirituality that make you who you are?

Apache

The Southwest has three major Apache reservations: New Mexico's Jicarilla Apache Reservation (http://jicarillaonline.com; population 2500), and Arizona's San Carlos Apache Reservation (www.sancarlosapache.com; population 9100) and Fort Apache Reservation, home to the White Mountain Apache Tribe (www.wmat.nsn.us; population 11,900).

The name Jicarilla (hek-a-*reh*-ya) comes from Spanish and means 'little basketmaker.' In addition to artistic basketry, the tribe is known for beadwork, leatherwork and pottery; the tribal headquarters in Dulce, NM, has a small museum. All the Apache tribes descend from Athabascans who migrated from Canada around 1400. They were nomadic hunter-gatherers who became warlike raiders, particularly of Pueblo tribes and European settlements, and they fiercely resisted relocation to reservations.

Today, the San Carlos and Fort Apache Reservations are among the poorest and youngest: over 50% live below the poverty line, unemployment hovers around 16%, the median *household* income is $17,000, and the median age is 22.

Havasupai

The Havasupai Reservation (www.havasupaitribe.com; population 450) abuts Arizona's Grand Canyon National Park (p198) beneath the canyon's south rim. Reservation access is legendary: the small tribe's one village, Supai, can only be reached by an 8-mile hike or a mule or helicopter ride from road's end at Hualapai Hilltop.

Havasupai (hah-vah-*soo*-pie) means 'people of the blue-green water,' and tribal life has always been dominated by the Havasu Creek tributary of the Colorado River on which they live. Reliable water meant the ability to irrigate fields, which led to a season-based village lifestyle. The deep Havasu Canyon also protected them from others; this extremely peaceful people basically avoided Western contact until the 1800s. Today, the tribe relies on tourism, and Havasu Canyon's three gorgeous waterfalls draw a steady stream of visitors.

The tribe is related to the Hualapai. Their Havasupai language is a Hokan (or Pai) dialect and is vigorously maintained, even though it's only been a written language for a few decades.

Hopi

The Hopi Reservation (www.nau.edu/~hcpo-p; population 6600) occupies more than 1.5 million acres in the middle of the Navajo Reservation. Most Hopi live in 11 villages at the base and on top of three mesas jutting from the main Black Mesa; Old Oraibi, on Third Mesa, is considered (along with Acoma Pueblo) the continent's oldest continuously inhabited settlement. Like all Pueblo peoples, the Hopi are descended from the Ancestral Puebloans (formerly known as Anasazi), and thus trace their Southwest roots back over 2000 years. They are the only Pueblo tribe to speak a Uto-Aztecan dialect.

Who needs Vegas? Since the 1990s, over 25 Native American tribes have opened nearly 40 casinos and gambling halls across Arizona and New Mexico.

Why 'Indian Country'? Arizona has five of the top 10 most populated reservations; Arizona and New Mexico are both top-five states for Indian population; and Phoenix has the largest proportion of Indians among US cities.

One of the best museums devoted to Southwest Native American life and culture is Phoenix' Heard Museum (p156).

HOPI KACHINAS

In the Hopi religion, maintaining balance and harmony between the spirit world and our 'fourth world' is crucial, and the spirit messengers called kachinas (also spelled *katsinas*) play a central role. These supernatural beings are spirits of deities, animals and even deceased clan members, and they can bring rain, influence the weather, help in daily tasks and punish violators of tribal laws. They are said to live atop Southwest mountains; on the winter solstice they travel to the Hopi pueblos, where they reside until the summer solstice.

In a series of kachina ceremonies and festivals, masked dancers impersonate the kachinas; during these rituals, it is believed the dancers are inhabited by and become the kachinas. There are hundreds of kachina spirits: some are kindly, some fearsome and dangerous, and the elaborate, fantastical costumes dancers wear evoke the mystery and religious awe of these beings. In the 1990s, to keep these sacred ceremonies from becoming trivialized as tourist spectacles, the Hopi closed most to the public.

Kachina dolls (*tithu* in Hopi) are brightly painted, carved wooden figures traditionally given to young Hopi girls during certain kachina festivals. These religious icons are not toys; they are meant to help teach the girls about the kachinas, and they become treasured family heirlooms.

Over time, kachina figures became collector's items, and the Hopi now carve some as art meant for the general public. Today, the Navajo and others also carve kachina dolls, but the Hopi feel these could never accurately depict Hopi kachinas.

Hopi (*ho*-pee) translates as 'peaceful ones' or 'peaceful person,' and perhaps no tribe is more renowned for leading such a humble, traditional and deeply spiritual lifestyle. The Hopi practice an unusual, near-miraculous technique of 'dry farming'; they don't plow, but plant seeds in 'wind breaks' and natural water catchments. Their main crop is and has always been corn (which is central to their creation story), but they also grow beans, squash and melons, and herd sheep.

> The US contains over 4.3 million Native Americans (both full and part Indian, which is 1.5% of the US population). About 20% of Native Americans live on Southwest reservations.

Hopi ceremonial life is complex and intensely private, and extends into all aspects of daily living. Following the 'Hopi Way' is considered essential to bringing the life-giving rains, but the Hopi also believe it fosters the wellbeing of the entire human race. Each person's role is determined by their clan, which is matrilineal, and each clan has its own oral history and community responsibilities. Even among themselves, the Hopi keep certain traditions of their individual clans private.

The Hopi are skilled artisans; they are famous for pottery, coiled baskets and silverwork, as well as for their ceremonial kachina dolls.

Hualapai

> To volunteer or donate, consider Adopt a Native Elder (www.anelder.org), which aids traditional Diné on the Navajo Reservation. They also sell handwoven Navajo rugs, with all proceeds going directly to the weavers.

The Hualapai Reservation (http://hualapai-nsn.gov/; population 1350) occupies around a million acres along 108 miles of the Grand Canyon's south rim. Hualapai (*wah*-lah-pie) means 'people of the tall pines'; because this section of the Grand Canyon was not readily farmable, the Hualapai were originally seminomadic, gathering wild plants, particularly piñon nuts, and hunting small game.

Today, forestry, cattle ranching, farming and tourism are the economic mainstays. The tribal headquarters are in Peach Springs, AZ, which was the inspiration for 'Radiator Springs' in the animated movie *Cars*. Hunting, fishing and rafting are the reservation's prime draws, but the Hualapai have recently added a unique tourist attraction: Skywalk (p214).

Navajo

The Navajo Reservation (www.discovernavajo.com; population 175,000) is by far the largest and most populous in the US. Also called the Navajo

Nation and Navajoland, it covers 17.5 million acres (over 27,000 sq miles) in Arizona and parts of New Mexico and Utah. Using a Tewa word, the Spanish dubbed them 'Navajos' to distinguish them from their kin the Apache, but Navajo (*nah*-vuh-ho) call themselves the Diné (dee-*nay*; 'the people') and their land Dinétah.

Nationwide, there are about 300,000 Navajo, making it the USA's second-largest tribe (after the Cherokee), and the Navajo's Athabascan tongue is the most spoken Native American language, despite its notorious complexity. In the Pacific Theater during WWII, Navajo 'code talkers' sent and received military messages in Navajo; Japan never broke the code, and the code talkers were considered essential to US victory.

Like the Apache, the Navajo were feared nomads and warriors who both traded with and raided the Pueblos and who fought settlers and the US military. They also borrowed generously from other traditions: they acquired sheep and horses from the Spanish, learned pottery and weaving from the Pueblos, and picked up silversmithing from Mexico. Today, the Navajo are renowned for their woven rugs, pottery and inlaid silver jewelry, as well as for their intricate sandpainting, which is used in healing ceremonies.

The reservation has significant mineral reserves – Black Mesa, for instance, contains the USA's largest coal deposit, perhaps 21 billion tons – and modern-day mining of coal, oil, gas and uranium has been an important, and controversial, economic resource. Mining has depleted the region's aquifer, contaminated water supplies (leading, some claim, to high cancer rates), and impacted sacred places.

Tribal headquarters are in Window Rock, AZ, and the reservation boasts numerous cultural and natural attractions, including Monument Valley (p224), Canyon De Chelly National Monument (p224), Navajo National Monument (p223) and Antelope Canyon (p219) among others.

For decades, traditional Navajo and Hopi have successfully thwarted US industry efforts to strip mine sacred Big Mountain, but the fight continues. Black Mesa Indigenous Support (www.blackmesais.org) tells their story.

Paiute

The Kaibab-Paiute Reservation (www.kaibabpaiutetribal.com; population 260) is on the Arizona–Utah border. The Kaibab (*cay*-bob) are a band of Southern Paiute (*pie*-oot) who migrated to the Colorado Plateau around 1100. They were peaceful hunter-gatherers who avoided European contact longer than most Southwest tribes. They speak a Shoshone dialect of the Uto-Aztecan language family and are renowned basketmakers.

Today, they are another very poor, young tribe (nearly 60% live below the poverty line and the median age is 22). Their reservation runs a public campground and contains Pipe Spring National Monument (p220); the Kaibab-Paiute worked with the US park service to create the museum's rich displays on Native American life.

In From Sand Creek, *Acoma poet Simon Ortiz creates an unusual, riveting amalgam of poetry and history, sorrow and hope. It's a politically engaged, spiritually centered vision of Indian America.*

Pueblo

New Mexico contains 19 Pueblo reservations (see p282). Four reservations lead west from Albuquerque: Isleta, Laguna, Acoma and Zuni. Fifteen pueblos fill the Rio Grande Valley between Albuquerque and Taos: Sandia, San Felipe, Santa Ana, Zia, Jemez, Santo Domingo, Cochiti, San Ildefonso, Pojoaque, Nambé, Tesuque, Santa Clara, Ohkay Owingeh (or San Juan), Picuris and Taos.

Naturally, these tribes are as different as they are alike, and any generalization trails exceptions. For instance, while most speak a dialect of Tanoan (either Tewa, Tiwa or Towa), others speak Keresan, and the Zuni language is wholly unrelated. Nor does sharing a linguistic heritage mean that Pueblo tribes share bloodlines, custom or history.

Cochiti Pueblo is known for its high-quality double-sided aspen drums. Legend has it that Cochiti drum-makers were always sought after, and the drum forms the Cochiti tribal seal today.

Nevertheless, the term 'pueblo' (Spanish for 'village') is a convenient shorthand for what these tribes do share: all are believed to be ultimately descended from the Ancestral Puebloans and to have inherited their architectural style and their agrarian, village-based life – often dramatically perched atop mesas.

The original apartment living, pueblos are unique among American Indians. These adobe structures can have up to five levels, connected by ladders, and are built with varying combinations of mud bricks, stones, logs and plaster. In the central plaza of each pueblo is a kiva, an underground ceremonial chamber that connects to the spirit world. Not all the original pueblos have survived; Taos, one of the best preserved, was designated a World Heritage Site in 1992.

A legacy of missionaries, Catholic churches are prominent in the pueblos, and many Pueblo Indians now hold both Christian and native religious beliefs. This unmerged, unconflicted duality is a hallmark of much of Pueblo, and in fact Native American, modern life.

> Not all pueblos have websites, but available links and introductions to all are provided by the Indian Pueblo Cultural Center (www.indianpueblo.org; p294).

Tohono O'odham

The Tohono O'odham Reservation (www.itcaonline.com/tribes_tohono .html; population 9800) is the largest of four reservations that make up the Tohono O'odham Nation in the Sonoran Desert in southern Arizona. Tohono O'odham (*to*-ho-no oh-*oh*-dum) means 'desert people' (their Spanish name, Papago, is still sometimes used). The tribe was originally seminomadic, moving between the desert and the mountains with the seasons. They were famous for their calendar sticks, which were carved to mark important dates and events, and they remain well known for their baskets and pottery. Today, the tribe runs two casinos and the Mission San Xavier del Bac (p247) in Arizona; tribal headquarters are in Sells.

Ute

The Southwest has three main Ute (pronounced *yoot*) reservations: the Uintah and Ouray Reservation (www.utetribe.com; population 3150) in northeastern Utah; the Ute Mountain Reservation (www.utemountainute.com; population 1650) in southwestern Colorado; and the Southern Ute Reservation (www .southern-ute.nsn.us; population 1640) in southern Colorado.

Along with the Navajo and Apache tribes, Utes helped drive the Ancestral Puebloans from the region in the 1200s. By the time of European contact, seven Ute tribes occupied most of present-day Colorado and Utah (named for the Utes). In the 16th century, Utes eagerly adopted the horse and became nomadic buffalo hunters and livestock raiders, leading to a sometimes warlike life similar to Plains Indians. The Ute language is a Shoshone branch of Uto-Aztecan.

> Families predominate on reservations, which is partly why the median age for Native Americans living on tribal lands is about 25 (far younger than the US average of 36).

With over 4.5 million acres, the contemporary Uintah and Ouray Reservation is the second largest in the US. Rather than tourism, ranching and oil and gas mining are the tribe's main industries; tribal headquarters are in Fort Duchene, UT.

The Ute Mountain Utes (who call themselves the Weeminuche) are known for their guided tours of Mancos Canyon in Ute Mountain Tribal Park, which includes petroglyphs and cliff dwellings. Their reservation abuts Mesa Verde National Park (p391) and their tribal headquarters are in Towaoc, CO.

Like most Southwest tribes, the Southern Ute Reservation relies in part on casinos for income; in 2009, they will open a new casino four times larger than the current Sky Ute Casino in Ignacio, CO (the tribal headquarters).

LOCAL VOICES: DON MOSE – BRIDGING TWO WORLDS

Now 62, Navajo Don Mose is a teacher and educator who has dedicated his life to preserving his native language and culture. Currently living in Mexican Hat, UT, Don was born and raised in Piñon, AZ, 'smack in the middle of Navajoland.'

As a child, Don attended a government-sponsored reservation boarding school, where, he says, 'I remember being punished for speaking Navajo with my brother. That didn't stop me. When I had to learn English, it was put on to me by force – but who says I couldn't speak my own language?'

Don's parents eventually sent him to Salt Lake City and then to Phoenix to complete high school. 'My mom and dad were great believers in education. They thought if I could learn and maintain my way of life, the traditional life, and also go out and get an education, learn as much as you can from the Anglo people – because to have both is unique. That is the philosophy I brought back to the reservation. You combine the two cultures together.'

'Back in the 1970s there was only a handful of Navajo people themselves who knew how to read and write the language. It was a culture shock, a rude awakening. I heard this Navajo lady speak, and she said, "In five to ten years, we will lose our language." That was 20 years ago, and since then it's been rebuilding, rebuilding.'

Don has helped by developing school curriculum, such as bilingual and cultural programs ('coyote tales, mythology, creation stories, you name it'). Another program uses 'Navajo materials – weaving, beading, and basketmaking – to teach math.' His next goal is to include Navajo in the computer-based Rosetta Stone language course.

Don says with a laugh, 'Navajo is the hardest language in the world to learn, besides Chinese. There's something like 20 ways of saying 'to run' in Navajo. So you know I got my work cut out for me.'

Don frets that 'Navajo has become a second language to our young people,' but he's optimistic. 'Just about every school on the reservation has some kind of a Navajo language program now, and with government and tribal leaders behind it, it's going to grow bigger.'

Don says, 'A lot of people look at us as a real downtrodden and poor people. But to the Navajo people, you're not poor if you have the things that are sacred to you, which for us are the six sacred mountains, our homeland. To have lots and lots of money, sure that's great, but if you don't have your language, if you don't have your culture or spirituality, if you don't know your clan, then you are the poor man. When you look at us, you think, gosh how can people live like this? But that keeps us humble. We're not as bad off as everybody thinks we are. We're trying to live the best we can to stay in harmony and balance with Mother Earth and Father Sky.'

And the Navajo Nation's greatest resource? 'We're producing a lot of good intelligent young people, coming from our own schools now, and they want culture. I really believe there was a purpose for native peoples to be placed on this earth. Now is the time to take that education the Anglo way, take your traditional culture, place them together, and solve problems. That's what my hopes are.'

ARTS

Native American art is as essential to the Southwest as sagebrush, rattlesnakes and slot canyons. In the geometries of Pueblo pottery and Navajo rugs, we feel human hands making sense of this terraced, transcendent landscape. In fact, Native American art nearly always contains ceremonial purpose and religious significance; the patterns and symbols are not merely pretty, but are woven with spiritual meaning that provides an intimate window into the heart of Southwest peoples.

In addition, by purchasing arts from Native Americans themselves, visitors have a direct, positive impact on tribal economies, all of which now depend in part on tourist dollars. Many tribes run craft outlets and galleries, usually in their main towns, or maintain lists of reputable sellers.

The Indian Arts & Crafts Board (www.doi .gov/iacb) publishes a directory of Native American–owned businesses, certifies expensive craft items (always ask to see a certificate) and punishes deceptive merchants.

Pottery & Basketry

Pretty much every Southwest tribe has pottery and/or basketry traditions, making these crafts especially rich for cultural exploration. Originally, each tribe and even individual families maintained distinct styles, but modern potters and basketmakers readily mix, borrow and reinterpret classic designs and methods.

Pueblo pottery is perhaps most acclaimed of all. Initially, local clay determined color, so that Zia pottery was red, Acoma white, Hopi yellow, Cochiti black and so on. Santa Clara is famous for its carved relief designs, and San Ildefonso for its black-on-black style, which was revived by world-famous potter Maria Martinez. The Navajo and Ute Mountain Utes also produce well-regarded pottery.

Pottery is nearly synonymous with village life, while more portable baskets were often preferred by nomadic peoples. Among the tribes who stand out for their exquisite basketry are the Jicarilla Apache (whose name means basketmaker), the Kaibab-Paiute, the Hualapai, and the Tohono O'odham. Hopi coiled baskets, with their vivid patterns and kachina iconography, are also notable.

> Many tribes have weaving traditions, and New Mexico has created a 'fiber arts trail' (www.nmfiberarts.org) that gathers these varied artisans together.

Navajo Weaving

Navajo legend is that Spider Woman taught humans how to weave, and she seems embodied today in the iconic sight of Navajo women patiently shuttling handspun wool on weblike looms, creating the Navajo's legendary rugs (originally blankets), so tight they held water. Preparation of the wool and sometimes the dyes is still done by hand, and finishing a rug takes months (occasionally years). At one time, rug design indicated origin, but certain classic designs – such as Ganado Red, Two Grey Hills and Yei – are now geographically liberated and reproduced by all Navajo.

Authentic Navajo rugs are expensive, and justifiably so, ranging from hundreds to thousands of dollars. They are not average souvenirs but artworks that will last a lifetime, whether displayed on the wall or the floor. Take time to research, even a little, so you recognize when quality matches price.

> To start learning about Navajo rugs, visit www.gonavajo.com/navajoart. To see traditional weaving demonstrations, visit the Hubbell Trading Post (p226) in Ganado, AZ.

Silver & Turquoise Jewelry

Jewelry using stones and shells has always been a native tradition; silverwork did not arrive until the 1800s, along with Anglo and Mexican contact. In particular, Navajo, Hopi and Zuni became renowned for combining these materials with inlaid-turquoise silver jewelry. In addition to turquoise, jewelry often features lapis, onyx, coral, carnelian and shells.

Fake Native American jewelry, using synthetic turquoise and manufactured in Southeast Asia, is now big business. Authentic jewelry is often stamped or marked by the artisan, and items may come with an Indian Arts & Crafts Board certificate; always ask. Price may also be an indicator: a high tab doesn't guarantee authenticity, but an absurdly low one probably signals trickery. A crash course can be had at the August Santa Fe Indian Market (p318).

> Links to Native American tribal websites can be found at www.usa.gov/Government/Tribal_Sites/index.shtml and at Nativewiki (www.nativewiki.org).

Contemporary Art & Literature

In addition to preserving their culture, Southwest Native American artists use sculpture, painting, film, literature and more to reflect and critique modernity. This list barely scratches the surface.

Well-loved Navajo painter RC Gorman created now-iconic, flowing portraits of Native American women, while Navajo artist Shonto Begay creates impressionist canvases that engage the dilemmas of reservation life.

Sculptor, poet and filmmaker Nora Naranjo-Morse, from Santa Clara Pueblo, is best known for her ceramic figures, bronze sculptures and explorations of modern Pueblo culture. Hopi Victor Masayesva Jr creates moody, experimental photos and films that wrestle with Hopi myth and life (see his documentary *Imagining Indians*, 1992).

Among Southwest Native American writers, N Scott Momaday is preeminent; his Pulitzer Prize–winning *House Made of Dawn* (1968), about a Pueblo youth, launched a wave of Native American literature. Leslie Marmon Silko, from Laguna Reservation, is equally lauded; read *Ceremony* (1977) and *Gardens in the Dunes* (1999). Other notable Southwest Native American writers include Paula Gunn Allen and Carol Lee Sanchez.

Eclectic, personal, gritty: *Legends of the American Desert* by Alex Shoumatoff is an odd job, a painterly, historical travelogue that wryly captures this strange, prickly peopled country.

ETIQUETTE

Appropriate reservation etiquette involves two things. The first is asking about and following any specific rules. Almost all tribes ban alcohol, so don't crack open a beer. Some ban pets and restrict cameras, and all require permits for camping, fishing and other activities. Tribal rules may be posted at the reservation entrance, or visit the tribal office or the reservation's website (most are listed in this chapter).

The other thing is attitude and manner. When you visit a reservation, you are visiting a unique culture with perhaps unfamiliar customs. Be courteous, respectful and open-minded, and don't expect locals to share every detail of their lives. Native Americans welcome visitors, but the almost constant, high-season parade of well-meaning scrutiny would exhaust anyone.

The People by Stephen Trimble is as comprehensive and intimate a portrait of Southwest native peoples as you'd hope to find, bursting with Native American voices and beautiful photos.

Ask First, Document Later Some tribes restrict cameras and sketching entirely; others allow cameras and sketching, but they may charge a fee, or restrict them at ceremonies or in certain areas. *Always ask before taking pictures or drawing.* If you want to photograph a person, ask permission first; a tip is polite and often expected.

NATIVE AMERICAN DANCING

One art that has grown tremendously in recent decades is Native American dancing. Dancing is now something of a pan-Indian cultural expression, connecting all tribes at the same time that dancers – in stunning feathered and beaded regalia and dramatic face paint – celebrate their specific heritage. Don't miss an opportunity to witness one of these spectacular events, but note that not all occasions are the same.

Ceremonial or ritual religious dances are, as you might expect, serious occasions, and many are closed to the general public (pueblos can close on short notice). They may be puberty rites or rain dances, but ceremonials are in essence no different than a Catholic mass: they are spiritual, reverential community experiences. When these ceremonies are open to the public, some tribes (like the Zuni) require visitors to attend an orientation first; always contact the tribes to confirm arrangements.

Social dances are typically cultural, as opposed to religious, events. They are much more relaxed and often open to the public. They occur during powwows, festivals, rodeos and other times, both on and off the reservation. Intertribal dance competitions (the lively 'powwow trail') are quite popular, but the dancing may tell a story or be just for fun, to celebrate a tribe or clan gathering.

Social dances may charge an admission, and Native American food, crafts and music are often sold. Intertribals may even include times when everyone, even you the tourist, is invited to join the dance. Photography may be permitted, but as always, get permission from (and tip) any individuals.

Of course, Native Americans also perform dances strictly for the public as theater or art. Though these may lack community flavor, they are authentic and wonderful.

Though its exact boundaries are debatable, the Southwest contains roughly 10% of the USA's over 560 federally recognized tribes (those enjoying government-to-government relations).

Pueblos Are not Museums At pueblos, it's easy to forget that these incredible adobe structures still house people. But they do. Public buildings will be signed; if a building isn't signed, assume it's private. Don't open any old door, and certainly don't climb around. Kivas are nearly always off-limits.

Ceremonies Are not Performances Treat ceremonies like church services; watch silently and respectfully, without talking, clapping or taking pictures, and wear modest clothing. Powwows are more informal, but remember: unless they're billed as theater, ceremonies and dances are for the tribe, not you.

Privacy and Communication Many Native Americans are happy to describe their tribe's general religious beliefs, but not always or to the same degree, and details about rituals and ceremonies are often considered private. To avoid seeming rude, always ask before discussing religion and respect each person's boundaries. Also, Native Americans consider it polite to listen without comment; silent listening, given and received, is another sign of respect.

Food & Drink

Gourmands usually don't consider the Southwest when it comes to eating, but food is this region's best-kept secret. From fancy fusion to cowboy campfire, vegan to steak, organic to greasy spoon, Rocky Mountain oysters to Frito pies, eating in the Southwest should be an experience as eclectic and diverse as the region's culture and landscape. To get a feel for what we're saying, try a bowl of spicy green chile stew and a fresh lime margarita – both New Mexican staples – in an artsy Santa Fe café. Or stop by a gas station in southern Colorado and be surprised by the most tasty homemade tamales you've ever sampled, delivered hot from the oven of the little Mexican grandma who hand delivers them each morning. Grab a greasy green chile cheeseburger, fries and a vanilla coke at a mom-and-pop diner on Route 66 in Arizona. Or visit Las Vegas, America's latest foodie hot spot, where the top restaurants are acclaimed not only for their cutting-edge creations crafted by the best chefs in the industry, but also for their extravagant decor.

Three ethnic groups, the Spanish, Mexicans and Americans, influence Southwestern food culture. Spain and Mexico controlled territories from Texas to California well into the 19th century, and when they officially packed up, they left behind their cooking style and many of their best chefs. The American pioneers who claimed these states also contributed to the Southwest style of cooking. Much of the Southwest is considered cattle country, and whether you are in Phoenix, Flagstaff or Las Vegas you're pretty much guaranteed a good steak. What's cool about grilling meat in the Southwest – whether a Mexican-style fajita or Arizona-grown tenderloin – is it's often done over a mesquite fire. The tree is native to the region, and grilling over it infuses the meat with a delicious smoky flavor – known as mesquite.

> For a collection of native recipes including ones for Navajo and Zuni breads, as well as Indian tacos and tamales, check out www.aniwaya.org.

> Some of the most delicious, spicy and fresh tamales in the Southwest are found at gas stations off highways. Local women rise at dawn to bake and then deliver the flavor-packed Mexican staple.

STAPLES & SPECIALTIES

Huevos rancheros is the quintessential Southwestern breakfast; eggs prepared to order are served on top of two fried corn tortillas, loaded with beans and

---

EATING GREEN IN THE SOUTHWEST

Organic cooking is the in way to eat in America these days, and the Southwest is eager to please in the healthy noshing department. Numerous restaurants throughout the five-state region are dedicated to serving only organic, and when possible buying local, which helps their community self-sustain. The restaurants listed below offer three of the most unique, ecofriendly and wholesome eating experiences in the Four Corners region.

Hells Backbone Grill (Boulder, UT; p449) It takes four hours on a lonely, potholed stretch of road to reach Boulder, home to the super-remote foodie outpost Hells Backbone (www.hellsbackbonegrill.com), but those who make the drive find the reward at the end well worth the trip. The restaurant is sustainable, growing most of its bounty on its two-acre organic farm. The vegetables are divine, and include sweet beets, tender carrots and turnips with just the right sour kick. Owner Jen Spalding says her goal for the restaurant is to evoke a little bit of provincial France in off-the-grid Utah.

Tara's Organic (Santa Fe, NM; p323) Ice cream is what to order at Tara's Organic (www.tarasorganic.com), a downtown Santa Fe eatery where the ingredients are locally grown – the lavender comes from Los Poblanos, a small town near Albuquerque, and the green chiles are harvested on an Espanola farm.

Center Café (Moab, Utah; p435) Locals in the know ride Moab's sick slickrock in the morning, then head over the Center Café (www.centercafemoab.com) at exactly 3:30pm, when the organic tapas feast begins. The ingredients are always super-fresh and when possible locally procured – the asparagus and bacon comes from an organic farm in town, the wine from a vineyard just down the road.

WE DARE YOU

The Southwest may not be known for having crispy insects or pig anus on the menu, but the region does have one unique creation that's just as difficult to stomach: the 'Rocky Mountain oyster.' Don't get tricked by the name; this treat has nothing to do with mollusks. Nope, a Rocky Mountain oyster is 100% beef, and it's not just any part of the cow: it's the bull's testicles. Yup, you heard that right. Order this regional delicacy and you'll be dining on a pair of deep-fried, breaded and seasoned testicles, which sort of taste like liver-flavored chewy calamari. Mmmm, delish…

potatoes, sprinkled with cheese, and served swimming in chile. Breakfast burritos are built by stuffing a flour tortilla with eggs, bacon or chorizo, cheese, chile and sometimes beans.

A Southwestern lunch or dinner will probably start with a big bowl of corn chips and salsa. Almost everything comes with beans, rice and your choice of warm flour or corn tortillas, topped with chile, cheese and sometimes sour cream. Blue corn tortillas are one colorful New Mexican contribution to the art of cooking. Guacamole is also a staple, and many restaurants will mix the avocado, lime, cilantro (coriander), tomato and onion creation right at your table!

John Middelkoop's documentary *Beans from God: the History of Navajo Cooking* examines the significant role that food plays in Navajo spiritual life.

Steak & Potatoes

Home, home on the range, where the ranches and the steakhouses reign supreme. Have a deep hankerin' for a juicy slab of beef with a salad, baked potato and beans? Look no further than the Southwest. In Utah, the large Mormon population influences culinary options – good, old-fashioned American food like chicken, steak, potatoes, vegetables, homemade pies and ice cream prevail.

Mexican & New Mexican Food

Mexican food is often hot and spicy, but it doesn't have to be. If you don't like spicy food, just go easy on the salsa and you should be fine. There are some distinct regional variations in the Southwest. In Arizona, Mexican food is of the Sonoran type, with specialties such as *carne seca* (dried beef). Meals are usually served with refried beans, rice, and flour or corn tortillas; chiles are relatively mild. Tucsonans refer to their city as the 'Mexican food capital of the universe,' which, although hotly contested by a few other places, carries a ring of truth. Colorado restaurants serve Mexican food, but they don't insist on any accolades for it.

New Mexico's food is different from, but reminiscent of, Mexican food. Pinto beans are served whole instead of refried; *posole* (a corn stew) may replace rice. Chiles aren't used so much as a condiment (like salsa) but more as an essential ingredient in almost every dish. *Carne adobada* (marinated pork chunks) is a specialty.

From the sweet red bell pepper to the brutish jalapeño, smoky chipotle and potent serrano, chiles are carefully cultivated. Flourishing where lesser plants fail, they are revered as much for their health benefits as their bite.

Native American Food

Modern Native American cuisine bears little resemblance to that eaten before the Spanish conquest, but it is distinct from Southwestern cuisine. Navajo and Indian tacos – fried bread usually topped with beans, meat, tomatoes, chile and lettuce – are the most readily available. Chewy *horno* bread is baked in the beehive-shaped outdoor adobe ovens *(hornos)* using remnant heat from a fire built inside the oven, then cleared out before cooking.

Most other Native American cooking is game-based and usually involves squash and locally harvested ingredients like berries and piñon nuts. Overall it's difficult to find, especially in Southwestern Colorado, Utah and Las Vegas. Your best bets for good grub are festival food stands, powwows, rodeos, Pueblo feast days, casino restaurants or people's homes at the different pueblos.

Exceptions include Albuquerque's Indian Pueblo Cultural Center (p294), the Metate Room (p394) in Southwestern Colorado, Tewa Kitchen (p288) near Taos Pueblo and the Hopi Cultural Center Restaurant & Inn (p228) on the Hopi Reservation.

Fruit & Vegetables

Beyond the chile pepper, Southwestern food is characterized by its use of *posole*, *sopaipillas* (deep-fried puff pastry) and blue corn. *Posole*, Spanish for hominy, is dried or frozen kernels of corn processed in a lime solution to remove the hulls. It's served plain, along with pinto beans, as a side dish. Blue corn tortillas have a heartier flavor than the more common yellow corn tortillas. Pinto beans, served either whole or refried, are a basic element of most New Mexican dishes.

Corn is ground and patted into tortillas or made into *masa* (slightly sweet corn dough), then elaborately folded into corn husks with a filling to make tamales. Or it's soaked in lye until tender and used in a rich stew called *posole*.

Beans, long the staple protein of New Mexicans, come in many colors, shapes and preparations. They are usually stewed with onions, chiles and spices and served somewhat intact or refried to a creamy consistency. Avocados are a delightful staple, made into zesty guacamole. 'Guac' recipes are as closely guarded and vaunted by cooks as their bean recipes.

Nouvelle Southwestern Cuisine

An eclectic mix of Mexican and Continental (especially French) traditions began to flourish in the late 1970s and it continues to grow. Try innovative combinations such as chiles stuffed with lobster or barbecued duck tacos. But don't expect any bargains here. Southwestern food is usually inexpensive, but as soon as the chef tacks on a 'nouvelle' tag, the tab soars as high as a crested butte.

Generally speaking, cities such as Phoenix, Tucson, Santa Fe and Albuquerque have the most nouvelle Southwestern restaurants.

DRINKS

In the Southwest it's all about the tequila. Margaritas are the alcoholic drink of choice, and synonymous with this region, especially in heavily Hispanic New Mexico, Arizona and Southwestern Colorado. Margaritas vary in taste depending on the quality of the ingredients used, but all are made from tequila, a citrus liquor (Grand Marnier, Triple Sec or Cointreau) and either fresh squeezed lime or premixed Sweet & Sour.

Our perfect margarita includes fresh squeezed lime (say no to the ultra-sugary and high-carb packaged mix), a high-end tequila (skip the gold and go straight to silver or pure agave – we like Patron or Herrendura Silver) and Grand Marnier liquor (better than sickly sweet Triple Sec). Ask the bartender to add a splash of orange juice if your drink is too bitter or strong.

Margaritas are either served frozen, on the rocks (over ice) or straight up. Most people order them with salt. Traditional margaritas are lime flavored, but these days the popular drink comes in a rainbow of flavors including mango, strawberry and peach. Flavored margaritas are best ordered frozen. To find out where you can get a killer margarita, see p26.

Locally brewed beers are also popular in this region, and people like to gather after work for a drink at their local microbrewery – a pub where beer is produced in-house. Microbreweries are abundant throughout the Southwest, and many of the beers are also sold in local grocery and liquor stores. Many

Green chile is to New Mexicans what breath is to life – essential. Chiles are picked green, roasted in special barrel-shaped contraptions then sold fresh at roadside stands, farmers markets and grocery stores statewide in September and October.

Not all chiles are picked – those left on the plant are allowed to mature to a deep ruby red, then strung on the *ristras* which adorn walls and doorways throughout the Southwest.

New Mexico harvests more than 30,000 acres of chiles annually, predominantly in the southwestern town of Hatch, where just about every restaurant (including McDonald's) offers green chile as a side.

GREEN CHILE STEW

Hungry ahead of your scheduled departure? Green chile stew is perhaps the ultimate expression of chile cuisine, and most certainly the pride of every New Mexican cook. It's also the only proven cure for the common cold. Although this recipe may be best saved for when you are more acclimated to the cuisine, the daring will go ahead and give it a try. Begin preparing your taste buds today.

Green Chile Recipe

½ lb ground beef, pork or turkey
½ lb boneless sirloin, cubed
4 cups chicken broth
½ cup beer
2 lbs fresh green chiles, roasted, peeled and chopped
1 tomato, chopped
1 medium onion, chopped
1 clove garlic, minced
½ cup fresh cilantro (coriander), chopped
1½ tsp oregano
2½ tsp cumin
¹/₈ cup fresh parsley, chopped
1 tsp salt
1 tsp pepper

In a large pot, sauté ground meat and sirloin until done. Remove from pot. Add onions, garlic and cilantro to pot and cook for three to five minutes or until onions are soft. Add chicken broth, beer, green chiles and tomato. Bring to a boil and then reduce to a simmer. Add meat, oregano, cumin, parsley, salt and pepper. Simmer for two hours, stirring occasionally.

---

microbrews are considered 'big beers' – meaning they have a high alcohol content. If you want to get tipsy fast, order a barley wine–style beer, which is often 11% (an average beer is around 5%). See p34 for an itinerary that takes you to a series of brewpubs.

> Because they were considered such a hot commodity, chile peppers were once used as currency.

There are three things a good wine grape needs: lousy soil, lots of sunshine and dedicated caretakers, all of which New Mexico has. For a full run-down of its 33 producers, contact the **New Mexico Wine Growers Association** (☎ 505-899-3815, 866-494-6366; www.nmwine.com). La Chiripada Winery (p332), with a shop on the Taos plaza, is our choice for regional vineyards, serving a fabulous riesling and cabernet sauvignon.

If you're looking for something nonalcoholic you'll find delicious espresso shops in the bigger cities and sophisticated small towns – in rural Arizona or Nevada you're likely to get nothing better than stale, weak diner coffee, however. Santa Fe, Phoenix, Durango, Truth & Consequences and Tucson all have excellent coffee shops with comfortable couches for reading or studying. Basically, if the Southwestern town has a college, it will have a good coffee shop. That's a regional given.

> In New Mexico, the last place you'd expect, Gruet (www.gruetwinery.com) produces arguably the best affordable champagne in the country.

CELEBRATIONS

Santa Fe offers many upscale food-related events, including the Wine & Chile Fiesta (p319). Smaller New Mexico festivals, no less charming, include Grant's Chile Fiesta (p276), Hillsboro's Apple Festival (p358) and Cloudcroft's Cherry Festival (p368).

At Christmastime, though, the really good food comes rolling out. Families get together for big tamale-making parties, *biscochitos* (traditional cookies made with anise) are baked by the hundreds and specially spiced hot chocolate is served.

For centuries, Pueblos have really known how to throw a ceremony. Feast days, replete with dances, pole climbs, races and whatnot, are topped off with great food. The biggest events are noted throughout the book; they're mostly in New Mexico.

For more unusual culinary happenings, visit Springdale's green Jell-O sculpture competition (p469) or Roswell's New Mexico Dairy Day (p375) with its cheese-sculpting competition. In Las Cruces, they make the world's largest enchilada at the Whole Enchilada Fiesta (p363).

WHERE TO EAT & DRINK

From fine cafés to roadside trailers, you will find delicious regional food – for anywhere from $2 to $100 per person! Breakfast will run $3 to $10, depending on whether you're at a retro diner or a culinary hot spot. Lunch should be $4 to $10ish. You can get a good dinner in a pleasant, though not fancy, restaurant for $15 to $25 per person, without tax, tip or drinks. In posh big-city restaurants and swanky resorts, it's easy to fork out over $50 per person. For a breakdown of the price categories used in our reviews, see p523.

Unless you're deep in the desert or the mountains, you're never far from food. In cities and on highways, some fast-food restaurants are open 24 hours a day. For general restaurant opening and closing hours, see p520. There are variations on this theme, though. Some restaurants serve breakfast all day. Many places are open for lunch *and* dinner, continuing to serve meals through the afternoon. Some restaurants serve a lighter, less formal menu until midnight or 1am. Some restaurants close on Monday. Utah restaurants are generally closed on the Lord's Day (that'd be Sunday).

If you're looking for quality regional grub, ask the locals where they're chowing down. Places that gussy themselves up are unlikely to be your best bets for authentic cuisine.

Once known for its cheap all-you-can eat buffets, the Las Vegas of today has done a good job of shedding its greasy-spoon past and is by far the most sophisticated dining city in the Southwest, packed with almost as many critically acclaimed restaurants as casinos. These extravagant eating holes, popular with the Hollywood crowd, are known for serving cutting-edge creations by the best chefs in the country.

Las Vegas isn't the only place for posh noshing. Santa Fe is right on her stiletto heels, leading the charge into haute cuisine with a stellar line-up of restaurants like the Coyote Café, Geronimo and Ristra (for these and more Santa Fe restaurants, see p321). For those looking to spend a little less, this art town also offers a host of reasonably priced eateries like the Shed (p322), which serves damn near the best New Mexican fare in the state as far as we're concerned, and the Cowgirl BBQ & Western Grill (p323), which manages to combine barbecue and Mexican with stupendous results – order the brisket quesadilla with green chiles and topped with homemade guacamole.

The Phoenix metro area is another regional eating mecca with the biggest selection of chow holes in Arizona. Celebrities and food snobs alike flock to the restaurants in Scottsdale's swanky resorts for a fusion feast created by some of America's top chefs. Try Vincent on Camelback (p166) for the top gourmet fare in Phoenix. For something a bit simpler, head to Los Dos Molinos (p166). This popular Mexican restaurant is a family affair, with several generations working the kitchen and tables. Their motto is 'some like it hot' and locals line up outside the door.

Go nearly south of the border to the university town of Tucson to sample the best Mexican food in Arizona. The *mole* in this funky place is stupen-

In *The Red Chile Bible: Southwestern Classic & Gourmet Recipes,* authors Kathleen Hansel and Audrey Jenkins educate fellow gourmands about how best to utilize the fiery gem so that their palates can live to tell the story.

The 1974 movie *Alice Doesn't Live Here Anymore* chronicles a woman who takes a job at Mel's Diner in Phoenix, AZ, and must cope with his attitudes towards women and some hilarious coworkers.

dous, and the restaurant that does it best is Café Poca Cosa (p243), which is also known for its super-authentic Old Mexican cooking. Tucson is also filled with plenty of coffee, beer and sandwich shops catering squarely to the budget college market.

The top town for foodies in Southwestern Colorado is Durango, which offers quite a few award-winning restaurants to choose from. Durango is also the unofficial microbrew capital of the Southwest, featuring four different breweries. The Ska Brewing Company (p389) is our favorite.

Microbrews are even catching on in Mormon Utah, a traditionally dry state due to religious morals. You can now wet your whistle with a microbrew at Ray's Tavern (p440) and Eddie McStiff's (p435).

Finding a cocktail in Sin City is as easy as placing a five-dollar bet. But if you're itching for something a little more cosmopolitan than the casino floor, visit Jay Z's slick – and the city's hottest – pimp lounge, the 40/40 Club (p125). For something a bit more glam, sip your cocktail under the moonlight at the Palms' futuristic penthouse Moon (p126), which has a surreal moon roof that retracts. Glass-tiled floors change colors with the beat of the music, whether hip-hop, rock or pop.

VEGETARIANS & VEGANS

Most metro area eateries offer at least one veggie dish, although few are devoted solely to meatless menus. These days, fortunately, almost every larger town has a natural-food grocer. In fact, they're popping up throughout the Southwest faster than weeds in a compost pile. That said, you may go wanting in smaller hinterland towns, where beef still rules. In that case, your best bet is to assemble a picnic from the local grocery store.

'Veggie-heads' will be happiest in New Mexico and Arizona; go nuts (or more specifically, go piñon). Thanks to the area's long-standing appeal for hippie types, vegetarians and vegans will have no problem finding something delicious on most menus, even at drive-thrus and tiny dives. There's one potential pitfall, though: traditional Southwestern cuisine uses lard in beans, tamales, *sopaipillas* (deep-fried puff pastry) and flour (but not corn) tortillas, among other things. Be sure to ask – often, even the most authentic places have a pot of pintos simmering for vegetarians.

HABITS & CUSTOMS

Folks in the Southwest observe standard US habits, etiquette and customs regarding eating and serving food. Invariably, American-sized portions are 'super-sized.' If you're invited to dinner in someone's home, bring a gift (wine or chocolates) and don't overstay your welcome.

COOKING COURSES

Cooking classes are becoming increasingly popular in America, a pattern that's starting to catch on in the Southwest. Amateur chefs on holiday should try the Santa Fe School of Cooking (p317).

EAT YOUR WORDS

You'll probably encounter some different cuisine and preparations in the Southwest than you're accustomed to. Take a gander at this list so that you don't end up eating something meaty or deep-fried unless you want to.

Main Dishes

burrito (or burro) – soft flour tortilla folded around a choice of chicken, beef, chile, bean or cheese filling. A breakfast burrito is stuffed with scrambled eggs, potatoes and ham.
carne adobada – pork chunks marinated in a spicy chile and herb sauce, then baked

---

You can't visit Albuquerque without ordering a Frito pie – a messy concoction of corn chips, beef chile, cheese and sour cream. You can find it in restaurants and it's always served at city festivals.

From growing to roasting, www.chili-pepper-plants.com contains everything you need to know about how to cool it down and spice it up.

carne seca – beef that has been dried in the sun before cooking

chile relleno – chile stuffed with cheese and deep-fried in a light batter

chimichanga – burrito deep-fried to make the tortilla crisp

enchilada – rolled corn tortilla stuffed with a choice of sour cream and cheese, beans, beef or chicken, and smothered with a red (or green) chile sauce and melted cheese.

fajitas – marinated beef or chicken strips grilled with onions and bell peppers, and served with tortillas, salsa, beans and guacamole

flauta – similar to a burrito but smaller and tightly rolled rather than folded, and then fried

huevos rancheros – fried eggs on a soft tortilla, covered with chile sauce and melted cheese, and served with beans

mole – mildly spicy, dark sauce of chiles flavored with chocolate, usually served with chicken

posole – corn stew; may be spicy and contain meat

refried beans – thick paste of mashed, cooked pinto beans fried with lard

taco – crispy, fried tortilla, folded in half and stuffed with a combination of beans, ground beef, chiles, onions, tomatoes, lettuce, grated cheese and guacamole

tamale – slightly sweet corn dough *(masa)* stuffed with a choice of pork, beef, chicken, chile or olives (or nothing) and wrapped in a corn husk before being steamed

tortilla – pancake made of unleavened wheat or corn flour. They stay soft when baked, become crisp when fried, and form the basis of most Mexican dishes. Small pieces, deep-fried, become the crispy tortilla chips served with salsa as an appetizer in many Mexican restaurants.

tostada – flat (ie open-faced) taco

The Santa Fe School of Cooking Cookbook, by Susan Curtis, shares recipes from the Southwest's seminal cooking school.

Snacks & Desserts

fry bread – deep-fried Native American bread; doughy, slightly greasy and altogether delicious. It can be served as a dessert – laced with honey or sugar – or as a main course, topped with chile, cheese, beans, rice and maybe chicken.

guacamole – mashed avocado seasoned with lime juice and cilantro (coriander), optionally spiced with chopped chiles and other condiments

nachos – tortilla chips covered with melted cheese and other toppings

salsa – cold dip or sauce of chopped chiles, pureed tomatoes, onions and other herbs and spices

sopaipilla – deep-fried puff pastry served with honey as a dessert, or, in New Mexico, plain as an accompaniment to the main course

Environment   David Lukas

The Southwest is a place of dramatic surprises and contrasts. While everyone thinks immediately of deserts and cacti, you may also encounter alpine tundra and verdant marshes in this region. What's surprising is the close proximity of these contrasting habitats. In the Santa Catalina Mountains (p239) outside Tucson, for example, you can ascend from searing desert to snow-blanketed fir forests within 30 miles, the ecological equivalent of driving 2000 miles from southern Arizona to Canada.

The desert itself is anything but monotonous; look closely and you will discover everything from fleet-footed lizards to jewel-like wildflowers. The Southwest's four distinct desert zones, each with its own unique mixes of plants and animals, are superimposed on an astonishing complex of hidden canyons and towering mountains. One of the best parts of the Southwest is that the land has an open and inviting feel – meaning that all of its components, geologic and ecological, may be readily enjoyed by attentive visitors.

The often-used term 'slickrock' refers to the fossilized surfaces of ancient sand dunes.

THE LAND
Geologic History

Although the Southwest is now an inland desert, it started out as a coastal region along the young North American continent. Washed by advancing and retreating seas, the region was eventually built up, as uplift and an accumulation of sediments pushed the ocean's edge westward to its modern location along the Pacific coast. This story is spectacularly told in the colorful, exposed layers of rock throughout Utah, Arizona and New Mexico. Most of the visitor centers in the region's national parks and monuments have excellent displays that help explain this geologic story.

It may be hard to imagine now, but the Southwest was once inundated by a succession of seas that alternately left behind evidence of deep bays, shallow mudflats and coastal sand dunes. During this time North America was a young continent on the move, evolving slowly and migrating northward from the southern hemisphere over millions of years. Extremely ancient rocks (among the oldest on the planet) exposed in the deep heart of the Grand Canyon show that the region was underwater two billion years ago, and younger layers of rocks in southern Utah reveal that this region was continuously or periodically underwater until about 60 million years ago.

Pages of Stone: Geology of the Grand Canyon & Plateau Country National Parks and Monuments by Halka and Lucy Chronic is an excellent way to understand the Southwest's diverse landscape.

At the end of the Paleozoic era (about 286 million years ago), a collision of continents into a massive landmass known as Pangaea deformed the earth's crust and produced pressures that uplifted an ancestral Rocky Mountains. Though this early mountain range lay to the east, it formed rivers and sediment deposits that began to shape the Southwest. In fact, erosion leveled the range by 240 million years ago, with much of the sediment draining westward into what we now call Utah. Around the same time, a shallow tropical sea teeming with life, including a barrier reef that would later be sculpted into Carlsbad Caverns (p378), covered much of southern New Mexico.

For long periods of time (between episodes of being underwater), much of the Southwest may have looked like northern Egypt today: floodplains and deltas surrounded by expanses of desert. A rising chain of island mountains to the west apparently blocked the supply of wet storms, creating a desert and sand dunes that piled up thousands of feet high. Now preserved as sandstone, these dunes can be seen today in the famous Navajo sandstone cliffs of Zion National Park (p463).

This sequence of oceans and sand ended around 60 million years ago as North America underwent a dramatic separation from Europe, sliding westward over a piece of the earth's crust known as the East Pacific plate and leaving behind an ever-widening gulf that became the Atlantic Ocean. This collision, named the Laramide Orogeny, resulted in the birth of the modern Rocky Mountains and uplifted an old basin into a highland known today as the Colorado Plateau. Fragments of the East Pacific plate also attached themselves to the leading edge of the North American plate, transforming the Southwest from a coastal area to an interior region increasingly detached from the ocean.

In contrast to the compression and collision that characterized earlier events, the earth's crust began stretching in an east–west direction about 30 million years ago. The thinner, stretched crust of New Mexico and Texas cracked along zones of weakness called faults, resulting in a rift valley where New Mexico's Rio Grande now flows. These same forces created the stepped plateaus of northern Arizona and southern Utah.

Increased pulling in the earth's crust between 15 and eight million years ago created a much larger region of north–south cracks in western Utah, Arizona and Nevada known as the Basin and Range province. Here, parallel cracks formed hundreds of miles of valleys and mountain ranges that fill the entire region between the Sierra Nevada and the Rocky Mountains.

During the Pleistocene glacial period, large bodies of water accumulated throughout the Southwest. Utah's Great Salt Lake (p490) is the most famous remnant of these mighty ice age lakes. Basins with now completely dry, salt-crusted lake beds are especially conspicuous on a drive across Nevada.

For the past several million years the dominant force in the Southwest has probably been erosion. Not only do torrential rainstorms readily tear through soft sedimentary rocks, but also the rise of the Rocky Mountains generates large powerful rivers that wind throughout the Southwest, carving mighty canyons in their wake. Nearly all of the contemporary features in the Southwest, from arches to hoodoos, are the result of weathering and erosion.

Geographic Makeup of the Land

If the Southwest could be said to have a geographic heart, many people would agree that it's the Colorado Plateau – an impressive and nearly impenetrable 130,000-sq-mile tableland lurking in the corner where Colorado, Utah, Arizona and New Mexico join. Formed in an ancient basin as a remarkably coherent body of neatly layered sedimentary rocks, the plateau has remained relatively unchanged even as the lands around it were compressed, stretched and deformed by powerful forces in the earth's crust.

Perhaps the most powerful testament to the plateau's long-term stability is the precise layers of sedimentary rock stretching back two billion years. In fact, the science of stratigraphy – the reading of earth history through its rock layers – stemmed from work at the Grand Canyon, where an astonishing set of layers have been laid bare from the Colorado River cutting across them. Throughout the Southwest, and on the Colorado Plateau in particular, layers of sedimentary rock detail a rich history of ancient oceans, coastal mudflats and arid dunes.

All other geographic features of the Southwest seem to radiate out from the plateau. To the east, running in a north–south line from Canada to Mexico, are the Rocky Mountains. Dominating the landscape of northern New Mexico, these towering mountains are a sanctuary for aspens and were once home to grizzly bears. The Rocky Mountains are the source of the mighty Colorado River, which gathers on the mountains' high slopes and cascades

For an insight into how indigenous peoples used this landscape, read *Wild Plants and Native Peoples of the Four Corners,* by William Dunmire and Gail Tierney.

Naturalist Terry Tempest Williams' bestselling book *Refuge* is a compelling personal insight into Mormon culture and the natural history of the Great Salt Lake.

CRYPTOBIOTIC CRUSTS: WATCH YOUR STEP!

Not many people pay attention to dirt, but in recent years cryptobiotic crusts have begun to attract attention and concern. These living crusts cover and protect desert soils, literally gluing sand particles together so they don't blow away. Cyanobacteria, one of the earth's oldest life forms, start the process by extending mucous-covered filaments into dry soil. Over time these filaments and the sand particles adhering to them form a thin crust that is colonized by algae, lichen, fungi and mosses. This crust plays a significant role in desert food chains, and also stores rainwater and reduces erosion.

Unfortunately, the thin crust is easily fragmented under heavy-soled boots and tires. Once broken, the crust takes 50 to 250 years to repair itself. In its absence, winds and rains erode desert soils, and much of the water that would nourish desert plants is lost. Many sites in Utah, in particular, have cryptobiotic crusts. Visitors to the Southwest have an important responsibility to protect these crusts by staying on established trails.

---

downward across the Southwest to its mouth in the Gulf of California. East of the Rocky Mountains, the eastern third of New Mexico grades into the Llano Estacado – a local version of the vast grasslands of the Great Plains.

In Utah, a line of mountains known collectively as the Wasatch Line bisects the state nearly in half, with the eastern half on the Colorado Plateau, and the western half in the Basin and Range province. This western province is comprised of numerous north–south mountains and valleys formed by a stretching of the earth's crust. It encompasses all of Nevada, plus western Arizona and the land from southern Arizona into the southwestern corner of New Mexico. Within these mountains and valleys there is scarcely any potable water, making this an extremely difficult region to cross for early explorers and wagon trains.

Northern Arizona is highlighted by a spectacular set of cliffs called the Mogollon Rim that run several hundred miles to form a boundary between the Colorado Plateau to the north and the highland region of central Arizona. The mountains of central Arizona decrease in elevation as you travel into the deserts of southern Arizona.

Landscape Features

The National Landscape Conservation Society's website (www.discovernlcs.org) describes Southwestern monuments, historic trails, scenic rivers and conservation areas.

Part of the fun of visiting the Southwest is learning to recognize diagnostic features of the landscape. In fact, it would be impossible to miss them because the area is mostly devoid of trees, and rocks stick out like sore thumbs. Plus the Southwest is jam-packed with one of the world's greatest concentrations of remarkable rock formations.

One reason for this is that the region's many sedimentary layers are so soft that rain and erosion readily carve them into fantastic shapes. But the full story is a bit more complicated because not any old rain will do. It has to be hard rain that is fairly sporadic. Frequent rain would simply wash the formations away, and between rains there have to be long arid spells that keep the eroding landmarks intact.

What makes landscape viewing so ultimately rewarding in the Southwest are the unbelievable ranges of colors. Scientists will tell you how the colors derive from the unique mineral composition of each rock type, but most visitors to the parks are content to stand on the rim of the Grand Canyon (p198) or Bryce Canyon (p453) and simply watch the breathtaking play of light on the orange and red rocks.

This combination of color and soft rock is best seen in badlands, where the rock crumbles so easily you can actually hear the hillsides sloughing away. The result is an otherworldly landscape of rounded knolls, spires and folds painted in outrageous colors. Excellent examples can be found in the Painted Desert of Petrified Forest National Park (p264), at Capitol Reef National Park (p443) or in the Bisti Badlands south of Farmington, New Mexico.

More elegantly sculptured and durable versions are called hoodoos. These towering, narrow pillars of rock can be found throughout the Southwest, but are magnificently showcased at Bryce Canyon National Park (p453). Although formed in soft rock, these precarious spires differ from badlands because parallel joints in the rock create deeply divided ridges that weather into rows of pillars. The outstanding examples at Bryce are further accentuated wherever layers of resistant limestone sit atop the pillars and prevent them from crumbling.

Under special circumstances, sandstone may form fins and arches. At Arches National Park (p436), where there's a remarkable concentration of these features, it's thought they resulted from a massive salt deposit that was laid down by a sea 300 million years ago. Squeezed by the pressure of overlying layers, this salt body apparently domed up then collapsed, creating a matrix of rock cracked along parallel lines. Erosion along deep vertical cracks left behind fins and narrow walls of sandstone that sometimes partially collapse to create freestanding arches.

Streams cutting through resistant sandstone layers form natural bridges, which are similar in appearance to arches. Three examples of natural bridges can be found in Natural Bridges National Monument (p419). These formations are the result of meandering streams that double back on themselves to cut at both sides of a rock barrier. At an early stage of development these streams could be called goosenecks as they loop across the landscape. Perhaps the Southwest's most famous example can be found at the Goosenecks State Park (p419).

The Rio Grande of New Mexico flows along a unique formation called a rift valley. Like the famous Rift Valley in Africa, this formation is the result of divergent forces breaking apart the overlying earth's crust. In New Mexico, the rift originated about 30 million years ago and the area along this zone of stretching dropped by as much as 25,000ft. The rift has obviously filled in considerably since then, but it remains low enough to chart the river's course.

Many of the Southwest's characteristic features are sculpted in sandstone. Laid down in horizontal layers like stacks of pancakes, these rocks create distinctive features such as flat-topped mesas. Surrounded by sheer cliffs, mesas represent a fairly advanced stage of erosion where all of the original landscape has been stripped away except for a few scattered outposts that tower over everything else. The eerie skyline at Monument Valley (p224 and p418) on the Arizona–Utah border is a classic example.

Where sandstone layers remain fairly intact, as in the ponderous walls of Zion National Park (p463), it's possible to see details of the ancient dunes that created the sandstone. As sand dunes were blown across the landscape millions of years ago they formed fine layers of cross-bedding that can still be seen in the rocks at Zion. Wind-blown ripple marks and tracks of animals that once walked the dunes are also preserved. Modern sand dunes include the spectacular dunes at White Sands National Monument (p369), where shimmering white gypsum crystals thickly blanket 275 sq miles. Here you can find living examples of features that are fossilized in sandstone rocks everywhere else in the Southwest.

Although the sedimentary rocks of the Colorado Plateau are unique for their degree of horizontality (a measure of the region's long-term stability), compression of the earth's crust also created some folds that are known as monoclines. Layers of folded rock are recognized by their tilted or even

Arches National Park has more than 200 sandstone arches.

A summer thunderstorm in 1998 increased the flow of Zion's Virgin River from 200 cubic feet per second to 4500, scouring out canyon walls 40ft high at its peak flow.

vertical appearance, and one of the best examples in the world is the 100-mile-long Waterpocket Fold (p444) in Capitol Reef National Park.

Looking beneath the surface, the 85-plus caves at Carlsbad Caverns National Park (p378) provide further proof that tropical seas once covered the region. These caves are chiseled deep into a massive 240-million-year-old limestone formation that was part of a 400-mile-long reef similar to the modern Great Barrier Reef of Australia.

Ecological Provinces

The Southwest includes all four types of desert found in North America, and although they look similar to the uninitiated, each of the four is remarkably different. Not only are the climatic conditions unique to each type, but the rugged, inhospitable nature of the landscape means that plants and animals must adapt to local conditions and may consequently have very limited ranges specific to each desert.

Located to the north is the Great Basin Desert, a high, cold desert that receives much of its precipitation in the form of winter snows and lies in the rain shadow of the Sierra Nevada and coastal ranges of California, which deprive the region of life-giving rainstorms. Utterly dominated by vast stands of unpalatable shrubs such as sagebrush and shadscale, this desert supports little life. The Great Basin Desert covers most of Nevada and Utah (except for the mountains in the center and northeast corner of Utah) and small portions of northern Arizona.

Lying just to the south, the closely related Mojave Desert barely extends into Arizona as a finger reaching upstream along the arid depths of the Grand Canyon. This desert includes some of the driest and hottest places in North America because it sits in a region where warm, descending air sucks up extra moisture. The Mojave Desert is home to drought-tolerant specialists such as creosote bushes and yuccas.

Much of southern Arizona is occupied by the Sonoran Desert, the richest North American desert in terms of plants and animals, beautiful examples of which can be found around Tucson. This is a land of giant saguaros and organ-pipe cacti. Perhaps because it receives rainfall during both the winter and summer seasons, this region is able to support many forms of life.

The Chihuahuan Desert is a Mexican desert that extends northward into south-central New Mexico and the southwest borderlands of Texas. Unlike the Great Basin, this desert receives much of its precipitation from summertime monsoons that move inland from the Gulf of Mexico. Enclosed by two Mexican mountain ranges and sitting on an elevated plateau, this desert province is fairly distinct from the other three desert types. One of its most characteristic plants is the agave.

The Southwest offers more than just deserts. Numerous mountain ranges are scattered throughout the region, including some high-elevation peaks and upland areas that have more in common with Canada than the deserts at their feet. Entire ranges are cloaked in aspen groves and verdant spruce-fir forests. Some mountains, such as the San Francisco Peaks north of Flagstaff, AZ, or the La Sal Mountains east of Moab, UT, are even high enough to support alpine tundra.

Geology of the Grand Canyon

Arizona's Grand Canyon (p198) is the best-known geologic feature in the Southwest and for good reason: not only is it built on a scale so massive it dwarfs the human imagination, but it also records two billion years of geologic history – a huge amount of time considering the earth is just 4.6 billion years old. The canyon itself, however, is young, a mere five to

Edward Abbey shares his desert philosophy and insights in his classic *Desert Solitaire: A Season in the Wilderness*, a must-read for desert enthusiasts and conservationists (see p438).

For the most comprehensive introduction to the Arizona desert, check out the excellent *A Natural History of the Sonoran Desert*, edited by Steven Phillips and Patricia Comus.

GETTING GROUNDED WITH ROCKS: A GEOLOGY PRIMER

All rocks are divided into three major types – sedimentary, igneous and metamorphic. Sedimentary rocks dominate the landscape of the Colorado Plateau and elsewhere in the Southwest. They form when sediments and particles cement together over time. When deposited by wind or water, sediments generally settle in horizontal layers that tell geologists a lot about the conditions under which they were formed. Limestone is a type of sedimentary rock that is composed almost entirely of calcium carbonate, which acts like a strong cement until softened by water. Sandstone consists of sand particles that stack poorly, leaving lots of room for calcium carbonate to penetrate, making this a very hard and durable rock. At the opposite end of the spectrum from limestone, mudstone (which includes shale) consists of flaky particles that stack so closely together that they leave little room for binding cement. Thus mudstone is often very soft and breakable.

Igneous rocks originate underground as molten magma. They may cool deep underground or erupt to the surface as lava or volcanic ash. Across the Southwest, volcanic outcrops are typically recent in origin. The region's best-known volcanic feature, New Mexico's Shiprock (p353), is only 12 million years old. Rarely encountered among the monolithic sedimentary rocks of the Colorado Plateau, volcanic features reach their greatest diversity and number in New Mexico.

Metamorphic rocks start out as either sedimentary or igneous rocks, then are transformed by exposure to intense heat or pressure, especially where the earth's crust buckles and folds into mountain ranges. Metamorphic rocks usually remain underground except where overlying layers of rock have eroded away. Examples include recently exposed outcrops in the bottom of the Grand Canyon, and mountain ranges in western Utah and Arizona known as turtlebacks because they rose to the surface after sediments slid off.

six million years old. Carved by the powerful Colorado River as the land bulged upward, the 277-mile-long canyon reflects the differing hardness of the 10-plus layers of rocks in its walls. Shales, for instance, crumble easily and form slopes, while resistant limestones and sandstones form distinctive cliffs.

The layers making up the bulk of the canyon walls were laid during the Paleozoic era, 570 to 245 million years ago. These formations perch atop a group of one- to two-billion-year-old rocks lying at the bottom of the inner gorge of the canyon. Between these two distinct sets of rock is the Great Unconformity, a several-hundred-million-year gap in the geologic record where erosion erased 12,000ft of rock and left a huge mystery.

The oldest rocks in the canyon are dark gray Vishnu schist and pinkish Zoroaster granite that formed when sediments and volcanic ashes showered into a shallow tropical sea. These were later compressed into metamorphic rock as the earth buckled and uplifted into a mighty mountain range that eventually eroded away. Between 1.2 billion and 825 million years ago the area was covered once again by an ocean that rose and fell more than 18 times, leaving deposits that metamorphosed into a rock unit named the Grand Canyon Supergroup. Above the Supergroup lies the Great Unconformity, and above that 225 million years of rocks were laid down by a long succession of marine, freshwater and desert environments. Whenever deeper waters prevailed, fine-grained clays and deep-sea oozes settled to the ocean floor to become thinly layered shales and limestones. As sea levels fell, coastal deltas, mudflats and swamps collected sediments that transformed into siltstones and sandstones. Well-known examples of these particular layers include Redwall and Kaibab limestones, the Hermit and Bright Angel shales, and the Coconino and Tapeats sandstones. Unlike the dark-colored rocks of the inner canyon, these upper layers are distinct in being pale buff or orangish.

The North Rim of the Grand Canyon is 1200ft higher than the South Rim.

WILDLIFE

The Southwest's desolate landscape doesn't mean it lacks wildlife – on the contrary. However, the plants and animals of North America's deserts are a subtle group and it takes patience to see them, so many visitors will drive through without noticing any at all. While a number of species are widespread, others have adapted to the particular requirements of their local environment and live nowhere else in the world. Deep canyons and waterless wastes limit travel and dispersal opportunities for animals and plants as well as for humans, and all life has to hunker down carefully in order to survive this place. It's easy to hurtle through in the comfort of a modern, air-conditioned vehicle, but only when you leave the confines of your car will you fully encounter this landscape and its many inhabitants.

Animals

REPTILES & AMPHIBIANS

An estimated nine million free-tailed bats once roosted in Carlsbad Caverns (p378). Though reduced in recent years, the evening flight is still one of the premier wildlife spectacles in North America.

While most people expect to see snakes and lizards in a desert, it's less obvious that frogs and toads find a comfortable home here as well. But on a spring evening, the canyons of the Southwest may fairly reverberate with the calls of canyon tree frogs or red-spotted toads. With the rising sun, these are replaced by several dozen species of lizards and snakes that roam among rocks and shrubs. Blue-bellied fence lizards are particularly abundant in the region's parks, but visitors can always hope to encounter a rarity such as the strange and venomous Gila monster. Equally fascinating, if you're willing to hang around and watch for a while (but never touch or bother), are the Southwest's many colorful rattlesnakes. Quick to anger and able to deliver a painful or toxic bite, rattlesnakes are placid and retiring if left alone (see also p543).

BIRDS

Over 400 species of birds can be found in the Southwest, bringing color, energy and song to every season. There are blue grosbeaks, yellow warblers and scarlet cardinals. There are massive golden eagles and tiny vibrating calliope hummingbirds. In fact, there are so many interesting birds that it's the foremost reason many people travel to the Southwest. Springtime is particularly rewarding as songbirds arrive from their southern wintering grounds and begin singing from every nook and cranny.

One recent arrival at the Grand Canyon is at the top of everyone's list of must-see wildlife. With a 9ft wingspan, the California condor looks more like a prehistoric pterodactyl than any bird you've ever seen. Kids squeal with delight and adults whoop with excitement as these birds swoop back and forth over canyon viewpoints. Pushed to the brink of extinction, these unusual birds are staging a minor comeback at the Grand Canyon. After several decades in which no condors lived in the wild, a few wild pairs are now nesting on the canyon rim.

Fall provides another bird-watching highlight when sandhill cranes and snow geese travel in long skeins down the Rio Grande Valley to winter at the Bosque del Apache National Wildlife Refuge (p355). And although the Great Salt Lake looks like a salty wasteland, it is in fact one of North America's premier sites for migrating birds, with millions of ducks and grebes stopping each fall to feed on tiny brine shrimp before continuing their southward journey.

MAMMALS

Sadly, the Southwest's most charismatic wildlife species were largely exterminated by the early 1900s. First to go was the grizzly bear. Long gone are the thundering herds of buffalo. Silent are the nights, whereas once upon a time howling wolves would send shivers down your spine. Absent are the mysterious tropical jaguars that crossed the border out of Mexico. Vanished with hardly a trace are the prairie dogs (actually small rodents) that once numbered in the billions and were North America's most abundant mammal.

Like the California condor, however, some species are being reintroduced into their former ranges. A small group of Utah prairie dogs were successfully released in Bryce Canyon National Park (p453) in 1974. Mexican wolves were released in the midst of public controversy into the wilds of eastern Arizona in 1998. And bighorn sheep and elk are being reintroduced to new areas.

Mule deer still roam as widely as ever, and coyote are seen and heard nearly everywhere. Small numbers of elk, pronghorn antelope and bighorn sheep inhabit their favorite habitats (forests for elk, open grasslands for pronghorns and rocky cliffs for bighorns), but it takes a lot of luck or some sharp eyes to spot these creatures. Even fewer people will observe a mountain lion, one of the wildest and most elusive animals in North America. These large cats are fairly common but shy away from any human contact.

Collared peccaries live in the arid deserts of southern Arizona and New Mexico. These hairy, piglike animals with tusks move in large packs, and females with young may aggressively charge humans. Long-tailed coatis, relatives of the raccoon, also travel in groups in the same region. They have long noses that help them track down small food items.

Plants

Although the Southwest is largely a desert region, the presence of many large mountain ranges creates a remarkable diversity of niches for plants. Perhaps the best way to begin understanding the plants of this region is to understand life zones and the ways each plant thrives in its favored zone. First developed in 1889 by C Hart Merriam after visiting the Grand Canyon, the life zone concept is now used worldwide.

The largest aspen tree in Utah weighs 13 million pounds, and has 47,000 stems arising from a single root system that covers 106 acres.

At the lowest elevations, generally below 4000ft, high temperatures and lack of water create a desert zone where drought-tolerant plants such as cacti, sagebrush and agave survive. Many of these species have greatly reduced leaves to reduce water loss, or hold water like a cactus to survive long hot spells.

At mid-elevations, from 4000ft to 7000ft, conditions cool a bit and more moisture is available for woody shrubs and small trees. In much of Nevada, Utah, northern Arizona and New Mexico, piñon pines and junipers blanket vast areas of low mountain slopes and hills. Both trees are short and stout to help conserve water. Piñon pines have short, paired needles and pitchy cones loaded with nutritious seeds (pine nuts!). Junipers have leaves that are reduced to scales and bluish rounded cones that resemble little berries.

Nearly pure stands of stately, fragrant ponderosa pine are the dominant tree at 7000ft on many of the West's mountain ranges. In fact, this single tree best defines the Western landscape and many animals rely on it for food and shelter; timber companies also consider it their most profitable tree. Ponderosa pines are easily recognized by their sweet-smelling bark, large cones and long needles in sets of three.

Many of the Southwest's most common flowers can be found in *Canyon Country Wildflowers*, by Damian Fagan.

High mountain, or boreal, forests composed of spruce, fir, quaking aspen and a few other conifers are found on the highest peaks in the Southwest. This is a land of cool, moist forests and lush meadows with brilliant wildflower displays. Quaking aspen is easily identified by its smooth white bark and shimmering leaves that turn fluorescent red and orange in the fall. Spruce is a Rocky Mountain tree that hopscotches into the Southwest on high mountaintops. To confirm this tree's identity, grasp a branch and feel for sharp, spiny-tipped needles that prick your hand.

Perhaps the biggest surprises of all are the incredibly diverse flowers that appear each year in the deserts and mountains of the Southwest. These include desert flowers that start blooming in February, and late summer flowers that fill mountain meadows after the snow melts or pop out after summer thunderstorms wet the soil. At times, the displays of flowers can be more overwhelming than your first glimpse of the Grand Canyon – you just have to find them at the right moment. Visitors' favorite flowers include red columbines with their bright yellow centers and red long-spurred tubes, crimson monkey flowers that brighten remote desert oases with a flash of unexpected color, and yellow evening primroses whose four large papery petals emerge in the evening like delicate origami.

A fully hydrated giant saguaro can store more than a ton of water.

Some of the largest and grandest flowers belong to the Southwest's 100 or so species of cacti; these flowers are one of the reasons collectors seek out cacti for gardens and homes. The claret-cup cacti is composed of small cylindrical segments that produce brilliant red flowers in profusion from all sides of their prickly stems. Even a 50ft-tall giant saguaro, standing like a massive column in the desert, has prolific displays of fragrant yellow flowers that grow high on the stem and can only be reached by bats.

NATIONAL & STATE PARKS

The National Park Service has a website with links to sites for every park and monument at www.nps.gov.

One of the most fabulous concentrations of national parks, wildlife refuges and monuments in all of North America can be found in the Southwest. While many visitors head for these stellar landmarks, equally interesting (though less crowded) attractions can be found in smaller state parks and wildlife sanctuaries throughout the region. Try to include a mix of both in your trip and learn more about what the Southwest has to offer.

ENVIRONMENTAL ISSUES

In an arid landscape like the Southwest, it comes as little surprise that many of the region's most important environmental issues revolve around water, and when push comes to shove nature gets the short end of the deal when water is scarce (as has been happening in recent years). Drought has so severely impacted the region that researchers are now warning that 110-mile long Lake Mead may run dry by 2021, leaving an estimated 12 to 36 million people in cities from Las Vegas to Los Angeles and San Diego in dire need of water.

Read Marc Reisner's *Cadillac Desert: The American West and Its Disappearing Water* for a thorough account of how exploding populations in the West have utilized every drop of available water.

Construction of dams and human-made water features throughout the Southwest has radically altered the delicate balance of water that sustained life for countless millennia. Dams, for example, halt the flow of warm waters and force them to drop their rich loads of life-giving nutrients. The Glen Canyon Dam on the Colorado River now captures nearly all of the 380,000 tons of sediment that used to flow annually down the Grand Canyon. These sediments once rebuilt floodplains, nourished myriad aquatic and riparian food chains, and sustained the life of ancient endemic fish that now flounder on the edge of extinction. In place of rich annual floods, dams now release cold waters in steady flows that favor the introduced fish and weedy plants that have overtaken the West's rivers.

In other areas, the steady draining of aquifers to provide drinking water for cows and sprawling cities is shrinking the water table and drying up unique desert springs and wetlands that countless animals once depended on during the dry season (see boxed text, p80). Cows further destroy the fragile desert crust with their heavy hooves, and also graze on native grasses and herbs that are soon replaced by introduced weeds. Unfettered development around the region's many cities and communities is increasingly having the largest impact, as uniquely adapted habitats are bulldozed to make room for more houses. Virtually every productive valley bottom in the Southwest has been dramatically

NATIONAL & STATE PARKS

Park	Features	Activities	Page
Arches NP	sandstone arches, diverse geologic formations	hiking, camping, scenic drives	p436
Black Canyon of the Gunnison NP	rugged deep canyon, ancient rocks	rock climbing, rafting, hiking, horseback riding	p402
Bosque del Apache NWR	cottonwood forest along Rio Grande, abundant cranes & geese each winter	birding	p355
Bryce Canyon NP	eroded hillsides, red & orange hoodoos & pillars	camping, hiking, scenic drives, stargazing, cross-country skiing	p453
Canyon de Chelly NM	ancient cliff dwellings, canyons, cliffs	hiking and backpacking (guided only), horseback riding, scenic overlooks	p224
Canyonlands NP	sandstone formations at confluence of Green & Colorado Rivers	rafting, camping, mountain biking, backpacking	p421
Capitol Reef NP	buckled sandstone cliffs along the Waterpocket Fold	mountain biking, hiking, camping, wilderness solitude	p443
Carlsbad Caverns NP	underground cave system, limestone formations, bat flight in evening	ranger-led walks, spelunking (experienced only), backpacking	p378
Dinosaur NM	fossil beds along Yampa & Green Rivers, dinosaur fossils & exhibits	hiking, scenic drives, camping, rafting	p512
Grand Canyon NP	canyon scenery, geologic record, condors, remote wilderness	rafting, hiking, camping, mountain biking	p198
Grand Staircase-Escalante NM	desert wilderness, mountains, canyons, wildlife	mountain biking, hiking, camping, solitude	p450
Great Basin NP	desert mountains, canyons, wildlife, fall colors	hiking, camping	p140
Mesa Verde NP	Ancestral Puebloan sites	hiking, cross-country skiing	p391
Monument Valley Navajo Tribal Park	desert basin with sandstone pillars & buttes	scenic drive, guided tours, horseback riding	p224
Natural Bridges NM	premier examples of stone architecture	hiking, camping, sightseeing	p419
Organ Pipe Cactus NM	Sonoran Desert, cactus bloom May & Jun	cactus viewing, scenic drives, mountain biking	p246
Petrified Forest NP	Painted Desert, fossilized logs	scenic drives, backcountry hiking	p264
Red Rock Canyon NCA	unique geologic features close to Las Vegas, waterfalls	scenic drives, hiking, rock climbing	p131
Saguaro NP	desert slopes, giant saguaro, wildflowers, Gila woodpeckers, wildlife	cactus viewing, hiking, camping	p238
San Pedro Riparian NCA	40 miles of protected river habitats	birding, picnicking, fishing, horseback riding	p256
Sunset Crater Volcano NM	recent & dramatic volcanic landscape	hiking, sightseeing	p197
White Sands NM	white sand dunes, specially adapted plants & animals	scenic drives, limited hiking, moonlight bicycle tours, range of walks	p369
Zion NP	sandstone canyons, high mesas	hiking, camping, scenic drives, backpacking, rock climbing	p463

NP – National Park; NM – National Monument; NCA – National Conservation Area; NWR – National Wildlife Refuge

altered by cows or development; these were once the most important habitats for birds and mammals. Arizona's San Pedro River is a notable exception that shows what's possible when a natural area is left intact – almost half of the bird species in North America have been recorded in this relatively tiny area!

THE DESERT LIFE   *Kim Grant*

Desert conditions comprise 70% of the Southwest, overwhelmingly shaping the people and lives of all who dwell there. Folks who survive under the harsh privation of these lands are often cast as mythical individualists. And Southwesterners do not disappoint.

Triculturalism presents difficulties to a homogenized understanding of the way each group sees the challenges of desert living within the context of their own culture and heritage. But the Southwestern ethos has been shaped by this very survival.

In a practical sense, the most compelling daily challenge is, quite simply, a lack of water. From the time when the Hohokam dug primitive irrigation canals to the early 1900s when legislation allowed dam building – to the detriment of historical sites and natural ecological areas – the pursuit and control of water has shaped the history of the Southwest. Ongoing struggles persist today between Native American groups vying for land rights; legion battle lines are drawn between environmental groups and industry.

Mother Nature is not cooperating to alleviate the epic struggle for water. Drought and forest fires have been persistent. Conservation efforts have, at best, a cursory impact, as cities such as Albuquerque and Phoenix continue to spread like a horizontal mushroom cloud.

For the observant, the four deserts – Mojave, Chihuahuan, Great Basin and Sonoran – are far from a wasteland. Slow down to witness a complex ecosystem that's light-years from the ordinary, juicy with cacti, playful jackrabbits, reclusive desert sheep and radiant flowers. When spring snow melts, runoffs provide enough moisture for efficient and adaptive flora to survive the driest seasons. So too are human inhabitants efficient and matter-of-fact about desert living, accepting cyclical deprivations in exchange for bursts of drama – only seen by an initiated eye.

Tamarisk was introduced from Eurasia to help stabilize stream banks, but this wispy streamside tree now covers more than one million acres in the Southwest and is a serious weed.

On mountain slopes high above the desert floor, forests are being cut at an unsustainable rate. The region's stately pine and fir forests have been largely converted into thickets of scrawny little trees. The cutting of trees and building of roads in these environments can further dry the soil and make it harder for young trees and native flowers to thrive, plus injuries to an ecosystem in an arid environment take a very long time to heal.

Down in the Grand Canyon one of the thornier perennial issues is the daily onslaught of planes and helicopters zooming back and forth on commercial sightseeing tours. In 2007, there were an estimated 70,000 flights into the Grand Canyon, mostly during the summer months, when you can expect to see a plane every two minutes in the busiest areas. Responding to a high level of visitor complaints, not to mention the fact that federal law mandates 'natural quiet' within the national park boundaries, a coalition of agencies is expected to issue an environmental impact statement and ruling sometime in 2008 on how to regulate these flights.

Arizona Wilderness Coalition's website (www .azwild.org) documents its ongoing efforts to inventory and secure new wilderness areas throughout the region.

Although there are too many examples of these issues to count, it's also worth noting a few triumphs. For instance, the Malpais Borderlands Group, a handful of ranchers on the southern border of Arizona and New Mexico, has successfully pushed for sound ranching techniques. The group's leader, William McDonald, a fifth-generation rancher from Douglas, AZ, was honored with a MacArthur Foundation Genius Award in 1998. And (hope beyond hope) there is a serious, growing discussion about the possibility of taking down the Glen Canyon Dam. Local environmental groups continue to fight on behalf of these and other issues throughout the Southwest, but everything depends on how the waves of newcomers moving to the Southwest will vote and contribute to the future of this marvelous region.

Southwest USA Outdoors

Skiing in Arizona? Scuba diving in New Mexico and Nevada? The answer to both is yes! The Southwest serves up as dizzying an array of outdoor experiences as you will find anywhere else in America. OK, so there's no ocean, but there is dam diving. And there's no surfing, but there are plenty of big lake shorelines sandy enough to double for a sunbathing beach – Tahoe, anyone?

Cowboys and girls will delight in galloping through Nevada's Great Basin, and if they arrive at the right time, they'll get to witness another of the Southwest's miracles: after a spring rainstorm this lonely brown desert gains splotches of color when the cactus bloom and brighten the arid land with bold pink, red and orange flowers.

Along with all these unexpected activities, the Southwest offers an all-you-can-play buffet of more mainstream outdoor pursuits. There is mountain biking atop slick red rock slabs in Moab, white-water rafting down the Grand Canyon's rollercoaster rapids and snowboarding through powder bowls in Telluride or Tahoe.

So whether you are on foot or on skis, in the saddle or on a bike, off the grid or at a lush spa, it's time to kick up some dust (or powder), flex and lengthen your physique, soothe your muscles, fill your eyes with more than you thought possible and allow the landscape to overwhelm you. Because at the end of the day, when you get down to business, it's the Southwest's mind-blowing scenery that makes its outdoor adventures so awesome.

> *Ski* (www.skimag.com) and *Skiing* (www.skiingmag.com) magazines give details on conditions, resorts and events.

SNOW SPORTS

All five states offer snow sports on some level. Yes, you can even ski in Arizona. Southwestern Colorado is riddled with fabulous ski resorts, while the Lake Tahoe area reigns in Nevada. In New Mexico head to the steeps at Taos and in Utah the resorts outside Salt Lake City – they were worthy of hosting the Winter Olympic Games!

Downhill Skiing & Snowboarding

Endless vistas, blood-curdling chutes, sweet glades and ricocheting half-pipes: downhill skiing and boarding is epic whether you're hitting fancy resorts or local haunts. The season lasts from late November to April, depending on where you are.

> Visit www.coloradoski.com when trying to decide where to ride powder in the state. The website lists 'ski and stay' specials, and provides resort details and snow reports.

Salt Lake City and nearby towns hosted the 2002 Winter Olympics, and have rip-roaring routes to test your metal edges. Slopes are not crowded at Snowbasin (p506), where the Olympic downhill races were held. The terrain here is, in turns, gentle and ultra-yikes. Nearby Alta (p494) is the quintessential Utah ski experience: unpretentious and packed with powder fields, gullies, chutes and glades.

New Mexico's Taos Ski Valley (p343) is easily one of the most challenging mountains in the US, while the Santa Fe Ski Area (p316), just 15 miles outside town, allows you the chance to ski in the morning and shop Canyon Rd galleries come afternoon.

In Colorado you'll want to head to Telluride (p397) or Crested Butte (p403). Both are wonderfully laid-back old mining towns turned ski towns, offering the opportunity to ride some of the best powder in the state by day, then chill in some of the coolest old saloons and groove to live music

DAM DIVING IN THE SOUTHWEST

The Southwest USA has always been a bit of a rebel. This is cowboy and Indian country after all, home to the Wild West of lore and birthplace of the nuclear bomb. So it's no surprise that when locals and researchers decided they wanted to scuba dive in New Mexico, Arizona and Nevada, this region figured out a way for them to do it, despite being a thousand miles from the closest ocean.

How? Enter the National Park Service's Submerged Resources Center (SRC), an elite group of underwater archaeologists based in Santa Fe. The SRC team dive in dams around the region.

Why? The region's dams are filled with all sorts of archaeological wonders, from a crashed B-29 bomber to sandstone towers and ancient cliff dwellings, all of which have been covered up by the harnessing of nearly all the Southwest's water supplies by dams. So scientists descend into these huge artificial bodies of water to catalog and maintain these submerged artifacts.

Dam diving isn't limited to research trips, however. Tourists with scuba certification can participate too. A host of dive shops lead tours, which provide adventurous divers with an opportunity to explore some of the least visited dive sites in the US. And we have to admit, it's pretty damn cool to experience familiar regional artifacts in a totally different environment – it's another surreal Southwestern experience.

'There's a definite wow factor, like you're really descending into another world, which you are,' SRC archeologist Dave Conlin says. 'The dive communities are based around small mom-and-pop-shops, so there's an insider feel.'

Indeed many of the shops are located in small towns, and the surge in diving popularity has helped sustain their sagging economies, making this sport not only unusual but also economically friendly. It's also super green. By diving in an artificial setting – ie not on a living reef – you're taking the most ecofriendly option. You can't do much damage by accidentally slapping your fin against an abandoned old bomber, but you can kill a number of living organisms in a reef with just one swipe.

Here are our favorite Southwestern dive sites:

■ **Blue Hole, NM** (p279) This crystal-clear 81ft-deep artesian well is the number-one dive spot in the Southwest – some American colleges even take classes here. It's located 117 miles east of Albuquerque, water temperatures average in the mid-60s year-round – even when it's snowing – and the gorgeous blue water leads into a 131ft-long submerged cavern, which feels, well, cavernous. Blue Hole is just a few minutes off of historic Route 66 (US 40). Call the **Santa Rosa Dive Center** (☎ 505-472-3370; www.santarosanm.com; Hwy 40/US66, Blue Hole) to set up a dive. The shop is next to the hole.

■ **Colorado River & Lake Mead, AZ** Two dives are offered here: a river dive for novices and a trip to the bottom of Lake Mead for the truly adventurous (and experienced). The first dive is a shore-entry river dive that follows the Colorado River's swift-moving current downstream from Hoover Dam. The water here is up to 70ft deep. You should be looking for the rare humpback suckerfish. To dive in Lake Mead you will need to present expert technical diving certification. If you have the right card, however, this is one of the most interesting dives in America. Above the dam at Lake Mead, divers can explore the fuselage of a mostly intact B-29 bomber that crash-landed into Lake Mead in 1948 but was only located in 2001. Visit **Sin City Scuba** (Map pp104-5; ☎ 702-558-5361; www.sincityscuba.com; 3540 W Sahara Ave, Suite 553, Las Vegas) in Vegas to hook up either trip. It costs $465 to dive the bomber (www.divethe bomber.com) – yes, it's expensive, but it's a once-in-a-lifetime opportunity to relive this region's Cold War history – and a National Park Service–preserved site. River dives start at $150.

■ **Glen Canyon, UT** The beauty hidden behind Lake Powell's waters is phenomenal – entire sandstone towers and once dusty desert ground are now surrounded by water and inhabited by schools of hungry fish. It's a mesmerizing sight to see the natural world taken to this other level. Visit **Twin Fin** (☎ 928-645-3114; www.twinfin.com; 811 Vista Ave, Page, AZ) to set up a half-day trip – it costs $190.

after dark. For something completely local and as low-key as Colorado gets, check out family-run Wolf Creek (p384). Some swear it's home to the best powder in the state – it's not unusual for it to be above your waist in the steep tree-glades.

The Lake Tahoe area, straddling the Nevada–California border, is home to nearly a dozen ski and snowboard resorts. See p147 for more.

And then there's Arizona. Yes, you can ski. The snow isn't anything to write home about, but the novelty value may be. Head to the Arizona Snowbowl (p193) outside Flagstaff.

Ski areas generally have full resort amenities, including lessons and equipment rentals (although renting in nearby towns can be cheaper). Got kids? Don't leave them at home when you can stash them at ski school for a day. For 'ski, fly and stay' deals check out web consolidators and the ski areas' own websites.

Cross-Country & Backcountry Skiing

Backcountry and telemark skiing are joining cross-country skiing and snowshoeing as alternative ways to explore the untamed Southwestern terrain.

A must-ski for cross-country aficionados? Head to Utah's serene Soldier Hollow (p508), the Nordic course used in the 2002 Winter Olympics. It's accessible to all skill levels.

The North and South Rims of the Grand Canyon both boast cross-country trails. The North Rim is much more remote. On the south side, you'll find 18 miles of easy-to medium-difficulty groomed and signed trails within the Kaibab National Forest (p211).

The San Juan Hut Systems (p399) consist of a great series of shelters along a 206-mile route from Telluride, CO, to Moab, UT – the scenery is pretty fantastic too.

If you're an advanced skier looking for knock-your-socks-off adventure, definitely consider a heli-skiing adventure with Telluride Helitrax (see boxed text, p399).

HIKING

Conveniently, it's always hiking season somewhere in the Southwest. When temperatures hit the 100s in Phoenix, cooler mountain trails beckon in Utah and New Mexico. When highland paths are blanketed in snow, southern Arizona tenders balmy weather. Parks near St George in southwestern Utah offer pleasant hiking possibilities well into midwinter. Of course, hardy and experienced backpackers can always don cross-country skis or snowshoes and head out for beautiful wintertime mountain treks.

Planning

More and more people venture further from their cars and into the wilds these days, adding another reason beyond logistics for careful planning. Some places cap the number of backpackers due to ecological sensitivity or limited facilities. Reservations are essential in highly visited areas such as the Grand Canyon (p198), and during the busy spring and fall months in more seasonal areas like Canyonlands National Park (p421). Consider going to the less heavily visited Bryce Canyon National Park (p453), or Bureau of Land Management (BLM) lands and state parks, for a backpacking trip during busy months. Not only are they less restrictive than the national parks, but usually you can just show up and head out.

Backcountry areas are fragile and cannot support an inundation of human activity, especially insensitive and careless activity. The key is to minimize your impact, leave no trace of your visit and take nothing but photographs

The US Olympic ski team has its headquarters at Utah Olympic Park (p500) in Park City, UT, and this is one of the few places where tourists can pay to try the Olympic sports of ski jumping, bobsledding and luge.

With more than 300 golf courses, Arizona was ranked the number-one golf destination in North America in 2007 by the International Association of Golf Tour Operators – good for the tourism board but bad for environmentalists.

and memories. To avoid erosion and damage stay on main trails and use common sense and responsible backcountry ethics.

Safety

The climate is partly responsible for the epic nature of the Southwestern landscape. The weather is extraordinary in its unpredictability and sheer, pummeling force – from blazing sun to blinding blizzards and deadly flash floods. When there's too much water – the amounts necessary to scour slot canyons smooth – you'll drown. Too little water combined with unforgiving heat leads to crippling dehydration (see p542). A gallon (3.8L) of water per person per day is the recommended minimum in hot weather. Sun protection (brimmed hats, dark glasses and sunblock) is vital to a desert hiker. Know your limitations, pace yourself accordingly and be realistic about your abilities and interests. If a hot shower, comfortable mattress and clean clothes are essential to your wellbeing, don't head out into the wilderness for five days – plenty of day hikes offer access to quite stunning locations.

Solo travelers should always let someone know where they are going and how long they plan to be gone. At minimum, use sign-in boards at trailheads or ranger stations. Travelers looking for hiking companions can inquire or post notices at ranger stations, outdoors stores, campgrounds and hostels.

MOUNTAIN BIKING & CYCLING

As with hiking and backpacking, perfect cycling weather can be found any time of year in different parts of the Southwest. Southern Arizona is a perfect winter destination; Tucson (p234), considered a bicycle-friendly city, has many bike lanes and parks with bike trails. In spring and fall, Utah's Moab (p426) is an incredibly popular destination for mountain bikers wanting to spin their wheels on scenic slickrock trails. The area around Durango, CO, also has numerous trails (see boxed text, p387).

Local bike shops in all major and many minor cities rent bikes and provide maps and information. Visitor information offices and chambers of commerce usually have brochures with detailed trails maps. See p536 for info on rules, costs and so on.

Following are some choice mountain-biking spots.

Black Canyon of the Gunnison National Park

A dark, narrow gash above the Gunnison River leads down a 2000ft-deep chasm that's as eerie as it is spectacular. Head to the 6-mile-long South Rim Rd, which takes you to 11 overlooks. To challenge your senses, cycle along the smooth pavement running parallel to the rim.

The nearest town to this area is Montrose. For more info contact **Black Canyon of the Gunnison National Park** (☎ 970-249-1915; www.nps.gov/blca; 7-day admission per vehicle $8). See also p402.

Carson National Forest

Carson contains an enormous network of mountain-bike and multiuse trails between Taos, Angel Fire and Picuris Peak. The nearest town is Taos (p332), where you can rent bikes from **Gearing Up Bicycle Shop** (Map p333; ☎ 575-751-0365; 129 Paseo del Pueblo Sur; ☺ 9am-6:30pm) for $35 per day. For more info contact **Carson National Forest** (☎ 505-758-6200; www.fs.fed.us/r3/carson).

Four Corners Area

The Cortez area offers outstanding mountain-bike trails through piñon and juniper woodland over slickrock mesa. Be sure to try the 26-mile trail from

---

Along with archives that reach far and wide, www .cyberwest.com lists the region's best hiking, biking and skiing locations.

Adventures on America's Public Lands, edited by Mary Tisdale and Bibi Booth, flushes out the best-kept secrets of the American West.

Ben Guterson's *Seasonal Guide to the Natural Year* details when and where to catch the peak periods for flowers blooming, flocks migrating and the rituals of mating.

FLASH FLOODS: A DEADLY DESERT DANGER

Flash floods, which occur when large amounts of rain fall suddenly and quickly, are most common during the 'monsoon months' from mid-July to early September, although heavy precipitation in late winter can also cause these floods. They occur with little warning and reach a raging peak in a matter of minutes. Rainfall occurring miles away is funnelled from the surrounding mountains into a normally dry wash or canyon, and a wall of water several feet high can appear seemingly out of nowhere. There are rarely warning signs – perhaps you'll see some distant rain clouds – but if you see a flash flood coming, the only recommendation is to reach higher ground as quickly as possible.

Floods carry a battering mixture of rocks and trees and can be extremely dangerous, and a swiftly moving wall of water is much stronger than it appears. At only a foot high, it will easily knock over a strong adult. A 2ft-high flood sweeps away vehicles.

Especially during the monsoon season, heed local warnings and weather forecasts. Avoid camping in sandy washes and canyon bottoms, which are the likeliest spots for flash floods. Campers and hikers are not the only potential victims; every year foolhardy drivers driving across flooded roads are swept away. Flash floods usually subside fairly quickly. A road that is closed will often be passable later on the same day.

Dove Creek to Slick Rock along the Dolores River. Another good ride begins at the Sand Canyon archaeological site west of Cortez and follows a downhill trail west for 18 miles to Cannonball Mesa near the state line.

The nearest town to this area is Cortez (p394), where bike rental is available from **Kokopelli Bike & Board** (☎ 970-565-4408; www.kokopellibike.com; 30 W Main St; per day $20). For more info contact **Colorado Plateau Mountain Bike Trail Association** (☎ 702-241-9561).

Kaibab National Forest

Ride all or part of the still-evolving Arizona Trail, a 24-mile (one-way) trip to the south boundary of the Tusayan Ranger District in Kaibab National Forest (p211). It's an excellent, relatively easy ride. Tusayan Bike Trail is a moderate ride on an old logging road. The trailhead is 0.3 miles north of Tusayan on the west side of Hwy 64/180. Another 16 miles from the trailhead, Grandview Lookout has an 80ft fire tower with fabulous views. Three interconnected loops offer 3-, 8-, and 9-mile round trips.

It costs $20 per vehicle, $10 for bicyclists and pedestrians, for a seven-day pass on the trail. For more info contact the **Tusayan Ranger Station** (☎ 928-638-2443; www.fs.fed.us/r3/kai).

Moab

Bikers from around the world come to pedal the steep slickrock trails and challenging 4WD roads winding through woods and into canyon country around Moab (p426). The legendary Slickrock Trail is for experts only. This 12.7-mile, half-day loop will kick your butt. Intermediate riders can learn to ride slickrock on Klondike Bluffs Trail, a 15.6-mile round trip that passes dinosaur tracks. For a family-friendly ride, try the 8-mile Bar-M Loop.

Full-suspension bikes start at around $30 a day at **Rim Cyclery** (Map p429; ☎ 435-259-5333; www.rimcyclery.com; 94 W 100 N, Moab) – check out its museum.

San Juan Hut System

The 206-mile **San Juan Hut System** (☎ 970-626-3033; www.sanjuanhuts.com; huts per night $25) route stretches from Telluride (p397) west to Moab (p426), and is very popular with mountain bikers. The peaks surrounding Telluride offer awesome single-track routes and stupendous scenery. Beginners should try the 2-mile-long River Trail that connects Town Park with Hwy 145. For more

Visit www.go-utah.com/Moab/Biking and www.discovermoab.com/biking.htm for excellent Moab biking info. Both have loads of easy to access pictures, ratings and descriptions about specific trails.

Check out www.sanjuanhuts.com for info on the awesome 206-mile biking route between Telluride, CO, and Moab, UT – don't worry, you can ride it in stretches.

of a workout, continue up Mill Creek Trail, west of the Texaco gas station near where River Trail ends, and turn around at the Jud Wiebe Trail (which is for hikers only).

ROCK CLIMBING

If Dr Seuss had designed a rock-climbing playground, it would look a lot like the Southwest: a surreal landscape filled with enormous blobs, spires, blobs on spires and soaring cliffs. While southern Utah seems to have the market cornered on rock climbing, the rest of the region isn't too shabby when it comes to the vertical scene. Just keep an eye on the thermometer – those rocks can really sizzle during summer. Help keep climbing spaces open by respecting access restrictions, whether they are set by landowners harried by loud louts, or by endangered, cliff-dwelling birds that need space and silence during nesting season.

Otherwise, make a swift approach to central Arizona's Granite Mountain Wilderness, which attracts rock climbers in warmer months. Pack your rack for the rocky reaches of Taos Ski Valley, or pack your picks for the Ouray Ice Park, where a 2-mile stretch of the Uncompahgre Gorge has become world renowned for its sublime ice formations. Southwestern Utah's Snow Canyon State Park offers more than 150 bolted and sport routes. Zion Canyon has some of the most famous big-wall climbs in the country, including Moonlight Buttress, Prodigal Son, Touchstone and Space Shot. In southeastern Utah, Moab and Indian Creek make awesome destinations.

CAVING & CANYONEERING

Much of the Southwest's most stunning beauty is out of sight, sitting below the earth's surface in serpentine corridors of stone that make up miles of canyons and caves. Visit Carlsbad Caverns National Park (p378) and not only will you feel swallowed whole by the planet, you'll be amply rewarded with a bejeweled trove of glistening, colorful formations.

Canyoneering adventures vary from pleasant day hikes to multiday technical climbing excursions. Longer trips may involve technical rock climbing, swimming across pools, shooting down waterfalls and camping. Many experienced canyoneers bring inflatable mattresses to float their backpacks on as well as to sleep on.

Arizona and Utah offer some of the best canyoneering anywhere. The first canyoneers in the huge gashes of the Colorado Plateau were Native Americans, whose abandoned cliff dwellings and artifacts mark their passage. See for yourself at the many-fingered Canyon de Chelly (p224), accessible with a Navajo guide intimately familiar with its deep mazes.

The Grand Canyon (p198) is the mother of all canyoneering experiences, attracting thousands to its jaw-dropping vistas.

Then there are slot canyons, hundreds of feet deep and only a few feet wide. These must be negotiated during dry months because of the risk of deadly flash floods. Always check with the appropriate rangers for weather and safety information. The Paria Canyon, carved by a tributary of the Colorado River on the Arizona–Utah border, includes the amazing Buckskin Gulch, a 12-mile-long canyon, hundreds of feet deep and only 15ft wide for most of its length. Perhaps the best-known (though now highly commercialized) slot canyon is Antelope Canyon, near Lake Powell. You can also drive through magical Oak Creek Canyon (p188), with dramatic red, orange and white cliffs sweetened with aromatic pine. A nimbus of giant cottonwoods crowd the creek.

Zion National Park (p463) offers dozens of canyoneering experiences for day hikers and extreme adventurers, with weeping rocks, tiny grottoes, hanging gardens and majestic, towering walls.

Search for wilderness areas, wildlife refuges and trails at www.publiclands.org. You can also buy recreation permits, books and maps.

In *Between a Rock and a Hard Place*, Aron Ralston recounts his harrowing tale of amputating his arm with a pocketknife after getting trapped by a boulder while hiking an isolated Utah slot canyon alone.

Questions about critters, cacti and the best places to roam on the range are answered in the *Audubon Field Guide to the Southwestern States*.

WATER SPORTS

Few places in the US offer as much watery diversity as the Southwest. Bronco-busting rivers share the territory with enormous lakes and sweet trickles that open into great escapes. Whatever your interest, ability or experience, there are trips to fit your whim and watery toys of choice (raft, kayak or canoe). There are also numerous lakes throughout the Southwest to take a dip in.

White-Water Rafting & Kayaking

White-water rafting and kayaking – be it wild or mild – are the region's biggest water draws. The granddaddy of rafting trips is running the Colorado River through Arizona's Grand Canyon (p205). But if you don't have the time, cash or complete lack of fear needed to run the Grand, there are plenty of other rivers to try. Our pick would be Cataract Canyon (p430) through Canyonlands National Park. The rapids are almost as exciting as those in the Grand, but the trip is cheaper and takes less time.

For something a bit gentler, but still adrenaline-pumping, try rafting the Taos Box (p317) in New Mexico. Here you'll ride the Rio Grande through a steep-sided canyon – it's gorgeous.

In Utah, Moab (p430) serves as the hub for the state's most bashing rapids – more than a dozen outfitters run trips here. If you're disabled but want to run white water, head to Salt Lake City–based Splore (p428), which runs white-water adventures in the area.

In Southwestern Colorado the main white-water action takes place on the Animas River near Durango (p388).

If you would rather enjoy the views in real time instead of fast-forward, try a mellow float along the placid Green River in northeast Utah. It is another ideal gentle trip for canoes and follows John Wesley Powell's 1869 route.

Boating

Near the California–Arizona state line, a series of dammed lakes on the lower Colorado River is thronged with boaters year-round. Area marinas rent canoes, fishing boats, speedboats, water-skiing boats, jet skis and windsurfers. On the biggest lakes – especially Arizona's Lake Powell (p219) in the Glen Canyon National Recreation Area near the Grand Canyon and Lake Mead (p132) in the Lake Mead National Recreation Area near Las Vegas – houseboat rentals sleep six to 12 people and allow exploration of remote areas difficult to reach on foot.

The thrill of speed mixed with alcohol makes high-use houseboat areas dangerous for kayakers and canoeists. If you're renting a big rig, take the same care with alcohol as you would when driving a car. Check speed limits because of high-traffic or erosion dangers. Carbon monoxide emitted by houseboat engines is a recently recognized threat. Colorless and odorless, the

> Lake Powell contains about 8.5 trillion gallons of water and has 1960 miles of coastline, more than the coastline from Seattle to San Diego.

> Although it only took six million years for the Colorado River to erode the Grand Canyon, some of the rocks on the bottom of the canyon are two billion years old.

SLEEPING UNDER THE STARS: OVERNIGHT RAFT TRIPS

Calling all river rats... If you have the opportunity, there's no better place to do an overnight rafting trip than the Southwest. The Grand Canyon is the most famous multiday jaunt, but there are raft and camping adventures on rivers of all classes throughout the region.

So what's the lure? Well, it's pretty simple. Nothing quite matches sharing a campfire-cooked meal to the sound of lapping water, then sleeping under the stars on a sandy river bank. There is no more exhilarating experience than being jolted awake by the explosion of the day's first rapid minutes after you stepped into the raft, when you're still cold, stiff and bleary-eyed, or loving the way the sun's rays begin to warm the river as the early morning gives way to midday and the easier rapids become warm enough to float through on your back.

RANKING RAPIDS

White-water rapids are rated on a class scale of I to V, with Class V being the wildest and Class I being nearly flat water. Most beginner trips take rafters on Class III rivers, which means you'll experience big rolling waves and some bumps along the way, but nothing super technical. In Class IV water you can expect to find sharp drops, big holes (meaning giant waves) and stronger undertows, making it a bit rougher if you get thrown off the boat. Class V rapids are the baddest of all and should only be attempted by those with previous white-water experience, and who are strong swimmers – you should expect to be thrown out of the boat, and perhaps sucked under for a few moments. You'll need to know what to do and not panic.

Tip: if you do get thrown, float through the rapid, lying on your back – your life vest will keep you afloat. Point your feet downriver and keep your toes up. Protect your head and neck with your arms (don't leave them loose or they can get caught in rocks).

Of course the difficulty of the rafting will depend a lot on the kind of trip you're on – it's much harder to kayak a Class V rapid than it is to ride it out in a motorized platoon boat or even in one being oared by a professional. If you aren't a world-class kayaker, but want more interaction beyond being rowed down the river, try a paddle trip. On these, each person in the boat paddles, following the directions barked by the experienced guide at the helm of the ship.

The I to V class system applies to all Southwestern rivers except for a portion of one. The part of the Colorado River running through the Grand Canyon is just too wild to play by traditional rules, and hence requires a scale system – from Class I to Class X – all its own to classify its 160-plus rapids. Many of the Grand's rapids are ranked Class V or higher; two merit a perfect 10.

---

deadly gas is heavier than air and gathers at water level, creating dangerous conditions for swimmers and boaters. In recent years, several swimmers have drowned after being overcome by carbon monoxide.

Swimming & Tubing

> The single biggest drop on the Colorado River through the Grand Canyon is at Lava Falls – here the river plummets 37 stomach-churning feet in 300 yards.

Most lakes, and many reservoirs, in the Southwest allow swimmers. The exception will be high-traffic areas of the bigger lakes, where swimming is very dangerous due to the number of motor boats. It's not unusual to see locals swimming in rivers during the hot summer months, and tubing on creeks throughout the Southwest is popular. If you happen to see a bunch of people riding down a creek outside of your town, and wish to join, just ask where they go for their tires – where there's tubing in this region there is usually an entrepreneurial chap renting tubes from his van in the nearest parking lot. Swimming in lakes and rivers is generally free – although if you are in a state or national park or on a reservoir you may have to pay an entrance fee to enter the property itself, whether you choose to jump in the water or not.

HORSEBACK RIDING

Cowboys and Indians, the Pony Express, stagecoaches, cattle drives and rodeo riding – the legends are legion in the Southwest.

OK. You probably aren't looking to win the Derby, but horseback riding is quite popular in this region. Adventures range from one-hour rides for beginners (or experienced riders who just want to gallop a horse again) to multinight horse-packing trips with wranglers, cooks, guides and back-country camping. Another possibility is staying at a ranch where visitors go horseback riding on a daily basis, and the comforts of a bed and shower await at the end of each day.

> Check out www.dude ranches.com or www .ranchweb.com if your idea of a Southwestern vacation includes a week playing cowboy in the country.

Many towns have stables and offer horseback rides. During the winter, southern Arizona has delightful riding weather. Cattle drives, sunset dinner rides and horse-drawn wagon dinners are all popular options at stables around the region. There's nothing quite like seeing the stunning Monument Valley in Arizona just like John Wayne did: from the back of a horse.

Southwest with Kids
Jennifer Denniston

You've stuffed the bags and car with sunscreen, Frisbee, cooler, water sandals, hiking boots and hats. You've expounded eloquently to the kids about John Wesley Powell's one-armed exploration of the Colorado River and the age of dinosaurs, and have read books about Mormons, cowboys, trappers and miners. You've watched John Wayne and Clint Eastwood movies and have patiently explained that yes, roadrunners really do exist, and no, they don't say 'beep-beep.' You've got a plan, an itinerary, a schedule.

But now you've been in the car for hours, belting out *Grease* tunes and playing car bingo, and the whining and bickering in the backseat is beginning to give you a headache. You remember the guy at the gas station talking about petroglyphs out here somewhere, so you turn down a road you think he mentioned, and soon the pavement ends. Discussions ensue about flat tires and what if someone gets hurt out here in the middle of nowhere? A creek runs along the dirt road, and cottonwoods shade your drive. You pull over, pile out, stretch. One kid digs out the fly-rod, the littlest cautiously approaches the shallow water. It's hot and dusty, and there's nobody around for miles. Hours pass, and you never do find those petroglyphs. In fact, you don't find much of anything.

No, you probably won't make it to that national park tomorrow and no, you definitely won't pull into a motel in time for dinner and a swim. You may not even have a chance to wipe the red dirt off their faces. But when you put the kids to bed, perhaps carrying their exhausted bodies from the car, remember it's the journey, not the destination. We can tell you where to go and what to do with the kids, and there's plenty to recommend, but in the end, the best part of the iconic American Southwest is its Nothing.

For more on traveling with little ones, check out Lonely Planet's *Travel with Children*.

BRINGING THE KIDS

Long drives, unforgiving desert landscapes and stifling summer heat can be a challenge for parents. The rewards, however, can be found in the most mundane of activities – an afternoon splashing in a creek in New Mexico's Jemez Mountains (p302), picnicking on the edge of the Grand Canyon in Kaibab National Forest (p211), watching an old Western on the big screen at Parry Lodge's Old Barn Playhouse (p474) in Kanab, UT. To make it even more enticing, the region's geology, human history and wildlife, accessible in concrete ways at every turn, make the Southwest as educational as it is fun – kids learn without even trying.

Planning Ahead

Perhaps the most difficult part of a family trip to this region will be deciding where to go and avoiding the temptation to squeeze in too much. Distances are deceptive, and any one state could easily fill the standard two-week family vacation. While it's tempting to plan a loop that has you hopping from historical site to Native American pueblo, from white-water rafting to gold panning, resist the urge to do too much. You'll return home with photographs of places you can't remember, Utah will blur with Arizona, and the kids will come away with a desperate aversion to the car.

Instead, choose a handful of primary destinations, such as major cities, national parks and centers for outdoor recreation, to serve as the backbone of

Children aged five to 17 can participate in more than 100 programs, ranging from Outdoor Yoga to the Outdoor Leadership Challenge, from African Rhythms to Mountain Photography, at the well-respected Telluride Academy (www.tellurideacademy.com) in Colorado.

TOP 10 PLACES OF INTEREST ALONG THE WAY

■ Petrified Forest National Park (AZ; p264)

■ Lees Ferry (AZ; p217)

■ Goblin Valley State Park (UT; p440)

■ Tent Rocks National Monument (NM; p302)

■ Thanksgiving Point (UT; p485)

■ Lake Mead and Hoover Dam (NV; p132)

■ Slide Rock State Park (AZ; p189)

■ El Morro National Monument (NM; p275)

■ Capulin Volcano National Monument (NM; p349)

■ Snow Canyon State Park (UT; p478)

---

your trip. Then sit down with the map and connect these dots with a flexible driving plan that includes potential stops at several places of interest. Book rooms at the major destinations and make advance reservations for horseback rides, rafting trips, scenic train rides and educational programs or camps, but allow a couple of days between each to follow your fancy.

While the Southwest offers many particularly kid-friendly cities, including Salt Lake City (p480), Santa Fe (p306) and Flagstaff (p189), its real charm lies in its small towns and vast expanses of nothingness. A few days in Taos, NM (p332), Bisbee, AZ (p252), Prescott, AZ (p175), Park City, UT (p498), Kanab, UT (p472), or a handful of mountain towns in Southwestern Colorado can rejuvenate the bodies and spirits of even the most scheduled family.

Small-town festivals, rodeos and state fairs can be an excellent umbrella under which to plan your trip. Some to consider are Salt Lake City's Days of '47 (p486); the annual Navajo Nation Fair (p227); Fiesta de los Vaqueros in Tucson (p240); the Great American Duck Races (p361) in Deming, NM; and any of Telluride's music festivals (p398). In New Mexico, especially, many Native American festivals and ceremonial dances are open to the public. See individual reservations and pueblos for details.

Throughout this book, we've used the child-friendly icon (🏊) to indicate attractions, sleeping and eating options that are geared toward families, to help make planning your trip a cinch.

Local arboretums, zoos, aquariums and museums offer fantastic family activities and educational children's programs – even if you don't live in town, you can register online.

What to Bring

Hands down, the most important thing for any parent to remember when traveling with kids is that treasured stuffed octopus your child sleeps with or the music box they fall asleep listening to every night. Whatever it is that helps your child sleep, absolutely do not forget it. Put post-it notes on the coffeepot, the kitchen sink, the door, the car's steering wheel, everywhere. Just don't forget it.

Beyond that, you will find most anything you need in any major city and in most small towns as well.

If you plan on hiking, you'll want a front baby carrier (for children under one) or a backpack (for children up to about four years old) with a built-in shade top. These can be purchased or rented from outfitters throughout the region (see listings in regional chapters). Older kids need sturdy shoes and, for playing in streams, water sandals.

Other things you'll want include towels (for playing in rivers, streams and lakes between destinations), rain gear, a snuggly fleece or heavy sweater

Nothing dampens little ones' travel spirits more than real or imagined boo-boos – always carry a first-aid kit with Benadryl, calamine (or similar anti-itch ointment), Neosporin, Band-Aids, tweezers (for desert pricklies) and children's Tylenol.

(even in summer, desert nights can be cold – if you're camping, bring hats) and bug repellent. To avoid children's angst at sleeping in new places and to minimize concerns about bed configurations, bring a Pak 'n Play for infants and sleeping bags for older children.

Flying

Children under two fly free on most airlines when sitting on a parent's lap. Remember to bring a copy of your child's birth certificate – if the airline asks for it and you don't have it, you won't be able to board. Ask about children's fares, and reserve seats together in advance. Other passengers have no obligation to switch seats and sometimes have no qualms about refusing to do so. Southwest Airlines' open seating policy helps avoid this.

Consider carefully before opting for the cheapest flight regardless of itinerary. It may be that the cost to you and your kids of arriving at your destination at midnight or having three connections is not worth the monetary savings. And always bring plenty of entertainment – portable DVD players with headphones are popular with some families – and snacks.

Ridin' the Rails

A ride on Amtrak, with its 2nd-floor glass-domed observation deck, tiny sleeper rooms and formal dinners, enchants young ones and can be an excellent alternative to hours strapped in a car seat. See p535 for details.

Alternatively, children and adults alike enjoy scenic rides on classic trains, many of them with vintage steam engines. Consider the following:

- Cumbres & Toltec Scenic Railway (p351)
- Durango & Silverton Narrow Gauge Railroad (p387)
- Grand Canyon Railway (p261)
- Heber Valley Historic Railroad (p508)
- Nevada Northern Railway (p139)
- Santa Fe Southern Railway (p318)
- Virginia & Truckee Railroad (p146)

Just Can't Wait to Get on the Road Again

While few parents feel compelled to belt out Willie Nelson's ode to the road, the right frame of mind, careful planning of the route and some smart packing can not only minimize backseat whining but make the drive as much a part of the trip as the destination.

Try not to squeeze too much in. Endless hours in the car rushing from site to site and hotel to hotel can result in grumpy, tired kids and frustrated parents. Stop often and stay flexible. Sometimes the best times on road trips are those moments when you're not doing much of anything but pulling to the side of the road and poking around. Bring sunshades for the windows, snacks, water, and a football, soccer ball or Frisbee – any grassy area or meadow is a potential playing field.

When restlessness sets in, surprise the kids with a trip bag filled with books on the Southwest, a special treat, a car-friendly toy and a game. Bring a journal, an enlarged Xeroxed map and colored pencils for each child. Kids can follow along on their map as you drive, drawing pictures on it of what they see and do, and record the trip in their journal. Remember favorite CDs, or more conveniently an iPod and an iTrip (car speaker connector). Books on CD (most rental cars do not have tape players) from your local library can help pass the hours as well.

Every state has different car seat regulations (see p93). Most car-rental agencies rent rear-facing car seats (for infants under one), forward-facing seats (from one to four or up to a certain height/weight) and boosters for

Discovery Programs (www.musnaz.org/education/discovery.html) at the well-recommended Museum of Northern Arizona in Flagstaff offer fantastic summer camps for children aged three to 18.

Go to www.grandcanyon.org or www.museumofnewmexico.org for an excellent listing of regionally focused children's picture, activity and chapter books.

Bathrooms are few and far between on the Southwest's highways and byways. Prepare kids for the possibility of potty stops behind a cactus, and always bring toilet paper!

$10 per day, but you must reserve these in advance. Clarify the type of seat when you make the reservation, as each is suitable for specified ages and weights only.

Catching Your Zs

Most hotels and motels offer cribs and roll-away beds, sometimes for a minimal fee. Ask about bed configurations, suites, adjoining rooms and rooms with microwaves or refrigerators. While many hotels allow children to stay free with adults, some can charge as much as $90 extra per night – always ask. Folks with babies should ask for rooms with bathrooms or closets large enough to set up a Pak 'n Play.

Full-scale resorts with kids' programs, lovely grounds, full service and in-house babysitting can be found throughout the region, but particularly in Phoenix and, to a lesser degree, Tucson. There are far fewer resorts in New Mexico – try Bishop's Lodge Resort & Spa (p321) in Santa Fe and the Native American–owned Hyatt Tamaya (p285), on the Santa Ana Pueblo, just north of Albuquerque. For the real Western-immersion cowboy experience, complete with trail rides through the chamisa, cattle wrangling and beans 'n' corn bread round the fire, consider a stay at a dude ranch, such as the Flying E Ranch (p174) in Wickenburg, AZ.

If it's late, you're tired and you don't want any surprises, head to a chain motel. Hilton perches at the high end of the scale, while Motel 6 and Super 8, usually the least expensive, offer minimal services, and Best Western is notoriously inconsistent. Best bets are Holiday Inn Express, Fairfield Inn & Suites and Radisson.

Finally, even the most novice campers will find beautiful campsites in national and state forests and parks throughout the region to be perfect for car-camping. You can't beat the flexibility and price, and kids love it.

Chow Time

While the Southwest offers the usual fast-food suspects, you may find yourself driving mile after mile, hour after hour without a neon-lit fast-food joint anywhere. Be prepared with snacks and, if appropriate, a cooler packed with picnic items.

Go to www.kidsinvegas.com for a complete listing of kid-friendly places in Las Vegas.

Renting a house or condominium (particularly popular at ski resorts) gives parents space after little ones are asleep and can be economical. Try Vacation Rentals by Owner at www.vrbo.com.

CATCH A FLICK '50S-STYLE

The first drive-in movie theater in the USA opened in June 1933 in Camden, NJ, and by the late '50s there were almost 5000 drive-ins in the United States. Today, in the age of multiscreen Cineplex America, only a handful still exist. Open spring and summer only, most don't charge for children 12 and under. So bring a cooler, snacks and a lawn chair and catch a flick under the desert sky '50s-style.

Apache Drive-In Arizona (☎ 928-425-4511; US Hwy 60, Globe); New Mexico (☎ 505-325-3925; 1411 W Apache St, Farmington)

DeAnza Drive-In Theater (☎ 520-745-2240; 1401 S Alvernon Way, Tucson, AZ)

Fiesta Drive-In (☎ 575-885-4126; San Jose Blvd, Carlsbad, NM) See p377.

Fort Union Drive-In (☎ 505-425-9934; 3300 7th St, Las Vegas, NM) See p279.

Motor-Vu Drive-In (☎ 801-394-1768; 5368 S 1050 W, Ogden, UT) See p506.

Redwood Drive-In Theater (☎ 801-973-7088; 3688 S Redwood Rd, Salt Lake City, UT)

Scottsdale Six Drive-In (Map pp158-9; ☎ 602-949-9451; 8101 E McKellips Rd, Scottsdale, AZ) See p170; in the Greater Phoenix area.

West Wind Glendale Nine Drive-In (☎ 623-939-9715; 5650 N 55th Ave, Glendale, AZ) In the Greater Phoenix area.

CAR SEAT LAWS

Arizona law requires that children five years old and younger sit in a car seat except on public transportation. New Mexico and Nevada require children under 60lb, and five- and six-year-olds who have outgrown their car seat, to ride in a booster seat. In Colorado, children aged four to six and under 55in tall must sit in a booster, but they can ride in a pick-up truck bed if the tailgate is closed and they are sitting down. Utah law requires children under eight years old to sit in a car seat or booster; children who are not yet eight but are taller than 57in can use the car seat belt alone.

Don't sacrifice a good meal or attractive ambience because you have kids. All but a handful of upscale restaurants welcome families and many provide crayons and children's menus. To avoid the dilemma of yet another fried meal, ubiquitous on kids' menus, create your own kid's meal – simply ask for small adaptations to the standard menu, such as grilled chicken with no sauce, a side of steamed vegetables or rice with soy sauce.

LAS VEGAS & NEVADA

Sin City with kids? Seems counterintuitive, almost laughable, but the city best known for white-hot lights and red-hot nights gave itself a makeover in the early '90s to become more family-friendly. Though it has since regained its original mojo as a destination for gamblers and swingers, Vegas still offers families a crazy, full-throttle, Americana kind of place to hunker down for a couple of days. State law prohibits people under 21 from being in gaming areas, and several casinos ban strollers, but a simple walk down the strip or a ride on the elevated train can be entertainment enough. Think of it as the sensory overload of Disney World without Mickey and with more seductive princesses. If you bring your wallet, a sense of humor and an open mind, Las Vegas won't disappoint.

While most Vegas stage shows offer decidedly adult entertainment, a handful are appropriate for families. Excalibur's Tournament of Kings (p108) features real horses, battling knights and medieval damsels in distress. Of the five Cirque du Soleil shows, Kà (p127) and Mystere thrill young audiences. Finally, in true Vegas over-the-top style, the nightly free Viva Vision light-and-sound show in downtown's Fremont St (p112) features 12.5 million lights under a four-block canopy.

For high-speed thrills, head to Adventuredome at Circus Circus (p108), the roller coasters at New York-New York (p109) and Speed (p110), at Sahara. A green screen takes you over the city, snatching the toupee off an Elvis impersonator, grabbing a bag of money in a casino – that kind of thing – and you bring home a DVD of your cyber-adventures. *Star Trek* fans (and future recruits) head to Star Trek: the Experience (p114) at the Las Vegas Hilton. Other kid-friendly spots include the Shark Reef (p109) at Mandalay Bay, the glass-encased MGM Grand Lion Habitat (p116) and Lake Las Vegas (p116).

Of course, there's more to Nevada than Las Vegas. Consider a visit to Great Basin National Park (p140), Valley of Fire State Park (p134) or a few days in Reno (p143) and Lake Tahoe (p147) – little fans of fast cars won't want to miss the National Automobile Museum (p143).

ARIZONA

The most famous of all Southwestern destinations is Grand Canyon National Park (p214). While both rims offer opportunities for kids to hit the trails, the North Rim and the bordering Kaibab National Forest are particularly popular

Kids love New Mexico's trademark *sopaipillas* – puffy fried dough dripping with honey and served with the meal to cut the chile's kick – but will want their chile on the side!

In Japanese restaurants, try miso soup (maybe hold the seaweed or scallions) with an extra rice bowl of cubed tofu to mix in – healthy, filling, tasty and no more than a few dollars.

SOUTHWEST WITH PETS *Becca Blond*

Traveling with pooch? It's not always easy. In fact, sometimes it can seem more difficult than riding in the car with two screaming kids – all that panting and hot doggie breath right in your face. Your horse is tired, and wants a carrot. Where can he sleep for the night? And what about if you have a bird or cat? First off, don't worry. When it comes to pet-friendly travel destinations, overall the Southwest is one of the best, as long as you pay attention to a couple of rules. Don't immediately tie your dog up outside the first restaurant you see. Instead ask about the local laws. For instance, if you tied your dog up outside a restaurant in Santa Fe while you ate at the restaurant, you could end up with a hefty fine; however, many shops allow dogs inside – it's something about pets and food that doesn't mix in this sitting.

More and more hotels accept pets these days, although some charge extra per night, others make you leave a deposit and still others have weight restrictions – less than 35lb is usually the standard. To not get hit with an extra $50 in dog-room fees, call the hotel in advance. Best Westerns are the most friendly of the chains toward dogs, with no weight limits or extra fees. One of the most unique pet-friendly options in the Southwest is in Santa Fe: head to the swank Ten Thousand Waves Japanese Resort & Spa (p321). The spa pampers humans with hot-stone massages and private mineral soaking tubs, while doggies get to choose from custom-sized beds, bones and treats.

If you're traveling with a horse, there are a couple of places that will accept your four-legged friend. One of our favorites is Echo Basin Ranch (p390), a low-key and affordable ranch just outside Mancos in Southwestern Colorado.

Dogs love to run, and you'd think there'd be no better place for you both to enjoy the outdoors than national park and forest land. But check first before you let your pet off the leash – many forests and park lands have restrictions on dogs. Other places, however, such as Kaibab National Forest (p211), near the Grand Canyon's isolated North Rim, are doggie paradise. Dogs are allowed to run off-leash, and there are loads of trails meandering through aspen-strewn meadows. It's also a good place to park the horse trailer and saddle up. In Albuquerque, many folks take their dogs on the Bosque Trail, which runs along a ditch parallel to the Rio Grande. Wide and flat, and sometimes filled with shallow, calm water, it's a great place to stretch your pet's legs (and your own). If you have a horse, this is a popular horseback-riding trail as well.

In Utah, Kanab (p472) is easily the pet-friendliest town in the region. It is home to the Best Friends Animal Sanctuary, a no-kill rescue center that's become famous for rehabilitating Michael Vick's pit bulls and for being featured on the popular TV show *Dogtown*. Just about every hotel – and even a few restaurants – allow dogs. Moab (p426) is another good town for pet-friendly

with families who enjoy the outdoors. Its shaded trails and higher altitude entice travelers intent on escaping the desert heat, there are plenty of meadows where children can run around, away from the danger of the rim, and it's almost guaranteed that you'll see mule deer or wild turkeys. See Lonely Planet's *Grand Canyon National Park* for more on traveling to the park with children.

For those with the time and willingness to explore the unpolished reality of the American West, a trip to the Navajo and Hopi Reservations, including the private and isolated Hopi communities of First, Second and Third Mesas (p228), Canyon de Chelly (p224) and the eerie landscape of Monument Valley (p224), can be a highlight. Kachina dances on the reservation are often open to the public, and tribe members sometimes personally invite visitors to other ceremonies.

Several old mining towns have successfully reinvented themselves as tourist destinations. In Wickenburg (p174), you can pan for gold at the Vulture Mine before settling into a Western-style hotel room. Tombstone (p250), a National Historic Landmark, embraces its Wild West past with daily shoot-outs at the OK Corral.

Flagstaff, with excellent parks, a pedestrian-friendly downtown and plenty to do in the area, is an exceptionally kid-friendly town and well worth a

Many casino hotels have height restrictions at pools, so ask when making reservations. The wave machine at Mandalay Bay, while certainly enticing, scrapes little knees – we like the multipool complex at MGM Grand.

lodging in Utah. If you need to stay in Salt Lake City, the Hotel Monaco (p486) pampers dogs, cats and even birds with a toy and souvenir water bowl upon check-in.

Colorado has always been a pet-friendly state, and the southwestern corner is no exception. With lots of wild open spaces, it is also filled with dog-loving towns such as Durango (p386), where pooches are allowed in nearly all the shops; Telluride (p397), where you'll see many canines chilling outside in the bar; and Silverton (p405), where dogs frequently wander the unpaved streets at their leisure.

In Arizona, the energy in Sedona (p181) is as positive for your dog as it is for you. Several high-end resorts here compete to outdo each other with pet-pampering packages. If it's your dog's birthday, why not treat him to the Rouge & Pooch Package at the ultraswank Sedona Rouge Hotel & Spa (p186)? It includes turndown service with special biscuits and other frivolities. At equally luxe El Portal (p186), an intimate adobe hacienda, dogs of all sizes are welcomed with special beds and a basket full of treats.

Overall, Nevada is less pet friendly than other Southwestern states. You won't see too many dogs in Las Vegas, but if you venture way north to do your gambling in Reno, you can board your pup at Circus Circus (p144). Otherwise, you'll probably have the best luck getting your dog a bed at one of the budget chains – try Motel 6.

If you're planning a long day in the car, vets recommend stopping at least every two hours to let your dog pee, stretch their legs and have a long drink of water. If your dog gets nervous or nauseated in the car, it is safe and effective to give her Benadryl (or its generic equivalent) to calm her down. The vet-recommended dosage is 1mg per pound. We've used this on Duke – he gets very anxious in cars – and it really works.

The following websites have helpful pet-travel tips:

www.hsus.org/pets/pet_care/caring_for_pets_when_you_travel Top tips on travel with pets from the Humane Society; the site links to an online index of pet-friendly hotels.

www.horsetrips.com Traveling with a horse? Check out this site, which offers a state-by-state directory of horse-friendly motels, campgrounds and even B&Bs that will take care of your horse and you. The distance calculator is handy.

www.bestfriends.org The website for the Best Friends Animal Sanctuary may have you driving to Kanab just to adopt, but it also has a wealth of general info.

Also see p34 for an itinerary tailored for people traveling with pets.

few days' visit. Explore ancient Puebloan cliff dwellings at Walnut Canyon National Monument (p262), splash around in Oak Creek in nearby Sedona (p181) and catch an outdoor movie in Flagstaff's town square.

Outside Tucson, kids can see javelinas, bobcats and other local desert animals at the excellent Arizona-Sonora Desert Museum (p237). The compact Reid Park Zoo (p240) is another Tucson must for animal lovers. Old Tucson Studios (p238), once a film set, features shoot-outs and Wild West events galore. South of the city, relax in the quiet town of Patagonia (p249), spelunk at the magnificent Kartchner Caverns State Park (p255) and check out cacti at the stark and beautiful Organ Pipe Cactus National Monument (p246).

Intimate fields, cheap tickets and easy access to the players attract baseball fans young and old to Phoenix' spring training. See Phoenix for Children (p162) for other family-friendly fun in this popular tourist city.

Most public libraries offer children's rooms, story hours and weekend events – perfect for a rainy afternoon. Our favorites include those in Flagstaff, AZ (p190), Corrales, NM (p295), and Salt Lake City, UT (p482).

NEW MEXICO

In Santa Fe, the Museum of International Folk Art (p310) is particularly suited to kids. Though small, the Santa Fe Children's Museum (p318) features a pleasant outdoor activity area, and the bronze statues outside the galleries on Canyon Rd (p314) tickle little ones' imaginations. Take a day trip to the

---

TOP FIVE NATIVE AMERICAN SITES FOR FAMILIES

- Bandelier National Monument (NM; p304)
- Taos Pueblo (NM; p287)
- Acoma Pueblo (NM; p283)
- Mesa Verde National Park (CO; p391)
- Canyon de Chelly National Monument (AZ; p224)

Georgia O'Keeffe country of Abiquiú (p329) for a hike, or head to Chimney Rock at lovely Ghost Ranch (p329).

While most folks zoom through Albuquerque on their way somewhere else, families may want to stick around for a couple of days. Pack a lunch and ride to the top of the Sandia Mountains on the Sandia Peak Tramway (p294), get a bug's-eye view at the Rio Grande Botanic Gardens' (p296) Children's Fantasy Garden, and take in an outdoor concert at the Albuquerque BioPark (p296).

Several spots south of Albuquerque are well worth the drive. You can slide down soft sand dunes at White Sands National Monument (p369), descend 1567ft into Carlsbad Caverns (p378) and re-emerge to watch 250,000-plus bats exit en masse for their evening feast, and explore the remarkably undisturbed Ancestral Puebloan sites at Gila Cliff Dwellings (p361) in the spectacular Gila National Forest. Truth or Consequences (p356), with its hot springs and hole-in-the-wall charm, makes a fun place to kick around, and nearby Elephant Butte Lake (p357) is great for swimming, boating and fishing.

The Mineral Museum (p355) in Socorro wows kids with the state's largest collection of minerals, fossils and geological oddities. Older kids interested in outer space will enjoy the New Mexico Museum of Space History and the Tombaugh Imax Theater & Planetarium in Alamogordo (p366), as well as a trip to quirky Roswell (p373), the self-prescribed UFO capital of the world.

Peruse New Mexico Kids, available at grocery stores, museums, restaurants and bookstores (free), to find out what's going on for kids in Santa Fe, Taos and Albuquerque.

SOUTHWESTERN COLORADO

A surprising number of small-town gems with historic charm, easy access to the outdoors and a decidedly crunchy granola tone cluster in Southwestern Colorado; any one of them makes an excellent base for families. Take a few days, clear the itinerary and feel your blood pressure ease in that Colorado Rocky Mountain high in lovely Durango (p386), in tiny Silverton (p405), a National Historic Landmark set at 9318ft, or in Ouray (p404), with its stunning scenery and natural hot springs.

One of our favorite family destinations is Telluride (p397), a low-key alternative to glitzy Aspen and Vail. Telluride's Town Park makes a great place to hang year round, with a kids' fishing pond, a pleasant playground and access to a river walking trail. In the winter, ice skate or sled down the park's Firecracker Hill.

For intimate skiing with smaller crowds, head to under-the-radar Wolf Creek Ski Area (p384).

Ten Thousand Waves (p321), a Japanese health spa featuring private hot tubs nestled amongst the piñon trees in Santa Fe, welcomes children with child-size kimonos and kid-friendly snacks.

UTAH

Like the rest of the Southwest, much of Utah's draw for families is its spectacular landscape and the resultant breadth of outdoor recreation. National parks in the south, including Bryce Canyon (p453), Capitol Reef (p443), Canyonlands (p421) and Arches (p436), offer fantastic hiking, biking and rafting through classic red rock country, and it's easy to pass days and weeks enjoying the mountains, meadows and streams of the Wasatch Mountains (p492).

Just outside Salt Lake City, Big and Little Cottonwood Canyons (p494) offer lift-served hiking, and even little ones enjoy the boardwalk nature trail to Silver Lake (p497). For those looking for fast fun in the sun, the alpine slide at Snowbird (p496) twists and turns down 1300ft.

Houseboating on Lake Powell (p219) is hugely popular, as is rafting on the Colorado River from Moab (p430) and canoeing from Green River (p439).

Of the many ski resorts, Park City Mountain Resort (p501) attracts families with its convenient location and abundance of easy trails. At Soldier Hollow (p508), the cross-country ski course used in the Olympics is groomed and accessible to all levels; children also love the snow-tubing hill (p508).

Don't miss the excellent Utah Field House of Natural History (p512) in otherwise drab Vernal, and dinosaur enthusiasts will love the kitschy Ogden Eccles Dinosaur Park (p506).

There's lots for tots in Salt Lake City. Discovery Gateway (p485), the city's children's museum, is great and older kids enjoy the Clark Planetarium (p484) downtown. On a hot day, play in the Olympic Snowflake Fountain (p484) and enjoy an evening picnic and outdoor concert at the Gallivan Center (p489).

At the Wheeler Historic Farm (p485), kids can milk cows, churn butter and feed animals. Animal-lovers will also enjoy the Hogle Zoo (p485) and the Tracy Aviary (p485). Finally, This is the Place Heritage Park (p484), a 450-acre living history village, shows kids first-hand what it was like to live in Mormon-pioneer Utah. The park features special events, day camps (four-day sessions) and dinner theater.

Kids love the whimsical sculptures at the Shidoni Foundry (p316) north of Santa Fe – pack a picnic and head to the stream bank at the far end of the garden.

Performances at Santa Fe's Lensic Performing Arts Theater (p325) are often well suited to families, with children's plays, spirited dance troupes and holiday specials.

Las Vegas & Nevada

You know you're in Nevada when even gas stations have slot machines.

Like an ambitious starlet vying for your affections, fabulous Las Vegas is a wild ride, an outrageous fantasyland that promises to never let you down. In Sin City, fate is decided by the spin of a roulette wheel. All that glitters is often fool's gold in this high-octane desert oasis, where the poor feel rich and the rich lose thousands. Glamor's sweet stench is thicker than a blue-haired grandmother's cigarette smoke as she feeds dollar bills into the hot, hot slots, slugging gin and tonics and wearing a cleavage-revealing top that looks so wrong and yet so right. It's nearing dawn outside, but you wouldn't know it because the casinos' lights are brighter than an atomic-bomb blast.

When you tire of the ding-ding-ding of the slot machines, every road leaving Las Vegas leads through the desert's amazing wind- and water-carved landscapes. Or starting from Reno, aka 'the biggest little city in the world,' escape west to emerald Lake Tahoe on the California border; drive south to Nevada's capital, Carson City, and into the hills of Virginia City, where the Comstock Lode was struck in 1859; north across the vast *playas* of the Black Rock Desert; or east into the Basque-flavored cowboy country around Winnemucca and Elko.

Wherever you travel in the Silver State, remember that Nevada is weird. Anything can happen in a place where alien UFOs, atomic-weapons testing grounds and the 'Loneliest Road in America' are all part of the surreal landscape.

HIGHLIGHTS

■ **Best Place to be Sinful**
Even if gambling isn't your style, cut loose and visit Las Vegas' world-famous Strip (p107)

■ **Oddest Small Town**
It's a toss-up between time-warped Virginia City (p146) and Elko (p141), with its Basque restaurants, brothels and cowboy poetry festival

■ **Coolest Escape**
Hit the fairytale ski slopes and summer beaches of Lake Tahoe (p147) or drive up Wheeler Peak in Great Basin National Park (p140)

■ **Best Place to Get Lost**
Follow eerily deserted US Hwy 50, the 'Loneliest Road in America' (p137), through Nevada's heartland

■ **Hottest Place to be Seen**
Literally, it's the annual Burning Man 'experiment' (p148)

History

What history, you ask. Looking around, you are to be forgiven. Unlike the rest of the ruin-laden Southwest, traces of early history are scarce in the Silver State.

Early Native Americans lived in small bands and made seasonal migrations between mountains and valleys. Uto Aztecan–speaking Southern Paiutes inhabited the region around Las Vegas. Shoshone tribes lived in the east. The Northern Paiutes occupied much of the northwest, while Lake Tahoe was Washoe country.

Mid-19th-century trappers and traders on the Spanish Trail blazed through the USA's last frontier to be explored by Anglos. Jedediah Smith left what is now Utah in 1826 and traveled through the Mojave Desert into California, becoming one of the first Europeans to set foot in present-day Nevada. In 1843–44, US Army officer John Fremont made expeditions to extensively map the territory, which became part of the USA after Mexico's defeat in 1848.

In 1855, Mormon missionaries built and then abandoned a fort in the Las Vegas valley, where a natural-springs oasis flowed. In 1859, the richest vein of silver ever discovered in the USA, the Comstock Lode, was struck at Virginia City, which became the most notorious boomtown in the West. President Abraham Lincoln ratified Nevada as a state in 1864.

By the turn of the 20th century, plans had been made to link Los Angeles and Salt Lake City by train. In January 1905, the final spike, a golden one, was driven into the railroad line outside Jean, near the California border. On May 15, 1905, land lots were auctioned off in a frenzy to miners, ranchers and LA land speculators.

Once the dust settled, the city of Las Vegas was officially founded. Gambling dens, brothels and saloons soon sprang up beside the tracks, especially in Las Vegas' infamous Block 16 red-light district, which survived Nevada's bans on gambling and the supposedly 'dry' years of Prohibition.

In 1931, the state legalized gambling and dropped the divorce residency requirement to six weeks, guaranteeing an influx of taxable tourist dollars. The construction of Hoover Dam, completed in 1935, helped ease the economic pain of the Great Depression. Soon after WWII, the Cold War justified the Nevada Test Site. Monthly above-ground atomic blasts shattered casino windows in Las Vegas, while the city's official 'Miss Atomic Bomb' beauty queen graced tourism campaigns.

The federal government's grip on Nevada's public lands (it now owns an estimated 87%) was fiercely contested during the so-called 'Sagebrush Rebellion' of the late 1970s. Several Western states, Nevada foremost among them, banded together to force the federal government to relinquish control of all public lands within their borders. Their efforts largely failed, but fierce debates over land rights continue today.

Despite rapid growth, Nevada is sparsely populated, and its enormous potential for outdoor adventure activities and ecotourism is largely untapped. Most of the state's development has been at the cost of the environment, such as ever-expanding casino hotels and more heavily irrigated golf courses, a travesty in this parched desert state.

Climate

Across northern Nevada, peaks are covered by snow (the Spanish word 'nevada' means 'snow-capped') during winter, usually November to April. Much of southern Nevada is desert plateau that receives little annual rainfall. Each year Las Vegas enjoys more than 300 sunny days and averages just 4in of precipitation. The mercury hovers above 100°F during summer (locals say it's a dry heat, but it feels unbearably humid), while overnight temperatures dip below freezing, so always bring along a jacket. Winters are milder in the south than in the north, which can freeze solid for months at a time, but it's still cold

---

FAST FACTS

Population 2,565,382
Area 110,540 sq miles
State nickname The Silver State
Website www.travelnevada.com
Sales tax 6.5%
Average temps low/high Las Vegas Jan 36/56°F, Jul 78/104°F
Las Vegas to Reno 450 miles, 8 hours
Las Vegas to Great Basin National Park 310 miles, 5½ hours
Las Vegas to Grand Canyon, AZ 275 miles, 4½ hours
Las Vegas to St George, UT 125 miles, 2 hours
Las Vegas to Moab, UT 460 miles, 6½ hours

NEVADA

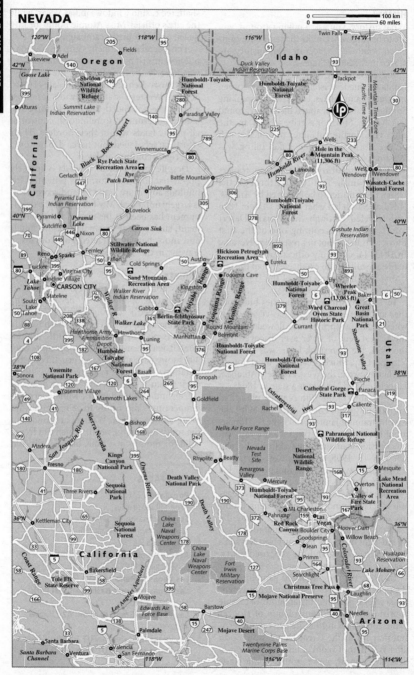

in Las Vegas during January, especially when strong winds blow. In spring and summer, thunderstorms can cause flash floods in the desert, even on the Strip!

Time Zone

Nevada runs on Pacific Time (eight hours behind GMT). That's one hour behind Utah, New Mexico and, during winter, Arizona. Otherwise, when daylight saving time applies (p529), Nevada and Arizona are in sync.

Information

The **Nevada Commission on Tourism** (☎ 800-638-2328; www.travelnevada.com) distributes an essential free state map at Nevada Welcome Centers:
Boulder City (☎ 702-294-1252; 100 Nevada Hwy, off US Hwy 93; ☷ 8am-4:30pm) Near Hoover Dam.
Laughlin (☎ 702-298-3321; 1555 Casino Dr, south of NV Hwy 163; ☷ 8am-5pm Mon-Fri, 8:30am-5pm Sat & Sun)
Mesquite (☎ 702-346-2702, 877-637-7848; 460 N Sandhill Blvd, off I-15 exit 122; ☷ 8am-4:30pm) Near the Utah border.

National & State Parks

At Great Basin National Park (p140), glaciers, ancient bristlecone pine trees and underground caves await exploration by the border with Utah. Near Las Vegas and Laughlin, Lake Mead National Recreation Area (p133) is a popular fishing, boating, swimming and weekend-camping destination. Much of Nevada's wild outback – for example, Red Rock Canyon (p131), Valley of Fire State Park (p134) and the Spring Mountains (p134) – is overseen by other governmental agencies:
Bureau of Land Management (BLM; ☎ 775-861-6400; www.nv.blm.gov; 1340 Financial Blvd, Reno; ☷ 9am-4:30pm Mon-Fri) BLM operates eight field offices across Nevada.
Humboldt-Toiyabe National Forest (☎ 775-331-6444; www.fs.fed.us/r4/htnf) USDA Forest Service manages nine ranger districts in Nevada.
Nevada Division of State Parks (☎ 775-684-2770; http://parks.nv.gov; 901 S Stewart St, Carson City) Manages two dozen historic sites and outdoor recreation areas, mostly around Las Vegas, Reno and in eastern Nevada.

For outdoor recreational trails throughout the state, visit www.nvtrailmaps.com.

Nevada Scenic Routes

For those who love wild and lonely places, almost all of Nevada's back roads are scenic routes. Nicknamed the 'Loneliest Road

in America,' famous Hwy 50 (p137) bisects the state. Request the *Hwy 50 Survival Guide* from the **Nevada Commission on Tourism** (☎ 800-638-2328; www.travelnevada.com) to find out how to get a free souvenir pin and a signed certificate from the governor. Plenty of shorter scenic routes abound in Nevada. The Las Vegas Strip (p107) is the USA's only nighttime scenic byway. Around Las Vegas, Red Rock Canyon (p131), the Valley of Fire (p134), Lake Mead (p132) and the Spring Mountains (p134) all have scenic drives, too. Lesser-known routes around Nevada include Lamoille Canyon Rd (p141), in the Ruby Mountains outside Elko; stairway-to-heaven Angel Lake Rd (p142) via Wells; and, near Reno, the Pyramid Lake Scenic Byway (p147) and the Mt Rose Hwy (p147), which winds down to Lake Tahoe. More rugged 4WD dirt roads race across the *playas* of the Black Rock Desert (p147), north of I-80. Truly in the middle of nowhere, the Extraterrestrial Hwy (p137) passes by infamous 'Area 51.'

Getting There & Around

Most drivers speed across Nevada on interstate highways I-80 or I-15. It takes less than two hours to drive 125 miles from Primm, on the California state line, to Mesquite near the Utah border via I-15; the best overnight stop along this route is Las Vegas. On I-80, it takes about 5½ hours to drive 400 miles from Reno to Wendover on the Utah state line; Winnemucca and Elko are the most interesting places to pull off for a night's sleep. US Hwy 95 may be the quickest route between Las Vegas and Reno, but it's still a full day's drive without much to see or do along the way. Likewise, the Great Basin Hwy (US Hwy 93) starting from Las Vegas and heading north to the I-80 corridor, can be a tedious trip; sleep over in Ely and detour to Great Basin National Park. Interstate speed limits range from 65 to 75mph, while Nevada highway traffic moves at 55 to 70mph. For road conditions, call ☎ 877-687-6237 or visit www.nvroads.com.

Las Vegas' McCarran International Airport (p130) frequently has cheap flights to the rest of the USA, from international gateway hubs as well as smaller regional airports. Car rentals in Las Vegas are more expensive than elsewhere in the Southwest. Greyhound (p535) bus and Amtrak (p535) train services are limited in Nevada, and hardly useful for getting around. Amtrak's *California Zephyr* follows

I-80 across northern Nevada, stopping in Reno, Winnemucca and Elko en route to Chicago from San Francisco Bay. **Hertz** (☎ 800-654-3131; www.hertz.com) rents cars at the downtown Reno train station.

For more information on transportation throughout the Southwest, see p536.

LAS VEGAS

pop 552,500 / elev 2178ft

Las Vegas is the ultimate escape. Time is irrelevant here. There are no clocks, just never-ending buffets and ever-flowing drinks. Look, there's a bum bumming cigarettes from a Prada-clad starlet. A bible-toting Elvis and a giddy couple that just pledged eternity in the Little White Wedding Chapel. A drunk guy surviving on his last dollar, and another hawking his first hip-hop album. A porn star saunters by a nightclub's velvet rope. Blink, and you'll miss it. Sleep? Fuhgeddaboutit.

The city demands a suspension of disbelief. So don't take it too seriously. Do like locals do: admit the city has its flaws, but learn to love it. Nothing here is built to last anyway. Change can be as sudden and unpredictable as the secret implosion of a vintage casino hotel after midnight. Like the shifting sand dunes of the Mojave Desert that surround the city, what's hot and what's not here can change in an instant.

An oasis in the middle of a final frontier, Sin City exists chiefly to satisfy the needs and desires of its visitors. Attracting almost 40 million tourists each year (more than the holy city of Mecca), Las Vegas is the USA's fastest-growing metro area and a last liberal port of opportunity for countless modern Americans seeking a fast fortune.

HISTORY

Contrary to Hollywood legend, there was much more at this dusty desert crossroads than railroad tracks, gambling dens and tumbleweeds the day mobster Ben 'Bugsy' Siegel rolled in and opened a glamorous, tropical-themed casino under the searing sun.

In 1829 Rafael Rivera, a scout for a Mexican trading expedition, became the first European to find the valley's natural spring, after which it became known as *las vegas* ('the meadows'). Hell-bent on doing God's work in Indian country, Mormon missionaries arrived from Salt Lake City in 1855, but abandoned their small fort just three years later. After the Civil War ended, the fort became a flourishing ranch.

The completion of a railroad linking Salt Lake City to Los Angeles in 1905 speared Las Vegas into the modern era. Quickie weddings and divorces, legal prostitution and championship boxing carried the city through the Great Depression. New Deal projects like Hoover Dam flowed into southern Nevada's coffers through WWII, which brought a huge air-force base, plus a paved highway to LA.

In 1941 Thomas Hull opened the Strip's first casino hotel, El Rancho Vegas. A building spree sparked by the Flamingo in 1946 led to mob-backed tycoons upping the glitz ante at every turn. Big-name entertainers such as Frank Sinatra, Liberace and Sammy Davis Jr arrived on stage at the same time as topless French showgirls in the 'Fabulous Fifties.'

Sin City started to clean up its act, starting with desegregation of the Strip in 1960. The high-profile purchase of the Desert Inn in 1966 by eccentric billionaire Howard Hughes gave the gambling industry a much-needed patina of legitimacy. The debut of the MGM Grand in 1973 signaled the dawn of the era of the corporate-owned 'megaresort,' and a building bonanza along the Strip that's still going on today. Every decade since has made Vegas more of a boomtown than ever before.

In 1999, Las Vegas voters picked criminal defense lawyer Oscar Goodman to be their mayor. The alleged 'barrister to butchers,' as a *Las Vegas Review-Journal* editorial once described him, has been a tireless proponent of the need to redevelop the city's rotten downtown core into a vital mixed-use area. Despite attempts at diversification, tourism and gambling still drive the Las Vegas economy.

ORIENTATION

Two interstate highways (I-15 and US Hwy 95) bisect the town. If it's your first visit, and you're driving, arrive at night so you can pull over before reaching city limits and admire the neon lights. Then, take the first exit and cruise the Strip, a four-mile stretch of Las Vegas Blvd.

I-15 parallels the entire length of the Strip, beginning near the Luxor's black pyramid and running north to the Stratosphere Tower. Downtown lies at the north end of Las Vegas Blvd, with the Fremont Street Experience streaking down the middle of historic Glitter Gulch. A desolate area along Las Vegas Blvd known as the 'Naked City' links downtown with the Strip.

More casino hotels are east of the Strip along Paradise Rd by the University of Nevada, Las Vegas (UNLV) campus; west of I-15, mostly along Flamingo Rd; and east of downtown on the Boulder Hwy. The outlying metro area consists of mini-malls and sprawling suburbs, like fast-growing Henderson and Summerlin.

Disorientation is a constant risk, whether searching for your hotel room, wending your way through a purposefully confusing casino, or just trying to remember where you parked the car. McCarran International Airport is southeast of the Strip, off I-215. Greyhound buses arrive downtown at the Plaza. For local transportation, see p130.

INFORMATION
Bookstores
Gamblers Book Shop (Map p112; ☎ 702-382-7555; www.gamblersbook.com; 630 S 11th St; ☺ 9am-5pm Mon-Sat) Stocks almost every book ever written about Las Vegas.

Get Booked (Map pp104-5; ☎ 702-737-7780; www .getbooked.com; 4640 S Paradise Rd; ☺ 10am-midnight Sun-Thu, to 2am Fri & Sat) In the LGBT-oriented Fruit Loop east of the Strip, pick up *QVegas* (www.qvegas.com) and *Out Las Vegas* (www.outlasvegas.com) magazines here.

Reading Room (Map pp104-5; ☎ 702-632-9374; Mandalay Place, 3930 Las Vegas Blvd S; ☺ 8am-11pm Sun-Thu, to midnight Fri & Sat) Indie bookshop for local-interest titles, guidebooks and maps.

Emergency
Police (☎ 911, non emergency 311)
Rape Crisis Hotline (☎ 702-366-1640)

Internet Access
At hotels, high-speed internet access (wireless or wired) usually costs more than $10 per 24 hours. Free wi-fi hotspots are found at some chain coffee shops and off-Strip at the airport and convention center. Cheap internet cafés are found inside souvenir shops on the Strip. If you didn't bring your laptop, try:

FedEx Kinko's (www.fedexkinkos.com) Downtown (Map p112; ☎ 702-383-7022; 830 S 4th St; per min 10-30¢; ☺ 7am-9pm Mon-Fri, 9am-5pm Sat; 🖳); East of the Strip (Map pp104-5; ☎ 702-951-2400; 395 Hughes Center Dr; per min 10-30¢; ☺ 24hr; 🖳)

Internet Resources
Cheapo Vegas (www.cheapovegas.com) Cheeky comments on the 'Sensational Strip' and 'Dingy Old Downtown.'
Las Vegas Logue (www.lasvegaslogue.com) Celebrity gossip, breaking headlines and reviews.
Only Vegas (www.visitlasvegas.com) The city's official tourism site.
Raw Vegas (www.rawvegas.tv) Programming 24/7, from daily news to reality vlogs.
VEGAS.com (www.vegas.com) Encyclopedic info – but watch out for advertorials.

Media
The conservative daily *Las Vegas Review-Journal* (www.lvrj.com) is Nevada's largest newspaper, publishing Friday's *Neon* entertainment guide. Free alternative tabloid weeklies include *Las Vegas Weekly* (www .lasvegasweekly.com) and *Las Vegas CityLife* (www.lasvegascitylife.com). Available in hotel rooms and at the airport, free tourist magazines like *Las Vegas Magazine + Showbiz Weekly* and *What's On* contain valuable discount coupons and listings of attractions, entertainment, nightlife, dining and more.

Medical Services
Harmon Medical Center (Map pp104-5; ☎ 702-796-1116; www.harmonmedicalcenter.com; 150 E Harmon Ave; ☺ 24hr) Discounts for uninsured patients; limited translation services.
University Medical Center (Map p112; ☎ 702-383-2000, emergency 702-383-2661; 1800 W Charleston Blvd; ☺ 24hr) Nevada's most advanced trauma center.
Walgreens The Strip (Map pp104-5; ☎ 702-739-9645; 3765 Las Vegas Blvd S; ☺ 24hr); Downtown (Map p112; ☎ 702-385-1284; 495 E Fremont St; ☺ 24hr) Call for prescription pharmacy hours.

Money
Every casino and bank and most convenience stores have ATMs. Fees imposed by casinos for foreign-currency exchange and ATM transactions are much higher than at banks.
American Express (Map pp104-5; ☎ 702-739-8474; Fashion Show, 3200 Las Vegas Blvd S; ☺ 10am-9pm Mon-Fri, to 8pm Sat, noon-6pm Sun) Currency exchange at competitive rates.

TIPPING
Dealers expect to be tipped (or 'toked') only by winning players, typically with a side bet that the dealer collects if the bet wins. Buffet meals are self-serve, but leave a dollar or two

LAS VEGAS & NEVADA

THE STRIP

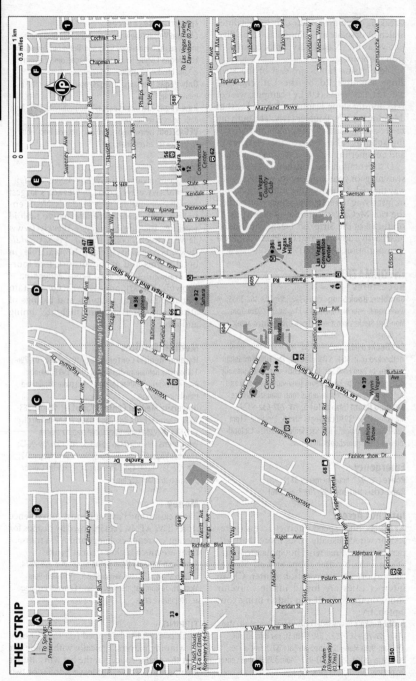

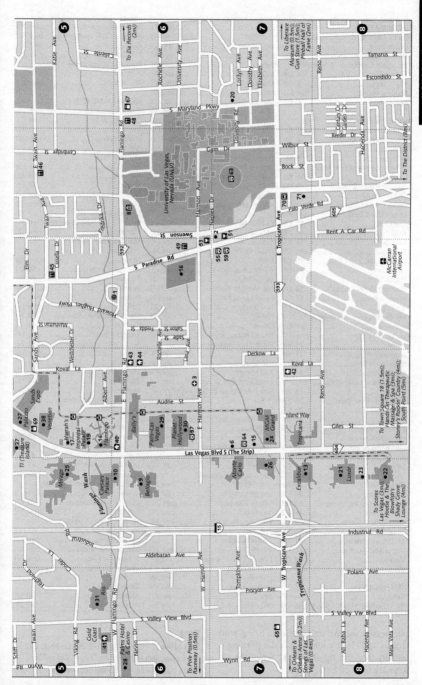

LAS VEGAS & NEVADA

per person for the waitstaff who bring your
drinks and clean your table. Valet parking is
usually free, but tip at least $2 when the car
keys are handed back to you.

Post

Post office Downtown (Map p112; 201 Las Vegas Blvd S
8:30am-5pm Mon-Fri); Strip Station (Map pp104-5;
3100 S Industrial Rd; 8:30am-5pm Mon-Fri)

LAS VEGAS IN...

One Day

Cruise the Strip, then hit the megaresorts for a taste of high-roller action. Ride the double-decker Deuce bus or the monorail between casinos, with stops for noshing and shopping. Zoom up the **Stratosphere** (p110) to try its thrill rides. After dinner at a star chef's **restaurant** (p121), catch a late **show** (p126), then party till dawn.

Two Days

Nobody's an early riser in Vegas. Shake off the Rabelaisian fête of the night before at a bunch **buffet** (p122). Indulge at a **spa** (p116) or chill poolside at your hotel – it's going to be another late night. Roll west to **Red Rock Canyon** (p131) for sunset. After a catnap, imbibe cocktails at an **ultra lounge** (p125) before hitting the **clubs** (p126).

Three Days

Sleep in again, then spend the afternoon **shopping** (p128) or at one of Vegas' **quirky attractions** (p117). Head downtown after dark to see where it all began. Visit the trippy **Fremont Street Experience** (p112) and the al-fresco **Neon Museum** (p113). After midnight, let it ride on the Strip one last time, grabbing a bite or a nightcap at the Peppermill's **Fireside Lounge** (p125) before sunrise.

Four Days

Don't even think about it.

Tourist Information

Las Vegas Convention & Visitors Authority (LVCVA; Map pp104-5; ☎ 702-892-0711, 877-847-4858; www .visitlasvegas.com; 3150 Paradise Rd; ⏱ 8am-5pm) Helpful hotline (6am to 9pm), but a not-so-helpful office opposite the convention center.

SIGHTS

The action in Vegas centers on casinos, but there are some fine museums and also thrill rides and amusements guaranteed to get your adrenalin pumping. The major tourist areas of the city are safe. However, Las Vegas Blvd between downtown and the Strip gets shabby, while Fremont St becomes unsavory too far east of Las Vegas Blvd. Avoid walking alone after dark.

The Strip

Ever more spectacular and more of a spectacle, the world-famous (or rather, infamous) Strip is constantly reinventing itself. As the cliché goes, it's an adult Disneyland, dealing nonstop excitement. Every megaresort is an attraction, with plenty on offer besides gambling. Open for business 24/7/365 is the rule at casino hotels – many places don't even bother with locks on their doors. Unless otherwise noted here, sights listed alphabetically below don't charge admission, offer free valet (tip $2) and self-service parking, are on the double-decker Deuce bus line and are wheelchair-accessible.

BELLAGIO

Built by Steve Wynn on the site of the legendary Dunes casino hotel, and inspired by a lakeside Italian village, the beautiful **Bellagio** (Map pp104-5; ☎ 702-693-7111; www.bellagio.com; 3600 Las Vegas Blvd S) is Vegas' original opulent, if parvenu, pleasure *palazzo*. Visitors are first dazzled by the choreographed dancing fountain show every 15 to 30 minutes during the afternoon and evening. Beyond the resort's glass and metal porte cochere are a few haute restaurants, a swish shopping concourse, a European-style casino and the **Bellagio Gallery of Fine Art** (☎ 702-693-7871, 877-957-9777; adult/student $17/12; ⏱ 10am-6pm Sun-Thu, to 9pm Fri & Sat), which showcases temporary exhibits by world-class modern artists. The highlight of the hotel lobby is Dale Chihuly's sculpture composed of 2000 hand-blown glass flowers in vibrant colors. Real flowers, cultivated in a gigantic on-site greenhouse, brighten countless ornate vases throughout the property. Near the lobby, the conservatory and botanical garden boast ostentatious seasonal floral arrangements, unbelievably installed by crane through a soaring 50ft ceiling.

BY THE BOOK

Except for poker, all casino games pit the player against the house, which always has a statistical edge. Over the long haul, you're guaranteed to lose everything you gamble. As such, think of gambling only as entertainment – for which you *do* pay a fee. Some casinos offer introductory lessons in poker, blackjack, craps and the like. You may ask the dealer for help and advice, for example, the odds on a particular bet at craps, or what the strategy is for the blackjack hand you've just been dealt. If you're winning, it's polite to give your dealer a 'toke' (tip).

Speaking of vices, prostitution is illegal only in Clark and Washoe Counties (including Las Vegas and Reno). Legalized, heavily regulated brothels are found in Nevada's more rural counties. Don't expect a romantic Old West bordello, though; most are just a few double-wide trailers behind a scary barbed-wire fence on the side of a lonesome highway. For a real-life peek behind the scenes, read Alexa Albert's highly conflicted *Brothel: Mustang Ranch and Its Women* or catch an episode of HBO's tacky *Cathouse*.

CAESARS PALACE

Thanks to ongoing megabucks renovations, **Caesars** (Map pp104–5; ☎ 702-731-7110; www.caesars .com; 3570 Las Vegas Blvd S) is redefining its swanky self, and it remains as impressive and quintessentially Vegas as ever. When it debuted in 1966, this Greco-Roman fantasyland captured the world's attention with its full-size marble reproductions of classical statuary and its cocktail waitresses clothed as goddesses. Bar girls continue to roam the gaming areas in skimpy togas, and the fountains are still out front – the same ones daredevil Evel Knievel made famous by jumping them on a motorcycle on December 31, 1967. Two imperial-sized casinos proffer over 100 card tables and thousands of slots, plus a state-of-the-art race and sports book with giant-screen TVs. The Colosseum showroom hosts mega-concerts. Stroll through the Forum Shops (p128), with its aquarium and odd animatronic fountain shows.

CIRCUS CIRCUS

On the bedraggled North Strip, you can't miss the enormous clown-shaped marquee or the tent-shaped, gaudily striped big top. From the outside, **Circus Circus** (Map pp104–5; ☎ 702-734-0410; www.circuscircus.com; 2880 Las Vegas Blvd S) looks pretty cheesy – and it *is*. Yet there's still some fun to be had here by all ages. Suspended above the casino is the Circus Circus Midway, where acrobats, contortionists and trapeze artists freely perform daily every 30 minutes until midnight. The revolving carousel of the Horse-a-Round Bar, made infamous by gonzo journalist Hunter S Thompson's *Fear and Loathing in Las Vegas*, has views of the stage. Cacophonous Slots A' Fun (p117) is

just a drunken stumble away. Out back of the casino hotel, the indoor amusement park, **Adventuredome** (☎ 702-794-3939; www.adventure dome.com; day pass over/under 48in tall $25/15, per ride $4-7; ⏰ hours vary), is packed with thrills. Must-rides include the double-loop, double-corkscrew Canyon Blaster and the Sling Shot packing 4Gs. Tamer garden-variety carnival rides are popular with wee ones.

EXCALIBUR

Faux drawbridges and Arthurian legends aside, the medieval caricature castle known as **Excalibur** (Map pp104–5; ☎ 702-597-7777; www.ex calibur.com; 3850 Las Vegas Blvd S) epitomizes gaudy Vegas. Down on the Fantasy Faire Midway are buried ye-olde carnival games, with joystick joys and motion-simulator ridefilms hiding in the Wizard's Arcade. The dinner show, *Tournament of Kings,* is more of a demolition derby with hooves than a flashy Vegas production.

FLAMINGO

Back in 1946, the **Flamingo** (Map pp104–5; ☎ 702-733-3111; www.flamingolasvegas.com; 3555 Las Vegas Blvd S) was the talk of the town. Its original owners – all members of the New York mafia – shelled out millions to build this unprecedented tropical gaming oasis in the desert. Mobster Benjamin 'Bugsy' Siegel named it after his girlfriend, a dancer named Virginia Hill called 'The Flamingo' for her red hair and long legs. Today, it isn't quite what it was back when its janitorial staff wore tuxedos; think more *Miami Vice,* less *Bugsy.* It's maniacally crowded inside the casino, where there are some low-limit tables and slots, plus free gambling lessons. Drop by during the madhouse afternoon happy hours to sling back massive margaritas in souvenir glasses. Out back is a wildlife habitat with magnificent gardens where Chilean flamingos and African penguins wander, and 15 acres of meandering pools, waterfalls and waterways are filled with swans, exotic birds and ornamental koi.

LUXOR

Only a faint echo of Egypt's splendid ancient city, the landmark **Luxor** (Map pp104-5; ☎ 702-262-4000; www.luxor.com; 3900 Las Vegas Blvd S) has a 40-billion-candlepower beacon visible to astronauts in outer space that shoots up out of its jet-black pyramid. Out front is a 10-story crouching sphinx and a sandstone obelisk etched with hieroglyphics. The interior is adorned with huge Egyptian statues of guards, lions and rams; sandstone walls with hieroglyphic-inscribed tapestries and grand columns; and an audacious replica of the Great Temple of Ramses II. The confusingly laid out casino has a sub-par spread of table games and slot machines.

MANDALAY BAY

Almost everything at **'M-Bay'** (Map pp104-5; ☎ 720-632-7777; www.mandalaybay.com; 3950 Las Vegas Blvd S) is a spectacle, if you know where to look. There's rock-star karaoke at House of Blues (p126), a headless Lenin statue at Red Sq (p125), world-class championship boxing at the events center (p127), vintage burlesque at Forty Deuce (p126), a constellation of star chefs' restaurants, and sky-high Mix (p125) lounge atop THEhotel (p120), where couples escape to the bathhouse (p116) spa. High-stakes gamblers will appreciate the classy casino, which feels almost as limitless as the credit line needed to play here, especially in the shark-infested poker room. Speaking of cartilaginous creatures, M-Bay's **Shark Reef** (Map pp104-5; ☎ 702-632-4555; adult/child $16/11; ☽ 10am-11pm, last entry 10pm) is a walk-through aquarium that's home to thousands of submarine beasties, with a shallow petting pool for young 'uns. Rare and endangered toothy reptiles on display include the world's last remaining golden crocodiles. Admission includes a free audio guide, or pay extra for a behind-the-scenes tour ($8). M-Bay is connected to Luxor by eclectic Mandalay Place (Map pp104–5) shopping mall.

MGM GRAND

With over 5000 rooms, the $1 billion **MGM Grand** (Map pp104-5; ☎ 702-891-1111; www.mgmgrand.com; 3799 Las Vegas Blvd S) retains the 'world's largest hotel' title. Owned by movie mogul Metro Goldwyn Mayer, the shimmering emerald-green 'City of Entertainment' co-opts themes from classic Hollywood movies. The casino consists of one gigantic circular room with an ornate domed ceiling and replicated 1930s glamor. The gaming areas – equal in size to four football fields – offer the full spectrum of stingy slots and table games, plus a race and sports book with VIP skyboxes next to a hot poker room. Out front, it's hard to miss the USA's largest bronze statue, a 100,000lb lion that's 45ft tall, perched on a pedestal ringed by fountains and Atlas-themed statues. Popular attractions include a lion habitat (p116), an arena (p127) for headliner concerts and sports events, and a deluxe assortment of eating and entertainment venues.

MIRAGE

With a tropical setting replete with a huge atrium filled with jungle foliage and soothing cascades, the **Mirage** (Map pp104-5; ☎ 702-791-7111; www.mirage.com; 3400 Las Vegas Blvd S) captures the imagination. Circling the atrium is a vast Polynesian-themed casino, which places gaming areas under separate roofs to envoke intimacy, including a popular high-limit poker room. Real and faux tropical plants add to the casino's elegant splendor. Don't miss the 20,000-gallon saltwater aquarium, with 60 species of critters hailing from Fiji to the Red Sea (including puffer fish, tangs and pygmy sharks), in the hotel registration area. Out front in the lagoon, a fiery faux volcano erupts hourly after dark until midnight, inevitably bringing traffic on the Strip to a screeching halt.

NEW YORK–NEW YORK

Give me your tired, huddled (over a Wheel of Fortune slot machine) masses. The frenetic mini-megapolis **New York–New York** (Map pp104-5; ☎ 702-740-6969; www.nynyhotelcasino.com; 3790 Las Vegas Blvd S) features scaled-down replicas of the Empire State and Chrysler Buildings, the Brooklyn Bridge and the Statue of Liberty, with a Coney Island–style roller coaster wrapped around the exterior. Claustrophobes, beware: this Disneyfied version of the Big Apple can get even more crowded than the real deal. The crowded casino attracts a mélange of mostly frat-boy humanity. Slews of slots and gaming tables are set against a backdrop of famous

'Nu Yawk' landmarks. Eateries and shops hide behind colorful facades from Park Ave, Greenwich Village and Times Sq. Upstairs, kids dig the Coney Island Emporium (p116) arcade. For cool virtual-reality sports arcade games, head to the upper level of ESPN Zone sports bar.

PARIS–LAS VEGAS

Adorned with fake Francophonic signs like 'Le Buffet,' **Paris–Las Vegas** (Map pp104–5; ☎ 702-946-7000, 877-796-2096; www.parislv.com; 3655 Las Vegas Blvd S) is a Gallic caricature that strives to capture the essence of the grande dame by re-creating her landmarks. Cut-rate likenesses of the Hotel de Ville, Opéra, Arc de Triomphe, Champs-Élysées and even the river Seine frame the property.

Just as in the French capital, the signature attraction is the **Eiffel Tower Experience** (Map pp104–5; ☎ 702-946-7000; adult/child $9/7; ☒ 10am-1am, weather permitting). Ascend in a glass elevator to the observation deck for panoramic views of the Strip, notably the Bellagio's dancing fountains. How authentic is the half-scale tower? Gustave Eiffel's original drawings were consulted, but the 50-story replica is welded rather than riveted together. It's also fireproof and engineered to withstand a major earthquake.

SAHARA

The Moroccan-themed **Sahara** (Map pp104–5; ☎ 702-737-2111, 888-696-2121; www.saharavegas.com; 2535 Las Vegas Blvd S) is one of the few old-Vegas carpet joints that have survived the megaresort onslaught. The *Arabian Nights* theme continues inside the casino, guarded by severe-looking statues of Middle Eastern sultans. Dealers hustle a unique variety of card games, with pretty bad odds. More compelling are the thrill rides, **Las Vegas Cyber Speedway & Speed** (Map pp104–5; ☎ 702-737-2111; single-ride/day pass $10/22; ☒ open at 10am daily, closing time varies). Speed is an electromagnetic roller coaster that slingshots to a top speed of 70mph, while the cyber-speedway Indy and Nascar simulators are so authentic they excite real Formula One drivers. Nearby, the Nascar Café displays monstrous 'Carzilla,' the world's largest stock car, designed by Dale Earnhardt Jr.

STRATOSPHERE

Standing over 100 stories, the three-legged **Stratosphere** (Map pp104–5; ☎ 702-380-7777; www.strato

spherehotel.com; 2000 Las Vegas Blvd S) is the tallest building west of the Mississippi. At its base is a lackluster casino with all the appeal of a redneck trailer park. What the place lacks in attitude, it makes up for in altitude, though. Atop the tapered **tower** (adult/child $14/10; ☒ 10am-1am Sun-Thu, to 2am Fri & Sat) is a revolving restaurant, a circular bar, and indoor and outdoor viewing decks offering the most spectacular 360-degree panoramas in town. To get there, ride the USA's fastest elevators, which ascend 108 floors in 37 ear-popping seconds. Up top, queue for adrenaline-pumping **thrill rides** (per ride $12-13, all rides incl elevator $28-34; ☒ 10am-1am Sun-Thu, to 2am Fri & Sat). Take your pick from Big Shot, which straps riders into completely exposed seats that zip up and down the pinnacle; Insanity, which dangles them over the tower's edge into thin air and spins them around; and xScream, a real dud. The rides don't operate in strong wind or rain.

TI (TREASURE ISLAND)

Yo, ho, whoa: although traces of the original swashbuckling skull-and-crossbones theme linger at this **casino hotel** (TI; Map pp104–5; ☎ 702-894-7111; www.treasureisland.com; 3300 Las Vegas Blvd S), TI's shift from family-friendly to bawdy and oh-so naughty epitomizes Vegas' efforts to put the 'sin' back in 'casino.' One-armed Playboy bandits have replaced the playful pirates, plastic doubloons and chests full o'booty. Visitors approach the property via a wood-bottomed bridge with hemp-rope supporting sides (for that 'authentic' piratey feel!) spanning artificial Sirens' Cove, where the spiced-up Sirens of TI show stages a mock sea battle between sultry temptresses and renegade freebooters, as their two ships – a Spanish privateer and a British frigate – face off on schedule, usually several times nightly.

VENETIAN
This facsimile of a doge's **palace** (Map pp104-5; ☎ 702-414-1000; www.venetian.com; 3355 Las Vegas Blvd S), inspired by the splendor of Italy's most romantic city, features roaming mimes and minstrels in period costume, hand-painted ceiling frescoes and full-scale reproductions of the Italian port's famous landmarks. Flowing canals, vibrant piazzas and stone walkways attempt to capture the spirit of La Repubblica Serenissima, reputedly the home of the world's first casino. In a city filled with spectacles, the Venetian is surely one of the most spectacular. Take a romantic gondola ride (adult/child/private $15/7.50/50) outdoors or through the Grand Canal Shoppes (p128). Notice that the Strip's skyline has a different look these days, now that the Venetian's sister resort, Palazzo (Map pp104–5), has opened next door, with even more elite shops and celebrity chefs' restaurants.

WYNN LAS VEGAS
Steve Wynn's signature (literally, his name is written in script across the top, punctuated by a period) **casino hotel** (Map pp104-5; ☎ 702-770-7000, 877-321-9966; www.wynnlasvegas.com; 3131 Las Vegas Blvd S) stands on the site of the imploded 1950s-era Desert Inn. The curvaceous, copper-toned 50-story tower exudes secrecy – the entrance is obscured from the Strip by an artificial mountain of greenery. Inside, the resort comes alive with vibrant colors, inlaid flower mosaics, natural-light windows, lush foliage and waterfalls. The sprawling casino is always crowded, especially the poker room that attracts punters

and pros. Acclaimed director Franco Dragone created Wynn's dreamy production show, *La Rêve*, in a specially constructed theater-in-the-round, where a million-gallon pool doubles as the stage.

Downtown
Downtown remains the heart and soul of old Vegas. The city's original quarter is often preferred by serious gamblers, and the smoky, low-ceilinged casinos have hardly changed over the years. As attractions, they've got little to offer nongamblers, not to mention kids, but their close proximity to one another is a plus. Most have self-parking garages (free three-or four-hour maximum stay if you validate your parking stub inside the casino at the cashier's cage). The double-decker Deuce bus stops near Fremont St.

DOWNTOWN ARTS DISTRICT
On the **First Friday** (☎ 702-384-0092; www.firstfriday -lasvegas.org) of each month, a carnival of 10,000 art lovers, hipsters, indie musicians and hangers-on descend on Las Vegas' downtown arts district. These giant monthly block parties feature gallery openings, performance art, live bands and tattoo artists. The action revolves around the **Arts Factory** (Map p112; ☎ 702-676-1111; 101-109 E Charleston Blvd), **Commerce Street Studios** (Map p112; ☎ 702-678-6278; 1551 S Commerce St) and the **Funk House** (Map p112; ☎ 702-678-6278; 1228 S Casino Center Blvd). For event schedules and shuttle bus info, visit the First Friday website.

BINION'S
This old-school **casino hotel** (Map p112; ☎ 702-382-1600; www.binions.com; 128 E Fremont St) is best known for its 'zero limit' betting policy and for being the birthplace of the World Series of Poker. Benny Binion, a savvy horse

---

FINDING VINTAGE VEGAS

Pay your respects to 1940s mobsters by rolling the dice at the classic **Flamingo** (p108) casino hotel, then ride a roller coaster through the 1950s **Sahara** (opposite) marquee and watch showgirls kick up their heels at **Jubilee!** (p127). Detour east of the Strip to the outlandish **Liberace Museum** (p117). Head downtown to Glitter Gulch to see where it really all began. Stroll down Fremont St, past the open-air galleries of the **Neon Museum** (p113). Sidle up to a low-limit table inside the 100-year-old **Golden Gate** (p112) casino hotel or a classy carpet joint like the **Golden Nugget** (p113). Play some poker in the back room at **Binion's** (above), where the no-limit tradition of the World Series of Poker began. Finish the night with a tiki cocktail at the Peppermill's **Fireside Lounge** (p125).

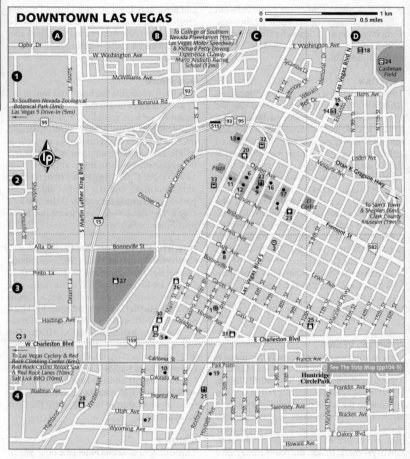

DOWNTOWN LAS VEGAS

trader, once quipped 'An honest deal makes its own friends.' Sadly, he has moved up to that great casino up in the sky, and his namesake gambling hall doesn't live up to his legend anymore.

FREMONT STREET EXPERIENCE

Streaking down the center of Vegas' historic Glitter Gulch gambling district, this five-block **pedestrian mall** (Map p112; ☎ 702-678-5600; www .vegasexperience.com; Fremont St, btwn Main St & Las Vegas Blvd) is topped by an arched steel canopy. Hourly from dusk until midnight, the 1400ft-long canopy turns on a six-minute light-and-sound show enhanced by 550,000 watts of wraparound sound and 12.5 million synchronized LEDs. The shows are ridiculously

cheesy, but mesmerizing enough to stop passersby in their tracks, especially drunks. Even better, the misting system built into the canopy provides cool relief on hot days.

GOLDEN GATE

A gambling hall and hotel has stood on the corner of Fremont and Main Sts since 1906, one year after the whistle-stop railway town of Las Vegas was founded. Drop by this snug **casino** (Map p112; ☎ 702-385-1906; www.goldengate casino.net; 1 E Fremont St), with its lively craps tables and double-deck blackjack being dealt to the herky-jerky sounds of old-fashioned piano music, to try one of the famous 99¢ shrimp cocktails and see the antique one-armed bandits on display near the deli.

GOLDEN NUGGET

Looking like a million bucks, this **casino hotel** (Map p112; 702-385-7111, 800-846-5336; www.golden nugget.com; 129 E Fremont St) has set the downtown benchmark for extravagance since opening in 1946. Thanks to Botox-like injections of style by impresario Steve Wynn, Fox's *Casino* reality TV-show stars Tim Poster and Tom Breitling and Landry's corp, it's still at the top of its class. No brass or cut glass was spared inside the swanky casino, known for its nonsmoking poker room; the RUSH Lounge, where live local bands play; and Gold Diggers nightclub upstairs for drinking, dancing and views of the Fremont Street Experience. Don't miss the gigantic 61lb Hand of Faith, the world's largest gold nugget, around the corner from the hotel lobby.

MAIN STREET STATION

This surprisingly elegant neo-Victorian **casino hotel** (Map p112; 702-387-1896; www.mainstreetcasino .com; 200 N Main St) is adorned throughout with notable *objets d'histoire*. Pick up a free *Guide to Artifacts, Antiques & Artworks* pamphlet from the hotel registration desk, then look for the art-nouveau chandelier from a Parisian opera house, stained-glass windows taken from movie star Lillian Gish's mansion, and even a graffiti-covered chunk of the Berlin Wall. The Pullman Grille (p124) is built around an ornate carved oak fireplace from a Scottish castle. A short walk south on Main St stands Buffalo Bill Cody's private rail car, which he used to travel the USA with his Wild West Show.

NEON MUSEUM

Plaques tell the story of each sign at these al-fresco **galleries** (Map p112; 702-387-6366; www .neonmuseum.org) of restored vintage neon signs. Look for the flashy 40ft-tall chap on horse-back, along with sparkling genie lamps, glowing martini glasses, 1940s motel marquees and more. For now, the biggest assemblages are found at the **Neonopolis** (450 E Fremont St), on the 3rd St cul-de-sac just north of Fremont St and at the old fort (see below). The permanent museum is a work in progress, although tours of its neon-sign boneyard, usually at noon and 2pm Tuesday through Friday, are available by advance reservation.

OLD LAS VEGAS MORMON FORT STATE HISTORIC PARK

Engaging for historians, these dusty adobe **ruins** (Map p112; 702-486-3511; http://parks.nv.gov /olvmf.htm; 500 E Washington Ave; adult/child $3/2; 8am-4:30pm Mon-Sat) mark the spot where Las Vegas was settled by Mormon missionaries in 1855. The visitor center showcases artifacts and photos from the early days. Outside are replicas of the first crops grown by Las Vegas Ranch, which resurrected the crossroads settlement after Mormons abandoned it.

East of the Strip
ATOMIC TESTING MUSEUM

During the atomic heyday of the 1950s, gamblers and tourists picnicked on downtown casino rooftops while mushroom clouds rose on the horizon. Buy your tickets to find out more about this unusual historical period at

LAS VEGAS & NEVADA

LOCAL VOICES: BONNIE FOGEL

Las Vegas resident and businesswoman Bonnie Fogel is a member of the advisory board for downtown's Neon Museum (p113).

Why did you become involved with the Neon Museum? I just liked the project, because it's art that is indigenous to Las Vegas. It's ours. Neon signage is what Las Vegas is all about. And somebody had the foresight to say, 'Hey, we can't lose this. This is a treasure.'

What's happening at the museum these days? We were able to rescue the La Concha Motel, designed by architect Paul Revere Williams, the first African American member of the American Institute of Architects. I think it's an important step for Las Vegas to think about its environment and preserving its buildings. The land on the Strip is so valuable that architecture doesn't get saved. It just gets torn down, then something else gets built.

What's the best thing about living in Las Vegas? What's the biggest challenge? People here are very interesting. For the most part, everyone is from somewhere else, and everyone has a story. It's still sort of the Wild West, and there are a lot of risk-takers. For me, the biggest frustration is that this is a new city, one that's still catching up to its growth.

Any last thoughts? All of the neon here is for everybody.

a replica of a Nevada Test Site guard station, then spend hours browsing this enormous Smithsonian-affiliated **museum** (Map pp104-5; ☎ 702-794-5161; www.atomictestingmuseum.org; 755 E Flamingo Rd; adult/child $12/9; ☒ 9am-5pm Mon-Sat, 1-5pm Sun), which also examines the long-term environmental effects of atomic testing. Watch black-and-white footage inside the Ground Zero Theater, mimicking a concrete test bunker.

STAR TREK: THE EXPERIENCE
Cruise on impulse power through the Museum of the Future exhibit, featuring authentic props, then queue for the live-action motion-simulator rides: 'Borg Invasion 4-D' and the classic 'Klingon Encounter' aboard – where else? – the starship *Enterprise*. 'Secrets Unveiled' tours go behind the scenes of this $70-million interactive **attraction** (Map pp104-5; ☎ 888-462-6535; www.startrekexp.com; Las Vegas Hilton, 3000 Paradise Rd; adult/child $43/36, incl tour $75/68; ☒ noon-8:30pm, ticket desk opens 11:30am; ☒). Stop by Quark's Bar & Restaurant to devour some 'Flaming Ribs of Targ' or to knock back a 'Phaser Shot' or two. The Deep Space Nine Promenade sells stuffed tribbles, alien ale and autographed collectibles found nowhere else in the Alpha quadrant.

HARD ROCK
Beloved by SoCal visitors, this trés-hip **casino hotel** (Map pp104-5; ☎ 702-693-5000; www.hardrockhotel .com; 4455 Paradise Rd) is home to one of the world's most impressive collections of rock 'n' roll memorabilia, including Jim Morrison's hand-

written lyrics to one of the Door's greatest hits and leather jackets from a who's who of famous rock stars. The Joint (p126) concert hall, Body English nightclub and Rehab summer pool parties attract a pimped-out, sex-charged crowd flush with celebrities.

West of the Strip
SPRINGS PRESERVE
On the site of the natural springs (which ran dry in 1962) that fed *las vegas* ('the meadows'), where southern Paiutes and Spanish Trail traders camped, and later Mormon missionaries and Western pioneers settled the valley, this educational **complex** (off Map pp104-5; ☎ 702-822-7700; www.springspreserve.org; 333 S Valley View Blvd; adult/child $19/11, admission to gardens & trails by donation; ☒ 10am-6pm, trails close at dusk; ☒) is an incredible trip through historical, cultural and biological time. Start your visit in the OriGen Experience museum, with its Natural Mojave and People of the Springs historical exhibits. The touchstone is the Desert Living Center, demonstrating sustainable architectural design and everyday ecoconscious living. Interpretive trails and gardens are worth a dalliance, as are the botanical gift shop and Wolfgang Puck's ecocafé.

PALMS
Equal parts sexy and downright sleazy, the **Palms** (Map pp104-5; ☎ 702-942-7777; www.palms.com; 4321 W Flamingo Rd) attracts loads of big-name celebrities (hint to the gossip-column obsessed: Paris Hilton and Britney Spears are just a few of the famously beautiful people who like to

shack up here) as well as a younger, mostly local crowd. Glam to the max, its restaurants, lounges and nightclubs are some of the hottest in town, especially now that the Playboy Club has been reborn here. The casino holds its own, with full-pay video-poker slots, table games, two poker rooms (one low-limit, one for whales) and a race and sports book with interactive TVs and specialty wagers. Other highlights at the Palms include a fabulous spa; a leather-clad tattoo studio; a 14-screen movie theater with IMAX capabilities; and a 1200-seat showroom, the Pearl (p126).

RIO

Craving *carnaval*? At night, the festive **Rio** (Map pp104-5; ☎ 702-777-7777; www.playrio.com; 3700 W Flamingo Rd) puts on the hourly free *Masquerade Show in the Sky*, a corny spectacle of floats, clowns, musicians and dancers. You can even ride along and have a souvenir photo taken in one of the floats ($13, reservations required). Forget about fun and games, though, in the cut-throat poker room, home of the World Series of Poker finals (p118). Ringed around the casino and its slot machines are outstanding buffets, plus the Chippendales Theater for bachelorette parties and Lucky Strike Lanes (right).

POLE POSITION RACEWAY

Dreamed up by Nascar and Supercross champs and modeled on Formula 1 road courses, this European-style **raceway** (off Map pp104-5; ☎ 702-227-7223; www.racep2r.com; 4175 S Arville St, off W Flamingo Rd; membership $5, race $22-25; ☯ 10am-midnight Sun-Thu, to 1am Fri & Sat) boasts the USA's fastest indoor go-karts (up to 45mph). Speed demons must be at least 48in/56in tall to drive the junior/adult karts. An upstairs viewing room has billiards tables, arcade games and plasma-screen TVs.

Greater Las Vegas
CLARK COUNTY MUSEUM

On the valley's outskirts, this humble but jam-packed historical **museum** (off Map p112; ☎ 702-455-7955; 1830 S Boulder Hwy, Henderson; adult/child $1.50/1; ☯ 9am-4:30pm; ♿) merits a quick stop en route to Hoover Dam. Explore images of Las Vegas as an ancient sea, Native American camp and Western frontier town, then step onto Heritage St and walk through early-20th-century houses, an antique railroad depot and a garden of indigenous desert plants.

RICHARD PETTY DRIVING EXPERIENCE

If you've got a need for speed, this **driving experience** (off Map p112; ☎ 702-643-4443, 800-237-3889; www.1800bepetty.com; Las Vegas Motor Speedway, 7000 Las Vegas Blvd N, off I-15 exit 54; rides from $149; ☯ hours vary) is your chance to ride shotgun during a Nascar-style qualifying run. Speeds in the 600-horsepower stock cars reach up to 150mph. Also based at the Speedway, **Mario Andretti Racing School** (off Map p112; ☎ 877-722-3527; http://andrettiracing.com) offers cheaper ride-along opps.

ACTIVITIES
Bowling & Billiards

Bowling is a big-time pastime in Las Vegas, as is shooting stick.

Cue Club (Map pp104-5; ☎ 702-735-2884; Commercial Center, 953 E Sahara Ave; per hr $10.50; ☯ 24hr) Swim with sharks at Vegas' largest pool hall.

Hootie & the Blowfish's Shady Grove Lounge (off Map pp104-5; ☎ 702-263-7777; Silverton Casino Lodge, 3333 Blue Diamond Rd; ☯ 24hr) Coin-op miniature bowling inside a shiny silver Airstream trailer.

Lucky Strike Lanes (Map pp104-5; ☎ 702-777-7999; Rio, 3700 W Flamingo Rd; ☯ 11am-3am, over-21s only after 9pm) Glam bowling alley with pin-up posters, a finger-lickin' menu of bar food and buckets of beer. Expect a wait.

Red Rock Lanes (off Map p112; ☎ 702-797-7467; Red Rock Casino Resort Spa, 11011 W Charleston Blvd; ☯ 24hr; ♿) Deluxe PBA-tour bowling alley, with 72 lanes, plasma-screen TVs, pool and shuffleboard tables, dartboards, a video-game arcade and VIP suites with bottle service.

Golf

For discounts and last-minute bookings, try: **Las Vegas Preferred Tee Times** (☎ 877-255-7277; www.lvptt.com).

Angel Park (☎ 702-254-4653, 888-446-5358; www.angelpark.com; 100 S Rampart Blvd; green fees $25-155) Two Arnold Palmer-designed championship courses, plus the par-three 'Cloud Nine' course that's part lit for night play.

Badlands (☎ 702-363-0754; www.badlandsgc.com; 9119 Alta Dr; green fees $45-180) The ultimate bad-ass desert challenge, with ball-chewing turf and unforgiving layouts.

Las Vegas Paiute Golf Resort (☎ 702-658-1400, 800-711-2833; www.lvpaiutegolf.com; 10325 Nu-Way Kaiv Blvd, off US Hwy 95 exit Snow Mountain Rd; green fees $59-220) Scenic Pete Dye–designed courses in the Spring Mountains.

Royal Links (☎ 702-450-8123, 888-427-6678; www.royallinksgolfclub.com; 5995 E Vegas Valley Dr; green fees $55-275) Inspired by the British Open's famous greens. Tiger Woods set the record here, scoring 67.

Tournament Players Clubs Las Vegas (☎ 702-256-2500; www.tpc.com; 9851 Canyon Run Dr; green fees $30-235) A PGA tour stop, the naturalistic, minimal-irrigation Canyons course is also an Audubon-certified cooperative sanctuary.

Rock Climbing

For beginners' indoor walls, drop by Circus Circus' Adventuredome (p108), New York–New York's ESPN Zone (p109) or **GameWorks** (Map pp104-5; ☎ 702-432-4263; Showcase Mall, 3785 Las Vegas Blvd S; rock climbing $10; ☉ 10am-midnight Sun-Thu, to 1am Fri & Sat). The **Red Rock Climbing Center** (off Map p112; ☎ 702-254-5604; 8201 W Charleston Blvd; day pass $10-15, belay check $5, equipment rental $8; ☉ 10am-10pm Mon-Fri, 9am-9pm Sat & Sun; ♿) offers 100ft wall climbs, radical roof routes and plenty of bouldering opps, including for kids; perfect your skills here before heading to Red Rock Canyon (p131).

Spas & Gyms

The Strip's spas are perfect for pampering. Day-use fees ($20 to $45) are usually waived with a treatment (minimum $75). Most spas have fitness centers; workout attire and gym shoes are required.

bathhouse (Map pp104-5; ☎ 877-632-9636; www.mandalaybay.com; THEhotel at Mandalay Bay, 3950 Las Vegas Blvd S; ☉ 6am-9:30pm) A multimillion-dollar minimalist temple, it offers 'aromapothecary' massage oils, ayurvedic herbal baths and plunge pools.

Canyon Ranch SpaClub (Map pp104-5; ☎ 702-414-3600; Grand Canal Shoppes, 3355 Las Vegas Blvd S; ☉ 5:30am-10pm) Health-conscious place offers over 100 different treatments and activities, including a rock-climbing wall. Also at the Palazzo.

Hands On Therapeutic Massage & Spa (off Map pp104-5; ☎ 702-614-6222; www.massagelasvegas.com; Cancun Resort, 8335 Las Vegas Blvd S) Recommended by five-star concierges, these traveling therapists can bring the massage table direct to your hotel room (by appointment only).

Qua Baths & Spa (Map pp104-5; ☎ 702-731-7776, 866-782-0655; www.harrahs.com/qua; Caesars Palace, 3570 Las Vegas Blvd S; ☉ 6am-8pm) Social spa-going is encouraged in the tea lounge, herbal steam room and arctic ice room, where dry-ice snowflakes fall.

Water Sports

On the way to Lake Mead (p132), artificial Lake Las Vegas resort is an oasis in summer. Rent kayaks, jet-skis and sailboats from **MonteLago Village Marina** (☎ 702-564-4700; www.montelagovillage.com), where one-hour yacht cruises depart most weekends. During winter, an ice-skating rink opens on the lake. **Gondola**

Adventures (☎ 877-446-6365; www.gondola.com; 1-2hr cruise per couple $135-195) sells romantic champagne-and-chocolate, picnic-lunch and sunset-dinner trips. It's a 40-minute trip from the Strip: take I-215 eastbound to Lake Mead Dr, then turn left onto Lake Las Vegas Parkway.

COURSES

It's Yoga (Map pp104-5; ☎ 702-798-9642; www.itsyogalasvegas.net; 4634 S Maryland Pkwy; ☉ hours vary) Near UNLV's campus, sunny studio offers drop-in classes in dynamic styles, from pranic power to dragon vinyasa.

Stripper 101 (Map pp104-5; ☎ 702-260-7200; www.stripper101.com; Planet Hollywood, 3667 Las Vegas Blvd S; tickets from $40; ☉ hours vary) In a cabaret setting complete with strobe lights, cocktails and feather boas, these pole-dancing classes are popular with bachelorettes. Don't worry, though: no nudity is allowed. Bring comfy workout clothes and a pair of high heels to practice in.

LAS VEGAS FOR CHILDREN

Since sin is 'in' again, few places in Vegas now bill themselves as family-friendly. State law prohibits anyone under 21 from loitering in gaming areas. Many properties actively discourage kids by prohibiting strollers. The only casino hotels on the Strip that cater to children are Circus Circus (p108) and Excalibur (p108). That said, there are still plenty of things to see and do with youngsters. Don't miss Mandalay Bay's Shark Reef (p109). Beyond arcades and amusement rides, teenagers will likely be bored out of their minds. For more advice from a parent who has taken her own children to Las Vegas, see p93.

Coney Island Emporium

The highlight of NY–NY's gargantuan video arcade and amusement center is the **roller coaster** (Map pp104-5; ☎ 702-740-6969; New York–New York, 3790 Las Vegas Blvd S; games from 50¢, roller coaster $12.50, re-ride $6; ☉ 11am-11pm Sun-Thu, 10:30am-midnight Fri & Sat; ♿). This four-minute ride includes lots of stomach-dropping dipsy-dos, high-banked turns, a 540-degree spiral and stellar Strip views, plus a heartline twist-and-dive maneuver, producing a sensation similar to the one felt by fighter pilots during a barrel roll. Your head and shoulders will take a helluva beating, though. Hold on tight and secure loose valuables in the lockers out front.

MGM Grand Lion Habitat

Inside the casino, this glass-walled **habitat** (Map pp104-5; ☎ 702-891-7777; www.mgmgrand.com; MGM

Grand, 3799 Las Vegas Blvd S; admission free; 11am-10pm;) showcases up to six magnificent felines daily, all descendants of the movie company's original mascot. The big cats live on a ranch outside town, and only two are allowed in the enclosure simultaneously. Big cats often sprawl above onlookers' heads inside the see-through walkway tunnel. The kid-friendly, tropical-themed Rainforest Café is nearby.

Pinball Hall of Fame

Next to a discount cinema east of the Strip, this interactive **museum** (off Map pp104-5; www.pinball museum.org; 3330 E Tropicana Ave at S Pecos Rd; admission free, games 25-50¢; 11am-11pm Sun-Thu, to midnight Fri & Sat;) is more fun than any slot machines. Take time out to read the handwritten curatorial cards explaining the history behind the 200-plus vintage pinball, video-arcade and carnival-sideshow games dating from the 1950s to the '90s. Best of all, profits from every quarter you drop here go to charity.

College of Southern Nevada Planetarium

Young scientists will love the multimedia shows and 'skywatch' astronomy programs at this small **planetarium** (off Map p112; 702-651-4759; www.csn.edu/planetarium; 3200 E Cheyenne Ave, east of I-15 exit 46; adult/child $6/4; shows usually 6pm & 7:30pm Fri, 3:30pm & 7:30pm Sat;). Show up early to get a seat (no latecomers allowed). Weather permitting, the observatory telescopes open for public viewing after the late show. You can buy astronaut ice cream, space pens, constellation charts and model rocketry kits in the attached astronomy **store** (5-8pm Fri & 3-8pm Sat).

Southern Nevada Zoological-Botanical Park

Near Texas Station casino hotel, this small **zoo** (off Map p112; 702-647-4685; www.lasvegaszoo.org; 1775 N Rancho Dr; adult/child $7/5; 9am-5pm;) takes care of Canadian river otters, African fossas, ostriches, swamp wallabies, Barbary apes and every type of venomous snake found in southern Nevada. Kids can feed some critters (not the snakes, of course), while adults look over the rare bamboo, cycad and gem displays. Go online for discount admission coupons.

ONLY IN VEGAS

After trying all of the outrageous experiences listed below, foxy ladies can also sign up for Stripper 101 (opposite) classes.

Imperial Palace

The blue neon-roofed pagoda facade and faux–Far East theme are unbelievably hokey, but the zany atmosphere inside the **casino** (Map pp104-5; 702-731-3311; www.imperialpalace.com; 3535 Las Vegas Blvd S; admission free; 24hr) is quite all right. Award-winning celebrity impersonators (see Legends in Concert, p127) do double-duty as 'dealertainers,' jumping up from the blackjack tables to show off their song-and-dance skills on the casino's main stage, starting at noon until the wee hours. Elvis fans, rejoice: the King never leaves the building.

Slots A' Fun

For cheap booze, cheap eats and cheap thrills, it's tough to beat this lowbrow **casino** (Map pp104-5; 702-734-0410; 2890 Las Vegas Blvd S; admission free; 24hr). Grab a coupon book at the door, give the giant slot machine a free spin, and scarf down a few 75¢ beers and $1 half-pound hot dogs. Then kick back, relax and enjoy the laughable lounge acts.

Liberace Museum

For true kitsch fans and connoisseurs of extravagance, this bizarre memorial **museum** (off Map pp104-5; 702-798-5595; www.liberace.org; 1775 E Tropicana Ave; adult/child $12/8; 10am-5pm Mon-Sat, 1-5pm Sun, tour schedule varies) is a must-do. An outlandish tribute to 'Mr Showmanship,' there's a hand-painted Pleyel on which Chopin played; a Rolls-Royce convertible covered entirely in mirror tiles; and a wardrobe exhibit full of feathered capes and million-dollar furs. It's simply too much, dahling.

Gun Store

Attention, wannabe Schwarzeneggers: this high-powered **shop** (off Map pp104-5; 702-454-1110; www.thegunstorelasvegas.com; 2900 E Tropicana Ave; 9am-6:30pm) offers live submachine gun rounds and pistol rentals to fire off in its indoor video-training range, not to mention the massive cache of weapons for sale. Tuesday is ladies' day. Check the website for coupons.

Viva Las Vegas Wedding Chapel

Even if you're not contemplating tying the knot, it's worth a peek inside this little assembly-line **wedding chapel** (Map p112; 702-384-0771, 800-574-4450; www.vivalasvegasweddings.com; 1205 Las Vegas Blvd S; wedding packages from $201; hours vary) of loooovvvee to see if anyone is getting married. The public is welcome to attend, and

---

MARRIAGES MADE IN SIN CITY

Whether it's a planned affair or a spur-of-the-moment decision, Las Vegas offers dozens of different places to tie the knot, ranging from the traditional little white wedding chapels to over-the-top fantasies. You can be married by an Elvis impersonator or outdoors after a helicopter landing at the bottom of the Grand Canyon.

Everyone must first get a marriage license ($55) from the **County Marriage Bureau** (Map p112; ☎ 702-671-0600; www.accessclarkcounty.com/depts/clerk/Pages/marriage_information.aspx; 201 Clark Ave; ☽ 8am-midnight). There's no waiting period and you don't need a blood test. Civil ceremonies are performed by a judge between 8am and 10pm daily, including holidays.

Once you have a marriage license in hand, it's off to the chapel for most folks. Choices for the perfect spot to say 'I do' are endless. Expect to pay from $200 for an ultra-basic wedding service, including a limo ride to the chapel. Don't expect much ceremony, though: there's probably another couple, hearts bursting with love, in line right behind you.

Be advised that Valentine's Day and other holidays are crush times for Vegas wedding chapels; plan ahead if you want to say your vows at peak times. You can apply for a marriage license up to a year in advance and make wedding-chapel reservations in advance online.

---

ceremonies are simulcast online. The themed weddings are as kitschy as all get-out, too, from Elvis' 'Blue Hawaii' and 'Pink Caddy' to the adagio acrobatics of 'Viva du Cirque.'

TOURS

It's easy enough to tour the Strip on your own via monorail or bus or on foot, but these companies offer more unique experiences. Check online for frequent promotions.

Gray Line (☎ 702-384-1234, 800-634-6579; www.gray linelasvegas.com; 4½hr bus tour $45) Popular nighttime 'Neon Light' bus tour, plus daytime tours around town and to Hoover Dam (p132) and Red Rock Canyon (p131).

Haunted Vegas Tours (Map pp104-5; ☎ 702-737-5540; www.hauntedvegastours.com; Greek Isles, 305 Convention Center Dr; 2½hr show & tour $56) A campy sideshow begins a tell-all bus tour visiting Bugsy at the Flamingo casino hotel, creepy Liberace's café, the 'Motel of Death' and more.

Jubilee! Backstage Tour (☎ 702-967-4567, 800-237-7469; Bally's, 3645 Las Vegas Blvd S; 1hr tour with/without show ticket $10/15; ☽ 11am Mon, Wed & Sat) Be astounded by technical trivia on a behind-the-scenes tour led by a real showgirl or chorus boy. For a review of the show, see p127.

Papillon Grand Canyon Helicopters (☎ 702-736-7243, 888-635-7272; www.papillon.com; McCarran Executive Terminal, 275 E Tropicana Ave) Flightseeing tour operator offers luxury Grand Canyon tours. Its 10-minute 'Neon Nights Express' jetcopter flyover of the Strip (adult/child from $64/44) is popular.

Vegas Mob Tour (Map pp104-5; ☎ 866-218-4935; www .vegasmobtour.com; Greek Isles, 305 Convention Center Dr; 2½hr tour & film $56) Nighttime bus tour delves into the mafia underworld of Sin City's past, including celebrity scandals, mobster assassinations and other dirty laundry.

FESTIVALS & EVENTS

For more information about special events, contact the LVCVA (p107).

Chinese New Year (www.lvchinatown.com) Lunar new year celebrations in January/February.

Nascar Weekend (www.nascar.com) Rabid race fans descend on the Las Vegas Motor Speedway (p127) in early March.

St Patrick's Day Fremont St throws a party and parade every March 17.

UNLVino (www.unlvino.com) Not-for-profit wine tasting extravaganza in mid-April.

Viva Las Vegas (www.vivalasvegas.net) Ultimate rockabilly weekend downtown in mid-April.

Lei Day (www.alohavalley.com) A Polynesian and Pacific Rim block party downtown around May 1.

Helldorado Days (www.elkshelldorado.com) Historic Old West hoedown, rodeo and barbecue near Fremont St in May.

World Series of Golf (www.worldseriesofgolf.com) Ingeniously combines golf with high-stakes poker in mid-May.

CineVegas (www.cinevegas.com) Sin City's film festival lights up the Palms (p114) in mid-June.

World Series of Poker (www.worldseriesofpoker.com) High rollers, casino dealers, Hollywood celebs and internet stars vie for millions from early June to mid-July.

DefCon (www.defcon.org) USA's largest conclave of underground computer hackers in mid-August.

Vegoose (www.vegoose.com) Zany indie music and arts festival with costumed partying over Halloween weekend.

Professional Bull Riders World Finals (www .pbrnow.com) Fast and furious gallopin' giddy-up at Sam Boyd Stadium in October/November.

Aviation Nation (www.aviationnation.org) Top-gun military and civilian air show at Nellis Air Force Base happens in November.

National Finals Rodeo (www.nfrexperience.com) Ten days of cowboy hoopla at the Thomas & Mack Center in December.
New Year's Eve The Strip sees the biggest crush of humanity this side of Times Sq.

SLEEPING

Rates fluctuate wildly according to demand. If you arrive midweek, rooms go for up to 50% less than on weekends. Rates skyrocket during big conventions and major holidays like Valentine's Day and New Year's Eve. The best deals are often found via hotel websites rather than through discount travel websites.

Whatever you do, don't arrive without a reservation, at least for the first night. You'd be amazed how often every standard room in town is occupied. During the biggest special events (opposite), even Laughlin (p229), 100 miles away in Arizona, is booked solid. Book as far in advance as possible. **TravelWorm** (☎ 888-700-8342; www.travelworm.com) often has last-minute rooms available.

Be prepared that casino-hotel rooms are typically lacking the basic amenities found at motels and hotels across the Southwest (eg they have no coffee makers, mini fridges, complimentary internet access or free local or toll-free telephone calls). A 'resort' fee of $5 up to $20 per night may apply. Valet (tip at least $2) and self-parking are free.

The Strip
BUDGET

Few places on the Strip offer budget accommodations. The cheapest tend to be the most child-friendly.

Circus Circus (Map p104-5; ☎ 702-691-5950, 800-634-3450; www.circuscircus.com; 2880 Las Vegas Blvd S; r $45-205; 🅿 👶 🖵 wi-fi) Most rooms at this family favorite have love seats. Suites, like clowns, come in varying shapes and sizes. Many motel-style Manor rooms out back by the RV park have mini fridges.

Stratosphere (Map p104-5; ☎ 702-380-7777, 888-212-0093; www.stratospherehotel.com; 2000 Las Vegas Blvd S; r $45-210; 🅿 👶 🖵 wi-fi) Warning! Your room is *not* in the landmark tower (p110) but rather in a much smaller, overcrowded building at the base of the spire. Guests enjoy free tower admission before noon.

Sahara (Map pp104-5; ☎ 702-737-2111, 888-696-2121; www.saharavegas.com; 2535 Las Vegas Blvd S; r $45-360; 🅿 🖵 wi-fi) A delightfully tacky Moroccan theme pervades this vintage Vegas casino. It

doesn't churn up a lot of excitement, but the simple hotel rooms are a bargain, and it's on the monorail line.

MIDRANGE

Many of these places would belong in the luxury bracket elsewhere, but Vegas is a city hell-bent on excess.

Luxor (Map p104-5; ☎ 702-362-4000, 888-777-0188; www.luxor.com; 3900 Las Vegas Blvd S; r $70-370; 🅿 🖵 wi-fi) With vaguely art-deco Egyptian furnishings and marble bathrooms (no tubs), Luxor's pyramid rooms let you ride unusual high-speed elevators, called 'inclinators,' which travel at a 39-degree angle. Avoid lower-floor rooms above LAX nightclub. Newer high-rise tower rooms may also have better views.

New York–New York (Map pp104-5; ☎ 702-740-6969, 866-815-4365; www.nynyhotelcasino.com; 3790 Las Vegas Blvd S; r $70-480; 🅿 🖵 wi-fi) The cheapest digs are rather tiny (just what one would expect in NYC), but pay more for a stylish Park Ave Deluxe and you'll have plenty of legroom. Avoid noisy lower-level rooms facing the roller coaster.

TI (Treasure Island) (Map pp104-5; ☎ 702-894-7111, 800-288-7206; www.treasureisland.com; 3300 Las Vegas Blvd S; r $90-390; 🅿 🖵 wi-fi) The micro rooms here feel deceptively expansive, thanks to floor-to-ceiling windows and airy earth tones. Recent grown-up additions include poolside cabanas and a huge party hot tub.

ourpick MGM Grand (Map pp104-5; ☎ 702-891-7777, 800-929-1111; www.mgmgrand.com; 3799 Las Vegas Blvd S; r $80-500, ste from $150; 🅿 👶 🖵 wi-fi) There's plenty to choose from at the world's largest hotel (5000-plus rooms), but is bigger better? That depends, but top-drawer restaurants, a sprawling pool complex and a monorail station always make it a good bet. Standard hotel rooms have blah decor, so stay in the minimalist-modern West Wing instead. Signature suites, with Jacuzzi tubs, kitchenettes and sometimes step-out balconies, are serene oases.

Mirage (Map pp104-5; ☎ 702-791-7111, 800-374-9000; www.mirage.com; 3400 Las Vegas Blvd S; r $85-699; 🅿 🖵 wi-fi) Gone is the four-star hotel's original tropical theme, replaced by chic, contemporary rooms with bold color palettes, plush patterned rugs, plasma-screen TVs and stereos with iPod docks:

Also recommended:
Bill's Gamblin' Hall & Saloon (Map pp104-5; ☎ 702-737-7111, 888-227-2279; www.barbarycoastcasino.com;

LAS VEGAS & NEVADA

COOL POOLS

- **Hard Rock** (opposite) Seasonal swim-up blackjack and Tahitian-style cabanas at the hip Beach Club, a constant throbbing (literally, there are underwater speakers!) meat-market party, especially during summer-only 'Rehab' pool parties.

- **Mirage** (p119) Lush tropical pool is a sight to behold, with waterfalls tumbling off cliffs, deep grottos and palm-tree studded islands for sun bathing. Feeling flirty? Check out the topless Bare lounge.

- **Mandalay Bay** (p109) Splash around an artificial sand-and-surf beach built from imported California sand and boasting a wave pool, lazy-river ride, casino and DJ-driven topless Moorea Beach Club.

- **Caesars Palace** (p108) Corinthian columns, overflowing fountains, magnificent palms and marble-inlaid pools make the Garden of the Gods Oasis divine. Goddesses proffer frozen grapes in summer, including at the topless Venus pool lounge.

- **Palms** (opposite) Where glam style meets mod design: stone-and-metal cabanas with Astroturf carpeting, blackjack tables under a glass-bottomed pool, and a waterfall bar. During summer, look for Ditch Fridays.

3595 Las Vegas Blvd S; r $69-330; wi-fi) The Strip's worst-kept budget-friendly secret. Parking is difficult.

Flamingo (Map pp104-5; ☎ 702-733-3111, 800-732-2111; www.flamingolasvegas.com; 3555 Las Vegas Blvd S; r $85-325; 🐾 💻 wi-fi) Book a seriously upgraded GO room, or don't go.

Mandalay Bay (Map pp104-5; ☎ 702-632-7777, 877-632-7800; www.mandalaybay.com; 3950 Las Vegas Blvd S; r $110-380; 🐾 💻 wi-fi) Stylishly remodeled rooms and suites look effortlessly luxurious, plus there's a popular pool and artificial beach.

TOP END

Impeccable service, 24/7 can-do concierge pampering and expedited check-in are par for the course. Booking online can score deep discounts.

THEhotel at Mandalay Bay (Map pp104-5; ☎ 702-632-7777; www.mandalaybay.com; Mandalay Bay, 3950 Las Vegas Blvd S; ste $150-540; 🐾 💻 wi-fi) Kick back with your entourage at THEhotel, at least for the moment. Enter the high-ceilinged lobby adjacent to Mandalay Bay, and you'll feel a world away from the Strip. Expansive suites come with wet bars, plasma-screen TVs, deep soaking tubs and cosmo NYC-chic decor. Nonsuite THEdeluxe rooms aren't so worth it.

Bellagio (Map pp104-5; ☎ 702-693-7111, 888-987-6667; www.bellagio.com; 3600 Las Vegas Blvd S; r $169-570; 🐾 💻 wi-fi) Once the belle of the ball, the nouveau-riche Bellagio is still lavishly and artistically designed. Do rooms look small? That's because bathrooms are oversized. Luxurious lake-view suites front the resort's dancing fountains.

Wynn Las Vegas (Map pp104-5; ☎ 702-770-7100, 877-321-9966; www.wynnlasvegas.com; 3131 Las Vegas Blvd S; r $199-515, ste from $289; 🐾 💻 wi-fi) Deluxe five-diamond resort rooms are bigger than some studio apartments, with high-thread-count linens, flat-screen high-definition TVs, Turkish towels and lots of little luxuries. Salon suites enjoy floor-to-ceiling windows and VIP check-in.

Venetian (Map pp104-5; ☎ 702-414-1000, 877-883-6423; www.venetian.com; 3355 Las Vegas Blvd S; ste $199-1000; 🐾 💻 wi-fi) The 700-sq-ft 'standard' suites are anything but. In fact, they're among the Strip's largest and most luxurious, with oversized Italian marble baths and sunken living rooms. The Venezia Tower and all-suites Palazzo next door boast concierge levels with pampering perks.

Downtown

Avoid rent-by-the-hour fleapits by sticking close to the Fremont Street Experience (p112).

ourpick **Main Street Station** (Map p112; ☎ 702-387-1896, 800-713-8933; www.mainstreetcasino.com; 200 N Main St; r $40-120; wi-fi) For a more intimate experience, try this 17-floor hotel tower with marble-tile foyers and Victorian sconces in the hallways. Bright, cheery hotel rooms with plantation shutters are as handsome as the casino (p113).

California (Map p112; ☎ 702-385-1222, 800-634-6255; www.thecal.com; 12 E Ogden Ave; r $40-120; 🐾) Tropical flair and a rooftop pool make it popular with visitors from Hawaii. Airy rooms have white plantation shutters, mahogany furnishings and marble baths.

Golden Nugget (Map p112; ☎ 702-385-7111, 800-846-5336; www.goldennugget.com; 129 E Fremont; r $59-125; ☒ ☐ wi-fi) This royal jewel has newfound panache. Ample standard rooms, with half-canopy beds and marble everywhere, are downtown's best. Outside by the lavish pool area, a three-story water slide plunges through a 200,000-gallon shark tank.

East of the Strip

Don't get stuck at chain cheapies near the airport or the city's convention center.

Hard Rock (Map pp104-5; ☎ 702-693-5544, 800-473-7625; www.hardrockhotel.com; 4455 Paradise Rd; r $109-450; ☒ ☐ wi-fi) Everything about this boutique hotel spells stardom. French doors reveal limited views, and brightly colored Euro-minimalist rooms feature souped-up stereos and plasma-screen TVs. The hottest action revolves around the lush Beach Club.

Platinum Hotel & Spa (Map pp104-5; ☎ 702-365-5000, 877-211-9211; www.theplatinumhotel.com; 211 E Flamingo Rd; ste $119-770; ☒ ☐ wi-fi) Avoid the casino scene at this luxury nongaming, nonsmoking resort hotel, where each of the enormous suites has a full kitchen and pull-out sofa bed.

Also recommended:

Motel 6 Tropicana (Map pp104-5; ☎ 702-798-0728, 800-466-8356; www.motel6.com; 195 E Tropicana Ave; s/d from $42/47; ☒ ☖ wi-fi) Basic, thin-walled rooms a reasonable walk from the Strip. Kids stay free; small pets OK.

Super 8 Motel (Map pp104-5; ☎ 702-794-0888, 800-800-8000; www.super8.com; 4250 Koval Lane; d from $79; ☒ ☖ wi-fi) Adjacent to Ellis Island Casino & Brewery, varying-quality rooms at least have coffeemakers. Pet surcharge $15.

West of the Strip

The Orleans, Rio and Gold Coast casino hotels provide free shuttles to the Strip.

Orleans (off Map pp104-5; ☎ 702-365-7111, 800-675-3267; www.orleanscasino.com; 4500 W Tropicana Ave; r $65-175; ☒ ☐ wi-fi) Tastefully appointed French-provincial rooms are good-value 'petite suites.' There's a free-access fitness center for guests in the spa, on-site childcare, a movie theater, a bowling alley and a live-music pub.

Palms (Map pp104-5; ☎ 702-942-7777, 866-942-7770; www.palms.com; 4321 W Flamingo Rd; r $109-459, ste from $209; ☒ ☐ wi-fi) Britney Spears spent her *first* wedding night here. Standard rooms are generous, as are tech-savvy amenities. Request

an upper floor to score a Strip view. Playpen suites are tailored for bachelor and bachelorette parties, or escape to the high-rise Palms Place.

Also recommended:

Gold Coast (Map pp104-5; ☎ 702-367-7111, 800-331-5334; www.goldcoastcasino.com; 4000 W Flamingo Rd; r $30-145; ☒ ☐ wi-fi) Flat-screen TVs, in-room coffeemakers and free local and toll-free telephone calls.

Rio (Map pp104-5; ☎ 702-777-7777, 866-746-7671; www.riolasvegas.com; 3700 W Flamingo Rd; ste $90-410; ☒ ☐ wi-fi) Spacious mini suites accommodate a jackass frat-boy crowd.

Greater Las Vegas

It's worth staying on the city's outskirts, if you score a deal. Most of these hotels offer free Strip shuttles.

Sam's Town (off Map p112; ☎ 702-456-7777, 800-897-8696; www.samstownlv.com; 5111 Boulder Hwy, east of I-515/US Hwy 93/US Hwy 95 exit 69; r $40-275; ☒ ☐ wi-fi) Ranchers, locals and RVers flock to this Wild West casino hotel, which neopunk band the Killers named their sophomore album after. Texas-sized rooms face a kitschy indoor garden or the city's neon lights.

South Point (off Map pp104-5; ☎ 702-796-7111, 866-791-7626; www.southpointcasino.com; 9777 Las Vegas Blvd S; r $60-300; ☒ ☖ ☐ wi-fi) Popular with cowboys for its equestrian center, this budget-deluxe casino hotel is a short drive south of the Strip, near the outlet mall. With rooms this big and beds this divine, who needs a suite? Perks include a spa, a cineplex and a bowling center.

Red Rock Casino Resort Spa (off Map p112; ☎ 702-797-7777, 866-767-7773; www.redrocklasvegas.com; 11011 W Charleston Blvd, off I-215 exit 22; r $125-575; ☒ ☖ ☐ wi-fi) For adventurous types who want the best of Vegas' urban jungle and its vast outdoor desert playground, this stylish place rocks. After a hard day's play, retreat to your ultra-modern room or the indulgent spa. Look for above-par restaurants and family-friendly amusements, too.

EATING

Sin City is an unmatched culinary adventure. Celebrity chefs have taken up residence in nearly every casino, with the latest invasion from France. With so many star-struck tables to choose from, stakes are high, and there are many overhyped eating gambles.

Cheap buffets and meal deals still exist, but if you're arriving from other cities in the Southwest, you may be stunned by the cost of

---

BELLY-BUSTING BUFFETS

When it comes to groaning boards, the adage 'you get what you pay for' was never truer. Most large casino hotels in Nevada lay on all-you-can-eat buffets, offering a bonanza of food at low prices. As anyone who has ever 'done' a buffet knows, it's both a blessing and a curse.

Look before you buy. Not all buffets are created equal. No host should stop you from perusing the offerings before putting down your money. Better buffets feature live-action cooking stations. Among the starring dishes at megaresorts are shrimp, lobster claws, carved-to-order meats, fresh fruit, and house-made breads and desserts.

On the Strip, expect to pay $7 to $15 for a breakfast buffet, $15 to $20 for lunch and $20 to $40 or more for dinner or weekend champagne brunch. Queues can be excruciatingly long, although line passes may be available for hotel guests and casino player's club members. Otherwise, plan on showing up early (eg before noon for Sunday brunch).

Vegas' most popular buffets, all of which are open for three round meals a day (unless otherwise noted), include the following:

- **The Buffet** (Map pp104–5; ☎ 702-770-7000, 877-321-9966; www.wynnlasvegas.com; Wynn Las Vegas, 3131 Las Vegas Blvd S)

- **Le Village Buffet** (Map pp104–5; ☎ 702-946-7000; www.parislv.com; Paris–Las Vegas, 3655 Las Vegas Blvd S)

- **Spice Market Buffet** (Map pp104–5; ☎ 702-785-9005; Planet Hollywood, 3667 Las Vegas Blvd S)

- **The Buffet** (Map pp104–5; ☎ 702-693-7111; www.bellagio.com; Bellagio, 3600 Las Vegas Blvd S)

- **Todai Japanese Seafood Buffet** (Map pp104–5; ☎ 888-800-8284; Miracle Mile Shops, Planet Hollywood, 3663 Las Vegas Blvd S)

- **Sunday Gospel Brunch** (Map pp104–5; ☎ 702-632-7600; www.hob.com; House of Blues, Mandalay Bay, 3950 Las Vegas Blvd S; adult/child $39/20; ⓨ seatings 10am & 1pm Sun) Buy tickets a couple of days in advance.

---

eating out in Las Vegas. It's slim pickings for vegetarians, though most places have a few dishes on the menu, and buffet salad bars are always safe.

Make reservations for more expensive restaurants as far in advance as possible, especially if you're here on a weekend. The dress code at most upscale eateries is business casual. At the most famous places, jackets and ties are preferred for men.

Every casino has a 24-hour café, often with breakfast available around the clock and 'grave-yard' specials from 11pm to 6am. Weekend champagne brunch buffets normally serve from 7am to 4pm. Dinner finishes around 10pm (11pm on Friday and Saturday nights).

The Strip

Vegas' casino restaurants alone could be fodder for an entire book; here are some favorites, but there are many, many more.

BUDGET

Inexpensive eateries are an anomaly on the Strip.

Luv-It Frozen Custard (Map pp104–5; ☎ 702-384-6452; 505 E Oakey Blvd; items $2-5; ⓨ 1-10pm Tue-Thu, 1-11pm Fri & Sat; ⚇) A local mecca since 1973, Luv-It's handmade concoctions are creamier than ice cream. Flavors change daily, so you'll be tempted to go back. Try a chocolate-dipped Luv Stick bar or double-thick milkshake. Cash only.

'Wichcraft (Map pp104–5; ☎ 702-891-3166; MGM Grand, 3799 Las Vegas Blvd S; meals $4-10; ⓨ 10am-6pm Sun-Thu, to 8pm Fri & Sat; ⚇) Cafeteria creates gourmet hot and cold sandwiches, such as grilled cheddar with smoked ham and baked apples, or plain ol' PB&J for kids. Salads, soups and fresh fruit are happy add-ons, as are whoopie-pie desserts.

Stripburger (Map pp104–5; ☎ 702-258-1211; Fashion Show, 3200 Las Vegas Blvd S; items $4-10; ⓨ 11:30am-1am Sun-Thu, to 2am Fri & Sat; ⚇) Outside the mall, a silver diner-in-the-round serves up all-natural beef, chicken, tuna and veggie burgers, with stupendous atomic cheese fries, thick milkshakes and gigantic cocktails.

Village Eateries (Map pp104–5; ☎ 702-740-6969; New York–New York, 3790 Las Vegas Blvd S; meals $6-18; ⓨ daily, hours vary; ⚇) Greenwich Village is bursting with tasty, budget-saving options, from gourmet sausage and fish-and-chips shops to an old-fashioned deli, a tequila-soaked Tex-Mex cantina and a Chinese kitchen serving dim sum and veggie-friendly tofu dishes.

MIDRANGE

Although the Strip is seriously overpriced, these places deliver tastes we crave.

Wolfgang Puck Bar & Grill (Map pp104-5; ☎ 702-891-3000; MGM Grand, 3799 Las Vegas Blvd S; mains $13-35; ☒ 11:30am-10:30pm Mon-Thu, to 11:30pm Fri-Sun) Truffled potato chips with blue cheese, skirt-steak skewers with creamy celery salad and wood-fired pizzas are as thrilling as the New World wine list at this ultra-contemporary Californian bistro.

Olives (Map pp104-5; ☎ 702-693-8181; Bellagio, 3600 Las Vegas Blvd S; mains $16-52; ☒ lunch & dinner) Bostonian chef Todd English dishes up homage to the life-giving fruit. Flatbread pizzas, house-made pastas and flame-licked meats get top billing. Patio tables overlook Lake Como. Good wine list.

Payard Bistro (Map pp104-5; ☎ 702-731-7292; Caesars Palace, 3570 Las Vegas Blvd S; breakfast & lunch $16-25, prix-fixe dinner $45-60; ☒ 6:30am-11:30am & noon-7:30pm, desserts-only after 9pm) Operated by third-generation chocolatier Françoise Payard, this exquisite place offers fresh takes on bistro classics and outrageously indulgent dessert-only dinner menus with artisan cheeses, fruits, nuts and sweet confections. Take-out pastry and espresso bar.

Isla Mexican Kitchen (Map pp104-5; ☎ 702-894-7111; TI, 3300 Las Vegas Blvd S; mains $18-35; ☒ 4pm-11pm Sun-Thu, to midnight Fri & Sat) Inventive Mexican-born chef Richard Sandoval creates a fusion of south-of-the-border tastes, like lobster spiked with serrano chiles and passion fruit. Call on Isla's tequila-bar goddess to help decipher the bounteous menu of agave elixirs, including artful margaritas unlike any you've ever had before.

StripSteak (Map pp104-5; ☎ 702-632-7414; Mandalay Bay, 3950 Las Vegas Blvd S; mains $22-69; ☒ dinner) Famed seafood chef Michael Mina has dived into the competitive world of Vegas steakhouses. An exceptional menu of Angus and Kobe beef delightfully detours from tradition, with the likes of duck fat fries, spicy green-papaya salad and epicurean mini-doughnuts for dessert.

Social House (Map pp104-5; ☎ 702-894-7777; TI, 3300 Las Vegas Blvd S; mains $24-44; ☒ 5pm-midnight daily, late-night menu midnight-2am Thu-Sun) While the *panko-*crusted crab cakes, lemongrass shrimp and tamarind short ribs may not always hit the right notes, the ubertrendy setting with shoji-papered windows and a Strip-view patio with bonsai trees does.

David Burke (Map pp104-5; ☎ 702-414-71111; Venetian, 3355 Las Vegas Blvd S; mains $29-52; ☒ dinner) David Burke's whimsical, tongue-in-cheek, globally flavored nouveau cuisine makes this under-the-radar find mostly sweet, with the only sour note being the haphazard service. Full menu at the bar.

RM Seafood (Map pp104-5; ☎ 702-632-9300; Mandalay Place, 3930 Las Vegas Blvd S; mains $27-62; ☒ café lunch & dinner, restaurant dinner) From ecoconscious chef Rick Moonen, modern American seafood dishes, such as Cajun popcorn and Maine lobster, come with comfort-food sides (like gourmet mac 'n' cheese), a raw shellfish and sushi bar, and a 'biscuit bar' serving savory salads.

TOP END

Look for even more famous chefs' restaurants at the new Palazzo resort.

Alex (Map pp104-5; ☎ 702-770-3300; Wynn Las Vegas, 3131 Las Vegas Blvd S; prix-fixe menu $140-235; ☒ dinner) Alessandro Stratta stretches his wings at this haute French Rivieran restaurant, with high-concept dishes like frog legs with garlic custard or roasted scallops with pink grapefruit, plus some Asian influences. Desserts triumph.

Restaurant Guy Savoy (Map pp104-5; ☎ 702-731-7286; Caesars Palace, 3570 Las Vegas Blvd S; tasting menu $190-290; ☒ dinner Wed-Sun) If this three-star Michelin chef's high-flying modern French tasting menus would leave you broke, just perch at the Bubble Bar for elegant champagne and appetizers, perhaps artichoke black-truffle soup or oysters in ice *gelée.*

Downtown

Fremont St is the stronghold of ravenous, penny-pinching omnivores.

Florida Café (Map p112; ☎ 702-385-3013; Howard Johnson's, 1401 Las Vegas Blvd S; mains $5-16; ☒ 7am-10pm) Don't let the bus-stop advertisements all over town dissuade you from the authentic shredded steak, fried pork and seasoned chicken with yellow rice. *Café con leche*, flan and *batidos* (tropical shakes) are superb.

Second Street Grill (Map p112; ☎ 702-385-3232; Fremont, 200 E Fremont St; mains $19-35; ☒ dinner Mon & Thu-Sun) At this unabashedly rococo gem, chef Rachel Bern flies in the seafood fresh from Hawaii. You can score a 16oz T-bone steak with all the trimmings for under 20 bucks, too.

Vic & Anthony's (Map p112; ☎ 702-385-7111; Golden Nugget, 129 E Fremont St; mains $21-46; ☒ 5-11pm) An outpost of the Houston steakhouse, here blood-red curtains and high-backed leather chairs complement a menu of serious classics like grain-fed Midwestern beef and Maine lobster with creamed spinach and Lyonnaise potatoes on the side.

Pullman Grille (Map p112; ☎ 702-387-1896; Main Street Station, 200 N Main St; mains $23-45; ☉ dinner Wed-Sun) The clubby Pullman features Black Angus beef and Pacific Rim seafood specialties amid gorgeous carved wood paneling. The centerpiece is a 1926 rail car, now a cigar lounge.

Also recommended:

Golden Gate (Map p112; ☎ 702-385-1906; 1 E Fremont St; ☉ 11am-3am) Famous 99¢ shrimp cocktails (supersize 'em for $2.99).

Binion's Snack Bar (Map p112; ☎ 702-382-1600; Binion's, 128 E Fremont St; items $2-6; ☉ 10am-10pm Sun-Thu, to midnight Fri & Sat) Old-fashioned burgers and juicy cherry-pie slices.

Grotto (Map p112; ☎ 702-385-7111; Golden Nugget, 129 E Fremont St; mains $13-30; ☉ 11:30am-10:30pm Sun-Thu, to 11:30pm Fri & Sat) Wood oven–fired pizzas and 200-bottle wine list available at the bar until 1am.

East of the Strip

There are many more choices besides the Hard Rock's overpriced eateries.

Firefly (Map pp104-5; ☎ 702-369-3971; Citibank Plaza, 3900 Paradise Rd; small dishes $4-10, large dishes $11-20; ☉ 11:30am-2am Sun-Thu, to 3am Fri & Sat) Firefly is always hopping. Taste traditional Spanish tapas, like chorizo clams and *patatas bravas*, while the bartender pours sangria and flavor-infused mojitos. Turntablists spin some nights.

Paymon's Mediterranean Café (Map pp104-5; ☎ 702-731-6030; 4147 S Maryland Pkwy; mains $8-20; ☉ 11am-1am Sun-Thu, to 3am Fri & Sat; **V**) One of the city's few veggie spots serves baked eggplant with fresh garlic, baba ganoush, tabbouleh and hummus. Carnivores should try the kebab sandwich, gyros or rotisserie lamb. The adjacent Hookah Lounge is a tranquil spot to chill with a water pipe and fig-flavored cocktail.

San-Toki Korean BBQ & Shabu Bar (Map pp104-5; ☎ 702-732-8654; 4480 Paradise Rd; mains $8-25; ☉ 5pm-4am) At this classy Korean barbecue joint across the street from the Hard Rock, boisterous friends gather around sizzling grills, DIY fondue-style hot pots and potent bottles of *soju* (potato liquor).

Also recommended:

Red Mango (Map pp104-5; ☎ 702-795-0004; 4480 Paradise Rd; items $2.50-5; ☉ 11:30am-1am; ☝) All-natural frozen-yogurt shop is addictive.

Harrie's Bagelmania (Map pp104-5; ☎ 702-369-3322; 855 E Twain Ave; items from $1.50, mains $4-8; ☉ 6:30am-3pm; ☝) Kosher deli and NYC-style bakery are best for breakfast.

Hofbräuhaus (opposite) Get a good taste of Munich and wash it down with imported German brews.

West of the Strip

Pan-Asian delights await in the Spring Mountain Rd strip malls of Chinatown.

N9NE (Map pp104-5; ☎ 702-933-9900; Palms, 4321 W Flamingo Rd; mains $26-43; ☉ dinner) At this hip steakhouse heavy with celebs, a dramatic dining room centers on a champagne and caviar bar. Chicago-style aged steaks and chops keep coming, along with everything from oysters Rockefeller to Pacific sashimi.

Alizé (Map pp104-5; ☎ 702-951-7000; Palms, 4321 W Flamingo Rd; mains $36-68; ☉ dinner) André Rochat's top-drawer gourmet room is named after a gentle Mediterranean trade wind. The panoramic floor-to-ceiling views (enjoyed by every table) are stunning, just like the haute French cuisine. A huge wine-bottle tower dominates the room.

Also recommended:

Veggie Delight (Map pp104-5; ☎ 702-310-6565; 3504 Wynn Rd; items $4-8; ☉ 11am-8pm; **V**) Buddhist-owned, Vietnamese-flavored vegetarian/vegan kitchen mixing up chakra color-coded Chinese herbal tonics.

Artem (Eliseevsky) (off Map pp104-5; ☎ 702-247-8766; 4825 W Flamingo Rd; dishes $9-18; ☉ 5pm-1am Tue-Sun) Like a *Doctor Zhivago* set, with live Russian singers on weekends; Cirque du Soleil performers dine here.

Greater Las Vegas

On day trips to Red Rock Canyon, look up these off-Strip stars.

Salt Lick BBQ (off Map p112; ☎ 702-797-7535; www.redrocklasvegas.com; Red Rock Casino Resort Spa, 11011 W Charleston Blvd; mains $9-24; ☉ 11am-10pm; ☝) An authentic barbecue joint hailing from Driftwood, TX gets a big thumbs-up for its slow-smoked pork ribs and succulent beef brisket with filling sides like smoked mac 'n' cheese and coleslaw.

our pick **Hash House a Go Go** (off Map pp104-5; ☎ 702-804-4646; 6800 W Sahara Ave; mains $12-27; ☉ 7:30am-2pm daily, dinner Mon-Sat; ☝) Fill up on this SoCal import's 'twisted farm food,' which has to be seen to be believed. The pancakes are as big as tractor tires, while farm-egg scrambles and house-made hashes could knock over a cow.

Rosemary's (off Map pp104-5; ☎ 702-869-2251; 8125 W Sahara Ave; dinner mains $30-42, 3-course prix-fixe menu

$55; ⊙ lunch Mon-Fri, dinner daily) Words fail to describe the epicurean ecstasy you'll encounter here. Yes, it's a very long drive from the Strip. But once you bite into heavenly offerings like Texas BBQ shrimp with Maytag blue cheese 'slaw, you'll forget about everything else. Wine and beer pairings make each course sublime.

DRINKING

Most booze consumption in Vegas takes place while staring down slot machines. Nevertheless, the Strip's casinos, plus many other bars and ultra lounges around the city, offer plenty of diversity, so you'll never be left out to dry.

40/40 Club (Map pp104-5; ☎ 702-638-4040; Palazzo, 3265 Las Vegas Blvd S; cover after 11pm $10-30; ⊙ noon-5am) Rags-to-riches rapper Jay-Z has brought his empire of ultraluxe hybrid sports bars and nightclubs to the Strip. VIP rooms are pimped out, and so is the cigar lounge.

ghostbar (Map pp104-5; ☎ 702-942-7777; 55th fl, Palms, 4321 W Flamingo Rd; cover $10-20; ⊙ 8pm-4am) A clubby crowd, often thick with celebs, packs this sky-high ultra lounge. DJs spin pop and hip-hop mash-ups while hoochie mamas and wannabe gangstas sip overpriced cocktails amid 360-degree panoramas and sci-fi decor.

Pussycat Dolls Lounge (Map pp104-5; ☎ 702-731-7873; Caesars Palace, 3570 Las Vegas Blvd S; cover $10-30; ⊙ 8pm-4am Tue-Sat) Lingerie-clad ladies do a little aerial swinging, rub-a-dub-dub in a tub and flaunt sexy song-and-dance numbers at this SoCal import.

Mix (Map pp104-5; ☎ 702-632-9500; 64th fl, THEhotel at Mandalay Bay, 3950 Las Vegas Blvd S; cover after 10pm $20-25; ⊙ 5pm-2am Sun-Thu, to 4am Fri & Sat) THE place to grab sunset cocktails. The glassed-in elevator has amazing views, and that's before you even glimpse the mod interior design and soaring balcony.

Revolution Lounge (Map pp104-5; ☎ 702-692-8383; Mirage, 3400 Las Vegas Blvd S; cover some nights $10-20; ⊙ 8:30pm-4am) At this psychedelic Beatles-themed ultra lounge with interactive art tables, DJs spin down-tempo house, Brit pop, hip-hop and musical fusion to mash-ups of classic rock and '80s new wave.

Trader Vic's (Map pp104-5; ☎ 702-405-4700; Miracle Mile Shops, 3663 Las Vegas Blvd S; ⊙ restaurant & bar 11:30am-midnight Mon-Thu, 11am-midnight Fri-Sun, lounge 9pm-4am Mon & Thu-Sat) The legendary Polynesian tiki bar that first formulated the Mai Tai cocktail has been laudably reinvented on the Strip, right down to the bamboo walls and zebra-print furnishings. Palm trees wave over a 2nd-floor patio, where DJs spin ear-tickling electronica.

Beauty Bar (Map p112; ☎ 702-598-1965; 517 E Fremont St; cover $5-10; ⊙ hours vary) At the salvaged innards of a 1950s New Jersey beauty salon, swill a cocktail while you get a makeover demo or chill out with the hip DJs and live local bands. Then walk around the corner to the Downtown Cocktail Room, a speakeasy.

Fireside Lounge (Map pp104-5; ☎ 702-735-4177; Peppermill, 2985 Las Vegas Blvd S; ⊙ 24hr) The Strip's most unlikely romantic hideaway is inside a retro coffee shop. Courting couples flock here for the low lighting, sunken fire pit and cozy nooks built for supping a Scorpion and other tiki drinks.

Hofbräuhaus (Map pp104-5; ☎ 702-853-3227; 4510 Paradise Rd; ⊙ 11am-11pm Sun-Thu, to midnight Fri & Sat) This Bavarian beer hall and garden is a replica of the original in Munich. Celebrate Oktoberfest year-round with premium imported suds, trademark *gemütlichkeit* (congeniality), fair *frauleins* and live oompah bands nightly.

Double Down Saloon (Map pp104-5; ☎ 702-791-5775; 4640 Paradise Rd; no cover; ⊙ 24hr) You just gotta love a dive whose tangy, blood-red house drink is named 'Ass Juice.' The jukebox vibrates with New Orleans jazz, British punk, Chicago blues and surf-guitar king Dick Dale. Monday is the Bargain DJ Collective night, with live local bands after 10pm other nights. Cash only.

New York–New York (Map pp104-5; ☎ 702-740-6969; 3790 Las Vegas Blvd S; ⊙ hours vary) Dueling pianos at the Bar at Times Square, perfectly poured pints and Celtic bands at Nine Fine Irishmen, big-screen sports TVs in the ESPN Zone, and prized American microbrews at Pour 24 upstairs.

Also recommended:

Romance at Top of the World (Map pp104-5; ☎ 702-380-7711; 107th fl, Stratosphere Tower, 2000 Las Vegas Blvd S; no cover, elevator ride $14; ⊙ 4pm-1am Sun-Thu, to 2am Fri & Sat) Smooth jazz and elevated martinis atop the tower.

Napoleon's (Map pp104-5; ☎ 702-946-7000; Paris–Las Vegas, 3655 Las Vegas Blvd S; ⊙ 4pm-2am) Be whisked away to a never-neverland of 19th-century France, with overstuffed sofas and over 100 types of bubbly, including vintage Dom Perignon.

Red Square (Map pp104-5; ☎ 702-632-7407; Mandalay Bay, 3950 Las Vegas Blvd S; ⊙ 5pm-2am) Heaps of Russian caviar, a solid ice bar and over 200 frozen vodkas, infusions and cocktails.

Triple 7 Brewpub (Map p112; ☎ 702-387-1896; Main Street Station, 200 N Main St; ☉ 24hr) Diehard sports fans and a crusty crowd of gamblers frequent this cavernous downtown brewpub.

ENTERTAINMENT
Nightclubs

Little expense has been spared to bring clubs inside casino hotels on par with NYC and LA in the area of wildly extravagant hangouts. Most are open 10pm to 4am later in the week; cover charges average $20 to $40.

Moon (Map pp104-5; ☎ 702-942-6832; 53rd fl, Fantasy Tower, Palms, 4321 W Flamingo Rd) Just a short glass-and-mirror elevator ride away from the Playboy Club, this futuristic penthouse has a surreal moon roof that retracts. Glass-tiled floors change colors with the beat of the music, whether hip-hop, rock or pop.

Tao (Map pp104-5; ☎ 702-388-8588; Grand Canal Shoppes, Venetian, 3355 Las Vegas Blvd S) Downstairs from the bistro and the giant Buddha's head, near-naked go-go girls covered by strategically placed flowers splash in bathtubs. On the risqué dance floor, Paris Hilton lookalikes forgo enlightenment and bump-and-grind to hip-hop instead.

Krāve (Map pp104-5; ☎ 702-836-0830; Miracle Mile Shops, 3663 Las Vegas Blvd S) Drawing a mixed crowd, it's the hottest gay nightclub in town, and the only one on the Strip. A glam warehouse-sized dance space is packed wall-to-wall with hard bodies and VIP cabanas. Stay for Saturday after-hours parties.

Forty Deuce (Map pp104-5; ☎ 702-632-9442; Mandalay Place, 3930 Las Vegas Blvd S) A speakeasy vibe pervades this petite, yet classily opulent club, where you can feast your eyes on smoking-hot traditional burlesque acts backed by a brassy, three-piece jazz combo or a rock band.

Polly Esther's (Map pp104-5; ☎ 702-889-1980; Stratosphere, 2000 Las Vegas Blvd S) A retro-minded chain megaclub with nostalgic rooms themed from the 1970s to the 2000s. Short lines pull in a ghetto-fabulous crowd that couldn't care less if you're wearing Manolo Blahniks or Pumas.

Drai's (Map pp104-5; ☎ 702-737-7801; Bill's Gamblin' Hall & Saloon, 3595 Las Vegas Blvd S; ☉ midnight-8am Wed-Sun) Feel ready for an after-hours scene straight outta Hollywood? Things don't really get going until 4am, when DJs spinning progressive discs keep the fashion plates content. Dress to kill.

Pirahna (Map pp104-5; ☎ 702-379-9500; www.gipsylv .net; 4633 Paradise Rd; cover up to $25) The lesbigay universe of the Fruit Loop orbits this two-story club, designed with aquariums, waterfalls and

fireplaces. For sexy tête-à-têtes, slip inside 8½ Ultra Lounge.

Gipsy (☎ 702-731-1919; 4605 S Paradise Rd; cover $5-10) Next door to Pirahna, Gipsy is a longer-running, but more rundown gay dance club that also hosts ladies' nights.

Also recommended:

The Bank (Map pp104-5; ☎ 702-693-8300; Bellagio, 3600 Las Vegas Blvd S) VIP booths lavishly layered around a multitiered dance floor, where pop and hip-hop mix.

Jet (Map pp104-5; ☎ 702-792-7900; Mirage, 3400 Las Vegas Blvd S) A sophisticated club, with flickering candles and seductive side lounges for hip-hop and deep house beats.

Poetry (Map pp104-5; ☎ 702-369-4998; Forum Shops, Caesars Palace; 3500 Las Vegas Blvd S) DJs spin hip-hop for rappers and movie stars in a faux luxe-life mansion setting.

Stoney's Rockin' Country (off Map pp104-5; ☎ 702-435-2855; 9151 Las Vegas Blvd S; cover after 8pm Fri & Sat $10; ☉ 7pm-5am Tue-Sat) Vegas' biggest country-and-western dance hall and saloon offers bikini bull riding and free two-steppin' lessons. Yeehaw!

Live Music

Contact these live-music venues directly for ticket prices and show times.

House of Blues (Map pp104-5; ☎ 702-632-7600; www .hob.com; Mandalay Bay, 3950 Las Vegas Blvd S) Blues is the tip of the hog at this Mississippi Delta juke joint, showcasing modern rock, pop and soul. Seating is limited, so show up early if you want to take a load off. Sightlines are good, and the outsider folk art is ubercool.

The Joint (Map pp104-5; ☎ 702-693-5066; www.hardrock hotel.com; Hard Rock, 4455 Paradise Rd) Concerts at this intimate venue (capacity 1400) feel like private shows, even when the Killers or Coldplay are in town. Most shows are standing-room only, with reservable VIP balcony seats upstairs.

The Pearl (Map pp104-5; ☎ 702-944-3200; www.palms .com; Palms, 4321 W Flamingo Rd) Modern rock acts like Gwen Stefani and Morrissey have burned up the stage at this 2500-seat concert hall with brilliant acoustics, hooked up to a state-of-the-art recording studio for live albums.

Also recommended:

Just Jazz (Map pp104-5; ☎ 702-650-0432; 1000 E Sa-hara Ave; no cover, 2-drink min at tables) East Coast–style jazz club with a speakeasy vibe.

Sand Dollar Blues Lounge (Map pp104-5; ☎ 702-871-6651; 3355 Spring Mountain Rd, enter off Polaris Ave; cover $5-10) Dive bar with live blues nightly after 10pm.

Production Shows

Some say it's a crime to leave town without seeing a show. But it's really not: most casino stage shows are minimal-plot productions with a lame variety of song, dance and magic acts. We've listed only a few established, well-reviewed shows here.

You can buy same-day discount tickets for a variety of shows at **Tix 4 Tonight** (☎ 877-849-4868; www.tix4tonight.com; Fashion Show, 3200 Las Vegas Blvd S; 🕑 11am-8pm), with additional locations on the Strip and downtown, or from **Tickets 2Nite** (Map pp104-5; ☎ 702-939-2222; www.tickets2nite.com; Showcase Mall, 3785 Las Vegas Blvd S; 🕑 11am-9pm), which accepts phone orders between 10:30am and 6pm.

LOVE (Map pp104-5; ☎ 702-792-7777, 800-963-9634; www.cirquedusoleil.com; Mirage, 3400 Las Vegas Blvd S; tickets $69-150; 🕑 7pm & 10pm Thu-Mon; 👶) Another smash hit from Cirque du Soleil, which has a dizzying number of shows on the Strip, LOVE started off as the brainchild of the late George Harrison. It psychedelically fuses the musical legacy of the Beatles with the troupe's aerial acrobatics and dancing in a 360-degree theater.

Phantom (Map pp104-5; ☎ 702-414-9000, 866-641-7469; www.venetian.com; Venetian, 3355 Las Vegas Blvd S; tickets $69-158; 🕑 7pm Mon-Sat, 9:30pm Mon & Sat; 👶) A $40-million, gorgeous theater mimics the 19th-century Parisian opera house where Andrew Lloyd Weber's musical story of a doomed love triangle takes place. Vegas-only special effects include fireworks and an onstage lake.

Kà (Map pp104-5; ☎ 702-891-7777, 877-880-0880; www.ka.com; MGM Grand, 3799 Las Vegas Blvd S; adult $69-150, child $35-75; 🕑 7pm & 9:30pm Tue-Sat; 👶) Cirque du Soleil's sensuous story of imperial twins, mysterious destinies, love and conflict is a hot ticket. Instead of a stage, there's a grid of moving platforms elevating a frenzy of martial arts–inspired performances.

Crazy Horse Paris (Map pp104-5; ☎ 702-891-7777, 800-880-0880; www.mgmgrand.com; MGM Grand, 3799 Las Vegas Blvd S; tickets $49-59; 🕑 8pm & 10:30pm Wed-Mon) Za, za, zoom. The 100% red room's intimate bordello feel oozes sex appeal. Onstage, balletic dancers straight from Paris' Crazy Horse Saloon perform provocative cabaret numbers interspersed with voyeuristic and humorous *l'art du nu* vignettes.

Legends in Concert (Map pp104-5; ☎ 702-794-3261, 877-777-7664; www.imperialpalace.com; Imperial Palace, 3535 Las Vegas Blvd S; adult $50-60, child $35-45; 🕑 7:30pm & 10pm Mon-Sat; 👶) Vegas' top pop-star impersonator show features real talent (no lip-synching allowed). Video screens show concert clips of the real-life performers, while dancers boogie up a VH1 storm.

Jubilee! (Map pp104-5; ☎ 702-967-4567, 800-237-7469; www.ballyslasvegas.com; Bally's, 3645 Las Vegas Blvd S; tickets $48-110; 🕑 7:30pm & 10:30pm Sat-Thu) It's a cheesy showgirl production that Vegas wouldn't be Vegas without. Expect flashy costumes, twinkling rhinestones and enormous headdresses and knockers on display, with less-than-exciting filler acts. For backstage tours, see p118.

Comedy & Magic Shows

Big-name comedians often headline at the Hilton, Flamingo, Caesars Palace and Golden Nugget casino hotels.

The Improv (Map pp104-5; ☎ 702-369-5223; Harrah's, 3475 Las Vegas Blvd S; admission $29; 🕑 8:30pm & 10:30pm Tue-Sun) NYC's well-established showcase spotlights touring stand-up headliners *du jour*.

Second City (Map pp104-5; ☎ 702-733-3333, 800-221-7299; Flamingo, 3555 Las Vegas Blvd S; admission $49; 🕑 8pm Thu-Tue, 10pm Thu, Sat & Sun) For the best-value sketch comedy acts in the city, try this national chain theater, which goes totally 'scriptless' for Saturday's late show.

Mac King (Map pp104-5; ☎ 702-369-5222; Harrah's, 3475 Las Vegas Blvd S; tickets $25; 🕑 1pm & 3pm Tue-Sat; 👶) With lots of PG-13 laughs and sleight-of-hand thrown in, King's bag of tricks includes baiting a live goldfish with a Fig Newton cookie.

Cinemas

Check **Fandango** (☎ 800-326-3264; www.fandango.com) for show times and more theater locations.

Las Vegas 5 Drive-In (off Map p112; ☎ 702-646-3565; 4150 W Carey Ave, off N Rancho Dr; adult/child under 12 $6/free; 🕑 gates open 6:30pm or 7pm; 👶) Old-fashioned place screens up to five double-features daily. Bring your buddies, grab a bucket of popcorn and put your feet up on the dashboard – ah, heaven.

Town Square 18 (off Map pp104-5; ☎ 702-362-7283; Town Square, 6587 Las Vegas Blvd S; adult/child $10/6.25) Swanky off-Strip cineplex offers digital projection and XL stadium seating.

Sports

Although Vegas doesn't have any professional sports franchises, it's a sports-savvy town. You can wager on just about anything at casinos' race and sports books – the Hilton has the world's largest, but Caesars Palace's is darn close.

For auto racing, including Nascar, Indy racing, drag and dirt-track races, check out the mega-popular **Las Vegas Motor Speedway** (Map p112; ☎ 702-644-4444, 800-644-4444; 7000 Las Vegas Blvd N, off I-15 exit 54).

World-class boxing draws fans from all over the globe to:

Mandalay Bay Events Center (Map pp104-5; ☎ 877-632-7800; www.mandalaybay.com; Mandalay, 3950 Las Vegas Blvd S) Boxing, ultimate fighting; 12,000 seats.

MGM Grand Garden Arena (Map pp104-5; ☎ 877-880-0880; www.mgmgrand.com; MGM Grand, 3799 Las Vegas Blvd S) Boxing, tennis; 17,000 seats.

Orleans Arena (off Map pp104-5; ☎ 888-234-2334; www.orleansarena.com; Orleans, 4500 W Tropicana Ave) Boxing, ice hockey, motorsports and more; 9000 seats.

Thomas & Mack Center (Map pp104-5; ☎ 702-739-3267, 866-388-3267; www.unlvtickets.com; UNLV campus, S Swenson St at Tropicana Ave) Wrestling, boxing and pro rodeo events; 18,000 seats.

Spend a lazy summer afternoon watching the minor-league **Las Vegas 51s** (Map p112; ☎ 702-386-7200; www.lv51.com; Cashman Field, 850 Las Vegas Blvd N; tickets $8-13; ☼ Apr-Aug) play ball north of downtown. If you adore bitchy, buxom girls on wheels, the **Sin City Rollergirls** (Map pp104-5; www.lasvegasderbygirls.com; Las Vegas Roller Hockey Center, 953 E Sahara Ave; ☼ hours vary) are a tough-as-nails roller-derby team.

Strip Clubs

Prostitution may be illegal, but plenty of places offer the illusion of sex on demand. Lap dances cost from $20. Unescorted women are usually not welcome at popular strip clubs, including the following.

Scores Las Vegas (off Map pp104-5; ☎ 702-367-4000; 3355 S Procyon St; cover $30; ☼ 24hr) NYC chain that Howard Stern raves about in a mini replica of Caesars Palace. Look for Hollywood celebs, pro athletes and a premium cigar menu.

Crazy Horse Too (Map pp104-5; ☎ 702-382-8003; 2476 Industrial Rd; cover $20; ☼ 24hr) Not even the FBI's 'Operation G-Sting' (aka 'Strippergate') could keep the doors of this legendary gentleman's club closed. Porn star Jenna Jameson started here.

Sapphire (Map pp104-5; ☎ 702-796-6000; 3025 S Industrial Rd; cover $20; ☼ 24hr) Just about everything is larger than life at Vegas' biggest adult entertainment complex. For ladies, the Men of Sapphire shake their booties upstairs on weekends.

Olympic Garden (Map pp104-5; ☎ 702-385-9361; 1531 Las Vegas Blvd S; cover $30; ☼ 24hr) Wins high marks from topless-club aficionados – and the nickname 'Silicone Valley' from the competition. Studs strip upstairs for ladies only Wednesday through Sunday nights.

SHOPPING

Consumption here is as conspicuous as dancing fountains in the middle of the desert. Upscale international haute purveyors cater to cashed-up clientele, selling catwalk fashions fresh off the runway and antique diamonds once worn by royalty. Of course, you'll also find truckloads of kitsch, naughty novelties and awful art.

The Strip has the highest-octane shopping action, concentrated in megaresorts and malls, where unique boutiques are scarce. Downtown you'll find gambling souvenirs, showgirl wigs and feather boas, along with antique, vintage and thrift stores. Cruise west of the Strip for XXX adult goods and trashy lingerie. East of the Strip, near UNLV, Maryland Parkway is chock-a-block with hip, bargain-basement shops catering to college students.

Shopping Malls & Arcades

Casino shopping malls and arcades are open from 10am until 11pm Sunday through Thursday, until midnight Friday and Saturday.

Forum Shops (Map pp104-5; ☎ 702-893-4800; 3500 Las Vegas Blvd S) Franklins fly out of Fendi bags faster at Caesars' fanciful re-creation of an ancient Roman market, housing 160 catwalk designer emporia. Get your photo taken inside a Ferrari at the Exotic Cars showroom.

Grand Canal Shoppes (Map pp104-5; ☎ 702-414-4500; Venetian, 3355 Las Vegas Blvd S) Living statues and mezzo-sopranos stroll along the cobblestone walkways of this Italianate indoor mall, winding past 85 upscale shops like BCBG, Burberry, Godiva, Jimmy Choo and Sephora.

Shoppes at Palazzo (Map pp104-5; ☎ 702-607-4300; Palazzo, 3325 Las Vegas Blvd S). Next door to Grand Canal, Palazzo is anchored by Barneys New York.

Wynn Esplanade (Map pp104-5; ☎ 702-770-7000; 3131 Las Vegas Blvd S) Wynn has lured high-end retailers like Oscar de la Renta, Jean-Paul Gaultier, Chanel and Manolo Blahnik to a 75,000-sq-ft concourse of consumer bliss. After you hit the jackpot, take a test drive at the Penske-Wynn Ferrari/Maserati dealership.

Miracle Mile Shops (Map pp104-5; ☎ 888-800-8284; Planet Hollywood, 3663 Las Vegas Blvd S) Sleekly redesigned mall is a staggering 1.5 miles long. Stand-outs include Bettie Page, for vintage-styled clothing; Brits H&M and Ben Sherman; LA denim king True Religion; and Vegas' own rock-star boutique, Stash.

Las Vegas Premium Outlets (Map p112; ☎ 702-474-7500; 875 S Grand Central Pkwy) Discount-shopping outlet mall features high-end names such as Armani Exchange, Calvin Klein, Dolce & Gabbana, Guess and Max Studio, alongside casual everyday brands like Levi's.

Hard Rock (Map pp104–5; ☎ 702-693-5000; 4455 Paradise Rd) The casino hotel's gift shop has limited-edition rock 'n' roll collectibles, but why stop there? Love Jones has imported lingerie. Rocks, a 24-hour jewelry store, sells diamonds anytime.

The District (off Map pp104–5; ☎ 702-564-8595, 877-564-8595; Green Valley Ranch, 2240 Village Walk Dr, Henderson, off I-215 exit Green Valley Pkwy) Along this open-air promenade find unique children's shop Along Came a Spider, one-of-a-kind women's clothing boutiques Pink and Chelsea, and West Coast outdoor outfitter REI.

Not Just Antiques Mart (Map p112; ☎ 702-384-4922; 1422 Western Ave; ☽ 10am-6pm Mon-Sat, noon-6pm Sun) It's a one-stop antique-shopping extravaganza in the downtown arts district. Look for art-deco estate jewelry, casino memorabilia and vintage tiki ware. Upstairs there's a quaint tearoom.

Clothing & Jewelry

Fred Leighton: Rare Collectible Jewels (Map pp104–5; ☎ 702-693-7050; Via Bellagio, 3600 Las Vegas Blvd S; ☽ 10am-midnight) Many Academy Awards night adornments are on loan from the world's most prestigious collection of antique jewelry. Unlike at the uptight NYC outlet, they might let you try on finery that once belonged to royalty.

Buffalo Exchange (Map pp104–5; ☎ 702-791-3960; 4110 S Maryland Pkwy; ☽ 10am-8pm Mon-Sat, 11am-7pm Sun) Trade in your nearly new garb for cash or credit at this savvy secondhand chain. They've combed through dingy thrift-store stuff and culled only the best 1940s to '80s vintage fashions, clubwear and designer duds.

The Attic (Map p112; ☎ 702-388-4088; 1018 S Main St; ☽ 10am-5pm Mon-Thu, to 6pm Fri, 11am-6pm Sat) A $1 'lifetime pass' is required to enter this vintage emporium, but it's worth it, even if you don't buy. Be mesmerized by fabulous hats and wigs, hippie-chic clubwear and lounge-lizard furnishings. The 1st floor is mostly furnishings. Upstairs is a smaller pre-1950s selection and a cool retro coffee bar for Greek grub.

Valentino's Zootsuit Connection (Map p112; ☎ 702-383-9555; 906 S 6th St; ☽ 11am-5pm Mon-Sat) A sweet (and stylish!) husband and wife team outfit party-goers with upscale vintage apparel: fringed Western wear and felt hats, plus glamorous dresses. Rentals and custom swinging zootsuits are a specialty.

Sheplers (off Map p112; ☎ 702-454-5266; Sam's Town, 5111 Boulder Hwy; ☽ 10am-10pm) Since 1899, this reliable Western outfitter has everything needed to outfit cowboys and cowgirls, from blue jeans and button-down shirts to felt fur hats and embroidered ostrich-skin boots.

Music & Books

For bookstores, see p103.

Zia Records (off Map pp104–5; ☎ 702-735-4942; 4225 S Eastern Ave; ☽ 10am-midnight) Calling itself the 'last real record store,' here you can dig up a demo by Vegas' next breakout band (who needs the Killers anyway?). Live in-store performances happen on a stage with the warning sign: 'No moshing allowed.'

Naughty Novelties

In a town with this many strip clubs, it should come as little surprise that the adult-apparel business is ba-bah-booming.

Adult Superstore (Map pp104–5; ☎ 702-798-0144; 3850 W Tropicana Ave; ☽ 24hr) This enormous, well-lit porn warehouse has more pussies than the SPCA: toys, books, magazines, videos, tasteful 'marital enhancement products' and titillating accessories. The XXX arcade is upstairs.

Déjà Vu Love Boutique (Map pp104–5; ☎ 702-731-5652; 3275 Industrial Rd; ☽ 10am-4am) Hit this party-colored sex shop for quick pick-me-ups like passion-fruit lube, a bouncy paddle or an adult DVD for your hotel room.

Strings of Las Vegas (off Map pp104–5; ☎ 702-873-7820; 4970 Arville St; ☽ noon-8pm Mon-Sat) All those hard-working sexy women and beefy guys obviously don't have time to make their own G-strings and tasseled undies. This industrial strip-mall warehouse outfits them from head to toe, with almost nothing in between.

Weird & Wonderful

Gamblers General Store (Map p112; ☎ 702-382-9903; 800 S Main St; ☽ 9am-6pm) It boasts one of the largest inventories of slot machines in Nevada, with new models and beautiful vintage machines, plus loads of souvenir gambling paraphernalia.

Rainbow Feather Dyeing Co (Map p112; ☎ 702-598-0988; www.rainbowfeatherco.com; 1036 S Main St; ☽ 9am-4pm Mon-Fri, to 1pm Sat) Where to satisfy that showgirl's feather-boa fetish? Need turkey, chicken, duck, goose, pheasant, ostrich or peacock quill fans? Find a fabulous selection in every possible hue here.

Houdini's Magic Shop (Map pp104-5; ☎ 702-798-4789; Forum Shops, 3500 Las Vegas Blvd S) The legendary escape artist's legacy lives on at this shop packed with gags, pranks, magic tricks and authentic Houdini memorabilia. Magicians perform, and each purchase includes a free private lesson.

Imperial Palace Auto Collections (Map pp104-5; ☎ 702-794-3174; www.autocollections.com; Imperial Palace, 3535 Las Vegas Blvd S; adult/child $7/3; ⊙ 9:30am-9:30pm) The entire lot on display is for sale on consignment (sorry, no test drives) at this indoor antique and collectibles lot on the 5th floor of the parking garage. Print out free-admission coupons from the website.

Bonanza Gifts Shop (Map pp104-5; ☎ 702-385-7359; 2440 Las Vegas Blvd S; ⊙ 11am-midnight) If it's not the 'World's Largest Gift Shop,' it's damn close. The amazing kitsch selection of overpriced souvenirs includes entire aisles of dice clocks, snow globes, tacky T-shirts and shot glasses.

GETTING THERE & AWAY
Air
Las Vegas has direct flights from most US cities, as well as some Canadian, Mexican, European and Asian gateways. During peak periods (eg holidays, weekends), vacation packages including airfare and accommodations can be fair deals.

Handy to the South Strip, **McCarran International Airport** (LAS; Map pp104-5; ☎ 702-261-5211; www.mccarran.com; 5757 Wayne Newton Blvd; wi-fi) offers free internet access; ATMs, currency-exchange booths and a bank; a post office; a 24-hour fitness center (day pass $10); and a kids' play area. Left-luggage lockers are unavailable post–September 11. Most domestic airlines use Terminal 1; international, charter and some domestic flights use Terminal 2. A free, wheelchair-accessible tram links outlying gates. Short-term metered parking costs 25¢ per 10 minutes.

Bus & Train
Long-distance Greyhound (p535) buses arrive at a downtown **bus station** (Map p112; ☎ 702-384-9561; Plaza, 200 S Main St). The nearest Amtrak (p535) station is in Kingman, AZ (see p259). Greyhound may provide connecting Thruway motor coach service to Las Vegas ($27 to $34, 2¾ to four hours).

Megabus (Map pp104-5; ☎ 877-462-6342; www.megabus.com; cnr E Tropicana Ave & S Swenson St) offers three daily express buses to/from downtown LA (Union Station), taking four to five hours each way. Fares vary from $1.50 to $35, depending on how far in advance you book a seat. From the Megabus station, take a taxi or CAT bus 201 ($1.25, 15 minutes) to the Strip or ride CAT bus 109 downtown ($1.25, 25 to 50 minutes).

Car & Motorcycle
The main roads into and out of Las Vegas are I-15 and US Hwy 95. US Hwy 93 leads southeast from downtown to Hoover Dam; I-215 goes by McCarran International Airport. It's a 165-mile drive (2½ hours) to Utah's Zion National Park, 275 miles (4½ hours) to Arizona's Grand Canyon Village and 270 miles (four hours) to Los Angeles. Along the I-15 corridor to/from California, Highway Radio (98.1FM, 99.5FM) broadcasts traffic updates every 30 minutes.

For car rental companies and policies, see p537. Booking ahead is essential on weekends, with the airport usually being cheaper than the Strip or downtown. For something glamorous, ring **Rent-A-Vette** (Map pp104-5; ☎ 702-736-2592, 800-372-1981; www.rent-a-vette.com; 5021 Swenson St). Corvettes and exotic convertibles easily fetch $200 or more per day. **Las Vegas Harley-Davidson** (Map pp104-5; ☎ 702-431-8500, 888-218-0744; www.lvhd.com; 2605 S Eastern Ave) rents Harleys from $90 to $155 per day, including unlimited mileage, 24-hour roadside assistance, a helmet and a rain suit.

GETTING AROUND
Gridlock along the Strip makes navigating the city's core a chore. The best way to get around is on foot, along with the occasional air-con taxi, monorail or bus ride.

To/From the Airport
Taxi fares to Strip hotels – 30 minutes in heavy traffic – run $10 to $15 (to downtown, average $20), cash only. Fare gouging ('long-hauling') through the airport connector tunnel is common; ask your driver to use surface streets instead. Most airport shuttles operate from 8am to midnight, but some run 24 hours; they charge $6 per person to the Strip, $7.50 to downtown or off-Strip hotels. If you're traveling light, CAT bus No 109 ($1.25, 30 to 60 minutes) runs downtown 24/7. Between 5am and 2am, CAT bus 108 ($1.25, 40 to 55 minutes) also heads downtown, stopping at

the Las Vegas Convention Center, Hilton and Sahara monorail stations.

Car & Motorcycle

Traffic often snarls, especially during morning and afternoon rush hours and at night on weekends around the Strip. Work out in advance which cross street will bring you closest to your destination and try to utilize alternate routes like Industrial Rd and Paradise Rd. Tune to 970AM for traffic updates. If you're too drunk to drive, call **Designated Drivers** (☎ 702-456-7433; ☯ 24hr) to pick you up and drive your car back to your hotel; fees vary, depending on mileage.

Public Transportation

The fast, frequent **monorail** (☎ 702-699-8200; www.lvmonorail.com; 1-/2-ride ticket $9/5, 24/72hr pass $15/40, child under 6 free; ☯ 7am-2am Mon-Thu, to 3am Fri-Sun) stops at the MGM Grand, Bally's/Paris–Las Vegas, Flamingo/Caesars Palace, Harrah's/Imperial Palace, Las Vegas Convention Center, Las Vegas Hilton and Sahara stations. A discounted six-ride ticket ($20) can be used by multiple riders.

Citizens Area Transit (CAT; ☎ 702-228-7433, 800-228-3911; www.catride.com; 24hr pass $5; ☯ most routes 5am-2am) operates dozens of local bus lines (one-way fare $1.25) and double-decker 'The Deuce' buses ($2), which run 24/7 along the Strip to and from downtown. Cash only (exact change required).

Many off-Strip hotels offer guests free shuttle buses to/from the Strip. A free public shuttle connects the Rio casino hotel to Harrah's Las Vegas, Bally's/Paris–Las Vegas and Caesars Palace every 30 minutes from 10am to 1am, sometimes later on Friday and Saturday nights. A free tram connects TI (Treasure Island) and the Mirage, and also Excalibur, Luxor and Mandalay Bay.

Taxi

It's illegal to hail a cab on the street. Taxi stands are found at casino hotels and malls. A 4.5-mile lift from one end of the Strip to the other runs $12 to $16, plus tip. Fares (cash only) are metered: flagfall is $3.30, plus $2.20 per mile and 20¢ per minute while waiting. By law, the maximum number of passengers is five, and all companies must have at least one wheelchair-accessible van. Call **Desert Cab** (☎ 702-386-9102), **Western Cab** (☎ 702-736-8000) or **Yellow/Checker/Star** (☎ 702-873-2000).

AROUND LAS VEGAS

Las Vegas is the antithesis of a naturalist's vision of America, yet it's close to some spectacular outdoor attractions. For iconic desert landscapes, Red Rock Canyon and Valley of Fire State Park are just outside the city limits. Mt Charleston is a small-time, year-round resort, offering hiking and camping during summer and skiing and snowboarding in winter. Straddling the Arizona–Nevada state line are Hoover Dam, just outside Boulder City, and the cool oases of Lake Mead National Recreation Area, all within easy striking distance of Las Vegas. Laughlin (p229) is less than two hours' drive away.

Organized Tours

Hoover Dam package deals can save ticketing headaches, while adventure outfitters ease logistical hassles for many of these excursions. Some tours include free pick-ups and drop-offs from Strip casino hotels. Check Vegas' free tourist magazines for discounts. Dozens of travel agents sell tours, but it's best to book directly with these recommended companies:

Black Canyon River Adventures (☎ 702-294-1414, 800-455-3490; www.blackcanyonadventures.com; Hacienda Hotel & Casino, off US Hwy 93, Boulder City; adult/child $83/51) Motor-assisted Colorado River raft floats launch beneath Hoover Dam, with stops for swimming and lunch.

Boulder City Outfitters (☎ 702-293-1190, 800-748-3702; www.bouldercityoutfitters.com; 1631 Industrial Rd, Boulder City; kayak/mountain-biking & hiking tours $63/100, canoe & kayak rentals per day $35-55, mountain-bike rental per half-day from $25) Guided kayak tours launch beneath Hoover Dam; DIY shuttles are available.

Escape Adventures (☎ 800-596-2953; www.escape adventures.com; weekend trips from $399) Escape the neon jungle for single-track mountain-biking, hiking and multisport tours of Red Rock Canyon, the Mojave Desert and beyond.

Gray Line (☎ 702-384-1234, 800-634-6579; www.gray linelasvegas.com; tours $52-112) Bus and boat excursions to Red Rock Canyon, Hoover Dam and Lake Mead.

Hike This! (☎ 702-393-4453; www.hikethislasvegas .com; tours $79-109) Private and group hiking and rock-scrambling tours around Red Rock Canyon.

RED ROCK CANYON

The startling contrast between Las Vegas' artificial neon glow and the awesome natural forces in this **national conservation area** (☎ 702-515-5350; www.blm.gov/nv; day-use per car/bicycle $5/2;

scenic loop 6am-5pm Nov-Feb, to 7pm Mar & Oct, to 8pm Apr-Sep) can't be exaggerated. Created about 65 million years ago, the canyon is more like a valley, with a steep, rugged red rock escarpment rising 3000ft on its western edge, dramatic evidence of tectonic-plate collisions.

A 13-mile, one-way scenic drive passes some of the canyon's most striking features, where you can access hiking trails and rock-climbing routes, or simply be mesmerized by the vistas. Stop at the **visitor center** (☎ 702-515-5350; 8:30am-4:30pm), for its natural-history exhibits and information on hiking trails, rock-climbing routes and 4WD routes. **Red Rock Canyon Interpretive Association** (☎ 702-515-5361/5367; www.redrockcanyonlv.org) operates the non-profit bookstore there and organizes activities, including birding and wildflower walks (advance reservations may be required).

Call ahead to reserve guided horseback tours led by **Cowboy Trail Rides** (☎ 702-387-2457; www.cowboytrailrides.com; off Hwy 159; tours $79-339;). Mountain biking is allowed only on paved roads, not dirt trails. Rent bikes at **Las Vegas Cyclery** (off Map p112; ☎ 702-596-2953; www.lasvegas cyclery.com; 8221 W Charleston Blvd; per day from $30; 10am-6pm Mon-Fri, 9am-6pm Sat, 10am-4pm Sun) in suburban Summerlin or at **McGhie's Bike Outpost** (☎ 702-875-4820; www.bikeoutpost.com; 16 Cottonwood Dr; per day from $35, tours from $109; hours vary) in Blue Diamond, near 125 miles of single-track trails in the Cottonwood Valley and Black Velvet areas.

To get here from the Strip, take I-15 south, exit at Blue Diamond Rd (NV Hwy 160), and drive westward, veering right onto NV Hwy 159. On the return trip, keep driving east on Hwy 159, which becomes Charleston Blvd. About 2 miles east of the visitor center off NV Hwy 159 is a **campground** (☎ 702-515-5350; tent & RV sites $10; Sep-May), offering first-come, first-served sites with water and vault toilets.

SPRING MOUNTAIN RANCH STATE PARK

South of Red Rock Canyon's scenic loop drive, a side road leaves Hwy 159 and enters the petite **Spring Mountain Ranch State Park** (☎ 702-875-4141; entry $5; 8am-dusk, visitor center 10am-4pm), abutting the cliffs of the Wilson Range. The ranch was established in the 1860s and has had various owners, including Vera Krupp (of the German industrialist family) and eccentric billionaire Howard Hughes. Popular with picnicking families on weekends, today it's a verdant place, with white fences and

an old red ranch house, which has historical exhibits. Call for schedules of guided ranch tours, moonlight canyon hikes and outdoor summer theater performances.

LAKE MEAD & HOOVER DAM

Even those who challenge, or at least question, the USA's commitment to damming the US West have to marvel at the engineering and architecture of the Hoover Dam. Set amid the almost unbearably dry Mohave Desert, the dam towers over Black Canyon and provides electricity for the entire region.

Hoover Dam created Lake Mead, which boasts 700 miles of shoreline, while Davis Dam created much smaller Lake Mohave, which straddles the Arizona border. Black Canyon, the stretch of the Colorado River just below Hoover Dam, links the two lakes. All three bodies of water are included in the Lake Mead National Recreation Area, created in 1964. The Colorado feeds into Lake Mead from Grand Canyon National Park, and rafting trips through the canyon finish on the east end of the lake.

Orientation & Information

US Hwy 93 crosses Hoover Dam about 45 minutes southeast of Las Vegas. For Hoover Dam traffic restrictions, call ☎ 888-248-1259. Expect delays of 30 minutes or more crossing the dam by car until the US Hwy 93 bypass is finished. Visitors to Lake Mead will find most services in Boulder City, a small town just west of the dam. The main towns at the south tip of Lake Mohave are Laughlin and Bullhead City, AZ (see p229).

Alan Bible Visitor Center (☎ 702-293-8990; Lakeshore Scenic Dr, off US Hwy 93; 8:30am-4:30pm) In Nevada, 5 miles west of Hoover Dam.

Katherine Landing Ranger Station (☎ 928-754-3272; off AZ Hwy 68, Bullhead City; 8:30am-4pm) In Arizona, 3 miles north of Davis Dam.

Sights

HOOVER DAM

A statue of bronze winged figures stands atop Hoover Dam, memorializing those who built the massive 726ft concrete structure, one of the world's tallest dams. Originally named Boulder Dam, this New Deal public works project completed ahead of schedule and under budget in 1936 was the Colorado River's first major dam. Thousands of men and their families, eager for work in the height of the Depression, came to Black Canyon and worked in excruciating conditions – dangling hundreds of feet above the canyon in 120°F desert heat. Hundreds lost their lives.

Today guided tours begin at the **visitor center** (☎ information 702-293-8321, reservations 702-992-7990, 866-998-3427; www.usbr.gov/lc/hooverdam; US Hwy 93; admission $8, incl power-plant tour adult/child/senior $11/9/9, all-inclusive tour $25; ☑ 9am-5pm, to 6pm in summer, last ticket sold 45min before closing), where a video screening features original footage of the construction. Then take an elevator ride 50 stories below to view the dam's massive power generators, each of which alone could power a city of 100,000 people. Zoom back up top for a self-paced tour of flood-preventing spillways, exhibit halls and outdoor points of interest. When you tire of admiring the view and pretending to jump the railing (no terrorist jokes, please – that sort of thing is taken *very* seriously around here), make a beeline for the refrigerated gift shop to pick up unique novelties for your loved ones: 'Got Power?' T-shirts, 'Dam Proud to Be an American' bumper stickers – you name it, bub.

HOOVER DAM MUSEUM

You'll enjoy the dam tour more if you stop at this small but engagingly hands-on **museum** (☎ 702-294-1988; www.bcmha.org; 1305 Arizona St, Boulder City; adult/child/senior $2/1/1; ☑ 10am-5pm Mon-Sat, noon-5pm Sun; ♿) first. It's upstairs at the historic Boulder Dam Hotel, where Bette Davis, FDR and Howard Hughes once slept. Exhibits focus on Depression-era America and the tough living conditions endured by the people who came to build the dam. A 20-minute film features historic footage of the project.

Activities

For motorized float trips and guided kayaking tours launching below Hoover Dam, see p131. Popular year-round activities in **Lake Mead National Recreation Area** (☎ 702-293-8906; www.nps.gov/lame; 5-day entry pass $5; ☑ 24hr) include swimming, fishing, boating, waterskiing and kayaking. The main scenic drive winds north along Lakeshore Dr and Northshore Rd, passing viewpoints, hiking and birding trailheads, beaches and bays, and full-service marinas. Because water levels vary, what was a beach one year may be a desert the next. In fact, recent studies suggest that due to climate change and the region's unquenchable thirst for water, Lake Mead may dry up entirely by 2021. **Fish Vegas** (☎ 702-293-6294; www.fishvegas.com; guided tours 1-2 people from $300) Chartered fishing trips

on Lake Mead. Go online for Cap'n Mike's monthly fishing reports and news.

Lake Mead Cruises (☎ 702-293-6180; www.lakemeadcruises.com; 90min midday cruise per adult/child $22/10; ☑ noon & 2pm) Kid-friendly tours on triple-decker, air-con, Mississippi-style paddle wheelers; depart from Hemenway Harbor.

Las Vegas Boat Harbor (☎ 702-293-1191; www.boatinglakemead.com; Hemenway Harbor) Most marinas on Lake Mead rent personal watercraft, power boats and water-sports equipment.

Sleeping

Inside the national recreation area, **Lake Mead Lodge** (☎ 702-293-2074, 800-752-9669; www.sevencrown.com; Lakeshore Dr; d $65-95, kitchen ste $120-180) is a basic motel at a busy marina. On Lake Mohave, **Cottonwood Cove Motel** (☎ 702-297-1464; www.cottonwoodcoveresort.com; r $65-115) has rooms with sliding glass doors overlooking a swimming beach. First-come, first-served **NPS campgrounds** (☎ 702-293-8906; tent & RV sites $10) are found on Lake Mead at Boulder Beach, Callville Bay, Echo Bay and Las Vegas Bay. Private campgrounds offering RV sites with full hookups are scattered around both lakes' shores.

Boulder City's main drag is lined with yesteryear motels. **El Rancho Motel** (☎ 702-293-1085; www.elranchoboulder.com; 725 Nevada Hwy; r $70-110; ☐ wi-fi), which has some kitchenettes and may accept pets for a surcharge, is comfier than most. The **Sands Motel** (☎ 702-293-2589; 809 Nevada Hwy; r $59-79) is a friendly, family-owned 1950s place providing clean, simple rooms.

Eating

In downtown Boulder City, **Milo's** (☎ 702-293-9540; 538 Nevada Way; dishes $4-18; ☑ 11am-10pm Sun-Thu, to midnight Fri & Sat) serves fresh sandwiches, salads and gourmet cheese plates at sidewalk tables outside the wine bar. Order home-cooked classic Italian pasta dishes and meatier fare, with tiramisu afterward, at **Le Bistro Cafe** (☎ 702-293-7070; 1312 Nevada Hwy; mains $12-18; ☑ dinner).

You'll find only basic restaurants at the Temple Bar, Boulder Beach and Echo Bay marinas on Lake Mead, and at Cottonwood Cove and Katherine Landing on Lake Mohave. Other lakeshore marinas have convenience stores for snacks and drinks.

Getting There & Away

From the Strip, take I-15 south to I-215 east to I-515/US 93 and 95 and continue over

Railroad Pass, staying on US Hwy 93 past Boulder City. As you approach the dam, park in the multilevel parking lot ($7, cash only; open 8am to 6pm) before you reach the visitor center. Or continue over the Arizona state line and park for free on the roadside (if you can find a space), then walk back over the top of the dam to the visitor center.

VALLEY OF FIRE STATE PARK

On the north edge of Lake Mead, this **park** (☎ 702-397-2088; http://parks.nv.gov/vf.htm; entry $6; ⏲ 24hr) is a masterpiece of desert scenery, a fantasyland of wondrous shapes carved in psychedelic sandstone by the erosive forces of wind and water. Several petroglyphs throughout the park are a reminder of early Native Americans. **Elephant Rock**, the **Seven Sisters** and **Beehives** are among the most intriguing rock formations. Stop at the **visitor center** (☎ 702-397-2088; ⏲ 8:30am-4:30pm), which has educational exhibits, sells books and maps, and has information about ranger-led activities like guided hikes, fossil hunting and stargazing. Take the winding scenic side road out to **White Domes**, an 11-mile round trip. En route you'll pass **Rainbow Vista**, followed by the turn-off to **Fire Canyon** and **Silica Dome** (incidentally, where Captain Kirk perished in *Star Trek: Generations*). Spring and fall are the best times to visit; daytime summer temperatures typically exceed 100°F. The valley is at its most fiery at dawn and dusk, so consider grabbing a first-come, first-served site in the **campgrounds** (tent & RV sites $14). The fastest way here from Las Vegas is to drive I-15 north to NV Hwy 169, taking about an hour.

MT CHARLESTON

Up in the Humboldt-Toiyabe National Forest, the Spring Mountains form the western boundary of the Las Vegas valley, with higher rainfall, lower temperatures and fragrant pine, juniper and mahogany forests. It's a total escape from the desert valley, and it's usually about 30°F cooler at these elevations, too.

From Las Vegas, take I-15 north to US Hwy 95 north to NV Hwy 157 (Kyle Canyon Rd) and drive uphill. Just past the NV Hwy 158 turn-off and campground, the **information station** (☎ 702-872-5486; www.fs.fed.us/r4/htnf; Kyle Canyon Rd; ⏲ hours vary) has free trail guides, brochures and outdoor activity information.

DETOUR: LOST CITY

The little **Lost City Museum** (☎ 702-397-2193; 721 S Moapa Valley Blvd, Overton; adult/senior $3/2, child under 18 free; ⏲ 8:30am-4:30pm) tells the story of the 'lost' Pueblo Grande de Nevada that existed on this site until around AD 1150. Exhibitions of excavated ruins inside the museum are almost as captivating as the Pueblo Revival–style building itself, constructed of sun-dried adobe bricks by the Civilian Conservation Corps during the 1930s. Out back you can peek inside replicas of Native American dwellings. To find the museum, drive 8 miles along NV Hwy 169, north of the Valley of Fire State Park turn-off from Lake Mead.

Curve left onto Old Park Rd to keep heading up the mountain. The **village** of Mt Charleston gives access to several hikes, including the demanding 16.6-mile round-trip **South Loop Trail** up Charleston Peak (elevation 11,918ft), starting from Cathedral Rock picnic area. The easier, 2.8-mile round-trip **Cathedral Rock Trail** offers canyon views.

Mt Charleston Lodge (☎ 702-872-5408, 800-955-1314; www.mtcharlestonlodge.com; 1200 Old Park Rd; cabins $145-260) has a chalet-style **dining room** (⏲ 8am-9pm Sun-Thu, 8am-10pm Fri & Sat) and rustic, romantic log cabins with fireplaces, whirlpool tubs and private decks.

Heading back downhill, turn left onto Hwy 158, a curvy alpine road that passes even more trailheads and **campgrounds** (☎ reservations 518-885-3639, 877-444-6777; www.recreation.gov; tent & RV sites $15-25; ⏲ mid-May–Oct, some year-round). At NV Hwy 156 (Lee Canyon Rd), turn either right to return to US Hwy 95 or left to reach **Las Vegas Ski & Snowboard Resort** (☎ 702-385-2754, snow report 702-593-9500; www.skilasvegas.com; half-day pass adult/child under 13 $45/25; ⏲ usually mid-Nov–Apr; ♿), which has four lifts, 11 trails (longest run 3000ft) and a half-pipe and terrain park for snowboarding. Surprised? Don't be. 'Nevada' is derived from the Spanish word for snow, and over 120in of the powdery stuff falls on these slopes each year. Equipment and clothing rentals are first-come, first-served.

PRIMM & JEAN

Southern Californians zooming along I-15 may mistake the bright lights of **Primm**

(☎ 800-386-7867; www.primmvalleyresorts.com; off I-15 exit 1; r from $32) for a suburb of Las Vegas. No such luck, although Primm does have casino hotels, 24-hour restaurants, a gas station and an outlet-shopping mall. Inside Primm Valley Resort, you can inspect the fateful 1934 getaway car of the notorious Bonnie and Clyde. Next door, Buffalo Bill's features amusement **rides** ($3-7), including Desperado, one of the USA's tallest and fastest roller coasters. Country music megastars perform at the Star of the Desert Arena.

At **Jean**, about 10 miles east of the California border, take the NV Hwy 161 exit and drive west 7 miles to the almost-ghost town of **Goodsprings**, where the tin-roofed **Pioneer Saloon** (☎ 702-874-9362; ⏰ 11am-late) dates from 1913. Riddled with bullet holes, it still serves up cold beers atop an antique cherrywood bar. Admire the vintage poker table and movie-star memorabilia before heading back to the interstate. From Jean, it's another half-hour's drive to Las Vegas.

MESQUITE
pop 19,200 / elev 1610ft
Just over an hour's drive northeast of Las Vegas via I-15, **Mesquite** (☎ 877-637-7848; www.visitmesquite.com) is another Nevada border town stuffed full of casino hotels, all banking on slot machine–starved visitors from Utah and Arizona. Near the **Mesquite Fine Arts Center & Gallery** (☎ 702-346-1338; 15 W Mesquite Blvd; admission free; ⏰ 10am-4pm Tue-Sat), the **Virgin Valley Heritage Museum** (☎ 702-346-5705; 35 W Mesquite Blvd; admission free; ⏰ 10am-4pm Tue-Sat) displays pioneer and Native American artifacts.

Escape the casinos by overnighting at the **Falcon Ridge Hotel** (☎ 702-346-2200; www.falconridgehotel.com; 1030 W Pioneer Blvd; d $70-100; 🖳 wi-fi), not too far from **Buffalo's Southwest Cafe** (☎ 702-346-1818; Red Hill Commons, 796 W Pioneer Blvd; mains $7-15; ⏰ 10am-10pm) and sports bar. **Sips & Dips Coffeehouse** (☎ 702-346-6963; 355 W Mesquite Blvd; items $3-10; ⏰ 7am-3pm Mon-Sat; wi-fi) serves homemade soups, sandwiches and ice cream. Try the 'Mesquite Mudd' concoction, fueled with six shots of espresso.

On the Arizona Strip, about halfway between Mesquite and St George, UT (p475), detour off I-15 (exit 18) into the **Virgin River Canyon Recreation Area** (☎ 435-688-3200; www.blm.gov/az; entry free), where hiking trails and a developed campground (tent and RV sites $8) await.

GREAT BASIN
Geographically speaking, nearly all of Nevada lies in the Great Basin – a high desert characterized by rugged mountain ranges and broad valleys that extends into Utah and California. Far from Nevada's major cities, this land is largely empty, textured only by peaks covered by snow in winter. It's big country out here – wild, remote and quiet. Anyone seeking the 'Great American Road Trip' will savor the atmospheric small towns and quirky diversions tucked away along these lonely highways. Each of the main routes used by drivers to cut across the state is described here, covering interesting places to stop along the way, plus some unusual detours.

ALONG HWY 95
US Hwy 95 runs vaguely north–south through western Nevada. Although it's hardly a direct route, it's the fastest way to get from Las Vegas to Reno – and still, it's a full day's drive of 450 miles, so get an early start. The highway zigzags to avoid mountain ranges and passes through old mining centers that are not much more than ghost towns today.

Nevada Test Site
About 65 miles northwest of Las Vegas, starkly scenic US Hwy 95 rounds the Spring Mountains and passes a side road signposted 'To Mercury.' Behind barbed wire lies the Nevada Test Site, where over 900 atmospheric and underground nuclear explosions were detonated between 1951 and 1992. Free public bus **tours** (☎ 702-295-0944; www.nv.doe.gov/nts/tours.htm) depart monthly, usually from Las Vegas' Atomic Testing Museum (p113), but you must apply for reservations months in advance. At the site's western edge is **Yucca Mountain** (☎ 702-821-8687; www.ymp.gov), which the Department of Energy has controversially selected as a high-level nuclear waste repository. Call ahead to ask about public-tour schedules.

Beatty
pop 1200 / elev 3320ft
It's another hour's drive northwest to broken-down Beatty, the northeastern gateway to Death Valley National Park. The **chamber of commerce** (☎ 775-553-2424, 866-736-3716; www.beattynevada.org; 119 Main St; ⏰ 9:30am-2:30pm Tue-Sat) is downtown. Four miles west of town, off NV Hwy 374, is the mining ghost town

of **Rhyolite** (www.rhyolitesite.com; donation appreciated; 24hr), where you can see a 1906 'bottle house' and the skeletal remains of a three-story bank. Next door, the bizarre **Goldwell Open Air Museum** (702-870-9946; www.goldwell museum.org; admission free; 24hr) stars Belgian artist Albert Szukalski's spooky *The Last Supper*. Five miles north of town, past the sign for Angel's Ladies brothel, **Bailey's Hot Springs** (775-553-2395; entry $5, tent/RV sites $15/18; 8am-8pm) offers private mineral pools at a 1906 former railroad depot.

Goldfield & Tonopah

Another hour's drive further north, **Goldfield** became Nevada's biggest boomtown after gold was struck here in 1902. A few precious historic structures survive today, including the Goldfield Hotel; a restored firehouse, now a museum; and the county courthouse, with its Tiffany lamps. Another survivor, the rough-and-tumble **Santa Fe Saloon** (775-485-3431; 925 N 5th Ave; hours vary) is a hoary watering hole.

Almost 30 miles further north, huge mine headframes loom above **Tonopah**, a historic silver-mining town that clings to its remaining population in a bereft yet beautiful setting. The **Central Nevada Museum** (775-482-9676; 1900 Logan Field Rd; admission free; 10am-1pm & 2-5pm Wed-Sun) has a good collection of Shoshone baskets, early photographs, mining relics and mortician's instruments. The **Tonopah Historic Mining Park** (775-482-9274; 520 McCulloch Ave; adult/child $5/3; 9am-5pm daily Apr-Sep, 10am-4pm Wed-Sun Oct-Mar) lets you explore an underground tunnel and peer into old silver-mine shafts. At night, it's dark enough for **stargazing** (www.tonopahstartrails.com).

If you end up stuck here, almost halfway between Las Vegas and Reno, **Tonopah Station** (775-482-9777; www.tonopahstation.com; 1137 S Main St; r from $65; restaurant 24hr; wi-fi) casino hotel dishes up cheap grub and has live entertainment most weekends. Comfier **Best Western Hi-Desert Inn** (775-482-3511; www.bestwestern.com; r from $80; wi-fi) accepts pets.

From Tonopah, it's almost a two-hour drive to Hawthorne, passing the NV Hwy 361 turn-off at Luning for a side trip to Berlin-Icthyosaur State Park (p139). A different scenic drive from Tonopah follows NV Hwy 376 about 100 miles north to US Hwy 50 through the pastoral Big Smoky Valley. On the way, there are interesting stops and side trips to the old mining towns of Round Mountain

and Manhattan. A rough road crosses the Toquima Range to Belmont ghost town.

Hawthorne
pop 3300 / elev 4431ft

The desert surrounding Hawthorne is oddly dotted with concrete bunkers storing millions of tons of explosives from a WWII-era military ammunition depot, which has been partially redone as a nine-hole **golf course** (775-945-1111; green fees $20-25). The **Mineral County Museum** (775-945-5142; 400 10th St; 11am-5pm Tue-Sat) has limited displays on mining and early pioneers. Hungry yet? Locals adore **Maggie's Restaurant & Bakery** (775-945-3908; 785 E St; meals $5-15; 7am-8:30pm). Otherwise, there's always the faded **El Capitan Resort & Casino** (775-945-3321, 800-922-2311; www.elcapitanresortcasino.com; 540 F St; meals from $5, r $50; restaurant 24hr;), which may accept pets.

Heading north, Hwy 95 traces the shrinking shoreline of **Walker Lake State Recreation Area** (775-867-3001; admission free; 24hr), a popular picnicking, swimming, boating and fishing spot that's evaporating fast. On Walker River Indian Reservation near the village of Schurz, the highway splits: US Hwy 95 barrels north through Fallon (p138) to I-80, heading eastbound to Utah. Alt-US Hwy 95 is the scenic route to Reno, joining I-80 westbound at Fernley.

ALONG HWY 93

US Hwy 93 is the oft-deserted route from Las Vegas to Great Basin National Park, a 300-mile trip taking over five hours. Coming from Arizona, Hwy 93 crosses Hoover Dam, then hits Las Vegas and joins I-15 for more than 20 miles before diverging north. The highway truly heads into the wild then, passing by mining ghost towns and wide open rangeland populated by more head of cattle than humans.

Pahranagat Valley

North of I-15, US Hwy 93 parallels the eastern edge of the Desert National Wildlife Range, where bighorn sheep can be spotted. About 90 miles outside of Las Vegas, the road runs by **Pahranagat National Wildlife Refuge** (775-725-3417; www.fws.gov/desertcomplex/pahranagat; admission free; 24hr), where spring-fed lakes surrounded by cottonwoods are a major stopover for migratory birds. Free undeveloped campsites line the east shore of Upper Lake, 4 miles south of Alamo.

DETOUR: AREA 51 & THE EXTRATERRESTRIAL HWY

Die-hard UFO fans and conspiracy theorists won't want to miss the way-out-there trip to Area 51, where some believe secret government research into reverse-engineering alien technology takes place.

Coming from Tonopah, drive east along US Hwy 6 for 50 miles, then follow NV Hwy 375, aka the 'Extraterrestrial Hwy,' for another hour to the roadside pit-stop of Rachel. Have burgers and beer at the **Little A'le'Inn** (☎ 775-729-2515; www.littlealeinn.com; 1 Old Mill Rd, Alamo; meals from $5, RV sites with hookups $12, r $40-140; ☺ 8am-10pm). Its gift shop sells alien bobbleheads, self-published books and hand-drawn maps of the area.

Sky-watchers gather farther east at the 29-mile marker on the south side of Hwy 375. There stands the mysterious black (now white) mailbox marking the beginning of a dirt road into Groom Lake's military base. Warning! Only travel as far as the base boundary, which is marked by signs but no fences. Otherwise, you'll be arrested and fined hundreds of dollars (or worse).

For a virtual visit to Area 51, surf to www.dreamlandresort.com.

Caliente & Pioche

Past Alamo and Ash Springs, US Hwy 93 leads to a junction, where you turn east through some desolate countryside to **Caliente**, a former railroad town with a Mission-style 1923 railway depot. Family-owned **Hansen's Fine Dining** (☎ 775-726-3215; 127 N Spring St; mains $10-17; ☺ dinner) neighbors Pioneer Pizza. At press time, the **hot springs** that gave the town its Spanish name were closed. South of town via NV Hwy 317, **Rainbow Canyon** is known for its colorful cliffs and petroglyphs.

Fifteen miles north of Caliente, just past the turn-off to Panaca, **Cathedral Gorge State Park** (☎ 775-728-4460; entry $4, tent & RV sites $10; ☺ visitor center 9am-4pm) is one of Nevada's little-known scenic treasures, featuring rows of natural spires and buttresses. Miller Point Overlook has sweeping views, with several easy hikes into narrow side canyons and campsites next to badlands-style cliffs.

A few miles farther on, take the loop off US Hwy 93, then follow the high road into **Pioche** (☎ 775-962-5544; www.piochenevada.com), a 19th-century silver-mining town overlooking Lake Valley. In 1873, a Nevada newspaper lambasted Pioche as 'a synonym for murder and lawlessness throughout the state.' To learn more about the town's wilder days, visit the **Lincoln County Museum** (☎ 775-962-5207; 69 Main St; admission free; ☺ 10am-4pm) and the **Million Dollar Courthouse** (☎ 775-962-5544; 69 Lacour St; admission free; ☺ 10am-4pm Apr-Oct). The **Overland Hotel & Saloon** (☎ 775-962-5895; www.overlandhotelnv.com; 85 Main St; r $49-109) and the circa-1920s **Silver Café** (☎ 775-962-5124; 97 Main St; mains $5-15; ☺ 8am-7pm Sun-Thu, to 8pm Fri & Sat) are pretty much the only games in town.

East of US Hwy 395, take a backcountry drive along NV Hwy 372 to **Spring Valley State Park** (☎ 775-962-5102; entry $4, tent & RV sites $10) or **Echo Canyon State Park** (☎ 775-962-5103; entry $4, tent & RV sites $6), both offering boating and fishing on artificial reservoirs.

North to Hwy 50 & I-80

US Hwy 93 continues north for 80 miles to US Hwy 50, heading east to Great Basin National Park (p140) or west to Ely (p139), either about a two-hour drive from Pioche. From Ely, Hwy 93 continues north for 2½ hours to Wells (p142) on I-80. Along the way, Alt-Hwy 93 diverges east to Wendover (p142), on the Utah border, just over two hours from Ely. North of Wells, Hwy 93 climbs into the mountains and crosses the Idaho border at Jackpot, a small casino town frequented by out-of-state gamblers.

ALONG HWY 50

On the 'Loneliest Road in America' barren brown desert hills collide with big blue skies. The highway goes on forever, crossing solitary terrain. Towns are few and far between, with the only sounds the whisper of wind or the rattle-and-hum of a truck engine. Once part of the coast-to-coast Lincoln Hwy, US Hwy 50 follows the route of the Overland Stagecoach, the Pony Express and the first transcontinental telegraph line. It's two hours' drive from Fallon to Austin, another longish hour to Eureka, and a further 1½ hours to the bright lights of Ely, a welcoming overnight stop. From Ely, it's just over an hour to Great Basin National Park near the Utah border, which alone is worth the entire trip.

Fallon

pop 8800 / elev 3960ft

Look up into the sky and you might spot an F-16 flying over Fallon, home of the US Navy's 'Top Gun' fighter-pilot school. Dragsters and classic hot rods compete at the **Top Gun Raceway** (☎ 775-423-0223; www.topgunraceway.com; tickets $8-35) between March and November.

Besides the usual pioneer relics, the **Churchill County Museum & Archives** (☎ 775-423-3677; www.ccmuseum.org; 1050 S Maine St; admission free; ☒ 10am-5pm Mon-Sat, noon-5pm Sun, closes 1hr earlier Dec-Feb) also displays an interesting replica of a Paiute hut and sponsors twice-monthly guided tours ($1) of Hidden Cave. The cave is near **Grimes Point Archaeological Area** (☎ 775-885-6000; www.blm.gov/nv; admission free; ☒ 24hr; ☒), about 10 miles east of Fallon, where a marked trail leads past boulders covered by Native American petroglyphs. Northeast of town, off Stillwater Rd (NV Hwy 166), **Stillwater National Wildlife Refuge** (☎ 775-428-6452; www.fws.gov/stillwater; admission free; ☒ 24hr) is a haven for over 280 species of birds, best seen during the **Spring Wings Festival** (www.springwings.org) in mid-May. Free primitive campsites are available.

Motels line Williams Ave. **Best Western Fallon Inn** (☎ 775-423-6005; www.bestwestern.com; 1035 W Williams Ave; r from $76; ☒ wi-fi) honestly *is* the best. Home-style cookin', including an unadvertised ham-and-eggs special, is served at the **Depot Diner** (☎ 775-423-2411; 875 W Williams Ave; meals $5-19; ☒ 8am-9pm), inside an early-20th-century railway station that has been turned into a casino.

Sand Mountain Recreation Area

About 25 miles southeast of Fallon off US Hwy 50, this **recreation area** (☎ 775-885-6000; www.blm.gov/nv; admission free; ☒ 24hr) boasts sand dunes that 'sing,' occasionally producing a low-pitched boom. The best time to hear it is on a hot, dry evening when the dunes are not covered with screeching off-road vehicles and whooping sandboarders. Pony Express station ruins have been excavated at the small Sand Springs Desert Study Area. Designated campsites with vault toilets (no water) are free. Near the Sand Mountain turn-off from US Hwy 50, look for the solar-powered **Loneliest Phone in America**. Another half-hour's drive east, past Middlegate but before the junction with NV Hwy 722, the **Old Shoe Tree** stands on the north side of the road. Dozens of knotted pairs of sneakers have been tossed over the

branches of a giant cottonwood. There was even a pair of roller skates hanging up there when we last drove by.

Cold Springs

Midway between Fallon and Austin, there's a historical marker on the south side of the highway. There a windswept 1½-mile walking path leads to the haunting ruins of **Cold Springs Pony Express Station**, built in 1860 but quickly replaced by a stagecoach stop and then the transcontinental telegraph line. It's just about the best place on US Hwy 50 to be carried away by the romance of the Old West. In fact, the mountain vistas alone are worth stopping for, at least to stretch your legs. A mile further east, the modernized, solar-powered **Cold Springs Station** (☎ 775-423-1233; www.coldspringsstationnv.com; 52300 Austin Hwy; RV sites $10-20, r $40-50) has a family diner and a basic motel offering pet-friendly rooms.

Austin

pop 340 / elev 6575ft

Although it looks pretty interesting after hours of uninterrupted basin-and-range driving, there's not much to this mid-19th-century boomtown – really, just a few frontier churches and atmospherically decrepit buildings along the short main street. At the town's western edge, **Stokes Castle**, a three-story, pseudo-Roman stone tower folly, was built in 1897. Enclosed by a chain-link fence and long since abandoned, it boasts amazing views over Reese Valley.

What most people come to Austin for is to play outdoors. Mountain biking is insanely popular; the **chamber of commerce** (☎ 775-964-2200; www.austinnevada.com; 122 Main St; ☒ 9am-noon Mon-Thu) can recommend routes. The **USDA Forest Service Austin Ranger District office** (☎ 775-964-2671; www.fs.fed.us/htnf; 100 Midas Canyon Rd, off US Hwy 50; ☒ 7:30am-4:30pm Mon-Fri) has info on camping, hiking trails and scenic drives, including the trip to **Toquima Cave**, where you can see rock art by ancient Shoshones. Take US Hwy 50 east of Austin about 12 miles to the NV Hwy 376 junction and turn south, then left at the signpost near the 99-mile marker. Continue southeast on Forest Rd 001 for 12 miles past **Spencer Hot Springs** to the cave.

Austin has a few budget motels and B&Bs. Try the friendly **Pony Canyon Motel** (☎ 775-964-2605; 30 Main St; r $40-50) or **Union Street Lodging B&B** (☎ 775-964-2364; 69 Union St; r $65-95). Inside

---

DETOUR: BERLIN-ICTHYOSAUR STATE PARK

Near the ghost town of Berlin (born 1896, died 1911) the fossilized remains of half a dozen ichthyosaurs have been found. The **park** (☎ 775-964-2440; entry $4, campsites & RV sites $8; ☺ hours vary) is about a 90-minute drive from US Hwy 50. Head south of Middlegate on NV Hwy 361, then east over the Paradise Range via NV Hwy 844, just north of Gabbs, which may be impassable due to weather.

The town itself is kept in a state of 'arrested decay,' meaning it's not being restored but is prevented from further deterioration. Follow the self-guided interpretative trail, then walk uphill to the excavation site of the ichthyosaurs, carnivorous marine reptiles who lived here 225 million years ago, when this area was the western edge of the North American continent.

If you're feeling adventurous, follow backloads to **Ione**, a remote ghost town. Slake your thirst at the Ore House Saloon, where you can ask Fly, the proprietor, for advice about which rough dirt roads will take you back to civilization and paved NV Hwy 122 (old Hwy 50).

---

a former hotel moved here in pieces from Virginia City in 1863, the **International Cafe & Saloon** (☎ 775-964-1225; 59 Main St; meals $4-18; ☺ 6am-8pm) is one of Nevada's oldest buildings. The **Toiyabe Cafe** (☎ 775-964-2220; 150 Main St; items $3-10; ☺ 6am-2pm Oct-Apr, 6am-9pm May-Sep) is known for its breakfasts.

North of US Hwy 50 at Hickison Summit, about 24 miles east of Austin, **Hickison Petroglyph Recreation Area** (☎ 775-635-4000; www .blm.gov/nv; admission & camping free; ☺ 24hr; ♿) has panoramic lookout points; a self-guided, ADA-accessible trail for viewing the petroglyphs; and a primitive campground (vault toilets, no water).

Eureka
pop 1300 / elev 6481ft

In the late 19th century, $40 million worth of silver was extracted from the hills around Eureka. Pride of place goes to the **county courthouse** (☎ 775-237-5540; 10 S Main St; admission free; ☺ 8am-5pm Mon-Fri), with its handsome pressed-tin ceilings and walk-in vaults, and the beautifully restored **opera house** (☎ 775-237-6006; 31 S Main St), also dating from 1880, which hosts an art gallery and summer folk-music concerts. The **Eureka Sentinel Museum** (☎ 775-237-5010; 10 S Bateman St; admission free; ☺ 10am-6pm Tue-Sat Nov-Apr, 10am-6pm daily May-Oct) displays yesteryear newspaper technology and some colorful examples of period reportage. Budget motels and cafés line Main St. The **Best Western Eureka Inn** (☎ 775-237-5247; www.bestwestern.com; 251 N Main St; r $100, pet fee $15; ♨) is comfortable, although better-value accommodations await in Ely, just 80 miles away. The family-owned **Pony Espresso Deli** (☎ 775-237-7663; 101 Bullion St; ☺ 5am-2pm Mon-Sat) cures its own meats, stuffs

its own sausages and bakes fresh doughnuts, cinnamon buns and fruity turnovers.

Ely
pop 4000 / elev 6437ft

The biggest town for miles around, Ely deserves an overnight stop. Its old downtown has beautiful regional history murals and awesome vintage neon signs.

East of downtown's gambling strip, marked by the 1929 Hotel Nevada and Jailhouse Casino, the **White Pine County Tourism & Recreation Board** (☎ 775-289-3720; www.elynevada .net; 150 Sixth St; ☺ 8am-5pm Mon-Fri) provides visitor information.

Ely was established as a mining town in the 1860s, but the railroad didn't arrive until 1907. The **East Ely Railroad Depot Museum** (☎ 775-289-1663; 1100 Ave A; adult/child $4/2; ☺ hours vary) inhabits the historic depot. There the **Nevada Northern Railway** (☎ 775-289-2085, 866-407-8326; www.nevadanorthernrailway.net; adult/child from $27/15; ☺ Apr-Dec) offers excursion rides on trains (adult/child from $27/15) pulled by historic steam engines. Call for schedules.

Off US Hwy 93 south of town via signposted dirt roads, **Ward Charcoal Ovens State Historic Park** (☎ 775-728-4460; http://parks.nv.gov/ww.htm; entry $4, tent & RV sites $10, yurt $20) protects a half-dozen beehive-shaped structures dating from 1876 that were once used to make charcoal to supply the silver smelters.

Good-value motels abound in Ely. Bottom-of-the-barrel **Motel 6** (☎ 775-289-6671; www.motel6 .com; 777 Ave O; r $40-50; ♨) accepts pets. The **Hotel Nevada** (☎ 775-289-6665, 888-406-3055; www .hotelnevada.com; 501 Aultman St; r $35-125; wi-fi) has tiny rooms above a smoky casino that come loaded with old-fashioned appeal, if not charm. The peaceful **Bristlecone Motel** (☎ 775-289-8838, 800-497-7404; 700 Ave I; r $50-75; wi-fi) has enormous rooms. Near the depot, the **Steptoe Valley Inn** (☎ 775-289-6991; www.steptoevalleyinn.com; 220 E 11th St; s/d/tr $81/90/99) is a twee Victorian B&B inside a former grocery store.

Ely's casinos have mostly ho-hum eateries, some open 24 hours. The **Silver State Restaurant** (☎ 775-289-8866; 1204 Aultman St; meals from $6; ☽ 6am-9pm) is an authentic diner-style coffee shop, where the waitresses call you 'hun' and comfort food is the only thing on the menu (cash only). **La Fiesta** (☎ 775-289-4114; 700 Ave H; mains $8-15; ☽ 11am-9pm) has tasty Mexican fare.

Great Basin National Park

Near the Nevada–Utah border, this uncrowded **national park** (☎ 775-234-7331; www.nps.gov/grba; admission free; ☽ 24hr) encompasses 13,063ft Wheeler Peak, rising abruptly from the desert, creating an awesome range of life zones and landscapes within a very compact area. The peak's narrow, twisting scenic drive is open only during summer, usually from June through October. Hiking trails near the summit take in superb country made up of glacial lakes, groves of ancient bristlecone pines (some over 5000 years old) and even a permanent ice field. The summit trail is an 8.2-mile round-trip trek, with a vertical ascent of nearly 3000 feet.

Back below, the main park **visitor center** (☽ 8am-4:30pm, extended hr summer) sells tickets for guided tours ($4 to $10) of **Lehman Caves**, which are brimming with limestone formations. The temperature inside is a constant 50°F, so bring a sweater. Call ahead for reservations or buy your ticket at the visitor center as soon as you arrive at the park, because there can be a long wait for the next available tour, if they're not already sold out. A dirt 2WD road nearby leads to the Baker Creek trailhead, from where hikers can make an 11-mile circuit around Baker and Johnson Lakes. This road is typically accessible from May through November.

In winter, much of the park is covered in snow. Because the upper roads are not plowed, access is limited except for backcountry skiers or snowshoers. The park's four developed **campgrounds** (tent & RV sites $12) are open during summer; only Lower Lehman Creek is available year-round. Next to the visitor center, a simple café stays open from May through October. The nearby village of Baker has a gas station, a basic restaurant and sparse accommodations.

ALONG I-80

I-80 is the old fur trappers' route, following the Humboldt River from northeast Nevada to Lovelock, near Reno. It's also one of the earliest emigrant trails to California. Transcontinental railroad tracks reached Reno in 1868 and crossed the state within a year. By the 1920s, the Victory Hwy traveled the same route, which later became the interstate. Although not always the most direct route across Nevada, I-80 skirts many of the Great Basin's steep mountain ranges. It's a 410-mile border-to-border run, taking 5½ hours or more. Overnight stops in the Basque-flavored country around Elko or Winnemucca will give you a true taste of cowboy life.

Lovelock

pop 1900 / elev 3982ft

Most travelers speed right by the small town of Lovelock, a 90-minute drive northeast of Reno. Behind the **Pershing County Courthouse** (☎ 775-273-7213; 400 S Main St; ☽ 8am-5pm Mon-Fri), inspired by Rome's pantheon, you can symbolically lock your passion on a chain for all eternity in **Love Lock Plaza** (www.loverslock.com). At the 1874 **Marzen House** (☎ 775-273-4949; 25 Marzen Lane; admission free; ☽ 1:30-4pm May-Oct), a small historical museum displays mementos of local sweetheart Edna Purviance, Charlie Chaplin's leading lady. Seek shelter at the **Covered Wagon Motel** (☎ 775-624-8506, 800-709-4796; www.lovelockmotel.com; 945 Dartmouth Ave; r $50-70; wi-fi), which is entirely nonsmoking. A country-style diner, the **Cowpoke Cafe** (☎ 775-273-2444; 995 Cornell Ave; meals from $5; ☽ 6am-8pm Tue-Sat, to 3pm Sun-Mon) serves homemade desserts. **Sturgeon's Casino** (☎ 775-273-2971; 1420 Cornell Ave; meals $5-19; ☽ 24hr) never closes.

Unionville & Around

This rural late-19th-century ghost town's big claim to fame is that Mark Twain tried his hand (albeit unsuccessfully) at silver mining here. Take a stroll by the writer's old cabin and the Buena Vista schoolhouse, pioneer cemetery and old-fashioned covered bridge. **Old Pioneer Garden B&B** (☎ 775-538-7585; 2805 Unionville Rd; r incl breakfast $75-95) arranges dinner for guests upon request; reservations required, cash only. It's just over an hour's drive from Lovelock: drive east on I-80, then take NV Hwy 400 south for approximately 17 miles, veering right onto the signposted dirt road into the canyon. Off I-80 in Imlay, a few miles west of the Unionville turn-off, **Thunder Mountain** is a folk-art sculp-

> **WHAT THE...?**
>
> Seven miles west of Lovelock, **Giant Tufa Park** sports a group of calcium carbonate spires that grew in the ancient Lake Lahontan. To get there from the town center, drive north on Merdian Rd for 1½ miles, then turn west (left) on Pitt Rd for about 2½ miles. Look for an unmarked gravel road on your right and follow it for about a mile. The park will soon be reconstructed as a golf course, so hurry up and see it while you still can.

ture garden. Built by a WWII veteran and self-proclaimed Native American chief, it's full of curious figures, concrete sculptures and recycled junkyard finds. Further west along I-80, **Rye Patch State Recreation Area** (☎ 775-538-7321; www.parks.nov.gov; entry $4, tent & RV sites $10) offers swimming, fishing and boating.

Winnemucca
pop 7500 / elev 4230ft

The biggest town on this stretch of I-80, Winnemucca has been a travelers' stop since the days of the Emigrant Trail. Named after a Paiute chief, it's also a center for the state's Basque community, descended from 19th-century immigrant shepherds.

The old-fashioned downtown area is full of antique shops. The **Winnemucca visitor center** (☎ 775-623-2225, 800-962-2638; www.winnemucca.nv.us; 30 W Winnemucca Blvd; 🕑 8am-5pm Mon-Fri) houses the Buckaroo Hall of Fame, full of cowboy art and folklore. Pick up a self-guided walking tour brochure of historic buildings downtown, and ask about horseback riding at local ranches, the Basque cultural festival in June and rodeo events throughout the year. North of the river in a former church, the **Humboldt County Museum** (☎ 775-623-2912; 175 Museum Lane; admission free; 🕑 10am-noon Mon-Fri, 1-4pm Mon-Sat) shows off antique cars, farming implements and beautiful Paiute baskets.

East of town, off Highland Dr at the end of Kluncy Canyon Rd, the **Bloody Shins Trails** are part of a burgeoning mountain biking trail system. Stop by the **BLM Winnemucca Field Office** (☎ 775-623-1500; www.blm.nv.gov; 5100 E Winnemucca Blvd; 🕑 7:30am-4:30pm Mon-Fri) for more information.

About 50 miles north of town, the Santa Rosa Mountains offer rugged scenery, hiking

trails and camping in the **Humboldt-Toiyabe National Forest**. A scenic drive follows NV Hwy 290, off US Hwy 95, up the Paradise Valley, where the **Stonehouse Country Inn** (☎ 775-578-3530; www.stonehouse.freeservers.com; r incl breakfast $60-90) offers peaceful stays in a cozy farmhouse surrounded by cottonwoods. Before heading out, inquire about road conditions at the **USFS Santa Rosa ranger station** (☎ 775-623-5025; www.fs.fed.us/r4 /htnf; 1200 E Winnemucca Blvd; 🕑 8am-4:30pm Mon-Fri).

Over halfway between Reno and Elko, Winnemucca's main drag has abundant motels and a few casino hotels with 24-hour restaurants. Family-owned **Town House Motel** (☎ 775-623-3620, 800-243-3620; www.townhouse-motel .com; 375 Monroe St; r $50-75; wi-fi) has tidy budget rooms equipped with microwaves and mini-fridges. For big breakfasts and lunches, the **Country Kitchen Café** (☎ 775-623-0800; 35 E Winnemucca Blvd; meals $4-8; 🕑 breakfast & lunch Mon-Sat) is beloved for its home-baked breads and desserts. An authentic mid-20th-century diner, **The Griddle** (☎ 775-623-2977; 460 W Winnemucca Blvd; meals $5-10; 🕑 6am-2pm) cooks up crispy hash browns and omelets with a Spanish sauce. **Delizioso Global Coffee** (☎ 775-625-1000; 508a W Winnemucca Blvd; items $2-5; 🕑 5am-5pm Mon-Fri, 6am-1pm Sat; wi-fi) brews fine espresso. **Ormachea's** (☎ 775-623-3455; 180 Melarkey St; meals $17-30; 🕑 dinner Tue-Sun) is a Basque family-style dinner house.

Elko
pop 16,700 / elev 5050ft

Though small, Elko is the largest town in rural Nevada and a center of cowboy culture, with a calendar of Western cultural events and a museum big on buckaroos, stagecoaches and the Pony Express. The other cultural influence is Basque; in fact, Basque shepherds and Old West cattlemen had some violent conflicts over grazing rights in the late 19th century. The **visitor center** (☎ 775-738-4091, 800-248-3556; www.elkocva.com; 1405 Idaho St; 🕑 hours vary) is inside a historic ranch house.

The **Northeastern Nevada Museum** (☎ 775-738-3418; 1515 Idaho Ave; adult/child $5/1; 🕑 9am-5pm Mon-Sat, 1-5pm Sun) has excellent displays on pioneer life, Pony Express riders, Basque settlers and modern mining techniques. Free monthly tours of the nearby Newmont gold mine usually start here; call ☎ 775-778-4068 for reservations. Aspiring cowboys and cowgirls should visit the **Western Folklife Center & Wiegland Gallery** (☎ 775-738-7508; www.westernfolklife.org; 501 Railroad St; admission free; 🕑 10am-5:30pm Mon & Wed-Fri,

10:30am-5:30pm Tue, 10am-5pm Sat), which hosts the remarkable popular **Cowboy Poetry Gathering** in January. The **National Basque Festival** (☎ 775-738-9957; www.elkobasque.com) is held around July 4, with games, traditional dancing and even Elko's own 'Running of the Bulls.'

South of Elko, the **Ruby Mountains** (www.ruby mountains.org) are a superbly rugged range, nicknamed Nevada's alps for their prominent peaks, glacial lakes and alpine vegetation. The village of **Lamoille** has basic food and lodging, and one of the most photographed rural churches in the USA. Just before the village, Lamoille Canyon Rd branches south, following the forested canyon for 12 miles past cliffs, waterfalls and other glacial sculptures to the Ruby Crest trailhead at 8800ft. If you miss the short summer hiking season, try **Ruby Mountain Heli-Ski** (☎ 775-753-6867; www.helicopterskiing.com). For backcountry information, stop by the **USDA Forest Service Mountain City Ranger District** office (☎ 775-738-5171; www.fs.fed.us/htnf; 2035 Last Chance Rd, off NV Hwy 227; 7:30am-4:30pm Mon-Fri).

A popular overnight stop for truckers and travelers, Elko has over 2000 rooms that fill up fast, especially on weekends. Chain motels and hotels line Idaho St, particularly east of downtown. Options range from the cost-conscious, pet-friendly **Rodeway Inn** (☎ 775-738-7152; www .choicehotels.com; 736 Idaho St; r $50-90; wi-fi) to the upscale **Holiday Inn Express** (☎ 775-777-0990; www .hiexpress.com; 3019 Idaho St; r incl breakfast $90-180; wi-fi). Run by an artistic couple, **Once Upon a Time B&B** (☎ 775-738-1200; 537 14th St; r incl breakfast $65-95) offers Old West Victorian–styled rooms, most with shared bathroom, and may accept pets.

For Basque food, downtown's **Star Hotel & Restaurant** (☎ 775-753-8696; 246 Silver St; meals $15-25; lunch Mon-Fri, dinner Mon-Sat) gets the best marks. Mexican-spiced **La Fiesta** (☎ 775-738-1622; 780 Commercial St; meals $8-20; 11am-10pm) packs in locals, as does **Cowboy Joe** (☎ 775-753-5612; 376 5th St; items $2-6; 5am-5:30pm Mon-Fri, 5:30am-3pm Sat, 7am-noon Sun; wi-fi), serving strong espresso. Hit the casinos for unlimited buffets and 24-hour coffee shops.

Wells
pop 1400 / elev 5630ft
Sports fans should know that heavyweight boxer Jack Dempsey started his career here, as a bouncer in the local bars. After strolling around the rough-edged **Front Street historic district** today, you can imagine how tough that job must've been. The **Trail of the '49ers**

Interpretive Center (☎ 775-752-3540; www.wells nevada.com; 395 S 6th St; hours vary) tells the story of mid-19th-century pioneers on the Emigrant Trail to California.

Southwest of town, scenic byway NV Hwy 231 heads into the mountains, climbing alongside sagebrush, piñon pine and aspen trees past two **campgrounds** (☎ 877-444-6777; www .recreation.gov; tent sites $12-22; Jun-Oct). After 12 miles, the road stops at cobalt-blue **Angel Lake** (8378ft), a glacial cirque beautifully embedded in the East Humboldt Range. Along NV Hwy 232, farther south of Wells, a large natural window near the top of **Hole in the Mountain Peak** (11,306ft) is visible from the road.

West Wendover
pop 4900 / elev 4450ft
If you just can't make it to Salt Lake City tonight, another two-hour drive on I-80 east of the Utah border, stop in West Wendover, where ginormous **casino hotels** (☎ 800-537-0207; www.wendoverfun.com; r $55-140) with 24-hour restaurants line Wendover Blvd, which continues east into the town of Wendover, UT. The state line is painted across the road by the towering 1950s-era cowboy statue of Wendover Will. Over on the Utah side, **Historic Wendover Airfield** (www.wendoverairbase.com; 345 Airport Apron, Wendover; admission by donation; 8am-6pm) is a top-secret WWII-era USAF base, where the Enola Gay crew trained for dropping the atomic bomb on Japan. The **Bonneville Speed Museum** (☎ 775-664-3138; 1000 E Wendover Blvd, Wendover; adult/child $2/1; 10am-6pm Jun-Nov) documents attempts to set land speed records on the nearby Bonneville Salt Flats, where 'Speed Week' time trials in the third full week of August draw huge crowds every year.

CAPITAL COUNTRY

A vast sagebrush steppe, the western corner of the state is carved by mountain ranges and parched valleys. It's also the place where modern Nevada began. It was the site of the state's first trading post, pioneer farms and the famous Comstock silver lode, which spawned Virginia City, financed the Union during the Civil War and earned Nevada its statehood. Today, Reno and the state capital, Carson City, have little of the Wild West rawness still extant in the Black Rock Desert, reached via Pyramid Lake. For pampering all-seasons getaways, it's a short drive up to emerald Lake Tahoe, right on the California border.

RENO

pop 211,000 / elev 4498ft

It's still a little rough around the edges, but there's a vibrancy to this northern Nevada town, a mere 45-minute drive from Lake Tahoe. In the past, visitors flocked only to Reno's smorgasbord of casinos, but the construction of a white-water park has raised the stakes for outdoor enthusiasts, and pockets of hipness are emerging throughout the Truckee River arts district with edgy galleries, bars and cafés.

Orientation & Information

Downtown's main artery, Virginia St, with most of the casinos, is wedged between the I-80 and the Truckee River. South of the river, the street continues for several miles of motels, malls and more casinos. The city of Sparks is 4 miles east of Reno via I-80.

Some coffee shops and bars (p145) offer free wi-fi, as do local buses (p145).

Police (☎ 775-334-2550; 199 E Plaza St) For non-emergencies.

Post office (☎ 800-275-8777; 50 S Virginia St; ☒ 7:30am-5:15pm Mon-Fri)

Reno Gazette-Journal (www.rgj.com) Daily newspaper.

Reno News & Review (www.newsreview.com/reno) Free alternative tabloid weekly.

Reno-Sparks Convention & Visitors Authority (☎ 775-827-7600, 800-367-7366; www.visitrenotahoe.com; Reno Town Mall, 4001 S Virginia St; ☒ 8am-5pm Mon-Fri) Also has an airport desk.

St Mary's Regional Medical Center (☎ 775-770-3000, emergency 775-770-3188; 235 W 6th St; ☒ 24hr)

Sundance Bookstore (☎ 775-786-1188; 1155 W 4th St; ☒ 9am-9pm Mon-Fri, 10am-6pm Sat & Sun) Indie bookstore hosts author events.

Sights

CASINOS

Few of Reno's casinos have the flash of Vegas, though some do try. All are wheelchair-accessible and open 24 hours. The Circus Circus, Eldorado and the Silver Legacy casino hotels are connected by a skywalk.

With its giant, candy-striped big top, family-friendly **Circus Circus** (☎ 775-329-0711; www.circuscircusreno.com; 500 N Sierra St) offers free circus acts and harbors a gazillion carnival games. The stalwart **Silver Legacy** (☎ 775-325-7401; 407 N Virginia St) is dominated by a mock-19th-century mining rig, lit up by an hourly sound-and-

light show inside a 180ft-high dome. A bit further on, **Eldorado** (☎ 775-786-5700; 345 N Virginia St) has a kitschy Fountain of Fortune featuring Neptune and his nymphets.

South across the train trench, rub a Blarney Stone for good luck before heading inside **Fitzgerald's** (☎ 775-785-3300; 255 N Virginia St), with its dopey 'lucky leprechaun' theme and the cheapest buffet in town. It's near the landmark **Reno Arch**, built in the 1920s, which proclaims Reno the 'Biggest Little City in the World.' **Harrah's** (☎ 775-786-3232; 219 N Center St) was founded by Nevada gambling pioneer William Harrah in 1946.

Closer to the river, the **Club Cal Neva** (☎ 775-954-4540; 38 E 2nd St) has seen better days but enjoys a reputation for loose slots. A block east is the ritzy Tuscan-themed **Siena** (☎ 775-327-4362; 1 S Lake St).

South of downtown, the outrageous **Peppermill** (☎ 775-826-2121; 2707 S Virginia St) has blindingly bright, almost psychotropic neon lights. Not far away, **Atlantis** (☎ 775-825-4700; 3800 S Virginia St) has an equally trippy setting of waterfalls, tiki huts and palm trees. Over in Sparks, **John Ascuaga's Nugget** (☎ 775-356-3300; 1100 Nugget Ave) is a legendary pioneer.

NEVADA MUSEUM OF ART

In an architecturally impressive building, inspired by the geologic formations of the Black Rock Desert, this **art museum** (☎ 775-329-3333; www.nevadaart.org; 160 W Liberty St; adult/child/student $10/1/8; ☒ 10am-5pm Tue-Sun, to 8pm Thu; wi-fi) has a floating staircase leading to galleries showcasing works related to the American West and temporary exhibits. There's a great café for post-cultural refueling.

NATIONAL AUTOMOBILE MUSEUM

At the engaging **museum** (☎ 775-333-9300; www.automuseum.org; 10 S Lake St; adult/child $10/4; ☒ 9:30am-5:30pm Mon-Sat, 10am-4pm Sun; ☒) stylized street scenes illustrate over a century's worth of automobile history. One-of-a-kind vehicles include James Dean's 1949 Mercury from *Rebel Without a Cause*, Elvis' 1973 Cadillac, a 24-karat gold–plated DeLorean and Buckminster Fuller's experimental 1934 Dymaxion.

Activities

Mere steps from the casinos, the Class II/III rapids of **Truckee River Whitewater Park** (☎ 775-334-2262; www.cityofreno.com; admission free) inject action into the middle of downtown, with year-round kayaking and kid-friendly tubing in summer. **Tahoe Whitewater Tours** (☎ 775-787-5000; 400 Island Ave) rents tubes and kayaks (from $25) and leads guided tours. Next to the Grand Sierra Resort, **Ultimate Rush Park** (☎ 775-786-7005; www.ultimate rushpark.com; 2500 E 2nd St; ☾ from 11am daily, weather permitting) has a 180ft-tall 'skycoaster' that's like bungee-jumping, sky-diving and hang-gliding all at once ($25, re-ride $10), along with bumper cars and miniature golf. Back downtown, the **Rink on the River** (☎ 775-334-6268; 10 N Virginia St; adult/youth $5/3, skate rental $2; ☾ hours vary) opens for ice skating in winter, when many hotels offer Lake Tahoe (p147) stay-and-ski packages.

Festivals & Events

Reno River Festival (www.renoriverfestival.com) Adrenaline junkies compete in mid-May.

Reno Rodeo (www.renorodeo.com) A Wild West rodeo in mid-June.

Tour de Nez (www.tourdenez.com) The 'coolest bike festival in America' in mid-June.

Hot August Nights (www.hotaugustnights.net) Catch the American Graffiti vibe with hot rods and rock 'n' roll in early August.

Best in the West Nugget Rib Cook-Off (www.nugget ribcookoff.com) The world's best ribmeisters face off in early September in Sparks.

Great Reno Balloon Race (www.renoballon.com) Mass ascension of hot-air balloons in early September.

National Championship Air Races & Air Show (www.airrace.org) Biplanes, jets and WWII fighters test their aerial mettle in mid-September.

Sleeping

Virginia St brims with cheap 'no-tell' motels south of the river. Casino hotels are a more inviting option.

Silver Legacy (☎ 775-325-7401, 800-687-8733; www .silverlegacyreno.com; 407 N Virginia St; r midweek/weekend from $45/90; ⊇ ▢ wi-fi) All trimmed up in mahogany and brass, this giant takes up two city blocks. Victorian-themed rooms are crisp and comfortable; those with views cost more.

Harrah's (☎ 775-786-3232, 800-427-7247; www .harrahsreno.com; 219 N Center St; r midweek/weekend from $60/100; ⊇ ▢ wi-fi) It's just about the fanciest place downtown, in a gold-embossed kind of way. A marble entryway leads to the West Tower, where art-deco rooms have plenty of class – and, more importantly, quiet.

Peppermill (☎ 775-826-2121, 800-648-6992; www .peppermillreno.com; 2707 S Virginia St; r midweek/weekend from $65/99; ⊇ ▢ wi-fi) The Tuscany Tower is almost a mini Bellagio, while the turquoise-and-black Peppermill Tower rides the retro wave with its tacky turquoise-and-black color scheme. Perks include an outdoor pool and a fitness center ($10 per day).

Siena (☎ 775-327-4362, 877-743-6233; www.sienareno .com; 1 Lake St; r $90-180; ⊇ ▢ wi-fi) You won't need to navigate the casino action to check into this contemporary boutique hotel with riverside rooms. An out-of-the-way location is a drawback, but there's a day spa, a wine bar and a Sunday champagne brunch buffet.

Also recommended:

Circus Circus (☎ 775-329-0711, 800-648-5010; www .circusreno.com; 500 N Sierra St; r midweek/weekend from $45/79; ⊇ 👶 ▢ wi-fi) Garish, inexpensive rooms. Dogs are allowed in 'Hound Hotel' kennels ($10 per day).

Hampton Inn (☎ 775-336-2222; www.hamptoninn reno.com; 10599 Professional Circle, off Hwy 395; r incl breakfast $119-189; ⊇ 👶 ▢ wi-fi) Stay away from the casino madness in quiet, comfy and well-equipped rooms.

Eating

Reno's dining scene goes far beyond the casinos, each of which has a 24-hour coffee shop and an all-you-can-eat buffet. Many of the best places are not even downtown.

Pho 777 (☎ 775-323-7777; 201 E 2nd St; dishes $5-8; ☾ 10am-9pm) A popular Vietnamese noodle shop just off the casino strip serves up bowls and bowls of steamy soup. The basic decor is a reprieve from the glitz and glare a block away.

Pneumatic Diner (☎ 775-786-8888; 2nd fl, Truckee River Lodge, 501 W 1st St; dishes $6-8; ☾ 11am-11pm Mon-Fri, 9am-11pm Sat, 8am-11pm Sun; Ⓥ) Under salvaged neon lights, this groovy little off-the-beaten path place off Ralston St, has meatless and vegan comfort food and desserts to tickle your inner two-year-old.

Silver Peak Grill & Taproom (☎ 775-284-3300; 135 N Sierra St; mains $8-16; ☾ 11am-midnight) Downtown outpost hums with the chatter of happy locals settling in with microbrews and great eats, from wild-mushroom pizza to barley-crusted chicken sandwiches and lamb burgers topped with kalamata olives.

Sezmu (☎ 775-327-4448; 670 Mt Rose St; mains $19-28, 4-course tasting menu $50; ☾ dinner Thu-Mon) Delightful, intimate and creative neighborhood bistro serving haute seasonal dishes, from chipotle sweet-potato chips to baked cod with lemon-creamed spinach. Call ahead for reservations and directions.

Harrah's Steakhouse (☎ 775-788-2929; Harrah's, 219 N Center St; lunch mains $10-17, dinner mains $28-38; ☾ lunch Mon-Fri, dinner daily) Sporting old-fashioned elegance and amazing service, Reno's top-voted steakhouse does right by tradition, from T-bone steaks and lobster tails to tournedos of buffalo Rossini topped by *foie gras*. Flavored soufflés and boxed truffles are available for dessert.

Lulou's (☎ 775-329-9979; 1470 S Virginia St; mains $34-48; ☾ dinner Tue-Sat) At this arty gourmet eatery on an otherwise drab stretch, bold canvases hang on brick walls and creative chefs fuss over modern American and Eurasian concoctions in the open kitchen. Reservations essential.

Also recommended:

Süp (☎ 775-324-4787; 719 S Virginia St; dishes $4-8; ☾ 11am-4pm Mon-Sat; **V**) Six daily house-made soups, plus sandwiches and salads.

Peg's Glorified Ham & Eggs (☎ 775-329-2600; 420 S Sierra St; dishes $7-10; ☾ 6:30am-2pm; ⚤) Retro diner with arguably the best breakfast in town.

Santa Fe Hotel (☎ 775-323-1891; 235 N Lake St; meals $19-24; ☾ dinner Tue-Sun) Hearty Basque dinners served family style behind Harrah's.

Drinking & Entertainment

Every casino has its watering holes, but there's much more to Reno after dark. Free live bands play at Harrah's Plaza, facing Virginia St, during summer.

Jungle Java & Jungle Vino (☎ 775-329-4484; 246 W 1st St; ☾ 6am-10pm Sun-Thu, to midnight Fri & Sat) Tiny, smoke-free wine bar with a Technicolor mosaic floor, Parisian café tables and art-clad walls is the boozy, late-night cousin of Jungle Java coffeehouse next door. A light menu suits carnivores and vegans.

Chocolate Bar (☎ 775-337-1122; 475 S Arlington Ave; ☾ 11:30am-midnight) Sinfully delicious hot spot enjoys most-favorite status with Reno scenesters for its wicked chocolate-themed drinks, urban-chic decor and awesome desserts.

BuBinga Lounge (☎ 775-786-5700; Eldorado, 345 N Virginia St; cover varies; ☾ 9pm-4am Tue & Thu-Sat) At this sexy ultra lounge, DJs pull in an eye-candy crowd with a pulsating mix of house and hip-hop. If the crammed dance floor is just too much, chill at the Eldorado's Brew Brothers brewpub, with live bands nightly.

Fireside Lounge (☎ 775-826-2121; Peppermill, 2707 S Virginia St; ☾ 24hr) The choicest seats at Reno's most plush make-out spot orbit a fireplace. Look for late-night drink specials and free happy-hour appetizers (4pm to 7pm weekdays).

Tronix (☎ 775-333-9696; 303 Kietzke Lane, off US Hwy 395 exit 67; ☾ 10am-3am Mon-Thu, 24hr Fri & Sat) East of

downtown, this LGBT video dance bar features karaoke and ladies' nights midweek, and weekend DJs and after-hours parties.

Also recommended:

Imperial Bar & Lounge (☎ 775-324-6399; 150 N Arlington Ave; ☾ from 11am daily) Fashionable gastropub inhabiting a relic of the past, with an excellent beer list and pool tables (no slots).

Roxy's (☎ 775-786-5700; Eldorado, 345 N Virginia St; ☾ from 5:30pm daily) Swanky casino restaurant-bar mixes up over 100 different knock-out martinis.

Tonic Lounge (☎ 775-337-6868; 231 W 2nd St; live-music cover $5-15; ☾ 5pm-late) Downtempo locals' spot where jazz musicians perform and eclectic DJs spin.

Getting There & Around

The **Reno/Tahoe International Airport** (RNO; ☎ 775-328-6400; www.renoairport.com; 2000 E Plumb Lane, off US Hwy 395 exit 65; wi-fi) is 4 miles southeast of downtown. Greyhound (p535) buses arrive at a downtown **bus station** (☎ 775-322-2970; 155 Stevenson St; ☾ 5am-10pm Fri-Mon, 6am-10pm Tue-Thu). Amtrak's *California Zephyr* (p535) stops at a downtown **train station** (☎ 775-329-8638; 280 N Center St; ☾ 8:15am-5pm).

Many hotels offer free airport shuttles. A taxi from the airport to downtown costs at least $15. **RTC Ride** (☎ 775-348-7433; single-ride/24hr pass $1.75/4) bus 14 connects the airport with downtown's CitiCenter station at E 4th and Center Sts. The free Sierra Spirit bus loops around downtown and to the Nevada Museum of Art approximately every 10 minutes from 7am until 9pm daily.

CARSON CITY

pop 55,300 / elev 4600ft
Handsome antique buildings and tree-lined streets abound in Nevada's pleasant state capital. The casinos are surprisingly sedate, and there are historical museums worth discovering. US Hwy 395 from Reno becomes the town's main drag, called Carson St. Look for the Cactus Jack neon sign letting you know you've reached downtown. About a mile further south, the **Carson City Convention & Visitors Bureau** (☎ 775-687-7410, 800-638-2321; www.visitcarson city.com; 1900 S Carson St; ☾ 9am-4pm Mon-Fri, to 3pm Sat & Sun) has information about mountain-biking trails and hands out a historical walking-tour map of the Kit Carson Trail, with interesting podcasts that you can download online.

Built in 1870, the **Nevada State Capitol** (☎ 775-687-5030; cnr Musser & Carson Sts; admission free; ☾ 8am-5pm) is complete with a silver-covered dome symbolizing its 'Silver State' status. The original senate chamber now houses a museum of statehood paraphernalia. Housed inside the 1869 US Mint building, the **Nevada State Museum** (☎ 775-687-4810; 600 N Carson St; adult/child $5/free; ☒ 8:30am-4:30pm) puts on rotating exhibits of Native American, frontier and mining history. Train buffs shouldn't miss the **Nevada State Railroad Museum** (☎ 775-687-6953; 2180 S Carson St; adult/child $4/3; ☒ 8:30am-4:30pm), displaying some 65 train cars and locomotives, most pre-dating 1900. For made-in-Nevada artisan crafts, shop at the **Brewery Arts Center** (☎ 775-883-1976; www.breweryarts.org; 449 W King St; ☒ 10am-4pm Mon-Sat).

In the leafy historic district, **Bliss Bungalow** (☎ 775-883-6129; www.blissbungalow.com; 408 W Robinson St; r incl breakfast $115-155; wi-fi) has genteel early-20th-century charm in each of its five rooms. **Comma Coffee** (☎ 775-883-2662; 312 S Carson St; dishes $4-8; ☒ 7am-6pm Mon & Wed-Thu, to 10pm Tue & Fri & Sat; wi-fi), an art-filled café and live-music venue, invites lingering. Though it looks rickety from the outside, the Old West–style barbecue steakhouse, **Red's Old 395 Grill** (☎ 775-887-0395; 1055 S Carson St; mains $8-30; ☒ 11am-10pm), cooks up giant juicy burgers and grill plates, and boasts an impressive beer list.

VIRGINIA CITY
pop 938 / elev 6620ft
About 25 miles south of Reno, this national historic landmark was the site where the legendary Comstock Lode was struck, sparking a silver bonanza that began in 1859 and stands as one of the world's richest strikes. At its peak, this high-flying, rip-roaring boomtown had over 30,000 residents. Newspaperman Samuel Clemens, alias Mark Twain, vividly captured the Wild West shenanigans in a book called *Roughing It*.

With its wooden sidewalks, well-preserved 19th-century Victorian buildings and hokey 'museums,' Virginia City feels almost like a frontier theme park, though it's still fun to visit.

The **visitor center** (☎ 775-847-4386, 800-718-7587; www.virginiacity-nv.org; 86 S C St; ☒ 10am-4pm) stands on the town's main drag, inside the historic Crystal Bar. Nearby is the **Mark Twain Bookstore** (☎ 775-847-0454; 111 S C St; ☒ hours vary).

The **Nevada Gambling Museum** (☎ 775-847-9022; 50 S C St; admission $1; ☒ 10am-5pm Oct-Mar, to 6pm Apr-Sep) displays antique slot machines, ingenious cheating devices and guns, while the old-fashioned **Way It Was Museum** (☎ 775-847-0766; 113 N C St; adult/child $3/free; ☒ 10am-6pm) offers historical background on mining the lode. After visiting **Chollar Mine** (☎ 775-847-0155; 615 S F St; 30min tour adult/child $7/2; ☒ 1-5pm Easter-Oct), stop by the **Mackay Mansion** (☎ 775-847-0173; 129 D St; admission $3; ☒ 11am-6pm) to see how the mining elite once lived.

From May through October, the **Virginia & Truckee Railroad** (☎ 775-847-0380; www.virginiatruckee.com; F & Washington Sts; 35min narrated tour adult/child $8/4; 🚻) offers vintage steam-train excursions. The **International Camel Races**, which began as a practical joke, have been going on for 50 years. Watch hopeful dromedaries galumphing towards the finish line as enormous crowds cheer them on in mid-September. The human-powered **Outhouse Races** are staged in October. If you're interested in forking into cooked cows' testicles (p64), the **Mountain Oyster Fry** is held around St Patrick's Day.

A mile south of town via NV Hwy 342, the **Gold Hill Hotel & Saloon** (☎ 775-847-0111; www.goldhillhotel.net; 1540 Main St; r $55-225) claims to be Nevada's oldest hotel. Inside an 1870s boarding house, **Sugarloaf Mountain Motel** (☎ 775-847-0551; 430 S C St; r $60-100) is just as historical, as is the more luxurious, antique-filled **Chollar Mansion B&B** (☎ 775-847-9777, 877-246-5527; www.chollarmansion.com; 565 S D St; r incl full breakfast $135), a nonsmoking inn where the views go on forever.

Virginia City has several touristy places to eat. **Mandarin Garden** (☎ 775-847-9288; 5 N C St; dishes $6-10; ☒ 11am-9:30pm Tue-Sun, 4-9pm Mon; Ⓥ) serves tasty noodle and rice plates. **Cafe del Rio** (☎ 775-847-5151; 394 S C St; mains $12-26; ☒ hours vary) cooks up Tex-Mex fare and steaks.

The various routes to Virginia City from Reno (take NV Hwy 341 southeast of US Hwy 395) or Carson City (take NV Hwys 341 and 342 north of US Hwy 50) all offer spectacular mountain views.

GENOA
pop 248 / elev 4788ft
This pretty village at the edge of Carson Valley, beneath the Sierra Nevada mountains, was the first European settlement at the western edge of the former Utah Territory. In 1851 a mostly Mormon group established a trading post to provision emigrant groups for the final leg of the trip to California. The **Genoa Saloon** claims to be the oldest bar in the state (since 1863), and it certainly looks the part. The **Genoa Courthouse Museum** (☎ 775-782-4325; 2304 Main St; adult/child $3/2; ☒ 10am-4:30pm May-Oct) contains the original jail and a collection of woven Washo

baskets. The **Mormon Station State Historic Park** (☎ 775-782-2590; museum $2; ⊙ 9am-5pm mid-May–mid-Oct) displays more pioneer-era artifacts. About 2 miles south of town, off NV Hwy 206, **David Walley's Hot Springs & Spa** (☎ 775-782-8155; www .davidwalleys.com; 2001 Foothill Rd; pools, sauna & work-out room day pass $20; ⊙ hours vary) offers a respite from traveling Nevada's dusty roads.

PYRAMID LAKE

A piercingly blue expanse in an otherwise barren landscape, Pyramid Lake is a stunning sight. About 30 miles northeast of Reno, on the Paiute Lake Indian Reservation, the lake is popular for recreation and fishing. Its shores are lined with beaches and interesting tufa formations. Nearer its east side, iconic pyramidlike Anaho Island is a bird sanctuary for American white pelicans. Permits for **day use** (entry $6), **overnight camping** (per vehicle $9) in primitive sites and **fishing** (per person $9) are available at the **tribal ranger station** (☎ 775-476-1155; www.plpt .nsn.us; 2500 Lakeview Dr, Sutcliffe; ⊙ 8am-6pm Mon-Thu, 10am-8pm Fri & Sat, hours vary winter), on NV Hwy 446 in Sutcliffe, accessible from Sparks via NV Hwy 445. Traveling south along the lakeshore, the road passes more sandy beaches and a tribal museum and visitor center near the village of Nixon, the tribal headquarters. Take NV Hwy 447 south to rejoin I-80 near Fernley.

BLACK ROCK DESERT

North of Pyramid Lake, NV Hwy 447 continues straight as an arrow for about 60 miles to the dusty railway town of Gerlach, with a gas station, a motel, a café and a few bars. Its is motto 'Where the pavement ends, the West begins.' **Bruno's Country Club** (☎ 775-557-2220; 445 Main St; meals $6-15; ⊙ hours vary) is famous for its meaty ravioli in cheese sauce. Outside Gerlach, world land-speed records have been set on the dry, mud-cracked *playas* of the **Black Rock Desert** (☎ 775-557-2900; www.blackrockfriends.org). Although most people only visit during the Burning Man festival (see boxed text, p148), this vast wilderness is primed for outdoor adventures year-round. Drop by Gerlach's small museum for information and advice before heading out. The popular 4WD trip to High Rock Canyon should only be attempted when dirt-road conditions are bone dry. Primitive campsites (tent/RV sites $10/12) and hot springs await at **Soldier Meadows Ranch** (☎ 775-849-1666; www.soldiermeadows.com; r $40-75, meals $12-20), a 65-mile trip northeast of Gerlach.

LAKE TAHOE

The sun shines on Lake Tahoe, straddling the California–Nevada state line, three out of every four days in each year, making it ideal for outdoor pursuits of all stripes. Swimming, boating, kayaking, windsurfing and other water-based activities are popular. So are hiking and camping among the horned peaks surrounding the lake. Winter brings bundles of snow, perfect for hitting the slopes at over a dozen skiing and snowboarding resorts.

The lake's mostly undeveloped eastern shore lies entirely within Nevada. To explore the California side, consult Lonely Planet's *California*.

Information

The **Blue Lake Tahoe Visitors Information Center** (☎ 775-588-5900 ext 351, 800-288-2463; www.bluelake tahoe.com; 169 US Hwy 50, Stateline; ⊙ 9am-5pm) and the **Incline Village/Crystal Bay Visitors Bureau** (☎ 775-832-1606, 800-468-2463; www.gotahoenorth.com; 969 Tahoe Blvd; ⊙ 8am-5pm Mon-Fri, 10am-4pm Sat & Sun) provide tourist info and make lodging reservations.

Sights

Reservations are required to visit eccentric San Francisco playboy George Whittell's **Thunderbird Lodge** (☎ bus tours 800-468-2463, cruises 888-867-6394 ext 3; www.thunderbirdlodge.org; adult/child from $32/16; ⊙ Jun-Sep, schedule varies). Tours include a trip down a 600ft tunnel to the infamous Card House, where the dearly departed George once played poker with the likes of Howard Hughes. The only ways to get to the lodge are by shuttle bus or catamaran cruise.

The big casinos are on the Nevada side at Stateline, near South Lake Tahoe. Las Vegas it sure ain't, but there are plenty of bad-odds blackjack tables and slot machines to part you from your hard-earned cash. The major casino hotels, Harrah's, Harvey's, MontBleu and Horizon, offer live entertainment. On the north shore, west of Incline Village at Crystal Bay, the 1920s Cal-Neva Lodge was built directly on top of the state line. Historically, the casino was a hangout for Hollywood celebs, politicians and entertainers, most famously Rat Pack member and one-time owner Frank Sinatra.

Activities

Ritzy Incline Village is the gateway to **Diamond Peak** (☎ 775-832-1177; www.diamondpeak.com; 1210 Ski Way; half-day pass adult/child $37/29, equipment rental $25-35; ♿) ski resort, a good place to learn. From the

BURNING MAN

Every year for a week before Labor Day, upwards of 30,000 euphoric individuals trek from all parts of the country (and world) to this same spot in the Nevada desert. It's one part survivalist camping experience, one part art festival, one part rave party, one part moneyless community experiment, and all parts freedom of expression and costume and libido and self.

It started in 1986 with a handful of friends gathering on a San Francisco beach to erect an 8ft effigy of a 'man' to burn. Within a few years their little ritual was drawing hundreds, then thousands. Its current home is Black Rock City, the name given to the enormous functioning 'city' that springs up in the Nevada desert, out of nowhere, for one precious week every year, then vanishes completely. 'Earth Guardians' and the recycling camp encourage festival-goers to adhere to 'leave no trace' principles and to recycle their junk as installation art.

Tickets ($210 to $295) for Burning Man go on sale in January, and must be purchased in advance via www.burningman.com, which has helpful FAQs and a first-timers' survival guide. You have to supply your own everything: food, water, camping gear, bike (mandatory to get around the *playa*), inebriants and SPF30. Just remember that if you go, you participate. There are no 100% spectators at this experimental spectacle.

top of the mountain you'll have a 360-degree panorama of desert, peaks and lake. Northeast of the village off NV Hwy 431 (Mt Rose Hwy), **Mt Rose Wilderness** offers miles of unspoiled terrain. A 9.6-mile round-trip trail leads steeply to the Mt Rose summit (10,778ft), starting along a well-trodden section of the multi-use, 165-mile **Tahoe Rim Trail** (www.tahoerimtrail.org) that circles the lake. Farther up Hwy 431, **Mt Rose** (☎ 775-849-0704, 800-754-7673; www.mtrose.com; 22222 Mt Rose Hwy; lift ticket incl round-trip shuttle adult/child $65/40, equipment rental $20-50) ski resort has Tahoe's highest base elevation (8260ft), and the newly opened expert terrain (the Chutes) delivers some screamers along its north-facing steeps.

Further down the eastern shore, busy **Lake Tahoe-Nevada State Park** (☎ 775-831-0494; http://parks.nv.gov/lt.htm; entry $2-8) has beautiful beaches and access to miles of backcountry trails for hiking, mountain biking, backpacking and horseback riding. At the park's southern end, near the US Hwy 50–NV Hwy 28 junction, **Spooner Lake** is popular for catch-and-release fishing, picnicking and cross-country skiing. Spooner Lake is also the start of the famous **Flume Trail**, a holy grail for experienced mountain bikers. You can rent bikes, reserve return shuttles and get information and maps at the trailhead from **Flume Trail Mountain Bikes** (☎ 775-749-5349; www.flumetrail.com; rentals per day $43-49, shuttles from $10).

Tours

Lake Tahoe Cruises (☎ 775-589-4906, 800-238-2463; www.zephyrcove.com; Zephyr Cove Marina, 750 Hwy 50; scenic cruises adult/concession from $39/18; 🚻) plies the 'big blue' year-round, courtesy of old-fashioned paddle wheelers. A narrated two-hour trip crosses to Emerald Bay on the lake's western shoreline in California.

Sleeping & Eating

Lake Tahoe gets jam-packed during summer, around holidays and on winter weekends, when prices soar and reservations are essential. In winter, many properties, including the Stateline casino hotels (all of which have restaurants and bars), offer stay-and-ski packages. Most other accommodations cluster in South Lake Tahoe across the California–Nevada border. At Incline Village, the ultraluxe **Hyatt Regency Lake Tahoe** (☎ 775-832-1234, 800-633-7313; www.hyatt.com; 111 Country Club Dr; r $190-1195; 🚻 🛁 💻 wi-fi), where the spa is bigger than the casino, resembles an elegant Arts and Crafts–style lodge. At the resort's Lone Eagle Grille, the lounge overlooks a private beach with idyllic sunset views and serves killer margaritas.

Getting There & Away

If you're driving, snow chains may be required anytime between late fall and early spring. For road condition updates, call ☎ 877-687-6237 (Nevada) and ☎ 800-427-7623 (California). **South Tahoe Express** (☎ 866-898-2463; www.southtahoeexpress.com; adult/child $24/12.50) runs almost a dozen daily buses between Reno's airport and Stateline casino hotels, taking 1½ to 2½ hours each way.

Arizona

Ask an African school child, a Taiwanese businessman or a London secretary what epitomizes the USA, and they'll likely mention the Grand Canyon. They'll describe a cowboy-and-Indian scene from a shoot-'em-up Western or a car commercial featuring fiery red rocks, pale sandy deserts, big green cacti and galloping horses. They might not be able to pinpoint Arizona on a map, or even link the vivid images to the state, but the blockbuster scenery is so well known, so cliché Wild West, it easily holds its own. Like a young Hollywood starlet whose name you can't remember, identity is secondary – what's important is her famous face.

Ask an American about the Grand Canyon state, and they'll talk about the stereotypes: silky golf courses and retirement communities, strip-mall cities and hotter-than-hell summer heat.

But ask an Arizonan about their state, and they'll wax lyrical on its hidden treasures. There'll be talk of tiny desert outposts where you expect nothing but find everything. They'll say the Grand Canyon is certainly grand, but there's so much more – rivers to raft, mountains to ski, mining towns to explore. They'll talk about a historical legacy as proud as it is sad and tell you Arizona has the third-largest Native American population in the 50 states. They'll speak about poverty and racism and how their ancestors were forced onto barren reservations. But there will be an upbeat tone when describing places where visitors can learn about Native American culture, taste mouthwatering fry bread and shop for handcrafted turquoise jewelry.

HIGHLIGHTS

- **Best Welcome with Open Arms**
  Meet the iconic symbols of the Southwest at Saguaro National Park (p238), home to a thriving colony of the majestic many-armed cacti and their relatives

- **Best Whispers of the Past**
  Beautiful and mysterious Canyon de Chelly National Monument (p224) is a sacred footprint of a vanished people – the Ancestral Puebloans – and a living monument to the trials and survival of the Navajo Nation

- **Best Photo Excursion**
  The solitary crimson buttes of Monument Valley Navajo Tribal Park (p224) touch the heart and soul no matter how many times you've seen them in movies or on TV

- **Best Place to Escape the Crowds**
  Marvel at nature's creativity at Chiricahua National Monument (p226), called 'land of standing up rocks' by the Apache warriors that used to hide among them

- **Best Shangri-La**
  Hike down to oasis-like Havasu Canyon (p212), a remote offshoot of the Grand Canyon, to splash in turquoise swimming holes and get pummeled by waterfalls

ARIZONA

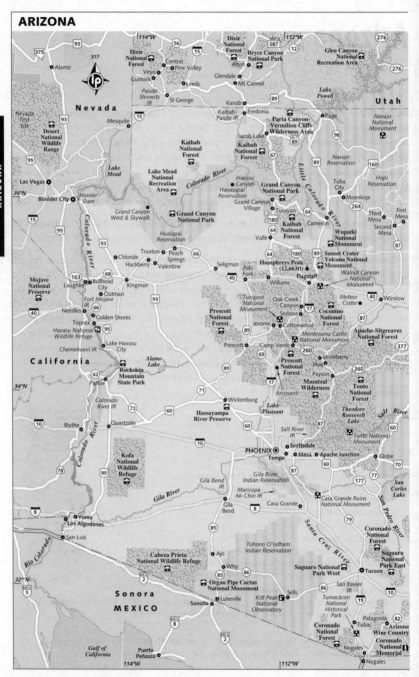

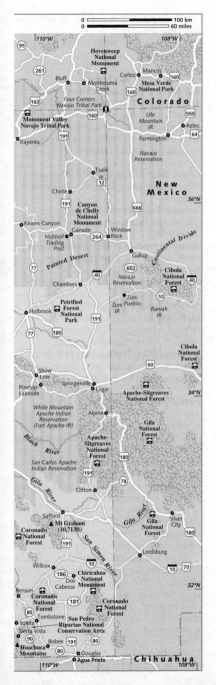

History

Native American tribes inhabited Arizona for centuries before Spanish explorer Francisco Vásquez de Coronado launched an expedition there from Mexico City in 1540. Settlers and missionaries followed in his wake, and by the mid-19th-century the US controlled Arizona. The Indian Wars, in which the US Army battled Native Americans to protect settlers and claim land for the government, officially ended in 1886 with the surrender of Apache warrior Geronimo.

Railroad and mining expansion grew and people started arriving in ever larger numbers. After President Theodore Roosevelt visited Arizona in 1903, he supported the damming of its rivers to provide year-round water for irrigation and drinking, thus paving the way to statehood: in 1912 Arizona became the last of the 48th contiguous US states to be admitted to the Union.

Today it's a state in transition. Scarcity of water remains among the foremost issues for Arizona lawmakers as the state has become the fastest growing in the country.

Climate

Arizona's highest mountains may be snow-capped in winter (December through March), but most of the state actually receives practically no rainfall. During summer (June to August), daytime temperatures often soar well above 100°F; it's a dry heat, but it's still uncomfortable. Summer rainstorms – called monsoons – come out of nowhere around August and September. The rain may turn dry riverbeds into raging torrents within minutes, so never camp in washes and ask about conditions before entering canyons.

Winters in northern Arizona are often freezing cold and places such as Flagstaff and Williams see quite a bit of snow on the ground. Some roads, most notably Hwy 67 to the Grand Canyon North Rim, are closed. Southern Arizona is milder, with daytime highs of around 70°F common in Phoenix, Yuma and even Tucson.

That said, fall and spring see less extreme temperatures, making these periods the best time for exploring Arizona.

Time Zone

Arizona is on Mountain Time (seven hours behind GMT), but is the only Western state not to observe daylight saving time from

---

ARIZONA FAST FACTS

Population 6.4 million

Area 114,000 sq miles

State nickname Grand Canyon State

Website www.arizonaguide.com

Sales tax 5.6%

Average temps low/high Phoenix Jan 41/66°F, Jul 80/105°F

Phoenix to Grand Canyon South Rim 230 miles, 3½ hours

Phoenix to Tucson 116 miles, 1¾ hours

Phoenix to Monument Valley 320 miles, 5½ hours

Page to Nogales 450 miles, 7 hours

Kingman to Holbrook 240 miles, 3¼ hours

---

spring to fall. The exception is the Navajo Reservation, which – in keeping with those parts of the reservation in Utah and New Mexico – does observe daylight saving time (although the small Hopi Reservation, which it surrounds, doesn't).

Information

Arizona Department of Transportation (www.dot .state.az.us) Road closures and other transportation details.

Arizona Heritage Traveler (www.arizonaheritage traveler.org) Sights, attractions and events with a cultural and historical slant, plus a useful itinerary builder.

Arizona Office of Tourism (☎ 866-275-5816; www .arizonaguide.com) Statewide tourist information.

Arizona State Government (www.az.gov) Official website.

National & State Parks

Gaping canyons, towering cacti, ancient cliff dwellings, crumbling Spanish missions, volcanic landscapes, scenic lakes, mysterious caverns and outlandish rock formations are among the sites that enjoy protection as national, state or tribal parks in Arizona. The Grand Canyon, of course, enjoys veritable cult status, but the iconic red buttes and spires of Monument Valley Navajo Tribal Park (p224) and the army of cacti at Saguaro National Park (p238) also get plenty of visitors. Some of the most evocative sites are in remote corners of the state, such as the ancient dwellings in idyllic Canyon de Chelly National Monument (p224) or the bizarre wonderland of rocks at Chiricahua National Monument (p226). The biggest stunner among the nearly three dozen state parks is Kartchner Caverns

Sate Park (p255), with its ethereal, multihued limestone formations.

For information on Arizona's state parks check out www.pr.state.az.us.

Arizona Scenic Routes

Arizona is crisscrossed by dozens of scenic roads, many more than we have space to list. For additional ideas, see www.byways.org and www.arizonascenicroads.com.

Grand Canyon North Rim Parkway (Hwy 67) Runs from Jacob Lake south to the North Rim via the pine, fir and aspen of Kaibab National Forest (p218).

Historic Route 66 from Topock to Seligman The longest uninterrupted remaining stretch of original Mother Road (p255).

Jerome to Sedona (Hwy 89A) Tremendous views of the Mogollon Rim and a grand welcome to Red Rock Country (p174).

Monument Valley (Hwy 163) Stupendous drive past crimson monoliths rising abruptly from the barren desert floor northeast of Kayenta (p224).

Oak Creek Canyon (Hwy 89A) Winds northeast from Sedona through dizzyingly narrow walls and dramatic rock cliffs before climbing up to Flagstaff (p174).

Sky Island Parkway Traverses ecozones equivalent to a trip from Mexico to Canada as it corkscrews up to Mt Lemmon (9157ft), northeast of Tucson (p239).

Vermilion Cliffs to Fredonia (Hwy 89A) Climbs through the remote Arizona Strip from fiery red Vermilion Cliffs up the forested Kaibab Plateau (p217).

Getting There & Around

The main east–west vein cutting across northern Arizona is the 400-mile stretch of I-40, which roughly follows the path of Historic Route 66. It's the one to take if you're headed for the Grand Canyon or Navajo Reservation. The towns with the best tourism infrastructure are Kingman, Williams and Flagstaff.

I-10 enters western Arizona at Blythe and travels for about 400 miles to New Mexico via Phoenix and Tucson. South of Phoenix, the I-8 coming west from Yuma joins the I-10.

The I-8 is the most southerly approach from California, and trust us, it's a lonely highway indeed. Cell-phone reception, FM radio, lodging and gas are practically nonexistent along the 120 intrusion-free desert miles between Yuma and Gila Bend. The same is pretty much true of the Navajo Reservation in the state's northeast corner, the Apache Reservations east of Phoenix between I-10 and I-40, and the I-10 west of Phoenix.

Phoenix' Sky Harbor International Airport (p170) and Las Vegas' McCarran International Airport (p130) are major gateways for Arizona, but Tucson also receives its share of flights. Smaller airports in Flagstaff, Prescott, Yuma and Kingman are served primarily by regional carriers.

Greyhound buses run several times daily along the major highways, connecting cities large and small, but they don't serve national parks or off-the-beaten track destinations, which is why you'll pretty much need your own wheels to get around.

Amtrak runs two train routes through Arizona. The *Southwest Chief* travels between Chicago and Los Angeles daily with stops in Flagstaff, Holbrook, Williams and Kingman. The *Sunset Limited* makes three trips a week between Los Angeles and New Orleans with stops in Yuma, Tucson and Benson.

For more information on transportation throughout the Southwest, see p536.

GREATER PHOENIX

pop 3.3 million / elev 1200ft

To tell the truth, Phoenix is a tough place to love at first. A conglomeration of some 20 cities zippered together by freeways, it's a vast, not particularly pretty, checkerboard of shopping malls, cookie-cutter subdivisions, fancy resorts, golfing greens, fast-food eateries and gas stations. There's just something artificial about this urban mirage that has desert lapping on all sides like some waterless ocean.

Well, don't lose faith. There's much more than meets the eye. Relaxed sophistication is Phoenix' hallmark. A cowboy hat and jeans are rarely out of place; a tie seldom required. With more than 300 days of sunshine, its nickname – 'Valley of the Sun' – couldn't be more appropriate. And lest you think that it's a cultural wasteland, let it be known that Phoenix has not only an opera, a symphony and several theaters, but also two of the state's finest museums – the Heard Museum and the Phoenix Art Museum. There are plenty of art galleries and even a growing local arts scene. Sports also play a big part of the culture in this city that fields teams in the national football, baseball and ice hockey leagues and is dotted with more than 230 golf courses (10 of them public). Never mind all that water…

So ignore the Botox babes, Hummer-driving '$30,000 millionaires' and dogs in cashmere turtlenecks and plunge right in to discover the many-layered charms of this sun-kissed oasis. Hey, David Spade, Alice Cooper and Stevie Nicks like it here! And so might you.

HISTORY

The Hohokam people lived here as early as 300 BC and developed a complex system of irrigation canals, only to mysteriously abandon them around AD 1450. Until the 1911 completion of the Theodore Roosevelt Dam, northeast of town on the Salt River, modern Phoenix didn't amount to much more than a desert outpost. Once the dam was built, however, the region began to boom. The Central Arizona Project (CAP), a controversial $4 billion undertaking completed in the early 1990s, brought more water to the region from the Colorado River via a series of canals and pipelines that runs 336 miles from Lake Havasu to Tucson.

ORIENTATION

Greater Phoenix – also referred to as the Valley throughout this chapter – may be vast and amorphous, but the areas of visitor interest are pretty much limited to three or four communities. Phoenix is the largest city and combines a business-like demeanor with a burgeoning cultural scene and top-notch sports facilities. Southeast of here, student-flavored Tempe (tem-*pee*) is a lively district hugging 2-mile-long Tempe Town Lake. Further east it segues smoothly into ho-hum Mesa, which has a couple of interesting museums. North of Phoenix, Paradise Valley and Scottsdale are both ritzy enclaves. While the former is mostly residential, Scottsdale is known for its cutesy old town, galleries and lavish resorts.

Other towns, including Chandler to the southeast and Glendale to the northwest, are thriving residential and manufacturing communities.

INFORMATION
Bookstores

Bookmans (www.bookmans.com; 9am-10pm; wi-fi) Mesa (Map p154; ☎ 480-835-0505; 1056 S Country Club Dr); Phoenix (Map pp158-9; ☎ 602-433-0255; 8034 N 19th Ave) Bibliophiles' indie mecca with neighborhood vibe, events and aisle after aisle of new and used books, mags and music. Pet-friendly. Free wi-fi.

Changing Hands (Map p154; ☎ 480-730-0205; 6428 S McClintock Dr, Tempe) *Publisher Weekly*'s 2007 Bookstore

ARIZONA

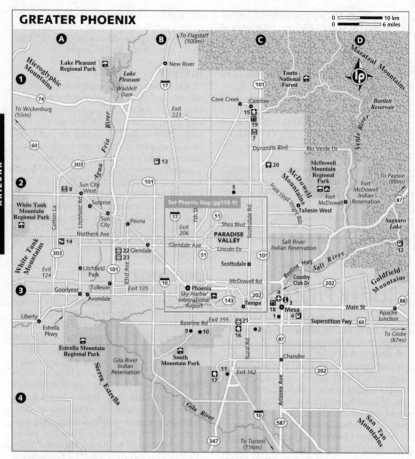

of the Year has used, new, hard-to-find and out-of-print books and magazines, plus lots of events.

Wide World of Maps Phoenix (Map pp158-9; ☎ 602-279-2323; 2626 W Indian School Rd); Scottsdale (Map pp158-9; ☎ 602-279-2323; 7325 E Frank Lloyd Wright Blvd) Fine selection of maps and guidebooks.

Emergency

Police (Map p160; ☎ 602-262-6151; 620 W Washington St, Phoenix)

Internet Access

Central Phoenix Library (Map p160; ☎ 602-262-4636; www.phoenixpubliclibrary.org; 1221 N Central Ave, Phoenix; ⊙ 9am-9pm Mon-Thu, 9am-6pm Fri & Sat, noon-6pm Sun; 🖳 wi-fi) Free internet; see website for additional locations.

Media

Also see the listings under Entertainment, p169.

Arizona Republic (www.azcentral.com) Major daily newspaper.

KJZZ 91.5 fm (http://kjzz.org) National Public Radio (NPR).

Phoenix Magazine (www.phoenixmag.com) Glossy lifestyle monthly.

Phoenix New Times (www.phoenixnewtimes.com) Free alternative news, lifestyle and listings paper.

Medical Services

Arizona Dental Association (☎ 800-866-2732) Free dentist referrals.

Banner Good Samaritan Medical Center (Map pp158-9; ☎ 602-239-2000; www.bannerhealth.com;

1111 E McDowell Rd, Phoenix) 24-hour emergency room. See website for additional Valley hospitals and clinics.

VCA Animal Referral & Emergency Center of Arizona (Map p154; ☎ 480-898-0001; 1648 N Country Club Dr, Mesa) 24-hour emergency pet care.

Money

American Express (Map pp158-9; ☎ 602-468-1199; cnr Camelback Rd & 24th St, Phoenix) At Biltmore Fashion Park.
TravelEx (Map pp158-9; ☎ 602-275-8767; Terminal 4, Sky Harbor International Airport, Phoenix)

Post

Downtown post office (Map p160; ☎ 602-253-9648; 522 N Central Ave, Phoenix)

Telephone

Greater Phoenix has three telephone area codes: ☎ 480, ☎ 602 and ☎ 623. You need to dial the area code even if you're in it.

Tourist Information

Downtown Phoenix Visitor Information Center (Map p160; ☎ 602-254-6500, 877-225-5749; www .visitphoenix.com; 125 N 2nd St, Suite 120; ☉ 8am-5pm Mon-Fri) The Valley's most complete source of tourist information.
Mesa Convention & Visitors Bureau (Map p154; ☎ 480-827-4700, 800-283-6372; www.mesacvb.com; 120 N Center St; ☉ 8am-5pm Mon-Fri)
Scottsdale Convention & Visitors Bureau (Map pp158-9; ☎ 480-421-1004, 800-782-1117; www.scotts dalecvb.com; 4343 N Scottsdale Rd, Suite 170; ☉ 8am-5pm Mon-Fri) Inside the Galleria Corporate Center.
Tempe Convention & Visitors Bureau (Map pp158-9; ☎ 480-894-8158, 800-283-6734; www.tempecvb .com; 51 W 3rd St, Suite 105; ☉ 8:30am-5pm Mon-Fri)

SIGHTS

Since the Phoenix area is so spread out, attractions are broken down by community in this guide.

Phoenix

At first glance, Downtown Phoenix appears to be all buttoned-up business and bureaucracy (the state capitol is here), but there's actually plenty of partying going on in its cultural venues, sports stadiums, bars and restaurants. There's even a small alternative art scene. Free DASH buses ply its main streets from Monday to Friday.

HERITAGE & SCIENCE PARK

Downtown is unapologetically modern except at **Historic Heritage Square** (Map p160; ☎ 602-262-5071; 115 N 6th St; admission free; ☉ 24hr). Blend out the surrounding skyscrapers and imagine thundering hooves and creaking stagecoaches as you amble around this cluster of stately Victorians. Join a tour of the 1895 **Rosson House** (tours adult/child/senior $5/2/4; ☉ 10am-4pm Wed-Sat, noon-4pm Sun) or take the tots to the **Arizona Doll & Toy Museum** (☎ 602-253-9337; cnr 7th & Monroe Sts; adult/child $3/1; ☉ 10am-4pm Tue-Sat, noon-4pm Sun Sep-Jul; ♿) in the nearby 1901 Stevens House. The 1912 schoolroom with a cast of antique dolls squeezed behind the wooden desks is adorable.

For an in-depth grounding in regional history – Pima Indians to the present – head over to the **Phoenix Museum of History** (Map p160; ☎ 602-853-2734; www.pmoh.org; 105 N 5th St; adult/child/concession $6/3/4; ☉ 10am-5pm Tue-Sat). If the artifact-filled display cases don't capture your imagination, the city's first jail and quirky 'Beer Bottle' sidewalk might just do the trick.

Too quaint? Make a beeline to the **Arizona Science Center** (Map p160; ☎ 602-716-2000; www .azscience.org; 600 E Washington St; adult/concession $9/7; ☉ 10am-5pm; ♿), a high-tech temple of discovery with 300-odd hands-on exhibits and live demonstrations. Learn icky things about your colon, investigate the mystery of gravity, explore the changing temporary exhibits, then

ARIZONA

ARIZONA

PHOENIX IN...

Driving distances are ginormous in Greater Phoenix, so don't pack too much into a day and pad your travel time for traffic.

One Day

Fuel up for the day at **Matt's Big Breakfast** (p165), then head to the **Heard Museum** (p156) for a primer on Southwestern tribal history, art and culture. If you've got the time and inclination for another museum, pop into the nearby **Phoenix Art Museum** (p156) before enjoying a light lunch at its **Arcadia Farms Café** (p166). If it's not too hot, take a prickly post-prandial stroll through the exquisite **Desert Botanical Garden** (p157); otherwise, steer towards your hotel pool or **Waterworld Safari** (p163) to relax and chill. Wrap up the day with an aperitif at **Kazimierz** (p168) before reporting to dinner at **Cowboy Ciao** (p167) or **Canal at Southbridge** (p167).

Two Days

On the morning of day two, head to **Taliesin West** (p157) to learn about the warped if fertile mind of architectural great Frank Lloyd Wright, then grab a fat sandwich at the **Orange Table** (p167) before browsing the galleries and souvenir shops of **Old Town Scottsdale** (p157). In the afternoon, share a couples' massage at the Avania Spa at **Hyatt Regency Scottsdale Resort & Spa** (p165) or VH Spa at **Hotel Valley Ho** (p164), then get all dressed up for a gourmet dinner at **Kai Restaurant** (p167). Families might prefer a tour of eccentric **Mystery Castle** (p161) followed by casual cuisine at **Chelsea's Kitchen** (p166).

---

wind down the day with a movie at the on-site **IMAX Theatre** (adult/concession $8/7) or the recently overhauled **Planetarium** (adult/child/senior $8/7/7).

HEARD MUSEUM

This extraordinary **museum** (Map pp158-9; ☎ 602-252-8848; www.heard.org; 2301 N Central Ave; adult/child/student/senior $10/3/5/9; ☷ 9:30am-5pm; ☀) is a magical mystery tour through the history, life, arts and culture of Native American tribes in the Southwest. It emphasizes quality over quantity and is one of America's best museums of its kind.

The permanent collection includes centuries' worth of kachina dolls, pottery, textiles, baskets, sculpture and jewelry that have changed surprisingly little from ancient times to today. Learn more about individual tribes at the interactive 'We Are! Arizona's First People' exhibit in a beautifully muraled giant hall. Most disturbing is the 'Boarding School Experience' gallery about the controversial federal policy of removing Native American children from their families and sending them to remote boarding schools in order to 'Americanize' them. There's also a special kids' gallery and temporary exhibitions, including those showcasing contemporary Native American artists. Guided tours run at noon, 1:30pm or 3pm (no extra charge) and audioguides are available for $3. Also check

out the busy events schedule and the superb gift shop.

Selections from the Heard's vast collection are also displayed at two new satellite museums, the **Heard Museum North** (Map p154; ☎ 480-488-9817; 32633 N Scottsdale Rd; adult/child/student/senior $5/2/2/4; ☷ 10am-5pm Mon-Sat, noon-5pm Sun) in Scottsdale and the **Heard Museum West** (Map p154; ☎ 623-344-2200; 16126 N Civic Center Plaza; adult/child/student/senior $5/2/2/4; ☷ 9:30am-5pm Tue-Sun) in the western suburb of Surprise.

PHOENIX ART MUSEUM

An Aladdin's cave of paintings and sculpture stretching across the ages and borders, the **Phoenix Art Museum** (Map p160; ☎ 602-257-1880; www.phxart.org; 1625 N Central Ave; adult/child/concession $10/4/8, 3-9pm Tue free; ☷ 10am-9pm Tue, 10am-5pm Wed-Sun; ☀) is Arizona's premier repository of fine art. Galleries teem with works by Claude Monet, Diego Rivera and Georgia O'Keefe alongside plenty of lesser-known practitioners. If you've got kids in tow, take them to the ingeniously crafted miniature period rooms in the Thorne Rooms and borrow a family audioguide or a KidPack filled with puzzles and activities. Hands-on types can get artsy in the PhxArtKids Gallery (check out www.phxartkids.org to plan your visit).

Grown-ups might want to join the free guided tours at 1pm and 2pm. The museum's contemporary Arcadia Farms Café (p166) is a great place to grab a bite, and not only for museum-goers.

DESERT BOTANICAL GARDEN

If you're all malled and museumed out, this inspirational **garden** (Map pp158-9; ☎ 480-941-1225; www.dbg.org; 1201 N Galvin Pkwy; adult/child/student/senior $10/4/5/9; ☼ 8am-8pm Oct-Apr, 7am-8pm May-Sep) is a great place to reconnect with nature. Paths lead past an astonishing variety of desert denizens, including Seussian-shaped organ-pipe cacti and modest-looking shrubs that send up ethereally beautiful flowers. It's all pretty dazzling year-round, but no more so than during December's nighttime *luminarias* when plants are draped in miles of twinkling lights.

The surrounding **Papago Park** has picnic areas and jogging, mountain biking and equestrian trails, along with a children's fishing pond.

PUEBLO GRANDE MUSEUM & ARCHAEO-LOGICAL PARK

Excavations at the Hohokam village of Pueblo Grande have yielded many clues about the daily lives of these ancient people famous for building such a well-engineered 1000-mile network of irrigation canals that some modern canals simply follow their paths.Study this fascinating culture at the small **museum** (Map pp158-9; ☎ 602-495-0901; www.pueblogrande.com; 4619 E Washington St; adult/child/senior Mon-Sat $2/1/1.50, Sun free; ☼ 9am-4:45pm Mon-Sat, 1-4:45pm Sun), then use your new knowledge to make sense of the park's excavations, which include a ball court, a ceremonial platform and a section of the original canals.

Scottsdale

In the north Valley, Scottsdale hovers above Phoenix like a haughty lady, sparkling with self-confidence fuelled by good looks, charm and money. She drives a big SUV, has probably had some plastic surgery, and adores shopping and the good life. She's also got plenty in store for visitors, including a pedestrian-friendly downtown, chic hotels and a vibrant food and nightlife scene. A free trolley links Old Town Scottsdale with Scottsdale Fashion Square mall via the new Scottsdale Waterfront, a retail and office complex on the Arizona Canal.

OLD TOWN SCOTTSDALE

Compared to the usual Phoenix sprawl, Old Town Scottsdale, centered on Brown Ave

and Main St, feels a lot snugger. It's great for strolling and can almost be forgiven for playing the Old West theme to the hilt. Expect cutesy buildings – some old, some not – with covered sidewalks and stores hawking mass-produced 'Indian' jewelry, wind chimes and Western art. One of the buildings with genuine history is the Little Red School House, now home of the **Scottsdale Historical Museum** (Map pp158-9; ☎ 480-945-4499; www.scottsdalemuseum .com; 7333 Scottsdale Mall; admission free; ☼ 10am-5pm Wed-Sun Oct-May, 10am-2pm Wed-Sun Jun & Sep), whose exhibits are well meaning but ho-hum.

In a cleverly adapted ex–movie theater, the **Scottsdale Museum of Contemporary Arts** (Map pp158-9; ☎ 480-874-4666; www.smoca.org; 7374 E 2nd St; adult/child/student $7/free/5; ☼ 10am-5pm Tue-Wed & Fri-Sat, 10am-8pm Thu, noon-5pm Sun) showcases global art, architecture and design, including James Turrell's otherworldly 'Skyspace' in the sculpture garden. The museum is part of the local performing arts center along with the Orange Table (p167) café.

NORTHERN SCOTTSDALE

Love him or not, there's no denying that Frank Lloyd Wright was one of the seminal American architects of the 20th century. **Taliesin West** (Map p154; ☎ 480-860-2700; www.franklloydwright .org; 12621 Frank Lloyd Wright Blvd; adult/child $18/5; ☼ 9am-5pm) was Wright's desert home and studio, built between 1938 and 1940. Still home to an architecture school and open to the public for guided tours, it's a prime example of organic architecture with buildings incorporating elements and structures found in nature. The most popular tour is the 90-minute **Insights Tour** (adult/child/student/senior $32/20/29/29; ☼ half-hourly 9am-4pm Nov-Apr, hourly 9am-4pm May-Oct) during which guides pied-piper you to Wright's office with its

> ### TICKETS TO SAVINGS
>
> Besides the usual discounts (see p521), you also can trim expenses by purchasing the **ShowUp Now Pass** (www.showupnowpass .com) online or at any visitor center. The Golden Triangle Pass (adult/child 3-12 yr $24/9) is good for one entry to the Heard Museum, Phoenix Art Museum and Desert Botanical Garden, while the Total Access Pass ($49.50/25.50) provides admission to 11 other attractions, including Taliesin West. Both are valid over a nine-day period.

lonelyplanet.com

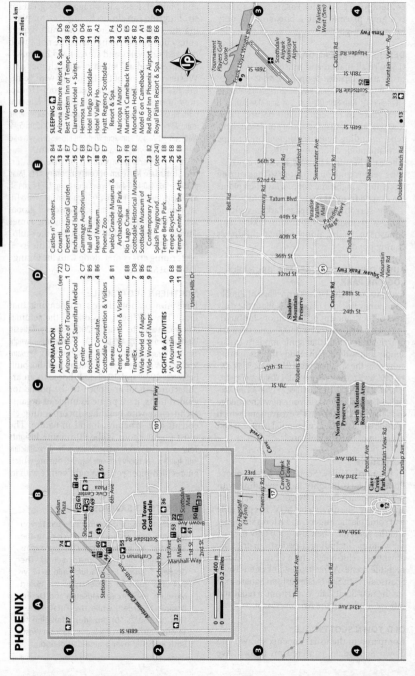

PHOENIX

ARIZONA

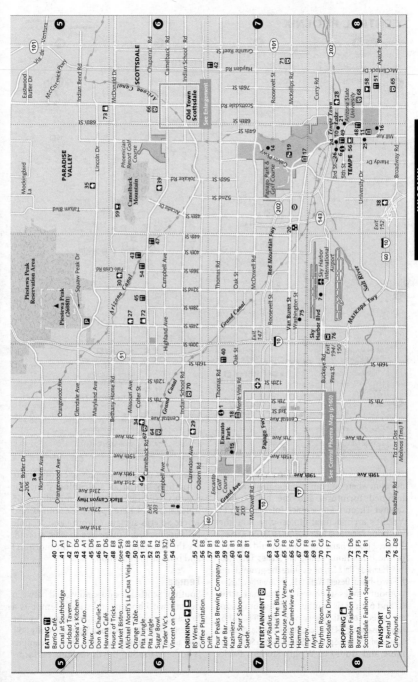

ARIZONA

CENTRAL PHOENIX

slanted canvas roof, the grand stone-walled living room where you can sit on original Wright-designed furniture, and the half-sunken Cabaret Theater. For a quick introduction to Wright's architectural philosophy, take the one-hour **Panorama Tour** ($27/10/23/23; 10:15am, 12:15pm, 2:15pm); hard-core fans should sign up for the three-hour **Behind the Scenes Tour** ($60; 9:15am Mon, Thu & Sat) or explore the grounds on the two-hour **Desert Walk** ($33; 10am Nov-Apr).

About 9 miles southwest of here, via Cactus Rd and 64th St, is another architectural marvel called **Cosanti** (Map pp158-9; 480-948-6145; www.arcosanti.org; 6433 E Doubletree Ranch Rd; donation appreciated; 9am-5pm Mon-Sat, 11am-5pm Sun). The home and studio of Wright student Paolo

Soleri, this unusual complex of cast-concrete structures served as a stepping stone for Soleri's experimental Arcosanti village, 65 miles north of here (p171). Cosanti is also where Soleri's signature bronze and ceramic bells are crafted. You're free to walk around, see the bells poured (usually in the morning) and browse the gift shop.

Tempe

South of Scottsdale and sandwiched between downtown Phoenix and Mesa, Tempe is a fun and energetic district, enlivened by the 51,000 students of **Arizona State University** (ASU; www.asu.edu). Founded in 1885, the vast campus is home to the Sun Devils stadium, perform-

WHAT THE...?

Equal parts Mexican hacienda, Native American cliff dwelling and psychedelic sand castle, the 18-room **Mystery Castle** (Map p154; ☎ 602-268-1581; 800 E Mineral Rd; adult/child $5/3; ⏰ 11am-4pm Thu-Sun Oct-May or by appointment) was constructed in the 1930s and '40s by Boyce Luther Gulley for his daughter Mary Lou. It's an eccentric contraption of stone, recycled telegraph poles, adobe and whatever else he could scavenge, held together by a mix of sand, cement, calcium and goat's milk. Mary Lou still lives in the house, but is now too frail to conduct the tours herself. Call ahead to make sure it's open at all.

ance venues, galleries and museums. It's also taken a leadership role in the eco-movement in striving to become a 'living laboratory' for sustainability.

Places to check out include the **ASU Art Museum** (Map pp158-9; ☎ 480-965-2787; http://asu artmuseum.asu.edu; admission free; ⏰ 11am-5pm Tue-Sat & 1-5pm Sun year-round, until 9pm Tue during school year), which has great art from throughout the Americas – Alaska to Argentina. For architecture fans, the circular **Gammage Auditorium** (Map pp158-9; ☎ 480-965-3434; www.asugammage.com; cnr Mill Ave & Apache Blvd; admission free, tickets from $20; ⏰ 1-4pm Mon-Fri Oct-May), Frank Lloyd Wright's last major building, is a major point of pilgrimage. A popular performance venue, it stages primarily Broadway-style musicals and shows.

Mill Ave (Map pp158-9), situated along the campus' western edge, is Tempe's main drag and lined with restaurants, bars and a mix of national chains and indie boutiques. It's a fine place to browse for old vinyl and vintage dresses and you can even sign up for two hours of free wi-fi along here and on campus. For cool metro and mountain views, huff it up for half a mile to the top of **'A' Mountain** (Map pp158-9), so-called because of the giant letter 'A' painted there by ASU students, but officially known as Tempe Butte or Hayden Butte. The trailhead is on E 3rd St, near Mill Ave.

Mill Ave spills into **Tempe Town Lake** (Map pp158-9; www.tempe.gov/lake), a 2-mile-long recreational pond created by reclaiming the long-dry Salt River in the 1990s. Have a picnic at

Tempe Beach Park and watch kids letting off steam at the waterfalls, rock slides and shallow pools of the ingenious **Splash Playground** (admission free; ⏰ Apr-Sep; 👶). There's no swimming in the lake, but **Rio Lago Cruise** (Map pp158-9; ☎ 480-517-4050; www.riolagocruise.com; 80 W Rio Salado Pkwy) rents boats and operates lake tours. Free outdoor concerts and festivals bring crowds to the park on weekends. The lakeshore has also become a much sought-after residential area and numerous condo, loft and apartment towers have sprouted here in recent years, as has the shiny new lakefront **Tempe Center for the Arts** (Map pp158-9; www.tempe.gov/tca).

To get around downtown Tempe, use the free FLASH shuttle bus.

Mesa

Founded by Mormons in 1877, Mesa is one of the fastest-growing cities in the nation and the third-largest city in Arizona with a population of around 500,000. Its main cultural attraction is the **Arizona Museum of Natural History** (Map p154; ☎ 480-644-2230; www.azmnh.org; 53 N MacDonald St; adult/child/student/senior $8/4/6/7; ⏰ 10am-5pm Tue-Fri, 11am-5pm Sat, 1-5pm Sun), which counts animated dinosaurs, an eight-cell territorial jail, a prehistoric Hohokam village and a replica Spanish mission among its many displays and interactive exhibits. Also in Mesa is the **Arizona Museum for Youth** (Map p154; ☎ 480-644-2468; www.arizonamuseumforyouth .com; 35 N Robson St; admission $5; ⏰ 10am-4pm Tue-Sat, noon-4pm Sun; 👶), whose primary mission is to get little ones excited about fine art through hands-on activities. There's even a special room for toddlers where they can play with giant crayons or build their own colorful garden.

About 20 miles south, on the Gila River Indian Reservation, the **Rawhide Western Town & Steakhouse** (Map p154; ☎ 480-502-5600; www.rawhide .com; 5700 W N Loop Rd; admission free, per attraction or show $4, unlimited day pass $15; ⏰ 5:30-9pm Mon-Thu, noon-9pm Fri-Sun, closed Mon & Tue May-Dec; 👶) is a re-created 1880s frontier town theme park. You can test your mettle on a mechanical bull, a stubborn burro or an amenable camel; ride a cutesy train or a stagecoach; pan for gold; get married in jail; help the sheriff arrest your rascal kids; watch a stunt show; and all sorts of other hokey-but-fun shenanigans. The steakhouse has rattlesnake and Rocky Mountain oysters (bull testicles; see p64) for adventurous eaters and mesquite-grilled slabs of beef for everyone else, usually accompanied by music and entertainment.

ARTYTOWN

It may not have the mystique of Santa Fe or the cachet of New York, but Phoenix has almost imperceptibly worked its way up the ladder of art cities that matter. Scottsdale in particular teems with galleries laden with everything from epic Western oil paintings to cutting-edge sculpture and moody Southwestern landscapes. Every Thursday evening, some 100 of them keep their doors open until 9pm for **Art Walk** (www.scottsdalegalleries.com), which centers on Marshall Way and Main St.

The vibe is edgier and the setting more urban during **First Fridays** (www.artlinkphoenix.com; ⏱ 6-10pm), which draws up to 20,000 people to the streets of downtown Phoenix on the first Friday of every month, primarily for art but also for music, poetry slams and other events. Stop by the Central Phoenix Library (p154) to nab a brochure, map and shuttle-bus schedule before joining the fun.

ACTIVITIES
Hiking & Mountain Biking

Hiking may not be an obvious activity to get your kicks in Phoenix, but trust us, a walk on the 'wild side' feels like taking a micro-vacation from the mad urban bustle. Check http://phoenix.gov/PARKS/hikemain.html for park details or consult *Day Hikes and Trail Rides in and Around Phoenix* by Roger and Ethel Freeman for further ideas.

Nature intersects with civilization at **South Mountain Park** (Map p154; ☎ 602-495-0222; Central Ave, Phoenix; ⏱ 5am-11pm), a local favorite for exercise kicks and, at 25 sq miles, larger than Manhattan. The 51-mile trail network (leashed dogs allowed) dips through canyons, over grassy hills and past granite walls, offering city views and access to Native American petroglyphs. There's an interpretive center near the Central Ave entrance.

If you prefer picking your way around saguaros, ocotillos and other local cacti, head to **Piestewa Peak** (Map pp158-9; ☎ 602-262-7901; Squaw Peak Dr, Phoenix; ⏱ 6am-11pm), previously known as Squaw Peak and renamed for local Native American soldier Lori Piestewa who was killed in Iraq in 2003. The trek to the 2608ft summit is hugely popular with the tight-buns brigade and the park can get jammed on winter weekends. Parking lots northeast of Lincoln Dr between 22nd and 24th Sts fill early. Dogs are allowed on some trails.

Another urban playground, on the Valley's western edge, is the 46-sq-mile **White Tank Mountain Regional Park** (Map p154; ☎ 623-935-2505; www.maricopa.gov/parks/white_tank; 13025 N White Tank Mountain Rd; per vehicle $6; ⏱ 6am-8pm Sun-Thu, 6am-10pm Fri & Sat). Better known as the White Tanks, it drapes across dramatic canyon landscape and is zigzagged by 26 miles of trails, including a grueling one to the top of the 4018ft summit. The park entrance is about 20 miles west of I-17 via Dunlap/Olive Ave.

All three parks have suitably challenging trails designated for mountain bikers. If you need wheels, **Airpark Bicycle Center** (Map p154; ☎ 480-596-6633; 3498 E Monte Cristo Ave, Scottsdale) and **Tempe Bicycles** (Map pp158-9; ☎ 480-446-3033; http://tempebicycle.com; 405 W University Dr, Tempe) rent all sorts of bicycles from $25 to $75 per 24 hours.

Horseback Riding

For explorations on horseback, **Ponderosa Stables** (Map p154; ☎ 602-268-1261; www.arizona-horses .com; 10215 S Central Ave, Phoenix; 1-/2-hr rides $28/48) leads rides through South Mountain Park (left). Reservations required.

Tubing

Floating down the Salt River in an inner tube is loads of fun, and it's also a great way to relax and cool down on a hot summer day. **Salt River Recreation** (Map p154; ☎ 480-984-3305; www .saltrivertubing.com; 1320 N Bush Hwy; tubes & shuttle $12, cash only; ⏱ 9am-7:30pm May-Sep; ♿) takes you down the Lower Salt River through the stark Tonto National Forest. The launch is in northeast Mesa, about 15 miles north of Hwy 60 on Power Rd. Floats are two, three or five hours long, including the shuttle bus ride back, and weekends can get superbusy. Kids must be at least 4ft tall and at least eight years old. If you want to bring a cooler along, you'll need to rent an extra tube. Alcohol is permitted, but glass containers are not.

PHOENIX FOR CHILDREN

Phoenix is a great family town, with plenty to keep the little tykes occupied. If your child loves animals, head to the **Phoenix Zoo** (Map pp158-9; ☎ 602-273-1341; www.phoenixzoo.org; 455 N Galvin Pkwy, Phoenix; adult/child/senior $14/6/9; ☼ 9am-5pm Oct-May, 7am-2pm Mon-Fri & 7am-4pm Sat & Sun Jun-Sep; ⚑). A wide variety of critters, including some rare ones, are housed in several distinct and natural-looking environments. Don't miss the petting zoo.

If that's too tame, make the trip out to the private **Wildlife World Zoo** (Map p154; ☎ 623-935-9453; 16501 W Northern Ave, Litchfield Park; adult/child $17/9; ☼ 9am-5pm; ⚑) to feed giraffes and view kangaroos, tigers, antelopes and other exotic creatures, many of them endangered. It's 35 miles northwest of downtown Phoenix. A new aquarium was expected to open in late 2008.

Back in town, next to the Phoenix Zoo in fact, is the **Hall of Flame** (Map pp158-9; ☎ 602-275-3473; www.hallofflame.org; 6101 E Van Buren St, Phoenix; adult/child/student/senior $6/1.50/4/5; ☼ 9am-5pm Mon-Sat, noon-4pm Sun; Ⓟ ⚑). Kids get to don firefighter gear, climb around a genuine fire engine and examine more than 90 fully restored fire-fighting machines and related paraphernalia from 1725 to today.

Preschoolers will likely be enthralled by the adorable singing, talking and dancing puppets of the **Great Arizona Puppet Theater** (Map p160; ☎ 602-262-2050; www.azpuppets.org; 302 W Latham St, Phoenix; adult/child $8/6; ⚑). The repertory includes classic fairy tales like *Little Red Riding Hood* and original shows like *The Monkey & the Pirate*.

Take your pint-sized thrill-seekers to the **Enchanted Island** (Map pp158-9; ☎ 602-254-1200; www.enchantedisland.com; 1202 W Encanto Blvd, Phoenix; single-ride tickets $1, unlimited rides day-pass over/under 54in tall $12.50/7.50; ☼ hours vary; ⚑), a low-key amusement park with plenty of cute rides that'll keep the single-digit set entertained for a couple of hours. It's surrounded by Encanto Park, a fine spot for picnics.

Older kids will likely get more out of **Castles n' Coasters** (Map pp158-9; ☎ 602-997-7575; www.castlesncoasters.com; 9445 E Metro Pkwy, Phoenix; unlimited rides Sat & Sun $21, activities individually priced Mon-Fri; ☼ hours vary; ⚑), a big amusement park by the Metrocenter Mall about 20 miles northwest of downtown, near exit 207 off I-17. From chickens to brave-hearts, there's a coaster for everyone, plus a watery log ride, a magic carpet ride, and other thrills and attractions, including miniature golf courses and video arcades.

To cool off in summer, **Waterworld Safari** (Map p154; ☎ 623-581-1947; http://phoenix.golfland.com; 4243 W

Pinnacle Peak Rd, Glendale; over/under 48in tall $24/19.50, toddlers/seniors $3/19.50; ☼ 10am-8pm Mon-Thu, 10am-9pm Fri & Sat, 11am-7pm Sun Jun-Aug; ⚑) has scores of pools, tube slides, wave pools, waterfalls, floating rivers and other splash zones. It's in Glendale, 2 miles west of I-17 at exit 217, about 30 miles northwest of downtown Phoenix.

In Mesa, about 13 miles southeast of downtown, **Golfland Sunsplash** (Map p154; ☎ 480-834-8319; http://mesa.golfland.com; 155 W Hampton Ave, Mesa; admission varies by activity; ☼ 10am-10pm Mon-Thu, 10am-midnight Fri & Sat, noon-10pm Sun; ⚑) has year-round miniature golf, a huge video game arcade, a laser tag arena (like paintball, only with lasers), a bumper boat lagoon and a go-cart racetrack. The Sunsplash water park is open from June to August.

FESTIVALS & EVENTS

The most popular event in Phoenix is the **Fiesta Bowl football game** (☎ 480-350-0900; www.fiestabowl.org) held on New Year's Day at the University of Phoenix Stadium (Map p154). It's preceded by one of the largest parades in the Southwest.

The **Arizona State Fair** (☎ 602-252-6771; www.azstatefair.com) lures folks to the Arizona State Fairgrounds (Map p160) during the first two weeks of October with typical rodeo and midway action.

SLEEPING

From basic motels to ritzy resorts, the Valley's hundreds of places to stay have one thing in common – prices plummet in summer when the mercury rises. Chain motels outnumber everything else in town, and many are represented by a dozen or more properties scattered around the Valley. B&Bs are few and far between. Greater Phoenix is famous for its lavish resorts, which aren't just places to sleep but destinations within themselves.

Phoenix

HI Phoenix Hostel (Map p160; ☎ 602-254-9803; http://home.earthlink.net/~phxhostel; 1026 N 9th St; dm $18-25, d $30-45; Ⓟ 🖳 wi-fi) Chalked thank-you notes grace the facade of this homey 14-bed hostel in a working-class residential neighborhood, and relaxing garden nooks buffer the front and back yards. Kitchen and common areas close during the day. Check-in is from 5pm to 10pm. It's closed in August.

San Carlos Hotel (Map p160; ☎ 602-253-4121, 800-528-5446; www.hotelsancarlos.com; 202 N Central

Ave; r $90-190; (P) (wi-fi) Monroe, Bogart and Gable were among the Hollywood royalty that shacked up in what once ranked among the most illustrious hotels in Phoenix. Today, this 1928 downtown property has lost much of its luster and rooms are snug by modern standards. Still, it's a friendly place and a solid choice if you're trying to avoid a chain and can't afford a resort.

Maricopa Manor (Map pp158-9; ☎ 602-274-6302, 800-292-6403; www.maricopamanor.com; 15 W Pasadena Ave; r $130-240; (P) (wi-fi) This intimate urban B&B is a popular retreat with both vacationers and business folk. Rooms are tucked into three 1920s and '30s casitas framing a seasonal pool and pretty gardens with trickling fountains. Privacy is key: there's no social hour and the gourmet breakfast is delivered to your room.

Clarendon Hotel + Suites (Map pp158-9; ☎ 602-252-7363; www.theclarendon.net; 401 W Clarendon Ave; r incl breakfast $150-290; (P) (wi-fi) This sassy lifestyle hotel scores points with trendy, design-minded travelers who love the dark custom furniture and original art in pleasingly minimalist rooms. The aptly named Oasis pool is a perfect bliss-out station with underwater music, massage jets and waterfalls. Superperk: free local, national and – get this – international calls.

Royal Palms Resort & Spa (Map pp158-9; ☎ 602-840-3610; www.royalpalmsresortandspa.com; 5200 E Camelback Rd; r $190-400, ste $210-3500; (P) (wi-fi) If this ultraposh boutique resort feels like a private mansion, it's because that's how it started out: as the winter retreat of New York industrialist Delos Cook. It's a hushed and elegant place spiked with antiques and surrounded by flowery gardens and palms imported from Egypt. Pets can go Pavlovian for soft beds, personalized biscuits and walking services.

Arizona Biltmore Resort & Spa (Map pp158-9; ☎ 602-955-6600, 800-950-0086; www.arizonabiltmore.com; 2400 E Missouri Ave; r & ste $380-2300; (P) (wi-fi) With architecture inspired by Frank Lloyd Wright, the Biltmore is perfect for connecting to the magic of yesterday when Irving Berlin penned 'White Christmas' in his suite and Marilyn Monroe splashed around in the pool. It boasts over 700 discerning units, two golf courses, several pools, a spa, a kids' club and more such luxe touches. Pooches get pampered with welcome treats and keepsake bowls and placemats, but wi-fi only works in the lobby and by the main pool.

Scottsdale

Motel 6 on Camelback (Map pp158-9; ☎ 480-946-2280; www.motel6.com; 6848 E Camelback Rd; r $40-85; (P)) You want to say you spent the night in Scottsdale but are not a member of FWS (fat-wallet society)? No problem, as long as you don't mind shacking up at this well-kept, if predictably basic, national chain. It's only a Frisbee toss from Scottsdale Fashion Square mall and a quick drive from Old Town. Pets OK.

Hermosa Inn (Map pp158-9; ☎ 602-955-8614, 800-678-8946; www.hermosainn.com; 5532 N Palo Cristi Rd; r incl breakfast $140-460, villa $310-700; (wi-fi) Step inside and you'll instantly understand why this boutique hotel is called 'hermosa' (Spanish for beautiful). Steeped in history, the adobe ranch began as the private home and studio of cowboy artist Lon Megargee. Today, the 35 rooms and casitas give off soothing vibes thanks to Spanish Colonial decor that makes perfect use of color and proportion, just like Megargee's paintings. Excellent restaurant, but no pool. Pets OK.

Hotel Indigo Scottsdale (Map pp158-9; ☎ 480-941-9400, 800-980-6429; www.scottsdalehiphotel.com; 4415 N Civic Center Plaza; r $180-400; (P) (wi-fi) This outpost for cashed-up hipsters boasts all the expected hot-spot trappings, from outdoor fire pits to the club music in the lobby, fancy toiletries and plasma TVs. The sumptuous bedding is the perfect hangover prevention after a night of cavorting and, if not, there's always the outdoor pool or gym to clear your head. Dogs are not only welcome, there's even a special package (from $180) that includes treats and clean-up bags.

Marriott's Camelback Inn (Map pp158-9; ☎ 480-948-1700, 800-242-2635; www.camelbackinn.com; 5402 E Lincoln Dr; r $300-550; (P) (wi-fi) The guest loyalty quotient is quite impressive at this 120-acre resort that niftily capitalizes on its 1936 pedigree yet keeps you comfortable with the full range of mod cons. Rooms in Southwestern adobe buildings scattered across a desert landscape come with microwaves, bathrooms that don't skimp on size, and private balconies perfect for taking some quiet time out. Kids can romp on the playground and the basketball court, and Rover is welcome too.

Hotel Valley Ho (Map pp158-9; ☎ 480-248-2000, 866-882-4484; www.hotelvalleyho.com; 6850 E Main St; r $320-610; (P) (wi-fi) Midcentury modern gets a 21st-century twist at this jazzy joint that once bedded Bing Crosby, Natalie Wood and Janet Leigh. Bebop music, upbeat desk staff and eye-magnets like the 'ice fireplace' nicely recapture the Rat Pack–era vibe, and the theme travels well to the balconied rooms. The pool is great, but don't ignore the VH Spa, whose expert staff definitely puts the 'treat' in 'treatments.' Ain't that swell? Fido stays free and gets doggie amenities.

Hyatt Regency Scottsdale Resort & Spa (Map pp158-9; ☎ 480-444-1234, 800-233-1234; www.hyatt.com; 7500 E Doubletree Ranch Rd; r $320-625; P ☺ ⓖ 🖵 wi-fi) If you're in town to see the sights, you've got a problem: there's simply no reason to leave this luxe and lush property. Swimming? How about an entire water park with multiple pools and hot tubs, a sandy beach and a huge waterslide. Indian culture? Swing by the Native American educational room. Golf? How do 27 holes sound? Drop the little ones at kids' camp while indulging in a holistic spa treatment choreographed to your body's internal clock. Views? Stunning. Only the rooms could use an update, but that was supposed to happen in 2008.

Mondrian Hotel (Map pp158-9; ☎ 480-308-1100; www.mondrianscottsdale.com; 7353 E Indian School Rd; r $395-695; P ☺ 🖵 wi-fi) Paris Hilton has slept at this signless fashionista favorite, which has an esoteric Garden of Eden theme. Crisp rooms feature a ruby-red apple and giant wall-mounted TVs but no other amenities, not even a coffeemaker. The two pools, two bars and restaurant are all epicenters of cool, so don't forget those oversized sunglasses.

ourpick Boulders Resort (Map p154; ☎ 480-488-9009, 866-397-6520; www.theboulders.com; 34531 N Tom Darlington Dr; casitas $400-800, villas from $600; P ☺ 🖵 wi-fi) Tensions evaporate the moment you arrive at this desert oasis that blends nearly imperceptibly into a landscape of natural rock formations – and that's even before you've put in a session on the massage table or steam room at the ultraposh on-site Golden Door Spa. Basically, everything here is calculated to take the edge off travel, making it a perfect destination for recovering from jet lag or rediscovering your significant other. For extra privacy, book an individual casita to which you will be whisked on a golf cart, past the 18-hole Jay Morris–designed championship golf course.

Tempe

Best Western Inn of Tempe (Map pp158-9; ☎ 480-784-2233; 670 N Scottsdale Rd; r incl breakfast $50-150; P ☺ 🖵) Dependable as a well-worn shoe, this well-kept contender sits right next to the busy 202 freeway but within walking distance from Tempe Town Lake. Get a room facing the lake and you should be fine. ASU and lively Mill Ave are within staggering distance. Perks include a free airport shuttle, but the pool is only flow resistance.

Red Roof Inn Phoenix Airport (Map pp158-9; ☎ 480-449-3205; www.redroofinn.com; 2135 W 15th St; r $65-85; P ☺ wi-fi) A recent face-lift has elevated this basic chain contender a couple of notches on the comfort ladder, although it's still pretty sparse in the amenities departments (no hair dryers). If you want a microwave and refrigerator, opt for a deluxe room. Cribs and rollways are free. Small pets OK.

InnSuites (Map p154; ☎ 480-897-7900, 800-842-4242; 1651 W Baseline Rd; r incl breakfast $70-140; P ☺ wi-fi) Shopaholics, hang on to your wallet: this property sits right across from the Arizona Mills mall. If you can't resist, there's plenty of space in your Southwest-styled room to store your loot. Amenities include a big TV, refrigerator, microwave and an above-average breakfast. Pets OK.

Sheraton Wild Horse Pass Resort & Spa (Map p154; ☎ 602-225-0100, 888-218-8989; www.wildhorsepassresort .com; 5594 W Wild Horse Pass Blvd, Chandler; r $370-1000; P ☺ ⓖ 🖵 wi-fi) It sure is peaceful out here on the Gila River Indian Reservation, especially at sunset when you might spy the eponymous wild horses silhouetted against the South Mountains. Owned by the Gila River tribe, this 500-room resort is a stunning alchemy of luxury and Native American traditions. The domed lobby is a mural-festooned roundhouse. Tribal elders relate ancient legends around the fire pit. The spa offers Blue Coyote wraps. Kai Restaurant (p167) serves indigenous Southwestern cuisine. That, plus two 18-hole golf courses, an equestrian center, tennis courts, sumptuous rooms, and whatever else one needs for a great getaway. Even pets are treated like royalty.

EATING

Phoenix has the biggest selection of restaurants in the Southwest: from fast food to ultrafancy, it's all here. Reservations are recommended at the posher places.

Phoenix

Matt's Big Breakfast (Map p160; ☎ 602-254-1074; 801 N 1st Ave; dishes $6-8; ⏱ 6:30am-2:30pm Tue-Sun) Lines are usually out the door at this honest-to-goodness greasy spoon souped up with orange retro tables and swingin' classic chairs. The name is the game here. The hungry-man breakfast – omelettes to waffles to griddlecakes – could well last you through supper.

Los Dos Molinos (off Map pp158-9; ☎ 602-243-9113; 8646 S Central Ave; mains $8-14; ⓨ lunch & dinner Tue-Sat) In a Santa Fe–style hacienda once owned by Hollywood cowboy star Tom Mix, this popular Mexican restaurant is a family affair, with several generations working the kitchen and tables. Their motto is 'some like it hot,' so ask them to go easy on the hot sauce unless you want to audition as a fire-eater. Avoid weekends when two-hour waits are not uncommon.

Delux (Map pp158-9; ☎ 602-522-2288; 3146 E Camelback Rd; dishes under $10; ⓨ lunch & dinner) The mirrored walls, communal table and unisex bathrooms may scream 'trendy,' but deep down this is just a postmodern patty-and-bun joint. The panini and salads are also good, but we're partial to the two-fisted Delux Burger made with Niman Ranch beef and piled high with Gruyère and blue cheese, applewood-smoked bacon, caramelized onion and arugula.

Pizzeria Bianco (Map p160; ☎ 602-258-8300; 623 E Adams St; pizza $10-14; ⓨ dinner Tue-Sat) It's no secret: James Beard–winner Chris Bianco makes the best pizza in town and maybe even all of America, if food writer Ed Levine and Oprah are to be believed. Hype aside, the thin-crust pies truly are tasty, but since the pizzeria doesn't take reservations you better start lining up at 4pm to snag one of the 42 seats in this converted early-20th-century machine shop.

Havana Café (Map pp158-9; ☎ 602-952-1991; 4225 E Camelback Rd; lunch $8-15, dinner $12-28; ⓨ lunch & dinner) The fragrant black bean soup, juicy roast pork sandwich and aromatic *pollo cubano* (Cuban chicken) are all testament to the authenticity of this colorful and contemporary Cuban kitchen that also makes a mean minty mojito. Grazers can pick from a couple of dozen small plates.

Arcadia Farms Café (Map p160; ☎ 602-257-2191; 1625 N Central Ave; mains $11-15; ⓨ 10am-5pm Tue-Sun) One of the nicest museum cafés for our money, the Arcadia at the Phoenix Art Museum (p156) uses only seasonal organic ingredients for its light yet satisfying lunches. Palate pleasers include any of the gourmet sandwiches, the creative crepes or the crispy crab cakes.

Cheuvront Restaurant & Wine Bar (Map p160; ☎ 602-307-0022; 1326 N Central Ave; mains $12-26; ⓨ lunch Mon-Fri, dinner daily) It's a sophisticated spot, but don't worry if you can't tell your pinot noir from your pinot grigio. Each dish, including such menu stars as red-wine-smothered short ribs and orange-glazed salmon, comes with its own wine recommendation. Or just pair an entire flight of wines with a sampling of exquisite cheeses and pâtés. Ken Cheuvront, Arizona's first openly gay politician (currently a state senator), owns the place.

Chelsea's Kitchen (Map pp158-9; ☎ 602-957-2555; 5040 N 40th St; mains $12-27; ⓨ lunch & dinner daily, brunch Sun) Brick walls, lofty industrial looks and leather booths: this casual place wouldn't be out of place in New York's Chelsea, but the cuisine is distinctly Western-inspired. Burgers, salad and tacos all make appearances, but we're partial to the organic meats tanned to juicy perfection in the hardwood rotisserie.

Barrio Café (Map pp158-9; ☎ 602-636-0240; 2814 N 16th St; mains $17-24; ⓨ lunch Sun & Tue-Fri, dinner Tue-Sun) Barrio's T-shirts are emblazoned with '*comida chingona*,' which translates as 'f…ing good food.' Crude, maybe. To the point, definitely. Barrio makes Mexican food at its most creative; how many menus featuring guacamole spiked with pomegranate seeds or goat-milk-caramel-filled *churros* (stick-shaped doughnuts) have you seen?

Vincent on Camelback (Map pp158-9; ☎ 602-224-0225; 3930 E Camelback Rd; lunch $11-16, dinner around $30; ⓨ lunch & dinner Mon-Sat) You may never have heard of chef Vincent Guerithault, but in Phoenix he's a household name. His secret? Ingenious French spins on Southwestern cuisine. Try such flavor-packed creations as corn ravioli with truffle oil or thyme-infused rack of lamb, and definitely leave room for a signature soufflé (try the one with Grand Marnier). For more casual gourmets, Vincent recently opened the Market Bistro behind the original restaurant. It's especially buzzy on Saturday mornings from fall to spring when a tiny but immensely popular gourmet and farmers market takes over the parking lot.

Scottsdale

Pita Jungle (Map pp158-9; ☎ 480-922-7482; 7366 E Shea Blvd; dishes $3-9; ⓨ 11am-10pm; ⓥ) One bite and you're hooked by the tangy hummus, crispy falafel and chicken shwarma at this upbeat joint that's on the radar of tousled students as much as frenzied families. Herbivores can happily fill their tummies with tofu, tempeh and veggie burgers.

Sugar Bowl (Map pp158-9; ☎ 480-946-0051; 4005 N Scottsdale Rd; dishes $4-9; ⊗ 11am-10pm Sun-Thu, 11am-midnight Fri & Sat; ⚲) When the kids tire of shopping, get them their ice-cream fix at this pink-and-white Valley institution, which has been working its frozen magic since the '50s. If you want more substantial fare, there's a whole menu of sandwiches and salads to choose from.

Orange Table (Map pp158-9; ☎ 480-424-6819; 7373 E Scottsdale Mall; dishes $4.50-12.50; ⊗ 7am-10pm Tue-Sat, 7am-3pm Sun & Mon; **V**) Service is perfunctory, but that's the only downside to this jazzy joint tucked behind the Scottsdale Performing Arts Center. Spice up your mornings with jalapeño-pecan pancakes or join the lunchtime crowd of museum patrons, business folk and cool kids for a sandwich feast. With three dozen wholesome varieties, you will find a favorite. Guaranteed.

Carlsbad Tavern (Map pp158-9; ☎ 480-970-8164; 3313 N Hayden Rd; mains $10-25; ⊗ lunch & dinner) Popular with a youngish, fast-forward crowd, this place lets you indulge in tequila shrimp, lobster enchiladas and other consistently delicious New Mexican fare until 2am. Sit on the patio or in the batty cavernous interior.

Canal at Southbridge (Map pp158-9; ☎ 480-949-9000; 7144 E Stetson Dr, Suite 250; mains $11-28; ⊗ 11am-midnight) Substance meets style at this ultrahip boîte accented by velvety booths, a fashion runway and an audiovisual wall. Your palate will be racking up frequent-flyer miles with chef Justin Beckett's fine-tuned food flights. Expect first-class ingredients, presentation and service in such dishes as fluffy sweetcorn cakes, buttery short ribs and even a $30 lobster sandwich.

Don & Charlie's (Map pp158-9; ☎ 480-990-0900; 7501 E Camelback Rd; dishes $14-26; ⊗ dinner) The pork and beef ribs are fall-off-the-bone tender and the barbecue sauce smoky just so at this noisy eatery filled with sports memorabilia and photographs. Portions are huge and come with various sides, including chopped liver. Don't crinkle your nose – it's surprisingly tasty.

Trader Vic's (Map pp158-9; ☎ 480-248-2000; 6850 E Main St; mains $17-38; ⊗ dinner) Part of the renaissance at the Hotel Valley Ho (p164), this venerable Polynesian restaurant will make you feel like you're on a South Pacific shore leave. Order a Mai Tai (Trader Vic's supposedly invented it) before delving into the long menu full of such palate ticklers as beef

cho-cho (served on a flaming mini-hibachi), macadamia-nut-encrusted mahimahi or any dish slow-cooked to perfection in the Chinese wood-fired oven.

Cowboy Ciao (Map pp158-9; ☎ 480-946-3111; 7133 E Stetson Dr; mains lunch $9-16, dinner $20-32; ⊗ lunch & dinner) It's perky vibes all around in this mood-lit cantina where dishes are a veritable cauldron of textures and flavors. The elk loin, for instance, is paired with crunchy hazelnut pesto, creamy mushroom risotto and a rich cabernet demi-glace. Sometimes it works, sometimes it's too complex for comfort.

Luc's Restaurant at El Pedregal (Map p154; ☎ 480-488-9009; 34631 N Tom Darlington Dr; mains $26-39; ⊗ dinner) Consider yourself luc-ky to dine at Luc's (inexplicably pronounced 'lucks'), where dishes are like jewels – polished and beautiful. Stars on the Asian-influenced menu include *ishiyaki* (beef and fish cooked on a heated stone at the table) and lamb chops drizzled with prosciutto caper sauce. The decor exudes big-city sophistication with Murano glass bubble chandeliers and amazing wall mosaics depicting mythological Greek figures.

Tempe

Pita Jungle (Map pp158-9; ☎ 480-804-0234; 1250 E Apache Blvd; dishes $3-9; ⊗ 9am-10pm; **V**) The original 'jungle' is funky industrial, serves the same deliciously healthy fare as its younger Scottsdale brother (opposite), but gets more of a student crowd.

Michael Monti's La Casa Vieja (Map pp158-9; ☎ 480-967-7594; 1 S Mill Ave; lunch $7-12, dinner $12-40; ⊗ lunch & dinner) This been-here-forever restaurant in a mazelike adobe hacienda filled with antiques is strong on grilled meats and atmosphere. Careful: don't OD on their homemade 'Roman' bread before the main event.

House of Tricks (Map pp158-9; ☎ 480-968-1114; 114 E 7th St; lunch $8-12, dinner $23-34; ⊗ lunch & dinner) No, they don't do magic, but Robin and Robert Trick will still wow you with their eclectic contemporary American menu that borrows influences from the Southwest, the Med and Asia. The trellised garden patio usually buzzes with regulars and drop-ins, but the tables inside the vintage cottages are equally charming.

ourpick Kai Restaurant (Map p154; ☎ 602-225-0100; 5594 W Wild Horse Pass Blvd, Chandler; mains $35-49, 8-course tasting menu $175; ⊗ dinner Tue-Sat) Kai takes Native American cuisine to unsuspected heights by using traditional crops grown along the Gila

ARIZONA

River. Dinners here are like fine tapestries with such dishes as tribal black cod wrapped in shaved cedar planks or caramelized red mullet with cereal of chia seeds striking just the right balance between adventure and comfort. Service is unobtrusive yet flawless, the wine list handpicked and the smart room decorated with Native American art. Dress nicely (no shorts or hats). It's at the Sheraton Wild Horse Pass Resort & Spa (p165) on the Gila River Indian Reservation.

Mesa

Landmark (Map p154; ☎ 480-962-4652; 809 W Main St; mains lunch $8-12, dinner $16-28; ☒ lunch & dinner, closes 7pm Sun) If you worship at the culinary altar of steaks and prime rib, you'll want to make the pilgrimage to this converted 1908 Mormon church that's been a family-owned local mainstay for decades. Lighter eaters, meanwhile, have an entire 'Salad Room' with over 100 items to graze on ($14).

DRINKING

Posh watering holes are found in the most unlikely of spots in the Phoenix area, some hidden amid chain stores in strip malls. Scottsdale has the greatest concentration of trendy bars and clubs, while Tempe attracts the student crowd.

Kazimierz (Map pp158-9; ☎ 480-946-3004; www .kazbar.net; 7137 E Stetson Dr, Scottsdale; ☒ 2:30pm-2am) With an entrance through the alley and a sign saying only 'The Truth is Inside,' this wine cave feels like a swanky '20s speakeasy, only the air here is rather genteel, grown-up and devoid of debauchery. The sofas are as soft as the music and the wine list as long as a Tolstoy novel: with 3000 global bottles to choose, you'll want to (and happily can) rely on your server's recommendation.

Four Peaks Brewing Company (Map pp158-9; ☎ 480-303-9967; 1340 E 8th St, Tempe; ☒ 11am-2am) Beer lovers rejoice: you're in for a treat at this quintessential neighborhood brewpub in a cool Mission Revival–style building. The strong Scottish ale is a bestseller, but also try lesser-known brews such as Kölsch, which originates in Cologne, Germany, and seasonal styles like the spicy pumpkin porter.

Coffee Plantation (Map pp158-9; ☎ 480-829-7878; 680 S Mill Ave, Tempe; ☒ 6am-midnight) If in Tempe, train your java radar to this regional retort to Starbucks, whose high-octane espresso and lattes have kept ASU students fueled for well over a decade. Pastries and light meals are also served.

Alice Cooper'stown (Map p160; ☎ 602-253-7337; 101 E Jackson St, Phoenix) Yes, this 'jock-and-rock'-themed beer hall really is the original shock rocker's (and Phoenix resident's) baby. On game days, it floods with giddy fans toasting their teams playing at the nearby US Airways Center and Chase Field. Come anytime for drinks specials and to tackle the 'Big Unit' (a 2ft hot dog), one of the most popular items on the tongue-in-cheek menu.

Greasewood Flat (Map p154; ☎ 480-585-9430; 27375 N Alma School Pkwy, Scottsdale; ☒ 11am-11pm) Lest you think Scottsdale is all flash and no grit, come to this rustic ex-stagecoach stop to find out otherwise. It's a beer-garden-sized outdoor pub where rough-and-tumble types – cowboys, bikers, real-estate agents – gather around the smoky barbecue and knock back the whisky as if the Gold Rush never ended. Cash only.

Rusty Spur Saloon (Map pp158-9; ☎ 480-425-7787; 7245 E Main St, Scottsdale) Yee-haw it up with the grizzled Budweiser crowd gathered for good times, cheap drinks and twangy country bands that've been around the block once or twice. It's in an old bank building that closed during the Depression; the old vault now holds liquor instead of greenbacks.

Amsterdam (Map p160; ☎ 602-258-6122; 718 N Central Ave, Phoenix; ☒ 4pm-2am Sun-Thu, 4pm-4am Fri & Sat) Say hello to the gargoyles at this fun, cool and friendly bar with its over-the-top medieval decor. It's a big player with the gay scene, but everybody's welcome to hang on the patio and sample the mind-boggling martini menu (300 last we checked). Check out 'Martini & Manicure Monday.'

BS West (Map pp158-9; ☎ 480-945-9028; 7125 E 5th Ave, Scottsdale; ☒ 2pm-2am) A high-energy gay video bar and dance club in the Old Town Scottsdale area, this place has pool tables and a small dance floor and hosts karaoke on Thursdays and Sundays.

Suede (Map pp158-9; ☎ 480-970-6969; 7333 E Indian Plaza, Scottsdale) The walls and furniture are covered in suede, *of course*, at this ultrachic art-deco-style lounge-cum-restaurant, which is a good spot to launch a night on the razzle. The best seats for swilling that martini (pinkie raised and all) are by the patio fireplace.

Also recommended:

Roosevelt Tavern (Map p160; ☎ 602-254-2561; 816 N 3rd St, Phoenix; ☒ Tue-Sun) Handcrafted beer, choice wines and comfort food in a historic building.

Jade Bar (Map pp158-9; ☎ 480-948-2100; 5700 E McDonald Dr, Sanctuary on Camelback Mountain Resort, Paradise Valley) Best place to sip a cantaloupe martini while watching the sun set over the sparkling valley.

Drift (Map pp158-9; ☎ 480-949-7474; 4341 N 75th St, Scottsdale) Funky tiki lounge has one of the city's best happy hours (4pm to 7pm Monday to Friday).

Compass Lounge (Map p160; ☎ 602-252-1234; 24th fl, Hyatt Regency Hotel, 122 N 2nd St; ☽ 5:30pm-midnight) Rotating lounge lures romantics grateful for the mellow lighting and low sound levels.

ENTERTAINMENT

The entertainment scene in Phoenix is lively and multifaceted, if not particularly edgy. You can hobnob with high society at the opera or symphony, mingle with the moneyed at a chic nightclub, or let your hair down at a punk concert in a local dive. Spectator sports are huge.

These publications will help you plug into the local scene in no time:

Arizona Republic Calendar (www.azcentral.com/ent/calendar) The Thursday edition of this major daily newspaper includes a special section with entertainment listings.

College Times (www.ecollegetimes.com) Freebie geared towards – would you have guessed? – college kids.

Get Out (www.getoutaz.com) Free weekly tabloid paper with Arizona-wide entertainment news and listings.

Phoenix New Times (www.phoenixnewtimes.com) The best of the bunch, this alternative free weekly is published on Thursday and available citywide.

Nightclubs & Live Music

Myst (Map pp158-9; ☎ 480-970-5000; 7340 E Shoeman Lane, Scottsdale; cover $10-40; ☽ 10pm-2am Wed, Fri & Sat) Once past the picky bouncers it's all about dancing with friendly folks and sipping the signature apple 'tartinis' at this party palace and its adjoining sister club, Ballroom. Global DJs hit the decks in this stylized space teeming with wrinkle-free hotties and hangers-on. Guys – dress up or you'll be riding the velvet rope for a long time.

Rhythm Room (Map pp158-9; ☎ 602-265-4842; 1019 E Indian School Rd, Phoenix; ☽ Tue-Sun) Kick-ass blues is king at this local favorite, although jazz, swing and other sounds occasionally invade the schedule. Cover charges range from a few dollars for local bands (usually early in the week) to about $30 for big-name touring acts on weekends. Bonus: the fingerlickin' barbecue shack in the parking lot.

Homme (Map pp158-9; ☎ 602-234-3023; 138 W Camelback Rd, Phoenix; cover $5-10; ☽ 10pm-2am) DJs whip the crowd into a frenzy with different sounds nightly, from goth and industrial Wednesdays to house Fridays and electro Saturdays. The hot 'n' heavy vibe draws unpretentious party-hearty locals, including gays and queens. For drinkies, try the Dum Dum Tini embellished by a lollipop.

Axis/Radius (Map pp158-9; ☎ 480-970-1112; 7340 E Indian Plaza, Scottsdale; cover $10, women free on Thu; ☽ Thu-Sat) This megaplush posing and preening pen is another entry in Scottsdale's growing cadre of state-of-the-art lounge-club combos. It's full of shiny, happy and barely legal hotties who may be too busy seeing and being seen to actually have a good time. Gotta love the LED panels and chilly liquid nitrogen fog, though.

Improv (Map pp158-9; ☎ 480-921-9877; www.improv.com; 930 E University Dr, Tempe; cover $10-25; ☽ Thu-Sun) Part of a national chain, this club delivers an assembly line of yucks from new talent and today's hottest stand-up comics. The two-item minimum purchase (food or drink, in addition to the cover charge) is strictly enforced.

Char's Has the Blues (Map pp158-9; ☎ 602-230-0205; 4631 N 7th Ave, Phoenix; no cover Mon-Thu, cover Fri-Sun) Dark and intimate, this blues grotto packs 'em in with solid acts most nights of the week but somehow still manages to feel like a well-kept secret. Play pool or darts or share your sorry tales with another blues brother.

Clubhouse Music Venue (Map pp158-9; ☎ 480-968-3238; 1320 E Broadway Rd, Tempe; cover $8-20) This bastion of indie sounds is known for bookers with a knack for catching upwardly hopeful bands before their big break. Kasabian, Blindside and the Young Dubliners have all played before 600-capacity crowds.

Cinemas

For show information check any of the listings publications. The Phoenix area teems with fancy-pants multiplexes, but there are a few indie theaters left. Tickets for most theaters can be purchased on the theaters' websites or at www.movietickets.com.

Harkins Camelview 5 (Map pp158-9; ☎ 480-947-8778; 7001 E Highland Ave, Scottsdale; adult/child/senior $9.50/5.50/6.50) This top flick magnet for indie types presents stimulating and off-beat fare from overseas and homegrown underground filmmakers, plus handpicked Hollywood blockbusters.

IMAX Theatre (Map p154; ☎ 480-897-1453; www.imax.com/tempe; 5000 Arizona Mills Circle, cnr Priest & Baseline Rds,

Tempe; adult/child/senior $14.50/11.50/12.50) At Arizona Mills mall, this megascreen presents everything from family-friendly nature films to the amazing U2 live-action 3D concert film.

Scottsdale Six Drive-In (Map pp158-9; ☎ 602-949-9451; 8101 E McKellips Rd, Scottsdale; adult/child under 12 $6/free) Drive-ins are a dying breed, but this one still lets you enjoy a double-bill of recent-release flicks in the comfort (and privacy) of your car.

Performing Arts

The following are the most acclaimed venues and companies in Phoenix. Not much goes on during summer.

Phoenix Symphony (Map p160; ☎ 602-495-1999, 800-776-9080; www.phoenixsymphony.org; 75 N 2nd St, Phoenix) Arizona's only full-time professional orchestra plays classics and pops, mostly at Symphony Hall, from September to May.

Arizona Opera (Map p160; ☎ 602-266-7464; www.azopera.com; 75 N 2nd St, Phoenix; ☉ Oct-Apr) The state ensemble produces five operas per season, usually favorites such as Mozart's *Magic Flute* and Verdi's *La Traviata*. Performances are at Symphony Hall.

The **Herberger Theater Center** (Map p160; 222 E Monroe St, Phoenix) has two stages shared by three resident companies: **Arizona Theatre Company** (☎ 602-256-6995; www.aztheatreco.org), the state's leading ensemble; the **Actors Theatre** (☎ 602-252-8497; www.atphx.org) for more experimental, fringe productions; and the **Center Dance Ensemble** (☎ 602-252-8497; www.centerdance.com), which specializes in modern dance. The Gammage Auditorium (p160) on the ASU Tempe campus presents primarily crowd-pleasing plays and musicals.

Sports

Phoenix has some of the nation's top professional teams, and tickets for the best games sell out fast.

Arizona Cardinals (☎ 602-379-0102; www.azcardinals.com; 1 Cardinals Dr, Glendale) In 2006 this National Football League (NFL) team moved from Tempe to the brand-new and architecturally distinguished University of Phoenix Stadium (Map p154) in the western Valley city of Glendale. The season runs from fall to spring.

Arizona Diamondbacks (☎ 602-462-6500; www.arizona.diamondbacks.mlb.com; 201 E Jefferson St, Phoenix) This major-league baseball team won the World Series in 2001 and plays at Chase Field (Map p160) in downtown Phoenix.

Arizona Rattlers (☎ 602-379-2333; www.azrattlers.com; 201 E Jefferson St, Phoenix) An arena football team, the Rattlers were the 1994 and 1997 world champions, and hold games between May and August at the US Airways Center (Map p160).

Phoenix Coyotes (☎ 480-563-7825; www.phoenixcoyotes.com; 9400 Maryland Ave, Glendale) Right next to University of Phoenix Stadium is the Jobing.com Arena (Map p154), where this National Hockey League (NHL) team (currently coached by one of its co-owners, Wayne Gretzky) plays from December to March.

Phoenix Mercury (☎ 602-252-9622; www.wnba.com/mercury; 201 E Jefferson St, Phoenix) The women's National Basketball Association (NBA) team became champions in 2007 and play professional basketball from June to September at the US Airways Center (Map p160).

Phoenix Suns (☎ 602-379-7900; www.suns.com; 201 E Jefferson St, Phoenix) The current team of basketball legend Shaquille O'Neill (since 2008), the NBA Suns puts in appearances at the US Airways Center (Map p160) from December to April.

SHOPPING

The question is not so much what to buy (you can buy just about anything) but where to go. Old Town Scottsdale is known for its art galleries and Southwestern crafts shops. Apart from its stellar museum, the Heard Museum (p156) has the best bookshop about Native Americans and the most authentic and expensive selection of Native American arts and crafts. Mill Ave in Tempe has a nice mix of indie and chain boutiques.

Mall culture is huge in the Valley. You may not like 'em but, trust us, the air-con does give them a certain allure on hot summer days. Some of the most upscale shopping is done at the **Scottsdale Fashion Square** (Map pp158-9; cnr Camelback & Scottsdale Rds, Scottsdale) and the even more exclusive **Biltmore Fashion Park** (Map pp158-9; cnr Camelback Rd & 24th St, Phoenix). Both provide a good selection of restaurants. One of the fancier outdoor malls, featuring lots of boutiques and galleries, **Borgata** (Map pp158-9; 6166 N Scottsdale Rd, Scottsdale) was designed to look like a medieval Italian town.

GETTING THERE & AWAY

Sky Harbor International Airport (Map pp158-9; ☎ 602-273-3300; http://phoenix.gov/aviation; wi-fi) is 3 miles southeast of downtown Phoenix and served by 20 airlines, including United, American, Delta and British Airways. Its three terminals (Terminals 2, 3 and 4; Terminal 1 was demolished in 1990) and the parking lots are linked by the free Airport Shuttle Bus.

Greyhound (Map pp158-9; ☎ 602-389-4200; 2115 E Buckeye Rd) runs direct buses to Tucson ($19, two hours, seven daily), Flagstaff ($29, five daily), Albuquerque ($94.50, 10 hours, three daily) and Los Angeles ($73, eight hours, eight daily), among other cities. Valley Metro's Red Line and No 13 buses link the airport and the Greyhound station.

GETTING AROUND
To/From the Airport
All international car-rental companies have offices at the airport. Also here is **EV Rental Cars** (Map pp158-9; ☎ 877-387-36825; www.evrental.com; 201 S 24 St), which specializes in ecofriendly hybrids and natural-gas vehicles.

The citywide door-to-door shuttle service provided by **Super Shuttle** (☎ 602-244-9000, 800-258-3826) costs about $6 to downtown Phoenix, $10 to Tempe, $15 to Mesa and $16 to Scottsdale.

Three taxi companies serve the airport: **AAA Cab** (☎ 602-437-4000), **Allstate** (☎ 602-275-8888) and **Discount** (☎ 602-266-1110). The charge is $5 for the first mile and $2 for each additional mile; from the airport there's a $1 surcharge and $15 minimum fare.

The airport is directly linked to downtown Phoenix and Tempe by the Red Line bus. Starting in 2009, a free shuttle bus will ferry passengers to 44th and Washington Sts where they can hop on the new Valley Metro Light Rail line (see below).

Car & Motorcycle
Greater Phoenix is a huge metropolitan sprawl, so getting around efficiently means spending some time behind the wheel. The network of freeways, most of them built in the last 10 years, is starting to rival Los Angeles and so is the intensity of traffic. Always pad your sightseeing day for traffic jams. The I-10 and US 60 are the main east–west thoroughfares, while the I-17 and SR51 are the major north–south arteries. Loops 101 and 202 link most of the suburbs. Parking is plentiful outside of the downtown area.

Public Transportation
Valley Metro (☎ 602-253-5000; www.valleymetro.org) operates buses all over the Valley and, at press

time, was expected to inaugurate a 20-mile light rail line linking north Phoenix with downtown Phoenix, Tempe/ASU and downtown Mesa in late 2008. Fares are $1.25 per ride (no transfers) or $2.50 for a day pass. Free trip planning is available by phone and online. FLASH buses operate daily around ASU and downtown Tempe, while the Scottsdale Trolley loops around downtown Scottsdale, both at no charge. Free DASH buses roam around downtown Phoenix, but only on weekdays.

CENTRAL ARIZONA

Much of the area north of Phoenix lies on the Colorado Plateau and is cool, wooded and mountainous. Square mile by square mile, it's draped with the most diverse and scenic quilt of sites and attractions in all of Arizona. You can clamber around a volcano, channel your inner goddess on a vortex, hike through sweet-smelling canyons, drive beneath dramatically sculpted crimson cliffs, schuss down alpine slopes, admire 1000-year-old Native American dwellings, and delve into Old West and pioneer history. The main hub, Flagstaff, is a lively and delightful college town and gateway to the Grand Canyon South Rim. Summer, spring and fall are the best times to visit.

PHOENIX TO FLAGSTAFF
It's no secret that the best way to get from A to B isn't always the shortest and that's certainly true when traveling from Phoenix to Flagstaff.

You can make the trip between the two in just over two hours if you put the pedal to the metal on I-17. Opt for one of the more leisurely routes along Hwys 87 or 89, though, and you'll be rewarded with beautiful scenery and intriguing sites along the way.

Along I-17
The I-17 freeway is a straight 145-mile shot to Flagstaff. Fast? Yes. Scenic? Not so much, as it inconveniently bypasses the nicest pockets this region has to offer. Still, there are a few worthwhile sights to make you ease off the pedal if you pick this route.

ARCOSANTI
Two miles east of I-17 exit 262 (Cordes Junction; 65 miles north of Phoenix), **Arcosanti**

(☎ 928-632-7135; www.arcosanti.org; suggested donation for tours $8; ☽ tours 10am-4pm) is an architectural experiment in urban living that's been a work in progress since 1970. The brainchild of ground-breaking architect and urban planner Paolo Soleri, it is based on Soleri's concept of 'arcology,' which seeks to create communities in harmony with their natural surroundings. Other goals include minimizing the use of energy, raw materials and land, and reducing waste and environmental pollution. Radical when conceived in the 1960s, Soleri's ideas now seem on the cutting edge in this age of urban sprawl and global warming. If and when it is finished, Arcosanti will be a self-sufficient village for 5000 people with futuristic living spaces, large-scale greenhouses and solar energy.

Hour-long tours take you around the site and provide background about the project's history and design philosophy. A gift shop sells the famous bronze bells cast at the foundry in Cosanti (p160), near Phoenix. Overnight accommodations are available (singles/doubles from $30/40), but often book out well in advance. Also on offer are week- and month-long seminars, concerts and other events.

CAMP VERDE & FORT VERDE STATE HISTORIC PARK

Camp Verde was founded in 1865 as a farming settlement only to be co-opted soon after by the US Army who built a fort here to prevent Indian raids on Anglo settlers. Tonto Apache chief Chalipun surrendered here in April 1873. Today, the town's **Fort Verde State Historic Park** (☎ 928-567-3275; www.azparks.gov; 125 E Hollamon St; adult/child under 14 $2/free; ☽ 8am-5pm) offers an authentic snapshot of frontier life in the late 19th century. Exploring the well-preserved fort, you'll see the officer's and doctor's quarters, sprint down the parade grounds and study displays about military life and the Indian Wars. Staff occasionally dress up in period costume and conduct living history tours. To get here, take exit 287 off I-17, go south on Hwy 260, turn left at Finnie Flat Rd and left again at Hollamon St.

Among the handful of motels in town, the independent Western-themed **Territorial Town Inn** (☎ 928-567-0275, 866-567-0275; 628 S Main St; r $52-90) is a good spot to spend the night. The **Days Inn & Suites** (☎ 928-567-3700; 1640 W Hwy 260; r incl breakfast $50-100; 🛋) allows pets.

OUT OF AFRICA WILDLIFE PARK

Take a walk on the wild side at this **animal park** (☎ 928-567-2840; www.outofafricapark.com; 4020 N Cherry Rd, Camp Verde; adult/child 3-12/senior $32/20/28; ☽ 9:30am-5pm Wed-Sun, last admission 4pm), an odd if entertaining mix of zoo, circus and theme park. Close encounters with slithering anacondas and boas are as much part of your visit as Tiger Splash, the most popular show in which the magnificent creatures leap into a pool in pursuit of plastic toys and balloon bags. On a jeep safari you get to train your camera on grazing giraffes, lazing lions and romping rhinos. All in all, more than 400 formerly wild animals make their home here. Take I-17 exit 187 and head towards Cottonwood on Hwy 260 for about 3 miles, then hook a left on Verde Valley Justice Center Rd.

MONTEZUMA CASTLE NATIONAL MONUMENT

Like nearby Tuzigoot (p181), **Montezuma Castle** (☎ 928-567-3322; www.nps.gov/moca; adult/child under 16 $5/free, combination pass with Tuzigoot National Monument $8; ☽ 8am-6pm Jun-Aug, 8am-5pm Sep-May; ♿) is a stunningly well-preserved 1000-year-old Sinagua cliff dwelling. The name refers to the splendid castlelike location high on a cliff; early explorers thought the five-story-high pueblo was Aztec and hence dubbed it Montezuma. A **museum** interprets the archaeology of the site, which can be spotted from a short self-guiding, wheelchair-accessible trail. Entrance into the 'castle' itself is prohibited, but there's a virtual tour on the website. Access the monument from I-17 exit 289, drive east for 0.5 miles, then turn left on Montezuma Castle Rd.

Montezuma Well (admission free; ☽ 8am-6pm Jun-Aug, 8am-5pm Sep-May) is a natural limestone sinkhole 470ft wide, surrounded by both Sinaguan and Hohokam dwellings. Water from the well was used for irrigation by the Native Americans and is still used today by residents of nearby Rimrock. Access is from I-17 exit 293, 4 miles north of the Montezuma Castle exit. Follow the signs for another 4 miles through McGuireville and Rimrock.

North on Hwy 87

A considerably more scenic route takes you northeast out of Phoenix on Hwy 87 (the Beeline Hwy) to Payson, just below the sheer cliffs of the Mogollon Rim. From here, hook northwest on Hwy 260 via Pine and

Strawberry to the I-17. Then you can either head straight up north for the quick 55-mile trip to Flagstaff or take the more circuitous and slower 60-mile drive continuing on Hwy 260 to Cottonwood (p180) and from there north to Sedona (p181) and Oak Creek Canyon (p188) before reaching Flagstaff.

PAYSON & THE MOGOLLON RIM
pop 14,800 / elev 5000ft
Payson's nearly perfect climate (coolish summers and not-too-cold winters) has made the town a popular retirement spot. Just 94 miles north of Phoenix, it attracts Phoenicians by the thousands hoping to seek relief from stifling summer heat. Founded by gold miners in 1882, Payson was once a ranching and logging center but today considers tourism its main draw. The main drags are a curious, but unappealing, mix of strip malls and antique shops. However, the surrounding Tonto National Forest provides numerous opportunities for hiking, swimming, fishing and hunting, and is the main reason to visit.

Orientation & Information
Hwy 87, which connects Payson to Phoenix, is the main commercial drag. For camping and other information, contact the following:
Rim Country Regional Chamber of Commerce (☎ 928-474-4515; www.rimcountrychamber.com; 100 W Main St; ☾ 8am-5pm Mon-Fri & 10am-2pm Sat year-round, 8am-2pm Sun Apr-Oct)
Tonto National Forest Payson Ranger Station (☎ 928-474-7900; www.fs.fed.us/r3/tonto; 1009 E Hwy 260; ☾ 8am-5pm Mon-Fri)

Sights & Activities
Aside from a few antique shops, the main attraction in Payson itself is the **Rim Country Museum** (☎ 928-474-3483, www.rimcountrymuseums .com; 700 Green Valley Pkwy; adult/child under 12/student/ senior $3/free/2/2.50; ☾ noon-4pm Wed-Mon). It lays out the region's history in several buildings, including a 1930 forest ranger station, but is of particular interest to fans of Western novelist Zane Grey, who penned many famous works here in the 1920s, including *Under the Tonto Rim*. A replica of Grey's cabin displays exhibits on the man and his work (the original burned down in 1990).

The area's biggest tourist attraction, though, is **Tonto Natural Bridge State Park** (☎ 928-476-4202; adult/child under 13 $3/free; ☾ 8am-7pm May-Aug, 8am-6pm Apr, Sep & Oct, 9am-5pm Nov-Mar). Tucked into

a tiny, forested valley about 10 miles northwest of Payson proper, it protects the largest natural travertine bridge in the world: 183ft high, 150ft wide and 400ft long. Formed from calcium carbonate deposited over the years by mineral-laden spring waters, it actually looks more like a tunnel than a freestanding arch. It… It… Obviously, it's difficult to describe so you'll just have to see it yourself! Steps and trails drop you down into the canyon for close-ups of waterfalls, travertine formations and the 'tunnel' itself. Trails are steep and rocky, so wear sturdy shoes.

The park entrance is 3 miles off Hwy 87; the final stretch of the access road is precipitous and winding. Heavy snow may close the park in winter.

For something different, try hiking the quiet forests surrounding Payson in the company of llamas, which carry your gear. **Fossil Creek Llama Ranch** (☎ 928-476-5178; hikes from $65) offers two-hour to all-day llama treks as well as wellness courses, spiritual retreats and a goat petting zoo (it also makes its own goat cheese). It's a lovely place to spend the night in a teepee or a yurt ($85 per unit).

Sleeping & Eating
Ponderosa Campground (☎ 877-444-6777; www.rec reation.gov; campsites $15; ☾ mid-Apr–Oct) This USFS spot is 12 miles northeast of Payson on Hwy 260 and has 60 tent and RV sites as well as drinking water and toilets, but no showers. For other area campgrounds, check with the ranger station.

Best Western Payson Inn (☎ 928-474-3241; www .bestwesternpaysoninn.com; 801 N Beeline Hwy; r incl breakfast $70-150; ⓦ wi-fi) Dependable and good value, this 99-room property in a mock-Tudor building has modern-looking rooms (get a deluxe for extra space). Rates include a modest breakfast. Children under 17 stay free and pets are welcome.

Roadrunner Espresso (☎ 928-472-7229; 511 S Beeline Hwy; sandwiches $6; ☾ 6am-5pm Mon-Sat, 8am-3pm Sun; wi-fi) This relative newcomer has already become a local favorite for powering up with strong mochas and a mouthwatering assortment of pastries, bagels and sandwiches.

Cucina Paradiso (☎ 928-468-6500; 500 N Hwy 87; lunch $8-10, dinner $13-30; ☾ lunch & dinner Tue-Sun) It's not a fancy place, but the pizzas are loaded with tasty toppings and calamari fans will enjoy the spicy *fra diavolo* preparation. Quite possibly the best food in town.

ARIZONA

ARIZONA

North on Hwy 89

The longest but most rewarding route from Phoenix to Flagstaff is via Hwys 89/89A (ALT 89), which follows a sight-packed old stagecoach route. Pick up Hwy 89 in the Old West town of Wickenburg, about an hour northwest of Phoenix. From here, Hwy 89 climbs up into the pine-scented Prescott National Forest to the elegant former territorial capital of Prescott. Cut over on Hwy 89A to Jerome, a rough-and-tumble mining town turned artist colony, and pass through Cottonwood and Clarkdale, terminus of the nostalgic Camp Verde Railroad. Further north, Sedona and the rock formations of Red Rock Country exude their otherworldly glow as though transplanted from Mars. From here, Flagstaff is just a short, breathtaking drive away via the sculpted cliffs of Oak Creek Canyon. The total trip is about 200 miles and should be done in a minimum of two days – it's better over three or four.

The rest of this section is structured following this route.

WICKENBURG

pop 5100 / elev 2093ft

What do Kate Moss, Rush Limbaugh, Elle MacPherson and Cindy McCain have in common? All have been to Wickenburg to beat an addiction or disorder. Like so many Arizona towns, Wickenburg's genesis is a tale of prospectors, gold mines and ranchers. When those industries lost steam, guest ranches started flourishing, drawing people in search of the romance of the Old West. Today, the one-time 'dude ranch capital of the world' still hosts weekend wranglers, but (quietly and discreetly) it has evolved into a 'rehab capital.' Fortunately, in the downtown area the Old West spirit is very much alive thanks to Western storefronts, palm trees and a dome of blue sky. The climate is pleasant anytime but summer.

Information

The **chamber of commerce** (☎ 928-684-5479, 800-942-5242; www.wickenburgchamber.com, www.outwickenburgway.org; 216 N Frontier St; ☽ 9am-5pm Mon-Fri, 10am-2pm Sat & Sun) offers info and a map of a historic walking tour. The **library** (☎ 928-684-2665; 164 E Apache St; ☽ 9am-5:30pm Mon, 10:30am-7pm Tue, 9am-5:30pm Wed-Fri, 8am-noon Sun; ⊕) has free internet.

Sights & Activities

The **Desert Caballeros Western Museum** (☎ 928-684-2272; www.westernmuseum.org; 21 N Frontier St; adult/child under 16/senior $7.50/free/6; ☽ 10am-5pm Mon-Sat, noon-4pm Sun) has a world-class collection of American Western artists, including key works by Frederic Remington, George Catlin and Maynard Dixon, along with history exhibits, minerals and Native American artifacts. Downstairs is a nifty recreation of an Arizona streetscape c 1915. Changing exhibitions keep things dynamic.

Locals like to point out the 19th-century **Jail Tree**, to which outlaws were chained in the late 1800s.

Normally the Hassayampa River flows underground, but in the **Hassayampa River Preserve** (☎ 928-684-2772; admission $5; ☽ 7am-11am Fri-Sun mid-May–mid-Sep, 8am-5pm Wed-Sun mid-Sep–mid-May) it shows off its crystalline shimmer. This is one of the few riparian habitats remaining in Arizona and a great place for birders to go gaga over 240 feathered resident and migrating species – from hawks to cuckoos. It's on the west side of Hwy 60, 3 miles south of town. There's a visitor center where you can pick up information and maps.

A bit further south, the venerable **Vulture Mine** (☎ 602-859-2743; Vulture Mine Rd; admission $7; ☽ 8am-4pm) spat out lots of gold between 1863 to 1942, but today is merely an embalmed ghost town. Short self-guided tours take you past the main shaft, the blacksmith shop and other dusty old buildings. Head west on Hwy 60, turn left onto Vulture Mine Rd and follow it for 12 miles. Pets on leash OK.

Sleeping & Eating

Los Viajeros (☎ 928-684-7099, 800-915-9795; 1000 N Tegner St; r $80-100; ⊕ wi-fi) For a motel, this place does better than most in the charm department. We especially like the pale-colored furniture in good-sized, balconied rooms with small refrigerators. There's a pool for relaxing and a spa to soak saddle sores.

Flying E Ranch (☎ 928-684-2690, 888-684-2650; www.flyingeranch.com; 2801 W Wickenburg Way; d $310-390; ⊕ ⊕) This down-home working cattle ranch in the Hassayampa Valley is a big hit with families and gets plenty of repeaters. Rooms are Western-themed and rates include activities and three square family-style meals daily. It's open to guests from November to April, with two- or three-night minimum stays. Two-hour horseback rides cost $35. There's no bar; BYOB.

Rancho de los Caballeros (☎ 928-684-5484; www.sunc.com; 1551 S Vulture Mine Rd; r $400-620; ⊕ ⊕) With an 18-hole championship golf course, exclusive spa, special kids' program and fine dining, this 20,000-acre ranch feels more 'Dallas' than 'Bonanza.' The lovely main lodge – with flagstone floor, brightly painted furniture and copper fireplace – gives way to cozy rooms decked out stylishly with Indian rugs and handcrafted furniture. Dinner is a dress-up affair, but afterwards you can cut loose in the saloon with nightly cowboy music. Open to guests mid-October to mid-May.

Screamer's Drive-In (☎ 928-684-9056; 1151 W Wickenburg Way; dishes $4-6; ☺ 6am-8pm Mon-Sat, 10:30am-8pm Sun) If you've got a hankering for a big, juicy burger, this '50s-style diner (not really a drive-in) will quickly put you in a state of contentment. Indoor and outdoor seating.

Pony Espresso (☎ 928-684-0208; 223 E Wickenburg Way; dishes $4-7; ☺ 7am-8pm Mon-Fri, 8am-6pm Sat & Sun) Get comfy with a cappuccino on the overstuffed sofas of this funky little coffee shop with cheerful red walls and lots of books and chess tables. Scones, brownies and sandwiches provide sustenance.

Anita's Cocina (☎ 928-684-5777; 57 N Valentine St; mains $5-10; ☺ 10:30am-9pm) This local favorite is perfect for winding down the day south-of-the-border-style. Think margaritas, burritos, tacos and all the other faves.

House of Berlin (☎ 928-684-5004; 169 E Wickenburg Way; dishes $10-16; ☺ lunch Wed-Sun, dinner Tue-Sun) Schnitzels with noodles and warm apple strudels – you'll find them all at this homey Germanic lair along with stuffed cabbage rolls, pork chops and other continental classics from Henry Wickenburg's home country.

Getting There & Away

Wickenburg is about equidistant (60 miles) from Phoenix and Prescott off Hwy 60. There is no bus service. Coming from Kingman and I-40, you can reach it via Hwy 93, which runs a lonely 105 miles to Wickenburg. It's dubbed **Joshua Tree Forest Parkway** because pretty much the only living things growing here are those spiny bushes that are a member of the lily family.

PRESCOTT

pop 41,500 / elev 5346ft

Mile-high Prescott (pronounced 'press-kit') is a positively delightful little town – tidy, compact and joyfully prosperous. Founded by gold prospectors in 1864, it has a pedigree as Arizona's first territorial capital, but

somehow doesn't quite fit the state persona. Sure, it boasts saloons, vintage hotels and a downtown with tons of colorful history (think hard-core drinking, brothels and gunfights), but the shaded tree-lined square, outstanding stock of Victorian buildings, European-style sidewalk cafés, a growing arts community and upscale boutiques imbue it with a gentility and respectful air that perennially charms the socks off visitors.

Best of all, Prescott combines historic authenticity with some of the most gorgeous scenery the state has to offer. The boulder-strewn Granite Dells rise to the north, while in the west the landmark Thumb Butte sticks out like the tall kid in your third-grade picture. And to the south, the pine-draped Bradshaw Mountains form part of the Prescott National Forest.

Information

Library (☎ 928-777-1500; 215 E Goodwin St; ☺ 9am-5:30pm Mon, Fri & Sat, 9am-9pm Tue-Thu, 1-5pm Sun; ☐ wi-fi) Free internet.

Main post office (☎ 928-778-1890; 442 Miller Valley Rd)

Police (☎ 928-777-1988; 222 S Marina St)

Prescott National Forest office (☎ 928-443-8000; 344 S Cortez St; ☺ 8am-4:30pm Mon-Fri) Info on camping, hiking and more in the national forest.

Tourist office (☎ 928-445-2000, 800-266-7534; www .visit-prescott.com; 117 W Goodwin St; ☺ 9am-5pm Mon-Fri, 10am-2pm Sat) Information and pamphlets galore, including a handy free walking tour pamphlet of historical Prescott.

Yapapai Regional Medical Center (☎ 928-445-2700; 1003 Willow Creek Rd)

Sights

HISTORIC DOWNTOWN

Montezuma St west of Courthouse Plaza was once the infamous **Whiskey Row**, where 40 drinking establishments supplied suds to studs; ie rough-hewn cowboys, miners and wastrels. A devastating 1900 fire destroyed 25 saloons, five hotels and the red-light district, but several early buildings remain. Many are still bars, mixed in with boutiques, galleries (see boxed text, p176) and restaurants. The columned **County Courthouse** anchoring the elm-shaded plaza dates from 1916 and is particularly pretty when sporting its lavish Christmas decorations. **Cortez St**, which runs east of the plaza, has become a hive of antique and collectible stores, as well as home to **Ogg's**

WHISKEY ROW TO GALLERY ROW

There's still plenty of drinkin' and dancin' going on in Whiskey Row's fine historic saloons, but more recently the infamous strip has taken on a second life as Gallery Row. Standouts include **Arts Prescott Gallery** (☎ 928-776-7717; www.artsprescott.com; 134 S Montezuma St), a collective of 22 local artists working in all media, including painting, pottery, illustration and jewelry. Prices are quite reasonable. Deeper pockets are required at **Van Gogh's Ear** (☎ 928-776-1080; www.vgegallery.com; 156 S Montezuma St), where you can snap up John Lutes' ethereal glass bowls, Dale O'Dell's stunning photographs or works by three dozen other nationally known artists making their home in the Prescott area. A great time to sample Prescott's growing gallery scene is during the monthly **4th Friday Art Walk** (www.artthe4th.com).

Hogan (☎ 928-443-9856; 111 N Cortez St), with its excellent selection of Native American crafts and jewelry, mostly from Arizona tribes.

Buildings east and south of the plaza escaped the 1900 fire. Some are Victorian houses built by East Coast settlers and are markedly different from adobe Southwestern buildings. Look for the fanciest digs on Union St, where cowboy artist John Coleman makes his home at No 211 and No 217 is the ancestral Goldwater family mansion (yes, of Barry Goldwater fame). Manicured Mt Vernon St is also worth a stroll or drive.

MUSEUMS

The **Sharlot Hall Museum** (☎ 928-445-3122; www.sharlot.org; 415 W Gurley St; adult/child $5/free; 10am-5pm Mon-Sat, noon-4pm Sun May-Sep, 10am-4pm Mon-Sat, noon-4pm Sun Oct-Apr) is Prescott's most important museum, although the name is really a misnomer. It's named for its 1928 founder, pioneer woman Sharlot Hall (1870–1943), but is actually a general historical museum highlighting Prescott's period as territorial capital. A small exhibit in the lobby commemorates Miss Hall, who distinguished herself first as a poet and activist before becoming Territorial Historian. In 1924, she traveled to Washington DC to represent Arizona in the Electoral College dressed in a copper mesh overcoat provided by a local mine. There would be no mistaking that Arizona was the 'Copper State!' The coat and her cactus leaf hat are part of the modest displays.

The most interesting of the nine buildings making up this museum campus is the 1864 **Governor's Mansion**, a really big log cabin where Hall lived in the attic until her death. It's filled with a hodgepodge of memorabilia from guns to opium pipes and letters. Outside, the Rose Garden pays homage to Arizona's pioneer women. The museum hosts numerous special events, including a cowboy poetry gathering, an art market and living history tours. The website has all the details.

Seven miles north of town, en route to Jerome, the **Phippen Museum** (☎ 928-778-1385; www.phippenartmuseum.com; 4701 Hwy 89; adult/child under 12/concession $5/free/4; 10am-4pm Tue-Sat, 1-4pm Sun) was named after cowboy artist George Phippen and hosts changing exhibits of celebrated Western artists (including Prescott resident John Coleman), along with contemporary art depicting the American West.

Built like an Indian pueblo, the **Smoki Museum** (☎ 928-445-1230; www.smokimuseum.org; 147 N Arizona St; adult/child under 12/student/senior $5/free/3/4; 10am-4pm Tue-Sat, 1-4pm Sun) trains the spotlight on Southwestern Native American history and artifacts dating from the prehistoric to the present. By the way, the correct pronunciation is 'smoke-eye.'

Activities

Quiz the tourist office staff or, better still, the rangers at Prescott National Forest office (p175) for ideas on hikes, climbs, picnic areas and fishing holes. If you only have time for a short hike, get a moderate workout and nice views of the town and mountains on the 1.75-mile **Thumb Butte trail**. The trailhead is about 4 miles west of downtown Prescott on Gurley St, which changes to Thumb Butte Rd.

There are five lakes within a short drive of town, but the most scenic for our money is **Watson Lake**, where the eerily eroded rock piles of the Granite Dells reflect in the crystalline stillness. About 4 miles north of town, off Hwy 89, the lake is great for boating, picnicking and bouldering. Summer tent camping is $10. **Lynx Lake**, 4 miles east on Hwy 69 then 3 miles south on Walker Rd, offers fishing, hiking, camping and small-boat rental (summer only).

North of town, the **Granite Mountain Wilderness** attracts rock climbers in the warmer months. It also has a fishing lake, camping grounds and hiking trails. To reach it, bear left on Iron Springs Rd from Grove Ave downtown, then turn right on unpaved USFS Rd 347 and continue another 4 miles.

Festivals & Events

Prescott has a packed year-round events calendar. See www.visit-prescott.com for the full scoop.

Territorial Days Arts & Crafts Show (☎ 928-445-2000) Arts, crafts, demonstrations, performances, food and general merriment for the entire family on the second weekend in June.

World's Oldest Rodeo (☎ 928-445-3103; www.worlds oldestrodeo.com) Prescott celebrates its frontier heritage with bronco busting (since 1888), a parade and an arts and crafts fair during the week before July 4.

Sleeping

Don't expect any lodging bargains in Prescott, although if you're not too picky you might find rooms for $70 in one of the indie motels on the outskirts of town. With its many Victorians, it's no surprise that Prescott is B&B terrain. Check out www.prescottbb.com for links to area inns.

Point of Rocks RV Park (☎ 928-445-9018; www .pointofrockscampground.com; 3025 N Hwy 89; RV sites $25; wi-fi) About 4 miles north of town, this lovely, quiet campground is tucked up amongst beautiful granite boulders behind Watson Lake. Most sites are level, tree-shaded and have full hookups. Pets OK.

Hotel St Michael (☎ 928-776-1999, 800-678-3757; www.stmichaelhotel.com; 205 W Gurley St; r incl breakfast $70-130; wi-fi) This popular 1900 hotel puts you within staggering distance of the saloons on Whiskey Row. It has 72 delightfully old-fashioned rooms, including three family units with three double beds. Rates include a full cooked-to-order breakfast in the downstairs bistro, though unfortunately it's only served until 9am.

Hotel Vendome (☎ 928-776-0900, 888-468-3583; www.vendomehotel.com; 230 S Cortez St; r incl breakfast $100-180; wi-fi) With charm dating back to 1917, this historic hotel features quaint and smallish rooms with lace curtains, quilts and other old-fashioned touches. Room 6 has a clawfoot tub. The hosts are friendly and the cozy wooden bar is an inviting place for a drink.

Pleasant Street Inn (☎ 928-445-4774, 877-226-7128; www.pleasantbandb.com; 142 S Pleasant St; r $125-175; wi-fi) This lovingly kept Victorian with its forest-green shingle siding sits on a genteel residential street, but is only three blocks from downtown action. There are just four units, including two suites (one with fireplace, the other with private deck), all decorated differently in a refreshingly uncluttered style.

Rocamadour B&B (☎ 928-771-1933, 888-771-1933; 3386 N Hwy 89; r $140-190; wi-fi) Mike and Twila used to run a château hotel in France and they've brought back not only some elegant furniture but also a healthy dose of *savoir vivre* to their new Granite Dells outpost. Breakfasts are leisurely gourmet affairs where the conversation flows as freely as the coffee. Highly recommended.

Hassayampa Inn (☎ 928-778-9434, 800-322-1927; www.hassayampainn.com; 122 E Gurley St; r incl breakfast $150-250; wi-fi) One of Arizona's most elegant hotels when it opened in 1927, today the restored inn has many original furnishings, hand-painted wall decorations and a lovely dining room. The 68 rooms vary, but all include rich linens and sturdy dark-wood furniture. The cheapest are on the smallish side, while the most expensive come with spa tubs. It has an on-site restaurant, the Peacock Room & Bar (p178).

Eating & Drinking

Sweet Tart (☎ 928-443-8587; 125 N Cortez St; dishes $5-10, dinner $45; 🕑 7am-4pm Tue-Sat, 8am-3pm Sun, dinner Sat) How sweet it is to discover this cheery patisserie-café whose high ceiling, textured walls and spacious velour booths radiate big-city style. The preservative-free pastries steal the show, but you'd be a fool not to try the healthy gourmet sandwiches or crunchy salads. Attending the prix-fixe Saturday dinner feels almost like being at a party with friends.

Raven Café (☎ 928-717-0009; 142 N Cortez St; dishes $5-12; 🕑 7:30am-11pm Mon-Sat, 8am-3pm Sun; wi-fi) This cool, loftlike spot changes stripes from daytime coffee hangout for chatty moms, web surfers and people catching up on their reading, to after-dark pub with live music and 32 beers on tap. The mostly organic menu is small but the sweet-potato fries are famous.

Palace (☎ 928-541-1996; 120 S Montezuma St; mains $8-20; 🕑 lunch & dinner) Kick open the swinging doors and be time-warped back to the 19th-century Whiskey Row days, when the Earp brothers used to knock 'em back with Doc Holliday at the huge Brunswick bar. There are plenty of framed photos and Old West memorabilia, including antique gambling devices, to distract you from your pint of Palace Red. Skip the food.

El Gato Azul (☎ 928-445-1070; 316 W Goodwin St; tapas $4-9, mains $8-22; ☷ lunch Mon-Sat, dinner daily) Spanish for 'blue cat,' this kitty is small and merry and hides out right by the historic Granite Creek. It will have you purring for creative tapas (black-bean cakes to sunflower-encrusted goat cheese) or filling Spanish-Southwestern mains. In warm weather, snag a patio table under the trees.

Murphy's (☎ 928-445-4044; 201 N Cortez St; dishes $10-25; ☷ lunch & dinner daily, brunch Sun) In an 1890 building, Murphy's highlights its pedigree as a dry-goods store with displays of yesteryear's tins and boxes on the built-in shelves. It attracts a grown-up clientele, including politicians and editors, with its classic and satisfying American menu that reminds us of the simple goodness of a roast prime rib or rotisserie chicken.

Peacock Room & Bar (☎ 928-778-9434; Hassayampa Inn, 122 E Gurley St; breakfast $6.50-11, lunch $10-14, dinner $18-32; ☷ breakfast, lunch & dinner) The stuffily stylish dining room at the Hassayampa Inn (p177) is famous for its classic American dinners, but we actually like it best before noon. Eggs Sardou (with spinach), *huevos rancheros* (a Mexican fried-egg dish with chile sauce and cheese) and lemon-soufflé pancakes should get your day off to a scrumptious start. Locals also like to unwind with after-work cocktails at the bar, which hums with sweet live jazz Wednesday to Saturday evenings.

Matt's Saloon (☎ 928-778-9914; 112 S Montezuma St) This dark and woodsy honky-tonk is similar in appearance to the Palace (p177), but has, in fact, only been around since the 1960s. Buck Owens and Waylon Jennings used to perform live back then and today it's still Prescott's kickiest two-stepping place.

Getting There & Away

Prescott's tiny airport is about 9 miles north of town on Hwy 89 and is served by US Airways from Phoenix and from Las Vegas via Kingman.

Prescott Transit Authority (☎ 928-445-5470; 820 E Sheldon St) runs buses to/from Phoenix airport ($29 to $32, 2½ hours, 16 daily) and Flagstaff ($22, 1½ hours, daily). **Shuttle U** (☎ 800-304-6114; www.shuttleu.com; 1505 W Whipple St) runs the same route on an almost identical schedule ($31, 2½ hours, 16 daily).

JEROME

pop 340 / elev 5400ft

Precipitous Native American cliff dwellings aside, Jerome enjoys the most spectacular setting of any settlement in Arizona. Wedged into steep Cleopatra Hill, it resembles those higgledy-piggledy Mediterranean hamlets clinging to a rocky hillside. Well, at least from afar. Close-ups reveal a history solidly rooted in the Old West. Jerome was home of the unimaginably fertile United Verde Mine, nicknamed the 'Billion Dollar Copper Camp.' It was also the wickedest town in the West, teeming with brothels, saloons and opium dens. When the mines petered out in 1953, Jerome went from boom to bust instantly and saw its population plummet from 15,000 to just 100 stalwarts practically overnight. But then came the '60s and scores of hippies with a keen eye for the latent charm of this virtual ghost town. They snapped up crumbling buildings for pennies, more or less restored them and, along the way, injected a dose of artistic spirit that survives to this day. In fact, Jerome lays claim to having the nation's highest number of artists per capita. Judging by the number of galleries, we wouldn't doubt it.

Quaint as it is, the most memorable aspect of Jerome is its panoramic views of the Verde Valley, embracing the fiery red rocks of Sedona and culminating in the snowy San Francisco Peaks. Sunsets? Ridiculously romantic, trust us.

More than a million visitors – most of them day-trippers and weekend warrior bikers – spill into Jerome each year, but somehow the tiny town doesn't feel like a tourist trap. Far from over-gentrified, many buildings still wear their weathered mantle of time and grime with stubborn pride, despite having been turned into souvenir shops, restaurants, saloons and B&Bs. To experience Jerome's true magic, spend the night. Who knows, you might even see a ghost. This is, after all, 'Arizona's ghost capital.'

Information

Chamber of Commerce (☎ 928-634-2900; www .jeromechamber.com; Hull Ave near 1st Ave; ☷ 10am-4pm summer) Offers tourist information.

Library (☎ 928-639-0574; 600 Clark St; ☷ noon-6pm Mon, 10am-9pm Tue, noon-8pm Wed, 10am-8pm Thu, noon-9pm Fri, 10am-2pm Sun; ☐ wi-fi) Free internet.

Police (☎ 928-634-8992; 305 Main St)

Post office (☎ 928-634-8241; 120 Main St)

Sights

Jerome's colorful history comes to life (sort of) at the **Mine Museum** (☎ 928-634-5477; 200 Main

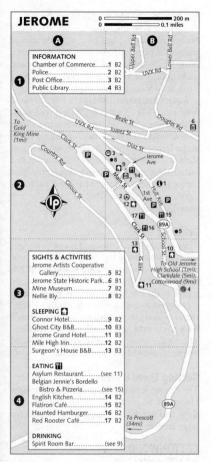

Kids will likely get a bigger kick out of the rambling **Gold King Mine** (☎ 928-300-1292; adult/child $5/3; ☀ 9am-5pm; ⚒), a miniature ghost town a mile north of Jerome. Walk among rusting mining equipment, then explore the walk-in mine and make friends with the rabbits and chickens that roam around free.

Back in town, there's a good number of fine galleries mixed in with the usual souvenir schlock shops. A good place to start is **Jerome Artists Cooperative Gallery** (☎ 928-639-4276; www.jeromeartistscoop.com; 502 Main St), where about 30 local artists working in pottery, painting, jewelry and other media sell their creations at very fair prices. Another cool place is **Nellie Bly** (☎ 928-634-0255; www.nellieblyscopes.com; 136 Main St), an Aladdin's Cave of kaleidoscopes in all shapes and sizes.

Downhill, the **Old Jerome High School** now harbors two dozen artist studios and galleries. Many are open to the public most days, but the best time to visit is during the **Jerome Art Walk** (www.jeromeartwalk.com) on the first Saturday of the month from 5pm to 9pm.

Sleeping

Accommodations are as eccentric as the town itself, featuring antique flourishes and quaint decor.

Mile High Inn (☎ 928-634-5094; www.jeromemile highinn.com; 309 Main St; r shared/private bathroom incl breakfast $85/125) Having gone through stints as a bordello and a hardware store, the Mile High has been reborn as a snug B&B whose seven newly remodeled rooms have such unusual furnishings as a tandem chair and a lodgepole bed. The ghost of the former madam supposedly haunts the latter room, called Lariat & Lace. Breakfast is served at the downstairs restaurant until a hangover-friendly noon.

Connor Hotel (☎ 928-634-5006, 800-523-3554; www .connorhotel.com; 164 Main St; r $90-165; wi-fi) This rambling 1898 haunt has 12 restored rooms that convincingly capture the Victorian period with such touches as pedestal sinks, flowery wallpaper and a pressed-tin ceiling. It's above the popular Spirit Room Bar (p180), which has live music on weekends; rooms 1 to 4 get most of the bar noise.

Ghost City B&B (☎ 928-634-4678, 888-634-4678; www.ghostcityinn.com; 541 Main St; r $95-145) In an 1898 building fronted by a creaky front porch, this is the kind of place that looks like it would have a resident ghost or two, but don't worry, it's owned by Jerome's police chief Allen Muma

St; adult/child/senior $2/free/1; ☀ 9am-4:30pm), which doubles as a gift shop. The more interesting items are non-mining related, such as a Chinese laundry machine, gambling equipment and the Colt pistol used by a local marshal to gun down three vigilantes on Main St back in the day.

Another treat for history buffs is the **Jerome State Historic Park** (☎ 928-634-5381; www.pr.state.az.us; adult/child $3/free; ☀ 8am-5pm). This state park preserves the 1916 mansion of eccentric mining mogul Jimmy 'Rawhide' Douglas. Recently updated exhibits offer insight into the town's mining heyday. Take a gander… The state park is best reached via Douglas Rd off Hwy 89; the turnoff is about 0.5 miles south of downtown Jerome.

and his wife Jackie. Each room has a different theme, from the cowboy-inspired Western room to the more girly Verde Valley room with an antique brass bed and killer views.

Surgeon's House B&B (☎ 928-639-1452, 800-639-1452; www.surgeonshouse.com; 101 Hill St; r incl breakfast $120-195) Built in 1917, this adorable place has just three suites with lots of space, great views and handpicked furnishings. The owner, Andrea, has published several cookbooks so you can expect the buffet-style breakfast to be worth writing home about. The coolest asset, though, is the back garden, with lounge chairs, a koi pond and a profusion of plants. Pet rates are $45 per night.

Jerome Grand Hotel (☎ 928-634-8200, 888-817-6788; www.jeromegrandhotel.com; 200 Hill St; r $120-450; wi-fi) If the walls of this legendary restaurant-hotel combo could talk, the stories would make you laugh, blush and cry. Built as a hospital in 1926, the haunted mansion is aging gracefully and remains full of charming touches, including a creaky old elevator. If possible, get a 3rd-floor balcony room for otherworldly valley and mountain views. Otherwise, enjoy same from the nostalgic Asylum Restaurant (right).

Eating

Flatiron Café (☎ 928-634-2733; 416 Main St; dishes $3-8; 🕑 breakfast & lunch) Get your caffeine fix, a freshly pressed juice or a healthy sandwich for the road at this teensy café.

Red Rooster Café (☎ 928-634-7087; 363 Main St; dishes $5-10; 🕑 breakfast & lunch) Cheerfully decorated with yellow walls and a golden pressed-tin ceiling, this bistro serves inspired, homemade lunch fare. The charmingly named Fatti Boombalatti (white lasagna with black forest ham and caramelized onions) is the signature dish.

English Kitchen (☎ 928-634-2132; 119 Jerome Ave; dishes $5-10; 🕑 breakfast & lunch) Arizona's oldest continually operating restaurant (since 1899) was originally Chinese-owned (and allegedly an opium den at one time) but is now a destination for belly-filling American breakfasts and homemade pies.

Haunted Hamburger (☎ 928-634-0554; 410 N Clark St; dishes $6-13; 🕑 breakfast, lunch & dinner) Perched high on a hill and often jammed elbow-to-elbow, this patty-and-bun joint is definitely a candidate for 'burger king' in town. It serves Mexican food and pricier steak and chicken dishes, but why bother?

Belgian Jennie's Bordello Bistro & Pizzeria (☎ 928-639-3141; 412 Main St; dishes $10-18; 🕑 lunch & dinner Wed-Sun) Would you like the Quickie, the 6-inch Piece or maybe the superhot Tijuana Tina? Naughty, naughty, but hey, what do expect from a place that's named after one of Jerome's most famous madams? The pizzas really are quite good, but there's also an excellent New York Strip Steak for 'real men.'

Asylum Restaurant (☎ 928-639-3197; 200 Hill St; dinner mains $18-29; 🕑 lunch & dinner) Deep-red walls, lazily twirling fans, gilded artwork and views, views vault this venerable dining room at the Jerome Grand Hotel (left) to the top of the town's restaurant heap. Order the roasted butternut squash soup with cinnamon-lime crème and the prickly pear barbecue pork tenderloin and you'll see what we mean. Superb wine list too.

Drinking

The bar at Asylum Restaurant is a genteel place for a cocktail, but if you truly want to let your hair down, head to the **Spirit Room Bar** (☎ 928-634-8809; 166 Main St). No matter whether you sip a pint at the bar, shoot some pool, strike up a conversation with some (friendly) Harley riders or study the bordello scene mural, you'll have a fine time at this dark, old-time saloon. There's live music on weekend afternoons and open-mike night on Wednesdays.

Getting There & Away

To reach Jerome from Prescott follow Hwy 89A north for 34 miles. The drive is slow and windy and not recommended for large trailers.

COTTONWOOD

pop 9200 / elev 3320ft

Named for the graceful trees on the banks of the Verde River, Cottonwood doesn't knock it out of the ballpark when it comes to scenery and charm, but it's a convenient and cheaper base for exploring the area, including Sedona (16 miles northeast) and Jerome (9 miles west). The main approach is via Hwy 89A, a faceless, busy thoroughfare. Fortunately, things get a little more Western-flavored in Old Town Cottonwood along Main St with its covered sidewalks. For information go straight to jail, home of the **Old Town Visitor Center** (☎ 928-634-9468; 1101 N Main St; 🕑 9am-4pm Mon-Sat), or stop by the **chamber of commerce** (☎ 928-634-7593; www.cottonwood.verdevalley.com; 1010 S Main St; 🕑 9am-5pm).

To learn a bit about the town, pay a visit to the **Clemenceau Heritage Museum** (☎ 928-634-

2868; 1 N Willard St; admission by donation; 9am-noon Wed, 11am-3pm Fri-Sun), whose old schoolroom, period furniture and a superb and realistic model railroad diorama make for a nostalgic flashback to yesteryear.

The Verde River runs through **Dead Horse Ranch State Park** (928-634-5283; 675 Dead Horse Ranch Rd; day-use per vehicle $6, tent/RV sites from $12/19), which offers picnicking, fishing, nature trails and a playground as well as campsites, some with hookups, and hot showers.

Cottonwood is the land of motels, mostly of the chain variety, but prices are as low as you'll find in the area.

Named after a local mine, **Little Daisy Motel** (928-634-7865; www.littledaisy.com; 34 S Main St; r $50-55) won't spoil you with frilly extras but is an excellent choice if all you're longing for is a good night's sleep after a long day on the road. Pets OK.

The best bang for your buck in town is **View Motel** (928-634-7581; www.theviewmotel.com; 818 S Main St; r $50-65;). A professionally run motel, it delivers the views its name promises. Rooms are clean, if back to basics. There's even a hot tub for you to relax in while the rug rats splash around the heated outdoor pool or romp around the play area. Pets OK.

Super 8 Cottonwood (928-639-7581; 800 S Main St; r from $60; wi-fi) is the most dependable among Cottonwood's chain motels thanks to the lovely manager couple who works hard to inject some personality into blandness. Breakfast is minimal.

The vintage gas pumps at **Willy's Burgers & Shakes** (928-634-6648; 749 N Main St; dishes $4-8.50; 11am-7pm Mon-Sat, 11am-3pm Sun) are relics of this classic 1950s diner's earlier incarnation as a gas station. Today you can fuel up with bulging burgers and frothy milkshakes made with Häagen-Dazs. Alternatively, knock-your-socks-off coffee, crispy croissants and fresh salads and sandwiches keep **Old Town Café** (928-634-5980; 1025 N Main St; dishes $4-10; 8am-3pm Tue-Sat) packed at all hours.

You wouldn't really expect an old Chicago vibe – dark, cozy, woodsy – in ho-hum Cottonwood, but **Nick's Italian Steak & Crab House** (928-634-9626; 925 N Main St; mains $11-46; dinner) gets it right. Same goes for the grilled steaks, preferably smothered in mushrooms and onions. The line often snakes out the door for the early-bird specials.

Right by Dead Horse Ranch State Park is **Blazin' M Ranch** (928-634-0334, 800-937-8643;

www.blazinm.com; adult/child under 12/senior $35/25/33). Here you can yee-haw with the rest of them at gut-busting chuckwagon suppers paired with rootin' tootin' cowboy entertainment. It's hokey, but kids big and small seem to love it. Call for dates and reservations.

CLARKDALE

About 4 miles northwest of Cottonwood on SR 260 (Main St, then Broadway), Clarkdale was a company town built in 1914 to process ore from the mines in nearby Jerome. Today it's best known as the terminus of the **Verde Canyon Railroad** (928-639-0010, 800-293-7245; www.verdecanyonrr.com; 300 N Broadway; adult/child under 12/senior $55/35/50). Vintage FP7 engines pull climate-controlled passenger cars on leisurely four-hour narrated round-trips into the splendid canyon north of Cottonwood Pass, traveling through roadless wilderness with views of red-tinged rock cliffs, riparian areas, Native American sites, wildlife and, from December to April, bald eagles. The midpoint is Perkinsville, a remote ranch where scenes from *How the West Was Won* were filmed; the train returns the way it came, over bridges and trestles. Views far surpass that of the Grand Canyon Railway. Trains leave at 1pm daily, with some extra departures in season. Reservations required.

Squatting atop a ridge about 2 miles north of Clarkdale, **Tuzigoot National Monument** (928-634-5564; www.nps.gov/tuzi; adult/child $5/free, combination ticket with Montezuma Castle National Monument $8; 8am-6pm Jun-Aug, 8am-5pm Sep-May), a Sinaguan pueblo like nearby Montezuma (p172), is believed to have been inhabited from AD 1000 to 1400. At its peak as many as 225 people lived in its 110 rooms, including a couple of dozen on the upper level. Stop by the visitor center to examine tools, pottery and other artifacts dug up from the ruin, then trudge up a short, steep trail (not suitable for wheelchairs) for memorable views of the Verde River Valley.

Birders will want to make the short trek to a viewpoint over the **Tavasci Marsh** to train their binoculars on such species as the least bittern, the Yuma clapper rail and the belted kingfisher. Arizona's largest spring-fed marsh away from the Colorado River is an official Audubon Society Important Bird Area.

SEDONA
pop 11,300 / elev 4500ft

You won't see tower rock formations the color of Sedona's anywhere else on earth. They truly blaze with incandescent crimson, cinnamon, gold and orange, and if the sun hits just right, it seems as though they're actually lit from within by gigantic blowtorches.

With spindly towers, grand buttes and flat-topped mesas carved in crimson sandstone, Sedona can easily hold its own against national parks in terms of beauty. In countless Western flicks the scenery has provided a jaw-dropping backdrop for those riding tall in the saddle. The drive into town will have you humming the theme of *The Magnificent Seven*.

Though Sedona was founded in the 19th century, the discovery of energy vortices here in the 1980s turned this once-modest settlement into a bustling New Age destination (see boxed text, p186). Today the combination of 'spiritual cauldron' and red-rock majesty entrances everyone from retirees to artists and tourists year-round.

Orientation

In navigating around Sedona, you need to know about the 'Y' – the junction of Hwys 89A and 179. North of here, pedestrian-friendly Uptown is chockablock with restaurants, shops, galleries, hotels and tour offices. West of the Y, Hwy 89A jogs west and turns into a long stretch of generic strip malls barreling through West Sedona. South of the Y, Hwy 179 runs past the cute but faux arts and crafts village of Tlaquepaque (t'*lah*-key-*pah*-key), before continuing on to the Village of Oak Creek. There's an off-leash dog park at the northwest corner of Carruth Dr and Soldiers Pass Rd.

Information

Beware of time-share agencies and other businesses masquerading as 'tourist offices.'
Library (☎ 928-282-7714; 3250 White Bear Rd; ☯ 10am-8pm Mon & Wed, 10am-6pm Tue & Thu, 10am-5pm Fri & Sat, noon-5pm Sun; 🖥 wi-fi) Free internet.
Medical center (☎ 928-204-3000; 3700 W Hwy 89A) 24-hour emergency services.
Police (☎ 928-282-3100; 102 Roadrunner Dr)
Post office (☎ 928-282-5351; 160 Coffee Pot Dr; ☯ 10am-7pm Mon-Sat)
USFS ranger station (☎ 928-203-7500; www.redrock country.org; 8375 Hwy 179; ☯ 8am-4:30pm Mon-Fri) Just south of the Village of Oak Creek. Ask for the free *Red Rock Country Recreation Guide*.
Visitor center (☎ 928-282-7722, 800-288-7336; www .visitsedona.com) South Gateway (Tequa Plaza, 7000 Hwy 179, Village of Oak Creek; ☯ 8:30am-5pm); Uptown (331 Forest

Rd; ☯ 8:30am-5pm Mon-Sat, 9am-3pm Sun) Brochures galore, Red Rock Passes (see boxed text, opposite) and lodging information. Also sells the Sedona SuperPass, a $10 booklet of discount coupons for meals, tours, theater, massages, astrology reports, museums and lots of other places and services.
Well Red Coyote (☎ 928-282-2284; 3190 W Hwy 89A) Much-beloved indie bookstore with well-edited selection, workshops and readings.

Sights & Activities
From the wild to the mild, Sedona's got something for everyone.

SCENIC DRIVES
If you're pushed for time, one way to see a lot of country is with your own four wheels. Right in town, the short drive up paved Airport Rd opens up panoramic views of the valley. At sunset, the rocks blaze a psychedelic red and orange that'll have you burning up the pixels in your digicam. Airport Mesa is the closest vortex to town.

Any time is a good time to drive the winding 7-mile **Red Rock Loop Rd**, which is all paved bar one short section and gives access to Red Rock State Park (below) as well as Red Rock Crossing/ Crescent Moon Picnic Area (day-use $8). A small army of photographers usually gathers at the crossing at sunset to record the dramatic light show unfolding on iconic **Cathedral Rock**, another vortex. There's also swimming in Oak Creek. Access is via Upper Red Rock Loop Rd off Hwy 89A, 4 miles west of the Y.

For a breathtaking loop, follow Dry Creek Rd to **Boynton Pass Rd**, turn left, then left again at Forest Rd 525. It's mostly paved but there are some lumpy unpaved sections. The route passes two of the most memorable rock formations, Vultee Arch and Devil's Bridge. Extend this trip by turning right on FR 525 and taking in the Palatki ruins (opposite).

If you're four-wheeling it, head to the breathtakingly scenic but unpaved 12-mile **Schnebly Hill Rd**, which bounces off Hwy 179 near Oak Creek and ends up at I-17 exit 320. It's closed in winter.

RED ROCK STATE PARK
This **park** (☎ 928-282-6907; www.azstateparks.com; Lower Red Rock Loop Rd; per vehicle $6; ☯ 8am-7pm May-Aug, 8am-6pm Apr & Sep, 8am-5pm Oct-Mar) has an environmental education center, a visitor center, picnic areas next to Oak Creek and six family-friendly hiking trails in a riparian habitat amid gorgeous scenery. Ranger-led activi-

ties include nature and bird walks (usually at 10am daily) and moonlight hikes from April to October. The park is 5.5 miles west of the Y along Hwy 89A, then 3 miles left on Lower Red Rock Loop Rd.

PALATKI HERITAGE SITE

Thousand-year-old Sinagua cliff dwellings and rock art are good-enough reasons to brave the 9-mile dirt road leading to this enchantingly located **archaeological site** (☎ 928-282-3854; admission free; ☽ 9:30am-3pm) on the edge of the wilderness. There's a small visitor center and two easy trails suitable for strollers but not for wheelchairs. Reservations are required. True ruin groupies should ask here about exploring the **Honanki Ruins**, a further 3 miles north.

To get to the site, follow Hwy 89A west of the Y for about 10 miles, then hook a right on FR 525 (Red Canyon Rd, a dirt road) and follow it 8 miles north to the parking lot.

CHAPEL OF THE HOLY CROSS & BUDDHIST STUPAS

The aesthetic value of wedging a concrete church **chapel** (☎ 928-282-4069; ☽ 9am-5pm Mon-Sat, 10am-5pm Sun) into red rock spires is certainly debatable, but there's no denying that it's quite a spectacular sight. Step inside if only to enjoy the views of the Bell Rock formation. To get here, head 3 miles south on Hwy 179 and turn left on Chapel Rd.

Another example of sacred architecture can be admired across town in the West Sedona hills at the **Amitabha Stupa** (☎ 928-300-4435; www.stupas.org), a consecrated Buddhist shrine set quite stunningly amid piñon and juniper pine and the ubiquitous rocks. There's a smaller stupa further down and an entire park is being planned. Heading along Hwy 89A west from the Y, turn right on Andante Dr, left on Pueblo Dr, then head up the gated trail on your right.

Activities
HIKING & MOUNTAIN BIKING

To truly commune with Sedona's out-of-this-world beauty, get away from the town bustle and onto a trail. There are dozens of them, from easy-as-pie jaunts to multiday treks. Frankly, it's hard to pick a bad one, but if you want some advice, drop by the visitor center or the ranger station to find one that matches your fitness level, interests and time frame. If you're planning multiple hikes, consider picking up a copy of the widely available *Sedona Hikes* by Richard and Sherry Mangum. Spring and fall are the best seasons, though hiking is possible year-round. Simply stick to the higher elevations in summer and the desert in winter. Finally, always pack plenty of water and sunscreen.

Although mountain bikes are verboten in the wilderness area, the biking in and around Sedona is awesome, with lots of single-track trails carving through canyons, forest and desert. A good ride for moderately fit first-timers is 23-mile Schnebly Hill Rd (off Hwy 179), even though the awe-inspiring views may make it hard to keep an eye on the trail. For other ideas, plumb the guys at local bike shops. The following outfits all sell trail maps, rent and repair gear and offer guided tours:

Bike & Bean (☎ 928-284-0210; www.bike-bean.com; 6020 Hwy 179) About 5 miles south of town. Rental rates start at $25 per hour and $40 all day.

Mountain Bike Heaven (☎ 928-282-1312; www.mountainbikeheaven.com; 1695 W Hwy 89A) Bike rentals start at $12.50/40 per hour/day.

Sedona Sports (☎ 928-282-1317; www.sedonasports.com; 251 Hwy 179) Rentals from half/full day cost $25/35.

HORSEBACK RIDING

Channel your inner hombre and ride 'em, cowboy. **M Diamond Ranch** (☎ 928-300-6466; www.mdiamondranch.com; 1-/2-hr rides $69/90; ☽ Mon-Sat; ☗) is a working cattle ranch that takes small

> ### RED ROCK PASS
>
> If you want to park anywhere in the forest surrounding Sedona, you'll need to buy a Red Rock Pass, which is available at the visitor centers, the ranger station and vending machines at some trailheads and picnic areas. Passes cost $5 per day or $15 per week and must be displayed in the windshield of your car. You don't need a pass if you're just stopping briefly for a photograph or to enjoy a viewpoint, or if you have an America Beautiful pass. For additional details, see www.redrockcountry.org. Passes are not valid at other fee areas, including state parks, national monuments and the day-use areas of Banjo Bill, Crescent Moon, Call of the Canyon and Grasshopper Point; the latter charge $8 per vehicle.

ARIZONA

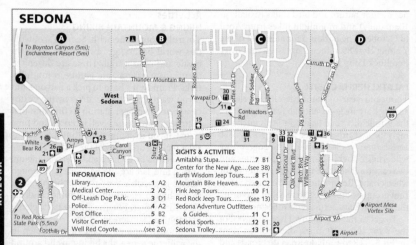

SEDONA

SIGHTS & ACTIVITIES
Amitabha Stupa	7 B1
Center for the New Age	(see 38)
Earth Wisdom Jeep Tours	8 F1
Mountain Bike Heaven	9 C2
Pink Jeep Tours	10 F1
Red Rock Jeep Tours	(see 13)
Sedona Adventure Outfitters	
& Guides	11 C1
Sedona Sports	12 E1
Sedona Trolley	13 F1

INFORMATION
Library	1 A2
Medical Center	2 A2
Off-Leash Dog Park	3 D1
Police	4 A2
Post Office	5 B2
Visitor Center	6 E1
Well Red Coyote	(see 26)

groups of people on trail rides through eye-candy countryside. Before and afterwards, everybody loves mingling with Elvis the Goat, Timmie the Dog and the rest of the ranch animals who all live in Beaver Creek, about 30 minutes from town. Staff will give you a ride from your hotel.

Tours

Sedona's stunning scenery is the backdrop for many a rugged adventure, and numerous tour operators stand by to take you there. Bumpy off-road jeep tours are the most popular and not only kids will howl with glee as you bounce around like Punch and Judy on acid. Guided hikes, mountain-bike or horseback trips are other options, or you can board a balloon for a gentle float. Some companies expect a minimum of four participants and charge more per person for smaller groups.

Crossing Worlds (☎ 928-649-3060, 800-350-2693; www.crossingworlds.com) Offers tours on Hopi, Navajo and other Native American cultures, and Sedona vortices. Tours last anywhere from 2½ hours to multiple days. A 2½-hour vortex tour starts at $80.

Earth Wisdom Jeep Tours (☎ 928-282-4714; www .earthwisdomtours.com; 293 N Hwy 89A) Groovy jeep tours with a metaphysical bent and Native American focus. Journey to vortices and sacred Indian sites and don't simply enjoy the views but meditate on them. Tours from $49 to $98.

Evening Sky Tours (☎ 928-203-0006; www.evening skytours) Journey to the universe and view planets, stars, galaxies and nebula with the naked eye and through large Dobsonian telescopes. Ninety-minute tours cost $45 to $60, depending on group size. Kids are $20.

Northern Light Balloon Expeditions (☎ 928-282-2274, 800-230-6222; www.northernlightballoon.com) Spend about one hour floating in the air at sunrise ($195 per person), then get a buzz on during the champagne picnic back on solid ground.

Pink Jeep Tours (☎ 928-282-5000, 800-873-3662; www.pinkjeep.com; 204 N Hwy 89A) This local institution runs three different thrilling and often funny, if bone-rattling, off-road tours lasting from 1½ hours (adult/child $45/34) to four hours ($106/80) and, yes, you'll be tooling around in a pink jeep.

Red Rock Jeep Tours (☎ 928-282-6667; www .redrocktours.com; 270 N Hwy 89A) Guides in cowboy garb take you on mild to wild jeep adventures; this is the only company going out to the historic Soldier Pass Trail (adult/child $64/48). Also does horseback and hiking tours.

Sedona Adventure Outfitters & Guides (☎ 928-204-6440; www.sedonahiking.com; 2020 Contractors Rd) Offers all sorts of outdoor adventures, from hikes to the top of Cathedral Rock to tubing Oak Creek and kayaking on Lynx Lake. Tours range from $48 to $91.

Sedona Trolley (☎ 928-282-4211; www.sedonatrolley .com; 270 N Hwy 89A; adult/child $11/5, both tours $20/10; ☽ 10am-5pm) Choose from two narrated tours, both lasting 55 minutes and departing on the hour. 'Sedona Highlights' covers Tlaquepaque Arts & Crafts Village and the Chapel of the Holy Cross, while 'Seven Canyons Scenic' runs to West Sedona and Boynton Canyon.

Festivals & Events

Sedona's festival schedule is fantastic, but the town is often swamped with people during these times.

Red Rocks Music Festival (☎ 877-733-7257; www .redrocksmusicfestival.com) Symphonies, chamber music,

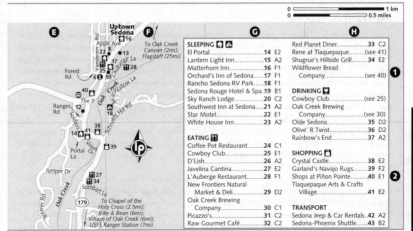

tango, flamenco, opera – you never know what's on the menu for one week in late August.

Sedona Jazz on the Rocks (☎ 928-282-1985; www .sedonajazz.com) Big-name musicians on the last September weekend. Book early.

Sedona Arts Festival (☎ 928-204-9456; www .sedonaartsfestival.org) Fine arts, crafts, music and nonstop entertainment in early October.

Sleeping

Sedona has beautiful B&Bs, creekside cabins and full-service resorts, but few chain motels and thus few bargains; budget options are limited. Cheaper lodging may be available in Cottonwood (p180) and Camp Verde (p172). Between May and October, Sedona often gets booked out on weekends.

BUDGET

Rancho Sedona RV Park (☎ 928-282-7255, 888-641-4261; www.ranchosedona.com; 135 Bear Wallow Lane; RV sites $40-55; wi-fi). The closest campground to town, Rancho Sedona has 84 sites (mostly full hookups) shaded by sycamore and cottonwood trees, an adult-only section by the creek, plus laundry, showers and a store. Dispersed camping is not permitted in Red Rock Country. For camping in Oak Creek Canyon, see p188.

White House Inn (☎ 928-282-6680; www.sedonawhite houseinn.com; 2986 W Hwy 89A; r $50-100; wi-fi) Friendly management gives this humble motel an edge and makes it a great choice for pennywise nomads. Behind purple doors await clean, good-sized rooms; those on the upper floor

of the back building even have private patios with red-rock views. Pets OK.

Star Motel (☎ 928-282-3641; 295 Jordan Rd; r $66-76; wi-fi) At these prices you won't find candy on your pillow, but who cares so long as the bed is clean, the shower strong and the refrigerator handy for chilling those sunset beers. Bakeries, cafés and eateries are just a hop, skip and jump away.

MIDRANGE

Sky Ranch Lodge (☎ 928-282-6400, 888-708-6400; www .skyranchlodge.com; Airport Rd; r $80-160; 🐾) Sedona is not lacking in the looks department, but from up here, on six lushly landscaped acres 500ft above the town, rock country truly reveals itself in all its eye-popping glory. Rooms, though lacking none of the standard amenities, will make less of a lasting impression. Spend the extra money and get a Rim View Room.

Matterhorn Inn (☎ 928-282-7176; www.matterhorninn .com; 230 Apple Ave; r $90-180; 🐾) The best thing about the 23 rooms at this Uptown motel are the private balconies with stunning red-rock vistas, so who cares if the decor is less than inspiring. The outdoor pool and Jacuzzi are nice for post-hike unwinding. Pets: $10 per day per pet.

Orchard's Inn of Sedona (☎ 928-282-2405, 800-341-6075; www.orchardsinn.com; 254 N Hwy 89A; r $100-240; 🐾 💻 wi-fi) Set back from the street but smack-dab in Uptown Sedona, this 41-room inn is a charmer and deservedly popular. You'll have fantastic postcard-perfect views of Cleopatra Hill and the reclining 'Snoopy' formation from your private patio, and the 3rd-floor units come with gas fireplaces.

THE SPIRIT OF SEDONA

Fancy having your chakras aligned, your aura photographed, your Ayurvedic doshas analyzed or your body detoxed with an ionic footbath? Come to Sedona, spiritual power center and mecca of the New Age movement. Native American tribes have long considered the area a sacred place, but Sedona's contemporary spirituality didn't arrive in full force until 1987, the year of the **Harmonic Convergence**. On August 16, 1987, thousands of people descended upon the town to usher in a new era of global awakening, peace and love. Some of them planted themselves in front of the Bell Rock formation, waiting for it to open and expose a spaceship. The UFO never came, but New Age pilgrims did and continue to do so to this day.

New Age beliefs are an alchemy of Eastern and Western spirituality, religion and mysticism along with contemporary scientific findings and quackery. The faithful seek to reach a higher consciousness by integrating mind, spirit and body, hoping that ultimately such personal efforts will transform the world at large.

You can't miss the New Age stores in town – many of them have the word 'crystal' in their names. The oldest and best of them is the **Center for the New Age** (☎ 520-282-2085; www.sedo nanewagecenter.com; 341 Hwy 179), which is full of friendly, enlightened people and a good place to start dipping into metaphysical waters. It's truly a one-stop esoteric supermarket with a huge selection of books, crystals, healing stones, angels and other paraphernalia, along with an extensive menu of services, including palmistry, reflexology and crystal healing, plus all those mentioned at the start of this box. It also offers vortex tours.

Vortices are sites where the earth's energy is believed to be highly concentrated, sort of like acupressure points on the earth's body. Sensitive types pick up this energy, feel it resonate in their bodies, and achieve greater clarity, healing and awareness as a result. The four best-known vortices are **Bell Rock**, near the Village of Oak Creek east of Hwy 179; **Cathedral Rock**, near Red Rock Crossing; **Airport Mesa**, along Airport Rd; and **Boynton Canyon**. Local maps show these four main sites, though some individuals claim that others exist.

Southwest Inn at Sedona (☎ 928-282-3344, 800-483-7422; www.swinn.com; 3250 W Hwy 89A; r incl breakfast $120-240; 🔁 🖳 wi-fi) Eco-principles are heartily embraced at this oasis of charm where you'll retreat to high-ceilinged rooms filled with energy-saving devices, gas fireplaces and the full range of amenities. The bold colors of the Southwest decor neatly match the stunning rock country views (get an upper unit).

Lantern Light Inn (☎ 928-282-3419, 877-275-4973; www.lanternlightinn.com; 3085 W Hwy 89A; r $130-195; guesthouse 2/4 persons $220/300) This charming four-unit inn with lovely gardens and quaint Euro-style courtyard rooms is excellent value for those tired of big resorts and generic chains. Proprietors Ed and Kris are fall-over-backwards friendly and will happily help you get the most out of your Sedona stay. Check-in is only on Thursday, Friday and Saturday nights and rates for those days include an ample breakfast. You're free to continue your stay through the week at reduced rates and without breakfast.

TOP END
Sedona Rouge Hotel & Spa (☎ 928-203-4111, 866-312-4111; www.sedonarouge.com; 2250 W Hwy 89A; r $280-360;

🔁 wi-fi) Although on the main highway, this classy and artistic place beautifully channels the sultry mood of southern Spain with kaleidoscopic tile-work, fountains and a blend of contemporary and exotic furniture. On balmy nights, the rooftop terrace invites stargazing by the fire pit. For travelers visiting with dogs there's the Rouge & Pooch Package ($530), which includes special K-9 biscuits, a turn-down service and other such frivolities.

El Portal (☎ 928-203-9405, 800-313-0017; www .elportalsedona.com; 95 Portal Lane; r $280-550; 🔁 wi-fi) Everything in this intimate adobe hacienda is a brilliant alchemy of materials, textures and color, from the river-rock fireplace and original Craftsman furniture to the vaulted log-beam ceiling. The ambience is so serene and soothing you may be tempted to ditch your vortex-hopping plans. All dogs are welcome and even get a special bed and a treats basket.

Enchantment Resort (☎ 928-282-2900, 800-826-4180; www.enchantmentresort.com; 525 Boynton Canyon Rd; r from $450; 🔁 🔥 🖳 wi-fi) The name is the game at this country-club-style resort that's so exclusive you must have room, dinner or spa reservations to even enter the driveway.

Tucked into Boynton Canyon, rooms with private patios sprawl across the extensive grounds. Active types can head on a canyon hike, splash around the pool or play some tennis, while relaxation comes in the form of saunas and, most famously, the exquisite Mii Amo spa. Rid yourself of your deepest worries in the Crystal Grotto or turn into Gumby on the massage table. Camp Coyote keeps kids ages four to 12 socialized and busy.

Eating

Sedona's cuisine scene may not be cutting edge, but traveling foodies will find plenty to satisfy their appetite, and not only in the upscale restaurants. In fact, the spectrum of dining options is fantastic, with enough variety to keep vegetarians and health nuts happy. Fast-food chains, on the other hand, are refreshingly rare.

BUDGET

New Frontiers Natural Market & Deli (☎ 928-282-6311; 1420 W Hwy 89A; sandwiches $5; ☯ 8am-8pm) A health nut's nirvana, this natural foods store has it all, from hormone-free meats to freshly squeezed peanut butter. Deli dabblers can pick from creamy soups, made-to-order sandwiches and fresh salads.

Wildflower Bread Company (☎ 928-204-2223; Shops at Piñon Pointe, cnr Hwys 89A & 179; dishes $5-10; ☯ breakfast, lunch & dinner) Yummy bread alert – carbophobes beware! Any time is a good time to feed grumbling tummies at this regional bakery and deli chain, but lines are definitely longest at lunchtime. The healthful sandwiches are a good picnic choice if you're hitting the hiking trail.

Coffee Pot Restaurant (☎ 928-282-6626; 2050 W Hwy 89A; dishes $5-11; ☯ 6am-2pm) Hollywood diva Jane Russell used to own the building, but this breakfast institution is delightfully unglamorous. It consistently wins top marks with locals and visitors, although the mind-boggling 101 omelette selection may present a mental hurdle for morning grumps.

D'Lish (☎ 928-203-9393; 3190 W Hwy 89A; dishes $6-12; ☯ 11am-8pm; Ⓥ) Waist-watchers and enlightened eaters crowd this buzzy, contempo organic-vegetarian-raw café to munch on tamari-glazed walnut burgers, raw zucchini pasta, delicious hummus platters and other guilt-free fare.

Raw Gourmet Café (☎ 928-282-2997; 1595 W Hwy 89A; mains $6.50-12.50; ☯ 11am-8pm Mon-Sat, 11am-6pm Sun; Ⓥ wi-fi) Wake up and smell the patchouli at this all-raw, all-organic, all-the-time New Age café where you can sink your teeth into a Vortex Pizza and pick around the Cosmic Rainbow Salad. For the ultimate energy kick, snort some clean air at the Oxygen Bar and get a crunchy Magic Healing Bar for your next vortex foray.

MIDRANGE

Red Planet Diner (☎ 928-282-6070; 1655 W Hwy 89A; dishes $9-14; ☯ 10am-11pm) For an out-of-this-world dining experience, stop at this '50s-themed diner where pasty aliens float through the space as decorative busts of Mr Spock and Obi-Wan Kenobi look on. Grill food (with a fair number of vegetarian choices) rules this Roswellian roost.

Oak Creek Brewing Company (☎ 928-204-1300; 2050 Yavapai Dr; dishes $9-15; ☯ lunch & dinner) Beer-lovers will want to make the pilgrimage to this microbrewery, which has been racking up the medals at various beer festivals for ages. The nutty brown ale packs a punch, while the Hefeweizen is a fabulous post-trail refresher. They pair well with the gastropub fare, including delicious spicy wings. There's a more upscale (and touristed) outpost at Tlaquepaque village.

Picazzo's (☎ 928-282-4140; 1855 W Hwy 89A; slices $4, pizzas $9-16.50; ☯ 11am-9pm) Pizza purists might shudder at the unorthodox toppings, but clued-in devotees gobble 'em up like M&Ms. If chicken-bacon-gorgonzola or chipotle-barbecue-beef don't tickle your fancy, you can always design your own. Nice touch: the mouthwash dispenser in the bathroom.

Javelina Cantina (☎ 928-203-9514; 671 Hwy 179; dishes $9-17; ☯ lunch & dinner) Perennially popular with both locals and tourists, this fun, feel-good place does respectable Mexican and Southwestern food, including tasty grilled fish tacos and unusual but good enchiladas stuffed with potato, cheese and spinach. Depending on your point of view, the tropical sunset mural complements or clashes with the fantastic rock panorama.

Cowboy Club (☎ 928-282-4200; 241 N Hwy 89A; lunch $9-16, dinner $15-25; ☯ lunch & dinner; ☝) At the home of the 'famous' prickly pear margarita, you can follow up your rattlesnake skewer and cactus fries appetizer with a buffalo burger (or filet mignon, if you wish) while perusing the eclectic Western-themed wall decor. Kids are welcomed with crayons and coloring placemats in the yee-haw tavern section but not in the adjacent Silver Saddle Room for the silver-spoon crowd.

TOP END

Rene at Tlaquepaque (☎ 928-282-9225; Tlaquepaque Arts & Crafts Village, Hwy 179; lunch $9-16, dinner $22-42; ☺ lunch & dinner) A sentimental favorite with locals and repeat visitors, romantic Rene infuses classic French cuisine with Southwestern touches. It does meat best (lamb is a specialty), but even lunches go well beyond the sandwich-burger-salad routine with such selections as chicken-stuffed crepes pompadour and basil-crusted salmon.

Shugrue's Hillside Grill (☎ 928-282-5300; 671 Hwy 179; lunch $9-18, dinner $25-30; ☺ lunch & dinner) With panoramic views and an outdoor deck to enjoy them, this restaurant is perfect if you want top-drawer food but don't feel like dressing up. Fresh fish prepared in umpteen ways is just one reason this place is perennially packed to the gills. At lunchtime, the spinach and wild mushroom quiche is so feistily flavored, even manly men will love it.

L'Auberge Restaurant (☎ 928-282-1667; 301 L'Auberge Lane; dinner mains $32-44; ☺ breakfast, lunch & dinner) The chef at this romantic dining shrine overlooking Oak Creek knows his lexicon of world cuisine but seems to be especially fond of French classics such as sautéed foie gras, roast pheasant and the lunch staple *croque monsieur* (grilled ham and cheese sandwich). For the full survey, go for the six- or eight-course tasting menu. Dress nicely.

Drinking & Entertainment

Locals under 30 jokingly call Sedona 'Slow-dona' when it comes to nightlife and head straight for Flagstaff (p196) for a good time. However, if you feel like guzzling your Corona in company without leaving town, try the Cowboy Club (p187), the Oak Creek Brewing Company (p187) or any of the fine establishments following.

Olde Sedona (☎ 928-282-5870; 1405 W Hwy 89A) There's always something rockin' at this restaurant-bar, from Monday's poker night and jam session to karaoke and live bands on weekends.

Rainbow's End (☎ 928-282-1593; 3235 W Hwy 89A) This roadhouse has been a local fixture since the 1950s and has the scarred-wood bar and worn pool tables to prove it. Live bands, playing everything from country to rock to

Top 40, heat up the action on Friday and Saturday nights.

Full Moon Saloon (☎ 928-284-1872; 7000 Hwy 179) This friendly pub in the Village of Oak Creek has the funnest karaoke in town, along with pool tournaments, happy hour (from 3:30pm to 6:30pm) and other party-people magnets. Best of all, it's open to 2am. Go wild!

Olive' R Twist (☎ 928-282-1229; 1350 W Hwy 89A) If you prefer getting liquefied on martinis, check out this stylish lounge where James Bond's favorite libation comes in 24 varieties. In summer, there may be live music on the fireplace patio.

Shopping

Shopping is a big draw in Sedona, and visitors will find everything from exclusive boutiques to T-shirt shops. Uptown along Hwy 89A is the place to go souvenir hunting, while the new **Shops at Piñon Pointe** (www.theshopsathyattpinon pointe.com; cnr Hwys 89A & 179; ☺ 10am-6pm) development embraces a cluster of exclusive galleries and boutiques. Art is also the main focus of **Tlaquepaque Arts & Crafts Village** (☎ 929-282-4838; www.tlaq.com; 336 Hwy 179; ☺ 10am-5pm), a tastefully re-created Mexican village with fountain, courtyards and cobbled lanes, just south of the Y. Across the street is **Crystal Castle** (☎ 928-282-5910; 313 Hwy 179); it's one of several stores selling New Age books and gifts. Continuing south, **Garland's Navajo Rugs** (☎ 928-282-4070; 411 Hwy 179) has the area's best selection of rugs, as well as other Native American crafts.

Getting There & Around

The closest major airport to Sedona is Phoenix' Sky Harbor International Airport (p170), which is served by the **Sedona-Phoenix Shuttle** (☎ 928-282-2066, 800-448-7988; www.sedona -phoenix-shuttle.com; one way/round-trip $45/85) nine times daily in about 2½ hours, traffic permitting. It drops off and picks up at the Super 8 Motel, 2545 W Hwy 89A. Call to make reservations.

Sedona Jeep & Car Rentals (☎ 928-282-8700; www .sedonajeeprentals.com; 3009 W Hwy 89A) can outfit you with a jeep for backcountry exploration for $145 per four hours and $225 per 24 hours.

OAK CREEK CANYON

For something truly magical, follow Hwy 89A from Sedona into Oak Creek Canyon. It's a surreally scenic drive that won't soon be forgotten. The canyon is at its narrowest here, and the crimson, orange and golden cliffs at their most dramatic. Pine and sycamore cling to the canyon sides and the air smells sweet and romantic. Giant cottonwoods clump along the creek, providing a scenic shady backdrop for trout-fishing and swimming and turning a dramatic golden in fall. Unfortunately, traffic can be brutal in summer, so pack plenty of patience.

About 2 miles into the drive, **Grasshopper Point** (day-use $8) is a great swimming hole. Another splash zone awaits a further 5 miles north at **Slide Rock State Park** (☎ 928-282-3034; www.azstateparks.com; per vehicle Sep-May $8, Jun-Aug $10; ☾ 8am-7pm Jun-Aug, 8am-6pm Sep-Oct, 8am-5pm Nov-Feb, 8am-6pm Mar-Apr), a historic homestead and apple farm along Oak Creek. Short trails ramble past old cabins, farming equipment and an apple orchard, but the park's biggest draw is the natural rock slides you can swoosh down on into the creek. Water quality can be an issue, but it's tested daily; call the hotline at ☎ 602-542-0202. This park gets jam-packed in summer, so come early or late in the day to avoid the worst congestion.

About 13 miles into the canyon, the road embarks on a dramatic zigzag climb, covering 700ft in 2.3 miles. Pull into **Oak Creek Vista** and whip out your camera to capture the canyon from a bird's-eye perspective. A small visitor center is open seasonally, and there's a year-round Native American arts and crafts market.

Beyond here, the highway flattens out and reaches I-17 and Flagstaff in about 8 miles.

The USFS operates five developed campgrounds along N Hwy 89A:

Bootlegger (campsites $18; ☾ mid-Apr–Oct) Nine miles from Sedona; 10 sites first-come, first-served.

Cave Springs (campsites $20; ☾ mid-Apr–mid-Sep) Thirteen miles; 81 sites, 11 reservable, rest first-come, first-served.

Manzanita (campsites $18; ☾ year-round) Six miles; 18 sites, 11 reservable, rest first-come, first-served.

Pine Flat East (campsites $20; ☾ Apr–mid-Oct) 13 miles; 21 first-come, first-served sites.

Pine Flat West (campsites $20; ☾ early Mar-late Oct) Also 13 miles; 37 sites, 18 reservable.

All of these campgrounds have toilets and, except for Bootlegger, water. Cave Springs also has coin-operated showers. All but Bootlegger and Manzanita can accommodate RVs. Cave Springs, Manzanita and Pine Flat West accept **reservations** (☎ 877-444-6777; www.recreation.gov) for

some of their sites. The rest are first-come, first-served. For weekends, show early on Friday morning or forget snagging a spot.

The family-owned **Forest Houses Resort** (☎ 928-282-2999; www.foresthousesresort.com; 9275 N Hwy 89A; r $90-145; ☾ mid-Mar–Dec) has been an Oak Creek fixture for decades. The 14 cabins do show some wear and tear, but all is forgotten when soaking up the peaceful vibe amid groves of sycamore and alders. All units are fully equipped and come with fireplace and kitchen, but no maid service. Two-night minimum stay. Pets OK.

Huddled amid woodland 8 miles north of Sedona, **Junipine Resort** (☎ 928-282-3375, 800-742-7463; www.junipine.com; 8351 N Hwy 89A; r weekday/weekend $200/260 Mar-Oct, discounts Nov-Feb; wi-fi) has 50 spacious, thoughtfully decorated one- and two-bedroom 'creekhouses' (read: glorified cabins) with kitchens, living rooms, fireplaces and decks. Some come with lofts; others have creekside views, hot tubs or both. Make sure you get an updated one. The on-site restaurant serves good food, so you don't need to brave the meandering highway to get a bite to eat.

Eight miles into the canyon, **Garland's Oak Creek Lodge** (☎ 928-282-3343; www.garlandslodge.com; 8067 N Hwy 89A; cabins $225-275; ☾ May–mid-Nov) is a sweet place combining the rustic elegance of your uncle's manse, the cheerful warmth of your parents' home and the casual comforts of your best friend's pad. Rates include a full hot breakfast, cocktails and a gourmet dinner made from organic produce grown right on the premises. Perfect for adults who crave quiet, service and authenticity, but it's often booked solid. Call for places made available by cancellations, especially on weekdays.

FLAGSTAFF
pop 65,000 / elev 6900ft

Flagstaff is a gal who likes to break the rules. She's good at mocking – redefining even – that Arizona stereotype of searing temps, sandy deserts and loads of golfing retirees. She's got mountains and winter snow. Heck, there's even skiing. Older folks? She doesn't know them all too well. She's not opposed; it's just that she runs with a younger, liberal-minded crowd. That would be the college crowd attending Northern Arizona University (NAU). She likes to sip microbrews, chill in coffeehouses, listen to bands (this is the live-music capital of northern Arizona) and dance the night away in throbbing clubs. And she really digs the outdoors, from hiking to mountain biking to skiing.

Sheepherder Thomas Forsyth McMillan first settled in Flagstaff in early 1876, but it was the arrival of the railroad in 1882 that really put the town on the map. Cattle and sheep ranching became economic mainstays, and the surrounding forests formed the basis of a small logging industry.

Today, tourism is the major economic stimulant of this dynamic little city. The cool summer temperatures attract Arizonans; it's 141 freeway miles north of Phoenix, 25 slow rural highway miles north of Sedona and under a two-hour drive from the Grand Canyon.

Orientation

Old Route 66 – here called Santa Fe Ave – is the main east–west drag and runs parallel to the railway tracks (over 100 freight trains come through every day). Historic downtown drapes across 14 blocks north of the Amtrak station, which also houses the visitor center. South of the tracks things get increasingly more student-flavored the closer you get to the NAU campus. **Thorpe Park Bark Park** (Map p191; 191 N Thorpe Rd) is a dog park with benches and a water fountain.

Information

BOOKSTORES
Bookmans (Map p191; ☎ 928-774-0005; 1520 S Riordan Ranch St; ☯ 9am-10pm; wi-fi) Indie book and music mini-chain cum neighborhood café.

EMERGENCY
Police (Map p191; ☎ 928-556-2316; 911 E Sawmill Rd)

INTERNET ACCESS
Biff's Bagels (Map p192; ☎ 520-226-0424; 1 S Beaver St; per hr $5; ☯ 7am-3pm Mon-Sat, 8am-2pm Sun) Internet access, bagels and coffee.
Library (Map p192; ☎ 928-779-7670; 300 W Aspen Ave; ☯ 10am-9pm Mon-Thu, 10am-7pm Fri, 10am-6pm Sat; 🖳 wi-fi) Free internet.

MEDICAL SERVICES
Flagstaff Medical Center (Map p191; ☎ 928-779-3366; 1200 N Beaver St) 24-hour emergency room.
Walk-In Medical Care (Map p191; ☎ 928-527-1920; 1110 E Rte 66, Suite 100; ☯ 8am-8pm Mon-Fri, 10am-4pm Sat & Sun; wi-fi) Urgent-care clinic.

Westside Veterinary Clinic (Map p191; ☎ 928-779-0148; 963 W Rte 66, Suite 230) 24-hour emergency pet care.

POST
Post office (Map p191; ☎ 928-714-9302; 2400 Postal Blvd)

TOURIST INFORMATION
Coconino National Forest Supervisor's Office (Map p191; ☎ 928-527-3600; 1824 S Thompson St; ☯ 8am-4:30pm Mon-Fri) Info on camping, hiking and mountain biking in the forest.
Visitor center (Map p192; ☎ 928-774-9541, 800-842-7293; www.flagstaffarizona.org; 1 E Rte 66; ☯ 8am-5pm Mon-Sat, 9am-4pm Sun) Inside the historic Amtrak railway station; offers information on lodging and dining along with free maps and brochures.

Sights

Most of Flagstaff's major sights are a few miles outside the downtown area, so you'll need to have your own car or hop on a Mountain Line Transit bus (p197).

MUSEUM OF NORTHERN ARIZONA

If you have time for only one sight in Flagstaff, come here. In an attractive stone building set in a pine grove, this excellent **museum** (Map p191; ☎ 928-774-5213; www.musnaz.org; 3101 N Fort Valley Rd; adult/child/student/senior $7/4/5/6; ☯ 9am-5pm) rivals Phoenix' Heard Museum in the depth and breadth of local Native American exhibits – it's an essential introduction if you're planning further forays into Indian country. A walk-through will open your eyes about numerous tribal facets, from archaeology to history, geology to the arts. Don't miss the splendid collections of Hopi kachina dolls (p56), basketry, ceramics and Navajo textiles. The museum is about 3 miles north of downtown Flagstaff.

LOWELL OBSERVATORY

A key sight for hobby astronomers and tech-minded types, this venerable **observatory** (Map p191; ☎ 928-233-3211; www.lowell.edu; 1400 W Mars Hill Rd; adult/child/student/senior $6/3/4/5; ☯ 9am-5pm Mar-Oct, noon-5pm Nov-Feb) a mile west of downtown has provided a window on the universe since 1894. There are plenty of fascinating exhibits and a state-of-the-art space theater, but most people come to see the 1896 24in **Clark Telescope**, through which Clyde Tombaugh first spotted Pluto in 1930. Although demoted from planet to being merely the largest object

ARIZONA

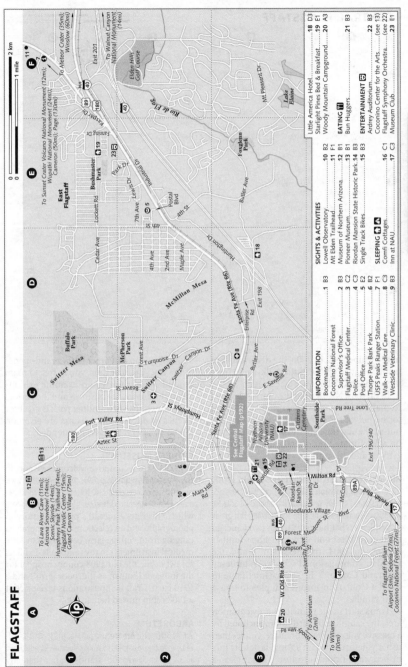

FLAGSTAFF

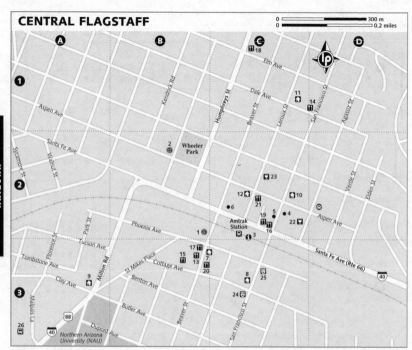

CENTRAL FLAGSTAFF

in the Kuiper Belt in 2006, the distant sphere is still included on the Pluto Walk, a trail tracing a scale model of our solar system.

In the '60s, NASA used the Clark Telescope to map the moon. On clear nights, it opens to the public for stargazing (call for hours), but in the daytime the only way to see it is on a 30-minute tour offered hourly between 1:15pm and 4:15pm.

RIORDAN MANSION STATE HISTORIC PARK
The **Riordan Mansion** (Map p191; ☎ 928-779-4395; www.pr.state.az.us; 409 W Riordan Rd; adult/child $6/2.50; ⏰ 8:30am-5pm May-Oct, 10:30am-5pm Nov-Apr) is a great example of what happens when two Chicago boys head West and strike it rich as lumber barons. In 1904, brothers Tim and Mike Riordan commissioned Charles Whittlesey of Grand Canyon's El Tovar Hotel fame to build a Craftsman-inspired duplex to house their families.

Tours start in the mansion's only common area, the cabinlike Billiard Room anchored by a massive volcanic stone fireplace. Guides then usher you through Tim's wing, tastefully furnished with Stickley furniture, Tiffany glass, a

Steinway piano and other fancy brand-names of the era. After the tour, you're free to roam around Mike's house and examine exhibits about the family, the business and the period. In summer, the surrounding park is great for picnics or daydreaming. Tours are given on the hour; reservations recommended.

PIONEER MUSEUM
A 1929 steam locomotive welcomes visitors to the **Pioneer Museum** (Map p191; ☎ 928-774-6272; www .arizonahistoricalsociety.org; 2340 N Fort Valley Rd; adult/child under 12/student/senior $3/free/2/2; ⏰ 9am-5pm Mon-Sat), which illustrates Flagstaff's pioneer history in photographs and an eclectic mix of memorabilia ranging from vintage farm equipment to early medical instruments to toys and dolls. Exhibits sprawl inside the old 1908 county hospital for the indigent (known as the 'poor farm') and a 1910 barn. Craft demonstrations take place at a 1908 cabin moved here in 1967.

ARBORETUM
At 7150ft, the **Arboretum** (off Map p191; ☎ 928-774-1442; www.thearb.org; 4001 S Woody Mountain Rd; adult/child $6/3; ⏰ 9am-5pm Apr-Oct) stands higher than any

other botanical garden in the country. We don't know what kind of 'miracle grow' they put in their soil, but the 200 acres are home to an incredible diversity of 2500 plant species, and this despite a growing season of just 75 days. Two short wood-chip trails meander beneath ponderosa pines, passing a herb garden, native plants, vegetables and wildflowers, opening up fabulous views along the way. Bring a picnic, catch a guided tour (11am and 1pm) or observe the antics of hawks, owls, falcons and other rambunctious raptors in daily shows at noon and 2pm.

Activities

If you didn't bring your own gear, **Peace Surplus** (Map p192; ☎ 928-779-4521; 14 W Rte 66) and **Aspen Sports** (Map p192; ☎ 928-779-1935; 15 N San Francisco St) rent backpacks, sleeping bags and tents as well as skis in winter.

HIKING & MOUNTAIN BIKING

The mountains and forests around Flagstaff offer scores of hiking and mountain-biking trails. Ask at the Coconino National Forest Supervisor's Office (p190) for maps and information or pick up a copy of the recently updated *Flagstaff Hikes* by Richard and Sherry Mangum.

The closest hiking to town is the steep, 3-mile one-way trek up 9299ft **Mt Elden**; the trailhead is just past the ranger station on Hwy 89. Arizona's highest mountain, the 12,663ft **Humphreys Peak** north of Flagstaff in the San Francisco Peaks, is a reasonably straightforward though strenuous summer hike. The trail begins at the Arizona Snowbowl (right) and winds through forest, coming out above the timberline. The elevation, steepness and loose footing make for a breathless ascent, but the views make it worthwhile. It is 4.5 miles one way; allow six to eight hours round-trip.

Absolute Bikes (Map p192; ☎ 928-779-5969; www .absolutebikes.net; 18 N San Francisco St) has the scoop

on the biking scene. The shop offers mountain-, road- and children's-bike rentals (from $15 per day), as well as trail maps and info. It also sells equipment and does repairs. **Single Track Bikes** (Map p191; ☎ 928-773-1862; 575 W Riordan Rd) offers similar services.

SKIING & SNOWBOARDING

The only ski resort in the northern part of the state, **Arizona Snowbowl** (off Map p191; ☎ 928-779-1951, snow report 928-779-4577; www.arizonasnowbowl .com; Snowbowl Rd; lift ticket half-/full-day adult $40/48, child $26/21) is small but lofty, with four chairlifts servicing 32 runs (beginner through expert) between 9200ft and 11,500ft. There's also a terrain park. Day lodges offer rentals, lessons and meals, and there are cabins for overnight lodging ($80 to $100 Stay & Ski packages available). The season is dependent on snowfall, which varies dramatically, so check ahead. Arizona Snowbowl is 7 miles northwest of Flagstaff along Hwy 180, then another 7 miles on Snowbowl Rd; chains or 4WD may be required, but ski buses are available.

If downhill isn't your style, cross-country skiing is offered at the **Flagstaff Nordic Center** (off Map p191; ☎ 928-220-0550; www.flagstaffnordiccenter.com; Hwy 180; trail pass $10-15). The season is short (call to see if the center is open), but there are 25 miles of groomed trails, skiing lessons, rentals and food. It's located 15 miles northwest of Flagstaff.

SCENIC SKYRIDE

To escape the summer heat, hop on the chairlift at the Arizona Snowbowl (above) for the 25-minute **Scenic Skyride** (off Map p191; ☎ 928-779-1951; adult/child/teen/senior $10/free/6/8; ⏱ 10am-4pm daily mid-Jun–Aug, 10am-4pm Fri-Sun Sep–mid-Oct) up the extinct volcano to an elevation of 11,500ft. A short trail leads to an observation point and café from where you'll enjoy the most sweeping views in the state. See if you can glimpse the Grand Canyon in the far distance.

ARIZONA

Sleeping

Flagstaff provides the best budget and moderately priced lodging in this region. Unlike in southern Arizona, summer is high season. Note that many hotels are right next to the train tracks and those freight trains run all through the night.

BUDGET

Basic motels line Route 66 parallel to the railway, especially the 3-mile stretch east of downtown and near NAU southwest of downtown. The cheaper places don't have soundproof rooms.

Grand Canyon International Hostel (Map p192; ☎ 928-779-9421, 888-442-2696; www.grandcanyonhostel.com; 19 S San Francisco St; dm incl breakfast $17-19, s/d incl breakfast $34-41; ☐ wi-fi) This indie hostel, one of the best in Arizona, is capably helmed by Lisa and Johnny who welcome pennywise nomads of all ages and stripes. Their historic, Southwest-flavored building has plenty of facilities, including a laundry and kitchen. Thumbs up, too, for their reasonably priced Grand Canyon and Sedona tours. Book early, especially in summer and for the private rooms.

Dubeau Hostel (Map p192; ☎ 928-774-6731, 800-398-7112; www.grandcanyonhostel.com; 19 W Phoenix Ave; dm incl breakfast $17-19, s/d incl breakfast $34-41; ☐ wi-fi) Sociable types might feel more comfortable at the Grand Canyon's sister property, where a jukebox, pool tables and Foosball attract a livelier (occasionally rowdy) crowd. The decor is '50s retro, but otherwise amenities are similar. Book early, especially in summer and for the private rooms.

Highland Country Inn (Map p192; ☎ 928-774-5041; www.highlandcountryinn.com; 223 S Milton Rd; r incl breakfast $60-120; wi-fi) This well-kept standard motel has recently had a date with a paint bucket and is a clean and adequate budget choice. Rates include a small breakfast.

There's plenty of camping in the surrounding Coconino National Forest. The USFS ranger station and the visitor center (p190) have a complete list. In town, your best bet is **Woody Mountain Campground** (Map p191; ☎ 928-774-7727, 800-732-7986; www.woodymountaincampground.com; 2727 W Rte 66; tent/RV sites $20/28; ☺ Apr-Oct; ☒) with 146 mostly tree-shaded sites as well as a playground and coin laundry.

MIDRANGE

Weatherford Hotel (Map p192; ☎ 928-779-1919; www.weatherfordhotel.com; 23 N Leroux St; r shared bathroom $50-70, private bathroom $85-130) If you like quirk and character by the bucket and don't mind the occasional ghost, you'll dream sweetly at this 1898 gem. Once northern Arizona's finest hotel, it's now a venerable landmark with eight snug, low-frills rooms (three must share one bathroom) and two larger, newly spiffed up ones on the 2nd floor with clawfoot tubs, air-con and phones. The downstairs bar, Charly's (p196), has good drinks prices and live bands on occasion.

Hotel Monte Vista (Map p192; ☎ 928-779-6971, 800-545-3068; www.hotelmontevista.com; 100 N San Francisco St; r Nov-Apr $70-140, May-Oct $75-170; wi-fi) Many of the 50 rooms and suites at this hotel are named after the old-time film stars who slept in them, Humphrey Bogart, Clark Gable and Jane Russell included. Rooms have been restored to their 1920s glory, and are comfortable and old-fashioned. As befits a place with such a pedigree, it is haunted – but only by friendly spirits, we are told.

Inn at NAU (Map p191; ☎ 928-523-1616; http://home.nau.edu/hrm/theinn; cnr San Francisco St & McCreary, Bldg 33; r incl breakfast $80-120; ☐ wi-fi) This top-value property on the university campus is Flag's worst-kept secret. Operated by the School of Hotel & Restaurant Management, it welcomes you to 19 stylish, ecofriendly rooms with heavenly mattresses and the usual range of amenities. Rates include a generous breakfast spread and no taxes are charged. It's closed during school breaks.

Little America Hotel (Map p191; ☎ 928-779-7900, 800-865-1401; www.littleamerica.com/flagstaff; 2515 E Butler Ave; r $100-190; ☒ ☖ wi-fi) 'Little' is not the word that comes to mind at this perennial pleaser set amid a sprawling ponderosa pine forest with 2 miles of trails. In fact, with four separate two-story wings, several restaurants, an outdoor pool, a fitness room and a playground, it feels more like a resort than a motel. A great choice for families, not least because of the big rooms.

Comfi Cottages (Map p191; ☎ 928-774-0731, 888-774-0731; www.comficottages.com; 1612 N Aztec St; cottages $135-280; ☖) Self-caterers, families and those in need of plenty of privacy will love shacking up in these cute 1920s cottages in a residential area a mere hop, skip and jump from downtown. Unexpected perks include a fridge stocked with breakfast foods, a barbecue and bikes. Some weekends and holidays may require a minimum stay.

Starlight Pines Bed & Breakfast (Map p191; ☎ 928-527-1912, 800-752-1912; www.starlightpinesbb.com; 3380 E

Lockett Rd; r $145-170) A great find if you're not the type in need of plenty of privacy, this B&B has just four romantic rooms with fireplaces, 6ft clawfoot tubs, Stickley furniture and Tiffany lamps. Hosts Richard and Michael prepare an awesome breakfast and will even serve it in bed (extra fee).

TOP END

Inn at 410 (Map p192; ☎ 928-774-0088, 800-774-2008; www.inn410.com; 410 N Leroux St; r incl breakfast $150-250; 🖳 wi-fi) All 10 good-sized rooms at this enchanting B&B bulge with character and eclectic furnishings. Choices include the bright Sunflower Fields room with antique wicker rocking chairs and the Mexican-flavored Sonoran Serenade with four-post bed and tiled fireplace. Mattresses are so magnetic you'll be in danger of missing the divine three-course breakfast inexplicably served from 8am to 9am only.

Eating
BUDGET

Macy's (Map p192; ☎ 928-774-2243; 14 S Beaver St; dishes $4-8; 🕑 6am-10pm; wi-fi) Students, outdoorsy types and caffeine-lovers hunker down at wooden tables in this been-there-forever hangout owned by an opera aficionado. Pies, cakes, brownies and other sweet treats are home-made and taste it, while the small menu features wheat-, meat- and dairy-free dishes but without sacrificing a lick to the taste gods.

Karma (Map p192; ☎ 928-774-6100; 6 E Rte 66; sushi rolls $5-7; 🕑 lunch & dinner) A trendy sushi bar with low lights, black lacquer tables and scented bar candles, Karma has lots of yummy rolls and combos to choose from, as well as noodle dishes and tempuras. You can quite literally feel the trains rumbling past across the street.

La Bellavia (Map p192; ☎ 928-774-8301; 18 S Beaver St; dishes $6-9; 🕑 breakfast & lunch) A great place to combat hunger pangs or hangovers, this homey, country-style café has been an enduring local breakfast favorite for decades. Benedicts to burritos, plus a long list of sandwiches for lunch (many with a healthful bent), should all get you off to a carb-fuelled start of the day.

Flagstaff Brewing Company (Map p192; ☎ 928-773-1442; 16 E Rte 66; dishes $6-10; 🕑 noon-2am) Mounted skis and a dangling boat give this brewpub a fun, outdoorsy vibe. The Stinkburger is an excellent vampire (or date) repellent, but there are also plenty of safer choices, including pizzas and salads.

Fratelli Pizza (Map p192; ☎ 928-774-9200; 119 W Phoenix Ave; pizzas from $7; 🕑 lunch & dinner) Watch the pizza acrobats toss and twirl the dough into submission before tucking it in the stone deck oven for perfectly crispy thin crusts. Topping-wise you can go classic or try the Route 66 bestseller with grilled chicken, roasted red peppers, barbecue sauce and other goodies. Best pizza in town!

Bun Huggers (Map p191; ☎ 928-779-3743; 901 S Milton Rd; meals under $8; 🕑 10:30am-1am) How can you resist a place with a name like that? We just had to try, and we weren't disappointed. Juicy, big and mesquite-grilled, these are simply the best burgers in town, bar none. Self-service.

MIDRANGE & TOP END

Beaver Street Brewery (Map p192; ☎ 928-779-0079; 11 S Beaver St; dishes $8-12; 🕑 lunch & dinner) Perfect on a chilly night, grab a pint of hoppy Rail Head Red and plan your next day's adventure by the pot-bellied stove. Grub is burger, pizza and sandwiches kicked into high gear – margarita chicken anyone? The attached billiard room with its heavy wooden bar stays open till 1am (2am on weekends). Cool beer garden with mountain views in summer.

Pasto (Map p192; ☎ 928-779-1937; 19 E Aspen Ave; mains $9-21; 🕑 lunch Mon-Fri, dinner daily) Italian food gets a contemporary twist at this candlelit cove with its copper ceiling and exposed brick walls. There are some interesting pasta dishes, but the chef's talent truly shines when it comes to more complex mains, such as squab (young pigeon) with roast apples and spaghetti squash. The six-course tasting menu for two is a steal at $60.

Josephine's (Map p192; ☎ 928-779-3400; 503 N Humphreys St; lunch $9-13, dinner $20-30; 🕑 lunch Mon-Sat, dinner daily) Josephine's features a casual yet upscale atmosphere in a 1911 Arts and Crafts bungalow with an outdoor patio and two fireplaces. It's run by siblings Tony and Jill (and named in honor of their mother) and offers a menu that mixes and matches culinary influences from around the world – from Mexico to the Mediterranean. Crab cakes and chipotle barbecue beef sandwiches are among the standout lunch choices.

our pick Brix (Map p192; ☎ 928-213-1021; 413 N San Francisco St; mains $23-31; 🕑 dinner Mon-Sat year-round, lunch Mon-Sat May-Oct) Classy and romantic, Brix delivers fine dining with a casual twist and scores big with patrons keen on seasonal, farm-fresh fare prepared with panache and creativity. Regionally sourced produce and meats find their destiny in such big-flavored plates as crispy duck breast with fingerling potatoes and roasted pear and mizuna salad. The artisanal cheese selection is a killer coda to a fabulous meal.

Cottage Place (Map p192; ☎ 928-774-8431; 126 W Cottage Ave; mains $24-36; ☽ dinner Wed-Sun) Tables at this pretty, intimate dining shrine are a hot commodity with dating couples, birthday celebrants and other special-occasion types. The ambience is fairly formal and grown-up, and so is the continental food, which is dependable if not exactly mould-breaking. Reservations are highly recommended.

Drinking & Entertainment

Flagstaff likes to party. It's a college town, so when school's in session the bars are packed with kids as well as skiers, locals and passers-through. From quiet bars to live-music joints and rowdy pubs, Flagstaff is as big on variety as the microbrews it produces. For listings, check the *Sundial* (the *Arizona Daily Sun*'s Friday entertainment supplement) and Thursday freebie *Flagstaff Live!* (www.flaglife.com).

Flagstaff Brewing Company (Map p192; ☎ 928-773-1442; 16 E Rte 66; ☽ noon-2am) Handcrafted brews and live music in a rustic ski-lodge setting. What more could you ask for? Well, Flag Brew also has a daily happy hour (4pm to 7pm Monday to Friday) when the kick-ass pints go for just $3, as well as decent food (p195) and a head-spinning single malt menu (over 100 at last count).

Mogollon Brewing Company (Map p192; ☎ 928-773-8950; 15 N Agassiz St) A wrinkle-free party-happy crowd makes this brewpub one of the most happening places in town. The back room morphs into a club with a dance floor and large stage where punchy local and national bands play most nights. The owners also operate Arizona's only distillery, the High Spirits Distillery, famous for its prickly pear vodka.

Charly's (Map p192; ☎ 928-779-1919; 23 N Leroux St) Inside the historic Weatherford Hotel (p194), this upbeat place buzzes with all sorts of folks, from wide-eyed tourists to tousled ski bums to preppy college kids, all drawn by a no-nonsense ambience, crackling fireplaces and cheap drinks. Plus it's one of the best places in town to catch up on the local live-music scene.

Rendezvous (Map p192; ☎ 928-779-6971; 100 N San Francisco St; wi-fi) The latest addition to the Hotel

Monte Vista (p194) goes from cozy coffee bar to soft-lit, chatty martini lounge as soon the as the moon lurches over the horizon. Try the Hot Monte, a sinful mélange of espresso, chocolate, milk, cayenne and cinnamon.

Museum Club (Map p191; ☎ 928-526-9434; 3404 E Rte 66; ☽ 11am-2am) This venerable Route 66 log-cabin roadhouse has been a Flagstaff fixture since 1931 and today is *the* place to kick up your heels and do the two-step and other country-and-western moves, often to live bands. It's a wacky place that started out as a taxidermy museum and is still filled with stuffed animals, which is why locals know it as the 'Zoo.' It's worth a look-see even in the daytime. Mondays are karaoke nights.

Mad Italian (Map p192; ☎ 928-779-1820; 101 S San Francisco St) Across the street from Mia's, the Mad Italian is much loved among NAU students for its ambience and atmosphere and is one of the best local spots to drink, dance and shoot some pool. On most nights there's a DJ playing dance music, but occasionally there is a live band. If you don't like large, fun-loving crowds, avoid going on the weekends.

Mia's Lounge (Map p192; ☎ 928-774-3315; 26 S San Francisco St) Formerly the Boardwalk, Mia's Lounge opened in late 2007 and has quickly become a Flagstaff hotspot for local bands. The atmosphere is laid-back and draws visitors, students and locals from all walks of life.

Uptown Billiards (Map p192; ☎ 928-773-0551; 114 N Leroux St) Uptown is upscale, at least by Flagstaff standards, so expect a mix of suits, sweethearts and post-college friends chalking up the cues over beers. Forget about shooting straight if you dip too deeply into the extensive whiskey and vodka menu.

Coconino Center for the Arts (Map p191; ☎ 928-779-2300; 2300 N Fort Valley Rd; ☽ 9am-5pm Tue-Sat & during events) Flagstaff's cultural and artistic hub showcases work by local artists along with performances, festivals and fundraisers.

Flagstaff Symphony Orchestra (Map p191; ☎ 928-523-5661; www.flagstaffsymphony.org) With only seven performances between September and April, you'll have to be lucky to be in town for one, but if you are, it's well worth a go. Concerts are held in the Ardrey Auditorium on the NAU campus.

Getting There & Around

US Airways Express operates several daily flights to and from Phoenix into **Flagstaff Pulliam Airport** (off Map p191; ☎ 928-556-1234; 6200 S Pulliam Dr), located about 4 miles south of town off I-17. More commercial flights may be available in the future thanks to a 2007 runway extension.

Amtrak's *Southwest Chief* stops in Flagstaff on its daily run between Chicago and Los Angeles.

Greyhound (Map p192; ☎ 928-774-4573; 399 S Malpais Lane) stops in Flagstaff en route to and from Albuquerque ($59, 6½ hours, three daily), Las Vegas ($55, 5½ hours, twice daily), Los Angeles ($87.50, 11 hours, two direct daily) and Phoenix ($29, 2¾ hours, five daily).

Flagstaff Express (☎ 928-225-2290, 800-563-1980; www.flagstaffexpress.com) offers shuttles to the Grand Canyon ($19) and Phoenix' Sky Harbor International Airport ($29). Call to arrange pickup.

Mountain Line Transit (☎ 928-779-6624; www .mountainline.az.gov) runs five local bus routes Monday through Saturday for $1 per ride. Pick up a map at the visitor center. The mobility-impaired should contact the company's on-call VanGo service.

For a taxi, call **Friendly Cab** (☎ 928-774-4444) or **Sun Taxi** (☎ 928-774-7400).

FLAGSTAFF TO GRAND CANYON

There are three ways to get to the Grand Canyon South Rim from Flagstaff. Most people take Hwy 180 through the San Francisco Peaks, a very scenic drive that can get busy in summer and treacherous in winter when it's safer to head west on I-40 and then catch Hwy 64/180 north in Williams (p260). Williams, a cute Route 66 town, is also the departure point of the historic Grand Canyon Railway.

A good way to avoid traffic and wait times at the South Entrance altogether is by arriving via the East Entrance. From Flagstaff, follow Hwy 89 north, perhaps stopping to check out Sunset Crater Volcano National Monument and Wupatki National Monument, then cut

west on Hwy 64 just south of Cameron. This route is just a little bit longer, but avoids the worst of the traffic and the drive along the eastern rim is extremely pretty. For an intimate overture to the 'Big Ditch,' pull over at the Little Colorado River Gorge overlook off Hwy 64 a few miles east of the park entrance. It's on the Navajo Reservation and Native Americans often sell crafts and jewelry from booths.

Cameron

Tiny, windswept Cameron sits on the western edge of the Navajo Reservation, about 22 miles north of Wupatki National Monument and just north of the Hwy 64 turnoff to the East Entrance of the Grand Canyon South Rim. There's not much to it other than the very active **Historic Cameron Trading Post & Lodge** (☎ 928-679-2231, 800-338-7385; www.camerontradingpost .com; RV sites $15, r Jun-Oct $100-180, Nov-May $60-160; wi-fi), which includes a restaurant serving Mexican and Navajo food, a market, a large gift shop selling quality Native American crafts, a gallery and gardens. If you're spending the night, views of the Little Colorado River Gorge from your private balcony are a wonderful prelude to your Grand Canyon adventure. Rooms are spacious and feature handcarved furniture, Southwestern art and all mod cons. Pets stay for $15.

Sunset Crater Volcano National Monument
elev 8029ft

A series of fiery eruptions between AD 1040 and 1100 created the 1000ft-high **Sunset Crater** (☎ 928-526-0502; www.nps.gov/sucr; adult/child $5/free; ☼ sunrise-sunset), the youngest of the volcanoes on the Colorado Plateau. At the revamped **visitor center** (☼ 8am-5pm May-Oct, 9am-5pm Nov-Apr) you can study up on the eruption and its dramatic effect on the lives of local Native Americans.

ARIZONA

DETOUR: LAVA RIVER CAVE

For a cool hike (especially in summer), head underground to this 0.75-mile pitch-black **lava tube**, where the temperature is about 40°F year-round. Formed some 700,000 years ago by molten rock, you can still see evidence of the lava flow in the frozen ripples of the floor. Wear sturdy boots and bring at least a couple of flashlights. It's not a long walk but it'll take longer than you think (budget an hour minimum). Admission is free and access is year-round, but roads are closed in winter, so you have to cross-country ski or snowshoe it in. To get there from Flagstaff, travel north on Hwy 180 for 9 miles, turn left on Forest Rd 245 (at milepost 230) for 3 miles, left again on Forest Rd 171 for 1 mile and one more left on Forest Rd 171B. Call ☎ 928-526-0866 for more information.

Kids especially will enjoy creating their own earthquake, taking a virtual tour of the volcano's summit or borrowing a free Discovery Pack that contains binoculars, a magnifying lens, a field guide and other items useful in unraveling the monument's mysteries.

The volcano itself is closed to hiking, but the 1-mile, partly wheelchair-accessible, **Lava Flow Trail** takes you around its base through cinder fields and frozen lava rivers.

The nearest campground is the USFS-operated **Bonito** (☎ 928-526-0866; tent & RV sites $16; ☺ May–mid-Oct) across from the Sunset Crater visitor center.

From Flagstaff, take Hwy 89 north for 12 miles, turn right on the Sunset Crater/ Wupatki Loop Rd and continue 2 miles to the visitor center. Tickets are also good for admission to Wupatki National Monument. Together, the two monuments make an excellent day trip from Flagstaff, covering 80 miles round-trip.

Wupatki National Monument

Fans of *Easy Rider* may recognize the landscape of **Wupatki National Monument** (☎ 928-679-2365; www.nps.gov/wupa; adult/child $5/free; ☺ sunrise-sunset), about 18 miles north of Sunset Crater Volcano National Monument via the Loop Rd, from the movie's opening scenes. Admission at Sunset is also good at Wupatki, and vice-versa.

The site protects ancient pueblos constructed in the aftermath of the volcano's eruption in the 11th century. It differs from other such settlements in that rooms are free-standing rather than built into a cliff or cave, indicating trading links with people from the south.

Start your visit at the excellent **visitor center** (☺ 9am-5pm), whose exhibits were recently brought into the 21st century and now feature a model pueblo room, computer simulations and games. As at Sunset Crater, kids can borrow Discovery Packs to intensify the visit.

From the visitor center, a half-mile loop trail leads to and through **Wupatki Pueblo**, the largest in the park with more than 100 rooms. Four other pueblos are easily accessible from the road, but to see the remote mesa-top **Crack-in-Wall Pueblo**, you'll need to join a strenuous but spectacular ranger-led 16-mile overnight trip. These are only in April and October, cost $50 per person and are limited to 13 people selected by lottery. Check the website for details.

GRAND CANYON REGION

No matter how much you read about the Grand Canyon or how many photographs you've seen, nothing really prepares you for the sight of it. One of the world's Seven Natural Wonders, it's so startling familiar and iconic – the equivalent of the Eiffel Tower in the Southwest – you can't take your eyes off it. The canyon's immensity, the sheer intensity of light and shadow at sunrise or sunset, even its very age, scream for superlatives.

At about two billion years old – half of Earth's total life span – the layer of Vishnu schist at the bottom of the canyon is some of the oldest exposed rock on the planet. And the means by which it was exposed is of course the living, mighty Colorado River, which continues to carve its way 277 miles

---

GREENING THE GRAND CANYON

Mitigating the impact of tourist traffic to protect the canyon and to insure visitor enjoyment has been an ongoing concern for the park service. Shuttles serving three routes on the South Rim encourage visitors to get out of their cars and reduce traffic. Additionally, the Greenway Plan that has been put into (slow) motion will eventually create a network of multi-use, accessible paths linking key points on the South Rim with Tusayan outside the park's South Entrance. Four miles of Greenway trails are already in use. The first section is part of the Rim Trail, stretching east from Yavapai Observation Station past Mather Point to Pipe Creek Vista. The second section connects Canyon View Information Plaza in the eastern Grand Canyon Village with the central Village near El Tovar Hotel.

As for noise pollution, scenic canyon flyovers have been restricted to specific corridors and are limited to certain hours of the day; none are allowed below the rim (except at Grand Canyon West).

ARIZONA

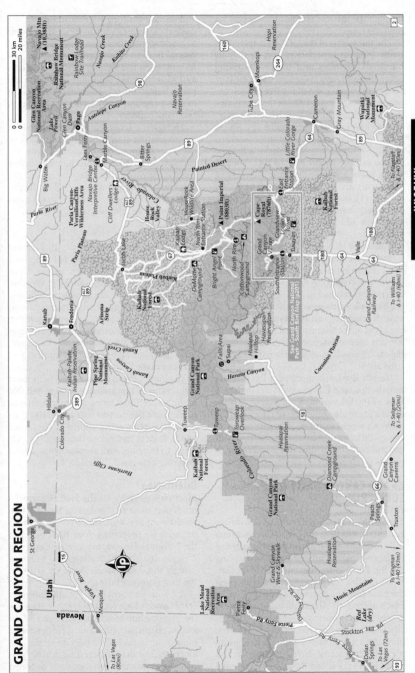

GRAND CANYON REGION

0 — 30 km
0 — 20 miles

To Las Vegas
(80mi)

Navajo Mtn
▲ (10,388ft)

Rainbow Bridge
National Monument

Rainbow Lodge
Site Trailhead

Navajo Creek

Kaibito Creek

Hopi
Reservation

Moenkopi

160

Glen Canyon
National Recreation
Area

Glen Canyon
Dam

Lake
Powell

Page

98

264

Navajo
Reservation

Tuba City

Gray Mountain

Cameron

Wupatki
National
Monument

Antelope Canyon

Glen Canyon

89

Bitter
Springs

Painted Desert

Little Colorado
River Gorge

East
Entrance
Station

64

89

To Flagstaff
& I-40 (50mi)

Big Water

Lees Ferry

Marble Canyon

Cliff Dwellers
Lodge

Paria Canyon-
Vermilion Cliffs
Wilderness Area

Navajo Bridge
Interpretive Center

ALT
89

Colorado River

House
Rock
Valley

House Rock
Wildlife Area

North Rim
Entrance Station

Kaibab
Lodge

▲ Point Imperial
(8803ft)

Cape
Royal (7876ft)

Grand
Canyon
Village

Tusayan

Grandview
Lookout
Tower

South Entrance
Station

Cottonwood
Campground

North Rim

Bright Angel
Point

Kaibab
National
Forest

180

Valle

64

180

Paria River

Paria Plateau

Jacob Lake

Kaibab Plateau

67

DeMotte
Campground

Paria
Plateau

ALT
89

89

Kanab

Fredonia

Arizona
Strip

Kaibab
National
Forest

See Grand Canyon National
Park – South Rim Map (p201)

Grand Canyon
Railway

To Williams
& I-40 (60mi)

Coconino
Plateau

Kaibab-Paiute
Indian Reservation

Pipe Spring
National Monument

389

Kanab Canyon

Kanab Creek

Hualapai
Hilltop

Supai

Falls Area

Grand Canyon
National Park

Havasu Canyon

Havasupai
Reservation

Hildale

Colorado City

St George

15

Utah

Nevada

Virgin River

Mesquite

Tuweep

Tuweep

Toroweap
Overlook

Kaibab
National
Forest

Colorado River

Hualapai
Reservation

18

Diamond Creek
Campground

Grand
Canyon
Caverns

66

Peach
Springs

Truxton

To Seligman
& I-40 (50mi)

To Williams

Hurricane Cliffs

Grand Canyon
National Park

Grand Canyon
West & Skywalk

Pierce
Ferry

Lake Mead
National
Recreation
Area

Pierce Ferry Rd

Hualapai
Reservation

Peach Springs

Diamond Bar Rd

Stockton Hill Rd

Music Mountains

Red
Lake
(dry)

Dolan
Springs

93

To Las
Vegas (72mi)

To Kingman
& I-40 (43mi)

To Kingman
& I-40 (20mi)

2

through the canyon as it has for the past six million years.

The three rims of the Grand Canyon offer quite different experiences and, as they lie hundreds of miles and hours of driving apart, they're rarely visited on the same trip. Summer is when most of the five million annual visitors arrive, and 90% of them only visit the South Rim (below), which offers easy-access viewpoints, historic buildings, Native American ruins and excellent infrastructure.

If it's solitude you seek, make a beeline for the remote North Rim (p214). Though it has fewer and less-dramatic viewpoints, its charms are no less abundant: at 8200ft elevation (1000ft higher than the South Rim), its cooler temperatures support wildflower meadows and tall, thick stands of aspen and spruce.

Run by the Hualapai Nation and not part of Grand Canyon National Park, Grand Canyon West (p213) is newly famous for its Skywalk, the controversial glass bridge jutting out over the rim that debuted in 2007. Critics consider the Skywalk sacrilege and a harbinger of unwise development on the fragile West Rim, but most agree that its construction will be a much needed financial shot in the arm for the casino-less Hualapai Nation to keep their tribe afloat.

Despite the amusement-park feel that can tinge both Grand Canyon West and the South Rim, all it takes to restore one's sense of wonder is a pause along the rims to refocus on the canyon's jagged features. The more time you can spend to form your own connection with this majestic chasm, the more it will reveal to you its subtle beauty and grandeur.

GRAND CANYON NATIONAL PARK – SOUTH RIM
elev 7200ft

The South Rim is where the Grand Canyon reveals itself at its best, and worst. Every summer camera-toting day-trippers clog its roads and trails, few making any effort beyond ogling the Big Ditch from the rimside viewpoints. So why is this rim so popular? Easy access is the most obvious reason: it's a mere 60 miles north of the I-40. Abundant infrastructure is another. This is where you'll find an entire village worth of lodging, restaurants, bookstores, libraries, a supermarket and a deli. Shuttles ply along two scenic drives, and the flat and paved Rim Trail allows the mobility-impaired

and stroller-pushing parents to take in the dramatic sweeping canyon views. If you want to venture into the inner gorge, you'll have several trails to choose from or you can just let a mule do the walking. Several museums and historic stone buildings illuminate the park's human history, and rangers lead a host of daily programs on subjects from geology to resurgent condors.

Though the accessibility of the South Rim means sharing your experience with others, there are many ways to commune with the canyon and its wildlife, and enjoy its sublime beauty, one on one. Escaping the crowds can be as easy as taking a day hike below the rim or merely tramping a hundred yards away from the parking lot of a scenic overlook.

Climate
On average, temperatures are 20°F cooler on the South Rim than at the bottom of the Grand Canyon. In summer, expect highs in the 80s and lows around 50°F. Weather is cooler and more changeable in fall, and snow and freezing overnight temperatures are likely by November. January has average overnight lows in the teens and daytime highs around 40°F. Winter weather can be beautifully clear, but be prepared for snowstorms that can cause havoc.

The inner canyon is much drier, with about eight inches of rain annually, around half that of the South Rim. During summer, temperatures inside the canyon soar above 100°F almost daily, often accompanied by strong hot winds. Even in midwinter, the mercury rarely drops to freezing, with average temperatures hovering between 37°F and 58°F.

Orientation
Most visitors arrive via the **South Entrance**, 80 miles northwest of Flagstaff on Hwy 64/180. Avoid summer wait times of 30 minutes or more by prepaying your park ticket at the National Geographic Visitor Center in Tusayan (p210), which allows you to cruise smugly through a special lane. Or arrive at the East Entrance instead.

A few miles north of the South Entrance, **Grand Canyon Village** (or simply the 'Village') is the primary hub of activity. Here you'll find lodges, restaurants, two of the three developed campgrounds, the backcountry office, the visitor center, shuttles, medical clinic, a bank, grocery store and other services. Coin-operated

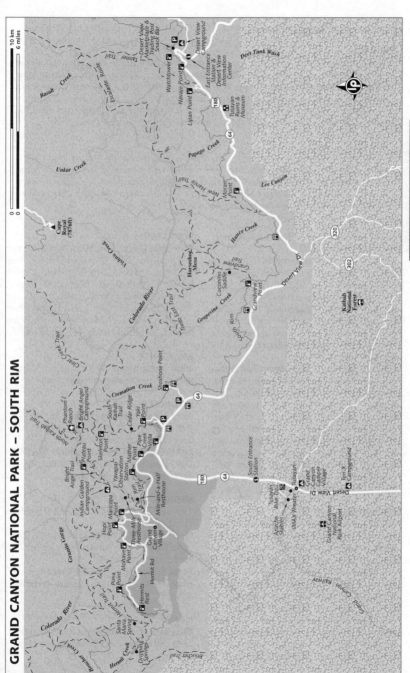

GRAND CANYON NATIONAL PARK – SOUTH RIM

ARIZONA

ARIZONA

GRAND CANYON SOUTH RIM IN...

One Day

Catch a predawn shuttle to see the sun come up at **Yaki Point** (p210), then head back to the Village for coffee and pastries at the **Deli at Marketplace** (p209). Swing by the **Canyon View Information Plaza** (p203), stroll the **Rim Trail** (p203) from Mather Point to **Yavapai Observation Station** (p203), then make a beeline to **El Tovar Dining Room** (p209) to beat the lunchtime crowds. In the afternoon, catch the shuttle to **Hermits Rest** (p210) and hike about 10 minutes down the **Hermit Trail** (p205) to look for ancient fossil beds, then catch the sunset at Hopi Point.

Two Days

Follow the one-day itinerary, capping the day with dinner in the elegant **Arizona Room** (p209) and an overnight stay in the Village (book well ahead). In the morning of day two, hop on the back of a **mule** (p205) for the seven-hour round-trip trek to Plateau Point. Wrap up your Grand Canyon adventure with a drive east along Desert View Dr, stopping at viewpoints, the **Tusayan Ruins & Museum** (p203) and the **Watchtower** (p203).

---

showers and laundry facilities are located next to Mather Campground.

West of the Village, **Hermit Rd** follows the rim for 8 miles, ending at Hermits Rest. Seven pullouts along the way offer spectacular views; from those at Mohave and Hopi Points you can spot three Colorado River rapids. Interpretive signs explain the canyon's features and geology. From March to November, the road is closed to private vehicles and accessible only by tour or free shuttle bus.

In the opposite direction, **Desert View Dr** meanders 25 miles to the **East Entrance** on Hwy 64, passing some of park's finest viewpoints, picnic areas, the Tusayan Ruins & Museum and the Watchtower. A campground, snack bar, small information center and general store are in Desert View, right by the entrance. Also here is the park's only gas station, which offers 24-hour pay-at-the-pump service from April to September. Gas stations in Tusayan are closer to the Village and open year-round.

Information

Park admission is $25 per vehicle or $12 per person if arriving on foot or by bicycle; it's valid for seven days at both rims. Bus and train passengers may pay a lesser fee or have it included in the tour price. Upon entering, you'll be given a map and *The Guide*, an incredibly useful newspaper thick with additional maps, the latest park news and information on ranger programs, hikes and park services. It also lists current opening hours of restaurants and businesses. Since these change seasonally, they are not listed in this book.

BOOKSTORES

The **Grand Canyon Association** (www.grandcanyon .org) publishes over 350 books, maps, trail guides and videos, which are sold at park bookstores at Yavapai Observation Station, Tusayan Museum, Kolb Studio, the Desert View Information Center and Hermits Rest gift shop. Books 'n' More at Canyon View Information Plaza has the biggest selection.

EMERGENCY

Grand Canyon Garage (☎ 928-638-2631; 🕑 8am–5pm) 24-hour towing and minor repairs.

INTERNET ACCESS

Grand Canyon Community Library (☎ 928-638-2718; per 50min $3; 🖳) Behind the garage in a little brown building, in the central Village.

Park Headquarters Research Library (☎ 928-638-7768; 1 Village Loop; 🕑 8am–noon & 1-4:30pm Mon-Thu & alternate Fri; 🖳 wi-fi) Free internet.

MEDICAL SERVICES

The nearest hospital is 80 miles south in Flagstaff (p189).

Clinic (☎ 928-638-2551; Clinic Rd, off Center Rd, Grand Canyon Village; 🕑 daily Mar-Oct, Mon-Fri Nov-Feb) Provides walk-in medical care.

Dental Service (☎ 928-638-2395; Grand Canyon Village; 🕑 9am-7pm Mon-Sat, 10am-4pm Sun) Located at the clinic.

MONEY

Chase Bank (Market Plaza, Grand Canyon Village) Can handle most of your money needs and also has a 24-hour ATM.

POST

Post office (☎ 928-638-2512; Market Plaza, Grand Canyon Village) Stamp vending machine is accessible from 5am to 10pm.

TOURIST INFORMATION

Canyon View Information Plaza (☎ 928-638-7644; www.nps.gov/grca; eastern Grand Canyon Village) Main ranger-staffed visitor center with lecture hall; outdoor displays and bulletin boards provide information about lodging, weather, tours, talks etc.

Desert View Information Center (☎ 928-638-7893; East Entrance)

Sights

The Grand Canyon's natural splendor is of course the prime draw, but to enrich your trip it pays to visit the park's cultural and architectural sites. Some of the most important buildings were designed by noted architect Mary Jane Colter to complement the landscape and reflect the local culture. Unless otherwise noted, sights are in the Village.

YAVAPAI OBSERVATION STATION

Views don't get much better than those unfolding behind the plate-glass windows of this little stone building at Yavapai Point, where handy panels identify and explain the various formations before you. Another reason to swing by is the superb geology exhibit that'll deepen your understanding of the canyon's multilayered geological palimpsest.

KOLB STUDIO

Photographers Ellsworth and Emery Kolb arrived at the Grand Canyon from Pennsylvania in 1902 and made a living photographing parties going down the Bright Angel Trail. Because there was not enough water on the rim to process the film, they had to run 4.5 miles down the trail to a spring at Indian Garden, develop the film and race back up in order to have the pictures ready when the party returned. Eventually, they built a small **studio** (☎ 928-638-2771) on the edge of the rim, which has since been expanded and now holds a small bookstore and an art gallery with changing exhibits.

HOPI HOUSE

A beautiful Colter-designed stone building, Hopi House has been offering high-quality Native American jewelry, basketwork, pottery and other crafts since its 1904 opening. The structure was built by the Hopi from native stone and wood, inspired by traditional dwellings on their reservation.

TUSAYAN RUINS & MUSEUM

Near the East Entrance, 22 miles east of the Village, you'll come across what's left of the nearly 900-year-old Ancestral Puebloan settlement of Tusayan. Only partially excavated to minimize erosion damage, it's less impressive than other such ruins in the Southwest. A small **museum** (⊙ 9am-5pm) displays pottery, jewelry and 4000-year-old twig animal figurines.

WATCHTOWER

Scramble to the top of Colter's stone **tower** (☎ 928-638-2736) at Desert View and pat yourself on the back for having reached the highest spot on the rim (7522ft). Unparalleled views take in not only the canyon and the Colorado River but also the San Francisco Peaks, the Navajo Reservation and the Painted Desert. The Hopi Room has festive murals depicting the snake legend, a Hopi wedding and other scenes.

Activities
HIKING

In order to truly experience the majesty of the canyon, get out of the car and onto a hiking trail. It may look daunting, but there are options for all levels of skill and fitness. Though summer is the most popular season for day hikes (despite oppressively hot 100°F-plus temperatures below the rim), experienced canyon hikers know that it's much more pleasant to hike in the spring and fall, when there are also significantly fewer visitors.

The easiest and most popular is the **Rim Trail**, which is quite literally a 'walk in the park.' It connects a series of scenic points and historical sights over 13 miles from Pipe Creek Vista to Hermits Rest. The section of the Rim Trail between Pipe Creek Vista and Maricopa Point is paved, and mostly wheelchair accessible. It's possible to catch a shuttle bus to a viewpoint, walk a stretch, then catch the next shuttle back or onward. The 3 miles or so winding through the Village are usually packed, but crowds thin out further west.

Heading down into the canyon means negotiating supersteep switchbacks. The most popular is the **Bright Angel Trail**, which is wide, well graded and easy to follow. Starting in

ARIZONA

BACKCOUNTRY ACCESS

If you think Grand Canyon views are impressive from the rim, wait till you get down below. Even day hikes are rewarding, but for the full wilderness immersion, consider an overnight trip to the canyon bottom. Now, these are not for sissies! You'll need to be in good shape, plan and pack carefully, and be prepared for steep trails and extreme temperatures. In summer, the inner gorge can be hotter than Satan's hoof. But imagine the rewards: walking the sandy banks of the Colorado River, exploring the side canyon tributaries, sleeping beneath the vast swath of stars and listening to the nightly serenade of chirping frogs.

Most overnight backpacking trips go from the South Rim to the river and then return because rim-to-rim trips involve a tedious four- to five-hour shuttle ride (p217). Most people spend two nights below the rim (p207) – either two nights at Bright Angel Campground or Indian Garden Campground, or one night at each. If you do arrange a shuttle, you could add a night at Cottonwood Campground on the way up to the North Rim. If your time is limited, a one-night trip is also rewarding. If you prefer a bed to a sleeping bag, make reservations at the canyon-bottom Phantom Ranch (p208) at least a year in advance.

Overnight hikes require a **backcountry permit**. Although the park issues 13,000 of them each year, demand far exceeds available slots. If you're caught camping in the backcountry without a permit, expect a hefty fine and possible court appearance.

Permits cost $10, plus an additional $5 per person per night, and are required for all backcountry use unless you've got a reservation at Phantom Ranch. The fee is nonrefundable and payable by check or credit card. Reservations are accepted in person or by mail or fax beginning the first day of the month, four months prior to the planned trip. For detailed instructions and to download the permit request form, go to www.nps.gov/grca and click on the Quicklink for Backcountry Hiking.

Alternatively, contact the **Backcountry Information Center** (☎ 928-638-7875; fax 928-638-2125; ✆ 8am-noon & 1-5pm Mon-Fri) and ask them to mail out the form. If you arrive without a permit, hightail it to the center, near Maswik Lodge, and get on the waiting list. You must show up daily at 8am to remain on the list, but you'll likely hear your name called within one to four days, depending on the season and itinerary.

the Village, right by Kolb Studio, it's a heavily trafficked route that's equally attractive to first-time canyon hikers, seasoned pros and mule trains. But the din doesn't lessen the sheer beauty. The steep and scenic 7.8-mile descent to the Colorado River is punctuated with four logical turnaround spots, including two resthouses offering shade and water. The first resthouse is about 1.5 miles, the second 3 miles down the trail. Day hikers and first-timers should strongly consider turning around at one of them or otherwise hitting the trail at dawn to safely make the longer hikes to Indian Garden or Plateau Point (9.2 and 12.2 miles round-trip, respectively). Hiking to the Colorado for the day is not an option.

One of the park's prettiest trails, the **South Kaibab Trail** combines stunning scenery and adventurous hiking with every step. The only corridor trail to follow a ridgeline, the red-dirt path allows for unobstructed 360-degree views. It's steep, rough and wholly exposed, which is why rangers discourage all

but the shortest of day hikes during summer. A good place to turn around is **Cedar Ridge**, reached after about an hour. It's a dazzling spot, particularly at sunrise, when the deep ruddy umbers and reds of each canyon fold seem to glow from within. During the rest of the year, the trek to **Skeleton Point**, 1.5 miles beyond Cedar Ridge, makes for a fine hike – though the climb back up is a beast in any season. The South Kaibab trailhead is 4.5 miles east of the Village on Yaki Point Rd and can only be reached by shuttle or the Hikers' Express leaving from Bright Angel Lodge around dawn (stopping at the Backcountry Information Center).

One of the steepest trails in the park, dropping 1200ft in the first 0.75 miles, **Grandview Trail** is also one of the finest and most popular hikes. The payoff is an up-close look at one of the inner canyon's sagebrush-tufted mesas and a spectacular sense of solitude. While rangers don't recommend the trek to **Horseshoe Mesa** (3 miles, four to six hours) in summer (there's no water on the very exposed trail, and the climb out is a doozy), it's not overly long and certainly doable for strong hikers strapped with a hydration system and hiking early or late in the day. For a shorter but still rewarding option, hike as far as **Coconino Saddle**. Though it's only 1.5 miles round-trip, it packs a quick and precipitous punch as you plunge 1600ft in less than a mile. With the exception of a few short level sections, the Grandview is a rugged, narrow and rocky trail. The trailhead is at Grandview Point, 12 miles east of the Village on Desert View Dr.

The wilderness **Hermit Trail** descends into pretty Hermit Canyon via of a cool spring. It's a rocky trip down, but if you set out early and take it slow, it offers a wonderfully serene hike and glimpses into secluded corners. Day hikers should steer towards **Santa Maria Spring** (5 miles round-trip) or to **Dripping Springs** via a spur trail (6.5 miles round-trip). The upper section of the Hermit is well shaded in the morning, making it a cool option in summer. The trailhead is at the end of its namesake road, 8 miles west of the Village. Although the road is only accessible via shuttle bus during the summer peak season, overnight backpackers are permitted to park near the trailhead year-round.

CYCLING & MOUNTAIN BIKING

Bicycles are allowed on paved roads and the short section of Greenway Trail that runs between Canyon View Information Plaza and Grand Canyon Village. Keep your ear open for news on paths to be constructed, eventually leading south to Tusayan and east to Desert View.

Hermit Rd offers a scenic 16-mile round-trip ride west to Hermits Rest. Keep in mind that shuttles ply this road every 10 to 15 minutes between March and November. They are not permitted to pass cyclists, so you'll have to pull over each time one drives by.

The ride along Desert View Dr towards the East Entrance (50 miles round-trip) is largely shuttle-free but sees a lot of car traffic in summer. Just off Desert View Dr, the 1-mile dirt road to Shoshone Point is an easy, nearly level ride that ends at a secluded panoramic vista – a rare spot for escaping South Rim crowds.

Options outside the park include Kaibab National Forest (p211), just south, which offers several mountain-biking trails.

MULE RIDES

Mule trips down into the canyon are fun, but more tiring than you might think. It's a bumpy ride on a hard saddle, and unless you're a regular horse rider, you *will* be saddle sore.

Rides depart daily from the corral west of Bright Angel Lodge. The seven-hour **day trip** (per person $148) goes down the Bright Angel Trail to Indian Garden for a lunch break before continuing on to Plateau Point. Hop down and enjoy the view of the Colorado River before the 6-mile return trip. **Overnight trips** (one/two people for 1 night $401/709 or 2 nights $566/946) head 10 miles down via the Bright Angel Trail to Phantom Ranch and up 8 miles on the South Kaibab Trail. Rates include lodging and food.

Riders must be at least 4ft 7in tall, speak fluent English and weigh less than 200lbs. At the corral you'll be given a small bag to store a change of clothes, a bathing suit and some personal items. Wranglers won't let you saddle up unless you wear a hat tied to your head, a long-sleeved shirt and long pants. Sunglasses must also be secured to your head. Water is provided, but eat something before leaving – it's a long, tiring ride to lunch.

To book a mule trip more than 24 hours and up to 13 months in advance, contact **Xanterra** (☎ 303-287-2757, 888-297-2757; www.xanterra.com). If you get to the park without a reservation, stop by the Bright Angel Lodge transportation desk and see what's available. If it's all booked up, sign the waiting list, show up at 6:15am the following day and hope for a cancellation.

WHITE-WATER RAFTING

Rafting the Colorado – the 'King Kong' of North American rivers – is an epic, adrenaline-pumping adventure. The biggest single drop at Lava Falls plummets 37 stomach-churning feet in just 300yd. But roller-coaster thrills are only the beginning. The canyon's true grandeur is best grasped looking up from the river, not down from the rim. Its human history comes alive in ruins, wrecks and rock art. You can hike to mystical grottos and waterfalls, explore ethereally lit slot canyons and view wildlife in its native habitat.

Commercial trips vary in length from three days to three weeks and in the type of watercraft used. Motorized pontoon rafts are the most stable and generally the least scary option. The huge inflatable boats seat eight to 16 passengers and go twice as fast as oar or paddle boats. Oar boats are more exciting and common. Rowed by an experienced guide, they provide good stability but feel more like a raft.

A fun and intimate alternative is to float in a river dory, a small, elegant hard-shelled rowboat for four passengers that's a lot speedier than a raft. Still, if it's thrills you're after, book a trip in an inflatable raft, which has you, your raft-rat-shipmates and a guide paddling all at once. You're going to get wet and maybe even thrown out of the raft, but not to worry – your experienced guide will know exactly what to do.

At night you'll be camping under stars on sandy beaches (gear provided). It's not as primitive as it sounds – guides are legendary not only for their white-water acumen but also for their culinary skills.

It takes about two or three weeks to run the entire 279 miles of river through the canyon. Shorter sections of around 100 miles take four to nine days. Expect to pay between $250 and $350 per day and book at least six months in advance. Recommended outfitters:

Arizona River Runners (☎ 602-867-4866, 800-477-7238; www.raftarizona.com) Runs trips on 35ft motorized boats and oar boats.

Oars (☎ 209-736-2924, 800-346-6277; www.oars.com/grandcanyon) Operates 18ft inflatable rafts and 17ft rigid dories.

Outdoors Unlimited River Trips (☎ 928-526-4546, 800-637-7238; www.outdoorsunlimited.com) Specializes in paddle trips.

It's not a good idea to raft the Colorado on a private trip unless you really know what you're doing (remember that 37ft drop?). You also need a permit issued by annual lottery. For details, visit www.nps.gov/grca and click on the Quicklink for River Permits. For information on the rapids classification system, see p88.

TOP FIVE WAYS TO GET AWAY FROM IT ALL

- Arrive through the East Entrance
- Take the 1-mile trail to Shoshone Point
- Walk along the rim just east of Pima Point or east of Mather Point
- Hike into the canyon on the steep and narrow Hermit Trail to Santa Maria Spring
- Camp at Desert View Campground rather than Mather Campground

---

RANGER-LED ACTIVITIES
Rangers are fonts of information which they happily share in free programs. Their talks cover everything from fossils to birds to Native Americans, while their hikes deepen your understanding of the canyon's geology and history. *The Guide* newspaper and the displays outside Canyon View Information Plaza list the latest offerings.

Grand Canyon for Children

Kids will have a field day at the park, and we're not just talking about mule-riding and rafting. Throughout summer, rangers run lots of exciting and free activities certain to create lasting memories. See *The Guide* for what's on during your stay, and remember that rangers are not baby-sitters: you must accompany your child at all times.

The Junior Ranger program for kids from four to 14 is the most popular. Pick up an activity book at the visitor center, complete three pages and attend a ranger program, then get sworn in as a junior ranger and receive a certificate and badge.

Aspiring naturalists aged nine to 14 can borrow a **Discovery Pack** containing binoculars, hand lens, field guides and other tools. Kids attend a 90-minute ranger-led program before heading off with their families to complete the activities in their field journal. Completion earns a Discovery Pack patch.

Active types can earn the Dynamic Earth patch by joining a ranger-led **Adventure Hike**, either down the Hermit Trail for close-ups of fossils or to Pima Point to learn about the canyon's geological mysteries.

In the **Way Cool Stuff for Kids** and **Kids Rock!** Programs, which are geared to kids aged six to 12, rangers use hands-on activities to teach about ecology and wildlife. For example, the ranger builds a forest with the children, who pretend to be trees, grasses, bees and other plants and animals.

Even the littlest ones can get in on the fun during **Story Time Adventure** held on the rim-facing porch of El Tovar Hotel.

Tours
COACH TOURS
First-time visitors can keep the overwhelm factor at bay by joining a narrated bus tour. Tours travel west to Hermits Rest (two hours, $20) and east to Desert View (four hours,

---

TOP SOUTH RIM OVERLOOKS

- **Desert View** Climb to the top of the Watchtower and wave down at the river.
- **Hopi Point** Catch huge sunset views.
- **Lipan Point** Creeks, palisades, rapids and sunrises.
- **Mohave Point** For a look at the river and three rapids.
- **Yaki Point** A favorite point to watch the sunrise warm the canyon's features.

$35; combination tour $45), stopping at key viewpoints. Stop by the transportation desk at any lodge or ask the El Tovar concierge for the latest schedule and tickets. Kids under 16 ride for free.

FLIGHT-SEEING

Fixed-wing airplane and helicopter flyovers at the Grand Canyon launch year-round from Tusayan and Las Vegas. Numbers, routes and altitudes of these flights are heavily regulated by the Federal Aviation Administration (FAA) to keep air and noise pollution at a minimum. Consider a ride aboard Eco-Star helicopters, which are quieter, or skip flying altogether and get a much cheaper virtual bird's-eye view at the IMAX Theatre (p210) in Tusayan.

Each of the following companies offers several options, and prices are fairly competitive, starting at about $115 for a 45-minute flight.

Air Grand Canyon (☎ 928-638-2686, 800-247-4726; www.airgrandcanyon.com)

Grand Canyon Airlines (☎ 866-235-9422; www.grandcanyonairlines.com)

Maverick Helicopters (☎ 888-261-4414; www.airstar.com) Uses Eco-Star copters.

Papillon Grand Canyon Helicopters (☎ 928-638-2419, 800-528-2418; www.papillon.com)

Sleeping

Pitch a tent in one of three campgrounds or enjoy a solid roof in the six hotels ranging from no-frill motels to luxurious lodges. **Xanterra** (☎ 303-297-2757, 888-297-2757; www.grandcanyonlodges.com) operates all park lodges, as well as Trailer Village. Reservations are accepted up to 13 months in advance and should be made as early as possible. For same-day bookings

call the **South Rim Switchboard** (☎ 928-638-2631). Summer rates we've quoted below usually drop 10% or 20% in winter. Children under 16 stay free, but cribs and cots are $10 per day.

If everything in the park is booked up, consider hightailing it to Tusayan (7 miles south; p210), Valle (30 miles south; p211) or Williams (60 miles south; p260). Campers can pitch a tent for free in the surrounding Kaibab National Forest (p211).

CAMPING
On the Rim

Desert View Campground (☎ 928-638-7893; www.nps.gov/grca; campsites $12; ☺ May–mid-Oct, subject to weather) In a piñon-juniper forest near the East Entrance, this first-come, first-served campground is quieter than Mather Campground in the Village, with nicely spread-out sites that insure a bit of privacy. The best time to secure a spot is midmorning, when people are breaking camp. Facilities include toilets and drinking water, but no showers or hookups. There's a small all-day cafeteria/snack shop and a general store stocked with basic camping supplies, beer and wine.

Mather Campground (☎ 877-444-6777; www.recreation.gov; Grand Canyon Village; campsites $18; ☺ year-round) Though Mather has over 300 campsites, it's a surprisingly pleasant and relatively quiet place to pitch a tent. Sites are shaded and fairly well dispersed, and the flat ground offers a comfy platform for your tent. You'll find pay showers, laundry facilities, drinking water, toilets, grills and a small general store; a full grocery store is a short walk away. Reservations are accepted from March through mid-November – the rest of the year it's first-come, first-served.

Trailer Village (☎ 888-297-2757, same-day reservations 928-638-2631; www.xanterra.com; Grand Canyon Village; campsites $30; ☺ year-round) As the name implies, this is basically a trailer park with RVs lined up tightly at paved pull-through sites amid a rather barren, dry patch of ground. Check for spots with trees on the far north side. You'll find picnic tables and barbecue grills, but showers are a quarter-mile away at Mather Campground.

Below the Rim

Stays at any of the three campgrounds below the rim require a backcountry overnight permit (see p204). **Indian Garden Campground** has 15

ARIZONA

sites and is 4.6 miles down the Bright Angel Trail, while **Bright Angel Campground** is on the canyon floor near Phantom Ranch, some 9.3 miles via the Bright Angel Trail. Both are ranger-staffed and have water and toilets. **Cottonwood Campground** is halfway up the North Kaibab Trail to the North Rim, about 16.6 miles from the South Rim; see p215.

LODGES

Phantom Ranch (per bunk $37; year-round) It ain't luxury, but after a day on the trail, even a bunk is likely to feel heavenly when finally arriving on the canyon floor. These are spread across cozy private cabins sleeping four to 10 and single-sex dorms outfitted for 10 people. Rates include bedding, soap, shampoo and towels, but meals are extra (breakfast $18.50, dinner $25 to $39) and must be reserved when booking your bunk. You're free to bring your own food and stove, though. Snacks, limited supplies, beer and wine are also sold. Without a reservation, try showing up at the Bright Angel Lodge transportation desk before 6am and hope to snag a canceled bunk.

Bright Angel Lodge & Cabins (Grand Canyon Village; r $76-86, cabins $106-166; year-round) Designed by Mary Jane Colter, this 1935 log-and-stone lodge on the ledge delivers historic charm by the bucket and has the nicest rooms on the South Rim except for those at El Tovar Hotel. Public spaces, though, are busy and lack the quiet, rustic elegance of Bright Angel's stately neighbor. If you're economizing, get a basic double (no TV, just a bed, desk and sink) with shared bathrooms down the hall. Cabins are brighter, airier and have tasteful Western character; the most expensive have rim views.

Maswik Lodge (Grand Canyon Village; cabins & south rooms $86, north rooms $162; year-round) A quarter-mile from the rim, Maswik Lodge is named for the Hopi kachina who guards the canyon. It's comprised of 16 modern two-story buildings set in the woods; rooms are of the standard motel variety. Rooms at Maswik North feature private patios, air-con, cable TV, high ceilings and forest views, while those at Maswik South are smaller, with fewer amenities and forgettable views. Amenities include a sports bar with pool table and big-screen TV. The cramped cabins are available in the summer only.

Yavapai Lodge (Grand Canyon Village; r west/east $102/146; Apr-Oct) The largest South Rim property is little more than your basic motel,

but it's close to the Canyon View Information Plaza and the grocery store, post office and bank at Market Plaza. The 178 basic but spotless rooms are stretched out amid a peaceful forest. Yavapai East rooms are pricier because they have air-con.

Kachina Lodge & Thunderbird Lodge (Grand Canyon Village; r $162-172; year-round) Beside the Rim Trail between El Tovar Hotel and Bright Angel Lodge, these drab lodges resemble elementary schools and offer large but uninspired rooms with two queen beds, full bathroom and TV. It's definitely worth spending an extra $10 bucks for a rimside room; with any luck you'll score one with partial canyon views! Kachina guests check in at El Tovar; Thunderbird guests at Bright Angel.

El Tovar Hotel (Grand Canyon Village; d $166-256, ste $306-406; year-round) Yup, Albert Einstein slept here and so did Teddy Roosevelt, and despite a recent renovation, this rambling 1905 wooden lodge hasn't lost a lick of its genteel historic patina. Even if you're not checking into one of the 78 rooms, swing by the hotel for its replica Remington bronzes, stained glass and exposed beams or to admire the stunning canyon views from its wide porches, martini in hand. Standard rooms are on the small side, so those in need of elbow room should go for the deluxe. For families or groups of more than three adults, a suite works out cheaper than multiple double rooms. All offer casual luxury and high standards of comfort.

Eating & Drinking

Food at Grand Canyon Village can be as fancy as dinner at El Tovar or as casual as grabbing a sandwich from the deli counter. There's a well-stocked grocery store at Market Plaza and a smaller one near the East Entrance. Rooms rarely have refrigerators, so bring a cooler for your food. Hours listed here are for summer and may vary in slower seasons.

Maswik Cafeteria (928-638-2631; Maswik Lodge; mains $5-10; 6am-10pm) Yes, it's a cafeteria so don't expect much charm, but the food is actually surprisingly good, reasonably priced and not too greasy. Get pizzas, burgers, tacos, pasta or other simple dishes from hot-food stations to fill the belly and a prepacked salad for vitamin kicks.

Bright Angel Restaurant (928-638-2631; Bright Angel Lodge; mains $8-13; 6:30am-10pm) Families love this busy, down-home coffee shop for its casual vibe and kid-friendly menu. However,

NIGHTLIFE IN THE GRAND CANYON

The park isn't exactly nightlife central, but if you've still got energy at the end of the day, there are a few places to cut loose.

On the South Rim, the patio off the bar at **El Tovar Dining Room** (below) is a great spot to sit with a prickly pear margarita and watch people strolling along the rim. Inside is a dark and cozy lounge, with big cushioned chairs and stained-glass windows. Sports fans can catch a game on the big-screen TV at the **Maswik Lodge** (opposite) sports bar. The dark, windowless bar at the **Bright Angel Lodge & Cabins** (opposite) doesn't offer much in the way of character, but it's fun to look at the historic photos on the bar. All bars close at 11pm, and drinks are prohibited along the rim itself.

On Thursday nights park employees head to Tusayan, just outside the park's South Entrance, for drinking, dancing and live entertainment at the **Grand Hotel** (☎ 928-638-3333, Hwy 64). Some opt to catch the latest scores at the popular sports bar in the **Best Western Grand Canyon Squire Inn** (p210), which also features a video arcade, pool tables and a bowling alley.

Night times are slower still at the North Rim. The only bar is the **Rough Rider Saloon** (p217), where you can study the Teddy Roosevelt memorabilia while sipping your chardonnay. You're also free to take your drink to the back of the Grand Canyon Lodge verandah or to your room.

ARIZONA

with no canyon views and only perfunctory service, it's the least appealing of the rim's three table-service restaurants.

Arizona Room (☎ 928-638-2631; Bright Angel Lodge; mains lunch $8-10, dinner $9-25; ☷ lunch Mar-Oct, dinner mid-Feb–Dec) A winning marriage of casual and upscale, this lovely restaurant serves continental fare – steak, chicken, fish – in a grand old-fashioned dining room with antler chandeliers and panoramic windows overlooking the canyon. Since it doesn't take reservations, there's a veritable stampede at 4:30pm when doors open for dinner. By 4:40pm you may be looking at an hour wait which you can spend taking in the vistas on the outside porch.

El Tovar Dining Room (☎ 928-638-2631; El Tovar Hotel; mains lunch $11-16, dinner $19-32; ☷ breakfast, lunch & dinner) There's something comfortably old-school about the linen-draped tables, dark wood and big picture windows of this venerable dining room. The service is excellent and the menu inspired. Portobello napoleon with tomato-fennel coulis? Yum. Reservations are required for dinner. To snag a table at lunchtime, arrive before the Grand Canyon Railway train pulls in at 12:15pm. The adjacent cocktail lounge is busy for afternoon cocktails and après-dinner drinks.

Other options:

Canyon Café (☎ 928-638-2631; Yavapai Lodge; dishes $5-9; ☷ 6am-10pm) Similar setup to Maswik Cafeteria; makes boxed lunches to go.

Deli at Marketplace (☎ 928-631-2262; Market Plaza, Grand Canyon Village; dishes $5-8; ☷ 7am-8pm) Fresh sandwiches and picnic goodies to go, plus pizza and fried chicken.

Desert View Trading Post Snack Bar (☎ 928-638-2360; Desert View; dishes $3-8; ☷ 8am-6pm) Snack bar by the East Entrance serves breakfast, burgers and other predictable basic fare.

Getting There & Away

Most people arrive at the canyon in a private vehicle or on a tour, but it's also possible to reach the park by public transportation.

AIR

Grand Canyon Express (☎ 702-433-1677, 800-940-2550; www.airvegas.com) operates daily flights from Boulder City, near Las Vegas, to Grand Canyon National Park Airport (one way $179) at Tusayan, 6 miles south of the Village. From Phoenix' Sky Harbor International Airport, **Open Road Tours** (☎ 602-997-6474, 800-766-7117; www.openroadtours.com) runs shuttles to Flagstaff (one way/round-trip $42/76), with onward service to the Grand Canyon ($27/54) via Williams. Rates don't include the reduced park entrance fee of $6.

BUS

The closest Greyhound bus station is in Flagstaff (p197). From here, Open Road Tours runs shuttles to the Grand Canyon (see above).

The only public transportation to the North Rim is by Trans-Canyon Shuttle, which leaves the South Rim at 1:30pm and arrives at 6pm. See p217 for details.

ARIZONA

CAR & MOTORCYCLE

Most people arrive via the park's busy South Entrance, but the East Entrance off Hwy 64 is only 10 miles further from Flagstaff; there's usually no wait and your first views of the canyon will be more dramatic and peaceful.

TRAIN

Amtrak's *Southwest Chief* makes a daily run between Chicago and Los Angeles, with stops at Flagstaff and Williams. From the latter, railroad buffs can continue their journey in style aboard the historic Grand Canyon Railway (p261). Otherwise, hop on the Open Road Tours shuttle bus (one way/round-trip $17/34) in Williams.

Getting Around
TO/FROM THE AIRPORT

Canyon Airport Shuttle serves the South Rim and its lodges hourly for $5 per person. Cabs cost $10 for two people, with each additional person $5; kids under 16 are free. Everyone must pay the reduced $6 park entrance fee. For 24-hour taxi service, call ☎ 928-638-2631, ext 6563.

SHUTTLES

Once at the rim, there's no good reason to use your car again because all services and points of interest are easily accessible via free and frequent shuttles. Three color-coded routes depart at 15-minute intervals during the day, and half-hourly from one hour before sunrise until daylight, and from dusk until one hour after sunset.

Village Route (Blue) Loops around Grand Canyon Village making stops at the Canyon View Information Plaza, Yavapai Point, Market Plaza, the Backcountry Information Center, hotels, restaurants, campgrounds and parking lots. It does not stop at the medical clinic.

Hermits Rest Route (Red) Runs along the western rim via Hermit Rd from March through November when the road is closed to private vehicles.

Kaibab Trail Route (Green) Provides service along the eastern rim via Desert View Dr, then turns onto the side road leading to Yaki Point, which is closed to private vehicles year-round.

TUSAYAN
pop 562 / elev 6612ft

Tusayan's main raison d'être is being only 7 miles south of Grand Canyon Village. Otherwise, it has all the ho-hum charm and personality you'd expect of a half-mile-long strip mall. Still, its hotels and eateries are a welcome sight if everything in the park is booked up solid. Mind you, even Tusayan gets busy in summer, so don't count on finding vacancies.

While in town, swing by the **National Geographic Visitor Center** (☎ 928-638-2468; www .explorethecanyon.com; 118 Hwy 64), which has racks of brochures, interactive exhibits and helpful staff to help you chart your Grand Canyon experience. You can also prepay your park admission here, which entitles you to use a special entry lane and thumb your nose at all those other cars stuck in the wait line. There's no extra charge.

To whet your appetite, plop into a plush seat at the center's **IMAX Theater** (adult/child $13/10; ⏲ 8:30am-8:30pm Mar-Oct, 10:30am-6:30pm Nov-Feb) for the terrific *Grand Canyon: Discovery & Adventure*. With exhilarating white-water rafting scenes and virtual-reality drops off canyon rims, this 34-minute movie plunges you into the history and geology of the canyon through the eyes of ancient Native Americans, explorer John Powell and a soaring eagle.

SLEEPING

All motels are along Hwy 64/180, and there are many more than those listed here. Reservations are recommended, especially in summer when rates are exorbitant for what are basically motel rooms. They usually drop 50% or more from November to March. Camping in the forest is free as long as you're at least 0.25 miles from the highway.

Grand Canyon Camper Village (☎ 928-638-2887, 877-638-2887; tent sites $20, RV sites $36-46; ⏲ Mar-Oct; ♿) The shadeless dirt sites on this private campground on the east side of Hwy 64/180 and north of the airport would probably not be your first choice, but they're safe and quiet and there's a playground to keep the kids busy while you're taking that nice hot shower.

Red Feather Lodge (☎ 928-638-2414, 800-538-2345; www.redfeatherlodge.com; r incl breakfast $90-160; ♿ 🖳 wi-fi) With more than 200 rooms, chances of finding a berth is better here than at most area lodgings. If you need space, opt for a room in the newer three-story hotel with elevator and interior doors. Quarters are more cramped in the adjacent motor lodge, which is also where they usually put people traveling with pets ($10 fee).

Best Western Grand Canyon Squire Inn (☎ 928-638-2681, 800-622-6966; www.grandcanyonsquire;

r $105-195; ⌕) The lobby is a promising overture, but not all rooms can carry the tune. Standard doubles in a two-story 1973 annex don't win kudos for their size or decor, but those in the main hotel are quite nice. Facilities-wise it's more like a resort, complete with bowling alley, pool tables, video arcade, beauty salon, fitness room, tennis courts and outdoor pool.

Canyon Plaza Quality Inn & Suites (☎ 928-638-2673, 866-698-2012; www.grandcanyonqualityinn.com; r $120-230; ⌕ ☐ wi-fi) You'll feel well taken care of at this subtly Southwestern-styled property where days might end with poolside chilling or soaking in an 18ft hot tub. The deluxe guestrooms are docked to a patio or balcony and are big enough for families. For even more space, get a suite.

EATING
Tusayan has its share of fast-food chains, plus these locally beloved eateries.

Jennifer's Bakery & Internet Café (☎ 928-638-3433; Grand Canyon Village Shops; dishes $3-9; ☻ 7am-10pm Apr-Oct, 7am-5pm Nov-Mar; ☐) Kick-start your day with breakfast and high-octane coffee, then pick up a fresh sandwich for a rimside picnic lunch. This is where forest rangers come to grab a bite and escape the tourists.

Sophie's Mexican Kitchen (☎ 928-638-1105; mains $6-10; ☻ 11am-9pm) Cheap and cheerful with bright turquoise walls and Southwestern accents, this tiny nosh spot makes back-to-basics Mexican for gringos – nothing too hot, nothing too spicy. Locals like it, making it a friendly, low-key alternative to the bigger, tourist-oriented restaurants in town and on the rim.

We Cook Pizza & Pasta (☎ 928-638-2278; dishes $10-16; ☻ 11am-10pm; ♿) It ain't New York, but all the expected pastas and pizzas are accounted for at this cavernous, busy joint where you order, take a number and chomp down at one of the big tables. Bonus: the children's portions, vegan pizzas (topped with soy cheese) and the ice-cream shop next door.

VALLE
At first sight Valle, about 25 miles south of the park, is just a cluster of businesses ganging up on the intersection of Hwys 64 and 180. At second sight, there's the **Planes of Fame Air Museum** (☎ 928-635-1000; www.planesoffame.org; 755 Mustang Way, junction of Hwys 64 & 180; adult/child under 12 $6/2; ☻ 9am-5pm), a small treasure trove

of vintage warbirds and civilian aircraft, many of them still ready for the skies. A key exhibit is General Douglas MacArthur's personal Lockheed that also served in the Berlin Airlift.

And then there's one of those wacky roadside attractions that make traveling around America so much fun. **Flintstones Bedrock City** (☎ 928-635-2600; tent/RV sites $13/17; admission $5; ☻ Mar-Oct) is both a campground and a well-worn, low-tech theme park where you can hobnob with Fred and Wilma, admire a Flintmobile, clamber around painted dinos or munch on a 'bronto burger.' Kids, kitsch-lovers and Flintstone fans will be in heaven. The campground itself is barren and windswept, but at least you'll be able to take a shower. Well-behaved dogs may be off-leash.

More solid lodging is provided by the family-owned **Grand Canyon Inn** (☎ 928-635-9203, 800-635-9203; www.grand-canyon-inn.com; 317 Hwy 64; r $50-100; ⌕), which is little more than a basic pit stop, but with clean rooms and a heated outdoor pool for summertime plunging. It's next to the gas station and minimart. Children under 12 stay free.

KAIBAB NATIONAL FOREST
No canyon views, but no crowds either. Divided by the Grand Canyon into two distinct ecosystems, this 1.6-million-acre **forest** (www.fs.fed.us/r3/kai) offers a peaceful escape from the park madness. Thick stands of ponderosa pine dominate the higher elevations, while piñon pine and juniper create a fragrant backdrop further down. Sightings of elk, mule deer, turkeys, coyotes and even mountain lions and black bears are all possible.

Hwy 64/180 slices through 60 miles of forest between the South Rim and Williams (p260), offering access to outdoor recreation at its finest. There's a ranger station in Tusayan (☎ 928-638-2443), but the best place to pick up maps and information is at the visitor center in Williams.

There are literally hundreds of miles of **hiking trails** to explore, and dogs are allowed off-leash as long as they don't both anyone. **Mountain biking** is possible after the snowmelt, roughly between April and November. A popular, moderate ride is along the Tusayan Bike Trail, actually an old logging road. The trailhead is 0.3 miles north of Tusayan on the west side of Hwy 64/180. It's 16 miles from the trailhead to the Grandview Lookout Tower, an 80ft-high fire tower with fabulous views. If you don't want to ride all that way, three inter-connected loops offer 3-, 8- and 9-mile round-trips. From the lookout you can continue on the easy and still-evolving 24-mile Arizona Trail. In the winter the USFS maintains 21 miles of **cross-country skiing** trails.

Apache Stables (☎ 928-638-2891; www.apachestables .com; Hwy 64; 1-/2-hr rides $46/86) offers one- and two-hour horseback rides through the forest (no canyon views). You can also ride your pony on a one-hour evening trek to a campfire and re-turn by wagon ($56) or go both ways by wagon ($26). Either way, you must bring your own food (think hot dogs and marshmallows) and drinks. The stables are about 1 mile north of Tusayan; to get to them, turn west on Moqui Dr (Forest Service Road 328) off Hwy 64/180 and it'll be a quarter-mile down on your left.

There's free backcountry camping through-out the forest as well as seven first-come, first-served developed campgrounds, including **Ten-X Campground** (☎ 928-638-2887; campsites $10; May-Sep) in a lovely woodsy setting about 2 miles south of Tusayan. The 70 sites are gener-ously spaced and equipped with picnic tables, fire rings and barbecue grills; amenities include water and toilets, but no showers or hookups.

HAVASUPAI RESERVATION & HAVASU CANYON
pop 450

In the heart of the Havasupai Reservation, about 195 miles west of the South Rim, the hidden valley around **Havasu Canyon** has four gorgeous spring-fed waterfalls and inviting azure swimming holes. The falls lie 10 miles below the rim, 2 miles past Supai, the only Native American village within the Grand Canyon and accessible only via a moderately challenging hiking trail. Trips require an over-night stay in Supai, which must be arranged before setting out. Do not try to hike down and back in one day – it's dangerous and won't give you enough time at the falls.

Orientation & Information

The well-maintained trail to Supai and Havasu Canyon descends from Hualapai Hilltop, about a 60-mile drive north of Route 66 via Hwy 18. Spend the night before either in Peach Springs (p259) or in one of the motels along Route 66 (p259).

Information is available from the **Havasupai Tourist Enterprise** (☎ 928-448-2141; www.havasupaitribe

.com). There's a $35 entrance fee and $5 environ-mental care fee that's refundable if you pack out trash. Campers must pay the fee when checking in at the **camping office** (7am-7pm Apr-Oct, 8am-5pm Nov-Mar), while lodge guests have it added to their bill. Dogs cost $20 and must be supervised.

The local post office distributes mail by pack animals and postcards mailed from here bear a special postmark to prove it. Recreational drugs – including alcohol – and nude swimming are not allowed. A small clinic can handle basic medical emergencies.

Sights & Activities

The 8-mile **Hualapai Trail** to Supai from Hualapai Hilltop is a serenely beautiful moderate hike that takes between three and five hours. The first waterfall, 75ft-high **Navajo Falls**, is just a mile beyond Supai. Next comes **Havasu Falls**, a mesmerizing cascade hopscotching 100ft into a sparkling blue swimming hole framed by cottonwoods. A quarter-mile further on is **Havasu Campground**, from where the trail heads on to **Mooney Falls**, which tumbles 200ft into another turquoise pool. To get to the swimming hole, you must climb through two tunnels and descend a very steep trail (chains provide welcome handholds). Travertine walls tower over the creek and falls. After a picnic and a swim, you can continue another 2 miles to **Beaver Falls**. The Colorado River is 5 miles beyond, but the trek is difficult and actively discouraged by the Havasupai.

Sleeping & Eating

Supai offers two sleeping options, which must be reserved well ahead of time. Right in the village, **Havasupai Lodge** (☎ 928-448-2111; www.ha vasupaitribe.com; r $145) has spacious motel rooms with showers, air-con and canyon views, but no TVs or telephones. A village café serves meals and the general store has a small range of groceries.

It's a further 2-mile trek to **Havasupai Campground** (☎ 928-448-2121; www.havasupaitribe.com; campsites $17), which has 340 primitive creek-side sites stretched for three-quarters of a mile between Havasu and Mooney Falls. Facilities include picnic tables, pit toilets and a water spring (purify it before drinking), but no show-ers. Fires are not permitted; gas stoves are.

Getting There & Around

The signed turnoff to Hualapai Hilltop is 7 miles east of Peach Springs off Route 66. After

62 miles across barren desert the road dead-ends in a parking area, where there are stables and the trailhead, but no other services.

If you don't want to hike to Supai, you can arrange for a horse to carry you in and out. Rides to the lodge are $70/120 one way/round-trip; the fee to the campground is $75/150. Your baggage travels by pack mule (duffel bags are recommended). Horses depart Hualapai Hilltop between 10am and noon year-round. Call the lodge or campground (wherever you'll be spending the night) in advance to arrange a ride.

The fastest way down is provided by **Airwest Helicopters** (☎ 623-516-2790; one-way $85; ☺ 10am-1pm Mon, Thu, Fri & Sun mid-Mar–mid-Oct, 10am-1pm Sun & Fri mid-Oct–mid-Mar). They don't take reservations; you sign up when you arrive at the parking lot. Call Havasupai Tourist Enterprise before you arrive to be sure the helicopter is running.

HUALAPAI RESERVATION & GRAND CANYON WEST
elev 4300ft

The Hualapai tribe owns nearly a million acres of land along 108 miles of the Colorado River in the far southwestern reaches of the Grand Canyon. In 2007 the reservation grabbed headlines with the opening of the much-hyped, controversial, but most certainly intriguing **Skywalk**, a horseshoe-shaped, glass-floored walkway jutting over the rim some 3500 vertigo-inducing feet above the canyon bottom. It's the latest gimmick in a development known as **Grand Canyon West** (GCW), financed by Las Vegas entrepreneur David Jing.

The remote attraction is about 50 miles east of Hwy 93 and 73 miles north of Kingman.

Although the Hualapai consider the canyon sacred, they agreed to this partnership as a much-needed revenue-generating strategy for their struggling 2500-member tribe. They'd tried their hand at gaming back in the '90s, but with Las Vegas so close the venture was preprogrammed for failure. So this time they decided to not only bet the farm, but quite literally the canyon. Will the gamble pay off? The jury's still out. For a local take, see our interview with Hualapai Indian Robert Bravo Jr (below).

Orientation & Information
If you arrive in your own vehicle, you must pay $20 to park in a big lot next to the visitor center, where you can book a variety of packages to see the canyon. This is the only way to experience GCW; you cannot drive around on your own.

Sights & Activities
As of now, crowds are refreshingly small at **Grand Canyon West** (GCW; ☎ 702-878-9378, 877-716-9378; www.destinationgrandcanyon.com; ☺ 7am-7pm mid-Mar–Oct, 7am-4:30pm Nov–mid-Mar), partly because of its remoteness and partly because of the cost involved in experiencing it. Most visitors are day-trippers from Las Vegas taking advantage of being a mere 120 miles from the canyon instead of 280 miles to the South Rim. Views here may not be quite as sublime, but that's only in comparison: you'll definitely be burning up those pixels big-time.

LOCAL VOICES: ROBERT BRAVO JR

Robert is a Hualapai Indian and Special Projects & Operations Manager at Grand Canyon West (GCW). When we caught up with him, his biggest job was to find water at the rim so it will no longer have to be piped in from 36 miles away.

What are some common misconceptions people might have about GCW and the Hualapai?
A lot of people say that we're raping and pillaging our land. We've got 108 miles along the Canyon and about 997,000 acres and we've only set aside 9,000 of those acres for development: less than 1%! We've got one of the 'Seven Natural Wonders of the World.' And we take good care of it.

What makes GCW different from other parts of the canyon? We're the only place in the entire canyon where you can experience it by land, by water and by air – all in one day!

What's your favorite spot in the canyon? Guano Point where you get a 360-degree view. I like to just sit up there on that high rock and think about where I am and who I am and then just look for that expression of awe on people's faces.

What do you want people to take away with them when they leave? Fine memories. And a little more awareness of who we are. I'd like people to say 'The Hualapai know what they're doing. They're protecting their land and everything they do is done for the people of their tribe.'

The basic package tour – the Hualapai Legacy ($30) – entitles you to use the hop-on, hop-off shuttle that comes around at 15-minute intervals and makes four stops: **Hualapai Ranch**, a faux cowboy town; **Guano Point**, a truly magnificent 360-degree viewpoint reached after a 10-minute clamber up a pile of rocks; **Indian Village**, a cluster of traditional dwellings; and, of course, the **Skywalk**.

To set foot onto the Skywalk, which doesn't actually hover above the Grand Canyon but over a side canyon, you need to fork over an additional $30, making the experience a rather pricey proposition. After depositing all your belongings in a locker ($1), you get to walk out 70ft beyond the rim and gaze 3500ft beneath your feet with nothing but a thick panel of glass between you and eternity. It's a dizzying, even thrilling effect once you get your vertigo under control.

sSince GWC is not part of the Grand Canyon National Park, the Hualapai are free to offer helicopter rides below the rim, an impressive if apocalyptically noisy experience. The six-minute flights land at the bottom, where you board a 20-minute pontoon ride along the muddy Colorado River before heading back up ($160).

Other optional add-ons include a trip in a Hummer (30-/60-minute rides $60/90), horseback rides (30-/90-/180-minute rides $60/80/100) and meals ($12).

Sleeping & Eating

As of now, the only way to spend the night at GCW is at the rustic **Hualapai Ranch Cabins** (☎ 702-878-9378, 877-716-9378; www.destinationgrand canyon.com; per person $130). Rates include dinner, breakfast and the Hualapai Legacy package, but not the Skywalk.

A gourmet restaurant is planned, but for now eating at the canyon is a pretty mediocre experience. Meal vouchers are $12 and good at the **Hualapai Ranch** dining room, which serves ribs, pot pie, steak and other Western fare; at **High Point Café** at Guano Point, which has grilled chicken, barbecue beef, corn and awesome views; and at the **Skywalk Café**, where you can fill your tummy with hot dogs, noodle soup and rice bowls.

Getting There & Away

There is no public transportation to Grand Canyon West, but several tour operators run day trips by bus or plane from Las Vegas.

If you're driving in from Vegas, follow Hwy 93 south to the Dolan Springs turnoff, from where it's about 50 miles to GCW. Follow Pierce Ferry Rd for 28 paved miles, then turn right onto Diamond Bar Rd. The first 14 miles are unpaved and not suitable for RVs, with conditions ranging from excellent to abysmal and a particularly nasty pebbly stretch. Watch out for sharp rocks. The route itself is lovely, meandering through thick Joshua tree forest and a narrow canyon towards a colorful mountain range. The last 7 miles are a smooth paved ride. Tribal spokespeople have assured us that the entire road will be fully paved by late 2009. Keep us posted!

Coming from Kingman, take Stockton Hill Rd north, which meets Pierce Ferry Rd after 42 miles. Turn right and follow the directions outlined above. Directions from other towns are detailed at www.destination grandcanyon.com.

If you don't feel up to driving, **Grand Canyon West Express** (☎ 702-260-6506) offers a round-trip shuttle service from a park-and-ride area for $10. Call at least a day ahead for reservations and parking directions.

GRAND CANYON NATIONAL PARK – NORTH RIM
elev 8200ft

On the Grand Canyon's North Rim, solitude reigns supreme. There are no shuttles or bus tours, no museums, shopping centers, schools or garages. In fact, there isn't much of anything here beyond a classic rimside national park lodge, a campground, a motel, a general store and miles of trails carving through sunny meadows thick with wildflowers, willowy aspen and towering ponderosa pines. Amid these forested roads and trails, what you'll find is peace, room to breathe and a less fettered Grand Canyon experience.

At 8200ft, the North Rim is about 10°F cooler than the south – even on summer evenings you'll need a sweater. The lodge and all services are closed from mid-October through mid-May. Rambo types can cross-country ski in and stay at the campground (p216).

Orientation & Information

Park admission is $25 per vehicle or $12 per person if arriving on foot or by bicycle; it's valid for seven days at both rims. Upon entering, you'll be given a map and *The Guide* (see p202). The entrance to the North Rim is 24 miles south of Jacob Lake on Hwy 67. From here, it's another 20 miles to the Grand Canyon Lodge, where you'll find a restaurant, deli, saloon, postal window and gift shop, as well as the **North Rim Visitor Center** (☎ 928-638-7864; www.nps.gov/grca; ◷ 8am-6pm). About a mile up the road, next to the campground, are a **general store** (◷ 7am-7pm), laundry facilities, fee showers, a gas station and the **North Rim Backcountry Office** (☎ 928-638-7875; ◷ 1-5pm). To contact the Grand Canyon Lodge front desk, the saloon, gift shop, gas station or general store, call the **North Rim Switchboard** (☎ 928-638-2612). The closest ATM is in Jacob Lake.

Sights & Activities
BRIGHT ANGEL POINT
The short and easy paved trail (0.3 miles) to Bright Angel Point is a canyon must. Beginning from the back porch of the Grand Canyon Lodge, it goes to a narrow finger of an overlook with unfettered views of the mesas, buttes, spires and temples of Bright Angel Canyon. That's the South Rim, 11 miles away, and beyond it the San Francisco Peaks near Flagstaff. It's popular for sunrise and sunset walks, but visit after dusk for unparalleled stargazing. Note that, although paved, steep inclines and rocky spots make this trail dangerous for strollers and prohibitive to wheelchairs.

HIKING & BACKPACKING
The 1.5-mile **Transept Trail**, a rocky dirt path with moderate inclines, meanders north from the lodge through aspens to the North Rim Campground (p216). The winding **Widforss Trail** follows the rim for five miles with views of canyon, meadows and woods, finishing at Widforss Point. The trailhead is 1 mile west of Hwy 67, or 2.7 miles north of the lodge.

The steep and difficult 14-mile **North Kaibab Trail** is the only maintained rim-to-river trail and connects with trails to the South Rim near Phantom Ranch. The trailhead is 2 miles north of Grand Canyon Lodge. There's a parking lot, but it's often full soon after daylight. An informal **hikers' shuttle** (first/additional passengers $7/5) departs around 5:30am and 6:30am, but you need to sign up the night before.

If you just want to get a flavor of inner-canyon hiking, walk 0.75 miles down to **Coconino Overlook** or 2 miles to the **Supai Tunnel**. More ambitious day hikers can continue another 2 miles to the waterfall of **Roaring Springs**, which is also a popular mule-ride destination.

Take the short detour to the left, where you'll find picnic tables and a pool to cool your feet. Seasonal water is available at the restrooms.

If you wish to continue to the river, plan on camping overnight (backcountry permit required, see p204) at Cottonwood Campground (p208), some 2 miles beyond Roaring Springs. It's a beautiful spot with seasonal drinking water, pit toilets, a phone and a ranger station, but the 11 campsites are not shaded.

From the campground, it's a gentle downhill walk along Bright Angel Creek to the Colorado River. Phantom Ranch (p208) and the Bright Angel Campground (p208) are 7 and 7.5 miles respectively below Cottonwood.

Rangers suggest three nights as a minimum to enjoy a rim-to-river-to-rim hike, staying at Cottonwood on the first and third nights and Bright Angel on the second. Faster trips would be an endurance slog and not much fun.

Hiking from the North Rim to the South Rim requires a ride on the Trans-Canyon Shuttle to get you back (see p217 for details).

MULE RIDES
Canyon Trail Rides (☎ 435-679-8665; www.canyonrides .com; Grand Canyon Lodge) offers one-hour mule trips ($30) to a rim overlook, and half- or full-day trips into the canyon along the North Kaibab Trail. The full-day, seven-hour trip ($125, minimum age 12 years) to Roaring Springs departs at 7:25am. Lunch and water are provided. Half-day trips ($65, minimum age 10 years) to Supai Tunnel leave at 7:25am and 12:30pm. Unlike mule rides on the South Rim, trips usually don't require reservations; just drop by the Mule Desk inside the lodge. Credit cards are not accepted.

CROSS-COUNTRY SKIING
Once the first heavy snowfall closes Hwy 67 into the park, you can cross-country ski the 44 miles from Jacob Lake to the rim and camp at the campground (no water, pit toilets). It's a serenely beautiful route that takes about three days. Make sure you are well prepared, fit and comfortable in severe weather conditions. Camping is permitted elsewhere on the North Rim with a backcountry permit, available from rangers year-round.

SCENIC DRIVES
Driving on the North Rim involves miles of slow, twisty roads through dense stands

ARIZONA

ARIZONA

GRAND CANYON NORTH RIM IN...

One Day

Arrive at the rim as early as possible and get your first eyeful of the canyon from **Bright Angel Point** (p215). If you didn't bring a picnic, grab a sandwich at the **Deli in the Pines** (p217), then spend the rest of the morning hiking through meadows and aspen on the **Widforss Trail** (p215). In the afternoon, drive out to **Point Imperial** (p216), soak up the view, then backtrack and head out on **Cape Royal** (p216) road. Return to **Grand Canyon Lodge** (p216), grab a coffee and relax in a rough-hewn rocker on the verandah before pointing the wheels back north.

Two Days

Follow the one-day itinerary, wrapping the day up with dinner and a good night's sleep at the **Grand Canyon Lodge** (p216). On day two, hike down the **North Kaibab Trail** (p215) as far as Roaring Springs for a picnic with a side of stunning views. Chill your feet in a cool pool before making the trek back to the top. Don't have buns of steel? Let a **mule** (p215) do the walking.

---

of evergreens and aspen to get to the most spectacular overlooks. From Grand Canyon Lodge, drive north for about 3 miles, then take the signed turn east to Cape Royal and Point Imperial and continue for 5 miles to a fork in the road called the 'Y.'

From the Y it's another 15 miles south to **Cape Royal** (7876ft) past overlooks, picnic tables and an Ancestral Puebloan site. A 0.6-mile paved path, lined with piñon, cliffrose and interpretive signs, leads from the parking lot to a natural arch and Cape Royal Point, arguably the best view from this side of the canyon.

Point Imperial, the park's highest overlook (8803ft), is reached by following Point Imperial Rd from the Y for an easy 3 miles. Expansive views include Nankoweap Creek, the Vermilion Cliffs, the Painted Desert and the Little Colorado River.

The dirt roads to **Point Sublime** (34 miles round-trip; an appropriately named 270-degree overlook) and **Toroweap** (122 miles round-trip; a sheer-drop view of the Colorado River 3000ft below) are rough, require high-clearance vehicles and are not recommended for 2WDs. While they certainly offer amazing views, they require navigating treacherous roads and if your goal is absolute solitude, you might be disappointed. The dirt road to Point Sublime starts about 1 mile west of Hwy 67, 2.7 miles north of Grand Canyon Lodge (look for the Widforss Trail sign). It should take about two hours to drive the 17 miles each way. Toroweap is reached via BLM Rd 109, a rough dirt road heading south off Hwy 389, 9 miles west of Fredonia. The one-way trip is 61 miles and should take at least two hours.

Sleeping

Accommodations on the North Rim are limited to one lodge and one campground.

North Rim Campground (☎ 928-638-7814, 800-365-2267; www.recreationgov.com; campsites $18) This campground, 1.5 miles north of the lodge, offers shaded sites on level ground blanketed in pine needles. Sites 11, 14, 15, 16, 18 and 19 overlook the Transept (a side canyon) and cost $25. There's water, a store, a snack bar, coin-op showers and laundry facilities, but no hookups. Reservations are accepted up to six months in advance.

Grand Canyon Lodge (☎ 480-998-1981, 877-386-4383; www.grandcanyonlodgenorth.com; r $107, cabins $111-156; 🛉) Walk through the front door of Grand Canyon Lodge into the lofty sunroom and there, framed by picture windows, is the canyon in all its glory. Rooms are not in the lodge itself, but in rustic cabins sleeping up to five people. The nicest are the bright and spacious Western cabins, made of logs and buffered by trees and grass. Reserve far in advance; children under 16 sleep free. About 0.5 miles up the road are 40 simple motel rooms, each with a queen bed.

If these two options are fully booked, try snagging a room at the **Kaibab Lodge** (☎ 928-638-2389; www.kaibablodge.com; r $95-155), on Hwy 67 about 6 miles north of the park entrance; it also has a restaurant. Nearby is the first-come, first-served **DeMotte Campground** (campsites $10) with 23 primitive sites. There's also free dispersed camping in the surrounding Kaibab National Forest. Otherwise, you'll find more options another 60 miles north in Kanab, UT (p473).

Eating & Drinking

Deli in the Pines (☎ 928-638-2612; dishes $3-8; ⏱ 7am-8pm) This small cafeteria adjacent to the lodge serves surprisingly good food, although the menu is limited to sandwiches, pizza and a few more simple items.

Rough Rider Saloon (☎ 928-638-2612; ⏱ 5:30am-11pm) For a drink and browse of Teddy Roosevelt memorabilia, pop by this small saloon. Lug your beer to the stone patio behind the lodge, where rough-hewn rocking chairs face the rim and a blazing fire on chilly nights. Rangers offer talks. Espresso drinks and breakfast pastries are served in the early morning.

Grand Canyon Lodge Dining Room (☎ 928-638-2612; mains $9-20; ⏱ breakfast, lunch & dinner) Some people get belligerent if they can't get a window seat, but the canyon-view windows are so huge it really doesn't matter where you sit. The menu includes buffalo steak and vegetarian options, but don't expect any culinary memories. Reservations are not accepted.

Getting There & Around

The only access road to the Grand Canyon North Rim is Hwy 67, which closes with the first snowfall and reopens in spring after the snowmelt (exact dates vary).

Although only 11 miles from the South Rim as the crow flies, it's a grueling 215-mile, four- to five-hour drive on winding desert roads between here and Grand Canyon Village. You can drive yourself or take the **Trans-Canyon Shuttle** (☎ 928-638-2820; one way/round-trip $70/130, no credit cards), which departs from Grand Canyon Lodge at 7am daily to arrive at the South Rim at 11:30am. Reserve at least two weeks in advance.

ARIZONA STRIP

Wedged between the Grand Canyon and Utah, the Arizona Strip is one of the state's most remote and sparsely populated regions. Only about 3000 people live here, in relative isolation, many of them members of the Fundamentalist Church of Latter-Day Saints (FLDS), who defy US law by practicing polygamy. In 2005, authorities cracked down on FLDS headquarters in Colorado City, Arizona, and nearby Hildale, Utah. A couple of years later, church leader Warren Jeffs was sentenced to 10 years in prison for being an accessory to rape. Many members have since relocated to Eldorado, Texas. For more on the subject, see p480 and our interview

with former FLDS member Carolyn Jessop on p479.

Only one major paved road – Hwy 89A – traverses the Arizona Strip. It crosses the Colorado River at Marble Canyon before getting sandwiched by the crimson-hued Vermilion Cliffs to the north and House Rock Valley to the south. Scan the skies for California condors, an endangered species recently reintroduced to the area. Desert scrub gives way to piñon and juniper as the highway climbs up the Kaibab Plateau to enter the Kaibab National Forest. At Jacob Lake, it meets with Hwy 67 to the Grand Canyon North Rim (p214). Past Jacob Lake, as the road drops back down, you'll get stupendous views across southern Utah.

Marble Canyon & Lees Ferry

About 14 miles past the Hwy 89/89A fork, Hwy 89A crosses the Navajo Bridge over the Colorado River at Marble Canyon. Actually, there are two bridges: a modern one for motorists that opened in 1995, and a historical one from 1929. Walking across the latter you'll enjoy fabulous views down Marble Canyon to the northeast lip of the Grand Canyon. The **Navajo Bridge Interpretive Center** (☎ 928-355-2319; ⏱ 9am-5pm Apr-Oct) on the west bank has good background info about the bridges as well as the area and its natural wonders. Keep an eye out for California condors (p218).

Just past the bridge, a paved 6-mile road veers off to the fly-fishing mecca of Lees Ferry. Sitting on a sweeping bend of the Colorado River, it's in the far southwestern corner of Glen Canyon National Recreation Area (p219) and a premier put-in spot for Grand Canyon rafters. Fishing here requires an Arizona fishing license available at local fly shops and outfitters such as **Marble Canyon Outfitters** (☎ 928-645-9235, 800-533-7339; www.leesferryflyfishing.com).

Few visitors realize that Lees Ferry was named for John D Lee, the leader of the 1857 Mountain Meadows Massacre, in which 120 emigrants from Arkansas were brutally murdered by Mormon and Paiute forces. To escape prosecution, Lee moved his wives and children to this remote outpost, where they lived at the **Lonely Dell Ranch** and operated the only ferry service for many miles around. Lee was tracked down and executed in 1877, but the ferry service continued until the Navajo Bridge opened in 1929. You can walk around

---

CALIFORNIA CONDORS AT VERMILION CLIFFS

California condors are imposing creatures, but pretty they ain't. Bright pink or orange featherless heads perch on chunky black bodies about twice the size of your Thanksgiving turkey. Their wingspan is longer than an NBA player is tall. But see them in the sky and they're as graceful and balletic as Rudolf Nureyev in his prime.

The tale of the California condor is a tale of survival. In prehistoric times, condors patrolled the skies across the entire continent, feeding on carcasses of mastodons, camels and saber-toothed cats. When these species died out, the birds retreated to a stronghold along the Pacific Coast from Canada to Mexico, surviving primarily on large sea mammals. But by 1982, shrinking habitats, egg collecting, DDT pollution and lead poisoning had brought the species to the verge of extinction, with only 22 birds remaining in the wild. So zoologists from the Los Angeles Zoo and the San Diego Wild Animal Park scooped them up, put them in captive breeding programs and hoped for the best.

Fortunately, this sorry tale has a happy ending. Since 1987, the condor population has climbed steadily back up to just over 300 birds. In 1996, six of them were released at Arizona's Vermilion Cliffs, a rugged and remote escarpment between Marble Canyon and Jacob Lake, whose caves, ledges and inaccessible cliffs provide ideal nesting conditions. By 2007, more than 60 birds were again flapping their enormous wings. In summer, they can sometimes be spotted at the Grand Canyon South Rim, but chances of seeing them year-round are greatest at their release site off Hwy 89A. Turn right onto House Rock Valley Rd (BLM Rd 1065, about 13 miles past Cliff Dwellers Lodge) and drive about 3 miles to a kiosk and viewing area.

Lonely Dell Ranch and have a picnic amid the stone house and the log cabins.

On a small hill, **Lees Ferry Campground** (campsites $12) has 54 riverview sites along with drinking water and toilets but no hookups. Public coin showers are at **Marble Canyon Lodge** (☎ 928-355-2225, 800-726-1789; Hwy 89A; 1br s/d $58/68, 2br $74, apt $145) a half-mile west of Navajo Bridge, which has 45 rooms and suites as well as a restaurant, store and bar. Other options include the rustic but comfortable **Lees Ferry Lodge** (☎ 928-355-2231, 800-451-2231; Hwy 89A; d $55-100), 3 miles west of Navajo Bridge, which has 12 rooms plus a restaurant and bar with 100 international beers.

Jacob Lake

From Marble Canyon, Hwy 89A climbs 5000ft over 40 miles to the Kaibab National Forest and the oddly lakeless outpost of Jacob Lake. All you find is a motel with a restaurant, a gas station and the USFS **Kaibab Plateau Visitor Center** (☎ 928-643-7298; 8am-5pm May-Oct). From here Hwy 67 runs south for 44 miles past meadows, aspen and ponderosa pine to the Grand Canyon North Rim. The only facilities between Jacob Lake and the rim are the Kaibab Lodge (p216), North Rim Country Store and DeMotte Campground (p216), about 18 miles south.

Camping is free in the national forest or you can try **Jacob Lake Inn** (☎ 928-643-7232; www

.jacoblake.com; r $75-135), which has no-frills cabins with tiny bathrooms, run-down motel rooms and spacious doubles in the modern hotel-style building. There's also a **restaurant** (6:30am-9pm) with a great bakery and ice-cream counter. Pets welcome.

Kaibab Lodge Camper Village (☎ 928-643-7804; Hwy 67; campsites $12-23; mid-May-Oct), a mile south of Jacob's Lake, has more than 100 sites for tents and RVs.

Fredonia
pop 1100 / elev 4925ft

The main town in the Arizona Strip is postage-stamp-sized Fredonia, some 30 miles northwest of Jacob Lake. The only reason to put on the brakes is if you can't find lodgings in or closer to the Grand Canyon North Rim. Otherwise, push on to Kanab (p472), 7 miles north in Utah, which has much better tourist infrastructure. Fredonia has the **Kaibab National Forest District Headquarters** (☎ 928-643-7395; 430 S Main St; 8am-5pm Mon-Fri), where you can pick up info on hiking and camping in the forest.

The nicest quarters in town are at the **Juniper Lodge** (☎ 928-643-7752; www.juniperlodge .info; 465 S Main St; r $60), which also operates the town's only restaurant, the **Sage House Grill** (mains $5-22; breakfast, lunch & dinner). It serves '$7 bucks salads,' '$8 bucks sandwiches' and '$12 bucks dinner.'

PAGE & GLEN CANYON NATIONAL RECREATION AREA

An enormous lake tucked into a landlocked swath of desert? You can guess how popular it is to play in the spangly waters of **Lake Powell**. The country's second-largest reservoir and part of the **Glen Canyon National Recreation Area** (☎ 928-608-6200; www.nps.gov/glca; 7-day pass per vehicle $15) was created by the construction of Glen Canyon Dam in 1963. To house the scores of workers, an entire town called Page was built from scratch near the dam. Now a modern town with hotels, restaurants and supermarkets, it's a handy base for lake visitors.

Straddling the Utah–Arizona border, the 186-mile-long lake has 1960 miles of empty shoreline set amid striking red-rock formations, sharply cut canyons and dramatic desert scenery. Lake Powell is famous for its houseboating, which appeals hugely to families and college students alike. Though hundreds of houseboats ply its waters at any given time, it's possible to explore its secluded inlets, bays, coves and beaches for days with hardly seeing anyone at all.

Unfortunately, the reservoir's future is in grave danger because of a protracted drought that has sent water levels to below 50% of capacity since 1999, exposing petroglyphs, arches, caves, dino tracks and other previously submerged features. Although the 2008 snow pack was about 20% above average, it's quite literally a drop in the bucket as demand for water in thirsty cities such as Phoenix, Las Vegas and Los Angeles continues to grow. For more on the subject, see www.livingrivers.org.

Orientation

The gateway to Lake Powell is the small town of Page (population 6800), which sits right next to Glen Canyon Dam in the far southwest corner of the recreation area. Hwy 89 (called N Lake Powell Blvd in town) forms the main strip.

Aramark (☎ 800-528-6154; www.lakepowell.com) runs five of the lake's six marinas, including the often frenetic **Wahweap Marina** (☎ 928-645-2433), 6 miles north of Page. The only other marina on the Arizona side is the much more peaceful **Antelope Point Marina** (☎ 928-645-5900, ext 5), which opened in 2007 on the Navajo Reservation, about 8 miles east of Page. Marinas rent boats, kayaks, jet skis and water skis and have stores, restaurants and other services.

Information

Digital Lands (☎ 928-645-2241; 40 S Lake Powell Blvd; per hr $6; ☿ 10am-10am; 💻) Internet access.

Hospital (☎ 928-645-2424; 501 N Navajo Dr)

Library (☎ 928-645-4270; 479 S Lake Powell Blvd; ☿ 10am-8pm Mon-Thu, 10am-5pm Fri & Sat; 💻 wi-fi) Free internet.

Visitor center (☎ 928-645-2741; 608 Elm St; ☿ 8am-6pm Mon-Sat Apr-Jun, 7am-7pm daily Jul-Oct, 8am-5pm Mon-Fri Nov-Mar)

Sights

ANTELOPE CANYON

Unearthly in its beauty, **Antelope Canyon** (www.navajonationparks.org/htm/antelopecanyon.htm) is a hotspot slot canyon on the Navajo Reservation a few miles east of Page and open to tourists by Navajo-led tour only. Wind and water have carved sandstone into an astonishingly sensuous temple of nature where light and shadow play hide and seek. Less than a city block long (about a quarter-mile), its symphony of shapes and textures are a photographer's wet dream. Lighting conditions are best around mid-morning between April and September, but the other months bring smaller crowds and a more intimate experience.

Four tour companies offer trips into upper Antelope Canyon; **Antelope Slot Canyon Tours** (☎ 928-645-5594; www.antelopeslotcanyon.com; 55 S Lake Powell Blvd), owned by Chief Tsotsie, is recommended. The 90-minute sightseeing tour costs $29, while the 2½-hour photographic tour is $46; both include the $6 Navajo Permit Fee. The company also offers tours to lesser-known Cathedral Canyon.

JOHN WESLEY POWELL MUSEUM

In 1869 one-armed John Wesley Powell led the first Colorado River expedition through the Grand Canyon. This small **museum** (☎ 928-645-9496; www.powellmuseum.org; 64 N Lake Powell Blvd; admission $5; ☿ 9am-5pm mid-Feb–mid-Dec) displays memorabilia of early river runners, including a model of Powell's boat, and photos and illustrations of his excursions.

GLEN CANYON DAM

At 710ft tall, Glen Canyon Dam is the nation's second-highest concrete arch dam – only Hoover Dam is higher, by 16ft. Guided 45-minute tours departing from the **Carl Hayden Visitor Center** (☎ 928-608-6404; ☿ 8am-5pm Mar–mid-May, Sep & Oct; 8am-6pm mid-May–Aug) take you deep inside the dam via elevators. Tours run every

ARIZONA

DETOUR: PIPE SPRING NATIONAL MONUMENT

Fourteen miles southwest of Fredonia on Hwy 389, **Pipe Spring** (☎ 928-643-7105; www.nps.gov/pisp; adult/child $5/free; 🕑 7am-5pm Jun-Aug, 8am-5pm Sep-May) is quite literally an oasis in the desert. Visitors can experience the Old West amid cabins and corrals, an orchard, ponds and a garden. In summer, rangers and costumed volunteers re-enact various pioneer tasks. Tours (on the hour and half-hour) let you peek inside the stone **Winsor Castle** (🕑 8am-4:30pm Jun-Aug, 9am-4pm Sep-May), and there's also a small **museum** (🕑 7am-5pm Jun-Aug, 8am-5pm Sep-May) that examines the turbulent history of local Paiutes and Mormon settlers.

---

half-hour from 8:30am to 4pm in summer (less frequently the rest of the year). Displays and videos in the visitor center tell the story of the dam's construction and offer technical facts on water flow, generator output etc. The dam is a short drive north of Page via Hwy 89.

RAINBOW BRIDGE NATIONAL MONUMENT
On the south shore of Lake Powell, about 50 miles by water from Wahweap Marina, **Rainbow Bridge** (☎ 928-608-6404; www.nps.gov/rabr; admission $4) is the largest natural bridge in the world at 290ft high and 275ft wide. A sacred Navajo site, it resembles the graceful arc of a rainbow. Most visitors arrive by boat (below), but experienced backpackers can also drive along dirt roads to access two unmaintained trails (each 28 miles round-trip) on the Navajo Reservation. Tribal permits are required. Check with the **Navajo Parks & Recreation Department** (☎ 928-871-6647; www.navajonationparks .org) on how to obtain one.

Activities
BOATING & CRUISES
Marinas rent kayaks (single/double $26/32 per day in peak season, June to August), 19ft powerboats ($375), wakeboards ($41), kneeboards ($27) and other toys. From Wahweap Marina, **Aramark** (☎ 800-528-6154; www.lakepowell .com) offers boat cruises to Rainbow Bridge (all day adult/child $124/84 April to October; half day $81/50 mid-June to October). Because of low water levels, seeing the arches is no longer possible from the boat but involves a 2-mile round-trip hike. Dinner cruises, sunset cruises and trips to Navajo Canyon (adult/child $59/35) and the waterside of Antelope Canyon ($38/23) are also offered.

HIKING & MOUNTAIN BIKING
Ask at the Page visitor center (p219) or the Carl Hayden Visitor Center (p219) at Glen Canyon Dam for information and maps of the area's many hiking and mountain-biking trails. **Lakeside Bikes** (☎ 928-645-2266; 12 N Lake Powell Blvd) rents mountain bikes for $25 per day.

The most popular hike is the 1.5-mile round-trip trek to the overlook at **Horseshoe Bend**, where the river wraps around a dramatic stone outcropping to form a perfect U. Though it's short, the sandy, shadeless trail and moderate incline can be a slog. Toddlers should be secured safely in a backpack, as there are no guardrails at the viewpoint. The trailhead is south of Page off Hwy 89, just across from mile marker 541.

The 15-mile **Rimview Trail**, a mix of sand, slickrock and other terrain, bypasses the town and offers views of the surrounding desert and Lake Powell. While there are several access points (pick up a brochure from the museum or chamber of commerce), a popular starting point is behind Lake View School at the end of N Navajo Dr.

Sleeping
You can camp anywhere along the Lake Powell shoreline for free as long as you have a portable toilet or toilet facilities on your boat.

Page-Lake Powell Campground (☎ 928-645-3374; www.pagecampground.com; 849 S Coppermine Rd; tent/RV sites $18/23; 🏊) At this campground just out of town you'll find RV sites with hookups, a few tent sites, a newly revamped indoor pool and hot tub, a store, laundry facilities and showers.

Debbie's Hide-A-Way (☎ 928-645-1224; www .debbieshideaway.com; 117 8th Ave; ste $40-160; 💻) The owners encourage you to feel right at home – throw a steak on the grill, leaf through a book or just hang out with other guests among the roses and fruit trees. In 2007 the rooms received a much-needed face-lift, with new tiles, paint and carpet, and all have kitchens. There are free laundry facilities.

Lulu's Sleep Ezze Motel (☎ 928-608-0273, 800-553-6211; 105 8th Ave; r $50-65; 🕑 mid-Mar–Oct; wi-fi)

Seven bright and newly renovated rooms share a small patio with two large tables, rattan umbrellas, two barbecues and pebble landscaping.

Days Inn (☎ 928-645-2800; 961 N Hwy 89; r $60-140, ste $70-190; 🕹 ⬜ wi-fi) The best value among the chains, this immaculate property has handsome, mod-con-equipped rooms, as well as some cool, oversized suites with Jacuzzis for two. Rates include a continental breakfast. Children under 18 stay free. Pets cost $10.

Canyon Colors B&B (☎ 928-645-5979, 800-536-2530; www.canyoncolors.com; 225 S Navajo Dr; r $85-120; 🕹) For a little more character, check into this two-room B&B, about 6 miles from the lakeshore. Rooms have refrigerators, fireplaces, a sitting area and stuffed animals. In the back yard there is a small grassy area, a patio with a barbecue for guest use, and a raised pool.

Lake Powell Resort (☎ 928-645-2433; www.lake powell.com; 100 Lake Shore Dr; RV sites $32, r $140-180; 🕹 ⬜ wi-fi) Six miles north of Page and right on the lake, this ecofriendly resort (a member of the Green Hotel Association) has fairly basic rooms, some with unbeatable views. A small pool perches on red rocks and overlooks the water, and huge windows in the dining room offer panoramic views. The concierge can arrange boat tours and rentals.

Eating & Drinking

Bean's Coffee (☎ 928-645-6858; 644F N Navajo Dr; dishes $3-7; 🕒 breakfast & lunch; wi-fi) While the coffee runs weak, this tiny café serves good breakfast burritos and sandwiches that make great picnic lunches to go.

Slackers (☎ 928-645-5267; 635 Elm St; sandwiches $3.50-8.50, mains $11-18; 🕒 lunch & dinner) At lunchtime lines can be long at this upbeat patty-and-bun joint that serves burgers, beer, sandwiches and giggles. Order from the huge chalkboard menu, then wait for your grub to be delivered to your booth or an outside table.

Ranch House Grill (☎ 928-645-1420; 819 N Navajo Dr; dishes $6-11; 🕒 6am-3pm) *The* breakfast joint, the Ranch offers good food, huge portions and fast service. After a three-egg omelette and two huge pancakes, you won't need to stop for lunch.

Blue Buddha Sushi Lounge (☎ 928-645-2161; 544 N Navajo Dr; dishes $7-15; 🕒 dinner Tue-Sat) Big-city sophistication in hard-scrabble Page? It's hard to believe, but Buddha delivers with cool design, a jazzy vibe and interesting – if unconventional – sushi creations such as the Dam Roll

(seared beef tenderloin paired with yellowtail). Enter through the alley off Dam Plaza.

Dam Bar & Grille (☎ 928-645-2161; 644 N Navajo Dr; lunch $6-12, dinner $7-25; 🕒 lunch & dinner) Raft guides recommend this place for its dependable pub fare and microbrewery vibe. If you're really hungry, try the Dam Big Burger, a one-pounder with fries for $12. The patio is pleasant on summer evenings, despite the strip-mall view.

Fiesta Mexicana (☎ 928-645-4082; 125 S Powell Blvd; mains $8-17; 🕒 lunch & dinner) It's always fiesta time at this cheerful cantina where the *cerveza* (beer) is cold and the portions ample enough to share. The seafood enchilada is a big fat bonanza of shrimp, crab meat, scallops and calamari.

Getting There & Around

Page is served by Hwy 89 from Flagstaff (135 miles). Coming from Monument Valley, you can cut over on Hwy 98 (100 miles).

Great Lakes Airlines (☎ 928-645-1355, 800-554-5111; www.greatlakesav.com) offers flights between Page Municipal Airport and Phoenix, Prescott, Show Low and Sierra Vista (Arizona), as well as Denver (Colorado) and Farmington (New Mexico).

NAVAJO RESERVATION

pop 88,000

John Wayne galloping into the sunset amid fiery red buttes. The Marlboro Man gazing towards a horizon of towering cliffs. Forrest Gump running along a lonely highway. Even if we've never been there, images from the Navajo Reservation have been deeply etched into our collective memory by movies and TV. At 27,000 sq miles the Navajo Reservation is the country's largest, spilling over into the neighboring states of Utah, Colorado and New Mexico. Most of this land is as flat as a calm sea and barren almost without relief until – all of a sudden – Monument Valley's crimson red buttes rise before you or you come face to face with ancient history at the cliff dwellings at Canyon de Chelly and Navajo National Monuments. Elsewhere you can walk in dinosaur tracks or be mesmerized by the shifting light of hauntingly beautiful Antelope Canyon (p219).

While it's true that this remote northeastern corner of the state embraces some of Arizona's most photogenic and iconic landscapes, there's also plenty of evidence of the poverty, depression

ARIZONA

and alcoholism that ravish Native American communities to this day. You'll see it in rusting, ramshackle trailers, or in crumbling social services buildings in small nowhere towns, or in the paucity of stores and businesses.

Many Navajo rely on the tourist economy for survival. You can help keep their heritage alive by staying on reservation land, purchasing their crafts or trying their foods such as the ubiquitous Navajo taco (p64).

For historic background on the Navajo, see p56. Tips on reservation etiquette can be found on p61.

Information

Unlike Arizona, the Navajo Reservation observes daylight saving time. The single best source of information for the entire reservation is the **Navajo Tourism Office** (☎ 928-871-6436; www.discovernavajo.com).

Getting There & Around

You really need your own wheels to properly explore this sprawling land. Gas stations are scarce and fuel prices are higher than outside the reservation.

The only public transportation is provided by the **Navajo Transit System** (☎ 928-729-4002, 866-243-6260; www.navajotransit.com), but services are geared towards local, not tourist, needs. It operates daily buses on seven routes, including one that goes from Tuba City to Window Rock via the Hopi Reservation. There's also service between Kayenta, near Monument Valley, to Window Rock via Chinle and Tsaile near Canyon de Chelly; and from Window Rock to Gallup in New Mexico.

TUBA CITY

pop 7300 / elev 4936ft

A small outpost in nowhere land, at the intersection of Hwys 160 and 264, hard-scrabble Tuba City would be skippable were it not for its new and excellent museum on Navajo culture. The town itself sits on Navajoland but was named for 19th-century Hopi chief Tuve (or Toova). It's a good base if you're headed for the Hopi mesas (p227).

Open since June 2007, the engaging multimedia **Explore Navajo Interactive Museum** (☎ 928-640-0684; www.explorenavajo.com; cnr Main St & Moenave Rd; adult/child/senior $9/6/7; ⏰ 10am-8pm Mon-Sat, noon-8pm Sun) is a perfect introductory stop for your reservation explorations and will deepen your understanding of the land, its people and their traditions. You'll learn why the Navajo call themselves the 'People of the Fourth World,' the difference between male and female hogans (traditional homes of the Navajo) and what the Long Walk was all about. Such aspects of contemporary life as education, the role of the elders and the popularity of rodeo, are all addressed in creative ways that will appeal to everyone from school kids to grizzled travel veterans.

Visits wrap up in the historic **Tuba Trading Post**, which dates back to the 1880s and sells authentic Native American arts and crafts.

Grey Hills Inn (☎ 928-283-4450; cnr Hwy 160 & Warrior Dr; r $45-55; wi-fi), a student training facility in a converted high-school dormitory, has good-sized, carpeted rooms with one, two or three beds, plus cable TV and phones. Bathrooms, though, require a trek down the hall.

As comfy as things get on the reservations, the modern and well-maintained **Quality Inn** (☎ 928-283-4545, 800-644-8383; www.explorenavajo.com; cnr Main St & Moenave Rd; r $90-120; 🖳 wi-fi) welcomes you with a cozy lobby with fluffy sofas and historical photographs; pet rates are $10. Room rates include breakfast at the popular next-door **Hogan Restaurant** (☎ 928-283-5260; cnr Main St & Moenave Rd; mains $7-15; ⏰ breakfast, lunch & dinner), which has an extensive menu of Southwestern,

---

WHAT THE...?

It stretches the imagination that once upon a time – say a cool 65 million years ago – dinosaurs roamed this empty and barren part of Arizona, which, back then, was blanketed by lush forest. Much to the delight of dino fans, some of these critters left their fossilized tracks in the desert floor about 5 miles west of Tuba City off Hwy 160. A crude sign beckons you to turn onto a dirt track where Native Americans are waiting by a roadside stand, eager to show you the best Jurassic tracks for a tip (they may ask for as much as $15 per person for the short tour, but feel free to give them whatever you wish). If you prefer exploring on your own, look for three-toed footprints about 10in to 12in wide left by a creature called Dilophosaurus. And yes, *Jurassic Park* fans, that's the beast that lunches on Dennis Nedry's character in the first movie.

Navajo and American dishes. For your cappuccino fix or web-surfing session, swing by **Hogan Espresso & More** (cnr Main St & Moenave Rd).

Kate's Café (☎ 928-283-6773; cnr Main St & Edgewater Dr; dishes $3-10; ☺ breakfast, lunch & dinner) is a popular diner in an adobe building. Kate has a large breakfast menu, lunchtime sandwiches and seafood, steak and pasta plates at dinner.

NAVAJO NATIONAL MONUMENT
elev 7300ft

The sublimely well-preserved Ancestral Puebloan cliff dwellings of Betatkin and Keet Seel are protected as the **Navajo National Monument** (☎ 928-672-2700; www.nps.gov/nava; Hwy 564; admission free; ☺ 8am-5pm late May-Sep) and can only be reached on foot. It's no walk in the park, but there's truly something magical about approaching these ancient stone villages in relative solitude. The site is administered by the National Park Service, which controls access and maintains a visitor center 9 miles north of Hwy 160 at the end of paved Hwy 564. For a distant glimpse of Betatkin follow the easy Sandal Trail about half a mile from the center. There's a free campground, with 31 first-come, first-served sites, and water nearby.

Betatkin, which translates as 'ledge house,' is reached on a ranger-led 2.5-mile hike departing from the visitor center daily at 8:20am and 11am between June and September. Groups are limited to 25 people. Ranger availability and weather permitting, there's also a tour at 10am during the other months; be sure to phone ahead. Carry plenty of water; it's a tough slog back up to the canyon rim.

The 8.5-mile trail to the astonishingly beautiful **Keet Seel** is steep, strenuous and involves crossing sand gullies and shallow streams, but it's well worth the effort. The trail is open from late May to early September and requires a backcountry permit reservable up to five months in advance. Do call early since daily access is limited to 20 people; alternatively show up early on the day and hope for cancelations. You hike on your own but are met at the pueblo by a ranger who will take you on a tour. Most hikers stay at the primitive campground down in the canyon, which has composting toilets but no drinking water.

KAYENTA
pop 5300 / elev 5641ft

'Kayenta' is Navajo for 'bog hole' and, trust us, the town is about as appealing as one. It's not really a town at all: more like a bunch of businesses and a few trailer homes clustered around the junction of Hwys 160 and 163. Frankly, the only thing it's got going is being the closest town to Monument Valley, some 20 miles away. As such, it does have the kind of infrastructure road-trippers need: gas stations, motels, restaurants, a supermarket, a bank with ATM and, as a bonus, even a tiny movie theater. The **visitor center** (☎ 928-697-3572; Hwy 160), in a neat hogan-shaped building, keeps erratic hours and presents dances and other cultural events in summer.

The Burger King near the junction has a well-meaning but minimal exhibit on the Navajo Code Talkers. **Roland's Navajoland Tours** (☎ 928-697-3524) and **Sacred Monument Tours** (☎ 435-727-3218; www.monumentvalley.net) offer vehicle, hiking and horseback riding tours through Monument Valley.

A dearth of options sends prices sky-high in summer when demand at the three main chain motels exceeds capacity. Rates drop by nearly half in the slower seasons.

A step up from run-of-the-mill motels, the **Hampton Inn** (☎ 928-697-3170; www.monumentvalleyonline.com; junction Hwys 160 & 163; r incl breakfast $70-140; ⬛ wi-fi) boasts a restaurant, Native American decor and an outdoor pool perfect for chilling after a day on the dusty roads. Kids under 18 stay free. Pets OK.

The largest hotel in town, **Holiday Inn** (☎ 928-697-3221; www.holidayinnkayenta.com; junction Hwys 160 & 163; r $80-150; ⬛ ⬛ ⬛ wi-fi) is a winning respite from the road with 164 rooms, a separate splash pool and a decent restaurant where kids eat free.

Recently spruced up, **Best Western Wetherill Inn** (☎ 928-697-3231, 800-528-1234; 1000 Main St/Hwy 63; r incl breakfast May–mid-Oct $122, mid-Oct–Apr $65-80; ⬛ ⬛ wi-fi) has 54 standard-issue rooms hued in an appealing color scheme. All have refrigerators and there's an indoor pool as well.

Behind the Wetherill Inn, **Golden Sands Cafe** (☎ 928-697-3684; Hwy 163; lunch $4.50-11, dinner $8.50-19; ☺ 7am-8pm Mon-Fri, 7am-3:30pm Sat & Sun) is a friendly-feeling roadhouse with authentic Old West touches and a casual menu of American and Navajo dishes.

Amigo Cafe (☎ 928-697-8448; Hwy 163; breakfast & lunch $5-8, dinner $7-15; ☺ 10:30am-8pm Mon-Fri, 8am-8pm Sat) is an unassuming pit stop run by a Mexican family where you can fortify yourself on ginormous burritos, enchiladas and other staples.

ARIZONA

ARIZONA

MONUMENT VALLEY NAVAJO TRIBAL PARK

Like a classic movie star, Monument Valley has a face known round the world. Her fiery red spindles, sheer-walled mesas and grand buttes have starred in flicks and commercials, and have been featured in magazine ads and picture books. You might not know her name, but you've likely seen her photo framed in your neighbor's living room.

Monument Valley's epic beauty is heightened by the drab landscape surrounding it. One minute you're in the middle of nowhere, just sand and rocks and infinite sky, then suddenly you're transported to a fantasyland of crimson sandstone towers soaring skyward up to 1200ft. It's a superlative sensory experience.

Long before the land became part of the Navajo Reservation, the valley was home to Ancestral Puebloans, who abruptly abandoned the site some 700 years ago. When the Navajo arrived a few centuries ago, they called it 'Valley Between the Rocks.' Today, Monument Valley straddles the Arizona–Utah border and is traversed by Hwy 163.

The most famous formations are conveniently visible from the rough 17-mile dirt road looping through **Monument Valley Navajo Tribal Park** (☎ 435-727-3287; adult/child under 10 $5/free; ☻ 6am-8:30pm May-Sep, 8am-4:30pm Oct-Apr). It's usually possible to drive it in your own vehicle, even standard passenger cars, but expect a dusty, bumpy ride. There are multiple overlooks where you can get out and snap away or browse for trinkets and jewelry offered by Navajo vendors. Most of the formations have whimsical names like the Mittens, Eagle Rock, Bear & Rabbit and Elephant Butte. Budget at least 1½ hours for the drive, which starts from the visitor center at the end of a 4-mile paved road off Hwy 163 at Goulding. There's also a restaurant, a tour desk and the new View Hotel, which was still under construction at press time. (Note that National Parks and Golden Eagle Passes are not accepted for admission into the park.)

The only way to get off the road and into the backcountry is by taking a **Navajo-led tour** on foot or horseback or by vehicle. Rates start at $40. You'll see rock art, natural arches and coves such as the otherworldly 'Ear of the Wind,' a bowl-shaped wall with a nearly circular opening at the top. Guides shower you with details about the life on the reservation, movie trivia and whatever else comes to mind. Tours leave frequently in summer, less so in winter; inquire at the visitor center. Outfitters in Kayenta and at Goulding's Lodge also offer tours.

The only hiking trail you are allowed to take without a guide is the **Wildcat Trail**, a 3.2-mile loop trail around the West Mitten formation. The trailhead is at the picnic area, about a half-mile north of the visitor center.

By the time you're reading this, the new **View Hotel** (www.monumentvalleyview.com) next to the visitor center should have opened; call ☎ 435-727-3470 or check the website to find out more. For additional accommodation and food options, see Kayenta (p223).

The 100 campsites of the tribally operated **Mitten View Campground** (campsites Apr-Sep $10, Oct-Mar $5) are available first-come, first-served and fill quickly in summer. There are toilets, coin-op hot showers (closed in winter) and water, but no hookups.

The historic **Goulding's Lodge** (☎ 435-727-3231; www.gouldings.com; r mid-Mar–mid-Nov $123-180, mid-Nov–mid-Mar $73-80; ☒ wi-fi) delivers million-dollar views from private balconies attached to 62 modern, motel-style rooms dressed in appealing Southwest color and patterns. Amenities include a DVD player so you can watch one of the locally shot Westerns available for rent ($5). **Goulding's campground** (tent/RV sites $24/38) comes with a slew of comforts, including full hookups, hot showers and a laundromat. Campers are welcome to use the lodge's indoor pool. The campground is open year-round, but with limited service from November to mid-March.

Goulding's restaurant, **Stagecoach Dining Room** (mains $10-22; ☻ breakfast, lunch & dinner), is a replica of a film set built for John Ford's 1949 Western *She Wore a Yellow Ribbon*. Get a vitamin kick from the salad bar before tucking into the steaks or Navajo tacos piled high with chile and cheese. At lunchtime it often swarms with coach tourists.

CANYON DE CHELLY NATIONAL MONUMENT

It's a near soundless world, this remote and beautiful multipronged Canyon de Chelly (pronounced 'd-*shay*'), far removed from time and space. Inhabited for 5000 years, it shelters prehistoric rock art and 1000-year-old Ancestral Puebloan dwellings built into sheltering alcoves.

Today, Canyon de Chelly is private Navajo land administered by the NPS. The name itself is a corruption of the Navajo word *tsegi*, which means 'rock canyon.' The Navajo arrived in the canyon in the 1700s and used it for farming and as a stronghold and retreat for their raids on other tribes and Spanish settlers. But if these cliffs could talk, they'd also tell stories of great violence and tragedy. In 1805, Spanish soldiers killed scores of Navajo hiding deep in the canyon in what is now called Massacre Cave. And in 1864, the US Army – led by Kit Carson – drove thousands of Navajos into the canyon and starved them into surrendering, then forced the survivors to march 300 miles – the Long Walk – to Fort Sumner in New Mexico. Four years later, the Navajos were allowed to return.

Today, about 80 Navajo families still raise animals and grow corn, squash and beans on the land, allowing you a glimpse of traditional life. Only enter hogans with a guide and don't take photographs without permission.

Orientation & Information

The mouth of the canyon is about 3 miles east of **Chinle**, where services include motels, a gas station, a supermarket, a bank with ATM and fast-food outlets. En route to the canyon you'll pass the **visitor center** (☎ 928-674-5500; www.nps.gov/cach; ☻ 8am-5pm), which has information on guides and tours. Scenic drives skirting the canyon's northern and southern rim start nearby. Both are open year-round and, aside from one hiking trail, the only way to see the canyon without joining a guided tour.

Sights & Activities

If you only have time for one trip, make it the **South Rim Drive**, which runs along the main canyon and has the most dramatic vistas. The 16-mile road passes six viewpoints before dead-ending at the spectacular Spider Rock Overlook, with views of the 800ft free-standing tower atop of which lives Spider Woman. The Navajos say that she carries off children who don't listen to their parents! Budget about two hours for the round-trip, including stops.

For the most part, **North Rim Drive** actually follows a side canyon called Canyon del Muerto. It has four overlooks and ends at the Massacre Cave Overlook, 15 miles from the visitor center. The road continues 13 miles to the town of **Tsaile** (say-*lee*), where Diné College has an excellent museum as well as a library and bookstore with a vast selection of books about the Navajo.

Bring binoculars and water, lock your car and don't leave valuables in sight when taking the short walks at each scenic point. The lighting for photography on the north rim is best in early morning and on the south rim in late afternoon.

Tours

Entering the canyon maze is an amazing experience as walls start at just a few feet but rise dramatically, topping out at about 1000ft. At many stops, Navajo vendors sell jewelry and crafts, usually at prices much lower than at the trading posts. Summer tours can get stifling hot and mosquitoes are plentiful, so bring a hat, sunscreen, water and insect repellent.

HIKING

With one exception, you need a guide in order to hike anywhere in the canyon. Several authorized Navajos usually hang around the visitor center and rangers will happily help you make arrangements and obtain the necessary (free) permit. Guides charge $15 per hour for groups of up to 15 with a three-hour minimum. Overnight trips can be arranged as well. Rangers sometimes lead free half-day hikes in summer.

Otherwise, the steep and stunning **White House Trail** is your only option. Narrow switchbacks drop 550ft down from the White House Overlook on the South Rim Drive, about 6 miles east of the visitor center. It's only 1.25 miles to the stupendous White House Ruin, but coming back up is strenuous, so carry plenty of water and allow at least two hours. In summer, start out early or late in the day to avoid the worst of the heat.

HORSEBACK RIDING

Justin's Horse Tours (☎ 928-674-5678; www.justinshorserental.com), at the mouth of the canyon, has horses available year-round for $15 per person per hour plus $15 an hour for the guide (two-hour minimum). **Totsonii Ranch** (☎ 928-755-6209; www.totsoniiranch.com), about 1¼-mile beyond the end of the pavement on South Rim Drive, charges the same. The most popular ride is the four-hour round-trip to Spider Rock. Both companies also arrange overnight trips starting at $200.

FOUR-WHEEL DRIVING

It's a tough slog, but if you have a 4WD with high clearance you may drive yourself into the canyon accompanied by an authorized Navajo guide, several of whom usually vie for customers by the visitor center. They charge $15 per hour for one vehicle and $5 for each additional vehicle with a three-hour minimum. Heavy rain in late summer or ice in winter may make the roads impassable.

If you prefer to have someone else doing the driving, consider a tour offered by **Thunderbird Lodge Tours** (☎ 928-674-5841; www.tbirdlodge.com), based at the Thunderbird Lodge (below). They use Suburbans for small groups or, in summer, open-top heavy-duty 6WD propane-fuelled US army Korean War troop carriers. Locals call these 'shake-n-bake' tours. Half-day trips leave at 9am and 1pm or 2pm and cost $43/33 for adults/children. All-day tours ($70, no discounts) operate from March to November and include a picnic lunch.

Check with the visitor center for additional tour operators.

Sleeping & Eating

Lodging near the canyon is limited and often booked solid in summer, so plan ahead.

Cottonwood Campground (campsites free) Near the visitor center, this NPS-run campground has 93 primitive sites on a first-come, first-served basis. Water is available from April to October, and there are restrooms but no hookups or showers.

Spider Rock Campground (☎ 928-674-8261, 877-910-2267; www.spiderrockcampground.com; tent/RV sites $10/15, hogans $29-39; wi-fi) This Navajo-run campground 12 miles from the visitor center along South Rim Drive is surrounded by piñon and juniper trees. It has solar-heated showers ($2.50) and free wi-fi and the owner sells drinking water, snacks, espresso drinks and firewood. Tent rentals are $9. In winter, you can stay in a hand-built hogan. Pets are OK.

Thunderbird Lodge (☎ 928-674-5841, 800-679-2473; www.tbirdlodge.com; d Mar-Oct $111, Nov-Feb $69; wi-fi) The closest lodging to the canyon entrance, this all-Navajo-staffed member of the Green Hotels Association has 73 rooms with TV and phone, most of them in a pink adobe lodge. The cafeteria (open from 6:30am to 9pm, with shorter winter hours), though nicely decorated with Navajo rugs and art from the adjacent gift shop, offers very mediocre American and Navajo food. There's also a nice grassy area that's great for kids or just hanging out reading.

Other options:

Best Western Canyon de Chelly Inn (☎ 928-674-5875, 800-327-0354; www.canyondechelly.com; r $80-

120; ☒ wi-fi) In Chinle but still close to the canyon, this property has an indoor pool, restaurant and sauna.

Holiday Inn (☎ 928-674-5000; www.holidayinnchinle.com; r $70-140; ☒ ☖ wi-fi) Half a mile west of the visitor center, you'll find modern rooms, a restaurant and a heated outdoor pool. Kids eat and stay free.

GANADO & HUBBELL TRADING POST
elev 6300ft

Widely respected merchant John Lorenzo Hubbell established this **trading post** (☎ 928-755-3475; www.nps.gov/hutr; admission free; ☺ 8am-6pm May-early Sep, 8am-5pm mid-Sep–Apr) in 1878 to supply Navajos returning from Fort Sumner with dry goods and groceries. Now run by the NPS, it still sells food, souvenirs and local crafts. Navajo women often give weaving demonstrations inside the visitor center. Hubbell himself was an avid collector of these woolen artworks as you'll discover on a tour of his house (adult/child $2/free), given at the top of the hour.

The post is in the village of Ganado, about 30 miles south of Chinle/Canyon de Chelly and 40 miles north of the I-40.

WINDOW ROCK
pop 3500 / elev 6900ft

The tribal capital of Window Rock is a bustling little place at the intersection of Hwys 264 and 12, near the New Mexico border. The namesake rock is a nearly circular arch high up on a red sandstone cliff in the northern part of town. At its base is the new **Navajo Veterans Memorial Park** (☎ 928-871-6647; admission free; ☺ 8am-5pm), whose layout is patterned after a medicine wheel. Also worth a quick peek are the nearby beautifully mural-festooned **Navajo National Council Chambers** (8am-noon & 1-5pm Mon-Fri), where tribal delegates hold legislative sessions

The sleek and modern **Navajo Nation Museum** (928-871-7941; cnr Hwy 264 & Loop Rd; admission by donation; 8am-5pm Mon & Sat, 8am-8pm Tue-Fri) looks more imposing and interesting than it really is, with temporary shows that are hit or miss. The tribal library is here as well, as is a tourist desk where you can pick up information about the entire reservation. Nearby, cougars, elk, Gila monsters and other native animals are on display in the small **zoo & botanical park** (928-871-6573; admission free; 10am-5pm Mon-Sat), which is nicely set amid sandstone pinnacles known as the Haystacks.

For a superb selection of Navajo jewelry and crafts, swing by the **Navajo Arts & Crafts Enterprise store** (NACE; 928-871-4090; Hwy 264) next to the Quality Inn. Established in 1941, NACE is wholly Navajo operated and guarantees the authenticity and quality of its products.

The **Navajo Nation Fair** (www.navajonationfair.com) held in early September is a weeklong blowout with rodeos, the Miss Navajo Nation pageant, song and dance, livestock shows, horse races, a chile cook-off and lots of other events.

Rooms at the **Quality Inn Navajo Nation Capital** (928-871-4108; www.qualityinnwindowrock.com; 48 W Hwy 264; r incl breakfast $83-125; wi-fi) are nothing fancy, but we liked the Southwestern motif. The hotel's biggest asset, though, is the falling-over-backwards staff. Rates include a tummy-filling breakfast in the reasonably priced restaurant serving Navajo, American and Mexican fare all day long. Pets OK.

Three miles west of town, in quiet St Michaels, the **Navajoland Days Inn** (928-871-5690; 392 W Hwy 264; r from $70;) features clean, nondescript digs along with an indoor pool, sauna and exercise room. Pets cost $15.

HOPI RESERVATION

pop 11,000 / elev 7200ft

Did you know that the 'center of the universe' is actually in the middle of nowhere? At least that's how it may seem to visitors traversing the dazzlingly forbidding expanse of high desert that is the Hopi Reservation, a 2410-sq-mile island floating in the Navajo Reservation. To the Hopi, Arizona's oldest and most traditional tribe, this remote terrain is not merely their homeland but the hub of their spiritual world. The 11,000 members of this intensely religious tribe greatly cherish their privacy and would just as soon be left alone on the trio of insular, fingerlike mesa tops where they've lived for eons.

Because of their isolated location, the Hopi have received less outside influence than other tribes and have limited tourist facilities. Aside from ancient Walpi on First Mesa and Old Oraibi on Third Mesa, villages don't hold much appeal for visitors. Once you've toured these two and stopped at the Hopi Cultural Center, there isn't much more to do than to shop. Fortunately, the Hopi are extremely accomplished artists and craftspeople and it's well worth stopping at several shops along the main highway to peruse handmade baskets, kachina dolls (p56), overlay silver jewelry and pottery.

ORIENTATION

Eleven of the 12 Hopi villages lie at the base or on the top of three mesas named rather prosaically First Mesa, Second Mesa and Third Mesa by early European explorers. They are linked by Hwy 264 along with the non-Hopi village of Keams Canyon. Narrow and often steep roads lead off the highway to the mesa tops. The 12th village is Moenkopi, about 45 miles to the west near Tuba City.

INFORMATION

Make your first stop the **Hopi Cultural Center** (928-734-2401; www.hopiculturalcenter.com) on Second Mesa to pick up information and get oriented. Information may be also be obtained from the **Hopi Tribe Cultural Preservation Office** (928-734-3612; 8am-5pm Mon-Fri) in Kykotsmovi (Third Mesa). Each village has its own rules for visitors, which are usually posted along the highways, but generally speaking, any form of recording, be it camera, video or audiotape, or even sketching, is strictly forbidden. This is partly for religious reasons but also to prevent commercial exploitation by non-Hopis. Alcohol and other drug use is also prohibited.

As with the rest of Arizona (and different from the surrounding Navajo Reservation), the Hopi Reservation does not observe daylight saving time in summer. The climate is harsh – ungodly hot in summer and freezing cold in winter – so come prepared either way.

Hopi prefer cash for most transactions. ATMs are found at the Hopi Cultural Center, the Circle M store on Hwy 264 in Polacca (First Mesa), the McGee Shopping Center in Keams Canyon, and Secakuku Supermarket in Second Mesa at the junction of Hwys 264 and 87.

There's a **hospital** (☎ 928-738-0911) with emergency care in Polacca. For other emergencies, call the **BIA police** (☎ 928-738-2233).

Gas is cheaper outside the reservation, but there are filling stations in Keams Canyon and Kykotsmovi.

SIGHTS
First Mesa

Three villages squat atop this mesa and another village, nontraditional **Polacca**, hugs its base. The road up is steep; if you're here by RV, leave it in Polacca and walk. The first village is **Hano**, which blends imperceptibly into **Sichomovi**, where you'll find the community center at **Ponsi Hall** (☎ 928-737-2262; ☽ 9:30am-4pm Apr-Oct, 10am-2pm Nov-Mar). From here, local guides lead tours (adult/child $8/3) of the tiny village of **Walpi**, preceded by an introduction to Hopi culture and belief systems. The most dramatic of the Hopi enclaves, Walpi dates back to AD 1200 and clings like an aerie onto the mesa's narrow end. Sandstone-colored stone houses seem to organically sprout from the cliffs. These days, their only inhabitants are a few old ladies who live without plumbing or electricity, just like in the old days.

Outside Ponsi Hall, local artisans sell pots, kachinas and *piki* (a wafer-thin, dry rolled bread made from blue-corn meal) at fair prices.

Second Mesa

On Second Mesa, some 10 miles west of First Mesa, the **Hopi Cultural Center Restaurant & Inn** (☎ 928-734-2401; www.hopiculturalcenter.com) is as visitor-oriented as things get in Hopiland. It provides food and lodging, and there's also the small **Hopi Museum** (☎ 928-734-6650; adult/child $3/1; ☽ 8am-5pm), whose historical photographs, baskets, pottery and other craft items may hold your interest for about a half-hour. To browse for quality silverwork and other crafts, visit the **Hopi Arts & Crafts Guild** (☎ 928-734-2463).

Second Mesa has three villages of which the oldest, **Shungopavi**, is famous for its snake dances, where dancers carry live rattlesnakes in their mouths. **Mishongnovi** and **Sipaulovi** sometimes have Social or Butterfly dances open to the public.

Third Mesa

The tribal capital of **Kykotsmovi** (☎ 928-734-2474) sits below Third Mesa with **Batavi** and **Old Oraibi** up on top. The latter has been inhabited since AD 1200 and vies with Acoma Pueblo in New Mexico for the title of the USA's oldest continuously inhabited village. Park next to crafts shops near the village entrance and visit on foot. On the highway leading to Oraibi is the **Monongya Gallery** (☎ 928-734-2344), which has a good crafts selection.

TOURS

Since Hopi culture, history and traditions aren't easily accessible, you may want to join a guided tour to learn more about this fascinating culture. Tours are led by knowledgeable Hopi guides who will share their stories, introduce you to local artists and take you to archaeological and petroglyph sites only accessible with a guide. Bertram Tsavadawa of **Ancient Pathways** (☎ 928-734-9544, 928-797-8145; ancientpathways4@hotmail.com) and Gary Tso of **Left-Handed Hunter Tour Company** (☎ 928-734-2567; lh hunter58@hotmail.com) are recommended. Prices depend on tour length and group size.

FESTIVALS & EVENTS

Each village decides whether to allow non-Hopis at ceremonial dances. Some of the Kachina dances, held between January and July, are closed affairs, as are the famous Snake or Flute dances in August. It's much easier to attend Social dances and Butterfly dances, held late August through November. For upcoming festivities, check with the community development offices at each village:

Kykotsmovi (☎ 928-734-2474)
Mishongnovi (☎ 928-737-2520)
Shungopavi (☎ 928-734-2262)
Sichomovi & Walpi (☎ 928-734-2670)
Sipaulovi (☎ 928-734-7135)

When attending these ceremonies, be respectful. For details on etiquette, see p61.

SLEEPING & EATING

The reservation's only **hotel** (☎ 928-734-2401; d mid-Mar–mid-Oct $100, mid-Oct–mid-Mar $75) is part of the Hopi Cultural Center. Reservations are essential, especially in summer when its

33 modern if bland rooms usually book out. The **restaurant** (breakfast & lunch $4-10, dinner $10-17; ⓨ breakfast, lunch & dinner) is your chance to try such tasty Hopi treats as *noqkwivi* (lamb and hominy stew) served with blue-corn fry bread. Less adventurous palates will find a salad bar and the usual American fare to ease hunger pangs.

West of here, at the junction of Hwys 264 and 87, **LKD's Diner** (☎ 928-737-2717; meals under $10; ⓨ lunch & dinner Mon-Sat) serves Hopi tacos, burgers and a few Mexican dishes.

GETTING THERE & AWAY

The Hopi mesas are about 50 miles east of Tuba City and 85 miles west of Window Rock via flat and largely uneventful Hwy 264. Three roads enter the reservation from I-40 in the south. Coming from Flagstaff, the closest approach is by heading east on I-10 to Winslow, then cutting north on Hwy 87 (130 miles). From Winslow it's 70 miles via Hwy 87 and from Holbrook 80 miles on Hwy 77. Buses operated by **Navajo Transit System** (☎ 928-729-4002, 866-243-6260; www.navajotransit.com) pass through on their daily route between Tuba City and Window Rock.

WESTERN ARIZONA

Arizona may not be on the ocean but it does have a 'West Coast.' At least that's what wily marketers have dubbed the 1000-mile stretch of Colorado River that forms the state's boundary with California. After emerging from the Grand Canyon, the river gets tamed by a series of megadams, most famously Hoover Dam (p132). In winter migratory flocks of birds arrive from frigid northern climes. The winged variety seeks out riverside wildlife refuges, while the two-legged 'snowbird' species packs dozens of dusty RV parks, especially in Yuma. Although summers are hellishly hot, the cool Colorado brings in scores of water rats and boaters seeking relief from the heat in such places as Lake Havasu and Laughlin.

LAUGHLIN & BULLHEAD CITY

pop 40,000 / elev 540ft

Vegas on the cheap. The 'un-Vegas.' The 'anti-Sin City.' Laughlin, Nevada, has been called many names, and that's just fine with the little city founded in 1964 by gaming impresario Don Laughlin, a high-school dropout from Minnesota. On the banks of the Colorado River, across from Bullhead City in Arizona, this is still a place of $30 rooms, $1.99 steak breakfasts and free entertainment. The image of 'good, clean fun' (no leggy showgirls, no sleazy types touting escort services) is a winner with the blue-haired set and, increasingly, budget-strapped families looking for an inexpensive getaway.

Across the river, Bullhead City, or 'Bull,' began as a construction camp for Davis Dam, built in the 1940s 2 miles upstream to control water releases from Hoover Dam. Today, the town survives primarily because of the Laughlin casinos and provides little, if any, reason to make you stop.

Skip either town in summer when temperatures often soar to a merciless 120°F.

Information

The **Bullhead Area Chamber of Commerce** (☎ 928-754-4121; 1251 Hwy 95; ⓨ 8am-5pm Mon-Fri, 8:30am-5pm Sat & Sun) and the **Laughlin visitor center** (☎ 702-298-3321, 800-284-4546; www.visitlaughlin.com; 1555 S Casino Dr; ⓨ 8am-5pm Mon-Fri, 8:30am-5pm Sat & Sun) have area info, including copies of the *Entertainer*, a weekly guide to the Laughlin casino scene.

Nevada time is one hour behind Arizona in winter, but on the same time zone in summer (Arizona doesn't observe daylight saving time).

Activities

If you're not a gambler or you need a break from the blackjack table, the Colorado River is your best bet for noncasino diversions. A landscaped **River Walk** links the casinos, while on-the-water options include hour-long floats aboard a faux stern-wheeler (adult/child $8/6), 90-minute jaunts to the base of Davis Dam (adult/child $10/6) or six-hour boat tours through scenic Topock Gorge to London Bridge at Lake Havasu City (p230; adult/child $52/32). All major casinos also rent jet skis and other water craft.

Sleeping

Laughlin's big hotel-casinos are fantastic value with spacious doubles starting at $30 during midweek and $40 on weekends. All are on Casino Dr, which parallels the river.

Aquarius Casino Resort (☎ 800-662-5825, 702-298-5111; www.aquariuscasinoresort.com; 1900 S Casino Dr; r $30-40; 🅿 🖳) New investors hope they're ushering in the 'Age of Aquarius' as this

1900-room casino (formerly the Flamingo Laughlin) is undergoing a gradual makeover. Public areas look pretty nice already, especially the waterfall lobby and the Splash Cabaret with free nightly entertainment. Alas, the pool area seems mired in more concrete than Hoover Dam, but rooms were getting a much-needed revamp when we visited. Rates may go up.

Tropicana Express (☎ 702-298-4200, 800-243-6846; www.tropicanax.com; 2121 S Casino Dr; r $30-90; 🖳 🕭) The 1500-room ex–Ramada Express has zoomed into the 21st century without ditching its family-friendly train theme (there's a free miniature choo-choo and even the pool is locomotive-shaped). The new rooms could give Vegas a run for its money with chocolate-brown contemporary furniture, leather headboards and pillow-top mattresses.

Golden Nugget (☎ 702-298-7111, 800-950-7700; www.goldennugget.com/laughlin; 2300 S Casino Dr; r midweek/weekend from $40/70; 🖳 🖳 wi-fi) This is the casino on which Vegas mogul Steve Wynn cut his teeth back in 1989. The latest owners of this 300-room 'boutique casino' have sunk big bucks into creating an intimate but classy experience with tropical-themed rooms, a palm-tree-flanked riverfront pool and above-average eateries.

Harrah's (☎ 702-298-4600; www.harrahslaughlin .com; 2900 S Casino Dr; r from $40; 🖳 🖳) The most appealing feature of hulking Harrah's is the private, family-friendly swimming beach in a cove on the river. Rooms at the three-tower behemoth are fine but generic. Spend a little extra for river views or risk overlooking the depressing parking lot. It's about a mile south of the other casinos.

Eating & Drinking

All casinos feature multiple restaurants, usually including a buffet, a 24-hour café and an upscale steakhouse, along with bars and lounges.

Boiler Room (☎ 702-298-4000; 2100 S Casino Dr; dishes $7-15; 🕑 food 11am-10pm Sun-Thu, 11am-11pm Fri & Sat) This lively brewpub at the Colorado Belle casino goes for a '20,000 Leagues Under the Sea' decor and is funky enough to stand out even in Laughlin. The open kitchen prepares delish wood-fired pizzas, burgers and tasty ribs.

Saltgrass Steakhouse (☎ 702-298-7111; 2300 S Casino Dr; mains $15-27; 🕑 dinner Mon-Sat, 7am-10pm Sun) Surrender helplessly to your inner car-

nivore at this river-view Wild West–themed restaurant at the Golden Nugget. The yummy cuts of Angus beef are the way to go, but char-grilled chicken and fish also put in menu appearances.

Losers Lounge (☎ 702-298-2535; 1650 S Casino Dr) Shuffle and jive to live bands playing chart music at this bar and dance-club fixture at the Riverside Resort. Posters and pics of famous 'losers' decorate the walls. Now that's one hall of fame you don't want to be in.

Hideout (☎ 702-299-0008; 2311 S Casino Dr; 🕑 24hr) For a local-flavored beer and cocktail scene drop by this sports bar with eight plasma TVs, drinks specials and Friday night karaoke.

Getting There & Away

The only commercial flights into Bullhead City/Laughlin Airport are those on the **Sun Country Airlines** (☎ 800-359-6786; www.suncountry .com) service from Minneapolis. Las Vegas' McCarran International Airport is about 100 miles north of town and linked to Laughlin by **River City Shuttle** (☎ 928-854-5253; www.rivercity shuttle.com) three times daily ($50 one way, 1¾ hours).

LAKE HAVASU CITY

pop 58,000 / elev 575ft

Lake Havasu City has all the unreal charm of a manufactured community. It also has London Bridge. Yes, that would be the original gracefully arched bridge that spanned the Thames from 1831 until 1967 when it was quite literally falling down (as predicted in the old nursery rhyme) and put up for sale. On the other side of the world, Robert McCulloch was busy developing a master-planned community on Lake Havasu and badly in need of some gimmick to drum up attention for his project. Bingo! McCulloch snapped up the London Bridge for a cool $2.46 million, dismantled it into 10,276 slabs and reassembled it in the Arizona desert. The first car rolled across in 1971.

Listed in the *Guinness World Records* as the 'world's largest antique,' London Bridge may be one of Arizona's most incongruous tourist sites, but it's also among its most popular. Day-trippers come by the busload to walk across it and soak up faux British heritage in the kitschy-quaint English Village. The lake itself is the other major draw. Formed in 1938 by the construction of Parker Dam, it's much beloved by water rats, especially students on Spring Break (roughly March to May) and summer-heat refugees from Phoenix and beyond.

Information

The **visitor center** (☎ 928-855-5655, 800-242-8278; www .golakehavasu.com; 420 English Village; 🕒 8:30am-4pm Mon-Sat; 💻 wi-fi) has all the need-to-know info.

Sights & Activities

Once you've snapped pics of London Bridge, you'll find that most of your options are water related. Several companies offer boat tours (from around $40) from English Village. Options include one-hour narrated jaunts, day trips and sunset tours, and can usually be booked on the spot.

The best beach in town is **London Bridge Beach**, in the county park off West McCulloch Blvd (behind the Island Inn hotel). The park has lots of palm trees, a sandy beach and bridge views.

Action Adventure Rentals (☎ 928-854-5377) and **Blue Water Rentals** (☎ 928-855-7171), both in the English Village, rent a variety of boats from paddle crafts ($16 per day) to 220ft pontoon boats ($220 per day). With no speed limits, the lake is Arizona's aquatic autobahn.

Canoes and kayaks can be rented from $25 a day from **Western Arizona Canoe & Kayak Outfitter** (Wacko; ☎ 928-715-6414; www.azwacko.com; 770 Winston Pl). The company also offers tours ($45) of Topock Gorge (p256), a relaxing way to spend an afternoon floating past cacti and rocky crags.

ARIZONA

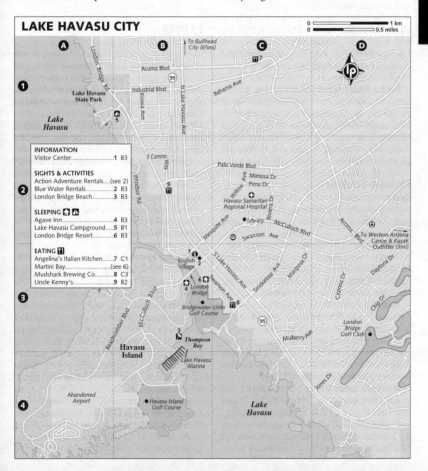

LAKE HAVASU CITY

INFORMATION	
Visitor Center........................1	B3

SIGHTS & ACTIVITIES	
Action Adventure Rentals....(see 2)	
Blue Water Rentals................2	B3
London Bridge Beach............3	B3

SLEEPING	
Agave Inn.............................4	B3
Lake Havasu Campground....5	B1
London Bridge Resort...........6	B3

EATING	
Angelina's Italian Kitchen......7	C1
Martini Bay.......................(see 6)	
Mudshark Brewing Co..........8	C3
Uncle Kenny's.......................9	B2

If you'd rather spend your time four-wheeling through the desert, check out **Safari Tours** (☎ 928-486 1891; adult/concession $35/20), which runs 3½-hour trips to lesser-visited natural sites, including Whipple Wash Gorge and Palm Canyon View.

Sleeping

Rates fluctuate tremendously from summer weekends to winter weekdays. The cheapest properties line Acoma Blvd.

Lake Havasu Campground (☎ 928-855-2784; www .pr.state.az.us; 699 London Bridge Rd; tent/RV sites from $15/19) This recently upgraded beach and camping area has showers, boat-launch facilities and new hookups. Day-use costs $10 per vehicle.

ourpick Agave Inn (☎ 928-854-2833, 888-898-4328; www.agaveinn.com; 1420 McCulloch Blvd; r $80-190; wi-fi) This sassy new boutique hotel hits on all cylinders. Rooms are hip and contempo and most have private patios with views of London Bridge. A waterfront restaurant and cocktail lounge should be open by the time you're reading this.

London Bridge Resort (☎ 928-855-0888, 888-503-9148; www.londonbridgeresort.com; 1477 Queens Bay Rd; ste $100-300; ⚐ ☐ wi-fi) A replica of a British 1762 royal coach greets you at this popular all-suite property. It's a good choice if you want pools, nightclubs, bars and restaurants all under one roof.

Eating & Drinking

Restaurants and bars line a half-mile stretch of McCulloch Blvd between Smoketree Ave and Acoma Blvd. Other options include the following:

Uncle Kenny's (☎ 928-680-7100; 362 London Bridge Rd; dishes $4-8; ♥ 6am-2pm) Grab a booth and join famished locals for soul-sustaining omelettes, *huevos rancheros* and other breakfast favorites. Lines are freakishly long on Sunday.

Mudshark Brewing Co (☎ 928-453-2981; 210 Swanson Ave; dishes $6.50-20; ♥ lunch & dinner) At this bustling brewpub you'll be surrounded by copper vats and a happy crowd downing fresh and hand-crafted brews, from low-carb lager to a spicy Belgian-style ale. The well-priced menu even features a Kobe beef burger ($12.50).

Angelina's Italian Kitchen (☎ 928-680-3868; 2137 W Acoma Blvd; mains $8-20; ♥ dinner Tue-Sat) If you like your Italian food as if mama was behind the stove, you'll like this hole-in-the-wall on an industrial stretch east of downtown. It's cluttered and some of the patrons may be ec-

centric, but the home-cooked Italian weaves together pungent flavors like fine tapestry.

Martini Bay (☎ 928-855-0888; 1477 Queens Bay Rd; small plates $6-14, mains $17-32; ♥ dinner) A stylish place at the London Bridge Resort, Martini Bay attracts friends, lovebirds and trendy families. Grazers can pick around the small-plate menu, pretending not to be tempted by blue-corn-crusted red snapper or key-lime marinated marlin.

Getting There & Away

Lake Havasu is on Hwy 95, about 20 miles south of the I-40. There's no public transportation, but **River City Shuttle** (☎ 928-854-5253; www.rivercityshuttle.com) runs buses to Las Vegas' McCarran International Airport three times daily ($65 one way, 3¼ hours).

PARKER

pop 3100 / elev 417ft

This teensy townlet, some 30 miles south of Lake Havasu, hugs a 16-mile stretch of Colorado River known as the Parker Strip. All hell breaks lose in late January when the engines are revved up for the **Best in the Desert Parker 425**, an off-road race that lures up to 100,000 speed freaks. Contact the **chamber of commerce** (☎ 928-669-2174; www.parkertourism.com; 1217 California Ave; ♥ 8am-5pm Mon-Fri) for the lowdown.

Lake Havasu was formed by **Parker Dam**, 15 miles north of town. It may not look it, but this is in fact the world's deepest dam, with 73% of its structural height of 320ft buried beneath the original riverbed. Water- and jet-skiing, fishing, boating and tubing are popular here, and there are plenty of concessionaires along the Parker Strip.

Buckskin Mountain State Park (☎ 928-667-3231; www.pr.state.az.us; per vehicle $8), tucked along a mountain-flanked bend in the Colorado River some 11 miles north of Parker, has great family-friendly infrastructure, with a playground, swimming beach, basketball court, café and grocery store (summer only). **Campsites** (tent & RV sites $19-25) are first-come, first-served. Tenters should head another mile north for quieter, more scenic desert camping at the park's **River Island Unit** (☎ 928-667-3386; tent sites $14-25).

South of Parker, the Colorado River Indian Reservation is inhabited by members of the Mohave, Chemehuevi, Navajo and Hopi tribes. Their stories, along with amazing handicrafts (the basket collection is famous), come to life at the **Colorado River Indian Tribes Museum** (☎ 928-669-9211; cnr Mohave Rd & 2nd Ave; admission by donation; ◷ 8am-5pm Mon-Fri, 10am-3pm Sat).

There aren't really any great properties in town, but if you must spend the night, the all-purpose, tribal-owned **Blue Water Resort & Casino** (☎ 928-669-7000; www.bluewaterfun.com; 13000 Resort Dr; r $50-140; ▨ ▯ wi-fi) is probably your best bet. The nicest rooms overlook the river marina.

For honest-to-goodness home-cooked meals, stop by **Coffee Ern's** (☎ 928-669-8145; 1720 S California Ave; meals under $10), which feeds hungry bellies 24/7. Another grub-alicious option is the **Hole-in-the-Wall** (☎ 928-669-9755; 904 S California Ave; dishes $4-8; ◷ breakfast, lunch & dinner), a no-nonsense coffee shop.

Parker is 35 miles south of Lake Havasu via Hwy 95.

YUMA
pop 87,000 / elev 200ft

Yuma isn't actually in it, but the 2007 remake of the 1957 classic *3:10 to Yuma* has likely increased the name recognition of this sprawling city at the confluence of the Gila and Colorado Rivers. It's the blazing-hot birthplace of farmworker organizer César Chávez and the winter camp of some 70,000 snowbirds craving Yuma's sunny skies, mild temperatures and cheap RV park living. There ain't too much here for the rest of us to ease off the gas pedal, although recent efforts to revitalize the snug historic downtown have met with some success.

Information

For maps and information, stop by the **visitor center** (☎ 928-783-0071; www.visityuma.com; 377 S Main St; ◷ 9am-5pm Mon-Fri, 9am-2pm Sat May-Oct, 9am-6pm Mon-Fri, 9am-4pm Sat, 10am-2pm Sun Nov-Apr).

Sights

Attraction number one is the **Yuma Territorial Prison State Historic Park** (☎ 928-783-4771; www.pr.state.az.us; 1 Prison Hill Rd; adult/child $4/free; ◷ 8am-5pm) on a bluff above the Colorado River. Between 1876 and 1909, it housed 3069 of Arizona's most feared criminals, including 29 women. The cells, main gate and guard tower offer a glimpse of convict life, making this a grim, mildly historic, offbeat attraction suitable for the whole family (no pets).

In downtown, the **Yuma Art Center** (☎ 928-373-5202; www.yumafinearts.com; 254 S Main St; suggested donation $3; ◷ 10am-5pm Tue-Thu & Sat, 10am-7pm Fri, 1-5pm Sun) presents contemporary art in four galleries and also houses artist studios and a gift shop. It's next to the beautifully restored 1911 Historic Yuma Theater, which hosts concerts and theater from November to March.

About 10 miles south of town, the Cocopah maintain a well-presented **museum** (☎ 928-627-1992; www.cocopah.com; cnr County 15 & Ave G, Somerton; admission free; ◷ 8am-5pm Mon-Fri) featuring the tribe's traditions, clothing, beadwork, tribal games, tattoos and depictions of warriors.

Sleeping & Eating

Yuma has plenty of chain-brigade contenders, mostly along the highway.

La Fuente Inn & Suites (☎ 928-329-1814, 877-202-3353; www.lafuenteinn.com; 1513 E 16th St; r incl full breakfast $87-119; ▨ ▯) For more character try this place, where pretty gardens wrap around a modern, Spanish Colonial style building. The evening social hour is great for mingling with fellow guests over free wine.

Lutes Casino (☎ 928-782-2192; 221 Main St; dishes $3-6; ◷ 9am-8pm) You won't find slots or poker at this 1940s hangout, just old-school domino players and cool movie and advertising memorabilia. To show you're in the know, order the 'especial' – a burger topped with a sliced hot dog. Tums not included.

River City Grill (☎ 928-782-7988; 600 W 3rd St; mains $15-22; ◷ lunch Mon-Fri, dinner daily) Chic, funky and gourmet, the River has scrumptious crab cakes and brie-stuffed chicken, as well as mouthwatering vegetarian mains.

Julieanna's Patio Café (☎ 928-317-1961; 1951 W 25th St; lunch $7-14, dinner $19-26; ◷ lunch Mon-Fri, dinner Mon-Sat) Amadeus and Max, a couple of resident macaws, preside over this cheerful lair with its tropical patio and original art. The Caesar salad, prepared tableside, is a trademark dish.

Getting There & Away

Yuma Airport (☎ 928-726-5882; www.yumainternationalairport.com; 2191 32nd St) has daily flights to Phoenix, Los Angeles, Las Vegas and Salt Lake City. **Greyhound** (☎ 928-783-4403; 170 E 17 Pl) runs two direct buses daily to Phoenix ($29, four hours), while Amtrak's *Sunset Limited* makes a brief stop thrice weekly on its run between Los Angeles ($38, six hours) and New Orleans ($133, 43 hours).

SOUTHERN ARIZONA

Way down south by the Mexican border the skies are big and blue. This is a land of Stetsons and spurs, where cowboy ballads are sung around the campfire and thick steaks sizzle on the grill. It's big country out here, beyond the confines of bustling college-town Tucson, where long, dusty highways slide past rolling vistas and steep, pointy mountain ranges. A place where majestic saguaro cacti, the symbol of the region, stretch out as far as the eye can see. Some of the Wild West's most classic tales were begot in small towns like Tombstone and Bisbee, which still attract tourists by the thousands for their Old West vibe. The desert air here is hot, sweet and dry by day, cool and crisp at night. This is a land of stupendous sunsets, a place where coyotes still howl under starry, black-velvet skies.

TUCSON

pop 518,800 / elev 2389ft

An energetic college town, Tucson (*too*-sawn) is attractive, fun-loving and one of the most culturally invigorating places in the Southwest. Set in a flat valley hemmed in by craggy, odd-shaped mountains, Arizona's second-largest city smoothly blends Native American, Spanish, Mexican and Anglo traditions. Distinct neighborhoods and 19th-century buildings give a rich sense of community and history not found in more modern and sprawling Phoenix. Some major construction and gentrification in the historic downtown notwithstanding, you'll likely find Tucson easier to navigate and a more satisfying base. This is a town rich in Hispanic heritage (more than 20% of the population is of Mexican or Central American descent), so Spanish slides easily off most tongues and high-quality Mexican restaurants abound. The eclectic shops toting vintage garb, scores of funky restaurants and dive bars don't let you forget Tucson is a college town at heart, home turf to the 37,000-strong University of Arizona (U of A).

Although it's fun to wander around the colorful historic buildings and peruse the shops, Tucson's best perks are found outside town. Whether you yearn to hike past giant cacti in the beautiful Saguaro National Park, watch the sun set over the rugged Santa Catalina Mountains or check out the world-class Arizona-Sonora Desert Museum, a stray beyond city limits is bound to please just about anyone.

Orientation

Downtown Tucson and the historic district are east of I-10 exit 258. About a mile northeast of downtown is the University of Arizona campus; 4th Ave is the main drag here, packed with cafés, bars and interesting shops.

Though the freeway will remain open, a number of I-10 on- and off-ramps will be closed for construction through spring 2010. The **Arizona Department of Transportation** (www .i10tucsondistrict.com) posts up-to-the-minute route updates.

Information

BOOKSTORES

Antigone Books (Map p239; ☎ 520-792-3715; 411 N 4th Ave; ☯ 10am-7pm Mon-Thu, 10am-9pm Fri & Sat, noon-5pm Sun) Great indie bookstore with a feminist slant.
Bookmans (Map p236; ☎ 520-325-5657; 1930 E Grant Rd; ☯ 9am-10pm; wi-fi) Well-stocked Arizona indie chain cum locals' hangout.

EMERGENCY

Police (Map p239; ☎ 520-791-4444; 270 S Stone Ave)

INTERNET ACCESS

Library (Map p239; ☎ 520-791-4393; 101 N Stone Ave; ☯ daily; ▢ wi-fi) Free internet.

MEDIA

The local newspapers are the morning *Arizona Daily Star*, the afternoon *Tucson Citizen* and the free *Tucson Weekly* published on Thursday, chock-full of great entertainment and restaurant listings. *Tucson Lifestyle* is a glossy monthly mag.

MEDICAL SERVICES

Tucson Medical Center (Map p236; ☎ 520-327-5461; 5301 E Grant Rd) 24-hour emergency services.
Veterinary Specialty Center (Map p235; ☎ 520-795-9955; 4909 N La Canada Dr) 24-hour emergency pet care.

POST

Post office (Map p236; ☎ 520-629-9268; 825 E University Blvd, Suite 111)

TOURIST INFORMATION

Coronado National Forest Supervisor's Office (Map p239; ☎ 520-388-8300; Federal Bldg, 300 W Congress St; ☯ 8am-4:30pm Mon-Fri)

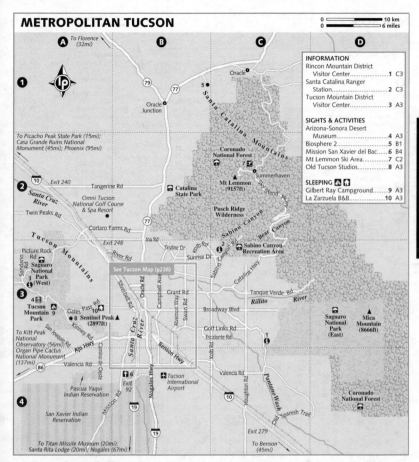

METROPOLITAN TUCSON

0 _____ 10 km
0 _____ 6 miles

INFORMATION
Rincon Mountain District
　Visitor Center.....................1 C3
Santa Catalina Ranger
　Station...............................2 C3
Tucson Mountain District
　Visitor Center.....................3 A3

SIGHTS & ACTIVITIES
Arizona-Sonora Desert
　Museum..............................4 A3
Biosphere 2.............................5 B1
Mission San Xavier del Bac.....6 B4
Mt Lemmon Ski Area..............7 C2
Old Tucson Studios................8 A3

SLEEPING
Gilbert Ray Campground........9 A3
La Zarzuela B&B....................10 A3

ARIZONA

Tucson Convention & Visitors Bureau (Map p239; ☎ 520-624-1817, 800-638-8350; www.visittucson .org; 110 S Church Ave, Suite 7199) Ask for its free *Official Visitors Guide*.

Sights & Activities

Most of Tucson's blockbuster sights, including the Saguaro National Park and the Arizona-Sonora Desert Museum, are on the city outskirts. The downtown area and 4th Ave near the university are compact enough for walking.

For avid explorers the Tucson Attractions Passport ($15) may be a ticket to savings. It's available through www.visittucson.org /visitor/attractions/passport or at the visitor center and entitles you to two-for-one tickets or other discounts at dozens of major muse-

ums, attractions, tours and parks throughout southern Arizona.

DOWNTOWN TUCSON

Don't let all that messy construction stop you from exploring historic downtown. A good place to start is the **Tucson Museum of Art & Historic Block** (Map p239; ☎ 520-624-2333; www.tucson museumofart.org; 140 N Main Ave; adult/child/student/senior $8/free/3/6; ☺ 10am-4pm Tue-Sat, noon-4pm Sun), which complements its respectable collection of pre-Columbian, Western and contemporary art with often excellent traveling exhibits and a superb gift shop. Works are displayed in the modern main building and five historic ones, including the 1854 Casa Cordova, one of the Tucson's oldest buildings.

ARIZONA

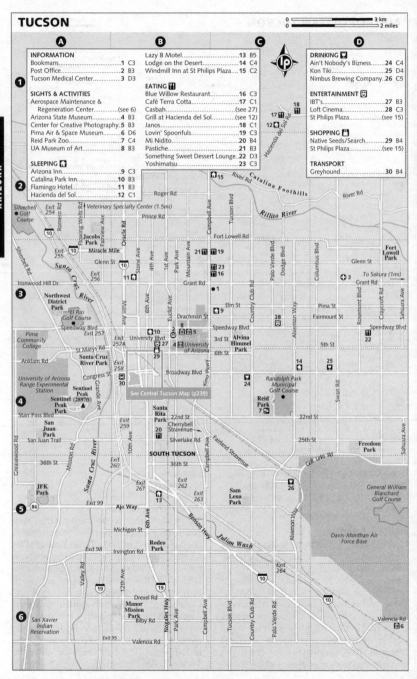

TUCSON

0 _____ 3 km
0 _____ 2 miles

A

INFORMATION
Bookmans.................................1 C3
Post Office................................2 B3
Tucson Medical Center.............3 D3

SIGHTS & ACTIVITIES
Aerospace Maintenance &
   Regeneration Center............(see 6)
Arizona State Museum..............4 B3
Center for Creative Photography.5 B3
Pima Air & Space Museum........6 D6
Reid Park Zoo...........................7 C4
UA Museum of Art....................8 B3

SLEEPING
Arizona Inn...............................9 C3
Catalina Park Inn.....................10 B3
Flamingo Hotel........................11 B3
Hacienda del Sol.....................12 C1

B

Lazy 8 Motel...........................13 B5
Lodge on the Desert................14 C4
Windmill Inn at St Philips Plaza..15 C2

EATING
Blue Willow Restaurant............16 C3
Café Terra Cotta......................17 C1
Casbah..................................(see 27)
Grill at Hacienda del Sol........(see 12)
Janos......................................18 C1
Lovin' Spoonfuls....................19 C3
Mi Nidito................................20 B4
Pastiche.................................21 B3
Something Sweet Dessert Lounge..22 D3
Yoshimatsu.............................23 C3

C

DRINKING
Ain't Nobody's Bizness........24 C4
Kon Tiki.................................25 D4
Nimbus Brewing Company..26 C5

ENTERTAINMENT
IBT's.....................................27 B3
Loft Cinema..........................28 C3
St Philips Plaza....................(see 15)

SHOPPING
Native Seeds/Search.............29 B4
St Philips Plaza....................(see 15)

TRANSPORT
Greyhound............................30 B4

BEATING BOREDOM ON THE I-8

If you're driving east of Yuma on the I-8, bring some good music or an audiobook for the lonely 120-mile stretch through largely intrusion-free desert to Gila Bend. For a sugar rush, grab a date shake at **Dateland** (☎ 928-454-2772; exit 87; ✆ 6am-10pm), a family-style diner near an actual date oasis. Admire prehistoric rock art at the **Painted Rock Petroglyph Site**, an interpreted trail about 9 miles north off exit 102. In Gila Bend, check out the gorgeously kitsch '60s-era **Space Age Lodge** (☎ 928-683-2273; exit 119, 401 E Pima St; mains $7-12), complete with flying saucer and space-themed murals (redone after a 1998 fire). The diner serves American and Mexican standards.

The museum complex is part of the **Presidio Historic District** (Map p239), which embraces the site of the original Spanish fort and a ritzy residential area once nicknamed 'Snob Hollow.' It teems with restored 19th-century mansions, but the original fort is completely gone, although there's a short reconstructed section at the corner of Church Ave and Washington St. Shoppers should steer towards **Old Town Artisans** (Map p239; 201 N Court Ave), a block-long warren of adobe houses filled with galleries and crafts stores set around a lush and lovely courtyard café.

A couple of blocks south of Alameda St, Congress St is the main downtown drag and home to the newly spiffed-up art-deco **Fox Theatre** (p244), a 1930s beauty with fluted golden columns, water fountains and a giant sunburst mural radiating from the ceiling.

Past Cushing St is the **Barrio Histórico District**, which was an important business district in the late 19th century and is now home to funky shops and galleries in brightly painted adobe houses. Don't miss **El Tiradito** (Map p239; 221 S Main Ave), a quirky, crumbling 'wishing shrine' with a bizarre story of passion and murder. Legend has it a young herder was killed by his father-in-law after getting caught making love to his mother-in-law and is now buried where he fell. These days, pious locals bring flowers and burn candles praying for their wishes to come true.

4TH AVENUE

Linking historic downtown and the university, 4th Ave is one of a rare breed: a hip yet alt-flavored strip with a neighborhood feel and not a single chain store. The stretch between 9th St and University Blvd is lined by lively restaurants, coffeehouses, bars, galleries, tattoo parlors, and indie boutiques and vintage stores of all stripes (see p244).

The best time to visit 4th Ave is during the two annual street fairs held for three days in

mid-December and early March. See www .fourthavenue.org for details.

UNIVERSITY OF ARIZONA

The University of Arizona campus houses excellent museums, including the internationally renowned **Center for Creative Photography** (Map p236; ☎ 520-621-7968; www.creativephotography .org; 1030 N Olive Rd; donations appreciated; ✆ 9am-5pm Mon-Fri, noon-5pm Sat & Sun), which presents changing, high-caliber exhibits and administers the archives of Ansel Adams.

At the adjacent **UA Museum of Art** (Map p236; ☎ 520-621-7567; www.artmuseum.arizona.edu; admission free; ✆ 9am-5pm Tue-Fri, noon-4pm Sat & Sun) you can clap eyes on 500 years of European and American paintings and sculpture featuring such heavy hitters such as Rembrandt, Goya, Matisse and Picasso.

Another delight is the **Arizona State Museum** (Map p236; ☎ 520-621-6302; www.statemuseum .arizona.edu; 1013 E University Blvd; suggested donation $3; ✆ 10am-5pm Mon-Sat, noon-5pm Sun), which focuses on the cultural history of the Southwestern tribes, from Stone Age mammoth hunters to the present, and has much-envied collections of minerals, indigenous pottery and Navajo textiles.

ARIZONA-SONORA DESERT MUSEUM

To say that this is Tucson's most outstanding **museum** (Map p235; ☎ 520-883-2702; www.desert museum.org; 2021 N Kinney Rd; adult/child $10/2; ✆ 8:30am-5pm Oct-Feb, 7:30am-5pm Mar-Sep) isn't really telling the whole story. It's really a zoo, a botanical garden and a museum combined in one – a trifecta of treats that'll keep young and old entertained for easily half a day. All sorts of desert denizens, from precocious coatis to playful prairie dogs, make their home in natural enclosures hemmed in by invisible fences. The grounds are thick with desert plants, and docents are on hand to answer questions as you wander around. There are two walk-through aviaries, a mineral exhibit inside a cave (kids love that one!) and an underground exhibit with windows into ponds where beavers, otters and ducks frolic. Strollers and wheelchairs are available, and there's a gift shop, art gallery, restaurant and café. The museum is off Hwy 86, about 12 miles west of Tucson, near the western section of Saguaro National Park.

SAGUARO NATIONAL PARK

They have arms, noses and other...shall we say...protuberances. They shake your hand, tell you to stop, wave at you or draw a gun on you. 'They' are ribbed saguaro (sah-*wah*-ro) cacti, majestic sentinels of the Southwest, an entire army of which is protected in this **national park** (☎ 520-733-5100; www.nps.gov/sagu; 7-day pass per vehicle $10; ☼ 7am-sunset). Their foot soldiers are the spidery ocotillo, the fluffy teddy bear cactus, the green-bean-like pencil cholla and hundreds of other plant species.

Saguaros grow slowly, taking about 15 years to reach a foot in height, 50 years to reach 7ft and almost a century before they begin to take on their typical many-armed appearance. The best time to visit is April, when the saguaros begin blossoming with lovely white blooms – Arizona's state flower. By June and July, the flowers give way to ripe red fruit that local Native Americans use for food.

Saguaro National Park is divided into two units separated by 30 miles and the city of Tucson. Both are equally rewarding and it's not necessary to visit them both. Note that trailers longer than 35ft and vehicles wider than 8ft are not permitted on the parks' narrow scenic loop roads.

The larger section is the **Rincon Mountain District**, about 15 miles east of downtown. The **visitor center** (Map p235; ☎ 520-733-5153; 3693 S Old Spanish Trail; ☼ 9am-5pm) has information on day hikes, horseback riding and backcountry camping. The latter requires a permit ($6 per site per day) and must be obtained by noon on the day of your hike. The meandering 8-mile **Cactus Forest Scenic Loop Drive**, a paved road open to cars and bicycles, provides access to picnic areas, trailheads and viewpoints.

Hikers pressed for time should follow the 1-mile **Freeman Homestead Trail** to a grove of massive saguaro. For a full-fledged desert adventure, head out on the steep and rocky **Tanque Verde Ridge Trail**, which climbs to the summit of Mica Mountain

(8666ft) in 18 miles (backcountry camping permit required).

West of town, the **Tucson Mountain District** has its own **visitor center** (Map p235; ☎ 520-733-5158; 2700 N Kinney Rd; ☼ 9am-5pm). The **Scenic Bajada Loop Drive** is a 6-mile graded dirt road through cactus forest that begins 1.5 miles north of the visitor center. Two quick, easy and rewarding hikes are the 0.8-mile **Valley View Overlook** (awesome at sunset) and the half-mile **Signal Hill Trail** to scores of ancient petroglyphs. For a more strenuous trek we recommend the 7-mile **King Canyon Trail**, which starts 2 miles south of the visitor center near the Arizona-Sonora Desert Museum.

OLD TUCSON STUDIOS

Nicknamed 'Hollywood in the Desert,' this old movie set of Tucson in the 1860s was built in 1939 for the filming of *Arizona*. Hundreds of flicks followed, bringing in an entire galaxy of stars, including Clint Eastwood, Harrison Ford and Leonardo DiCaprio. Now a Wild West theme park, it's mostly mom, pop, buddy and sis who are shuffling down the dusty streets of **Old Tucson Studios** (Map p235; ☎ 520-883-0100; www.oldtucson.com; 201 S Kinney Rd; adult/child 4-11 $17/11; ☼ 10am-6pm). Shootouts, stagecoach rides, saloons, sheriffs and stunts are all part of the hoopla awaiting visitors. The studios are a few miles southeast of the Arizona-Sonora Desert Museum off Hwy 86.

PIMA AIR & SPACE MUSEUM

An SR-71 Blackbird spy plane, JFK's Air Force One and a massive B-52 bomber are among the stars of this extraordinary private aircraft **museum** (Map p236; ☎ 520-574-0462; www.pimaair.org; 6000 E Valencia Rd; adult/child Jun-Oct $11.75/8, Nov-May $13.50/9; ☼ 9am-5pm, last admission 4pm). Allow at least two hours to wander through hangars and around the airfield where 275 'birds' trace the evolution of civilian and military aviation. If that's too overwhelming, consider joining the free 90-minute walking tour offered at 10:15am daily (also 11:45am Saturday and Sunday) or shell out an extra $5 for the one-hour tram tour departing at 10am, 11:30am, 1:30pm and 3pm.

Hardcore plane-spotters should call ahead to book space on the one-hour bus tour of the nearby 309th **Aerospace Maintenance & Regeneration Center** (Amarg; Map p236; adult/child $6/3; ☼ Mon-Fri) – aka the 'boneyard' – where some 5000 aircraft are mothballed in the dry desert air. You don't need to pay museum admission

ARIZONA

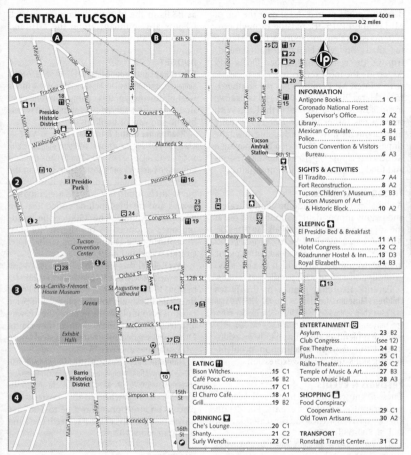

CENTRAL TUCSON

to join this tour, but discounted combination tickets are available, as are combo tickets with the Titan Missile Museum (p247).

SANTA CATALINA MOUNTAINS

The Santa Catalinas northeast of Tucson are the best loved and most visited among the region's mountain ranges. You need a **Coronado Forest Recreation Pass** ($5 per vehicle per day) to park anywhere in the mountain area. It's available at the USFS **Santa Catalina ranger station** (Map p235; ☎ 520-749-2861; 5700 N Sabino Canyon Rd; ☉ 8am-4:30pm) at the mouth of Sabino Canyon, which also has maps, hiking guides and camping information.

Sabino Canyon (Map p235; www.sabinocanyon.com; 5900 N Sabino Canyon Rd), a lush, pretty and shaded

mini-gorge, is a favorite year-round destination for both locals and visitors. Narrated hop-on, hop-off tram tours along the Sabino Canyon Trail (adult/child $7.50/3) depart every half hour for a 45-minute, nine-stop loop with access to trailheads and riverside picnic areas. It's nicest in the afternoon when the sun plays hide and seek against the canyon walls. A non-narrated shuttle ($3/1) provides access to Bear Canyon and the trailhead to Seven Falls, which has picnic sites and swimming but no facilities. From the falls, the trail continues up as high as you want to go.

A great way to escape the summer heat is by following the super-scenic **Sky Island Parkway** (Map p235; officially called Catalina Hwy), which meanders 27 miles from saguaro-dappled desert to pine-covered forest near the top of Mt Lemmon (9157ft), passing through ecosystems equivalent to a journey from Mexico to Canada. Budget at least three hours roundtrip. Of the vista points, Babad Do'ag and Aspen are the most rewarding.

In winter, Mt Lemmon has the southernmost **ski area** (Map p235; ☎ 520-576-1400; Catalina Hwy; adult/child $32/14; ⊙ mid-Dec–Mar) in the USA. With snow levels rather unpredictable, it's really more about the novelty of schussing down the slopes within views of Mexico than having a world-class alpine experience. Rentals, lessons and food are available on the mountain.

Tucson for Children

A global menagerie including giant anteaters and pygmy hippos delights young and old at the small and compact **Reid Park Zoo** (Map p236; ☎ 520-791-4022; 1030 S Randolph Way; adult/child/senior $6/2/4; ⊙ 9am-4pm; ♿). Cap a visit with a picnic in the surrounding park, which also has playgrounds and a pond with paddleboat rentals.

Parents also sing praises of the **Tucson Children's Museum** (Map p239; ☎ 520-792-9985; 200 S 6th Ave; adult/child/senior $7/5/5; ⊙ 10am-5pm Tue-Sat, noon-5pm Sun year-round, plus 10am-5pm Mon Jun–mid-Aug; ♿), which has plenty of engaging, hands-on exhibits that stimulate the imagination, problem-solving skills and creative expression.

Festivals & Events

Tucson knows how to party and keeps a year-round schedule of events. For details check www.visittucson.com/calendar or call ☎ 800-638-8350.

The **Tucson Gem and Mineral Show** (☎ 520-332-5773; www.tgms.org), in early February, is the largest of its kind in the world and sends room rates soaring. The **Fiesta de los Vaqueros** (Rodeo Week; ☎ 520-741-2233, 800-964-5662; www.tusconrodeo.com), held the last week of February for over 80 years, brings world-famous cowboys to town and features a spectacular parade with Western-themed floats and buggies, historic horse-drawn coaches, folk dancers and marching bands.

Sleeping

Tucson's gamut of lodging options rivals Phoenix' for beauty, comfort and location. Rates plummet as much as 50% between June and September, making what would otherwise be a five-star megasplurge an affordable getaway. If it's quaintness you're after, you'll love those old-time mansions resuscitated as B&Bs in the historic downtown district. Chains are abundant along the I-10 and around the airport.

BUDGET

Gilbert Ray Campground (Map p235; ☎ 520-877-6000; Kinney Rd; tent/RV sites $10/20; P) About 13 miles west of downtown, this campground has 130 first-come, first-served sites along with water, but no showers or hookups.

Roadrunner Hostel & Inn (Map p239; ☎ 520-628-4709, 520-940-7280; www.roadrunnerhostel.com; 346 E 12th St; dm/r incl breakfast $22/45; P 🖳 wi-fi) Cultural and language barriers melt faster than snow in the desert at this small and friendly hostel. The guest kitchen and TV lounge are convivial spaces and freebies include coffee, tea and a waffle breakfast. The 1900 adobe building once belonged to the sheriff involved in capturing the Dillinger gang at the Hotel Congress (below) in 1934.

Lazy 8 Motel (Map p236; ☎ 520-622-3336, 888-800-8805; www.lazy8motel.com; 314 E Benson Hwy, exit 261; r incl breakfast $36-70; P 🖳 wi-fi) If you can forgo Frette linens and designer toiletries for a slim price tab, this is your place. It's right off the freeway and truly as sparklingly clean as they claim. Other perks: a decent-sized pool, a steakhouse with salad bar and free breakfast.

Flamingo Hotel (Map p236; ☎ 520-770-1910, 800-300-3533; www.flamingohoteltucson.com; 1300 N Stone Ave; r incl breakfast $50-70; P 🖳 wi-fi) A classic 1950s motel festooned with old film posters, this place is an affectionate homage to Tucson's movie history. Elvis fans pay heed: the King stayed in room 102.

MIDRANGE

Hotel Congress (Map p239; ☎ 520-622-8848, 800-722-8848; www.hotelcongress.com; 311 E Congress St; r $70-120; P 🖳 wi-fi) This beautifully restored 1919 hotel is a bohemian vintage beauty and a beehive of activity, mostly because of its popular café, bar and club (p243). Infamous bank robber John Dillinger and his gang were captured here during their 1934 stay when a fire broke out at the hotel. Many rooms have period furnishings, rotary phones and wooden radios. Ask for a room at the far end of the hotel if you're noise-sensitive. Pets are welcome.

Windmill Inn at St Philips Plaza (Map p236; ☎ 520-577-0007, 800-547-4747; www.windmillinns.com; 4250 N Campbell Ave; r incl breakfast $80-220; P 🖳 wi-fi) Modern, efficient and friendly, this place is a family favorite thanks to spacious two-room suites (no charge for kids under 18), free continental breakfast (delivered to your room, if you wish), board games and a lending library, a heated pool and free bike rentals. It's opposite a small, upscale mall with a couple of eateries. Pets stay free.

Santa Rita Lodge (off Map p235; ☎ 520-625-8746; www.santaritalodge.com; 1218 S Madera Canyon; casita/cabin $92/112; **P**) If you want a nature base that's reasonably close to the city, this haven in Madera Canyon might be the ticket. It's 35 miles south of downtown via the I-19 and a birder magnet between March and May. Free-standing cabins sleep up to four and have a private back porch, while the casitas have more of a motel feel.

El Presidio Bed & Breakfast Inn (Map p239; ☎ 520-623-6151, 800-349-6151; www.bbonline.com/az/elpresidio; 297 N Main Ave; ste incl breakfast $120-155; **P** wi-fi) Smack dab in the Presidio Historic District, this sedate Victorian adobe mansion exudes irresistible 'old lady' charm with its fresh flowers, quilted beds, fine china and tchotchkes throughout. Each of the four units has a separate sitting room and two have kitchenettes. Days start with a full breakfast and end with complimentary drinks and snacks.

Catalina Park Inn (Map p236; ☎ 520-792-4541, 800-792-4885; www.catalinaparkinn.com; 309 E 1st St; r $140-170; **P** wi-fi; ☼ closed mid-Jul–mid-Sep) Hosts Mark Hall and Paul Richard have poured their hearts and hard-earned cash into restoring this 1927 Med-style villa. Each of the six rooms exudes a different vibe, from the oversized and over-the-top peacock-blue-and-gold Catalina Room to the white and uncluttered East Room with iron canopy bed. The cacti and desert garden has lots of little corners for lazy afternoon cat naps.

TOP END

Hacienda del Sol (Map p236; ☎ 520-299-1501, 800-728-6514; www.haciendadelsol.com; 5601 N Hacienda del Sol Rd; r $165-465; **P** ☼ ☐) An elite hilltop girls' school built in the 1920s, this refuge has artist-designed Southwest-style rooms and teems with special touches like carved ceiling beams and louvered exterior doors to catch the courtyard breeze. Having been on the radar of Spencer Tracy, Katharine Hepburn and other legends, you'll know you're sleeping with history. Fabulous restaurant, too (see p243).

Royal Elizabeth (Map p239; ☎ 520-670-9022, 877-670-9022; www.royalelizabeth.com; 204 S Scott Ave; r $185-285; **P** ☼ ☐ wi-fi) Nostalgia and high-tech merge smoothly at 'The Liz,' as she is lovingly called

by her owners Chuck and Jeff. This femme fatale among boutique B&Bs woos you with splendid antiques, elaborate woodwork, a sweet garden with heated pool and even a guest kitchen. Rooms boast an alphabet soup of gadgets, including TV, VHS, DVD, CD and MP3, and calls are free throughout North America via internet phone.

Lodge on the Desert (Map p236; ☎ 520-325-3366, 800-456-5634; www.lodgeonthedesert.com; 3-6 N Alvernon Way; r $200-340; **P** ☼ ☐ wi-fi) A gracefully aging 1930s resort, this lush, pet-friendly retreat focuses on relaxation. Rooms are in hacienda-style casitas flanked by cacti and palm trees and decorated in charmingly modern Southwest style. Many units have beamed ceilings or fireplaces. Dogs are allowed on the restaurant patio.

La Zarzuela B&B (Map p235; ☎ 520-884-4824, 888-848-8225; www.zarzuela-az.com; 455 N Camino de Oeste; r $275-300; ☼ closed mid-Jun–mid-Sep; **P** ☼ ☐ wi-fi) If you entertain fantasies of escaping to a remote artsy hideaway, this gorgeous adult-only mansion in the foothills is your place. It has five spacious casitas splashed in bold colors and with wide-open terrace and porch views.

Arizona Inn (Map p236; ☎ 520-325-1541, 800-933-1093; www.arizonainn.com; 2200 E Elm St; r $320-550; **P** ☼ ☐) Lest you accuse us of ageism, let it be known that this pink grande dame is still lovely. However, it could probably use a little nip and tuck to keep up with the times. As it is, the mature gardens and old Arizona grace not only provide a respite from city life but also from the 21st century. Sip coffee on the porch, take high tea in the library, lounge by the small pool or join in a game of croquet, then retire to rooms furnished in antiques and quality repros.

Eating

Tucson's cuisine scene delivers a flavor-packed punch in everything from family-run 'nosherias' to five-star dining rooms. Intricately spiced and authentic Mexican and Southwestern fare is king here and much of it is prepared freshly with regional ingredients. Steaks, often grilled over a mesquite-wood fire, also have their loyal fan clubs. Health nuts and herbivores, meanwhile, will find the best selection of organic and meat-free cafés and markets here in all of Arizona. And of course there's also plenty of sushi parlors, Thai eateries, American diners and fast-food outlets. We've listed some locals' favorites, but for

more options, consult www.tucsonoriginals
.org, an affiliation of local and independently
owned restos.

BUDGET

Casbah (Map p236; ☎ 520-740-0393; 628 N 4th Ave;
dishes $5-11; ✇ 9am-10pm Mon-Thu, 9am-11pm Fri & Sat;
wi-fi) Beyond the 400-year-old wooden portal from Afghanistan lies Tucson's grooviest
hippie-style teahouse-cum-café. The patchouli
hangs thickly in the Bedouin-tent-style back
patio where you can loll on thick pillows, sip
organic tea or munch on homemade vegan
chile or a tempeh Reuben sandwich. Local
performers entertain most nights.

Grill (Map p239; ☎ 520-623-7621; 100 E Congress St;
mains $6-25; ✇ 24hr) In the wee hours this divey
downtown diner gets howling with night
owls hoping to restore balance to the brain.
Squeeze into a red booth and keep an eye out
for that cute drummer you just saw at the club
up the street. Just don't let the moth-eaten
animal heads freak you out.

Bison Witches (Map p239; ☎ 520-740-1541; 526
4th Ave; sandwiches $7; ✇ 11am-1am) Bring a mon-
ster appetite or forget about finishing the
whopping sandwiches at this funky deli-bar.
Everything's made fresh and with good and
healthy ingredients like grilled meats, avocado
and sprouts. The back patio is more for the
smoking and drinking crowd.

Other good budget eats:

Mi Nidito (Map p236; ☎ 520-622-5081; 1813 S 4th Ave;
dishes $4.50-9; ✇ lunch & dinner) Authentic Mexican
fare enjoyed by Bill Clinton, Enrique Iglesias and regular
'Joes' like us.

Something Sweet Dessert Lounge (Map p236;
☎ 520-881-7735; 5319 E Speedway Blvd; desserts $5-7;
✇ 5pm-midnight) Death by chocolate, tarts, fruit pies,
cheesecake or Big A$$ Brownie – pick your sweet poison.
No booze.

MIDRANGE

Lovin' Spoonfuls (Map p236; ☎ 520-325-7760; 2990 N
Campbell Ave; lunch $6-8, dinner $8-11; ✇ 9:30am-9pm
Mon-Sat, 10am-3pm Sun; Ⓥ) Burgers, country-fried
chicken, meatloaf, salads – the menu reads like
those at your typical café but there's one big
difference: no animal products will ever find
their way into this vegan haven. Outstandingly
creative choices include the cashew-mushroom
pâté and the adzuki bean burger.

Blue Willow Restaurant (Map p236; ☎ 520-795-
8736; 2616 N Campbell Ave; mains $8-14; ✇ breakfast,
lunch & dinner) If you've greeted the day with

bloodshot eyes, get back in gear with high-
octane coffee, energy-restoring omelettes or
a fiery chorizo scramble at this beloved local
institution. Fresh pasta, bulging sandwiches,
meat-free choices and daily specials keep the
place packed through dinnertime. The patio
is heated in winter.

Yoshimatsu (Map p236; ☎ 520-320-1574; 2660 N
Campbell Ave; dishes $8-17; ✇ lunch & dinner; Ⓥ) Billing
itself as a 'healthy Japanese eatery,' Yoshimatsu
uses mostly organic foods, eschews MSG and
offers lots of vegetarian and vegan options.
Order a bento box, steamy soup or rice bowl
at the counter and eat in the woodsy front
tavern, or get table service at the separate and
more intimate sushi café in back.

El Charro Café (Map p239; ☎ 520-622-1922; 311 N Court
Ave; mains $8-18; ✇ lunch & dinner) The buzz is con-
stant in this rambling hacienda where the Flin
family has been making innovative Mexican
food nonstop since 1922. They're particularly
famous for the *carne seca*, sundried lean beef
that's been reconstituted, shredded and grilled
with green chile and onions. The fabulous
margaritas pack a Pancho Villa punch.

Caruso (Map p239; ☎ 520-624-5765; 434 4th Ave; mains
$9-12; ✇ lunch & dinner Tue-Sun) Caruso the cook has
left as much of a mark on the local culinary
scene as Caruso the tenor has on the world
of opera. Linguine with clam sauce, chicken
parmigiano and crispy-crust pizza have fed
tummies and souls since the 1930s. If you're
on a romantic mission, skip the garlic bread
but do book a patio table.

Pastiche (Map p236; ☎ 520-325-3333; 3025 N Campbell
Ave; mains $10-27; ✇ 11:30am-midnight Mon-Fri, 4:30pm-
midnight Sat & Sun) The name is the game at this
ambitious, artsy and bustling bistro where
dishes from the Middle East, France, Italy
and Asia team up to form the quintessential
American menu. Wallet- or waist-watchers
can order the bistro portions and still walk
away fed and happy.

Sakura (Map p236; ☎ 520-298-7777; 6534 E Tanque
Verde Rd; lunch $8-12, dinner $12-26; ✇ lunch Mon-Fri,
dinner daily) Usually packed to the gills, this
Japanese restaurant will satisfy purists with
its fresh eel and tuna, the squeamish with its
baked California roll, and meat-eaters with
its *teppan* (fun tableside chopping and pyro-
technics). The Sakura Boat featuring 32 pieces
is great for sharing and there's even a 'Karate
Kids' menu for pint-sized Samurai.

Café Terra Cotta (Map p236; ☎ 520-577-8100; 3500 E
Sunrise Dr; mains $16-22; ✇ lunch & dinner Tue-Sun) This

restaurant gets consistently high marks for its wood-fired pizza, spicy pork tenderloin and upscale Southwestern fare. The small-plate starters are so appetizing that many people order a couple and skip the main.

Café Poca Cosa (Map p239; ☎ 520-622-6400; 110 E Pennington St; mains $16-25; ☑ lunch & dinner Tue-Sat) At this award-winning Nuevo-Mexican bistro a Spanish-English blackboard menu circulates between tables because dishes change twice daily. It's all freshly prepared, innovative and beautifully presented. The undecided can't go wrong by ordering the Plato Poca Cosa and letting chef Suzana D'avila decide. Great margaritas, too.

TOP END

Grill at Hacienda del Sol (Map p236; ☎ 520-529-3500; 5601 N Hacienda del Sol Rd; Sunday brunch $32, mains $26-42; ☑ dinner daily, brunch Sun) The sunset views compete with the smart, grown-up ambience, the Spanish Colonial decor and, of course, the exquisitely composed nouvelle Southwestern cuisine featuring herbs, veggies and fruit grown on site. Oenophiles have an extensive wine list to slobber over. Reservations are required.

Janos (Map p236; ☎ 520-615-6100; 3770 E Sunrise Dr; mains $28-50, tasting menu $85; ☑ dinner Mon-Sat) Even in the pantheon of Southwestern gourmet eateries, this is a standout. French-trained James Beard Award–winner Janos Wilder is a veritable wizard in creating Southwestern compositions with that certain *je ne sais quoi*. His dining room at the Westin La Paloma overlooks the entire valley and is perfect for big, long romantic meals.

Drinking

Nimbus Brewing Company (Map p236; ☎ 520-745-9175; 3850 E 44th St) Brewmeisters at Nimbus, a cavernous purple warehouse space, make ale like Mattel makes Barbies: one in every color – blonde, brown, red, dark. No matter what type you prefer, it's likely to be a smooth guzzle. The taproom has a distinctive monkey theme in keeping with the brewery's cheeky logo.

Shanty (Map p239; ☎ 520-623-2664; cnr 4th Ave & 9th St) This friendly pub staple is all about friends, conversation, free popcorn, shooting pool and, of course, good beer. And boy, have they got beer. You'd need weeks to quaff your way through the menu, which features Czech pilsner, Boddington's and obscure brews from

Nicaragua and Kenya. Smoking is permitted on the patio.

Che's Lounge (Map p239; ☎ 520-623-2088; 346 N 4th Ave) If everyone's favorite revolutionary heart-throb was still in our midst, he wouldn't have charged a cover either. A slightly skanky but hugely popular watering hole with $1 drafts, a huge wraparound bar and local art gracing the walls, this college hangout rocks with live music Saturday nights.

Surly Wench (Map p239; ☎ 520-882-0009; 424 4th Ave) This bat cave of a watering hole is often packed with pierced pals soaking up $1.50 bottles of Schlitz in careless quantities, giving the pinball machine a workout or bopping heads to deafening punk, thrash and alt-rock bands.

Kon Tiki (Map p236; ☎ 520-323-7193; 4625 E Broadway Blvd) Never mind the strip-mall setting. Once inside this tropical tiki tavern with its reed roof and palm fronds you'll feel like you've apparated straight to Tahiti. Drinks look girly, but don't be fooled: the trademark 'Scorpion' will sneak up on your brain cells without warning.

Ain't Nobody's Bizness (Map p236; ☎ 520-318-4838; 2900 E Broadway Blvd, Suite 118) In a shopping plaza, this has long been Tucson's favorite lesbian bar. Escape the chaos around the pool tables and on the dance floor by heading to the quiet room for a long get-to-know-you chat.

Entertainment

The free *Tucson Weekly* has comprehensive party listings, but for downtown-specific info pick up the *Downtown Tucsonian*, also gratis. Another good source is www.aznightbuzz.com. Congress St in downtown and 4th Ave near the university are both busy party strips.

NIGHTCLUBS & LIVE MUSIC

Club Congress (Map p239; ☎ 520-622-8848; 311 E Congress St; cover $3-10) Skinny jeansters, tousled hipsters, aging folkies, dressed-up hotties – the crowd at Tucson's most happening club inside the grandly aging Hotel Congress (p240) defines the word eclectic. And so does the musical line-up, which usually features the finest local and regional talent.

Rialto Theater (Map p239; ☎ 520-798-3333; 318 E Congress St; cover $10-35) This gorgeous 1920 vaudeville and movie theater has been reborn as a top venue for live touring acts – rock to hip hop, flamenco to swing, plus the odd comedian; basically anyone too big to play at Club Congress across the street.

ARIZONA

Plush (Map p239; ☎ 520-798-1298; cnr 4th Ave & 6th St; club cover $5) Plush is another club to watch when it comes to catching cool bands from LA, Seattle, Chicago and beyond. There's usually a line-up of two or three holding forth in the main room where the light is mellow and the sound is not. Head to the pub-style lounge in front to rest eardrums between sets.

IBT's (Map p236; ☎ 520-882-3053; 616 N 4th Ave; no cover) At Tucson's most sizzling gay fun house, the theme changes nightly – from drag shows to techno dance mixes to karaoke. Chill on the patio, check out the bods, or sweat it out on the dance floor.

Asylum (Map p239; ☎ 520-882-8949; 121 E Congress St; cover $5) If you worship at the altar of goth and industrial, put on your black thrift-shop threads, nailpolish and eyeliner and have yourself committed to this dark and edgy downtown den. Free bands on Friday and nightly drinks and food specials should leave you with enough change for an early am burger at the Grill (p242) across the street.

CINEMAS & PERFORMING ARTS

It's always worth checking out what's on at the deco **Fox Theatre** (Map p239; ☎ 520-624-1515; www.foxtucsontheatre.org; 17 W Congress St), a gloriously glittery venue for classic and modern movies, music, theater and dance.

For indie, art-house and foreign movies head to **Loft Cinema** (Map p236; ☎ 520-322-5638; 3233 E Speedway Blvd).

In April, May, September and October, jazz fans gather for free outdoor concerts at **St Philips Plaza** (Map p236; 4280 N Campbell Ave) on Sunday nights.

The **Arizona Opera** (☎ 520-293-4336; www.azopera .org) and **Tucson Symphony Orchestra** (☎ 520-792-9155; www.tucsonsymphony.org) perform between October and April at the **Tucson Music Hall** (Map p239; 260 S Church Ave). The **Arizona Theatre Company** (☎ 520-622-2823; www.arizonatheatre.org), meanwhile, puts on shows from September to April at the **Temple of Music & Art** (Map p236; 330 S Scott Ave), a renovated 1920s building.

Shopping

Old Town Artisans (Map p239; 201 N Court Ave) in the Presidio Historic District (p237) is a good destination for quality arts and crafts produced in the Southwest and Mexico. Also recommended is **St Philips Plaza** (Map p236; 4280 N Campbell Ave), where standouts include the **Obsidian Gallery** (☎ 520-577-3598) for art and jewelry, **Bahti Indian Arts** (☎ 520-577-0290) for Native American wares, and the **Turquoise Door** (☎ 520-299-7787) for stunning baubles.

For fun, eclectic shopping, you can't beat 4th Ave, where there's a great cluster of vintage stores between 8th and 7th Sts. **Food Conspiracy Cooperative** (Map p239; 412 4th Ave) is great for stocking up on organic produce and products, while the beautiful **Native Seeds/Search** (Map p236; 526 4th Ave) sells rare seeds of crops traditionally grown by Native Americans, along with quality books and crafts.

Getting There & Away

Tucson International Airport (Map p235; ☎ 520-573-8000; www.tucsonairport.org) is 15 miles south of downtown and served by 13 airlines with daily flights to such destinations as Las Vegas, Los Angeles, San Diego and New York.

Greyhound (Map p236; ☎ 520-792-3475; 471 W Congress St) and its partners run up to 10 direct buses to Phoenix ($19, two hours) among other destinations.

The *Sunset Limited* train, operated by **Amtrak** (Map p239; ☎ 800-872-7245; www.amtrak.com; 400 E Toole Ave), comes through on its way west to Los Angeles ($38, 10 hours, three weekly) and east to New Orleans ($133, 37 hours, three weekly).

Getting Around

All major car-rental agencies have offices at the airport. **Arizona Stagecoach** (☎ 520-889-1100; www.azstagecoach.com) runs shared-ride vans into town for about $18 per person. A taxi from the airport to downtown costs around $20 to $25. Taxi companies include **Yellow Cab** (☎ 520-624-6611) and **Allstate Cab** (☎ 520-881-2227).

Ticet operates five free shuttle lines throughout central Tucson. The most useful route is the Red Line, which goes from downtown along 4th St to the University of Arizona. Pick up a free route map at the **Ronstadt Transit Center** (Map p239; cnr Congress St & 6th Ave). This is also the main hub for the public **Sun Tran** (☎ 520-792-9222; www.suntran.com) buses serving the entire metro area. Fares are $1, or $2 for the day pass.

TUCSON TO PHOENIX

If you just want to quickly travel between Arizona's two biggest cities, it's a straight 120-mile shot on a not terribly inspiring stretch of the I-10. However, a couple of rewarding side trips await those with curiosity and a little more time on their hands.

Picacho Peak State Park

Distinctive Picacho Peak (3374ft) sticks out from the flatlands like a desert Matterhorn, about 40 miles northwest of Tucson. The westernmost battle of the American Civil War was fought in this area, with Arizona Confederate troops killing two or three Union soldiers before retreating to Tucson and dispersing, knowing full well that they would soon be greatly outnumbered.

The battle is reenacted every March with much pomp, circumstance and period costumes. The **state park** (☎ 520-466-3183; www.pr.state .az.us/parks; I-10, exit 219; per vehicle Jun-Aug $3, Sep-May $6; ◷ 8am-10pm) provides year-round **camping** (tent/RV sites Jun-Aug $10-15, Sep-May $12-22), picnicking and hiking trails, including two to the summit. Fixed ropes and ladders aid hikers, but no technical climbing is involved.

Biosphere 2

Built to be completely sealed off from Biosphere 1 (that would be Earth), **Biosphere 2** (Map p235; ☎ 520-896-6200; www.b2science.org; 32540 S Biosphere Rd; adult/child/senior $20/13/18; ◷ 9am-4pm) is a 3-acre campus of glass domes and pyramids containing five ecosystems: a tropical ocean, mangrove wetlands, a tropical rainforest, savannah and a coastal fog desert. In 1991, eight biospherians were sealed inside for a two-year tour of duty from which they emerged thinner but in pretty fair shape. Although this experiment was ostensibly a prototype for self-sustaining space colonies, the privately funded endeavor was engulfed in controversy. Heavy criticism came after the dome leaked gases and was opened to allow a biospherian to emerge for medical treatment. After several changes in ownership, the sci-fi-esque site is now a University of Arizona–run earth science research institute. Public tours take in the biospherians' apartments, farm area and kitchen, the one-million gallon 'tropical ocean' and the 'technosphere' that holds the mechanics that made it all possible.

Biosphere 2 is near Oracle, about 30 miles north of Tucson via Hwy 77 (Oracle Rd) or 30 miles east of the I-10 (exit 240, east on Tangerine Rd, then north on Hwy 77). No pets.

Casa Grande Ruins National Monument

Built around AD 1350, Casa Grande (Big House) is one of the country's largest Hohokam structures with 11 rooms spread across four floors and mud walls several feet thick. Preserved as a **national monument** (☎ 520-723-3172; www.nps.gov/cagr; 1100 W Ruins, Dr, Coolidge; adult/child $5/free; ◷ 8am-5pm), it's in reasonably good shape, partly because of the strange metal awning that's been canopying it since 1932. The visitor center has exhibits about the Hohokam society and Casa Grande itself, including a model of what the place may have originally looked like. Ranger-led 30-minute tours are available between November and April.

The ruins are about 70 miles northwest of Tucson. Leave the I-10 at exit 211 and head north on Hwy 87 towards Coolidge and follow the signs. Don't confuse the monument with the modern town of Casa Grande, west of the I-10.

WEST OF TUCSON

West of Tucson, Hwy 86 cuts like a machete through the Tohono O'odham Indian Reservation, the second largest in the country. Although this is one of the driest areas in the Sonora Desert, it's an appealing drive for anyone craving the lure of the lonely highway with only the occasional cactus for cops to hide behind. Listen for the sounds of the desert – the howl of a coyote, the rattle of a snake. The skies are big, the land vast and barren. Gas stations, grocery marts and motels are sparse, so plan ahead and carry plenty of water and whatever else you need.

Kitt Peak National Observatory

Dark and flawlessly clear night skies make remote **Kitt Peak** (☎ 520-318-8726; www.noao.edu/kpno; Hwy 86; admission by donation; ◷ 9am-3:45pm) a perfect site for one of the world's largest observatories. Just west of Sells, 56 miles southwest of Tucson, this 6875ft-high mountaintop is stacked with two radio and 23 optical telescopes, including one boasting a staggering diameter of 12ft.

There's a visitor center with exhibits and a gift shop but no food. Guided one-hour **tours** (adult/child $4/2.50; ◷ 10am, 11:30am & 1:30pm) take you inside the building housing the telescopes, but alas you don't get to peer through any of them. To catch a glimpse of the universe, sign up for the **Nightly Observing Program** (adult/student/senior $39/34/34; ◷ Sep–mid-Jul), a three-hour $5

ARIZONA

stargazing session starting at sunset and limited to 20 people. This program books up weeks in advance but you can always check for cancellations when visiting. And dress warmly! It gets cold up there.

There's no public transportation to the observatory, but **Adobe Shuttle** (☎ 520-745-5940) runs vans out here from Tucson. There's a minimum fee of $150, good for up to three people; additional persons cost $45 each.

Organ Pipe Cactus National Monument

Anyone seeking solitude beneath big blue open skies will love the crowdless scenery of this huge and exotic **park** (☎ 520-387-6849; www.nps.gov/orpi; Hwy 85; per vehicle $8; ☉ 24hr) along the Mexican border. It's a gorgeous, forbidding land that supports an astonishing number of animals and plants, including 26 species of cacti, first and foremost its namesake organ-pipe. A giant columnar cactus, it differs from the more prevalent saguaro in that its branches radiate from the base. Organ-pipes are common in Mexico but very rare north of the border. The monument is also the *only* place in the USA to see the senita cactus. Its branches are topped by hairy white tufts, which give it the nickname 'old man's beard.' Animals that have adapted to this arid climate include bighorn sheep, coyotes, kangaroo rats, mountain lions and the piglike javelina. Your best chances to encounter wildlife are greatest in the early morning and evening. Walking around the desert by full moon or flashlight is another good way to catch things on the prowl, but wear boots and watch where you step.

Winter and early spring, when Mexican gold poppies and purple lupine blanket the barren ground, are the most pleasant seasons to visit. Summers are shimmering hot (above 100°F) and bring monsoon rains between July and September.

ORIENTATION & INFORMATION

The only paved road to and within the monument is Hwy 85, which travels 26 miles south from the hamlet of Why to Lukeville, near the Mexican border. After 22 miles you reach the **visitor center** (☉ 8am-5pm), which has information, drinking water, books and exhibits. Ranger-led programs run from January to March.

DANGERS & ANNOYANCES

Rubbing up against the Mexican border, this remote monument is a popular crossing for undocumented immigrants and drug smugglers,

and large sections of it are closed to the public. A steel fence intended to stop illegal off-road car crossings marks its southern boundary. In 2002, 28-year-old ranger Kris Eggle, for whom the visitor center is named, was killed by drug traffickers while on patrol in the park. Call ahead or check the website for current accessibility.

SIGHTS & ACTIVITIES

Two scenic drives are currently open to vehicles and bicycles, both starting near the visitor center. The 21-mile **Ajo Mountain Drive** takes you through a spectacular landscape of steep-sided, jagged cliffs and rock tinged a faintly hellish red. It's a well-maintained but winding and steep gravel road navigable by regular passenger cars (not recommended for RVs over 24ft long). If you prefer to let someone else do the driving, ask at the visitor center about ranger-led van tours available from January to March. The other route is **Puerto Blanco Drive**, of which only the first 5 miles are open, leading to a picnic area and overviews.

Unless it's too hot, the best way to truly experience this martian scenery is on foot. There are several **hiking trails**, ranging from a 200yd paved nature trail to strenuous climbs of over 4 miles. Cross-country hiking is also possible, but bring a topographical map and a compass and know how to use them – a mistake out here can be deadly. Always carry plenty of water, wear a hat and slather yourself in sunscreen.

SLEEPING & EATING

The 200 first-come, first-served sites at **Twin Peaks Campground** (tent/RV sites $12) by the visitor center are often full by noon from mid-January through March. There's drinking water and toilets, but no showers or hookups. Tenters might prefer the scenic if primitive **Alamo Canyon Campground** (campsites $8), which requires reservations at the visitor center. There's no backcountry camping because of illegal border crossings.

No food is available in the monument, but there's a restaurant and a small grocery store in Lukeville. The closest lodging is in **Ajo**, about 11 miles north of Why, on Hwy 85.

SOUTH OF TUCSON

From Tucson, the I-19 is a straight 60-mile shot south through the Santa Cruz River Valley to Nogales on the Mexican border. A historical trading route since pre-Hispanic times, the highway is unique in the US because distances are posted in kilometers – it was built at the time when there was a strong push to go metric. Speed limits, though, are posted in miles!

Though not terribly scenic, I-19 is a ribbon of superb cultural sights with a bit of shopping thrown into the mix. It makes an excellent day trip from Tucson. If you don't want to backtrack, follow the much prettier Hwys 82 and 83 to the I-10 for a 150-mile loop.

Mission San Xavier del Bac

About 8 miles south of Tucson on the I-19 (take exit 92), the ornate twin towers of this **mission** (Map p235; ☎ 520-294-2624; www.sanxaviermission.org; 1950 W San Xavier Rd; donations appreciated; 🕑 7am-5pm) rise from the dusty desert floor like a dazzling mirage. Nicknamed 'White Dove of the Desert,' the original mission was founded by Jesuit missionary Father Eusebio Kino in 1700 but was mostly destroyed in the Pima uprising of 1751. Its successor was gracefully rebuilt in the late 1700s in a harmonious blend of Moorish, Byzantine and Mexican Renaissance styles. Carefully restored in the 1990s with the help of experts from the Vatican and still religiously active, it's one of the best preserved and most beautiful Spanish missions in the country.

Nothing prepares you for the extraordinary splendor behind its thick walls. Your eyes are instantly drawn to the wall-sized carved, painted and gilded retable behind the altar, which tells the story of creation in dizzying detail. In the left transept the faithful line up to caress and pray to a reclining wooden figure of St Francis, the mission's patron saint. Metal votive pins shaped like body parts have been affixed to his blanket, offered in the hope of healing.

A small museum explains the history of the mission and its construction. Native Americans sell fry bread, jewelry and crafts in the parking lot.

Titan Missile Museum

Cold War history comes frighteningly alive at this original Titan II missile site, where a crew of two stood at the ready 24/7 to launch a nuclear warhead within seconds of receiving a presidential order. The Titan II was the first liquid-propelled Intercontinental Ballistic Missile (ICBM) that could be fired from below ground and could reach its target –

halfway around the world or wherever – in 30 minutes or less. On alert from 1963 to 1986, this is the only one of 54 Titan II missile sites nationwide that has been preserved as a **museum** (☎ 520-574-9658; www.titanmissilemuseum.org; 1580 W Duval Mine Rd; adult/child/senior $8.50/5/7.50; 🕑 9am-5:30pm Nov-Apr, 9am-5pm May-Oct). The one-hour tours (last tours an hour before closing), which are usually led by retired military types, are both creepy and fascinating. Walking through several 3-ton blast doors you enter the belly of the beast – the Control Room – where you experience a simulated launch before seeing the actual (deactivated, of course) 103ft-tall missile still sitting in its launch duct. Exhibits in the small museum demonstrate how the US government trivialized the dangers of nuclear war. Particularly sinister is the 'duck and cover' instructional video shown to school children.

The museum is 24 miles south of Tucson, off I-19 exit 69.

Tubac

Tubac, about 45 miles south of Tucson, started as a Spanish fort set up in 1752 to stave off Pima attacks. These days, the tiny village depends entirely on cashed-up tourists dropping money for crafts, gifts, jewelry, souvenirs, pottery and paintings peddled in its 100 or so galleries and shops. Compact and lined with handsome adobe-style buildings, it's an attractive place to poke around for an hour or so.

The fort here is all but gone, but you can view its foundations at the **Tubac Presidio State Historic Park** (☎ 520-398-2252; www.pr.state.az.us/parks; adult/child $3/free; 🕑 8am-5pm), a distinctly underwhelming experience. Fortunately, the attached museum has some worthwhile exhibits, including Arizona's oldest newspaper printing press from 1859.

For maps and information, swing by the **Tubac Visitor Center** (☎ 520-398-2704; www.tubacaz.com; 4 Plaza Rd, Suite E; 🕑 9am-4pm; wi-fi) near the village entrance, just behind the **Tubac Deli & Coffee Co** (☎ 520-398-3330; 6 Plaza Rd; dishes $4-7; 🕑 6:30am-8pm). Across the street is the **Old Tubac Inn** (☎ 520-398-3161; 7 Plaza Rd; lunch $6-11, dinner $10-20; 🕑 lunch & dinner), where you can enjoy delicious mesquite-smoked barbecue in a homey dining room or on the patio with iron furniture.

Once the shops close around 5pm, Tubac practically turns into a ghost town. For a quiet night, check in at the **Tubac Country Inn** (☎ 520-398-3178; www.tubaccountryinn.com; 13 Burruel St; r incl

ARIZONA

breakfast $110-160; wi-fi), an uncluttered five-room B&B where a generous continental breakfast is delivered right to your doorstep.

Tumacácori National Historic Park

In 1691 Father Eusebio Kino and his cohort arrived at the Pima settlement of Tumacácori and quickly founded a mission to convert the local Native Americans. However, repeated Apache raids and the harsh winter of 1848 drove the last priests out, leaving the complex to crumble for decades. Only 3 miles south of Tubac, its hauntingly beautiful ruins are now a **national historic park** (☎ 520-398-2341; www.nps.gov/tuma; I-19, exit 29; per person $3; 🕑 9am-5pm). Self-guided tours (ask for the free booklet) start at the visitor center, which also has a few exhibits. Skip the naive 15-minute video, but do visit the church with its unfinished bell towers and faded murals in the sanctuary.

Skip also the snack places opposite the mission and from the national historic park towards Tubac to the **Wisdoms Café** (☎ 520-398-2379; 1931 E Frontage Rd; dishes $6-16; 🕑 11am-3pm & 5-8pm). At this local institution (since 1944), the Mexican-themed menu heavily touts the signature 'fruit burros' (a fruit-filled crispy tortilla rolled in cinnamon and sugar).

Another roadside attraction is **Santa Cruz Chili & Spice** (☎ 520-398-2591; 1868 E Frontage Rd; 🕑 8am-5pm), a spice factory in business for over 60 years.

Nogales

pop 21,000 / elev 3865ft

The I-19 dead-ends at the US–Mexican border in Nogales, at the narrowest part of the Santa Cruz Valley. Founded in 1880 as a trading point, its history is inseparable from that of Nogales, Sonora, right across the border. For decades the only physical division between the two was a barbed-wire fence, but that all changed in 2007 when a 2.8-mile-long heavy metal wall was put up to deter illegal immigration and drug smuggling.

Both towns lack traditional tourist attractions and most people visit to buy cheap cigarettes, booze and trinkets on the Mexican side. US dollars and credit cards are accepted everywhere, and bargaining is the rule of land. Pharmaceuticals are considerably less expensive too, but note that in addition to a US doctor's prescription, you also need one from a Mexican doctor or risk getting busted by Mexican police. Many pharmacies can make referrals to a local doctor who will write one for a small fee.

Bars and clubs often crawl with revelers under 21 who are taking advantage of Mexico's legal drinking age, which is 18. With some venues advertising $20 all-you-can-drink deals, binge drinking is a common phenomenon.

See the boxed text (p250) for customs and immigration information.

ORIENTATION & INFORMATION

I-19 goes straight to the border crossing, avoiding downtown Nogales, Arizona, altogether. To go through the town center, take exit 4 and follow Mariposa Rd east past chain motels, supermarkets and fast-food outlets. Turn right on Grand Ave, which cuts through the increasingly Mexican-flavored downtown, culminating at the border crossing.

Hospital (☎ 520-285-3000; 1171 W Target Range Rd) 24-hour emergency services.

Library (☎ 520-287-3343; 518 N Grand Ave; 🕑 Mon & Wed 9:30am-6pm, Tue & Thu 9.30-7pm, Fri 9am-5pm, Sat 9am-4pm; 💻 wi-fi) Free internet.

Nogales-Santa Cruz County Chamber of Commerce (☎ 520-287-3685; www.thenogaleschamber.com; 123 W Kino Pkwy; 🕑 9am-4pm Mon-Fri, 9am-1pm Sat) Enthusiastic staff provides information about both Nogales and travel into Mexico. It's on a little dead-end street near the intersection of Grand Ave and Patagonia Hwy (Hwy 82).

Police (☎ 520-287-9111; 777 N Grand Ave)

Post office (☎ 520-287-9246; 300 N Morley Ave)

US Immigration (☎ 520-287-3609) At the border.

SLEEPING & EATING

Look for US chain motels, including a Motel 6 and a Holiday Express, along Mariposa Rd.

El Dorado Inn (☎ 520-287-4611; www.eldoradoinnsuites.com; 884 N Grand Ave; r $70-100; 🏊 💻) The best of the independent downtown cheapies, El Dorado has clean, adequate rooms, including business suites with big desks and spacious family suites with balconies. There's even a decent gym to burn off that megaburrito you had for lunch.

Esplendor Resort at Rio Rico (☎ 520-281-1901, 800-288-4746; www.hhandr.com/esplendor; 1069 Camino Caralampi; r $110-160; 🏊 💻) On a hilltop about 12 miles north of town (I-19 exit 17), this is a lovely secluded resort decorated in Spanish Colonial style and festooned with colorful tiles. Rooms are tasteful and cozy. An 18-hole golf course is a short drive away and there are facilities for tennis and horseback riding in the mountains.

Hacienda Corona de Guevavi (☎ 520-287-6502, 888-287-6502; www.haciendacorona.com; r $175-225; 🏊 wi-fi)

This hidden gem is fit for a duke, or perhaps we should say 'the Duke,' aka John Wayne, who used to stay here when it was under a previous owner. Now in the capable hands of Wendy and Phil, this B&B is an enchanting retreat with dreamy mountain views, vintage courtyard murals and lovingly furnished rooms. In summer, concerts take place on the lovely grounds.

El Zarape (☎ 520-287-3920; 964 N Grand Ave; mains $4-7; ☼ breakfast, lunch & dinner) For authentic Mexican on the US side, join families, soldiers and cowboys for heaping plates of chimichanga, burritos and chilaquiles at this cafeteria-style nosh spot opposite Denny's. The homemade flour tortillas are among the best we've ever had.

Bella Mia (☎ 520-761-3535; 204 W Mariposa Rd, Suite 6; mains $9-20; ☼ lunch & dinner) If Mexican doesn't agree with you, you'll likely be satisfied with the antipasti, pasta, fish and meat dishes of this congenial trattoria across from Motel 6. There's even a special 'bambino' (kids) menu with all dishes priced at $5.

La Roca Restaurant (☎ 520-313-6313; Calle Elias 91; mains $12-24; ☼ 11am-midnight) It's well worth the trouble of crossing the border to indulge in an unexpectedly exquisite candlelight dinner at this popular Sonoran restaurant built partly into the rocky cliffs. Kick back with a fresh lime margarita while making up your mind between the chicken mole, the garlic shrimp or other worthy menu candidates. After crossing the border, walk straight for about 300ft, cross the railroad tracks to your left and look for a narrow side street along the base of a cliff. The restaurant is about 100ft down this road.

GETTING THERE & AWAY

Greyhound (☎ 520-287-5628; www.greyhound.com; 35 N Terrace Ave) operates bus services to Tucson (from $9, 1¼ hour, four daily) and Phoenix ($26, 4 hours, four daily).

PATAGONIA HWY & ARIZONA WINE COUNTRY

pop 880 / elev 4050ft

Nogales is the gateway to Hwy 82, aka the Patagonia Hwy, which rumbles through rolling hills, open range, wine country and bird refuges to link up 70 miles later with Hwy 80 near Tombstone. Tall grass sways in the breeze and lazy cattle graze in fields dotted with the occasional windmill. If the land looks familiar it's because you've probably seen it on film. More than 50 movies were filmed in this area, including *Red River* and *Oklahoma*. It's truly a road

less traveled and a great way to get away from it all and perhaps taste a bit of Arizona wine. Didn't know they grew grapes down here? OK, so it's not the Napa Valley and there are only seven wineries thus far, but thanks to a special microclimate, the grapes are thriving.

Most wineries are open for free public tastings from Friday to Sunday but one that's open daily is the spooky-cool **Arizona Vineyards** (☎ 520-287-7972; ☼ 10am-6pm), about 15 miles along the highway. The tasting room is as dark and dank as Dracula's den and filled with wacky flea-market furnishings and burning incense. Labels are called Rattlesnake Red and Sweet Killer Bee.

To find out about the other wineries, drop by the **visitor center** (☎ 520-394-0060, 888-794-0060; www.patagoniaaz.com; 307 McKeown Ave; ☼ 10am-5pm Mon-Sat, 10am-4pm Sun) in sleepy Patagonia, about 4 miles further on. It's in the Mariposa Book & Gift Shop, one block off Hwy 82.

A surprisingly cultured ranching outpost with tree-lined streets and old adobe buildings, Patagonia is trying hard to become an art destination, although there's not yet that much art. But with quaint B&Bs, good restaurants and a handful of nearby wineries, it's a favorite weekend getaway for Tucsonans looking for rural quaintness.

Grab a java at **Gathering Grounds** (☎ 520-394-2097; 319 McKeown Ave) or treat yourself to gourmet pizza at the **Velvet Elvis Pizza Company** (☎ 520-394-2102; 292 Naugle Ave; dishes $6.50-16, slice $7, pizza $22; ☼ 11:30am-8:30pm Thu-Sun), which is a veritable shrine to the King. If you like it enough here to spend the night, try the artsy **Duquesne House** (☎ 520-394-2732; 357 Duquesne St; r $75) in an 1898 ex-boarding house for miners. It has six old-fashioned units each with its own entrance, sitting room and porch.

About 20 miles east of Patagonia, **Callaghan Vineyards** (☎ 520-455-5322; www.callaghanvineyards.com; 336 Elgin Rd; ☼ 11am-3pm Fri-Sun) is widely considered the area's best winery. To get here, head south on Hwy 83 at the village of Sonita, then east on Elgin Rd. Elgin Rd skirts other wineries before arriving at the **Village of Elgin Winery** (☎ 520-455-9309; www.elginwines.com; 471 Elgin Rd; ☼ 10am-5pm). The quality of the varietals isn't as good, but tastings take place in a 1898 brothel.

Backtrack to Hwy 82 and continue east. Not long after the road crosses the San Pedro Riparian National Conservation Area (p256), it arrives at **Fairbank**, on the east bank of the San Pedro River. The most rewarding of the

ARIZONA

CROSSING THE MEXICAN BORDER

If you just want to visit Mexico for the day, park on the US side (border-adjacent lots on Crawford St and Terrace Ave charge about $4 a day) and walk through immigration.

As of January 31, 2008, US and Canadian citizens must present either a passport, or a government-issued photo ID (eg a driver's license) and proof of citizenship (eg a birth certificate or a certificate of naturalization) in order to return to the United States. Other nationals must carry their passport and, if needed, visas for entering Mexico and reentering the US. Regulations change frequently, so get the latest scoop at www.cbp.gov.

Driving across the border is a serious hassle and only worth it if you're planning a longer sojourn in Mexico. At the border or at the checkpoint 13 miles south of it, you need to pick up a free Mexican tourist card. US or other nations' auto insurance is not valid in Mexico and we strongly suggest you buy Mexican insurance on the US side of the border; rates range from $10 to $20 per day, depending on coverage and your car's age and model.

US citizens and permanent residents over the age of 21 may bring 1L of alcohol, 200 cigarettes or 100 cigars, and $800 worth of gifts back into the US without paying duty. Other nationals over 21 may bring 1L of alcohol, 200 cigarettes or 50 cigars or 3lbs (1.35kg) of smoking tobacco, and $100 worth of gifts back to the US.

---

area's many ghost towns, it boomed in the 1880s as a railroad outpost for Tombstone, 9 miles away. It has plenty of evocatively ruined buildings, including a saloon and a post office. The restored one-room schoolhouse now holds a **visitor center** (☟ 9:30am-4:30pm Fri-Sun).

TOMBSTONE

pop 1500 / elev 4539ft

Stories this good just can't be made up. The year was 1877 and a rip-roaring, brawling, silver-mining town was about to be born. Despite friends' warnings that all he would find was his own tombstone, prospector Ed Schieffelin braved the dangers of Apache attack and struck it rich. He named the strike Tombstone and a legend was born. You've heard the stories about hard-drinking miners, gambling desperados, 'shady ladies,' quick-to-draw cowboys – tales of fortunes won and lost. This is the town of the infamous 1881 shootout at the OK Corral, when Wyatt Earp, his brothers Virgil and Morgan and their friend Doc Holliday gunned down outlaws Ike Clanton and Tom and Frank McLaury. The fight so caught people's imagination, it not only made it into the history books but also onto the silver screen, many times. Just watch the 1993 *Tombstone*, starring Kurt Russell and Val Kilmer, to get you in the mood.

Most boomtowns went bust but Tombstone declared itself 'too tough to die.' Tourism was the new silver and as the Old West became en vogue, Tombstone didn't even have to reconstruct its past. By 1962 the entire town was a National Historic Landmark. Yes, it's a tourist trap, but a delightful one and a fun place to find out how the West was truly won.

Information

Library (☎ 520-457-3612; cnr 4th & Toughnut Sts; ☟ 8am-noon & 1-5pm Mon-Fri; 🖳 wi-fi) Free internet.
Police (☎ 520-457-2244; 313 E Fremont St)
Post office (☎ 520-457-3479; 100 Haskell St)
Tombstone Chamber of Commerce (☎ 520-457-3929, 888-457-3929; cnr 4th & Allen Sts; ☟ 9am-5pm)

Sights

Walking around town is free, but you'll pay to visit most attractions.

OK CORRAL

Site of the famous gunfight, the **OK Corral** (☎ 520-457-3456; www.ok-corral.com; Allen St btwn 3rd & 4th Sts; admission $7.50, without gunfight $5.50; ☟ 9am-5pm) is the heart of both historic and touristic Tombstone. It has models of the gunfighters and other exhibits, including CS Fly's early photography studio and a recreated 'crib,' the kind of room where local prostitutes would service up to 80 guys daily for as little as 25 cents a pop. Fights are reenacted at 2pm (with an additional show at 3:30pm on busy days).

Tickets are also good next door at the **Tombstone Historama**, a 25-minute presentation of the town's history using animated figures, movies and narration (by Vincent

Price). Don't forget to pick up your free copy of the Tombstone *Epitaph,* reporting on the infamous shootout.

The historic newspaper office is now the **Tombstone Epitaph Museum** (☎ 520-457-2211; cnr 5th & Fremont Sts; admission free; 9:30am-5pm).

The losers of the OK Corral – Ike Clanton and the McLaury brothers – are buried (in row 2), along with dozens of other desperados, at **Boothill Graveyard** off Hwy 80 about a quarter-mile north of town. The entrance is via a gift shop but admission, thankfully, is free. Some headstones are twistedly poetic. The one of George Johnson, who was 'hanged by mistake' in 1882, reads:

He was right
We was wrong
But we strung him up
And now he's gone

TOMBSTONE COURTHOUSE STATE HISTORIC PARK

Seven men were hanged in Tombstone's courthouse courtyard, and today a couple of nooses dangle ominously from the recreated gallows. Inside the rambling Victorian **building** (☎ 520-457-3311; 223 Toughnut St; adult/child $4/free; 8am-5pm) you can poke around an eclectic bunch of items relating the reality of frontier justice. Check out the tax licenses for the prostitutes and the doctor's bullet-removal kit.

STAGED SHOOTOUTS

These days, lawlessness in Tombstone takes the form of rip roarin' shootouts reenacted by various gunslinger troupes throughout the day. It's so delightfully hokey, it's worth every penny. Apart from the 2pm show at the OK Corral, there are daily shows at **Helldorado Town** (☎ 520-457-9035; cnr 4th & Toughnut St) and at the Six Gun City restaurant and saloon (p252). Stop by the chamber of commerce for current times.

BIRD CAGE THEATER

Back in the 1880s, this **theater** (☎ 520-457-3421; 517 E Allen St; adult/child/senior $10/7/9; 8am-6pm) was Tombstone's wicked one-stop sin pit. Besides onstage shows, it was a saloon, dance hall, gambling parlor and a home for 'negotiable affections.' In fact, the very name derives from the 14 compartments lining the upper floor of the auditorium – like boxes at the opera –

where the 'soiled doves' entertained their customers. The entire place is stuffed with dusty old artifacts that bring the period to life, including a faro gambling table, a big black hearse, a fully furnished crib and a creepy 'merman,' a mythological creature that's half man, half fish. Yeah. And of course, the theater is haunted.

ROSE TREE MUSEUM

In April, the world's largest rosebush puts on an intoxicating show in the courtyard of this **museum** (☎ 520-457-3326; cnr 4th & Toughnut Sts; adult/child $5/free; 9am-5pm), a beautifully restored Victorian home still owned by the Macia family and brimming with their memorabilia, including a 1960 photograph showing the matriarch with Robert Geronimo, son of the Apache chief.

Festivals & Events

Tombstone events revolve around weekends of Western hoo-ha with shootouts (of course!), stagecoach rides, fiddling contests, 'vigilette' fashion shows, mock hangings and melodramas. The biggest event is **Helldorado Days** (third weekend in October). Other events include **Territorial Days** (variable dates in March), **Wyatt Earp Days** (Memorial Day weekend), **Vigilante Days** (second weekend in August) and **Rendezvous of the Gunfighters** (Labor Day weekend).

Sleeping

Properties increase their rates during special events, when reservations are recommended.

Best Western Lookout Lodge (☎ 520-457-2223, 877-652-6772; www.bestwesterntombstone.com; 801 N Hwy 80; r $60-190;) Up on a hill, about five minutes from town, this newly renovated property gets high marks for its spacious room overlooking the Dragoon Mountains, its Ranch 22 restaurant and the pretty gardens. Very pet-friendly.

Victorian Gardens B&B (☎ 520-457-3677, 800-952-8216; 211 Toughnut St; r $65-75) Next to the courthouse, this respectable-looking B&B actually hides a delightfully checkered past involving gamblers, corrupt judges and, of course, ghosts. Decked out with hardwood floors, lead-glass windows and a frilly parlor, it's popular for weddings and even has its own chapel.

ourpick Larian Motel (☎ 520-457-2272; www.tomb stonemotels.com; 410 E Fremont St; r $70-90; wi-fi) This one's a rare breed: a motel with soul, thanks to the personalized attention from proprietor Gordon, cute retro rooms named for historical characters (Doc Holliday, Curly Bill, Wyatt Earp) and a high standard of cleanliness. Children under 14 stay free.

Katie's Cozy Cabins (☎ 520-457-3963; 16 W Allen St; r $90-110) Four new cabins sleeping up to six people make a nice base for exploring Tombstone and the surrounding area. The upstairs lofts have a double bed, while the rooms below have a couple of bunks for the kiddies.

Tombstone Boarding House B&B (☎ 520-457-3716, 877-225-1319; www.tombstoneboardinghouse.com; 108 N 4th St; r $100-120) The five bedrooms have private entrances, pastel decor and Old West Victoriana. The on-site restaurant, the Lamplight Room (below), is one of the best in town.

Eating

It's a tourist town, so don't expect any culinary flights of fancy. In keeping with its Old West theme, the food is mostly standard American and Mexican.

Longhorn Restaurant (☎ 520-457-3405; cnr Allen & 5th Sts; dishes $5-15; ⏰ breakfast, lunch & dinner) The original 'Bucket of Blood Saloon,' this was where Virgil Earp was shot dead from a 2nd-floor window in 1881. Enjoy a cowboy breakfast or spike your cholesterol with the 40oz steak.

Six Gun City (☎ 520-457-3827; cnr 5th & Toughnut Sts; mains $8-20; ⏰ breakfast, lunch & dinner) Munch on hearty steaks, ribs or sandwiches while Tombstone's 'toughest' cowboys shoot it out at this spit-and-sawdust place. Margaritas are just $2 all day long.

Nellie Cashman's (☎ 520-457-2212; cnr 5th & Toughnut Sts; dishes $9-19; ⏰ breakfast, lunch & dinner) Nellie was a tough Irishwoman who brooked no nonsense but helped out many a down-and-out miner. This 1878 restaurant serves comfy family cooking in a quietly charming dining room. Kids love the foot-long hot dogs and half-pound burgers with all the fixin's starting at $6.

Lamplight Room (☎ 520-457-3716; 108 N 4th St; dishes $11-17; ⏰ lunch & dinner) Part of the Tombstone Boarding House B&B (above), this living-room-style restaurant is big on charm and character. The menu features old-fashioned comfort food – pork loin roast, fettuccine alfredo, chicken cordon bleu – in ample-sized portions. And yes, it also serves Mexican food. On Friday and Saturday nights a classical guitarist provides a background serenade.

Drinking

There's little more to do in the evening than to go on a pub crawl – or make that a saloon stagger.

Crystal Palace Saloon (☎ 520-457-3611; cnr 5th & Allen Sts) This lively saloon was built in 1879 and has been completely restored. It's a favorite end-of-the-day watering hole with Tombstone's costumed actors or anyone wanting to play outlaw for a night.

Big Nose Kate's (☎ 520-457-3107; 417 E Allen St) Full of Wild West character, Doc Holliday's girlfriend's joint features some great painted glass, historical photographs and live music in the afternoons. Down in the basement is the room of the Swamper, a janitor who dug a tunnel into the silver mine shaft that ran below the building and helped himself to buckets of nuggets. Or at least so the story goes…

Getting There & Away

Tombstone is 24 miles south of the I-10 via Hwy 80 (exit 303 towards Benson/Douglas). The Patagonia Hwy (Hwy 82) links up with Hwy 80 about 3 miles north of Tombstone. There is no public transport into town.

BISBEE

pop 6100 / elev 5300ft

Wedged between the steep and narrow walls of Tombstone Canyon, Bisbee is a delightful little town, clean, trim and historical. Oozing old-fashioned ambience, its fine early-19th-century brick buildings line narrow twisting streets and house classy galleries, splendid restaurants and charming hotels. A darling of moviemakers, it has stood in not only as itself, but also as New York and Greece.

Bisbee built its fortune on ore found in the surrounding Mule Mountains. Between 1880 and 1975, underground and open pit mines coughed up copper in sumptuous proportions, generating more than $6 billion worth of metals. Business really took off in 1892 when the Phelps Dodge Corporation, which would soon hold a local monopoly, brought in the railroad. By 1910 the population had climbed to 25,000, and with nearly 50 saloons and bordellos crammed along Brewery Gulch, Bisbee quickly gained a reputation as the liveliest city between El Paso, Texas, and San Francisco, California.

In 2007, Phelps Dodge was acquired by Freeport-McMoRan, which is planning to re-open mining operations in Bisbee, a controversial move, to say the least. It's anybody's guess what this will mean for this thriving community whose residents are a charming mix of aging miners, hippies, artists and folks just wanting to leave big-city life behind. Better visit now before it's too late.

Orientation & Information

Hwy 80 runs through the center of town. Most businesses are found in the Historic District (Old Bisbee), along Main St and near the intersection of Howell and Brewery Aves. Many businesses close from Monday to Wednesday.

Bisbee Visitor Center (☎ 520-432-3554, 866-224-7233; www.discoverbisbee.com; 2 Copper Canyon Plaza; ☽ 9am-5pm Mon-Fri, 10am-4pm Sat & Sun)

Copper Queen Hospital (☎ 520-432-5383; 101 Cole Ave)

Library (☎ 520-432-4232; 6 Main St; ☽ noon-7pm Mon, 10am-7pm Tue & Wed, 10am-5pm Thu & Fri, 10am-2pm Sat; ☐ wi-fi) Free internet.

Police (☎ 520-432-2261; 35 Hwy 92)

Post office (☎ 520-432-2052; 6 Main St)

Sights & Activities

Walking through Old Bisbee, up winding back alleys, steep staircases and café- and shop-lined Main St, is a delight in itself. For sweeping views, walk up OK St above the southern edge of town. A path at the top leads to a hill where locals have built colorful shrines filled with candles, plastic flowers and pictures of the Virgin Mary.

Back in town, don't miss a spin around the **Bisbee Mining & Historical Museum** (☎ 520-432-7071; www.bisbeemuseum.org; 5 Copper Queen Plaza; adult/child/senior $7.50/3/6.50; ☽ 10am-4pm), a Smithsonian affiliate in the 1897 former headquarters of the Phelps Dodge Corporation. It does an excellent job at delineating the town's past, the changing face of mining – from the hammer-and-chisel era to today's open-pit procedures – and the use of copper in our daily lives. You even get to 'drive' a shovel with a dipper larger than most living rooms.

Armed with such knowledge, a tour of the **Queen Mine** (☎ 520-432-2071; 119 Arizona St; adult/child $12/5; ☽ 9am-3:30pm) will be much more rewarding. Don miners' garb, grab a lantern and take the mine train deep into the chilly

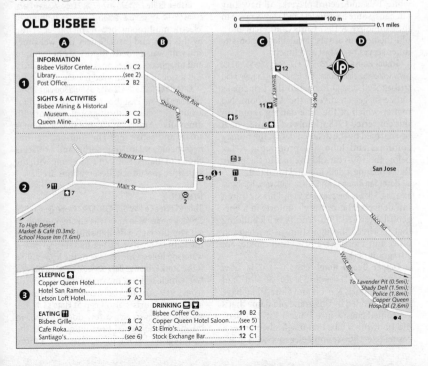

OLD BISBEE

0 — 100 m
0 — 0.1 miles

INFORMATION
Bisbee Visitor Center.................**1** C2
Library....................................(see 2)
Post Office.............................**2** B2

SIGHTS & ACTIVITIES
Bisbee Mining & Historical
 Museum................................**3** C2
Queen Mine............................**4** D3

SLEEPING 🛏
Copper Queen Hotel.................**5** C1
Hotel San Ramón.....................**6** C1
Letson Loft Hotel.....................**7** A2

EATING 🍴
Bisbee Grille...........................**8** C2
Cafe Roka...............................**9** A2
Santiago's..............................(see 6)

DRINKING ☕ 🍺
Bisbee Coffee Co......................**10** B2
Copper Queen Hotel Saloon......(see 5)
St Elmo's...............................**11** C1
Stock Exchange Bar..................**12** C1

To High Desert Market & Café (0.3mi); School House Inn (1.6mi)

Subway St

Main St

San Jose

To Lavender Pit (0.5mi); Shady Dell (1.5mi); Police (1.8mi); Copper Queen Hospital (2.6mi)

ARIZONA

earth's belly (bring warm clothes). To see the aftermath of open-pit mining, drive a half-mile south to the **Lavender Pit**, an immense stair-stepped hole in the ground that produced about 600,000 tons of copper between 1950 and 1974.

Tours

To get the scoop on the town's turbulent past, join a fun and engaging **walking tour** with local historian Michael London, an eccentric bearded character who looks like he's just walked off a movie set. The one-hour tours cost $10 and leave daily from the visitor center.

Sleeping

Bisbee is refreshingly devoid of chain hotels with most lodging in historic hotels or B&Bs. Weekends often fill up early, so come mid-week if you don't have a reservation.

our pick Shady Dell (☎ 520-432-3567; www .theshadydell.com; 1 Douglas Rd; rates $50-165) Yes, it's a trailer park, but with a deliciously retro twist: each 'unit' for rent is an original 1950s travel trailer, meticulously restored and outfitted with period accoutrements such as black-and-white TVs and record players. All have tiny kitchens, some have toilets, but showers are in the bathhouse. A 1947 Chris Craft yacht and a tiki-themed bus are also available. The on-site diner serves breakfast and lunch.

School House Inn (☎ 520-432-2996, 800-537-4333; www.schoolhouseinnbb.com; 818 Tombstone Canyon; r incl breakfast $80-150; wi-fi) Report to the Principal's Office or get creative in the Art Room. No matter which of the nine darling rooms in this converted 1918 school you choose, you'll be charmed by the detailed decor, the homey comforts and John, the proprietor. Relax below the 160-year-old live oak in the patio. Rates include a delicious full breakfast.

Hotel San Ramón (☎ 520-432-1901; www.hotelsanra mon.com; 5 Howell Ave; r $85-145; wi-fi) This six-room inn delivers 21st-century comforts in a gorgeously restored 19th-century brick building that has lived through stints as a telegraph office and a tortilla factory. Fresh cookies are a fragrant perk.

Copper Queen Hotel (☎ 520-432-2216; www .copperqueen.com; 11 Howell; r $90-200; 🍸 wi-fi) Paul Newman, Boris Karloff and Gore Vidal have all been bedded by this grand old dame that's welcomed guests since 1902. It's still a splendid find with a vibe that magically marries a casual late-19th-century elegance with mod-

ern amenities. Rooms vary in size and comfort, so preview before you pick.

Letson Loft Hotel (☎ 520-432-3210, 877-432-3210; www.letsonlofthotel.com; 26 Main St; r $120-185; wi-fi) Urban sophistication meets Victorian quaintness at this sweet eight-room boutique inn in a sensitively restored 19th-century building. Original touches like exposed adobe and brick walls add character to high-ceilinged rooms with flat-screen TV but no phones.

Eating

High Desert Market & Café (☎ 520-432-6775; 203 Tombstone Canyon; dishes $4-8; 🕒 7am-7pm) This cheerful nosh spot serves breakfast and fresh and custom-made sandwiches and salads opposite the Iron Man, a 1935 socialist-aesthetic statue of a manly, bare-chested miner. Its shelves are stocked with local and imported produce and products.

Santiago's (☎ 520-432-1910; 1 Howell Ave; mains $8-15; 🕒 lunch & dinner) Upbeat and contempo, cheerful Santiago's lays on Mexican charm with a trowel. Try the family specialty: *chilorios* (tacos filled with pork marinated in orange citrus ancho chile).

Bisbee Grille (☎ 520-432-6788; 2 Copper Queen Plaza; mains $8-18; 🕒 lunch & dinner) Fancy a helping of 'electric mushrooms' or a 'B Hill Burger'? Drop by this cozy and casual eatery that welcomes you with warm woods, historical photographs and imaginative takes on American standards. Get a side of beer-battered fries to share.

Cafe Roka (☎ 520-432-5153; 35 Main St; dinner $15-25; 🕒 dinner Thu-Sat) Past the art-nouveau steel door awaits this sensuously lit grown-up spot with innovative American cuisine that is at once smart and satisfying. The four-course dinners include salad, soup, sorbet and a rotating choice of mains. You can't go wrong with the signature roast duck. Reservations are key.

Drinking

Bisbee Coffee Co (☎ 520-432-7879; 2 Copper Queen Plaza; 🕒 6:30am-9pm; wi-fi) has javas strong enough to get you through a double shift on the tourist track. In its heyday, Bisbee had several dozen watering holes. One that keeps the legacy alive is the **Stock Exchange Bar** (☎ 520-432-9924; 15 Brewery Ave), which still has the original stock boards from 1919. An often boisterous mix of thirsty locals and tourists also keep **St Elmo's** (☎ 520-432-5578; 36 Brewery Ave), a few doors down, in business. The signed beer mugs behind the cash register belong to regulars. For a more genteel drinking experience, head over to the **Copper Queen Hotel Saloon** (☎ 520-432-2216; www .copperqueen.com; 11 Howell). Its porch is a quaffing perch for balmy nights.

Getting There & Away

Bisbee is about 50 miles south of the I-10 (exit 303 towards Benson/Douglas) and 25 miles south of Tombstone and only about 10 miles north of the Mexican border. There is no public transport to town.

BENSON & AROUND

pop 4700 / elev 3580ft

A railway stop since the late 1800s, Benson is best known as the gateway to the famous Kartchner Caverns, among the largest and most spectacular caves in the USA. This wonderland of spires, shields, pipes, columns, soda straws and other ethereal formations has been five million years in the making, but miraculously wasn't discovered until 1974. In fact, its very location was kept secret for another 25 years in order to prepare for its opening as **Kartchner Caverns State Park** (☎ reservations 520-586-2283, information 520-586-2410; Hwy 90; adult/child Rotunda Tour Oct-Jul $19/10, Aug-Sep $17/9, Big Room Tour mid-Oct–mid-Apr $23/13; ☽ tours 8:20am-4:20pm). Two 90-minute tours are available, both equally impressive. The Big Room Tour closes to the public around mid-April because that's when a colony of migrating female cave myotis bats starts arriving from Mexico to roost and give birth to pups in late June. Moms and baby bats hang out until mid-September before flying off to their wintering spot. While a bat nursery, the cave is closed to the public. Tours often sell out far in advance, so make reservations – online or by phone – early. The entrance is 9 miles south of I-10, off Hwy 90, exit 302.

About 15 miles east of Benson, in Dragoon, the private, nonprofit **Amerind Foundation** (☎ 520-586-3666; www.amerind.org; 2100 N Amerind Rd; adult/child/senior $5/3/4; ☽ 10am-4pm Tue-Sun) exhibits Native American artifacts, history and culture from tribes from Alaska to Argentina, from the Ice Age to today. The Western gallery has exceptional works by such renowned artists as Frederic Remington and William Leigh. It's right off I-10 exit 318.

The complex is near Texas Canyon in the **Little Dragoon Mountains**, which is known for its clumps of giant and photogenic granite boulders. For a closer look swing by the historic **Triangle T Guest Ranch** (☎ 520-586-7533; www .triangletguestranch.com; 4190 Dragoon Rd), where you can arrange horseback rides (from $30), enjoy refreshments in the saloon (mains $6 to 27) or spend the night in fairly basic cabins ($120 to $225). Tenters can set up among the rocks for $20.

Lodging in Benson is mostly about chain motels, which cluster off I-10 exits 302 and 304. For a trip to the 'twilight zone,' snag one of the four space-themed rooms at the hilltop **Astronomer's Inn** (☎ 520-586-7906; www .astronomersinn.com; 1311 S Astronomers Rd; r incl breakfast $105-210) at the Vega-Bray Observatory a few miles southeast of town. Optional nighttime sessions of telescope- and binocular-aided stargazing start at $145.

For soul-sustaining grub try **Galleano's** (☎ 520-586-3523; 601 W 4th St; breakfast $3-8, lunch & dinner $7-17; ☽ breakfast, lunch & dinner), a homey little place that dishes up heaps of Italian and American favorites.

Greyhound (☎ 520-586-3141; 680 W 4th St) buses stop in town on their runs along I-10. Amtrak's *Sunset Limited* comes through thrice weekly on its run between LA and New Orleans.

ROUTE 66 TO NEW MEXICO

Ah, Route 66. The Mother Road. Main Street of America. For down-on-their-luck Okies and post-WWII baby boomers, this 2200-mile ribbon linking Chicago and Los Angeles was the highway of dreams leading to the Promised Land. It came into its own during the Depression, when scores of Dust Bowl refugees slogged westwards in their beat-up old jalopies. During the fuzzy-dice era of the 1950s, Americans took their newfound optimism and wealth on the road, essentially inventing the modern driving vacation. The era of 'getting your kicks on Route 66' was born. But doom was just on the horizon in the form of the new interstate road system. By 1984, Route 66 was history.

Today, Arizona is home to several sections of this legendary highway where you can still get a taste of old-school motoring. Miles of open, windblown road are interrupted by wacky roadside attractions and plenty of vintage pop culture from '50s diners to '30s motor courts. It's a blast from the past all

ARIZONA

FLIGHTFUL ENCOUNTERS OF THE BIRDING KIND

Southeast Arizona is prime turf for that most peculiar human species called 'the birder.' They arrive here by the thousands, especially in spring and fall, outfitted with big binoculars, eagle eyes, endless patience and a bird log. And no wonder: skies here are crowded with more than half of the bird species in North America. You can watch them fly and feed, coo and quack, mate and roost. 'This area sits at an ecological confluence of the Sonoran Desert, the Chihuahuan Desert, the Sierra Madre of Mexico and the Rocky Mountains and so it draws separate bird families from all these different regions,' explains Tony Battiste, a retired cop and avid birder who, together with his wife Julie, runs **Battiste's B&B** (☎ 520-803-6908; www.battistebedandbirds.com; 4700 E Robert Smith Lane; r $135-150; wi-fi) just off Hwy 92 about 15 miles south of **Sierra Vista**. They've counted more than 50 bird species in their backyard alone and each spring host a nesting elf owl that has become a local attraction.

Birding is big business. According to the US Fish and Wildlife Service, 46 million Americans spend $32 billion each year in pursuit of feathered friends. It's fairly cheap, low-impact, not physically taxing, puts you close to nature and, let's face it, those birds are darn pretty. Like the elegant trogon, a multihued beauty with a red breast, yellow beak and green back that's one of the avian superstars around here. 'Bird-watchers want the unusual and this is where they find it. Mexican jay, elegant trogon, fire-striped sparrow, red-faced warbler – they're all rare north of the Mexican border,' says Battiste. The Huachuca Mountains south of Sierra Vista, where Battiste lives, is a birding mecca. **Ramsey Canyon Preserve** (☎ 520-378-2785; www.nature.org; adult/child $5/free; ☽ 8am-5pm daily Feb-Oct, 9am-4pm Thu-Mon Nov-Jan), owned by the Nature Conservancy, is famous for its 14 hummingbird species and astonishing diversity of earthbound wildlife, including the endemic leopard frog, coatis, ringtails and deer. Two trails lead up into the canyon. The 0.7-mile nature loop is quite easy, and the longer Hamburg Trail climbs high into the Huachucas. Free guided nature walks are offered at 9am Tuesday, Thursday and Saturday March to October. Note that access is limited to 23 parking spaces.

If you can't snag a spot here head south on Hwy 92 to Miller or Carr Canyon or east to the **San Pedro Riparian National Conservation Area** (☎ 520-439-6400; www.blm.gov). About 95% of Arizona's riparian habitat has disappeared, victim to overgrazing, logging and development. 'The San Pedro River corridor is crucial to migratory birds,' says Battiste. About 350 bird species, many of them endangered, 84 mammal species and nearly 41 species of reptiles and amphibians have been recorded along the 40-mile stretch of the San Pedro River within the conservation area. It's the healthiest riparian ecosystem in the Southwest.

The **visitor center** (☽ 9:30am-4pm) in the 1930s San Pedro House, reached by driving 6 miles east on Fry Blvd from Sierra Vista, provides access to hiking trails. Guided nature walks are offered on weekends. There's another parking area further south where Hereford Rd cross the river. Backcountry camping costs $2 per person per night and there are self-pay stations at trailheads.

If you're not camping, base yourself at Battiste's, one of the eight other area B&Bs or in a motel in Sierra Vista, a modern town dominated by the Fort Huachuca military base. For help or details, contact the **Sierra Vista visitor center** (☎ 520-417-6960, 800-288-3861; www.visitsierravista .com; 3020 E Tacoma St; ☽ 8am-5pm Mon-Fri, 9am-4pm Sat).

---

right, where decades collide and time often seems to stand still.

Turn-by-turn driving directions are available for free at www.historic66.com. Each year the **Historic Route 66 Association of Arizona** (www.azrt66.com) organizes an annual 'Fun Run' motorcade from Seligman to Golden Shores. The 2006 animated feature film *Cars* is set in the fictional Route 66 town of Radiator Springs.

CALIFORNIA TO KINGMAN

Coming from California, Route 66 enters Arizona at Topock, near the 20-mile **Topock Gorge**, a dramatic walled canyon that's one of the prettiest sections of the Colorado River. It's part of the **Havasu National Wildlife Refuge** (☎ 760-326-2853), a major habitat for migratory and water birds. Look for herons, ducks, geese, blackbirds and other winged creatures as you raft or canoe through the gorge. There are plenty of coves and sandy beaches for picnics and sunning. Companies renting boats include **Jerkwater Canoe & Kayak** (☎ 928-768-8192; www.jerkwater.com; canoe/kayak per person $40/55) in Topock. Rates include boat rental for the 17-mile float from Topock to Castle Rock and the return shuttle.

North of here, in **Golden Shores**, you can refuel on gas and grub before embarking on a rugged 20-mile trip to the terrifically crusty former gold-mining town of **Oatman**, cupped by pinnacles and craggy hills. Since the veins of ore ran dry in 1942, the little settlement has reinvented itself as a movie set and unapologetic Wild West tourist trap, complete with staged gun fights (daily at noon) and gift stores named Fast Fanny's Place and the Classy Ass. And speaking of asses, there are plenty of them (the four-legged kind, that is) roaming the streets and shamelessly begging for carrots (sold at $1 per bag). Stupid and endearing, they're descendents from pack animals left behind by the early miners.

Squeezed among the shops is the 1902 **Oatman Hotel**, a surprisingly modest shack where Clark Gable and Carole Lombard first shagged (presumably) on their wedding night in 1939. You can no longer stay, but feel free to scamper up the off-kilter staircase and sneak a peek. Clark apparently returned quite frequently to play cards with the miners in the downstairs saloon, which is awash in one-dollar bills (some $40,000 worth by the barmaid's estimate). The attached restaurant serves a mean buffalo burger ($7) and homemade potato chips they call 'burro ears.'

Beyond Oatman, keep your wits about you as the road twists and turns past tumbleweeds, saguaro cacti and falling rocks as it travels over **Sitgreaves Pass** (3523ft) and corkscrews into the rugged Black Mountains before arriving in Kingman.

KINGMAN
pop 25,900 / elev 3345ft

Among Route 66 aficionados, Kingman is known as the main hub of the longest uninterrupted stretch of the historic highway, running from Topock to Seligman. Most people, though, regard the town as little more than a pit stop. Too bad. Spend a mere hour or two and you'll be walking among early-20th-century buildings, including the former Methodist church at 5th and Spring St where Clark Gable and Carole Lombard tied the

knot back in 1939. Or learn about hometown hero Andy Devine, who had his Hollywood breakthrough as the perpetually befuddled driver of the eponymous *Stagecoach* in John Ford's Oscar-winning 1939 movie.

These days, Kingman is pinning its hopes on becoming the gateway to Grand Canyon West (p213), about 73 miles northeast of here. Much energy is also being channeled into resuscitating the historic downtown along Beale St, where coffeehouses, antique stores and galleries are gradually replacing the thrift and schlock shops. Kingman is worth keeping an eye on.

Orientation & Information
Route 66 barrels through town as Andy Devine Ave. Near its western end is the excellent **Powerhouse Visitor Center** (☎ 928-753-6106, 866-427-7866; www.kingmantourism.org; 120 W Andy Devine Ave; 🕙 9am-6pm Mar-Oct, 8am-5pm Nov-Feb) and, parallel to it, up-and-coming Beale St. Supermarkets, gas stations and other businesses line up along northbound Stockton Hill Rd, which is also the road to take for Grand Canyon West.

Sights & Activities
The 1907 powerhouse that contains the visitor center also houses the **Route 66 Museum** (☎ 928-753-9889; www.kingmantourism.org; 120 W Andy Devine Ave; adult/child/senior $4/free/3; 🕙 9am-6pm Mar-Oct, 8am-5pm Nov-Feb), which has a charmingly put-together collection of memorabilia. Admission here also gets you into the **Mohave Museum of History & Arts** (☎ 928-753-3195; www.mohavemuseum.org; 400 W Beale St; adult/child/senior $4/free/3; 🕙 9am-5pm Mon-Fri, 1-5pm Sat), a warren of rooms filled with extraordinarily eclectic stuff. All sorts of regional topics are dealt with, from the Hualapai to mining history and Andy Devine. It's old-fashioned, sure, but heck, they're making the most with meager funds, so give 'em a break. Kids get to clamber around a 1923 wooden caboose, while grown-ups may well be enthralled by the documentary on Route 66.

In summer locals flock to **Hualapai Mountain Park** (☎ 928-681-5700; www.mcparks.com; day-use $5) for picnics, hiking and wildlife-watching amid cool ponderosa pine and aspen.

Festivals & Events
Historic Route 66 Fun Run (☎ 928-753-5001; www.azrt66.com) Vintage car rally from Seligman to Topock on the first weekend in May.
Andy Devine Days (☎ 928-753-4003) Week-long party with parades, rodeo and dances in late September.

DETOUR: CHIRICAHUA NATIONAL MONUMENT

Cutting an arrow-straight swath south from the I-10 past fields of swaying blond grass, fence-trapped tumbleweeds and the virtual ghost town of Dos Cabezas, Hwy 186 provides no clue as to the natural treasure hiding in the mountains beyond. Pronounced 'cheery-cow-wha,' **Chiricahua National Monument** (☎ 520-824-3560; www.nps.gov/chir; Hwy 181; adult/child $5/free) is one of Arizona's most unique and evocative landscapes; a wonderfully rugged yet whimsical wonderland. Rain, thunder and wind have chiseled volcanic rocks into fluted pinnacles, natural bridges, gravity-defying balancing boulders and soaring spires reaching skyward like totem poles carved in stone. The remoteness made Chiricahua a favorite hiding place of Apache warrior Cochise and his men. Today it's attractive to birds and wildlife: bobcats and bears are often sighted on the hiking trails. Keep a lookout for deer, coatis and javelinas.

Past the entrance, the paved **Bonita Canyon Scenic Drive** climbs 8 miles to Massai Point at 6870ft, passing several scenic pullouts and trailheads along the way. RVs longer than 29ft are not allowed beyond the **visitor center** (☯ 8:30am-4:30pm), which is about 2 miles along the road.

To explore in greater depth, lace up your boots and hit the trails. Eighteen miles of hiking trails range from easy, flat 0.2-mile loops to strenuous 7-mile climbs. A hikers' shuttle bus leaves daily from the visitor center at 8:30am, going up to Massai Point for $2. Hikers return by hiking downhill.

If you're short on time, hike the **Echo Canyon Trail** at least half a mile to the Grottoes, an amazing 'cathedral' of giant boulders where you can lie still and enjoy the wind-caressed silence. The most stupendous views are from **Massai Point**, where you'll see thousands of spires positioned on the slopes like some petrified army.

Bonita Campground (campsites $12), near the visitor center, has 22 first-come, first-served sites that often fill by noon. There's water, but no hookups or showers. Wilderness camping is not permitted inside the monument, but there is a USFS campground about 5 miles up Pinery Rd, which is near the park entrance station.

The monument is about 37 miles off I-10 at Willcox.

Sleeping

Kingman has plenty of motels along Andy Devine Ave north and south of the I-40. Rates start at about $30 per double, but the cheapest places are dingy and popular with down-on-their-luck long-term residents. Inspect before committing.

Hualapai Mountain Park (☎ 928-681-5700, 877-757-0915; www.mcparks.com; Hualapai Mountain Rd; tent/RV sites $12/20, cabins $45-110) Camp among granite rock formations and ponderosa pine at this pretty county park, some 15 miles south of town.

Hotel Brunswick (☎ 928-718-1800; www.hotel-brunswick.com; 315 E Andy Devine Ave; s $35, r/ste with bathroom $65/95; wi-fi) Thanks to its young, energetic owners, Jason and Jen, this 1909 'haunted' jewel is a winning cocktail of historic grandeur and modern amenities. Cash-strapped solo travelers can shack up in one of 12 superbasic cowboy/girl singles, which share four bathrooms; other rooms come with TV and private facilities. Rates include breakfast.

Hualapai Mountain Resort (☎ 928-757-3545; 4525 Hualapai Mountain Rd; r $75-95) Rooms won't make you swoon, but the juicy steak in the attached restaurant (mains $18 to $35) just might. Keep an eye out for friendly elk that like to graze near the property. Pets OK.

Hampton Inn & Suites (☎ 928-692-0200; 1791 Sycamore Ave; r incl breakfast $110-190; 🐾 🖥 wi-fi) The best lot among the chains, the Hampton has clean and spacious rooms and is a good choice for families. There's a small outdoor pool for cooling off after a day on the road.

Eating & Drinking

Mr D'z Route 66 Diner (☎ 928-718-0066; 105 E Andy Devine Ave; dishes $4-13; ☯ 7am-9pm) Get your *American Graffiti* fix at this modern-vintage diner with its hot-pink and turquoise color scheme and cool memorabilia. Oprah herself gave thumbs up to its cheeseburgers, onion rings and signature root-beer float when stopping by in 2006. Breakfast is served all day.

Dambar Steakhouse (☎ 928-753-3523; 1960 E Andy Devine Ave; lunch $5-12, dinner $10-28; ☯ lunch & dinner; 👶) This local landmark serves giant steaks in the Old West bad-boy environs and keeps the kiddies happy with coloring placemats and crayons. Local characters hang out at the spit-and-sawdust saloon with cow-hide tablecloths, especially during happy hour (3pm to 7pm).

Hubbs Café (☎ 928-718-1800; 315 E Andy Devine Ave; mains $22-45; ☺ dinner Mon-Sat) At the Hotel Brunswick, Hubbs exudes Southwest gentility with its draped chairs and fine old pressed-tin ceiling. It does mostly continental standards with occasional flavor excursions to Asia or the Mediterranean. Afterwards it's bottoms up at the adjacent Mulligan's Bar.

Beale Street Brews (☎ 928-753-4004; 418 E Beale St; ☺ 6am-6pm Sun-Thu, 8am-10pm Fri & Sat; wi-fi) This cute indie coffee shop draws local java cognoscenti with its potent lattes, live music and poetry nights.

Getting There & Away
Kingman Airport (☎ 928-757-2134; 7000 Flightline Dr, Rte 66) is 6 miles northeast of town. US Airways Express flies between Kingman and Phoenix twice daily Monday to Friday. **Greyhound** (☎ 928-757-8400; 3264 E Andy Devine Ave) runs several buses daily to Phoenix ($39, 5½ hours), Las Vegas ($29, 2¾ hours), Flagstaff ($35, 2½ hours), Los Angeles ($65, 9½ hours) and other cities. **Amtrak's** westbound *Southwest Chief* stops at 12:40am, the eastbound at 3:03am.

AROUND KINGMAN
Chloride
pop 250 / elev 4200ft
The hills surrounding Chloride, some 20 miles northwest of Kingman, once spewed forth tons of silver, gold, copper and turquoise from as many as 75 mines. These days, this peaceful semi-ghost town is inhabited by quirky locals who create bizarre **junk sculptures** and proudly display them outside their ramshackle homes. You can post a letter in Arizona's **oldest continuously operating post office** (since 1862) or snap a picture of yourself behind bars at the crumbling **jail**. Up in the hills, reached via a super-rough 1.5-mile dirt road, are Roy Purcell's psychedelic **rock murals**. If you don't have a 4WD, hike up or risk a busted axle. Two gunfighting troupes stage rip-roarin' **shoot'em-ups** at high noon on Saturdays. One of them are the ultimate 'guns and roses,' the world's all-girl Wild Roses of Chloride.

For maps and information, talk to Allen at the **Mine Shaft Market** (☎ 928-565-4888; 4940 Tennessee Ave; ☺ 8am-5pm Mon-Sat, 9am-5pm Sun).

When the sun goes down and the stars come out, you'll feel the true Wild West spirit.

Bonnie and John operate a few simple but cozy adobe-walled rooms with squeaking mattresses at the **Sheps Miners Inn** (☎ 928-565-4251; 9827 2nd St; r $35-65). It's right behind **Yesterdays** (☎ 928-565-4251; 9827 2nd St; mains $7-20; ☺ from 11am Mon-Fri, 8am Sat & Sun), their restaurant and Western saloon, with creaky wooden floors, vintage gas pumps and hand-painted murals. It serves hearty American grub, international beers and toe-tapping live music nightly.

KINGMAN TO WILLIAMS
Past Kingman, Route 66 arcs north away from the I-40 for 115 dusty miles of original Mother Road through scrubby, lonely landscape. It merges with the I-40 near Seligman, then reappears briefly as Main St in Williams. Gas stations are rare, so make sure you've got enough fuel. The total distance to Williams is 130 miles.

Kingman to Peach Springs
The first of several tiny settlements is teensy **Hackberry**, where highway memorialist Robert Waldmire lures passers-by with his much loved **Old Route 66 Visitor Center** (☎ 928-769-2605; admission free; ☺ 9am-5pm) inside an eccentrically decorated gas station. Vintage pumps and cars faded in the desert heat, old toilet seats and rusted-out ironwork adorn the 1934 general store and dusty parking lot. It's a lovely spot for a cold drink and souvenirs. Keep going and you'll pass through the blink-and-you'll-miss-them towns of **Valentine** and **Truxton**.

Peach Springs
The tribal capital of the Hualapai Reservation (p213), tiny Peach Springs is also a jumping-off point for the only one-day rafting excursions on the Colorado River. This is the same tribe that operates Grand Canyon West, about 55 miles northwest of here via what locals have dubbed 'Buck-and-Doe-Rd.' It's beautiful, but don't even think about taking it without a 4WD.

If you plan to travel off Route 66 on the Hualapai Reservation, you need to buy a permit ($15) at the **Hualapai Office of Tourism** (☎ 928-769-2219, 888-255-9550) at the Hualapai Lodge. This is also where you arrange raft trips operated by **Hualapai River Runners** (☎ 928-769-2219, 888-255-9550; ☺ Mar-Oct). Packages ($320) include transportation from the lodge to the river at Diamond Creek via a bone-jarring 22-mile track (the only road anywhere to the bottom of the

ARIZONA

canyon), the motorized-raft trip to Pierce Ferry landing, a helicopter ride out of the canyon and the bus ride back to Peach Springs.

With a permit, you're also allowed to drive yourself to **Diamond Creek**, where you'll find a beach, picnic tables and first-come, first-served riverside **campsites** (per person incl permit $25; ☽ year-round) with pit toilets and picnic tables but no drinking water. It gets extremely hot and buggy in summer.

The modern **Hualapai Lodge** (☎ 928-769-2230, 888-255-9550; 900 Rte 66; r $90-100; 🖳 🖳) is the only place to stay in Peach Springs and, quite oddly, has a saltwater swimming pool and hot tub. The attached **Diamond Creek Restaurant** (mains $8-19; ☽ 6am-8pm) serves American standards. Lodging/rafting packages are available.

Grand Canyon Caverns

Nine miles past Peach Springs, a plaster dinosaur welcomes you to the **Grand Canyon Caverns & Inn** (☎ 928-422-3223; www.grandcanyoncaverns.com; Rte 66 at Mile Marker 115; 1hr tour adult/child $15/10; ☽ 8am-6pm May-Sep, 10am-4pm Oct-Apr; 🖳 🖑), a cool subterranean retreat from the summer heat. An elevator drops 210ft underground to artificially lit limestone caverns and the skeletal remains of a prehistoric ground sloth. If you've seen other caverns, these might be underwhelming, but kids still seem to get a kick out of a visit. The complex also includes a **campground** (tent/RV sites $15/30) amid junipers and a basic **motel** (r $85; 🖳 🖳). The **restaurant** (mains $5-15; ☽ 7am-7pm) is a nice little roadside spot with a small playground and serves burgers and fried food. Note that, despite the name, Grand Canyon Caverns has nothing to do with the Grand Canyon itself.

Seligman
pop 700

Some 23 miles of road slicing through rolling hills gets you to Seligman, a town that takes its Route 66 heritage seriously thanks to the Delgadillo brothers, who for decades have been the Mother Road's biggest boosters. Juan sadly passed away in 2004, but octogenarian Angel and his wife Vilma still run **Angel's Barbershop** (☎ 928-422-3352; www.route66giftshop.com; 217 E Rte 66). OK, so he doesn't cut hair anymore, but the barber's chair is still there and you can poke around for souvenirs and admire license plates sent in by fans from all over the world. If Angel is around, he's usually happy to regale you with stories about the Dust Bowl era. He's seen it all.

Angel's madcap brother Juan used to rule prankishly supreme over the **Snow Cap Drive-In** (☎ 928-422-3291; 301 E Rte 66; dishes $4-8; ☽ Mar-Nov), a Route 66 institution now kept going by his sons Bob and John. The crazy decor is only the beginning. Wait until you see the menu featuring cheeseburgers with cheese and 'dead chicken'! Beware the fake mustard bottle…

The best sit-down restaurant in town is the **Roadkill Café & OK Saloon** (☎ 928-422-3554; 502 W Rte 66; dishes $10-20; ☽ 7am-9pm), which has an all-you-can-eat salad bar and juicy steaks and burgers amid suitably vintage decor. It's within stumbling distance of the **Historic Route 66 Motel** (☎ 928-422-3204; 500 W Rte 66; r $50-70). Rooms have had a recent date with a paint bucket and feature a TV, refrigerator and new mattresses. If they're full, there are plenty of other choices, including the **Deluxe Inn** (☎ 928-422-3244; r $50; wi-fi).

WILLIAMS
pop 2800 / elev 6762ft

The railroad town of Williams has all the charm and authenticity of 'Main Street America.' Its historical center is a pastiche of Victorian-era brick houses harking back to a proud but bawdy frontier past and 1950s motels from the Route 66 heyday, some still sporting original neon signs. An excellent launch pad for the Grand Canyon South Rim, 60 miles north of here, Williams delivers a lot of things the park doesn't: inexpensive lodging, no-nonsense eateries, coffeehouses and shops. It's also the southern terminus of the Grand Canyon Railway, a vintage train and major tourist attraction in its own right.

Orientation & Information

Most businesses are along Route 66, which slices through the historic district as a one-way street headed east. Traffic headed west travels along the parallel Railroad Ave.

Java Cycle Coffee (☎ 928-635-1117; 326 W Rte 66; ☽ 6am-sunset; 🖳 wi-fi) Louise's lair has strong coffee and free wi-fi.

Library (☎ 928-635-2263; 113 S 1st St; ☽ 9am-5pm & 6-8pm Tue-Thu, 9am-5pm Fri, 9am-1pm Sat; 🖳 wi-fi) Free internet.

Police (☎ 928-635-4461; 501 W Rte 66)

Post office (☎ 928-635-4572; 120 S 1st St)

Visitor center (☎ 928-635-4061, 800-863-0546; www .williamschamber.com; 200 W Railroad Ave; ☽ 8am-6:30pm) Inside the historical train depot, this center has books for sale, free pamphlets and exhibits on the Kaibab National Forest. A USFS ranger is also usually on hand.

Williams Health Care Center (☎ 928-635-4441; 301 7th St; ☸ 8am-8pm) Emergency care.

Sights & Activities

There are plenty of opportunities for hiking and biking in nearby Kaibab, Coconino and Prescott National Forests. Ask at the visitor center for maps and information.

Children love the critter interaction going on at the **Grand Canyon Deer Farm** (☎ 928-635-4073, 800-926-3337; www.deerfarm.com; 6769 E Deerfarm Rd; adult/child $7.50/4.50; ☸ 9am-6pm mid-Mar–mid-Oct, 10am-5pm mid-Oct–mid-Mar), about 8 miles east of Williams, off I-40 exit 171. Deer, goats, reindeer, wallabies and even a baby camel are happy to be petted and, in some cases, fed.

In winter, the new **Elk Ridge Ski Area** (☎ 928-814-5038; www.elkridgeski.com; adult/child all-day lift tickets $27/20, all-day tubing pass $10/7; ☸ 9:30am-4:30pm Fri-Mon) has a small hill for skiing and snowboarding as well as two fun 200ft tubing runs.

Sleek, shiny and humming like a well-oiled machine, the **Grand Canyon Railway** (☎ 928-773-1976, 800-843-8724; www.thetrain.com; Railway Depot, 200 W Railroad Ave) makes the trip from Williams to the Grand Canyon South Rim in 2¼ hours. Cars are either pulled by historic steam or diesel locomotives and come in five classes, from the fussily restored 1923 Harriman-style Pullman cars (adult/child round-trip $65/35) to the luxurious Parlor cars where you can sip champagne on an open-air platform while the train trundles through ponderosa pines ($170).

Trains depart Williams at 10am; the return train pulls out at 3:30pm, giving you a little over three hours at the rim. To set the mood, departures are preceded by a Wild West shootout, a banjo player roams the aisle, and robbers may hold up the train (don't worry, the sheriff has things under control). Various lodging packages are available. See the website for details.

Sleeping

Rates listed here can drop by half in winter. Reservations are advised in summer unless you arrive by early afternoon.

Grand Motel (☎ 928-635-4601, 877-635-4601; www.thegrandmotel.com; 234 E Rte 66; r incl breakfast from $52) OK, so it's not exactly 'grand,' but instead this 1936 motel is a bargain with 15 rooms dressed in Route 66 vintage flair yet equipped with mod cons. Rates include a small breakfast, served on the patio if the weather gods play along.

Canyon Country Inn (☎ 928-635-2349, 877-405-3280; www.thecanyoncountryinn.com; 442 W Rte 66; r incl breakfast $54-80) Not really a B&B and not a motel – it's something in between and very reasonably priced to boot. Rooms range from snug to spacious, but the Southwestern-style quilts and teddy bears add homey touches and the generous continental breakfast is a pleasing perk.

Grand Canyon Hotel (☎ 928-635-1419; thegrandcanyonhotel.com; 145 W Rte 66; dm $20, r with shared bathroom $60, with private bathroom $70-80; wi-fi) This charming European-style hotel-hostel combo occupies an 1891 building right on Route 66. Themed rooms reflects the spirit of yesteryear, be it the pink Boudoir Room, the Missouri Room with brass bed or the Asian Room with paper umbrellas. The dorm sleeps six.

Canyon Motel (☎ 928-635-9371, 800-482-3955; www.thecanyonmotel.com; 1900 E Rodeo Rd; r $70-133; wi-fi) Fans of retro motels, camp, the romance of the rails and families will be charmed by Kevin and Shirley and their unique property where you can spend the night in a vintage caboose or rail car. They're snug but cute and outfitted with all standard motel amenities, including TVs and microwaves. The stone cottages are less distinctive but comfortable enough.

Red Garter Bed & Bakery (☎ 928-635-1484, 800-328-1484; www.redgarter.com; 137 W Railroad Ave; r incl breakfast $120-145; wi-fi) To return to Williams' wicked past, book into this bordello-turned-B&B where the ladies used to hang out the windows to flag down customers. Wake up to the aroma of pastries made in the on-site bakery and served at breakfast. Innkeeper John Holst is an expert on the town and its history and usually happy to get out a map and clue you in.

And then we have:

Railside RV Ranch (☎ 928-635-4077, 888-635-4077; www.railsidervranch.com; 877 Rodeo Rd; tent/RV sites $17/32; ☐ wi-fi) Full-service spot with coin showers, laundry rooms, playground and summertime movies.

FireLight B&B (☎ 928-635-0200, 888-838-8218; www.firelightbandb.com; 175 W Mead Ave; r $150-250; wi-fi) Classy Tudor-style home with such lovebird-friendly touches as private whirlpool tubs for two, canopy beds and fireplaces.

Eating & Drinking

At no risk of snagging a Michelin star, Williams' culinary scene features plenty of creative and healthy options alongside Betty Crocker–inspired country cooking. For groceries, drop by **Safeway** (☎ 928-635-0500; 637 W Rte 66; ☸ 5am-10pm).

Cruiser's Café 66 (☎ 928-635-2445; 233 W Rte 66; dishes $7-16; ☸ lunch & dinner) In a 1930s gas station this

Americana diner plays up the roadster theme big time. Chevy fins dangle above racing-car red and inky black booths, while the ceiling is sheathed in shiny tin. Dogs are allowed at the outdoor tables.

Pine Country Restaurant (☎ 928-635-9718; 107 N Grand Canyon Blvd; lunch $4-7.50, dinner $8-13; ❤ breakfast, lunch & dinner) It's an old-school country kitchen, but after one too many beers at Sultana's, the greasy comfort food will quickly restore balance to the brain. Get a slice of the homemade pies – from apple blueberry to baked pineapple coconut – for the road.

Red Raven (☎ 928-635-4980; 135 W Rte 66; lunch $6-10, dinner $10-22; ❤ lunch & dinner Tue-Sun) This relative newcomer brings urban creativity to down-homey Williams. At lunchtime locals favor the freshly made wraps, sandwiches and squirty Baja tacos, but dinners are more haute. Don't miss the Southwest egg rolls drizzled with velvety chipotle sauce – they're veritable flavor bombs.

World Famous Sultana Bar (☎ 928-635-2028; 301 W Rte 66; ❤ 10am-2am) Back during Prohibition, boozers on a mission would steal down to the basement for bootleg liquor and gambling. Today, you can guzzle your brew legally, play pool, meet colorful locals and keep an eye on the stuffed mountain lion. Sometimes there's live music.

Also recommended:

Pancho McGillicuddy's (☎ 928-635-4150; 141 W Railroad Ave; mains $6-14; ❤ 11am-10pm; wi-fi) Good-time old-time cantina with Mexican food, loud music and a long tequila and margarita menu (more than 40 tequilas and 20 different flavors of margaritas).

Pizza Factory (☎ 928-635-3009; 214 W Rte 66; dishes $5-10; ❤ lunch & dinner) Pies are piled high with tasty toppings and the red-checkered floors add a cheery touch.

Getting There & Around

Amtrak's *Southwest Chief* stops on the outskirts of Williams, but there's a shuttle connecting the station to the Grand Canyon Railway depot downtown. The eastbound train to Chicago comes through at 5:20am, the westbound to Los Angeles at 10:33pm.

Open Road Tours (☎ 928-226-8060, 800-766-7117; www.openroadtours.com) runs two daily shuttles to the Grand Canyon (adult/child $22/17) and Flagstaff ($17/12), as well as a connecting shuttle from Flagstaff to Phoenix' Sky Harbor International Airport ($42/30).

WILLIAMS TO HOLBROOK

East of Williams, much of Route 66 has been absorbed into the I-40, but one place to get a nostalgia kick is along the so-called **Deer Farm Loop** (I-40 exit 167). This is where Route 66's signature two-lane concrete highway with 'thumpty-thump' expansion cracks alternates with older red-dirt roadbed, which may be impassable in winter or during heavy rains. Scattered beside are photo-worthy gas station, café and motel ruins. Rejoin I-40 at Bellemont (exit 185).

I-40 barrels into the spirited Flagstaff (p189), a cultured college town that's still Old West at heart. East of here, mountain views soon flatten out into relentlessly featureless prairie. Fortunately, there are a number of worthwhile spots to break the boredom. Besides those mentioned below, you'll also pass the Route 66 ghost towns of Twin Arrows, a long-closed trading post and café, and Two Guns, where a gas station and a clutch of ruined buildings decompose quietly in the desert sun.

Walnut Canyon National Monument

The near vertical limestone walls of the forested **Walnut Canyon** (☎ 928-526-3367; www.nps.gov/waca; ❤ 9am-5pm) don't look like a particularly inviting place to settle. However, about 1000 years ago the hardy Sinagua people, ancestors of the Hopi, braved mother nature by building cliff dwellings below overhangs and into shallow natural caves.

Until a series of rock slides closed the access trail in December 2007 you could get close-ups of 25 of the rooms. It's anybody's guess when it will reopen, so in the meantime you can only catch distant glimpses from the visitor center and the short, wheelchair-accessible **Rim Trail**. Admission is waived until the main trail reopens.

The monument is 11 miles southeast of Flagstaff off I-40 exit 204.

Meteor Crater

The wooly mammoths and ground sloths that slouched around northern Arizona 50,000 years ago must have got quite a nasty surprise when a fiery meteor crashed into their neighborhood, blasting a hole some 550ft deep and nearly 1 mile across. Today the privately owned **crater** (☎ 928-289-2362; www.meteorcrater .com; adult/child/senior $15/7/13; ❤ 7am-7pm Jun–mid-Sep,

8am-5pm mid-Sep–May) is a major tourist attraction with exhibits about meteorites, crater geology and the Apollo astronauts who used its lunar-like surface to train for their moon missions. You're not allowed to go down into the crater, but guided one-hour rim walking tours depart from 9:15am to 2:15pm (free with admission). Don't get too excited: it's really just a big hole in the ground. The crater is about 6 miles off I-40 exit 233, 35 miles east of Flagstaff and 20 miles west of Winslow. There's also a year-round **campground** (☎ 928-289-5898; tent/RV sites $25/27) with showers, laundry, a Subway and a gas station.

Winslow
pop 10,000 / elev 4880ft

'Standing on a corner in Winslow, Arizona…' Sound familiar? Thanks to the Eagles' catchy '70s tune *Take It Easy* (written by Jackson Browne and Glenn Frey), lonesome little Winslow is now a popular stop on the tourist track. In a small **park** (www.standinonthecorner.com; 2nd St & Kinsley Ave) on Route 66 you can pose with a life-sized bronze statue of a hitchhiker backed by a charmingly hokey trompe l'oeil mural of that famous girl – oh Lord! – in a flatbed Ford. Up above, a painted eagle poignantly keeps an eye on the action, and sometimes a red antique Ford parks next to the scene. In 2005 a fire gutted the building behind the mural, which was miraculously saved. If enough funds materialize, the city plans on expanding the park, adding an amphitheater, neon signs, lawns and benches with Cadillac fins.

INFORMATION
The **chamber of commerce** (☎ 928-289-2434; www.winslowarizona.org; 101 E 2nd St; ⏰ 8am-5pm Mon-Fri) has the usual tourist info but may be moving to the Historical Hubbell Trading Post at 2nd St and Campbell Ave. The **library** (☎ 928-289-4982; 420 W Gilmore St; ⏰ Tue-Sat; 🖳) offers free internet.

SIGHTS & ACTIVITIES
For a window on Winslow's past, swing by the **Old Trails Museum** (☎ 289-5861; 212 Kinsley Ave; donations appreciated; ⏰ 10am-4pm Tue-Sat) in a 1921 bank building with original tile-work, marble counters and a vault.

Homolovi Ruins State Park (☎ 928-289-4106; www.pr.state.az.us; per vehicle $5, tent/RV sites from $10/14), three miles northeast of Winslow via Hwy 87 (exit 257), hugs the Little Colorado River. Short hikes access petroglyphs and partly excavated ancient Native American ruins. Download a free podcast audio tour from the website.

One of the desert's most beautiful overlooks is at **Little Painted Desert County Park** (☎ 928-524-4251), about 10 miles further north on Hwy 87. Perfect for a sunset picnic!

SLEEPING & EATING
Winslow is a handy base for the Hopi Reservation (p227), some 60 miles northeast of here. About a dozen old motels, some run-down, are found along Route 66, charging rates from $30. In comparison, **La Posada** (☎ 928-289-4366; www.laposada.org; 303 E 2nd St; r $100-150) is most definitely another fine sight to see (or stay at). An impressively restored 1930 hacienda designed by star architect *du jour* Mary Jane Colter, it was the last great railroad hotel built for the Fred Harvey Company along the Santa Fe Railroad. Elaborate tile work, glass-and-tin chandeliers, Navajo rugs and other details accent its rustic Western-style elegance. They go surprisingly well with the splashy canvases of Tina Mion, one of the three preservation-minded artists who bought the run-down place in 1997. The small, period-styled rooms are named for illustrious former guests, including Albert Einstein, Gary Cooper and Diane Keaton. Pets cost $10.

Even if you're not staying at La Posada, treat yourself to the best meal between Flagstaff and New Mexico at its **Turquoise Room** (lunch $9-12, dinner $16-33; ⏰ breakfast, lunch & dinner). Dishes have updated Southwestern flair, and there's a children's menu as well. A cheaper alternative is the cheerful family-run **Casa Blanca Café** (☎ 928-289-4191; 1201 E 2nd St; dishes $5-10; ⏰ lunch & dinner), which has served big plates of Mexican fare since 1942.

GETTING THERE & AWAY
Greyhound stops at McDonald's at 1616 N Park Dr, but tickets are not sold at this location. The *Southwest Chief* stops daily (westbound at 7:50pm, eastbound at 6:09am) at the unstaffed **Amtrak station** (501 E 2nd St).

HOLBROOK
pop 4900 / elev 5080ft

Holbrook was once one of the wickedest towns in the Old West with a reputation as being 'too tough for women or churches.'

There ain't much to make you ease off the accelerator, but if you have time drop by the **Navajo County Historical Museum** (☎ 928-524-6558; donations appreciated; ⊗ 8am-5pm Mon-Fri, 8am-4pm Sat & Sun). It's inside the 1898 county courthouse, a gracefully aging heap of bricks whose Perry Mason–era courtroom still hosts hearings. Downstairs, curator Steve and his Chihuahua named Peewee preside over an amiably eclectic collection of Wild West memorabilia. A creepy highlight is the old county jail whose windowless cells were still in use until 1976.

The same building doubles as the **visitor center** (⊗ 8am-5pm Mon-Fri, 8am-4pm Sat & Sun) and hosts free Native American dances at 7pm in summer. Photography is permitted. If you're interested in Holbrook's lawless history, pick up a self-guided walking tour map that takes in such places as the Bucket of Blood Saloon and the Blevins House, where a 1888 shootout between the local sheriff and the Blevins cattle-rustler gang left three men dead in less than 60 seconds.

It's illegal to collect petrified wood inside the Petrified Forest National Park (right), but there are several rock shops in Holbrook where you can purchase pieces of the fossilized wood. The most famous is the **Rainbow Rock Shop** (☎ 928-524-2384; 101 Navajo Blvd), easily recognized by its seven massive dinosaur sculptures. A small fee (about $1) is charged if you just want your picture taken. For the best selection and quality, though, stop by **Jim Gray's Petrified Wood Co** (☎ 928-524-1842; www.petrifiedwoodco.com; cnr of Hwys 77 & 180), about 2 miles south of town. Pieces range from $1 to $10,000. A small museum stars Wild Bill, a 2.9-million-year-old alligator fossil, and there's also a neat petrified wood waterfall.

Most of Holbrook's motels line Navajo Blvd and Hopi Dr between I-40 exits 286 and 289. Hopi Dr parallels the railroad tracks and suffers from nighttime train noise.

Thanks to new owners, the 124 rooms of the basic standby **Motel 6** (☎ 928-524-6101; 2514 Navajo Blvd; r $40-45; ⊛) are getting a thorough makeover, so definitely ask to stay in a new one.

Devotees of Route 66 schlockabilia will love to snooze in one of the 15 concrete teepees at **Wigwam Motel** (☎ 928-524-3048; www.galerie-kokopelli .com/wigwam; 811 W Hopi Dr; r $48-58), each outfitted with restored 1950s hickory log-pole furniture and retro TVs but no phones (cell phones work OK). Americana at its finest!

If you've got deeper pockets, try the modern **Holiday Inn Express** (☎ 928-524-1466; 1308 Navajo Blvd; r $100-120; ⊛ ⊡ wi-fi), which has an indoor pool and laundry. Pets are an extra $25.

Full of Western memorabilia, the **Butterfield Stage Co Steak House** (☎ 928-524-3447; 609 W Hopi Dr; mains $10-25; ⊗ dinner) delivers the region's best steaks at good prices. You'll find reasonably authentic Italian fare at the locally recommended **Mesa Italiana** (☎ 928-524-6696; 2318 E Navajo Blvd; mains lunch $8-12, dinner $10-17; ⊗ lunch & dinner).

Greyhound (☎ 928-524-3832; www.greyhound.com; 101 Mission Lane) stops at the Circle K.

HOLBROOK TO NEW MEXICO

East of Holbrook, Route 66 barrels on as I-40 for 70 miles before entering New Mexico just beyond Lupton. The only attraction to break the monotony of the road is the section cutting through the Painted Desert with the Petrified National Forest on your right (south).

Petrified Forest National Park
elev 5472ft

Forget about green. The 'trees' of the Petrified Forest are fragmented, fossilized logs scattered over a vast area of semidesert grassland. Sounds boring? Not so. First, many are huge – up to 6ft in diameter – and at least one spans a ravine to form a natural bridge. Second, they're beautiful. Take a closer look and you'll see extravagantly patterned cross-sections of wood shimmering in ethereal pinks, blues and greens. And finally, they're ancient, 225 million years old, making them contemporaries of the first di-

---

DETOUR: ROCK ART RANCH

For an off-the-beaten-path adventure, steer your trusty wheels along a dirt road to the remote **Rock Art Ranch** (☎ 928-288-3260), a working cattle farm owned by Brantley Baird. Baird leads year-round tours of isolated **Chevelon Canyon**, considered one of the finest Native American petroglyph sites in the Southwest. Thousands of stick figures, animals, flute players and geometric shapes have been etched into the red sandstone walls over the centuries. The ranch itself houses a museum of pioneer, cowboy and Ancestral Puebloan artifacts. Call ahead for reservations, directions and rates, which depend on group size; if it's just two of you, budget about $25 each.

nosaurs that leapt onto the scene in the Late Triassic period.

The trees arrived via major floods, only to be buried beneath silica-rich volcanic ash before they could decompose. Groundwater dissolved the silica, carried it through the logs and crystallized into solid, sparkly quartz mashed up with iron, carbon, manganese and other minerals. Uplift and erosion eventually exposed the logs. Souvenir hunters filched thousands of tons of petrified wood before Teddy Roosevelt put a stop to the madness and made the forest a national monument in 1906 (it became a national park in 1962). Scavenge some today and you'll be looking at fines and even jail time.

Aside from the logs, the park also encompasses Native American ruins and petroglyphs, plus an especially spectacular section of the Painted Desert north of the I-40.

Petrified Forest National Park (☎ 928-524-6228; www.nps.gov/pefo; per vehicle $10; ☼ 7am-7pm Jun-Aug, 8am-5pm Sep-May), which straddles the I-40, has an entrance at exit 311 off I-40 in the north and another off Hwy 180 in the south. A 28-mile paved scenic road links the two. To avoid backtracking, westbound travelers should start in the north, eastbound ones in the south.

A 20-minute video describing how the logs were fossilized runs regularly at the **Painted Desert Visitor Center** (☼ 7am-7pm Jun-Aug, 8am-5pm Sep-May), near the north entrance, and the **Rainbow Forest Museum** (☼ 7am-7pm Jun-Aug, 8am-5pm Sep-May) near the South Entrance. Both have bookstores, park exhibits and rangers that hand out a free map and information pamphlet.

The scenic drive has about 15 pullouts with interpretive signs and some short trails, but there's no need to stop at each and every one in order to appreciate the park. Two trails near the southern entrance provide the best access for close-ups of the petrified logs: the 0.6-mile **Long Logs Trail**, which has the largest concentration, and the 0.4-mile **Giant Logs Trail**, which is entered through the Rainbow Forest Museum and sports the park's largest log.

A highlight in the center section is the 3-mile loop drive out to **Blue Mesa**, where you'll be treated to 360-degree views of spectacular badlands, log falls and logs balancing atop hills with the leathery texture of elephant skin. Nearby, at the bottom of a ravine, hundreds of well-preserved petroglyphs are splashed across **Newspaper Rock** like some prehistoric bulletin board. Hiking down is verboten, but free spotting scopes are set up at the overlook.

There's more rock art at **Puerco Pueblo**, but the real attraction here is the partly excavated 100-room ruins that may have been home to as many as 1200 people in the 13th century.

North of the I-40, you'll have sweeping views of the **Painted Desert**, where nature presents a hauntingly beautiful palette, especially at sunset. The most mesmerizing views are from **Kachina Point** at the **Painted Desert Inn** (admission free; ☼ 9am-5pm year-round), an old adobe turned museum adorned with impressive Hopi murals.

Kachina Point is also the trailhead for wilderness hiking and camping. There are no developed trails, water sources or food, so come prepared. Overnight camping requires a free permit available at the visitor centers.

There are no accommodations within the park and food service is limited to snacks available at the visitor centers. The closest lodging is in Holbrook (p263).

ARIZONA

New Mexico

Strewn with boughs of blood-red *ristras* and earth-tone adobes and smelling of sage, piñon and roasting green chile, the 'Land of Enchantment' is like nowhere else in the country.

Home of the atomic bomb, Billy the Kid, the world's most famous UFO crash site and America's only Hispanic governor, New Mexico is also adding hot tourism destination to its resume. Who's coming? Hollywood production companies (seems everyone is shooting a movie here these days), Richard Branson (he's planning to launch tourists into outer space from his Virgin Galactic Spaceport in 2010) and more than 15 million visitors a year (not all from this planet).

DH Lawrence, Georgia O'Keeffe and the Coen brothers all found inspiration in the ethereal backdrop of mesas, mountains and desert, and the unique light of New Mexico. Art is everywhere, whether you're buying Navajo weaving direct from a Madrid artist's studio or stocking up on cheesy alien souvenirs in Roswell. Sophisticated and historic, Santa Fe is America's number-one art destination, but Wild West Silver City and New-Age Truth or Consequences offer off-the-grid alternatives for quirky gallery-hopping.

Don't be surprised if strangers say hello on the street. New Mexicans are a friendly lot, and community is paramount. Even the smallest middle-of-nowhere towns have at least one restaurant doubling as a meeting place for family and friends spread far across this sparsely populated state. And nowhere else in American will you find cultural diversity like this – Anglo, Hispanic and Native American traditions are woven together to create one dynamic quilt.

HIGHLIGHTS

- **Best Hot Springs**
  The hot waters at Ojo Caliente (p330) soothe the mind and heal bodily ailments in a gorgeous cliffside location – don't miss drinking from the Lithia spring

- **Best Undiscovered Single Track**
  Bike a high-desert single track across sandstone mesas just outside Gallup (p270)

- **Best Spot for Solitude**
  Camp amid gypsum and yucca by huge, empty dunes at White Sands National Monument (p369)

- **Best Overall Town**
  All-adobe Santa Fe (p306) is filled with fabulous art, culture and architecture, plus it serves the tastiest green chile and fresh margaritas around

- **Best Off-the-Grid Town**
  Head south to New-Age Truth or Consequences (p356)

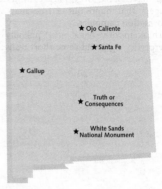

★ Ojo Caliente

★ Santa Fe

★ Gallup

★ Truth or Consequences

★ White Sands National Monument

NEW MEXICO FAST FACTS

Population 1.9 million

Area 121,356 sq miles

State nickname Land of Enchantment

Website www.newmexico.org

Sales tax 5%

Average temps low/high Santa Fe Jan 15/43°F, Jul 54/86°F

Albuquerque to Las Cruces 223 miles, 3½ hours

Albuquerque to Salt Lake City 622 miles, 9 hours

Gallup to Tucumcari 311 miles, 4½ hours

Santa Fe to Roswell 192 miles, 3 hours

Santa Fe to Taos 70 miles, 1 hour

History

People roamed the land here as far back as 10,500 BC, but by Francisco Vasquez de Coronado's arrival in the 16th century, Pueblos were the dominant communities found here. Santa Fe was established as the colonial capital in 1610, after which Spanish settlers and farmers fanned out across northern New Mexico, and missionaries began their often violent efforts to convert the area's Puebloans to Catholicism. Following on from a successful revolt, Native Americans then occupied Santa Fe until 1692 when Diego de Vargas recaptured the city.

In 1851 New Mexico became US territory. Native American wars, settlement by cowboys and miners, and trade along the Santa Fe Trail further transformed the region, and the arrival of the railroad in the 1870s created an economic boom.

Painters and writers set up art colonies in Santa Fe and Taos in the early 20th century. In 1943 a scientific community descended on Los Alamos and developed the atomic bomb. The dawn of the 21st century has been history-making for New Mexico. Bill Richardson, the country's first, and only, Hispanic governor was elected in 2002. President Clinton's former Secretary of Energy, Richardson, a Democrat, has created many positive initiatives for New Mexico during his time in office, including raising the minimum wage well above the national average and building the movie industry in his state. He ran for president in the Democratic primaries in 2007, but dropped out of the race after losing significant number of primaries.

Climate

Because the altitude in New Mexico ranges from 3000ft to 13,000ft, temperatures can vary wildly. What you can depend on, no matter the season, is about 300 days a year of sun and dry air. The southern desert receives less than 10in of rain annually, but when it rains (usually in late summer), thunderstorms are intense. Mountainous areas near Taos receive quite a bit of snow (anywhere from about 200in to 300in per winter), while the Sacramento Mountains in Southern New Mexico average about 180in.

Time Zone

New Mexico is on Mountain Time (seven hours behind GMT) and observes daylight saving time.

Information

All About New Mexico (www.psych.nmsu.edu/~linda/chilepg.htm) Links to practically everything imaginable about New Mexico, from outdoor recreation to where to buy chile products.

New Mexico CultureNet (www.nmcn.org) Articles about the artists, writers and history of New Mexico, with events listings of the most enriching sort.

New Mexico Department of Tourism (www.newmexico.org) Information and links to accommodations, attractions and other useful sites.

Santa Fe New Mexican (www.santafenewmexican.com) Online visitor information and top local stories from Santa Fe's newspaper.

State of New Mexico (www.newmexico.gov) Facts, stats and state government sites, plus links to public transportation, USGS and street maps, and other official business.

National & State Parks

Unique geological features and ancient ruins pepper the New Mexico landscape,

NEED TO KNOW

New Mexico added a second area code in late 2007, although for the next few years you will still be able to dial ☎ 505 anywhere in the state and be rerouted to the new ☎ 575 area code. In general the ☎ 505 area code will be used in Northwestern New Mexico along with the cities of Santa Fe, Albuquerque, Los Alamos and Las Vegas, although existing businesses will be allowed to keep their ☎ 505 area code in other areas should they wish.

NEW MEXICO

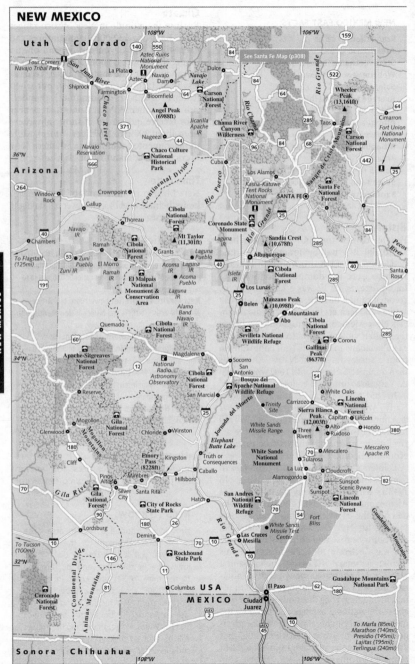

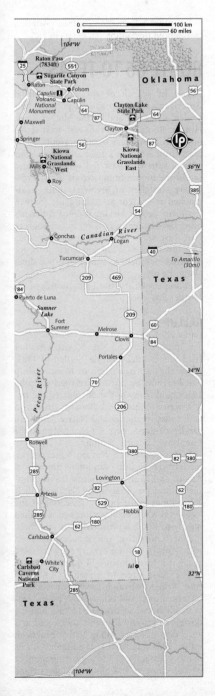

often bathed in crystalline light against the backdrop of a bright-blue sky. Southeastern New Mexico boasts the stark rolling dunes of White Sands National Monument (p369) and the cave system of Carlsbad Caverns National Park (p378). In the Southwest, Gila National Forest (p360) offers backpackers a natural playground and a springboard to visit cliff dwellings and hot springs. Nearby Bosque Del Apache National Wildlife Refuge (p355) is a winter home for endangered whooping cranes. To the north, Bandelier National Monument (p304) offers 50 sq miles of canyons and hiking trails. Northwestern New Mexico holds some of the country's most inspiring ancient Indian sites, including the massive Puebloan buildings at Chaco Culture National Historical Park (p348) and Aztec Ruins National Monument (p353), connected to Chaco by a 30ft-wide ancient road.

At **New Mexico State Parks** (www.nmparks.com) you can search by park to find a list of facilities, fishing guides and other resources.

New Mexico Scenic Routes

One way to explore New Mexico is to travel some of the 24 state-designated scenic byways, which are dedicated to preserving and promoting historic, cultural or natural assets located on or near them. The four routes mentioned here have been selected as National Scenic Byways. For more information, visit www.byways.org. Another official scenic byway worth checking out is the Turquoise Trail (p303).

Santa Fe Trail This trail made it possible for wagon trains to roll westward, and their wagon ruts still remain at Fort Union National Monument. From Santa Fe (p306), travel north on Hwy 25 to lovely Las Vegas (p277), then take Hwy 518 east to Hwy 161, south to Hwy 25 and north to Hwy 21 to gunslinging Cimarron (p348). From here take Hwy 64 north to the ranching center of Raton (p349) and Colorado. The eastern spur heads through Clayton (p350) and into Oklahoma. Allow a couple of days to explore this route.

Jemez Mountain Trail This trail makes for a picturesque day trip from Santa Fe through its national forest. Take Hwy 4 east past the famous labs at Los Alamos (p304) and past Bandelier National Monument (p304) before taking Hwy 126 west toward mountainous Cuba. Then head east on Hwy 44 through the Jemez Indian Reservation, and east on Hwy 4 back to Santa Fe.

Billy the Kid This looped byway pays tribute to the Wild West (allow at least two days). Travel from Capitan, home of the original Smokey Bear, east on Hwy 48 to Ruidoso

> **DID YOU KNOW?**
>
> New Mexico shares a border with Mexico and five states – Arizona, Colorado, Utah, Texas and Oklahoma.

(p369), west on Hwy 70 then east on Hwy 380 towards Lincoln (p372), where Billy the Kid made his last stand.

El Camino Real The 'Royal Highway of the Interior Land' follows the Rio Grande from Santa Fe through Bernalillo, down Hwy 47 south to San Miguel Mission and Socorro (p355), past the startling beauty of Elephant Butte Lake (p357), to the hot-springs haven of Truth or Consequences (p356), past chile-laden Hatch, the university town of Las Cruces (p361) and onward to the Texas border. Allow a few days for this drive.

Getting There & Around

Most travelers fly into Albuquerque International Sunport (ABQ; p301), but you may also fly into El Paso International Airport (ELP) in adjacent Texas – it's about 266 mile (around four hours) drive between the two cities.

Public transportation options are extremely limited in New Mexico, even in large cities, so plan on renting a car. The two major interstates in New Mexico are I-25 (north–south, including through Santa Fe, Truth or Consequences and Las Cruces) and I-40 (east–west, passing through Grants and Gallup), which intersect in Albuquerque. The historic Route 66 parallels I-40 throughout the state. Other major routes across New Mexico include I-10, which runs east–west from Las Cruces to the Arizona border and all the way to Los Angels, 760 miles to the west. If you're looking for aliens or earthships, take the 'extraterrestrial highway,' Hwy 285 from Carlsbad to Roswell, then continue north for 262 miles to Taos.

Greyhound buses travel to most New Mexico towns and are the cheapest option. But in smaller towns, they may run only once a day, or a couple of times a week. Be sure to check the schedule.

Amtrak provides a passenger train service on the *Southwest Chief*, which runs between Chicago and Los Angeles, and stops in Raton, Las Vegas, Lamy, Albuquerque and Gallup. The *Sunset Limited* stops in Deming on its way from Florida to Los Angeles. A Native American guide hops aboard between Albuquerque and Gallup to provide insightful commentary.

For more information on transportation throughout the Southwest, see p536.

ROUTE 66 TO TEXAS

Those in search of the quintessential Americana road trip should pop on their golden oldies mix and hit the Mother Road. Historic Route 66/I-40 runs east–west across northern New Mexico and presents a real blast from America's road-trip days. Your wheels spin you past red mesa tops and sandstone buttes; tumbleweeds blow across lonely stretches of arrow-straight, heat-cracked pavement stretching on forever. For many people, kicking it down America's most famous highway is reason enough to visit. Just make sure to stop in the yesteryear towns, like Gallup and Tucumcari, for a malted milkshake in a mom-and-pop diner along the way.

Albuquerque also has a long stretch of the Mother Road; see p288.

GALLUP

pop 20,500 / elev 6515ft

The mother town on New Mexico's mother road seems stuck in time. Settled in 1881, when the railroad came to town, Gallup had her heyday during the road-tripping 1950s, and many of the dilapidated old hotels, pawn shops and billboards, mixed in with today's galleries and Native American handicraft stores, have not changed since the Eisenhower administration.

Just outside the Navajo Reservation, modern-day Gallup is an interesting mix of Anglos and Native Americans; it's not unusual to hear people speaking Navajo on their cell-phones while buying groceries at the local Wal-Mart. Gallup's tourism is limited mostly to Route 66 road-trippers and those in search of Native American history. Even with visitors, it's not exactly crowded, and at night it turns downright quiet.

The 'main street of America' (Route 66) runs straight through downtown Gallup's historic district and is lined with pretty, renovated light-red sandstone buildings housing dozens of kitschy souvenir shops and arts and crafts galleries selling Native American wares. Gallup is starting to capitalize on its outdoor attractions, and a growing number of rock climbers and mountain bikers come to challenge their bodies on surrounding sandstone buttes and red mesa tops.

Information

Chamber of Commerce (☎ 505-722-2228; www .gallupchamber.com; 103 W Hwy 66; ☿ 8am-5pm Mon-Fri) Next to the Gallup Cultural Center. Be sure to check out the permanent exhibit on the Navajo code-talkers of WWII.

Gallup Visitor Information Center (☎ 505-863-3841, 800-242-4282; www.gallupnm.org; 701 Montoya Blvd; ☿ 8am-5pm Mon-Fri) Grab a copy of the full-color, helpful – it has a good map – Gallup visitors guide, produced annually.

Hospital (☎ 505-863-7000; 1901 Red Rock Dr; ☿ 24hr emergency)

Library (☎ 505-863-1291; 115 W Hill Ave; ☿ 10am-6pm Mon-Fri; ▣) Free internet access.

Police (☎ 505-722-2231; 451 State Rd 564)

Post office (☎ 505-863-3491; 950 W Aztec)

Sights

All roads in downtown Gallup dead-end onto Route 66, which runs uninterrupted through town – take Exit 20 or 22 from Hwy 40 to access the best of Route 66 downtown. The **historic district** is lined with about 20 structures of historic and architectural interest, built between 1895 and 1938. Most are located along 1st, 2nd and 3rd Sts between Hwy 66 and Hill Ave and are detailed in a brochure found at the visitor center. Among these is the small **Gallup Historical Museum** (☎ 505-863-1363; 300 W Rte 66; admission by donation; ☿ 8:30am-3:30pm Mon-Fri), in the renovated, turn-of-the-19th-century Rex Hotel.

Downtown Gallup's centerpiece is the beautifully resorted **El Morro Theater** (☎ 505-726-0050; 207 W Coal Ave; ☿ hours vary). Built in 1926 as the town's showcase theatrical house, it reopened after massive renovations in 2006 as part of an effort to promote downtown business development. The grand old Spanish Colonial theatre – which only got central heating and air-con in the 2006 upgrade – now hosts Saturday movies and children's programs, and also does live theatre and dance.

The **Gallup Cultural Center** (☎ 505-863-4131; www .southwestindian.com; 218 E Rte 66; ☿ 8am-5pm) houses

NEW MEXICO

KICKIN' IT DOWN ROUTE 66

Never has a highway been so symbolic as Route 66. Snaking across the belly of America, this fragile ribbon of concrete pavement first connected the prairie capital of Chicago with the California dreamin' of Los Angeles in 1926. Along the way, lightning-bug towns sprouted up with neon signposts, motor courts and drive-ins, all providing the simple camaraderie of the road.

Called the 'Mother Road' in John Steinbeck's novel *The Grapes of Wrath*, Route 66 came into its own during the Depression years, when hundreds of thousands of migrants escaping the Dust Bowl slogged westward in beat-up old jalopies painted with 'California or Bust' signs. Meanwhile unemployed young men were hired to pave the final stretches of muddy road. They completed the job, as it turns out, just in time for WWII.

Hitchhiking soldiers and factory workers rode the road next. Then, amid the jubilant postwar boom, Americans took their newfound optimism and wealth on the road, essentially inventing the modern driving vacation. And so the era of 'getting your kicks on Route 66' was born. Traffic flowed busily in both directions.

But just as the Mother Road hit her stride, President Dwight Eisenhower, a US army general who had been inspired by Germany's autobahn, proposed a new interstate system for the USA. Slowly but surely, each of Route 66's more than 2200 miles was bypassed. Towns became ghost towns and traffic ground nearly to a halt. The highway was officially decommissioned in 1984.

A movement for preservation of the Mother Road resulted in the **National Historic Route 66 Association** (www.national66.com), a nonprofit alliance of federal, state and private interests. Every year another landmark goes up for sale, but more are rescued from ruin.

Today this phoenix-like highway relies on travelers daring enough to leave the interstate behind for a combination of blue-line highways and gravel frontage roads. You can still spy relics of the original road, stay in a jewel of a 1930s motor court, revel in sunsets over the Painted Desert or splash in the Pacific Ocean. This is not just your mother's Mother Road. It's yours.

New Mexico revels in all 475 miles of its Route 66 legacy. In addition to publishing a quarterly magazine, the active **New Mexico Route 66 Association** (☎ 505-224-2802; www.rt66nm.org; 1415 Central Ave NE, Albuquerque) has archives, news and event calendars on its website.

a small but well-done museum with Indian art, including excellent collections of both contemporary and old kachina dolls, pottery, sand painting and weaving. A 10ft-tall bronze sculpture of a Navajo code-talker honors the sacrifices made by many men of the Navajo Reservation in WWII. A tiny theatre screens films about Chaco Canyon and the Four Corners region.

Activities

Gallup's gaining a reputation as the kind of outdoors town where you can still get lost on the bike trails should you wish. Read: fewer crowds. Hikers should head six miles east of town to beautiful **Red Rock State Park** (☎ 505-863-1337; ⏱ 8am-4:30pm Mon-Fri, trading post 6:30am-5:30pm). It has a little museum with modern and traditional Indian crafts, a campground (opposite) and hiking trails. Try the 3-mile round- trip Pyramid Rock trail past amazing rock formations. From the 7487ft summit you can see as far as 50 miles on a clear day.

Mountain bikers can test their skills on the **High Desert Trail System**. It offers a variety of terrain for different skill levels, including plenty of sick, slick rock – try the loops off the main trail for the most challenging rides.

The trail system is 3 miles north of Gallup on Hwy 491 off the Chico/Gamerco Rd. Pick up maps at the tourist office.

The **Mentmore Rock Climbing Area** lets you challenge yourself with 50 different boltedtop-rope climbs and some free-climbing areas. Difficulty levels range from 5.0 to 5.13 – grab maps and info at the visitor center. You'll need your own gear and to know what you are doing. Reach the park via Exit 16 off I-40 – head north on County Rd 1.

Festivals & Events

Thousands of Native Americans and non-Indian tourists throng the streets of Gallup and the huge amphitheater at Red Rock State Park in the first week of August for **Inter-Tribal Indian Ceremonial Gallup**. The almost 90-year-old tradition includes a professional all-Indian rodeo, beautifully bedecked ceremonial dancers from many tribes and a powwow with competitive dancing. Book accommodations as far ahead as possible during this and several other annual events. Foremost among them is the **Navajo Reservation Fair** (first weekend in September), held in nearby Window Rock, Arizona (p226). The **Lions Club Rodeo**, in the third week in June, is the most professional

---

STRETCH YOUR LEGS: GALLUP MURAL WALK

Home to numerous outdoor murals depicting town life throughout the centuries, Gallup is further proof that New Mexico lives and breathes art. Painted over the last 80 years, the murals grace numerous downtown buildings, including the City Hall. Old and new, all are tasteful, and showcase Gallup's tricultural and distinctly Southwestern legacy and New Mexico's devout patronage of the arts in every form.

Gallup's original murals date back to the 1930s and were created during the Depression as part of President Franklin D Roosevelt's WPA program – an initiative to give out-of-work men jobs building and beautifying towns and parks on railway lines across the country. Some of the original murals can still be seen around town – check out the **McKinley County Courthouse** (213 Coal Ave).

The city takes pride in promoting the outdoor arts, and recently commissioned 12 local artists to paint new murals in central downtown. Eight have been completed and can be viewed on a short mural walk (about 10 blocks total). The murals range from abstract to realist and depict stories of peace and turmoil throughout Gallup's 126-year-old history. Although the murals are large, they don't distract from Gallup's historic aesthetics, rather they lend a different look to another small struggling Western town, and take the concept of a public gallery to an entirely different level.

Start your walk at the corner of W Aztec Ave and S 2nd St. The first mural, **Great Gallup** by Paul Newman and Steve Heil, is on the west-facing wall of the City Hall building and uses a variety of media to crate a graphic narrative of life in Gallup in panels – look for Native Americans on horseback in one, and a blue pick-up truck, so laboriously detailed it resembles an old photograph, in another. The **Gallup Inter-Tribal Indian Ceremonial Mural** by Irving Bahl is our other favorite mural. The last mural on the walk is found on the Ceremonial Building between 2nd and 3rd Sts on Coal Ave. It depicts Native American traditions and sacred Navajo symbols.

and prestigious of several area rodeos. Almost 200 colorful hot-air balloons take part in demonstrations and competitions at the **Balloon Rally** (first weekend in December) at Red Rock State Park (p182).

Local Native Americans perform social Indian dances at 7pm nightly from late June to early September, near the Amtrak Station.

Sleeping

Gallup has a number of chain and independent motels just off I-40 – including a Best Western and Holiday Inn. Follow the billboards or Route 66 outside of downtown for a few miles. A number of the motor lodges from the 1950s have gone out of business, but a couple are still open. Rooms cost between $45 and $125, except during Ceremonial week and other big events, when prices can double.

Red Rock Park Campground (☎ 505-722-3839; tent/RV sites $15/18) Plop your tent down in this beautiful setting with easy access to tons of hiking trails. Six miles east of town, it has showers, flush toilets, drinking water and a grocery store.

ourpick El Rancho (☎ 505-863-9311; www.el ranchohotel.com; 1000 E Hwy 66; r $65-118, ste $130; 🖳) Hollywood goes Native American futuristic at Gallup's best, and only, full-service historic lodging option. This town-center hotel with a neon facade was opened in 1937 and quickly became known as the 'home of the movie stars.' Many of the great actors of the '40s and '50s stayed here, including Humphrey Bogart, Katharine Hepburn and John Wayne, when he was filming Westerns in the area. El Rancho features a superb two-story open lobby decorated in rustic old National Park lodge style. Rooms are big, bright and decorated with eclectic Old West fashions. Pay the few extra dollars to say you've stayed in the hotel's presidential suite; room 103, named for Ronald Reagan, is not only massive, it's excellent value at just $130! The hotel has a restaurant and bar, which sometimes hosts bands. If El Rancho is full, the modern motel next door is under the same ownership. It has less interesting rooms for a few dollars less.

Eating & Drinking

Gallup is a good town to fill up your stomach – there are a number of restaurants and watering holes. Many restaurants in Gallup do not serve liquor, so read the review carefully if having beer with dinner is important. At the El Rancho Hotel, the 49ers Lounge offers drinks in an Old West setting and live music once a month. Stop by for the schedule.

Coffee House (☎ 505-726-0291; 203 W Coal Ave; mains $4-10; 🕒 7am-9:30pm Mon-Thu, 7am-11pm Fri & Sat, 7am-4pm Sun; wi-fi) With local art on the walls, overstuffed couches and newspapers, this restaurant has the feel of a small college-town hang-out. But there's no mistaking its Southwestern roots – the pressed-tin ceiling and historic building attest to that. As you might imagine, it serves strong espresso, chicken salads, soups, turkey sandwiches and homemade desserts.

El Rancho Restaurant (☎ 505-863-9311; 1000 E Hwy 66; breakfast & lunch $6-12, dinner $8-22; 🕒 breakfast, lunch & dinner; 🛇) This hotel restaurant is a trip. The menu seems to have been created way before the woman's rights movement: most of the 'leading lady' dishes at the movie-themed restaurant are of the fruit with sorbet or cottage cheese variety. Boys, you can sink your teeth into a hunk of beef – there are lots of steak and burger choices. Photos of old-time movie stars plaster the walls; heavy furniture dots the landscape. It's straight out of a movie set.

Genaro's Café (☎ 505-863-6761; 600 W Hill Ave; mains $6-12; 🕒 lunch & dinner Tue-Sun) This small, out-of-the-way place serves large portions of New Mexican food, but no alcohol. If you like your chile hot, you'll feel right at home here. And if you're up for a green chile cheeseburger, ask for chile on the side or your buns will become soggy really quickly – the burger swims in the green stuff.

Ranch Kitchen (☎ 505-722-2537; 3001 W Hwy 66; mains $6-15; 🕒 5am-9pm Tue-Sun) Almost everybody seems to stop by this longtime town favorite – must be the combination of reasonable prices, good food (barbecued and smoked meats, prime rib and the like) and the availability of beer and wine. Raised knotty pine ceilings and pine furniture set the bar higher than other places in town.

Earl's Family Restaurant (☎ 505-863-4201; 1400 E Hwy 66; mains $7-13; 🕒 breakfast, lunch & dinner; 🛇) The name says it all – Earl's is a great place to bring the kids. It has also been serving great green chile and fried chicken (but no alcohol) since the late 1940s. And the locals know it; the fast-food, diner-like place is packed on weekends. Perhaps you'll even get some shopping done here; Navajos sell goods at the eatery to tourists passing through.

NEW MEXICO

Oasis Mediterranean Restaurant (☎ 505-722-9572; 100 E Hwy 66; mains $8-20; ☯ 10am-9pm Mon-Sat; ☒) This pleasant gallery excels in conventional Mediterranean cuisine like baba ganoush, falafel and baklava, but also gets more creative with chicken dishes prepared with blazingly fresh components. It's a breath of fresh air in these parts.

Shopping

Gallup serves as the Navajo and Zuni peoples' major trading center, and is arguably the best place in New Mexico for top-quality goods at fair prices. Many trading posts are found downtown in the historic district on Hwy 66. See the boxed text, below, for info on visiting the Ellis Tanner Trading Co, a true Gallup experience.

Getting There & Around

The **Greyhound bus station** (☎ 505-863-3761), at the Amtrak building next to the cultural center, has four daily buses to Flagstaff, Arizona ($45, three hours) and Albuquerque ($27, 2½ hours) and beyond.

Amtrak (☎ 800-872-7245; www.amtrak.com; 201 E Hwy 66), which has an 'Indian Country Guide' pro-

---

GALLUP MUST-DO: ELLIS TANNER TRADING CO

If you've made it all the way to Gallup, go two miles further.

Just south of town is one of its most interesting shops. The **Ellis Tanner Trading Company** (☎ 505-863-4434; www.etanner.com; cnr Nizhoni & Hwy 602) is one of the Southwest's largest, functional traditional Indian trading posts. Owned by the same family, the Tanners, for four generations, it serves as a sort of combination of shop, bank and community meeting center for the local Navajo community – Gallup is just outside the Navajo Reservation. The parking lot of the huge complex is always packed with pick-up trucks out of which spill entire families who've driven hundreds of miles to sell, pawn or trade their wares.

Pass a row of worn leather saddles and into another world. The customers inside the main trading room speak a rainbow of languages, and you'll likely be one of the few non-Native faces here. Native Americans sit in groups on creaky wooden benches, catching up on the week's gossip, while waiting patiently for their turn at the trade counter. The walls are lined with art. On one side of the big room groceries and other hardware items line well-stocked shelves. Near the middle are arts and crafts materials – shepherds from the south trade raw wool for colorful rugs spun by northern weavers.

The Tanner family's trading began as many others did in the west, with a 'Mormon Calling.' Ellis Tanner, the 4th-generation owner who still runs the shop, described his great-grandfather's western odyssey – he followed Brigham Young when the Mormons settled Salt Lake City – to a local newspaper like this:

'He was sent out to set up small Mormon colonies. Each time he stayed a little longer. Finally, he set up a trading post in Tuba City and he didn't leave. The Navajos called him Hosteen Shush (Mr Bear). We had a family reunion out there, in Tuba City, two or three years ago. They're still using the same irrigation system today that he set up. Tanner Rapids, a tributary to the Grand Canyon, Tanner Wash, all that is named after Seth Tanner.

'My grandfather, Joe Tanner ('Shush Yazzae' or Little Bear in Navajo) also became a trader in Tuba City. He was a very good friend of the Chairman of the Navajo Reservation. Joe had a large family. Pretty soon we had several trading posts. Between my folks, the grand folks, my brothers, we've been all over the reservation with trading posts.'

Today Ellis is behind the trade counter at the Gallup trading post most mornings. When he's not, you could likely find him in his trading post's other main attraction. Located behind huge painted doors that once guarded an old Arizona copper mine, is the pawn room – Tanner's is one of the world's largest pawn dealers. From gorgeous turquoise necklaces to woven blankets, the pawn shop is filled with a treasure trove of Native American art in all mediums.

Whether you come for a bag of blue cornmeal or fresh fry-break, for turquoise stones, Navajo CDs or rare art, a visit to this market offers a chance to experience uniquely New Mexican, and specifically Native American, aspect custom – an honest-to-goodness old Indian trading post – not often seen in America today. We'd highly encourage supporting this sustainable homegrown initiative – 90% of the employees are Native American.

viding informative narration between Gallup and Albuquerque, runs an afternoon train to Albuquerque and a daily evening train to Flagstaff, Arizona.

SCENIC ROUTE 53

A great alternative way to reach Grants from Gallup is via Scenic Route 53. To get onto Route 53 from I-40 in Gallup cut south on Hwy 602. Running parallel to I-40, it is home to some of the coolest natural wonders and ancient history in the region. To really experience the out-of-this world landscape of lava tubes and red arches, traditional old New Mexican towns, volcanic craters and ice caves, you'll need to devote a full day to driving the route and exploring the attractions just off it.

Start your day a half-hour south of Gallup on Hwy 602. Turn east on Hwy 53 to begin. First up is **El Morro National Monument** (☎ 505-783-4226; www.nps.gov/elmo; adult/child $3/free; ☉ 9am-5pm, 9am-7pm in summer), 52 miles southeast of Gallup. Throughout history travelers have liked to leave their mark, as in 'Kim was here' – El Morro is proof positive of that. Also known as Inscription Rock, it's been a travelers' oasis for a few millennia. Well worth a stop, this 200ft sandstone outcrop is covered with thousands of carvings, from Pueblo petroglyphs at the top (c 1250) to inscriptions by Spaniard conquistadors and Anglo pioneers. Of the two trails that leave the visitor center, the paved, half-mile loop to **Inscription Rock** is wheelchair accessible. The unpaved, 2-mile **Mesa Top loop trail** requires a steep climb to the Pueblos. Trail access stops one hour before closing.

To camp, visit **El Morro RV Park & Cabins** (☎ 505-783-4612; Hwy 53; tent/RV sites $10/18, cabins $65-75). This NPS campground, with drinking water and pit toilets, is about a mile east of the visitor center and offers 26 sites and six cabins. Call ahead in the winter since it may be closed from October through April. El Morro's on-site **Ancient Way Café** (mains $6-10; ☉ breakfast, lunch & dinner; Ⓥ) serves home-cooked American, New Mexican and veggie specialties in simple wood environs. You can wake up in the morning with an espresso and eggs.

A few miles northwest of El Morro is Ramah, a true traditional old New Mexico town once typical of the region, but quickly vanishing. Ramah's Navajo population – the Native American residents are recognized as a chapter of the Navajo Reservation – have developed a sustainable local economy revolving

around sheep, weaving and other land-based traditions. The **Stage Coach Café** (☎ 505-783-4288; 3370 Bond St/Hwy 53; mains $6-10; ☉ 10am-6pm Mon-Sat, 10am-4pm Sun) is a good place to eat downtown. It offers great steaks, Mexican food and a giant selection of pies. Service is friendly.

Animal-lovers won't want to miss the **Wild Spirit Wolf Sanctuary** (☎ 505-775-3304; www.wildspirit wolfsanctuary.org; 378 Candy Kitchen Rd; tours adult/child $5/3; ☉ 10:30am-5pm Tue-Sun; ♿), 20 miles southeast of Ramah off Hwy 53. Home to rescued and captive-born wolves and wolf-dog mixes, the sanctuary offers six interactive walking tours per day, where you walk with the wolves – and get closer than you've imagined – that roam the sanctuary's large natural habitat enclosures. On the quarter-mile walk you'll learn more about conservation efforts, the sanctuary's mission and all about wolves – from behavior to what they like to eat. If you want to stay here overnight, primitive **camping** is available for $10 per night – you'll need all your own equipment and note that bathrooms are of the scoop and bury variety. Still, it's cool to camp out and hear the howl of wolves not far away.

After you've seen wolves, it's time for volcanic badlands. Visit the privately owned **Bandera Ice Cave** (☎ 505-783-4303, 888-423-2283; adult/child 5-12 $8/4; ☉ 8am-4:30pm), known to Pueblo Indians as Winter Lake, located 25 miles southwest of Grants on Hwy 53. Inside part of a collapsed lave tube, this is a large chunk of ice (tinted green because of Arctic algae) that stays frozen year-round – the ice on the cave floor is 20ft thick and temperatures never rise above 31°F!

Next up is **El Malpais National Monument** (☎ 505-285-4641; www.nps.gov/elma; Grants office, 123 E Roosevelt Ave, Grants; ☉ 8am-4:30pm Mon-Fri) Pronounced el mahl-pie-*ees*; which means 'bad land' in Spanish, the monument consists of almost 200 square miles of lava flows abutting adjacent sandstone. Five major flows have been identified; the most recent one is pegged at 2000 to 3000 years old. Prehistoric Native Americans may have witnessed the final eruptions since local Indian legends refer to 'rivers of fire.' Scenic Hwy 117 leads modern-day explorers past cinder cones and spatter cones, smooth *pahoehoe* lava and jagged aa lava, ice caves and a 17-mile-long lava tube system.

El Malpais is a hodgepodge of National Park Service (NPS) land, private land, conservation areas and wilderness areas administered by

NEW MEXICO

NEW MEXICO

the BLM. Each area has different rules and regulations, which change from year to year. The **BLM Ranger Station** (☎ 505-528-2918; Hwy 117; ◷ 8:30am-4:30pm), 9 miles south of I-40, has permits and information for the Cibola National Forest. The **El Malpais Information Center** (☎ 505-783-4774; www.nps.gov/elma; Hwy 53; ◷ 8:30am-4:30pm), 22 miles southwest of Grants, has permits and information for the lava flows and NPS land. Backcountry camping is allowed, but a free permit is required.

Though the terrain can be difficult, there are several opportunities for hiking through the monument. An interesting but rough hike (wear sturdy footwear) is the 7.5-mile (one way) **Zuni-Acoma Trail**, which leaves from Hwy 117 about 4 miles south of the ranger station. The trail crosses several lava flows and ends at Hwy 53 on the west side of the monument. Just beyond **La Ventana Natural Arch**, visible from Hwy 117 and 17 miles south of I-40, is the **Narrows Trail**, about 4 miles (one way). Thirty miles south of I-40 is **Lava Falls**, a 1-mile loop.

County Rd 42 leaves Hwy 117 about 34 miles south of I-40 and meanders for 40 miles through the BLM country on the west side of El Malpais. It passes several craters, caves and lava tubes (reached by signed trails) and emerges at Hwy 53 near Bandera Crater. Since the road is unpaved, it's best to have a high-clearance 4WD. If you go spelunking, the park service requires each person to carry two sources of light and to wear a hard hat. Go with a companion – this is an isolated area.

GRANTS

pop 8800 / elev 6400ft

Once a booming railway town, and then a booming mining town, today Grants is simply a strip on Route 66 with a couple of motels. The oncoming countrywide recession is already taking its toll on this small town – the coolest café has already closed, and eating options are now almost exclusively fast food. Log on to the Chamber of Commerce website and click on coffee houses, and you'll be politely informed: 'At this time there are no coffee houses in Grants. Maybe you should open one!'

The town is a convenient, inexpensive (albeit uninteresting) base for regional explorations, including down Hwy 53. Originally an agricultural center and railway stop founded in the 1880s, Grants experienced a major mining boom when uranium was discovered here in 1950.

Orientation & Information

Santa Fe Ave (business I-40, Hwy 118 or Route 66) is the main drag through town. It runs parallel and north of I-40 between exits 81 and 85.

Cibola National Forest Mount Taylor Ranger Station (☎ 505-287-8833; 1800 Lobo Canyon Rd; ◷ 8am-noon & 1-5pm Mon-Fri)

Grants Chamber of Commerce (☎ 505-287-4802, 800-748-2142; www.grants.org; 100 N Iron St; ◷ 9am-4pm Mon-Sat)

Sights & Activities

The **New Mexico Mining Museum** (☎ 505-287-4802; adult/child 7-18 $3/2; ◷ 9am-4pm Mon-Sat; ⚿) bills itself as the only uranium-mining museum in the world. Although the mine no longer operates because of decreased demand, it remains America's largest uranium reserve. The hands-on museum is made for kids, who will dig descending into the 'Section 26' mine shaft in a metal cage, then exploring the underground mine station.

The 11,301ft peak of **Mt Taylor** is the highest in the area, and the mountain offers great views and hiking. Head northeast on Lobo Canyon Rd (Hwy 547) for about 13 miles to where it changes into gravel USFS Rd 239. For a great view follow 239 and then USFS Rd 453 for another 3.3 miles to **La Mosca Lookout** at 11,000ft, about a mile northeast of Mt Taylor's summit.

Festivals & Events

In mid-February the **Mt Taylor Quadrathlon** (www.mttaylorquad.org) between Grants and Mt Taylor combines cycling, running, cross-country skiing and snowshoeing. Individuals and teams of two to four athletes compete. Then there's the **Fire & Ice Route 66 Bike Rally** (www.fireandicebikerally.com), a two-day Harley Davidson festival in mid-July with motorcycle rodeo events and live music. The **Chile Fiesta** (www.grants.org) in early October celebrates chile with a chile cook-off and other events.

Sleeping & Eating

Grants has a string of chains and fading old motor lodges on its main road, Route 66, which runs straight through town. Take your pick, or drive a little out of town to our favorite spot, the Cimarron Rose. As for food, if you don't want fast food from Taco Bell or McDonalds, then head to the hotels – most have some sort of steakhouse-themed restaurant inside. Otherwise, there's not much else to eat.

Coal Mine Campground (Lobo Canyon Rd; campsites $8; ☼ mid-May–late Sep) This pleasantly wooded place is 10 miles northeast of town and has a nature trail and flush toilets, but no showers.

`our pick` **Cimarron Rose** (☎ 505-783-4770; www .cimarronrose.com; 689 Oso Ridge Rd; ste $110-185) If you're looking for a peaceful alternative to the chains of Grants and Gallup, and want to stay green, pay a visit to the Cimarron Rose. Although it's 30 miles southwest of Grants, this B&B is conveniently located on Hwy 53 between El Malpais and El Morro in the Zuni Mountains. Cimarron Rose offers two Southwestern-style suites, with tiles, pine walls and hardwood floors (one has a kitchen). The innkeepers take pride in being ecofriendly. Rainwater is collected and used as utility water, and grey water is re-used to water trees. Two goats and a horse organically fertilize Cimarron's perennial gardens, which provide food and shelter for more than 80 species of birds.

New Mexico Steakhouse (☎ 505-287-7901; Best Western Inn & Suites, 1501 E Santa Fe Ave; mains $10-25; ☼ dinner) One of the better hotel steakhouses, this one is in the Best Western. It serves a variety of steaks, salads and potatoes as well as some New Mexican dishes. If you're in need of a stiff drink, there's a full service bar.

Getting There & Away

Greyhound (☎ 505-285-6268; www.greyhound.com) stops at 1700 W Santa Fe Ave and offers several daily buses to Albuquerque ($25, 1¼ hours), Flagstaff, Arizona ($60, 5½ hours) and beyond. Pay the driver in cash.

LAS VEGAS & AROUND
pop 14,600 / elev 6470ft

Long before they were discovering carnal pleasures in Las Vegas, NV they were dishing it out in the bordellos of America's original sin city, Las Vegas, NM. Sitting on the Santa Fe Trail, 19th-century Las Vegas was a true-blue outlaw town, a place where Billy the Kid and pal Vicente Silva (who once killed 40 people at one time) held court and Doc Holliday owned a saloon (although ultimately his business failed because he kept shooting at the customers).

A century and a half later, Las Vegas has grown into an elegant, sienna-tinted place with a lively social swirl (most of it radiating from its two small universities) that feels much more like a small town than New Mexico's third-largest city. More than 900 historic buildings grace its quaint downtown that's served as a Western backdrop for many a Hollywood picture – *Wyatt Earp, The Ballad of Gregorio Cortez* and most recently Oscar-winner *No Country for Old Men* – are just a few of the movies filmed here. Las Vegas isn't technically on Route 66 – although the town sits just off the original roadbed, now renamed US 84, and we include it here because it's always acted as a gateway to the route. Las Vegas also serves as gateway to two striking wilderness areas: the Pecos Wilderness (p317) and Las Vegas National Wildlife Refuge.

Home to the Comanche people for some 10,000 years, Las Vegas was established by the Mexican government in 1835, just in time to serve as a stop along the Santa Fe Trail and later the Santa Fe Railroad. It quickly grew into one of the biggest, baddest boomtowns in the West, and in 1846 the USA took possession of it.

Orientation & Information

Las Vegas is located on I-25, 65 miles east of Santa Fe. Hwy 85 or Grand Ave, which runs north–south, parallels the interstate and is the main thoroughfare.

Carnegie Public Library (☎ 505-454-1403; 500 National; ☼ 8am-5pm Mon-Wed & Fri, 8am-8pm Thu, 8am-noon Sat; ⌨) Free internet access.

Chamber of Commerce (☎ 505-425-8631, 800-832-5947; www.lasvegasnm.org; 701 Grand Ave; ☼ 9am-5pm Mon-Fri)

Hospital (☎ 505-426-3500; 104 Legion Dr; ☼ 24hr emergency)

Police (☎ 505-425-7504; 318 Moreno)

Post office (☎ 505-425-9387; 1001 Douglas Ave)

Santa Fe National Forest Ranger Station (☎ 505-425-3534; 1926 7th St; ☼ 8am-5pm Mon-Fri)

Sights & Activities
IN LAS VEGAS

The Chamber of Commerce publishes walking tours of various historic districts and beautiful neighborhoods surrounding the plaza and Bridge St. Around the historic center, note the lovely Plaza Hotel (p278); it was built in 1880 and is still in use.

The small but informative **City of Las Vegas Museum & Rough Rider Memorial Collection** (☎ 505-454-1401; 727 Grand Ave; admission free; ⊕ 9am-4pm Mon-Fri & 10am-3pm Sat year-round, plus noon-4pm Sun Apr-Sep) chronicles the fabled cavalry unit led by future US president Theodore Roosevelt in the 1898 fight for Cuba. More than one-third of the volunteer force came from New Mexico, and in this museum you'll see their furniture, clothes and military regalia.

At the **Santa Fe Trail Interpretive Center** (☎ 505-425-8803; 127 Bridge St; admission free; ⊕ 10am-4pm Mon-Sat) the local historically society displays an impressive collection of old photos and artifacts from Las Vegas' heyday as a rough-and-tumble trading post on the Santa Fe Trail. Guided tours are available.

NEAR LAS VEGAS

Five miles southeast of Las Vegas on Hwys 104 and 67, the 14-sq-mile **Las Vegas National Wildlife Refuge** (☎ 505-425-3581; Rte 1; admission free; ⊕ dawn-dusk) has marshes, woodlands and grasslands to which upwards of 275 bird species have found their way. Visitors can follow a 7-mile drive and walking trails.

The pretty **Villanueva State Park** (☎ 505-421-2957; per car per day $5, tent/RV sites $10/14), about 35 miles south of Las Vegas, lies in a red rock canyon on the Rio Pecos valley. A small visitor center and self-guided trails explain the area's history – it was once a main travel route for Indians and, in the 1500s, for the Spanish conquistadors. Head south on I-25 for 22 miles, then take Hwy 3 south for 12 miles. Tent and RV sites have showers.

En route along Hwy 3, you'll pass the Spanish colonial villages of **Villanueva** and **San Miguel** (the latter with a fine church built in 1805), surrounded by vineyards belonging to the **Madison Winery** (☎ 505-421-8028; Hwy 3; ⊕ 10am-4:30pm Mon, Tue, Thu & Fri, noon-4:30pm Sun), which has a tasting room. While here, don't miss **La Risa** (☎ 505-421-3883; Hwy 3; dishes $5-8; ⊕ 8am-8pm Mon-Sat, 8am-2pm Sun), a gourmet anomaly in the middle of nowhere, with homemade desserts, breads and pastries.

Montezuma, 5 miles northwest of Las Vegas on Hwy 65, is famous for Montezuma Castle, built in 1886 as a luxury hotel close to local hot springs. (It's now owned by the United World College and is under renovation.) The nearby natural **hot springs** (☎ 505-454-4200; Hwy 65; admission free; ⊕ 5am-midnight), just north of the college, reputedly have curative and therapeutic powers and are especially fabulous at night under the light of a full moon.

Festivals & Events

The four-day festivities surrounding the **Fourth of July** here are a colorful mix of Hispanic and Anglo festivities, and include Mexican folk music, dancing and mariachi bands. Other events include the **San Miguel County Fair** on the third weekend in August and a **Harvest Festival** (third Saturday of September) with music and food.

Sleeping

Inn on the Santa Fe Trail (☎ 505-425-6791, 888-448-8438; www.innonthesantafetrail.com; 1133 Grand Ave; r incl breakfast from $52; ▣) It looks a bit bland from the exterior, but rooms here are surprisingly modern posh, decorated in a lovely hacienda Southwestern-style with lots of white painted adobe and beautiful curves and high-quality polished wood furniture and ceiling beams. It also features a good restaurant, central courtyard and shaded grounds.

Plaza Hotel (☎ 505-425-3591, 800-328-1882; www.plazahotel-nm.com; 230 Old Town Plaza; r incl breakfast from $69; ▣) This is Las Vegas' most celebrated and historic lodging, and it's also excellent value. It was opened in 1882 and carefully remodeled a century later; plenty of architectural details abound. The elegant brick building now offers 36 comfortable antique-filled rooms.

Star Hill Inn (☎ 505-425-5605; www.starhillinn.com; 247 Las Dispensas Rd, Sapello; cottages $170-380) Astronomy buffs will dig this experience-based inn, where nights are spent looking through the lens of a telescope. North of Las Vegas, high in the Sangre de Cristos, it sits on 200 acres laced with hiking and cross-country skiing trails, and gets very little in the way of light pollution. So when owner Phil Mahon introduces you to the grandeur of the night sky, you'll get to see a million stars. The eight cottages are decorated Southwestern style (think kokapelli lamps and Navajo-inspired bedspreads with lots of bold stripes) and have fireplaces and kitchens; a two-night minimum is required. Since there are no stores nearby, you should bring along food to fully utilize the kitchens. Look for Star Hill in the tiny village of Sapello, 13 miles north of Las Vegas on Hwy 518.

Eating

Charlie's Spic & Span Bakery & Café (☎ 505-426-1921; 715 Douglas Ave; mains $4-9; ⊕ breakfast, lunch & dinner;

wi-fi) This Las Vegas institution has listened to the town's gossip for half a century now, and it remains the place for locals to hang out. To catch up over a cup of coffee (or vanilla latte) and New Mexican diner fare – think bean and cheese stuffed *sopaipillas*, pancake sandwiches and good old-fashioned hamburgers. Save room for dessert.

Super Chief Coffee Bar (☎ 505-454-1360; 514 Grand Ave; mains $4-19; ✹ breakfast & lunch; wi-fi) If you're hungry, it's worth getting off I-25 just to eat at this relatively new café serving healthy, organic fare and the best coffee in town. With big picture windows, plenty of chairs and newspapers, this is a place meant for lingering. But should you be in a hurry, Super Chief does 'design your own' sandwiches, soups or fresh salad to go. There's a used bookstore upstairs and free wi-fi, making it a popular local haunt.

Estella's Café (148 Bridge St; lunch mains $5-7, dinner mains $7-12; ✹ 11am-3pm Mon-Wed, 11am-8pm Thu-Fri, 11am-7pm Sat) Talk about stepping back in time – Estella's doesn't even have a phone! The restaurant does have a group of devoted patrons who come for the homemade red chile, *menudo* and scrumptious enchiladas. Owned by the Gonzalez family since 1950, this crowded gem is the best place in town for simple and tasty New Mexican food.

Blackjack's Grille (☎ 505-425-6791; Inn on the Santa Fe Trail, 1133 N Grand Ave; mains $13-20; ✹ dinner) In a small adobe courtyard lit by oil lamps, eating at Blackjack's is like hitting 21 on the card table. Serving excellent New Mexican cuisine in intimate white-tablecloth environs, this restaurant gets good marks for service, personality and best of all its fresh, simple food. Wash it down with a local microbrew or Agave wine cocktail. The grill is part of the Inn at the Santa Fe Trail, and guests receive a 10% discount.

Drinking & Entertainment
Cafés and coffee shops on Bridge St may have poetry readings or folk music.

Byron T Saloon (☎ 505-425-3591; 230 Old Town Plaza) Within the Plaza Hotel, this bar hosts live jazz, blues and country music on weekends.

Fort Union Drive-In (☎ 505-425-9934; 3300 7th St; per car $5; ✹ Thu-Sat May-Sep) One of New Mexico's few remaining drive-in movie theatres lies just north of town and has great views of the surrounding high desert. But you're supposed to be watching the flicks, remember?

Getting There & Around
TNM&O buses (☎ 505-425-8387, 505-243-4435; www.greyhound.com; 1901 W Grand) stop at Pino's Truck Stop several times a day on their way to Raton and Santa Fe.

Amtrak (☎ 800-872-7245; www.amtrak.com) runs a daily train between Chicago, Illinois, and Los Angeles, California, that stops in Las Vegas.

SANTA ROSA
pop 2500 / elev 4600ft
Scuba in Santa Rosa? Yup, that's right. Settled in the mid-19th century by Spanish farmers, Santa Rosa's modern claim to fame is, oddly enough, as the scuba-diving capital of the Southwest – see the boxed text, p82. There's not much else going on here, though.

Orientation & Information
Take exit 273 from Route 66/I-40 to reach downtown. The main street begins as Coronado St, then becomes Parker Ave through downtown, before becoming Will Rogers Dr when it passes exits 275 and 277. Most hotels and restaurants lie along the main thoroughfare, part of the celebrated Route 66.

The **Chamber of Commerce** (☎ 505-472-3763; www.santarosanm.org; 486 Parker Ave; ✹ 8am-5pm Mon-Fri) has more information.

Sights & Activities
One of the 10 best spots to dive in the country is, surprisingly, here in li'l ol' Santa Rosa. How could that be? Because of the bell-shaped, 81ft-deep **Blue Hole**. Fed by a natural spring flowing at 3000 gallons a minute, the water in the hole is both very clear and pretty cool (about 61°F to 64°F). It's also 80ft in diameter at the surface and 130ft in diameter below the surface. Platforms for diving are suspended about 25ft down. Visit the **Santa Rosa Dive Center** (☎ 505-472-3370; www.santarosanm.com; Hwy 40/US 66) to set up a dive. The shop is next to the hole.

Nine miles south of town along Hwy 91, tiny **Puerto de Luna** was founded in the 1860s and is one of the oldest settlements in New Mexico. The drive there is pretty, winding through arroyos surrounded by eroded sandstone mesas. In town you'll find an old county courthouse, a village church and a bunch of weathered adobe buildings. It's all quite charming, as long as you're not in a hurry to do something else.

The **Route 66 Auto Museum** (☎ 505-472-1966; www.route66automuseum.com; 2766 Rte 66; adult/child under 5 $5/free; ☉ 7:30am-7pm May-Aug, 7:30am-5pm Sep-Apr) pays homage to the mother of all roads. It boasts upwards of 35 cars from the 1920s through the 1960s, all in beautiful condition in its exhibit hall, and lots of 1950s memorabilia. It's a fun place; enjoy a milkshake at the '50s-style snack shack. If you're in the market for a beautifully restored old Chevy, the museum doubles as an antique car dealer.

Festivals & Events
In keeping with the Route 66 theme, the **Annual Custom Car Show** (held August or September) attracts vintage- and classic-car enthusiasts, as well as folks driving strange things on wheels. The **Santa Rosa Fiesta** (third week of August) is homespun, to say the least, with a beauty-queen contest and the bizarre, annual Duck Drop, for which contestants buy squares and then wait for a duck suspended over the squares to poop – if the poop lands on their square, they win cold cash.

Sleeping & Eating
Santa Rosa has numerous inexpensive old independent motels – a handful have been around since before I-40 was built – and more modern chains clustered around its I-40 exits. The town is home to nine long-established family-owned diners and roadside cafés, all with historic allure.

Budget 10 Motel (☎ 505-472-3454; 120 Hwy 54; r from $35) An inexpensive oldie that caters mainly to I-40 traffic, Budget 10 is a no-frills place, but it's clean and safe.

La Quinta Inn (☎ 505-472-4800; www.lq.com; 1701 Will Rogers Dr; r from $59; ☒ wi-fi) One of the best hotels in Santa Rosa, this La Quinta offers standard, slightly bland, but big, sunny and clean chain hotel–style rooms. What La Quinta lacks in uniqueness, it makes up in stunning city views – it sits at Santa Rosa's highest point. The heated indoor swimming pool, giant Jacuzzi and free wi-fi are plusses. Traveling with pet? La Quinta welcomes your pooch.

Silver Moon (☎ 505-472-3162; Will Rogers Dr; mains $5-15; ☉ breakfast, lunch & dinner) A trademark Route 66 eatery that first opened its doors in 1959, Silver Moon serves fantastic homemade *chile rellenos* and other tasty diner grub dressed up with a New Mexican twist. It's popular with travelers following Route 66's old roadhouse trail, as well as locals who

come for a morning coffee and a plate of bacon and eggs.

Comet II Drive-in (☎ 505-472-3663; 239 Parker Ave; dishes $5-10; ☉ 11am-9pm Tue-Sun) This classic drive-in offers options beyond the usual burgers and fries; instead it focuses on delicious Mexican fare with a Southwestern flair. Try the *carne adobada* and green chile enchiladas. It's a family run restaurant, and owners Johnny and Alice Martinez offer warm, friendly service.

our pick **Joseph's Bar & Grill** (☎ 505-472-3361; 865 Will Rogers Dr; mains $6-12; ☉ breakfast, lunch & dinner) Route 66 nostalgia lines the walls of this popular place, family owned since its inception in 1956. Many of the bountiful Mexican and American recipes have been handed down through the generations. Burgers and steaks are as popular as anything smothered in green chile. Joseph's also mixes the best margaritas on Route 66.

Getting There & Away
Santa Rosa's downtown is at exit 273 on Route 66/I-40. The town is about 120 miles east of Albuquerque.

TUCUMCARI
pop 5500 / elev 4080ft
The biggest town on I-40 between Albuquerque and Amarillo, Tucumcari is a ranching and farming town between the mesas and the plains. It's scenic and also home to one of the best-preserved sections of Route 66 in the country. Not surprisingly, it still caters to travelers with inexpensive motels, several classic pre-interstate buildings and souvenir shops like the Tee Pee Curios.

Orientation & Information
Tucumcari lies barely north of I-40. The main west–east thoroughfare between these exits is old Route 66, called Tucumcari Blvd through downtown. The principal north–south artery is 1st St. A **chamber of commerce** (☎ 505-461-1694; www.tucumcarinm.com; 404 W Tucumcari Blvd) keeps sporadic hours.

Sights & Activities
Drive the kids down Tucumcari's main street at night, when dozens of old neon signs cast a blazing glow. The bright, flashing signs are relics of Tucumcari's Route 66 heyday, when they were installed by business owners as a crafty form of marketing to get weary travelers to stop for the

DETOUR: WEST TEXAS BOUND

Pull off the highway and scramble to the top of any of the buttes in West Texas, squint your eyes just so, and you'll actually see a waterline: the ghost of an ancient ocean that deposited an eon's worth of corals, skeletons, shells and sediment that make up this blistering and beautiful landscape. The western reaches of this state are to many native Texans the quintessential Texas experience.

Here's where you'll find **Guadalupe Mountains National Park**, where, in the fall, **McKittrick Canyon** becomes one of the most scenic hiking areas in the park. **Pines Springs Campground** (campsites $8) sits next to the **visitor center** (☎ 915-828-3251; www.nps.gov/gumo; Hwy 62/180; ◷ 8am-4:30pm Mon-Fri).

Isolated at the state's far-western tip, **El Paso** is an unpretentious, bicultural city with a strong independent streak. Its historic heart is **San Jacinto Plaza**, which could easily pass for Mexico. For a self-guided walking tour, head to the **visitor center** (☎ 915-534-0601, 800-351-6024; www .visitelpaso.com; Santa Fe St; ◷ 8am-5pm Mon-Fri).

Across the Rio Grande lies **Ciudad Juarez**, Mexico's 4th-largest city. Though the US Border Patrol tries to keep the two countries neatly separated, Mexican culture has always been dominant in El Paso and Spanish is the default language. Don't forget your passport. About 32 miles east of El Paso, off US 62/180, **Hueco Tanks State Historic Site** has abundant wildlife and ancient pictographs. The 860-acre **park** (☎ 915-857-1135; www.tpwd.state.tx.us/park/hueco/) is also a magnet for rock climbers. To minimize impact on the fragile park, a daily visitor quota is enforced; call ahead.

Big Bend National Park is vast enough for a lifetime of discovery. A white-water rafting, mountain- biking and hiking paradise, it's also one of the least visited national parks, and for good reason: it's hot. The area around the park, surprisingly, is home to many artist retreats, historic hotels and quaint mountain villages. Its diverse geography makes for an amazing variety of wildlife. Stop at the main **visitor center** (☎ 432-477-2251; www.nps.gov/bibe; 7-day pass per car $15; ◷ 8am-6pm). The park's 110 miles of paved road and 150 miles of dirt road make scenic driving the most popular activity.

West of Big Bend you'll find **Terlingua**, one of Willie Nelson's favorite spots. Travelers and artists passing through tend to linger here. There are several excellent restaurants and a nice live-music scene. It's also one of the main jumping-off points for Big Bend.

West of Lajitas, FM 170 hugs the Rio Grande through spectacular and remote scenery. Known as the **Camino del Rio**, it winds its way for 50 miles to **Presidio**, a dreary border town. From there US Hwy 67 heads north to **Marfa**, home to the **Chinati Foundation** (☎ 432-729-4362; adult/child $10/5; ◷ tours 10am & 2pm Wed-Sun, book 2 weeks in advance), a sprawling complex of minimalist art founded by New York artist Donald Judd in 1986. The town's original fame came after James Dean, Elizabeth Taylor and Rock Hudson filmed *Giant* here in 1955. Everyone stays at the 1930s-era **Hotel Paisano** (☎ 866-729-3669; 207 N Highland; r from $100). Marfa is also known for the unexplained 'Marfa lights,' which flash across the desert sky on random nights. As yet, no one has figured out where they come from.

East of Marfa, **Marathon** is an artsy hamlet with art galleries, great eateries and the best place to sleep in Texas: the **Gage Hotel** (☎ 432-386-4205, 800-884-4243; www.gagehotel.com; 101 Hwy 90 W; r $84-325; ▣). Rooms are straight out of a Wild West pulp novel, with wide wooden blinds, saddles in the rooms and cowhides on the beds.

night. Today the old signs, with their Western motifs, make quite a sight after dark.

The town is also home to 23 life-size and larger **murals** recording Tucumcari's history throughout the decades. The pieces of art, which adorn buildings on and just north and south of Route 66, are the life work of local painters Doug and Sharon Quarles. Taking

the town's mural walk is a great way to stretch your legs and experience Tucumcari's Route 66 legacy. Grab a mural walking map off the chamber of commerce website (www.tucumcarinm.co m/visitors_guide).

Several rooms of the **Tucumcari Historical Museum** (☎ 505-461-4201; 416 S Adams St; admission $3; ◷ 8am-5pm Mon-Sat, 8am-6pm May-Sep) feature

NEW MEXICO

reconstructions of early Western interiors, such as a sheriff's office, a classroom and a hospital room. It's an eclectic collection, to say the least, displaying a barbed-wire collection alongside Indian artifacts.

Well worth a visit is the **Mesalands Dinosaur Museum** (☎ 505-461-3466; 222 E Laughlin St; adult/child $6/3.50; ☾ noon-5pm Tue-Sat Sep-Feb, 10am-6pm Tue-Sat Mar-Sep), which showcases real dinosaur bones and has hands-on exhibits. Casts of dinosaur bones are done in bronze (rather than the usual plaster of Paris), which not only shows fine detail, but also makes them works of art.

At the east end of town, the 770-acre **Ladd S Gordon Wildlife Preserve** (off Tucumcari Blvd) encompasses Tucumcari Lake. Wintering ducks begin arriving mid-October, and geese a month later. To reach it, take the gravel road north when you see the Motel 6.

Sleeping

Tucumcari has the usual number of chain motels spread along I-40. It also has a number of cool old independent motels on historic Route 66. There is also a KOA (campground franchise) a quarter mile east of I-40 at exit 355.

Historic Route 66 Motel (☎ 505-461-1212; www .tucumcarimotel.com; 1620 E Route 66; r incl breakfast from $25; wi-fi) When it comes to budget digs, you can't beat this historic, rather squat old motor-court motel with giant plate glass doors and mesa views. It's nothing splashy, but the 25 rooms are cheap and clean. Small dogs are welcome. A continental breakfast is served each morning.

our pick Blue Swallow Motel (☎ 505-461-9849; www.blueswallowmotel.com; 815 E Tucumcari Blvd; r from $59; wi-fi) Spend the night in this beautifully restored Route 66 motel listed on the State and National Registers of Historic Places, and feel the centuries melt away. The classic neon sign has been featured in many Route 66 articles and boasts that Blue Swallow offers a '100% refrigerated bar'. The place has a great lobby, friendly owners and vintage, uniquely decorated rooms. The Blue Swallow is so cool in fact, it has its own MySpace page: www .myspace.com/historicblueswallowmotel.

Eating & Drinking

Del's Restaurant (☎ 505-461-1740; 1202 E Tucumcari Blvd; mains $5-15; ☾ breakfast, lunch & dinner Mon-Sat) Del's is popular in these here parts for its menu of Mexican and American classic diner fare – burgers and burritos, as well as a hearty salad bar, lots of soup choices and take-away service if you'd rather dine from the comfort of your motel bed.

Pow-Wow Restaurant & Lizard Lounge (☎ 505-461-0500; Best Western Pow Wow Inn, 801 W Tucumcari Blvd; mains $7-20; ☾ breakfast, lunch & dinner) Big, juicy steaks, spicy Mexican and a long cocktail menu make Pow-Wow's one of the town's more popular restaurants despite being in the local Best Western. It has the added plus of doubling as a popular bar in this oft-quiet town. For weekend drinks and dancing, head to the attached Lizard Lounge to try two-steppin' to live country and western entertainment.

Getting There & Away

Tucumcari is at the crossroads of Historic Route 66, now I-40, and US Hwy 54. It is 110 miles from Amarillo, Texas, and 170 miles from Albuquerque, New Mexico.

NEW MEXICO PUEBLOS

New Mexico is home to 19 Native American pueblos, with the greatest concentration found just outside Santa Fe. For a comprehensive overview on visiting these Indian homes, stop by Albuquerque's Indian Pueblo Cultural Center (p294). Operated by the Pueblos themselves, it will give you an idea of what to expect from each distinct village. A historical museum here traces the development of Pueblo cultures; exhibits compare cultures through languages, customs and crafts; an art gallery features changing exhibits and a restaurant serves Pueblo fare.

Don't expect all Native American pueblos to be tourist attractions – many offer little for visitors outside of festival weekends. Instead, most serve simply as neighborhoods, complete with schools, shops and gathering places. Many of the pueblos are poor and the gritty realities of life are all too prevalent.

Most New Mexican pueblos make money by building casinos (you can gamble on the Indian reservations, but not elsewhere in the state). Note that most Pueblo casinos don't serve alcohol.

For more information on etiquette when visiting Indian reservations, see p61. Note that all the pueblos in this section are mapped on p54.

TOP FIVE PUEBLOS

With so many Native American pueblos to visit, you may have to prioritize what you want to see or you could spend months viewing these historic dwellings. Below are our top five choices for must-see pueblos.

- **Taos Pueblo** (p287) The most famous pueblo in New Mexico; make sure to eat fry bread at Tewa's Kitchen.
- **Zuni Pueblo** (below) Less touristy than other pueblos, go for the creative jewelry and wild scenery; it's 35 miles outside of Gallup.
- **Acoma Pueblo** (below) Dramatic mesa-top location; one of the oldest continually inhabited pueblos in America.
- **Nambé Pueblo** (p286) Nambé has long been a spiritual center for the Tewa-speaking tribes; today it is entered through a fantastic natural entryway.
- **Picuris Pueblo** (p287) Once one of the largest and most powerful pueblos in the state on the High Rd to Taos; visit the ruins from the old pueblo site and the exquisite 1770 church.

WESTERN NEW MEXICO PUEBLOS

There are three interesting pueblos in the western portion of the state.

Zuni Pueblo

pop 6500 / elev 6293ft

This pueblo, 35 miles south of Gallup, is well known for its jewelry, and you can buy beautiful pieces at little shops throughout the town along Hwy 53. Other than that, there's not much going on, which is precisely why you might want to spend a little time driving around its housing developments. It'll give you a hint of modern reservation life, albeit from the outside looking in. Information is available from the extremely helpful **Zuni Tourism Program Office** (☎ 505-782-7238; ☽ 8am-5:30pm), which dispenses photography permits. The office also offers daily tours, walking past stone houses and beehive-shaped mud ovens to the massive **Our Lady of Guadalupe Mission**, featuring impressive locally painted murals of about 30 life-size kachinas. The church dates from 1629, although it has been rebuilt twice since then.

The **Ashiwi Awan Museum & Heritage Center** (☎ 505-782-4403; Ojo Caliente Rd; admission by donation; ☽ 9am-5pm Mon-Fri) displays early photos and other tribal artifacts. They'll also cook traditional meals for groups of 10 or more ($10 per person) with advance reservations. Next door, **Pueblo of Zuni Arts & Crafts** (☎ 505-782-5531) sells locally made jewelry, baskets and other crafts.

The most famous ceremony at Zuni is the all-night **Shalak'o ceremonial dance**, held on the last weekend in December. The **Zuni Tribal Fair** (late August) features a powwow, local food, and arts and crafts stalls. To participate in any ceremony hosted by the Zuni community, you must attend an orientation; call the program office for more information.

The friendly **Inn at Halona** (☎ 505-782-4547, 800-752-3278; www.halona.com; 1 Shalaka Dr; r from $79), decorated with local Zuni arts and crafts, is the only place to stay on the pueblo. Since each of the eight pleasant rooms is very different, check out as many as you can to see which fits your fancy. Full breakfasts (for an extra fee) are served in the flagstone courtyard in the summer; room service is provided by a grocery store in the back. The inn is located behind Halona Plaza, south from Hwy 53 at the only four-way stop in town.

Acoma Pueblo

pop 3500 / elev 6400ft

Journeying to the top of 'Sky City' is like journeying into another world. There are few more dramatic mesa-top locations; the village sits 7000ft above sea level and 367ft above the surrounding plateau. It's one of the oldest continuously inhabited settlements in North America; people have lived in Acoma Pueblo since the 11th century. In addition to a singular history and a dramatic location, it's also famous for pottery, which is sold by individual artists on the mesa. There is a distinction between 'traditional' pottery (made with clay dug on the reservation) and 'ceramic' pottery (made elsewhere with inferior clay and simply painted by the artist), so ask the vendor.

NEW MEXICO

Visitors can only reach Sky City on guided tours, which leave from the **visitor center** (☎ 505-469-1052, 800-747-0181; tours adult/child 6-17 $10/7) at the bottom of the mesa. These tours are offered daily every 45 minutes, except for July 10 to July 13 and either the first or second weekend in October, when the pueblo is closed to visitors. Though you must ride the shuttle to the top of the mesa, you can choose to walk down the rock path to the visitor center on your own. It's definitely worth doing this.

Festivals and events include a **Governor's Feast** (February), a harvest dance on **San Esteban Day** (September 2) and festivities at the **San Esteban Mission** from December 25 to 28. Photography permits cost $10; no videos are permitted.

The Sky City visitor center is about 13 miles south of I-40 exit 96 (15 miles east of Grants) or I-40 exit 108 (50 miles west of Albuquerque).

Sky City Hotel (☎ 505-552-6123, 888-759-2489; www.skycityhotel.com; exit 102 off I-40; r from $75; 🏊), the pueblo's modern casino, has 132 motel-style rooms and suites dressed up in Southwestern decor. Amenities include live entertainment, dining options, room service and a pool.

Acoma Pueblo is 63 miles southwest of Albuquerque – take I-40 west to exit 108, then head south on Hwy 23.

Laguna Pueblo
pop 423 / elev 5807ft

From Albuquerque you can zoom along I-40 for 150 miles to the Arizona border in a little over two hours. But don't. Stop at the Indian reservation of Laguna, about 40 miles west of Albuquerque or 30 miles east of Grants. Founded in 1699, it's the youngest of New Mexico's pueblos and consists of six small villages. Since its founders were escaping from the Spaniards and came from many different pueblos, the Laguna people have a very diverse ethnic background.

The imposing stone and adobe **San José Mission** (☎ 505-552-9330; 🕘 9am-3pm Mon-Fri), visible from I-40, was completed in 1705 and houses fine examples of early Spanish-influenced religious art. It will beckon you off the interstate.

Main feast days include **San José** (March 19 and September 19), **San Juan** (June 24) and **San Lorenzo** (August 10 and Christmas Eve). Contact **Laguna Pueblo** (☎ 505-552-6654) for more information.

ALBUQUERQUE AREA PUEBLOS

There are a number of pueblos north of Albuquerque on the way to Santa Fe.

Isleta Pueblo
pop 2200 / elev 4887ft

This **pueblo** (☎ 505-869-3111), 16 miles south of Albuquerque at I-25 exit 215, is best known for its church, the **San Augustine Mission** (☎ 505-869-3398). Built in 1613, it's been in constant use since 1692. A few plaza shops sell local pottery, and there is gambling at the **Isleta Casino and Resort** (☎ 505-724-3800; www.islet-casino.com; 🕘 8am-4am Mon-Thu, 24hr Fri-Sun). On **Saint Augustine's Day** (September 4 and August 28), ceremonial dancing is open to the public.

Sandia Pueblo
pop 4400 / elev 5043ft

About 13 miles north of Albuquerque, this **pueblo** (☎ 505-867-3317; www.sandiapueblo.nsn.us; I-25 exit 234) was established around AD 1300. It opened one of the first casinos in New Mexico and subsequently used its wealth to successfully lobby for legislation preventing further development of Sandia Crest, the Sandia people's old sacred lands, appropriated by Cibola National Forest. The **Sandia Casino** (☎ 800-526-9366; www.sandiacasino.com; 🕘 8am-4am Mon-Thu, 24hr Fri-Sun) boasts an elegant outdoor venue, the Sandia Casino Amphitheater, hosting everything from symphony orchestras to boxing matches to Bill Cosby.

Bien Mur Marketplace (☎ 800-365-5400; www.bienmur.com; 100 Bien Mur Dr NE), across the road from the casino, claims to be the largest Native American–owned trading post in the Southwest, which is probably true. The tribe invites visitors to **Marketfest** (late October), when Native American artists show their stuff, as well as to corn dances during **Feast Day** (June 13).

Santa Ana Pueblo
pop 479 / elev 5300ft

This **pueblo** (☎ 505-867-3301; www.santaana.org; US 150) is *posh*. Really posh. It boasts two great **golf courses** (☎ 505-867-9464, 800-851-9469; www.santaanagolf.com; green fees $35-100), the Santa Ana Golf Club, with three nine-hole courses, and the extravagant Twin Warriors Golf Club, with 18 holes and waterfalls. **Santa Ana Star Casino** (☎ 505-867-0000; US 150; 🕘 8am-4am Sun-Wed, 24hr Thu-Sat) has a staggering buffet, 36 lanes of bowling and the opportunity to challenge

Rocko the Rooster to a $25,000 game of tic-tac-toe (watch out, he's good).

The **Stables at Tamaya** (☎ 505-771-6037; ⓨ 9:30am-3:30pm) offer trail rides and lessons ($75) through the woods, into which the pueblo has recently pumped millions of dollars for cleanup and restoration. And, lest you forget that this is not Beverly Hills west, there are **Corn Dances** (June 24 & July 26).

The luxurious **Hyatt Tamaya** (☎ 505-867-1234; www.tamaya.hyatt.com; 1300 Tayuna Trail; r from $195; ⓡ), hidden in the desert landscape with expansive views, has three pools, three restaurants and a small spa.

San Felipe Pueblo
pop 2100 / elev 5100ft

Though best known for the spectacular **San Felipe Feast Green Corn Dances** (May 1), this conservative Keres-speaking **pueblo** (☎ 505-867-3381; I-25 exit 252) now has a couple more claims to fame. The **Casino Hollywood** (☎ 505-867-6700; www.sanfelipecasino.com; I-25 exit 252; ⓨ 8am-4am Sun-Wed, 24hr Thu-Sat) isn't just for gambling – this themed venue takes full advantage of its location to pull in acts like Los Lobos and Julio Iglesias. Visitors are also invited to the **San Pedro Feast Day** (June 29), and occasionally the pueblo hosts an **Arts & Crafts Fair** in October.

Santo Domingo Pueblo
pop 2700 / elev 5185ft

This nongaming **pueblo** (☎ 505-465-2214; Hwy 22; ⓨ 8am-dusk) has long been a seat of Pueblo government – the All Indian Pueblo Council still meets here annually. Several galleries and studios at the pueblo abut the plaza in front of pretty 1886 **Santo Domingo Church**, with murals and frescos by local artists. The tribe is most famous for *heishi* (shell bead) jewelry, as well as the huge **Corn Dances** (August 4) and a wildly popular **Arts & Crafts Fair** in early September.

This pueblo is on Hwy 22, 6 miles northwest from I-25 exit 259, about halfway between Albuquerque and Santa Fe.

Cochiti Pueblo
pop 500 / elev 5300ft

About 10 miles north of Santo Domingo on NM 22, this **pueblo** (☎ 505-465-2244) is known for its arts and crafts, particularly ceremonial bass drums and storyteller dolls. Several stands and shops are usually set up around the plaza and mission (built in 1628); dances are held on the **Feast Day of San Buenaventura** (July

14 and December 25). There's no photography allowed here, but visitors can snap away at the **golf course**, considered the state's most challenging, or **Cochiti Lake**, favored by swimmers and non-motorized boaters.

SANTA FE AREA PUEBLOS
A quick glance at most maps reveals the region north of Santa Fe to be the heart of Pueblo Indian lands. The **Eight Northern Pueblos** (ENIPC; ☎ 505-852-4265) all lie within 40 miles of Española, some of which is on long-term lease from Santa Clara Pueblo. Together they publish the excellent *Eight Northern Indian Pueblos Visitors Guide*, available free at area visitor centers.

Many pueblos operate casinos, usually several miles from the main pueblo, which are generally open 8am to 4am Monday to Thursday morning, then stay open 24 hours through Sunday. Slots, craps, poker, shows and endless buffet tables are the big draws, but unlike casinos in Las Vegas, there's usually a gift shop selling high-quality pottery and other work by local artisans.

The pueblos themselves aren't really tourist attractions; they're towns, with schools, modern houses, post offices and whatnot. They are certainly a must-see, as you'll learn (or unlearn) a lot about Native American culture, and area artists in particular appreciate the traffic.

Begin by purchasing the required camera permits from either the visitor center, if there is one, or governor's office, where they may be able to point you toward galleries, guided tours and other areas of interest, if they're not too busy.

The Santa Fe area pueblos are all mapped on p328.

Tesuque Pueblo
pop 800 / elev 6000ft

Nine miles north of Santa Fe along Hwy 285/84 is **Tesuque Pueblo** (☎ 505-983-2667, 800-483-1040; Rte 5), whose members played a major role in the Pueblo Revolt of 1680. Today, the reservation encompasses more than 17,000 acres of spectacular desert landscape, including Aspen Ranch and Vigil Grant, two wooded areas in the Santa Fe National Forest. **San Diego Feast Day** (November 12) features dancing, but no food booths or vendors are allowed. There is an amazing flea market held here (see p327).

Pojoaque Pueblo
pop 2700 / elev 7000ft

Although this pueblo's history predates the Spaniards, it is known that a smallpox epidemic in the late 19th century killed many inhabitants and forced the survivors to evacuate. No old buildings remain. The few survivors intermarried with other Pueblo people and Hispanics, and their descendants now number about 200. In 1932, a handful of people returned to the pueblo and they have since worked to rebuild their people's traditions, crafts and culture.

The **Poeh Cultural Center & Museum** (☎ 505-455-3334; www.poehcenter.com; 🕑 10am-4pm Mon-Sat), on the east side of Hwy 84/285, features exhibits on the history and culture of the Tewa-speaking people. Next door, check out the large selection of top-quality crafts from the Tewa pueblos at the **visitor center** (☎ 505-455-9023; 96 Cities of Gold Rd).

The pueblo public buildings are 16 miles north of Santa Fe on the east side of Hwy 84/285, just south of Hwy 502. The annual **Virgin de Guadalupe Feast Day** on December 12 is celebrated with ceremonial dancing.

Nambé Pueblo
pop 1800 / elev 6200ft

Just driving into this **pueblo** (☎ 505-455-2036), through dramatically sculpted, multihued sandstone, is fantastic. NM 503, which leaves US Hwy 285/84 just north of Pojoaque to head into hills speckled with piñon, makes for a scenic addition to the High Rd to Taos.

Perhaps because of the isolated location (or inspirational geology), Nambé has long been a spiritual center for the Tewa-speaking tribes, a distinction that attracted the cruel attentions of Spanish priests intent on conversion by any means necessary. After the Pueblo Revolt and Reconquista wound down, Spanish settlers annexed much of their land.

Nambé's remaining lands have a couple of big attractions; the loveliest are two 20-minute hikes to **Nambé Falls** (per car per day $5). The steep upper hike has a photogenic overlook of the falls, while the easier lower hike along the river takes in ancient petroglyphs. The most popular attraction, however, is **Lake Nambé** (ranger station ☎ 505-455-2304; Hwy 101; per car per day $10; 🕑 7am-7pm Apr-Oct), created in 1974 when the US dammed the Rio Nambé, flooding historic ruins but creating a reservoir that attracts non-motorized boaters and trout lovers.

Public events include **San Francisco de Asis Feast Day** (October 4) and the **Catholic Mass and Buffalo Dance** (December 24).

San Ildefonso Pueblo
pop 1500 / elev 6000ft

Eight miles west of Pojoaque along Hwy 502, this ancient **pueblo** (☎ 505-455-3549; per car $4, camera/video/sketching permits $10/20/25; 🕑 8am-5pm) was the home of Maria Martinez, who in 1919, along with her husband, Julian, revived a distinctive traditional black-on-black pottery style. Her work, now valued at tens of thousands of dollars, has become world famous and is considered by collectors to be some of the best pottery ever produced.

Several exceptional potters (including Maria's direct descendants) work in the pueblo, and many different styles are produced, but black-on-black remains the hallmark of San Ildefonso. Several gift shops and studios, including the **Maria Poveka Martinez Museum** (admission free; 🕑 8am-4pm Mon-Fri), sell the pueblo's pottery. The **Pueblo Museum**, with exhibits on the pueblo's history and culture and a small store, is next to the visitor center.

Visitors are welcome to **Feast Day** (January 23) and **corn dances**, which are held throughout the summer.

Santa Clara Pueblo
pop 980 / elev 6800ft

The pueblo entrance is 1.3 miles southwest of Española on Hwy 30. Several galleries and private homes sell intricately carved black pottery. Stop first at **Singing Water Gallery** (☎ 505-753-9663; www.singingwater.com; Hwy 30; 🕑 11:30am-5pm), right outside the main pueblo. In addition to representing 213 of some 450 Santa Clara potters, owners Joe and Nora Baca also offer tours of the pueblo on weekends ($12), pottery demonstrations ($30) and classes, and can arrange feast meals ($15) with 48 hours' notice.

On the reservation at the entrance to Santa Clara Canyon, 5.7 miles west of Hwy 30 and southwest of Española, are the **Puye Cliff Dwellings**. Ancestors of today's Santa Clara Indians lived here until about 1500. The original carvings were cut into the Puye Cliffs on the Pajarito Plateau, and structures were later added on the mesas and below the cliffs. Because of a fire back in 2000, the cliff dwellings are not opened to the public but it's always subject to change.

Santa Clara Feast Day (August 12) and St Anthony's Feast Day (June 13) feature the Harvest and Blue Corn Dances. All are open to the public; the governor's office (☎ 505-753-7330; Hwy 30; 8am-4:30pm Mon-Fri) issues photo and video permits ($5).

Ohkay Owingh (San Juan) Pueblo
pop 6800 / elev 5600ft

Drive a mile north of Española on Hwy 68 and 1 mile west on Hwy 74 to get to this pueblo (☎ 505-852-4400), which is really no more than a bend in the road with a compact main plaza surrounded by cottonwoods. The pueblo was visited in 1598 by Juan de Oñate, who named it San Gabriel and made it the short-lived first capital of New Mexico. The original Catholic mission, dedicated to St John the Baptist, survived until 1913 but was replaced by the adobe, New England–style building that faces the main plaza. Adjacent to the mission is the Nuestra Señora de Lourdes Chapel, built in 1889. The kiva, shrines and some of the original pueblo houses are off-limits to visitors. There is a $5 fee for photography and for video cameras.

The Oke Oweenge Crafts Cooperative (☎ 505-852-2372; Hwy 74; 9am-4:30pm Mon-Sat) has a good selection of traditional red pottery, seed jewelry, weavings and drums. The on-site Silver Eagle Lounge serves alcohol and has live music nightly, while the Harvest Café (mains $1-12, buffet $6-10; 6:30am-10pm Sun-Thu, 6:30am-midnight Fri & Sat) has a great salad bar and $1 breakfast specials.

Public events include the Basket Dance (January), Deer Dance (February), Corn Dance (June 13), San Juan Feast Day (June 24) and a series of Catholic and traditional dances and ceremonies from December 24 to 26.

TAOS AREA PUEBLOS
The most famous pueblo of them all, Taos Pueblo, is here. Also in the area is the historically powerful Picuris Pueblo.

Picuris Pueblo
pop 86 / elev 7500ft

Located on the High Rd to Taos, this was once among the largest and most powerful pueblos in New Mexico. The Pikuri built adobe cities at least seven stories tall and boasted a population approaching 3000. After the Pueblo Revolt and Reconquista, when many retreated to Kansas rather than face De Vargas' wrath,

the returning tribe numbered only 500. Between raids by the Spanish and Comanches, that number continued to dwindle.

The governor's office (☎ 505-587-2519; photo/video permits $5/10; 8am-5pm Mon-Fri) can, with advance notice, help arrange guided pueblo tours that include their small buffalo herd, organic gardens, ruins from the old pueblo site and the exquisite 1770 San Lorenzo de Picuris Church. The unique tower kiva is off-limits to visitors but makes an impression even from the outside. The tribe's Picuris Pueblo Museum (☎ 505-587-1099) displays tribal artifacts and local art. The best time to visit the pueblo is during the popular San Lorenzo Feast Days (August 9 and 10), with food and craft booths, dances, races and pole climbs.

From Picuris Pueblo, follow Hwy 75 east and go north on Hwy 518 to connect with Hwy 68, the main road to Taos.

Taos Pueblo
pop 2300 / elev 7100ft

Whatever you do, don't miss it. Built around 1450 and continuously inhabited ever since, Taos Pueblo (☎ 505-758-1028; www.taospueblo.com; Taos Pueblo Rd; adult/child $10/5, photography or video permit $5; 8am-4pm) is the largest existing multistoried pueblo structure in the USA and one of the best surviving examples of traditional adobe construction. It's what all that pueblo-revival architecture in Santa Fe wants to be when it grows up. Note the pueblo closes for 10 weeks annually, starting in March.

One of New Mexico's largest and most spectacular Indian celebrations, San Geronimo Day (September 29 and 30) is celebrated with dancing and food. The huge Taos Pueblo Powwow (☎ 505-758-1028; www.taospueblopowwow.com; Taos Pueblo Rd; admission $5) in the second week of July features Plains and Pueblo Indians gathering for dances and workshops as this centuries-old tradition continues. Of all the pueblos in northern New Mexico, Taos Pueblo has the most events and celebrations open to the public.

Taos Mountain Casino (Map p342; ☎ 505-737-0777, 888-946-8267; www.taosmountaincasino.com; Taos Pueblo Rd; 8am-1am Sun-Wed, 8am-2am Thu-Sat) has less razzle-dazzle – not to mention smoke – than some casinos. In fact, this cozy alcohol- and cigarette-free spot is one of the nicest places around to blow your cash.

Several craftspeople sell fine jewelry, micaceous (an aluminum mineral found in local

NEW MEXICO

NEW MEXICO

FOLLOWING THE FIBER ARTS TRAIL

New Mexico's grassroots fiber arts trails are a perfect example of the state's effort to support sustainable arts-based tourism in rural communities. Developed by the state's Cultural Affairs department, the **New Mexico Fiber Arts Trails** (☎ 505-827-6490; www.nmfiberarts.org) are meant to put local weavers and fiber artists' shops on the map, and bring the market to them – it's not usual for New Mexican artists to drive hundreds of miles to sell their crafts, which not only causes financial hardship, but also puts strain on the family unit.

The concept is to cultivate interest and awareness of the state's rich and unique fiber arts heritage, as well as bring opportunities for artists to prosper without having to leave their home community. The state has put a lot of money into the initiative, and has created a fabulous glossy *New Mexico Fiber Arts Trails Guide*. The three main trails (including detours and spurs) are broken up by region. The **North Central Loop** includes stops in Tucumcari, Las Vegas, Taos, Chimayó, Santa Fe and Santa Rosa. The **North West Loop** starts in Albuquerque and heads northwest through Grants, then through the small town of Pine Hill on a back road to Gallup before heading north to Shiprock, then east across the top of New Mexico before cutting south back to Albuquerque. The **Southern Loop** is our favorite, and includes stops in Wild West Silver City, deep-south Las Cruces, New–Age Truth or Consequences and nuclear Alamogordo. It also traverses some of New Mexico's most wild country – wide open spaces where there's loads of room for hiking side trips (hint: tramping in remote Gila National Forest then taking a dip in the hot springs complements shopping perfectly). In total there are 71 stopping points along the three loops, representing the work of more than 200 New Mexican artists. Some stops are collectives, representing many artists, while others are working farms, studios, galleries and even suppliers.

We'd encourage exploring these unique trails. Not only do they allow you to get off the beaten path and experience New Mexico's gorgeous back roads and out-of-the-way places, but they also allow you to support rural communities directly by taking a piece of New Mexico's cultural tapestry home with you.

To find out specifics on fiber arts trails in northern and northwestern New Mexico, visit or call the **Española Valley Fiber Arts Center** (☎ 505-747-3577; www.evfac.org; 325 Paseo de Onate; ☷ hours vary) in Española, about 30 minutes north of Santa Fe. For southern trail info, visit the **Common Thread** (☎ 505-558-5733; 107 W Broadway St) in Silver City.

rocks) pottery and other arts and crafts at the main pueblo, which you can peruse after touring the place. You can also grab tacos and the most delicious chewy Indian fry bread ($3 to $5).

Just outside the pueblo, stop at the **Tony Reyna Indian Shop** (Map p342; ☎ 505-758-3835; Taos Pueblo Rd; ☷ 8am-noon & 1-6pm), which has a vast collection of arts and crafts from Taos and other tribes. Also see Shopping (p341) for more galleries that carry local artists' work.

Taos Indian Horse Ranch (Map p342; ☎ 505-758-3212, 800-659-3210; 1-/2-hr easy ride $55/95, 2hr experienced ride $125) offers riding trips through Indian land – experienced riders can go fast. It also does an overnight rafting/riding/camping trip – ring for details.

For food, everyone, and we mean everyone, heads to **Tewa Kitchen** (Map p342; ☎ 505-751-1020; Taos Pueblo Rd; mains $6-13; ☷ 11am-5pm Wed-Mon, 11am-7pm Jun-Aug). It's one of the few places in the state where you can sit down to a plate of Native treats like *phien-ty* (blue-corn fry bread stuffed with buffalo meat), *twa chull* (grilled buffalo) or a bowl of heirloom green chile grown on pueblo grounds.

Grab some green chile stew or an ice-cream cone at surprisingly good **Lucky 7s** (Map p342; Taos Mountain Casino; snacks $3-5; ☷ 10am-9pm Sun-Thu, 10am-10pm Fri & Sat), then settle into some blackjack or slots and stay a while.

ALBUQUERQUE

pop 801,900 / elev 5285ft

It's far too easy to ignore Albuquerque. She suffers in the sybaritic shadow of Santa Fe and doesn't engender the mystery of Taos. But if you want to understand New Mexico, don't ignore her. For she will, if given half a chance, introduce you to the spirit of the state. And you'll find that she's far more than the sum of her strip malls and legendary sprawl.

Albuquerque exists at the crossroads of I-25 and I-40, where drought and the manufacture of computer chips converge. Chances are, you will enter through her front door, the Sunport. (When was the last time you heard an airport called a Sunport?) Despite the adobe veneers on residences and commercial buildings, Albuquerque is a 'real' Western town (not a fictionalized Disneyfication, as its neighbor to the north is sometimes critically described) with a New Mexico–style independent streak.

Albuquerque doesn't give up her charms quickly, but they're right there, on a Nambé

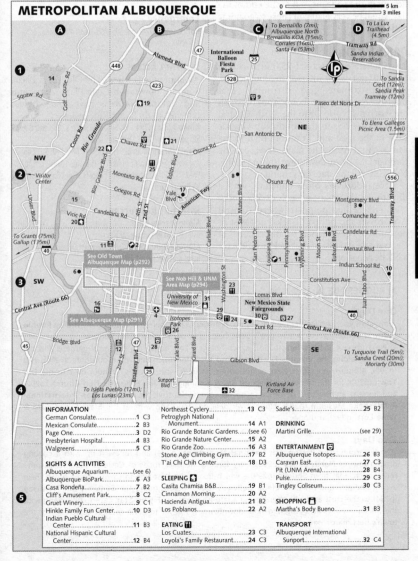

METROPOLITAN ALBUQUERQUE

INFORMATION		
German Consulate	1	C3
Mexican Consulate	2	B3
Page One	3	D2
Presbyterian Hospital	4	B3
Walgreens	5	C3

SIGHTS & ACTIVITIES		
Albuquerque Aquarium	(see 6)	
Albuquerque BioPark	6	A3
Casa Rondeña	7	B2
Cliff's Amusement Park	8	C2
Gruet Winery	9	C1
Hinkle Family Fun Center	10	D3
Indian Pueblo Cultural Center	11	B3
National Hispanic Cultural Center	12	B4

Northeast Cyclery	13	C3
Petroglyph National Monument	14	A1
Rio Grande Botanic Gardens	(see 6)	
Rio Grande Nature Center	15	A2
Rio Grande Zoo	16	A3
Stone Age Climbing Gym	17	B2
T'ai Chi Chih Center	18	D3

SLEEPING		
Casita Chamisa B&B	19	B1
Cinnamon Morning	20	A2
Hacienda Antigua	21	B2
Los Poblanos	22	A2

EATING		
Los Cuates	23	C3
Loyola's Family Restaurant	24	C3

Sadie's	25	B2

DRINKING		
Martini Grille	(see 29)	

ENTERTAINMENT		
Albuquerque Isotopes	26	B3
Caravan East	27	C3
Pit (UNM Arena)	28	B4
Pulse	29	C3
Tingley Coliseum	30	C3

SHOPPING		
Martha's Body Bueno	31	B3

TRANSPORT		
Albuquerque International Sunport	32	C4

NEW MEXICO

platter that's assumed a comforting patina. Hike La Luz trail or venture out to Kasha-Katuwe Tent Rocks; take the tram to Sandia Crest or mountain bike in Elena Gallegos; walk along irrigation ditches or the Rio Grande woods; shop for Western wear or Route 66 kitsch. And above all, begin a life-long love affair with green chile.

Albuquerque may not be the greatest beauty in the pageant, but at the end of the day, you'll be very glad you chose to go home with her.

ORIENTATION

Two interstate highways, I-25 (north–south) and I-40 (east–west), intersect in Albuquerque. An approximate grid surrounds that intersection, the major boundaries of which are Paseo del Norte Dr to the north, Central Ave (old Rte 66) to the south, Rio Grande Blvd to the west and Tramway Blvd to the east. Central Ave is the main street, passing through Old Town, downtown, the university, Nob Hill and the state fairground.

Street addresses often conclude with a directional designation, such as Wyoming NE. The center point is where Central Ave crosses the railroad tracks, just east of downtown. For instance, locations north of Central Ave and east of the tracks would have a NE designation.

INFORMATION
Bookstores
Page One (Map p289; ☎ 505-294-2026; www
.page1books.com; 11018 Montgomery Blvd NE; ☯ 9am-10pm Mon-Sat, 9am-8pm Sun) Huge and comprehensive selection of books.
UNM Bookstore (Map p294; ☎ 505-277-5451; Central Ave; ☯ 8am-6pm Mon-Fri, 10am-5pm Sat) On the south side of the campus on Central at Cornell.

Emergency
Police (Map p289; ☎ 505-768-2020; 400 Roma Ave NW)

Internet Access
Albuquerque is wired. The Old Town Plaza, Sunport, downtown Civic Plaza, Aquarium and Botanic Gardens have free wireless internet, as do Rapid Ride buses.
Kinko's (Map p294; ☎ 505-255-9673; 2706 Central Ave SE; per minute 20¢; ☯ 24hr; ☐)
Main Library (Map p291; ☎ 505-768-5140; 501 Copper Ave NW; ☯ 10am-6pm Mon & Thu-Sat, 10am-7pm Tue & Wed; ☐) Unlimited internet access after you purchase a $3 library card.

Internet Resources
Albuquerque Online (www.abqonline.com) Exhaustive listings and links for local businesses.
Albuquerque.com (www.albuquerque.com) Attraction, hotel and restaurant information.

ALBUQUERQUE IN...

One Day
Jump-start your belly with green chile from **Frontier** (p299), before heading to the **Indian Pueblo Cultural Center** (p294), where you'll get a head start on a primo pueblo education.

Next up visit the **BioPark** (p296), which boasts a zoo, aquarium, botanical gardens and na-ture trails along the bosque. Head back into town for lunch, and dine outdoors in **Nob Hill** (p299); Albuquerque's grooviest neighborhood is thick with eateries. Wander over to the **Old Town** (p292) for the afternoon. Walk off lunch admiring the **San Felipe de Neri Church** (p292) and ancient architecture or catching up on your snake trivia at the **American International Rattlesnake Museum** (p293). Linger over delicious food and wine at the **Slate Street Café & Wine Loft** (p298) at dinner.

Two Days
Wander around the **Petroglyph National Monument** (p294) and follow it up with a cooling driving tour of **North Valley** (p295) – try forging the back roads of Corrales. Indulge in some rolled enchiladas from **Sadie's** (p299) – which boasts the best sign in town – come lunch. Take a cool late-afternoon hike in **Elena Gallegos** (p295) before riding the **Sandia Peak Tramway** (p294) to the crest at dusk. After having a late-ish dinner at **Flying Star Café** (p299), hang with the 20-somethings at a watering hole downtown. It's never too late to start searching for the town's best margaritas.

ALBUQUERQUE

NEW MEXICO

City of Albuquerque (www.cabq.gov) Information on public transportation, area attractions and more.

Downtownabq.com (www.downtownabq.com) Dedicated to promoting this bourgening neighborhood.

Medical Services
Presbyterian Hospital (Map p289; ☎ 505-841-1234, emergency 505-841-1111; 1100 Central Ave SE; ⏲ 24hr emergency)
University Hospital (Map p294; ☎ 505-272-2411; 2211 Lomas Blvd NE; ⏲ 24hr emergency) Head here if you don't have insurance.
Walgreens (Map p289; ☎ 505-265-1548, 800-925-4733; 6201 Central Ave NE; ⏲ 24hr)

Post
Main post office (Map p291; ☎ 800-275-8777; 201 5th St SW)

Tourist information
Albuquerque Convention & Visitors Bureau (Map p291; ☎ 505-842-9918, 800-733-9918; www.itsatrip.org; 20 First Plaza; ⏲ 8am-5pm Mon-Fri)
Old Town Information Center (Map p292; ☎ 505-243-3215; 303 Romero Ave NW; ⏲ 9:30am-5pm, 9:30am-4:30pm Oct-Apr)

SIGHTS
Most of Albuquerque's top sites are concentrated in downtown and Old Town, a straight shot down Central Ave from Nob Hill and

UNM. Some of the best attractions, however – including the Indian Pueblo Cultural Center, Petroglyph National Monument and Sandia Peak Tramway – are more far-flung and most easily accessible by car.

Old Town

This neighborhood is best appreciated through a historical lens. These quaint adobe shops were not built 20 years ago to attract tourists – some have been here since 1706 when the first 15 Spanish families called the newly named Albuquerque their home. From the town's founding until the arrival of the railroad in 1880, Old Town Plaza was the hub of daily life. With many museums, galleries and original buildings within walking distance, this is the city's most popular tourist area. As you walk around, try to keep your mind's eye trained partly on the past. Imagine this area as it began, with a handful of hopeful families grateful to have survived a trek across hundreds, in some cases thousands, of miles of desert wilderness.

From mid-April to mid-November, the Albuquerque Museum runs informative and free guided **Old Town walking tours** (11am Tue-Sun mid-Apr–mid-Nov). The museum also publishes *Old Town: A Walking Tour of History and Architecture* that guides you to 17 historically significant structures, including **San Felipe de Neri Church** (Map p292; ☎ 505-243-4628; www.sanfelipe deneri.org; San Felipe Plaza; 7am-5:30pm daily, museum 10am-4pm Mon-Sat). The church dates from 1793

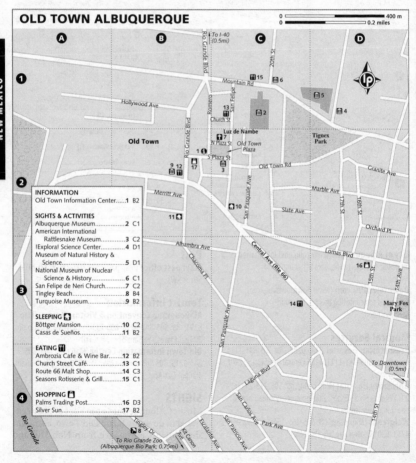

OLD TOWN ALBUQUERQUE

0 _____ 400 m
0 _____ 0.2 miles

NEW MEXICO

ONLY IN ALBUQUERQUE...

The **T'ai Chi Chih Center** (Map p289; ☎ 505-299-2095; www.taichichihassociation.com; Scottsdale Village, 3107 Eubank Blvd NE; ☒ call for class schedule) is the only one of its kind in the country to teach T'ai Chi Chih, a moving meditation originated by Albuquerque resident Justin Stone in 1974. It's not to be confused with T'ai Chi Chu'an, the ancient martial art with 108 poses; these movements focus on softness, continuity and circularity. Activating, balancing and circulating the Chi (or life force), the practice has a way of bringing into balance for each practitioner that which needs balancing. It's a tough concept to accept mentally until you try it for yourself. Over its relatively short life span, regular TCC practice has been shown to help all sorts of ailments, from arthritis and migraine headaches to osteoporosis and high blood pressure.

There are over 2200 teachers worldwide, and hundreds in the Albuquerque area. Maybe you'll get lucky and meet the originator, too, who often drops into the center to offer his wisdom.

---

and is Old Town's most famous photo op. Mass is given daily at 7am; Sunday Mass is at 7am, 10:15am and noon.

At the **Turquoise Museum** (Map p292; ☎ 505-247-8650; 2107 Central Ave NW; admission $4; ☒ 9:30am-3pm Mon-Sat) visitors get an enlightening crash course in determining the value of stones – from high quality to fakes.

If you've ever been curious about serpents, **American International Rattlesnake Museum** (Map p292; ☎ 505-242-6569; www.rattlesnakes.com; 202 San Felipe St NW; adult/child $3.50/2.50; ☒ 10am-5pm Mon-Sat, 1-5pm Sun) is the museum for you. It's possibly the most interesting museum in town, and you won't find more species of rattlesnake in one place anywhere else in the world. Come here for the lowdown on one of the world's most misunderstood snakes.

There's a great gallery featuring the work of New Mexican artists at the **Albuquerque Museum** (Map p292; ☎ 505-242-4600; www.albuquerque museum.com; 2000 Mountain Rd NW; adult/child $4/1, free 1st Wed of the month; ☒ 9am-5pm Tue-Sun). Family art workshops are offered on Saturdays at 2:30pm and gallery tours are given daily at 2pm.

The **National Museum of Atomic Nuclear Science & History** (Map p292; ☎ 505-245-2137; www.atomic museum.com; 1905 Mountain Rd NW; adult/child $5/4; ☒ 9am-5pm) has something for all ages. It features an impressive collection of nuclear weapons, exhibits on nuclear energy and interactive activities for children.

Downtown

As in many US cities, downtown isn't the epicenter for action that it was some decades ago, when Route 66 was a novelty and reason enough to set out from either coast in a big '55 Chevy. City planners and business owners have done a good job in recent years, though, of restoring some of that fab '50s neon and encouraging trendy restaurants, galleries, clubs and a multiplex theater. Drive through downtown just after it gets dark to glimpse America's past updated, and cruise through on Saturday night when Central Ave is jammed with 20-somethings cruising in low riders to see and be seen.

The **New Mexico Holocaust & Intolerance Museum** (Map p291; ☎ 505-247-0606; www.nmholocaust museum.org; 415 Central Ave NW; admission free; ☒ 11am-3:30pm Tue-Sat) emphasizes WWII exhibits, but there are plenty of powerful ones documenting genocides worldwide – from close-to-home Acoma to all-too-familiar Armenia.

Nob Hill & UNM Area

A fun and funky place to shop, eat, rent foreign films or see current ones, this stretch of Central Ave starts at UNM and runs east to about Carlisle Blvd. Mall-averse 20-somethings can scour colorful shops for something to wear; artists will find inspiration and supplies; and people of all ages with innovative style will find home furnishings ranging from enormous Mexican armoires to delicate Japanese lanterns.

There are 13 museums and galleries, along with loads of public art, packed onto the grounds of the **University of New Mexico** (UNM; Map p294; ☎ 505-277-5813; www.unm.edu; Central Ave NE). This adobe wonderland is also home to a performing arts center and the **Tamarind Institute**, which helped to save the art of lithography from extinction in the 1960s and '70s. Visit the **UNM Welcome Center** (Map p294; ☎ 277-1989; Las Lomas Rd; ☒ 8am-5pm Mon-Fri) for information and maps.

NEW MEXICO

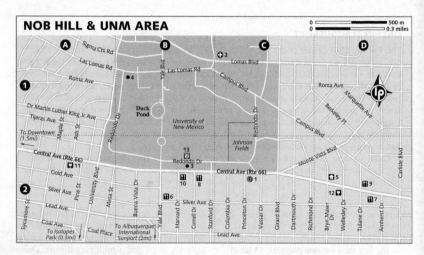

NOB HILL & UNM AREA

Metropolitan Albuquerque

Operated by the All Indian Pueblo Council, **Indian Pueblo Cultural Center** (Map p289; ☎ 505-843-7270; www.indianpueblo.org; 2401 12th St NW; adult/child $6/3; 🕐 9am-5pm) is a must-see even on the shortest of Albuquerque itineraries. The history exhibits are fascinating, and the arts wing features the finest examples of each pueblo's work. Do your homework here before considering any major purchases. The IPCC also houses a large gift shop and retail gallery. Along with serving Native New Mexican cuisine, the onsite **Pueblo Harvest Café** (mains $5-8; 🕐 8am-3pm Mon-Fri, 8am-5pm Sat & Sun; ⓥ 👶) has weekend art demonstrations, bread-baking demos and dances.

Sandia Peak Tramway (off Map p289; ☎ 505-856-7325; www.sandiapeak.com; Tramway Blvd; adult/child $15/10; 🕐 9am-9pm) is Albuquerque's most famous attraction (after the Indian Pueblo Cultural Center). At 2.7 miles, it's the world's longest aerial tram, rising from the desert floor to the top of 10,378ft Sandia Peak for spectacular views any time (but sunsets are particularly drop-dead brilliant).

In the historic Barelas neighborhood, the **National Hispanic Cultural Center** (Map p289; ☎ 505-246-2261; www.nhccnm.org; 1701 4th St SW; adult/child $3/ free, Sun free; 🕐 10am-5pm Tue-Sun) is a center for Hispanic visual, performing and literary arts. It has three galleries and the nation's premier Hispanic genealogy library.

Easily accessible off I-40, **Petroglyph National Monument** (Map p289; ☎ 505-899-0205; www.nps.gov /petr/home.htm; Unser Blvd; parking $2; 🕐 8am-5pm) offers hiking trails and picnic areas scattered throughout five (non-active) volcanic cones. Over 20,000 images have been sketched into shiny black volcanic rock by Native American peoples and early Spanish settlers.

There's a surprising amount of fine wine being made in these hills, and there are two particular standouts. **Gruet Winery** (Map p289; ☎ 505-821-0055; 8400 Pan American Fwy NE; 🕐 10am-5pm Mon-Fri, noon-5pm Sat) gives daily tours at 2pm and free tastings. **Casa Rondeña** (Map p289; ☎ 505-344-5911; 733 Chavez Rd NW; 🕐 10am-6pm Wed-Sat, noon-6pm

Sun) only gives tours during its July Lavender Festival and charges $3 for tastings.

South Valley and **North Valley** are traditional agricultural areas near the Rio Grande, characterized by open spaces, small ranches, farms, bosque (Spanish for woods) and acequia (historical irrigation ditches that also mark walking paths). Chickens and horses roam fields between historical adobe and wood-frame houses and newer developments. With a population nearly 80% Hispanic, the 39-sq-mile South Valley is bordered by I-25, I-40 and the West Mesa and volcanic cliffs.

North Valley is more mixed and upscale, with a reputation as affluent, pastoral, quiet and determined to keep it that way. Although it measures just 7 miles from downtown Albuquerque, it feels like a world away. This 100-sq-mile area is roughly bordered by I-40, I-25, the Rio Grande and the Bernalillo–Sandoval County line.

The village of **Corrales**, just north of North Valley, was established by Spanish settlers in 1710 but was home to Tewa Indians for centuries before that – they were practicing irrigated agriculture here 1300 years ago. Even more rural than North Valley, Corrales offers splendid strolling through the bosque and along acequia. Take NM 448 north into the village and then drive or walk along any side roads – most are unpaved and will reward with earthy scents of farms and open fields, horses, scampering rabbits and quail crisscrossing your path among 200-year-old adobes and modern replicas.

ACTIVITIES

Sandia Crest (see boxed text, below) is Albuquerque's playground, popular for skiing and hiking.

Elena Gallegos Picnic Area (off Map p289; ☎ 505-857-8334; Simms Park Rd; parking $2; ☼ 7am-7pm mid-Oct–mid-Apr, 7am-9pm mid-Apr–mid-Oct), in the foothills of the Sandias, is a popular jumping-off point for hiking, running and mountain-biking trails; some are wheelchair-accessible. Go early in the day before the overhead sun gets too hot, or at dusk to take advantage of the panoramic sunset views and watch the city lights begin twinkling below. Time your walk carefully, though, because darkness falls quickly after the sun sets and howling coyotes ring the park. They won't

NEW MEXICO

DETOUR: SANDIA CREST

Albuquerqueans always know which way is east thanks to 10,678ft Sandia Crest (off Map p289), sacred to Sandia Pueblo and well named for both its wavelike silhouette and the glorious pink (*sandia* is Spanish for 'watermelon') its granite cliffs glow at sunset. There are three ways to the top.

Beautiful 8-mile (one way) **La Luz Trail** (FR 444; parking $3) is the most rewarding, rising 3800ft from the desert, past a small waterfall to pine forests and spectacular views. It gets hot.

Sandia Peak Tramway (opposite) is the most extravagant route to the top; you can hike the La Luz up and take the tram down, hiking two more miles at the bottom on Tramway Trail to your car.

Finally you can drive, via NM 14, making a left onto Sandia Crest Rd (NM 165). The road is lined with trailheads and picnic spots (a daily $3 parking fee covers all of them), and low-impact camping ($3) is allowed by permit throughout Cibola National Forest. The choices are endless, but don't skip the easy 1-mile round trip to **Sandia Man Cave**, where the oldest human encampment in North America was discovered in 1936. Bring a flashlight.

At the top, the **Sandia Crest Visitor Center** (☎ 505-248-0190; NM 165; ☼ 8am-5pm, closed Sun Dec-Apr) offers nature programs daily; **Sandia Crest House** (☎ 505-243-0605; NM 165; dishes $3-8; ☼ 9:30am-sunset), in the same building, serves burgers and snacks. This is the jumping-off point for the exquisite **Sandia Crest Trail**, which heads 11 miles north and 16 miles south with incredible views; hike north along the ridgeline as long as you'd like to appreciate the best of them.

Take the trail 2 miles south, past **Kiwanis Cabin** rock house, to the tram terminal and **High Finance** (☎ 243-9742; lunch $8-12, dinner $16-42; ☼ 11am-9pm), which offers mediocre food and fabulous views.

This is also the site of **Sandia Peak Ski Park** (☎ 505-242-9052; www.sandiapeak.com; lift tickets adult/child $45/37; ☼ 9am-4pm Dec-Mar & Jun-Sep), a smallish but scenic ski area. In summer, the park has a bike and lift combo for $70 – you get a bike and lift pass to blaze those downhill runs all day long; note that bikes aren't allowed on the tram.

bother you, but if you're a fully fledged urbanite and unaccustomed to uninvited nighttime company, it might be unnerving.

Cycling is a major sport in Albuquerque, both for beginners and national-level competitors. Get outfitted at **Northeast Cyclery** (Map p289; ☎ 505-299-1210; 8305 Menaul NE; rentals per day $25) and head out. Download a useful city map at www.cabq.gov/bike to find dedicated off-road tracks along arroyos. To ride along the Rio Grande, park at the Albuquerque BioPark and follow the riverside trail north or south (the smell of green chiles roasting at local factories is best appreciated if you head south in October; the path is less urban if you head north).

Walking the irrigation ditches is a downright local thing to do. Get a decent city map from the visitor center (many hotels also have them) and find the thin blue lines branching out in North Valley from the Rio Grande between Montaño Rd and Paseo del Norte and around Rio Grande Blvd. Acequia are bordered by walking paths, a gift to early-morning risers who value cool morning temperatures in the summer.

Rock climbers itching to hit the wall will dig the **Stone Age Climbing Gym** (Map p289; ☎ 505-341-2016; www.stoneageclimbinggym.com; 4201 Yale Blvd; day pass $13; ☽ noon-10pm Mon-Fri, 10am-8pm Sat & Sun), offering 12,000 sq ft of professionally designed climbing terrain simulating a variety of real rock features. Walls cater to all skill levels and reach almost 30ft high, and there are two lead climbing stations and four bouldering areas to choose from. Equipment can be rented for $6 per day. If you're a novice and want to learn, try an intro class ($40). The gym is a great option, especially on rainy days when you don't feel like seeing another museum.

ALBUQUERQUE FOR CHILDREN

Albuquerque has tons on offer for kids – from hands-on museums to cool hikes.

To give your little one a lesson in astronomy or a chance to check out the latest educational IMAX flick on a five-story screen, visit the **Museum of Natural History & Science** (Map p292; ☎ 505-841-2800; www.nmnaturalhistory.org; 1801 Mountain Rd NW; adult/child $7/4; ☽ 9am-5pm, closed Mon Jan & Sep; ☀). It also has a number of kid-friendly activities and exhibits – children dig the Hall of Jurassic Supergiants and Dynatheater.

Hands-on science is the focus at the **!Explora! Science Center** (Map p292; ☎ 505-224-8300; www

.explora.mus.nm.us; 1701 Mountain Rd NW; adult/child $7/3; ☽ 10am-6pm Mon-Sat, noon-6pm Sun; ☀), where the preschool and tween set learn about chemical reactions, molecules and atoms through interaction – get the scoop on why bubbles can be blown while blowing them yourself.

Adults will get as much out of the **Albuquerque BioPark** (Map p289; ☎ 505-764-6200; www.cabq.gov/biopark; 903 10th St NW; adult/child for three parks $12/5, per park $7/3; ☽ 9am-5pm; ☀) as children. When the weather is nice, and you're traveling with family, the place is especially appealing for the combo ticket to three kid-friendly attractions: a zoo, an aquarium and a botanic gardens. It's a good-value way to stay entertained all day. Set on 60 shady acres along the Rio Grande, the park's **Rio Grande Zoo** is home to more than 250 species. There's a lot going on here: sea-lion feedings take place daily at 10:30am and 3:30pm, camel rides are offered in the spring and summer, and an entertaining summertime bird show happens at 11:30am and 2pm Wednesday through Sunday. Meanwhile the **Albuquerque Aquarium** boasts a 285,000-gallon shark tank.

On the flora side, visit the **Rio Grande Botanic Gardens** and let the kids marvel at the 10,000-sq-ft glass conservatory filled to the brim with Mediterranean and desert fauna. Special gardens events include the walk-through show **River of Lights** (late November to December) and a **Butterfly Pavilion** from May to September.

Tingley Beach (Map p292; admission free; ☽ sunrise-sunset; ☀) is connected to the aquarium and botanic gardens. This beloved open space includes fishing ponds stocked with rainbow trout, a children's pond and trails. You'll need a **fishing license** (day pass $17, annual $35), but fortunately they are sold on-site at the **gift shop** (☎ 505-248-8522; ☽ 9am-5pm). A little **train** (adult/child $2/1; ☽ 10am-3pm) connects the zoo, aquarium/botanic gardens and Tingley Beach; it runs approximately every half-hour.

When the kids have had enough learning (or they're hot), **Cliff's Amusement Park** (Map p289; ☎ 881-9373; www.cliffsamusementpark.com; 4800 Osuna NE; adult/child $22/19; ☽ Apr-Sep, hours vary; ☀) is a great reward. The park has about 25 rides, including a rollercoaster, the Water Monkey, a play area and other traditional favorites.

If the weather is not cooperating and you need to burn off some of your little one's energy, visit the **Hinkle Family Fun Center** (Map p289; ☎ 505-299-3100; www.hinklefamilyfuncenter.com;

12931 Indian School Rd NE; 5hr pass $39; ☾ noon-10pm Mon-Thu, noon-midnight Fri & Sat, 10am-10pm Sun; ♿), which keeps little ones of all ages amused with bumper cars, laser tag, mini-golf and a huge 'jungle play area' where kids can crawl and climb and slide around. Check online for almost constant promotions.

TOURS

The UNM Department of Continuing Education's **Story of New Mexico Program** (☎ 505-277-2527; www.dcereg.com) offers excellent lectures on all things New Mexico, as well as tours to Santa Fe and events like the Folk Art Market, Indian Market and opera, and gallery tours along the High Rd to Taos by top-notch guides like Sharon Niederman. Advance registration is required.

FESTIVALS & EVENTS

Friday's *Albuquerque Journal* (www.abqjournal.com) includes a venue section with an exhaustive listing of festivals and activities. The following are most notable.

Gathering of Nations Powwow (☎ 505-836-2810; www.gatheringofnations.com) Features dance competitions, displays of Native American arts and crafts, and the 'Miss Indian World' contest. Held in late April.

Gay/Lesbian/Bisexual/Transgender Pride (☎ 505-873-8084) All-inclusive, just like Albuquerque and Santa Fe. Mid-June.

Bernalillo Wine Festival (☎ 505-867-3311; admission $12) Locally produced wine and live music, staged about 15 minutes north of Albuquerque – a real treat if you're in town in early September.

New Mexico State Fair (☎ 505-265-1791; www.exponm.com) A biggie rodeo with live music; runs for 16 days in September.

International Balloon Fiesta (☎ 505-821-1000, 888-422-7277; www.balloonfiesta.org) The largest balloon festival in the world. You just haven't lived until you've seen a three-story-tall Tony the Tiger land in your hotel courtyard, which is exactly the sort of thing that happens for the nine-day festival between the first and second weekends in October.

SLEEPING

Although Albuquerque has about 150 hotels (all full during the International Balloon Fiesta and the Gathering of Nations), it's not exactly swimming in interesting non-motel lodging.

If you're looking for budget lodgings, inexpensive motels line Central Ave in metropolitan Albuquerque, concentrated around the I-25 on-ramp and east of Nob Hill. You can

score a room in the $35 to $45 range, but trust your gut as some are pretty sleazy. The best bets for midrange accommodations are the endless chain motels that hug I-25 and I-40.

Old Town

Casas de Sueños (Map p292; ☎ 505-247-4560; www.casasdesuenos.com; 310 Rio Grande Blvd SW; r incl breakfast $119-189; ♨ 🖳) This lovely and peaceful place with luscious gardens and a pool has 21 adobe casitas featuring handcrafted furniture and original artwork. Some casitas have a kitchenette, fireplace and/or private hot tub (a couple are even outside in a private garden).

Böttger Mansion (Map p292; ☎ 505-243-3639, 800-758-3639; www.bottger.com; 110 San Felipe St NW; r incl breakfast $140-250; wi-fi) This huge Victorian, built by German wool-exporter Charles Böttger in 1905, has been a Buddhist colony and boarding house. It currently has eight elegant rooms, including one suite, and is the most deluxe of the Old Town B&Bs.

Downtown

Route 66 Hostel (Map p291; ☎ 505-247-1813; 1012 Central Ave SW; dm $15, r from $20) With discounts for HI-USA members, this 42-person hostel is clean, fun, cheap and conveniently located between downtown and Old Town. A kitchen and library are available for guest use.

La Posada de Albuquerque (Map p291; ☎ 505-242-9090, 800-777-5732; www.laposada-abq.com; 125 2nd St NW; r $80-160) This 1939 downtown landmark is excellent value. It offers fine rooms, a relaxed bar with weekend jazz, and a classic coffee shop. It was completely renovated in 2006.

Mauger Estate B&B (Map p291; ☎ 505-242-8755, 800-719-9189; www.maugerbb.com; 701 Roma Ave NW; r $90-185; ♨ 🖳) Freshly cut flowers and stocked fridges are standard in the eight rooms at this restored Queen Anne house. The elegant place attracts the likes of Linda Rondstadt and Martin Sheen, but as the hosts are proud of saying, 'every guest is treated like a celebrity.' Breakfasts are delish, with carafes of fresh squeezed OJ and crusty bread. The city's Rapid Ride transit stops just a few blocks from this B&B.

Nob Hill & UNM Area

Hiway House (Map p294; ☎ 505-268-3971; 3200 Central Ave SE; s/d $35/40; 🐾 wi-fi) Hiway was once a prolific Southwest chain, and this was the last one built in the 1950s. Just beyond the heart of the UNM and Nob Hill neighborhood, it's a 60-room place with the original 1958 neon sign and colonial-style architecture, but has updated with wireless internet connections. Not the cleanest, but a decent budget bet.

Metropolitan Albuquerque

Albuquerque North Bernalillo KOA (off Map p289; ☎ 505-867-5227, 800-562-3616; www.koa.com; 555 Hill Rd, Bernalillo; tent site $21-33, RV site $30-52, cabin $37-56; ⓚ wi-fi) About 15 miles north of the Albuquerque city limits, the better of the city's two KOAs has wireless internet and is within easy exploring distance of city attractions.

Casita Chamisa B&B (Map p289; ☎ 505-897-4644; www.casitachamisa.com; 850 Chamisal Rd NW; r $85-95; ⓚ ▣) Accommodations here include a two-bedroom guesthouse equipped with a kitchenette and vibrant greenhouse, a large bedroom in the main house, and a studio with a kitchenette. The friendly host, Arnold Sargeant, offers valuable advice about area offerings and the archaeological site where the B&B is located.

Cinnamon Morning (Map p289; ☎ 505-345-3541; www.cinnamonmorning.com; 2700 Rio Grande Blvd NW; r $90-180; wi-fi) If you're traveling with lap-top, try this wired B&B near Old Town. It has four rooms and a two-bedroom guesthouse and an outdoor hot tub. Lots of Southwest charm and common areas make it a relaxing and homey place to slumber.

Hacienda Antigua (Map p289; ☎ 505-345-5399, 800-201-2986; www.haciendantigua.com; 6708 Tierra Dr NW; r $99-229; ⓚ) This eight-room inn is brimming with authentic New Mexican style. From the pale adobe walls to *vigas* (wooden roofing beams), Southwestern vacation expectations will be met.

ourpick Los Poblanos (Map p289; ☎ 505-344-9297, 866-344-9297; www.lospoblanos.com; 4803 Rio Grande Blvd NW; r $145-250) This six-room B&B, surrounded by gardens, lavender fields (blooming mid-June through July) and an organic farm, is a registered National Historic Place. Los Poblanos is a five-minute drive from Old Town and is within walking distance of the Rio Grande and open-space trails. Organic eggs and produce from the farm are served for breakfast, and rooms feature kiva fireplaces.

EATING

Albuquerque offers the region's widest variety of international cuisines while serving up some of the best New Mexican food anywhere. However, it's not a foodie destination like Santa Fe, and many restaurants geared to tourists are less than outstanding. Head to Nob Hill and browse the modest, family-owned joints serving excellent and authentic local cuisine and the cluster of colorful and (mostly) inexpensive restaurants until one catches your eye. You'll find Frito Pie on most menus; this concoction of red kidney bean and beef chile, cheddar cheese, onions and Frito chips is an Albuquerque original. At city festivals, it's what turkey legs are to the rest of the country – the vendor food of choice.

Old Town

The plaza is surrounded with average eateries serving average food at premium prices (it's the cost of convenience). Consider walking a few blocks for a better selection.

Route 66 Malt Shop (Map p292; ☎ 505-242-7866; 1720 Central Ave SW; mains $5; ⓧ lunch & dinner Mon-Sat; Ⓥ ⓚ) Bring the kids to this nostalgic and friendly place, tightly packed with 10 tables and four stools – up from just one table a few years ago. Make sure to try one of the awesome green chile cheeseburgers, washed down with a house-made root-beer float.

Church St Café (Map p292; ☎ 505-247-8522; 2111 Church St NW; mains $7-12; ⓧ 8am-4pm Sun-Wed, 8am-8pm Thu-Sat) The food is delicious, and the café is historical and the exception to the plaza rule. Try the Albuquerque roast beef, and the French dip with green chile on a flour tortilla.

Seasons Rotisserie & Grill (Map p292; ☎ 505-766-5100; 2031 Mountain Rd NW; lunch $7-14, dinner $14-28; ⓧ lunch Mon-Fri, dinner daily) With bright-yellow walls, high ceilings, fresh flowers and a creative menu, this contemporary place provides welcome relief from the usual Old Town atmosphere. Try the hearty red-chile-dusted chicken burgers or Baja tacos inside or on the rooftop cantina.

Ambrozia Café & Wine Bar (Map p292; ☎ 505-242-6560; 108 Rio Grande Blvd NW; mains $20-25; ⓧ 5-9pm Tue-Sat, 11am-2:30pm Sun) Ambrozia creates scrumptious contemporary global delicacies with local ingredients. Chef-owner Sam Etheride whips up his signature lobster corn dogs year-round, and the four-course Sunday brunch is dynamic (and good value at $20), with delicious choices like granola-crusted French toast, crab cake *huevos rancheros*, and tequila and red chile salmon. Can you say yum?

Downtown

ourpick Slate Street Café & Wife Loft (off Map p291; ☎ 505-243-2210; 515 Slate St; mains $5-13; ⓧ breakfast, lunch & dinner) This downtown establishment in the burgeoning Route 66 art district is usually packed with people who come to sample the clever Southwestern American fare in the café and drink merlot in the upstairs wine loft. The hottest new venue in Albuquerque is an intimate space made warm by the presence of a long red sofa, cozy armchairs and cocktail tables. The wine-tasting menu changes regularly and offers 30 different wines by the bottle from all over the world. Once a month the loft does tasting night ($15) from 5pm to 7pm, during which three comparable wines are paired with a plate of appetizers selected especially to complement them. A great new edition to the downtown Albuquerque scene.

Artichoke Café (Map p291; ☎ 505-243-0200; 424 Central Ave SE; mains $17-30; 🕙 11:30am-2:30pm Mon-Fri, 4:30-9:30pm Mon-Sat; **V**) Elegant and unpretentious, this popular bistro does creative gourmet cuisine with panache and is high on foodies' lists of Albuquerque's best.

Nob Hill & UNM Area
In the grand tradition of university neighborhoods, this is the best area for cheap, healthy and vegetarian meals. But you can also find a number of swanky places to nosh.

Satellite Coffee (Map p294; ☎ 505-254-3800; 2300 Central Ave SE; snacks $1-5; 🕙 6am-11pm Sun-Thu, 6am-midnight Sat; **V** wi-fi) Albuquerque's answer to Starbucks lies in these hip coffee shops, luring lots of laptop-toting regulars. Owned by the same brilliant folks who started the Flying Star; look for plenty of locations around town.

Frontier (Map p294; ☎ 505-266-0550; www.frontierrestaurant.com; 2400 Central Ave SE; mains $3-7; 🕙 24hr; 🚹 **V**) Get in line for enormous cinnamon rolls (made with, like, a stick of butter each!) and the best *huevos rancheros*. Period. The food, people-watching and Western art are all outstanding.

Annapurna (Map p294; ☎ 505-262-2424; 2201 Silver Ave SE; mains $6-8; 🕙 7am-8pm Mon-Sat, 10am-6pm Sun; **V**) This awesome vegetarian and vegan café has some of the freshest, tastiest healthy food in town, including delicately spiced ayurvedic delights that even carnivores love. Dishes are complemented by authentic East Indian (read: *real*) chai.

Il Vicino Pizzeria (Map p294; ☎ 505-266-7855; 3403 Central Ave NE; mains $6-8; 🕙 11am-11pm) Sure, you can come for simple traditional fare like wood-fired pizza, sandwiches and pasta. But the real bread and butter here is spectacular award-winning microbrewed beer, including the Wet Mountain IPA and Slow Down Brown.

Flying Star Café (Map p294; ☎ 505-255-6633; 3416 Central Ave SE; mains $6-12; 🕙 6am-11:30pm; 🚹 **V** wi-fi) This incredibly popular local chain draws flocks with innovative mains (look for homey fare like chicken pot pie and fish-and-chips), an extensive breakfast menu, sumptuous desserts, free wireless internet and creative, vibrant decor. It's pushed over the top of the groovy scale with organic, free-range and antibiotic-free ingredients. It's simply an Albuquerque must. And portions are humungous.

Metropolitan Albuquerque
The following Albuquerque choices are worth the little trek it takes to reach them.

Loyola's Family Restaurant (Map p289; ☎ 505-268-6478; 4500 Central Ave SE; mains $5-8; 🕙 6am-2pm Tue-Fri, 6am-1:30pm Sat, 7am-1:30pm Sun; 🚹 **V**) Pure Route 66 style baby, Loyola's has been serving fine, no-frills New Mexican fare since before there was even a song about the Mother Road.

our pick **Sadie's** (Map p289; ☎ 505-345-5339; 6230 4th St NW; mains $5-13; 🕙 10am-10pm Mon-Sat, 10am-9pm Sun; 🚹 **V**) Make sure to snap a photo in front of the sign at Sadie's that says, 'in 1897 in this location, nothing happened.' A massive place with a barn-like atmosphere, Sadie's is a local institution. One author makes this her first stop in Albuquerque – bar none. Recite along with us: 'a carafe of grand gold margaritas, please, and the enchilada dinner with blue corn, rolled, chicken, green vegetarian, no onions and a side of guac. Great. Thanks.'

Los Cuates (Map p289; ☎ 505-255-5079; 5016B Lomas Blvd NE; mains $7-10; 🕙 11am-9pm; 🚹 **V**) It's not unusual for lines to form out the door at this favorite joint serving huge plates of high-quality New Mexican cuisine – including meat-free options. Los Cuates changed ownership recently, but the food is still first-rate.

DRINKING
In addition to the places listed here, try the fabulous new Slate Street Café & Wine Loft (opposite) downtown– it offers monthly wine tasting and attracts an artsy crowd for pre- and post-theater noshing and sipping. Check out Il Vicino Pizzeria (left) for excellent microbrews. Bars are generally open from 4pm to 2am Monday through Saturday, and until midnight on Sunday.

Anodyne (Map p291; ☎ 505-244-1820; 409 Central Ave NW) An excellent spot for a game of pool,

NEW MEXICO

Anodyne is a huge space with book-lined walls, wood ceilings, plenty of overstuffed chairs, more than 100 bottled beers and great people-watching on Central Ave.

Martini Grille (Map p289; ☎ 505-255-4111; 4200 Central Ave SE) Often wins the vote for the best martinis and margaritas in Albuquerque. In addition to a brain-rocking alcoholic concoction, it has lively atmosphere.

Kelly's Brewery (Map p294; ☎ 505-262-2739; 3226 Central Ave SE; ⊗ 8am-midnight) Come here for patio dining, lots of local microbrews and 20-something's hanging out. On weekends there is live music.

Downtown Distillery (Map p291; ☎ 505-765-1534; 406 Central Ave SW) The Distillery boasts a casual crowd, pool and a jukebox, so you can be your own DJ.

Copper Lounge (Map p294; ☎ 505-242-7490; 1504 Central Ave SE) Recently voted one of the city's best 'ladies night out' spots, the Copper Lounge plays host to a friendly, mixed crowd.

ENTERTAINMENT

For a comprehensive list of Albuquerque's diverse nightspots and a detailed calendar of upcoming events, get *Alibi* (www.alibi.com), a free weekly published every Tuesday. The entertainment sections of Thursday evening's *Albuquerque Tribune* and the Friday and Sunday *Albuquerque Journal* are helpful, too.

Nightclubs & Live Music

Downtown has a great bar scene, and Nob Hill's scene is pretty good, too, because of UNM. The theme seems to be atomic alien.

Caravan East (Map p289; ☎ 505-265-7877; 7605 Central Ave NE) Put on your cowboy boots and 10-gallon hat and hit the dance floor to practice your line dancing and two-stepping at this classic Albuquerque country-and-western music bar. Live bands perform and the ambience is friendly.

El Rey (Map p291; ☎ 505-242-2353; www.elreytheater .com; 624 Central Ave SW) A fabulous venue for local and national rock, blues and country acts. Over the years, it's hosted such stars as Ella Fitzgerald, Etta James and Arlo Guthrie. It also does national poetry slams and occasionally hosts CD launch parties.

Launch Pad (Map p291; ☎ 505-764-8887; www .launchpadrocks.com; 618 Central Ave SW; ⊗ from 7pm) This retro-modern place is the hottest stage for local live music, and still allows smoking inside – wow, now that's old school.

Sauce/Liquid Lounge/Raw (Map p291; ☎ 505-242-5839; 405 Central Ave NW) A three-bars-in-one combo deal, this place has dancing and DJs spinning house music most nights, but it's not so loud that you can't just hang and talk. A popular and trendy spot, Sauce primarily serves very tasty gourmet pizza. The funky lounge in the back is a busy spot to hang out with a late-night drink.

Cinemas

Guild Cinema (Map p294; ☎ 505-255-1848; www.guild cinema.com; 3405 Central Ave NE; admission $8) This is the only independently owned, single-screen theater in town, and it always has great indie, avant-garde, Hollywood fringe, political and international features. Stick around when there are discussions following select films.

Performing Arts

Popejoy Hall (Map p294; ☎ 505-277-4569; www.unm tickets.com; Central Ave at Cornell St SE) and the historic **KiMo Theater** (Map p291; ☎ 505-768-3522; www.cabq .org; 423 Central Ave NW) are the primary places to see big-name national acts, as well as local opera, symphony and theater. The **Pit** (UNM Arena; Map p289; ☎ 505-925-5626; www.unmtickets .com; 1111 University Blvd SE) and **Tingley Coliseum** (Map p289; ☎ 505-265-1791; 300 San Pedro NE) host Albuquerque's major events.

The **New Mexico Ballet Company** (☎ 505-292-4245; www.nmballet.org; tickets $15-20) performs from October to April. The **New Mexico Symphony Orchestra** (☎ 505-881-8999; www.nmso.org; tickets $10-50) performs at various venues, including at the zoo (p296).

Sports

About those **Albuquerque Isotopes** (Map p294; ☎ 505-924-2255; www.albuquerquebaseball.com; Isotopes Park, Ave Cesar Chavez & University SE). First of all: yes, the city's baseball team really was named for the episode of *The Simpsons*, 'Hungry, Hungry Homer,' when America's favorite TV dad tried to keep his beloved Springfield Isotopes from moving to Albuquerque. The 'topes sell more merchandise than any other minor (and most major) league team. They sometimes win, too.

Albuquerque Scorpions (☎ 505-265-1791; www .scorpionshockey.com) play hockey at Tingley Coliseum (above). The **UNM Lobos** (☎ 505-277-4569; www.unm.edu) football squad packs the Pit, but it's the women's basketball and volleyball teams that carry the banner to playoffs and national championships.

SHOPPING

For Native American crafts and informed salespeople, stop by the **Palms Trading Post** (Map p292; ☎ 505-247-8504; 1504 Lomas Blvd NW; ☽ Mon-Sat), while the **Silver Sun** (Map p292; ☎ 505-242-8265; 2042 South Plaza NW) is a reputable spot for turquoise.

Another good spot to stroll (it lacks the touristy feel of Old Town) is around the university and in Nob Hill. If you walk east from the university down and around Central Ave, where you'll find an eclectic mix of shops (from a tattoo parlor to a herbal medicine shop to a toy store) until you reach the Nob Hill Shopping Center at Carlisle. Among the hip shops on Central Ave is **Martha's Body Bueno** (Map p294; ☎ 505-255-1122; 3901 Central Ave NE), which specializes in handmade beauty supplies and lingerie. Also don't miss **hey jhonny!** (Map p294; ☎ 505-256-9244; 3418B Central Ave SE), Albuquerque's most sophisticated home furnishing store, offering Buddha and Balinese art for every budget.

GETTING THERE & AWAY
Air

New Mexico's largest airport, the **Albuquerque International Sunport** (Map p289; ☎ 505-244-7700; www.cabq.gov/airport; 2200 Sunport Blvd) offers free wireless internet and is served by multiple airlines and car-rental companies, as well as private shuttles that run from the Sunport and downtown Albuquerque to Santa Fe and points north.

Bus

The **Albuquerque Bus Transportation Center** (Map p291; 300 2nd St SW) is home to Greyhound and **TNM&O** (☎ 505-243-4435, 800-231-2222), which offers two morning buses to Santa Fe ($12) and Taos ($30).

Train

Amtrak's *Southwest Chief* stops at **Albuquerque Amtrak Station** (Map p291; ☎ 505-842-9650, 800-872-7245; 214 1st St SW; ticket office ☽ 10am-5pm), from which daily trains run between Chicago and Los Angeles, with stops in Lamy and Las Vegas, New Mexico.

GETTING AROUND
To/From the Airport

The Sunport is served by the No 50 ABQ Ride bus. The **Airport Shuttle** (☎ 505-865-1234) and **Sunport Shuttle** (☎ 505-883-4966, 505-866-4966; www.sunportshuttle.com) both run 24 hours a day. Fares range from $5 to $60, depending on where you're headed. Expect to pay $14 one way to Old Town and $12 to downtown. Shuttles also run frequently to Santa Fe; see p327 for more.

Bicycle

Contact **Parks & Recreation** (☎ 505-768-2680; www.cabq.gov/bike) for a free map of the city's elaborate system of bike trails, or go to the website. All ABQ Ride buses are equipped with front-loading bicycle racks.

Bus

ABQ Ride (Map p291; ☎ 505-243-7433; www.cabq.gov /transit; 100 1st St SW; adult/child $1/35¢; ☽ 6am-8pm Mon-Thu, 6am-2:30am Fri & Sat, check website for Sunday routes) is a public bus system covering most of Albuquerque on weekdays and major tourist spots daily. Maps and schedules are available on the website; three-day passes ($4) are available at the main office. Exact change is required when buying tickets on board. Rapid Ride buses (which run on hybrid diesel engines and have free wireless internet!) offer access to the BioPark, downtown, Nob Hill, the fairgrounds and Old Town.

Car & Motorcycle

Albuquerque is an easy city to drive around. Streets are wide and there's usually metered or even free parking within blocks, or sometimes steps, from wherever you want to stop.

New Mexico's largest city is also motorcycle friendly – the town has its share of biker bars and you are more likely to hear a 'hog' thundering down the street than not.

Taxi

In general you must call for a taxi, though they do patrol the Sunport, Amtrak and bus station. Both companies charge about $5 for the first mile and $2.30 per mile thereafter.
Albuquerque Cab (☎ 505-883-4888)
Yellow Cab (☎ 505-247-8888, 800-657-6232)

ALBUQUERQUE TO SANTA FE

There are three main routes connecting New Mexico's two major cities: it takes a speedy hour to get from Albuquerque to Santa Fe along the semi-scenic I-25; at least 90 minutes

DETOUR: JEMEZ MOUNTAIN TRAIL

Get off I-25 at US 550 and roll along a passionless 25-mile stretch of scrub past Santa Ana Pueblo and then **Zia Pueblo** (☎ 505-867-3304; US 550), where the state's official symbol was first designed; it's famed for its August 15 Feast Day, Christmas Buffalo and Crow Dances. When you reach San Ysidro, head north on NM 4 into paradise. Detour, perhaps, to **Ponderosa Valley Winery** (☎ 505-834-7487; www.ponderosawinery.com; 3171 Hwy 290; ☺ 10am-5pm Tue-Sat, noon-5pm Sun) for a bottle of late-harvest riesling or pinot noir.

That's about when you enter the **Jemez Mountains** proper. A ragged expanse of moody grays and cool evergreens rise from the brilliant red desert; this is all that remains of the world's largest volcano – they've found pieces of it in Texas. Meander through sculpted formations and the melting ruins of abandoned pueblos along the Jemez River, which is fed by snowmelt and hot springs bubbling up from the still-molten heart of this strange and beautiful wilderness.

The **Walatowa Visitor Center** (☎ 505-834-7235; 7413 Hwy 4; ☺ 8am-5pm) at **Jemez Pueblo** is excellent and houses the **Museum of Pueblo Culture** (admission free). Across the road, **Jemez Red Rocks** hosts food stands on summer weekends, plus a powwow in late May.

The pretty village of **Jemez Springs** was built around a cluster of springs, as was the ruined pueblo at **Jemez State Monument** (☎ 505-829-3530; NM 4; adult/child $3/free; ☺ 8:30am-5pm, closed Tue Dec-Apr). You can experience the waters yourself at rustic **Jemez Springs Bath House** (☎ 505-829-3303; www.jemezspringsbathhouse.com; 62 Jemez Springs Plaza; per hr $15-20; ☺ 10am-8pm), with private tubs, massages and more.

Locals love the hot water at Jemez' **Giggling Springs** (☎ 505-829-9175) where you can soak in private hot springs for $15 an hour. It's across the road from the **Laughing Lizard Inn** (☎ 505-829-3108; www.thelaughinglizard.com; NM 4; r $70), which has great rooms and an attached **café** (mains $5-11; ☺ 5-8pm Thu-Fri, 11am-8pm Sat, 11am-5pm Sun, limited hours in winter) with live music on weekends. There are a handful of restaurants in Jemez Springs, including a good deli.

Before leaving town, take time out to inspect **Soda Dam**, a warm waterfall that's enveloped boulders with bizarre mineral deposits, and **Battleship Rock**, a dramatic trailhead and fishing spot.

on the much lovelier NM 14, the Turquoise Trail; or a day (or better, two) to meander through the stunning Jemez Mountains.

ALONG I-25

There are a couple of stops off the highway. See p284 for info on area pueblos.

Kasha-Katuwe Tent Rocks National Monument

Kasha-Katuwe Tent Rocks National Monument is a beloved weekend hiking spot for Santa Fe and Albuquerque residents and their canine companions. And if you're driving I-25 between the two cities, we suggest making the time to visit the bizarre and beautiful Tent Rocks, often referred to by New Mexicans as 'the Hoodoos' for their strange light-orange, sometimes tiger-striped, cone-like shape. When volcanic ash erupted from the nearby Jemez Mountain volcanoes, it was sculpted into teepee-like formations and steep-sided, narrow canyons. Visitors can hike up a dry riverbed through the piñon-covered desert to the formations, where sandy paths weave through the rocks and canyons. You'll need a couple of hours to drive the desert dirt road to get here and to hike around a bit, but it's well worth it. Take I-25 exit 264; follow Hwy 16 west to Hwy 22.

Coronado State Monument

After exiting I-25 onto US 550, you'll pass **Coronado Campground & State Monument** (☎ 505-980-8256; US 150; tent/RV sites $8/18, parking at monument $3; ☺ 8:30am-5pm Wed-Mon), which has shelters for shade, showers ($4), interpretive trails and a visitor center. You'll encounter the ruins of **Kuau'a Pueblo** (☎ 505-867-5351; US 150; admission free; ☺ 8am-5pm Wed-Sun). It's not exactly Chaco Canyon, but the murals are considered the finest example of pre-contact mural art in North America: various Pueblo gods (Kachinas) are depicted as personifications of nature, including the Corn Mother, who gave the Pueblo people corn. The murals have been artfully restored inside the visitor center and underground kiva.

Legends of New Mexico Museum & !Traditions! Festival Marketplace

This independent **museum** (☎ 505-867-8600; Budaghers exit 257 off I-25; adult/child $5/free; ♥ 10am-4pm Thu-Mon) spotlights the state's most famous visitors and residents – from Billy the Kid to Bill Gates, and the Roswell aliens to Smokey Bear. When they say it's a tribute to multiculturalism, they mean it. The marketplace on the same grounds features shops, galleries and a restaurant at which everything is either made in New Mexico or historically sold in the state.

TURQUOISE TRAIL

The Turquoise Trail has been a major trade route since at least 2000 BC, when local artisans began trading Cerrillos turquoise with communities in present-day Mexico. Today it's the scenic back road between Albuquerque and Santa Fe, lined with quirky communities and other diversions.

Cedar Crest

Located to the northeast of Albuquerque, on the eastern side of the Sandia mountains, and just a bit up Sandia Crest Rd (NM 165) from Cedar Crest, the **Tinkertown Museum** (☎ 505-281-5233; www.tinkertown.com; 121 Sandia Crest Rd; adult/child $3/1; ♥ 9am-6pm Apr-Nov; ♿) is an inspiring assortment of detailed towns, circuses and other scenes that come alive with a quarter. Woodcarver and wisdom collector Ross J Ward built it and surrounded it with antique toys, junque (aka fancy junk) and suggestions that you eat more mangoes naked.

The nearby **Museum of Archaeology** (☎ 505-281-2005; 22 Calvary Rd, off NM 14; adult/child $3.50/1.50; ♥ noon-7pm May-Oct; ♿) has an 'archaeological site' outdoors (kids dig this) and local Indian artifacts inside. It also runs the adjacent **Turquoise Trail Campground** (tent/RV sites $15/25, cabins $30-50), which has hot showers and cool shade. There's national forest access for guests.

Madrid

Madrid (pronounced *maa*-drid) is about 30 miles south of Santa Fe on Hwy 14. A bustling company coal-mining town in the 1920s and '30s, it was all but abandoned after WWII. In the mid-1970s, the company's heirs sold cheap lots to tie-dyed wanderers who have built a thriving arts community with galleries and wacky shops. It's not nearly as mellow as you'd think, attracting more bikers than New Agers, but that's just part of the appeal.

There are dozens of galleries and shops in this one-horse town, but pay special attention to **Fuse Arts** (☎ 438-4999; 2878 NM 14), with its first-rate abstractions; **Seppanen & Daughters Fine Textiles** (☎ 505-424-7470; 2879 NM 14), with its tactile and colorful Oaxaca, Navajo and Tibetan rugs; and **Range West** (☎ 505-474-0925; 2861 NM 14), with its elegant water fountains carved from monolithic granite chunks.

The **Old Coal Mine Museum** (☎ 505-438-3780; 2814 NM 14; adult/child $4/free; ♥ 10am-5pm) preserves plenty of old mining equipment, pretty much right where the miners left it. It also hosts the **Madrid Melodrama & Engine House Theatre** (adult/child $10/4; ♥ 3pm Sat & Sun May-Oct), starring a steam locomotive and lots of Wild West desperados, scoundrels and vixens, and stories that leave you feeling good. Admission includes a six-shooter loaded with marshmallows to unload at the villains.

Visit the 1919 **Mine Shaft Tavern** (☎ 505-473-0743; 2846 NM 14; dishes $5-11; ♥ noon-12pm) to meet locals, listen to live music on weekends and experience the 'longest stand-up bar in New Mexico.' The bar was built in 1946 and has been Madrid's favorite attraction ever since.

Mama Lisa's Cafe (☎ 505-471-5769; NM 14; snacks $6-10; ♥ 11am-4:30pm Fri-Sun) serves good quesadillas and a great red chile chocolate cake.

Overnight at **Madrid Lodging** (☎ 505-471-3450; www.madridlodging.com; 14 Opera House Rd; d $110-130; wi-fi), which has two two-room suites and an outdoor hot tub in well-tended, colorfully painted environs.

Cerrillos

Just a few miles north of Madrid on Hwy 14, about 25 miles from Santa Fe, Cerrillos is a photographer's dream. With unpaved streets threading through an adobe Old West town relatively unchanged since the 1880s, this is the home of the first mine in North America, built to extract turquoise around AD 100.

Cerrillos Turquoise Mining Museum & Petting Zoo (☎ 505-438-3008; 17 Waldo St; admission $2; ♥ 9am-sunset, can vary), a top-drawer roadside attraction, packs five rooms with Chinese art, pioneer-era tools, mining equipment dating to 3000 BC, bottles and antiques excavated from an abandoned area hotel, and anything else the owners thought was worth displaying. For $2 more you can feed the goats, llamas and unusual chickens.

NEW MEXICO

Broken Saddle Riding Co (☎ 505-424-7774; www
.brokensaddle.com; off County Rd 57; rides $55-90) offers
one- to three-hour horseback rides through
juniper-dotted hills and abandoned mines.
Along the way, you'll learn about local history and geology; don't forget a camera
to capture the spectacular views. It's open
by appointment.

BANDELIER NATIONAL MONUMENT

Because of its convenient location and spectacular landscape, Bandelier is an excellent
choice for folks interested in ancient pueblos. Rio Grande Puebloans lived here until
the mid-1500s. Although none of the sites
are restored, there are almost 50 sq miles of
protected canyons offering backpacking trails
and camping. The **Ceremonial Cave**, 140ft above
the canyon floor and reached by climbing four
ladders, is a highlight of a visit to Bandelier.
Mesa-top **Tsankawi**, an unexcavated site 13
miles north of the **visitor center** (☎ 505-672-3861;
Hwy 4; ☯ 8am-6pm) on Hwy 4, provides good
views and a steep 2-mile long trail.

The **park** (www.nps.gov/band; per car $10; ☯ 8am-
4:30pm, 8am-5pm late Jun–early Sep), 12 miles from
Los Alamos, has a good **bookshop** (☎ 505-672-
3861) that sells trail maps and guidebooks.

Juniper Campground (campsites $10), set among
the pines near the monument entrance, offers
about 100 campsites, drinking water, toilets,
picnic tables and fire grates, but no showers
or hookups. Free backcountry camping is allowed but permits must be obtained in person
from the visitor center.

LOS ALAMOS
pop 18,300 / elev 7400ft

In a stunning natural locale, Los Alamos
hugs the national forest and is set on mesas
overlooking the desert. It offers a fascinating
dynamic in which souvenir T-shirts printed
with atomic explosions and 'La Bomba' wine
are sold next to books on Pueblo history and
wilderness hiking. It's where some of the
smartest scientists in the world – and their
families – live alongside hippie artists trying
to get back to nature.

Orientation

Built on long thin mesas separated by steep canyons, Los Alamos has a confusing layout. The
main entrance from the east is Hwy 502, which
branches into the east–west streets of Canyon
Rd, Central Ave and Trinity Dr – these are the
main streets of town. Central Ave and Canyon
Rd form an oval enclosing the heart of town.
Canyon and Central merge on the west side
of town as Canyon Rd and meet back up with
Trinity at Hwy 501. The highway veers around
past the Los Alamos National Laboratory towards Bandelier National Monument and
turns into Hwy 4. Got that?

Information

Chamber of Commerce (☎ 505-662-8105, 800-444-
0707; www.visit.losalamos.com; 109 Central Park Sq;
☯ 9am-5pm Mon-Fri, 9am-4pm Sat, 10am-3pm Sun)
Forest Service (☎ 505-667-5120; 475 20th St;
☯ 8am-4pm Mon, Wed & Fri)
Hospital (☎ 505-662-4201; 3917 West Rd; ☯ 24hr)

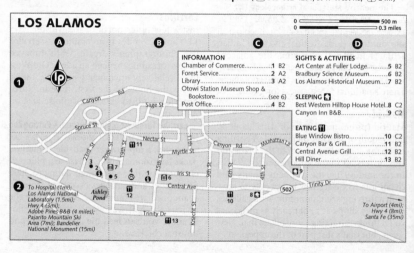

LOS ALAMOS

0 — 500 m
0 — 0.3 miles

INFORMATION		
Chamber of Commerce	1	B2
Forest Service	2	A2
Library	3	A2
Otowi Station Museum Shop & Bookstore	(see 6)	
Post Office	4	B2

SIGHTS & ACTIVITIES		
Art Center at Fuller Lodge	5	B2
Bradbury Science Museum	6	B2
Los Alamos Historical Museum	7	B2

SLEEPING 🏠		
Best Western Hilltop House Hotel	8	C2
Canyon Inn B&B	9	C2

EATING 🍴		
Blue Window Bistro	10	C2
Canyon Bar & Grill	11	B2
Central Avenue Grill	12	B2
Hill Diner	13	B2

Library (☎ 505-662-8250; 2400 Central Ave; ◷ 9am-6pm Mon-Sat; ▢) Free internet access.

Otowi Station Museum Shop & Bookstore
(☎ 505-662-9589; 1350 Central Ave; ◷ 8am-5pm Mon-Fri, 9am-6pm Sat, 11am-6pm Sun) A fine selection of science and regional books.

Post office (☎ 505-662-2071; 1808 Central Ave)

Sights & Activities

On July 16, 1945 a flash in the New Mexico desert forever changed the world. In that single moment, later said to be the most important event of the 20th century, scientists released energy equal to all the bombs dropped on London by Nazi Germany. Soon thereafter, on August 6 and August 9, 1945, the cities of Hiroshima and Nagasaki were destroyed by the first atomic bombs used in warfare.

You can't actually visit the Los Alamos National Laboratory, where the first atomic bomb was conceived, but you can visit the well-designed **Bradbury Science Museum** (☎ 505-667-4444; www.lanl.gov/museum; Central Ave; admission free; ◷ 10am-5pm Tue-Sat), which covers atomic history through more than 40 high-tech interactive exhibits and galleries. A children's section features hands-on activities including computer programs and videos.

Pop-culture artifacts from the atomic age are on display at the interesting **Los Alamos Historical Museum** (☎ 505-662-4493; www.losalamos.com/historicalsociety; 1921 Juniper St; admission free; ◷ 9:30am-4:30pm Mon-Sat, 11am-5pm Sun). It also features exhibits on the social history of life 'on the hill' during the secret project. Pick up one of the self-guided downtown walking-tour pamphlets. The **Art Center at Fuller Lodge** (☎ 505-662-9331; www.artfulnm.org; 2132 Central Ave; ◷ 10am-4pm Mon-Sat) mounts mixed-media shows of local and national artists. Fuller Lodge, built in 1928 to serve as the dining hall for the local boys' school, was purchased by the US government for the Manhattan Project. Inside are two small but good museums.

Ever wanted to ski down the rim of a volcano? Look no further, **Pajarito Mountain Ski Area** (☎ 505-662-5725, 888-662-7669; www.skipajarito.com; lift ticket adult/child $45/29; ◷ Fri-Sun Dec-Mar), 7 miles west of downtown, offers 40 runs – from easy groomers to challenging mogul steeps – plus a terrain park for snowboarders.

Sleeping

Canyon Inn B&B (☎ 505-662-9595; www.canyoninnbnb.com; 80 Canyon Rd; r $70) Catering to folks working at the labs, this B&B provides breakfast fixings so that guests can prepare the meals whenever they rise.

Adobe Pines B&B (☎ 505-661-8828; www.losalamoslodging.com; 1601 Loma Linda Dr; s/d $78/88; wi-fi) Adobe Pines offers five distinct rooms in an adobe building. Each is a little different. Try the 2nd-floor East Room, which comes with a king-size bed, private sitting area and a balcony to enjoy the city lights by evening or Jemez Mountains in day. The Sun Room has plate-glass doors, a wooden four-poster bed and white linens, giving it airy appeal.

Best Western Hilltop House Hotel (☎ 505-662-1118; www.bestwesternlasalamos.com; 400 Trinity Dr; r from $89; 🐾 ▢ wi-fi) The most posh hotel in Los Alamos is popular with business travelers and tourists looking for upmarket chain consistency. Guests are greeted with a welcome drink in the hotel lounge and rooms are spacious, with lots of amenities. There is a workout room and spa onsite. The La Vista Restaurant serves American and Italian dishes (mains $7 to $15) by a row of floor-to-ceiling windows. Breakfast is included. Best of all? Your dog stays free.

Eating & Drinking

Most of the chain hotels also have restaurants. Try La Vista at the Best Western if you're looking for something last-minute and quick.

Canyon Bar & Grill (☎ 505-662-3333; 163 Central Park Sq; mains $5-12; ◷ 11am-2am Mon-Sat, 11am-midnight Sun) The best place in town for a beer and basic bar grub does a great green chile cheeseburger. You won't find any glitz or Southwestern affectations here, but the local hangout has a long bar, pool table, live music and dancing on Friday and karaoke on Thursday.

Blue Window Bistro (☎ 505-662-6305; 813 Central Ave; lunch $8-9, dinner $8-21; ◷ lunch & dinner) On the north side of the shopping center, this brightly colored café offers lunchtime gyros and poached salmon, and dinners like Southwestern chicken and double-cut pork chops.

Hill Diner (☎ 505-662-9745; 1315 Trinity Dr; dishes $8-10; ◷ 11am-8pm) Those craving some home-cooked American classics, like chicken-fried steak and white country gravy, won't be disappointed by the adequate array of American diner fare served daily at this popular and inexpensive place.

Central Avenue Grill (☎ 505-662-2005; 1789 Central Ave; mains $10-18; ◷ lunch & dinner) For a more upscale and contemporary setting try this spot with high ceilings and big windows that open onto downtown Los Alamos. It serves satisfying dishes like shrimp fajitas, green-curry chicken and Asian-spiced salmon. At night Central Ave turns into a lively après-dark scene, when diners move from the marble tabletops to the big oak wood dance floor to shake their booties to live tunes. It stays open late.

ESPAÑOLA

pop 9700 / elev 5578ft

Founded by Don Juan de Oñate in 1598 as the first state capital, today Española is something of an anti–Santa Fe. We won't lie, Española doesn't feel like a pretty place; life is hard for many residents, with one in five people living below the poverty line. America's methamphetamine epidemic has hit Española especially hard. The DEA frequently busts labs around here – the city is surrounded by farmland, which is a favorite spot for cooks – and the city has the dubious honor of being one of the top spots in the USA when it comes to drug overdoses.

Yet despite the hardships facing its residents, Española is also home to many proud and optimistic people. Farmers-market organizers are purchasing a site with highly coveted water rights where a kids' demonstration garden and friendly gathering spot will water the soul of the community. Town celebrity Monica Lovato, a champion super flyweight boxer highly ranked by the World Boxing Council, brings hope and a great example to kids coming up behind her.

Cluttered with hair salons, fast-food restaurants, *tacquarias* and abandoned, crumbling old adobes, Española's location, framed by the Jemez Mountains and Trucas Peak, is stunning. Most of the surrounding country is farmland, much of it deeded in the 17th century to Hispanic land-grant families. Anchored to the north and south by two casinos, Española has less expensive lodging than neighboring Santa Fe. Plus this little town knows how to cook mean green chile – one restaurant here is so good, it's considered the best in the state.

Eating & Drinking

Ranchito San Pedro B&B (☎ 505-753-0583; www.janhart.com; Hwy 581; cabins $98) If you're planning to make Española your base for exploring northern New Mexico, then book in here; there's a three-night minimum, but it's very good value. It's a self-described adobe 'art dude ranch,' in a pleasant pastoral neighborhood. This is a relaxing place that's also pet-friendly.

Rancho de San Juan (☎ 505-753-6818; www.ranchodesanjuan.com; 34020 Hwy 285; r & ste $275-675) If you've got the dough, try sleeping here, just north of town. This little gem features first-class rooms, a spa, great service and a spectacular setting for dining on New Mexican classics at two nightly settings. Even if you can't afford to stay, it's worth coming to eat (mains $35). Considered the number-one restaurant in New Mexico by many, Rancho de San Juan is so good that locals drive from Santa Fe just to dine. Duck arrives at the table cooked with Chinese spices, drizzled with a blood orange glaze, served with pineapple and rice pilaf. Add an impressive wine list and a Chocolate Oblivion Tart ($10) for one heavenly meal.

Angelina's Restaurant (☎ 505-753-8543; 1226 N Railroad Ave; dishes $6-11; 🕑 7am-9pm) A popular dining option, where locals come for the finest organic lamb burritos ($7) in the land, along with a host of other delicious New Mexican specialties.

Getting There & Away

The town sits at the junction of US 84/285 (Santa Fe Hwy) leading southeast to Santa Fe; NM 30 (Los Alamos Ave) running southwest to Santa Clara Pueblo, Los Alamos and Bandelier; US 84 (Oñate St) heading northwest to Abiquiú and Ghost Ranch; NM 76 (Santa Cruz Rd; High Rd to Taos), the back road to Taos, going through Chimayó; N Riverside Dr/NM 68 heading north out of town as the Low Rd to Taos; and S Riverside Dr US 84/285 heading southeast to Santa Fe.

SANTA FE

pop 62,200 / elev 7000ft

Welcome to Santa Fe, a city that makes its own rules, yet never forgets its long and storied past. The country's second-oldest state capital city – she recently celebrated her 400th birthday – is a bewitching place where centuries-old umber adobes are set against a dramatic backdrop of the Sangre de Cristo Mountains. From art to opera, fusion food to world-class resorts and sick single-track bike trails through high desert mountains, everything Santa Fe does, she does with color and flair. Centered on a grassy plaza dating from 1610, Santa Fe is a gorgeous medley of hot green chile, wizened Native American faces selling turquoise jewelry on the plaza, warm adobe architecture, fiery red ristras, fabulous art, enchanting churches and sage-scented high-desert air. And she is known for her efforts to keep sacred traditions and centuries-old celebrations of the heart, belly, art and soul alive for generations to come.

The city is home to a motley crew of characters, including yuppie gringo artists, New Age hippie transplants, Spanish families that have called the city home for centuries, illegal Mexican immigrants trying to eke out a living laying brick for new adobe houses, reclusive ex-Hollywood producers and ageless movie stars. All have come for the privacy and space.

Despite the problems facing all urban areas – gangs, poverty, racial tensions – Santa Fe remains a beacon of progressive thought and creative culture in New Mexico and the USA. The UN named it 'most creative city' in 2005, a cool honor for a city that is committed to the arts like nowhere else in the country and strives hard to keeps its history alive through sacred traditions forged hundreds of years ago. Don't miss Christmas Eve on Canyon Rd, or the renowned Indian Market in August.

ORIENTATION

Cerrillos Rd (I-25 exit 278), a 6-mile strip of hotels and fast-food restaurants, enters town from the south; Paseo de Peralta circles the center of town; St Francis Dr (I-25 exit 282) forms the western border of downtown and turns into US 285, which heads north toward Los Alamos and Taos. Alameda follows the canal east–west through the center of town, and Guadalupe St is the main north–south street through downtown. Most downtown restaurants, galleries,

NEW MEXICO

SANTA FE IN...

Two Days

After breakfast at kid-friendly **Café Pasqual's** (p322), take in the plaza – particularly the excellent offerings of the **Museum of Fine Arts** (p311), the **Palace of the Governors** (p311) and the Native American jewelry out front. Also make sure to check out the miraculous staircase at the **Loretto Chapel** (p314). All your official tourist duties are over, and it's not even noon.

Have a cheap lunch (save your cash for the art) at **Del Churro Saloon** (p322), then take a walk down **Canyon Rd** (see boxed text, p314), stopping at numerous galleries along the way. Have an afternoon espresso or tea pick-me-up at **Downtown Subscription** (p321), the coffee house of choice for artists and writers, then head to the Shed (p322) for excellent green chile enchiladas, margaritas and fresh guacamole. Continue drinking after dark on the heated porch of **Ore House** (p324), right on the plaza. We think they do the best margs in Santa Fe.

The next morning, it's up and at 'em at **Tia Sophia's** (p322). Make reservations at **Ten Thousand Waves** (see boxed text, p321), then catch the M-line to **Museum Hill** (p310), where you can't skip the **Museum of International Folk Art** (p310). When you've had your fill of museums, grab your bike or lace up your walking shoes and head to the **South Dale Ball Trails** (p316) for some exercise. Now you deserve to relax with a hot stone massage and than a soak in a hillside hot tub at **Ten Thousand Waves** (see boxed text, p321), while watching the moon rise over Santa Fe. Finally it's time to head back to your hotel, the **Inn & Spa at Loretto** (p320). Order room service and just enjoy the kiva fireplace in your room, or spend the evening sipping port in the fabulous Southwestern lobby bar, listening to live acoustic guitar by the roaring fireplace. Ready to move here yet?

Three Days

After two days in Santa Fe, it's time to take a day trip. Hop onto US 285/84 north and spend the morning at the fabulous **Tesuque Flea Market** (p327) searching for cowboy boots and other gems, before stopping for a lunch of prepared-at-your-table guacamole and fajitas on the patio at **Gabriel's** (p324). Continue on NM 502 toward **Los Alamos** (p304), pausing at the **Bradbury Science Museum** (p305) to learn all about WMDs – it's a blast. Then it's back to Santa Fe for a dinner of barbecue brisket quesadillas and a Mescal margarita at the **Cowgirl BBQ & Western Grill** (p323). End your evening listening to live music at the **Second Street Brewery** (p324) in the up-and-coming Railyard District.

NEW MEXICO

SANTA FE

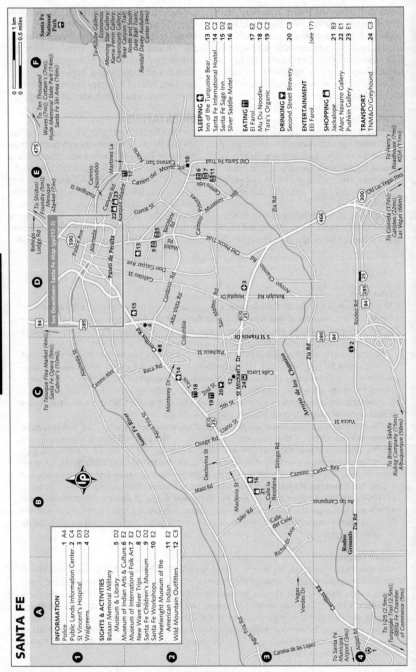

INFORMATION
Police.................................1 A4
Public Lands Information Center..2 C4
St Vincent's Hospital.............3 D3
Walgreens..........................4 D2

SIGHTS & ACTIVITIES
Bataan Memorial Military
  Museum & Library................5 D2
Museum of Indian Arts & Culture..6 E2
Museum of International Folk Art..7 E2
New Wave River Trips.............8 C2
Santa Fe Children's Museum.......9 D2
Wheelwright Museum of the
  American Indian.................10 E2
Santa Fe Workshops...............11 E2
Wild Mountain Outfitters.........12 C3

SLEEPING 🛏
Inn of the Turquoise Bear.........13 D2
Santa Fe International Hostel......14 C2
Santa Fe Sage Inn.................15 D2
Silver Saddle Motel................16 B3

EATING 🍴
El Farol...........................17 E2
Mu Du Noodles.....................18 C2
Tara's Organic....................19 C2

DRINKING 🍷
Second Street Brewery.............20 C3

ENTERTAINMENT 🎭
EEl Farol.........................(see 17)

SHOPPING 🛍
Jackalope.........................21 B3
Marc Navarro Gallery..............22 E1
Pushkin Gallery...................23 E1

TRANSPORT
TNM&O/Greyhound...................24 C3

museums and sites are either on or east of Guadalupe St and are within walking distance of the plaza, in the center of town.

INFORMATION
Bookstores
Collected Works (Map pp312-13; ☎ 505-988-4226; 208B W San Francisco St) Though small, this independently owned store has a good selection of regional, travel and general-interest books.

Downtown Subscription (Map pp312-13; ☎ 505-983-3085; 376 Garcia St) Next door to Garcia Street Books, this has the best newsstand in town and is where the writers come to browse.

Garcia Street Books (Map pp312-13; ☎ 505-986-0151; www.garciastreetbooks.com; 376 Garcia St) Shelves packed with heavily illustrated art and architecture books plus lots of rare and unusual offerings could have you perusing for hours.

Travel Bug (Map pp312-13; ☎ 505-992-0418; www.mapsofnewmexico.com; 839 Paseo de Peralta) For travel books and practically every map you could ever need.

Emergency
Police (Map p308; ☎ 505-955-5000; 2515 Camino Entrada)

Internet Access
CD Café (Map pp312-13; ☎ 505-986-0735; 301 N Guadalupe St; per hr $10; 🖳) Sip coffee or listen to CDs while you surf.

Santa Fe Public Library (Map pp312-13; ☎ 505-955-6781; 145 Washington Ave; 🕑 10am-9pm Mon-Thu,

10am-6pm Fri & Sat, 1pm-5pm Sun; 🖳) Make reservations for a free half-hour of internet access.

Medical Services
St Vincent's Hospital (Map p308; ☎ 505-983-3361; 455 St Michael's Dr) Has 24-hour emergency care.
Walgreens (Map p308; ☎ 505-982-4643; 1096 S St Francis Dr) A 24-hour pharmacy.

Money
It's a tourist town, and all-too-convenient ATMs are everywhere. **Wells Fargo** (Map pp312-13; ☎ 505-984-0424; 241 Washington Ave) changes foreign currency.

Post
Post office (Map pp312-13; ☎ 800-275-8777; 120 S Federal Place)

Tourist Information
New Mexico State Parks (Map pp312-13; ☎ 505-476-3355; www.nmparks.com; 141 E De Vargas St; 🕑 8am-4pm Mon-Fri) This office has information on all state parks and recreation areas, but doesn't reserve campsites.

New Mexico Tourism Bureau (Map pp312-13; ☎ 505-827-7336; www.newmexico.org; 491 Old Santa Fe Trail; 🕑 8am-5pm; 🖳) Housed in the historic 1878 Lamy Building (site of the state's first private college), this friendly place has flyers, information, a hotel reservation line, free coffee and even free internet access on one slow computer.

Public Lands Information Center (Map p308; ☎ 505-438-7542; www.publiclands.org; 1474 Rodeo Rd; 🕑 8:30am-4:30pm Mon-Fri) This place is very helpful,

NEW MEXICO

LOCAL MAGIC: CHRISTMAS EVE ON CANYON RD
On the night before Christmas, Santa Fe is an ethereal site. The city's thousands of adobe buildings glow a warm yellow from the lights of thousands of *farolitos* – real candles nestled in greased brown paper bags – lining streets, entranceways and even the roofs of the adobe homes and shops.

Walking down Santa Fe's most famous gallery avenue, Canyon Rd, on Christmas Eve is a uniquely Santa Fe experience, and in our book a magical must. There's something overwhelmingly graceful and elegant about the taste of the frosty air, the look of miles of glowing pathways of tiny candles and comradely quiet, the way the night sky meets softly lit gallery windows filled with fine art.

The magic comes partly from the intoxicating sights and scents of small piñon and cedarwood bonfires that line the road, offering guiding light and unforgettable memories. Partly it's a few equestrians prancing on horseback, jingle bells jingling, clackity-clacking along the narrow street, evoking memories of early Santa Feans who led their burros up the 'Road of the Canyon' to gather firewood in mountain forests. Partly it's the silhouettes of 250-year-old adobes softly lit by rows of twinkling *farolitos*.

Dress warmly and beat the crowds by arriving early, say by 6pm. You'll still be able to walk the road without mobs at this point. As night falls, the streets fill with human revelers and their canine friends, all giddy with the Christmas spirit. Small groups of carolers sing remarkably in tune. Join them, then pop into a gallery for a cup of spiced cider and a quick perusal of post-communist Russian art to warm up.

with maps and information on public lands throughout New Mexico.

Santa Fe Chamber of Commerce (Map p328; ☎ 505-983-7317; www.santafechamber.com; ☾ 8am-5pm) Inconveniently located at the Cerrillos exit from I-25, in the Premium Outlet Mall, this chamber has information for residents and visitors.

Visitor Center (Map pp312-13; ☎ 505-955-6200, 800-777-2489; www.santafe.org; 201 W Marcy St; ☾ 8am-5pm Mon-Fri) Conveniently located at the Sweeny Convention Center.

SIGHTS

While you're here in one of the top-rated arts towns in the United States, plan to spend time in some of the city's museums. Choices range from confrontational, political, Native American art to eye-popping modern art to Spanish and international folk art. In 2005, the UN officially designated Santa Fe one of the world's premier Creative Cities, the first US city to be so recognized.

Most museums are clustered in two primary locations – around the downtown plaza and on **Museum Hill** where four excellent museums, a research library and a recommended café all are linked by a sculpture-lined trail. Since it's almost 3 miles southwest of the plaza, unless you're really up for the walk, take the M Line – a Santa Fe Trails bus geared toward visitors – that winds through historical neighborhoods.

Many museums and other attractions offer discounts to senior citizens and discounts or free admission to New Mexico residents, at least on certain days of the week. Also, log on to www.museumhill.org for special-events calendars and links to all four Museum Hill institutions.

The Plaza

Santa Fe's plaza is the heart of the town, and dates back to the city's beginning in 1610. Between 1821 and 1880 the plaza served as the end of the Santa Fe Trail, and traders from as far away as Missouri drove here in their wagons laden with goods. Today, Native Americans sell their jewelry and pottery along the wall of the Palace of the Governors, kids skateboard and play hacky sack and tourists weighed down with cameras and purchases wander through the grassy center on their way to the next shop, museum or margarita. If you're hungry, the food stalls here are a great place to grab a snack.

Museums of New Mexico

This is a collection of four very different **museums** (☎ 505-827-6463; single museum adult/child $8/free, 4-day pass to all 4 museums adult/child $18/free; ☾ 10am-5pm Tue-Sun), two of them on Museum Hill and two on the plaza, also offer seminars, musical events and a variety of guided tours with historic or artistic focuses, many designed for children. Both the Palace of the Governors and Museum of Fine Arts, the two located on the plaza, are free on Friday from 5pm to 8pm. All the museums have fabulous gift shops.

On Museum Hill, the **Museum of International Folk Art** (Map p308; ☎ 505-476-1200; www.moifa.org; 706 Camino Lejo) houses more than 100,000 objects from more than 100 countries and is arguably the best museum in Santa Fe. The exhibits aren't simplistically arranged behind glass

---

TOP TIP: SHOPPING FOR NATIVE AMERICAN ART IN SANTA FE

The best place for shopping is the under the *portales* (overhangs) in front of the Palace of Governors. This is where the Native Americans come – some as far as 200 miles a day – to sell their gorgeous handmade jewelry. The artists selling their wares here are part of a state initiative that allows Native American artists to sell jewelry and art in front of the palace. It's a tradition that began in the 1880s, when Tesuque artisans began meeting the train with all manner of wares. Today up to 1200 members, representing almost every New Mexican tribe, draw lots for the 76 spaces under the vigas each morning. Those lucky enough to procure the desirable spots spread their wares – bracelets, pendants, fetishes and thick engraved silver wedding bands – on colorful woven Navajo blankets, covering the hard 17th-century sidewalks on which they sit between 8am and around 2pm Monday through Saturday. Turquoise and silver are materials of choice, but you'll find many other regional stones in a rainbow of colors. The artists are generally a friendly lot, happy to tell you the story behind each piece in his or her open-air gallery – and most are one-of-a-kinds. Not only are the prices better (don't barter though, unless it's suggested, as many artists find this insulting) here than in a store, but the money goes directly back to the source, the artist.

RAILYARD RENAISSANCE

Santa Fe is about to get even more cultured. Or at least that's what the **Railyard District** developers are hoping. Either way, starting around August 2008, the city's historic Railyard District – the railroads were the first to promote tourism to New Mexico back in the 19th century – will emerge from years of planning and construction to be the city's next oasis of arts, entertainment and recreation, aimed at a hip, young urban market. A post-grunge industrial neighborhood spread over 50 acres of land just south of the hip Guadalupe District (on Guadalupe St), the Railyard is the city's largest development project in decades.

It's already home to a number of cool shops, not to mention Santa Fe's best brew pub (**Second Street Brewery**, p324, which has rocking live acts most nights of the week) and a 400-year-old irrigation ditch, **Acequia Madre**, which was built by Spanish farmers and still flows in years of normal rainfall. It's also home to the **Santa Fe Southern Railway** (p318), which runs both passenger and freight trains from the historic depot. The improved Railyard District will also boast new museums and galleries and become the permanent home of Santa Fe's ever-popular farmers market – currently held in a parking lot off the Plaza. A movie theater, shops, restaurant and living and work spaces for artists are also planned. The southern portion of the neighborhood will be left semi-wild as a giant park with shady areas, paths, outdoor performance space, a crafty children's playground and lots of native gardens.

cases; the historical and cultural information is concise and thorough; and a festive feel permeates the rooms. The Hispanic wing displays religious art, tin work, jewelry and textiles from northern New Mexico and throughout the Spanish colonial empire, dating from the 1600s to the present.

The **Museum of Fine Arts** (Map pp312-13; ☎ 505-476-5072; www.museumofnewmexico.org; 107 Palace Ave; ⊙ tours 1:30pm) features works by regional artists and sponsors regular gallery talks and slide lectures. It was built in 1918, and the architecture is an excellent example of the original Santa Fe–style adobe. With more than 20,000 pieces – including collections of the Taos Society of Artists, Santa Fe Society of Artists and other legendary collectives – it's a who's who of the geniuses who put this dusty town on par with Paris and New York.

The **Palace of the Governors** (Map pp312-13; ☎ 505-476-5100; www.museumofnewmexico.org; 100 Palace Ave) is one of the oldest public buildings in the country. Built in 1610 by Spanish officials, it housed thousands of villagers when the Indians revolted in 1680 and was home to the territorial governors after 1846. Since 1909 the building has been a museum, with more than 17,000 historical objects reflecting Santa Fe's Indian, Spanish, Mexican and American heritage. Volunteers lead free, highly recommended palace tours throughout the day; call for exact times.

The **Museum of Indian Arts & Culture** (Map p308; ☎ 505-476-1250; www.miaclab.org; 710 Camino Lejo)

opened in 1987 to display artifacts unearthed by the Laboratory of Anthropology, which must confirm that any proposed building site in New Mexico is not historically significant. Since 1931 it has collected over 50,000 artifacts. Rotating exhibits explore the historical and contemporary lives of the Pueblo, Navajo and Apache cultures.

Georgia O'Keeffe Museum

The renowned painter first visited New Mexico in 1917 and lived in Abiquiú, a village 45 minutes northwest of Santa Fe, from 1949 until her death in 1986 (see boxed text, p330). Possessing the world's largest collection of her work, this **museum** (Map pp312-13; ☎ 505-946-1000; www.okeeffemuseum.org; 217 Johnson St; adult/child $8/free; ⊙ 10am-5pm Sat-Thu, 10am 8pm Fri, galleries closed Wed Nov-Jun) showcases the thick brushwork and luminous colors that don't always come through on ubiquitous posters; take your time to relish them here firsthand. Housed in a former Spanish Baptist church with adobe walls that have been renovated to form 10 sky-lighted galleries.

St Francis Cathedral

Jean Baptiste Lamy was sent to Santa Fe by the pope with orders to tame the Wild Western outpost town through culture and religion. Convinced that the town needed a focal point for religious life, he began construction of this cathedral in 1869. Lamy's story has been immortalized in Willa Cather's book *Death*

NEW MEXICO

DOWNTOWN SANTA FE

NEW MEXICO

INFORMATION
CD Cafe.................................1 D2
Collected Works.....................2 E3
Downtown Subscription..........(see 43)
Garcia Street Books................(see 43)
New Mexico State Parks..........3 F5
New Mexico Tourism Bureau......4 F5
Post Office............................5 F2
Santa Fe Public Library............6 F3
Travel Bug............................7 H4
Visitor Center........................8 F2
Wells Fargo...........................9 G2

SIGHTS & ACTIVITIES
Absolute Nirvana Spa & Tea
   Room...............................10 H4
Avanyu Spa..........................(see 33)
Georgia O'Keeffe Museum........11 E3
High Desert Angler.................12 D5
Institute of American Indian
   Arts Museum......................13 F4
Loretto Chapel......................14 F4
Melo Velo Cycles...................15 F4
Museum of Fine Arts...............16 F3
Palace of the Governors...........17 F3
St Francis Cathedral................18 G4
San Miguel Mission.................19 F5
Santa Fe Mountain Sports........20 D6
Santa Fe School of Cooking.....(see 70)
Santa Fe Southern Railway
   Depot...............................21 C5
Santuario de Guadalupe..........22 D4
SITE Santa Fe.......................23 C6
Spa Terre.............................(see 27)
State Capitol.........................24 F5

SLEEPING
Garrett's Desert Inn.................25 F5
Hotel St Francis......................26 F4
Inn & Spa at Loretto...............27 F4
Inn of the Anasazi...................28 F3
Inn of the Five Graces.............29 F5
Inn of the Governors...............30 E4
Inn on the Alameda.................31 H4
La Fonda..............................32 G4
La Posada de Santa Fe.............33 H4
Old Santa Fe Inn....................34 E4

EATING
Al Di La...............................35 E4
Andiamo!.............................36 D5
Bert's La Tacqueria.................37 D2
Café des Artistes...................38 H5
Café Pasqual's......................39 F4
Cantina at the Coyote Café.......40 E4
Compound...........................41 H5
Cowgirl BBQ & Western Grill.....42 D4
Del Churro Saloon..................(see 30)
Downtown Subscription............43 H6
French Pastry Shop.................(see 32)
Geronimo.............................44 H5
Railyard Restaurant & Saloon....45 C5
Ristra..................................46 D4
Santa Fe Farmers Market..........47 C6
SantaCafé............................48 G2
Shed...................................49 G3
Tia Sophia's.........................50 E3
Tomasita's............................51 C5
Winter Market.......................52 C5
Zia Diner.............................53 D4

DRINKING
Belltower Bar.........................(see 32)
Dragon Room Bar...................54 F5
Evangelo's............................55 F3
La Fiesta Lounge....................(see 32)
Ore House............................56 F3
Sleeping Dog Tavern...............57 F3

ENTERTAINMENT
Cowgirl BBQ & Western Grill....(see 42)
Lensic Performing Arts Theater..58 E3
Santa Fe Playhouse.................59 F5
Santa Fe Symphony.................(see 58)
Vanessie of Santa Fe...............60 D3
Warehouse 21.......................61 C5
Willie's Blues Bar...................62 D4

SHOPPING
78th St Gallery......................63 H4
Bodhi Bazaar.........................64 D4
Garcia Street Books................(see 43)
Gerald Peters Gallery...............65 H5
Linda Durham Contemporary
   Art.................................66 G6
Nambe Foundry Outlet............67 F3
Nathalie..............................68 H5
Nedra Mateucci Galleries.........69 G6
Plaza Mercado.......................70 F3
Seret & Sons........................71 E4

TRANSPORT
Santa Fe Trails......................72 F3

N Guadalupe St

Paseo de Peralta

Jose

Park Ave

60

Footbridges
Park   Alameda

W Water St

Alto St

Maynard

Barela

Closson St

Pacheco

Casados

Don Felix

Agua Fria St

Dudrow St

Debruri St

W De Vargas

Aztec St

64 53

62

S Guadalupe St

Montezuma

Romero St

Railroad
District

21

51

Garfield

Sandoval

W Manhattan Ave

45

12

Read

W Manhattan Ave

Cerrillos Rd

61

52

23

Hickox St

20

Paseo de Peralta

St Francis Dr

47

W Gomez Rd

Don Diego

Don Cubero

Gomez Rd

@
37

46

42

36

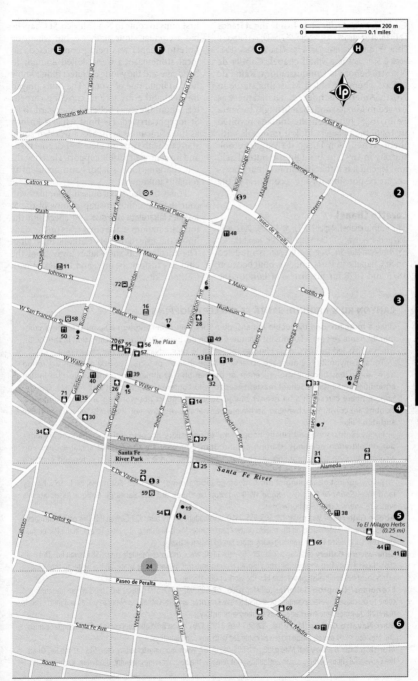

Comes for the Archbishop. Inside the **St Francis Cathedral** (Map pp312-13; ☎ 505-982-5619; 131 Cathedral Place; ☻ 8am-5pm, mass 7am & 5pm Mon-Sat, 8am, 10am, noon & 5pm Sun) is a small chapel, Capilla de Nuestra Señora la Conquistadora, Reina de la Paz, where the oldest Madonna statue in North America is housed. The statue was carved in Mexico and then brought to Santa Fe in 1625, but when the Indians revolted in 1680, the villagers took it into exile with them. When Don Diego de Vargas retook the city in 1692, he brought the statue back, and legend has it that its extraordinary powers are responsible for the reconquest of the city.

Loretto Chapel

The gothic **chapel** (Map pp312-13; ☎ 505-982-0092; www .lorettochapel.com; 207 Old Santa Fe Trail; admission $3; ☻ 9am-6pm May-Sep, 9am-5pm Oct-Apr) is modeled on St Chapelle in Paris, and was built between 1873 and 1878 for the Sisters of Loretto, the first nuns to come to New Mexico. St Chapelle has a circular stone staircase, but when the Loretto Chapel was being constructed, no local stonemasons were skilled enough to build one and the young architect didn't know how to build one of wood. The nuns prayed for help and a mysterious traveling carpenter, whom the nuns believed afterward to be St Joseph, arrived. He built what is known as the Miraculous Staircase, a wooden spiral staircase with two complete 360-degree turns and no central or visible support. He left without charging for his labors and his identity remains unknown.

Today the chapel is a museum popular with tourists who come to snap photos of the **St Joseph's Miraculous Staircase** and check out the intricate stations of the cross casts on the walls lining the aisle to the very Catholic main altar. The adjacent gift shop takes away from the church's historic beauty, and is packed with Catholic kitsch.

CANYON RD & AROUND: SANTA FE GALLERY-HOPPING

Once a footpath used by Pueblo Indians, then the main street through a Spanish farming community, Santa Fe's most famous art avenue, Canyon Rd, began its current incarnation in the 1920s, when artists led by Los Cincos Pintores moved in to take advantage of the cheap rent.

Today Canyon Rd is a must-see attraction. More than 90 of Santa Fe's 300 galleries are found here, and it has become the epicenter of the nation's healthiest art scene. From rare Indian antiquities to Santa Fe School masterpieces to wild contemporary work, it's all for sale. Gallery-hopping here can seem a bit overwhelming, so we'd suggest not worrying and just wandering. Exhibits are constantly changing, so have a peek in the window; you'll quickly tell what you like and don't like.

Friday nights are a particularly happy time to go gallery-hopping – that's when the galleries put on glittering openings, starting around 5pm. Not only are these great social events, you also can browse while nibbling on cheese, sipping chardonnay or sparkling cider and chatting to the artist.

Below are just a sampling of our Canyon Rd (and around) favorites. For more, pick up a handy (and free) *Santa Fe & Canyon Road Walking Map* or check out the Santa Fe Gallery Association's website, www.santafegalleries.net.

Adobe Gallery (off Map p308; ☎ 505-955-0550; www.adobegallery.com; 221 Canyon Rd) This gallery includes pieces by the 'Five Matriarchs' of the pueblo pottery renaissance: Maria Martinez, Margaret Tofoya, Maria Nampeyo, Lucy Lewis and Helen Cordero, among many other famed Indian artisans.

Chiaroscuro Gallery (off Map p308; ☎ 505-992-1100; www.chiaroscurosantafe.com; 558 Canyon Rd) This sophisticated and often abstract collection moved recently into this glorious large space, all the better to showcase extravagant yet minimalist modernism like the work of Udo Noger.

Economos/Hampton Galleries (off Map p308; ☎ 505-982-6347; 500 Canyon Rd) This is where museums come to purchase fantastic examples of ancient Native American art, pre-Columbian Mexican pieces and much, much more, all crammed onto two huge floors swirling with history.

Marc Navarro Gallery (Map p308; ☎ 505-986-8191; 520 Canyon Rd) Collectors come to find antique Spanish and Mexican silver pieces, including jewelry studded with onyx and amethyst.

Morning Star Gallery (off Map p308; ☎ 505-982-8187; www.morningstargallery.com; 513 Canyon Rd) Of all the Canyon Rd shops dealing Indian antiquities, this remains the best: weavings, jewelry, beadwork, kachina dolls

The chapel is one of the top places to get married in Santa Fe (it's non-denominational). After the ceremonies (which are not open to the public, and consequently, should someone rent the chapel for a wedding when you plan on visiting, it will be closed for a few hours) the newlyweds are often led across the plaza to the tunes and dancing of a colorfully costumed mariachi band, a true Santa Fe tradition – snapping a few photos makes up for the annoyance of having to wait to see the special staircase.

San Miguel Mission

The original construction of this **mission** (Map pp312-13; ☎ 505-983-3974; 401 Old Santa Fe Trail; admission $1; ☘ 9am-5pm Mon-Sat, 10am-4pm Sun, mass 5pm Sun) was started in 1625, and it served as a mission church for the Spanish settlers' Tlaxcalan Indian servants, who had been brought from Mexico. Though considered the oldest church in the United States, much

of the original building was destroyed during the Pueblo Revolt of 1680, and it was rebuilt in 1710, with new walls added to what remained.

Santuario de Guadalupe

The adobe **church** (Map pp312-13; ☎ 505-988-2027; 100 Guadalupe St; admission free; ☘ 9am-4pm Mon-Sat) is the oldest extant shrine to Our Lady of Guadalupe, the patroness of the poor in Mexico. It was constructed between 1776 and 1796 near the end of the Camino Real, a 1500-mile trading route from Mexico that ended in Santa Fe. There have been several additions and renovations since. The oil-on-canvas Spanish baroque *retablo* (altar painting) inside the chapel was painted in Mexico in 1783 by José de Alzíbar. For the trip to Santa Fe, the painting had to be taken apart and transported up the Camino Real in pieces on mule back. Look closely to see the seams where the painting was put back together.

and even a few original ledger drawings are just some of the stars at this stunning gallery, which specializes in pre-WWII Plains Indian ephemera. Some artifacts here are finer than those in most museums – like the 1775 Powhoge ceramic storage jar that sold for $225,000 and the 1860 Nez Perce war shirt that went for $220,000.

Pushkin Gallery (Map p308; ☎ 505-982-1990; www.pushkingallery.com; 550 Canyon Rd) Owned by the family of poet Alexander Pushkin, this gallery shows Russian masters including Nikolai Timkov and Vasily Golubev, who are outshone by newcomer Alexy Smirnov Vókressensky; museum-quality Orthodox icons and lacquer boxes are also on display.

The following galleries are off Canyon Rd, but worth visiting for their unique mediums and creations.

78th St Gallery (Map pp312-13; ☎ 505-820-0250; www.78thstreet.gallery.com; cnr Alameda St & Delgado Ave) Open by appointment only, this gallery just off Canyon Rd features unique paintings by local and international artists that focus on color, movement and spirit. Also check the website.

Gerald Peters Gallery (Map pp312-13; ☎ 505-954-5700; www.gpgallery.com; 1011 Paseo de Peralta) Santa Fe's preeminent restaurant and real-estate tycoon Gerald Peters' gallery, two blocks from Canyon Rd, carries a collection of fine art that few museums can touch, with all the Southwest masters: Nicolai Fechin, Charles Russell, Edward Borein, Woody Gwyn and many, many more. The back room has treasures the Museum of Fine Arts can't even afford.

Linda Durham Contemporary Art (Map pp312-13; ☎ 505-466-6600; www.lindadurham.com; 1101 Paseo de Peralta) Representing emerging and mid-career artists working in all media, this gallery focus on stimulating, elegant and original pieces that represent contemporary issues in culture, society and politics. Good-value investment pieces are often scored here.

Nedra Matteucci Galleries (Map pp312-13; ☎ 505-982-4631; www.matteucci.com; 1075 Paseo de Peralta) The Taos Society is on display at this top gallery, which shows the best work of Joseph Henry Sharp, Ernest Blumenschein and the rest of the gang. Don't miss the beautiful gardens out back, which have monumental sculptures in stone and bronze, including work by *Vietnam Women's Memorial* designer Glenna Goodacre.

Ted Flicker Sculpture (www.tedflicker.com) Open by appointment only – check the website to set things up. Ted's unique bronze sculptures focus on truth and beauty; many are inspired by his wife Barbara. Flicker is the writer and director of the 1967 comedic classic *The President's Analyst,* and the creator of the popular 1970s TV show *Barney Miller.*

NEW MEXICO

Other Attractions

Primarily showing work by students and faculty of the esteemed four-year **Institute of American Indian Arts Museum** (Map pp312-13; ☎ 505-983-8900; www.iaia.edu; 108 Cathedral Place; adult/child $8/4; ☻ 9am-5pm), this place also features the finest offerings of Native American artists from tribes across the US. It's an excellent place to see beautiful art and understand its role in Native American culture.

In 1937 Mary Cabot established the **Wheelwright Museum of the American Indian** (Map p308; ☎ 505-982-4636; www.wheelwright.org; 704 Camino Lejo; admission by donation; ☻ 10am-5pm Mon-Sat, 1-5pm Sun), part of Museum Hill, to showcase Navajo ceremonial art. While its strength continues to be Navajo exhibits, it now includes contemporary Native American art and historical artifacts. The gift store offers an extensive selection of books and crafts.

The **State Capitol** (Map pp312-13; ☎ 505-986-4589; cnr Paseo de Peralta & Old Santa Fe Trail; ☻ guided tours 10am & 2pm Mon-Fri), locally referred to as the Roundhouse, is the center of New Mexico's government and was designed after the state symbol, the Zia sign. It also has one of the best (free) art collections in New Mexico. Self-guided tours are possible.

An enormous, whitewashed space, the 8000-sq-ft **SITE Santa Fe** (Map pp312-13; ☎ 505-989-1199; www.sitesantafe.org; 1606 Paseo de Peralta; adult/student $10/5, free Sun; ☻ 10am-5pm Wed, Thu & Sat, 10am-7pm Fri, noon-5pm Sun, tours 6pm Fri, 2pm Sat & Sun) is a nonprofit art museum dedicated to presenting world-class contemporary art to the community. From radical installation pieces to cutting-edge multimedia exhibitions, this hybrid museum-gallery takes art to the next level. It also hosts wine-splashed openings, artist talks, movie screenings and performances of all kinds.

Five miles north of Santa Fe in Tesuque, the **Shidoni Foundry** (Map p328; ☎ 505-988-8001; Bishop's Lodge Rd) is an 8-acre apple orchard devoted to bronze sculptures. Founded in 1971, it has evolved into a world-renowned fine art casting facility and showplace. A gallery hosts changing exhibits, and there is a year-round outdoor sculpture garden on the lawn. Every Saturday, you can watch 2000°F molten bronze being poured into ceramic shell molds, one of several steps in the complex lost-wax casting technique.

ACTIVITIES

Although Santa Fe's museums, churches, galleries and shops are absolutely top notch, visitors do not live by art appreciation alone. Get thee to the great outdoors. Several sporting shops dispensing information, providing guides and renting equipment for outdoor activities include **Santa Fe Mountain Sports** (Map pp312-13; ☎ 505-988-3337; 607 Cerrillos Rd) and **Wild Mountain Outfitters** (Map p308; ☎ 505-986-1152; 815 St Michaels Dr).

Skiing

The **Santa Fe Ski Area** (☎ 505-982-4429, snow report 505-983-9155; www.skisantafe.com; lift ticket adult/child $54/39; ☻ 9am-4pm late Nov-Apr) is a half-hour, very scenic and winding drive from the plaza up Hwy 475. Recently expanded, it has a brand-new super chair that rides you to one of the highest summits in North America (12,075ft). Briefly admire the 80,000 sq miles of desert and mountain vistas, then fly down powder glade shoots, steep bump runs or long groomers. The resort caters to families and expert skiers alike with its varied terrain. On weekends from June through August and for a couple weeks during fall foliage, the chairlift is open (one way/round trip $7/10). There's also an expansive system of hiking trails.

Cottam's (off Map p308; ☎ 505-982-0495; Hyde Park Rd), on the way to the slopes, has reasonable prices on ski-gear packages (adult/child $27/15) and also rents snowshoes ($12).

There are numerous cross-country ski trails in the Jemez Mountains and the Santa Fe National Forest. Contact the Public Lands Information Center (p309).

Mountain Biking

Some of the best intermediate single track in New Mexico is found on the **North and South Dale Ball Trail System**, which encompass more than 20 miles of paved and unpaved bike and hiking trails through some of Santa Fe's most exclusive neighborhoods and features fabulous views of unspoiled mountains and deserts. Trails vary in length and difficulty – the **South Dale Ball Trails** are the most challenging. To get to the south trails follow Upper Canyon Rd north to the well-signed parking lot at Cerro Gordo Rd – there is a great **dog park** across the street from here. The ride from this parking lot is our favorite, but beware it starts with a super-long, hard and rocky single-track climb, followed by a series of harrowing switchbacks. You'll be rewarded richly, however, with loads of supreme isolation and outstanding views.

The 10-mile **Windsor Trail** traverses part of the North Dale Ball Trail System and is one of the most popular intermediate bike treks in the state. The scenery – particularly in the fall and winter – is outstanding. The route begins at Little Tesuque in Hyde Park and climbs steadily upward to serve as the spine of several other multiuse trails, including the bike-friendly Chamiza Loops.

Race the trains on the **Santa Fe Rail Trail**. Beginning at the Santa Fe Southern Railway Depot, this 18-mile trail follows the rail line clear to Lamy. The trail is unpaved until you hit Agua Fria St, then paved the rest of the way, though mountain bikers can take a dirt turnoff at the intersection with US 285 to avoid following CR 33 into Lamy.

If you need to rent a ride, visit **Melo Velo Bicycles** (Map pp312-13; ☎ 505-982-8986; www.sunmountain bikeco.com; 102 E Water St, El Centro gallery; rentals per hr/day $9/45; ☻ 9:30am-5pm Mon-Sat, 10am-4pm Sun). It also has information about trails throughout the region and offers half-day to 10-day tours.

White-Water Rafting

Santa Fe's white-water rafting outfits head to tiny Pilar for rafting on the Rio Grande between Santa Fe and Taos. The renowned Class IV **Taos Box**, which traverses 16 miles of spectacular wilderness gorge, is fantastically fun but not for the faint of heart – rafters must be at least 12 years old and experienced. If you want thrilling waves without as much chance of spills, then try the Class III **Racecourse**, also on the Rio Grande. It's fine for kids over 6. The Class III **Rio Chama** is often rafted as a multiday trip with camping supplies and food included. The day trips, through dramatic Rio Grande Gorge, are great excursions and are easily arranged from May through October.

New Wave River Trips (Map p308; ☎ 505-984-1444, 800-984-1444; www.newwaverafting.com; 1101 Cerrillos Rd; ☻ 9am-5pm) is one of the most popular outfitters in Santa Fe. It runs the Taos Box ($115) and also does a half-day trip down the Racecourse (adult/child $52/42). To amp up the excitement factor on either trip, trying running the river in a 'funyak,' an inflatable kayak that leaves the driving up to you. New Wave also offers overnight rafting trips – check the website for more info.

Hiking

Just walking around Santa Fe can be quite strenuous because of the 7000ft elevation. Spend a day or two acclimatizing before rushing off into the mountains of the **Santa Fe National Forest**, immediately to the east of town. The heart of the national forest is the undeveloped **Pecos Wilderness**, with trails leading to several peaks over 12,000ft. Nearly 1000 miles of trails, forming a complex web, are suitable for short hikes and multiday backpacking trips.

Weather changes rapidly in the mountains and summer storms are frequent, especially in the afternoons, so check weather reports; hike prepared. The trails are usually closed by snow in winter, and higher trails may be closed through May.

Maps and thorough area hiking information is available from the very helpful Public Lands Information Center (p309).

The most immediately accessible hiking trails are found on the city's Dale Ball Trail System just east of downtown. There are parking lots and maps on Hyde Park Rd and Upper Canyon Rd – see opposite.

Also in the vicinity, **Hyde Memorial State Park** (Map p328; ☎ 505-983-7175; Hwy 475; per car per day $5), northeast of Santa Fe near the ski base, offers a number of hikes. Try the 5-mile Borrego-Bear Wallow Loop to Tesuque Creek, which starts at the north end of Hyde Memorial State Park.

Protecting 135 acres along the acequia of Santa Fe Canyon, just 4 miles from the plaza, the **Randall Davey Audubon Center** (off Map p308; ☎ 505-983-4609; www.nm.audubon.org; 1800 Upper Canyon Rd; trail use $2; ☻ 9am-4pm Mon-Fri, 9am-2pm Sat) has information on the juniper and piñon forest's coyotes, bobcats and other wildlife. It's near the trailhead for the 3-mile **Bear Canyon Trail**, which leads into the steep-sided canyon.

Fishing

New Mexico's truly outstanding fishing holes are better accessed from Taos (p332) and the Enchanted Circle, but there are plenty of opportunities around Santa Fe, including Abiquiú, Nambé Lakes and Rio Chama. You'll need a license – available at tack shops like the **High Desert Angler** (Map pp312-13; ☎ 505-988-7688; www .highdesertangler.com; 451 Cerrillos Rd; ☻ 8am-6pm Mon-Sat & 11am-4pm Sun Jun-Aug, 10-am-6pm Mon-Sat Sep-May), which also sells a large selection of gear and offers guided excursions to private streams (one/two people from $275/350). A one-day, state-required license is $22.

COURSES

If you develop a love for New Mexican cuisine, try cooking lessons at the **Santa Fe School of Cooking** (Map pp312-13; ☎ 505-983-4511; www.santafeschool

NEW MEXICO

ofcooking.com; Plaza Mercado), which specializes in Southwestern cuisine. Class are three hours long and cost between $60 and $80, including the meal.

Santa Fe Workshops (Map p308; ☎ 505-983-1400; www.santafeworkshops.com; Mt Carmel Rd) help you develop your inner Ansel Adams awareness at week-long traditional photography and digital imagery workshops (classes $795 to $1200). Meals and lodging are extra.

SANTA FE FOR CHILDREN

Check *Pasatiempo*, the Friday arts and entertainment section of the *Santa Fe New Mexican*, for its 'Bring the Kids' column, which has a rundown on area events for children. Also look for the free local newspaper, *New Mexico Kids*, published six times a year, for great day-by-day event calendars.

The **Santa Fe Children's Museum** (Map p308; ☎ 505-989-8359; www.santafechildrensmuseum.org; 1050 Old Pecos Trail; admission $8; ☺ 10am-5pm Wed-Sat, noon-5pm Sun; ♿) features hands-on exhibits on science and art for young children, but adults will enjoy it as well. The museum runs daily two-hour programs (usually at 10am or 2:30pm), led by local scientists, artists and teachers, which tackle subjects like solar energy and printmaking.

The amazing Museum of International Folk Art (p310) has a fantastic big indoor play area with books, Lego and other toys. It is perfect rainy-day entertainment for your little one.

If you're traveling with a budding thespian, check out the backstage tours of the Santa Fe Opera (p325) during opera season. They are interesting, and free for folks under 17.

Most restaurants, except those that are seriously upscale, are happy to host your kids, and most have special menus – but only the Cowgirl BBQ & Western Grill (p323) has a playground *and* a full bar. One of Santa Fe's top breakfast spots, Café Pasqual's (p322), is also very child friendly.

If you want to get out on your own, **Magical Happenings Babysitting** (☎ 982-9327) can have sitters stay with your kids in your hotel room; it's $16 an hour for one child or $18 an hour for two, with a four-hour minimum, and reservations should be made in advance, particularly during the high season.

TOURS

Several companies offer walking and bus tours of Santa Fe and northern New Mexico. Others organize guided trips to the pueblos, as well as air tours and biking, hiking, rafting and horseback-riding trips.

A Well-Born Guide/Have PhD, Will Travel (☎ 505-988-8022; www.swguides.com; tours from $18) If the name doesn't lure you in, then the tours will. Run by Stefanie Beninato, an informative local historian who has a knack for good storytelling, these lively trips receive excellent feedback from past participants. Stefanie offers a variety of themed hikes and walks around Santa Fe, which focus on everything from bars and former brothels to ghosts, architecture and, of course, art. One of the unique tours is the Jewish legacy trip, which gets particularly good reviews from participants. Multiday trips around New Mexico are also offered.

Santa Fe Southern Railway (Map pp312-13; ☎ 505-989-8600; www.sfsr.com; 410 S Guadalupe St; ☺ 9am-5pm Mon-Sat, 11am-5pm Sun) Offers several scenic rides using the old spur line. The most popular run, a four-hour day trip (adult $32 to $55, child $18 to $42), takes you past the Galisteo Basin and to the fairly ghostly town of Lamy. Several other themed trips are also offered.

FESTIVALS & EVENTS

The **Santa Fe Visitors Bureau** (www.santafe.org) provides an excellent list of events, musical and theatrical productions and museum shows. Some of the biggies include the following.

ART Feast (www.artfeast.com) Eat your way around Santa Fe's galleries during this weekend-long festival (late February) that incorporates, art, food, wine and fashion and benefits art programs for Santa Fe children.

Pride on the Plaza (www.santafehra.org) Drag queens, parades, floats, a film festival, music, comedy and more; area bars and restaurants throw special bashes for a full week in mid-June when everyone flies the rainbow flag.

Rodeo de Santa Fe (☎ 505-471-4300; www.rodeo desantafe.org; admission $8-30) For more than half a century, wranglers, ranchers and cowpokes, along with plenty of rhinestone cow-persons, have been gathering to watch those bucking broncos, clowns in barrels, lasso tricks and fancy shooting. A pre-rodeo parade takes it all downtown. Held in late June.

Santa Fe Indian Market (☎ 983-5220; www.swaia.org) Only the best get approved to show their work at this world-famous juried show (held the weekend after the third Thursday in August), where more than 1000 artists from 100 tribes and pueblos exhibit. As if that's not enough, 100,000 visitors converge on the plaza, at open studios, gallery shows and the Native Cinema Showcase (www

.ccasantafe.org). Get there Friday or Saturday to see pieces competing for the prestigious top prizes (they get snapped up by collectors), but wait until Sunday if you want to try bargaining.

Spanish Market (☎ 505-982-2226; www.spanish market.org) Traditional Spanish Colonial arts, from *retablos* and *bultos* to handcrafted furniture and metalwork, make this juried show in late July an artistic extravaganza, second only to the Indian Market. Another Spanish Market is held in early December at the Sweeny Convention Center.

Santa Fe Fiestas (☎ 505-988-7575; www.santafe fiesta.org) Two weeks of events in early September celebrate the September 4, 1692, resettlement of Santa Fe, including concerts, a carnival, parades, a candlelight procession and the torching of Will Shuster's Zozobra (a 50ft-tall wooden man).

Wine & Chile Fiesta (☎ 505-483-8060; www .santafewineandchile.org) It's a gourmet's fantasy fiesta, with wine tastings and fine cuisine; dinner events sell out early. Late September.

Las Posadas On December 24, all of Santa Fe is illuminated with *farolitos*; carolers and revelers chow *biscochitos*, drink hot chocolate and make merry.

SLEEPING

Rates vary from week to week and day to day. Generally, January and February offer the lowest rates – cut by as much as 50% from what's listed here. September, October, March and April generally have midrange rates. In December and during the summer (particularly during Indian Market in August and on opera nights), expect to pay premium prices. Make reservations well in advance. Remember: prices do not include taxes and other add-ons of 11% to 15%.

Many agencies can help with reservations, including **Santa Fe Stay** (☎ 505-820-2468, 800-995-2272; www.santafestay.com), specializing in home stays, ranch resorts and casitas.

Most of the low-budget and national chain options line Cerrillos Rd between I-25 and downtown. There are a number of great midrange options.

When it comes to luxury accommodations, Santa Fe has more than its share of intimate hotels and posh B&Bs ready to cater to your every whim. Book through an internet consolidator for the best rates.

The Santa Fe National Forest (p317) and the Pecos Wilderness (p317) also have numerous camping sites. Stop by the Public Lands Information Center (p309) for maps and detailed information.

The Plaza & Canyon Rd

Hotel St Francis (Map pp312-13; ☎ 505-983-5700; www.ho telstfrancis.com; 210 Don Gaspar Ave; r $75-150; ▣) Rates are pretty good for being plaza-side, but this hotel's glory days were the 1930s and '40s. Still, guest rooms still whisper elegance in a decadently aging old European way and the trademark afternoon tea continues in the lobby.

Garrett's Desert Inn (Map pp312-13; ☎ 505-982-1851; www.garrettsdesertinn.com; 311 Old Santa Fe Trail; r $80-175; ▣ wi-fi) An old motor court–style place, Garret's has been popular with travelers for half a century now. Rooms have been recently renovated, and now boast a Southwestern theme. The heated pool is a plus. Families can book into one of the large suites.

Old Santa Fe Inn (Map pp312-13; ☎ 800-745-9910; www .oldsantafeinn.com; 320 Galisteo St; r $90-205; ▣ wi-fi) Just a few blocks from the plaza, rates vary wildly depending on season and occupancy. Rooms are a bit tight, but nicely decorated. The breakfast burrito bar is fabulous in the morning.

Inn of the Governors (Map pp312-13; ☎ 505-982-4333; www.innofthegovernors.com; 101 W Alameda; r $129-190; ▣ ▣ wi-fi) You can't beat the location, just blocks from the plaza. Rooms are elegantly decorated with kiva fireplaces, warm-hued bedspreads and Southwestern-style doors and windows. It's an intimate place to slumber. Don't miss the adjoining Del Churro Saloon, with some of the cheapest eats downtown.

Inn on the Alameda (Map pp312-13; ☎ 505-984-2121; www.innonthealameda.com; 303 E Alameda St; r from $175; ▣ ▣) Handmade furniture, kiva fireplaces, luxe linens, elegant breakfasts and afternoon wine-and-cheese receptions bring B&B-style elegance to a pleasantly efficient hotel. The staff can also arrange cooking classes, fly-fishing, outdoor adventures and more, all with local experts. The inn is perfectly positioned between Canyon Rd and the plaza. Small dogs are welcome for an extra $20 per night.

La Posada de Santa Fe (Map pp312-13; ☎ 505-986-0000, 866-331-7625; www.laposada.rockresorts.com; 330 E Palace Ave; r from $175; ▣ ▣ wi-fi) World-class service puts this hotel in a league of its own. Your every need is catered to on this beautiful, shady, six-acre property a few blocks from the plaza. Elegantly furnished adobe casitas are outfitted with gas fireplaces. More historical (and smaller) rooms, some with views, are located in the Staab House. Onsite Avanyu Spa (see boxed text, p320) is deservedly fabulous, while the cigar-friendly Staab House Lounge (open 11:30am to 11pm) is a

NEW MEXICO

local favorite for its leather-chaired ambience and single-malt scotch.

Inn of the Anasazi (Map pp312-13; ☎ 800-688-8100; www .innoftheanasazi.com; 113 Washington Ave; r $200-525; 🖳 wi-fi) Ancient blends seamlessly with ultra-modern in this elegant, Navajo-themed property. For a deal as well as a boost, try the Better Business Package ($200), which includes a night's lodging, a power breakfast, laundering and an optional session with a Native American mystic.

La Fonda (Map pp312-13; ☎ 800-523-5002; www.lafonda santafe.com; 100 E San Francisco St; r from $225; 🐾 🖳 wi-fi) Staff artist Ernest Martinez has been painting thousands of windows and other fixtures since 1954, giving La Fonda its unique folk-art character. Claiming to be the original 'Inn at the end of the Santa Fe Trail,' here since 1610, the hotel also features Southwest murals and paintings commissioned in the 1920s and '30s. The top-floor luxury suites in La Terraza are lovely, and sunset views from the rooftop Belltower Bar (p324) are the best in town.

our pick Inn & Spa at Loretto (Map pp312-13; ☎ 505-988-5531; www.hotelloretto.com; 211 Old Santa Fe Trail; r from $250; 🐾 🖳 wi-fi) Modeled after the Taos Pueblo, this gorgeous old hotel just got a total redo. Rooms are luxurious and larger than average, with a Native American theme that includes warm woven rugs covering Frette linens on beds and local art hanging on dark-red walls. Modern amenities include iPod docking sta-

tions and huge flat-screen TVs. Bathrooms are fabulous with Spanish-style tiles in the tubs and huge ivory and black sinks. Have a drink in the lobby bar and look up at the ceiling – each panel is hand-painted. The on-site Baleen Restaurant (dishes $8 to $42) is celebrated for its seafood and discerning wine list, while the pampering at SpaTerre (see boxed text, below) is world renowned.

Inn of the Five Graces (Map pp312-13; ☎ 505-992-0957; www.fivegraces.com; 150 E De Vargas St; ste $295-750) Much more than an ordinary luxury getaway, this exquisite, exclusive gem offers an upscale gypsy-style escape. Sumptuous suites are decorated in a lavish Persian/Indian/Asian fusion theme, complete with fireplaces, beautifully tiled kitchenettes and a courtyard behind river-rock walls.

Cerrillos Rd & Metro Santa Fe

Santa Fe International Hostel (Map p308; ☎ 505-988-1153; santafehostel@quest.net; 1412 Cerrillos Rd; dm $15, r $25-35; 🖳 wi-fi) If you're looking for a true-blue old hippie hostel, you can't beat this experience in communal living. It's not the cleanest place in Santa Fe, but it's definitely the cheapest. Guests can stay in a private room for just $25 (no taxes; the hostel is nonprofit) as long as they do an assigned daily chore. There's an entire fridge full of donated free food – when we visited, sushi,

---

TOP FIVE SPAS

Many Santa Fe spas offer spectacular natural settings and mountain views and world-class pampering. Below are our top choices.

Absolute Nirvana Spa & Tea Room (Map pp312-13; ☎ 505-983-7942; www.absolutenirvana.com; 106 Faithway St; 🕐 10am-6pm Sun-Thu, 10am-8pm Fri & Sat) Rose-petal baths and sumptuous Indonesian- and Thai-style massage ($150 to $220) await you here.

Avanyu Spa (Map pp312-13; ☎ 505-986-0000; www.laposada.rockresorts.com; 330 E Palace Ave; 🕐 7am-8pm) Choose from sophisticated massage techniques, including craniosacral therapy, polarity, reiki and shiatsu ($115 to $185) at this swanky spot within the La Posada de Santa Fe Hotel.

ShàNah Spa & Wellness (off Map p328; ☎ 505-983-6377; www.bishopslodge.com; 1297 Bishops Lodge Rd; 🕐 8am-8pm) This Bishop's Lodge spa has a watsu pool for floating shiatsu ($105), two outdoor massage gardens and indoor services too. General services cost $105 to $145.

SpaTerre (Map pp312-13; ☎ 505-988-5531; www.innatloretto.com; 211 Old Santa Fe Trail; 🕐 9am-9pm) Melt your cares away at this Inn at Loretto's spa with Native American–themed decor and absolutely delectable massages with herbs and aromatherapy ($115 to $225).

Ten Thousand Waves (off Map p308; ☎ 505-992-5025; www.tenthousandwaves.com; 3451 Hyde Park Rd; communal tubs $15, private tubs $20-27 per person, premium private tub $59; 🕐 9:15am-9:30pm daily except 4-9:30pm Tue Jul-Oct, 10:15am-8:30pm Mon & Wed-Thu, 4-8:30pm Tue, 9:15am-9:30pm Fri-Sun Nov-Jun) This gorgeous Japanese spa offers a host of attractive public and private outdoor soaking tubs, kitted out in a smooth Zen style with cold plunges and saunas. A host of treatments from prenatal, hot stone and Thai massages to herbal wraps are offered. Massages start at $85.

pizza and sandwiches were all up for grabs. If you need a spic-and-span room, even the manager admits you'd do better elsewhere. But if you're just looking for a cheap sleep, and don't mind a little dirt (as guests are responsible for most of the cleaning, the place can get grimy). Rooms are simple but big, with metal beds and fading but freshly washed linens. Dorms have private bathrooms. The hostel is on the bus line to town, and the garden is perfect for chilling with a beer. The only downer is it tends to attract some transients. Cash only.

Rancheros de Santa Fe Campground (Map p328; ☎ 505-466-3482, 800-426-9259; 736 Old Las Vegas Hwy; tent/RV sites $20/32; ⊙ Mar-Oct; ⊠ ▣ wi-fi) Seven miles southeast of town, off exit 290 from I-25 North, Rancheros has nice views, a convenience store and wireless internet. Plus its sites are shady and big.

Silver Saddle Motel (Map p308; ☎ 505-471-7663; www.motelsantafe.com; 2810 Cerrillos Rd; r from $45; ▣) One of the rustic subjects of the 1988 documentary film *Motel*, Silver Saddle is your best budget bet. Inspired Southwestern comfy-rustic decor, including some with attractively tiled kitchenettes and lots of kitschy appeal, make this Americana at its finest.

Santa Fe Sage Inn (Map p308; ☎ 505-982-5952; www.santafesageinn.com; 725 Cerrillos Rd; r $65-125; ⊠ ▣ wi-fi) This newly refurbished (bargain) gem has great curb appeal, a stylish, cheerful interior and wireless internet, all within walking distance of the plaza. Plus it's pet friendly.

Ten Thousand Waves Japanese Resort & Spa (off Map p308; ☎ 505-982-9304; www.tenthousandwaves.com; 3451 Hyde Park Rd; r $99-279) Pets get pampered as well as guests at Santa Fe's favorite Japanese spa – doggies are welcomed with custom-sized beds, bones and treats! Humans will dig the 13 gorgeous, Zen-inspired freestanding guesthouses. Most come with fireplaces and either a deck or courtyard, and all are within walking distance of the mountainside hot tubs and massage cabins. Make reservations two months in advance. The spa is about 10 minutes' drive from the plaza.

Inn of the Turquoise Bear (Map p308; ☎ 800-396-4104; www.turquoisebear.com; 342 E Buena Vista St; r from $150) Visitors enjoy the quiet now, but this expansive adobe palace built by local legend Witter Bynner and domestic partner Robert Hunt was once home to legendary parties hosting Thornton Wilder, Robert Oppenheimer, Edna St Vincent Millay, Robert

Frost and many, many others. It's now a B&B surrounded by an acre of sculpted gardens, combining authentic ambience and modern amenities. It is, as always, straight-friendly, but remains a cozy place for gays and lesbians to relax in historic Santa Fe. The inn can arrange commitment ceremonies and weddings in the gardens. Pets are welcome.

Bishop's Lodge Resort & Spa (Map p328; ☎ 800-7419-0492; www.bishopslodge.com; 1297 Bishops Lodge Rd; r from $200; ▣ wi-fi) Come play (upscale) cow-girl on 450 acres of almost untouched piñon wilderness just 3 miles from the plaza. This family-friendly destination resort boasts huge, luxurious rooms and casitas, many with patios, kitchenettes, fireplaces and more. From yoga classes at its spa to a magnificent outdoor pool overlooking the mountains to horseback riding through the mountains, there truly is something for everyone. The on-site restaurant, Las Fuentes (breakfast and lunch $8 to $17, dinner $24 to $34) has a lavish Sunday brunch that has been voted best in Santa Fe. Free shuttles take you downtown.

EATING

Food is another art form in Santa Fe and it's as world class as the galleries. From spicy, traditional Southwest favorites to cutting-edge cuisine, it's all here. Reservations are always recommended for the more expensive venues, especially during summer and ski season. All Santa Fe restaurants and bars are nonsmoking.

Check for current reviews in the *Santa Fe Reporter*, which often has coupons for area eateries, or the free monthly *Local Flavor*, with reviews and news about area restaurants.

The Plaza & Canyon Rd
BUDGET

If you're on a budget downtown, one of the cheapest and tastiest places to eat lunch or an early dinner is the takeaway city-licensed stalls on the plaza lawn. The beef fajitas with fresh guacamole is our favorite. Tacos and burritos are also offered.

Downtown Subscription (Map pp312-13; ☎ 505-983-3085; 376 Garcia St; snacks $2-7; ⊙ 7am-7pm; Ⓥ) The coffee shop of choice for resident artists and writers. It does 31 types of tea, espresso, pastries and savory offerings, complemented by a truly spectacular newsstand and flagstone patio.

French Pastry Shop (Map pp312-13; ☎ 505-983-6697; La Fonda Hotel, 100 San Francisco St; mains $3-7; ⊙ breakfast

& lunch) Serving delicious French bistro food inside the La Fonda hotel, the French Pastry Shop does divine crepes – filled with everything from ham and cheese to strawberries and cream – along with a host of quiches, sandwiches, cappuccino and of course pastries. The French onion soup is the best in town.

Tia Sophia's (Map pp312-13; ☎ 505-983-9880; 210 W San Francisco St; mains $3-9; ⊙ 7am-2pm Mon-Sat; V ⊛) Local artists and visiting celebrities outnumber tourists at this longstanding Santa Fe favorite that's always packed. Breakfast is the meal of choice, with fantastic burritos and other Southwestern dishes. Lunch is pretty damn tasty too; try the perfectly prepared *chile rellenos*. The shelf of kids' books helps little ones pass the time.

Del Churro Saloon (Map pp312-13; ☎ 505-982-4333; Inn of the Governors, 101 W Alameda; mains under $6; ⊙ breakfast, lunch & dinner) It serves giant, inexpensive margaritas and delicious pub grub (try a burger or the cheese stuffed peppers) – it's no wonder Governor Bill Richardson chooses to dine here. Inside the Inn of the Governors hotel, this popular pub is an atmospheric place with copper-topped tables, lots of vegetation and a blazing fire in the winter. In summer the patio opens up and tables spill onto the sidewalk. It serves food well into the night.

MIDRANGE

La Cantina at Coyote Café (Map pp312-13; ☎ 505-983-1615; 132 Water St; mains $7-18; ⊙ 11:30am-9pm Apr-Oct; V) This lively rooftop cantina atop famed sister restaurant, Coyote Café, welcomes budget gourmets to sample chef Mark Miller's cut-rate creations. Try the Oaxacan chicken *mole* ($11), spit-roasted pork tacos with pineapple ($13) and the signature mango margarita ($8). Sunsets are fabulous.

The Shed (Map pp312-13; ☎ 505-982-9030; 113½ E Palace Ave; lunch $8-10, dinner $9-20; ⊙ 11am-2:30pm & 5:30-9pm Mon-Sat; ⊛ V) Just thinking about this place makes us drool. We can't get enough of the red and green chile–smothered chicken enchiladas. This family-run, James Beard Award–winning restaurant has been serving New Mexican fare in a atmospheric 1692 adobe since 1953. Spicy posole soup comes with many of the mains, and is excellent, as are the deserts and margaritas. In summer sit outside on the patio.

Al Di La (Map pp312-13; ☎ 505-983-6766; 227 Galisteo St; mains $9-15, pizzas from $16; ⊙ lunch & dinner; V) Locals swear this is the best authentic New York pizza

in town. Just walking into the casual restaurant, you're hit with a delicious array of smells. The place is usually packed, has a congenial atmosphere, nightly specials and quite a few pasta, meat and chicken dishes should you not want pizza. Call ahead and order takeaway to eat at your hotel. Alcohol is not served.

Café Pasqual's (Map pp312-13; ☎ 505-983-9340; 121 Don Gaspar Ave; breakfast & lunch $8-15, dinner $20-40; ⊙ 7am-3pm & 5:30-9pm; ⊛ V) Make reservations for dinner if you'd like, but definitely wait in line to enjoy the famous breakfasts. We highly recommend *huevos motuleños* ($12), made with eggs and black beans, sautéed bananas, feta cheese and more; *tamale dulce* ($12), a sweet corn tamale with fruit, beans and Mexican chocolate; or the enormous Durango ham-and-cheese omelet ($13). They're all served up in a festive, if crowded, interior. Grab a seat faster by sitting at the community table, where tourists and locals mix it up daily.

TOP END

El Farol (Map p308; ☎ 505-983-9912; 808 Canyon Rd; lunch $8-18, dinner $25-50; ⊙ 11:30am-late; ⊛ V) This popular restaurant and bar, set in a rustically authentic adobe, features live music nightly. Although El Farol does excellent steaks, most people come to sample chef James Campbell Caruso's tapas. The weekly Wednesday flamenco dinner show ($60) is lively and perfect for birthdays or special occasions. Kids will also dig it.

SantaCafé (Map pp312-13; ☎ 505-984-1788; 231 Washington Ave; lunch $10-14, dinner $18-38; ⊙ 11:30am-2pm Mon-Sat, 5:30-9pm daily; V) Chef David Sellars is practically an international celebrity because of dishes like roasted poblano *chile rellenos* with three-mushroom quinoa and chipotle cream ($19). Housed in an 1850s adobe built by the infamous Padre Gallegos, SantaCafé also boasts the best courtyard in town for summertime dining. Lunch is a deal, the wine list flawless and the dining room historical. In short, perfection.

Compound (Map pp312-13; ☎ 505-982-4353; 635 Canyon Rd; lunch $12-20, dinner $24-32; ⊙ noon-2pm Mon-Fri, 6-9pm daily; V) A long-time local foodie favorite, the Compound features the contemporary American creations of Mark Kiffin, recognized by the James Beard Foundation as the Best Chef of the Southwest in 2005. The acclaimed seasonal menu draws on the elegant flavors of Southwestern and Mediterranean cooking. Ingredients are always fresh, and the presentation perfect. Come when there's reason to celebrate – the wine list includes several top-notch champagnes.

Geronimo (Map pp312-13; ☎ 982-1500; 724 Canyon Rd; lunch $20-40, dinner $30-55; ⏰ 11:30am-2pm & 6-9:30pm Tue-Sun; **V**) If you can't afford Santa Fe's most exclusive restaurant for dinner, try the cheaper, but equally delicious, lunch menu. Chef Eric DiStefana cooks up a delicious fusion of Southwestern and global dishes in an elegant and romantic 1756 adobe home on Canyon Rd. Sit outside on the front porch in summer.

Coyote Café (Map pp312-13; ☎ 505-983-1615; www .coyotecafé.com; 132 Water St; mains $23-45; ⏰ 5:30-9pm; **V**) Superstar chef Mark Miller keeps serious foodies returning year after year for stellar interpretations of New Mexico cuisine. The menu at Santa Fe's most celebrated restaurant changes frequently, but must-try stand-bys include delicious griddled buttermilk corncakes with chipotle prawns and pecan-wood grilled dry-aged rib chop. Delish margaritas come in a rainbow of flavors.

Guadalupe St Area

Off the main square by a number of blocks, this funky little neighborhood is home to some quirky dining and drinking options often frequented by Santa Fe's young and hip crowd.

Santa Fe Farmers Market (Map pp312-13; ☎ 505-983-4098; cnr Cerrillos Rd & Guadalupe St; ⏰ 7am-noon Sat & Tue Apr-Nov) Local produce, much of it heirloom and organic, is on sale at these spacious digs alongside homemade goodies, inexpensive food, natural body products and arts and crafts.

Bert's La Taqueria (Map pp312-13; ☎ 505-988-5991; 416 Agua Fria St; mains $5-12; ⏰ 11am-2pm & 5-10pm Mon-Sat; ♿ **V**) Long-time local favorite Bert's recently moved into a big new location closer to the center of town. Thank goodness that affordable food – including Mexican, veggie dishes, burgers and delicious homemade salsa – is still the norm. Choose between a large outdoor patio near the aromatic open-air grill or colorful, contemporary and casual indoor seating.

Zia Diner (Map pp312-13; ☎ 505-988-7008; 366 S Guadalupe St; mains $6-12; ⏰ 11am-10pm) Voted Best Comfort Food by locals, this cozy diner is known for its meatloaf, buffalo burgers and yummy homemade pies. Have a beer and watch pink-haired hipsters and graying progressives coo over their blue-plate specials (served weekdays only). It's one of the few places open late on Sundays.

Tomasita's (Map pp312-13; ☎ 505-983-5721; 500 S Guadalupe St; dishes $6-12; ⏰ 11am-10pm Mon-Sat; ♿ **V**) Locals hate to admit it, but they love this tourist standby for its outstanding green chile, served atop excellent burritos, enchiladas and, on weekdays, huge $10 blue-plate specials. Save room for desert – *sopaipillas* with honey butter are included with the mains. It's a raucous place, perfect for families hauling exuberant kids. Prepare to wait; the restaurant is always packed.

Cowgirl BBQ & Western Grill (Map pp312-13; ☎ 505-982-2565; 319 S Guadalupe St; mains $8-13; ⏰ 11am-midnight Mon-Fri, 8:30am-midnight Sat, 8:30am-11pm Sun, bar until 2am Mon-Sat, until midnight Sun; **V**) A fun place for all ages, thanks to the great playground, wacky Western-style feminist flair, outside patio and live music after 9pm, this restaurant has fabulous food and awesome margaritas. Everything is tasty, but Cowgirl's is known for its barbecue brisket – order it in a quesadilla with green chile. After dark, order smoky mescal margaritas and play a game of pool in the new billiards room.

Railyard Restaurant & Saloon (Map pp312-13; ☎ 505-989-3300; 530 S Guadalupe St; mains $8-20; ⏰ lunch & dinner; **V**) Housed in a corrugated tin warehouse in the up-and-coming, gritty-artsy Railroad District, this conventional steaks-and-chops house also offers pastas, sandwiches and a bar menu. Service is good.

Ristra (Map pp312-13; ☎ 505-982-8608; 548 Agua Fria St; mains $20-40; ⏰ dinner) Ristra attracts a regular clientele who come for its casual intimacy and excellent food. The contemporary American menu is influenced by the flavors of France and the Southwest, and changes seasonally. The steaks here are always fantastic, the wine list is lengthy and there are plenty of bottles of bubbly to toast those special occasions.

Cerrillos Rd & Metro Santa Fe

These eateries are convenient if you are staying on the outskirts of town.

Tara's Organic (Map p308; ☎ 505-216-9759; 1807 2nd St; mains from $2; ⏰ 1pm-8pm Mon-Sat, 12-5pm Sun) Ice cream is what to order at Tara's Organic, after you've had your fill sampling the tasty lunch specials. All the ingredients are locally grown – the lavender comes Los Poblanos, a small town near Albuquerque, the green chiles are harvested on an Espanola farm. But back to the ice cream: Rosemary's combined caramelized pear and allspice is the latest in a stable of all natural ice-cream flavors that often taste as wild as the nearby mountains – sage anyone?

Bobcat Bite (Map p328; ☎ 505-983-5319; 420 Old Las Vegas Hwy; dishes $5-20; ☒ 11am-7:50pm Wed-Sat) Often voted as serving the Best Burger in Santa Fe by locals, this relaxed roadhouse beneath the neon really does an outstanding green chile cheeseburger ($7). The steaks are pretty darn good too.

Gabriel's (off Map p308; ☎ 505-455-7000; US Hwy 84/285; lunch dishes $7-8, dinner dishes $10-20; ☒ lunch & dinner) It's worth the 12-mile drive north of Santa Fe to eat at Gabriel's. The scenic patio and beautiful interior, hung with Miguel Martinez's art, are fabulous spots to enjoy fresh guacamole, made to order at your table, excellent New Mexican cuisine and even better ribs. Plan to drop by if you're headed to the flea market or points north.

Mu Du Noodles (Map p308; ☎ 505-983-1411; 1494 Cerrillos Rd; mains $15-20; ☒ dinner Mon-Sat; Ⓥ) Pan-Asian organic dishes like salmon dumplings, Vietnamese spring rolls and tofu laksa inspire lines out the door of this lovely spot; the noodles (of course) and specials are always recommended, and almost everything has a vegan version.

DRINKING

Talk to 10 residents and visitors and you'll get 10 different responses about where to find the best margarita. You'll just have to sample the lot to decide for yourself.

Second Street Brewery (Map p308; ☎ 505-982-3030; www.secondstreetbrewery.com; 2nd St) Santa Fe's favorite brewery is the perfect spot to stop for a pint after a long hike. It serves handcrafted English-style beers – brewed on the premises – and also offers a hearty selection of better-than-average pub grub. Sit outside on the big patio, or inside the brewery. There's live music nightly.

Belltower Bar (Map pp312-13; ☎ 505-982-5511; 100 E San Francisco St; ☒ 5pm-sunset Mon-Thu, 2pm-sunset Fri-Sun May-Oct) During summer this bar atop La Fonda hotel is the premier spot to catch one of those patented New Mexican sunsets while sipping a killer margarita. After dark, retire to the hotel's lobby Fiesta Bar for live country and folk music.

Dragon Room Bar (Map pp312-13; ☎ 505-983-7712; 406 Old Santa Fe Trail) This 300-year-old adobe is a consistent top fave for locals and Hollywood-famous visitors alike. Drop by for a signature Black Dragon margarita. Visit after 9pm on Tuesday, Thursday or Saturday if you want it served with live music (flamenco guitar, Latin jazz and the like).

Ore House (Map pp312-13; ☎ 505-983-8687; 50 Lincoln Ave) We think this place makes the best fresh lime (no sweet and sour) margarita in town, and with more than 40 different types to choose from, there's bound to be a margarita for everyone. Choose from the seats on the heated balcony overlooking the plaza or a table inside.

Sleeping Dog Tavern (Map pp312-13; ☎ 505-982-4335; 114 W San Francisco St) With live music Wednesday through Saturday, the Sleeping Dog is another good drinking option half a block off the plaza. Other nights you can relax with an ice-cold brew, shoot a game of pool, throw darts or catch up on the sport shown on big-screen TVs.

Evangelo's (Map pp312-13; ☎ 505-982-9014; 200 W San Francisco St) Everyone is welcome in this casual, rowdy joint owned by the Klonis family since 1971 (ask owner/bartender Nick about his father's unusual fame). Drop in, put on some Patsy Cline and grab a draft beer – it's the perfect escape from Plaza culture.

ENTERTAINMENT

Check the *Santa Fe Reporter* and the 'Pasatiempo' section of Friday's *New Mexican* for a thorough listing of what's going on in Santa Fe – clubs here change faster than the seasons.

Live Music & Dance Clubs

La Fonda (p320) and the Inn & Spa at Loretto (p320) are just two of many hotel bars offering live music most nights. Some of the most popular places to dance in Santa Fe these days are the restaurants, which throw weekly dance nights featuring everything from salsa to swing.

Willee's Blues Bar (Map pp312-13; ☎ 505-982-0117; www.willees.com; 401 S Guadalupe St; cover from $5 Wed-Sat) One of Santa Fe's last remaining dance clubs, Willee's offers live jazz and blues Wednesday through Saturday – everyone from John Lee Hooker Jr, Leon Russell and Rockin' Jake have performed. DJs spin a mix of tunes Monday through Wednesday nights. Willee's serves good bar food, should you need to soak up the booze.

El Farol (Map p308; ☎ 505-983-9912; www.elfarolsf .com; 808 Canyon Rd; cover $4-7) This popular restaurant gets hopping on Wednesday nights when there's salsa dancing until midnight (late by Santa Fe standards) to the tunes of local band Savor. Spanish guitar, jazz, international music and flamenco dances also happen throughout the month – check the website to see what's on the schedule when you're in town.

Cowgirl BBQ & Western Grill (Map pp312-13; ☎ 505-982-2565; 319 S Guadalupe St; cover $1-5) In addition to being a fine and rustic-with-a-vengeance venue for catching live shows (despite the name, they're rarely country), it also has microbrews, margaritas and a brand-new billiards room. In short, Cowgirl's is the local standby, or in many cases the first choice, for a night out.

Vanessie of Santa Fe (Map pp312-13; ☎ 505-982-9966; 434 W San Francisco St; ☎ 5:30-10:30pm) You don't really come to Vanessie for the food, though there's nothing wrong with it. No, the attraction here is the piano bar, featuring blow-dried lounge singers who bring Neil Diamond and Barry Manilow classics to life in their own special way. The place is packed most nights, and also does a variety of fundraisers for worthy causes – making you feel good about all that alcohol you're funneling down your throat.

Warehouse 21 (Map pp312-13; ☎ 505-989-4423; 1614 Paseo de Peralta; cover $5-10) This all-ages club and art center in a 3500-sq-ft warehouse is the perfect alcohol-free venue for edgy local bands, plus a fair number of nationally known acts, or for just showing off the latest in multihued hairstyles.

Performing Arts

Patrons from the world's most glittering cities are drawn to Santa Fe in July and August because of opera, chamber music, performance and visual arts, an area in which Santa Fe matches anywhere on the globe. The opera may be the belle of the ball – clad in sparkling denim – but it would be a shame to bypass other offerings unaware. Let the searchable, exhaustive **What's Happening in Santa Fe calendar** (www.santafeartsandculture.org), with links to online advance ticket sales, become your new best friend. Plan ahead to score coveted seats, lodging and gourmet meals.

Santa Fe Opera (Map p328; ☎ 505-986-5900, 800-280-4654; www.santafeopera.org; standing room $10, seats $25-160; ☎ late Jun-late Aug) Many come to Santa Fe for this and this alone: the theater is an architectural marvel, with nearly 360-degree views of wind-carved sandstone wilderness crowned with sunsets and moonrises, and at center stage the world's finest talent performs western civilization's masterworks. It's still the Wild West, though; you can even wear jeans – just try *that* in New York City.

Gala festivities begin two hours before the curtain rises, when the ritual tailgate party is rendered glamorous in true Santa Fe style right in the parking lot. Bring your own caviar and brie, make reservations for the buffet dinner and lecture ($50) or a picnic dinner ($35), or have your own private caterer – several customize the menu to the opera's theme – pour the champagne. **Prelude Talks**, free to all ticket holders, are offered in Stieren Orchestra Hall one hour and two hours before curtain to accommodate various dining schedules. Shuttles run to and from the event for $20 from Santa Fe and $35 from Albuquerque; reserve through the opera box office.

Youth Night at the Opera (1 adult & 2 children $35, 2 adults & 3 children $60, each additional child $8) offers families a chance to watch dress rehearsals a few nights each summer – one precedes the run of each of the season's operas – with brief talks aimed at audience members ages 6 to 22. **Backstage tours** (adult/child $5/free; ☎ 1pm Mon-Sat Jun-Aug) offer opportunities to poke around the sets, costume and storage areas.

Santa Fe Chamber Music Festival (☎ 505-982-1890; www.sfcmf.org; tickets $16-54, students $10; ☎ Jul-Aug) This is the other big cultural event, known for filling elegant venues like the Lensic with Brahms, Mozart and other classic masters. It's not just world-class acts like violinist Pinchas Zukerman and pianist Yuja Wang defining the season; top-notch jazz, world music and New Music virtuosos round out the menu.

Santa Fe Desert Chorale (☎ 505-988-2282, 800-244-4011; www.desertchorale.org; tickets $15-50, some free events) Twenty lauded professional singers from around the country come together in July, August and the winter holidays to perform everything from Gregorian chants and gospel to Renaissance madrigals and modern love songs at venues like St Francis Cathedral and Loretto Chapel.

Santa Fe Playhouse (Map pp312-13; ☎ 505-988-4262; www.santafeplayhouse.org; 142 E De Vargas St; tickets $20; ☎ 8pm Thu-Sat, 2pm Sun) The state's oldest theater company performs avant-garde and traditional theater and musical comedy. On Sunday admission is as much as you can afford – which gives Santa Fe's less privileged residents the chance to experience the theater.

Lensic Performing Arts Theater (Map pp312-13; ☎ 505-984-1370; www.lensic.com; 1050 Old Pecos Trail) A beautifully renovated 1930 movie house, the theater hosts eight different performance groups and a weekly classic film series, including the Santa Fe Symphony & Chorus.

SHOPPING

Besides the Native American jewelry sold directly by the artists under the plaza *portales* (see boxed text, p310), there are enough shops for you to spend weeks browsing and buying in Santa Fe. Many venues are gallery-and-

shop combos. The focus is mainly on art, from Native American jewelry to wild contemporary paintings. For the gallery lowdown, see the boxed text, p314.

El Milagro Herbs (off Map pp312-13; ☎ 505-820-6321; 1020 Canyon Rd) This little shop is stocked with goodies for your skin and body, mixed by a resident herbalist. We swear by the Desert Dweller Deep Moisturizing Lotion – it cures

---

LOCAL VOICES: TED FLICKER

Ted Flicker is the writer and director of the 1967 comic classic *The President's Analyst*, and the creator of the popular 1970s television show *Barney Miller*, which he says gave him the getaway money to leave Hollywood, move to Santa Fe and learn to sculpt.

Why did you leave Los Angeles and move to Santa Fe of all places? I left because it was no longer fun to make movies. I found it all greedy and ugly and I had huge success with *Barney Miller* and Barbara (my wife) and I counted our pennies and said we have enough… We visited Santa Fe and it was just beautiful. We moved here in 1986 after searching, and finding, our dream home. And we intend to live here until they carry us out.

What's so special about Santa Fe? (Barbara and I) love the light. We love the atmosphere. It is like not being in America and yet we are still there. There is no place in America that has architecture like here. One of the great things about Santa Fe is it's the classic American small town. Barbara and I go to restaurants and always run into people we know. We run into them on the sidewalk. And it's not pretentious.

So what got you into sculpting? I was introduced to a local sculptor and asked him to teach me. I went to his studio and he sat me down next to him and explained everything he was doing. I was fascinated. I went out and bought supplies right away and to my amazement I was good at it. I found it was my passion.

What medium do you sculpt in, and what do you create? I used to work mostly in bronze, but now I am working in a new medium called design cast. It lives outside, and my sculptures live outside all over my property, so this is good. Plus it has a different feel about it. It's much softer and much quicker to cast. I sculpt figurative pieces. Barbara is my biggest influence, and most of my sculptures are devoted to her beauty. I also sculpt figures of friends and artists who have been important in my life.

How did you and Barbara meet? We met at a movie-star wedding. George Peppard [Audrey Hepburn's love interest in *Breakfast at Tiffany's*] was marrying Elizabeth Ashley. People were dancing and I saw this beautiful woman in a white dress… I didn't get to talk to her that night, but the next day I was running an errand and I bumped into her. So I ran over and got her name and number… It was instant love. She is my soul mate. On our first date we talked about when we get married. Two weeks later we moved in together [and married shortly afterwards]. That was 42 years ago.

What is your favorite Santa Fe gallery? Linda Durham for contemporary. Gerald Peters for big-time art, especially Western.

Art is food in Santa Fe. Do you have a favorite restaurant? Ristra is always good. Especially when taking family and friends to dinner. The SantaCafé, Barbara and I just love. They have the best courtyard in town, so we eat there mostly in summer and fall.

Can you sum up New Mexico? New Mexico is one of those bad combinations of a poor state with very rich people. But it is still a very special place. In fact, the Native Americans believe that all of humanity started just 30 miles from Santa Fe in a very special place called Black Mesa. They say that people emerged from the earth here.

If you want to find out more about, or purchase, Ted Flicker's sculpture, visit him on the web at www.tedflicker.com.

even the driest skin. Also available are a host of herbal tinctures to boost your immune system or help you adjust to the high desert altitude.

Nambe Foundry Outlet (Map pp312-13; ☎ 505-988-3574; www.nambe.com; 104 W San Francisco St) A unique metal alloy that contains no silver, lead or pewter (but looks like silver), was discovered in 1951 to the north of Santa Fe, near Nambé. Fashioned into gleaming and elegant pieces, Nambeware designs are individually sandcast and have won national and international recognition.

Seret & Sons (Map pp312-13; ☎ 505-988-9151; 224 Galisteo St) Feel like you've stepped into an Asian or Arabian bazaar at this giant art and sculpture warehouse. It offers a vast and fascinating collection of fine carpets, giant stone elephants, Tibetan furniture, pillars and solid teak doors – of course getting all this home take a bit of effort (or shipping money), but it's fun just to browse.

Tesuque Flea Market (Map p328; US Hwy 84/285; ☯ 9am-4pm Fri, 8am-5pm Sat & Sun Mar-Nov) A tiny outdoor market a few minutes north of Santa Fe at Tesuque Pueblos, this is the mother of all flea markets, and where locals in the know come for everything from high-quality rugs, turquoise rings and clothing to the best used (read: broken in) cowboy boots in the state. And all for significantly less than you'll find them in town.

Nathalie (Map pp312-13; ☎ 505-992-1440; www.nathalie santafe.com; 503 Canyon Rd) Come here for the finest cowboy and cowgirl gear, including gemstone-studded gun holsters, handmade leather, denim couture and lingerie for that saloon girl with a heart of gold.

Bodhi Bazaar (Map pp312-13; ☎ 505-982-3380; 500 Montezuma St) Girls, shop your heart out at this top designer boutique in the Sanbusco Market Center in the heart of the Guadalupe district. Voted one of the top 12 boutiques in the USA by *Elle Magazine*, Bodhi has all the latest Diane von Furstenberg, Lamb and Missoni or check out the extensive denim collection.

Garcia Street Books (Map pp312-13; ☎ 505-986-0151; www.garciastreetbooks.com; 376 Garcia St) Scavengers are rewarded with excellent bargains as well as the town's best selection of art books, including such rarities as a deluxe limited edition of Elias Rivera's paintings ($4200).

Jackalope (Map p308; ☎ 505-471-8539; 2820 Cerrillos Rd) Essential pieces of Southwest decor can be yours for a song. Start with a cow skull like George O'Keeffe made famous, snap up a kiva ladder, add some colorful pottery and Navajo potholders and you'll be set. Don't leave without watching authentic prairie dogs frolic in their piñon enclosure.

GETTING THERE & AROUND

The **Santa Fe Municipal Airport** (SAF; Map p328; ☎ 505-955-2908; Airport Rd near NM 599) is a tiny airport, primarily a landing strip for private planes. Although there has been talk of daily flights to Fort Worth, Los Angeles and Salt Lake City on Delta or American Eagle, these had not started at the time of research. Most people fly in from Albuquerque. Shuttles run from the Albuquerque airport to Santa Fe hotels. Try **Sandia Express Shuttle** (☎ 888-775-5696; www.sandiashuttle.com; one way $25).

TNM&O/Greyhound (Map p308; ☎ 505-471-0008; St Michael's Dr) has three buses daily to Albuquerque ($15, 80 minutes) and two daily buses to Taos ($17, 1½ hours). **Twin Hearts Shuttle** (☎ 800-654-9456; www.twinheartsexpress.com) runs between Santa Fe and the Albuquerque Sunport Airport ($25), Taos ($35), Española ($25), Red River ($35) and Questa ($30) daily; make reservations in advance.

Santa Fe Trails (Map pp312-13; ☎ 505-955-2001; www .santafenm.gov; per ride adult/child $1/50¢, day pass $2; ☯ 6am-11pm Mon-Fri, 8am-8pm Sat, 10am-7pm Sun) is the country's first natural-gas city bus system. The bus depot is on Sheridan Ave between Palace and Marcy Aves. **Capital City Cab** (☎ 505-438-0000) provides a taxi service throughout town.

The **Amtrak** (☎ 800-872-7245; www.amtrak.com) *Southwest Chief* stops at Lamy; from here, buses continue 18 miles to Santa Fe.

AROUND SANTA FE

Don't get too comfortable in Santa Fe, because the region around New Mexico's capital city is why they call this state the 'Land of Enchantment.' Whether you take the High Rd or Low Rd (to Taos that is), get ready for iconic scenery. Red rocks, pine forest and high desert sage-scented air are abundant. This area also offers the state's best hot-spring resort, streams made for fly-fishing, endless hiking trails and small towns boasting unexpected treasures – from beautiful old adobe churches to weaving studios where the artists work and sells their loom-woven wares.

NEW MEXICO

NEW MEXICO

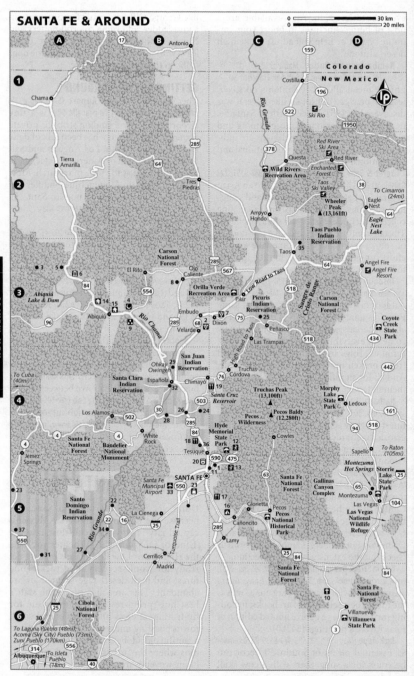

SANTA FE & AROUND

ABIQUIÚ

pop 500 / elev 6800ft

The tiny community of Abiquiú (sounds like barbeque), on Hwy 84 about 45 minutes' drive northwest of Santa Fe, is famous because the renowned artist Georgia O'Keeffe lived and painted here. With the Rio Chama flowing through farmland and spectacular rock formations, the ethereal landscape continues to attract artists, and many live and work in Abiquiú.

Sights & Activities

Georgia O'Keeffe died in 1986, at age 98, and her adobe house is open for limited visits. Her **foundation** (www.georgiaokeeffe.org) offers one-hour **tours** (505-685-4539; www.abiquiuinn.com/Tour .htm; tour $22; Tue, Thu & Fri Apr-Nov) of O'Keeffe's home, often booked months in advance, so plan ahead.

The spiritual landscape lures more than artists – two religious sanctuaries are perched in the hills. Muslims worship at **Dar Al Islam Mosque** (505-685-4515), an adobe mosque that welcomes visitors. From Hwy 84, take Hwy 554 (southeast of Abiquiú) towards El Rito, cross the Rio Chama, take your first left onto County Rd 155 and follow it for 3 miles. The mosque is up a dirt road on the right. Day visitors are welcome to join the monks in prayer at the **Christ in the Desert Monastery** (right); take Forest Service Rd 151, a dirt road off of Hwy 84 just south of Echo Amphitheater or 5 miles north of Ghost Ranch (right), and drive 13 beautiful miles.

The **Ghost Ranch Living Museum** (505-685-4333; www.ghostranch.org; US Hwy 84; 8am-5pm Tue-Sat), founded amid the colorful canyonlands as

the former 1766 Serrano Land Grant, was later dubbed Rancho de los Brujos (Ranch of the Witches) because of various eerie *X-Files*–style supernatural activity. This Presbyterian retreat offers lodging (below), classes and other activities for folks of any or no faith. Take the recommended 4-mile round-trip trek into **Box Canyon** or the popular 3-mile round-trip to **Chimney Rock**, with views of the Piedra Lumbre basin.

Surrounded by red rock and high-desert terrain, **Abiquiú Lake & Dam** (505-685-4371; Hwy 84; dawn-dusk) is a beautiful swimming spot.

Sleeping & Eating

Ghost Ranch (505-685-4333; www.ghostranch.org; US Hwy 84; tent/RV sites $16/23, dm incl board $45-70, dm with bathroom & board $80) This spectacular spot is where *City Slickers* was filmed. When space is available (seminar participants get first dibs), you can get a dorm bed here, including cafeteria-style meals made with locally raised meat and organic veggies grown on the farm.

Abiquiú Inn (505-685-4378, 800-447-5621; www .abiquiuinn.com; US Hwy 84; RV sites $18, r $89-149, 4-person casitas $189) An area institution, this sprawling collection of shaded adobes is peaceful and lovely; some spacious rooms have kitchenettes. The very professional staff also run the onsite Abiquiú Cafe (dishes $7 to $16). Stick to -the Middle Eastern menu – falafel, dolmas and gyros are all winners – and you can't go wrong.

Christ in the Desert Monastery (www.christdesert.org; off US Rte 84; r incl board suggested donation $50-75) When you really want to get away from it all, head west from US Hwy 84 onto the rough dirt Forest Service Rd 151, then follow it along the

NEW MEXICO

GEORGIA O'KEEFFE

Although classically trained as a painter at art institutes in Chicago and New York, Georgia O'Keeffe was always uncomfortable with traditional European style. For four years after finishing school, she did not paint, and instead taught drawing and did graphic design.

However, after studying with Arthur Wesley Dow, who shared her distaste for the provincial, O'Keeffe began developing her own style. She drew abstract shapes with charcoal, representing dreams and visions, and eventually returned to oils and watercolors. These first works caught the eye of her future husband and patron, photographer Alfred Stieglitz, in 1916.

In 1929 she visited Taos' Mabel Dodge Luhan Ranch and returned to paint 'The Lawrence Tree,' which still presides over the **DH Lawrence Ranch** (p343). O'Keeffe tackled the subject of the San Francisco de Asis Church in Ranchos de Taos, painted by so many artists before her, in a way that had never been considered: only a fragment of the mission wall, contrasted against the blue of the sky.

It was no wonder O'Keeffe loved New Mexico's expansive skies, so similar to her paintings' negative spaces. As she spent more time here, landscapes and fields of blue permeated her paintings. During desert treks, she collected the smooth white bones of animals, subjects she placed against that sky in some of her most identifiable New Mexico works.

Telltale scrub marks and bristle impressions divulge how O'Keeffe blended and mixed her vibrant colors on the canvas itself. This is in direct contrast to photographs of her work, which convey a false, airbrush-like smoothness. At the **Georgia O'Keeffe Museum** (p311), you can experience her work firsthand.

meandering Rio Chama for 13 inspirational miles to this isolated Benedictine monastery. Rates for the simple rooms, plus outrageous trails and peace and quiet, include vegetarian meals served without conversation – special medallions indicate your silent retreat. Chores are requested (not required) and include minding the gift shop or tending the garden.

Old Abiquiú B&B (☎ 505-685-4784; www.oldabiquiu.com; Hwy 84; r $60-95) This property, adjacent to the Poshuouinge church ruins and near a wildlife refuge on the south end of Hwy 84, offers three rooms (two with a kiva fireplace) nestled in the woods overlooking the river.

Bodes General Merchandise (☎ 505-685-4422; US Hwy 84; mains $5-7; ⏱ 6:30am-7pm Mon-Sat, 6:30am-6pm Sun) A true old-fashioned general store that's been in operation since 1919, Bodes is where to hang out with the locals and gossip over deli food.

Getting There & Away

Abiquiú is on Hwy 84, about 45 minutes' drive northwest of Santa Fe. It is best reached by private vehicle.

OJO CALIENTE

Billed as America's oldest health resort, **Ojo Caliente Mineral Springs** (☎ 800-222-9162; www.ojo calientespa.com; 50 Los Baños Dr; r $109-119, cottages $179-300, pool admission Mon-Fri $16, Sat & Sun $22, after 6pm

$12), which means 'hot eye' in Spanish, is our favorite high desert escape. It is a charmingly shabby-chic family-owned resort offering delightful casitas, five wonderful hot springs and absolutely gorgeous environs – think of towering, crumbly orangey sandstone monoliths set against a baby-blue New Mexico sky; after dark the lack of light pollution means you can float in the warm water and stare at a velvet canopy of a million stars arranged into hundreds of bright constellations. The on-site **Artesian Restaurant** (dishes $5-25) prepares organic and local ingredients three meals a day with aplomb. Everything is delicious.

The springs, which are open to day visitors, are considered sacred by Pueblo Indians. Due to an unusual trick of hydrogeology, each of the beautiful pools is fed by a different water source with different mineral contents. We love the indoor mineral-heavy Lithia spring, which has a kick – bring a bottle so you can take some home for sipping during depressing days. The soda spring is about as relaxing as it gets. The enclosed pool is full of steam and perfect for floating in the mist. It's meant to help relieve digestion problems. The iron spring is a euphoric cliffside pool. The floor is made from natural pebbles, which gently exfoliate your feet as you soak up the blood-cleansing and immune-boosting waters. In summer you can take a mud bath in the mud pool.

When you've had your share of soaking hit the sauna and steam room before indulging in one of the super-pampering **spa treatments** (massage $50-125, wraps $10-90, facials from $50, luxury packages from $125), a yoga class (Wednesday to Sunday) or hiking along one of the trails. If you're staying at the resort, admission to the pools is free. Check online for holiday and mid-week specials.

Other accommodations within walking distance of the springs include the slightly cheaper **Inn at Ojo** (☎ 505-583-9131; www.ojocaliente .com; Los Baños Dr; s/d $85/115), which is run by a former Los Alamos physicist, his wife and their daughter. It's a personable spot with uniquely decorated rooms that use 19th-century wardrobes as focal points.

For eats, try the **Mesa Vista Café** (☎ 505-583-2245; Hwy 285; dishes $4-7; ☾ breakfast, lunch & dinner; **V**), serving New Mexican diner food with lots of veggie options and a recommended red chile cheeseburger.

Ojo Caliente is located about 40 miles north of Santa Fe on Hwy 285. It's a pretty drive.

Both the Inn at Ojo and Mesa Vista Café are in the center of the tiny blink-and-you'll-miss it village of Ojo. The hot springs resort is a few minutes outside of town.

PECOS

When the Spanish arrived, this five-story pueblo with almost 700 rooms was an important center for trade between the Pueblo Indians of the Rio Grande and the Plains Indians to the east. The Spaniards completed a church in 1625, but it was destroyed in the Pueblo Revolt of the 1680s. The remains of the rebuilt mission, completed in 1717, are the major attraction. The pueblo itself declined, and in 1838 the 17 remaining inhabitants moved to Jemez Pueblo (see boxed text, p302).

At the **Pecos National Historical Park Visitor Center** (☎ 505-757-6414; www.nps.gov/peco; adult/child $3/free; ☾ 8am-5pm), a museum and short film explain more about the area's history. From Santa Fe, take I-25 east and follow signs; it's about 25 miles southeast.

HIGH ROAD TO TAOS

Go on, take the high road. One of two routes to Taos from Santa Fe, the more famous High Rd isn't necessarily any prettier (although beauty is relative here; both are gorgeous) than the faster Low Rd, but if you're interested in the fiber arts, you won't want to miss this route. Small towns along this route are filled with crumbling adobes, rusting pick-ups, graying snow in winter and sun-baked clay in summer; they often look half-abandoned, but look closely and you'll find they're rich in weaving and other Native American handicraft workshops. The road, which winds through river valleys, skirts high cartoonlike sandstone cliffs and edges past high mountain pine forests, passes numerous wood-carving and weaving studios-cum-shops.

Most people drive the High Rd north from Santa Fe (taking the Low Rd back, which we'd recommend) to Taos. To do so, take Hwy 76 from Española.

The High Rd is also home to one of New Mexico's largest and most influential pueblos, Picuris; see p287 for details.

Chimayó
pop 2900 / elev 6200ft

Chimayó is our favorite Santa Fe day trip, and a must-stop on this route. Originally established by Spanish families with a land grant, it is home to a fabulous old adobe church and an equally fabulous New Mexican restaurant. Whatever you do on the High Rd to Taos, don't miss a stop at the 1816 **Santuario de Chimayó** (☎ 505-351-4889; NM 76; admission free; ☾ 9am-5pm, mass 11am Mon-Sat & noon Sun). Legend has it that the dirt from the church has healing powers, and the back room is a shrine to its miracles, with canes, wheelchairs, crutches and other medical aids hanging from the wall. Kneel into a hole in the ground and smear some dirt on your ailing body. As many as 30,000 people make an annual pilgrimage to the church every spring on Good Friday.

The Oviedo family has been carving native woods since 1739, and today the **Oviedo Gallery** (☎ 505-351-2280; www.oviedoart.com; Hwy 76; ☾ 10am-6pm) is housed in the 270-year-old family farm. If you're interested in handloomed weaving, head to **Centinela Traditional Arts** (☎ 505-351-2180, 877-351-2180; www.chimayoweavers.com; NM 76; ☾ 9am-6pm Mon-Sat, 10am-5pm Sun). Irvin Trujillo, a 7th-generation Rio Grande weaver, whose carpets are in collections at the Smithsonian in Washington, DC, and the Museum of Fine Arts (p311) in Santa Fe, works out of and runs this cooperative gallery of 20 weavers. Naturally dyed blankets, vests and pillows are sold, and you can watch the artists weaving on handlooms in the back.

The most famous place for dinner is **Rancho de Chimayó** (☎ 505-351-4444; www.ranchodechimayo .com; 300 County Rd 98; dishes $8-16; ☾ 11:30am-9pm

NEW MEXICO

Mon-Fri, 8:30am-10:30am Sat & Sun, closed Mon Nov-Apr), serving classic New Mexican cuisine, courtesy of the Jaramillo family's famed recipes, and the perfect margarita.

Also highly recommended is the unpretentious **Casa Escondida** (☎ 505-351-4805; www.casaescondida.com; 64 County Rd 100; r $99-149), featuring eight beautiful rooms and a hot tub.

Truchas
pop 950 / elev 8400ft

Rural New Mexico at its most sincere is showcased in Truchas, a tiny town that looks as if it's seen better days. Truchas was originally settled by the Spaniards in the 18th century, and Robert Redford's *Milagro Beanfield War* was filmed here. It's easy to see why. The place looks like it's stuck in another century. Narrow roads, many unpaved, lead to yards of red dirt and crumbling adobe homes. Despite the obvious poverty, Truchas remains a determined little place that's worth supporting. Between the run-down homes are some wonderful little galleries, which double as workshops for local weavers and other artists. Don't miss the **Cordovas Handweaving Workshop** (☎ 505-689-2437; www.la-tierra.com/busyles; Main Truchas Rd), run by a friendly 4th-generation weaver named Harry. You can watch him weaving in between browsing his beautiful blankets, placemats and rugs. Opening hours are sporadic.

Rancho Arriba B&B (☎ 505-689-2374; www.ranchoarriba.com; Main Truchas Rd; s/d with shared bathroom $50/70, d $100; 🖳), in a rustic adobe farmhouse on the edge of Pecos Wilderness, has horses and wood stoves, and will arrange to cook you dinner in advance.

If you drive through town, rather than taking the turn for Taos, you'll find yourself winding into a mountain river valley, a creek and the trailhead to Truchas Peak (at 13,101ft, the second-highest peak in New Mexico) and the Carson Wilderness Area.

Las Trampas

Built in 1760 and constantly defended against Apache raids, the **Church of San José de Gracia** (Hwy 76; 🕙 9am-5pm Mon-Sat Jun-Aug) is considered one of the finest surviving 18th-century churches in the USA. Original paintings and carvings remain in excellent condition, and self-flagellation bloodstains from the Los Hermanos Penitentes (a 19th-century secretive religious order with a strong following in the northern mountains of New Mexico) are still visible.

LOW ROAD TO TAOS

People talk about the High Rd being so much more scenic than the so-called Low Rd that no one can fault you for having depressed expectations about this route. Fortunately, you'll be quite surprised at how scenic it is. Running along the Rio Grande River for much of the way, it's also an angler's paradise, with plenty of good fly-fishing spots. If you're traveling with your doggie, he'll appreciate getting out of the car and staring at the breathtaking desert-meets-mountain scenery or placing a paw in the rushing river that requires a rocky downhill scramble to reach. Bring a picnic lunch and stop at one of the tables perched above the Rio Grande. Keep an eye on the river in summer – you'll see dozens of tourist-packed white-water rafts rush by.

Fifteen miles north of Española, the **Black Mesa Winery** (☎ 505-852-2820, 800-852-6372; www.blackmesawinery.com; 1502 NM 68, Velarde; 🕙 10am-6pm Mon-Sat, noon-6pm Sun) offers tastings before the highway cuts through the apple orchards of Velarde and into the Rio Grande Canyon.

Take a slight detour east on Hwy 75 to the small farming community of **Dixon**, where there are a couple of galleries as well as the excellent **La Chiripada Winery** (☎ 505-579-4437, 800-528-7801; www.lachiripada.com; NM 75; 🕙 10am-5pm Mon-Sat, noon-5pm Sun), producers of our favorite inexpensive white wines (less than $20 a bottle; we like the riesling best). It offers tastings.

Seven miles further north, tiny **Pilar** is the base for summer white-water rafting – hence the prevalence of aforementioned rafts. Try an adventure with **Big River Raft Trips** (☎ 505-758-9711, 800-748-3746; www.bigriverrafts.com; cnr NM 68 & CR 570), which runs full-day and half-day floats ($60 to $125) as well as more thrilling trips down the Taos Box. The **Rio Grande Gorge Visitor Center** (☎ 505-751-4899; NM 68; 🕙 9am-4:30pm most days mid-Jan–Nov) has information on campsites and area hikes.

TAOS
pop 6500 / elev town 6950ft, ski base 9207ft

When it comes to natural graces, Taos delivers a trifecta: art, culture and beauty. It only takes a heartbeat to fall in love with this tiny and isolated town. Let your senses register the scent of sage in the air, the silver conch that decorates the belts and saddles of resident humans and horses, and that sweep of mesa cresting at the pointy, often white tips of Taos Mountain and you'll find yourself head over heels.

Don't think you're Taos' only lover, though. She's been stirring souls for centuries now with her kiss of canyons and dusty byways, her melding of New Age and ancient, and her perfect adobe pueblo, champagne powder ski slopes and fabulous restaurants.

The white man's love affair with Taos began on the cusp of the 20th century, when a lucky breakdown stranded a couple of artists in Taos. They stayed, and their reasons for staying soon got out; before too long an artists' enclave, drawn by light unencumbered by the weight of atmosphere, by colors at once subtle and brilliant, was

formed. Today the city is home to more than 80 galleries, and about 30% of people here call themselves artists.

The Native Americans knew Taos was special long before the artists, yuppies, neo-hippies and other mainstream dropouts showed up at her amazing natural doorstep. They knew Taos was one of those special places on earth, and built one of New Mexico's proudest and most magnificent pueblos, Taos Pueblo. The Taos Pueblo still stands strong and dignified, remaining a potent force in defining the culture and character of the adjacent city and ski resort.

Taos is also one of New Mexico's top tourism destinations, and visitors come to challenge themselves on her slopes, to shop for

NEW MEXICO

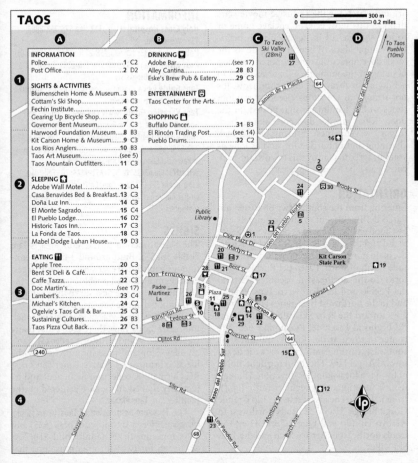

TAOS

INFORMATION
Police..1 C2
Post Office....................................2 D2

SIGHTS & ACTIVITIES
Blumenschein Home & Museum..3 B3
Cottam's Ski Shop.......................4 C3
Fechin Institute...........................5 C2
Gearing Up Bicycle Shop.............6 C3
Governor Bent Museum................7 C2
Harwood Foundation Museum.....8 B3
Kit Carson Home & Museum........9 C3
Los Rios Anglers.........................10 B3
Taos Art Museum.................(see 5)
Taos Mountain Outfitters...........11 C3

SLEEPING
Adobe Wall Motel.....................12 D4
Casa Benavides Bed & Breakfast..13 C3
Doña Luz Inn.............................14 C3
El Monte Sagrado......................15 C4
El Pueblo Lodge.........................16 D2
Historic Taos Inn.......................17 C3
La Fonda de Taos......................18 C3
Mabel Dodge Luhan House........19 D3

EATING
Apple Tree.................................20 C3
Bent St Deli & Café...................21 C3
Caffe Tazza...............................22 C3
Doc Martin's.......................(see 17)
Lambert's..................................23 C4
Michael's Kitchen......................24 C2
Ogelvie's Taos Grill & Bar..........25 C3
Sustaining Cultures....................26 B3
Taos Pizza Out Back..................27 C1

DRINKING
Adobe Bar..........................(see 17)
Alley Cantina............................28 B3
Eske's Brew Pub & Eatery..........29 C3

ENTERTAINMENT
Taos Center for the Arts............30 D2

SHOPPING
Buffalo Dancer..........................31 B3
El Rincón Trading Post.........(see 14)
Pueblo Drums............................32 C2

To Taos Ski Valley (28mi)
To Taos Pueblo (10mi)

Camino de la Placita
Camino del Pueblo
Brooks St
Public Library
Paseo del Pueblo Norte
Civic Plaza Dr
Martyrs La
Bent St
Kit Carson State Park
Don Fernando St
Padre Martinez La
Plaza
Ranchitos Rd
Ledoux St
Morada La
Kit Carson Rd
Quesnel St
Ojitos Rd
Paseo del Pueblo Sur
Siler Rd
Montoya St
Burch Ave
Los Pandos Rd

0   300 m
0   0.2 miles

NEW MEXICO

TOP TEN TAOS

- **Taos Ski Valley** (p343) For champagne powder, tree glades and now snowboarding!
- **El Monte Sagrado** (p339) For posh high-desert R&R.
- **Eske's Brew Pub** (p340) For green chile beer.
- **La Fonda de Taos** (p339) For a peak at DH Lawrence's Forbidden Art and fabulous rooms.
- **Adobe Bar** (p340) For a potent margarita and live music.
- **Taos Pueblo** (p287) For Native American festivals and delicious fry bread.
- **Earthship Rentals** (p338) For sleeping off the grid.
- **Rafting the Taos Box** (p337) For getting frustrations out on the river by riding down the Class IV run.
- **Rio Grande Gorge Bridge** (opposite) For the view.
- **Taos Plaza** (below) For wandering.

---

art and watch for the reclusive movie stars that call this most eclectic enclave home or to lose themselves in her mountain magic for a couple days. When in Taos, do as the locals do: embrace the time-honored tradition of living in the moment. Whatever needs to get done can always get done tomorrow. It's not strange to see shops closed at random times with a handmade sign posted on the door, 'Killer powder day, gone skiing, back tomorrow.' Yup, these residents are a casual, charming and unhurried lot, and as long as you can agree to play by this town's laid-back rules, you'll be a very happy camper.

ORIENTATION

Entering from the south, Hwy 68 turns into Paseo del Pueblo Sur, a strip of motels and fast-food chains. It changes briefly into Santa Fe Rd and then into Paseo del Pueblo Norte, the main north–south street in the town. One mile north of town, Paseo del Pueblo Norte forks: to the northeast it becomes Camino del Pueblo and heads toward Taos Pueblo, and to the northwest it becomes Hwy 64 and goes toward the Taos Ski Valley. Kit Carson Rd begins at Paseo del Pueblo Sur near the center of town at the Taos Plaza and runs southeast, turning into Hwy 64 as it heads toward Angel Fire. The 'blinking light' north of town is a focal point for directions (though it now functions as a regular traffic light); from it, Hwy 64 heads west to the Rio Grande Gorge Bridge, Hwy 522 heads northwest to Arroyo Hondo and Questa, and Hwy 150 heads northeast to Arroyo Seco and the Taos Ski Valley.

INFORMATION

Holy Cross Hospital (Map p342; ☎ 575-758-8883; 1397 Weimer Rd; ☉ 24hr)

Police (Map p333; ☎ 575-758-2216; 107 Civic Plaza Dr)

Post office (Map p333; ☎ 575-758-2081; Paseo del Pueblo Norte at Brooks St)

Taos Guide (www.taosguide.com) Click for an exhaustive list of easy-to-navigate links.

Taos Vacation Guide (www.taosvacationguide.com) Good site with sections in French, German and Spanish.

Taos Visitor Center (Map p342; ☎ 575-758-3873, 800-732-8267; www.destinationtaos.com; Paseo del Pueblo Sur at Paseo del Cañon; ☉ 9am-5pm)

Wired? (Map p342; ☎ 575-751-9473; 705 Felicidad Lane; per hr $7; ☉ 7am-7pm) Coffee shop with free wi-fi if you've got laptop; if not you can log on to their computers.

SIGHTS

The best attraction in the Taos area is **Taos Pueblo** (p287). Built around 1450 and continuously inhabited ever since, it is the largest existing multistoried pueblo structure in the USA and one of the best surviving examples of traditional adobe construction.

Otherwise, for a village that gets as much tourist traffic as Taos, there aren't that many sights to see. Wander historic **Ledoux St**, Taos' art alley. Stop and pose for a picture by the life-size bronzes by Native American artist RC Gorman. A collection of ancient and irregularly shaped adobes are centered on the picturesque **Taos Plaza**.

The **Museum Association of Taos** (www.taosmu seums.org) offers a six-museum pass ($25) and a six-museum ticket (adult/child $10/7 or $8/5 each for two) for area museums that represents great value; all the museums we list following are part of this deal. All museums have different hours, themes and single-entry prices.

Earthships

Definitely the coolest attraction in Taos. Innovative and off-the-grid, these **structures** (off Map p342; ☎ 575-751-0462; http://earthship.org; US Hwy 64; tour $5; ✆ 10am-4pm) are self-sustaining, environmentally savvy houses built with recycled materials like used automobile tires and cans. The community is the brainchild of architect Michael Reynolds, whose idea was to develop a building method that 'eliminates stress from both the planet and its inhabitants.' Buried on three sides by earth, the Earthships are designed to heat and cool themselves, make their own electricity and catch their own water. Sewage is decomposed naturally, and dwellers grow their own food. They are open daily for tours and are available for rental (p338). The tour office is located 1.5 miles past the Rio Grande Gorge Bridge on US Hwy 64 West.

San Francisco de Asis Church

Four miles south of Taos in Ranchos de Taos, this oft-photographed **church** (Map p342; ☎ 575-758-2754; St Francis Plaza; ✆ 9am-4pm Mon-Fri) was built in the mid-18th century and opened in 1815. It's been memorialized in numerous Georgia O'Keeffe paintings and Edward Weston photographs. Mass is held at 6pm the first Saturday of the month, and usually at 7am, 9am and 11:30am every Sunday (call to confirm).

Taos Art Museum & Fechin Institute

This **museum** (Map p333; ☎ 575-758-2690; www.fechin .com; 227 Paseo del Pueblo Norte; admission $5; ✆ 10am-4pm Wed-Sun) was home to Russian artist Nicolai Fechin, who emigrated to New York City in 1922 at age 42 and moved to Taos in 1926. Today his paintings, drawings and sculptures are in museums and collections worldwide. Between 1927 and 1933, Fechin completely reconstructed the interior of his adobe home, adding his own distinctly Russian woodcarvings. The Fechin house exhibits the artist's private collection, including much Asian art, and hosts occasional chamber music events. Five-day watercolor, sculpture and other arts workshops are offered from May to October at the nearby ranch.

Rio Grande Gorge Bridge

On US Hwy 64 about 12 miles northwest of Taos, the gorge bridge is the second-highest suspension bridge in the USA. Constructed in 1965, the vertigo-inducing steel bridge spans 500ft across the gorge and 650ft above the river below, and there's a walkway across it all. The views west over the emptiness of the

---

TAOS SOCIETY OF ARTISTS

In 1893 artist Joseph Henry Sharp first visited Taos to produce a group of illustrations depicting the pueblo for publication. Quite smitten with the scene, Sharp spread the word among his colleagues about his 'discovery,' and shortly afterward relocated here permanently.

Ernest Blumenschein, Bert Phillips and many more of his contemporaries followed, and in 1912 they, along with Oscar Berninghaus, Eanger Irving Couse and Herbert Dunton, established the Taos Society of Artists (TSA). The original six were later joined by other prominent painters including Lucy Harwood, the only female member, and Juan Tafiho Mirabol, a Taos Indian.

Early TSA paintings were inspired by the backdrop of the Sangre de Cristo Mountains as well as the buildings and people of Taos Pueblo. Set against the tonal shapes and neutral colors of earth, human figures act as anchors of color seen nowhere else in the desert. Pueblo architecture, with clusters of organic and sculptural block shapes reflecting the high desert light, also appealed to the Taos painters' artistic sensibilities.

The artists' styles were as diverse and experimental as the many philosophies of painting that defined the first half of the 20th century. From Sharp's illustrative and realistic approach and Blumenschein's impressionistic treatment of Southwestern themes to the moody art-deco spirit of Dunton's landscapes, the TSA portrayed the same subjects in infinite ways.

Only in later years would the TSA's contribution to modern art's development be fully recognized. Historically the paintings of the TSA are seen as a visual documentary of northern New Mexican cultures, which had not yet been so dramatically influenced by the industrial age.

Taos Plateau and down into the jagged walls of the Rio Grande are incredible.

Historic Homes

Kit Carson (1809–68) was the Southwest's most famous mountain man, guide, trapper, soldier and scout, and his home and life serve as an excellent introduction to Taos in the mid-19th century. The **Kit Carson Home & Museum** (Map p333; ☎ 575-758-4945; www.kitcarsonhome.com; Kit Carson Rd; adult/child $5/3; ⏰ 9am-5pm Jun-Sep, shorter rest of year) houses such artifacts as Carson's rifles, telescope and walking cane. Built in 1825 with 30in adobe walls and traditional territorial architecture, the home's 12 rooms are today furnished as they may have been during Carson's day, with exhibits on all periods of Taos history and mountain-man lore.

The 1797 **Blumenschein Home & Museum** (Map p333; ☎ 575-758-0505; 222 Ledoux St; adult/child $6/3; ⏰ 9am-5pm Jun-Sep, shorter rest of year) was the home of artist Ernest Blumenschein (one of the founding members of the Taos Society of Artists; see the boxed text, p335) in the 1920s. Today it's maintained much as it would have been when the Blumenscheins lived here. The period furniture is interesting, and the art is spectacular.

Harwood Foundation Museum

Housed in a historic mid-19th century adobe compound, the **Harwood Foundation Museum** (Map p333; ☎ 575-758-9826; www.harwoodmuseum.org; 238 Ledoux St; admission $7; ⏰ 10am-5pm Tue-Sat, noon-5pm Sun) features paintings, drawings, prints, sculpture and photography by northern New Mexican artists, both historical and contemporary. Founded in 1923, the Harwood has been run by the University of New Mexico since 1936 and underwent a major renovation

in 1997. It is the second-oldest museum in New Mexico, and one of its most important when it comes to art collections.

Millicent Rogers Museum

This **museum** (Map p342; ☎ 505-758-2462; www.millicentrogers.org; Millicent Rogers Museum Rd; admission $7; ⏰ 10am-5pm, closed Mon Nov-Mar), about 4 miles from the plaza, is filled with pottery, jewelry, baskets and textiles from the private collection of Millicent Rogers, a model and oil heiress who moved to Taos in 1947 and acquired one of the best collections of Indian and Spanish colonial art in the USA. You want to know what a top-quality squashblossom necklace is supposed to look like? Look no further. Also displayed are contemporary Native American and Hispanic artworks.

ACTIVITIES

Hike, bike, raft, ski, fish…the variety of outdoor activities in the Taos area is exhaustive; consult www.taosoutdoorrecreation.com for an online rundown of all your options.

In winter it's all about skiing, and most of the action takes place at the Taos Ski Valley, which is slightly confusingly not actually in the town of Taos; it's about 20 miles away. The ski (and newly minted snowboard) resort has a slew of lodging and eating options, so we've actually given it its own heading in this guide. Check out p343 for more on skiing in Taos.

Native Sons Adventures (Map p342; ☎ 575-758-9342; www.nativesonsadventures.com; 1033 Paseo del Pueblo Sur; ⏰ 7am-6pm) is a good source of information; it rents equipment and guides various trips. The huge **Taos Mountain Outfitters** (Map p333; ☎ 575-758-9292; www.taosmountainoutfitters.com; 114 S Plaza) rents and sells everything you need to get out and play. It also has loads of info on nearby hiking

---

SOMETHING DIFFERENT

Taos-based river outfitter, **Los Rios River Runners** (Map p342; ☎ 575-776-8854, 800-544-1181; www.losriosriverrunners.com; Hwy 68; ⏰ 8am-6pm) offers a unique twist on the classic three-day Chama River raft trip between El Vado and Abiquiú. For a (mere) $510 the company will arrange for an astronomer, archaeologist, yoga instructor, gourmet chef, local-lore storyteller or (new for 2008) herbalist to accompany you down the river. Book your candidate of choice and spend three days floating past perfect swimming holes, down Class III rapids, past towering vermilion cliffs and ancient Pueblo dwellings by day. Come dark, sit around the campfire and soak up your chile with a tutorial from your guru, which, depending on your tastes, could be anything from a lesson on the night sky to an riverside wine tasting or a discussion on the finer points of edible herbs.

trails, ranging from easy day hikes to overnight backcountry trips, and alpine mountain trails along rivers to awesome hikes along and through the Rio Grande Gorge. Many hikes begin near the Taos Ski Valley, 20 miles north of town.

White-Water Rafting

The major summertime attraction is white-water rafting in the Taos Box, the steep-sided cliffs that frame the Rio Grande. Busloads of rafters from Santa Fe go up to Pilar (p332), which can become a flurry of sunburned and screaming tourists. The best time to go is in May and June, when snowmelt keeps the rivers rapid, but it's warm enough to enjoy the splash. In town, contact **Los Rios River Runners** (Map p342; ☎ 575-776-8854, 800-544-1181; www.losrios riverrunners.com; Hwy 68; ☻ 8am-6pm), which runs trips for around $100. It also does half-day trips on the slightly less rabid Racecourse ($50) – make it more exciting by running it in an inflatable kayak where you're the sole driver.

Horseback Riding

Rio Grande Stables (off Map p342; ☎ 575-776-5913; www.lajitasstables.com/taos.htm; ☻ mid-May–mid-Sep), on the road to the ski valley, offers one- to three-hour trips ($45 to $135), all-day rides (including one to the top of Wheeler Peak) and combination horseback/rafting/camping treks they'll customize just for you. Rates start at $45 for one hour.

Fishing

Taos is ringed with stocked streams and lakes that draw adventuresome anglers (some choice spots require a rigorous hike to reach) and happy hooking, cutthroat and German brown trout. Many sites are within steps of your car door; some spots are fully wheelchair-accessible.

You must have a license to take advantage of all the fish; check with local outfitter and tackle shop **Los Rios Anglers** (Map p333; ☎ 575-758-2798; www.losrios.com; 126 W Plaza) for the scoop on this and good fishing spots. The company also runs a host of tailored guided trips – for beginners to experienced anglers – that take you to unspoiled private lands threaded with secret sparkling streams. Make reservations 48 hours in advance; day trips for one/two/three people cost $250/275/350.

Mountain Biking

Where else are you going to find biking this good, this close to the sky? Why bother looking elsewhere when an enormous network of mountain-bike and multi-use trails cover the region of the Carson National Forest between Taos, Angel Fire and Picuris Peak?

Standouts include the 9-mile **West Rim Trail** at Orilla Verde Recreation Area, suitable for strong beginners and intermediate cyclists to enjoy views of Rio Grande Gorge; and storied **South Boundary Trail**, considered one of the best mountain-bike trails in the nation – a 28-mile ride for experienced bikers.

If you want to really challenge yourself, try the 84-mile **Enchanted Circle** loop. It makes a fine regional road-bike circuit once you've acclimatized to the altitude.

For info, trails maps and rentals, visit **Gearing Up Bicycle Shop** (Map p333; ☎ 575-751-0365; 129 Paseo del Pueblo Sur; ☻ 9am-6:30pm). It rents mountain and hybrid bikes ($10/35/125 per hour/day/week), full-suspension bikes ($50 per day) and road bikes ($45).

TOURS

Historic Taos Trolley Tours (Map p342; ☎ 575-751-0366; www.taostrolleytours.com; cnr Paseo del Pueblo Sur & Paseo del Cañon; adult/child $33/10; ☻ 10:30am & 2pm) Offers two different tours aboard red trolleys from the visitor center. One visits Taos Pueblo, San Francisco de Asis and the plaza (where they'll also pick you up); the other takes in Millicent Rogers Museum and the Martinez Hacienda.

FESTIVALS & EVENTS

There are numerous athletic and cultural events all year, as well as visual arts workshops; the visitor center (p334) has details. **Christmas Holidays** in late December feature dances at Taos Pueblo (p287) and mass at San Francisco de Asis Church (p335). Christmas carolers and *farolitos* everywhere help keep everyone's spirits bright. Check out the boxed text, p341, for info on the green **Solar Music Festival** in June.

SLEEPING

Taos offers a wide variety of accommodation, from free camping in national forests to gourmet B&Bs in historic adobes. The village attracts visitors all year, though December to February and June to August are generally the high seasons.

Reservation services include the **Taos Association of Bed & Breakfast Inns** (☎ 800-939-2215; www.taos-bandb-inns.com) and **Taos Vacation Rentals** (☎ 800-788-8267; www.taosvacati onrentals.com).

Budget

Adobe Wall Motel (Map p333; ☎ 505-758-3972; 227 E Kit Carson Rd; r from $45) For almost 100 years, this mom-and-pop motel has offered affordable shelter to tired cowboys (and skiers). An old motor court–style place, rooms are slightly tattered, but the beds are decently comfortable and best of all, each room comes with a lovely, working kiva fireplace.

Hacienda Inn (Map p342; ☎ 505-758-8610; www .hacendainntaos.com; 1321 Paseo del Pueblo Sur; r $50-90) Three miles from the plaza, this family-owned and -operated place has been voted cleanest motel by the *Taos Valley Times*. Rooms are basic but big with Native American–influenced wood furnishings. Bathrooms are small, but the sink area separate from the toilet is convenient. There are multinight stay discounts in low season; dogs are welcome but cost $10 per night.

El Pueblo Lodge (Map p333; ☎ 800-433-9612; www .elpueblolodge.com; 412 Paseo del Pueblo Norte; r $55-125; 🖳) This place is right downtown, with big, clean rooms, some with kitchenettes and/or fireplaces, a pool, hot tub and fresh pastries in the morning. What's not to love?

Midrange

Enjoy a spacious, modern room on Paseo del Pueblo Sur or something more historic (read: nice but cramped) downtown. Folks who don't usually like B&Bs should note that many in Taos have private entrances and bathrooms, which gives you the same privacy as a hotel.

Laughing Horse Inn (Map p342; ☎ 800-776-0161; www.laughinghorseinn.com; 729 Paseo del Pueblo Norte; r $75-160; wi-fi) More like a hippie commune than a hotel, this unique inn offers one-of-a-kind rooms inside a meandering 120-year-old Spanish adobe hacienda. Furnished with everything from chile-shaped Christmas lights, piñon incense and hand-hewn furniture to a triple bunk with a sauna, most digs share bathrooms, but all are cool. A communal atmosphere continues with a hot tub under the stars and a huge penthouse. Each room captures the quirk of old Taos. Organic breakfast foods are available all day. Guests cook their own meals, which can sometimes turn into a delightful culinary mosaic of everyone's offerings.

American Artists Gallery House B&B (Map p342; ☎ 800-532-2041; www.taosbedandbreakfast.com; 132 Frontier Lane; r & ste $100-200; 🖳) Art flows here in ever-changing shows drawn from local galleries. George the peacock and lots of cats will be your inn-mates, while Jacuzzi suites will blow your mind. All rooms have wood-burning fireplaces. Creative breakfasts are legendary. It offers ski-and-stay packages that include lift tickets to Taos Ski Valley starting at $160 per person.

Mabel Dodge Luhan House (Map p333; ☎ 505-751-9686; www.mabeldodgeluhan.com; 240 Morada Lane; r $100-250) Every inch of this place exudes elegant meets rustic beauty. The 'Patroness of Taos,' Mabel Dodge Luhan (by equal measures graceful and grand, scandalous and unbearable) built this fabulous mansion to welcome everyone from Emma Goldman and Margaret Sanger to Carl Jung for a nice chat. You can sleep in rooms where Georgia O'Keeffe, Ansel Adams or Willa Cather once laid their heads, or where DH Lawrence added artful touches. It also runs art workshops – check the website for more.

Historic Taos Inn (Map p333; ☎ 800-826-7466; www .taosinn.com; 125 Paseo del Pueblo Norte; r $100-275; wi-fi) Parts of this National Register of Historic Places landmark date to the 17th century, which explains why it's not the plushest place in town. But it's still fabulous, despite the gradually settling adobe architecture. Perhaps it's the cozy lobby, heavy wood furniture and the sunken fireplace – or the classic restaurant Doc Martin's and lots of live local music at its famed Adobe Bar.

Old Taos Guesthouse (Map p342; ☎ 800-758-5448; www.oldtaos.com; 1028 Witt Rd; r $115-140; 🖳) This atmospheric treasure features spacious, old-world adobe rooms with undulating walls (just try to find a right angle here) and hand-carved wood furnishings and doors. Hidden away in a quiet residential neighborhood, the shady lawn and gardens beckon with inviting hammocks and 60-mile sunset views. The proprietors are seasoned adventurers and can point you toward great excursions.

our pick Earthship Rentals (off Map p342; ☎ 505-751-0462; US 64; r $125-175) Experience an off-grid night in a boutique-chic, solar-powered dwelling. A cross between organic Gaudi architecture and space-age fantasy, these sustainable dwellings are put together from recycled tires, aluminum cans and sand, with rain-catching and gray-water systems to minimize their footprint. Half-buried in a valley surrounding by mountains, they could be hastily camouflaged alien vessels – you never know…

Casa Europa (Map p342; ☎ 888-758-9798; www .casaeuropanm.com; 840 Upper Ranchitos Rd; r $175; wi-fi) Cool breezes provide the air-conditioning at this stunning 18th-century estate. Views of pastures and mountains are sublime. Euro-style antiques mix artfully with Southwestern-style pieces. Offers an elaborate breakfast and afternoon treats in summer, evening hors d'oeuvres in winter. Comfort, light and air define this welcoming spot.

Top End

Taos' finest options are in a quirky class by themselves and satisfy even the most pampered souls with style to spare. These luxurious retreats include exquisite antiques, evening wine tastings, multicourse breakfasts and all the saltillo-tiled elegance you'd want.

El Monte Sagrado (Map p333; ☎ 800-828-8267; www.elmontesagrado.com; 317 Kit Carson Rd; r $199-699; ☒ ☐ wi-fi) A lush oasis in the high desert, this lavishly decorated ecoresort has bright and cozy suites whimsically decorated with Native American, Mexican, Moroccan and Egyptian cultures in mind, all arranged around a flourishing courtyard irrigated with a gray-water system. It has an on-site spa, wi-fi internet access and plenty of package deals with the ski valley.

Doña Luz Inn (Map p333; ☎ 800-758-9187; www.stayin taos.com; 114 Kit Carson Rd; r $204; ☐) Your world will be framed only by the horizons at this 200-year-old inn. Rooms with adobe fireplaces, patios, kitchenettes and hot tubs range from the tiny La Luz to the three-level Rainbow Room suite, with a hot tub on the rooftop sundeck. All are decorated in colorful Spanish-colonial style, a cheerful clutter of Native American and Spanish colonial antiques, artifacts and art – lots of it sacred and all of it beautiful.

La Fonda de Taos (Map p333; ☎ 800-833-2211; www .hotellafonda.com; 108 S Plaza; r $239; ☐) This upscale hotel, formerly owned by notorious playboy Saki Karavas, just can't shake its sexy vibe – even the kiva gas fireplaces in the smallish, sensually angled suites seem like they're illuminating something that's up to no good. Perhaps it's the Forbidden Art collection of DH Lawrence, banned in 1929 Europe and displayed here to consenting adults, depicting, and perhaps inspiring, all sorts of sinful fun. No children under 13.

Casa Benavides Bed & Breakfast (Map p333; ☎ 505-758-1772, 800-552-1772; www.taos-casabenavides.com; 137 Kit Carson Rd; r $300; ☐) This romantic spot spans five buildings, and has lots of fireplaces, patios, balconies and gardens. Furniture is mostly antique and handmade, and shares space with artful treasures. Some rooms have kitchens.

EATING

Although there are some quality options around the plaza, that old rule of thumb still applies: the farther you get from the tourist epicenter, the better the food – or at least, the better the deal.

Budget

Caffe Tazza (Map p333; ☎ 505-758-8706; 122 Kit Carson Rd; goodies $2-6; ☺ 7am-7pm, until 9pm for events; ☝ Ⓥ) Tazza is more than just coffee drinks, Taos Cow hormone-free ice cream, healthy soups (go for the vegan green chile), homemade sandwiches, burritos and vegan desserts. This place packs its patio and cozy art-lined interior with crunchy-hipster Taoseños, who also participate in live music, open mics and readings.

Sustaining Cultures (Map p333; ☎ 505-751-0959; 114 Doña Luz St; mains $5-10; ☺ 9:30am-5:30pm Mon-Sat; ☝ Ⓥ) Some people can't start their day without a Wheatgrass Hopper from this New Age outpost. Although it's known for the best salad bar in town (open 11am to 3pm), should your Cancer moon ache for the avocado and cheese sandwich or your Taurus ascendant insist on the tempeh burger glazed with peanut sauce, there's still hope: tarot-card readers ($1 per minute) are usually available to assist you in these and other decisions.

Midrange

Bent Street Deli & Café (Map p333; ☎ 505-758-5787; 120 Bent St; breakfast & lunch $3-10, dinner $11-20; ☺ 8am-4pm Mon-Wed, 8am-9pm Thu-Sat, 10am-3pm Sun; ☝ Ⓥ) All three meals (and in-between snacks) are tasty, whether you're building your own sandwich or choosing one of 21 recommended combos and an array of irresistible sides. Dinner revolves around gourmet comfort food, while the rotating brunch menu is over the top.

Taos Pizza Out Back (Map p333; ☎ 505-758-3112; 712 Paseo del Pueblo Norte; slices $4-6, medium pies $18-23; ☺ 11am-9pm; ☝ Ⓥ) Pizza dreams come true with every possible ingredient under the sun at Taos' top pizza palace; for example, the recommended Vera Cruz has chicken breast and veggies marinated in a honey-chipotle sauce.

Slices are enormous, and crusts are made with organic flour. Out Back will also bake dough balls for kids, and has a great back patio.

Doc Martin's (Map p333; ☎ 505-758-1977; 125 Paseo del Pueblo Norte; breakfast & lunch $5-15, dinner $12-35; ⓨ breakfast, lunch & dinner) Hang out where Bert Philips (the Doc's bro-in-law) and Ernest Blumenschein cooked up the idea of the Taos Society of Artists. Sit by the kiva fireplace, pop a cork on one of the award-winning wines, dive into the *chile rellenos* ($12) and you'll be inspired to great things as well. Reservations recommended.

Graham's Grille (Map p342; ☎ 505-751-1350; www.grahamstaos.com; 106 Paseo del Pueblo Norte; mains $7-19; ⓨ lunch & dinner; Ⓥ) Locals say this is the best new restaurant in town. It serves honest, creative and nonfussy food in hip retro-mod environs – think lime-green walls, purple lightbulbs and starched white tablecloths. The menu features lots of sandwiches and salads, along with mac 'n' cheese and Frito pie bowls.

Michael's Kitchen (Map p333; ☎ 505-758-4178; 304C Paseo del Pueblo Norte; mains $8-13; ⓨ breakfast, lunch & dinner; ⓚ Ⓥ) OK, so it's a little touristy, but it's still an old local favorite in part because the energy is witty and entertaining, the food pretty darn good, and the in-house bakery produces goodies that fly out the door. Plus it serves the best damn breakfast in town, and you just may spot a Hollywood celebrity or two digging into a chile-smothered breakfast burrito.

Ogelvie's Taos Grill & Bar (Map p333; ☎ 505-758-8866; 103 E Plaza; lunch $8-11, dinner $10-26; ⓨ lunch & dinner; ⓚ Ⓥ) There's no place like the 2nd-floor patio for surveying the scene on the plaza. And there's nothing like the chicken *mole* for lunch ($11) or the garlic and black pepper rib-eye ($25).

Apple Tree (Map p333; ☎ 505-758-1900; 123 Bent St; mains $10-25; ⓨ lunch & dinner; ⓚ Ⓥ) Whether you've ordered a simple but elegant lunch or a gourmet twist on an old New Mexican classic (mango chicken enchilada), you'll want to savor your meal on the patio. The fancy surroundings in this historic adobe blend well with fine art, candles and a huge wine list. At lunch an abbreviated to-go menu wraps up simpler, but still stunning fare for a few dollars less than you'd pay to eat inside.

Top End
Stakeout Grill & Bar (Map p342; ☎ 505-758-2042; 101 Stakeout Dr, Rancho de Taos; mains $16-28; ⓨ dinner; Ⓥ) Steak and seafood prepared with a continen-

tal flair draw folks 8 miles south of town off NM 68. Patrons also come for the great wine list and the stellar sunset views of the Rio Grande Gorge from atop Outlaw Hill. (Yes, there were outlaws here at one point.) It's the most romantic place to dine around town.

Lambert's (Map p333; ☎ 505-758-1009; 309 Paseo del Pueblo Sur; mains $20-35; ⓨ 5-9pm; ⓚ Ⓥ) Winner of multiple Best of Taos awards, including best restaurant, Lambert's is a cozy local hangout where patrons sink deeply into sofas and conversation for hours on end. Lace curtains and subtle elegance make this atmospheric eatery a fine experience, whether you're digging into caribou, buffalo or the pepper-crusted lamb loin ($34).

DRINKING
Eske's Brew Pub & Eatery (Map p333; ☎ 505-758-1517; 106 Des Georges Lane; pub grub $6-10; ⓨ 4-10pm Mon-Thu, 11am-10pm Fri-Sun) This crowded hang-out rotates more than 25 microbrewed ales, from Taos Green Chile to Doobie Rock Heller Bock, to complement hearty bowls of Wanda's green chile stew and sushi on Tuesday. Live local music, from acoustic guitar to jazz, is usually free but national acts might charge a cover.

Alley Cantina (Map p333; ☎ 505-758-2121; 121 Terracina Lane; pub grub $6-14; ⓨ from 11:30am) It figures that the oldest building in Taos is a comfy bar, built more than three centuries ago by forward-thinking Native American capitalists as the Taos Pueblo Trading Post. Nowadays you can catch live music ranging from zydeco to rock and jazz almost nightly, but don't miss the Cullen Winter Blues band.

Adobe Bar (Map p333; ☎ 505-758-2233; Taos Inn, 125 Paseo del Pueblo Norte; ⓨ from noon) There's something about this place. There's something about the chairs, the Taos Inn's history, the casualness, the vibe and the tequila. It's true, the packed street-side patio has some of the state's finest margaritas, along with an eclectic line-up of great live music like Manzanares and Madi Soto – and there's almost never a cover.

Shadow's Lounge & Grill (Map p342; ☎ 505-751-9600; 330A Paseo del Pueblo Sur) Locals say this is the best sports bar in town. The popular place is also a top spot for mingling, serving cold beers and lots of atmosphere.

ENTERTAINMENT
Que Pasa (Map p342; ☎ 505-758-7344; 338 Paseo del Pueblo Sur; ⓨ 10am-6pm Mon-Sat, noon-5pm Sun) This

GOOD DAY SUNSHINE

Just as the Rio Grande Gorge opens up to engulf US Hwy 68 for the scenic climb into Taos, your radio will start to sputter. Don't put on that tired old CD; flip to KTAO 101.9 FM (www.ktao.com), broadcasting shows like 'Trash and Treasures' (where callers describe their wackiest for-sale items), Larry Torres' news and views from Taos Pueblo, and lots of great music.

KTAO has been doing it all with solar power since 1991, when station owner Brad Hockmeyer installed 50,000 watts worth of photovoltaic cells atop Mount Picuris. The station sponsors all the good old hippie jam-bands and doesn't worry too much about censorship – this is the liberal left and freedom of the press at its best.

The station sponsors events throughout the year, but the biggest bash is the **Solar Music Festival** (www.solarmusicfest.com), held the last weekend in June in Taos as a benefit for the **New Mexico Solar Energy Association** (www.nmsea.org). A free Solar Village sets up at the festival grounds, showcasing everything from the Los Alamos National Laboratory's solar-powered supercomputer to homemade solar cookers. Grab a cup of solar-percolated coffee and chat up alternative-energy lovers pitching straw-bale construction, solar cars that fool the UFO-watchers down in Roswell, passive solar design ('used at Taos Pueblo for a thousand years!') and of course the Taos Earthships.

You may even spot a protester or two outside carrying signs that ask, 'Solar energy is free, why does this cost admission?' Talk to them about the radical New Mexico solar scene – folks who seceded from the US government-affiliated **Solar Energy Industries Association** (www.seia.org) to protest US subsidies of fossil-fuel technologies. Ah, Taos, where there's even a counter-counterculture.

music store keeps a calendar of area events, and sells tickets to most of them.

Taos Chamber Music Group (☎ 505-758-0150; http://taoswebb.com/tcmg; tickets from $16) For classical and jazz, this group performs at venues throughout the region.

Taos Center for the Arts (TCA; Map p333; ☎ 505-758-2052; www.taoscenterforthearts.org; 133 Paseo del Pueblo Norte; tickets $5-30) In a remodeled 1890s adobe mansion, the TCA stages local and international performances of everything from chamber music to belly dancing to theater.

Storyteller Cinema (Map p342; ☎ 505-758-9715; 110 Old Talpa Cañon Rd; tickets adult/child $9/6) A few mainstream flicks and lots of artsy ones show at Taos' only movie house, right off Paseo del Pueblo Sur.

SHOPPING

Taos has historically been a mecca for artists, and the huge number of galleries and studios in and around town are evidence of this. Unfortunately, there are also a lot of T-shirt and coffee-mug shops (generally around the plaza).

Pueblo Drums (Map p333; ☎ 505-758-7929, 888-412-3786; www.pueblodrums.com; 110 Paseo del Pueblo Norte) This shop just off the plaza sells unique handmade drums by Phillip Martinez. Each is painted with a different Native American theme. The drums make beautiful gifts and come in all shapes and sizes.

El Rincón Trading Post (Map p333; ☎ 505-758-9188; 114 Kit Carson Rd) Dates back to 1909 when German Ralph Meyers, one of the first traders in the area, arrived. Even if you're not looking to buy anything, stop in here to browse through the dusty museum of artifacts, including Indian crafts, jewelry and Old West memorabilia.

Buffalo Dancer (Map p333; ☎ 575-758-8718; 103A East Plaza) One of the older outlets for Native American jewelry on the plaza, this store carries Rodney Concha's fine pieces plus other work in silver and semiprecious stones.

GETTING THERE & AROUND

Tiny **Taos Municipal Airport** (Map p342; ☎ 575-758-4995; Hwy 64) simply serves as a landing strip for personal planes.

Greyhound (Map p342; ☎ 575-758-1144, 800-231-2222; www.greyhound.com; 1386 Paseo del Pueblo Sur) has daily bus services to Albuquerque ($30, 2¼ hours) and Santa Fe ($20, 1½ hours), with stops at Pilar and Española.

The **Chile Line** (☎ 575-751-4459; one way/round trip 50¢/$1; ☽ 7am-7pm Mon-Sat) runs north–south along NM 68 between the Rancho de Taos post office and Taos Pueblo every 30 minutes, connecting to Greyhound buses. It also serves the ski valley and Arroyo Seco in winter. All buses are wheelchair-accessible.

AROUND TAOS

The area around Taos has fabulous skiing, cool little towns and some of the best scenery around. Driving the Enchanted Circle makes a fantastic day trip from Taos, while a night in little Arroyo Seco delivers rural New Mexican flavor and crisp high desert air. There's good fly-fishing around Red River, while Angel Fire is the place to head for serious skiing and a laid-back attitude.

ARROYO SECO
pop 1200 / elev 7100ft

For an unprocessed local flavor, a groovy plaza and a growing art scene, Arroyo Seco is the place to be. It's just 10 minutes north of Taos; there's not much to do in the center of town but you'll find plenty of ways to not do anything.

Backpackers will find their version of sleeping paradise at the popular, and extremely affordable, **Abominable Snowmansion** (☎ 575-776-8298; www.abominablesnowmansion.com; 476 Ski Valley Rd; dm $18, campsites $16, teepees & cabins $32, r $40-44; 🖳). This HI hostel boasts a cozy lodge, with clean (if a tad threadbare) private rooms, a wonderful campground with an outdoor kitchen, surprisingly nice cabins and a sweet and simple dorm room.

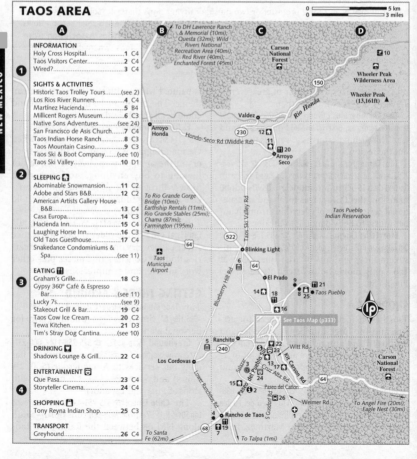

TAOS AREA

For something different – especially if you've got the kids – try sleeping in a teepee!

The **Adobe and Stars B&B** (☎ 575-776-2776, 800-211-7076; www.taosadobe.com; 584 Hwy 150; r incl breakfast $120-190; 🖳) has eight large, amazing rooms with working kiva fireplaces and private entrances, fabulous mountains visible through huge windows, and simply wonderful vibes. This could well be the best B&B in New Mexico.

Have breakfast where the locals do: **Gypsy 360° Café & Espresso Bar** (☎ 575-776-3166; 'downtown' Arroyo Seco; mains $6-13; 🕑 breakfast & lunch). It's right on the tiny plaza, has a sun-drenched patio and relaxing interior, and serves the most international menu in town – Vietnamese spring rolls, Japanese sushi, Indonesian satay and beer from all over the world.

On the way to out of town and towards the Taos Ski Valley, **Taos Cow Ice Cream** (☎ 505-776-5640; 485 Hwy 150; mains & cones $2-7; 🕑 7am-7pm) is famous for its tasty all-natural ice cream, baked goods, breakfasts and deli sandwiches.

TAOS SKI VALLEY
pop 56 / elev 9200ft

People move to New Mexico just to 'ski bum' at Taos for a couple years. Those who do say there's just something about the snow, challenging terrain and laid-back atmosphere that makes this mountain more of an addictive rush than cocaine.

Most visitors come in winter for the skiing and snowboarding. Once exclusive to skiers, Taos recently let snowboarders start riding its slopes. Offering some of the most difficult terrain in the USA, it's a fantastic place to zip down steep tree glades and jump cliffs into untouched powder bowls. Summer visitors to the village, which was once the rough-and-tumble gold-mining town of Twining, find an alpine wilderness with great hiking and cheap lodging.

Seasoned skiers luck out here, with more than half of the 70-plus trails at the **Taos Ski Valley** (☎ 866-250-7274; www.skitaos.org; half-/full-day lift ticket $47/63) ranked expert; the valley has more than 300in of all-natural powder annually, a peak elevation of 11,819ft and a 2612ft vertical drop. In addition to opening up to snowboarders, the resort recently added a skier-cross obstacle course to its popular terrain park. Check the resort website for ski-and-stay deals, including weeklong packages with room, board, lessons and lift tickets. At the beginning of the season there are often reduced-rate lift tickets and very good specials on offer.

In summer, several **hiking** trailheads are located along Hwy 150 to Taos Ski Valley and at the northern end of the Ski Valley parking lot.

When it comes to sleeping, high season is from Thanksgiving to Easter but there are dips in March and November and peaks during the holidays. From March to October, many lodges are closed, while those that are open offer excellent discounts.

Probably the best all-round option – with the best specials – is the giant **Snakedance Condominiums & Spa** (☎ 800-322-9815; www.snakedancecondos.com; 110 Sutton Pl; r $65-250; 🖳), which offers ski-lodge condo-style digs at the bottom of the lifts. It also has a restaurant, a bar, in-room massages and lots of other amenities, including a hot tub, a sauna and in-room kitchens.

Famous for its flame-roasted red and green chile, **Tim's Stray Dog Cantina** (☎ 505-776-2894; 105 Sutton Place; mains $4-12; 🕑 breakfast, lunch & dinner) is a ski institution. It serves fabulous northern New Mexican cuisine – the breakfast burritos are perfect fuel-up food – along with fresh margaritas and a big selection of bottled brews. The perfect après-ski or hiking hang-out.

To reach the valley, take Hwy 64 north out of Taos to the blinking light, and veer right on Hwy 150 toward Arroyo Seco. The 20-mile drive winds along a beautiful mountain stream, but during the winter, the Chile Line (p341) runs several times a day from downtown Taos.

DH LAWRENCE RANCH & MEMORIAL

In 1924, Mabel Dodge Luhan gave DH Lawrence's wife Frieda this 160-acre **ranch** (☎ 575-776-2245; www.unm.edu/~taosconf/links/lawrence.htm; admission free; 🕑 sunrise-sunset), now administered by the University of New Mexico, where the Lawrence-obsessed can pay their respects to the famed author of such classics as *Lady Chatterley's Lover*. While you are free to wander the grounds, you can't go into the cabins.

Lawrence and Frieda lived here for only a few months from 1924 to '25, along with artist Dorothy Brett, who accepted Lawrence's invitation to create 'Rananim,' a utopian society. Lawrence spent his time repairing the cabins, chopping wood, hiking the trails and (with the help of Frieda) fighting off the attentions of Dorothy and patron Mabel Dodge Luhan. He also managed to complete the novella *St Maw,* his biblical drama *David,* parts of *The Plumed Serpent* and other works in between. Relax beneath the **Lawrence Tree**, which brings in the O'Keeffe fans (yep, it looks just like her painting) and contemplate what he called 'the greatest experience I ever had from the outside world.'

Lawrence returned to Europe in 1925 and succumbed to tuberculosis in 1930. After Frieda moved back to Taos in 1934, she ordered his body exhumed and cremated, and had the ashes brought here. Luhan and Brett both showed up uninvited to help scatter said ashes, which, according to legend, prompted Frieda to finally dump the remains into a wheelbarrow full of wet cement, saying, 'Let's see them try to steal this!' According to one story, the cement was used to make the memorial's altar – ironic, as his personal symbol, the phoenix, rises therefrom.

Ascend the meandering paved walkway to the memorial, designed by Frieda's third husband, where the lump of concrete has been inscribed with DHL's initials and green leaves and yellow flowers. It's heartwarming, with a scandalous giggle, just like Lawrence would have wanted.

ENCHANTED CIRCLE

Unplug, sit back, unwind and absorb the beauty. There's a reason they call this 84-mile loop the Enchanted Circle, and you'll understand once you start driving – or to really experience the sublime natural nuances along this 84-mile stretch of pavement, ride it on your mountain bike. In warm weather, the route is popular with cyclists from around the world for its enchanting scenery and challenging altitude and terrain. Comprising NM 522, NM 38 and US 64, the scenic byway traverses alpine highlands that rise to 13,161ft Wheeler Peak, past crystalline lakes, pine forests scenically draped with feldspar and rolling steppes carpeted with windswept meadows. You're in marmot and elk country.

Most towns on the circuit (with the notable exception of Questa) are relatively young, founded in the 1880s gold rush by mostly Anglo settlers looking for the mother lode. It never quite panned out, however, and the abandoned mines and ghost towns are highlights of the trip.

Those settlers who remained turned to tourism, opening major ski resorts at Red River and Angel Fire; knickknack shops and adventure tours are probably the other two major employers. If you just do this as a drive, you may be a bit disappointed – folks around here are more likely to compare their rare world to the Bermuda Triangle than the tourist bureau's more evocative moniker. But take time to explore, and it will be one of the highlights of your trip.

Taos Net (www.enchantedcircle.org) has links to all area visitor centers; these links in turn link to outfitters, hotels and restaurants. **Taos Vacation Guide** (www/taosvacationguide.com) has a quick guide to sights along the way. Fill your gas tank in Taos, where it's cheaper, and allow at least a full day to make the journey. Better yet, spend the night along the way.

Questa
pop 1900 / elev 7670ft

Questa is a wonderfully un-themed community where local traditions overrule tourist initiatives. Primarily a mining town (the last vestige being the nearby molybdenum mine – it's the stuff used to help harden steel), it's also growing an enclave of artists, subsistence farmers and other organic types who are choosing to move off the grid. It's easy to see why. There's no way you can't appreciate the view: an alpine bowl glittering with lakes (it's possib;e to to rent ice-skates downtown during winter) and bright wildflowers, and spectacularly torn by the great chasm just north.

Questa's roots go back more than 400 years. It was once the northernmost settlement in the Americas when Spain held sway. Its name comes from a typo when the town was founded in 1842: it was meant to be called 'Cuesta,' meaning 'cliff, large hill', which would fit its looks perfectly, but thanks to a misspelling it became Questa!

The **Artesanos de Questa & Visitor Center** (☎ 575-586-0443; 41 NM 38) sells work by local artists, can recommend B&Bs, and will point you toward local artists' studios.

For sleeping, the **Kachina Motel** (☎ 575-586-0640; 2306 NM 522; r $80) is cute, clean and pretty basic but located right on the fish-filled Red River.

Grab a bite at the **Questa Café** (☎ 575-586-9631; 2422 NM 522; mains $4-12; ⏱ 6am-10pm Mon-Sat, 6am-3pm Sun), an expansive diner beloved for its Frito pie, chile cheese fries (go for red) and homemade deserts.

Wild Rivers Recreation Area

It seems every state has its own 'Grand Canyon' equivalent, and among the strong candidates in New Mexico is the 800ft-deep Rio Grande Gorge, carved into volcanic ash and surrounded by piñon-studded plugs of the ancient volcanoes that wrought this lonely place. Here the Rio Grande and the Red River, protected as 'Wild and Scenic' by Congress, merge. The Wild Rivers Recreation area provides access to the rim and to inside the gorge itself, offering Grand Canyon–style views, but without the crush of people. Just try finding this sort of peace on the rim of Arizona's claim to fame.

The **visitor center** (☎ 575-770-1600, 575-758-8851; NM 378; day-use $3; ☼ 10am-6pm Jun-Aug, limited hours Sep-May) has information about the park camping options. There are five semideveloped tent campgrounds ($10) with 22 spaces accessible by car. Four hiking trails lead to another 16 primitive riverside campsites ($5) at the bottom of the canyon. To reach them you'll have to drop down 800ft to the canyon floor. It's a sublime hike down – you'll feel as if you've entered another world, one that is perceptibly moister and cooler, where the vegetation is lushly green. Of course, getting back up the next morning is the challenging bit – bring plenty of water.

If you don't feel like a hike, drive the scenic 13-mile **Wild Rivers Backcountry Byway** loop for an impressive and visceral experience. La Junta provides the perfect spot for a picnic, overlooking the confluence of the twin gorges.

Red River

pop 492 / elev 8750ft

The cusp of the 19th and 20th centuries saw a pretty wild populace of gold miners and mountain men here, with saloons and brothels lining Red River's muddy thoroughfares. The early years of this century finds mountain men, and women as well, only this time tricked out in Gore-Tex instead of skins, and looking for a whole different kind of extracurricular activity – for the most part. When the hard-drinking miners' hopes were crushed by the difficulty of processing the ore, those who stayed realized that their outdoor paradise might appeal to flatlanders with income. Indeed.

The town appears as a cluster of cheerfully painted shops and chalets, gleaming in the high desert sun. Red River, ski resort for the masses, is decked out in German-peasant style with an Old West theme – you'd think it wouldn't work, but it does.

Six historic buildings, and lots of dilapidated mines, have been joined by a ski resort, adventure outfitters, ticky-tacky shops galore and, this being New Mexico, art galleries.

The **chamber of commerce** (☎ 800-348-6444; www.redrivernewmex.com; 100 E Main St; ☼ 8am-5pm Mon-Fri) publishes a comprehensive visitors guide with great information on the surrounding wilderness.

ACTIVITIES

Red River gets most of its tourism in the wintertime, when folks flock to the **Red River Ski Area** (☎ 800-331-7669; www.redriverskiarea.com; half-/full-day lift ticket $55/41). The resort caters to families and newbies with packages that include lessons and equipment or half-price weekends during the early season (beginning of December). Deals on multiday stays include accommodations at more than 30 area lodges, and your fourth day is usually free. Even if you're just a daytripper, Red River is about $20 cheaper than the average ski resort, and thanks to a huge investment in snow-making equipment, it's no longer restricted to mother nature's good mood – read: much more snow. Snowboarders and skiers alike should check out the terrain park complete with boxes and rails, specifically designed to lure you east from Angel Fire.

Are you traveling with your dog? Well he'll be grateful for a trip over to **Enchanted Forest** (☎ 800-966-9381; www.enchantedforestxc.com; NM 38; adult/teen/child $12/9/5; ☼ 9am-4:30pm Nov-Mar), where you can cross-country ski with your dog (well, unless he's really coordinated, we assume he'll stick to just running on four paws) on a designated pet-friendly 3-mile trail, or schuss with the humans on more than 20 miles of groomed trails near 9820ft Bobcat Pass at New Mexico's premier Nordic ski area. The views are spectacular and snowshoeing is encouraged. Special events include the illuminated Christmas Luminaria Tour, Moonlight Ski Tours (the Saturday before a full moon) and Just Desserts Eat & Ski (late February), when you'll ski from stand to stand as area restaurants showcase their sweet stuff.

In the summer, the kids won't want to miss the downtown **Frye's Old Town Shootout** (Main St; admission free; ☼ 4pm Tue, Thu & Sat Jun-Sep; ☝). It showcases the Second Amendment in all its ten-gallon-hat, buckskin-jacket glory, as good guys

NEW MEXICO

try to stop the bad guys from robbing a bank and end up in a faux showdown right in the center of town. From there, head out into the spectacular wilderness surrounding the strip.

Take NM 578 into the heart of the **Wheeler Peak Wilderness** for challenging but oh-so-worth-it hikes. **Horseshoe Lake Trail** leaves the Ditch Cabin Site for a 12-mile round-trip to the 11,950ft-high lake with good camping and fishing.

SLEEPING

Red River has more than 50 RV parks, lodges, B&Bs and hotels, many of which offer package deals with local outfitters and the ski area. Once the snow melts, this is the best place on the Enchanted Circle to bargain for a great room.

Copper King Lodge (☎ 800-727-6210; www.copper kinglodge.com; 307 East River St; r $59-179) Rough-hewn wood, rustic furnishings and a great backyard make these cabin-style apartments and condos with kitchenettes great value. But it's the hot tub next to the river that seals the deal. Rates vary wildly throughout the year.

Alpine Lodge (☎ 575-754-2952, 800-252-2333; www .thealpinelodge.com; 417 Main St; d $74-86, condos $185-312) This German-style Alpine lodge runs a slew of packages and specials – from college day discounts to stay-and-ski-free deals for kids. January bargain days, when rooms and lift

tickets are discounted, are also a good deal; check online for the latest or you'll lose out. Families and groups will want to stay in a chalet-style condo, which sleeps six or more. There are two hot tubs on the grounds, and the Red River runs right through it all.

EATING & DRINKING

Shotgun Willies (☎ 575-754-6505; cnr Main St & Pioneer Rd; mains $6-12; ⏲ 7am-7pm) Locals love this place serving the ultimate hangover sop-up, artery-clogging breakfast specials of fried eggs, meats and potatoes. The true house specialty is the barbecue, served by the pound. Order the brisket combo.

If you prefer a little line dancing with your barbecue, Red River is a favorite stop on the country and western music circuit. Catch live acts on weekends at venues around town, including **Bull o' the Woods Saloon** (☎ 575-754-2593; Main St).

Eagle Nest
pop 325 / elev 8300ft

This windswept high-plains town is a better place to explore the great outdoors if you can't take the tourist overkill of Red River. The tiny **chamber of commerce** (☎ 575-377-2420, 800-494-9117; www.eaglenest.org; Therma Dr; ⏲ 10am-4pm Tue-Sat) has reams of information.

DETOUR: VALLE VIDAL LOOP

In the mood for a longer drive through the highlands? Try the 173-mile Valle Vidal Loop, which departs the Enchanted Circle in Questa, heading north past the Wild Rivers Recreation Area on NM 522 and rejoining the road more traveled in Eagle Nest via US 64.

The bulk of the route is impassable during winter, and the washboard gravel road of FR 1950 is no picnic at the best of times – bring a spare tire. The northern gate to FR 1950 is closed April 1 to early June for elk calving season, while the southern gate closes January through March to let them winter in peace. The estimated 1800 elk are a major attraction the rest of the year and are best seen in the morning and evening.

Take NM 522 north past the El Rito turnoff, which accesses the elk-infested **Latir Peak Wilderness**, with mesas at 12,000ft and higher, administrated by the Questa Ranger District. Privately owned **Latir Lakes** (☎ 575-586-0542 for permits), eight alpine gems set into 12,700ft Latir Peak, are worth the hike that begins here.

Further north the **Urraca Wildlife Area** (☎ 575-476-8000; www.gmfsh.state.nm.us) has hiking and fishing. Just out of the small town of Costilla, NM 196 loses its cement and heads into a wilderness – where elk, wildcats and bears roam – that's sometimes called 'New Mexico's Yellowstone.'

FR 1950 follows stocked Rio Costilla, a fly-fisher's paradise and a great place to relax, and opens onto unlimited access to multiday backpacking adventures in the national forest.

Continue your journey into Carson National Forest, wending through meadows, forest, more elk, outstanding views of granite peaks and four developed campgrounds.

The route becomes blessedly paved again when you make a left onto US 64 for the drive back to Eagle Nest, where you rejoin the Enchanted Circle.

Three miles north of Eagle Nest on US 64, **Cimarron Canyon State Park** (☎ 888-667-2757; tent/RV sites $10/14) runs alongside a dramatic 8-mile stretch of scenic Cimarron River, hued in pine greens and volcanic grays. It also encompasses Horseshoe Mine, beaver ponds, lots of wildlife and fishing, and plenty of hikes.

For sleeping, try the **Laguna Vista Lodge** (☎ 505-377-6522, 800-821-2093; www.lagunavistalodge .com; 51 Therma Dr; r $125). It has spacious, beautiful rooms and amenities galore, including kitchenettes in the family suites and full kitchens in the lake-facing sportsmen's cabins. The on-site **Texas Reds Restaurant** (mains $7-20; ☺ dinner) serves steaks, lobster and burgers for $6 to $20. For drinks, visit the neighboring Laguna Vista Saloon. It's rustic, has all kinds of neat old stuff and the floors creak just like they did for the old-timers. The front doors of this 1880s-era building are among the most photographed icons in the valley.

Angel Fire
pop 1000 / elev 8382ft

Some love it, others hate it. But regardless, it remains one of New Mexico's more popular ski resorts. In summer a slew of hippie festivals draw baked refugees from lower elevations. No one can question the beauty of the surrounding mountains and valleys, and famous northern New Mexico light, even if the town looks a bit like a condo suite.

As if the 2077ft vertical drop and 450 acres of trails weren't enough, **Angel Fire Resort** (☎ 800-633-7463; www.angelfireresort.com; NM 434; half-/full-day lift ticket $44/59) recently underwent a massive $40-million retrofit, adding lifts, trails, snowbiking (on bikes with skis), snowskating (on skateboards without wheels), snowshoeing and a ski park just for kids, making this one serious winter wonderland.

The resort also boasts a Chris Gunnarson–designed, 400ft-long, competition-quality half-pipe with a wicked 26% grade.

In warmer weather golfers can test their skills on the third-highest-altitude 18-hole course in the USA – your ball will fly at the **Valle Escondido Golf Course** (☎ 575-758-3475; NM 64; 18 holes from $16; ☺ dawn-dusk). Cash only.

SLEEPING & EATING

NM 434, or Mountain View Blvd as it is known in town, is the main drag through Angel Fire and has a couple of other places to stay besides the ones listed here.

Angel Fire Resort (☎ 800-633-7463; www.angelfire resort.com; NM 434; r $150-300, ste from $250; ☒ ☒ ☐ wi-fi) Families will really dig the ski resort's lodging option. Parents can drop the kids off at childcare and hit the slopes just out front. The resort organizes loads of children's activities, especially in summertime, and also offers family-oriented packages. If you don't have the kids, it's still a nice place, with a ski chalet style. The concierge can arrange everything from golf to horse riding, plus it's big enough to not feel like kid central if you're not traveling with children. Three on-site restaurants mean you won't go hungry.

Elkhorn Lodge (☎ 575-377-2811; 3377 NM 434; r $165) This place has a central location, decks off all rooms, and suites that sleep six and feature kitchenettes. Rates drop in the off season.

Willie's Smokehouse & Grill (☎ 575-377-2765; Pinewood Plaza, 3453 Mountain View Blvd; mains $9-12; ☺ breakfast, lunch & dinner Mon-Sat) Head here for barbecued chicken, beef and pork, but if you want to do like the locals, order the burrito grande ($7); it's huge and delicious.

Roasted Clove (☎ 575-377-0636; www.roastedclove .com; 48 N Angel Fire Rd; mains $17-35; ☺ dinner Wed-Mon) This long-established restaurant is everyone's favorite fine dining: chipotle roasted chicken, sautéed wild mushrooms and mesquite-grilled filet are just a few of the gourmet dishes that you'll be pairing with a fine wine.

GETTING THERE & AROUND

Angel Fire is strung out along the northern terminus of NM 434, just south of the intersection with US 64. Continue on US 64 through the Carson National Forest back to Taos.

NORTHERN NEW MEXICO

New Mexico's wild north is home to wide-open, empty spaces. It is still dubbed 'Indian Country' and for good reason – huge swaths of land fall under the aegis of the Navajos, Pueblo, Zuni, Apache and Laguna tribes. This portion of New Mexico showcases remarkable ancient Indian sites alongside modern, solitary Native American settlements. Interspersed between sacred places like Chaco Canyon and Acoma Pueblo (see p283) are small rural towns where you can ride a scenic rail route in quaint Chama or fish for trout in the Navajo Dam.

NEW MEXICO

DETOUR: CHACO CULTURE NATIONAL HISTORICAL PARK & CUBA

Chaco, the center of a culture that extended far beyond the immediate area, was once a carefully engineered network of 30ft-wide roads. Very little of the road system is easily seen today, but about 450 miles have been identified from aerial photos and ground surveys. Clearly, this was a highly organized and integrated culture.

The **park** (per vehicle/bike $8/4; ☼ sunrise-sunset) contains massive and spectacular Puebloan buildings, evidence of 5000 years of human occupation, set in a remote high desert environment. The largest building, Pueblo Bonito, towers four stories tall and may have had 600 to 800 rooms and kivas. None of Chaco's sites have been reconstructed or restored. If you like isolation and using your imagination, few places compare.

All park routes involve rough and unpaved dirt roads, which can become impassable after heavy rains or snow. Park rangers prefer that visitors enter via Hwy 44/550 on the north side. About 3 miles south of the Nageezi Trading Post on Hwy 44/550 and about 50 miles west of Cuba, turn south at mile marker 112.5 on CR 7900, which is paved for 5 miles. Continue on the marked unpaved county road for 16 miles to the park entrance.

Park facilities are minimal – there's no food, gas or supplies. The nearest provisions are along Hwy 44, 21 miles from the **visitor center** (☎ 505-786-7014; www.nps.gov/chcu; ☼ 8am-5pm early Sep-late Jun, 8am-6pm late Jun-early Sep), where free backcountry hiking permits (no camping) are available. Inquire here about nighttime astronomy programs (April to October).

Ask at the visitor center, where you can also pick up water (it's the only place where water is available), about directions to the **Gallo Campground** (campsites $10), which operates on a first-come, first-served basis. There are no hookups, but toilets, grills and picnic tables are available. Bring your own wood or charcoal.

Mountainous Cuba, about 50 miles from the Chaco turnoff, is your closest hotel bet, with a number of motels catering to Chaco visitors on the town's main street.

For something different try the friendly **Circle A Ranch Hostel** (☎ 575-289-3350; www.circlearanch .info; off Hwy 550; dm from $20, r from $35; ☼ May–mid-Oct). A real gem, this place is set on 360 beautiful acres in the Nacimiento Mountains. The lovely old adobe lodge, which has exposed beams, grassy grounds, hiking trails and a classic kitchen, is a peaceful and relaxing place to hang out. Choose between private bedrooms (some with quilts and iron bedsteads) and shared bunk rooms. Look for the ranch 5 miles north of Cuba at the end of Los Pinos Rd.

CIMARRON
pop 917 / elev 6430ft

Cimarron has a wild past. It once served as a stop on the Santa Fe Trail, and a hang-out for gunslingers, train robbers, desperadoes, lawmen and other Wild West figures like Kit Carson, Buffalo Bill Cody, Annie Oakley, Wyatt Earp, Jesse James and Doc Holliday. The old St James Hotel alone saw the deaths of 26 men within its walls. Today, Cimarron is a peaceful and serene village with few street signs. Poke around to find what you need, or ask the friendly locals. The town is located on Hwy 64, 41 miles southwest of Raton (opposite) and 54 winding miles east of Taos. The **chamber of commerce** (☎ 575-376-2417; www.cimarronnm .com; Hwy 64) has an up-to-date website.

Most historic buildings lie south of the Cimarron River on Hwy 21, including the old town plaza, Dold Trading Post, the Santa Fe Trail Inn (which dates to 1854), Schwenk's Gambling Hall, a Wells Fargo Station and the old jail (1872).

Also here is the **St James Hotel** (☎ 575-376-2664, 800-748-2694; www.stjamescimarron.com; Hwy 21; historic r $90-120, modern r $60-100). A saloon in 1873, this well-known place was converted into a hotel in 1880 and renovated 100 years later. It's a toss-up between the 14 simple historic rooms or the modern annex, which has 10 rooms equipped with TVs and phones. Within the hotel, you'll find a decent midrange restaurant and a cozy bar with a pool table. Just for fun, count the bullet holes in the period pressed-tin ceiling. Dorothy, you're not in Kansas anymore.

Get away from it all by visiting the **Casa del Gavilan** (☎ 575-376-2246, 800-428-4526; www.casadel gavilan.com; Hwy 21; r incl breakfast $95-125). Set on 225 acres, it's a magnificent Pueblo Revival–style house built around 1908. The four double rooms are decorated with Southwestern antiques and art and come complete with high ceilings, vigas and thick adobe walls; the house is a treat. A two-room guesthouse sleeps up to four people.

RATON & AROUND
pop 7300 / elev 6668ft

It's probably time to get out of the car and stretch. Though Raton isn't a big tourist destination, the well-preserved town will hold your attention for a short stroll. Plus its attractively priced graceful old hotel makes it a bargain gem if you need to sleep.

Raton was founded with the arrival of the railroad in 1879 and quickly grew into an important railway stop and mining and ranching center. Upwards of 100 of the turn-of-the-19th-century buildings from this era have been preserved.

Orientation & Information

The city lies along I-25, 8 miles south of the Colorado state line. The main north–south thoroughfare is 2nd St, which runs parallel to and just west of I-25. The main east–west street is Hwy 64/87, called Tiger Dr west of 2nd St and Clayton Rd east of 2nd St. The **visitor center** (☎ 575-445-3689, 800-638-6161; www.raton.info; Clayton Rd; ☼ 8am-5pm Mon-Fri) has statewide information.

Sights & Activities

The small **historic district** along 1st, 2nd and 3rd Sts (between Clark and Rio Grande Aves) harbors over two dozen buildings. The great little **Raton Museum** (☎ 575-445- 8979; 2nd St; admission free; ☼ 9am-5pm Tue-Sat late Jun-early Sep, Wed-Sat Sep-May), housed in the 1906 Coors Building, is well worth a visit. Look for great photos, artifacts pertaining to Raton's mining days and illuminating information documenting the history of the Santa Fe Trail.

In the historic downtown, the 1915 **Shuler Theater** (131 N 2nd St) features an elaborate European rococo interior with excellent acoustics (it's still in operation). The foyer contains eight murals that were painted during the New Deal (1930s) by Manville Chapman, depicting the region's history from 1845 to 1895.

Note the reversed swastika signs (a Native American symbol of good luck) on top of the **International Bank** building, originally built in 1929 as the Swastika Hotel. The reversed swastika had been the symbol of one of the coal companies in Raton during the late 19th

NEW MEXICO

DETOUR: CAPULIN VOLCANO & FOLSOM MAN TERRITORY SCENIC DRIVE

Go ahead, support Raton's struggling economy and spend the night. That way you'll get to do this drive. A 50-mile loop through the high mountain plains above Raton, the Capulin Volcano and Folsom Man Territory Scenic Drive isn't just another stretch of pavement – it's also a history lesson (with volcanoes, which alone should be enticement enough to excite the kids).

America's most important archaeological discovery was made near the tiny town of Folsom, about 40 miles east of Raton. In 1908, George McJunkin, a local cowboy, noticed some strange bones in Wild Horse Arroyo. Cowboy that he was, he knew that these were no ordinary cattle bones. And so he kept them, suspecting correctly that they were bones from an extinct species of bison. McJunkin spoke of his find to various people, but it wasn't until 1926 to 1928 that the site was properly excavated, first by fossil bone expert Jesse Figgins and then by others.

Until that time, scientists thought that humans had inhabited North America for, at most, 4000 years. With this single find, the facts about the continent's ancient inhabitants had to be completely revised. Subsequent excavations found stone arrowheads in association with extinct bison bones dating from 8000 BC, thus proving that people had lived here for at least that long. These Paleo-Indians became known as Folsom Man.

Recent dating techniques suggest that these artifacts are 10,800 years old, among the oldest discovered on the continent, although it is clear that people have lived in the Americas for even longer.

The area is also known for its volcanoes. Rising 1300ft above the surrounding plains, **Capulin Volcano National Monument** is the easiest to visit. From the **visitor center** (☎ 575-278-2201; www.nps.gov/cavo; per car $5), a 2-mile road winds precariously up the mountain to the crater rim (which is 8182ft). There, a quarter-mile trail drops into the crater and a mile-long trail follows the rim. The entrance is 3 miles north of Capulin, which is 30 miles east of Raton on Hwy 87.

century, and it served as the town's unofficial logo until WWII. During the war, the reversed swastikas were covered with tarp and the hotel finally changed its name in 1943.

Sugarite Canyon State Park (☎ 575-445-5607; tent/RV sites $10/16), featuring two lakes stocked with rainbow trout, is situated in the pretty meadows and forests of the foothills of the Rockies, about 10 miles northeast of Raton. In winter, the 7800ft elevation is perfect for cross-country skiing. In summer, there are 15 miles of hiking trails that begin from a half-mile nature trail. To reach it, take Hwy 72 east out of Raton, then turn north onto Hwy 526; it's signposted about 7 miles north of here.

Sleeping & Eating

El Portal Hotel (☎ 575-445-3631; www.elportalhotel.com; 101 N 3rd St; r from $45) The best place to stay downtown, this wonderful turn-of-the-19th-century livery stable expanded in 1904 and turned itself into the Seaburg European Hotel. An interesting alternative to a plethora of standard issue motels, El Portal (as it's now known) offers 18 spacious antique-filled rooms (many with claw-foot bathtubs) and TVs.

Vermejo Park Ranch (☎ 575-445-3097; www.vermejoparkranch.com; Hwy 555; per person incl meals & activities around $350; ☐ wi-fi) Maintained by Ted Turner as a premier fishing and hunting lodge, this beautifully situated 920-sq-mile enterprise is about 40 miles west of Raton and offers fly-fishing clinics from June through August. As if to balance out the hunting and fishing aspects, the ranch also restores prairie dog habitats and encourages guests to observe a diverse array of wildlife – from elk and bison to bears and birds.

Park Ave Café (El Portal Hotel; mains $7-15; ☺ breakfast, lunch & dinner) New Mexico is known for having quirky cafés in her small towns; this is Raton's contribution. The restaurant's claim to fame is the chef, Marsha Merkel, who says she's cooked for both George Bushes, John Wayne, the king and queen of Sweden and Jimmy Dean. Quite a combination, which just happens to be what Merkel is good at – using unusual pairings of ingredients and flavors with excellent results.

Getting There & Away

Raton is right on I-25, eight miles south of the Colorado border. It is best reached by private vehicle. Please note that during winter snowstorms Raton Pass (just north of town) can be shut down, which means you may well be stranded in Raton for a night if you're trying to get to Colorado. It's happened to us.

CLAYTON & AROUND
pop 2500 / elev 5050ft

Ranches and prairie grasses surround Clayton, a quiet town with a sleepy Western feel on the Texas border. Near the Bravo Dome CO_2 Field (the world's largest natural deposit of carbon dioxide gas), Clayton is where infamous train robber Black Jack Ketchum was caught and hanged in 1901. The **Herzstein Memorial Museum** (☎ 575-374-2977; Methodist Episcopal Church, 2nd St at Walnut St; admission free; ☺ 1-5pm Tue-Sun) tells the story.

If you're moseying about these parts, you'll find over 500 dinosaur footprints of eight different species at **Clayton Lake State Park** (☎ 575-374-8808; www.claytonlakestatepark.com; Hwy 370; per car per day $5, tent/RV sites $10/16), 12 miles northwest of Clayton. The pretty lake also boasts swimming and camping.

Sometimes when you're in the mood for a detour to nowhere, there's nowhere to go. Not true here. Southwest of Clayton, in the most sparsely populated county in New Mexico, the

---

SUMMER DETOUR: CHAMA TO TAOS

This nearly 100-mile route makes a fabulous scenic way to get between Chama and Taos from late May through the first snows in mid-October. From Chama, take Hwy 84/64 about 11 miles south to see the spectacular cliffs in scenic **Brazos Canyon**. Just south of Los Brazos in Los Ojos, don't miss a visit to the famous **Tierra Wools** (☎ 575-588-7231, 888-709-0979; www.handweavers .com; 91 Main St; r $65-85), a 100-year-old weaving cooperative in a rustic, century-old building. On weekends, village artisans carry on the Hispanic weaving tradition, with hand-spinning, dyeing and weaving. In addition to a two-bedroom guesthouse, Tierra Wools also offers weaving classes (April to October).

From tiny TA (as Tierra Amarilla is locally know), head east on scenic Hwy 64 over a 10,000ft pass in the Tusas Mountains to Taos, 80 miles away.

Kiowa National Grasslands consist of high-plains ranch land – endless, vast and lonely. Farmed throughout the early 20th century, the soil suffered from poor agricultural techniques and it became useless, essentially blowing away during the dust-bowl years of the 1930s. The most visited section (though visitors are scarce) is **Mills Canyon**, north of Roy (with only a gas station and grocery store). About 10 miles northwest of Roy on Hwy 39, a signposted dirt road heads west another 10 miles to the **Mills Camping Area**, with free primitive camping but no drinking water. The river forms a small gorge here and the area is quite scenic.

While you're in the neighborhood, why not have a historic prairie frontier-style evening, with a meal (and perhaps a good night's sleep) at the 1890 **Eklund Hotel Dining Room & Saloon** (☎ 575-374-2551; 15 Main St; mains from $10; ☺ breakfast, lunch & dinner; wi-fi). The hotel has an elegant dining room and an Old West saloon with a beautifully carved bar. The 26 guest rooms (from $85) border on Spartan, but not in a bad way – we like the simplicity of the white bedspreads. All are newly renovated. Pay an extra $20 for the king suite with a Jacuzzi tub and access to the 2nd-floor balcony and a wet bar.

CHAMA
pop 1200 / elev 7880ft

When it comes to modern development, Chama moves about as fast as molasses. Only recently has the small mountain community of Chama been ever-so-slightly rediscovered, but even with its first-ever sidewalks, it still feels like an outpost. Sure, Indians lived and hunted here for centuries, and Spanish farmers settled the Chama River Valley in the mid-1700s, but it was the arrival of the Denver & Rio Grande Railroad in 1880 that really put Chama on the map. Although the railroad closed, the prettiest part later reopened as one of the most scenic train trips in the Southwest.

Today the colorful town is an oasis of green in the sage-scented high desert. With the Rio Grande and Rio Chama running through town, the valley is lush with emerald grasslands, purple peaks and chocolate gorges. It's a rather delicious feast for the eyes.

Orientation

East of the Jicarilla Reservation, Hwy 64 joins Hwy 84, crosses the Continental Divide and drops into Chama. Downtown is 1.5 miles north of the so-called Y-junction of Hwy 84/64 and Hwy 17.

Sights & Activities

The **Cumbres & Toltec Scenic Railway** (☎ 888-286-2737; www.cumbresandtoltec.com; adult/child $65/32) is both the longest (64 miles) and highest (over the 10,015ft-high Cumbres Pass) authentic narrow-gauge steam railroad in the USA. The train runs between Chama and Antonito and is a beautiful trip, particularly in September and October during fall foliage, through mountains, canyons and high desert. Some carriages are fully enclosed, but none are heated. Dress warmly. Whatever you do, make reservations two weeks in advance. There is a snack bar and rest room on board, and the train makes a lunch stop in Osier.

Several outfitters specialize in winter activities, including **Chama Ski Service** (☎ 505-756-2492; www.cvn.com/~porters), which can outfit you with skis and provide information on ski touring. It can also provide backcountry touring equipment including snowshoe rentals. **Cumbres Nordic Adventures** (☎ 888-660-9878; www.yurtsogood.com) offers backcountry ski tours in the snowy San Juan Mountains and deluxe backcountry yurt rentals for $100 to $115 per night.

Festivals & Events

Chama has a few events worth dropping in for, including the **Chama Chile Classic Cross-Country Ski Race** (early or mid-February), which attracts hundreds of competitors to 3.1-mile and 6.2-mile races; the **Chama Valley Music Festival** (every Friday and Saturday in July), which features national and international acts; and **Chama Days** (early August), which features a rodeo, firefighters' water fight and chile cook-off.

Sleeping & Eating

Foster Hotel (☎ 575-756-2296; 393 S Terrace Ave; s/d $45/53) If you're looking for local culture, look no further. Built in 1881 as a bordello, the hotel is the only building in Chama that wasn't wiped out by a massive fire in the 1920s. A few of the rooms are said to be so haunted that management doesn't rent them.

Elkhorn Lodge & Café (☎ 575-756-2105; www.elkhornlodge.net; Hwy 84; r from $45, cabins from $69) On the banks of the Rio Chama, Elkhorn offers blue-ribbon fly-fishing spots, chuckwagon barbecue dinners and old-time cowboy dances. Choose a simple but spacious motel room in

NEW MEXICO

the main log cabin or a freestanding cabin with a kitchenette (especially great for families).

Chama Trails Inn (☎ 575-756-2156, 800-289-1421; www.chamatrailsinn.com; 2362 Hwy 17; s/d from $60/65) This is more than another roadside motel, with 16 character-packed rooms with an abundance of handmade Southwestern furniture, local artwork and hand-painted tiles. A few rooms are further warmed with a gas fireplace. A communal hot tub and sauna come in handy after hiking.

High Country Restaurant & Saloon (☎ 575-756-2384; 2289 S Hwy 17; mains $8-20; ☷ lunch & dinner Mon-Sat, breakfast Sun) This Wild West saloon dishes up burgers, Mexican food, steak and seafood. It's probably the best all-round eating bet in town.

JICARILLA APACHE INDIAN RESERVATION
pop 3200

The Apache were relatively late arrivals in the Southwest, migrating from the north in the 14th century. The hawkish group took advantage of the more peaceful Pueblo peoples already living here. Indeed, the Zuni Indian word for 'enemy,' *apachu,* led to the Apache's present name. Jicarilla (pronounced hic-a-*ree*-ya) means 'little basket,' reflecting their great skill in basket weaving and other crafts. Apache crafts generally draw visitors to the 1360-sq-mile reservation, home to about 3200 Native Americans.

Tiny Dulce (☎ 575-759-3242 ext 218; ☷ 8am-5pm Mon-Fri), on Hwy 64 in the northern part of the reservation, is the tribal capital. Unlike at most reservations, alcohol is available. No permits or fees are needed to drive through the reservation, and photography is permitted.

NAVAJO DAM

Trout are jumpin' and visitors are floating. Navajo Lake, which stretches over 30 miles northeast and across into Colorado, was created by damming the San Juan River. At the base of the dam, there's world-class **trout fishing** from late June through September. You can fish year-round (although you'll need a permit), but catch-and-release regulations protect the stocks. The tiny community of Navajo Dam has several outfitters providing equipment, information and guided trips. Talk to the folks at **Born-n-Raised on the San Juan River, Inc** (☎ 575-632-2194; Hwy 173; half/full day from $210/275), based at Abe's Motel & Fly Shop; the guy who started these personalized trips – he now has guides working for him – has been fishing

the San Juan since he was a child. The more people in your group, the cheaper the trip.

River floating is also popular around here. Rent boats at the **Navajo Lake Marina** (☎ 575-632-3245) or the **Sims Mesa Marina** (☎ 575-320-0885) and put in at the Texas Hole parking lot at milepost 12 on Hwy 511. Then lazily float 2.5 miles to Crusher Hole. Ahhh.

The **Enchanted Hideaway Lodge** (☎ 575-632-2634; www.enchantedhideawaylodge.com; Hwy 173; ste & houses $65-200) rents a couple of drift boats ($125 daily). You can also stay the night. It's a friendly and low-key place with several highly recommended and pleasant suites as well as a private house and condos with kitchens and gas grills. The spacious Stone House, with a heavenly outdoor hot tub set in a grove of trees, is particularly nice; it's furnished with Southwestern flair and sleeps up to eight (each additional person over two costs $15). Poor fishermen can stay in the cost-effective fly room.

Anglers can also try the **Soaring Eagle Lodge** (☎ 800-866-2719; www.soaringeaglelodge.net; Hwy 173; s/d $100/140), which offers multi-night guided fishing tours and half- and full-board options (perfect for those wanting to devote all their waking hours to fishing). Nestled under the cliffs against the river, this beautiful and peaceful place has simple suites with kitchenettes. Try to get one of the units right on the river.

Visit **El Pescador** (☎ 575-632-5129; Hwy 173; mains $5-12; ☷ lunch & dinner) for standard, but decent, Mexican and American fare.

The BLM runs three **campgrounds** (with/without hookups $14/10). The biggest one is **Lake Pine River**, just past the dam on Hwy 511, with a visitor center and marina. About 10 miles south of the lake, **Cottonwood Campground** (Hwy 511) occupies a lovely spot under the cottonwoods on the river. It has drinking water and toilets but no showers.

AZTEC
pop 6000 / elev 5600ft

Although Aztec is primarily on the traveler's map because of the reconstructed Great Kiva at Aztec Ruins, the old downtown has several interesting turn-of-the-19th-century buildings, many on the National Register of Historic Places. Cruise the pleasant tree-lined residential district, too – although there's not really anywhere to spend the night (but the town is only 14 miles southeast of Farmington, where there are plenty of places to slumber).

If you're in the area, time a visit for the annual **Aztec Fiesta Days** (first weekend in June), with arts and crafts, food booths and a bonfire during which 'Old Man Gloom' is burned to celebrate the beginning of summer.

Hwy 516 from Farmington becomes Aztec Blvd in town and continues as Hwy 173 toward Navajo Dam State Park. For more details, visit the **visitor center** (☎ 888-838-9551; www .aztecnm.com; 110 N Ash; ☯ 8am-5pm Mon-Fri).

An alternative to the bigger and more visited sites like Chaco Culture National Historical Park (see boxed text, p348) and Mesa Verde National Park (p391), the 27-acre **Aztec Ruins National Monument** (☎ 505-334-6174; www.nps.gov/azru; admission $5; ☯ 8am-5pm Sep-May, 8am-6pm Jun-Aug) features the largest reconstructed kiva in the country, with an internal diameter of almost 50ft. Let your imagination wander as you sit inside the Great Kiva. Rangers give early-afternoon talks at the site (c AD 1100) about ancient architecture, trade routes and astronomy during the summer months. They're very informative.

The small but excellent **Aztec Museum & Pioneer Village** (☎ 505-334-9829; 125 N Main Ave; admission $4; ☯ 9am-5pm Mon-Sat Jun-Aug, 10am-4pm Mon-Sat Sep-May) features an eclectic collection of historical objects, including telephones, barbershop chairs and a great display of late-19th-century regional photographs. Outside, a small 'pioneer village' has original and replica early buildings, such as a church, jail and bank.

FARMINGTON & AROUND
pop 43,600 / elev 5400ft

Well sited for an overnight stay, the region's largest town serves as a pleasant base for excursions to nearby sites. Farmington itself has nice parkland on the San Juan River, a quaint downtown and some good trading posts, but most visitors hang around because they're visiting Shiprock and Aztec Ruins, within 20 miles of Farmington. It's also the best place to stay when visiting the remote and desolate Chaco Culture National Historical Park (see boxed text, p348), located about two hours' drive south of Farmington.

Information
Bureau of Land Management (☎ 505-599-8900; 1235 La Plata Hwy; ☯ 7:45am-4pm Mon-Fri) Take Hwy 64 west across La Plata River and head north on La Plata Hwy.

Carson National Forest Ranger Station (☎ 505-632-2956; Hwy 64, Bloomfield; ☯ 8am-4:30pm Mon-Fri) Fourteen miles east of town.
Hospital (☎ 505-325-5011; 801 W Maple St)
Post office (☎ 505-325-5047; 2301 E 20th St)
Visitors Bureau (☎ 505-326-7602, 800-448-1240; www.farmingtonnm.org; Farmington Museum at Gateway Park, 3041 E Main St; ☯ 8am-5pm Mon-Fri)

Sights & Activities
The coolest sight around these parts by far is outside of Farmington proper. **Shiprock**, a 1700ft-high volcanic plug and a lofty landmark for Anglo pioneers, is also a sacred site to the Navajo. It rises eerily over the landscape west of Farmington. It's certainly visible from Hwy 64, but there are better views from Hwy 666 – yes, people do stop to snap pictures of the signs (this stretch of highway was immortalized in Oliver Stone's classic movie, *Natural Born Killers*). Indian Hwy 13, which almost skirts its base, is another good photo-op area.

Farmington itself won't hold your attention for long, but if you need something to do, then the **Farmington Museum at Gateway Park** (☎ 575-599-1174; www.farmingtonmuseum.org; 3041 E Main St; suggested donation $2; ☯ 9am-5pm Mon-Sat) is the most worthy pause. It mounts national and juried regional art shows, and houses a permanent exhibit on the cultures and history of Farmington. After the Ancestral Puebloans departed the area, the Navajos and Utes moved in and were eventually followed by Anglo beaver-trappers and ranchers.

The Animas River waterfront and surrounding bosque has a developed 5-mile **River Corridor** that's pleasant to explore on foot or bike. You might not expect to play golf in these parts, but **Pinon Hills** (☎ 505-326-6066; www.farmington.nm.us) is one of the few public courses in the country with a five-star rating. To get here, take Butler Ave north to Sunrise Parkway and head west.

Festivals & Events
Farmington likes to celebrate. Watch for the **Invitational Balloon Festival & Riverfest** (late May); the week-long **Connie Mack World Series Baseball Tournament** (☎ 505-327-9673; 1101 N Fairgrounds Rd) in mid-August, featuring top amateur ballplayers and scouts from college and professional teams; the **Totah Festival** (Labor Day weekend), with juried Native American arts and crafts and a Navajo rug auction; and the **Northern Navajo Reservation Fair** (late September or early October), featuring a rodeo, powwow and

NEW MEXICO

traditional dancing. This fair is perhaps the most traditional of the large Indian gatherings and begins with the Night Way, a complex Navajo healing ceremony, and the *Yei Bei Chei* chant, which lasts for several days.

Sleeping

Knights Inn (☎ 575-325-5061; 701 Airport Dr; r from $45) This place, with 21 large rooms and weekly rates, has the cheapest, simplest and cleanest rooms in town. It fits the bill, nothing more, nothing less.

Silver River Spa Retreat & Adobe B&B (☎ 575-325-8219, 800-382-9251; www.silveradobe.com; 3151 W Main St; r $105-175) Three miles from downtown, this lovely two-room place offers a peaceful respite among the trees on the San Juan River. Fall asleep to the sound of the river, wake to organic blueberry juice and enjoy a morning walk to the prairie-dog village. The additional guest house is attractively rustic, and is made of adobe and timbers. It especially caters to golfers, with stay-and-play combos at a nearby municipal golf course.

our pick **Kokopelli's Cave** (☎ 575-325-7855; www .bbonline.com/nm/kokopelli; r $240) For something truly unique, sleep 70ft below the ground in this incredible 1650-sq-ft cave carved from La Plata River sandstone. Equipped with a kitchen stocked for breakfast and lunch, a VCR with videos and a hot tub, this spacious cave dwelling offers magnificent views over the desert and river. The isolation is magnificent. A 3-mile drive on dirt roads and a short hike is required to reach it.

Eating & Drinking

Three Rivers Eatery & Brewhouse (☎ 575-324-2187; 101 E Main St; mains $7-15; ☾ lunch & dinner; ♨) Managing to be both trendy *and* kid-friendly, this almost hip spot has good food and its own microbrews. Try the homemade potato skins or artichoke and spinach dip, but keep in mind that the steaks are substantial. Plenty of spiffy sandwiches (like a Thai turkey wrap) and soups (broccoli cheddar) are served at lunchtime.

Clancy's Pub (☎ 575-325-8176; 2703 E 20th St; mains $7-15; ☾ lunch & dinner; wi-fi) Popular with 20- and 30-somethings, Clancy's offers imported beers to wash down hamburgers, Mexican food and other pub grub. Get more exotic at the dinnertime sushi bar. Dine inside where the rock music is loud, or on their patio (unfortunately overlooking a strip). With laptop? There's free wi-fi in house.

Getting There & Away

TNM&O/Greyhound (☎ 505-325-1009; www.greyhound .com; 101 E Animas) has one or two daily buses to Albuquerque ($35, four hours) and Durango, Colorado ($15, 1¼ hours).

SOUTHERN NEW MEXICO

Southern New Mexico can resemble another planet, and truth be told, many folks believe its inhabitants just might be from outer space. Seriously though, the lower half of the state

---

DETOUR: VERY LARGE ARRAY RADIO TELESCOPE

In some remote regions of New Mexico, TV reception is little more than a starry-eyed fantasy. About 40 miles west of Socorro, though, 27 huge antenna dishes sprout from the high plains like a couch potato's dream come true. Actually, the 240-ton dishes comprise the National Radio Astronomy Observatory's **Very Large Array Radio Telescope** (VLA; 4 miles south of US 60 off Hwy 52; www.vla.nrao .edu; admission free; ☾ 8:30am-sunset). Together, they combine to form a very large eyeball peeking into the outer edges of the universe. It would take a 422ft-wide satellite dish to provide the same resolution that this Y-shaped configuration of 82ft-wide antennas offers the observatory.

Sure, the giant 'scope may reveal the relativistic electron movement in the heavens and allow geophysicists to wonder at the wobble of the earth on its axis…but what does it tell the rest of us? Well, without them, Jodie Foster never could have flashed forward into our future (or was it her past?) in the movie *Contact,* which was filmed here with a little help from Canyon de Chelly (p224). The radio waves collected by these enormous dishes have increased our understanding of the complex phenomena that make up the surface of the sun. They have given us a gander at the internal heating source deep within the interiors of several planets sharing our orbit. They provide us with just enough information to turn our concepts of time and space inside-out as we extrapolate the existence of varieties of matter that, sans satellites, might only exist in our imaginations as we spin through space on the head of this peculiar little blue-green globe.

looks a little lunar, encompassing vast open stretches of scrubland that extend flat, dusty and bright all the way to Mexico.

With the exception of the state's second-largest city, Las Cruces, residents here (mostly Hispanic) are few and far between. Southern New Mexico is the state's poorest region. But even though this half of the state looks empty from the outside, get up close and you'll find it's home to some of the most interesting attractions around. First off check out the ultra-cool (and quickly growing) hippie art towns of Truth & Consequences (home to great hot springs) and Silver City (home to Billy the Kid). Southern New Mexico is also home to the state's cheesy alien headquarters, Roswell, and has the dubious honor of being the place where the US government exploded the first atomic bomb – on the ironically named 'Highway of Death.'

Outdoor enthusiasts will have a field day camping amid the yucca and agave of the Chihuahuan Desert (I-10 cuts across it) at the bottom of the state or exploring the wilds of Gila National Forest, wild with backpacking and fishing adventures or hiking around the dazzling mounds of brightness that are towering dunes in White Sands National Park, one of New Mexico's stranger natural attractions. Spelunkers will have a blast in Carlsbad National Caverns.

SOCORRO
pop 8900 / elev 4585ft

A quiet and amiable layover, Socorro has a downtown with a good mix of buildings dating from the 1800s to the late 20th century. Its standout is a 17th-century mission. Most visitors are birders drawn to the nearby Bosque del Apache refuge.

Socorro means 'help' in Spanish. The town's name supposedly dates to 1598, when Juan de Onate's expedition received help from Pilabo Pueblo (now defunct). The Spaniards built a small church nearby, expanding it into the San Miguel Mission in the 1620s. With the introduction of the railroad in 1880 and the discovery of gold and silver, Socorro became a major mining center and New Mexico's biggest town by the late 1880s. The mining boom went bust in 1893. The New Mexico Institute of Mining and Technology (locally called Tech) offers postgraduate education and advanced research facilities here, and runs a mineral museum.

Information

The **chamber of commerce** (☎ 575-835-0424; www .socorro-nm.com; 101 Plaza; ☼ 8am-5pm Mon-Fri, 10am-noon Sat) is helpful.

Sights & Activities

Most of the **historic downtown** dates to the late 19th century. Pick up the chamber of commerce's walking tour, the highlight of which is the **San Miguel Mission** (☎ 505-835-1620; San Miguel Rd), three blocks north of the plaza. Although restored and expanded several times, the mission still retains its colonial feel and parts of the walls date back to the original building.

Most travelers are naturalists who descend on Socorro because of its proximity to the **Bosque Del Apache National Wildlife Refuge** (www .fws.gov/southwest/refuges/newmex/bosque; per car $5; ☼ dawn-dusk). About 8 miles south of town, the refuge protects almost 90 sq miles of fields and marshes, which serve as a major wintering ground for many migratory birds – most notably the very rare and endangered whooping cranes, of which about a dozen winter here. Tens of thousands of snow geese, sandhill cranes and various other waterfowl also call this place home, as do bald eagles. The wintering season lasts from late October to early April, but December and January are the peak viewing months and offer the best chance of seeing bald eagles. Upwards of 325 bird species and 135 mammal, reptile and amphibian species have been recorded here. From the **visitor center** (☎ 575-835-1828; ☼ 7:30am-4pm Mon-Fri, 8am-4:30pm Sat & Sun), a 15-mile loop circles the refuge; hiking trails and viewing platforms are easily accessible. To get here leave I-25 at San Antonio (10 miles south of Socorro) and drive 8 miles south on Hwy 1.

Festivals & Events

Socorro's **Balloon Rally** in late November is not to be missed; all participating balloonists line up on the street and inflate their balloons prior to a mass ascension. At the **49ers Festival** (third weekend of November), the entire town gets involved in a parade, dancing and gambling, while the **Festival of the Cranes** on the same weekend features special tours of Bosque del Apache, wildlife workshops and arts and crafts.

Sleeping & Eating

Economy Inn (☎ 575-835-4666; 400 California NE; r $40-60; ☒) There aren't a lot of options in

---

SOUTHWEST REGIONAL SPACEPORT: THE ULTIMATE SIDE TRIP

White Sands earned its nickname 'Birthplace of the Race to Space' in 1947, when humanity, courtesy of NASA's Werner von Braun, successfully hurled its first missile out past the stratosphere from among those rolling, pure white dunes. Today, thanks to Virgin Galactic CEO Sir Richard Branson, Governor Bill Richardson and lots of other pie-in-the-sky visionaries (not to mention state taxpayers who'll foot most of the projected $225 million bill), the world's first private spaceport has opened right next door.

Space tourism, till now restricted to adventurers willing to shell out US$2 million a pop aboard Russia's *Soyuz*, may well involve a simple 62-mile (straight up) add-on to your New Mexico vacation package. For just $200,000, you can book your flight on the VSS *Enterprise* online for a 90-minute ride in a plush cruiser with reclining seats, big windows and a pressurized cabin so you won't need space suits. The vessel is currently being built by legendary aerospace engineer Bob Rutan, whose *SpaceShipOne* was the first privately funded (by Microsoft cofounder Paul Allen) manned vehicle to reach outer space twice in a row, winning him the $10 million 2004 Ansari X-Prize.

It's not all about tourism, however. The Southwest Regional Spaceport (SRS), which is set to be renamed Spaceport America, has been used by UP Aerospace to launch cheap cargo carriers into low Earth orbit since 2006. The SRS is also the new home of the X-Prize competition, as well as other aerospace-themed expositions to be held throughout the year. But it's Virgin Galactic's maiden voyage, projected for early 2010, that promises to bring in the real press.

The New Mexico Office for Space Commercialization, founded by forward thinkers in 1994, estimates that the SRS will pump US$500 million into the state economy annually, primarily in the neighboring towns of Upham, Alamogordo and Truth or Consequences. Officials also hope to raise international awareness of New Mexico as a serious high-tech center: 'The planet will be watching as we reach for the stars,' says New Mexico tourism secretary Michael Cerletti.

'We might even be able to allow those aliens who landed at Roswell 50 years ago in a UFO a chance to go home,' adds Richard Branson.

---

town. Clean and reasonably well kept, most rooms here have microwaves and small refrigerators.

Socorro Springs Brewing Co (☎ 575-838-0650; 115 Abeyta Ave; mains $6-15; ☺ lunch & dinner) In the mood for a relatively sophisticated experience? Come to this renovated adobe joint for a really good clay-oven pizza, big calzones, decent pasta dishes, lots of salads and homemade soups. At times, the selection of brews can be on the minimal side. Whatever they're serving at the moment, though, is always smooth and tasty.

Owl Bar Café (☎ 575-835-9946; 215 San Antonio; dishes $6-15; ☺ breakfast, lunch & dinner Mon-Sat) It's worth the drive across I-10 to half a mile east of I-25 near San Antonio for the Owl Bar Café's green chile cheeseburgers. The sandwich is a potent mix of greasy beef, soft bun, sticky cheese, tangy chile, lettuce and tomato. It drips onto the plate in perfect burger fashion. Gossip hounds: this tiny town was the childhood home of hotelier Conrad Hilton – Paris Hilton's great-grand-daddy, that is.

Getting There & Around

Socorro is on I-25 about 75 miles (one-hour drive) south of Albuquerque. It is best reached via private vehicle.

The historic downtown is small and easily walkable and there is usually plenty of parking – your quarter buys a lot more time in the parking meters here, too.

TRUTH OR CONSEQUENCES & AROUND
pop 7300 / elev 4260ft

Home to a growing number of New Age hippies, off-the-grid artists and sustainable-living eco-warriors, kooky Truth or Consequences (T or C) is the quirkiest little town in New Mexico.

Situated on the banks of the Rio Grande, this high-desert oasis is hot property these days. And we're not just talking about the mineral-rich springs on which it was built and named (T or C was known as Hot Springs until 1950, when the town officially changed its name to match a popular radio game show in an effort to increase tourism). Half a century after T or C tried to become famous by changing its name, the moniker is finally catching on, but only because the town is kooky enough to match its name. T or C's latest publicity stunt? It's about to become the world's first commercial launch pad to outer space. Yup, you heard us, Richard Branson's Virgin Galactic is set to start blasting tourists off the planet from the nearby spaceport in 2010.

Space travel aside, T or C has also gained a reputation as the place for arty-holistic types to move, drop out and start a different journey – the geothermal energy here is supposedly comparable to Sedona's. In the last five years the town's population has soared, and the shabby-chic main drag is now filled with crystal shops, herbalists offices, yoga studios and a dozen eclectic art galleries and off-the-wall boutiques, the brain-children of the spiritual seekers, healers, writers and painters who came to find their vision.

Information

The **chamber of commerce** (☎ 575-894-3536; 400 W 4th St; ☺ 9am-5pm Mon-Fri, 9am-1pm Sat) and **Gila National Forest Ranger Station** (☎ 575-894-6677; 1804 N Date St; ☺ 8am-4:30pm Mon-Fri) have detailed information.

Sights & Activities

It won't take you more than an hour, but get your bearings in tiny T or C by strolling down Main St. Each day it seems another kooky art gallery or new herbal remedy shop opens, and it's fun to just walk and window-shop.

Also be sure to stop by the well-respected **Geronimo Springs Museum** (☎ 505-894-6600; 211 Main St; adult/student $3/1.50; ☺ 9am-5pm Mon-Sat). It's an extensive place with minerals, local art and plenty of historical artifacts ranging from prehistoric Mimbres pots to beautifully worked cowboy saddles. Exhibits also explain the details of the famous 1950 name change.

For centuries Indians, including Geronimo, have bathed in the area's mineral-laden **hot springs**. Long said to boast therapeutic properties, the waters range in temperature from 98°F to 115°F and have a pH of 7 (neutral).

Most of T or C's hotels and motels double as spas. As there are dozens of places to choose from, have a look at a couple of different spas to find your ideal relaxing spot. Massages and other treatments are usually available. Guests soak free.

The swankiest place to take a hot dip by far is **Sierra Grande Lodge & Spa** (p358), which added two new mineral baths and a holistic spa last year. The resort charges nonguests $25 for the first person, then $5 for each additional person in the party, to use its mineral springs.

For a more casual experience, try **Riverbend Hot Springs** (below), which offers six outdoor tubs by the river and a hippie hostel vibe. It costs between $10 and $15 per person to soak.

Just 20 miles north of T or C is the angler's paradise of **Elephant Butte Lake State Park** (☎ 575-744-5421; I-25; car per day $4, tent/RV sites $10/14). The state's largest artificial lake (60 sq miles), it's popular with day-trippers from T or C who come for waterskiing, windsurfing and, of course, fishing. The nearby **marina** (☎ 575-894-2041) rents tackle and boats (for fishing, pontoon and skiing). Spring and fall are best for fishing; guides will help you get the most out of your time for about $225 to $350 per day (for one to four anglers). Contact professional angler Randy Snyder, who operates recreational and instructional fishing tours through **Bass Busters** (☎ 575-894-0928; www.zianet.com/bassbusters), or Frank Vilorio, who works through **Fishing Adventures** (☎ 800-580-8992; www.stripersnewmexico.com) to make sure you take home your fill of striped bass.

Festivals & Events

The **T or C Fiesta**, held the first weekend in May, celebrates the town's 1950 name change with a rodeo, barbecue, parade and other events. The **Sierra County Fair** (late August) has livestock and agricultural displays, and the **Old Time Fiddlers State Championship** (third weekend in October) features country and western, bluegrass and mariachi music.

Sleeping & Eating

When it comes to places to get away, T or C is definitely taking off, but it's still not exactly happening by city standards – it's more of a make-your-own-fun type of place. Don't expect much in the way of nightlife or even lots of eating options. Still, the ones that exist are great. Think about booking ahead in summer.

Riverbend Hot Springs (☎ 575-894-7625; www.riverbendhotsprings.com; 100 Austin St; campsites/dm $20/24, r $40-100; wi-fi) Overseen by friendly hosts, this riverside hostel offers dormitory-style accommodation in cabins, trailers and teepees – you can also pitch a tent or camp in your car. Private rooms have kitchenettes, microwaves

NEW MEXICO

DETOUR: GHOSTLY MINING TOWNS

South of T or C, Hwy 152 west leads into silver country through **Hillsboro**, **Kingston** and **Santa Rita** (a ghost town). The slow but scenic road has some hairpin bends and crests at the Black Range at 8228ft Emory Pass, where a lookout gives views of the drier Rio Grande country to the east. A few miles beyond Emory Pass, the almost-ghost town of Kingston had 7000 inhabitants in its 1880s heyday as a silver-mining center, but now only a few dozen residents call it home. Nearby Hillsboro was revived by local agriculture after mining went bust. Today it's known for an **Apple Festival** on Labor Day, when fresh-baked apple pies, delicious apple cider, street musicians and arts and crafts stalls attract visitors. Have a sandwich at the **Barbershop Café** (☎ 575-895-5283; 200 Main St; mains $5-12; ☺ 11am-3pm Wed, Thu & Sun, 11am-8pm Fri & Sat), which also offers rooms (around $60), or stay at the **Enchanted Villa B&B** (☎ 575-895-5686; r from $65), with three rooms and a two-bedroom suite.

It's hard to miss the **Santa Rita Chino Open Pit Copper Mine**, which has an observation point on Hwy 152 about 6 miles from its intersection with Hwy 180. Worked by Indians and Spanish and Anglo settlers, it's the oldest active mine in the Southwest. The open pit mine is a staggering 1.5 miles wide, 1800ft deep and produces 300 million pounds of copper annually.

---

and coffeepots; several teepees sleep families and small groups. The hot-spring tubs are spread along the river.

Sierra Grande Lodge & Spa (☎ 575-894-6976; www .sierragrandelodge.com; 501 McAdoo St; r from $99; ☐ wi-fi) Chakras align at this oasis. A masterfully renovated 1920s lodge, Sierra Grande is T or C's most posh resort. Guest rooms and suites are luxe and tranquil, furnished with sophisticated touches and attention to detail; mineral-bath privileges (two new tubs opened last year) are included with the room. The holistic spa is offers a range of fabulous treatments and massages, including reiki.

Los Arcos (☎ 575-894-6200; 1400 N Date St; mains $15-25; ☺ dinner) T or C's 1960s-era steakhouse is the most upscale place to dine in town. Along with perfectly grilled steaks, it does a selection of (imported) lobster and shrimp and locally caught fish. Dine on the pleasant patio or within the hacienda-like interior.

Pine Knot Bar (☎ 575-894-2714; 1400 E Riverside Dr) Dance to a live Mexican band on weekends at this cocktail lounge; it's a popular local hang-out.

Getting There & Away

Greyhound/TNM&O (☎ 575-894-3649; www.greyhound .com) runs one or two daily buses north and south along I-25.

SILVER CITY & AROUND
pop 10,500 / elev 5938ft

Silver City's streets are dressed with a lovely mish-mash of old brick and cast-iron Victorians and thick-walled red adobe build-ings, and the place still emits a Wild West air. Billy the Kid spent some of his childhood here, and a few of his haunts can still be found mixed in with the new gourmet coffee shops, quirky galleries and Italian ice-cream parlors gracing its pretty downtown.

Once a rough-and-ready silver hub (and still a copper-mining town), Silver City is now attracting a growing number of adventure addicts who come to work and play in its surrounding great outdoors. With some 15 mountain ranges, four rivers, the cartoonish rock formations in City of Rocks State Parks and the action-packed Gila National Forest all in the vicinity, it's easy to understand the burgeoning love affair between visitors and this classic, Southwestern small town. Plus, as the home to Western New Mexico University, Silver City is infused with a healthy dose of youthful energy often lacking in this state.

Information

Chamber of Commerce (☎ 575-538-3785; www .silvercity.org; 201 N Hudson St; ☺ 9am-5pm Mon-Sat) Publishes a map with the city's galleries.

Library (☎ 575-538-3672; 515 W College Ave; ☺ 9am-5pm Tue, Wed & Fri, 9am-8pm Mon & Thu; ☐) Free internet access.

Medical center (☎ 575-538-4000; 1313 E 32nd)

Post office (☎ 575-538-2831; 500 N Hudson St)

Sights & Activities

The heart of this Victorian town is encom-passed by Bullard, Texas and Arizona Sts between Broadway and 6th St. The former Main St, one block east of Bullard, washed out during a series of massive floods in 1895. Caused by runoff from logged and overgrazed areas north of town, the floods eventually cut 55ft down below the original height of the street. In a stroke of marketing genius, it's now called **Big Ditch Park**.

The **Silver City Museum** (☎ 575-538-5921; www .silvercitymuseum.org; 312 W Broadway; admission free; ☷ 9:30am-4:30pm Tue-Fri, 10am-4pm Sat & Sun), ensconced in an elegant 1881 Victorian house, displays Mimbres pottery, as well as mining and household artifacts from Silver City's Victorian heyday. Its shop has a good selection of Southwestern books and gifts.

The **Western New Mexico University Museum** (WNMU; ☎ 575-538-6386; 1000 W College Ave; admission free; ☷ 9am-4:30pm Mon-Fri, 10am-4pm Sat & Sun) boasts the world's largest collection of Mimbres pottery, along with exhibits detailing local history, culture and natural history. The gift shop specializes in Mimbres motifs.

Seven miles north of Silver City along Hwy 15 lies **Pinos Altos**, established in 1859 as a gold-mining town. These days, it's almost a ghost town; its few residents strive to retain the 19th-century flavor of the place. Cruise Main St to see the log-cabin schoolhouse built in 1866, an opera house, a reconstructed fort and an 1870s courthouse.

Rounded volcanic towers create a cartoonish beauty in nearby **City of Rocks State Park** (☎ 575-536-2800; Hwy 61; per car $4, tent & RV sites $10-14). You can camp among the towers in secluded sites with tables and fire pits. A nature trail, drinking water and showers are available. The park is 33 miles southeast of Silver City – take Hwy 180 east to Hwy 61 south.

Visit **Gila Hike & Bike** (☎ 575-388-3222; 103 E College Ave; ☷ 9am-5:30pm Mon-Sat) for the scoop on regional single-track routes. Make sure to ask about the gorgeous new trail on Signal Peak, a mountain just above the town, with track through oaks and ponderosas and views all the way to Mexico. The shop also rents bicycles, snowshoes and camping equipment for exploring the region's outdoor attractions.

Sleeping

Most places to stay are outside of Silver City limits.

KOA (☎ 575-388-3351; www.koa.com; 11824 E Hwy 180; tent/RV sites $21/25, cabins from $45; ☷) Five miles east of town, this campground franchise is a clean, child-friendly option with a playground and coin laundry. The 'kamping kabins' are compact

but cute and good value, with all the necessities packed into the square wooden rooms. The place fills up in summer, so reserve ahead.

Palace Hotel (☎ 575-388-1811; www.zianet.com/pal acehotel; 106 W Broadway; r from $45; ☐) This venerable old hotel is the spot to slumber in Silver City. A restored 1882 hostelry, it has 19 rooms that vary from small (with a double bed) to two-room suites (with king- or queen-size beds) outfitted with refrigerators, microwaves, phones and TVs. All have old-fashioned Territorial-style decor.

Bear Creek Motel & Cabins (☎ 575-388-4501; www .bearcreekcabins.com; 88 Main St, Pinos Altos; cabins $110-160) Nestled under giant ponderosa pines just 7 miles north of Silver City, Bear Creek is a wonderful rugged wooden retreat. All 15 comfortable cabins (of varying size; some have two bedrooms and a kitchenette) are rustic, simple affairs with either fireplaces or wood-burning stoves. Soak your sore limbs in the big communal hot tub with hydrotherapy jets. Kids can try their luck at gold prospecting; the managers have gold pans for sifting through the silt at nearby Bear Creek.

Bear Mountain Lodge (☎ 575-538-2538; www .bearmountainlodge.com; 2251 Cottage San Rd; r $125-189) Tucked away on 178 acres next to the Gila National Forest, Bear Mountain Lodge (just outside of town) is operated by the Nature Conservancy. Rooms are in a large 1928 ranch house, and all 11 are decked out with Mission-style furniture and blue-and-white ceramic block tile in the bathrooms. Rates vary depending on room – each is different.

Eating & Drinking

Yankee Creek Coffeehouse (☎ 575-534-9025; 112 W Yankie St; coffee from $2; ☷ breakfast & lunch Mon-Sat) Wake up with gourmet coffee or a vanilla latte. Whatever caffeinated beverage you choose, it's bound to smell delicious and taste strong and fresh. Locally owned, Yankee imports coffee blends from around the world. Pastries and other snacks are served in casual environs.

Vicki's Deli & Eatery (☎ 575-388-5430; 107 W Yankie St; mains $5-9; ☷ breakfast & lunch Mon-Sat) With a roster of fresh feel-good food, vegetarian dishes, simple sandwiches, yummy Greek salads, stuffed grape leaves and other light meals, Vicki's is a long-time residential favorite. Dine outside in good weather. Check out the daily specials.

Silver City Brewing Co (☎ 575-534-2739; 101 E College Ave; mains from $6; ☷ lunch & dinner) If you're

NEW MEXICO

interested in the craft, ask to chat with the head brewer at this hands-on brewery that serves a range of homemade ales and lagers along with pizza, calzones and appetizers. The wings are good and spicy, and you can order a salad with your cheese, tomato and dough. It's near the university and popular with the college crowd.

Shevek & Mi (☎ 575-534-9168; 602 N Bullard St; mains $8-25; ✆ 10:30am-8:30pm Mon-Thu, 8:30am-10:30pm Fri & Sat, 8:30am-8:30pm Sun) Owned by a CIA-trained chef, this delightful eatery is at turns formal, bistro-like and patio-casual. It depends on which room you choose. Sunday brunch is decidedly New York, à la Upper West side; dinners range from Moroccan to Spanish to Italian. Enjoy the excellent selection of beer and wine.

Diane's Restaurant & Bakery (☎ 575-538-8722; 510 N Bullard St; mains $10-25; ✆ 11am-2:30pm & 5pm-8:30pm Tue-Fri, 9am-2pm Sat & Sun) Diane's is the local restaurant of choice, especially for weekend breakfasts. If you visit then, order the Hatch Benedict eggs; the house version of the original is doused with the region's beloved chile pepper. Diane's does a busy lunch trade during the week. The romantic appeal is upped at dinner, when there is dim lighting and white linen.

Buckhorn Saloon (☎ 575-538-9911; Main St, Pinos Altos; mains $12-25; ✆ dinner Mon-Sat) About 7 miles north of Silver City, this restored adobe eatery offers steaks (a house specialty) and seafood amid 1860s Wild West decor – try the buffalo burgers, they're fresh and tasty. The big stone fireplaces are warming. Live country music livens up the joint on Friday and Saturday.

Getting There & Around

Silver City sits just south of the junction of Hwy 180 and Rte 90 and is best reached via private transportation. Silver City is 115 miles from Las Cruces, the closest sizeable junction town. To get here from Las Cruces head west on US 10 then follow Hwy 180 all the way north to Silver City.

Downtown Silver City is small and walkable and street parking is plentiful. The town also serves as the gateway to the Gila National Forest (below), just north of town.

GILA NATIONAL FOREST

If you're looking for isolated and undiscovered, not to mention magnificent, these mountains have magic in spades. Northwest of

Silver City, Hwy 180 crosses the Continental Divide and winds through remote and wild country dotted with a few tiny communities. The Gila National Forest and Mogollon Mountains offer some excellent opportunities for remote and primitive backpacking, hiking, camping and fishing. The **ranger station** (☎ 575-539-2481; Hwy 180; ✆ 8am-4:30pm) a half-mile south of Glenwood has details.

From Glenwood head 5 miles east on Hwy 174 to the **Catwalk** – a trail enclosed by a wire cage hugging the cliff up narrow Whitewater Canyon. It follows water pipes built by miners in 1893. When the pipes needed repair, the miners walked along them (the 'Catwalk'). It's a short but worthwhile hike with some steep spots.

Mogollon, a semi-ghost town, lies 4 miles north of Glenwood and then 9 miles east on steep and narrow Hwy 159 (inaccessible during the winter). Once an important mining town, it's now rather deserted and empty, inhabited by only a few antique-like shops and, as is typical for middle-of-nowhere New Mexico, one proud little restaurant. This one is called the **Purple Onion** (☎ 575-529-2710; Main St; mains $5-10; ✆ breakfast & lunch Fri, Sat & Sun) and it claims to serve the best burger in New Mexico. We're not sure if it's the best, but it's pretty darn good, as are most of the homemade dishes at this friendly, weekend-only place.

The USFS maintains the **Bighorn campground** (admission free; ✆ year-round) in Gila National Forest, a quarter-mile north of Glenwood, with no drinking water or fee.

The area around **Reserve** on Hwy 180 is mainly settled by ranchers, cowboys and loggers who particularly loathe federal government interference and environmentalists. It's the kind of place where county officials passed a resolution urging every family to own a gun. This is about as close to the old Wild West as you'll get.

For serene outback forest slumber, rent one of the five stunningly situated **Casitas de Gila Guesthouse** (☎ 877-923-4827; www.casitasdegila .com; off Hwy 180, near Cliff; casitas $150-200) adobe-style casitas set on 90 acres of wilderness. Each unit has a fully stocked kitchen, plenty of privacy and one or two bedrooms. Stay a while and rates drop. There are telescopes, an outdoor hot tub and grills to keep you occupied. The guest house is about two hours from the Gila Cliff Dwellings, but practically right on top of the Gila National Forest.

Gila Cliff Dwellings

Mysterious, relatively isolated and accessible, these remarkable cliff dwellings look very much like they would have at the turn of the first century. Luckily, the cliffs are not crowded with visitors, so it will be easy for you to step back in time. The influence of the Ancestral Puebloans (p38) on the Mogollon culture is writ large. Take the 1-mile round-trip self-guided trail that climbs 180ft to the dwellings, overlooking a lovely forested canyon. Parts of the trail are steep and involve ladders. The trail begins at the end of Hwy 15, 2 miles beyond the **visitor center** (☎ 575-536-9461; admission $3; ⏲ 8am-5pm). Between the visitor center and trailhead are two small **campgrounds** with drinking water, picnic areas and toilets. They're free on a first-come, first-served basis and often fill on summer weekends. A short trail behind the campground leads to older dwellings.

Gila Hot Springs

Used by Indians since ancient times, these springs are 39 miles north of Silver City, within the **Gila Hotsprings Vacation Center** (☎ 575-536-9551; www.gilahotspringsranch.com; Hwy 15; tent/RV sites $12/17, r from $50). The pet-friendly resort (dogs can stay for an extra $5 per night) has simple rooms with kitchenettes in a giant red barn-like structure, along with camping sites and an RV park with a spa and showers fed by hot springs. Primitive camping is adjacent to the **hot pools** (hot pools $3, camping & hot pools $4). You can arrange horseback rides, guided fishing and wilderness pack trips and other outfitting services in advance through the center.

DEMING & AROUND

pop 15,300 / elev 4335ft

In the least populous of the state's four corners, Deming (founded in 1881 as a railway junction) is popular with retirees. It's surrounded by cotton fields on the northern edge of the Chihuahuan Desert. But if this is a desert, where does all the water come from for the family farms and ranches? It's tapped from the invisible Mimbres River, which disappears underground about 20 miles north of town and emerges in Mexico.

Although it has a good museum and nearby state parks, the real reason anyone comes to Deming is for the **Great American Duck Races**, held on the fourth weekend in August. Attracting tens of thousands of visitors, the late summer race is perhaps the most whimsical and popular festival in the state. The main event is the duck races themselves, which offer thousands of dollars in prize money. Anyone can enter for a $10 fee ($5 for kids), which includes 'duck rental.' Other wacky events include the Tortilla Toss (winners toss tortillas over 170ft), Outhouse Races and a Duckling Contest. As if that weren't enough, entertainment ranges from cowboy poets to local musicians, and there's a parade, hot-air balloons and food.

Run by the Luna County Historical Society, the **Deming Luna Mimbres Museum** (☎ 505-546-2382; 301 S Silver Ave; admission free; ⏲ 9am-4pm Mon-Sat, 1:30-4pm Sun, closed major holidays) has varied, interesting and well-displayed exhibits including a superb doll collection, Mimbres pots, vintage cars, liquor decanters, homemade quilts and, get this, a braille edition of *Playboy*.

Fourteen miles southeast of Deming via Hwys 11 and 141, **Rock Hound State Park** (☎ 505-546-6182; per car $4) is known for the semiprecious or just plain pretty rocks that can be collected here (there's a 15lb limit). You'll need a shovel and some rockhounding experience to uncover anything special; local experts suggest walking into the Little Florida Mountains for a while before beginning to look for rocks bearing (perhaps) agate, opal, jasper or quartz crystals. Don't know what you're looking for? Stop at the **Geolapidary Museum & Rock Shop** (☎ 505-546-4021; admission $1; ⏲ 9am-5pm Thu-Tue), 2 miles before the park entrance.

Room rates rise during duck races and the state fair (early October), when you need to make reservations. Probably the best bet in town, the **Grand Motor Inn** (☎ 505-546-2631; 1721 E Pine St; r $40; 🅿) offers discounts when it's slow. It's a decent spot to sleep, surrounded by grassy grounds.

Deming has a handful of good and simple Mexican-American restaurants, but **Si Senor** (☎ 575-546-3938; 200 E Pine St; mains $6-11; ⏲ 9:30am-8pm Mon-Sat, 10am-3pm Sun) is the best. Order *huevos rancheros* in the morning and a big deluxe platter with the works later in the day. Then go take a siesta.

Greyhound (☎ 505-546-3881; www.greyhound.com; 300 E Spruce St) runs two or three daily buses along the I-10 corridor.

LAS CRUCES & AROUND

pop 74,700 / elev 3890ft

At the crossroads of two major highways, I-10 and I-25, Las Cruces makes a great pit stop, once you get past the shock that this rural outpost is actually New Mexico's second-biggest city! Las Cruces and her sister city, Mesilla, sit in a blessed valley wedged between the sparkling waters of the Rio Grande and the fluted Organ Mountains. And there is something very special about the combination of bright white sunlight, glassy blue skies, flowering cacti, rippling red mountains and desert lowland landscape found here.

Las Cruces is an eclectic mix of old and young. The city is home to New Mexico State University (NMSU), whose 15,000-strong student body infuses it with a healthy dose of youthful liveliness, while at the same time its 350 days of sunshine, mild climate and 72 holes of golf are turning it into a dream retirement destination for the 65-plus crowd.

Mesilla is the perfect place to lose track of time. Let the centuries slide back as you wander its beautiful historic plaza surrounded by lovely 19th-century buildings adorned with colorful *ristras* and shops selling souvenirs ranging from cheap and kitschy to expensive.

Although it's becoming more popular, this region is far from prosperous. Las Cruces is a poor area of New Mexico, where residents get by cultivating chiles, corn, fruit and pecans on small family farms or they work at the nearby White Sands Missile Range.

Information

Convention & Visitors Bureau (☎ 800-343-7827; www.lascrucescvb.org; 211 N Water, Las Cruces) Loads of tourist info online.

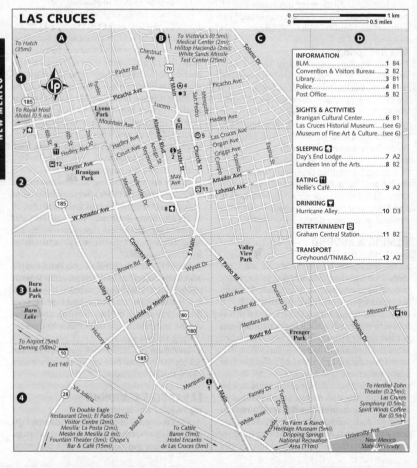

LAS CRUCES

INFORMATION	
BLM	**1** B4
Convention & Visitors Bureau	**2** B2
Library	**3** B1
Police	**4** B1
Post Office	**5** B2

SIGHTS & ACTIVITIES	
Branigan Cultural Center	**6** B1
Las Cruces Historial Museum	(see 6)
Museum of Fine Art & Culture	(see 6)

SLEEPING	
Day's End Lodge	**7** A2
Lundeen Inn of the Arts	**8** B2

EATING	
Nellie's Café	**9** A2

DRINKING	
Hurricane Alley	**10** D3

ENTERTAINMENT	
Graham Central Station	**11** B2

TRANSPORT	
Greyhound/TNM&O	**12** A2

Library (☎ 575-528-4000; 200 E Picacho Ave, Las Cruces; ☺ 10am-9pm Mon-Thu, to 6pm Fri & Sat, to 5pm Sun; ▣) Free internet access.

Medical Center (☎ 575-522-8641; 2450 S Telshor Blvd, Las Cruces; ☺ 24hr emergency)

Mesilla Visitor Center (☎ 575-647-9698; www .oldmesilla.org; Ave de Mesilla, Mesilla ☺ 9:30am-4:30pm Mon-Sat, 11am-3pm Sun)

Police (☎ 505-526-0795; 217 E Picacho Ave, Las Cruces)

Post office (☎ 575-524-2841; 201 E Las Cruces Ave, Las Cruces)

Sights

Four miles south of Las Cruces is her sister city, **Mesilla** (www.oldmesilla.org). Dating back 150 years (and looking pretty much the way it did back then), Mesilla is a charming old adobe town rich in culture and texture. Despite the souvenir shops and tourist-oriented restaurants, the Mesilla Plaza and surrounding blocks remain a step back in time. Wander a few blocks beyond the plaza to garner the essence of a mid-19th-century Southwestern border town of Hispanic heritage. Mesilla once served as a stop on the route to Mexico, and it saw its share of shady characters pass down its dusty streets – Billy the Kid stood trial for murder here. One highlight of a walk through town is visiting the **San Albino Church** on the plaza. The church, originally built of adobe in 1855, still offers masses today, both in English and Spanish. Outside the church is a memorial to parishioners who died in combat.

Both Mesilla and Las Cruces are home to a burgeoning fine arts and performing arts community, with more than 40 galleries and a number of theatrical and musical production companies scattered around the valley. What's neat about gallery hopping here is that many of the places double as the artist's studio and most are happy to chat with visitors about their passion. Find out more on arts, theater and dance at the **Branigan Cultural Center** (☎ 575-541-2155; 490-500 N Water St, Las Cruces; admission free; ☺ 8:30am-4:40pm Mon-Fri, 9am-1pm Sat). The center also houses the **Museum of Fine Art & Culture** and the **Las Cruces Historical Museum**, with small collections of local art, sculpture, quilts and historic artifacts.

Explore New Mexico's nuclear history with a visit to the **White Sands Missile Test Center Museum** (☎ 575-678-2250; www.wsmr-history.org; Bldg 200, Headquarters Ave; admission free; ☺ 8am-4pm Mon-Fri, 10am-3pm Sat & Sun), 25 miles east of Las Cruces

along Hwy 70. It represents the heart of the White Sands Missile Range, a major military testing site since 1945. The place also serves as an alternative landing site for the space shuttle. At the gate, tell the guard you are visiting the museum; you'll need to show your driver's license, proof of car insurance and car registration (or rental papers).

Festivals & Events

The **Whole Enchilada Fiesta**, from late September to early October, is the city's best-known event. It features live music, food booths, arts and crafts, sporting events, a chile cook-off, carnival rides and a parade. It culminates in the cooking of the world's biggest enchilada on Sunday morning. The **Fiesta of Our Lady of Guadalupe** (☎ 575-526-8171), held in the nearby Indian village of Tortugas from December 10 to 12, is different. Late into the first night, drummers and masked dancers accompany a statue of Mary in a procession from the church. On the following day, participants climb several miles to Tortugas Mountain for mass; dancing and ceremonies continue into the night in the village. The **Southern New Mexico State Fair & Rodeo**, from late September to early October, features a livestock show, auction, lively rodeo and country musical performances. The **International Mariachi Festival** (☎ 505-525-1735; www.lascrucesmariachi .org) in mid-November celebrates this folkloric dance with educational workshops and big-time performances.

Sleeping

Las Cruces has a dearth of hotel and motel chains. At the cheapest places you can score a room for as little as $40 (plus taxes); the average for a Best Western or Hampton-style motor lodge with an on-site restaurant and pool is around $80.

Day's End Lodge (☎ 575-524-7753; 755 N Valley Dr, Las Cruces; r $35-55) Smokers listen up: this place still lets you light up inside! For the majority who don't puff, you better sniff before paying. If the room is not smoky (and they do have designated nonsmoking rooms), Day's End provides a pleasant chain hotel experience with clean but faded rooms and fresh coffee in the morning. Rooms come with mini-fridges and HBO.

Royal Host Motel (☎ 575-524-8536; 2146 W Picacho Ave, Las Cruces; r $40-65; ☙) Pets are welcome (extra $10) at this downtown spot with 26 spacious

NEW MEXICO

rooms. It's a basic budget motel, but clean and friendly. An onsite restaurant, pool and free local calls win points.

Mesón de Mesilla (☎ 575-525-9212, 800-732-6025; www.mesondemesilla.com; 1803 Ave de Mesilla, Mesilla; r $65-140; 🏊) This stylish and graceful adobe house has 15 guest rooms with antiques, Southwestern furnishings and modern amenities. A short walk from the plaza, the 'boutique-style' house also has a lovely courtyard; attractive gardens surround the house. The honeymoon suite includes a full breakfast in the restaurant.

our pick Lundeen Inn of the Arts (☎ 505-526-3326, 888-526-3326; www.innofthearts.com; 618 S Alameda Blvd, Las Cruces; r $80-125, ste $99-155) This large, turn-of-the-19th-century Mexican Territorial–style inn is one of the nicest in its genre. The 20 thoughtfully decorated guestrooms are each unique and named for local artists. Our favorites are the Georgia O'Keeffe room, done up in black, white and gray with calla lilies on the mantle, and the very warm and Southwestern RC Gorman room. It boasts its own entrance, kiva fireplace and partial viga ceiling. The public areas are equally fantastic – check out the soaring pressed-tin ceilings in the great room decked out with old world Jacobean-style furniture and dark wood floors. There is an art gallery onsite.

Hilltop Hacienda (☎ 505-382-3556; www.zianet.com /hilltop; 2600 Westmoreland, Las Cruces; r from $90) Yes, the antique-filled rooms are comfortable and the B&B offers a common room with VCR and library. But it's the setting, on 18 acres atop a hill with breathtaking 360-degree mountain views, that's the real draw. Catch at least one sunset and sunrise here.

Hotel Encanto de Las Cruces (☎ 505-522-4300; 705 S Telshor Blvd, Las Cruces; r from $110; 🖳 🏊) This former Hilton is the city's best big hotel. It's a seven-story Mexican colonial structure that gets positive feedback for its 200 spacious rooms done up in warm Southwestern style. Shoppers: the hotel is across the street from New Mexico's biggest mall. Also on site is an exercise room, restaurant and lounge.

Eating

There are two main eating areas: Las Cruces and Mesilla. We've split the listings here to make your life a little easier. Located in the heart of the chile capital of the world, this area is home to some of the spiciest Mexican food in the state. Yum.

LAS CRUCES

Nellie's Cafe (☎ 505-524-9982; 1226 W Hadley Ave; mains $5-8; 🕙 8am-4pm Tue-Sat) Without a doubt the favored local Mexican restaurant, Nellie's has been serving homemade burritos, *chile rellenos* and tamales for decades now and garnered a dedicated following. The slogan here is 'Chile with an Attitude' and the food is deliciously spicy. It's small and humble in decor, but big in taste.

Spirit Winds Coffee Bar (☎ 575-521-1222; 2260 S Locust; mains $5-15; 🕙 breakfast, lunch & dinner) Join the university crowd for excellent cappuccino and gourmet tea, as well as good sandwiches, salads, soups and pastries, and some more substantial dishes come dinner. An eclectic gift and card shop and occasional live entertainment keeps the students, artsy types and business folks coming back.

Cattle Baron (☎ 575-522-7533; 790 S Telshor Blvd; mains $7-20; 🕙 lunch & dinner; 🧒) This restaurant serves the best fine steaks in town, cooked to order. If you're not into red meat, don't fear: the Baron offers a wide range of chicken, pasta and seafood options as well as a kid's menu. A good spot to bring the tots.

MESILLA

Chope's Bar & Café (☎ 575-233-3420; Hwy 28; mains $5-10; 🕙 lunch & dinner Tue-Sat) About 15 miles south of town and worth every second of the drive, Chope's is a southern New Mexican institution. It isn't anything to look at, but the hot chile will turn you into an addict within minutes. From *chile rellenos* to burritos, you've seen the menu before; you just haven't had it this good. The adjacent bar is loads of fun.

La Posta (☎ 575-524-3524; 2410 Calle de San Albino; mains $6-18; 🕙 lunch & dinner Tue-Sun) The area's most famous Mexican eatery is housed in an early-19th-century adobe house that predates the founding of Mesilla. A Butterfield stagecoach stop in the 1850s, today's restaurant claims to have the largest collection of tequila in the Southwest (with close to 100 varieties). Order enchiladas.

Double Eagle Restaurant (☎ 575-523-6700; 308 Calle de Guadalupe; mains $13-40; 🕙 lunch & dinner) Central courtyards, chandeliers and a 30ft bar are all fabulous assets to this upscale eatery, which serves delicious continental and Southwest cuisine in an elegant 19th-century Victorian and Territorial style setting. The restaurant is on the National Register of Historic Places;

make sure to walk off lunch with a stroll around the property.

Drinking & Entertainment

The *Bulletin*, a free weekly published on Thursday, has up-to-the-minute entertainment information.

El Patio (☎ 575-524-0982; plaza, Mesilla; ☺ bar until late) In an old adobe building, this historic place has been rocking Mesilla since the 1930s. It serves cocktails along with live rock and jazz.

Hurricane Alley (☎ 575-532-9358; 1490 Missouri Ave, Las Cruces) With live rock or DJs and dancing on weekends, this bar near the university is popular with the college crowd.

Graham Central Station (☎ 575-524-9131; 505 S Main St, Las Cruces; cover $2-20) Join the university students for a night of revelry at this four-in-one club buffet. Listen to big-name country artists, enter a shot-taking contest or dance like you're in Miami at a South Beach–themed lounge under the same roof. It's a bit of a meat market – college kids come here to hook up. But as long as you don't mind some old-fashioned American sleaze, it's a cheap place to get wasted. Nightly drink specials are seemingly mandatory.

Fountain Theater (☎ 575-524-8287; www.fountaintheater.org; 2469 Calle de Guadalupe, Mesilla; adult/student $7/6) Home of the nonprofit Mesilla Valley Film Society, this theater screens foreign and art films. Check out the website to see what's playing when you're in town.

The American Southwest Theater Company presents plays at the **Hershel Zohn Theater** (☎ 575-646-4515; McFie Circle; tickets $10-15)

on the NMSU campus, while the **Las Cruces Symphony** (☎ 575-646-3709; tickets $22) performs at the NMSU Music Center Recital Hall.

Getting There & Away

Greyhound/TNM&O (☎ 575-524-8518; www.greyhound.com; 490 N Valley Dr) has buses traversing the two interstate corridors (I-10 and I-25), as well as buses to Roswell and beyond.

Las Cruces Shuttle Service (☎ 800-288-1784; www.lascrucesshuttle.com) runs 12 vans daily to the El Paso International Airport ($38 one way, $15 to $30 for each additional person) and vans to Deming, Silver City and other destinations on request.

ALAMOGORDO & AROUND
pop 36,100 / elev 4350ft

Despite a dearth of amenities, Alamogordo (Spanish for 'fat cottonwood tree') is the center of one of the most historically important space and atomic research programs. If you're traveling with the kids in summer, it's worth coming here for Shuttle Camp at the Museum of Space History. It's a hands-on science lesson they won't soon forget. The city is also filled with lots of other kid-friendly attractions. There's not much for adults in Alamogordo, although the area around it is nice – check out the tiny art outpost of La Luz or the fine vineyard in equally small Tularosa, both nearby town.

White Sands Blvd (also called Hwy 54, 70 or 82) is the main drag through town and runs north–south. Addresses on North White Sands Blvd correspond to numbered cross-streets (thus 1310 N WSB is just north

NEW MEXICO

THE BLAST HEARD 'ROUND THE WORLD

On just two days a year (the first Saturday in April and October), the public is permitted to tour the **Trinity Site**, where the first atomic bomb was detonated on July 16, 1945, 35 miles west of Carrizozo. The eerie tour includes the base camp, the McDonald Ranch house where the plutonium core for the bomb was assembled, and ground zero itself. The test was carried out above ground and resulted in a quarter-mile-wide crater and an 8-mile-high cloud mushrooming above the desert. The radiation level of the site is 'only' 10 times greater than the region's background level; a one-hour visit to ground zero will result in an exposure of one-half to one millorentgen (mrem), two to four times the estimated exposure of a typical adult on an average day in the USA. Trinitite, a green, glassy substance resulting from the blast, is still radioactive, still scattered around and still must not be touched. Resist the urge to add it to your road-trip rock collection. This desolate area is fittingly called **Jornada del Muerto** (Journey of Death) and is overshadowed by 8638ft **Oscura Peak** (Darkness Peak on state maps). Call the **Alamogordo Chamber of Commerce** (☎ 505-437-6120, 800-826-0294; www.alamogordo.com) for information.

of 13th); addresses on South WSB are one block south of 1st.

Information

Hospital (☎ 575-439-6100; 2669 N Scenic Dr; ☻ 24hr emergency)

Library (☎ 575-439-4140; 10th St; ☻ 10am-8pm Mon-Thu, 10am-5pm Fri, 11am-5pm Sat, 1-5pm Sun; ☐) Free internet access.

Lincoln USFS National Forest Ranger Station (☎ 575-434-7200; 1101 New York Ave; ☻ 7:30am-4:30pm Mon-Fri)

Police (☎ 575-439-4300; 700 Virginia Ave)

Post office (☎ 575-437-9390; 30 E 12th St)

Visitor center (☎ 575-437-6120, 800-826-0294; www .alamogordo.com; 1301 N White Sands Blvd; ☻ 8am-5pm Mon-Fri, 9am-5pm Sat & Sun)

Sights & Activities

Alamogordo is a good place to bring the kids. The most important museum is the four-story **New Mexico Museum of Space History** (☎ 575-437-2840, 877-333-6589; www.spacefame.org; Hwy 2001; adult/child $6/4; ☻ 9am-5pm; ☻). Nicknamed 'the golden cube,' it looms over the town and has excellent exhibits on space research and flight. Its **Tombaugh IMAX Theater & Planetarium** (adult/child $6/4.50; ☻) shows outstanding films on anything from the Grand Canyon to the dark side of the moon, as well as laser shows and multimedia presentations on a huge wraparound screen. If your child has ever been interested in space travel, the museum runs a summer **Shuttle Camp** (per week/half-day $500/$85; ☻) for kids aged 7 through 17. The education-based science program includes some pretty cool features, including flight training in a cockpit simulator, field trips and other hands-on experiments. The week-long sleepover camp is great if you have the time, but even if you're just in town for a few days, it's worth checking out the half-day camp.

Established in 1898 as a diversion for railway travelers, the **Alameda Park & Zoo** (☎ 575-439-4290; 1021 N White Sands Blvd; adult/child 3-11 $2.20/1.10; ☻ 9am-5pm; ☻) is the oldest zoo west of the Mississippi. Small but well run, it features exotics from around the world, among them the endangered Mexican gray wolf. Best of all, it hasn't changed its admission prices in years.

Railroad buffs and kids flock to the **Toy Train Depot** (☎ 575-437-2855; 1991 N White Sands Blvd; admission $3; ☻ noon-5pm Wed-Sun; ☻), an 1898 railway depot with five rooms of train memorabilia and toy trains, and a 2.5-mile narrow-gauge train.

Wander around the historic center of town, east of N White Sands Blvd along and just off 10th St; the USFS building at 11th and New York houses Peter Hurd's *Sun and Rain* frescoes, painted in the early 1940s as part of the New Deal's WPA art program.

The small and thoroughly local **Tularosa Basin Historical Society Museum** (☎ 575-434-4438; www.alamogordomuseum.org; 1301 N White Sands Blvd; admission free; ☻ 10am-4pm Mon-Fri, 10am-3pm Sat, noon-3pm Sun) focuses on Mescalero Indians and the mining, railroad and logging industries. The museum's most cherished holding is a 47-star US flag, one of only a handful that exist because Arizona joined the USA just six weeks after New Mexico did.

Alamogordo's most attractive attractions lie outside the city limits. Head 4 miles north on Hwy 54 to the tiny art enclave of **La Luz**. Home to a motley crew of painters, writers and craftspeople who share a passion for creating artwork and living off the land, this wild outpost remains untouched by commercial tourism and is well worth a browse.

Continue north another ten miles to the attractive village of **Tularosa**. It's dominated by the 1869 St Francis de Paula Church, built in a simple New Mexican style. **Tularosa Vineyards** (☎ 575-585-2260; www.tularosavineyards.com; Hwy 54; ☻ 9am-5pm Mon-Sat, noon-5pm Sun) is a friendly and picturesque winery about 2 miles north of Tularosa. It offers daily afternoon tours and tastings.

When you've had your fill of vino, head back to Tularosa for lunch at Casa de Suenos (opposite). The trip from Alamogordo through La Luz to Tularosa and back, while only 9 miles long, can be stretched out to make a good half-day trip if you're in this area.

Sleeping & Eating

This town doesn't have much in the way of creativity – besides the places listed here there are many other chains scattered along White Sands Blvd.

Oliver Lee State Park (tent/RV sites $10/14) Developed and free dispersed camping is available in the Lincoln National Forest, particularly along forest roads branching off from Hwy 82 east of Alamogordo.

Alamogordo Roadrunner Campground (☎ 575-437-3003; 412 24th St; tent/RV sites $19/24, cabins from $35; ☻ ☻ ☐ wi-fi) This high-tech campground (yup, laptop owners can check their email

---

DETOUR: THREE RIVERS PETROGLYPH NATIONAL RECREATION AREA

The uncrowded **Three Rivers Petroglyph NRA** (☎ 575-525-4300; County Rd B30, off Hwy 54; per car $3, tent/RV sites $3/15) showcases 20,000 petroglyphs inscribed 1000 years ago by the Jornada Mogollon people. The 1-mile hike through mesquite and cacti offers good views of the Sacramento Mountains to the east and White Sands Monument on the horizon. Nearby is a pithouse in a partially excavated village. There are six camping shelters with barbecue grills (free), restrooms, water and two hookups for RVs. The **BLM** (☎ 575-525-4300; Marquess St, off Valley Dr) in Las Cruces has details.

The site is 27 miles north of Alamogordo on Hwy 54, and then 5 miles east on a signed road. If you want to rough it, a dirt road continues beyond the petroglyphs for about 10 miles to the Lincoln National Forest, where you'll find **Three Rivers Campground** (☎ 575-434-7200).

---

from the comfort of their sleeping bag) is great for families. It has a big playground, along with laundry facilities, a recreation room and swimming pool (plenty to keep kids of all ages busy). If you don't feel like sleeping on the ground, try one of the cute little cabins; they're compact wooden affairs with bunk beds. Grab hamburger patties and buns from the on-site grocery store and fire up the grill out front. Now that's posh camping.

Satellite Inn (☎ 575-437-8454; www.satelliteinn.com; 2224 N White Sands Blvd; r $44; ☏ ⬛) An old-school Alamogordo independent with simple and clean double rooms that have a microwave and refrigerator. Rooms are basic, but it's a bit more personal feeling than your typical roadside motel.

Best Western Desert Aire Motor Inn (☎ 575-437-2110; www.bestwestern.com; 1021 S White Sands Blvd; r from $64; ☏ ⬧) Recently remodeled, this chain hotel has standard-issue rooms and suites (some with kitchenettes), along with a sauna and whirlpool. In summer, the swimming pool is a cool sanctuary.

Plaza Pub (☎ 575-437-9495; cnr White Sands Blvd & 10th St; mains $5-7; ☻ lunch-late) A truly local place to kick back, this pub has good burgers and green chile stew along with a wide selection of beer. Come to shoot some pool and ponder the stuffed animal heads on the walls. On weekends, live bands draw scores of townies.

Margo's (☎ 575-434-0689; 504 E 1st St; mains $5-11; ☻ 10:30am-9pm Mon-Sat, 11am-8:30pm Sun) There's not much to look at inside but hey, when they offer such good Mexican cuisine at such good prices, who can complain? Family-owned since the early 1980s, Margo's has a robust and tasty combo plate.

Casa de Suenos (☎ 575-585-3494; 35 St Francis Dr, Tularosa; mains $5-15; ☻ lunch & dinner Mon-Fri, breakfast, lunch & dinner Sat & Sun) The restaurant is all done up with folk paintings from South of the Border; it's a festive place with a great outdoor patio. Its New Mexican cuisine is some of the best in the area and the lunchtime buffet is bountiful.

Compass Rose Brew Pub (☎ 575-434-9633; 2203 E 1st St; mains $10-20; ☻ lunch & dinner) If you're tired of green chile and beans, and are overcome by a desire for food with a German flair, try this slightly yuppyish place. Compass Rose has a great selection of brews (although they no longer brew their own) and fresh guacamole and salads.

Shooters Pizza & Patio Bar (☎ 575-443-6000; Hwy 70) Shooters has karaoke Monday through Wednesday; the line-up the rest of the week is hip-hop, country or Top 40. It's better for drinking than eating.

Getting There & Around

The **TNM&O bus station** (☎ 800-231-2222; www .greyhound.com; 601 N White Sands Blvd) has several daily buses to Albuquerque ($45, 4½ hours), Roswell ($30, 2½ hours), Carlsbad ($42, 4½ hours) and El Paso ($27, two hours). The **Alamo El Paso Shuttle** (☎ 575-437-1472, 800-872-2701; Best Western Desert Aire Motor Inn) has five buses daily to the El Paso International Airport ($40, 1½ hours).

CLOUDCROFT & AROUND
pop 700 / elev 8600ft

Nestled high in the mountains, Cloudcroft is paradise year-round. In winter there's snow tubing and snowmobiling across powder-soaked meadows and down canyons. In summer, at nearly two miles high, Cloudcroft offers refreshing respite from the surrounding desert heat, plus awesome hiking and biking. The town itself is a pleasant place to wander, with some early-19th-century buildings, a

NEW MEXICO

low-key mountain vibe and one of the top historic resorts in the Southwest. But where Cloudcroft really shines is the great outdoors, and most people visit to play in the surrounding peaks and forests.

Orientation & Information

Hwy 82 is the main drag through town; most places are on Hwy 82 or within a few blocks of it. Stop at the **chamber of commerce** (☎ 575-682-2733; www.cloudcroft.net; Hwy 82; ☯ 10am-5pm Mon-Sat) or **Sacramento Ranger Station** (☎ 575-682-2551; Chipmunk Ave; ☯ 7:30am-4:30pm Mon-Fri).

Sights & Activities

One of the world's largest solar observatories is near Sunspot, 20 miles south of Cloudcroft. Though it's primarily for scientists, tourists can take self-guided tours of the **Sacramento Peak Observatory** (☎ 575-434-7000; ☯ visitor center 10am-4pm) on Friday, Saturday and Sunday at 2pm during the summer. The drive to Sunspot, along the **Sunspot Scenic Byway**, is a high and beautiful one, with the mountains to the east and White Sands National Monument (opposite) to the west. From Cloudcroft, take Hwy 130 to Hwy 6563.

Hiking is popular here from April to November; outings range from short hikes close to town to overnight backpacking trips. Although trails are often fairly flat, the 9000ft elevation can make for some strenuous hiking if you are not acclimatized. The most popular day hike is the 2.6-mile **Osha Loop Trail**, which leaves Hwy 82 from a small parking area 1 mile west of Cloudcroft.

The Lodge Resort (right) has a beautiful nine-hole **golf course** (☎ 575-682-2098; admission from $20, cart rental per person $8) that is one of the highest and oldest in the USA. In the winter, the course is groomed for cross-country skiing. The Lodge also provides guided snowmobile and horse-drawn sleigh rides.

Trails in the Sacramento Mountains offer great mountain biking. **High Altitude** (☎ 575-682-1229; www.highaltitude.org; 310 Burro Ave; ☯ 10am-6pm Wed-Mon) rents bikes and points you towards the trails.

In winter, grab the lift up and race an inner tube down the hill at the **Triple M Mystical Mountain Snow Ski Area** (☎ 575-682-2205; www.triplemsnowplay.com; Sunspot Hwy, off Hwy 6563; ☯ Sat, Sun & holidays), 5 miles south of Cloudcroft. A day of tubing costs $20. It also runs guided one-hour snowmobile tours into nearby Lincoln Forest. Racing a snowmobile across a snow-

strewn meadow and down into a canyon is a breathtaking rush we'd highly recommend. If you are a pair (or family) rent a double snowmobile for $60 per hour – you pay by the snowmobile, not the person, so this works out to be a great deal. Riding solo costs $50 per hour; with less weight your snowmobile goes faster, making for a more exhilarating ride.

Festivals & Events

Autumn is celebrated with **Oktoberfest** (first weekend of October) and summer is celebrated with an annual **Cherry Festival** on the third Sunday in June. The nearby hills between Cloudcroft and Alamogordo are rife with cherry orchards.

Sleeping & Eating

Cloudcroft is blessed with some heavenly choices.

USFS Camping (☎ 575-682-2551; campsites $8-10; ☯ May–mid-Sep) Several USFS campgrounds are open in the summer only because of the elevation, though some may open earlier or later, with no services or fees, weather permitting. There are no RV hookups.

Raven Wind (☎ 505-687-3073; www.ravenwindranch .com; 1234 NM Hwy 24, Weed; r incl breakfast $85; ☐) If you happen to have your horse with you, he'd probably appreciate a stay at Raven Wind. Surrounded by the Lincoln National Forest about 28 miles from Cloudcroft, this ranch-style B&B offers plenty of long green grass for horses to munch, and boarding facilities for overnight stays. For humans, it's a serene place to just get away – and horseback riding can be arranged should you not be traveling with steed. Rooms are basic (this isn't a fancy place) but perfectly comfortable, and the rockers on the huge wraparound porch are fabulous. Unlike many B&Bs, this one is kid friendly. There's an in-house masseuse should you need some body work, and an outdoor hot tub for nighttime stargazing.

Lodge Resort & Spa (☎ 575-682-2566; www .thelodgeresort.com; 1 Corona Pl; r/ste from $100/185; ☒ ☐ wi-fi) One of the best historic hotels in the Southwest, this place is reason enough to visit Cloudcroft. A grand old Lodge built in 1899 as a vacation getaway for railroad employees, today it is a full-scale resort, with a pampering spa – with a sauna – where treatments are tailored to the customer, a wonderful restaurant, a golf course and beautifully maintained grounds. Try to get a room in the main Bavarian-style hotel; these are furnished with period and Victorian pieces. Pavilion rooms are a few blocks away in a separate, less attractive building.

New Mexico Skies (☎ 575-687-2429; www.nmskies .com; 1- & 2-bedroom apt from $150, 3-bedroom house from $250) Tucked against a national forest backdrop, this B&B rents high-powered stargazing equipment and amateur astronomers (in particular) will really enjoy staying here. Digs are in simple knotty-pine cottages or a family apartment. Advance reservations required.

Rebecca's (☎ 575-682-3131; 1 Corona Pl; mains $6-25; ⊗ breakfast, lunch & dinner) Stop by Rebecca's, at the Lodge, for the long-standing favorite Sunday brunch. It's equally good for other meals – this is by far the best food in Cloudcroft. Kick back on the outside deck, have a beer and check out the spectacular views of the mountains and the distant and shimmering White Sands National Monument. Then head inside for an elegant meal with good service and a menu that includes everything from steak tenderloin to cheese enchiladas.

Getting There & Away
Cloudcroft is about 20 miles east of Alamogordo on Hwy 82 and is best reached via private vehicle.

WHITE SANDS NATIONAL MONUMENT
These captivating windswept dunes are a highlight of any trip to New Mexico. Try to time a visit to the oasis-like and ethereal **White Sands** (www.nps.gov/whsa; 15 miles southwest of Hwy 82/70; admission $3) with sunrise or sunset (or both) when it's even more magical than normal. It's here that gypsum, a chalky mineral used in making plaster of Paris, covers 275 sq miles. From the **visitor center** (☎ 575-679-2599; ⊗ 8am-7pm Jun-Aug, 8am-5pm Sep-May), drive the 16-mile scenic loop into the heart of the dazzling white sea of sand – get out of the car and climb, romp, slide and roll in the soft dunes. Hike the Alkali Flat, a 4.5-mile (round-trip) backcountry trail through the heart of the dunes, or the simple 1-mile loop nature trail. **Backcountry campsites**, with no water or toilet facilities, are a mile from the scenic drive. Pick up permits ($3 per night) at the visitor center up to one hour before sunset.

RUIDOSO & AROUND
pop 4500 / elev 7000ft
You want lively in these parts? You want Ruidoso. Downright bustling in the summer

and big with punters at the racetrack, resort-like Ruidoso has an utterly pleasant climate thanks to its lofty and forested perch near the Sierra Blanca (12,003ft). Neighboring Texans and local New Mexicans escaping the summer heat of Alamogordo (46 miles to the southwest) and Roswell (71 miles to the east) are happy campers here (or more precisely, happy cabiners). The lovely Rio Ruidoso, a small creek with good fishing, runs through town. Summertime hiking and wintertime skiing at Ski Apache keep folks busy, as do a smattering of galleries.

Orientation & Information
Ruidoso is very spread out, with vacation homes tucked away on narrow streets sprawling into the surrounding mountains. Hwy 48 from the north is the main drag through town. This is called Mechem Dr until the small downtown area where it becomes Sudderth Dr, heading east to the Y-intersection with Hwy 70. Six miles north on Mechem Dr is the community of Alto, with more accommodations. The community of Ruidoso Downs is a separate village just east of Ruidoso on Hwy 70.

Both the **chamber of commerce** (☎ 800-253-2255; www.ruidoso.net; 720 Sudderth Dr; ⊗ 8:30am-5pm Mon-Thu, 9am-5pm Fri-Sun) and the **Lincoln National Forest Ranger Station** (☎ 575-257-4095; 901 Mechem Dr; ⊗ 7:30am-4:30pm Mon-Fri year-round, 7:30am-4:30pm Sat May-Oct) are helpful. The chamber's website translates into Spanish, Italian, German and French.

Sights
The fine **Hubbard Museum of the American West** (☎ 575-378-4142; www.hubbardmuseum.org; 841 Hwy 70 W; admission $6; ⊗ 9am-5pm) displays more than 10,000 Western-related items including Old West stagecoaches and American Indian pottery, and works by Frederic Remington and Charles M Russell. An impressive collection of horse-related displays, including a collection of saddles and the Racehorse Hall of Fame, lures horse-lovers.

The **Ruidoso Downs Racetrack** (☎ 575-378-4431; www.ruidosodownsracing.com; Hwy 70; admission free; ⊗ races Thu-Sun late May-early Sep) is one of the major racetracks in the Southwest. The big event is Labor Day's All American Futurity. The world's richest quarter-horse race has a purse of over $2 million. A track **casino** (⊗ 11am-11pm) features an all-you-can eat buffet ($7 to $15).

DETOUR: SMOKEY THE BEAR'S STOMPING GROUNDS

You've seen his likeness in state and national forests everywhere around the region. But did you know that Smokey the Bear was a real, live black bear cub and not just a sketch summoned from some designer's imagination? Once upon a time, he was found clinging to a tree, paws charred from a 17,000-acre forest fire in the Capitan Mountains. Nursed back to health, Smokey lived out the rest of his days in the National Zoo in Washington, DC, and became the poster bear for fire prevention. At the 3-acre **Smokey Bear Historical State Park** (☎ 575-354-2748; per day $1), set in the village of **Capitan**, 12 miles west of Lincoln, visitors can see the bear's grave and learn about fire prevention. Every Fourth of July, a **Smokey the Bear Stampede** features a parade, a rodeo, cookouts and other festivities. **Smokey the Bear Days**, celebrated the first weekend in May, includes a street dance, woodcarving contest, craft and antique car shows.

Stop for a bite at the family-owned **El Paisano Restaurant** (☎ 575-354-2206; 442 Smokey Bear Blvd; mains $5-10; ☽ lunch & dinner Tue-Sat), just east of town. Everything is homemade here, including the chips and tortillas, and it boasts fantastic green chile stew and salsa. Hours can be sporadic.

About 3000 Native Americans live on the 719-sq-mile **Mescalero Apache Indian Reservation**, which lies in attractive country 17 miles southwest of Ruidoso on Hwy 70. The nomadic Apache arrived in this area 800 years ago and soon became enemies with local Pueblo Indians. In the 19th century, under pressure from European settlement and with their mobility greatly increased by the introduction of the horse, the Apache became some of the most feared raiders of the West. Despite the name of the reservation, the Apache here are of three tribes: the Mescalero, the Chiricahua and the Lipan. The **Cultural Center** (☎ 575-464-4494; Chiricahua Plaza, off Hwy 70, Mescalero; ☽ hours vary) has an interesting exhibit about the Apache peoples and customs.

Activities

The best ski area south of Albuquerque is **Ski Apache** (☎ 575-336-4356; snow conditions 505-257-9001; www.skiapache.com; Hwy 48 exit 532; lift ticket adult/child $39/25), 18 miles northwest of Ruidoso on the slopes of beautiful Sierra Blanca Peak. It's not exactly world-class riding, but when it comes to affordability and fun, it's a very good choice. Plus, Ski Apache is home to New Mexico's only gondola.

Hiking is popular in warmer months. Try the 4.6-mile day hike from the Ski Apache area to Sierra Blanca Peak, an ascent of 2000ft. Take Trail 15 from the small parking area just before the main lot and follow signs west and south along Trails 25 and 78 to Lookout Mountain (11,580ft). From there an obvious trail continues due south for 1.25 miles to Sierra Blanca Peak. Several other trails leave

from the Ski Apache area; the ranger station in Ruidoso (p369) has maps and information for more adventurous trips, including the beautiful Crest Trail.

Rio Ruidoso and several national forest lakes offer good fishing. **Flies Etc** (☎ 505-257-4968; 2800 Sudderth Dr) has tackle and fishing licenses, and runs fly-fishing excursions.

Festivals & Events

The top-quality **Ruidoso Art Festival** (last full weekend in July) attracts thousands of browsing and buying visitors from all over the Southwest, while the **Golden Aspen Motorcycle Rally** on the third weekend of September draws 30,000 motorcycles riders. **Aspenfest** (first weekend in October) features a chile cook-off and a street festival, while the **Lincoln County Cowboy Symposium** (second weekend in October) features cowboy poetry, chuckwagon cooking and horse breaking. The fun continues at the Bavarian-themed **Oktoberfest**, held on the third weekend in October, with German food and beer, along with professional polka dancing and oompah bands. The annual Apache **Maidens' Puberty Ceremony** (July 4) takes place for about five days in early July and features a powwow, rodeo and arts and crafts demonstrations.

Sleeping

There are lots of area cabin rentals, but some of the ones in town are cramped. Most of the newer cabins are located in the Upper Canyon. Generally, cabins have kitchens and grills, and often fireplaces and decks. **Central Reservations of Ruidoso** (☎ 888-257-7577; www.casasderuidoso.com; 712 Mechem Dr; ☽ 8am-5pm) arranges condominium, cabin and lodge rentals. Although Ruidoso hotels are often referred to as 'lodges' or 'inns,' they're basically your standard motel.

Apache Motel (☎ 575-257-2986, 800-426-0616; www .ruidoso.net/apache; 344 Sudderth Dr; r from $50) These small basic rooms are clean; some have kitchenettes. A family unit is offered with fireplace and dining area.

Dan Dee Cabins (☎ 575-257-2165; www.dandeecabins .com; 310 Main Rd; cabins $85-199) One of the friendliest places to stay in New Mexico; 12 woodsy cabins are spread over five grassy and forested acres. Constructed at various times beginning in the 1940s, each one is unique, private and comfy. The cabins vary widely in size; the most expensive, Rainbow, has three bedrooms and sleeps up to six. Pets are welcome.

High Country Lodge (☎ 575-336-4321; www.high countrylodge.net; Hwy 48; r from $89; 🐾) Just south of the turnoff to Ski Apache, this funky older place welcomes you with three friendly (and sadly, wooden) bears. It offers a comfortable selection of rustic and basic two-bedroom cabins, each with kitchen, fireplace and porch. Other facilities include a sauna, hot tub and tennis courts.

Shadow Mountain Lodge (☎ 575-257-4886; www .smlruidoso.com; 107 Main St; r & cabins from $100) Geared toward couples, these immaculate rooms feature fireplaces and offer romantic allure. A wooden wraparound balcony overlooks the professionally landscaped grounds; the hot tub is tucked away in a gazebo. Individual cabins have Jacuzzi tubs and giant flat-screen TVs.

Inn of the Mountain Gods (☎ 800-545-9011; www .innofthemountaingods.com; 287 Carrizo Canyon Rd; r $129-299; 🐾 wi-fi) This luxury resort hotel on the Mescalero Apache Reservation (opposite) has surprisingly low rates – internet promotions can be even lower. Gamblers can feed slots at the casino, and guided fishing, paddleboat rentals and horseback riding are all just a concierge call away. Several restaurants, a nightclub, sports bar and a championship golf course are also onsite. It's fun for a night or two.

Also recommended:

Bonito Hollow Campground (☎ 575-336-4325; tent/RV sites $16/30, r & cabins $45; 😋 May–mid-Oct) Lots of options on the Bonita River.

Sitzmark Chalet (☎ 575-257-4140; www.sitzmark -chalet.com; 627 Sudderth Dr; r $60-90; 🖥 wi-fi) Simple motel with hot tub.

Best Western Swiss Chalet (☎ 575-258-3333; 1451 Mechem Rd; r $69-109; 🐾 wi-fi) Convenient to the ski slopes and forest; ask about ski-and-bike packages.

Eating

Hummingbird Tearoom (☎ 575-257-5100; 2306 Audeth Dr, Village Plaza; mains $5-7; 😋 lunch Mon-Sat; 🇻) This homey little place specializes in simple soups, salads and lunchtime sandwiches; delectable desserts and rich teas make a lovely afternoon diversion. The service is particularly attentive.

Cornerstone Bakery (☎ 575-257-1842; 359 Audeth Dr; mains up to $10; 😋 breakfast & lunch; 🇻) Stay around long enough and the Cornerstone may become your touchstone. Everything on the menu, from omelets to croissant sandwiches, is worthy. Locals are addicted.

Terraza Camanario (☎ 575-257-4227; 1611 Sudderth Dr; mains $5-13; 😋 lunch & dinner; 🇻) Aimed at the town's local Hispanic crowd, this Spanish-speaking Mexican restaurant serves authentic and delicious food. Order the guacamole to start – it's really good, and will help you forget how slow the service can be.

Casa Blanca (☎ 575-257-2495; 501 Mechem Dr; mains $6-20; 😋 lunch & dinner) Dine on Southwestern cuisine in a renovated Spanish-style house or on the pleasant patio in the summer. The *chile rellenos* is to die for. Not in the mood for Mexican? Order a big burger or the chicken fried steak.

Café Rio (☎ 575-257-7746; 2547 Sudderth Dr; pizza $10-25; 😋 lunch & dinner; 🧒 🇻) Thick-crust pizza, with your choice of toppings, is deservedly popular here, but the stuffed calzones and Greek offerings are also decent for a small-town restaurant. Wash it down with a big selection of international and seasonal beer.

Mountain Annie's (☎ 575-257-7982; 2710 Sudderth Dr; mains $10-25; 😋 dinner) This casual family-owned place serves hearty food – like steaks and barbecue, along with a big salad bar and even bigger smiles. It's a truly welcoming restaurant.

Texas Club (☎ 575-258-3325; 212 Metz Dr; mains $10-30; 😋 dinner Wed-Sun) One of the busiest and best restaurants in town, decorated with all the bigness you'd expect in a place that takes its name from Texas (think longhorns and cowboy hats), this place serves big tasty steaks and seafood. There is dancing and live entertainment on the weekends. Call for directions (it's a bit hidden) and reservations (it's often packed).

Drinking & Entertainment

Quarters (☎ 575-257-9535; 2535 Sudderth Dr) Dance the night away to live blues and rock on the big dance floor, or listen from a barstool or at one of the comfortable tables.

Spencer Theater for the Performing Arts (☎ 575-336-4800; www.spencertheater.com; 108 Spencer Rd, Alto; performances $20-40) In a stunning mountain venue, it hosts theatrical, musical and dance performances. Take Hwy 220 to Alto. Check the website for what's playing.

Flying J Ranch (☎ 505-336-4330; Hwy 48; adult/child 4-12 $20/10; ☺ daily May-Aug, Sat Sep-Oct) Families with little ones will love this place, as it delivers a full night of entertainment, not just dinner. Located 1.5 miles north of Alto, this 'Western village' stages gunfights and offers pony rides with their cowboy-style chuckwagon. Western music tops off the evening.

Getting There & Around

The **bus depot** (☎ 575-257-2660; www.greyhound .com; 138 Service Rd) serves buses heading to Alamogordo ($15, one hour), Roswell ($18, 1½ hours) and El Paso, Texas ($37, three hours), several times a day; buses to Carlsbad ($39, four hours) also leave daily.

LINCOLN

pop 70 / elev 5700ft

Fans of Western history won't want to miss little Lincoln. Twelve miles east of Capitan along the **Billy the Kid National Scenic Byway** (www .billybyway.com), this is where the gun battle that turned Billy the Kid into a legend took place.

It's hard to believe that in Billy the Kid's era Lincoln had a bustling population of nearly 900. Today it is essentially a ghost town, with only about 70 people living here. Those who do, however, are dedicated to preserving the town's 1880s buildings. Modern influences, such as souvenir stands, are not allowed in town, and the main street has been designated the **Lincoln State Monument**. It's a pretty cool place to get away from this century for a night.

Start at the **Anderson Freeman Visitor Center & Museum** (☎ 575-653-4025; Hwy 380; admission $6; ☺ 8:30am-4:30pm), where exhibits on the Buffalo soldiers, Apaches and the Lincoln County War explain the town's history. The admission price includes entry to the Tunstall Store (with a remarkable display of late-19th-century merchandise), the courthouse where the Kid escaped imprisonment, and Dr Wood's house, an intact turn-of-the-century doctor's home and office. The Tunstall Store and Dr Wood's house are closed from March to November.

LEGEND OF BILLY THE KID

So much speculation swirls. Even the most basic information about Billy the Kid tends to cast a shadow larger than the outlaw himself. Here's what we know, or don't. Most historians agree that he was born sometime in 1859, most likely in New York City (or Indiana or Missouri). He *may* be buried in **Old Fort Sumner** (p378, where his skull *may* have been stolen and *possibly* recovered) – that is, unless he colluded with his presumed assassin, Sheriff Pat Garrett, and lived to a ripe, old age…somewhere.

The Kid didn't start out as a murderer. His first known childhood crimes included stealing laundry and fencing butter. In the mid-1870s, about the time the teenage Billy arrived in New Mexico, the 400 residents of **Lincoln** (above) shopped at 'Murphy's,' the only general store in the region. In 1877, though, Englishman John Tunstall arrived and built a competing general store.

Within a year, Tunstall was dead, allegedly shot by Murphy and his boys. The entire region erupted in what became known as the **Lincoln County War**. Tunstall's most famous follower was a wild teenager named Henry McCarty, alias William Bonney, aka Billy the Kid. Over the next several months the Kid and his gang gunned down any members of the Murphy faction they could find. The Kid was captured or cornered a number of times but managed brazen and lucky escapes before finally being shot by Sheriff Pat Garrett near Fort Sumner in 1881, where he lies in a grave in a barren yard. Maybe.

Enough controversy still dangles over whether he conspired with Sheriff Garrett to fake his death that there is a movement afoot to exhume the body and do a little DNA testing. Brushy Bill Roberts of Hico, Texas, now deceased, claimed that he was actually the elusive outlaw. A man in his 70s claims that Sheriff Garrett's widow told him at the tender age of nine that the conspiracy was, in fact, the truth. Should they actually perform the tests and discover the truth, not only will it lay some portion of the legend to rest, but also forever cast a shadow of a doubt over the old saying, 'Dead men tell no tales.'

During the **Old Lincoln Days** (held the first full weekend in August), now in its sixth decade, musicians and mountain men, doctors and desperadoes wander the streets in period costume, and there are demonstrations of spinning, blacksmithing and other common frontier skills. In the evening there is the folk pageant, 'The Last Escape of Billy the Kid.'

The Kid supposedly spent the night at **Casa de Patrón B&B** (☎ 575-653-4676; www.casapatron.com; s/d from $82/92), an adobe boarding house that has been open since the 1860s! Seven rooms are located in the historic main house, adjoining casitas or a newer addition. Some have a fireplace or kitchenette; pick your preference.

The 19th-century adobe **Ellis Store Country Inn** (☎ 575-653-4609, 800-653-6460; www.ellisstore.com; NM 98, Hwy 380; r $90-$120) offers three antique-filled rooms (complete with wood stove) in the main house; five additional rooms are located in a historic mill on the property. Since dining options are limited in town, the host offers a six-course dinner ($75 per person) served in the cozy dining room Thursday to Saturday. Nonguests are welcome with a reservation.

Hurd Ranch Guest Homes (☎ 575-653-4331; www.wyethartists.com; 105 La Rinconada, San Patricio; casitas $125-250) is a 2500-acre, very rural place in San Patricio, about 14 miles south of Lincoln, that rents six lovely casitas by an apple orchard. Furnished with style and grace, and lots of original art, some units sleep up to six people. They are outfitted with modern conveniences. Owner and artist Peter Hurd runs the Hurd la Rinconada Gallery on the premises; he also shows the work of his relatives NC and Andrew Wyeth, his mother Henriette Wyeth and his father Michael Hurd. Pets can stay for $20 (per visit).

ROSWELL
pop 49,000 / elev 3649ft

Whether or not you're a true believer, a visit to Roswell is worth visiting to experience one of America's most enduring, eclectic and fanatical pop-culture phenomena. Sure it's about as cheesy as it gets for most of us, but conspiracy theorists and *X-Files* fanatics descend from other worlds into Roswell in real seriousness. Oddly famous as both the country's largest producer of wool and its UFO capital, Roswell has built a tourist industry around the alleged July 1947 UFO crash (see boxed text, p374), after which the military quickly closed the area and allowed no more information to filter

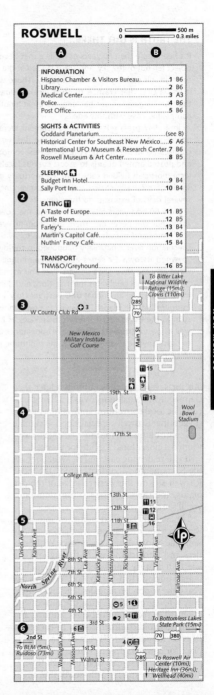

ROSWELL

INFORMATION	
Hispano Chamber & Visitors Bureau	1 B6
Library	2 B6
Medical Center	3 A3
Police	4 B6
Post Office	5 B6

SIGHTS & ACTIVITIES	
Goddard Planetarium	(see 8)
Historical Center for Southeast New Mexico	6 A6
International UFO Museum & Research Center	7 B6
Roswell Museum & Art Center	8 B5

SLEEPING	
Budget Inn Hotel	9 B4
Sally Port Inn	10 B4

EATING	
A Taste of Europe	11 B5
Cattle Baron	12 B5
Farley's	13 B4
Martin's Capitol Café	14 B6
Nuthin' Fancy Café	15 B4

TRANSPORT	
TNM&O/Greyhound	16 B5

NEW MEXICO

THE TRUTH IS OUT THERE....

It's been more than 60 years now since that heady summer of 1947, when an unidentified flying object fell out of the sky, and crash-landed in the desert near Roswell, and the little New Mexican town is still cashing in on the mystery. Those who believe aliens are out there are convinced it was a UFO that crashed the first week of July in that post-WWII baby-making summer, and that the US government has gone to great lengths to cover the crash up. They certainly have a compelling case with this one.

In a 1947 press release, the government identified the object as a crashed disk. A day later, however, it changed its story: now the disk was really just a weather balloon. The feds then confiscated all the previous press releases, cordoned off the area as they collected all the debris, and posted armed guards to escort curious locals from the site of the 'weather-balloon' crash. A local mortician fielded calls from the mortuary office at the government airfield inquiring after small, hermetically sealed coffins for preventing tissue contamination and degeneration after several days of exposure to the elements.

Now 60-odd years after the incident, the government is still tight-lipped, and Roswell is the story that will never die. There are frequent eyewitness accounts of flying saucers in the sky, and rumor and misinformation continue to swirl about the original crash, fueling all manner of speculation over what really happened in the desert that day. In the early 2000s, Roswell even spawned its own TV series about alien-mutant hybrid teenagers trying to survive as humans while keeping their alien powers alive and attempting to get home.

Now Roswell celebrates the assertions and denials, the mystery and the speculation surrounding the event, in an annual **UFO Festival** (July 1 to 4), which attracts upwards of 20,000 visitors from around the planet – Roswell is now synonymous with UFOs. Interplanetary-travel celebs such as the Duras sisters (known to Trekkies as Klingon warriors from the TV series *Star Trek*), as well as past astronauts, often make appearances. Besides enough lectures, films and workshops to make anyone's ears go pointy, the nighttime parade and alien-costume competitions are not to be missed.

---

out for several decades (although later they claimed it was a balloon). Was it a flying saucer? The local convention and visitors bureau suggest that Roswell's special blend of climate and culture attracted touring space aliens who wanted a closer look! Decide for yourself.

If you're driving east on Hwy 70/380 from the Sacramento Mountains, enjoy the view. Roswell sits on the western edge of the dry plains, and these are the last big mountains you'll see for a while.

The 'Staked Plains' extending east into Texas were once home to millions of buffalo and many nomadic Native American hunters. White settlers and hunters moved in throughout the late 19th century, and killed some 3.5 million buffalo during a two-year period. Within a few years, the region became desolate and empty; only a few groups of Comanche mixed with other tribes roaming the plains, hunting and trying to avoid confinement on reservations. Roswell, founded in 1871, served as a stopping place for cowboys driving cattle.

The main west–east drag through town is 2nd St and the main north–south thorough-fare is Main St; their intersection is the heart of downtown.

Information

BLM office (☎ 575-627-0272; 2909 W 2nd St; ☽ 7:30am-4:30pm Mon-Fri)

Hispano Chamber & Visitors Bureau (☎ 575-624-0889, 888-767-9355; www.roswell-usa.com; 426 N Main St; ☽ 8am-5pm Mon-Fri)

Library (☎ 575-622-7101; 301 N Pennsylvania Ave; ☽ 5-10pm Wed-Sun; ▯) Free internet access.

Medical Center (☎ 575-622-8170; 405 W Country Club Rd; ☽ 24hr emergency)

Police (☎ 575-624-6770; 128 W 2nd St)

Post office (☎ 575-623-7232; 415 N Pennsylvania Ave)

Sights & Activities

Serious followers of UFO phenomena (not to mention skeptics or the merely curious) will want to check out the **International UFO Museum & Research Center** (☎ 575-625-9495; www.iufomrc.org; 114 N Main St; admission free; ☽ 9am-5pm). Original photographs and witness statements form the 1947 Roswell Incident Timeline and explain the 'great cover-up.' The library claims to have the most comprehensive UFO-related materials in the world, and we have no reason to be skeptical.

On a more down-to-earth front, the excellent **Roswell Museum & Art Center** (☎ 575-624-6744; www.roswellmuseum.org; 100 W 11th St; admission free; 9am-5pm Mon-Sat, 1-5pm Sun) deserves a visit. Seventeen galleries showcase Southwestern artists including Georgia O'Keeffe, Peter Hurd and Henriette Wyeth. An eclectic mix of Native American, Hispanic and Anglo artifacts means there's something for everyone. A major focus of the museum is space research. The **Goddard Planetarium** is the reconstructed lab of Robert H Goddard, who launched the first successful liquid fuel rocket in 1926. Goddard spent more than a decade carrying out rocket research in Roswell. A variety of early rocketry paraphernalia is also on display.

Housed in the 1910 mansion of local rancher James Phelp White, the **Historical Center for Southeast New Mexico** (☎ 575-622-8333; 200 N Lea Ave; admission by donation; 1-4pm) is well worth seeing. It's on the National Register of Historic Places, and its interior has been carefully restored to its original early-20th-century decor with period furnishings, photographs and art.

Birders will want to bring their binoculars. Wintering water birds gather at the 38-sq-mile **Bitter Lake National Wildlife Refuge** (☎ 575-622-6755; www.fws.gov/southwest; Pine Lodge Rd; admission free; sunrise-sunset); many birds remain to nest in the summer. To reach the refuge, about 15 miles northeast of Roswell, follow the signed roads from either Hwy 380 or Hwy 285/70.

Festivals & Events

As you might imagine, Roswell has a couple of quirky festivals worth checking out. **New Mexico Dairy Day** (early June) features the Great Milk Carton Boat Race on Lake Van, 20 miles south of Roswell, as well as cheese-sculpting contests, 36ft-long ice-cream sundaes, games and sporting events. The **UFO Festival** (see boxed text, opposite) centers around alien-costume competitions and lectures about UFOs. The main annual event, though, is the **Eastern New Mexico State Fair** (☎ 575-623-9411) in early October, with rodeo, livestock and agricultural competitions and chile-eating contests.

Sleeping

Bottomless Lakes State Park (☎ 575-624-6058; Hwy 409; per car per day $5, tent/RV sites $10/17) Seven popular lakes in the area provide welcome relief from summer heat. These primitive campsites are among the best available. To reach them, drive 10 miles east of Roswell on Hwy 380, then 5 miles south on Hwy 409.

Budget Inn Hotel (☎ 575-623-6050; 2101 N Main St; r from $45;) Basic digs; the hot tub is a plus.

Heritage Inn (☎ 575-748-2552; www.artesiaheritageinn.com; 209 W Main St, Artesia; r incl breakfast from $84; wi-fi) The nicest place to stay is actually not in Roswell. If you're traveling between Roswell and Carlsbad and in the mood for slightly upscale digs (this is southeastern New Mexico, don't forget), this c-1900 establishment offers 11 Old West–style rooms in Artesia, about 36 miles south of Roswell.

Sally Port Inn (☎ 800-528-1234; 2000 N Main St; r from $95; wi-fi) This is as good as it gets in Roswell. This Best Western has limited spa facilities and standard-issue rooms (some with refrigerators and microwaves).

Eating

Martin's Capitol Café (☎ 575-624-2111; 110 W 4th St; mains $5-7; breakfast, lunch & dinner Mon-Sat) Although several inexpensive New Mexican and Mexican restaurants in town are good, this one is dependable.

Wellhead (☎ 575-746-0640; 332 W Main St, Artesia; mains $6-15; lunch & dinner Mon-Sat) If you're traveling between Roswell and Carlsbad, you'll find the region's best food and drink at this modern brewpub restaurant and bar. Housed in a 1905 building and reflecting the town's origins, it's decorated with an oil-drilling theme. Artesia is about 36 miles south of Roswell.

Farley's (☎ 575-627-1100; 1315 N Main St; mains $7-12; lunch & dinner) A boisterous barn-like place that stays open until 2am on Friday and Saturday, Farley's has something for everyone: burgers, pizza, chicken and ribs. It also has a big bar with pool tables and music.

Cattle Baron (☎ 505-622-2465; 1113 N Main St; mains $7-15; lunch & dinner) This efficient and friendly place specializes in consistently good and reasonably priced beef. With a name like that, whadaya expect? Still, the salad bar is stacked with enough veggies and beans to keep non-carnivores happy. Hang your spurs at the full bar before or after dinner.

Nuthin' Fancy Café (☎ 575-623-4098; 2103 N Main St; mains $9-16; breakfast, lunch & dinner) There is truth in advertising after all. For blue-plate specials and diner food, along with an espresso bar and upward of 15 beers on tap, nuthin' much compares.

NEW MEXICO

A Taste of Europe (☎ 575-624-0313; 1201 N Main St; mains $10-20; ☯ lunch & dinner Tue-Fri, dinner Sat, lunch Sun) For a relative united nations of continental and European cuisine choices, these tastes are a treat. Having said that, the menu leans heavily toward Italian dishes.

Getting There & Around

TNM&O/Greyhound (☎ 575-622-2510; www.grey hound.com; 1100 N Virginia Ave) has daily buses to Carlsbad ($22, 1½ hours), Albuquerque ($41, four hours) and beyond. From Tuesday to Saturday, a 7am bus heads to Santa Fe ($44, six hours).

CARLSBAD

pop 25,600 / elev 3120ft

When Carlsbad Caverns (p378) was declared a national monument in 1923, a trickle of tourists turned into a veritable flash flood. Today, hundreds of thousands of visitors come through annually. Carlsbad is situated on the Pecos River about 30 miles north of the Texas state line, and its main thoroughfare is Hwy 285, which becomes Canal St, then S Canal (south of Mermod St) and then National Parks Hwy at the southern end of town.

Information

BLM (☎ 575-234-5972; 620 E Greene St; ☯ 7:45am-4:30pm Mon-Fri)

Chamber of Commerce (☎ 575-887-6516; www .carlsbadchamber.com; 302 S Canal St; ☯ 9am-5pm Mon, 8am-5pm Tue-Fri, 9am-3pm Sat May-Sep)

Library (☎ 575-885-6776; 101 S Halagueno St; ☯ 10am- 8pm Mon-Thu, 10am-6pm Fri & Sat, 2-6pm Sun; 💻) Free internet access.

Medical Center (☎ 575-887-4100; 2430 W Pierce St; ☯ 24hr emergency)

National Parks Information Center (☎ 575-885-8884; 3225 National Parks Hwy; ☯ 8am-4:30pm Mon-Fri) Information on both Carlsbad Caverns National Park and Guadalupe Mountains National Park.

Police (☎ 575-885-2111; 405 S Halagueno St)

Post office (☎ 575-885-5717; 301 N Canyon St)

USFS Ranger Station (☎ 575-885-4181; 114 S Halagueno; ☯ 7:30am-4:30pm Mon-Fri) The Lincoln National Forest Guadalupe ranger station is located in the federal building at Halagueno and Fox Sts.

Sights & Activities

On the northwestern outskirts of town, **Living Desert State Park** (☎ 575-887-5516; 1504 Miehls Dr, off Hwy 285; adult/child 7-12 $5/3; ☯ 8am-8pm May-Aug, 9am-5pm Sep-Apr) is a great place to see and learn about cacti, coyotes and wildlife with evocative Southwestern names such as agave, javelina, ocotillo and yucca. The park has a good 1.3-mile trail that showcases different habitats of the Chihuahuan Desert.

The **Carlsbad Museum & Art Center** (☎ 575-887-0276; www.nmculture.org; 418 W Fox St; admission free; ☯ 10am-5pm Mon-Sat) displays Apache artifacts, pioneer memorabilia and art from the renowned Taos School.

Southwestern touches at the 1891 **Eddy County Courthouse** are also worth a look: the cattle brands of the most important local ranches are carved into the doorframes, and the interior ceilings boast heavy beams and ornate iron chandeliers.

A system of dams and spillways on the Pecos River created the 2-mile **Lake Carlsbad**, which has a pleasant 4.5-mile trail along its banks. At the north end of Park Dr (or at the east end of Church St), **Carlsbad Riverfront Park** has a beach and swimming area. At nearby **Port Jefferson** (☎ 575-887-8343; ☯ 10am-5pm Mon-Sat late May-early Sep, Sat & Sun Oct), you can rent a paddlewheel boat to tour the river.

Sleeping

The nearby national park and mild winters make this a year-round destination; always ask for the best rates. Sorry, folks, but it's mostly chain motels in Carlsbad. If none of the following sound appealing, there are many, many more on Canal St.

Carlsbad KOA (☎ 575-457-2000; www.carlsgadkoa .com; 2 Manthei Rd; tent/RV sites from $22/30, cabins $45; 🏊 🐕 wi-fi) On Hwy 285 about 12 miles north of Carlsbad, this KOA offers the choice of cozy 'kamping kabins' or grassy tent sites. There's a pool, game room, grocery store, laundry, playground and showers here. Ask friendly hosts Scott and Susan Bacher about free rides for the kids in a retired fire truck. The KOA is also dog friendly, going so far as to include a park especially for your canine companion.

Stage Coach Inn (☎ 575-887-1148; 1819 S Canal St; r from $40; 🏊) Of the budget motels on the main drag, the conventional one is the best, with an indoor hot tub and in-room refrigerators.

Best Western Stevens Inn (☎ 575-887-2851; 1829 S Canal St; r from $85; 🏊 wi-fi) Carlsbad's largest hotel has more than 200 rooms, some with kitchenettes or microwave/refrigerator combos.

Holiday Inn (☎ 575-885-8500; 601 S Canal St; r incl breakfast from $85; 🏊) This two-story place is the

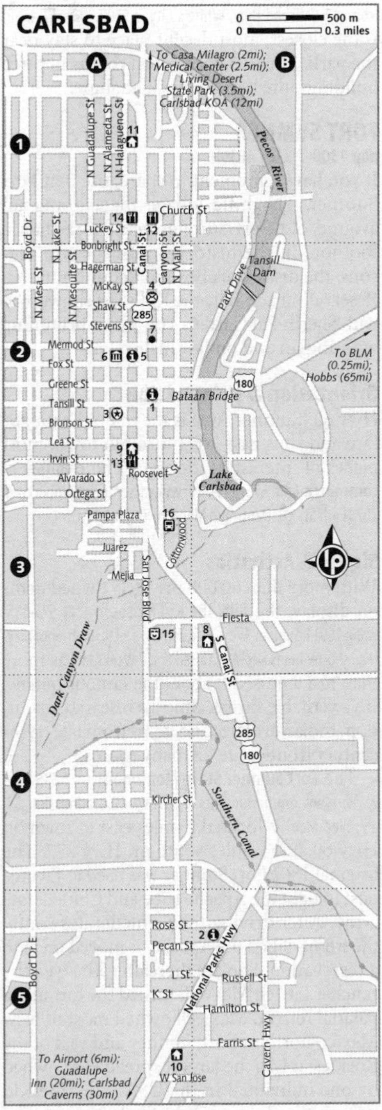

INFORMATION
Chamber of Commerce.......1 A2
Library.......(see 6)
National Parks Information Center.......2 B5
Police.......3 A2
Post Office.......4 A2
USFS Ranger Station.......5 A2

SIGHTS & ACTIVITIES
Carlsbad Museum & Art Center.......6 A2
Eddy County Courthouse.......7 A2

SLEEPING
Best Western Stevens Inn.......8 B3
Holiday Inn.......9 A2
Quality Inn.......10 A5
Stage Coach Inn.......11 A1

EATING
Blue House Bakery & Café.......12 A1
Lucy's.......13 A3
Red Chimney Pit Barbeque.......14 A1

DRINKING
Silver Spur Lounge.......(see 8)

ENTERTAINMENT
Fiesta Drive-In Theater.......15 A3

TRANSPORT
TNM&O/Greyhound.......16 A3

only full-service hotel downtown; rooms are spacious and have a faux Southwestern feel.

Casa Milagro (☎ 575-887-2188; www.casa-milagro-nm.com; 1612 N Guadalupe St; r from $95) Casa Milagro is a comfortable, turn-of-the-20th-century homestead on the edge of town, with five pleasant rooms that are the pride of the owner. Plan your day on the porch or stay a while and read.

Eating

Blue House Bakery & Café (☎ 575-628-0555; 609 N Canyon St; mains $3-9; 7:30am-3:30pm Mon-Sat) This sweet Queen Anne house perks the best coffee and espresso in this quadrant of New Mexico. Its baked goods are pretty darn good too. At lunchtime, the cheery place has good sandwiches made with fresh breads.

Lucy's (☎ 575-887-7714; 701 S Canal St; mains $5-10; lunch & dinner Tue-Sun) The most popular place in Carlsbad, Lucy's is usually packed with devoted locals *and* visitors. Apart from a great Mexican menu, Lucy's serves up tasty margaritas and a good selection of microbrews (and admittedly that may be one reason the place is jumpin').

Red Chimney Pit Barbeque (☎ 575-885-8744; 817 N Canal St; mains $7-12; lunch & dinner Mon-Fri) Barbecue aficionados will agree: Red Chimney has one of the most unusual sauces you'll ever encounter. It just may have you dreaming about secret ingredients.

Drinking & Entertainment

Silver Spur Lounge (☎ 575-887-2851; 1829 S Canal St) At the Best Western Stevens Inn, this is the place to come for country music.

Fiesta Drive-In Theater (☎ 575-885-4126; San Jose Blvd; per person from $5; Fri-Mon) By far the coolest après-dark thing to do in Carlsbad. Soak up some nighttime desert air, watch a blockbuster and experience a form of American entertainment that has almost disappeared. The Fiesta boasts three screens.

Getting There & Away

TNM&O/Greyhound (☎ 575-887-1108; www.grey hound.com; 1000 Canyon St) buses depart daily for Albuquerque ($50, five hours) and El Paso, Texas ($42, three hours).

CARLSBAD CAVERNS NATIONAL PARK

Drive for hours across the desert just to see a cave? But it's not just any cave; it's a truly astonishing and immense system of caves, one of the world's greatest. Once visitors get a glimpse, even the most skeptical are impressed. A visit is, without a doubt, a highlight of any Southwestern journey. But wait, there's more. The cave's other claim to fame is the 250,000-plus Mexican free-tail bat colony that roosts here from April through to October. Visitors flock here at sunset to watch them fly out to feast on a smorgasbord of bugs.

The park covers 73 sq miles and includes almost 100 caves. Visitors can take a 2-mile subterranean walk from the cave mouth to an underground chamber 1800ft long, 255ft high and over 800ft below the surface. Exploration for experienced spelunkers only continues at the awe-inspiring **Lechuguilla Cave**. With a depth of 1567ft and a length of about 60 miles, it's the deepest cave and third-longest limestone cave in North America.

The park entrance is 23 miles southwest of Carlsbad. A three-day pass for self-guided tours to the natural entrance and the Big Room (send a postcard from the lunchroom, 829ft below the surface!) costs $6 for adults and $3 for children. The **park** (☎ 800-967-2283; www .nps.gov/cave; 3225 National Parks Hwy; ☺ 8am-5pm mid-Aug–late May, 8am-7pm late May–mid-Aug) also has a spectrum of ranger-led tours ($7); call for advance reservations. If you want to scramble to lesser-known areas, ask about Wild Cave tours. The last tickets are sold two to 3½ hours before the visitor center closes. Wilderness backpacking trips into the desert are allowed by permit (free); the visitor center sells topographical maps of the 50-plus miles of hiking trails.

There is no accommodation within the park, but the comfortable, small and resort-like **Guadalupe Inn** (☎ 800-228-3767; www.bestwestern

.com; 17 Carlsbad Hwy, White's City; r $100; 🐾 🖳 wi-fi) is the closest, most decent place to stay near the park. It has 63 good-sized rooms in three buildings, the best being Guadalupe.

FORT SUMNER
pop 1300 / elev 4030ft

If you have a moment to spare, use it at Fort Sumner. The little village that sprang up around old Fort Sumner gets more than a footnote in the history books for two reasons: the disastrous Bosque Redondo Indian Reservation and Billy the Kid's last showdown with Sheriff Pat Garrett. The area is brimming with Indian and outlaw history.

Orientation & Information

Hwy 60 (Sumner Ave) is the main thoroughfare and runs east–west through town; most places of interest lie along it. The **chamber of commerce** (☎ 575-355-770; www.ftsumnerchamber.com; 707 N 4th St; ☺ 9am-4pm Mon-Fri) is helpful.

Sights & Activities

With more than 60,000 privately owned items on display, the **Billy the Kid Museum** (☎ 575-355-2380; 1601 E Sumner Ave; admission $5; ☺ 8:30am-5pm May-Nov, shorter hours Dec-Apr, closed first 2 weeks Jan) is more than just a museum about the famous outlaw. It's a veritable shrine, almost a research institution. Indian artifacts and items from late-19th-century frontier life fill many rooms.

The **Fort Sumner State Monument** (☎ 575-355-2573; www.nmmonuments.org; Hwy 272; admission $3; ☺ Wed-Mon) is located 2 miles east of town on Hwy 60 and 4 miles south on Hwy 272. The original 1862 Fort Sumner was used as an outpost to fight the Apache tribe and Confederate army. After driving the Confederates south, the troops killed the Apache or moved them to a reservation. Shortly thereafter, the wealthy rancher Lucien Maxwell turned the fort into a palatial retreat. Maxwell owned most of New Mexico north of Fort Sumner and east of the Rockies; it was the largest spread ever owned by one individual in the USA. Billy the Kid was visiting here on July 14, 1881, when he was shot and killed by Sheriff Pat Garrett. The original fort no longer stands, but a visitor center has interpretive exhibits. Several trails, including one to Navajo sites and one to the river, leave from the visitor center.

The **Old Fort Sumner Museum** (☎ 575-355-2942; Billy the Kid Rd; admission $4; ☺ 10am-5pm), with more local history and an emphasis on Billy the Kid, is located near the state monument. Behind the museum you'll find **Billy the Kid's Grave** and that of Lucien Maxwell. The Kid's tombstone is protected by an iron cage because 'souvenir hunters' kept trying to steal it.

Unusual atmospheric circulation patterns in the spring and fall bring NASA and international scientists to Fort Sumner to launch **weather balloons** carrying scientific research instruments 32 miles into the atmosphere. One inflates to the size of the Houston Astrodome at its highest elevation.

Festivals & Events

Old Fort Days, held on the second weekend in June, features various athletic events. The purse for the winner of the tombstone race, in which contestants must negotiate an obstacle course while lugging an 80lb tombstone, is $2000.

Sleeping & Eating

Sumner Lake State Park (☎ 575-355-2541; per car per day $5, tent sites $10-14) When the Pecos River was dammed, this artificial lake was created; primitive camping is available. To reach it, take Hwy 84 north for 11 miles, then Hwy 203 west for 6 miles. There is also free primitive camping near Bosque Redondo Lake, 2 miles south of town.

Sadie's Frontier Restaurant (☎ 575-355-1461; 510 Sumner Ave; dishes $5-10; ☺ 7:30am-8pm Thu-Mon) If you're passing through, pick up a homemade breakfast burrito or other simple but good New Mexican fare.

Getting There & Away

Fort Sumner is on Hwy 60, 84 miles north of Roswell, 45 miles southwest of Santa Rosa and 60 miles west of Clovis. It is best reached by private vehicle.

Southwestern Colorado

The story of Southwestern Colorado is a timeless classic. Part ghost story, part spaghetti Western, it's set to a spectacular backdrop of table-flat mesas and crumbling ruins, rugged peaks and wide open spaces. The plot spans centuries, toes the line between past and present, is complicated and never dull.

Indians and cowboys, yuppies and ski-bums, leathery-skinned mountain folk and mink-coated fast-talking transplants are the heroes and heroines of this destination that's perfect for history and adrenaline junkies alike. Experience a semblance of the heyday of the gold-mining towns as the boots of swanky cowgirls reverberate against planked wood floors in main-street saloons, and tourists ride the narrow-gauge railway from Durango to Silverton.

In the ruins of Mesa Verde National Park there's a mystery without conclusion, a tale of a civilization of Ancestral Puebloans who vanished without a trace around 1300. While in the mining haunts of Telluride, Durango and Ouray, you'll find the raw materials are here for a classic rags-to-riches tale, one that begins with fortune-seekers riding the rails west and ends with ski resorts and charming towns determined to keep their historical legacy alive. Yesteryear's bordellos may now be swanky restaurants and tourism may be the new gold, but step into an old saloon, where smoke and ragtime fill the air, and you'll be transported back in time.

Wherever you travel in Southwestern Colorado there's a grand adventure story to be had; you'll have to visit to explore further.

HIGHLIGHTS

- **Best Festival Town**
  You can't beat the mountain magic of Telluride (p397), especially during bluegrass and film-festival time

- **Top Place to Lose Track of Time**
  Spend the night in Silverton (p405), a real old-fashioned Wild West town, where streets remain unpaved and the four-wheel driving is stupendous

- **Best Adventure Town**
  Drop dead gorgeous Ouray (p404), in the heart of a box canyon, is an ice-climber's frozen dream

- **Best-Kept Secret**
  Wolf Creek Ski Area (p384) gets Colorado's best snow, crowds are unheard of and lift tickets are still affordable

- **Top Spot to Listen for the Ancestors' Whisper**
  Mesa Verde National Park (p391), where a civilization vanished around 1300

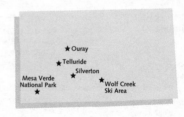

History

Six bands of Utes once resided in a vast area stretching between the Yampa and San Juan Rivers. When white miners entered their lands, the Utes did not give in so easily. Chief Ouray (1833–80), remembered for paving the way to peace between the two parties, actually had little choice but to eventually give up most of the Ute territory.

The mining era was launched with the discovery of gold west of Denver in 1859, but by the 1870s silver took center stage. Mountain smelter sites, such as Leadville and Aspen, turned into thriving population centers almost overnight.

Colorado relied heavily on its abundant natural resources, and the 20th century was an economically topsy-turvy time when mines shut and cities became ghost towns. The forecast turned sunnier in the 21st century. The Wild West came galloping back in the southwest corner of the state after many gone-bust silver towns cashed in on their century-old bad-boy days, reinventing themselves as Old West tourism cash cows, complete with unpaved streets, brothel lore and fabulous re-opened old saloons and hotels. Each year millions of visitors flock to Colorado's national parks, historic cities and 25 ski resorts. In fact, the state boasts the most terrain for skiing in North America. Along with tourism, the military and the high-tech industries are the major component of the state's economy – it is home to a number of high-profile defense-department establishments including the US Air Force Academy and NORAD.

Climate

Like elsewhere in the state, Southwestern Colorado's weather is fickle and changeable. The weather bureau might report snow, but you'll wake up to blue skies and warm temperatures. The San Juan Mountains dominate the region, and winter comes early. Temperatures drop dramatically in mid-September and higher elevations will usually see their first snowfall then. The heaviest snow begins to fall in mid-November and continues through April, when the mercury starts rising, although it can snow anytime – even in July! Summer temperatures can rise into the 80°F range at lower elevations, although you should always carry a sweater because nights are cool, no matter what the time of year. Southwestern Colorado sees plenty of sunshine, and though it may snow in July, you also get January days warm enough for a T-shirt!

Time Zone

Colorado is on Mountain Time (seven hours behind GMT) and observes daylight-saving time.

Information

Colorado Bureau of Land Management (☎ 303-239-3600; www.co.blm.gov) The state's plentiful natural beauty makes camping one of its best accommodation options. This site offers information on booking public campgrounds.

Colorado Travel & Tourism Authority (☎ 800-265-6723; www.colorado.com; PO Box 3524, Englewood, CO 80155) Provides statewide tourism information along with free state highway maps.

National & State Parks

Mesa Verde National Park (p391) is one of the Southwest's largest tourist draws. It's primarily an archaeological preserve with elaborate cliff dwellings abandoned by a civilization of Ancestral Puebloans around 1300. Just outside the Four Corners 'official' boundaries is Black Canyon of the Gunnison National Park (p402). One of the country's newest (and most eerie) parks, Black Canyon features a 2000ft chasm over the Gunnison River. Sheer walls, dizzying depths and narrow openings are all exhibited here. The region has numerous state parks as well as thousands of acres of land ripe for exploration in the San Juan National Forest.

For information on Colorado's national and state parks check out the following:

FAST FACTS

Population 4.9 million

Area 104,247 sq miles

State nickname Centennial State

Website www.colorado.com

Sales tax 2.9% state sales tax, plus individual city taxes up to 6%

Average temps low/high Durango Jan 12/40°F, Jul 51/85°F

Durango to Mesa Verde National Park 66 miles, 1 hour

Telluride to Ouray 50 miles, 1 hour

Durango to Denver 340 miles, 5 hours

Pagosa Springs to Santa Fe 155 miles, 2 hours

SOUTHWESTERN COLORADO

Colorado State Parks (☎ 303-470-1144; www.parks
.state.co.us) Information on state parks.
National Park Service (NPS; ☎ 303-969-2500; www
.nps.gov; Intermountain Region, 12795 Alameda Pkwy,
Denver, CO 80225) Comprehensive website with state-by-
state listings of national parks.

Southwestern Colorado Scenic Routes

One of the best ways to explore Southwestern
Colorado is by getting off the beaten path. The
state has 24 designated scenic byways and
hundreds of other less-traveled paths (some
less so than others). The Four Corners area
yields the greatest concentration of old mining roads in Colorado, and exploring these
back roads is more than just visually stunning.
You'll also glean a deeper understanding of
the region's complex and colorful history,
which stretches back more than 10 centuries.
A few suggestions for great drives follow, but
for more information on scenic byways visit
www.coloradobyways.org.

A demanding but fantastic drive, the 63-
mile Alpine Loop begins in Ouray (p404)
and travels east to Lake City – a wonderful
mountain hamlet worth stopping in – before
taking you back to its starting point. Along
the way you'll cross two 12,000ft mountain
passes, and swap pavement and people for
solitude, spectacular scenery, abandoned
mining haunts and the remote and rugged
heart of the San Juan Mountains. You'll need
a high-clearance 4WD vehicle and some
four-wheeling skill to conquer this drive;
allow six hours.

It's been more than eight centuries since
the Ancestral Puebloans, formerly known
as the Anasazi, disappeared without a trace
from the cliffside dwellings they built in and
around Mesa Verde National Park (p391),
and yet their mysterious disappearance is still
pondered today. If you're searching for clues,
the Trail of the Ancients – a 114-mile drive
along Hwy 145, Hwy 184 and US 160 – might
be a good place to start. Begin your journey
in Cortez (p394) and either head northwest
toward Hovenweep National Monument
(p418) on the Utah border (which, like Mesa
Verde, contains dense clusters of Ancestral
Puebloan dwellings) or southwest toward the
meeting point of Colorado, Utah, Arizona and
New Mexico: Four Corners. Either way, you'll
travel through arid moonscape terrain passing
cliff dwellings, pottery shreds and rock art.
Allow three hours for the drive.

WHAT THE... ?

When it comes to Colorado, there's some
local lingo you just must know. First, ask
what kind of microbrew (a locally produced
beer, usually made in small batches) is on
tap at the pub. And be careful before ordering the Rocky Mountain oysters – that's Old
West talk for fried bull testicles, something
we still can't appreciate after more than a
decade in the region!

The spectacular Imogene Pass 4WD
route connects Ouray (p404) with Telluride
(p397). The road is only 16 miles long, but
requires a high-clearance vehicle and takes
about three hours to drive in each direction.
Built in 1880, the old mining road is one of
the highest in the San Juan Mountains (the
pass summits at 13,114ft) and takes you by
two important mining sites. In Ouray, head
south on Main St and turn right on Bird
Camp Rd (City Rd 361). You will pass the
Bird Camp Mine, once one of the San Juan's
most prolific, before climbing high into the
mountains. Along the way you will have
to cross a stream or two, and at times the
road snakes precariously close to sheer cliff
drops, which can be a thrilling adrenaline
rush if you're an experienced four-wheeler.
Eventually the route opens up into high alpine meadows before reaching the summit
of Imogene Pass. Traveling down, towards
Telluride, you'll pass the abandoned Tomboy
Mine. Still littered with old mining paraphernalia, it once had a population as large
as present-day Ouray. The pass is only open
in summer.

The most beautiful way to reach Ouray
from Silverton in the summer is via Overton
Pass, technically a 4WD route, but accom-
plishable in a high-clearance car when it's
dry. Silverton local Doug Wall says locals call
it Subaru pass because 'going from Silverton
to Ouray in the summer you can get by in a
Subaru. Coming back's a bit more technical, but it's a beautiful drive.' It sure is. If
you're into exhilarating 4WD tracks, this is
arguably one of the best (and certainly the
most famous) in the state; especially appealing because it doesn't require super expertise
and relative beginners can conquer it when
starting from Silverton. The pass is only open
in summer.

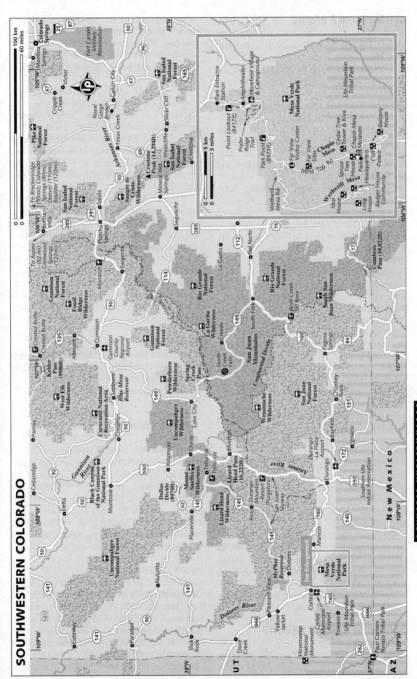

SOUTHWESTERN COLORADO

Getting There & Around

Southwestern Colorado is best seen by private vehicle. US 160, from Durango to Cortez and past Mesa Verde National Park, is the main east–west vein through the region, although it is far from the most gorgeous route in the state. US 50 also crosses the state from east to west but is further north than US 160. It hooks up Montrose with Pueblo, where you'll have access to I-25, which will take you north to Wyoming or south to New Mexico. Not as photogenic as other routes in the state, US 50 is nonetheless fast and convenient – both Gunnison and Salida have plenty of sleeping options and there are many gas stations along the route.

For true beauty, check out US 550, which runs north–south and connects Durango with Silverton, Ouray and Ridgeway. Known as the Million Dollar Hwy between Ouray and Silverton, this is one of the most beautiful drives in the Rocky Mountains and should not be missed. An alternative north–south option takes you from Cortez to Ridgeway via Dolores and, with a slight detour, Telluride. For this route follow Hwy 145 north until you reach Mountain Village where you can head east to Telluride – it's another stunning drive with lots of craggy grey peaks and dark-green forests. The road ends at Telluride, so you'll have to double back to get out. Once you do, continue north on Hwy 145 until you reach Placerville, where the road intersects with Hwy 62. Follow Hwy 62 northeast to Ridgeway and join up with US 550 again. The southwest portion of Colorado is also home to numerous scenic byways and 4WD tracks – see p382 for more on these alternate routes between cities.

Denver International Airport (see p531) is Colorado's main hub, although it's 300-plus miles northeast of Durango. However, from DIA you can catch a commuter plane to regional destinations such as Durango and Telluride.

Greyhound (☎ 800-231-2222; www.greyhound.com) has fixed routes throughout the region. **TNM&O** (☎ 719-635-1505; www.greyhound.com) is affiliated with Greyhound and serves the same lines through Colorado.

For more information on transportation throughout the Southwest, see p536.

PAGOSA SPRINGS & AROUND
pop 1600 / elev 7079ft

Even though the secret about the amazing powder at Wolf Creek Ski Area has been out of the bag (at least among Coloradans) for a decade now, the resort remains refreshingly low-key. It's just a down-home place where powder hounds from around the state come faithfully each winter to shred lots and lots of snow.

At the base of the continental divide, Pagosa Springs is the nearest town to Wolf Creek. It's an unpretentious little place with panoramic mountain views, soothing hot springs and a distinctly undiscovered vibe. It may not be the most bubbly or sophisticated place in Colorado, but it serves visitors and resident ski bums alike with a host of sleeping and eating options.

If snow riding isn't for you, don't sweat. Or rather do. Pagosa is as famous for its mineral springs as it is for its powder. Locals swear by the healing properties of the water after which Pagosa was named – the Ute word *'pagosh'* means 'healing waters.' The city's hot-spring pools certainly feel wonderful after a long day on the slopes or hiking trail. Make sure to check out the steam billowing out of vents in the San Juan River flowing past volcanic rock formations in the center of town.

Information

The **Pagosa Springs Area Chamber of Commerce** (☎ 970-264-2360; www.visitpagosasprings.com; 402 San Juan St; ☺ 9am-5pm Mon-Fri) operates a large visitor center located across the bridge from US Hwy 160.

Sights & Activities
HIKING

There is no shortage of hiking options during the summer months. Pagosa Springs is surrounded by the three-million-acre San Juan National Forest and backs up to Weminuche Wilderness Area, the largest continuous wilderness area in the USA. For details on the more than 500 hiking trails in the region, stop by the Pagosa Springs Area Chamber of Commerce visitor center (above).

WOLF CREEK SKI AREA

With more than 450in of snow per year, riding **Wolf Creek** (☎ 970-264-5629; www.wolfcreekski.com; lift ticket adult/child $48/26; ☺ Nov–mid-Apr) on a powder day feels like riding a tidal wave of snow. Located 25 miles north of Pagosa Springs on US 160, this family-owned ski area is one of Colorado's last and best-kept secrets – although locals have been flocking here for the past decade, it still hasn't caught on with the out-of-state crowd. Never crowded, and lacking the glitz and glamour of larger resorts, it's simply a laid-back, awesome place to ride. The powder can be waist-high after a big storm blows through. The five lifts service 50 trails, from wide-open bowls to steep tree glades.

HOT SPRINGS

For visitors to Pagosa Springs, soaking in the glorious riverside pools at the **Springs Resort** (☎ 970-264-4168; 165 Hot Springs Blvd; adult/child $17.25/9; ☉ 7am-11pm Sun-Thu, to 1am Fri & Sat) is de rigueur. The pool area is impressively decorated, using lots of natural materials to style its 18 different outdoor soaking tubs – some have tumbling waterfalls, others resemble Yellowstone's geysers. The pools front a tangerine Spanish-style mansion (now the changing area) on one side and the San Juan River on the other. Craggy peaks surround and the air is scented with pine. The healing, mineral-rich waters are drawn from the Great Pagosa Aquifer, which is the largest and deepest hot mineral spring in the world. Each pool is a different size and shape, but all are designed to look as

natural as possible, and the views are beyond stupendous. Temperatures vary from 83°F to 114°F – this last one is appropriately named 'the lobster pot!'

Night owls and those staying at the on-property resort and spa will love how late the pools stay open – 1am on weekends.

CHIMNEY ROCK ARCHAEOLOGICAL AREA

Stunning rock spires house Ancestral Puebloan ruins overlooking the Piedra River at this **archaeological area** (☎ 970-883-5359; tours $8; ☉ mid-May–Oct) 18 miles west of Pagosa Springs on Hwy 131. Recent research suggests the site was a Chacoan outlier that may have furnished timber to communities throughout the southwest. Another recent discovery suggests the twin pinnacles were used to observe lunar events. By the year 1125, the site, like others in the southwest, was abandoned, possibly because of drought.

Guided tours are the only way to visit the hundreds of structures, including the Great Kiva that once housed between 1200 and 2000 inhabitants. A fire lookout tower offers views of the excavated Chacoan sites perched high

---

DETOUR: LAKE CITY

Whichever way you choose to reach the scenically spectacular Lake City, it's worth the drive. Located on two scenic and historic byways – the Silver Thread (Hwy 149) and the 4WD-only Alpine Loop (see p382) – Lake City is a stress-free mountain community that makes the perfect summer day trip or romantic overnight from Pagosa Springs, located 112 miles to the south along Hwy 149. Art galleries and funky shops line the main drag, and there are all sorts of lodgings and delicious eating options around the Victorian-style historic downtown – check out the city's website, www.lakecity.com, for more.

If you happen to be in the region around the end of June, you'll be in for a real local experience. Every year the town celebrates Alfred Packer Days, making light of the life of the man who cannibalized members of his own hiking party in the nearby mountains in 1874. The totally offbeat festival includes a mystery-meat cook-off, a bone-throwing contest and, of course, coffin races down the main street.

The landscape around Lake City is as interesting as the tiny mountain town. **North Creek Falls** is south of Lake City over Spring Creek Pass. Hidden in a box canyon off Forest Rd 510, reached via Hwy 149 after crossing Springer Pass, the falls are some of the most beautiful in Colorado. The landscape surrounding the falls is relatively flat, and covered in prairie grasses, which serves as a stark contrast to the gushing water in the tight rocky canyon, making the falls seem even more impressive. The North Creek Falls sit at an elevation of more than 10,000ft and emit a wonderful crashing sound as the swiftly flowing Clear Creek rushes over a rocky ledge and tumbles 100 odd feet through the slot canyon and into the Rio Grande River below. Many say it takes their breath away – others say a picture is worth a thousand words, which is probably why it's one of the most photographed waterfalls in the state.

Lake City is primarily a summer destination, and when the high-country snows begin to pile up come November, most hotels and restaurants shut their doors until May. A few places do stay open year-round. Check the city's website for specifics.

on the rock formation. Two-hour walking tours leave daily in season at 9:30am, 10:30am, 1pm and 2pm.

Sleeping & Eating

Hotels here tend to be a bit less expensive than in nearby Durango.

San Juan Motel (☎ 970-264-2262; www.sanjuanmotel .net; 191 E Pagosa St; campsites for 2 people $20, r from $65; ⚘) This economical place has rooms in all shapes and sizes – some are rather outdated but perfectly fine for slumbering if you'd rather spend your cash on other pursuits; others are newer and up to modern motel standards. There are also a variety of cabins with or without kitchens, plus places to pitch a tent. This is a family-oriented option; facilities include a game room, laundry, a hot tub and ski packages at Wolf Creek. Pets are allowed for an extra $12.50 per night. The campsites sit in a meadow by the river and come with fire pits.

Inn at the Springs (☎ 970-731-3362; www.inn-at -the-springs.com; 596 Antero Dr; r from $85; ⚘) Four rooms share two bathrooms and there's also a bunked loft family room where kids under 12 stay free at Dave and Barbara Snyder's rustic guesthouse. The inn is a good deal, considering the (included) full breakfast and genial charm of the place. Don't miss out on a lazy daydream in the great room, with a huge river-rock fireplace, mountain views from picture windows, smooth wood walls and comfortable couches. Rooms are petite but cram a lot of good stuff into a small package even if the walls are too rough-hewn for the place to be considered luxurious. If you like bears, as we do, spend the night in the 'Bear Room', where you'll be joined by dozens of teddy bears – many homemade – even a bear-shaped phone. Horseback riding can be arranged.

Springs Resort (☎ 970-264-4168; www.pagosahot springs.com; 165 Hot Springs Blvd; r from $150; 🖳) Guests here enjoy all-you-can-hot-tub privileges in the hotel's top-notch hot springs, along with commendable rooms. The cheapest are nothing special, but you're paying for the healing waters. The deluxe rooms feature thicker mattresses, higher thread-count sheets, more floor space and kitchenettes. The terraced pink adobe hotel overlooking the banks of the San Juan also features a spa, offers ski packages and welcomes pets.

Elkhorn Café (☎ 970-264-2146; 438 Main St; mains $7-10; 🕑 breakfast, lunch & dinner) Serving Mexican fare that is spicy, filling and good, this is a popular spot with locals – the green chile is especially delicious. Stop by for a breakfast burrito before hitting the slopes. For those not in the mood for a stuffed *sopaipilla* (deep-fried puff pastry), the restaurant also does the usual American burger-and-fries fare.

JJ's Riverwalk Restaurant Pub (☎ 970-264-9100; 356 E Hwy 160; mains from $10; 🕑 lunch & dinner) Overlooking the San Juan River, JJ's has a great vibe, tasty food, a decent wine list and pleasant service. There are nightly dinner specials, including early-bird cheap meals and a nightly happy hour. In summer sit outside on the patio overlooking the river and watch the kayakers float by.

Getting There & Around

Pagosa Springs is at the junction of US 160 and US 84.

DURANGO

pop 14,800 / elev 6580ft

The darling of this region, Durango is nothing short of delightful. It's an archetypal old Colorado mining town filled with graceful hotels, Victorian-era saloons, and mountains dominating the periphery as far as the eye can see. It's a place seemingly frozen in time. The waitress slinging drinks at the scarred wooden bar is dressed straight out of the early 19th century. The antique-laden inn and the musician pounding ragtime on worn ivory keys add to the surrealism.

It's only after stepping into the classy stores and restaurants that you'll be reminded of the present day. There are dining options poised to charm the most critical of palates and a store for any desire, from outdoor apparel to fancy jewelry or funky retro garb. But if your appetite is still not whetted, dip into Durango's goody bag of adventures to get the heart really pumping. Meander through the historic district and listen for a shrill whistle, then watch the steam billow as the old train pulls in (opposite). Rent a bike and explore the trails, or get out the skis and head up the road for miles upon miles of powdery white bowls and tree-lined glades.

Orientation & Information

Most visitors' facilities are along Main Ave, including the 1882 Durango & Silverton Narrow Gauge Railroad Depot (at the south end of town). Motels are mostly north of the town center. The downtown is compact and easy to walk in a few hours.

Maria's Bookshop (☎ 970-247-1438; 960 Main Ave) A good general bookstore.

Mercy Medical Center (☎ 970-247-4311; 375 E Park Ave) Outpatient and 24-hour emergency care.

Post office (☎ 970-247-3968; 222 W 8th St)

Public library (☎ 970-385-2970; 1118 E 2nd Ave; ☐) Free internet access.

San Juan-Rio Grande National Forest Headquarters (☎ 970-247-4874; 15 Burnett Ct; ☺ 8am-5pm Mon-Sat) Offers camping and hiking information and maps. It's about a half-mile west on US Hwy 160.

Visitor center (☎ 800-525-8855; www.durango.org; 111 S Camino del Rio; ☺ 8am-5pm Mon-Fri) South of town, at the Santa Rita exit from US 550.

Sights & Activities
DURANGO & SILVERTON NARROW GAUGE RAILROAD

Climb aboard this steam-driven **train** (☎ 970-247-2733, 888-872-4607; www.durangotrain.com; adult/child $75/45) for a scenic 45-mile trip north to Silverton, a National Historic Landmark. The journey is best in fall, when the trees put on a magnificent show of colors. The train has been in continuous operation for 123 years, carrying passengers behind vintage locomotives and allowing them to relive the sights and sounds of yesteryear. The dazzling trip takes 3½ hours each way, and allows two hours for exploring Silverton. It is only offered from May through October (8:15am and 9am). In winter, the train runs to Cascade Canyon (adult/child $49/29) in the heart of the San Juan National Forest. The snowy landscape is stunning, and you'll learn about native flora and fauna while riding past an ultra-remote portion of the Animas River.

SKIING & SNOWBOARDING

The town's other main draw is **Durango Mountain Resort** (☎ 970-247-9000, 800-693-0175; www.durangomountainresort.com; lift ticket adult/child $60/32; ☺ mid-Nov–Mar), 25 miles north on US 550. The resort, also known as Purgatory, is one of the state's least expensive, offers 1200 skiable acres and boasts 260in of snow per

---

BREWS & BIKES IN DURANGO

Coloradoans take their beer-drinking seriously, but you won't catch locals drinking any of that hopped-up water that local beer giant Coors produces. No, Coloradoans regard beer the same way the French think of wine, and the state has a reputation for producing some gnarly micro (or small-batch) brews. These can range from hoppy to fruity but all tend to be strong on flavor. For serious punch, order a barley wine. The alcohol content can be as high as 12%!

Durango has become a microbrew mecca of sorts. Beer connoisseurs dig that this small town boasts four breweries serving and bottling more than two dozen local beers (many of which are sold in liquor stores across the state and country). Brewers from around the state gather at the Durango Mountain Resort for the **San Juan Brewfest** in September. Check www.durango mountainresort.com for details. The festival includes food, music and, of course, lots of beer. If you're in the neighborhood, this is a great way to experience Colorado mountain life during a brilliantly beautiful season.

For info on individual Durango breweries, see listings in the Eating and Drinking sections. One brewery, the Durango Brewing Co, doesn't have a tasting room, but you can sample its brews at most local restaurants and liquor stores.

Biking goes hand in hand with imbibing alcohol in Colorado, so it's little surprise a town supporting such a lively microbrew community would also be considered paradise to mountain bikers. Bike geeks take note: Durango is home to some of the world's best cyclists, like Ned Overend and Travis Brown. From steep single-tracks to scenic road rides, Durango has hundreds of trails to choose from. Some are well marked; others the locals like to keep secret (much in the manner of surf spots) and you'll have to do a bit of snooping if you want to hit pay dirt. For an easy ride, try the **Old Railroad Grade Trail**, a 12.2-mile loop that uses both US Hwy 160 and a dirt road following the old rail tracks. From Durango, take Hwy 160 west through the town of Hesperus. Turn right into the Cherry Creek Picnic Area, where the trail starts.

For something a bit more technical, try **Dry Fork Loop**, accessible from Lightner Creek just west of town. It has some great drops, blind corners and copious vegetation.

There are quite a few sports shops on Main Ave that rent mountain bikes.

year. Eleven lifts carry skiers and boarders to 85 different trails of varying difficulty, while two terrain parks offer plenty of opportunity to catch some big air. There's a 400ft half-pipe as well as rails, hits, drops and tabletops. Those interested in cross-country skiing can check out the Nordic Center across US 550 from the main base. There are 10 miles of groomed trails for all levels. The cost is $10 for adults, $8 for kids.

WHITE-WATER RAFTING

In spring and summer white-water rafting is one of the most popular sports in Durango.

Mild to Wild Rafting (☎ 970-247-4789; 50 Animas View Dr; trips from $55) is one of numerous companies around town offering Animas river-rafting trips. Beginners should check out the one-hour introduction to rafting, while the more adventurous (and experienced) run the upper Animas, which boasts Class III to V rapids.

Sleeping

Durango's best sleeping deals are found at the independent motels just north of town on US 550 (Main Ave), with the greatest concentration between 18th and 32nd Sts. Most places are very similar, with clean boxy rooms and swimming pools. Look for rates posted on big signs out front. Rooms go for around $40 in winter and $65 in summer.

Days End (☎ 970-259-3311; www.daysenddurango.com; 2202 N Main Ave; r from $42; 🛜 wi-fi) We get good feedback about this inexpensive motel on a small creek just north of town. Rooms are good value; even in summer they can cost under $50, and many come with king-size beds. The indoor hot tub and barbecue grills by the water are other positives. Tennis junkies can get their fix on the adjacent public courts. The motel offers ski discounts with Purgatory resort in winter. Pets are welcome, but there's a fee.

Siesta Motel (☎ 970-247-0741; 3475 N Main Ave; r from $50; 🐾) This family-owned hotel is another one of the town's cheaper options. It's a welcoming place offering spacious and comfortable rooms. There's a little courtyard with a barbecue grill, plus a grassy area with a slide for the kiddies to play on.

General Palmer Hotel (☎ 970-247-4747; www.generalpalmer.com; 567 Main Ave; r from $105; 🐾) A Victorian landmark from 1898, the hotel features pewter four-poster beds, quality linens and even a teddy bear for snuggling. Rooms are small but elegant, and if you tire of TV there's a collec-

tion of board games at the front desk. Check out the cozy library or the relaxing solarium.

Rochester House (☎ 970-385-1920; www.rochesterhotel.com; 721 E 2nd Ave; r $120-160; 🛜 wi-fi) Influenced by old Westerns (movie posters and marquee lights adorn the hallways) the Rochester is a little bit of old Hollywood in the New West. Rooms are spacious with vaulted ceilings. Two formal sitting rooms serving cookies and a breakfast room in an old train car are other perks at this pet-friendly establishment. If Rochester is full, try Leland House across the street – owned by the same folks, it has the same rates.

Blue Lake Ranch (☎ 970-385-4537; www.bluelakeranch.com; 16000 Hwy 140; r $125-325; wi-fi) Fishing enthusiasts will delight in the private trout-filled lake on this gorgeous property 16-miles north of Durango. Set on 200 secluded acres, it's the perfect place to just get away for a few days. Decked out with lush Southwestern decor – think Native American rugs and woven baskets, bright patterned pillows and whitewashed adobe kivas – this is one classy B&B. You'll get a full, delicious Southwestern breakfast in the morning – including tamales! Choose from casitas and cabins with fabulous mountain views, simpler rooms and cabins, and even a riverside home. Blue Lake is where to come for a dream country wedding or a romantic mini-break with your honey.

ourpick Strater Hotel (☎ 970-247-4431; www.strater.com; 699 Main Ave; r $200; 🐾) The interior of this lovely, old-world hotel is museum-worthy – check out the Stradivarius violin and the gold-plated commemorative Winchester rifle in the lobby. Romantic rooms feature antiques, crystal and lace. Beds are super comfortable with impeccable linens. It's a fantastic deal in winter, when king rooms can go for as little as $89. The hot tub is a major romantic plus: it can be reserved by the hour. Another romantic feature is the summertime melo-drama (theatre) the hotel runs.

Eating

Durango is full of great places to eat. Below is just a sample; walk around town for a few minutes and you'll stumble across many more.

Olde Tymers Café (☎ 970-259-2990; 1000 Main Ave; mains $4-10; 🕙 11am-10pm) Voted as having the best burger in Durango by the local paper, the Olde Tymers is popular with the college crowd, especially during $5 burger nights. Well-priced American classics at cozy booths under pressed-tin ceilings in a big open dining room or on the patio outside. Ask about the cheap daily specials.

East by Southwest (☎ 970-247-5533; 160 E College Dr; sushi $4-13, mains $12-24; ☿ lunch & dinner) Thai, Vietnamese, Indonesian and Japanese cuisine, including a full sushi bar, is served in a congenial low-key setting. The food is delicious and can be washed down with a creative martini or sake cocktail. Locals rave about this establishment.

Jean Pierre Bakery (☎ 970-385-0122; 601 Main Ave; mains $5-16; ☿ 8am-9pm) Visit this charming patisserie for a taste of France in Colorado. The mouthwatering delicacies are made from scratch. Don't miss the soup and sandwich lunch special ($12), which includes a sumptuous French pastry chosen from the large counter display. Well worth at least one meal.

Carver Brewing Co (☎ 970-259-2545; 1022 Main Ave; lunch $5-7, dinner $12-18; ☿ lunch & dinner) A local institution and longtime favorite among beer drinkers, this relaxed brewery churns out 1000 barrels of brew annually; enjoy a pint with burgers and sandwiches in the outdoor beer garden.

Steamworks (☎ 970-259-9200; 801 E 2nd Ave; mains $9-17; ☿ lunch & dinner) Industrial design meets ski lodge at this popular microbrewery with high sloping rafters and exposed pipes. There's a large bar area, separate dining room and a Cajun-influenced menu. The craft brews are excellent. DJs and live bands alternate to bring you nightly entertainment.

Randy's (☎ 970-247-9083; 152 E College Dr; dishes $20-25; ☿ dinner) A fine-dining establishment serving an eclectic menu of mainly seafood and steak, it's an intimate place just perfect for that special meal. Eat between 5pm and 6pm and get the same menu for $12 to $14. Happy hour runs from 5pm to 7pm and offers drinks and appetizer specials in the bar. Locals say this is the finest restaurant in town for top-end dining.

Ore House (☎ 970-247-5707; 147 E College Dr; dishes $20-30; ☿ dinner) The best steakhouse in town, with food served in casual and rustic environs. Order a hand-cut aged steak or the Ore House grubsteak ($40) with steak, crab leg and lobster; it's easily big enough for two. There's also a large wine cellar for making the perfect beverage selection.

Drinking

With a mix of college students, cowboys and ski bums, it's little surprise that Durango has an active night scene. Carver Brewing Co (left) and Steamworks (left) are popular after-dark watering holes.

ourpick Ska Brewing Company (☎ 970-247-5792; 545 Turner Dr) Big on flavor and variety, these are the best beers in town. The small, friendly tasting-room bar was once mainly a production facility, but over the years it has gained a loyal clientele and is usually jam-packed with locals chatting over an end-of-the-day pint. In fact, Ska has become so popular it's started running weekly barbecues with live music and free food – call ahead for dates. The brewers often double as bartenders, sharing knowledge of their craft, and the atmosphere remains refreshingly relaxed.

Diamond Belle Saloon (☎ 970-376-7150; 699 Main Ave) The perfect place to start (or end) an evening, this is a period place right down to the waitress dressed in Victorian-era garb – fishnets and garters with a feather in her hair. It's cozy and elegant, with a piano man who belts out ragtime tunes and takes requests from patrons. There are half-price appetizers and drink specials from 4pm to 6pm.

El Rancho (☎ 970-259-8111; 975 Main Ave) A bar with a long history, this place attracts loads of loyal locals who come to drink their whiskey well into the night. A dive with attitude, its long bar is made for serious boozing. Don't miss the mural on the outside, and there are pool tables in the back. El Rancho gets progressively rowdier as the night progresses.

Lady Falconburgh's (☎ 970-582-9664; 640 Main Ave) With the largest selection of microbrews and imports in the Four Corners region, it's no secret that this place is popular. There's a brick-and-brass theme, with original murals on the walls and more than 100 beers on offer – 38 of which are on tap. It's a great place for mingling. You won't feel out of place going here alone.

On the Patio (☎ 970-382-8554; 121 W Eighth St) This summer-only place in the heart of downtown is super popular on warm August nights when crowds gather around the big rooftop kiva to gossip and listen to light music played at conversation levels. Stop by just before sunset for a truly gorgeous cocktail experience. Pub grub is served but the ambience is the main draw.

Getting There & Around

Durango-La Plata County Airport (☎ 970-247-8143) is 18 miles southeast of Durango via US 160 and Hwy 172. **American Airlines** (www.aa.com) offers daily jet service to Dallas during ski season. Otherwise, you are on commuter turbo-prop plane that is much slower. **United Express** (www.united.com) has daily flights to Denver, while **America West** (www.americawest.com) serves Phoenix, AZ.

Greyhound/TNM&O (www.greyhound.com) buses run daily from the **Durango Bus Center** (☎ 970-259-2755; 275 E 8th Ave) north to Grand Junction and south to Albuquerque, NM.

Durango lies at the junction of US Hwy 160 and US Hwy 550, 42 miles east of Cortez, 49 miles west of Pagosa Springs and 190 miles north of Albuquerque in New Mexico.

MANCOS
pop 900 / elev 7000ft

A quick sprint through tiny Mancos and you'll think you've stumbled upon yet another Colorado ghost town. But slow down for a minute and wander amid the historic homes and landmark buildings and you'll be in for a great surprise. Sleeping and eating options are limited, but the ones that do exist are charming and eclectic. Mesa Verde National Park is just 7 miles to the west, so if visiting the park is on your itinerary, staying in Mancos makes an appealing alternative to Cortez's rather nondescript motels.

Historic displays and a walking-tour map are available at the **visitor center** (☎ 702-533-7434; www.mancosvalley.com; cnr Main St & Railroad Ave; ☒ 9am-5pm Mon-Fri). It also has information on outdoor activities and local ranches that offer horseback rides and Western-style overnight trips.

Sleeping

Mancos has some of Colorado's most interesting sleeping options. For more options than we could list here, visit www.mancosvalley.com.

Jersey Jim Lookout (☎ 800-525-8855; r $40; ☒ mid-May–mid-Oct) How about spending the night in a former fire-lookout tower? Standing 55ft above a meadow 14 miles north of Mancos at an elevation of 9800ft, this place is on the National Historic Lookout Register and comes with an Osborne Fire Finder and topographic map. The tower accommodates up to four adults (bring your own bedding) and must be reserved long in advance; there's also a two-night minimum stay. The reservation office opens on the first workday of March (1pm to 5pm) and the entire season is typically booked within days.

Enchanted Mesa Motel (☎ 970-533-7729; 862 W Grand Ave; r from $45; ☒) Hipper than most independent motels, with shiny lamps and solid wooden furniture that come standard along with king- and queen-size beds. There's a big playground out front for the kids. Best of all, you can play a game of pool while waiting for your whites to dry – there's a billiards table in the laundry room!

Echo Basin Ranch (☎ 970-533-7000; www.echobasin.com; 43747 County Rd M; cabins per night/week from $119/600) Traveling with horse? No problem. Stop for the night at Echo Basin Ranch, an affordable unnstructured dude ranch. The A-frame cabin accommodation is very cool (as long as you don't mind rustic, and by that we mean basic). We love the pitched roof and big windows – very Rocky Mountain high. The deluxe cabins are still not posh, but plenty comfortable, with multiple rooms and more artistic decor. There is at least a two-night minimum to stay here, and it is much cheaper (and in scale with what you pay for, amenities-wise) if you stay at least four nights. Dogs are welcome, and horses stay for $10 per night. The ranch offers a host of activities, from guided horseback riding to a putting green. The onsite restaurant and saloon mean you don't have to drive to eat – Echo Basin is about 7 miles from Mancos.

Eating & Drinking

Columbine Bar (☎ 970-533-7397; 123 W Grand Ave; mains $5) More than a century after Columbine Bar first opened its doors, the saloon – established in 1903 and one of Colorado's oldest continuously operating bars – is still going strong. Locals come for pints of ice-cold local brews and good pub food, but visitors will love the Old West feel this smoky old saloon oozes. The mounted animal heads keep watch as you shoot pool.

Absolute Baking Co (☎ 970-533-1200; 110 S Main St; mains $6-8; ☒ breakfast & lunch) The most happening spot in town, this café serves healthy and delicious homemade meals including wraps, salads, pastas and sandwiches. The amiable owners are rightly justified in advertising 'sublime breads…food with integrity.' Only organic flours and grains go into the fresh-baked breads and pastries. If you're in the market for a new read, the café has a decent collection of used books for sale; so grab a cup of coffee and just chill out.

Millwood Junction (☎ 970-533-7338; cnr Main St & Railroad Ave; mains $10-20; ☒ 4-10:30pm) This is a popular steak and seafood dinner joint. Folks from miles around come to Mancos on Friday night for the $14 seafood buffet. The restaurant often doubles as a club, showcasing live music.

Getting There & Away

Mancos is located right on Hwy 160, just 7 miles east of Mesa Verde National Park and 30 miles west of Durango. It is most easily accessed via private transportation.

MESA VERDE NATIONAL PARK

More than 700 years after its inhabitants disappeared, the mystery of Mesa Verde remains unsolved. It is here that a civilization of Ancestral Puebloans (see boxed text, p38) appears to have vanished into thin air in 1300. Today their last known home is preserved as Mesa Verde, a fascinating, if slightly eerie, national park. Anthropologists will love Mesa Verde, which is unique among American national parks in its focus on maintaining this civilization's cultural relics rather than its natural treasures.

Ancestral Puebloan sites are found throughout the canyons and mesas of the park, perched on a high plateau south of Cortez and Mancos. If you only have time for a short visit, check out the Chapin Mesa Museum (p392) and try a walk through the Spruce Tree House (p393), where you can climb down a wooden ladder into the cool chamber of a kiva.

Mesa Verde rewards travelers who set aside a day or more to take the ranger-led tours of Cliff Palace and Balcony House, (p392), explore Wetherill Mesa (p393), linger around the museum or participate in one of the campfire programs run at Morefield Campground (p394).

Preserving the Ancestral Puebloan sites while accommodating ever-increasing numbers of visitors continues to challenge the National Park Service (NPS). The NPS strictly enforces the Antiquities Act, which prohibits the removal or destruction of any antiquities and prohibits public access to many of the approximately 4000 known Ancestral Puebloan sites.

History

A US army lieutenant recorded the spectacular cliff dwellings in the canyons of Mesa Verde in 1849–50. The large number of sites on Ute tribal land, and their relative inaccessibility, protected the majority of these antiquities from pothunters.

The first scientific investigation of the sites in 1874 failed to identify Cliff Palace, the largest cliff dwelling in North America. Discovery of the 'magnificent city' occurred only when local cowboys Richard Wetherill and Charlie Mason were searching for stray cattle in 1888. The cowboys exploited their 'discovery' for the next 18 years by guiding both amateur and trained archaeologists to the site, particularly to collect the distinctive black-on-white pottery.

The shipping of artifacts overseas motivated Virginia McClurg of Colorado Springs to embark on a long campaign to preserve the site and its contents. McClurg's efforts led Congress to protect artifacts on federal land,

---

MESA VERDE IN A FEW HOURS...

If you've only got a couple of hours to spend in Mesa Verde National Park, then we'd suggest the following itinerary.

Hit up the Far View Visitor Center first to gather info from the helpful rangers. Next head to Spruce Tree House, reached via an easy walk without ladders or steps. This sheltered alcove, more than 200ft wide and almost 90ft deep, contains about 114 rooms and eight kivas once housing about 100 people. One kiva has a reconstructed roof and ladder for entry.

After your walk, get back in the car and drive the nearby 6-mile Mesa Top Rd circuit, which connects 10 excavated mesa-top sites, three accessible cliff dwellings and many vantage points to see inaccessible cliff dwellings from the mesa rim. You can see the Cliff Palace pretty well on this drive due to your location at the edge of the narrowing canyon. There are many stopping points along the way – some are more visually appealing than others.

Your last stop should be the Chapin Mesa, home to the largest cluster of Ancestral Puebloan settlements in the park. Before walking around, stop in at the Chapin Mesa Museum for the back story on the history you are about to experience.

with passage of the Antiquities Act establishing Mesa Verde National Park in 1906.

Orientation

The North Rim summit at Park Point (8571ft) towers more than 2000ft above the Montezuma Valley. From Park Point the mesa gently slopes southward to a 6000ft elevation above the Mancos River in the Ute Mountain Tribal Park. Parallel canyons, typically 500ft below the rim, dissect the mesa-top and carry the drainage southward. Mesa Verde National Park occupies 81 sq miles of the northernmost portion of the mesa and contains the largest and most frequented cliff dwellings and surface sites.

The park entrance is off US 160, midway between Cortez and Mancos. From the entrance, it's about 21 miles to park headquarters, Chapin Mesa Museum and Spruce Tree House. Along the way are Morefield Campground (4 miles), the panoramic viewpoint at Park Point (8 miles) and the Far View Visitor Center opposite the Far View Lodge and restaurant (about 11 miles). Towed vehicles are not allowed beyond Morefield Campground.

South from park headquarters, Mesa Top Rd consists of two one-way circuits. Turn left about a quarter mile from the start of Mesa Top Rd to visit Cliff Palace and Balcony House on the east loop. From the junction with the main road at Far View Visitor Center, the 12-mile mountainous Wetherill Mesa Rd snakes along the North Rim, acting as a natural barrier to tour buses and indifferent travelers. The road is open only from Memorial Day in late May to Labor Day in early September.

A map of Mesa Verde National Park can be found as an inset on p383.

Information

Park roads are open 8am to sunset, except Wetherill Mesa Rd, which closes at 4:30pm. Winter vehicle travel on Mesa Top Rd is subject to weather conditions. You may snowshoe or cross-country ski on the roadway when conditions permit.

Chapin Mesa Museum (☎ 970-529-4475) This museum (right) provides information on weekends when park headquarters is closed.

Far View Visitor Center (☎ 970-529-5036; ☉ 9am-5pm mid-Apr–mid-Oct) More comprehensive information is available at the Chapin Mesa Museum, but visitors must first stop at Far View to obtain the required tickets ($2.75) for tours of Cliff Palace, Long House or Balcony House.

Mesa Verde Museum Association (☎ 970-529-4445; Chapin Mesa Museum; ☉ 8am-6:30pm mid-Apr–mid-Oct, 9am-5pm mid-Oct–mid-Apr) Has an excellent selection of materials on the Ancestral Puebloan and modern tribes in the American Southwest.

Park Headquarters (☎ 800-449-2288, 970-529-4461; www.nps.gov/meve; 7-day park entry per vehicle $15, cyclists, hikers & motorcyclists $8; ☉ 8am-4:30pm Mon-Fri) Provides brochures and maps to each visitor. These are also available in French, Spanish and German.

Sights & Activities

CHAPIN MESA

There is no other place in Mesa Verde where so many remnants of Ancestral Puebloan settlements are clustered together, providing an opportunity to see and compare examples of all phases of construction – from pothouses to Pueblo villages to the elaborate multiroom cities tucked into cliff recesses. Pamphlets describing the most excavated sites are available at either the visitor center or Chapin Mesa Museum.

On the upper portion of Chapin Mesa are the **Far View Sites**, which are perhaps the most densely settled area in Mesa Verde after 1100. The large-walled Pueblo sites at Far View House enclose a central kiva and planned room layout that was originally two stories high. To the north is a small row of rooms and an attached circular tower that likely used to extend just above the adjacent 'pygmy forest' of piñon pine and juniper trees. This tower is one of 57 in Mesa Verde that may once have served as watchtowers, religious structures or astronomical observatories for agricultural schedules.

The **Chapin Mesa Museum** (☎ 970-529-4475; admission free; ☉ 8am-6:30pm mid-Apr–mid-Oct, to 5pm mid-Oct–mid-Apr) has exhibits pertaining to the park. It's a good first stop.

CLIFF PALACE & BALCONY HOUSE

Tickets are required for the one-hour guided tours of either **Cliff Palace** or **Balcony House** (admission $3; ☉ 9am-5pm Mar-Nov), on the east loop of Mesa Top Rd.

Foot access to Cliff Palace, the largest site in the park, resembles the approach taken by the Ancestral Puebloans – visitors must climb a stone stairway and four 10ft ladders. This grand representative of engineering achievement, with 217 rooms and 23 kivas, provided shelter for 250 people. Its inhabitants were without running water – springs across the canyon, below Sun Temple, were the most likely water sources. Use of small 'chinking' stones between the large blocks is strikingly similar to Ancestral Puebloan construction at distant Chaco Canyon.

A visit to Balcony House is quite an adventure and will challenge anyone's fear of heights or small places. You'll be rewarded with outstanding views of Soda Canyon, 600ft below the sandstone overhang that once served as the ceiling for 35 to 40 rooms. The Balcony House tour requires you to descend a 100ft-long staircase into the canyon, then climb a 32ft-tall ladder, crawl through a 12ft-long tunnel and climb an additional 60ft of ladders and stone steps to get out. It's the most challenging tour in the park but might just be the most rewarding, not to mention fun!

SPRUCE TREE HOUSE & MESA TOP RD
Near the park headquarters, an easy walk without ladders or steps leads to Spruce Tree House. This sheltered alcove, more than 200ft wide and almost 90ft deep, contains about 114 rooms and eight kivas once housing about 100 people. One kiva has a reconstructed roof and ladder for entry. During winter, when many portions of the park are closed, access to this site is by ranger-led tours only; see p394.

South from park headquarters, the 6-mile Mesa Top Rd circuit connects 10 excavated mesa-top sites, three accessible cliff dwellings and many vantages of inaccessible cliff dwellings from the mesa rim. It's open 8am to sunset.

WETHERILL MESA
The less-frequented western portion of Mesa Verde offers a comprehensive display of Ancestral Puebloan relics. The **Badger House Community** consists of a short trail connecting four excavated surface sites depicting various phases of Ancestral Puebloan development. For a complete chronological circuit, continue on the trail to **Long House**, the second-largest cliff dwelling in Mesa Verde National Park (for this you will first need to purchase a $2.75 ticket at the visitor center). The nearby **Step House**, which was initially occupied by Modified Basketmaker peoples residing in pithouses, later becoming the site of a Classic Pueblo–period masonry complex with rooms and kivas.

PARK POINT
The fire lookout at Park Point (8571ft) is the highest elevation in the park and of-fers panoramic views. To the north are the 14,000ft peaks of the San Juan Mountains; in the northeast are the 12,000ft crests of the La Plata Mountains; to the southwest, beyond the southward sloping Mesa Verde plateau, is the distant volcanic plug of Shiprock; and to the west is the prone humanlike profile of Sleeping Ute Mountain.

HIKING
Hiking is a great way to explore the park, but follow the rules. Backcountry access is specifically forbidden and fines are imposed on anyone caught wandering off designated trails or entering cliff dwellings without a ranger. Please respect these necessary regulations, so that the fragile and irreplaceable archaeological sights and artifacts remain protected for centuries to come.

When hiking in Mesa Verde always carry water and avoid cliff edges. Trails can be muddy and slippery after summer rains and winter snows, so wear appropriate footwear. Most park trails, except the Soda Canyon Trail, are strenuous and involve steep elevation changes. Hikers must register at the respective trailheads before venturing out.

The 2.8-mile **Petroglyph Loop Trail** is accessed from Spruce Tree House. It follows a path beneath the edge of a plateau before making a short climb to the top of the mesa, where you'll have good views of the Spruce and Navajo Canyons. This is the only trail in the park where you can view petroglyphs.

The 2.1-mile **Spruce Canyon Loop Trail** also begins at Spruce Tree House and descends to the bottom of Spruce Tree Canyon. It's a great way to see the canyon bottoms of Mesa Verde.

MOUNTAIN BIKING
Finding convenient parking at the many stops along Mesa Top Rd is no problem for those with bikes. Only the hardy will want to enter the park by bike and immediately face the grueling 4-mile ascent to Morefield Campground, quickly followed by a narrow tunnel ride to reach the North Rim. An easier option is to unlimber your muscles and mount up at Morefield, Far View Visitor Center or park headquarters.

SKIING & SNOWSHOEING
Winter is a special time in Mesa Verde. The crowds disperse and the cliff dwellings sparkle

in the snow. The skies are often blue and sunny and you may be the only person around. In recent years there has been enough snow to ski or snowshoe on most winter days after a snowstorm (although Colorado's dry climate and sunshine cause the snow to melt quickly). Before setting out, check the current snow conditions by calling ☎ 970-529-4461.

Two park roads have been designated for cross-country skiing and snowshoeing when weather permits. The **Cliff Palace Loop Rd** is a 6-mile relatively flat loop located off the Mesa Top Loop Rd. The road is closed to vehicles after the first snowfall, so you won't have to worry about vehicular traffic. Park at the closed gate and glide 1 mile to the Cliff Palace overlook continuing on past numerous other scenic stopping points.

The **Morefield Campground Loop Rds** offer multiple miles of relatively flat terrain. The campground is closed in winter, but skiers and snowshoers can park at the gate and explore to their heart's content.

Tours

The park concessionaire, **Aramark Mesa Verde** (☎ 970-529-4421; www.visitmesaverde.com; PO Box 277, Mancos, CO, 81328), offers guided tours to excavated pit homes, cliff dwellings and the Spruce Tree House daily from May to mid-October.

Introductory three-hour tours (adult/child $49/38) depart from Morefield Campground (below) at 8:30am and from Far View Lodge (right) at 9am. Afternoon tours include the Balcony House and depart the Far View Lodge at 1pm.

Sleeping & Eating

Nearby Cortez (right) and Mancos (p390) have plenty of midrange places to stay. Within the national park, visitors can stay in luxury at the lodge, or rough it camping. For something in between, rent one of the canvas tents with cots at Morefield Campground. An overnight stay in the park allows convenient access to the many sites during the best viewing hours, participation in evening programs and the sheer pleasure of watching the sun set over Sleeping Ute Mountain from the tranquility of the mesa top.

Morefield Campground (☎ 970-529-4421; campsites $20, canvas tents from $39; ☽ May–mid-Oct) With 445 campsites only 4 miles from the park entrance, this place has plenty of capacity for the peak season. Grassy tent sites at

Navajo Loop are conveniently located near Morefield Village (which offers a general store, gas station, restaurant, showers and laundry). If you want to camp but don't have a tent, Morefield offers the gourmet camper a big canvas tent, two cots and a lantern. Free evening campfire programs take place nightly from Memorial Day (late May) to Labor Day (early September) at the Morefield Campground Amphitheater.

Far View Lodge (☎ 800-449-2288, 970-529-4421; r $120-150, packages per couple $699; ☽ mid-Apr–Oct) Perched on the mesa-top 15 miles inside the park entrance, this tasteful pueblo-style lodge has 150 rooms done up in Southwestern style. The kiva rooms are a bit more expensive but are more personal with Navajo rugs on hardwood floors, big windows and customized wooden headboards. The cheapest rooms resemble your generic American chain. Regardless of style, the mesa views from the private balconies are stunning, with no TVs or phones to distract from the surroundings. Reserve in advance.

The lodge has all-inclusive two-night packages that include a welcome bottle of local wine, gourmet breakfast and dinner plus a private tour of the park's ancient ruins. Far View is pet friendly, but Fido will cost you an extra $10 per night (plus a $50 refundable damage deposit).

Far View Terrace (☎ 970-529-4421; dishes from $5; ☽ breakfast, lunch & dinner Apr-Oct) Immediately south of the visitor center, this self-service place offers reasonably priced meals. Don't miss their special – the Navajo Taco.

Metate Room (☎ 970-529-4421; Far View Lodge; dishes $15-30; ☽ dinner) This restaurant has an innovative menu inspired by Native American food and flavors. Native American artwork and spectacular views of the park and Four Corners region provide the ambience, while palates are titillated with mains like oven-roasted chicken breast with green chile stuffing and buffalo fajitas.

Getting There & Around

Mesa Verde is best seen by private vehicle. There is no public transportation in the park.

CORTEZ

pop 8900 / elev 6200ft

There's nothing particularly stunning or outright unique about Cortez, but its location, 10 miles west of Mesa Verde National Park, makes it a good lodging base for exploring the area. Plus Cortez is a hot spot for mountain biking, with hundreds of great single-track rides in its vicinity. Typical of small-town Colorado, downtown Cortez is lined with squat buildings housing shops selling hunting rifles, trinkets and surprisingly eclectic clothing; family-style restaurants dishing up homemade delicacies; and of course a good microbrewery. The outer edges of the town are jam-packed with independent motels and fast-food outlets. Far-off mountain vistas complete the picture.

Orientation & Information

Colorado Welcome Center (☎ 970-565-4048; 928 E Main St; ☷ 9am-5pm) Maps, brochures and some excellent pamphlets on local activities like fishing and mountain biking.

Post office (☎ 800-275-8777; 35 S Beech St)

Quality Book Store (☎ 970-565-9125; 34 W Main St) Sells travel books and maps and offers a good selection on local history and Native American cultures.

Southwest Memorial Hospital (☎ 970-565-6666; 1311 N Mildred Rd) Provides emergency services.

Sights & Activities

CROW CANYON ARCHAEOLOGY CENTER

The **center** (☎ 970-565-8975, 800-422-8975; www.crow canyon.org; 23390 Rd K; adult/child $50/25; ☷ 9am-5pm Wed & Thu Jun–mid-Sep), about 3 miles north of Cortez, offers a day-long educational program that visits an excavation site west of town. Programs teach the significance of regional artifacts and are an excellent way to learn about Ancestral Puebloan culture first-hand.

CORTEZ COLORADO UNIVERSITY CENTER & MUSEUM

Exhibits on the Ancestral Puebloans, as well as visiting art displays, make this **museum** (☎ 702-565-1151; 25 N Market St; admission free; ☷ 10am-9pm Mon-Sat May-Oct, to 5pm Nov-Apr) worthy of a visit if you have a few hours to spare.

Its **Cultural Park** is an outdoor space where Ute, Navajo and Hopi tribe members share their stories with visitors through dance and craft demonstrations.

Summer evening programs feature Native American dances six nights a week at 7:30pm, followed at 8:30pm by cultural programs that often feature Native American storytellers.

MOUNTAIN BIKING

The Four Corners area around Cortez offers some epic mountain-bike trails among piñon-juniper woodland and over the other-worldly 'slickrock' mesa. The dispersed sites at Hovenweep National Monument (p418) are ideal riding destinations. In fact, the roads are slightly better suited for biking than driving.

A good ride begins at the Sand Canyon archaeological site west of Cortez and follows a downhill trail west for 18 miles to Cannonball Mesa near the state line. If you're looking for a shorter ride, at the 8-mile mark the Burro Point overlook of Yellow Jacket and Burro Canyons is a good place to turn back. Test your skills riding the 27-mile **Stoner Mesa Loop**, a challenging intermediate to expert ride beginning with 8 miles of paved road along the west fork of the Dolores River. The tough part comes during the 7-mile dirt-road climb (you'll gain nearly 2000 feet in elevation) to the top of Stoner Mesa. When you reach the top, though, the views are splendid, and you'll be rewarded with a long, mellow downhill through amazing forests of aspens and open meadows. The last 2 miles are the most technical, consisting of an endless number of tight switchbacks and rock and root steps that take you down to the trailhead in a steep descent. Stoner Mesa is most beautiful in fall, when the aspens add a golden glow to the ride.

Pick up a copy of *Mountain and Road Bike Routes for the Cortez-Dolores-Mancos area*, available at the Colorado Welcome Center (left) and at local chambers of commerce. It provides maps and profiles for several road and mountain-bike routes. The friendly staff at **Kokopelli Bike & Board** (☎ 970-565-4408; www .kokopellibike.com; 30 W Main St; per day $20) are happy to talk trail with riders, and also rent and repair mountain bikes. The rental price includes helmet, air pump, water bottle and tools. For some pre-trip planning, visit the shop's website. It has great trail descriptions.

Sleeping

Cortez has heaps of budget motels along its main drag, and rates and rooms pretty much look the same at most. In winter, prices drop by almost 50%.

Sand Canyon Inn (☎ 970-565-8562, 800-257-3699; 301 W Main St; r from $65; ☷ wi-fi) Smack in the center of town, this is a pleasant motel with a sundeck and laundry facilities. Rooms are spotless and quite large, with a table and chairs. It's pet friendly. Guests receive 10% off at nearby Nero's Italian Restaurant.

Tomahawk Lodge (☎ 970-565-8521, 800-643-7705; www.angelfire.com/co2/tomahawk; 728 S Broadway; r from $65; ⊠) Friendly hosts welcome you at this clean, good-value place. It feels more personable than the average motel with unique Native American art on the walls. A few rooms allow pets.

Best Western Turquoise Inn and Suites (☎ 970-565-3778; www.bestwestern.com; 535 E Main St; r from $80; ⊠ ⚗) With two swimming pools to keep the young ones entertained, this is a good choice for families (kids stay free, and the restaurant has a kiddy menu). Rooms here are spacious, and bigger families can grab a two-room suite. If you're exploring Mesa Verde all day and just want an affordable and clean, if slightly bland, hotel to crash at night this comfortably laid out Best Western will do the trick.

Kelly Place Bed & Breakfast Lodge and Cabins (☎ 970-565-3125; www.kellyplace.com; 14663 Montezuma County Rd; r & cabins $80-175; ▣) This unique adobe-style guest lodge is situated on 40 acres of red rock canyon and Indian ruins 15 miles west of Cortez. Founded by a well-respected local botanist, the late George Kelly, the place still has fabulous orchards. Rooms are tasteful and rates include a full hot buffet breakfast. We like the adobe cabins, especially the one with a private flagstone patio and whirlpool tub. Kelly Place also offers horseback riding, cultural tours and archaeological programs. At night put a DVD on the big-screen TV in the communal lounge and chill with a glass of wine or a tasty microbrew – the lodge serves both.

Eating & Drinking

Tequila's Mexican Restaurant (☎ 970-565-6868; 1740 E Main St; mains $4-10; ⏰ lunch & dinner) Good-tasting food at bargain prices, that's what draws the crowds to Tequila's on any given night. The restaurant serves the usual Americanized Mexican staples, but does a great job with these. The chicken *mole*, seafood tacos and *carne asada* have all been declared excellent by more than one diner, as have the margaritas made with fresh lime juice. Expect to wait for a table on weekends.

Main Street Brewery & Restaurant (☎ 970-544-9112; 21 E Main St; mains $8-15; ⏰ lunch & dinner) The excellent German-style house-brewed beers are listed on the wall, right next to the cheery hand-painted murals at this cozy place. The large menu features everything from Southwestern cuisine to Mexican and Italian and includes the requisite burgers and pizzas. After dinner kick it up a notch in the downstairs game room, where you can enjoy a beer and some billiards.

Nero's Italian Restaurant (☎ 970-565-7366; 303 W Main St; mains $12-20; ⏰ dinner Mon-Sat) This solid Italian restaurant serves tasty food in intimate environs. The menu is extensive, offering all sorts of pasta, meat and poultry dishes. Eat between 5pm and 6pm to receive the reduced-price early-bird special.

Dry Dock Lounge & Restaurant (☎ 970-564-9404; 200 W Main St; mains $15; ⏰ lunch & dinner) Southwestern cuisine and lots of pasta and seafood are served in a ship-themed casual atmosphere. The menu is large and varied and offers a couple of lighter fare choices.

Getting There & Around

Cortez Municipal Airport (☎ 970-565-7458) is served by **United Express** (www.united.com), which has daily flights to Denver. The airport is 2 miles south of town off US 160/666.

Cortez is easier to reach by car from Phoenix, AZ, or Albuquerque, NM, than from Denver (379 miles away by the shortest route). East of Cortez, US Hwy 160 passes Mesa Verde National Park on the way to Durango – the largest city in the region.

DOLORES

pop 1100 / elev 7000ft

Scenic Dolores, sandwiched between the walls of a narrow canyon of the same name, offers history buffs a hearty meal of Native American artifacts, fishers the best angling in the southwest and romantic couples a charming place to rest their heads.

Information

Anasazi Heritage Center (☎ 702-882-4811; 27501 Hwy 184; admission $3; ⏰ 9am-5pm Mar-Nov, to 4pm Dec-Feb) Three miles west of town, with hands-on exhibits including weaving, corn grinding, tree-ring analysis and an introduction to the way in which archaeologists examine potsherds.

Dolores Visitor Center (☎ 702-882-4018, 800-807-4712; 421 Railroad Ave; ⏰ 9am-5pm Mon-Fri) Housed in a replica of the town's old railroad depot, it has regional information on lodging and outdoor activities.

Activities

Dolores is home to **McPhee Lake**, the second-largest body of water in Colorado. Covering

4470 surface acres and 50 miles of shoreline stretching north and west of town, McPhee Lake is one of the top fishing spots in the San Juan basin. Located in a canyon of the Dolores River, McPhee offers many angling spots accessible only by boat. In the lake's skinny, tree-lined side canyons, wakeless boating zones have been established to allow for awesome still-water fishing without the buzz and disturbance of motor craft. Talk about getting away from it all. With the best catch ratio in all of southwest Colorado – according to the state division of wildlife – it's a great place to teach younger anglers. Plus the surrounding mountain scenery is easy on the eye. Make sure you have a valid Colorado fishing license.

Sleeping & Eating

If you want to camp, you can find out about nearby sites in the San Juan National Forest from the USDA Forest Service (USFS) **Dolores Ranger Station** (☎ 970-882-7296; cnr 6th St & Central Ave; ⏲8am-5pm Mon-Fri). Otherwise, the **Dolores River RV Park** (☎ 970-882-7761; 18680 Railroad Ave; campsites $12, RV sites $20), located about 1.5 miles east of town, has pleasant sites.

Outpost Motel (☎ 970-882-7271, 800-382-4892; 1800 Central Ave; s/d $60/70, cabins $125) At the east end of town, it has small but clean rooms, as well as cabins. Some rooms have kitchenettes and the courtyard features a pleasant little wooden deck overlooking the Dolores River. The motel also takes RVs.

Rio Grande Southern Hotel (☎ 866-882-3026; www .rgshotel.com; 101 S Fifth St; r $80-100) By far the best sleeping option in town; step back in time at this graceful National Historic Landmark, where Norman Rockwell prints and an old-world front desk beckon guests. A cozy library and antique-filled guestrooms add to the charm. Bedrooms are small, but all four units are multiroom suites, so there's enough legroom. Try for Room 4, where Zane Gray is rumored to have stayed while writing *Riders of the Purple Sage*. A full breakfast is included.

Historic Rio Grande Southern Restaurant (mains $5-15; ⏲breakfast & lunch daily, dinner Wed-Sat) Onsite to the hotel, this is a good eating bet, regardless of whether you are here to sleep. Under the domain of Dolores' former mayor turned chef, Tommy Lux, it offers a solid a la carte American menu and does weekly specials including a fish fry and Chicago pizza night.

Old Germany Restaurant, Lounge & Beer Garden (☎ 702-882-7549; 200 S 8th St; mains $9-15; ⏲dinner Tue-Sat). For something other than the typical American pub grub a lot of restaurants serve, Old Germany has been dishing up platters of bratwurst and Wiener schnitzel for more than 20 years. Repeat customers swear it's the best German food in the region, and portions are large and fairly priced.

Getting There & Away

Dolores is 11 miles north of Cortez on Hwy 145, also known as Railroad Ave.

SAN JUAN SKYWAY

Drive the San Juan Skyway in late September or early October, when the aspen trees glow yellow, when there's a hint of snow and pine and cedar in the crisp air, and you'll feel your stress drift right out the window. Life's day-to-day tensions will get lost somewhere among the towering peaks, picturesque towns and old mines around each bend, or melt into the bright sun and intensely blue Colorado sky.

The 236-mile route takes you to the top of the world as it twists and turns past a series of 'fourteeners' (a Colorado term for peaks exceeding 14,000ft). The present blends into the past as you descend through rotting mines and ghost towns where time has worn away the surface, leaving just the shell behind. The air is heavy with history. Places like Telluride (below), Durango (p386) and Silverton (p405) tell a thousand colorful yarns of yesteryear, while an air of mystery and intrigue lingers over the ancestral homes of the Ancestral Puebloans at Mesa Verde (p391). The San Juan Skyway leads you past bubbling rapids ripe for rafting and quiet fishing spots on the Animas River. Bluegrass, jazz and folk music provide a summer soundtrack, when local towns host renowned festivals.

From Ridgeway follow US 550 south to Ouray and then over Red Mountain Pass to Silverton. Continue heading south of US 550 until you hit Durango. From here, you can head west on US 160 to the ruins at Mesa Verde, then head north on Rte 145 toward Telluride before following Rte 62 back to Ridgeway. To drive the entire byway, allow at least one or two days.

TELLURIDE

pop 2000 / elev 8750ft

It's been a hunting ground for the Utes, a mining mecca and a ghost town. But nowadays, folks flock to this archetypal mountain

TELLURIDE'S FABULOUS FESTIVALS

Telluride has two giant festivals each year. The wild, eclectic and totally tribal-feeling **Telluride Bluegrass Festival** (☎ 800-624-2422; www.bluegrass.com/telluride; 4-day pass $175) in late June sells out months in advance and attracts thousands for a weekend of top-notch rollicking bluegrass in a fantastic outdoor setting. It's one hell of a party, and one of those truly Colorado experiences that should be experienced at least once. The music line-up changes each year. Arrive early to scope out a grassy spot and set up the blanket and picnic basket. Stalls sell all sorts of food and local microbrews to keep you happy. When the sun goes down revelers kick it up a notch, dancing wildly to the day's most anticipated acts. Many folks choose to camp, and during the festival all nearby campgrounds require a concert pass to park your tent. The closest campgrounds, Telluride Town Park Campground (p400) and Warner Field – the big grassy area in the center of town, you can't miss it – which are within walking distance of the venue and close enough to hear the music, fill up first and cost $50 per person for a four-day pass (again, you must buy your camping pass way in advance to score a spot). If these options are sold out, you can camp at **Ilium Campground** (☎ 970-327-4261), a beautiful site on the river 7 miles west of Telluride that costs $45 per person including frequent shuttle service between the campsite and festival. There are numerous other campgrounds within 15 miles of Telluride that cost between $6 and $12 per site. All campgrounds fill up quickly during festival week, so arrive early. Tickets and camping passes can be purchased on the festival website, which, considering how quickly the festival sells out, is the first place to visit.

Telluride hosts the lesser-known – but locally more popular for that very reason – **Telluride Blues & Brews Festival** (www.tellurideblues.com) over a weekend in September. Dance to blues, funk, rock and gospel while sampling homegrown beers from 50 microbreweries during the Saturday grand tasting. At night, the festivities move into town, where spontaneous late-night jam sessions are known to break out at popular saloons.

Telluride's other major blow-out event is the increasingly popular and esteemed **Telluride Film Festival** (☎ 603-433-9202; www.telluridefilmfestival.com; admission $20-650; 🕑 early Sep). National and international films are premiered at venues throughout the town, and the event attracts big-name stars. The only way to guarantee you'll see your first-choice film is to purchase a pass. These start at $325 and include priority entrance to numerous screenings. Admission to individual films costs $20, but these tickets are only made available right before show time and passholders get first dibs. For more information on the relatively complicated pricing scheme visit the festival website.

town for outdoor adventures galore, fantastic festivals and an all-round laid-back feel. Easy on the eye, Telluride boasts not only a well-preserved Victorian downtown but also picture-perfect Colorado mountain views and a mellow vibe to match.

Orientation & Information

Colorado Ave, also known as Main St, is where you'll find most of the restaurants, bars and shops. The town's small size means you can get everywhere on foot, so leave your car at the intercept parking lot at the south end of Mahoney Dr (near the visitor center) or wherever you are staying.

From town you can reach the ski mountain via two lifts and the gondola. The latter also links Telluride with Mountain Village, the true base for the Telluride ski area.

Located 7 miles from town along Hwy 145, Mountain Village is a 20-minute drive east, but only 12 minutes away by gondola (free for foot passengers).

Ajax Peak, a glacial headwall, rises up behind the town to form the end of the U-shaped valley that contains Telluride. To the right (or south) on Ajax Peak, Colorado's highest waterfall, Bridal Veil Falls, cascades 365ft down; a switchback trail leads to a restored Victorian powerhouse atop the falls.

Bookworks (☎ 970-728-0700; 191 S Pine St) The town's biggest bookstore.

Telluride Medical Center (☎ 970-728-3848; 500 W Pacific Ave) Handles skiing accidents, medical problems and emergencies.

Telluride Sports (☎ 970-728-4477; 150 W Colorado Ave) Has topographical and USFS maps, sporting supplies and outdoor information.

Visitor center (☎ 970-728-3041, 800-525-3455; www
.telluride.com; 398 W Colorado Ave; 🕑 9am-5pm Mon-
Sat) Has loads of area information.

Activities

SKIING

Covering three distinct areas, **Telluride Ski Resort**
(☎ 970-728-6900, 866-287-5015; www.tellurideskiresort
.com; lift tickets $70) is served by 16 lifts. Much of
the terrain is for advanced and intermediate
skiers, but there's still ample choice for beginners. Locals say the best expert run is the
Plunge; try it if you're up for a truly hair-rising
descent. After a day on the mountain, head to
the Chair 8 Bar (p400) for après-ski drinks.

There are public cross-country trails in
Town Park, as well as along the San Miguel
River and the Telluride Valley floor west of
town. Instruction and rentals are available
from the **Telluride Nordic Center** (☎ 970-728-1114;
800 E Colorado Ave). Experienced Nordic skiers will
appreciate the **San Juan Hut System** (☎ 970-626-
3033; www.sanjuanhuts.com; huts per night $25), a series
of crude huts along a 206-mile route stretching from Telluride west to Moab in Utah. In
the summer these huts, which are equipped
with bunks and cooking facilities, are popular
with mountain bikers. Book well in advance,
as space goes quickly.

MOUNTAIN BIKING

Mountain biking is big news in Telluride. The
surrounding peaks offer awesome single-track
routes and, of course, stupendous scenery.

Beginners should try the easy and smooth
gravel **River Trail** that connects Town Park with
Hwy 145 for a total trail distance of about 2
miles. If you want a bit more of a workout,
continue up **Mill Creek Trail**, west of the Texaco
gas station near where the River Trail ends.
After the initial climb, the trail follows the
contour of the mountain and ends at the Jud
Wiebe Trail (hikers only), where you'll have
to turn back. To rent some gear, visit **Easy Rider
Mountain Sports** (☎ 970-728-4734; 101 W Colorado Ave),
which has a variety of bikes to choose from,
as well as maps and information.

HIKING

The **Bear Creek Trail** is slightly more than 2
miles and ascends 1040ft to a beautiful cas-
cading waterfall. From here, you can access
the strenuous **Wasatch Trail**, a 12-mile loop that
heads west across the mountains to **Bridal Veil
Falls** – Telluride's most impressive landmark.
The Bear Creek trailhead is at the south end
of Pine St, across the San Miguel River.

Sleeping

Telluride's lodging can fill quickly, and for the
best rates it's best to book online. Unless you're
planning to camp, however, don't expect much
in the budget category. Telluride's activities and
festivals keep it busy year-round.

Matterhorn Campground (☎ 970-327-4261; Hwy
145; campsites $10-14, vehicle pass $6; 🕑 mid-May–mid-
Sep) Ten miles south of Telluride, this USFS
campground has well-maintained sites as well

BARGAIN-BASEMENT HELI-SKIING

Heli-skiing is no longer reserved solely for the Richard Bransons of the adventure world. Thanks
to a new trip by **Telluride Helitrax** (☎ 970-728-8377; www.helitrax.net), even backpackers can afford
the thrill of riding virgin powder above the tree line. Called the Bear Creek Descent, this guided
trip ($285) is affordable – heli-skiing can cost into the thousands for a single day – because it
makes use of a remote, yet easily accessible, area right outside town accessed via a single lift
in the chopper.

One's all you need, though. After the bird leaves you hovering at 13,200ft on a ridge of Silver
Mountain, take a few minutes to admire the views around you – you'll be able to see nine
'fourteeners' in Colorado and mountains as far away as Utah. Then it's time to get after it. The
guided 4300-vertical-foot descent takes you on an exhilarating – this an expert-only trip – ride
that flies into an alpine bowl, over a sheer face, down two couloirs and through the glades before
dropping you directly into downtown Telluride. Rates include the rental of extra-fat skis, which
allow you to cut through waist-high powder with ease. Snowboarders will need their own gear –
you'll definitely want to bring a wide powder board or you'll be sure to get stuck. The best
snow is usually found in April – a little late in the season, we know, but typical of Colorado.
Helitrax usually runs trips between January and May, but this varies depending on snow levels
and avalanche danger, so check the website.

as shower and toilet blocks. It's a good option if you arrive during a festival and other lodging options are full.

Telluride Town Park Campground (☎ 970-728-2173; 500 W Colorado Ave; campsites $11; ⊙ mid-May–mid-Sep) Right in the center of town, it has 20 sites with shower access ($1.50 for a hot shower). It fills up quickly in the high season. There are many other campgrounds within 10 miles of town; check with the visitor center for more info.

Victorian Inn (☎ 970-728-6601; www.tellurideinn.com; 401 W Pacific Ave; r from $99; wi-fi) One of Telluride's better deals, it offers comfortable rooms (some with kitchenettes) plus a hot tub and dry sauna. Kids 12 and under stay free, and you can't beat the downtown location. A continental breakfast is included. Stay here from mid-November through December 20 and get $48 lift tickets. The Victorian offers $58 lift tickets (still a deal) for most of the rest of the season.

Hotel Columbia (☎ 970-728-0660; www.columbia telluride.com; r from $140; ❄) Each room at this charismatic place has a balcony, a fireplace and a mountain view. Bathrooms are larger than average and breakfast is included. Other highlights include a rooftop hot tub and fit-

ness room. Plus, the hotel is right across the street from the gondola and allows pets.

Inn at Lost Creek (☎ 970-728-5678; www.innatlost creek.com; 119 Lost Creek Lane, Mountain Village; r from $189; wi-fi) A boutique luxury hotel that manages to feel unpretentious and as comfortable as your own home. The Inn is perfectly poised at the bottom of Telluride's main lift, but despite the foot traffic outside, remains private. Service is personalized but not overbearing, and the rooms are impeccably decorated. Be sure to visit the two rooftop spas. Rates are reasonable value – check the website for packages.

Camel's Garden (☎ 970-728-9300; www.camelsgar den.com; 250 W San Juan; r from $275; ❄ wi-fi) This modern and luxurious choice is located at the base of the gondola. The lobby is filled with local artwork and the large rooms feature custom-crafted furniture and Italian marble bathrooms with oversized tubs. Don't miss the giant 25ft hot tub on the top level. The complex also features restaurants, bars and spa treatments – the Chair 8 Bar is a favorite with the après-ski crowd. You may be able to find a deal at this pricey place by booking through a consolidator like www.hotels.com.

Eating

Telluride's main street is packed with bars and eateries.

Baked in Telluride (☎ 970-728-4775; 127 S Fir St; mains $6-10; ⊙ 5:30am-10pm) A Telluride institution for the last 25 years, this is where everyone now heads for a fill-up on pizza, sandwiches, salads and calzones. The front deck is where to sit if you're looking to see or be seen, and the atmosphere is more than casual.

Excelsior Café (☎ 970-728-4250; 200 W Colorado Ave; mains $16-40; ⊙ dinner) One of Telluride's hottest restaurants, Excelsior gets rave reviews for its Parisian café meets jazzy wine-bar feel – exposed brick walls, low lights, bold art and comfortable couches are all decor rigueur. The menu is all over the board and includes everything from Moroccan lamb chops to Montana buffalo short ribs. If you don't have loads of cash, try the less expensive bar menu. It still offers plenty of tantalizing choices and gives you the opportunity to experience great wine, ambience and people-watching over the main street.

221 South Oak (☎ 970-728-9505; 221 S Oak St; mains $19-25; ⊙ dinner; Ⓥ) This is an intimate restaurant in a historic home, with a small but innovative menu mixing world flavors and yielding

---

TOP 10 TELLURIDE

- **Best Place for Pizza on the Porch**
  Baked in Telluride (right)

- **Best Martini**
  Cosmopolitan (opposite)

- **Best Late-Night Bar**
  Last Dollar Saloon (opposite)

- **Best Place to Drink Beer and Eat Wings**
  Smugglers Brewpub & Grille (opposite)

- **Best Ski Run**
  The Plunge, Telluride Ski Resort (p399)

- **Best Place to Play Pool and Pick Up People**
  New Sheridan Bar (opposite)

- **Best Après-Ski Bar** Chair 8 Bar, Camel's Garden (right)

- **Best Appetizer**
  Excelsior Café (right)

- **Best Place to Hear Live Music**
  Fly Me to the Moon Saloon (opposite)

- **Best Adrenaline-Pumping Adventure**
  Helicopter skiing with Helitrax (p399)

DETOUR: RICO

Check out Colorado's last frontier town, tiny Rico, an old mining haunt that refused to go bust after the gold ran dry. With a population of just 200, Rico is one of the state's last true Wild West towns. Visit in summer for fabulous fishing along the Dolores River (which conveniently runs through town). Anglers score big with cutthroat, rainbow and brown trout. You can also hike the 9-mile loop from the top of Lizard Head Pass to the base of Lizard Head Peak (check out www .fs.fed.us/r2/sanjuan for more on this hike), a crumbling 13,113ft tower of rock.

You can get grub and catch some shut-eye at the **Rico Hotel Mountain Lodge** (☎ 970-967-3000; www.ricohotel.com; 124 S Hwy 145; r incl breakfast $80), which offers comfortable rooms in a refurbished miners' boarding house. The on-site Argentine Grille serves delicious beef tenderloin tacos with mango, chile and cilantro. At night, unwind in the hot tub.

Rico is 40 miles north of Durango in Colorado's southwest corner. It is best reached by private vehicle.

---

excellent results. Dishes are meat, fish and seafood based with lots of fresh vegetables. A vegetarian menu is available upon request.

Cosmopolitan (☎ 970-728-1292; 300 W San Juan Ave; dishes from $20; ☽ dinner) Can you resist a menu that includes Himalayan yak rib eye and lobster corn dogs? Chef Chad Scothorn has won numerous awards for his culinary aptitude. Influenced by the cuisines of France, the Southwest and Thailand, the menu changes weekly – although some chef favorites are pretty much house staples – and the food is consistently delicious. Choose from more than 200 bottles of wine to complement your meal.

Drinking

Last Dollar Saloon (☎ 970-728-4800; 100 E Colorado Ave) For a splash of local color with your cocktail, head to this long-time town favorite. With the best selection of imported beers in town, as well as pool tables and darts, it's no wonder this creaky wooden bar is so popular.

Fly Me to the Moon Saloon (☎ 970-728-6666; 132 E Colorado Ave) Let your hair down and kick up your heels to the tunes of live music at the Fly Me to the Moon Saloon, the best place in Telluride to groove. During music-festival weekends, it's not unusual for bands to pop in here and play spontaneous late-night jam sessions and sip pints of locally made brews.

Smugglers Brewpub & Grille (☎ 970-728-0919; 225 South Pine St) Beer lovers will feel right at home at casual Smugglers, a great place to hang out in any season. With at least seven beers on tap, this brewpub is big on variety. And with the pint of the day only $2 between 3pm and 5pm, you can afford to sample the best it has. Food wise, it's known for its wings, and strangely, kids' menu.

New Sheridan Bar (☎ 970-728-3911; 231 W Colorado Ave) Most of this historic bar survived the waning mining fortunes even as the adjoining hotel was busy selling off chandeliers and finely carved furnishings to help pay the heating bills. These days, overdressed visitors occupy stools and chat about upcoming film releases next to the old-timers or young hippy girls – locals like to start their evenings here.

Getting There & Around

Commuter aircraft serve the mesa-top **Telluride Airport** (☎ 970-778-5051; www.tellurideairport.com), 5 miles east of town – weather permitting. At other times planes fly into Montrose, 65 miles north. **Telluride Express** (☎ 970-728-6000; www.tellu rideexpress.com) runs shuttles to Montrose airport (adult/child $42/20); call to arrange pick-up.

RIDGEWAY

pop 720 / elev 6895ft

More than a few classic Westerns were shot in and around this enticing 19th-century railway town, including *How the West Was Won* and *True Grit*. But don't let the rustic vibe fool you: Ridgeway has its share of swanky ranches, including one owned by fashion designer Ralph Lauren.

Fishing aficionados should head to **Ridgeway State Park & Recreation Area** (☎ 970-626-5822; 2855 US 550; admission free; ☽ dawn-dusk), 12 miles north of town. The reservoir here is stocked with loads of rainbow trout, as well as German brown, kokanee, yellow perch and the occasional large-mouth bass. There are also hiking trails and campsites.

The Southwestern adobe-style **Chipeta Sun Lodge & Spa** (☎ 970-626-3737; www.chipeta.com; 304

S Lena St; r from $160) is the best sleeping option. Rooms feature hand-painted Mexican tiles, rough-hewn log beds and decks with a view. It's very classy and upmarket, and there are wonderful public areas on the property. Have a read in the Great Room or a chat in the solarium, or head out to the hot tubs on the property for a quiet soak. The onsite spa features treatments developed by the Ute Indians and daily yoga classes. Check Chipeta's website for ski, soak and stay deals, where you can ride the slopes at Telluride, soak in the hot springs pools in Ouray and spend the night in Ridgeway.

Scenes from the movie *True Grit* were filmed at the appropriately named **True Grit** (☎ 970-626-5739; 123 N Lena Ave; mains $8-15; ⏰ lunch & dinner). This popular neighborhood pub is a kind of shrine to John Wayne, with his pictures and memorabilia hung on the walls. Burgers, sandwiches and tasty chicken fried steaks are on the menu.

Ridgeway is at the crossroads of US 550 and Rte 62 and a good spot from which to start a circular drive on the San Juan Skyway (see p397).

BLACK CANYON OF THE GUNNISON NATIONAL PARK

If the Four Corners region has whetted your appetite for Colorado's splendors and you're craving a bigger bite, then head to the elusive **Black Canyon of the Gunnison National Park** (☎ 970-249-1915; www.nps.gov/blca; 7-day admission per vehicle $8). Here a dark, narrow gash above the Gunnison River leads down a 2000ft-deep chasm that's as eerie as it is spectacular. No other canyon in America combines the narrow openings, sheer walls and dizzying depths of the Black Canyon, and a peek over the edge evokes a sense of awe (and vertigo) for most. Head to the 6-mile-long South Rim Rd, which takes you to 11 overlooks at the edge of the canyon, some reached via short trails up to 1.5 miles long (round trip). To challenge your senses, cycle along the smooth pavement running parallel to the rim's 2000ft drop-off. You definitely get a better feel for the place than if you're trapped in a car.

Mountain climbers can get their kicks in Black Canyon, although you'll need to know what you are doing and have your own equipment – this is not a place for beginners. Routes

IF YOU'VE GOT A FEW EXTRA DAYS IN COLORADO

So you've covered the southwestern corner of the state, but the place has entranced you so much you're just not quite ready to leave. If you're keen to explore a little further, much of the rest of the state (with the exception of the eastern plains: sorry, but they just can't compete with the adventure-laden mountains) is equally fabulous. Following are a few favorite destinations.

Aspen

Home to great skiing and beautiful alpine scenery, Aspen is Colorado's glitziest high-octane resort and plays host to some of the wealthiest skiers in the world – where else in Colorado can you shop at Prada or Gucci? The scenery, especially in the fall when the trees put on a spectacular display, is just extra-sugary eye-candy. The historic town is charming, and the rock stars that vacation here must like to party, because the bars are happening. Aspen is 150 miles southwest of Denver on Hwy 82.

Boulder

Tree-hugging hippies, Trustafarians, well-heeled young professionals and hard-drinking college kids give this town its unique, independent vibe. A long way from the conservative mindset found in much of Colorado, residents here take pride in saying they live in the 'People's Republic of Boulder.' The city has an ongoing love affair with the outdoors, and you'll see a constant slew of mountain bikers pedaling the main roads. Hang out on the pedestrian-only Pearl St Mall – packed with boutiques, restaurants and bars – and catch a street performance. Down a pint or two at one of the microbreweries or grab an inner tube and float down Boulder Creek on a hot summer day. Despite the city's reputation for partying, those not interested in overindulgence won't feel at odds. There are family-friendly places to sleep and eat, intimate dining options for that special night and loads of quiet hiking trails for afternoon escapes. Plus, the are not well charted, and even the easier climbs are still multipitch traditional routes in remote areas of the canyon.

If you are an experienced climber, this is your playground. The Black Canyon is home to Colorado's tallest vertical cliff, **Painted Wall**, measuring 2250ft from the bottom of the canyon and named for its fabulous marble stripes. There are a number of different climbing routes to the top of Painted Wall. Check the website for updates – when we visited, some routes were closed due to nesting raptors (it's a national park, so the animals should, and do, come first here). Most of the climbing in the park takes on the North and South Chasms, which measure 1820ft. For more info on specific routes and difficulty levels, visit the park's excellent website. The best literature on climbing in the park is *Black Canyon Rock Climbs* by Robbie Williams.

For a surrealistic experience, visit Black Canyon's South Rim in winter. The stillness of the snow-drenched plateau is broken only by the icy roar of the river at the bottom of the canyon, far, far below.

The park is 12 miles east of the US 550 junction on US 50. Exit at Hwy 347 – well marked with a big brown sign for the national park – and head north for 7 miles.

CRESTED BUTTE
pop 1500 / elev 8885ft

In a valley ringed by three wilderness areas, remote and beautiful Crested Butte is void of pretension. Despite being one of Colorado's best ski resorts (some say *the* best), it doesn't put on airs. There's nothing haughty, or even glossy, about the town – just lovely fresh mountain air, a laid-back attitude and friendly folk. During winter, it's all about the skiing on Mt Crested Butte, the conical mountain, strangely positioned in the centre of the valley floor. But during summer the wildflowers rule the grasslands around this charming hamlet – so much so that the Colorado State Senate officially recognized the town as the state's wildflower capital!

Most everything in town is on Elk Ave, including the **visitor center** (☎ 970-349-6438; www.crestedbuttechamber.com; 601 Elk Ave; ⊗ 9am-5pm).

---

ever-popular Rocky Mountain National Park is an easy day-trip away. Boulder is 30 miles north of Denver on Hwy 36.

Breckenridge
This resort town has a 19th-century mining feel and is full of young people looking to party (many migrate to 'Breck' after university to spend a few years 'ski bumming'). In fact the motto seems to be 'ride hard all day, drink hard all night.' But it's also a great place to bring the family. There's beginner terrain at the ski resort, the restaurants are kid-friendly and many hotels offer babysitting services. With four of Colorado's best snow-riding resorts less than an hour's drive away, Breckenridge, 80 miles west of Denver off I-70, makes an ideal regional base.

Colorado Springs
A very popular family vacation spot, Colorado's second-largest city sits in a picture-perfect location below famous Pikes Peak. It's a rather bizarre amalgam of evangelical conservatives, tourists and military installations, but it offers loads of tourist activities. Take a stroll through Garden of the Gods, with its towering red rock spires; ride the cog railroad to the top of Pikes Peak, where Katherine Lee Bates was inspired to write *America the Beautiful;* or wander the streets of historic Manitou Springs, home to scores of New Age shops and even a penny arcade. Colorado Springs is on I-25, 60 miles south of Denver.

Glenwood Springs
Located just outside a spectacular canyon, Glenwood Springs is a pleasurable place to kick up your heels. Aside from its world-famous hot springs, it offers tip-top road and mountain biking and loads of hiking trails. In the summer, raft Glenwood Canyon's Class III to IV white-water. The town is 150 miles west of Denver on I-70.

Activities

Crested Butte Mountain Resort (☎ 970-349-2333; www.skicb.com; lift ticket $70) sits 2 miles north of the town at the base of the impressive mountain of the same name. Surrounded by forests, towering pistes and the West Elk, Raggeds and Maroon Bells-Snowmass Wilderness Areas, the scenery is wet-your-pants beautiful. It caters mostly to intermediate and expert riders.

Crested Butte is also a mountain-biking mecca, full of excellent high-altitude singletrack trails. For maps, information and mountain-bike rentals visit the **Alpineer** (☎ 970-349-5210; 419 6th St).

Sleeping

Crested Butte International Hostel (☎ 970-349-0588; www.crestedbuttehostel.com; 615 Teocalli Ave; dm $25-38, r $65-95; 💻) If you're looking for the privacy of a hotel with the lively ambience of a hostel, then grab a room at this attractive hostel. The nicest private rooms have private bathrooms. Dorm bunks come with reading lamps and lockable drawers. The communal area is mountain rustic with a stone fireplace and comfortable couches. Rates vary dramatically by season, with fall being cheapest.

Elevation Hotel & Spa (☎ 970-349-2222; www.skicb.com; 500 Gothic Rd, Mt Crested Butte; r from $200; 🏊 💻 wi-fi) If you're more swank than budget, try this newly renovated hotel at the base of Crested Butte Ski Resort. Located just steps from a major chairlift, this hip and classy place offers oversized rooms and it's right by one of the main lifts, so you can ski back to your modern country-western abode. The appropriately named Atmosphere Restaurant is a trendy place to grab a meal, while the hotel's slope-side deck is the spot to drink a beer next to the fire pit and watch the snowboarders whiz by. Elevation is one of a number of hotels run by the ski resort. Be sure to check online for specials – during the beginning and end of the season ski-and-stay deals can go for as low as $109 per person.

Eating & Drinking

Cheap meals are served at the pleasant **Paradise Café** (☎ 970-349-6233; cnr 4th St & Elk Ave; mains $4-7; 🕑 breakfast & lunch).

Certainly not a secret, the **Secret Stash** (☎ 970-349-6245; 21 Elk Ave; mains $8-20; 🕑 5-9pm) is by far the most happening restaurant in Crested Butte, loved by locals. This enticing pizza and calzone joint has a hip interior where you can either sit on the floor upstairs or park yourself in a velvety chair on the lower level and catch up on all the gossip.

Crested Butte has an interesting music scene year-round. Check out the lively **Eldo** (☎ 970-349-6125; 215 Elk Ave), the town's stand-by bar of choice for locals and tourists alike. It does double duty as a microbrewery and a club, and is the spot where out-of-town acts play. Escape the chaos inside on the fabulous outside deck overlooking the main street below. The **Princess Wine Bar** (☎ 970-349-0210; 218 Elk St) is another good bet. It's an intimate joint, perfect for sitting and chatting. First-rate live music of the local singer-songwriter flavor is on show nightly.

Getting There & Away

Crested Butte's air link to the outside world is **Gunnison County Airport** (☎ 970-641-2304), located 28 miles south of the town. The **Alpine Express** (☎ 970-641-5074) shuttle bus meets all commercial flights in winter but requires reservations in summer. The fare to Crested Butte is $25.

The free **Mountain Express** (☎ 970-349-7318) connects Crested Butte with Mt Crested Butte every 15 minutes in winter, less often in other seasons; check times at bus stops.

By car, the trip from Ouray to Crested Butte takes a little less than three hours.

OURAY & THE MILLION DOLLAR HWY

pop 840 / elev 7760ft

No matter how many times you visit, Ouray's views slam you in the face every time. Sandwiched between imposing peaks, tiny Ouray just might be that little bit of paradise John Denver waxes lyrical about in *Rocky Mountain High*. Here the mountains don't just tower over you, they actually embrace you – the peaks leave barely a quarter-mile of valley floor in town!

Between Silverton and Ouray, US 550 is known as the Million Dollar Hwy because the roadbed fill contains valuable ore. One of the state's most memorable drives, it's a breathtaking stretch of pavement that passes old mine head-frames and larger-than-life alpine scenery – at some points the spectacular peaks are so close they seem ready to grab you. The road is scary when raining or snowing, so take extra care.

Information

The **visitor center** (☎ 970-325-4746; www.ouraycolorado.com; 1220 Main St; 🕑 9am-5pm) is at the hot-springs pool.

Sights & Activities

Ouray's stunning scenery isn't the only ace up the town's sleeve. For a healing soak, try the **Ouray Hot Springs** (☎ 970-325-4638; 1220 Main St; admission $9; ☺ 10am-10pm Jun-Aug, hours vary rest of yr). The crystal-clear natural spring water is free of the sulfur smells plaguing other hot springs around here, and the giant pool features a variety of soaking areas at temperatures from 96°F to 106°F. It is definitely one of the nicest public mineral springs in the region.

Climbing the face of a frozen waterfall can be a sublime experience. Head to the **Ouray Ice Park** (☎ 970-325-4061; www.ourayicepark.com; admission free; ☺ 7am-5pm mid-Dec–March) to try it yourself. This park spans a 2-mile stretch of the Uncompagre Gorge that has been dedicated to public ice climbing. The park is the world's first, and draws enthusiasts from around the globe to try their hand at climbs for all skill levels. For information on its festival, see below. **San Juan Mountain Guides** (☎ 970-325-4925; www.ourayclimbing.com; 2-day courses from $320) offers a weekend two-day introduction course. All equipment is included, but check out the website for dates. If you already know your stuff and just need to pick up gear, stop by **Ouray Mountain Sports** (☎ 970-325-4284; 722 Main St).

Festivals & Events

Ouray Ice Festival (☎ 970-325-4288; www.ourayicefestival.com) is held in January each year. This festival features four days of climbing competitions, dinners, slide shows and clinics. You can watch the competitions for free, but to check out the evening events you'll need to make a $15 donation to the ice park. Once inside you'll get free brews from popular Colorado microbrewer New Belgium.

Sleeping

Some of Ouray's lodges are destinations within themselves.

Amphitheater Forest Service Campground (☎ 877-444-6777; US 550; campsites $12) A mile south of town, this USFS campground has pleasant tent sites.

Historic Western Hotel, Restaurant & Saloon (☎ 970-325-4645; www.historicwesternhotel.com; 210 7th Ave; r $35-95) Old Wild West meets Victorian charm at this place, one of the largest remaining wooden structures on Colorado's western slope. It offers rooms for all budgets; the cheapest have shared bathrooms. The open-air 2nd-floor veranda commands stunning views of the Uncompahgre Gorge, while the Old West Saloon serves affordable meals and all sorts of drinks in a timeless setting.

Box Canyon Lodge and Hot Springs (☎ 800-327-5-80, 970-325-4981; www.boxcanyonouray.com; 45 3rd Ave; s/d from $70/80) Offers geothermal heated rooms that are spacious and accommodating. The real treat here is four wooden spring-fed hot tubs for guests, perfect for a romantic stargazing soak.

Wiesbaden (☎ 970-325-4347; www.wiesbadenhotsprings.com; cnr 6th & 5th Aves; r from $130; 🐾) The best bit about slumbering at this posh hotel is that guests can use the fantastic natural indoor vapor cave for free. Rooms are cozy and romantic in a European ski-lodge style. Outside you'll find a selection of hot spring pools. Couples should rent the private, clothing-optional soaking tub with a waterfall – it can be reserved for $35 per hour. The onsite Aveda salon provides relaxing massages and soothing facials to make your mountain detox complete.

Beaumont Hotel (☎ 970-325-7000; www.beaumonthotel.com; 505 Main St; r $180-350) Ouray's classiest lodging option, this small hotel offers 12 rooms elegantly appointed with period furnishings. Established in 1886, the hotel was closed for more than 30 years before undergoing extensive renovations and reopening five years ago. It also boasts a spa and three unique boutiques.

Eating

Silver Nugget Café (☎ 970-325-4100; 746 Main St; mains $7-20; ☺ 8am-9pm) A busy, contemporary eatery in a historic building, Silver Nugget features a very large breakfast menu as well as deli-style sandwiches at lunch. Dinner offerings include deep-fried Rocky Mountain rainbow trout, and liver and onions.

Tundra Restaurant at the Beaumont (☎ 970-325-7040; 505 Main St; mains from $20; ☺ 5-10pm) This elegant restaurant has won several awards for its wine cellar and does Thursday-evening tasting. Billing itself as serving 'High Altitude' cuisine, it focuses on regional specialties with great results.

Getting There & Around

Ouray is 24 miles north of Silverton along US 550 and best reached by private vehicle.

SILVERTON

pop 550 / elev 9318ft

A dozen odd years ago, when the last mine shut down, it seemed Silverton was destined to fade away into history. And for a while it did: tourists riding the Durango & Silverton Narrow Gauge Railroad were greeted with long-abandoned storefronts and shabby restaurants. You'd hardly believe that today.

Silverton, with in-your-face mountains covered in blankets of aspens, is Colorado's best rediscovered vintage gem and definitely worth visiting. Whether you're into snowmobiling, biking, fly-fishing or just basking in the sunshine, Silverton delivers. Plus it's literally in the middle of nowhere.

Silverton is a two-street town, and only one of these is paved. The main drag is called Greene St; it's where you'll find most businesses. Blair St, still unpaved, runs parallel to Greene and is a blast from the past. During the silver rush, Blair St was considered 'notorious' and home to thriving brothels and boozing establishments.

Although Silverton is a tourist town by day in summer, once the final choo-choo departs it turns back to local turf. Visit in the middle of the winter for a real treat – only the most hard-core residents stick around, and you'll find many of the T-shirt shops, and even hotels and restaurants, board up come first snowfall. Snowmobiles become a main means of transportation, and Silverton turns into a winter adventure playground for intrepid travelers.

Information

The **Silverton Chamber of Commerce & Visitor Center** (☎ 970-387-5654; Hwys 550 & 110; ⏲ hours vary) provides information about the town.

Sights & Activities

To see the region from the open back of a truck (don't worry, there are seats), contact **Historic San Juan Tours** (☎ 970-387-5716; historicsanjuantours@earthlink.com; 1148 Empire St; adult/child from $35/25; ⏲ Mar–Nov). The company offers a variety of tours that take you over the top of 13,000ft peaks, past ghost towns and historic mines, and through meadows of wildflowers.

If you want to explore the area's numerous back roads on your own, **Triangle Jeep Rental** (☎ 970-387-9990; www.trianglejeeprental.com; 864 Greene St; per day $140) will provide you with a jeep, a map and operating instructions. They're also happy to talk routes and tailor a trip to your comfort level. Popular routes include four-wheeling over high mountain passes to the towns of Telluride (p397) or Ouray (p404).

Other trails take you past well-preserved ghost towns and near historic mines.

In the winter, **Silverton Mountain** (☎ 970-387-5706; www.silvertonmountain.com; per day $100), 6 miles from town on Hwy 110, is a playground for advanced and expert skiers. The new kid on the block, it offers guided-only high-elevation skiing. The facility is an innovative and unusual offering at a base of 10,400ft. Included in the price are a guide, avalanche beacons, probe poles and shovels. Again, you really need to know your stuff before heading out – the easiest terrain here is comparable to skiing double blacks at other resorts.

Sleeping & Eating

Silverton has about half a dozen hotels and around the same number of restaurants – although you'll be hard pressed to find food after 8pm even in the summertime (not even the gas station stays open).

Bent Elbow (☎ 970-387-5775; 1114 Blair St; r $50-100) Smack in the middle of town, this place stays open year-round. Each of the quaint, good-sized guestrooms is decorated slightly differently, but all feature a Western flavor. Locals say the restaurant (mains $6 to $12) has the best chef in town. It's a cheerful dining room with a gorgeous old wood shotgun bar that serves Western American fare. In winter, the Bent Elbow arranges snowmobiling, guided ice-climbing and dog-sledding trips on nearby Molas Pass, a pristine wilderness area.

Red Mountain Motel & RV Park (☎ 970-382-5512; www.redmtnmotelrvpk.com; 664 Greene St; cabins from $58, r $68). This pet-friendly place stays open year-round, rents jeeps for $130 per day and runs snowmobile tours in the winter. The micro log cabins (they really are tiny, especially if you try to sleep four) stay warm and cozy and make good use of their limited space – ours came with a double bed, a bunk, a tiny TV with HBO and even a fully outfitted little kitchenette. The river, with good fishing, is just a few minutes' walk away.

Wyman Hotel & Inn (☎ 970-387-5372; www.the wyman.com; 1371 Greene St; r $105-180; ⏲ mid-Dec–Oct) In a handsome red-sandstone building, this hotel is on the National Register of Historic Places. Rooms are uniquely decorated with late-19th-century antiques and feature Victorian-era wallpaper and top-quality beds and linens. High ceilings and arched windows are the norm throughout the place. The price includes a full breakfast plus afternoon wine and cheese tasting.

Inn of the Rockies at the Historic Alma House (☎ 970-387-5336; www.innoftherockies.com; 220 E Tenth St; r from $110) Opened by a local named Alma in 1898, this inn has nine unique rooms furnished with Victorian antiques. The hospitality is first-rate and its New Orleans–inspired breakfasts, served in a chandelier-lit dining room, merit special mention. There's also a hot tub in the garden for soaking after a long day. Breakfast is included.

Mobius Cycles & Café (☎ 970-387-0770; 1321 Greene St; coffee & mains $3-5; ☯ 8am-5pm) For your morning latte and breakfast burrito, you'll want to visit this little café, which does the best espresso drinks – we especially liked the frozen ones – in town. Ask the proprietor, a young man named Winston Churchill, about the best biking in the area. He also does repairs.

Handlebars (☎ 970-387-5395; 117 13th St; dishes $10-20; ☯ May-Oct) Yes, it's a bit touristy, but you can't argue about the goodness of the baby-back ribs basted in this eclectic-looking restaurant's famous secret barbecue sauce. The decor, a mish-mash of old mining artifacts, mounted animal heads and cowboy memorabilia, gives this place a ramshackle museum-meets-garage-sale feel. After dinner, kick it up on the dance floor to the sounds of live rock and country music.

Pride of the West (☎ 970-387-5150; 1323 Greene St) Silverton's best bar. A gigantic, creaking, old, no-frills place, it's the kind of spot where locals gather late into the night, shooting the breeze at the long bar or playing a game of pool upstairs.

Getting There & Around

TNM&O (www.greyhound.com) buses stop in front of **Teki's Place** (1124 Green St). One-way train tickets to Durango or Weminuche Wilderness trailheads on the Durango & Silverton Narrow Gauge Railroad can be purchased at the **Silverton Depot** (☎ 970-387-5416; cnr 10th & Animas Sts; ☯ May-Oct). **Durango Transportation** (☎ 800-626-2066) operates a bus to Durango ($20, one hour, twice daily). By car, Silverton is 45 miles north of Durango via US 550.

Utah

Shhh, don't tell. We wouldn't want word to get out that this oft-overlooked state is really one of nature's most perfect playgrounds. In Utah you can raft, rock climb, rappel; fish, float, boat; ride a horse, ride a four-wheeler, ride a snowmobile; go off-road, off-trail, off-piste… More than 65% of the lands are public, part of 12 national parks and monuments, 41 state parks, six national forests and numerous wilderness and recreation areas.

In the southern red rock country, you can hike beneath spires and arches that seem to defy gravity, and past water- and wind-sculpted sandstone that resembles art. High above Salt Lake City, mountain bike the forested Wasatch Mountain slopes in summer and swoosh down world-class ski runs in winter. Further east, explore the ancient dinosaur digs and rock art sites. You don't even have to get out of your car for stunning vistas in Utah (though you should): scenic byways and backways lace the state.

The enticing land was also what drew the first Mormon pioneers to the territory in the mid-1800s; church members today make up 60% of the extremely polite population. Small rural towns can be quite conservative, but the rugged beauty has attracted outdoorsy independent thinkers as well. You're as likely to encounter a 1970s VW bus with a kayak on the top as a family minivan with a gaggle of clean-cut, formally dressed children spilling out.

So pull on your boots or rent a jeep: Utah's wild and scenic hinterlands are waiting to be explored. But that's just between you and me.

HIGHLIGHTS

■ **Most Outrageous Adventures**
Moab outfitters (p428) can arrange enough adrenaline for the most avid rafting, off-roading and slickrock mountain-biking junkie

■ **Best Spot for Solitude**
Get your 4WD in gear to explore ancient Native American lands southeast of Natural Bridges National Monument (p419) – darkest night skies in the lower 48

■ **Easiest to Reach Jaw-Dropping Viewpoint**
Dead Horse Point State Park (p426) overlooks serpentine river canyons, with 2-mile-high mountain ranges looming on the horizon

■ **Hippest Small Towns**
The tiny nearby towns of Torrey (p446) and Boulder (p448) have more than their fair share of liberal thinkers, and two great restaurants

■ **Top Scenic Drive**
Utah Hwy 12 (p448) curves past plummeting red rock canyons, giant cream-colored domes and deep-green alpine forests

Moab
Dead Horse ★
Point State Park ★
Torrey ★
★ Boulder
Highway 12 ★
★ Natural Bridges National Monument

UTAH

History

'This is the place!' Brigham Young exclaimed when he and Mormon pioneers arrived in Salt Lake Valley in 1847. Part of Mexico until 1848, Congress created the Utah Territory in 1850, named after the Native American Utes. Church leader Brigham Young, the first governor, encouraged believers to spread out and set down roots. (One group was so determined that it lowered its wagons by rope through a hole in the rock to continue on an impassible mountain trail; see p452.) Inevitable conflicts with the Utes arose, but in general, Mormon policy was to try to coexist and convert.

The first five petitions for statehood were rejected because of the Mormon practice of polygamy. A tense situation was suddenly settled in 1890 when church president Wilford Woodruff discontinued plural marriage as the official practice. (For more on polygamy, see p49.) About the same time, Utah's rugged country served as the perfect hideout for notorious Old West bad men, such as native son Butch Cassidy, and the last spike of the first intercontinental railroad was driven here.

Throughout the 20th century the influence of the Mormon Church, today called the Church of Jesus Christ of Latter-day Saints (LDS), was pervasive in state government. Though it's still a conservative state, there's evidence that LDS supremacy may be waning – only about 60% of today's population claims church membership (the lowest percentage to date). The urban/rural split may be more telling for future politics: about 75% of state residents now live along the urbanized Wasatch front surrounding Salt Lake City.

Climate

The state has a high-mountain-desert climate with four seasons; its average elevation is 6100ft. But before you make assumptions about temperature, check the elevation of the town you're traveling to. It's no surprise that the ski mountain resorts such as Park City are cooler than the desert valley towns such as St George. But Bryce Canyon National Park (8000ft at rim level) can be 10°F to 20°F cooler than the valleys of Zion Canyon National Park (4000ft), just 1½ hours away. Salt Lake City's average temperature is 28°F in January and 80°F in July. Fog blankets the valley around Salt Lake for extended periods in winter (to rise above the gray gloom, ascend the mountains). Evaporation from the nearby Great Salt Lake helps generate the 500in of snow that falls on the Wasatch Mountain front in winter.

Time Zone

Utah is on Mountain Time (seven hours behind GMT) and observes daylight saving time.

Information

Utah is pretty much a nonsmoking state. All lodgings are required to have nonsmoking rooms, and even most bars are smoke-free (exceptions are noted in the text). At campgrounds, 'tent sites' require a little walking, while 'campsites' are pull-up spaces suitable for trailers or tents (no electricity). Many grounds in the arid south do not have showers. 'Camping cabins' require you to bring linens, other cabins don't.

Natural Resources Map & Bookstore (Map p481; ☎ 801-537-3320, 888-882-4627; www.maps.state.ut.us; 1594 W North Temple St, Salt Lake City)

Public Lands Information Center (Map p481; ☎ 801-466-6411; www.publiclands.org; 3285 E 3300 South St, Salt Lake City; ⏰ 10:30am-7pm Tue-Sat) Inside REI's Salt Lake City store, this is a central source of information for all public lands (state parks, Bureau of Land Management sites, Forest Service Wilderness Areas) in Utah. Books and maps sold online.

US Geological Survey (USGS; ☎ 303-202-4700, 888-275-8747; www.usgs.gov) The best topographic and satellite maps; order by phone or online.

Utah Avalanche Center (www.avalanche.org/~uac) Snow and weather reports.

Utah Public Library (http://pioneer.utah.gov)

Utah Travel Council (Map p483; ☎ 800-200-1160, bookstore 801-538-1398; www.utah.com; Council Hall, 300

FAST FACTS

Population 2,550,000
Area 82,144 sq miles
State nickname Beehive State
Website www.utah.com
Sales tax 4.65%
Average temps low/high Park City Jan 7/30°F, Jul 44/71°F; St George Jan 27/54°F, Jul 68/102°F
Salt Lake City to Las Vegas, NV 687 miles, 11½ hours
Salt Lake City to Grand Canyon, AZ 515 miles, 8½ hours
Salt Lake City to Durango, CO 394 miles, 6½ hours

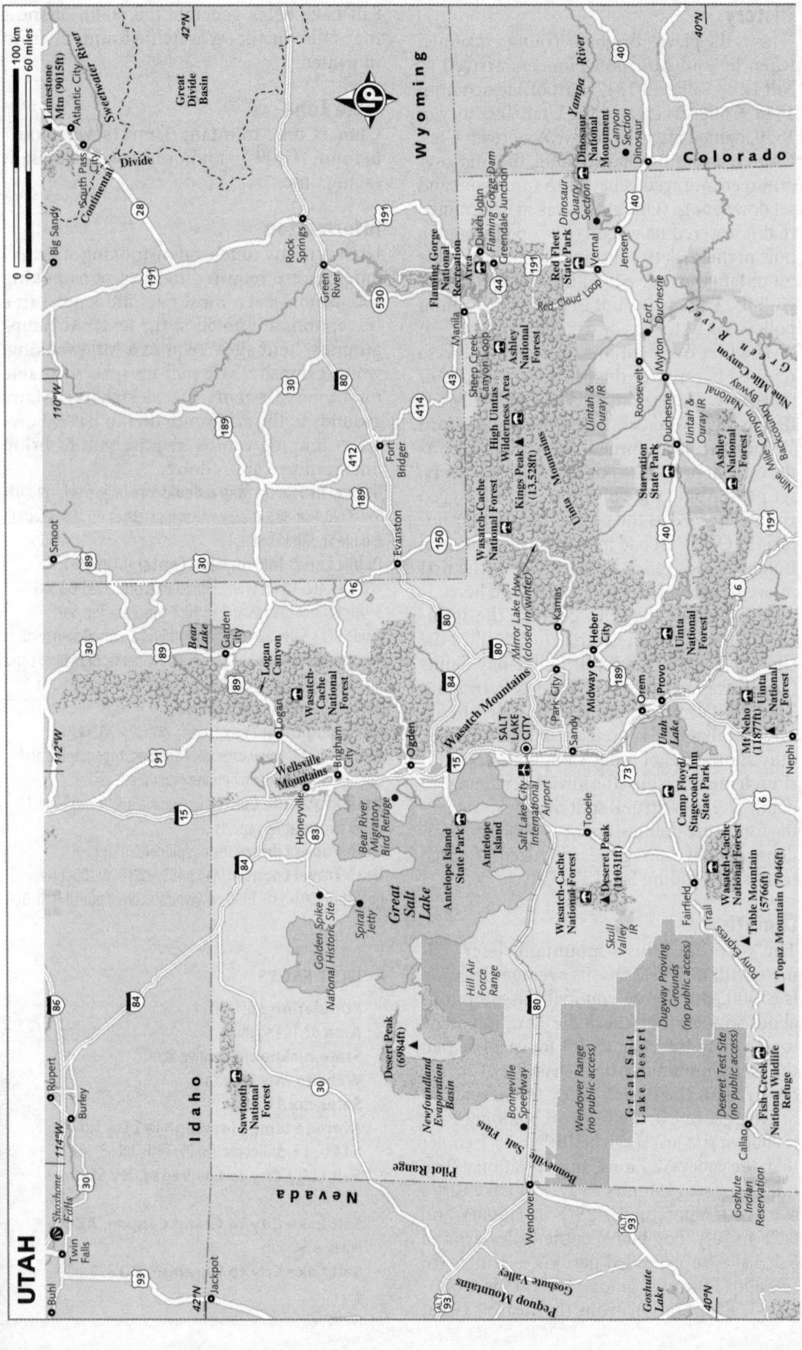
UTAH
0 100 km
0 60 miles
Idaho
Nevada
Wyoming
Colorado
42°N
40°N
110°W
112°W
114°W
Buhl
Twin Falls
Shoshone Falls
Jackpot
Burley
Rupert
Sawtooth National Forest
Pilot Range
Newfoundland Evaporation Basin
Desert Peak (6984ft)
Bonneville Salt Flats
Bonneville Speedway
Wendover
Pequop Mountains
Goshute Valley
Goshute Lake
Goshute Indian Reservation
Callao
Wendover Range (no public access)
Great Salt Lake Desert
Deseret Test Site (no public access)
Fish Creek National Wildlife Refuge
Hill Air Force Range
Dugway Proving Grounds (no public access)
Pony Express Trail
Topaz Mountain (7046ft)
Table Mountain (5766ft)
Wasatch-Cache National Forest
Fairfield
Skull Valley IR
Deseret Peak (11031ft)
Golden Spike National Historic Site
Spiral Jetty
Great Salt Lake
Antelope Island State Park
Antelope Island
Bear River Migratory Bird Refuge
Honeyville
Wellsville Mountains
Brigham City
Ogden
Salt Lake City International Airport
SALT LAKE CITY
Tooele
Camp Floyd/Stagecoach Inn State Park
Nephi
Mt Nebo (11877ft)
Uinta National Forest
Utah Lake
Orem
Provo
Sandy
Park City
Midway
Heber City
Kamas
Wasatch Mountains
Mirror Lake Hwy (closed in winter)
Logan
Logan Canyon
Wasatch-Cache National Forest
Bear Lake
Garden City
Smoot
Evanston
Fort Bridger
Wasatch-Cache National Forest
Kings Peak (13,528ft)
Uinta Mountains
High Uintas Wilderness Area
Sheep Creek Canyon Loop
Ashley National Forest
Manila
Flaming Gorge National Recreation Area
Dutch John
Flaming Gorge Dam
Greendale Junction
Red Cloud Loop
Red Fleet State Park
Vernal
Jensen
Dinosaur Quarry Section
Dinosaur National Monument
Canyon Section
Dinosaur
Yampa River
Uintah & Ouray IR
Roosevelt
Fort Duchesne
Myton
Duchesne
Starvation State Park
Ashley National Forest
Nine Mile Canyon National Backcountry Byway
Nine Mile Canyon
Green River
Rock Springs
Green River
Big Sandy
South Pass City
Atlantic City
Limestone Mtn (9015ft)
Sweetwater River
Continental Divide
Great Divide Basin
15
84
86
30
93
ALT 93
80
83
91
89
16
150
189
412
414
43
30
530
191
28
44
40
6
73
80

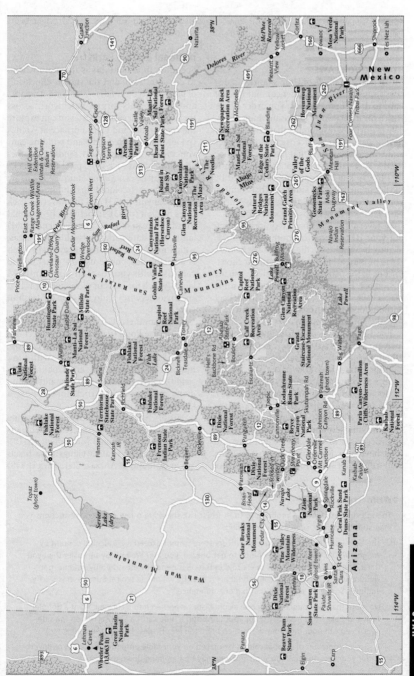

N State St, Salt Lake City; ⏰ 8am-5pm Mon-Fri, 10am-5pm Sat & Sun) Publishes the free *Utah Travel Guide;* the bookstore sells guides and maps.

UTAH LIQUOR LAWS

Much has been made of Utah's quirky liquor laws (a result of LDS influence), but it's not hard to drink in the state. If you order a beer with a meal, you won't notice anything amiss. The majority of restaurants that serve dinner have a partial liquor license and offer beer and wine. Restaurants that have a full liquor license serve also hard alcohol. The catch is that to drink at a 'restaurant' (as defined by the liquor board), even sitting at a bar counter, you have to order something to eat. Not to worry, $1 worth of chips and salsa counts.

A 'tavern' (or 'beer bar') requires nothing but your ID to drink (beer only, up to 3.2% alcohol by weight; see the boxed text, below). It can be hard to single out taverns, but choosing one of the many microbreweries is usually a good bet. Hybrids have developed, so some places have sections where you can drink beer without food and other areas where you have to order something to eat.

Food-free, full-alcohol bars and discos are 'private clubs' that require 'membership.' Obtaining membership can be as simple as signing your name to a paper slip, which counts as your private membership card, or paying up to $5 (both good for three weeks). Think of it as a cheap cover charge. Leave the Park City–Salt Lake City region and private clubs become few and far between.

Grocery stores sell 3.2% alcohol beer and malt beverages Monday through Saturday. State-run liquor stores (usually one per town), also closed on Sundays, sell stronger beer, wine and spirits.

National & State Parks

Spending time outdoors is the main reason to come to Utah, and the state is chock-full of parks to accommodate you. National parks and monuments form a patchwork across the south. From east to west, you can explore the rock arches and Fiery Furnace at Arches (p436), the steep red cliffs and winding canyons of Canyonlands (p421), sandstone domes and chunky red rock in Capitol Reef (p443), the vast expanses of Grand Staircase-Escalante (p450), sherbet-colored fins and hoodoos at Bryce Canyon (p453) and the towering rock faces of Zion (p463). In between lie national forests, Bureau of Land Management (BLM) lands, and state parks and wilderness areas, which means the majority of southern Utah is available for public use. In general, you can hike with your dog off-leash on BLM lands (watch for signs in recreation areas that specify otherwise). Fido must be on-leash in state parks.

Great southern Utah state parks include: Dead Horse Point (p426), where you get up-close views of a spectacular badland canyon; Coral Pink Sand Dunes (p474), with pink mounds of slippery sand; and Goblin Valley (p440), where you can climb over and around giant mushroom-like rock formations (a kids' favorite).

History buffs shouldn't miss the fascinating square towers built by Ancestral Puebloans at Hovenweep National Monument (p418). Other Native American dwellings and artifacts are to be found at Anasazi State Park (p448)

WHAT THE...?

Though drinking is not a problem in Utah (trust us), there are a few eccentric restrictions you may stumble across, such as the following:

■ The beer you get in a restaurant or grocery store cannot exceed 3.2% alcohol content by weight. Whoa...how am I ever going to get buzzed, you ask? Well it may be easier than you think. The alcohol content for beers sold in the US is generally measured by volume, not weight. So a '3.2' beer is actually about a 4% beer by volume (a typical Budweiser is 5% by volume). So there's really not that big of a difference.

■ No more than one ounce of any one alcohol can be poured into a cocktail. Want a double Jack and Coke? You have to ask for your drink and a 'side car' – a shot served on the side – which you can pour into your drink, then hand the empty glass back to the waiter.

■ A second container of alcohol cannot be placed on your table until the first one is removed. Order your second drink too soon and you may be slamming down the first.

WHAT'S A BLM?

Unless you've been to the American West, you've likely not heard of the **Bureau of Land Management** (BLM; www.blm.gov), a Department of the Interior agency that manages close to 300 million acres of public land. What does BLM mean for you in Utah? Outdoor fun. Unless otherwise posted, you can hike where you please on BLM lands. Unless you're in a special managed area (as posted), you can also pretty much camp where you please – as long as you stay on established roads to get there. Even campfires are OK, unless a fire danger is posted.

Look at a land usage map of Utah and you'll see how staggering this is. The BLM manages close to 23 million acres, making up 42% of the land in the state. It publishes topographic maps for the state, and the comprehensive *Utah State Explorer: BLM Map Edition* CD-ROM covers them all. For maps, BLM field office locations and information about BLM recreation, check out www .publiclands.org. Now get exploring!

---

outside Boulder and Edge of the Cedars State Park (p420) in Blanding. Unless otherwise noted, state park entry is free.

Water enthusiasts can explore Lake Powell by houseboat from Glen Canyon National Recreation Area (p441), or head to Utah's northeastern-most reaches for trout fishing and floating at Flaming Gorge National Recreation Area (p513).

For information on Utah's national and state parks contact the following:

BLM (☎ 801-539-4001; www.ut.blm.gov)
State Park Camping Reservations (☎ 801-322-3770, 800-322-3770; www.reserveamerica.com)
USDA Forest Service (USFS; ☎ 801-236-3400; www .fs.fed.us/r4/wcnf)
Utah State Parks & Recreation (☎ 801-538-7220; www.stateparks.utah.gov)

Utah Scenic Routes

Roads in Utah can be attractions in themselves. State-designated Scenic Byways (www .byways.org) twist and turn through the landscape, winding past stunning views. Getting there will take a little longer, but the roads are paved and the effort well rewarded (check out Hwys 9, 12, 14 and 95). On designated Scenic Backways, the grades are steeper, the turns tighter, the drop-offs more sheer, the roadbed unpaved and 4WD is often necessary. Driving the backways can be spectacular or scary; if you like roller coasters, you'll generally be OK.

Look for regional route suggestions in the Roads That Rule boxes at the beginning of sections, but know that there are far more back roads in Utah than we can list here. Buy a good road map and get going. Be warned that some counties maintain their backways better than others. Ask locals about conditions (and how often the roads are graded) and check the weather – snow can cover mountain passes while flowers bloom down below.

Some don't-miss drives to consider are listed following. Arguably Utah's most diverse and stunning route, the Hwy 12 (p448) Scenic Byway winds through rugged canyons on a 124-mile journey from before Bryce Canyon to near Capitol Reef. Towns along the way have free route guides available. If you traverse no other section, at least drive between Torrey and Boulder, where an incredible panorama of hardened dunes (think sand-covered monsters emerging from the earth) unfolds around mile marker 98.

Deep red cliffs loom above a red roadbed (made using local rock) as the 5-mile Kolob Canyons Rd (p463) scenic drive climbs up beside Taylor Creek in the less-visited, western section of Zion National Park. The intense color and frequent turnouts make this the best bet for those who want a lot of reward for little effort.

In the southeast corner of the state, Moki Dugway (Rte 261; p419) follows a narrow, twisting series of switchbacks to drop (or rise) 1000ft in a scant 3 miles. From the top there are views into Arizona; take the side route to the undulating Valley of the Gods at the base for the complete roller coaster experience.

East of Park City, Mirror Lake Hwy (Rte 150; p502), one of the state's most spectacular high-alpine roads, winds beneath 12,000ft peaks before dropping into Wyoming. Plan ahead – October through April tire chains or 4WD are required.

Heading north from Vernal into the northeastern Uintas Mountains, Flaming Gorge–Uintas Scenic Byway (Hwy 191; p513) is a drive and a geology lesson all in one.

TOP PICKS FOR PARKS

- Arches National Park (p436)
- Zion National Park (p463)
- Bryce Canyon National Park (p453)
- Dead Horse Point State Park (p426)
- Goblin Valley State Park (p440)

Interpretive signs indicate the age and significance of the exposed rock layers. Great spot for fall color and wildlife-watching, too.

Getting There & Around

Driving around the state can be quite a speedy affair. The three major interstate freeways have a 75mph limit, but people often go faster. If you're zipping south to north on I-15, say from Las Vegas to Salt Lake City (SLC), there aren't a lot of great stops. Cedar City is only 170 miles from Vegas, but has some good B&Bs and a great summer Shakespeare festival. Consider detouring east at St George on Hwy 9 and then following Hwy 89 north. It's slower going (365 miles, seven hours, St George to SLC, compared with 303 miles and 4¼ hours on the I-15), but you'll pass through some stunning red rock country.

Cruising in from Denver on I-70, make sure you get gas in Green River (345 miles, 5¼ hours) and have a burger at Ray's. The 104 miles between Green River and Salina is the largest stretch of US interstate with no services – no gas, no restaurants, nothing but a lonely rest stop for bathroom breaks.

You may not be trying to set any records on the I-80 trip west from SLC to the Nevada state line (120 miles, 1¾ hours), but you can stop at the Bonneville Salt Flats to see those who are. Continue along the interstate and you'll pass through Reno on the way to San Francisco (from SLC 737 miles, 10½ hours).

Smaller US highways post a maximum speed limit of 65mph. Remember that the state has some daunting geographic features. Don't assume that just because you see a road on a map that taking off cross-country will be quicker. Sheer drops, switchbacks and steep inclines are all part of the back road experience. In between are paved 'scenic byways' (Hwy 9, 12, 14, 95), with not-to-be-missed views around every turn.

Note that most towns in Utah follow a typical Mormon grid, in which numbered streets radiate from a central hub (or zero point), usually the intersection of Main and Center Sts. Compass points indicate where you are in relation to that hub; thus, 100 E 300 South is one block east and three blocks south of Main and Center. It's confusing at first, but you get used to it.

Getting from here to there:
Bryce Canyon National Park to Moab 282 miles, 4½ hours
Moab to Salt Lake City 234 miles, 4 hours
St George to Salt Lake City 303 miles, 4¼ hours
Zion National Park to Bryce Canyon National Park 77 miles, 2 hours

Salt Lake City International Airport (p489) is the state's main airport, but travelers use Las Vegas as an alternative. Amtrak train service links Salt Lake and Green River with LA and Chicago, but is little help in-state.

Bus service statewide isn't great either. Greyhound only goes to a handful of the biggest towns, and most of those are close to SLC. Getting to small towns and national parks, you definitely need a car. Salt Lake and Park City both have good public transportation systems, but pretty much nowhere else does. If you're leaving those cities, plan to drive, period.

For more information on transportation throughout the Southwest, see p536.

SOUTHEASTERN UTAH

Dusty and desolate, hot and hard-scrabble: parts of southeastern Utah were so forbidding that they were the last to be mapped in the continental US. Yet it's in this rocky corner of the Colorado Plateau that you can experience Earth's beauty at its most raw. Beyond the odd mountain or two, there's little vegetation to hide the handiwork of time, water and wind. Look for the effects of erosion in the red rock formations of Arches National Park, in the sheer-walled river canyons from Canyonlands National Park to Lake Powell and in the stunning buttes of Monument Valley. Moab is adventure central with as much four-wheeling, white-water rafting, outfitter fun as you can handle. Or you can lose the crowd while looking for Ancestral Puebloan rock art and dwellings in miles of undeveloped lands.

Note that many southeastern restaurants and shops – some motels even – are seasonal;

don't count on things being open outside the May to late-October main season.

BLUFF

pop 300 / elev 4380ft

Tiny tot Bluff isn't much more than a spot in the road. But a few great motels and a handful of restaurants, surrounded by stunning red rock, make it a cool little base for exploring the far southwestern corner of the state. From here you can easily reach Moki Dugway (30 miles), Monument Valley (47 miles) and Natural Bridges National Monument (61 miles), to mention just a few area sights, and you can explore the BLM wilderness to the northwest.

There's no visitor center here at the crossroads of Hwys 191 N and 163; you can check online at www.bluff-utah.org, but local business owners and staff are your best resource (they know the hikes better than an office worker could, anyway). To preserve the night sky, Bluff has no streetlights.

Sights & Activities

Other than eating, sleeping and a little trading post shopping, there's not much to do in the tiny town. Three miles west of Bluff off Hwy 163, follow Sand Island Rd to the easily accessible **Sand Island Petroglyphs** (on BLM land), which were created between 800 and 2500 years ago. The nearby boat launch is the starting point for San Juan River adventures.

Vaughn Hadenfeld of **Far Out Expeditions** (☎ 435-672-2294; www.faroutexpeditions.com) leads off-the-beaten-path day hikes to rock art and ruins. Vaughn has the trust of the Navajo

---

ROADS THAT RULE: SOUTHEASTERN UTAH

People come from around the world to drive in southeastern Utah. From paved desert highways for RV-cruising retirees to vertical slickrock trails for Jeepsters, there are drives for every taste. The Moab Information Center (p428) has free route guides.

■ **Utah's Trail of the Ancients** Starting at Monticello, make a counterclockwise loop past Native American ruins and Natural Bridges National Monument (p419) on Hwy 95, down an insanely steep switchbacked dugway on Hwy 261, past the stunning buttes of Valley of the Gods (p418), finishing in Bluff (above) on Hwy 163 in the sparsely populated southeast corner of the state (125 miles, allow three hours).

■ **Comb Wash Road** Straddling Comb Ridge, Comb Wash Rd (or CR 235) is a dirt track that runs for about 20 miles between Hwys 163 and 95 (parallel to Hwy 191) west of Blanding and Bluff. Views are fantastic (bring binoculars) and the ridge contains numerous ancient cliff dwellings. High-clearance 4WD vehicles recommended; in wet weather, this road is impassable.

■ **Colorado River Byway** From Moab, Hwy 128 follows the river northeast to Cisco, 44 miles away just off I-70. Highlights are Castle Rock, the 900ft-tall Fisher Towers, the 1916 Dewey Bridge (one of the first across the Colorado) and sightings of white-water rafters.

■ **La Sal Mountain Loop Road** This road heads south into the Manti-La Sal forest (p421) from 15 miles north of Moab, ascending switchbacks (long RVs not recommended) into the refreshingly cool forest, with fantastic views. You connect with Hwy 191, 8 miles south of Moab. The 67-mile (three to four hours) paved loop closes in winter.

■ **Potash Road Scenic Byway** The 15-mile, paved Potash Rd (Hwy 279) goes south from Hwy 191, 3 miles north of Moab. It's named for the potash extraction plant at the end. Highlights are petroglyphs, dinosaur tracks and area arches. Past the potash plant, you'll need a 4WD to reach Island in the Sky (p423) in Canyonlands.

■ **Kane Creek Boulevard** A paved road heading west from Moab passes petroglyphs and a rock-climbing area before becoming a gravel route into Kane Springs Canyon. After 14 miles, you ford the creek, which, depending on the weather, may be impassable. Then at 28 miles comes 4470ft Hurrah Pass, after which only 4WD vehicles can continue. The stupendous scenery includes views *up* to Dead Horse Point. (With a 4WD you can eventually end 50 miles beyond at Hwy 211, east of the Needles area of Canyonlands National Park.)

SOUTHEASTERN UTAH

0 — 30 km
0 — 20 miles

111°W
110°W
109°W

To Price (38mi)

Hill Creek Extension Uintah & Ouray Indian Reservation

To Grand Junction (CO) (23mi)

Cleveland
Huntington
10
Orangeville
Castle Dale
191
6

Price River

Colorado River

Colorado

39°W
39°W

Sego Canyon

Green River
Thompson Springs
Cisco
128

Gateway

To Salina (55mi)
50
70

To Grand Junction

Arches National Park

Castle Valley

La Sal Mountains

San Rafael Reef
San Rafael Swell
24
San Rafael Desert
San Rafael R
Green River
313
279
Moab
La Salle Mountain Loop Rd
141

Canyonlands National Park (Horseshoe Canyon)

Dead Horse Point State Park
Potash Rd
Anticline Overlook
Hole 'n the Rock

Manti-La Sal National Forest
Paradox
90

Goblin Valley State Park

Island in the Sky

Caineville
24
Hanksville

Canyonlands National Park

Needles Overlook
La Sal Junction
46
La Sal
191

To Capital Reef National Park (16mi)
95

Hans Flat Ranger Station

The Maze

38°W
38°W

Slick Rock

Burr Point
Henry Mountains

Henry Mountains

Glen Canyon National Recreation Area

The Needles

211

Newspaper Rock Recreation Area

Abajo Mtns
Abajo Peak 11,360ft
Monticello
491
Dove Creek

276

Hite Marina
95

Manti-La Sal National Forest

Natural Bridges National Monument

Edge of the Cedars State Park
Blanding

To Mesa Verde National Park (45mi)

Ticaboo

Butler Wash Ruins
Mule Canyon Ruins

Montezuma Canyon Rd

Hovenweep National Monument

Bullfrog Marina
Ferry
Lake Powell
Halls Crossing Marina

275
95

Grand Gulch Primitive Area

Cedar Mesa
261
Moki Dugway

Comb Wash Rd
Comb Ridge

262
Hatch Trading Post

Glen Canyon National Recreation Area
276

San Juan River

Valley of the Gods
191
Bluff
162
Montezuma Creek
Aneth
262

Muley Point Overlook
Sand Island Petroglyphs

Navajo Indian Reservation

Goosenecks State Park
163
Mexican Hat
191

Four Corners Navajo Tribal Park
41
37°W

Navajo Mtn 10,388ft
Oljato
Goulding's Lodge
Monument Valley

Monument Valley Navajo Tribal Park
160
Tes Nez Iah
Teec Nos Pos

6

37°W

Arizona

111°W
110°W
109°W

UTAH

GET OFF THAT TRAIL: IN SEARCH OF ANCIENT AMERICA

Ancestral Puebloan cliff dwellings, centuries-old rock art and artifacts – the southeastern corner of the state is a great place to explore ancient cultures. Don't miss the ruins at **Butler Wash** (p419), the tower dwellings at **Hovenweep** (p418) and the museum and kiva at **Edge of the Cedars State Park** (p420). But there's far more than that to explore: ruins and petroglyphs can be found all across BLM lands.

If you're an inexperienced hiker, or don't have a 4WD, your best bet is to hire a guide through an operator such as **Far Out Expeditions** (p415). If you're well aware that you need a gallon of water per person per day in the desert, then what are you doing still reading this? Get going!

Off Comb Wash Rd (linking Hwys 95 and 163) is a good place to start, as is Montezuma Canyon Rd, north of Hovenweep. Ask locals for tips (hint: you can also suss out the ruin symbols on the *Delorme Utah Atlas & Gazetteer*). Don't forget to bring a good topographic map.

A few things to keep in mind:

▪ Take only pictures – do not touch, move or remove any artifacts you find. Not only will this contaminate future study, it's against the law.

▪ Tread lightly – though the sandstone structures seem sturdy, climbing on building walls causes irreparable damage. Don't do it.

▪ Respect the spiritual and historical value of these places – they are sacred to many Native Americans.

▪ Leave no trace – pack out anything you pack in. You leave the least effect on the area's ecology if you walk on slickrock or in dry washes.

---

people, so you may be able to hike on tribal land. **Buckhorn Llama** (☎ 435-672-2466; www.llamapack.com) specializes in multiday pack trips into harder-to-reach wilderness. For a float through the canyons of the San Juan River, contact **Wild Rivers Expeditions** (☎ 435-672-2244; www.riversandruins.com).

Sleeping

Sand Island Campground (☎ 435-587-1500; www.blm.gov; Sand Island Rd; campsites $10; ☽ May-Oct) Shade and the San Juan River help cool things off at these 27 first-come, first-served sites. Pit toilets and drinking water available.

Recapture Lodge (☎ 435-672-2281; www.recapturelodge.com; Hwy 191; r incl breakfast $46-76; ☒) Locally owned and operated for eons, the staff here are super-knowledgeable. They help out with trip planning and present educational slide shows in season. There's plenty of shade around the rustic motel and on the 3½ miles of walking trails.

Desert Rose Inn (☎ 435-672-2303, 888-475-7673; www.desertroseinn.com; Hwy 191; r $69-99, cabins $89-109; wi-fi) Wood porches wrap around this dramatic, two-story, log motel at the far western edge of town. Quilts on every pine bed and supersized, exterior-access guest rooms make this a prime choice for comfort. Microwaves and mini-refrigerators.

Other options include the following:

Kokopelli Inn (☎ 435-672-2322; www.kokoinn.com; Hwy 191; r $45-57; wi-fi) Tiny 26-room motel; perfectly fine. Some pets OK.

Far Out Bunkhouse (☎ 435-672-2294; www.faroutexpeditions.com; cnr 7th East & Mulberry Sts; r $65-85) Two private six-bunk rooms with kitchen.

Eating

Comb Ridge Coffee (☎ 435-672-2279; Hwy 191; baked goods $2-4; ☽ 7am-3pm Tue-Sun) Locals line up to grab an espresso and a homemade muffin at this arty café-gallery.

Twin Rock Trading Post (☎ 435-672-2341; 913 E Navajo Twins Dr; mains $6-14; ☽ 7am-9pm) Try Indian fry bread with your three daily meals – as part of a breakfast sandwich, wrapped up as a Navajo taco at lunch or accompanying stew with dinner. Owner Craig Simpson is a font of local lore.

Cow Canyon (☎ 435-672-2208; cnr Hwys 191 & 163; mains $11-18; ☽ dinner Thu-Mon Apr-Oct) Don't miss having dinner in this rambling house where local ingredients star on a daily changing, world-food menu, with dishes such as Middle Eastern lamb and rice-stuffed onion. Good salads and vegetarian options are always available. A small gift shop up front sells rugs, baskets, pottery and jewelry.

Cottonwood Steakhouse (☎ 435-672-2282; cnr Main & 4th West Sts; mains $12-22; ☽ dinner Mar-Nov) Yee-haw!

UTAH

Sure it's a little touristy and overpriced, but you're paying for Wild West–style fun to go with your rib-eye steak, pardner.

HOVENWEEP NATIONAL MONUMENT

Since 1923 the six sets of **Ancestral Puebloan sites** that straddle the Utah–Colorado state line have been protected as a national monument. The area was home to a sizeable Native American population before abandonment in the late 1200s (perhaps because of drought and deforestation). The Square Tower Group and **visitor center** (☎ 970-562-4282; www.nps.gov/hove; park entrance per week $3; ☒ 8am-5pm, trails sunrise to sunset) are what people are generally referring to when speaking of Hovenweep. Pick up the interpretive guide (50¢), essential for understanding the unexcavated ruins.

Stronghold House is accessible from a paved path and from there you overlook the rest of the ruins. Most of the eight towers and unit houses you'll see were constructed between 1230 and 1275. The masonry skills it took to piece together such tall structures on such little ledges definitely inspires reflection. To get a closer look, you'll have to hike down into the canyon (and back up); follow the trail clockwise to see the ruins unfold around every corner.

A nice 30-site **campground** (campsites $10) with water and toilets (no electricity) is near the visitor center, but there's a whole lotta nothin' else out here. The closest store is the **Hatch Trading Post** (County Rd 414), an atmospheric white-brick building that sells a few sundries and some Native American crafts. Other than that, supplies are in Blanding (45 miles), Bluff (40 miles) and Cortez, CO (43 miles).

The best way to get here is on paved Hwy 262. From the turnoff east at Hwy 191 follow the signs; it's a 28-mile drive to the main entrance (past Hatch Trading Post). Ask for a map at the visitor center if you have a 4WD and plan to explore the more remote monument sites. Use caution traveling on any unpaved roads here: all become treacherous in wet weather. From Hovenweep, Mesa Verde National Park (p391) is 75 miles east in Colorado.

VALLEY OF THE GODS

Up and over, through and around, the unpaved road that leads through Valley of the Gods is like a do-it-yourself roller coaster – amid some mind-blowing scenery. In other states, this uncrowded **butte-filled valley** would be a national park, but such are the riches of Utah that here it is merely a BLM-administered area. Locals call it 'mini–Monument Valley.' The San Juan Visitor Center (p420) in Monticello passes out pamphlets identifying the sandstone monoliths and pinnacles that have been named over the years: **Seven Sailors, Lady on a Tub, Rooster Butte.**

The night sky here is incredible, making the free BLM camping (see boxed text, p413) among the rock giants a dramatic – if shade-free – prospect. Or you could spend a secluded night at one of the original ranches in the area, now the **Valley of the Gods B&B** (☎ 970-749-1164; www.valleyofthegods.cjb.net; off Hwy 261; r incl breakfast $85-115), 6.5 miles north of Hwy 163. Exposed wood-and-stone rooms have simple rustic beds. Water is trucked in and solar power is harnessed out of necessity here (leave your hair dryer at home).

A high-clearance vehicle is advised for driving Valley of the Gods (County Rd 242). This author's little Volkswagen GTI made it on a very dry day, but don't try it without a 4WD if it's rained recently. Allow an hour for the 17-mile loop connecting Hwys 261 and 163. The nearest services are in Mexican Hat, 7 miles southwest of the Hwy 163 turnoff.

MEXICAN HAT

pop 110 / elev 4244ft

The settlement of Mexican Hat is named after a **sombrero-shaped rock**, 3 miles northeast on Hwy 163. The town is little more than a handful of simple lodgings, a couple of places to eat and a store or two on the north bank of the San Juan River. The south bank marks the edge of the Navajo Reservation. Monument Valley is 20 miles to the south, Bluff 27 miles to the east. The cliffside **San Juan Inn** (☎ 435-683-2220, 800-447-2022; www.sanjuaninn.net; Hwy 163; r $70-80) perches high above the river. Motel rooms are pretty basic, but are the nicest in town. You can buy Navajo crafts, books and beer on site at the **trading post** (☒ 7am-9pm), and the year-round **restaurant** (mains $5-15; ☒ 7am-10pm) has the only full liquor license for at least 50 miles.

MONUMENT VALLEY

From Mexican Hat, Hwy 163 winds southwest and enters the **Navajo Reservation** and, after 22 miles, Monument Valley, on the Arizona state line. Though you'll recognize it instantly from TV commercials and Hollywood movies (remember where Forrest Gump stopped his cross-country run?), nothing compares with seeing the sheer chocolate-red buttes and colossal mesas for real. To get close, you must visit the **Monument Valley Navajo Tribal Park**. Goulding's Lodge is the motel-lodge-restaurant-grocery store-trading post-museum-movie house-gift shop-tour operator. For more, see p224.

GOOSENECKS STATE PARK

Near the southern end of Hwy 261, a 4-mile paved road heads west to Goosenecks State Park, a freely accessible lookout with yet more jaw-dropping views. From here you can see how, over time, the San Juan River snaked back on its course, leaving gooseneck-shaped spits of land untouched below. The serpentine path carved by years of running water is dramatically evident from above. The park itself doesn't have much to speak of: there are pit toilets, picnic tables and free campsites, but the frequent winds discourage staying long.

MOKI DUGWAY & AROUND

Ready for a ride? The Moki Dugway is a (roughly paved) hairpin-turn-filled section of Hwy 261 that descends 1100ft in just 3 miles (you ascend traveling north). Miners 'dug out' the extreme switchbacks in the 1950s to transport uranium ore. Today it's a way to Lake Powell, and to some hair-raising fun. Driving up is almost scarier, since you cannot see what's around the narrow corners; when driving down you at least have an overview. Either way, the dugway is not for anyone who's height sensitive (or for those in a vehicle more than 28ft long).

Don't miss **Muley Point Overlook** at the top of the dugway. The sweeping cliff-edge viewpoint looks south to Monument Valley and other stunning landmarks in Arizona. The turnoff isn't easy to spot heading north; look for the road that goes west at the top of the dugway. There are signs for those traveling south.

Follow Hwy 261 further to the wild and twisting canyons of **Cedar Mesa** and **Grand Gulch Primitive Area**, hugely popular with backcountry hikers. The BLM-administered area also contains hundreds of Ancestral Puebloan sites, many of which have been vandalized by pot hunters. (It bears repeating that all prehistoric sites are protected by law, and authorities are cracking down on offenders.) You can follow Kane Gulch Trail 4 miles down (600ft elevation change) to a view of **Junction Ruin cliff dwelling**. To hike in most canyons you need a $2 day-use permit ($8 overnight); some walk-ins are available at the **Kane Gulch Ranger Station** (Hwy 261, 4 miles south of Hwy 95; ☺ 8am-noon Mar-Nov), but the number of permits is limited from March to June 15 and September through October. Make advance reservations by calling the **Monticello Field Office** (☎ 435-587-1510). This is difficult country with primitive trails; the nearest water is 10 miles away at Natural Bridges National Monument.

NATURAL BRIDGES NATIONAL MONUMENT

In 1908 **Natural Bridges National Monument** (☎ 435-692-1234; www.nps.gov/nabr; admission $6; ☺ 7am-sunset, visitor center 8am-5pm) became Utah's first National Park Service (NPS) land. The highlight is a dark-stained, white sandstone canyon with three natural bridges.

The oldest, beautifully delicate **Owachomo Bridge**, spans 180ft and rises over 100ft above ground but is only 9ft thick. **Kachina Bridge** is the youngest and spans 204ft. **Sipapu Bridge** (286ft span) just misses out on the 'largest in US' title – that honor goes to Rainbow

---

DETOUR: BUTLER WASH & MULE CANYON RUINS

Driving along Hwy 95 between Blanding and Natural Bridges provides an excellent opportunity to see isolated Ancestral Puebloan ruins. No need to be a backcountry hiker here: it's only a half-mile hike to **Butler Wash Ruins** (14 miles west of Blanding), a 20-room cliff dwelling. Scramble over the slickrock boulders (follow the cairns) and you're rewarded with an overlook of the sacred kivas, habitation and storage rooms that were used c 1300.

Not as well preserved, the base of the tower, kiva and 12-room **Mule Canyon Ruins** (20 miles west of Blanding) are more easily accessed. Follow the signs to the parking lot just steps from the masonry remains. The pottery found here links the population (c 1000 to 1150) to the Mesa Verde group in southern Colorado. Butler Wash relates to the Kayenta group of northern Arizona. Both are on freely accessible BLM-administered land.

Bridge (290ft span), near Lake Powell. All three bridges are visible from a 9-mile winding loop road with easy access overlooks. Most visitors never venture below the canyon rim, but distances are short (the longest is just over half a mile one way) even if descents are steep. Getting to Sipapu Bridge involves stairs and ladders. Enthusiastic hikers can take a longer trail that joins all three bridges (8 miles). The elevation here is 6500ft; trails are open all year, but steeper sections may be closed after heavy rains or snow.

The 12 sites at the **campground** (campsites $10), almost half a mile past the visitor center, are fairly sheltered among scraggly trees and red sand. The stars are a real attraction staying here; the park has been designated an International Dark Sky Park and is one of the darkest in the country. There are pit toilets and grills; water is available only at the visitor center. The campground fills on summer afternoons, after which you are allowed to camp in the pullouts along Hwy 275. There is no backcountry camping. Towed trailers are not suitable for the loop drive.

The nearest services are in Blanding, 47 miles to the east. If you continue west on Hwy 95 from Natural Bridges, and follow Hwy 276, the services of Lake Powell's Bullfrog Marina are 140 miles away.

BLANDING
pop 3200 / elev 6000ft

Two specialized museums elevate small, agriculturally oriented Blanding beyond its totally dull name. Still, it's best to visit as a day trip, or en route between Bluff (22 miles) and Moab (75 miles). Both the motels and the (alcohol-free) restaurants are, well…bland.

Blanding Visitor Center (☎ 435-678-3662; www .blandingutah.org; cnr Hwy 191 N & 200 East; ☯ 9am-5pm Mon-Sat) puts out a guide that covers the whole region from Bluff to Natural Bridges. If you're here, the small pioneer artifact collection is worth a look.

More a museum than a park, **Edge of the Cedars State Park** (☎ 435-678-2238; www.stateparks.utah .gov; 660 W 400 North; admission $5; ☯ 9am-5pm) houses a treasure trove of ancient Native American artifacts and pottery gathered from all across southeastern Utah. Informative displays provide a good overview of area cultures. Outside you can climb down into a preserved ceremonial kiva built by the Ancestral Puebloans c 1100. The encroaching subdivision makes

you wonder what other sites remain hidden under neighboring houses.

Despite being born of owners Steven and Sylvia Czerkas' personal collection, the **Dinosaur Museum** (☎ 435-678-3454; 754 S 200 West; adult/child $2/1; ☯ 9am-5pm Mon-Sat mid-Apr–mid-Oct) is quite ambitious; the goal is to cover the complete history of the world's dinosaurs. Mummified remains and fossil replicas go a long way toward this goal, but most interesting is the collection of dinosaur-movie-related memorabilia.

If you just have to eat here, duck into the **Homestead Steak House** (☎ 435-678-3456; 121 E Center St; mains $6-16; ☯ lunch & dinner Mon-Sat) for generic all-American dishes, good salads and home-made breads. For a sweet treat with a side of novelty, head to **Old Bank Creamery** (☎ 435-678-2411; 30 W 100 South; ☯ 1-9pm Mon-Sat mid-Apr–mid-Oct) in a 100-year-old tiny stone bank. Try flavors such as cotton candy and peanut butter cup.

You can see Native American artists at work in the factory and buy their wares at **Cedar Mesa Pottery** (☎ 435-678-241; 333 S Main St; ☯ 9am-4:30pm Mon-Fri mid-Apr–mid-Oct).

MONTICELLO
pop 1900 / elev 7069ft

Greener and cooler than other towns in the region, Monticello (mon-ti-*sell*-o) sits in the foothills of the Abajo (or Blue) Mountains. This, the seat of San Juan County, covering the southeast corner of Utah, is the place to get area information before heading further south. Nearby, Manti-La Sal National Forest rises to 11,360ft at Abajo Peak. Monticello is 54 miles south of Moab and 47 miles north of Bluff. Befitting the area's religiousness, Hwy 666, which goes to Colorado, was officially renamed Hwy 491 in 2003.

The multi-agency **San Juan Visitor Center** (☎ 435-587-3235, 800-574-4386; www.southeastutah .com; 117 S Main St; ☯ 10am-4pm Mon-Fri Nov–mid-Mar, 8am-5pm daily mid-Mar–Oct) has extensive information on all public lands in southeastern Utah. (Note: many of its brochures are online as PDFs.) The **BLM Monticello Field Office** (☎ 435-587-2141; 435 N Main St; ☯ 9am-5pm Mon-Fri) is the place to inquire about backcountry hiking and to buy BLM topo maps. If you like to get way, way off the beaten path on multiday hikes, ask about the brilliantly empty Dark Canyon Primitive Area.

Southwest Ed-Ventures (☎ 435-587-2156, 800-525-4456; www.sw-adventures.org) runs learning vacations – rafting the San Juan River or Butler

Wash archaeological research trips, for example – in San Juan County. Proceeds support conservation education.

Hundreds of trail miles crisscross the 1.4-million-acre **Manti-La Sal National Forest** (www.fs.fed.us/r4/mantilasal), west of Monticello. Here spruce- and fir-clad slopes offer respite from the heat (expect a 10°F drop in temperature for every 1000ft you ascend) and spring wildflowers and fall color are a novelty in the arid canyonlands. Seven miles west of Monticello, oaks and aspens shade the 11 spots at the 8900ft-elevation **Buckboard Campground** (Forest Rd 105; campsites $10; ⊙ May-Sep) – one of many in the forest. Water and pit toilets are available. The San Juan Visitor Center has maps and campground lists.

In Monticello you're midway between Moab and Bluff; both have better places to stay but this *is* the closest town to the Canyonlands' Needles District. If low cost is a high priority, choose **Canyonlands Motel** (☎ 435-587-2266; 533 N Main St; r $45-65; ⓦ wi-fi). The synthetic spreads and veneer beds are standard cheap-motel issue, but there are mini-refrigerators and pet rooms. The one-story, exterior-access **Best Western Wayside Inn** (☎ 435-587-2266; 533 N Main St; r incl breakfast $70-87; ⓦ ⌨) isn't the newest of places, but it does give you more space. Family rooms have three queen beds, two sinks, a refrigerator and a microwave; some pets OK.

Peace Tree Juice Café (☎ 435-587-5063; 516 N Main St; mains $4-7; ⊙ 7am-5pm) is a great place for full breakfasts, organic espresso, smoothies or a healthy lunch wrap. Slow service hasn't stopped **Lamplight Restaurant** (☎ 435-587-2170; 655 E Central St; mains $7-18; ⊙ dinner Mon-Sat) from being the local choice for pasta, steaks and seafood.

From Monticello there's a back way (22 miles instead of the main route's 34 miles) to Canyonlands National Park – Needles District. Take County Rd 101 (Abajo Dr) west to Harts Draw Rd (closed in winter); after 17 scenic miles you join Hwy 211 near Newspaper Rock Recreation Area.

NEWSPAPER ROCK RECREATION AREA

This tiny, free recreation area showcases a single large sandstone rock panel packed with more than 300 **petroglyphs** attributed to Ute and Ancestral Puebloan groups during a 2000-year period. The many red rock figures etched out of a black 'desert varnish' surface make for great photos (evening sidelight is best). The site, about 12 miles along Hwy 211 from Hwy

191, is usually visited as a short stop on the way to the Needles section of Canyonlands National Park (8 miles further).

CANYONLANDS NATIONAL PARK

Vast serpentine canyons tipped with white cliffs loom high over the Colorado and Green Rivers, their waters a stunning 1000ft below the rim rock. Sweeping arches, skyward-jutting needles and spires, deep craters, blue-hued mesas and majestic buttes define the landscape. Canyonlands is Utah's largest national park, a 527-sq-mile vision of ancient earth. Overlooks are easy enough to reach. To explore further you'll need to contend with difficult dirt roads, great distances and a lack of water (even the visitor centers only have bottled). Despite its beauty, this is the least visited of all the major Southwestern national parks.

The Colorado and Green Rivers form a 'Y' that divides the park into three separate districts inaccessible to one another within the park – no bridges and few interior roads mean long drives to see the sights. Cradled atop the Y is the most developed and visited district, Island in the Sky (30 miles/45 minutes from Moab). Think of this as the overview section of the park, where you look down from viewpoints into the canyons that make up the other sections.

The thin hoodoos, sculpted sandstone and epic 4WD trails of the Needles District are 75 miles/90 minutes south of Moab. Serious skill is required to traverse the 4WD roads of the most inaccessible section, the Maze (130 miles/3½ hours from Moab). Horseshoe Canyon (100 miles/two hours from Moab), with one of the Southwest's most spectacular pictograph panels, is an unconnected unit northwest of the Maze. Roads are roughly graded but passable by 2WD when dry.

PERMITS

In addition to entrance fees, permits are required for overnight backcountry camping, backpacking, mountain biking, 4WD trips and river trips. Backpackers pay $15 per group (call for size limits). Day-use mountain bike or 4WD groups pay $30 for up to three vehicles. River trips cost $30 per group in Cataract Canyon, $20 for flat water trips. Horses are allowed on all 4WD trails. Permits are valid for 14 days and are issued on a space-available basis at the visitor center or ranger station where your trip begins. In spring and fall, you should reserve six months to two weeks

CANYONLANDS NATIONAL PARK

To Green River (35mi)

Arches Visitor Center

Arches National Park

Negro Bill Canyon Trail

(313)

Corona Arch • (279) ○ Moab

Kane Creek Blvd

Mineral Rd

Potash Rd

Dead Horse Point State Park

191

La Sal Mountains

To Hwy 24 (25mi)

Kayenta Campground

Visitor Center

Dead Horse Point Overlook

Anticline Overlook

Lower San Rafael Rd

Great Gallery • Horseshoe Canyon

Island in the Sky Visitor Center

Island in the Sky

Shafer Trail Rd

Upheaval Dome Overlook

Willow Flat Campground

Green River Overlook

• Aztec Butte

• Mesa Arch

White Rim Rd

Glen Canyon National Recreation Area

Murphy Point Overlook

White Rim Overlook

River

To Hwy 24 (35mi)

Murphy Hogback Campground

Grand View Point Overlook

Colorado

To Monticello (44mi)

Green River

Needles Overlook

Panorama Point Overlook

Hans Flat Ranger Station

Canyonlands National Park

Colorado River Overlook

Big Spring Canyon Overlook

Canyon Rims Recreation Area

Maze Overlook

Confluence Overlook

Slickrock Trail

Needles Outpost & Campground

Wind Whistle Campground

The Maze

Confluence

Cataract Canyon

Pothole Point

Needles Visitor Center

Cave Spring

Elephant Hill

Squaw Flat Campground

Chesler Park

The Needles

Salt Creek Canyon

Joint Trail

Druid Arch

Elephant Canyon Trail

Indian Creek Cliffs

211

Lake Powell

▲ Henry Mountains

Newspaper Rock Recreation Area

0 — 10 km
0 — 6 miles

---

ahead, by fax or mail, with the **NPS Reservations Office** (☎ 435-259-4351; fax 435-259-4285; www.nps.gov/cany/permits.htm; 2282 SW Resource Blvd, Moab, UT 84532; ☺ 8:30am-noon Mon-Fri). Designated camp areas abut most trails; open-zone camping is permitted in some places.

EMERGENCY

Cell phones work up high, but only satellite phones work in canyons. For search and rescue, contact the **Grand County Emergency Coordinator** (☎ 435-259-8115).

REGULATIONS

Four-wheel-drive vehicles, mountain bikes and street-legal motorbikes are permitted on dirt roads, but not ATVs. In the backcountry, campfires are allowed only along river corridors; use a fire pan, burn only driftwood or downed tamarisk, and pack out unburnt debris. Rock climbing is allowed, but not in Horseshoe Canyon, on any archaeological site or on any feature marked on USGS maps, except Washerwoman Arch. All climbing must be free or clean-aid climbing. The Needles' soft rock is unsuitable for climbing. Check with rangers.

TOURIST INFORMATION

Island in the Sky and the Needles District have visitor centers, listed in the respective sections following. If you have kids, ask about renting a Discovery Pack, which contains binoculars, a magnifying lens and a nature guide.

UTAH

Moab Information Center (p428) also covers the park.

Canyonlands Natural History Association (☎ 435-259-6003, 800-840-8978; www.cnha.org) Sells books for the NPS.

Canyonlands NPS Headquarters (☎ 435-259-7164; www.nps.gov/cany) For advance information.

Canyonlands – Island in the Sky

You'll apprehend space in new ways atop the appropriately named Island in the Sky, a 6000ft-high flat-topped mesa that drops precipitously on all sides, providing some of the longest, most enthralling vistas of any park in southern Utah. The island sits atop a sandstone bench called the White Rim, which indeed forms a white border 1200ft below the mesa top, 1500ft above the river canyon bottom. The 11,500ft Henry Mountains bookend panoramic views in the west, and the 12,700ft La Sal Mountains are to the east. You can stand beneath a sparkling blue sky and watch thunderheads inundating far-off regions while you contemplate applying more sunscreen.

Admission to Island in the Sky ($10 per car, $5 per motorcycle, pedestrian or cyclist) includes entry to Needles, too (keep your receipt). Watching the complimentary video at the **Island in the Sky Visitor Center** (☎ 435-259-4712; www.nps.gov/cany/island; Hwy 313; ☺ 8am-4:30pm Nov-Feb, 8am-6pm Mar-Oct) provides insight into the nature of the park. Get books, maps, permits and campground information here. Schedules are posted daily for ranger-led lectures and hikes on topics such as area geology. An overlook driving tour CD sells for $10 or rents for $5.

The visitor center sits 2 miles beyond the entrance station. From there, the road heads 12 miles to Grand View Point. Halfway there, a paved spur leads northwest 5 miles to Upheaval Dome. Overlooks and trails line each road. Most trails follow cairns over slickrock. Bring lots of water and watch for cliff edges!

SIGHTS & ACTIVITIES
Hiking & Backpacking
Several easy trails pack a lot of punch. Hike **Mesa Arch Nature Trail** (a half-mile loop) at sunrise, when the arch, dramatically hung over the very edge of the rim, glows a fiery red. A mile before Grand View Point, the **White Rim Overlook Trail** is a good spot for a picnic and a 1.8-mile round-trip hike. At the end of the road, the **Grand View Trail** follows a 2-mile round-trip course at rim's edge. Even if you don't hike, Grand View Point overlook is a must-see.

At **Upheaval Dome**, a half-mile spur leads to an overlook of a geological wonder that was possibly the result of a meteorite strike 60 million years ago. Back near the 'Y' in the road, the moderate 2-mile round-trip **Aztec Butte Trail** climbs slickrock to stellar views and an ancient granary.

Longer hikes off the mesa to the White Rim are strenuous, steep and require advance planning. There's one major, hard-to-follow backpacking route, the **Syncline Loop** (8.3 miles, five to seven hours). In summer the exposed trail gets blazingly hot. Most park rescues occur here, because day hikers get lost and/or run out of water. Talk to rangers before setting out.

Mountain Biking & Four-Wheel Driving
Blazed by uranium prospectors in the 1950s, primitive **White Rim Road** circles Island in the Sky. Accessible from the visitor center via Shafer Trail Rd, this 70-mile route is the top choice for 4WD and mountain-biking trips. It generally takes two to three days in a vehicle or three to four days by bike. Since the route lacks any water sources, cyclists should team up with a 4WD support vehicle or travel with an outfitter (see p428). Rangers patrol the route and provide help in a pinch; they also check permits. Stay on trails. Pick up *A Naturalist's Guide to the White Rim Trail* by David Williams and Damian Fagon.

SLEEPING
Seven miles from the visitor center, the first-come, first-served, 12-site **Willow Flat Campground** (tent sites $10) has vault toilets but no water. Bring firewood and don't expect shade. Arrive early to claim a site during spring and fall. Backcountry camping in the Island is mostly open zone (not in prescribed areas), but is still permit limited (see p421). An alternative is to camp nearby in Dead Horse Point State Park (p426), and Moab (p433) has numerous RV parks. The nearest food is in Moab.

Canyonlands – Needles District
Named for the spires of orange-and-white sandstone jutting skyward from the desert floor, the Needles District's otherworldly terrain is so different from Island in the Sky, it's hard to believe

UTAH

they're part of the same park. Despite having paved access roads, the Needles receives only half as many visitors as the Island. Why? It takes 90 minutes to drive from Moab, and once you arrive, you have to work harder to appreciate the wonders – in short, you have to get out of the car and walk. Expend a little energy though, and the payoff is huge: peaceful solitude and the opportunity to participate in, not just observe, the vastness of canyon country.

The **Needles Visitor Center** (☎ 435-259-4711; www.nps.gov/cany/needles; Hwy 211; 🕑 8am-4:30pm Nov-Feb, 8am-6pm Mar-Oct) has similar books and maps to the Island's one. Admission to the Needles District costs $10 per car, $5 per motorcycle, pedestrian or cyclist, and includes entry to Island in the Sky.

Needles Visitor Center lies 2.5 miles inside park boundaries and provides drinking water. From the visitor center, the paved road continues almost 7 miles to the Big Spring Canyon Overlook. Parking areas along the way access several sights, including arches, Ancestral Puebloan ruins and petroglyphs. Morning light is best for viewing the rock spires.

SIGHTS & ACTIVITIES

Hiking

The Needles has four short trails, totaling 4 miles, off the main road and easily doable in a day. They provide an overview of the region's human and geological history. None are wheelchair accessible. Cairns mark sections across slickrock. **Cave Spring Trail** (0.6-mile loop, easy to moderate) is popular with kids. Follow the trail to an abandoned cowboy camp, climbing ladders up slickrock; look for the haunting handprint pictographs on the last cave's walls. **Pothole Point Trail** (0.6-mile loop, easy) might bore little ones, but brainiacs love the biology of the potholes, which contain microorganisms that come to life after rainstorms and complete their lifecycles before the water evaporates. (Keep fingers out of water-filled potholes; oils from your hand kill the critters.)

Slickrock Trail (2.4-mile loop, moderate) scampers across slickrock to fabulous views across the canyon; on the return route, you face the district's needles and spires in the distance.

Needles is Canyonlands' premier backpacking destination; strong hikers can do the best trails in a day. If you venture off-trail, stay in washes or on slickrock to avoid trampling fragile cryptobiotic crust soil (living organisms). Take the **Chesler Park Loop** to get into and among the namesake needles formations. Combined with the slot-canyon-like **Joint Trail** it makes for an awesome 11-mile loop across desert grasslands, past towering red-and-white-striped pinnacles and between deep, narrow fractures, some only 2ft across. Elevation changes are mild, but the distance makes it a moderate to difficult day hike. Also consider the **Confluence Overlook Trail**, a moderate four- to six-hour round-trip from Big Spring Canyon trailhead, to see the silty Green River flow into the muddy-red Colorado. Many hikes connect in a series of loops, some requiring route-finding skills. For gorgeous scenery, the **Elephant Canyon Trail** (11-mile loop) to Druid Arch is hard to beat. The *National Geographic Trails Illustrated* Canyonlands map should suffice, but if you're inclined to wander, pick up a 7.5-minute quadrangle USGS map at the visitor center.

Mountain Biking & Four-Wheel Driving

Fifty miles of 4WD and mountain-biking roads crisscross Needles; off-roading is a main attraction here. Get your permit from the visitor center, check road conditions with rangers and stay on designated routes. Four-wheel-drive roads here require high-clearance vehicles (most off-the-lot SUVs don't count). Know what you're doing, or risk damaging your vehicle and endangering yourself. Towing fees run $1000 to $2000 – really. If you're renting a 4WD vehicle, check the insurance policy; you might not be covered here.

Elephant Hill (32-mile round-trip) is the most well-known and technically challenging route in the district, with steep grades and tight turns (smell the burning brakes and clutches). If you've always wanted to rock climb on wheels, you've found the right trail. Don't try this as your first 4WD or mountain-bike adventure. The route to the **Colorado River Overlook** is easy in a vehicle and moderately easy on a mountain bike; park and walk the final, steep 1.5-mile descent to the overlook. Following the district's main drainage, archaeology junkies love the rock art along the **Salt Creek Canyon Trail** (27-mile loop), which is moderately easy for vehicles, moderate for bikes.

Rock Climbing

About 16.5 miles along Hwy 211 driving toward the Needles District, look up. Even if you don't climb, it's fascinating to watch the experts scaling the narrow cliffside fis-

---

READ ALL ABOUT IT

The otherworldly beauty of Utah has moved many to words almost as eloquent as the nature itself: '…if the redrocks were cut would they bleed?' Terry Tempest Williams ponders in *Red: Passion and Persistence in the Desert*. In addition to reading the incomparable Edward Abbey (see boxed text, p438), turn to the following writers to help deepen your understanding of this impossible place:

Craig Childs (1967–) You'll never see a slot canyon in the same light again after reading the heart-thumping account of flash floods in *Secret Knowledge of Water*, a travelogue that follows naturalist Childs' travels through Utah deserts. His *House of Rain* explores ancient ruins in the Four Corners area.

Tony Hillerman (1925–) Many of Hillerman's whodunits take place on Navajo tribal lands similar to those in Utah and New Mexico around Monument Valley. Landscape and lore are always woven into his mysteries.

Everett Ruess (1914–34) Artist, poet and adventurer, Everett Ruess set out on his burro into the desert near the Escalante River Canyon at 20 years old, never to be seen again. He left behind scores of letters that paint a vivid portrait of life in canyon country before humans and machines. Pick up a copy of *Everett Ruess: A Vagabond for Beauty*, which includes his letters and an afterword by Edward Abbey.

Wallace Stegner (1909–93) A graduate of the University of Utah, Stegner became one of the classic writers of the American West. *Mormon Country* provides an evocative account of the land the Mormons settled and their history; *Big Rock Candy Mountain* is historical fiction that follows a couple's prosperity-seeking moves to Utah.

Terry Tempest Williams (1955–) Born and raised in Utah, Tempest Williams has been both poet and political advocate for the wilderness she loves. In addition to *Red*, an essay collection focused on southeastern Utah, check out *Refuge*, a lyrical elegy for her mother and the Great Salt Lake.

---

sures near **Indian Creek** (www.friendsofindiancreek.org). Experienced crack climbers, take note. There's a small parking lot from where you can cross the freely accessible Nature Conservancy and BLM grazing land.

SLEEPING & EATING

Backcountry camping (p421), in prescribed areas only, is quite popular, so it's hard to secure an overnight permit without advance reservation.

The first-come, first-served 27-site **Squaw Flat Campground** (☎ 435-719-2313, 435-259-4711; www .nps.gov/cany; campsites $15), 3 miles west of the visitor center, fills every day spring to fall. It has flush toilets and cold water. Chose side A, where many sites (12 and 14, for example) are shaded by juniper trees and cliffs. Maximum allowable RV length is 28ft.

If Squaw Flat is full, fret not. Immediately outside the park boundaries, the campground at **Needles Outpost** (☎ 435-979-4007; www.canyonlands needlesoutpost.com; Hwy 211; campsites $15; ☼ Apr-Nov) is an excellent alternative with showers (gasp!). Rock walls provide morning shade (especially at site 2) and, in general, sites are well spaced. Use of the extremely clean shower facilities costs $3 for campers, $5 for noncampers. Other amenities include flush toilets, fire rings, a dump station and a **store** (☼ 8am-6pm). In addition to selling limited groceries, beer,

ice, gasoline and propane, the store's **lunch counter & grill** (dishes $3-7; ☼ 8am-5pm) whips up breakfasts, burgers and such.

Canyonlands – Horseshoe Canyon

Way far west of Island in the Sky, Horseshoe Canyon shelters millennia-old Native American rock art. The centerpiece is the **Great Gallery** and its haunting Barrier Canyon–style pictographs from between 2000 BC and AD 500. The heroic, bigger-than-life-size figures are magnificent. Artifacts recovered here date back as far as 9000 BC. The Great Gallery lies at the end of a 6.5-mile round-trip hiking trail descending 750ft from the main dirt road. Plan on six hours. Rangers lead gallery hikes on Saturday and Sunday from April to October; contact the **Hans Flat Ranger Station** (☎ 435-259-2652; www.nps.gov/cany/horseshoe; ☼ 8am-4:30pm).

You can camp on BLM land at the trailhead, though it's really a parking lot. There is a single vault toilet, but no water. Take Hwy 191 north to I-70 west, then Hwy 24 south. About 25 miles south of I-70, past the turnoff for Goblin Valley State Park, turn east (left) and follow the gravel road 30 miles. From Moab the trip takes about two hours.

Canyonlands – The Maze

A 30-sq-mile jumble of high-walled canyons, the Maze is a rare preserve of true wilderness

UTAH

WHAT THE...?

An unabashed tourist trap 12 miles south of Moab, **Hole 'n the Rock** (☎ 435-686-2250; www.moab -utah.com/holeintherock; 11037 S Hwy 191; adult/child $5/4; ☼ 9am-5pm; ♿) is a 5000-sq-ft home-cum-cave carved into sandstone and decorated in knockout 1950s kitsch. What weren't owners Albert and Gladys Christensen into? He was a barber, a painter, an amateur engineer and a taxidermist. She was a cook (the cave once housed a restaurant) and lapidary jeweler who lived in the blasted-out home until 1974. The hodgepodge of metal art, old signs, small petting zoo and stores make it worth the stop, but you have to tour the surprisingly light home to believe it.

---

for hardy backcountry veterans. The colorful canyons are rugged, deep and sometimes completely inaccessible. Many of them look alike and it's easy to get turned around – hence the district's name. (Think GPS.) Rocky roads absolutely necessitate high-clearance, 4WD vehicles. (There may not be enough money on the planet to get you towed out of here. Wreckers won't even try.) Plan on spending at least three days, though a week is ideal. If you're inexperienced at four-wheel driving, stay away. Be prepared to repair your jeep and, at times, the road.

For predeparture advice and necessities, contact the **Hans Flat Ranger Station** (☎ 435-259-2652; www.nps.gov/cany/maze; ☼ 8am-4:30pm). The station is 130 miles (3½ hours) from Moab, and has a few books and maps, but no other services. Take Hwy 191 north to I-70 west, then Hwy 24 south. Hans Flat is 16 miles south of Horseshoe Canyon. The few roads into the district are poor and often closed with rain or snow; bring tire chains from October to April.

AROUND CANYONLANDS

The BLM **Canyon Rims Recreation Area** (☎ 435-259-2100; www.blm.gov/utah/moab; Needles Overlook Rd) to the east of the national park has two interesting overlooks, undeveloped hiking and backcountry driving. Turn west off Hwy 191 (32 miles south of Moab, 27 miles north of Monticello); a paved road leads 22 miles to **Needles Overlook** and a panorama of the park. Two-thirds of the way to the overlook, the gravel **Anticline Overlook Rd** stretches 16 miles north to a promontory with awesome views of the Colorado River.

Three miles after the Hwy 191 turnoff is **Wind Whistle Campground** (☎ reservations 877-444-6777; www.recreation.gov; campsites $10; ☼ Mar-Oct). The 20 well-spaced sites have fire rings and scenic vistas. Pit toilets; water available.

DEAD HORSE POINT STATE PARK

The views at Dead Horse Point pack a wallop, extending 2000ft down to the winding Colorado

River, up to the La Sal Mountains' 12,700ft peaks and out 100 miles across Canyonlands' mesmerizing stair-step landscape. (You might remember it from the final scene of *Thelma & Louise*.) If you thrive on rare, epic views, you're gonna love Dead Horse.

Leave Hwy 313, 4 miles north of Island in the Sky (30 miles from Moab). Toward the end of the drive, the road traverses a narrow ridge just 90ft across. Around the turn of the 20th century, cowboys used the mesa top as a sort of natural corral by driving wild horses onto it and blocking the ridge. The story goes that ranch hands forgot to release the horses they didn't cull; the stranded equines supposedly died with a great view of the Colorado River…

The **visitor center** (☎ 435-259-2614; www.state parks.utah.gov; admission $10; ☼ 8am-5pm) has great exhibits, shows on-demand videos and sells books and maps. Rangers lead walks and talks in summer. To escape the small (but sometimes chatty) crowds, take a walk around the mesa rim. Visit at dawn or dusk for the best lighting. The 21-site **Kayenta Campground** (☎ reservations 800-322-3770; www.stateparks.utah .gov; RV sites $20), south of the visitor center, provides limited water and a dump station. Reservations are accepted from March to October, but you can often secure same-day sites by arriving early. Fill RVs with water in Moab.

MOAB

pop 4800 / elev 4000ft

An island of civilization in a sea of stunning wilderness, Moab serves as a terrific base camp for area adventures. Hike in Arches or Canyonlands National Parks during the day, then come back to a comfy bed, a hot tub and your selection of surprisingly great restaurants at night. Here you can shop for groceries till midnight, browse the shelves at *two* indie bookstores, sit down for dinner at

9pm and still find several places open for a beer afterward. There's a distinct sense of fun here at 'Utah's Recreation Capital.' Rafting and riding outfitters based here take forays into national parks and onto public lands.

It was miners in search of 'radioactive gold,' ie uranium, that blazed a network of jeep roads, laying the groundwork for Moab to become a 4WD mecca. But neither mining nor the hundreds of Hollywood films shot here had as much influence on the character of Moab as the influx of youth-culture, fat-tire, mountain-bike enthusiasts. Development does come at a price though: chain motels and T-shirt shops line Main St; neon signs blot out the stars; the town gets overrun March through October; and the impact of all those feet, bikes and 4WDs on the fragile desert is a serious concern (use existing trails).

People here love the land, even if they don't always agree about how to protect it. If the traffic irritates you, just remember – you can disappear into the vast desert in no time.

Orientation & Information

Moab lies along an important Colorado River wildlife corridor, tucked beneath high rock walls. Hwy 191 becomes Main St through town. Refill water jugs at the Phillips 66 Station (corner Main St and 300 South), which provides a spigot. Alternatively go to Matrimony Springs (Hwy 128, 100yd east of Hwy 191 on the right). Note that

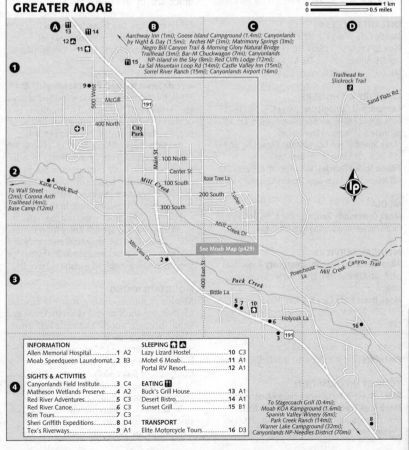

GREATER MOAB

0 ____ 1 km
0 ____ 0.5 miles

Aarchway Inn (1mi); Goose Island Campground (1.4mi); Canyonlands by Night & Day (1.5mi); Arches NP (3mi); Matrimony Springs (3mi); Negro Bill Canyon Trail & Morning Glory Natural Bridge Trailhead (3mi); Bar-M Chuckwagon (7mi); Canyonlands NP–Island in the Sky (8mi); Red Cliffs Lodge (12mi); La Sal Mountain Loop Rd (14mi); Castle Valley Inn (15mi); Sorrel River Ranch (15mi); Canyonlands Airport (16mi)

Trailhead for Slickrock Trail

Sand Flats Rd

500 West

McGill

191

400 North

City Park

Main St

100 North

Center St

Mill Creek

100 South

Rose Tree La

200 South

Tusher St

300 South

Mill Creek Dr

See Moab Map (p429)

Kane Creek Blvd

To Wall Street (2mi); Corona Arch Trailhead (4mi); Base Camp (12mi)

Mtn View Dr

2

400 East St

Pack Creek

Bittle La

Powerhouse La

Mill Creek Canyon Trail

5 7 10

6

3 191

Holyoak La

16

To Stagecoach Grill (0.4mi); Moab KOA Kampground (1.6mi); Spanish Valley Winery (6mi); Park Creek Ranch (14mi); Warner Lake Campground (32mi); Canyonlands NP–Needles District (70mi)

8

INFORMATION	
Allen Memorial Hospital	1 A2
Moab Speedqueen Laundromat	2 B3

SIGHTS & ACTIVITIES	
Canyonlands Field Institute	3 C4
Matheson Wetlands Preserve	4 A2
Red River Adventures	5 C3
Red River Canoe	6 C3
Rim Tours	7 C3
Sheri Griffith Expeditions	8 D4
Tex's Riverways	9 A1

SLEEPING	
Lazy Lizard Hostel	10 C3
Motel 6 Moab	11 A1
Portal RV Resort	12 A1

EATING	
Buck's Grill House	13 A1
Desert Bistro	14 A1
Sunset Grill	15 B1

TRANSPORT	
Elite Motorcycle Tours	16 D3

UTAH

many restaurants and some motels shut down (or limit hours) from late October through March.

BOOKSTORES

Arches Book Company (Map p429; ☎ 435-259-0782; 78 N Main St; ⏱ 7:30am-8pm) General bookstore, good fiction, green-tea smoothies.

Back of Beyond Books (Map p429; ☎ 435-259-5154; 83 N Main St; ⏱ 9am-5pm Nov-Mar, 9am-9pm Apr-Oct) Great selection of local trail guides, histories and nonfiction.

EMERGENCY

Cell phones work here, but not in canyons, where a satellite phone is essential.

Grand County Emergency Coordinator (☎ 435-259-8115) Search and rescue.

Police (Map p429; ☎ 435-259-8938; 115 W 200 South)

INTERNET ACCESS

Mondo Café (Map p429; ☎ 435-259-5551; McStiff's Plaza, 59 S Main St; per 5min 75¢; ⏱ 6:30am-7pm Nov-Feb, 6:30am-7pm Sun-Thu & 6:30am-9:30pm Fri & Sat Mar-Oct) Five internet terminals; free wi-fi.

LAUNDRY & SHOWERS

Canyonlands Campground (Map p429; ☎ 435-259-6848, 800-522-6848; www.canyonlandsrv.com; 555 S Main St) Showers $5; super well maintained.

Moab Speedqueen Laundromat (Map p429; ☎ 435-259-7456; 702 S Main St; ⏱ 8am-7pm)

Poison Spider Bicycles (Map p429; ☎ 435-259-7882; 497 N Main St; ⏱ 8am-8pm) Showers $3 per five minutes.

MEDIA

Moab Community Radio (89.7FM & 106.1FM) Tune in for alternative programming from folk to funk.

MEDICAL SERVICES

Allen Memorial Hospital Emergency Room (Map p427; ☎ 435-259-7191; 719 W 400 North) Emergency medical care.

Moab Immediate Care & X-Ray (Map p429; ☎ 435-259-5276; 267 N Main St; ⏱ noon-8pm) Non-emergency care.

POST

Post office (Map p429; ☎ 435-259-7427; 50 E 100 North)

TOURIST INFORMATION

BLM (☎ 435-259-2100; www.blm.gov/utah/moab)
Moab Area Travel Council (☎ 800-635-6622; www.discovermoab.com; PO Box 550, Moab, UT 84532; ⏱ 8am-5pm Mon-Fri) Advance information only.

Moab Happenings (www.moabhappenings.com) Free newspaper and website geared toward visitors.

Moab Information Center (Map p429; ☎ 435-259-8825; cnr Main & Center Sts; ⏱ 8am-8pm) Its comprehensive selection of books and maps covers all of southeastern Utah, including NPS, USFS, BLM and state park lands. Pamphlets on off-road trails, 4WD roads, rock art, movie location sites etc. Walk-in only.

Sights & Activities

Moab is a base for mountain bikers, white-water rafters, hikers, backcountry 4WD enthusiasts and visitors to Arches and Canyonlands National Parks. If you have a disability or are traveling with someone with a physical or mental disability, book a trip through **Splore** (☎ 801-484-4128; www.splore.org).

Between breakfast and dinner there's not much activity in Moab. On a rainy day, you might check out the dinosaur and mining exhibits at the **Dan O'Laurie Museum** (Map p429; ☎ 435-259-7985; www.grandcountyutah.net/museum; 118 E Center St; adult/child $2/free; ⏱ 10am-3pm Mon-Sat, noon-3pm Sun).

The Nature Conservancy oversees the 890-acre **Matheson Wetlands Preserve** (Map p427; ☎ 435-259-4629; www.nature.org; 934 W Kane Creek Blvd; admission free; ⏱ dawn-dusk) just west of town. Bring binoculars and bug spray. Guided birding walks begin at 8am Saturday, March to October.

Red Cliffs Lodge (off Map p427; ☎ 435-259-2002; Mile 14, Hwy 128; admission free; ⏱ 8am-10pm), 15 miles north of town, has a tasting room for its on-site winery. It also houses the Moab Museum of Film & Western Heritage, with Hollywood memorabilia from films shot in the area.

For some no-frills wine tasting, visit the surprisingly good **Spanish Valley Winery** (off Map p427; ☎ 435-259-8134; www.moab-utah.com/spanish valleywinery; Zimmerman Lane, off Stocks Dr; ⏱ noon-5pm Mon-Sat), 6 miles south of Moab on Hwy 191.

MOUNTAIN BIKING

Moab's mountain biking is world-famous. Challenging trails ascend steep slickrock and wind through woods and up 4WD roads. There's no place like it. Spring and fall are busiest. In summer start by 7am, otherwise it's too hot. Pick up *Above & Beyond Slickrock*, by Todd Campbell, or *Rider Mel's Mountain Bike Guide to Moab*. Avoid all off-trail riding and pack everything out (including cigarette butts).

Be sure to reserve rentals in advance. Full-suspension bikes start at around $40 per day. Shops are generally open from 9am to

MOAB

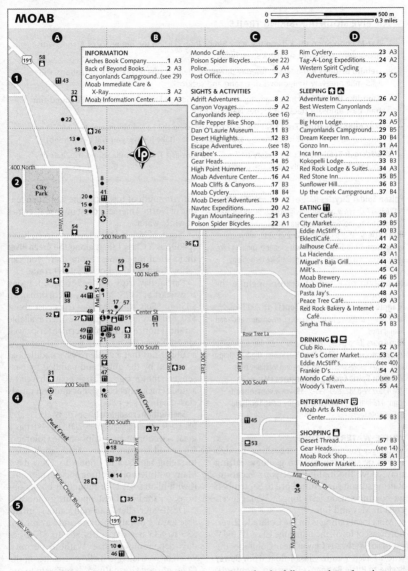

0 — 500 m
0 — 0.3 miles

INFORMATION
Arches Book Company.............1 A3
Back of Beyond Books..............2 A3
Canyonlands Campground..(see 29)
Moab Immediate Care &
  X-Ray...............................3 A2
Moab Information Center.......4 A3

SIGHTS & ACTIVITIES
Adrift Adventures.....................8 A2
Canyon Voyages.....................9 A2
Canyonlands Jeep................(see 16)
Chile Pepper Bike Shop.........10 B5
Dan O'Laurie Museum............11 B3
Desert Highlights....................12 B3
Escape Adventures.............(see 18)
Farabee's...............................13 B3
Gear Heads............................14 B5
High Point Hummer................15 A2
Moab Adventure Center.........16 A4
Moab Cliffs & Canyons...........17 B3
Moab Cyclery.........................18 B4
Moab Desert Adventures........19 A3
Navtec Expeditions.................20 A2
Pagan Mountaineering............21 A3
Poison Spider Bicycles............22 A1

Mondo Café............................5 B3
Poison Spider Bicycles.........(see 22)
Police....................................6 A4
Post Office.............................7 A3

Rim Cyclery...........................23 A3
Tag-A-Long Expeditions.........24 A2
Western Spirit Cycling
  Adventures..........................25 C5

SLEEPING
Adventure Inn.......................26 A2
Best Western Canyonlands
  Inn...................................27 A3
Big Horn Lodge.....................28 A5
Canyonlands Campground......29 B5
Dream Keeper Inn.................30 B4
Gonzo Inn............................31 A4
Inca Inn...............................32 A1
Kokopelli Lodge....................33 B3
Red Rock Lodge & Suites.......34 A3
Red Stone Inn.......................35 B5
Sunflower Hill.......................36 B3
Up the Creek Campground.....37 B4

EATING
Center Café..........................38 A3
City Market...........................39 B5
Eddie McStiff's......................40 B3
EklectiCafé...........................41 A2
Jailhouse Café.......................42 A3
La Hacienda.........................43 A1
Miguel's Baja Grill.................44 A3
Milt's..................................45 C4
Moab Brewery......................46 B5
Moab Diner..........................47 A4
Pasta Jay's...........................48 A3
Peace Tree Café....................49 A3
Red Rock Bakery & Internet
  Café.................................50 A3
Singha Thai..........................51 B3

DRINKING
Club Rio...............................52 A3
Dave's Corner Market............53 C4
Eddie McStiff's..................(see 40)
Frankie D's...........................54 A2
Mondo Café......................(see 5)
Woody's Tavern....................55 A4

ENTERTAINMENT
Moab Arts & Recreation
  Center...............................56 B3

SHOPPING
Desert Thread.......................57 B3
Gear Heads......................(see 14)
Moab Rock Shop...................58 A1
Moonflower Market...............59 B3

5pm year-round, and at least until 8pm from March through October. Full-day tours (including rentals) start at around $100.

For multisport tours, see the boxed text, p431. For biking, hiking or rafting shuttles, contact **Roadrunner Shuttle** (☎ 435-259-9402; www.roadrunnershuttle.com) or **Coyote Shuttle** (☎ 435-259-8656; www.coyoteshuttle.com).

Consider the following places for sales, gear and rental:

Chile Pepper Bike Shop (Map p429; ☎ 435-259-4688, 888-677-4688; www.chilepepperbikeshop.com; 550½ N Main St) Also does repairs.

Moab Cyclery (Map p429; ☎ 435-259-7423, 800-451-1133; www.moabcyclery.com; 391 S Main St) Runs tours, rents and shuttles.

TOP FIVE MOUNTAIN-BIKING TRAILS

■ **Bar-M Loop** Bring the kids on this easy 8-mile loop skirting the boundary of Arches, with great views and short slickrock stretches.

■ **Gemini Bridges** A moderate, full-day downhill ride past spectacular rock formations, this 13.5-mile one-way trail follows dirt, sand and slickrock.

■ **Klondike Bluffs Trail** Intermediates can learn to ride slickrock on this 15.6-mile round-trip trail, past dinosaur tracks to Arches National Park.

■ **Moonlight Meadow Trail** Beat the heat by ascending the La Sal Mountains to 10,600ft on this moderate 10-mile loop among aspens and pines (take it easy; you will get winded).

■ **Slickrock Trail** Moab's legendary trail will kick your ass! The 12.7-mile round-trip, half-day route is for experts only (as is the practice loop).

Poison Spider Bicycles (Map p429; ☎ 435-259-7882, 800-635-1792; www.poisonspiderbicycles.com; 497 N Main St) Road bikes, too. Good, cheap trail maps.

Rim Cyclery (Map p429; ☎ 435-259-5333; www.rim cyclery.com; 94 W 100 North) Moab's longest-running bike shop; includes a museum of mountain-bike technology.

Mountain bike tour operators include the following:

Magpie Adventures Cycling Tours (☎ 800-546-4245; www.magpieadventures.com) Canyonlands and road biking trips.

Rim Tours (Map p427; ☎ 435-259-5223, 800-626-7335; www.rimtours.com; 1233 S Hwy 191) Where the bike shops turn. Super-professional half-, one- and multiday trips.

Western Spirit Cycling Adventures (Map p429; ☎ 435-259-8732, 800-845-2453; www.westernspirit.com; 478 Mill Creek Dr) Closest to the trails. Local and nationwide tours.

WHITE-WATER RAFTING

Whatever your interest, be it bashing through rapids or studying canyon geology, rafting may prove the highlight of your vacation. Rafting season runs from April to September; jet-boating season lasts longer. Water levels crest in May and June.

Most local rafting is on the Colorado River, northeast of town, including the Class III to IV rapids of **Westwater Canyon**, near Colorado; the wildlife-rich 7-mile Class I float from **Dewey Bridge to Hittle Bottom** (no permit required); and the Class I to II **Moab Daily**, the most popular stretch near town (no permit required; expect a short stretch of Class III rapids).

Rafters also launch north of Moab to get to the legendary Class V rapids of **Cataract Canyon** (NPS permit required). This Colorado River canyon south of town and the Confluence is one of North America's most intense stretches of white water.

North of Moab, in the town of Green River (p439), is a Class I float along the **Green River** that's ideal for canoes. From there you can follow John Wesley Powell's 1869 route.

Partial-day trips cost $45 to $65; full-day trips start at $125. Multiday excursions run $350 to $800, while jet-boat trips cost about $70. Kids pay less. Day trips are often available on short notice, but book overnight trips well ahead. Know the boat you want: an oar rig is a rubber raft that a guide rows; a paddleboat is steered by the guide and paddled by passengers; motor rigs are large boats driven by a guide (such as jet boats). For more on rapids classification, see p88.

Sheri Griffith Expeditions (Map p427; ☎ 435-259-8229, 800-332-2439; www.griffithexp.com; 2231 S Hwy 191) has a great selection of river trips on the Colorado, Green and San Juan Rivers – from family floats to raging rapids, a few hours to a few days. Many outfitters offer rafting and can combine it with hiking, 4WD or mountain-biking options; see the boxed text, opposite for more.

Do-it-yourselfers can rent canoes, inflatable kayaks or rafts. Canoes and kayaks run $35 to $45 per day, rafts $65 to $130 per day, depending on size. Without permits, you'll be restricted to mellow stretches of the Colorado and Green Rivers; if you want to run Westwater Canyon or enter Canyonlands on either river, you'll need a permit. Contact the **BLM** (☎ 435-259-2100; www.blm.gov/utah/moab) or **NPS** (☎ 435-259-4351; www.nps.gov/cany/permits.htm).

Advanced rafters wanting to run Cataract Canyon, beyond the Confluence, will have to book a jet-boat shuttle. Two companies hold permits: Tex's Riverways (below) and Tag-A-Long Expeditions (below). Reserve equipment, permits and road and river shuttles way in advance. **Slickrock Air Guides** (☎ 435-259-6216; www .slickrockairguides.com) and **Redtail Aviation** (☎ 435-259-7421; www.redtailaviation.com) operate air shuttles for river trips.

River rental and shuttle operators include the following:

Black Dog Shuttle (☎ 800-241-2591; www.rr-ss.com) Transport only.

Canyon Voyages (Map p429; ☎ 435-259-6007, 800-733-6007; www.canyonvoyages.com; 211 N Main St) Rents and sells kayaks, canoes and rafts.

Red River Adventures (Map p427; ☎ 435-259-4046; www.redriveradventures.com; 1140 S Main St) Rentals and tours.

Red River Canoe (Map p427; ☎ 435-259-7722, 800-753-8216; www.redrivercanoe.com; 1371 N Hwy 191) Canoes only.

Tex's Riverways (Map p427; ☎ 435-259-5101; www .texsriverways.com; 691 N 500 West) Rents rafts and kayaks, and runs river shuttles.

HIKING

Don't limit yourself to the national parks. To see petroglyphs and two spectacular arches, hike the moderately easy **Corona Arch Trail** (trailhead 6 miles up Potash Rd). You may recognize Corona from a well-known photograph showing an airplane flying through it – this is one big arch! Plan on two hours for the 3-mile walk. The moderately easy **Negro Bill Canyon Trail** is a 2.5-mile walk along a stream. (The totally politically incorrect canyon name refers to a prospector who grazed his cows here in the 1800s.) Scoot down a shaded side canyon to find petroglyphs, then continue to the 243ft-wide **Morning Glory Natural Bridge**, at a box canyon. Plan on three to four hours. The trailhead is 3 miles north of Moab on Hwy 128. To escape summer's heat, head to the **La Sal Mountains** east of Moab and hike through white-barked aspens and ponderosa pines.

Canyonlands Field Institute (Map p427; ☎ 435-259-7750, 800-860-5262; http://canyonlandsfieldinst.org; 1320 S Hwy 191) leads all-ages nature hikes that are a wonderful introduction to the area.

FOUR-WHEEL DRIVING

If you go four-wheeling, stay on established routes. The desert looks barren, but it's a fragile landscape of complex ecosystems. Cryptobiotic crusts (see p72) may take a century to regenerate after one tire track (really). Moab Information Center has tons of route info. Several good companies lead 4WD and combination land/river trips; see the boxed text, left.

ALL-IN-ONE OUTFITTERS

Can't choose just one adventure? No worries. Scads of Moab outfitters will help you combine hiking with biking, rafting with horseback riding, off-roading with rafting. Do it all in one day or have your outfitter plan a multiday extravaganza. Most have stores that sell books and some gear.

Adrift Adventures (Map p429; ☎ 435-259-8594, 800-874-4483; www.adrift.net; 378 N Main St) It all started back in 1978 with rafting trips, and that's still what Adrift does best. But its helpful staff will arrange for you to be on the water in the morning and on a group 4WD tour in the afternoon.

Canyon Voyages (Map p429; ☎ 435-259-6007, 800-733-6007; www.canyonvoyages.com; 211 N Main St) Take a single or multiday guided raft river trip or make your own multisport package that includes kayaking, hiking and biking.

Escape Adventures (Map p429; ☎ 435-259-7423, 800-451-1133; www.escapeadventures.com; 391 S Main St) This Las Vegas–based company with green intentions (vegetable-oil-fueled support vehicles, solar-powered store, Leave No Trace group member…) organizes mountain biking and multiday multisport tours.

Moab Adventure Center (Map p429; ☎ 435-259-7019, 866-904-1163; www.moabadventurecenter.com; 225 S Main St) Truly your one-stop adventure shop. This megacenter arranges, alone or in combination, rafting trips, Hummer excursions, jeep rental, horseback riding, rock climbing, guided hikes, scenic flights and even national park bus tours.

Navtec Expeditions (Map p429; ☎ 435-259-7983, 800-833-1278; www.navtec.com; 321 N Main St) Comprehensive river excursions are led by dedicated local guides. Closed-vehicle 4WD tours are also available alone or in combo.

Tag-A-Long Expeditions (Map p429; ☎ 435-259-8946, 800-453-3292; www.tagalong.com; 452 N Main St) Detail-oriented and Moab-specific, Tag-A-Long is a good all-adventure outfitter. It offers flat-water jet boats, white-water rafting, land safaris, horseback riding, scenic flights, skydiving and more.

For a guided two- to four-hour thrill ride up the slickrock in a Hummer, call **High Point Hummer** (Map p429; ☎ 435-259-2972, 877-486-6833; www.highpointhummer.com; 281 N Main St; adult $65-89, child $39-55). It sets the standard for helpful service and also rents ATVs and leads ATV tours. **Coyote Land Tours** (☎ 435-259-6649; www .coyotelandtours.com) offers similar group outings in Hummer-like 4WDs, but it uses the very open, bright yellow Mercedes Benz Unimog off-road vehicles; you can't miss them.

Rather ride in a jeep? Nobody knows the backcountry like **Dan Mick's Guided Jeep Tours** (☎ 435-259-4567; www.danmick.com). Be warned that not everyone gets along so well with Dan: if he doesn't agree with your politics, he may push your buttons.

If you rent your own 4WD vehicle ($175 to $190 per day), remember that insurance policies may not cover off-roading damage. Rental agency hours are 7:30am to 7pm March through October, 8am to 5pm November through February. Reputable companies include the following:

Canyonlands Jeep (Map p429; ☎ 435-259-4413; www.canyonlandsjeep.com; Moab Adventure Center, 225 S Main St) Generally the cheapest; check internet specials.

Cliffhanger Jeep Rental (off Map p427; ☎ 435-259-2599; www.cliffhangerjeeprental.com; Aarchway Inn, 1551 N Hwy 191)

Farabee's (Map p429; ☎ 435-259-7494; www.moab jeeprentals.com; 401 N Main St)

ROCK CLIMBING & CANYONEERING

Rock climbers in town gravitate toward **Wall Street** (Moab's El Capitan; off Map p427), off Potash Rd, so it gets crowded. For information and gear, head to **Pagan Mountaineering** (Map p429; ☎ 435-259-1117; www.paganmountaineering.com; 59 S Main St, Suite 2) or **Gear Heads** (Map p429; ☎ 435-259-4327, 888-740-4327; www.gearheadsoutdoorstore.com; 471 S Main St).

You can also rappel into rivers and hike through slot canyons. Half-day canyoneering or climbing adventures run around $95 per person for two, full-day $150 per person. Locally owned **Desert Highlights** (Map p429; ☎ 435-259-4433, 800-747-1342; www.deserthighlights.com; 50 E Center St; trips $80-120) leads outstanding canyoneering and climbing trips high on personal attention. It's also the only outfitter with a permit to canyoneer in Arches' Fiery Furnace.

Also check out the following:

Moab Cliffs & Canyons (Map p429; ☎ 435-259-3317, 877-641-5271; www.cliffsandcanyons.com; 63 E Center St)

Moab Desert Adventures (Map p429; ☎ 435-260-2404; www.moabdesertadventures.com; 451 N Main St)

HORSEBACK RIDING

If you want to combine riding and white-water rafting, see the boxed text, p431. Otherwise, **Red Cliffs Lodge** (off Map p427; ☎ 435-259-2002, 866-812-2002; www.redcliffslodge.com; Mile 14, Hwy 128) guides half-day trail rides (March to November) around Castle Valley, north of town.

SKIING & SNOWSHOEING

The La Sal Mountains, which lord over Moab, receive tons of powder, just perfect for cross-country skiing, and there's a hut-to-hut ski system. To book the huts contact **Tag-A-Long Expeditions** (Map p429; ☎ 435-259-8946, 800-453-3292; www.tagalong.com; 452 N Main St). **Rim Cyclery** (Map p429; ☎ 435-259-5333; www.rimcyclery.com; 94 W 100 North) rents skis and **Gear Heads** (Map p429; ☎ 435-259-4327, 888-740-4327; www.gearheadsoutdoorstore.com; 471 S Main St) rents snowshoes; both provide trail maps.

OTHER ACTIVITIES

Moab's airport is 16 miles north of town on Hwy 191. Two companies run one-hour air tours ($125 per person): **Slickrock Air Guides** (☎ 435-259-6216; www.slickrockairguides.com) and **Redtail Aviation** (☎ 435-259-7421; www.redtailaviation .com). You can go skydiving or base-jumping with **Skydive Moab** (☎ 435-259-5867; www.skydive moab.com; tandem jump $189-229).

Base Camp (off Map p427; ☎ 435-260-1783; www .camelotlodge.com; off Kane Creek Blvd; per player $5), west of town, maintains an 18-hole, par 61 disc golf (Frisbee) course over canyons, slickrock and cactus-strewn meadows. Reservations essential; call for directions.

Festivals & Events

Moab loves a party. For calendars, contact the **Travel Council** (☎ 435-259-8825, 800-635-6622; www .discovermoab.com).

Skinny Tire Festival (☎ 435-259-2698; www.skinny tirefestival.com) Road cycling; first weekend in March.

Jeep Safari (www.rr4w.com) The week before Easter, more than 2000 4WD vehicles overrun town in the year's biggest event. Register early; trails are assigned.

Moonshadows in Moab (☎ 435-259-2698; www .moonshadowsinmoab.com) Bike riding by July moonlight.

Rumble in the Red Rocks Motocross (☎ 435-259-7814; www.racemoab.com) Motocrossers rev up in September.

Moab Fat Tire Festival (☎ 435-260-1182; www .moabfattirefest.com) One of Utah's biggest mountain-biking events with tours, workshops, lessons, competitions and plenty of music in October.

Moab Folk Festival (☎ 435-260-2488; www.moabfolk festival.com) Folk music and environmental consciousness combined. This November festival is 100% wind powered, venues are easily walkable and recycling's encouraged.

Sleeping

Rates given here are for March to October; prices drop by as much as 50% outside those months. Some smaller places close in winter. Cyclists: ask whether a property provides *secure* bike storage, not just bike storage (most have that). Most also have hot tubs for aching muscles, and motels have laundry facilities to clean up the trail dirt. For condos, try **Moab Central Reservations** (☎ 800-505-5343, 800-748-4386; http://moabutahlodging.com).

BUDGET
Hostels & Motels
Lazy Lizard Hostel (Map p427; ☎ 435-259-6057; www .lazylizardhostel.com; 1213 S Hwy 191; dm/s/d $9/23/26, cabins $35-47; 🖳) Many long-term residents hang out at this house and cabin compound south of town. The couches are frayed and the bunks worn, but there is a small kitchen and computer.

our pick **Red Stone Inn** (Map p429; ☎ 435-259-3500, 800-772-1972; www.moabredstone.com; 535 S Main St; r $55-70) See the simple, pine-paneled rooms with refrigerator, microwave, coffee makers and free wired internet access and you may think you've found the perfect budget digs. If the walls weren't so thin, you wouldn't be wrong. Guests have pool privileges at the Big Horn Lodge across the street. Some pets OK.

Adventure Inn (Map p429; ☎ 435-259-6122, 866-662-2466; www.adventureinnmoab.com; 512 N Main St; r incl breakfast $58-69; 🕑 Mar-Nov) Super-cute little motor court motel on the main drag. The lilac linens and fluffy green towels at this family-owned property feel like an upgrade. There's a picnic area on site; no hot tub.

Kokopelli Lodge (Map p429; ☎ 435-259-7615, 888-530-3134; www.kokopellilodge.com; 72 S 100 East; r $65-75; 🖳 wi-fi) Tucked away on a back street, you'll find this carefully tended, 1950s motel with eight rooms only. A sunset color exterior, pine posts and grassy yard all add character. Pet friendly.

Also recommended:

Inca Inn (Map p429; ☎ 435-259-7621; www.incainn.com; 570 N Main St; r incl breakfast $52-82; 🕑 Mar-Nov; 🐾) Swiss mom-and-pop motel hosts; spick-and-span rooms.

Red Rock Lodge & Suites (Map p429; ☎ 435-259-5431, 877-207-9708; www.red-rocklodge.com; 51 N 100 West; r $60-79) Old-West exterior, standard motel interior. Hot tub, high-speed internet access.

Camping
Fill up your water containers for free at Gear Heads outdoors store (opposite), which rents and sells tents and sleeping bags.

Goose Island Campground (off Map p427; ☎ 435-259-2100; www.blm.gov/utah/moab; Hwy 128; campsites $10) Ten no-reservation riverside BLM campgrounds lie along a 28-mile stretch of Hwy 128 that parallels the Colorado River. The 18-site Goose Island, just 1.4 miles from Moab, is the closest. Pit toilets, no water.

Up the Creek Campground (Map p429; ☎ 435-259-6995; 210 E 300 South; tent sites per one/two people $15/25) Within walking distance of downtown sits this fun, little hippy-hiker-vibe campground. Park in the lot and walk the shaded tent grove that fosters community. Showers $6; no fires.

Canyonlands Campground (Map p429; ☎ 435-259-6848, 800-522-6848; www.canyonlandsrv.com; 555 S Main St; tent sites $23, RV sites/ camping cabins $34/47; 🐾) Think old-growth trees and lots of shade at one of the longest-running local campgrounds, right downtown. RVs are lined up parking lot–like, but the tent area is separate. Showers, laundry, store and playground on site.

Other options include the following:

Warner Lake Campground (off Map p427; ☎ 435-587-2041, 888-444-6777; reservations www.recreation.gov; off La Sal Mountain Loop Rd; campsites $10; 🕑 Jun-Oct) In La Sal Mountains, 32 miles southeast (and 20°F cooler).

Moab KOA Kampground (off Map p427; ☎ 435-259-6682, 800-562-0372; www.moabkoa.com; 3225 S Hwy 191; tent sites/ RV sites $24/32, camping cabins $50; 🕑 Mar-Oct; 🐾 ♿ wi-fi) Pancake breakfasts, playground, games room and mini-golf. Pets welcome.

Portal RV Resort (Map p427; ☎ 435-259-2028, 800-574-2028; www.portalrvresort.com; 1261 N Hwy 191; RV sites $31-35; wi-fi) The place for luxury RVers. Showers; some pets OK.

MIDRANGE
Big Horn Lodge (Map p429; ☎ 435-259-6171, 800-325-6171; www.moabbighorn.com; 550 S Main St; r $80-95; 🐾 wi-fi) The two-story sibling across from Red Stone Inn has a heated pool and slightly more guest space. Paneled rooms with pine beds contrast with the reflective black-glass windows.

Base Camp (off Map p427; ☎ 435-260-1783; www .camelotlodge.com; off Kane Creek Blvd; r $100) On 50 rugged riverside acres beneath Hurrah Pass, the five-room Base Camp is a bona fide back-country lodge. Leave your high heels at home: the only way here is via 4WD or boat. Bike, jeep and ATV rental available.

Dream Keeper Inn (Map p429; ☎ 435-259-5998, 888-230-3247; www.dreamkeeperinn.com; 191 S 200 East; r incl breakfast $115-165; 🐾) Walk to restaurants from this immaculate mid-century ranch-house B&B. Native American textiles add to the refined design of six uncluttered rooms, and lush lawns surround a kidney-shaped pool.

Aarchway Inn (off Map p427; ☎ 435-259-2599, 800-341-9359; www.aarchwayinn.com; 1151 N Hwy 191; r $119-149; wi-fi) The activities desk will arrange all your outdoor adventures or rent you a jeep, but you can also hike nature trails from here at the northern end of town. Family suites and rooms with three queen beds are a great group choice. All rooms have microwaves, mini-refrigerators and lots of space.

Best Western Canyonlands Inn (Map p429; ☎ 435-259-2300, 800-528-1234; www.canyonlandsinn.com; 16 S Main St; r incl breakfast $139; 🐾 wi-fi) You can't get more central than staying at the crossroads of Main and Center Sts. It's a bit better maintained than the Best Western Greenwell Inn across the street, even if the room colors are a little garish Southwest.

Gonzo Inn (Map p429; ☎ 435-259-2515, 800-791-4044; www.gonzoinn.com; 100 W 200 South; r/ste $145/189; 🐾 wi-fi) Brushed metal-and-wood headboards, concrete shower stalls and '50s retro patio furniture make this Moab's hippest hotel. Standard rooms have king-size beds, while suites also have pull-out sofas. Some pets OK.

Also try:

Motel 6 Moab (Map p427; ☎ 435-259-6147, 800-466-8356; www.motel6.com; 1089 N Main St; r $80-99; 🐾) Multistory, interior-access motel; great red rock views.

Castle Valley Inn (off Map p427; ☎ 435-259-6012; www.castlevalleyinn.com; La Sal Mountain Loop Rd; r incl breakfast $95-170) Idyllic B&B, 15 miles northwest of town.

TOP END

Sunflower Hill (Map p429; ☎ 435-259-2974, 800-662-2786; www.sunflowerhill.com; 185 N 300 East; r incl breakfast $155-225; 🐾 wi-fi) Kick back in an Adirondack chair amid the manicured gardens of two inviting buildings – an early-20th-century home and a 100-year-old farmhouse. The 12 rooms at Sunflower have a sophisticated country sensibility. Breakfast may include scones, homemade jam, omelettes and freshly squeezed

juice, and there are snacks and beverages 24/7. Heated pool, hot tub.

Pack Creek Ranch (off Map p427; ☎ 435-259-5505; www.packcreekranch.com; cabins $165-225; 🐾) Eleven log cabins at this little Shangri-la in the mountains (14 miles southeast of Moab) sleep from four to 12 people. All have full kitchens, some have fireplaces, and a few allow pets.

Red Cliffs Lodge (off Map p427; ☎ 435-259-2002, 866-812-2002; www.redcliffslodge.com; Mile 14, Hwy 128; r $199-299; 🐾) Part dude ranch, part luxury motel, Red Cliffs has exceptionally comfy rooms with vaulted ceilings, kitchenettes and private patios (some overlook the river). Taste the wines made on site, go for a trail ride or arrange a rafting trip or ATV rental.

Sorrel River Ranch (off Map p427; ☎ 435-259-4642, 877-359-2715; www.sorrelriver.com; Hwy 128; r $339-459; 🐾 💻) Handmade log beds, custom-crafted lighting, exquisite linens – every in-room detail is perfect. The much-touted lodge restaurant (opposite) is a destination in itself. Southeast Utah's only AAA Four Diamond resort resides along the Colorado River (Mile 17), so everything from the decadent spa to the pool and hot tub has a waterfront view.

Eating

BUDGET

our pick Milt's (Map p429; ☎ 435-259-7424; cnr 300 South & 400 East; burgers $4-5; ⏰ 6am-8pm Mon-Sat) Pull up one of only a handful of stools at this tiny 50-year-old diner, or order through the screen window and eat under the tree. Locals come back often for the chile cheeseburgers, hand-cut fries and boffo milkshakes (try butterscotch-banana).

Stagecoach Grill (off Map p427; ☎ 435-259-6315; 2728 S Hwy 191; breakfast & sandwiches $4-8; ⏰ breakfast & lunch) Here's where the locals come to catch up on the gossip. The all-American food ain't fancy, but it'll stick to your ribs.

EklectiCafé (Map p429; ☎ 435-259-6896; 352 N Main St; breakfast & sandwiches $5-7; ⏰ breakfast & lunch; 💻 wi-fi) Soy-ginger-seaweed scrambled eggs anyone? This homey café lives up to its eclectic name. Come for organic coffee, curried wraps, vegetarian salads and such.

Jailhouse Café (Map p429; ☎ 435-259-3900; 101 N Main St; breakfast $7-8; ⏰ 7am-noon Mar-Oct) Sure, it's a cute tiny breakfast place with good advertising. But if there's a wait (and there usually is), know that there you can do just as well elsewhere.

For health food, visit the nonprofit **Moonflower Market** (Map p429; ☎ 435-259-5712; 39 E 100 North; ⏰ 9am-8pm Mon-Sat, 10am-3pm Sun).

Sandwich stops include the following:

City Market (Map p429; ☎ 435-259-5181; 425 S Main St; sandwiches $3-6; ⏰ 6am-midnight) Groceries, Starbucks and make-to-order deli.

Peace Tree Café (Map p429; ☎ 435-259-8503; 20 S Main St; wraps $4-8; ⏰ 8am-6pm Nov-Feb, 8am-8pm Mar-Oct) Fresh fruit smoothies and healthy wraps.

Red Rock Bakery & Internet Café (Map p429; ☎ 435-259-5941; 74 Main St; sandwiches $4-8; ⏰ 7am-6pm; 💻 wi-fi) Fat sandwiches on homemade bread.

MIDRANGE

Steaks are a good deal pricier (around $30) than anything else on the menu.

Moab Diner (Map p429; ☎ 435-259-4006; 189 S Main St; breakfast & sandwiches $6-8, mains $9-15; ⏰ 6am-9pm Mon-Sat) The Diner serves classic greasy-spoon fare with a Southwest twist. Don't miss the green chile sauce on your eggs at breakfast.

La Hacienda (Map p429; ☎ 435-259-6319; 574 N Main St; mains $9-14; ⏰ 11am-10pm) For big plates of straightforward Tex-Mex, 'La Ha' is Moab's long-running favorite. Whenever possible it uses local, hormone-free beef.

Moab Brewery (Map p429; ☎ 435-259-6333; 686 S Main St; dishes $9-16; ⏰ 11:30am-11pm Mar-Oct, 11:30am-9pm Nov-Feb) You don't have to eat when you drink at this busy microbrewery, but you should – the food is darn good and the menu selection's huge. Choose from gyro salad or salmon Caesar, St Louis ribs or Texas BBQ, turkey burger or tilapia, for example. Wash it all down with a site-made wheat beer.

Singha Thai (Map p429; ☎ 435-259-0039; 92 E Center St; dishes $10-16; ⏰ lunch & dinner Mon-Sat, dinner Sun) Locals rave about the curries and pad Thai, but the seafood specialties, such as the tilapia in coconut sauce, are quite good, too.

Miguel's Baja Grill (Map p429; ☎ 435-259-6546; 51 N Main St; dishes $10-18; ⏰ 5-10pm) Miguel's makes great fish tacos, just like in Baja. Surfside murals give the narrow place a lot of character.

Buck's Grill House (Map p427; ☎ 435-259-5201; 1393 N Hwy 191; mains $11-24; ⏰ dinner) Upscale contemporary Southwestern specialties, such as duck tamales with adobo and elk stew with horseradish cream, are what Buck's does best (there are veggie options, too). Don't miss the buffalo chorizo and cheese quesadilla. This is white tablecloth service for down-home food.

Also try the following:

Pasta Jay's (Map p429; ☎ 435-259-2900; 4 S Main St; lunches $5-11, mains $10-16; ⏰ 11am-9pm Nov-Feb, 11am-11pm Mar-Oct) Lunch specials are a bargain.

Eddie McStiff's (Map p429; ☎ 435-259-2337; 59 S Main St; dishes $11-17; ⏰ 5:30pm-midnight Mon-Fri, 11:30am-midnight Sat & Sun) The other brewhouse in town; always packed and popular with the fat-tire crowd.

Sunset Grill (Map p427; ☎ 435-259-7146; 900 N Hwy 191; mains $15-24; ⏰ dinner Mon-Sat) The view is the only draw here on a hill overlooking Moab.

TOP END

Formal dress is not required, but you'll want to change out of your bike shorts. Make reservations.

Red Cliffs Lodge (off Map p427; ☎ 435-259-2002; Mile 14, Hwy 128; sandwiches $6-10, mains $16-28; ⏰ lunch & dinner Mon-Sat, brunch Sun) Come before sunset: every table has a stunning view of red rock buttes and the river below. The Western-style dinner menu includes steaks and ribs. In nice weather, the outside patio is the place to be.

Center Café (Map p429; ☎ 435-259-4295; 60 N 100 West; small plates $6-11, mains $18-30; ⏰ dinner) The chef-owner at Center Café draws from regional American and Mediterranean influences to create his inspired cuisine. Main dishes might include sautéed shrimp with cheddar-garlic grits or pan-roasted lamb with balsamic-port reduction. By dining here you are supporting the local farmers market and youth garden. Budgeteers: come for the small plates served from 3pm to 6pm.

Sorrel River Grill (off Map p427; ☎ 435-259-4642; Sorrel River Ranch, Hwy 128; lunch mains $10-14, dinner mains $24-36; ⏰ lunch & dinner Mar-Oct, dinner Nov-Feb) Reserve ahead: dining at the River Grill is a hot, high-end ticket. The New American menu changes seasonally, but expect fresh seafood from the coast and, of course, a filet mignon. Service is superb, as are the sunsets over the red cliffs outside of town.

Desert Bistro (Map p427; ☎ 435-259-0756; 1266 N Hyw 191; mains $19-29; ⏰ dinner) Twinkling lights hang in the trees outside this old ranch-house-turned-restaurant. Inside, stylized preparations of game is the specialty; everything is made in-house. Great wine list, too.

Drinking

Skip Starbucks; instead sip shade-grown espresso at **Dave's Corner Market** (Map p429; ☎ 435-259-6999; 401 Mill Creek Dr; ⏰ 6am-10pm), owned by

UTAH

the mayor. Or get jacked on caffeine, check email, then play hackeysack with the dudes at **Mondo Café** (Map p429; ☎ 435-259-5551; McStiff's Plaza, 59 S Main St; ☼ 6:30am-7pm Nov-Feb, 6:30am-7pm Sun-Thu, 6:30am-9:30pm Fri & Sat Mar-Oct).

Of the two microbreweries, hikers and bikers guzzle pitchers at **Eddie McStiff's** (Map p429; ☎ 435-259-2337; 59 S Main St; dishes $8-17; ☼ 5:30pm-midnight Mon-Fri, 11:30am-midnight Sat & Sun). A mixed tourist and local crowd populates **Moab Brewery** (Map p429; ☎ 435-259-6333; 686 S Main St; ☼ 11:30am-11pm Mar-Oct, 11:30am-9pm Nov-Feb). Both also serve food.

Local bars (or 'private clubs,' with a cover-like charge) occasionally have music: meet area miners and ranchers at the rough-cut **Woody's Tavern** (Map p429; ☎ 435-259-9323; 221 S Main St); shoot pool or play horseshoes at **Frankie D's** (Map p429; ☎ 435-259-2654; 44 W 200 North); or boogie Friday and Saturday when the raucous **Club Rio** (Map p429; ☎ 435-259-6666; 100 W Center St) has DJs.

Entertainment

Great fun for kids and grandparents, **Canyonlands by Night & Day** (off Map p427; ☎ 435-259-2628, 800-394-9978; www.canyonlandsbynight.com; 1861 N Hwy 191; adult with/without dinner $59/49, child $49/39; ☼ Apr-Oct; ☝) runs a two-hour sunset boat trip on the Colorado with an optional barbecue beforehand.

A night of unapologetic tourist fun at **Bar-M Chuckwagon** (off Map p427; ☎ 435-259-2276, 800-214-2085; www.barmchuckwagon.com; Hwy 191; adult/child $25/12.50; ☼ Apr-Oct; ☝), 7 miles north of Moab, starts with a gunfight in a faux Western town. A cowboy dinner and Western-music show follows. Reservations recommended.

The **Moab Arts & Recreation Center** (Map p429; ☎ 435-259-6272; www.moabcity.state.ut.us/marc; 111 E 100 North) hosts everything from yoga classes to contra dances and poetry gatherings.

Shopping

Every few feet along Main St, there's a shop selling outdoorsy clothing and T-shirts; there's plenty of pottery and Native American trading post knickknacks to be had, too. Look for art and photography galleries on Center St, near the Main St intersection. From March to October, stores stay open until 10pm.

You can pick up a gorgeous hand-knitted scarf or bag, or buy supplies to do it yourself, at **Desert Thread** (Map p429; ☎ 435-259-8404; 90 E Center St). The **Moab Rock Shop** (Map p429; ☎ 435-259-7312; 600 N Main St) is a rock hound's paradise. If you're

after camping gear, go to **Gear Heads** (Map p429; ☎ 435-259-4327, 888-740-4327; 471 S Main St).

Getting There & Around

Moab is 235 miles from SLC via I-15, US Hwy 6 and US Hwy 191. **Bighorn Express** (☎ 888-655-7433; www.bighornexpress.com) operates a scheduled van service to and from the SLC airport. Alternatively, you can fly to Grand Junction, Colorado (115 miles northeast).

Twice daily, **Great Lakes Airlines** (☎ 800-554-5111; www.flygreatlakes.com) flies from Denver, CO to **Canyonlands Airport** (CNY; off Map p427; ☎ 435-259-7421; www.moabairport.com), 16 miles north of Moab via Hwy 191. **Roadrunner Shuttle** (☎ 435-259-9402; www.roadrunnershuttle.com) operates on-demand service to and from the Moab airport.

Greyhound (☎ 435-564-3421, 800-229-9424; www.greyhound.com) and **Amtrak** (☎ 435-872-7245, 800-872-7245; www.amtrak.com) serve Green River, 53 miles northwest of Moab. From there, ride Roadrunner Shuttle or Bighorn Express.

Rent motorcycles from **Elite Motorcycle Tours** (Map p427; ☎ 435-259-7621, 888-778-0358; www.moab.net/elitetours; 1310 Murphy Ln).

For hiking, biking or rafting shuttles, contact Roadrunner Shuttle or **Coyote Shuttle** (☎ 435-259-8656; www.coyoteshuttle.com).

ARCHES NATIONAL PARK

Giant windows and sweeping arcs of chunky sandstone frame snowy peaks and desert landscapes at Arches National Park. The park boasts the highest density of rock arches anywhere on Earth – more than 2500 in a 116-sq-mile area. You'll lose perspective on size at some, such as the thin and graceful Landscape Arch, which stretches more than 300ft across (one of the largest in the world). Others are tiny – the smallest only 3ft across. Once you train your eye, you'll spot them everywhere (like a game of 'Where's Waldo?'). An easy drive (some say too easy) makes the spectacular arches accessible to all. Fiery Furnace is a not-to-be-missed guided-tour-only area of the park, where you weave your way through narrow canyons and soaring finlike rocks.

Though they look stable, arches are forever in flux; eventually they all break and disappear. As you stroll beneath these monuments to nature's power, listen carefully, especially in winter, and you may hear spontaneous popping noises in distant rocks – it's the sound of arches forming. (If you hear popping noises *overhead*, however, run like the dickens!)

ARCHES NATIONAL PARK

0 —— 5 km
0 —— 3 miles

Orientation & Information

Enter off Hwy 191, 5 miles north of Moab. Admission is $10 per car, or $5 per motorcycle, bicycle or pedestrian. There's one main road, with two short spurs that lead to more major sights. The most popular stops lie closest to the visitor center. If you're tight on time, visit the Windows Section, off the first spur, where the formations are visible from the road.

Crowds are often unavoidable, and parking areas overflow on weekends, spring to fall. The NPS may eventually institute a shuttle. For now, to keep drivers from parking in dangerous or sensitive areas, rangers have stepped up ticketing for illegal parking. In summer arrive by 9am, when crowds are sparse and temperatures bearable, or visit after 7pm. Drive carefully; accidents occur when drivers focus on the scenery, not the road.

Stop first at the **visitor center** (☎ 435-719-2299; www.nps.gov/arch; ⏰ 7:30am-6:30pm Apr-Oct, 8am-4:30pm Nov-Mar) to see the informative video, check ranger-led activity schedules, reserve your tickets for a Fiery Furnace hike and buy maps. To buy books about the area in advance, con-

tact the **Canyonlands Natural History Association** (☎ 435-259-6003, 800-840-8978; www.cnha.org; 3031 S Hwy 191, Moab, UT 84532).

For search and rescue, contact **Grand County Emergency Coordinator** (☎ 435-259-8115). July highs average 100°F; carry at least one gallon of water per person.

Sights & Activities

SCENIC DRIVES

Salt Valley Rd is generally accessible to conventional vehicles (except when wet). It leaves the main road a mile before Devils Garden and heads 9 miles west to **Klondike Bluffs**. You'll get away from the crowds, but you won't be alone. From Klondike Bluffs, an unnamed, 10-mile 4WD dirt road doubles back to the scenic drive at Balanced Rock. Drive north to south (the northbound route tackles a steep and sandy climb that may be impassable).

From Balanced Rock, **Willow Flats Rd** leads west 8 miles to Hwy 191. Formerly the main route into the park, it requires a high-clearance or 4WD vehicle. The road doesn't offer any important features, just distant views and semisolitude. Check with rangers for up-to-date road conditions.

HIKING & BACKPACKING

Tight on time? The Windows Section has stunning arches that take little physical effort to reach. The 0.6-mile round-trip **Windows Trail** brings you up to the namesake formations. Stand beneath North Window and look out to the canyon views beyond, or frame North Window within South for a stunning picture. Don't forget Double Arch, right across the parking lot.

Book ahead for a **Fiery Furnace** guided hike, so you can explore the maze of spectacularly

---

ARCHES & BRIDGES

What's the difference between an arch and a bridge? Both form through erosion of sandstone. An arch forms when water freezes and expands in cracks, forming fins, like those in the Fiery Furnace at Arches. When portions of the rock break away underneath, an arch results. A bridge forms when water passes beneath sandstone, causing its erosion. But rivers dry up or change course, so it can sometimes become difficult to tell a bridge from an arch.

UTAH

IN DEFENSE OF THE DESERT

Passionate defender of the desert, author Edward Abbey (1927–89) became intimate with Arches National Monument in the 1950s, when he worked there as a seasonal ranger, pre–national park. Environmentalist? Anarchist? Was he a crank or just cranky? It's hard to pin Abbey down, but what's certain is that he cherished this land and championed its protection. His evocative prose has enticed countless readers to do the same. Many of his essay collections are set in part in Utah and all of them are filled with radical, raw and deadly serious humorous opinions.

In *Desert Solitaire: A Season in the Wilderness* (1969), an essay collection, Abbey wrote of his time in Arches, describing the simple beauty and subtle power of a vast landscape. Here, and in other books, he bemoaned (in colorful language) the government co-opting the wilderness, the paving of nature and the scourge of the automobile. He saw the takeover of the car as inevitable and ruinous. As he said in *Desert Solitaire:* 'In the first place, you can't see anything from a car; you've got to get out of the goddamned contraption and walk, better yet crawl, on hands and knees, over the sandstone and through the cactus. When traces of blood begin to mark your trail you'll see something, maybe.'

As one of the foremost Western writers, bringing to life the stark beauty of the canyonlands in southern Utah, Abbey undeniably attracted people seeking the very remoteness he wanted to preserve. Many of Abbey's fears have been realized – you need only arrive at Arches on a busy weekend and get stuck in a line of SUVs to know that he was, in his way, a prophet.

narrow canyons and giant fins. Buy tickets in person (adult $10, child $5) at the visitor center. Reserve up to seven days in advance for the two- to three-hour walks, offered morning and afternoon, April to October. Hikes fill two days ahead. If you're an accomplished hiker and want to go it alone, you must pay a fee, watch a video and discuss with rangers how to negotiate this confusing jumble of canyons before they'll grant you a permit.

The park's most famous hike is to **Delicate Arch**. You've seen this one before: it's the unofficial state symbol and is pictured on just about every piece of Utah tourist literature out there. To get there, drive 2.5 miles beyond **Balanced Rock**, a 3577-ton boulder sitting atop a spindly pedestal, like a fist shooting out of the earth. From there a spur road leads 2 miles to **Wolfe Ranch**, a well-preserved 1908 pioneer cabin. A footbridge crosses **Salt Wash** (near Native American rock art) and marks the beginning of the moderate, 3-mile round-trip trail to Delicate Arch. The trail ascends slickrock, culminating in a wall-hugging ledge. There are shorter look-out hikes, but it's well worth the trek to the arch itself. Tip: ditch the crowds by passing beneath the arch and dropping down the other side several yards (bring a picnic).

Many short hikes originate near the main park road. Just over 2 miles from the entrance is **Park Avenue**, a mile-long trail past a giant fin of rock reminiscent of a New York skyline. Kids love running through the **Sand Dune Arch**

(0.4-mile round-trip); from the same trailhead, walk across grassland for 1 mile to reach 60ft **Broken Arch.**

Nineteen miles from the visitor center, at the end of the paved road, **Devils Garden** marks the beginning of several hikes, from 2- to 7-mile round-trips, that pass nearly a dozen arches. The easy mile to **Landscape Arch** gets busy, but ahead, the trail gets less crowded and grows rougher.

Due to the fragility of the living cryptobiotic crusts (also called 'biological soil'; see p72), the park discourages backcountry hikes. If you're determined, there is the **Devils Garden Primitive Loop**; get a backcountry permit, available in person from the visitor center, and speak with rangers.

ROCK CLIMBING

Rock climbing is allowed only on unnamed features. Routes require advanced techniques. No permits are necessary. Ask about current regulations and route closures. For guided canyoneering into the Fiery Furnace, contact an outfitter such as Desert Highlights (p432) in Moab.

Sleeping & Eating

Devils Garden Campground (☎ 877-444-6777, 518-885-3639; www.recreation.gov; campsites $15) Don't expect much shade, just red rock and scrubby piñon trees at the park's only campground, 18 miles from the visitor center. A few of the sites at the top have La Sal Mountain views. From March to October, half the sites are available by reservation only; for same-day availability, check at the visitor center, not the campground. Facilities include water, picnic tables, grills and toilets, but no showers (available in Moab; see p428). RVs up to 30ft are welcome, but generator hours are limited to two hours in the morning, four in the evening.

No food is available in the park; again, Moab is the place. Stock up or dine out there.

Getting There & Around

The park has no shuttle system and no public buses run to the park. So, pretty much you need your own wheels. Moab Adventure Center (p431) runs bus tours into the park from Moab.

GREEN RIVER

pop 980 / elev 4100ft

A small-town, white-water rafting base, Green River has cheaper accommodations than Moab, 53 miles to the southeast. Settled in 1878, the town now relies mainly on tourism for income, as you can tell from the many motels. The only town of note along I-70 between Salina, UT (108 miles west), and Grand Junction, CO (102 miles east), Green River is a pit stop for travelers. It's also the 'world's watermelon capital,' and celebrates the harvest with the **Melon Days** festival in September.

Orientation & Information

The I-70 business loop north of the freeway between exits 158 and 162 becomes Main St. **Emery County Visitor Center** (☎ 435-564-3600, 888-564-3600; www.greenriverutah.com; 885 E Main St; ☻ 8am-8pm Mar-Oct, 8am-4pm Tue-Sun Nov-Feb) sells white-water rafting maps and guides, and is attached to the local museum.

Sights & Activities

The Colorado and Green Rivers were first explored in 1869 and 1871 by the legendary one-armed Civil War veteran, geologist and ethnologist John Wesley Powell. Learn about his amazing travels at **John Wesley Powell River History Museum** (☎ 435-564-3427; www.jwprhm .com; 885 E Main St; adult/child $3/1; ☻ 8am-8pm Apr-Oct, 8am-4pm Nov-Mar), which also has good exhibits on the Fremont Indians, geology and local history.

Shady **Green River State Park** (☎ 435-564-3633; www.stateparks.utah.gov; Green River Blvd; per car $5; ☻ 8am-10pm Mar-Oct, 8am-5pm Nov-Feb) has a boat launch and a nine-hole **golf course** (☎ 435-564-8882; 9/18 holes $10/20) with pro shop.

Crystal Geyser, about 9 miles south of town, erupts unpredictably from near the east bank of the Green River every 13 to 17 hours, sometimes shooting 100ft into the air for 30 minutes. Ask the visitor center for directions.

The river is flat between the park and the confluence of the Colorado River, making it good for float-it-yourself rafting and canoeing. (The current is deceptively strong; swim only with a life jacket.) Local outfits rent canoes and run easy rafting day trips for about $60 for adults and $40 for kids, including lunch and transportation. Outfitters include the following:

Colorado River & Trail (☎ 435-564-8170, 800-253-7328; www.crateinc.com) Tours only, no rentals.

Holiday Expeditions (☎ 435-564-3273, 800-624-6323; www.bikeraft.com; 1055 E Main St)

Moki Mac River Expeditions (☎ 435-564-3361, 800-284-7280; www.mokimac.com; 100 Silliman Ln) The biggest of the bunch.

Sleeping

Green River State Park (☎ reservations 800-322-3770; www.reserveamerica.com; campsites $15) The 42 green

---

DETOUR: SEGO CANYON

It's rare to see the **rock art** of three different ancient cultures on display all in one canyon, but that's precisely what you can do at Sego. The canyon itself is 4 miles north of I-70 at Thompson Springs (26 miles east of Green River). On the south-facing wall, the **Barrier Culture pictographs** are the oldest (at least 2000 years old); the wide-eyed anthropomorphic creatures take on haunted, mummy- or ghostlike appearances to modern eyes. The **Fremont petroglyphs** were carved about 1000 years ago. Many of the line art figures are wearing chunky ornamentation and headdresses (or antennae?). The third panel is from the 19th-century Utes; look for the horses and buffalo. If you drive half a mile further north up the canyon, you come to a little **ghost town**. The few buildings were deserted when a mining camp was abandoned in the 1950s.

and shady campsites in this riverfront park are open year-round. Water, showers and boat launch on site.

Shady Acres RV Park (☎ 435-564-8290, 800-537-8674; www.shadyacresrv.com; 350 E Main St; tent sites $20, RV sites $26-35, cabins $42; 🛉 wi-fi) Three playgrounds, 36 washers and dryers, an on-site grocery store and an RV wash make Shady Acres a family vacationer's dream. Air-conditioned camping cabins sleep four (bring linens).

Robbers Roost Motel (☎ 435-564-3452; www.robbers roost-motel.com; 225 W Main St; r $30-50; wi-fi) This small 1940s motel is family-owned and cared for. Rooms are basic, but it's a bargain. Park right outside your room.

Super 8 (☎ 435-564-8888; 1248 E Main St; r $59-74; 💻 wi-fi) A plain-Jane, interior-access motel that isn't far from the highway. Makes a good I-70 pit stop.

Best Western River Terrace (☎ 435-564-3401, 800-528-1234; www.bestwestern.com; 880 E Main St; r incl breakfast $80-90; 🐕 💻 wi-fi) Stay riverfront, with a full-service restaurant (great fudge). Roomy guest quarters have traditional darkwood veneer furniture (and super black-out curtains). Breakfast bar includes omelettes.

Eating & Drinking

Green River Coffee Co (☎ 435-564-3352; 115 W Main St; sandwiches $3-6; 🕑 7am-2pm; 💻 wi-fi) 'Friends don't let friends drink Starbucks,' or so says the cash register sign. The barista brews up various caffeine-laden drinks. Breakfast and lunch sandwiches available.

Ray's Tavern (☎ 435-564-3511; 25 S Broadway; burgers $5-7, steaks $12-22; 🕑 lunch & dinner) People flock to this local beer joint for the best hamburgers and fresh-cut French fries around. The steaks aren't bad either. On display are T-shirts rafters from all over have donated ('Rafters stay wet all day' is a fun one). Microbrews and a pool table round out the evening.

Buy groceries and deli sandwiches at **Melon Vine Food Store** (☎ 435-564-3228; 76 S Broadway; 🕑 8am-7pm Mon-Sat).

Other options:

Ben's Cafe (☎ 435-564-3352; 115 W Main St; mains $6-8; 🕑 lunch & dinner) Mexican-American.

Tamarisk Restaurant (☎ 435-564-8109; 870 E Main St; mains $9-16; 🕑 breakfast, lunch & dinner) Family restaurant next to the Best Western.

Getting There & Around

Greyhound (☎ 435-564-3421, 800-231-2222; www.grey hound.com), in the Rodeway Inn (525 E Main St),

goes to Grand Junction, CO ($29, one hour and 40 minutes). **Bighorn Express** (☎ 888-655-7433; www.bighornexpress.com) also stops at the Rodeway Inn; it runs vans to Salt Lake City ($59, 3½ hours) and Moab ($39, one hour).

Amtrak (☎ 435-872-7245, 800-872-7245; www.amtrak .com; 250 S Broadway) runs daily to SLC ($31, 4½ hours) and Denver, CO ($58 to $91, 10 hours). Green River is the only Amtrak stop in southeastern Utah.

GOBLIN VALLEY STATE PARK & AROUND

A Salvador Dali-esque melted-rock fantasy, a valley of giant stone mushrooms, an otherworldly alien landscape or the results of an acid trip the creator went on? No matter what you think the stadium-like valley of stunted hoodoos resembles, one thing's for sure – the 3654-acre **Goblin Valley State Park** (☎ 434-564-3633; Goblin Valley Rd; per car $7) is just plain fun. A few trails lead down from the overlooks to the valley floor, but after that there's no path to follow. You can climb down, around and even over the evocative 'goblins' (2ft- to 20ft-tall formations). Kids and photographers especially love it.

The 21-site **campground** (☎ 801-322-3770, reservations 800-322-3770; campsites $16) has water and showers, but little shade; it books up on most weekends. Further west off Goblin Valley Rd is BLM land – free camping, no services (stay on designated roads).

The park is about 46 miles southwest of Green River; from Hwy 24, a signed paved road leads 12 miles to the entrance. There is no visitor center (headquarters are officially at Green River State Park; p439), but the rangers at the **fee booth** (🕑 9am-5pm) are helpful.

Twenty miles south on Hwy 24 is **Hanksville** (population 350, elevation 4300ft). If you don't need gas, there's little reason to stop (better to stay in Green River, Torrey or at Lake Powell, depending where you're headed). The **BLM** (☎ 435-542-3461; 406 S 100 West; 🕑 8:30am-4:30pm Mon-Fri) has maps and information for surrounding lands, particularly the Henry Mountains. If you have to stay, **Whispering Sands Motel** (☎ 435-542-3238; www.hanksville.com/whisperingsands/motel.html; 90 S Hwy 95; r $45-60; 💻 wi-fi) is the town's nicest lodging (though that's not saying much). Before continuing south, fill up your car and carry your own food and water. There are no more services until you get to Bullfrog Marina (70 miles) or Mexican Hat (130 miles).

To the southwest, the majestic **Henry Mountains** (11,000ft) was the last range to be named and explored in the lower 48. Extremely remote and scenic, it boasts one of the country's remaining free-roaming, wild bison herds. Look for pronghorn antelopes, mule deer and bighorn sheep as well. There are two main access roads: from Hanksville, follow 1100 East street to the south, which becomes Sawmill Basin Rd; from Hwy 95, about 20 miles south of Hanksville, follow the Bull Mountain Scenic Backway west. Both are very rough and rocky dirt roads; flat tires are common and 4WD vehicles are highly recommended. Rangers patrol infrequently. It's so remote that the area was famous as a hiding place for outlaws such as Butch Cassidy.

GLEN CANYON NATIONAL RECREATION AREA & LAKE POWELL

In the 1960s, construction of a massive dam flooded Glen Canyon, forming the lake. Almost 50 years later, this is still an environmental hot-button topic, but generations of Western families have grown up boating here. Water laps against stunning, multihued cliffs that rise hundreds of feet; narrow channels and tributary canyons twist off in every direction.

Lake Powell stretches for more than 185 miles. Most of the watery way lies within Utah. However, Glen Canyon Dam itself, the main Glen Canyon National Recreation Area visitor center, the largest and most developed marina (Wahweap) and the biggest town on the lake (Page) are all in Arizona. For more on Arizona services, and sights such as Rainbow Bridge, see p219. In Utah, **Glen Canyon National Recreation Area** (entry per week $7) surrounds the lake. Primary access is 70 miles south of Hanksville; check in at the **Bullfrog Visitor Center** (☎ 435-684-7420; Hwy 276; 8am-5pm May-Sep) and get general info.

At the end of the road, **Bullfrog Marina** (☎ 435-684-3000; www.lakepowell.com; Hwy 276; 9am-4pm) rents out boats – 19ft runabouts ($375) and personal watercraft ($275) – by the day, but houseboats are really its big business. You can rent a 54ft boat that sleeps 12 for between $1800 and $2400 a week. Invest in the waterproof *Lake Powell Photomap* ($11) so you can pilot your craft to some great canyon hikes.

Landlubbers can spend the night at the marina's waterfront **Defiance House Lodge** (☎ 435-684-3000; www.lakepowell.com; Hwy 276; r $94-114; Mar-Oct) and eat at **Anasazi Restaurant** (☎ 435-684-3000; www.lakepowell.com; Hwy 276; breakfast $6-8, mains $8-16; breakfast, lunch & dinner Mar-Oct). The restaurant serves pretty standard all-American fare, but it does try to use local produce and sustainable practices. Also on site: a small convenience store, marine fuel and trailer parking. The 24-space **Painted Hills RV Park** (☎ 435-684-3000; www.lakepowell.com; Hwy 276; RV sites $34; Mar-Oct), with showers, is just up the road. The pavement is wide (50ft pull-thrus), but there's little ground cover.

Inland 12 miles or so from the marina, there are a couple of marine service-gas station-convenience store-deli complexes. **Ticaboo Lodge** (☎ 435-788-2110; Hwy 276; r $70-90; wi-fi) is a fine money-saving sleeping alternative. The big, interior-access motel rooms all have two queen beds and are quite tidy. The attached **Horney Toad Bar & Grill** (☎ 435-788-2434; breakfast $4-7, mains $6-14; breakfast, lunch & dinner Tue-Sun) is the local fave.

To continue south along Hwy 276, you have to take the **ferry** (☎ 800-528-6154; www.lakepowell.com; per car $20) to Hall's Crossing. The trip takes about 30 minutes and there are six crossings a day between 8am and 7pm, May to September. Hours cut back gradually in the fall and spring until only two boats run between 8am and 3pm, November through March.

Low lake levels in recent years closed the marina at **Hall's Crossing** (☎ 435-684-7000; www.lakepowell.com; 8am-4pm Mar-Oct). However, it is once again running a small store (variable hours) and doing a few houseboat rentals. Cottonwoods shade some of the 32 pull-thru waterfront spaces at the associated **Village Center Campground** (RV sites $34; Mar-Oct). Hite Marina remains closed.

SOUTHWESTERN UTAH

Wonder at the deep-crimson canyons of Zion National Park, hike among the delicate pink and orange minarets at Bryce Canyon, drive past the swirling yellow-white domes of Capitol Reef. Southwestern Utah is so spectacular that you can't go anywhere without tripping over a national park or forest, BLM wilderness or a state park; the vast majority of the territory has been preserved as public lands. The most recent addition, Grand Staircase-Escalante National Monument (GSENM) is both the largest and the least

SOUTHWESTERN UTAH

ROADS THAT RULE: SOUTHWESTERN UTAH

- **Loop-the-Fold** This 100-mile loop, half of which is on dirt roads generally accessible to 2WD passenger vehicles, provides a comprehensive overview of Waterpocket Fold (p444). A driving guide is for sale ($1) at the Capitol Reef National Park visitor center (below). West of the park, the segment of rocky valleys and twists on Hwy 12 (www.scenicbyway12.com), between Hwy 24 and Boulder, is one of the most striking drives in Utah. It only gets better after turning east along unpaved Burr Trail Rd to Strike Valley Overlook (35 miles east of Boulder). You can stop here and backtrack (recommended) or take the really rough Nottom-Bullfrog Rd (p445) north to finish the loop at Hwy 24.

- **Caineville Wash Road** Just west of Capitol Reef National Park, turn north off Hwy 24 to the otherworldly monoliths like Temple of the Sun and Temple of the Moon on Caineville Wash Rd. Continue on into the northern part of the park and Glass Mountain, a 20ft mound of fused selenite. Two-wheel drive is usually fine for the first 15.5 miles. With a 4WD you can make this a 58-mile Cathedral Valley loop along Hartnet Rd, which fords the Fremont River just before rejoining Hwy 24.

- **Hell's Backbone** The gravel-strewn 48 miles from Hwy 12 along Hell's Backbone Rd to Torrey is far from a shortcut. You'll twist, you'll turn, you'll ascend and descend hills, but the highlight is a single lane bridge atop an impossibly narrow ridge (for more, see p448).

- **Hwy 14** From Cedar City, this paved scenic route leads 42 miles over the Markagunt Plateau, ending in Long Valley Junction at Hwy 89. The road rises to 10,000ft with splendid views of Zion National Park to the south. Make sure you detour at Cedar Breaks National Monument (p462). Hwy 14 is kept open all year by snowplows, but snow tires or chains are required November to March.

---

charted. But the whole area is ripe for outdoor exploration, with narrow slot canyons to shoulder through, pink sand dunes to scale and wavelike sandstone formations worth seeking out.

To get to some of the most noteworthy sites can be quite a hike (and may require specialized gear). Elevation changes in the region – mountainous highs to desert lows – pose an additional challenge. In the end, any effort you make is usually more than equaled in pay-off by a stunning view of our eroding and ever-changing Earth.

Note that you'll average no more than 35mph to 50mph on scenic highways in the area.

CAPITOL REEF NATIONAL PARK

Giant slabs of chocolate-red rock and sweeping yellow sandstone domes dominate the landscape of Capitol Reef, which Fremont Indians called the 'Land of the Sleeping Rainbow.' The park's centerpiece is Waterpocket Fold, a 100-mile-long monocline – a buckle in the Earth's crust – that blocked explorers' westward migration like a reef blocks a ship's passage. Known also for its enormous domes,

one of which resembles Washington DC's Capitol Dome, the park has fantastic desert hiking trails, 800-year-old petroglyphs and a verdant 19th-century Mormon settlement with prolific fruit trees.

Orientation & Information

There's no fee to enter the park in general. Scenic Dr runs 9 miles south from the visitor center; entry costs $5 per car if you go beyond Fruita Campground. Pay at the self-service kiosk. All services – food, gas, medical – are based out of Torrey, 11 miles west. Capitol Reef National Park is southwest of I-70, 107 miles from Green River.

The narrow park runs north–south along Waterpocket Fold. Hwy 24 traverses its northern section. Capitol Reef's central region is the Fruita Historic District. To the far north lies Cathedral Valley, the least-visited section. Aside from Hwy 24 and Scenic Dr, other routes follow dirt roads bladed only four times a year. Check weather and road conditions before heading out.

The **visitor center** (☎ 435-425-3791; www.nps.gov/care; cnr Hwy 24 & Scenic Dr; ☺ 8am-6pm Mar-Oct, 8am-4:30pm Nov-Feb) is park headquarters and the only

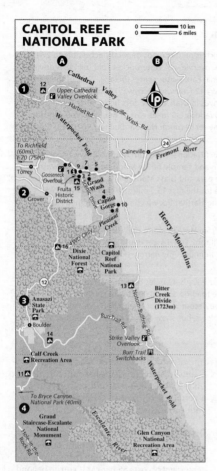

CAPITOL REEF NATIONAL PARK

0 ___ 10 km
0 ___ 6 miles

chaeologists that the Fremont Indians were a distinct group.

For area tours and outfitters, see Torrey (p446).

FRUITA HISTORIC DISTRICT

Fruita (*froo*-tuh) is a cool green oasis, where shade-giving cottonwoods and fruit-bearing trees line the Fremont River's banks. The first Mormon homesteaders arrived in 1880; Fruita's final resident left in 1969. Among the historic buildings, the NPS maintains 2700 cherry, apricot, peach, pear and apple trees planted by early settlers. Visit between June and October, and pluck ripe fruit from the trees, for free, from any unlocked orchard. Ask rangers or call the **fruit hotline** (☎ 435-425-3791). Pick only mature fruit; leave the rest to ripen. Near the orchards is a wonderful picnic area, with roaming deer and birds in the trees, a desert rarity.

Across the road from the blacksmith shop (just a shed with period equipment) is the **Ripple Rock Nature Center** (🕙 10am-3pm Mar-Oct; 🔥), a family-oriented learning center. The **Gifford Homestead** (🕙 10am-3pm Mar-Oct) reveals the day-to-day world of pioneer homesteads.

WATERPOCKET FOLD

Park boundaries roughly follow Waterpocket Fold. Scenic Dr parallels it; Hwy 24 crosses it (domes along Hwy 24, such as Navajo and Capitol Domes, are actually part of the fold). But the easiest way to see it is off Hwy 12; drive east from Boulder and ascend the Burr Trail Switchbacks (p452), then continue north for 3 miles to **Strike Valley Overlook**.

in-park source for information. Watch the short film, then ooh and aah over the 64-sq-ft park relief map, carved with dental instruments. Inquire about ranger-led programs.

Occasional summer thunderstorms pose a serious risk of flash floods. Always check weather with rangers at the visitor center. Bugs bite in May and June. Summer temperatures can exceed 100°F at the visitor center (5400ft), but it's cooler than Moab. If it's too hot, ascend to Torrey (10°F cooler) or Boulder Mountain (30°F cooler).

Sights & Activities

East of the visitor center on Hwy 24, look for the freely accessible roadside **petroglyphs**; these are the carvings that convinced ar-

SCENIC DRIVES

Numbered roadside markers on the paved **Scenic Drive** correspond to a driving tour available at the visitor center or online. The best of the 9-mile-long route is its last 2 miles between the narrow sandstone walls of Capitol Gorge. It'll knock your socks off. To continue south past Pleasant Creek, a 4WD vehicle is advised.

Nottom-Bullfrog Rd is a rough, rough road that heads south from Hwy 24 (5 miles east of Fruita) paralleling Waterpocket Fold. Thirty-two miles south, you can turn west toward Hwy 12 and the Burr Trail Switchbacks (see p452). Continue south and Nottom-Bullfrog Rd merges with the Burr Trail Rd to Lake Powell and Bullfrog Marina, another 35 miles away.

HIKING

Capitol Reef has little shade. Drink at least one quart of water every two hours of hiking and wear a hat. Distances listed are one way.

At the end of Scenic Dr is **Capitol Gorge Trail** (1 mile, easy); spur trails lead to **Pioneer Register**, where names carved in the rock date back to 1871, and **The Tanks**, giant water pockets. Look for the spur to the **Golden Throne** formation off Capitol Gorge Trail (another mile).

Also along Scenic Dr, a good dirt road leads to **Grand Wash Trail** (2.25 miles, easy), a flat hike between canyon walls that at one point tower 80 stories high but are only 15ft apart. You can follow an offshoot to **Cassidy Arch** (2 miles).

Hickman Bridge Trail (1 mile, moderate), a popular walk, includes a canyon stretch, a stunning natural bridge and wildflowers in spring. Mornings are coolest; it starts about 2 miles east of the visitor center.

Two miles west of the visitor center off Hwy 24, a short unpaved road heads to **Panorama Point** and **Gooseneck Overlook**, a dizzying 800ft-high viewpoint above serpentine Sulphur Creek. Afternoon light is best.

For **backcountry hikes**, ask for the information pamphlets at the visitor center or check online (hint: there are additional petroglyphs and pioneer graffiti to be found).

SWIMMING & WADING

Across the highway from Chimney Rock parking area (about 2 miles west of the visitor center), an easy trail leads to **Sulphur Creek**. Near the visitor center, hike up Sulphur Creek a mile to a large, shaded wading pool. Also wade along **Pleasant Creek**, at the end of Scenic Dr; get directions from rangers. Only wade in wide sections of calm water – and only if there's no flash-flood threat. Do not swim at the waterfall on the north side of Hwy 24, 4 miles east of the petroglyphs. Rocks are slippery and currents are strong. More accidents happen here than anywhere else in the park (usually compound fractures).

ROCK CLIMBING

Technical climbing is allowed without permits. Note that Wingate sandstone can flake unpredictably. Follow clean-climbing guidelines, and take all safety precautions. For details, check with rangers or see www.nps.gov/care.

CYCLING & MOUNTAIN BIKING

Scenic Dr works well for beginner and intermediate road riders; experienced mountain bikers love **Cathedral Valley**, though it's a muddy mess when wet. Start at Hartnet Rd (11.7 miles east of the visitor center on Hwy 24) or Caineville Wash Rd (18.6 miles east of the visitor center). Rent bikes in Torrey (p446).

Sleeping & Eating

Free primitive camping is possible year round at **Cathedral Valley Campground** at the end of River Ford Rd, and at **Cedar Mesa Campground**, about 23 miles south along Nottom-Bullfrog Rd. The terrific, 71-site **Fruita Campground** (Scenic Dr; campsites $10) sits alongside the Fremont River surrounded by orchards. First-come, first-served; water, no showers. In the summer high season, sites fill up by early afternoon.

The nearest motel lodging and dining are, again, in Torrey. Eighteen miles east on Hwy 24, stop in Caineville at **Mesa Market** (☎ 435-456-9146; Hwy 24; ☻ 7am-3pm Easter until the first frost) for straight-from-the-garden organic salads and

---

WATER, WATER EVERYWHERE

Hidden inside Capitol Reef's towering jumble of rocks and winding canyons are giant natural cisterns full of water. These caches are rare in this arid landscape. John Wesley Powell, the first Western explorer to encounter the reef, found the precious resource and nicknamed the monocline Waterpocket Fold.

freshly baked artisan bread from an outdoor stone-hearth oven. That's all it serves and it's delicious.

Getting Around

Buy gasoline in Torrey or Boulder. Bicycles are allowed on all park roads but not trails. **Wild Hare Expeditions** (☎ 435-425-3999, 800-304-4273; www .color-country.net/~thehare; 116 W Main St, Torrey) offers a trailhead taxi service that either drops you and picks you up at trailheads, or drops you at one trailhead and your vehicle at another.

TORREY

pop 170 / elev 6843ft

A quiet town built along a main street (Hwy 24), Torrey's primary industry is outdoor tourism. Capitol Reef National Park is only 11 miles east, Grand Staircase-Escalante National Monument is 40 miles south and national forests surround the town. In summer there's a whiff of countercultural sophistication in the air, but November to February the town shuts down. If you're here on the third weekend in July, don't miss the **Bicknell International Film Festival** (BIFF), just up Hwy 24. This wacky B-movie spoof on Sundance includes films, parties and the 'fastest parade in America.'

Torrey's small town center lies just west of the ugly prefab chain motels and gas stations at the junction of Hwys 24 and 12. Just about every motel and B&B on Main St sells handmade and Native American crafts.

Information

Freemont River/Loa Ranger District (☎ 435-836-2811; www.fs.fed.us/r4/fishlake; 138 S Main St, Loa; ☒ 9am-5pm Mon-Fri)
Local police (☎ 435-425-3791)
Sevier Valley Hospital (☎ 435-896-8271; 1000 N Main St, Richfield) Sixty miles west on I-70.
Teasdale Ranger Station (☎ 435-425-3702; www .fs.fed.us/dxnf; 138 E Main St, Teasdale; ☒ 9am-5pm Mon-Fri)
Wayne Community Health Center (☎ 435-425-3744; 128 S 300 West, Bicknell; ☒ 9am-5pm Mon-Fri, 9am-1pm Sat) Eight miles west on Hwy 24.
Wayne County Travel Council (☎ 435-425-3365, 800-858-7951; www.capitolreef.org; cnr Hwys 24 & 12; ☒ noon-7pm Apr-Oct)

Sights & Activities

Most visitors head for nearby national parks, but more than 300 miles of trails cover the mountainous **Fishlake National Forest**. Four-wheel drive roads lead north of town around Thousand Lake Mountain (11,306ft). Hwy 72, 17 miles west of town in Loa, is a paved route through the same area. **Fish Lake**, a giant trout fishery, is 21 miles northwest of Loa, off Hwy 25. Check with the Fremont River/Loa Ranger District office for info.

Part of the expansive **Dixie National Forest** contains Boulder Mountain (11,317ft) to the south of Torrey. Nearby are numerous fishable lakes and streams, as well as hiking, biking and ATV trails. Teasdale Ranger Station, 4 miles southwest, is the nearest contact.

TOURS & OUTFITTERS

Guides and outfitters cover the surrounding area well (Capitol Reef, the national forests, Escalante and beyond) and usually handle several types of activities; a full-day adventure runs from $80 to $120 per person. The outfitters' headquarters also serve as outdoor gear shops.

Hondoo Rivers & Trails (☎ 435-425-3519, 800-332-2696; www.hondoo.com; 90 E Main St) operates half- and one-day hikes, and fantastic horseback and vehicle trips. With a multiday hike, you could cover the whole southwest. Take a smooth and scenic back-roads drive with **Wild Hare Expeditions** (☎ 435-425-3999, 800-304-4273; www.color-country .net/~thehare; 116 W Main St), or choose one of the more rugged 4WD trips. Its hiking and driving outings last from two hours to two days.

In addition to 4WD and hiking packages, **Backcountry Outfitters** (☎ 435-425-2010; www.ride thereef.com; 677 E Hwy 24 at Hwy 12) also rents bicycles ($38 per day) and ATVs ($150 per day). Shuttles and guided bike, ATV and horseback rides available, too.

Thousand Lakes RV Park (☎ 435-425-3500, 800-355-8995; www.thousandlakesrvpark.com; Hwy 24), 1 mile west of Torrey, rents 4WD vehicles ($95 per day). For horseback riding call **Cowboy Homestead Cabins** (☎ 435-425-3414, 888-854-4871; www.cowboyhomesteadcabins.com; Hwy 12; half-day rides $85), 3 miles south of town.

Boulder Mountain Adventures & Alpine Angler's Flyshop (☎ 435-425-3660, 888-484-3331; www.fly-fishing -utah.net; 310 W Main St) will set you up for a day of fly-fishing; it also leads horseback riding and fishing tours.

Sleeping

Sandcreek RV Park (☎ 435-425-3577; www.sandcreekrv .com; 540 Hwy 24; tent sites/RV sites/cabins $13/21/28)

Pitch horseshoes, sip site-made espresso and hang out at this friendly campground with just 17 sites. Showers, laundry; pets OK.

Thousand Lakes RV Park (☎ 435-425-3500, 800-355-8995; www.thousandlakesrvpark.com; Hwy 24; tent sites/ RV sites $16/25, cabins $59-95; ☺ Apr-Oct; ☻ wi-fi) The 22 acres here are filled with facilities and services, including a heated swimming pool, gift shop, jeep rental and evening cook-out dinners ($13 to $19).

Austin's Chuckwagon Motel (☎ 435-425-3335, 800-863-3288; www.austinschuckwagonmotel.com; 12 W Main St; r $45-69, cabins $125; ☺ Apr-Oct; ☻ wi-fi) Rustic wood buildings ring the shady grounds of the town's best value-for-money motel. Standard rooms have two beds, and two-bedroom cabins have kitchens. Grocery and deli on site. Some pets OK.

Rim Rock Inn (☎ 435-425-3398, 888-447-4676; www .therimrock.net; 2523 E Hwy 24; r $49-79; ☺ Mar-Nov) East of Torrey, 1 mile from Capitol Reef, the Rim Rock is surrounded by red rock cliffs. This family-owned motel on 120 acres has basic rooms with great views. Good restaurants on site, too.

Pine Shadows Cabins (☎ 435-425-3939, 800-708- 1223; www.pineshadowcabins.net; 195 W 125 South, Teasdale; cabins $69-75) A fabulous hideaway, Pine Shadows shelters among piñon pines near trails at the end of the road. Vaulted ceilings and tons of windows brighten each 16ft by 28ft cabin (two beds and kitchenette).

Torrey Schoolhouse B&B (☎ 435-425-2116, 877-425-2116; www.torreyschoolhouse.com; 150 N Center St; r incl breakfast $115-150; ☺ Apr-Oct; wi-fi) Who knew schoolhouses were so large and rambling in 1914? The nine, light-colored rooms are pretty spacious and three classrooms have been turned into a large gathering space.

our pick **Lodge at Red River Ranch** (☎ 435-425-3322, 800-205-6343; www.redriverranch.com; 2900 W Hwy 24, Teasdale; r incl breakfast $140-215; ☐ wi-fi) In the grand old tradition of Western lodges, the great room here has a three-story open-beam ceiling, giant fireplace and timber walls adorned with Navajo rugs. Details are flawless – from the country quilts on high-thread-count sheets to the masonry of each room's wood-burning fireplace. The deep-red and cowboy motif of the 'Rodeo Room' is especially fun. Western bric-a-brac decorates the lodge's cozy dining room, where nonguests are welcome for breakfast and dinner. After supper, enjoy the star-filled sky from the outdoor hot tub.

Dixie National Forest runs several campgrounds, such as the 17-site **Pleasant Creek Campground** (Map p444; ☎ 435-425-3702; www.fs.fed .us/dxnf; Forest Rd 186, off Hwy 12; campsites $9; ☺ Jun-Oct), where ponderosa pines and an 8700ft elevation provide cool relief on Boulder Mountain. Camping is also available in Capitol Reef National Park (p445).

More options:

Torrey Trading Post (☎ 435-425-3716; www.torrey tradingpost.com; 75 W Main St; cabins $28) Two tidy cabins with shared bathroom; no air-con.

Best Western Capitol Reef Resort (☎ 435-425-3761, 888-610-9600; www.bestwesternutah.com; 2600 E Hwy 24; r $69-99; ☻ wi-fi) Surprising back balconies overlook rusty red cliffs.

Skyridge Inn (☎ 435-425-3222; www.skyridgeinn.com; 950 E Hwy 24; r incl breakfast $119-164) Country-elegant farmhouse B&B.

Eating & Drinking

Brink's Burgers Drive In (☎ 435-425-3710; 165 E Main St; burgers $4-7; ☺ 11am-9pm Mar-Oct) Order at the window for old-fashioned burgers, home-cut fries and thick milkshakes.

Capitol Reef Café (☎ 435-425-3271; 360 W Main St; breakfast $5-9, lunch & dinner mains $7-16; ☺ 7am-9pm Apr-Oct) *Gourmet* magazine has recognized the healthy, vegetable-heavy dishes here. Area trout and locally made pies are a hit.

Rim Rock Patio (☎ 435-425-3398; 2523 E Hwy 24; mains $6-10; ☺ lunch & dinner Apr-Oct, dinner Nov-Mar) Inventive pizzas, organic salads – and beer. Chugalug while you play darts or laze outside on a summer day.

Rim Rock Restaurant (☎ 435-425-3398; 2523 E Hwy 24; mains $11-25; ☺ dinner Mar-Nov) Grilled steaks, pastas and fish come with a million-dollar view of red rock cliffs.

our pick **Café Diablo** (☎ 435-425-3070; 599 W Main St; mains $20-24; ☺ dinner Apr-Oct) One of southern Utah's best, Café Diablo serves outstanding, highly stylized Southwestern cooking – including succulent vegetarian dishes – bursting with flavor and towering on the plate. For something you definitely won't find back home, try the rattlesnake cakes. Even if you order just appetizers ($9 to $11) and dessert, you won't leave hungry. Don't miss this one.

Linger over a latte on a comfy couch by the fire at Torrey's hip **Robber's Roost Books & Beverages** (☎ 435-425-3265; 185 W Main St; ☺ 9am-9pm Mon-Sat, 10am-3pm Sun May-Nov; ☐ wi-fi) or buy Utah-roasted brews at **Castle Rock Coffee &**

Candy (☎ 435-425-2100; cnr Hwys 12 & 24; ☻ 7am-7pm Apr-Oct; ☐ wi-fi).

Entertainment
Supporting the local arts scene, **Entrada Institute** (www.entradainstitute.org) hosts Saturday night events (concerts, readings and so on) at Robber's Roost Books & Beverages. **Wayne Theater** (☎ 435-425-3123; www.waynetheater.com; 11 E Main St, Bicknell) shows movies (on weekends) for a pittance and hosts the Bicknell International Film Festival in July.

HWY 12 – TORREY TO ESCALANTE
Hwy 12 (www.scenicbyway12.com) is a truly spectacular road, linking several national parks and small towns such as Boulder. Take advantage of pullouts and viewpoints to see how quickly and dramatically the land changes from wooded plateau to red rock canyon, from slickrock desert to alpine forest. Many consider the best section of the road to be the switchbacks and petrified sand dunes between Torrey and Boulder. Then again, the razor-thin Hogback Ridge between Escalante and Boulder is pretty stunning, too.

Boulder
pop 180 / elev 6593ft
From Torrey, you traverse 11,317ft-high Boulder Mountain before Hwy 12 rises into Boulder. Until 1940, this isolated outpost received its mail by mule. It's still so remote that the federal government classifies it as a 'frontier community.' Nevertheless, Boulder has some surprisingly progressively minded residents. The diverse population of down-to-earth folks ranges from artists and ecologists to farmers and cowboys. Hell's Backbone Grill has helped promote understanding by hosting community events such as ice-cream socials.

Lorded over by Boulder Mountain and surrounded by the GSENM, Boulder makes a great home base for outdoor activity, but has far fewer services than Torrey, 37 miles away. To learn more, visit www.boulder utah.com. The town shuts down November through March.

SIGHTS & ACTIVITIES
The pieced-back-together jars and jugs on display are just a few of the thousands and thousands of pottery shards excavated at the Coomb's Site in the 1950s. Today it's the petite **Anasazi State Park Museum** (☎ 435-335-7308; www .stateparks.utah.gov; Main St/Hwy 12; admission $4; ☻ 8am-6pm Jun-Aug, 9am-5pm Sep-May), where you can wander parts of the site itself, inhabited from AD 1130 to 1175. The ruins aren't as evocative as some in southeastern Utah, but the museum is well worth seeing for the re-created six-room pueblo, pottery gallery and exhibits about the Ancestral Puebloan (or Anasazi) peoples. There's a seasonal **BLM desk** (☎ 435-335-7382; ☻ 9am-5pm Apr-Oct) where you can talk to rangers and get backcountry road updates.

The ruggedly beautiful **Box-Death Hollow Wilderness Area** is BLM land that surrounds Hell's Backbone Rd (see boxed text, below). The stunning Burr Trail drive through GSENM (p452) also originates in Boulder.

Cofounder of the Southern Utah Wilderness Alliance, Grant Johnson and his **Escalante Canyon Outfitters** (ECO; ☎ 435-691-3037, 888-326-4453; www.eco hike.com; 2520 S Lower Deer Creek Rd; ☻ Mar-Nov) are the best for informative multiday hikes through the region. Don Montoya, curator at the Anasazi State Park Museum, runs the archaeo-hikes to Native American sites and rock art.

For super-smart geologic interpretation, most **Earth Tours** (☎ 435-691-1241; www.earth-tours .com; full-day tours $50-100; ☻ Mar-Nov) are run by a

---

DETOUR: HELL'S BACKBONE ROAD

To get a sense of just how remote Boulder actually is, take a drive up Hell's Backbone Rd toward the Box-Death Hollow Wilderness Area. Just west of town, at Mile 84, turn north off Hwy 12. Climbing steadily uphill for 14 miles along a gravel-and-dirt route, the sometimes-rough road reaches Hell's Backbone Bridge, a death-defying one-lane crossing above a plunging, yellow-and-orange slickrock canyon sure to give you vertigo. Cut the engine and get out. Wind funnels up the canyon, whistling through the pines, while giant crows float silently on the thermals. To the east, Boulder Mountain is carpeted with deep-green forests and stands of quaking aspen trees; in fall the aspens turn gold – a gorgeous sight. The rest of the drive passes mainly through woods as it continues 28 miles to Escalante, but the treat is the bridge. The road is open roughly April through October; check on road conditions at Anasazi State Park Museum.

COOKING UP A COMMUNITY

When partners and restaurateurs Jen Castle and Blake Spalding moved to Boulder in 2000, most of the residents in the insular community were of rural Mormon stock; no restaurant had ever gotten a license to serve liquor. But instead of yelling like their predecessors, they shared their vision of 'beautiful food in a beautiful country' coupled with financial reality. In the end, the town council approved a full liquor license, but they elected only to serve beer and wine out of respect. Since then, Hell's Backbone Grill (below) has enjoyed huge success. The restaurant has hired locally and invited the community in by hosting ice-cream socials and talent shows. At summer's end they team up with Boulder Mountain Lodge to host **Folksfest**, a concert festival and folk fair. All gate proceeds go toward a conservation easement for a public park. It's all about being good neighbors.

PhD professor who speaks in lay terms. Hikes venture into Waterpocket Fold and the like.

Go horseback riding from **Boulder Mountain Ranch** (☎ 435-335-7581; www.boulderutah.com/bmr; rides $35-118); call for directions. Or arrange a fishing trip with **Boulder Mountain Fly-fishing** (☎ 435-335-7306, 435-231-1823; www.bouldermountainflyfishing.com; ✆ Mar-Nov).

SLEEPING & EATING

Pole's Place (☎ 435-335-7422, 800-730-7422; www.boulderutah.com/polesplace; r $50-65 ✆ Mar-Oct) Small and simple, this mom-and-pop motel is lovingly and immaculately maintained. Limited TV channels.

Boulder Mountain Ranch (☎ 435-335-7480; www.boulderutah.com/bmr; Hell's Backbone Rd; lodge r $60-66, cabins $67-85; 🖳) Enjoy restful – and rustic – ranch life on 160 blissful acres adjacent to Box-Death Hollow Wilderness Area. No cookie-cutter kit cabins these: each is handcrafted to accommodate four to six in a basic bunk-and-bathroom configuration. The simple lodge rooms are up the hill in the main building (with wi-fi), where congenial hosts Sheri and Gary sometimes offer breakfast and dinner. Horseback riding available; some pets OK.

Boulder Mountain Lodge (☎ 435-335-7460, 800-556-3446; www.boulder-utah.com; cnr Hwy 12 & Burr Trail Rd; r $97-175; 🖳 wi-fi) Watch the birds flit by on the adjacent 15-acre wildlife sanctuary and stroll through the organic garden – Boulder Mountain Lodge has a strong eco-aesthetic. It's the ideal place for day-hikers who want to return to high-thread-count sheets, plush terry robes and Aveda bath products. Hell's Backbone Grill, on site, is a southern Utah must-eat. Hot tub; dogs welcome.

our pick **Hell's Backbone Grill** (☎ 435-335-7464; Boulder Mountain Lodge, cnr Hwy 12 & Burr Trail Rd; breakfast $4-8, mains $12-22; ✆ breakfast & dinner May-Sep,

dinner only Mar, Apr & Oct–mid-Nov) Along with Café Diablo in Torrey and Buffalo Bistro in Glendale, this restaurant makes up the triple crown of foodie destinations in southwestern Utah. Hell's Backbone serves soulful, earthy preparations of locally raised meats and organically grown produce from its own garden. Save room for desserts such as *chimayo*-chile ginger cake with butterscotch sauce. Dinner reservations are a must. For more on owners Jen Castle and Blake Spalding, see the boxed text, above.

Burr Trail Outpost & Grill (☎ 435-335-7503; cnr Hwy 12 & Burr Trail Rd; sandwiches $6-8; ✆ lunch & dinner Mar-Oct) The outpost is equal parts gallery, outfitter, restaurant and gathering place; beer and wine available.

Boulder Mesa Restaurant (☎ 435-335-7447; 155 E Burr Trail Rd; breakfast & sandwiches $6-9, mains $12-18; ✆ 8am-9pm) Whether the casual food here's any good depends on who's cooking that night. Breakfast is pretty safe.

Hills & Hollows Country Store (☎ 435-335-7349; Hwy 12; pizzas $11-17; ✆ 9am-7pm, gas 24hr) Persian rugs, health food and a bit of this and that are for sale at Hills. Out back it has a wood-fired oven where it bakes up cookies and cook-to-order organic pizzas.

Head of the Rocks

At Mile 70 on Hwy 12 pull off for one of Utah's most arresting roadside views at Head of the Rocks. The Aquarius Plateau lords over giant mesas, towering domes, deep canyons and undulating slickrock, all unfurling in an explosion of color. At Mile 73, you reach the singular **Kiva Koffeehouse** (☎ 435-826-4550; www.kivakoffeehouse.com; soups & pastries $2-5; ✆ 8am-4:30pm Wed-Mon Apr-Nov), built into the cliff with floor-to-ceiling glass walls over the plateau. Kiva also rents two cushy hideaway **cottage rooms** (r $170; wi-fi), also etched into the stone, with whirlpool tubs and fireplaces.

Escalante
pop 820 / elev 5600ft

Stock up on groceries and park information here in the 'largest' town on Hwy 12. Escalante lies roughly halfway between Bryce (50 miles) and Capitol Reef (76 miles) national parks, and is surrounded by Grand Staircase-Escalante National Monument (right). You'll find better eating and sleeping in Boulder (27 miles) and Torrey (65 miles), but Escalante is on the rise. Jointly operated by the BLM, the USFS and NPS, the **Escalante Interagency Office** (☎ 435-826-5499; www.ut.blm.gov/monument; 775 W Main St; ☽ 8:30am-5:30pm) is *the* source for information about area public lands.

Find books, maps, camping and hiking supplies, outfitter trips and tours, bike rental, pizza, high-speed internet access, coffee and liquor (a rarity round here) at the everything-to-everyone **Escalante Outfitters** (☎ 435-826-4266; 310 W Main St). For groceries, visit **Griffin's** (☎ 435-826-4226; 300 W Main St). There's more about the town's services at www.escalante-cc.com. The nearest medical care is in Panguitch (p458).

For top-notch, custom-tailored, all-day adventure hikes through GSENM, **Excursions of Escalante** (☎ 435-826-4714, 800-839-7567; www.excursions-escalante.com; Trailhead Café, 125 Main St; half-day trips $65-100; ☽ Mar-Nov) offers everything from easy photo walks to hard-core canyoneering.

Escalante Petrified Forest State Park (☎ 435-826-4466; http://stateparks.utah.gov/; day use $5; ☽ 7am-10pm) is about 2 miles northwest of town along Hwy 12. Check out the small 'forest' of petrified wood and the modest lake. The 22-site, reserveable **campground** (☎ 800-322-3770; www.recreation.gov; campsites $16) has wonderfully hot showers.

Pitch a tent or rent a cozy, heated camping cabin (shared bathroom) at oh-so-cute **Escalante Outfitters Bunkhouse Cabins** (☎ 435-826-4266; www.escalanteoutfitters.com; 310 W Main St; tent sites/RV sites/cabins $14/30/44; ☐ wi-fi). The family-owned **Circle D Motel** (☎ 435-826-4297; www.utahcanyons.com/circled.htm; 475 W Main St; r $35-55) has cheap and clean – if dated – rooms; some have a fridge and microwave. Pets are OK at both.

Colorful murals and earthy paint colors (think red clay or fiery sunset) define the suites at **Escalante's Grand Staircase Bed & Breakfast Inn** (☎ 435-826-4890, 866-826-4890; www.escalantebnb.com; 280 W Main St; r incl breakfast $135; ☐). Each suite has a seating area, and full French toast and

eggs–style breakfasts are served privately. High-speed internet; pets welcome.

House rentals include the following:
Wild West Retreat (☎ 435-826-4849, 866-292-3043; www.wildwestretreat.com; cnr 200 East & 300 South; d $120) A refurbished 1930s barn with hot tub.
La Luz Desert Retreat (☎ 435-826-4967, 888-305-4705; www.laluz.net; off 500 West; up to 4 people $175) Contemporary adobe home at the GSENM's edge; sleeps six.

For coffee, homemade croissants and local-beef burgers, visit **Trailhead Café** (☎ 435-826-4714, 800-839-7567; 125 E Main St; sandwiches $4-7; ☽ 8am-8pm Wed-Sun May-Oct; ☐ wi-fi). For granola and yogurt at breakfast and pizza and beer at lunch and dinner, visit **Esca-Latte Café** (☎ 435-826-4266; Escalante Outfitters, 310 W Main St; dishes $5-12; ☽ 8am-10pm Mar-Nov, 10am-6pm Tue-Sat Dec-Feb; ☐ wi-fi).

GRAND STAIRCASE-ESCALANTE NATIONAL MONUMENT

Nearly twice the size of Rhode Island, the 1.9-million-acre Grand Staircase-Escalante National Monument (GSENM) is the largest park in the Southwest and has some of the least visited, most spectacular scenery. Its name refers to the 150-mile-long geological strata that begins at the bottom of the Grand Canyon and rises 3500ft to Bryce Canyon and the Escalante River canyons. Together the layers of rock reveal 260 million years of history in a riot of color. Sections of the GSENM have so much red rock that the reflected light casts a pink hue onto the bottoms of clouds above.

Established in 1996 by President Bill Clinton, the monument is unique in that it allows some uses that would be banned in a national park (such as hunting and grazing, by permits), but allows fewer uses than other public lands to maintain its 'remote frontier' quality. Tourist infrastructure is minimal and limited to towns on the park's edges.

Orientation

The GSENM links the area between Bryce Canyon, Capitol Reef National Park and Glen Canyon National Recreation Area. Hwy 12 skirts the northern boundaries between Tropic, Escalante and Boulder. Hwy 89 arcs east of Kanab into the monument's southwestern reaches.

The park encompasses three major geological areas. The Grand Staircase is in the westernmost region, south of Bryce Canyon and west of Cottonwood Canyon Rd. The Kaiparowits

Plateau runs north–south in the center of the monument, east of Cottonwood Canyon Rd and west of Smoky Mountain Rd. Escalante Canyons lie at the easternmost sections, east of Hole-in-the-Rock Rd and south of the Burr Trail.

The visitor centers have good maps. The waterproof Trails Illustrated/National Geographic map *No 710 Canyons of the Escalante* is great, but to hike the backcountry you'll need USGS 7.5-minute quadrangle maps. Also consider the excellent guidebook *Hiking the Escalante* by Rudi Lambrechtse.

Information

There are no fees for the GSENM. Food, gas and lodging are available in Boulder, Escalante, Torrey and Kanab.

Big Water Visitor Center (☎ 435-675-3200; 100 Upper Revolution Way, Big Water; ☾ 9am-5:30pm Apr-Oct) Near Lake Powell.

Cannonville Visitor Center (☎ 435-826-5640; 10 Center St, Cannonville; ☾ 8am-4:30pm Apr-Oct) Five miles east of Tropic.

Escalante Interagency Office (☎ 435-826-5499; www.ut.blm.gov/monument; 775 W Main St, Escalante; ☾ 7:30am-5:30pm)

Grand Staircase-Escalante National Monument (☎ 435-826-5499; www.ut.blm.gov/monument; PO Box 225, Escalante, UT 84726) Write-ahead information.

Kanab Visitor Center (☎ 435-644-4680; 745 E Hwy 89, Kanab; ☾ 8am-4:30pm Apr-Oct, 8am-4:30pm Mon-Fri Nov-Mar) Southwestern section; park headquarters.

Dangers & Annoyances

Always check with rangers about weather and road conditions before driving or hiking. Slot canyons and washes are flash-flood prone. After heavy rain or snow, roads may be impassable, even with a 4WD. If it starts to rain while you're driving, *stop*. Storms pass and roads dry quickly, sometimes even within 30 minutes. Never park in a wash. Carry a gallon of water per person, wear a hat and sunscreen, and carry food, maps and a compass. Help in case of an emergency may be hard to find. Avoid walking on cryptobiotic crusts (p72), the chunky black soil that looks like burnt hamburger meat; it fixes nitrogen into the ground, changing sand to soil.

Sights & Activities

Learn how to survive in GSENM's forbidding wilderness by taking a seven-, 14- or 21-day wilderness course with the **Boulder Outdoor Survival School** (☎ 303-444-9779; www.boss-inc.com).

PARK POLITICS

The Grand Staircase-Escalante National Monument was created over the vehement objections of some residents and legislators, who had hoped to develop the area's mining potential. Locals have since learned to exploit the tourist economy, but don't be surprised to occasionally see a bumper sticker that says, 'If it's tourist season, why can't we shoot 'em?' Fret not: nobody's gonna take aim. But just to be safe, don't bring up land-use politics.

SCENIC DRIVES

Skutumpah & Johnson Canyon Rds

The most westerly route through the monument, the unpaved Skutumpah Rd heads southwest from Kodachrome Basin State Park, around the southern end of Bryce Canyon's Pink Cliffs. After 35 miles (two hours), Skutumpah Rd intersects with the 16-mile paved Johnson Canyon Rd, and passes the White Cliffs and Vermilion Cliffs areas en route to Hwy 89 and Kanab. For the best sightseeing, drive south to north. Four-wheel drive or high-clearance 2WD recommended.

Cottonwood Canyon Rd

This 46-mile scenic backway heads east, then south, from Kodachrome Basin State Park, emerging at Hwy 89 near Paria Canyon-Vermilion Cliffs Wilderness Area. It's the closest entry into GSENM from Bryce and an easy, sometimes rough drive, passable for 2WD vehicles (RVs not recommended). Twenty miles south of Hwy 12 you'll reach **Grosvenor Arch**, a yellow-limestone double arch, with picnic tables and restrooms.

The road continues south along the west side of the **Cockscomb**, a long, narrow monocline in the Earth's crust. The Cockscomb divides the Grand Staircase from Kaiparowits Plateau to the east; there are superb views. The most scenic stretch lies between Grosvenor Arch and **Lower Hackberry Canyon**, good for hiking. The road then follows the desolate Paria River valley toward Hwy 89.

Smoky Mountain Rd

A 78-mile dirt-and-gravel road (ATV or high-clearance 4WD only), this route takes over six hours. From Escalante, it crosses the rugged **Kaiparowits Plateau** and emerges at the Big

Water Visitor Center on Hwy 89, just west of Glen Canyon. The prime destination is **Alstrom Point**, 38 miles from Hwy 89, a plateau-top vantage point with stunning Lake Powell views.

Hole-in-the-Rock Rd

The scenery and history are wild along this 57-mile dirt-and-gravel road, from 5 miles east of Escalante to Lake Powell (four to five hours each way). It's passable by 2WD when dry, except for the last 7 miles, which requires 4WD. In 1879–80, Mormon pioneers followed this route on their way to settle in southeast Utah. Little did they know the steep walls of Glen Canyon on the Colorado River would block their path. More than 200 pioneers blasted and hammered through the cliff, creating a hole wide enough to lower 80 wagons; look for historic markers. The final stretch now lies submerged beneath Lake Powell.

If you don't drive the entire route, at least visit **Devils Garden** (12 miles in), where rock fists, orbs, spires and fingers rise 40ft above the desert floor. A short walk from the car leads atop giant sandstone slabs – kids love it. There's also good hiking. **Dry Fork** (26 miles in) has great slot canyons for hiking. It has no campgrounds or facilities, but dispersed camping is permitted with a backcountry permit (free). The main road stops short of **Hole-in-the-Rock**, but hikers can descend to **Lake Powell**, a rough, expert route doable in an hour – but you have to climb out, too.

Burr Trail Rd

The region's most immediately gratifying, dramatic drive, the initially paved Burr Trail Rd heads east from Boulder, crosses GSENM's northeast corner and, after about 30 miles, reaches Capitol Reef National Park, where the road becomes loose gravel. Just past the Deer Creek trailhead, the road enters **Long Canyon** beneath towering vertical red rock slabs. At the end of the canyon, stop for views of the **Circle Cliffs**, hanging like curtains above the undulating valley.

In Capitol Reef, the road meets the giant, angled buttes of hundred-mile-long Waterpocket Fold (p444). Just ahead, the **Burr Trail Switchbacks** follow an original wagon route through the fold. If returning to Boulder, first drive to the base of the switchbacks – the scale of the landscape will blow your mind. Another option is to turn north onto Nottom-Bullfrog

Rd and continue to Hwy 24 (32 miles), or south to Glen Canyon (35 miles), but the road is awfully rough and not good for 2WD.

HIKING

Along Hwy 12, **Upper Calf Creek Falls** (2-mile round-trip) is the GSENM's most accessible and popular moderate day hike. Start on the spur road between Miles 81 and 82 (22 miles northeast of Escalante). Cairns lead the way down a fairly steep slickrock trail past far-ranging views. When the trail splits, head toward the lovely pools and swimming hole on the upper trail.

Lower Calf Creek Falls (off Hwy 12 at Mile 75) is a longer, 6-mile round-trip on which you slog through sand to get to a 126ft waterfall. Allow about four hours. Along the way, you pass a campground, where there's a cool spot for playing in the water. There's a $2 fee for day use in the Calf Creek Recreation Area. Just west, an easy trail heads to **Escalante Natural Bridge** (2-mile loop), crisscrossing the Escalante River (wear sturdy footwear) and arriving at a 130ft-high, 100ft-long sandstone arch.

The most easily accessible slot canyons are at Dry Fork, 26 miles down Hole-in-the-Rock Rd from Hwy 12. Check with rangers for directions and conditions at the four slots: the **Narrows**, **Peekaboo Gulch**, **Spooky Gulch** and **Brimstone Gulch**. Don't climb up and out of slots, then jump down the other side, lest you get trapped below the smooth face you've descended.

GSENM is filled with hard-core **backcountry hikes**. Heading off-trail requires significant route-finding skills; GPS proficiency isn't enough. Know how to use a compass and a topographical map, or risk getting lost. Ask rangers about **Coyote Gulch**, off Hole-in-the-Rock Rd; **Escalante River Canyon**; **Boulder Mail Trail**; and the **Gulch**, off the Burr Trail.

TOURS & OUTFITTERS

Outfitters and guide services that operate in GSENM base themselves in Boulder (p448), Escalante (p450), Torrey (p446) and Kanab (p473).

Sleeping & Eating

Most sleeping and eating is done in Escalante, Boulder or Kanab. The GSENM website (www .ut.blm.gov/monument) lists suggested areas for free camping. Pick up the required permit at a visitor center. Remember: water sources must be treated or boiled; campfires are permitted only in certain areas (use a stove instead); and biting insects are a problem in spring and early summer. Watch for scorpions and rattlesnakes.

There are two developed campgrounds in the northern part of the monument. Beside a year-round creek, 15 miles east of Escalante, **Calf Creek Campground** (Map p444; ☎ 435-826-5499; www.ut.blm.gov/monument; Hwy 12; campsites $7) is surrounded by red rock canyons (hot in summer) and has 13 non-reserveable sites with drinking water available in summer. The campground is near the trailhead to Lower Calf Creek Falls. **Deer Creek Campground** (Map p444; ☎ 435-826-5499; www.ut.blm.gov/monument; Burr Trail; campsites $4; ☻ mid-May–mid-Sep), 6 miles southeast of Boulder, has four sites and no water, but sits beside a year-round creek beneath tall trees.

Getting Around

High-clearance 4WD vehicles are best, since many roads are unpaved and only occasionally bladed. (Most off-the-lot SUVs and light trucks are *not* high-clearance vehicles.) Heed all warnings about road conditions. Buy gasoline whenever you see it. Find stations in Tropic, Escalante, Boulder and Kanab.

Book hiker shuttles in advance. In the north contact **Excursions of Escalante** (☎ 435-826-4714, 800-839-7567; www.excursions-escalante.com); **Paria Outpost & Outfitters** (☎ 928-691-1047; www.paria .com) runs shuttles in the south.

BRYCE CANYON NATIONAL PARK

Graceful spires of pink, yellow, white and orange hoodoos stand like sentinels at the eroding edges of the vast plateau that is Bryce Canyon. Though the smallest of southern Utah's national parks, Bryce is the most visually stunning, particularly at sunrise and sunset when an orange wash sets the otherworldly rock formations ablaze with color. Unlike at other parks, it's relatively easy to get down into and among the rock formations here. On the canyon floor, hike among vanilla-scented cedar trees and towering pines while marveling at the elegant, ancient rock above.

Crowds come May to September, clogging the park's road (shuttle optional). For solitude, visit in winter. Though nighttime temperatures drop below freezing for more than 200 consecutive nights, days are mild and sunny, and snowcaps on the formations are stunning.

You can't visit Bryce Canyon National Park without noticing the townlike sleep-shop-eat-outfit complex, Ruby's Inn, just north of the park. The motel has been part of the landscape since 1919 when it was located at the canyon's rim. After the area was declared a national monument in 1923, owner Rueben Syrett moved his business north to his ranch, its current location.

Orientation

Bryce Canyon National Park is 77 miles east of Zion and 39 miles west of Escalante. Some services are just north of the park boundaries on Hwy 63; the nearest town is Tropic, 11 miles northeast on Hwy 12. Red Canyon recreation area is 13 miles west, and Kodachrome Basin State Park 22 miles east on Hwy 12.

Roughly shaped like a seahorse, the park is a compact 56 sq miles. It has one entrance, 3 miles south of Hwy 12, via Hwy 63. The park's 18-mile-long main road climbs from 8000ft at the entrance to 9115ft at Rainbow Point. To alleviate congestion mid-May to late September, the park operates a voluntary shuttle. Trailers are allowed only as far as Sunset Campground, 3 miles south of the entrance.

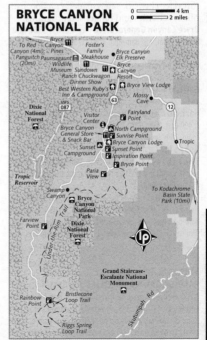

BRYCE CANYON NATIONAL PARK

BEST OF BRYCE

■ **Best Short Hike into the Canyon**
Navajo Loop Trail (opposite)

■ **Best Colored Rock** Bryce Amphitheater
(right) at sunrise

■ **Best Long Hike for Solitude Among the
Amphitheaters** Fairyland Trail (opposite)

■ **Best and Most Stunning Hoodoos,
Viewed from the Rim** Silent City from
Inspiration Point (right)

■ **Best Overlooked Sight** 1600-year-old
trees on Bristlecone Loop trail (opposite)

Bryce rim stays relatively cool (80°F) on summer days, but beware of altitude sickness. June and September are ideal; in July and August be prepared for thunderstorms and mosquitoes. Snow blankets the park in winter, but most roads are plowed. Several are designated for cross-country skiing and snowshoeing.

Information

Admission is $25 per car, $15 on foot or motorcycle. The park's newspaper, *Hoodoo*, lists hikes, activities and ranger-led programs.

Bryce Canyon General Store (☎ 435-834-5361; near Sunrise Point; ⏰ 8am-8pm Apr-Oct) Showers ($4) and laundry.

Bryce Canyon Natural History Association (☎ 435-834-4600; www.brycecanyon.org) Online book shopping.

Garfield County Travel Council (☎ 435-676-1160, 800-444-6689; www.brycecanyoncountry.com) Area info online.

Garfield Memorial Hospital (☎ 435-676-8811; 224 N 400 East, Panguitch) The nearest clinic and emergency room, 25 miles northwest.

Ruby's Inn (☎ 435-834-5341; www.rubysinn.com; 1000 S Hwy 63) Post office, grocery store, showers ($6), ATV rental, outfitter tours, free wi-fi and computer terminals ($1 for five minutes).

Visitor Center (☎ 435-834-5322; www.nps.gov/brca; Hwy 63; ⏰ 8am-8pm May-Sep, 8am-4:30pm Nov-Mar, 8am-6pm Apr & Oct) Maps and books, a great introductory film, and information on weather, roads and campsite availability.

Sights & Activities

PAUNSAGAUNT WILDLIFE MUSEUM

Live deer roam the yard at this barnlike **museum** (☎ 435-834-5555; www.brycecanyonwildlifemuseum .com; 1945 W Hwy 12; adult/child $6/3; ⏰ 9am-8pm Apr-Oct), with more than 400 taxidermied animals and a butterfly and bug room. Ask at the museum about scheduling a visit to see the live bull elk and buffalo at the associated 80-acre **Bryce Canyon Elk Preserve**, a mile north of Hwy 12 on Airport Rd.

RIM ROAD SCENIC DRIVE

The park's 18-mile-long main road roughly parallels the canyon rim. Navigate using the park brochure you receive at the entrance. Scenic overlooks lie on the east side (the left, as you head south). Avoid left turns on the very busy road by driving all the way to Rainbow Point, then turn around and work your way back, stopping at the pullouts on your right. Traffic is heaviest at the overlooks into Bryce Amphitheater. If you stop nowhere else, see the stunning Bryce Point.

From late May to early September, a free bus shuttle goes as far as Bryce Amphitheater. You can hop off and back on at viewpoints. Buses come every 15 minutes. The **Rainbow Point Tour** (Visitor Center; tours $5; ⏰ 10am & 2pm late May-Aug) is a three-hour narrated bus loop that goes to the end of Rim Rd and back, stopping at seven viewpoints en route.

BRYCE AMPHITHEATER

Bryce Amphitheater stretches from **Bryce Point** to **Sunrise Point**, where hoodoos stand like melting sandcastles in shades of coral and magenta, ochre and white, set against a deep-green pine forest. A shaft of sunlight suddenly breaking through clouds can transform the scene from grand to breathtaking. To best see the row after row of eroding sandstone fins nicknamed Silent City, head to **Inspiration Point**. The morning views at both **Sunset** and **Sunrise Points** ain't bad either.

HIKING

The views from the rim hikes are great, but the best thing about Bryce is that you can also experience the weirdly eroding hoodoos up close. Descents and ascents can be long and steep, and the altitude makes them extra strenuous. Take your time; most trails skirt exposed drop-offs.

The easiest hike is along the 0.5- to 5.5-mile-long (one-way) **Rim Trail**, which outlines Bryce Amphitheater from Fairyland to Bryce Points. Several sections are paved and wheelchair accessible, the most level being the half mile between Sunrise and Sunset Points. In the summer, you could easily take the shuttle to any one point and return from another instead of backtracking to a car.

The 1-mile **Bristlecone Loop**, at road's end near Rainbow Point, is an easy walk past 1600-year-old bristlecone pines, with 100-mile vistas. Outside main park boundaries (east of the entrance), off Hwy 12 at Mile 17, take the easy half-mile one-way walk to the year-round waterfall off **Mossy Cave Trail**, a summertime treat and frozen winter spectacle.

Many moderate trails descend below the rim. One of the most popular is **Navajo Loop Trail** (1.4 miles), which descends 521ft from Sunset Point and passes through the famous narrow canyon **Wall Street**. Combine part of the Navajo with the **Queen's Garden Trail** for an easier ascent. Once you hike up the 320ft to Sunrise Point, follow the rim trail back to your car (2.9-mile round-trip).

A good half-day hike (four to five hours) is the 8-mile round-trip **Fairyland Trail**, with a trailhead at Fairyland Point north of the visitor center. The tall hoodoos and bridges unfold best if you go in a clockwise direction. On trail there's a 700ft elevation change, plus many additional ups and downs. The 7-mile-long **Peekaboo Trail**, which leaves from Bryce Point, allows dogs and horses – not the best smelling in summer.

Only 1% of all visitors venture onto the **backcountry hikes**. You won't walk among many hoodoo formations here, but you will pass through forest and meadows with distant views of rock formations. And oh, the quiet. The 23-mile **Under-the-Rim Trail**, south of Bryce Amphitheater, can be broken into several athletic day hikes. The 11-mile stretch between Bryce Point and **Swamp Canyon** is one of the hardest and best. Get backcountry permits ($5) and trail info from rangers at the visitor center.

HORSEBACK RIDING

The park's only licensed outfitter is **Canyon Trail Rides** (☎ 435-679-8665; www.canyonrides.com; Bryce Canyon Lodge), which operates out of the park lodge. You can take a short, two-hour trip to the canyon floor ($40) or giddy-up for 3½ hours through the dramatic hoodoos on Peekaboo Trail.

You have two choices for horseback rides into the Dixie National Forest, including Red Canyon, where Butch Cassidy is rumored to have hung out, and the BLM lands surrounding Bryce. Check in at super-slick Ruby's Inn

for its frequent, well-organized **Red Canyon Rides** (☎ 435-679-8761, 800-679-5859; www.horserides .net; Ruby's Inn, 1000 S Hwy 63; ☽ Apr-Oct). Better yet, head 4 miles west of the Hwy 12/63 junction to the Bryce Canyon Pines motel. This mom-and-pop outfit runs the more personal **Red Canyon Trail Rides** (☎ 435-834-5441, 800-892-7923; http://brycecanyonmotel.com; Hwy 12; ☽ Mar-Nov). At both places there is a variety of time and trail options, but a half-day will cost about $65, and a full-day $100 (may include lunch).

RANGER-LED ACTIVITIES

Summer to early fall, rangers lead canyon-rim walks, hoodoo hikes, geology lectures, campfire programs and kids' ecology walks. If you're here when skies are clear and the moon's full, don't miss the two-hour **Moonlight Hike** among the hoodoos. Register same-day at the visitor center, but do so early.

TOURS & OUTFITTERS

Bryce Canyon Tours (☎ 435-834-5200, 800-432-5383; www.brycecanyonresort.com; Bryce Canyon Resort, 13500 Hwy 12; bus tours adult/child $26/12) leads 1½-hour sunrise and sunset minibus tours into the national park. It also rents ATVs ($100 per day) and runs guided ATV tours (one hour, $35) outside the park boundaries. In addition to similar ATV rentals and tours, **Ruby's Inn** (☎ 435-834-5341; www.rubysinn.com; 1000 S Hwy 63) also offers helicopter tours and mountain bike rental ($35 per day).

There's no commercial guided hiking at Bryce, but several companies lead Bryce to Zion bicycle tours. Try **Rim Tours** (☎ 435-259-5223, 800-626-7335; www.rimtours.com), **Western Spirit Cyclery** (☎ 435-259-8732, 800-845-2453; www.western spirit.com) or **Backroads Bicycle Adventures** (☎ 800-462-2848, 510-527-1555; www.backroads.com).

Festivals & Events

The park hosts no events, but Ruby's Inn does. In early February, **Bryce Canyon Winterfest** includes everything from cross-country skiing and snowmobiling to archery and snow sculpting. In August, the **Bryce Canyon Rim Run** follows a 6-mile course partially along a portion of the Bryce Canyon rim outside the park.

Sleeping

The park has one lodge and two campgrounds. Backcountry camping permits ($5) are available at the visitor center. Most travelers stay just north of the park near the Hwy 12/63 junction or 11 miles east in Tropic. A few more lodging options are available 13 miles west of the park around Red Canyon (opposite) and 24 miles southwest in Hatch (p463). Motels in Panguitch (p458), 24 miles west, are a last-ditch option.

INSIDE THE PARK

North Campground (☎ reservations 877-444-6777; www .recreation.gov; Bryce Canyon Rd; campsites $10) The 107-site NPS campground near the visitor center has laundry, showers, groceries, toilets and water. Loop C is the closest to the rim (sites 59 and 60 have great views, but little privacy). May 15 to September you can reserve ahead for $14.

Sunset Campground (Bryce Canyon Rd; campsites $10; ☾ Apr-Sep) More wooded than North Campground, no-reservation Sunset also has fewer amenities (for laundry, showers and groceries, visit North). It has toilets and water. During summer, the 101 sites 2 miles south of the visitor center fill by noon.

Bryce Canyon Lodge (☎ 435-772-3213, reservations 888-297-2757; www.brycecanyonlodge.com; Bryce Canyon Rd; r $108-136, cabins $126; ☾ Apr-Oct) Being in the park is the main attraction at the 1920s Bryce Lodge. Common spaces exude mountain charm, right down to the reproduction Hickory furnishings, but compared with other national park lodges, the '90s-ish motel rooms may disappoint. The central cabins have gas fireplaces, front porches and are in high demand. No TVs.

OUTSIDE THE PARK

Bryce Canyon Pines (☎ 435-834-5441, 800-892-7923; www.brycecanyonmotel.com; Hwy 12; tent sites/ RV sites $17/25, r $55-110; ☾ Apr-Nov; ☒) Looking for a mom-and-pop experience? It's not the newest of places, but this rambling white clapboard motel has been in the same family for ages. Standard rooms have simple beds with simple spreads; some have kitchenettes, but there is a restaurant. Four miles west of the Hwy 12/63 junction. Some pets OK.

Ruby's Inn Campground (☎ 866-866-6616; www .rubysinn.com; 1000 S Hwy 63; tent sites $22-29, tepees $28-40, RV sites $31-39, cabins $50-59; ☾ Apr-Oct; ☒) The 200 sites adjacent to all those services at Ruby's Inn (right) are certainly shady. Also under the pines is a heated campground swimming pool. Didn't bring your tent? Lay your sleeping bag in one of the tepees. Camping cabins sleep

four (double bunk beds); no linens. Showers on site.

Bryce View Lodge (☎ 435-834-5180, 888-279-2304; www.bryceviewlodge.com; r $60-80; ☾ Apr-Oct) Owned by the same folks as Best Western Ruby's Inn across the street, Bryce View is geared toward budget travelers. Rooms are smaller and less spiffy, but you have free access to Ruby's pool and hot tub.

Bryce Country Cabins (☎ 435-679-8643, 888-679-8643; www.brycecountrycabins.com; 320 N Main St, Tropic; cabins $65-145; wi-fi) Knotty-pine walls, log beds and bear appliqué comforters add lots of charm to the one- and two-bedroom cabins here. The log duplexes (new in '07) have kitchens and great cliff views off rear decks.

Bullberry Inn (☎ 435-679-8820; www.bullberryinn .com; 412 S Hwy 12, Tropic; r incl breakfast $85) Built in 1998 this farmhouse-style inn has great views and is an excellent alternative to motels. Owners make the bullberry jam they serve with homemade goodies at breakfast.

Best Western Ruby's Inn (☎ 435-834-5341, 866-866-6616; www.rubysinn.com; 1000 S Hwy 63; motel r $85-145, ste $140-190; ☒ ☐ wi-fi) At Ruby's Inn, you can take a helicopter ride, watch a rodeo, admire Western art, wash laundry, shop for groceries, fill up with gas, dine at restaurants and post a letter. You can even buy bottles of alcohol – maybe the rarest service of all. Oh, and you can sleep in a snappy modern motel room or a cushy family or whirlpool suite. In 2007, the 2300-acre resort was officially incorporated as Bryce Canyon City. 'The motel that became a town' may sound like a horror movie, but in fact, the gargantuan complex has been owned by the same local family since its inception in 1919.

Stone Canyon Inn (☎ 435-679-8611, 866-489-4680; www.stonecanyoninn.com; 1220 Stone Canyon Lane, Tropic; r incl breakfast $125-190; wi-fi) Ultracomfortable beds and whirlpool tubs coddle a hiker's weary muscles, and imaginative full breakfasts help you fuel up for the hike ahead. Innkeepers will arrange guided hikes, and horseback and ATV rides.

Also try the following:

Bryce Pioneer Village (☎ 435-679-8546, 800-222-0381; www.bpvillage.com; 80 S Main St, Tropic; tent sites/RV sites $17/18, r $55-75, cabins $55-85; ☾ Apr-Oct) Motel rooms, cabins and camping backing up to a cliff. Some pets OK.

Bryce Canyon Resort (☎ 435-834-5351, 800-834-0043; www.brycecanyonresort.com; cnr Hwys 12 & 63; r $80-139, cabins $65-105, ste $175; ☒) Ruby's Inn wannabe; tours and outfitting available.

Eating & Entertainment

Nobody comes to Bryce for the food. Expect chicken-fried steak, canned gravy, frozen peas… If you're vegetarian, BYOV or subsist on iceberg lettuce and soggy fries. There's a Subway at the intersection of Hwys 63 and 12.

INSIDE THE PARK

Bryce Canyon General Store & Snack Bar (☎ 435-834-5361; near Sunrise Point; dishes $3-7; ☽ 8am-8pm Apr-Oct) Sells basic supplies, hot dogs, drinks, sandwiches, chile, soup and pizza.

Bryce Canyon Lodge (☎ 435-834-5361; Bryce Canyon Rd; breakfast & sandwiches $6-10, dinner mains $15-21; ☽ breakfast, lunch & dinner Apr-Oct) Windows line the walls of the rustic main lodge dining room. Dinner mains try a bit too hard to be gourmet (apples and brie, trout almandine), but this is by far the best place around to eat. For breakfast and lunch, expect casual American fare. Dinner reservations essential.

OUTSIDE THE PARK

Clarke's Grocery (☎ 435-679-8633; 121 N Main St, Tropic; sandwiches $4-6; ☽ 7:30am-7pm Mon-Sat) Tropic's grocery store has a deli sandwich counter and homemade baked goods.

The Pizza Place (☎ 435-679-8888; 21 N Main St, Tropic; breakfast $4-9, pizzas $5-12; ☽ 7:30am-9pm Apr-Oct, dinner Thu-Sat Nov-Mar) Outdoor seating and good pizza make this Tropic's top spot for simple dining.

Bryce Canyon Pines (☎ 435-834-5441; Hwy 12; breakfast & lunch $4-8, dinner mains $10-18; ☽ 6:30am-9:30pm) Marked only by a yellow sign reading 'Restaurant,' the Pines serves meat-and-potatoes meals. It's known for its homemade soups and pies, which are heavy but pretty good. Four miles west of the Hwy 12/63 junction.

Foster's Family Steakhouse (☎ 435-834-5227; Hwy 12; breakfast & sandwiches $5-9, mains $10-22; ☽ 7am-10pm May-Sep, 4-9pm Oct-Apr) Skip the thin-cut steaks and iceberg-lettuce salads and stick to the diner-like menu items. Two miles west of the Hwy 12/63 junction.

Cowboy's Buffet & Steak Room (☎ 435-834-5341; Ruby's Inn, 1000 S Hwy 63; breakfast & sandwiches $5-10, mains $14-28; ☽ 6:30am-10pm) Yeah, it's national park priced, but the ribs-and-beef dinner buffet ain't bad. Even with the cavernous dining room, expect a wait.

Sundown Ranch Chuckwagon Dinner Show (☎ 435-834-5033; 139 W Hwy 12; dinner show adult/child $40/28; ☽ 5:45pm Apr-Oct; ♠) Yee-haw! Cowboy up for some pure kitschy fun. Ride in a covered wagon to the ranch for Western song and verse to go with your fire-cooked chicken and beans.

April to October, Ruby's Inn also has a fast-food diner open for lunch and dinner.

Getting Around

A car is the only way around from fall through spring. If you're traveling in summer, ride the voluntary **shuttle** (free; ☽ 9am-6pm late May-Sep), lest you find yourself unable to find parking. Leave your car at the Ruby's Inn or Ruby's Campground stops, and ride the bus into the park. The shuttle goes as far as Bryce Point; buses come roughly every 15 minutes. (Note: the park's Visitor Center parking lot fills up, too.) A round-trip without exiting takes 50 minutes. Tune to 1610AM as you approach Bryce to learn about current shuttle operations. The *Hoodoo* newspaper shows routes.

No trailers are permitted south of Sunset Point. If you're towing, leave your load at your campsite or in the trailer turnaround lot at the visitor center.

AROUND BRYCE CANYON NATIONAL PARK

Red Canyon

Deep ocher-red monoliths rise up roadside as you drive along Hwy 12, 10 miles west of the Bryce Canyon turnoff. The aptly named **Red Canyon** (☎ 435-676-8815; www.fs.fed.us/dxnf; Dixie National Forest) provides an easy look at eerie formations. A network of trails leads hikers, bikers and horseback riders deeper into the area. Legend has it that outlaw Butch Cassidy once rode here; a tough 8.9-mile hiking route, **Cassidy Trail**, bears his name.

Check out the excellent geologic displays and pick up trail maps at the **Visitor Center** (☎ 435-676-2676; Hwy 12; ☽ 9am-6pm Jun-Aug, 10am-4pm May & Sep). Several moderately easy hiking trails begin near the center: the 0.7-mile **Arches Trail** passes 15 arches as it winds through a canyon; the 1-mile **Pink Ledges Trail** winds through red rock formations. For a harder hike, try the 2.8-mile, two- to four-hour **Golden Wall Trail**.

A couple of outfitters (see p455) near the national park run horseback rides through Red Canyon. There are also excellent mountain-biking trails. The best is 7.8-mile **Thunder Mountain Trail** through pine forest and red rock. Rent a bike 12 miles east at **Ruby's Inn** (☎ 435-834-5341; www.rubysinn.com; 1000 S Hwy 63; half-/full-day

UTAH

rentals $25/40), which also rents car racks, but operates no shuttle.

Surrounded by limestone formations and ponderosa pines, no-reservation **Red Canyon Campground** (☎ 435-676-8815; www.fs.fed.us/dxnf; campsites $9; ☷ mid-May–Sep) is scenic. The 37 sites with flush toilets, showers and dump station are a great alternative to the Bryce Canyon National Park grounds.

Just west on Hwy 12, before the intersection of Hwy 89, **Harold's Place** (☎ 435-676-2350; www .haroldsplace.net; Hwy 12; r $55-70, cabins $65-75; ☷ Mar-Oct) has cozy, modern, knotty-pine-paneled cabins, motel rooms with high-speed internet, and a restaurant (breakfast and dinner) with trout on the menu. Also down the road, the shade-free **Red Canyon RV Park** (☎ 435-676-2690; www.redcanyon .net; 3279 Hwy 12; cabins with shared bathroom $22-28, RV sites $30) has really rustic cabins (bring linens) and RV sites that'll hold a 40-footer.

Kodachrome Basin State Park

Petrified geysers and dozens of red, pink and white sandstone chimneys – some nearly 170ft tall – resemble everything from a sphinx to a snowmobile at **Kodachrome Basin** (☎ 435-679-8562; www.stateparks.utah.gov; off Cottonwood Canyon Rd; admission $6), 9 miles south of Cannonville. Visit in the morning or afternoon, when shadows play on the red rock. Most sights are along hiking and mountain-biking trails. The moderately easy, 3-mile round-trip **Panorama Trail** gives the best overview. Be sure to take the side trails to **Indian Cave**, where you can check out the handprints on the wall (cowboys' or Indians'?), and **Secret Passage**, a short hike through a narrow slot canyon. **Angel Palace Trail** (1-mile loop, moderate) has great desert views from on high.

Charming, seasoned proprietors Bob and Miraloy Ott run **Trail Head Station & Cabins** (☎ Apr-Nov 435-679-8536, Dec-Mar 435-679-8787; www .brycecanyoninn.com; cabins incl park admission $85; ☷ Apr-Nov). In addition to renting out great little cabins inside the park (two double beds, microwave, mini-refrigerator, coffee maker), they also offer horseback rides at $16 per hour.

The 26 well-spaced sites at the park service **campground** (☎ reservations 800-322-3770; www.stateparks .utah.gov; campsites incl park admission $16) get some shade from juniper trees. Good hot showers, too.

PANGUITCH

pop 1485 / elev 6624ft

Roughly halfway between Las Vegas (234 miles) and Salt Lake City (245 miles),

Panguitch is a good place to spend the night en route. Founded in 1864, the town was historically a ranching and lumber town, but mom-and-pop motels have long been the number-one industry. This is the best place around to fill up on gas and groceries for Bryce Canyon National Park, 24 miles east.

Panguitch is the seat of Garfield County and hosts numerous festivals. Two of the best are in June: the **Quilt Walk Festival** celebrates pioneer history and **Chariots in the Sky** is a huge hot-air balloon festival.

Information

Garfield County Travel Council (☎ 435-676-1160, 800-444-6689; www.brycecanyoncountry.com; 55 S Main St; ☷ 9am-5pm Mon-Fri) Visitor center.

Garfield Memorial Hospital (☎ 435-676-8811; 224 N 400 East)

Local police (☎ 435-676-8807)

Panguitch City Library (☎ 435-676-2431; 25 S 200 East; ☷ 1-6pm Mon-Fri) Free internet.

Post office (☎ 435-676-8853; 65 N 100 West)

Powell Ranger Station (☎ 435-676-8815; www .fs.fed.us/dxnf; 225 E Center St; ☷ 8am-4:30pm Mon-Fri) Dixie National Forest camping and hiking info.

Sleeping

Hitch-n-Post (☎ 435-676-2436; 420 N Main St; tent sites/ RV sites $15/25; wi-fi) Small lawns and trees divide RV spaces; tent sites are in a grassy field, but still have barbecue grills. RV wash and heavy-duty laundry on site. Some pets allowed.

Panguitch KOA (☎ 435-676-2225; 555 S Main St; tent sites/RV sites $21/32, partial hookups $28; ☒ wi-fi) A big pool (open May through September) is one of the main draws at this attractive campground just south of the Hwys 89/12 junction.

Canyon Lodge (☎ 435-676-8292, 800-440-8292; www.colorcountry.net/~cache/; 210 N Main St; r $45-55; ☷ Apr-Oct) Love that vintage neon sign at this immaculate older motel with 10 rooms. The 30-something couple running the place is super helpful. Hot tub.

Purple Sage (☎ 435-676-2659, 800-241-6889; www .purplesagemotel.biz; 132 E Center St; r $65-85; ☷ Mar-Oct; wi-fi) Pillow-top mattresses and hardwood furnishings in Panguitch? Yep, that and an outdoor hot tub, too. Family rooms available.

Red Brick Inn (☎ 435-676-2141, 866-732-2745; www .redbrickinnutah.com; 11161 N 100 West; r incl breakfast $89) The 1920s Dutch colonial home that holds Panguitch's only B&B was once the town's hospital. Room styles vary from country gingham and Victorian frill to faux lakefront cabin.

DETOUR: HWY 89 – PANGUITCH TO PROVO

Driving Hwy 89 from Panguitch to Provo, as an alternative route from Southwestern Utah's national parks to SLC, you come across scenes of rural life, small communities and a few attractions. Forty-eight miles north of Panguitch, outside of Marysvale, the mineral-stained giant to your left is **Big Rock Candy Mountain**, named after a Burl Ives (and later Dorsey Burnette) song.

Take a detour five miles west on I-70 and you'll reach **Fremont Indian State Park & Museum** (☎ 435-527-4631; http://stateparks.utah.gov; 3820 W Clear Creek Canyon Rd; admission $5; ☼ 9am-5pm), which contains more than 500 panels of Fremont Indian rock art on 12 interpretive trails, one of the largest collections in the state. There's also a partially excavated Fremont village.

Back on Hwy 89, 11 miles north, Monroe is a quiet, conservative Mormon farming community with one (good) restaurant. The main draw, however, is the hippie-esque **Mystic Hot Springs** (☎ 435-527-3286; 475 E 100 North; campsites per person $15, cabins $35, day use $5; ▯), where the water runs out of the earth into old claw-foot tubs and small cobbled-together pools. Put up a tent or stay in one of the tiny historic cabins they've dragged here from around the state.

Every year in June, Manti, 61 miles north, hosts the **Mormon Miracle Pageant** (☎ 435-835-3000; www.mormonmiracle.com). Hundreds of thousands attend the dramatic presentations from the bible and Book of Mormon at the foot of the dominating Mormon Temple.

Yet more choices:

Horizon Motel (☎ 435-676-2651, 800-776-2651; www .horizonmotel.net; 730 N Main St; r $49-60; ☼ Mar-Nov; wi-fi) Small, old-fashioned place showing pride of ownership.

Color Country Motel (☎ 435-676-2386, 800-225-6518; www.colorcountrymotel.com; 526 N Main St; r $50-60; 🐾) Small pets OK.

Marianna Inn Motel (☎ 435-676-8844, 800-598-9190; www.mariannainn.com; r $50-75; wi-fi) Log furniture, big back deck.

Eating & Drinking

Apple Crate Café (☎ 435-676-8986; 445 E Center St; dishes $4-15; ☼ 7am-9:30pm) A chef from Las Vegas is hiding out here in the Big 4 Travel Center truck stop. Even his chicken-fried steak is a lighter and fresher interpretation of the standard.

  Grandma Tina's Spaghetti House (☎ 435-676-2377; 523 N Main St; dishes $5-15; ☼ 7am-10pm May-Sep, 7am-10pm Thu-Sun Oct-Mar) Serves Italian sausages and vegetarian pastas.

  Cowboy's Smokehouse BBQ (☎ 435-676-8030; 95 N Main St; dinner mains $18-28; ☼ 11:30am-9pm Mar-Oct) Sometimes you get good barbecue here, sometimes not. But there's country music Friday and Saturday nights, June to August.

Shopping

There's really only one street in town – Main St (go figure) – where grocery stores and bric-a-brac shops line up. Check out the **Scrappy Appleyard** (☎ 435-676-8677; 190 N Main St) for quilts and fabrics, and **Cowboy Collectibles** (☎ 435-676-8060; 57 N Main St) for Western antiques.

CEDAR CITY

pop 25,600 / elev 5800ft

Shakespeare in the desert. From June to October, southern Utah's second-largest town plays host to one heck of a theater festival honoring the bard. Every year, roughly 150,000 visitors come to see the plays, tour behind the scenes and attend nightly concerts. In Cedar City, if it's not one festival, it's another. Outdoors enthusiasts also stay here to hit the trails in nearby Cedar Breaks National Monument (p462) and ski or bike at Brian Head Resort (p462). Cedar City is 3000ft higher than St George, which means it's deliciously cool in summer. The town's also a good I-15 stop between Vegas and SLC.

Orientation & Information

Cedar City is on I-15, 55 miles from St George, 180 miles from Las Vegas and 260 miles from SLC. Bryce Canyon is 80 miles east and Zion's south entrance is 60 miles southeast. Most businesses front Main St.

BLM (☎ 435-586-2401; 176 E DL Sargent Dr; ☼ 7:45am- 4:30pm Mon-Fri) Manages the land west of I-15, which is known for wild horses.

Cedar City & Brian Head Tourism & Convention Bureau (☎ 435-586-5124, 800-354-4849; www.scenic southernutah.com; 581 N Main St; ☼ 8am-5pm Mon-Fri, 9am-1pm Sat) Free internet and wi-fi.

Cedar City Ranger Station (☎ 435-865-3200; 1789 N Wedgewood Ln; ☼ 8am-5pm Mon-Fri) Provides Dixie National Forest information.

Local police (☎ 435-586-2956; 10 N Main St)

Mountain West Books (☎ 435-586-3828; 77 N Main St; ☼ 9am-7pm Mon-Fri, 9am-6pm Sat)

Post office (☎ 435-586-6701; 333 N Main St)

Valley View Medical Center (☎ 435-868-5000; 1303 N Main St)

Zions Bank (☎ 435-586-7614; 3 S Main St; ☼ 9am-5pm Mon-Fri, 9am-1pm Sat) Currency exchange.

Sights & Activities

Mormon pioneers and their early mining attempts are commemorated at the **Iron Mission State Park** (☎ 435-586-9290; 635 N Main St; admission $3; ☼ 9am-6pm May-Sep, 9am-6pm Mon-Sat Oct-Apr) museum. Check out the 19th-century stagecoaches and buggies. Living history demos take place in summer.

Hiking and biking trails abound in the area. At the foot of 300 East, the recommended 8-mile, unpaved **C Trail** loop is strenuous. **Canyon Park** (cnr 400 East & College Ave) marks the start of the paved **Canyon Walking Trail** (3-mile round-trip) past painted cliffs along Hwy 14. **Cedar Cycle** (☎ 435-586-5210; www.cedarcyle.com; 38 E 200 South; ☼ 9am-5pm Mon-Fri, 9am-2pm Sat) repairs and rents bikes ($20 to $30 a day) and has trail information.

Festivals & Events

The play's the thing at Cedar City's main event, held annually at **Southern Utah University** (SUU; ☎ 435-586-7700; www.suu.edu; 351 W Center St) since 1962. The Tony Award–winning **Utah Shakespearean Festival** (☎ 435-586-7878, 800-752-9849; www.bard.org) presents three of the bard's plays, plus three other stage classics from mid-June to September. In the fall (mid-September to late October), it presents three more chestnuts – one Shakespearean, one straight and one musical. Productions are top quality, but it's the extras that draw the crowds. In summer, there are free seminars discussing the plays, free 'Greenshows' with Elizabethan minstrels, classes for credit, child care and more. In fall, there's a pumpkin festival, quilt gathering and classes.

Make reservations at least one to two weeks in advance; tickets cost from $26 to $60. Ask about last-minute seats at the **Courtesy Booth** (☎ 435-586-7790; 351 W Center St). A few last-row gallery tickets go on sale here the day of the performance; arrive early.

More festivities:

Utah Summer Games (☎ 435-865-8421; www.utahsummergames.org) A June mini-Olympics with 7600 amateur athletes, plus a rodeo.

Midsummer Renaissance Fair (☎ 435-586-3711; www.umrf.net) Renaissance entertainment in early July.

Neil Simon Festival (☎ 435-327-8673; www.simonfest .org) American plays staged mid-July to mid-August.

Cedar City Skyfest (☎ 435-867-5890; www.cedar cityskyfest.org) Hot-air balloons, kites and model rockets go off in September.

Sleeping

To do Cedar City right, reserve ahead and stay in one of its many B&Bs; no children under 12. Rates following are for the high season (March through October), but in-demand weekends during the Shakespearean Festival may cost more.

Cedar City KOA (☎ 435-586-9872; 1121 N Main St; tent sites/RV sites $25/39, cabins with shared bathroom $39-60; ⊠ wi-fi) Loads of extras here include a movie theater, full-service laundry and a snack bar. Bring linens for the one- and two-bedroom camping cabins. Some pets allowed.

Knights Inn (☎ 435-586-9916; 281 S Main St; r $50-65; ⊠ wi-fi) This near-downtown motel is next door to Sulli's Steakhouse. The building got a new coat of paint – inside and out – in 2007. Some pets OK.

Abbey Inn Motel (☎ 435-586-9966, 800-325-5411; www.abbeyinncedar.com; 940 W 200 North; r incl breakfast $66-86; ⊠ wi-fi) Dark wood furnishings offset jewel-toned linens at this traditional motel. Rooms have microwaves and mini-refrigerators.

Big Yellow Inn (☎ 435-586-0960; www.bigyellowinn .com; 234 S 300 West; r incl breakfast $79-109; ⊡ wi-fi) Two B&Bs in one: the Big Yellow itself is a Georgian revival grand dame with Victorian 2nd-story rooms and more lodgey-looking 1st-floor walk-outs. Guest quarters at Across the Street Inn (guess where it is?) have a lighter, more country feel, and DVD players instead of VCRs.

Amid Summer's Inn (☎ 435-586-6612; www.bards bandb.com; 140 S 100 West; r incl breakfast $99-149; ⊡ wi-fi) Given the plain exterior, there's a certain wow factor when you see the lavish tester canopy bed in the Enchanted Dream suite or the themed-out Captain's Quarters. (Yes, the owners are interior designers.)

Garden Cottage B&B (☎ 435-586-4919, 866-586-4919; www.thegardencottagebnb.com; 16 N 200 West; r incl breakfast $109-119) Vines stretch up the white stucco exterior and a riot of color blooms in the garden. Even the five precious rooms here are named for flowers. No room TVs.

Iron Gate Inn (☎ 435-867-0603, 800-808-4599; www .theirongateinn.com; 100 N 200 West; r incl breakfast $109-159; ⊡) Rambling porches and a big yard surround an 1897 house with large guest rooms. Enjoy your breakfast on the patio or at individual tables in the formal dining room.

Storybook Cottage (☎ 435-586-8057, 866-586-8057; www.storybookbnb.com; 218 S 100 West; r incl breakfast $110-135; ▨ wi-fi) Bard the cat welcomes you to this three-room B&B. Thoroughly modern fixtures, such as the Kohler pedestal sinks, in this 1920's cottage redo were chosen for their old-world feel.

And then there's the following:

Holiday Inn Express ☎ 435-865-7799, 888-465-4329; www.hiexpress.com; 1555 S Old Hwy 91; r $79-109; ▨ ▨ wi-fi) Modern motel rooms with an up-to-date look.

Marriott Springhill Suites (☎ 435-586-1685, 888-236-2427; www.marriott.com; 1477 S Old Hwy 91; r $99-159; ▨ wi-fi) Colorful contemporary suites.

Eating

How wonderful it would be if Cedar City had dining on par with its B&Bs and top-notch theater. But alas, poor Yorick, it doth not. Hours are usually extended variably during Shakespeare weekends.

Cafe Orleans (☎ 435-867-6437; 5 N Main St; sandwiches $6-10, mains $10-18; ☽ lunch & dinner) Two Louisiana restaurateurs moved here post–hurricane Katrina – to Cedar City's benefit. Authentic gumbos and étouffées are completely site made; veggie versions, too.

Garden House (☎ 435-586-6110; 164 S 100 West; lunch mains $6-10, dinner mains $12-22; ☽ lunch & dinner Mon-Sat) A character-filled home-turned-restaurant, Garden House is the locals' recommended eatery. Homemade soups, sandwiches, pastas and seafood dishes top the menu.

Milt's Stage Stop (☎ 435-586-9344; Cedar Canyon, Hwy 14; mains $13-25; ☽ dinner Mon-Sat) Trophy heads have been hanging on the wall here since Milt started grilling steaks and seafood in 1956.

Sullivan's Cafe (☎ 435-586-6761; 301 S Main St; dishes $6-12; ☽ 6am-10pm) serves diner food at its greasy best: big breakfasts, piled-high burgers and homemade meatloaf. Attached is **Sulli's Steakhouse** (mains $12-22; ☽ dinner), with a full bar and surf-and-turf menu.

Also try:

Bulloch Drug (☎ 435-586-9651; 91 N Main St; treats $2-5; ☽ 9am-9pm Mon-Fri, 9am-7pm Sat) Ice-cream sodas from a vintage 1940s fountain.

Pastry Pub (☎ 435-867-1400; 86 W Center St; dishes $3-7; ☽ 7:30am-10pm Mon-Sat) Pastries, sandwiches, shakes.

Main Street Grill (☎ 435-586-8389; 155 N Main St; dishes $5-9; ☽ breakfast & lunch) Waiters know every name; gossip served with the omelettes.

Entertainment

The Shakespeare Festival is the biggest game in town. Cedar City is pretty quiet otherwise.

Heritage Center (☎ 435-865-2882, 866-882-3327; www.heritagectr.org; 105 N 100 East) Home to the local orchestra, the Neil Simon festival and other theater events year round.

Groovacious Music Store (☎ 435-867-9800; www.groovacious.com; 171 N 100 West; ☽ 10am-9pm Mon-Sat) The local music store (with awesome vinyl) hosts concerts and other events. Every Thursday is open mic night (7pm to 9pm).

Grind Coffeehouse (☎ 435-867-5333; www.thegrindcoffeehouse.com; 19 N Main St; ☽ 7am-7pm Mon-Thu, 7am-midnight Fri & Sat, 8:30am-5pm Sun; ▨ wi-fi) Friday nights are for comedy improv, Saturday nights there's live music. Both are adults only, but note that there's no booze.

AROUND CEDAR CITY

As scenic drives go, **Hwy 14** is awesome. It leads 42 miles over the Markagunt Plateau, cresting at 10,000ft for stunning vistas of Zion National Park and Arizona. The surrounding area is part of **Dixie National Forest** (www.fs.fed.us/r4/dixie). For more information, check in with Cedar City Ranger Station (p459). Four-wheel drive or chains may be required November through April.

Hiking and biking trails, past the Cedar Breaks National Monument turnoff on Hwy 14, have tremendous views, particularly at sunset; they include the short (less than a mile one way) **Cascade Falls** and **Bristlecone Trails** and the 32-mile **Virgin River Rim Trail**. A signed turnoff 24.5 miles from Cedar City leads to jumbled **lava beds**.

Twenty-five miles east of Cedar City, boating and fishing are the activities of choice at **Navajo Lake**. You can rent a motor boat ($70 a day) or stay over in a historic 1920s cabin at **Navajo Lake Lodge** (☎ 702-646-4197; www.navajolakelodge.com; cabins $65-85; ☽ May-Oct). The rustic lodgings include bedding, but no refrigerators.

Five miles further east, **Duck Creek Visitor Center** (☎ 435-682-2432; ☽ 9am-4:30pm Memorial Day-Labor Day) provides information about fishing in the adjacent pond and stream. **Falcon's Nest Cabins** (☎ 435-682-2556, 800-240-4930; www.falconsnestcabins.com; cabins $90-110) is one of several lodges in the area. Cabins have big kitchens and sleep at least six. Some pets OK.

Continuing east on Hwy 14, follow the passable dirt road 10 miles south to **Strawberry Point**, for possibly the best views of all.

Fifteen miles south of Cedar City on I-15 is the spectacular Kolob Canyons section of Zion National Park; see opposite.

CEDAR BREAKS NATIONAL MONUMENT

Sculpted cliffs and towering hoodoos glow like neon tie-dye in a wildly eroded natural amphitheater encompassed by Cedar Breaks National Monument. The majestic kaleidoscope of magenta, salmon, plum, rust and ocher rises to a height of 10,450ft atop the Markagunt Plateau. The compact park lies 22 miles east and north of Cedar City, off Hwy 14. There are no cedar trees here, by the way: early pioneers mistook the evergreen junipers for cedars.

The monument's one road, Hwy 148, closes because of snow, November through April. Summer temperatures range from 40°F to 70°F; brief storms drop rain, hail and even powdery white snow. A small **visitor center** (☎ 435-586-9451; www.nps.gov/cebr/; park admission $3; ☷ 8am-6pm) opens from Memorial Day to Labor Day.

No trails descend into the breaks, but the park has five viewpoints off Hwy 148 and there are rim trails. **Ramparts Trail** – one of southern Utah's most magnificent trails – leaves from the visitor center. The elevation change on the 3-mile round-trip is only 400ft, but it can be tiring because of the high elevation. **Alpine Pond Trail** is a lovely, though less dramatic, 4-mile loop.

The first-come, first-served **Point Supreme Campground** (campsites $14; ☷ mid-Jun–Sep) has water and restrooms, but no showers; its 28 sites rarely fill.

BRIAN HEAD

pop 120 / elev 9700ft

The highest town in Utah, Brian Head towers over Cedar City, 35 miles southwest. 'Town' is a bit of an overstatement though; this is basically a ski resort. From Thanksgiving through April, snow bunnies come to challenge the closest slopes to Las Vegas (200 miles). For online info, check out www.brianheadutah .com. Cedar City & Brian Head Tourism & Convention Bureau (p459) is the closest tourism office.

Advanced skiers might grow impatient with the short trails (except on a powder day), but there's lots to love for beginners, intermediates and free-riders at **Brian Head Resort** (☎ 435-677-2035; www.brianhead.com; Hwy 143; day lift ticket adult/child $45/32). Lines are usually short and it's the only resort in Utah within sight of the red rock desert. The lowdown: 1320ft vertical drop, base elevation 9600ft, 500 acres.

A new bridge, finished in January 2008, provides an easy skiable link to all the lifts. Added at the same time were two new triple-chair high-speed lifts, for a total of eight. A highlight is the kickin' six-lane snow-tubing area (with surface lift), and there's a mini-terrain park for snowboarders. Friday and Saturday nights, ski under the lights from one lift ($12).

July to August, the elevation keeps temperatures deliciously cool. Ride the **summer chair-lift** (☷ 9:30am-4:30pm) up to 11,000ft for an alpine hike or mountain biking.

The resort's lodges and town's sports shops rent skis and snowboards ($27 to $32 per day). **Georg's Ski & Bike Shop** (☎ 435-677-2013; http://brianheadtown.com/georgs/; Hwy 143), by the bridge, also rents clothing, mountain bikes, cross-country skis and sleds. Forty-two miles of cross-country trails surround Brian Head, including semi-groomed trails to Cedar Breaks National Monument.

Public lands also have snowmobile trails: rent at **Ride-N** (☎ 435-310-0300; www.ride-n.com; Hwy 143), where a full day costs about $185, or take a guided snowmobile tour with **Thunder Mountain Sports** (☎ 866-677-2386; www.brianhead thunder.com; 539 N Hwy 143; 1½-hr tour $70).

Check the ski resort website for lodging/ski packages – two nights in Vegas, two nights in Brian Head can be under $200 per person. Local lodging is in condos ($85 to $450); contact **Brian Head Condo Reservations** (☎ 435-677-2045, 800-722-4742; www.brianheadcondoreservations.com; 356 S Hwy 143).

Cedar Breaks Lodge & Spa (☎ 888-282-3327, 435-677-4242; www.cedarbreakslodge.com; 222 Hunter Ridge Rd; r $100-290; ☢ ☐ wi-fi) runs time-share units as a hotel, with amenities such as a day spa and restaurant. **Bristlecone Log Cabins** (☎ 435-680-0871; www.brianhead cabins.com; homes $395) rents two beautiful 2500-sq-ft-plus homes; each has five queen beds.

The ski resort day lodges have fast-food stands. Get groceries at **Apple Annie's Country Store** (☎ 435-677-2040; The Mall, 259 S Hwy 143). Also in the Mall, the **Bump & Grind Café** (☎ 435-677-3111; 259 S Hwy 143; dishes $4-11; ☷ lunch & dinner daily, breakfast Sat & Sun) serves a variety of pastas and sandwiches. **Mountainview Pizza Pub** (☎ 435-677-2411; 508 N Hwy 143; sandwiches & pizzas $7-13; ☷ lunch & dinner Wed-Sun) is the place for a good homemade pie (of both the pizza and dessert variety); Utah beers on tap. **Double Black Diamond Steakhouse** (☎ 435-677-4242; Cedar Breaks Lodge, 222 Hunter Ridge Rd; mains $9-23; ⏲ dinner) serves sit-down American meals.

HWYS 89 & 9 – BRYCE TO ZION

In the days before freeways, US Hwy 89 was Utah's main north–south artery. If you like driving but hate the interstate, you'll love cruising the curvy roads passing red-rock vistas between Bryce and Zion. Most people pass by the tiny old towns along the way, which is all the better for you – there are some real restaurant gems and lodging treasures hidden here. Remember when reading distances that you'll average 35mph to 50mph along these roads.

Independent motels and a few eateries line up along Hwy 89 in **Hatch**, 25 miles southwest of Bryce. The settlement on the Sevier River attracts fly-fishers. The **Cottonwood Meadow Lodge** (☎ 435-676-8950; www.panguitchanglers; Mile 121, Hwy 89; r $90, cabins/house $150/175; wi-fi) owners will sell you lures from their fly-shop and fill you in on where to hook browns, rainbows and brookies. The restored pioneer homestead is also a great place to rest your head. There are several small rooms in the original house, a romantic log-and-mortar cabin and a larger pond-side house on the property. The best place to eat in town, 5 miles south of the lodge, is **Café Adobe** (☎ 435-735-4020; 16 N Main St; dishes $4-12; ⏲ 8am-9pm Mar–mid-Nov). Workers from Bryce Canyon travel here for gourmet hamburgers, interesting salads and sandwiches.

Further south, 50 miles from Bryce and 26 miles to Zion, **Glendale** is a historic little Mormon town founded in 1871. Today there's an excellent B&B and eclectic bistro to draw you in, but this is also an access point for Grand Staircase-Escalante National Monument (GSEMN). From Hwy 89, turn onto 300 North at the faded sign for GSENM; from there it turns into Glendale Bench Rd, which leads to Johnson Canyon and Skutumpah Rds (p451). Get your giddy-up going with a horseback ride ($20 per hour) from **Glendale KOA Campground** (☎ 435-648-2490; tent sites/ RV sites/ camping cabins $20/30/35; ⏲ May-Oct; ☒), 5 miles north on Hwy 89. It also has bicycle rental.

The seven-room **Historic Smith Hotel** (☎ 435-648-2156, 800-528-3558; www.historicsmithhotel.com; 295 N Main St, Glendale; r incl breakfast $44-80), c 1927, offers true rural hospitality. Pull up a cozy quilt among the antiques in your room, bubble

away in the whirlpool hot tub or roam the 2 acres of gardens and fruit trees (late summer, pick your own). Next door, **Buffalo Bistro** (☎ 435-648-2778; 305 N Main St, Glendale; burgers $7-10, mains $17-28; ⏲ 4-8pm Apr–mid-Nov) conjures up an Old West spirit with its breezy wooden porch and outdoor sizzling grill. Foodies come for the excellent wild boar and buffalo ribs. You might also try the rabbit and rattlesnake sausages, or vegetarian pastas. The gregarious owner-chef has a great sense of humor and sometimes hosts music and events, such as the Testicle Festival (Rocky Mountain oysters served), under the trees.

In Mt Carmel, the *Architectural Digest*–noted **Maynard Dixon Home & Studio** (☎ 435-648-2653; www.thunderbirdfoundation.com; Hwy 89; tours $20; ⏲ May-Oct) is where renowned Western painter Maynard Dixon (1875–1946) lived and worked in the 1930s and '40s. Docent-led tours are by appointment only. Look for the house at Mile 84 on Hwy 89, about 6 miles south of Glendale; it's easy to miss.

Boredom-prone families should consider staying 2 miles east of Zion at the **Zion Ponderosa Ranch Resort** (Map p464; ☎ 435-648-2700, 800-293-5444; www.zionponderosa.com; North Fork Rd; tent sites $45, cabins $69-160; ☒ ☒ ☒); activities on the 8000 acres include canyoneering, hiking, biking, ATV tours, horseback rides, basketball, tennis, swimming and more. The kid's day camp means parents can enjoy alone time. Comfy cabins, sleeping up to six, share spotless bathroom facilities. Ask about all-inclusive meal packages.

At **Zion Mountain Resort** (Map p464; ☎ 435-688-1039, 866-648-2555; www.zionponderosa.com; Hwy 9; cabins $120-140; ☒), the adventure set-up is similar, if a smidge fancier. Buffalo roam (and appear on the dinner menu) at this 6000-acre resort. Registration is 2.5 miles east of the Zion park entrance.

ZION NATIONAL PARK

The soaring red-and-white cliffs of Zion Canyon, one of southern Utah's most dramatic natural wonders, rise high over the Virgin River. But for all its initial awe-inspiring majesty, the park holds more delicate beauties as well – weeping rocks, tiny grottoes, hanging gardens, lush riverbanks and meadows of mesa-top wildflowers. The lush vegetation and low elevation give the magnificent rock formations here a whole different feel from the barren parks in the east.

Hiking Zion is fantastic, and challenging: there's nothing like the adrenaline rush from peering down from one of 22 switchbacks you've climbed up a cliffside, or the thrill of negotiating a stream-filled slot canyon.

Even Hwy 9, which winds through the southern part of the park, is a sight. Most of the park's 2.5 million annual visitors come from May to September. The main Zion Canyon section is jam-packed but fairly quiet in summer, since park shuttle use is mandatory. The Kolob Canyons section, 40 miles northwest by car, is less visited year-round.

Climate

Summers are hot (100°F is common); summer nighttime temperatures drop into the 60s. Beware of sudden cloudbursts from July to September. Winter brings some snow, but daytime temperatures increase to 50°F. Wildflowers bloom in May, as do the bugs; bring repellant.

Orientation

Zion's main entrance is 77 miles (two hours) southwest of Bryce. The park occupies 147,000 acres between I-15 in the northwest and Hwy 9 to the south. Three roads access the park: the main visitor center is on Hwy 9 and Zion Canyon Scenic Dr branches off near there. The desolate Kolob Terrace Rd, west of the visitor center, travels 35 miles north from Hwy 9 leading through BLM and park service lands. To the northwest, Kolob Canyons Rd

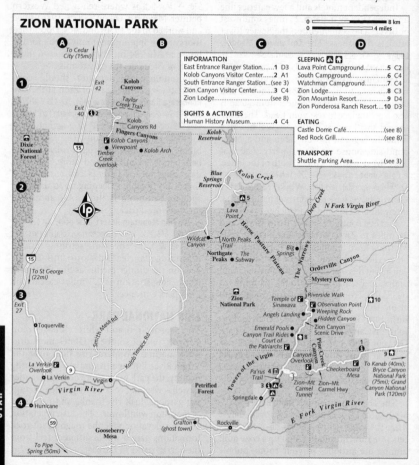

ZION NATIONAL PARK

INFORMATION		
East Entrance Ranger Station	1	D3
Kolob Canyons Visitor Center	2	A1
South Entrance Ranger Station	(see 3)	
Zion Canyon Visitor Center	3	C4
Zion Lodge	(see 8)	

SIGHTS & ACTIVITIES		
Human History Museum	4	C4

SLEEPING		
Lava Point Campground	5	C2
South Campground	6	C4
Watchman Campground	7	C4
Zion Lodge	8	C3
Zion Mountain Resort	9	D4
Zion Ponderosa Ranch Resort	10	D3

EATING		
Castle Dome Café	(see 8)	
Red Rock Grill	(see 8)	

TRANSPORT		
Shuttle Parking Area	(see 3)	

stretches east off I-15 and continues past an entrance gate and the second visitor center. No road within the park directly connects the main and Kolob Canyons sections.

Springdale (p468), an outdoorsy community full of motels, eclectic restaurants and shops, is just west of the visitor center on Hwy 9. Look there for tour outfitters and most services. St George (p475), 40 minutes southwest of both Zion and Kolob canyons, is the nearest city.

Information

Kolob Canyons Visitor Center (☎ 435-586-0895; Kolob Canyons Rd; ◷ 8am-4:30pm) Secondary visitor center at the northwest entrance.

Local police (☎ 435-772-3322)

Zion Canyon Visitor Center (☎ 435-772-3256; www .nps.gov/zion; Hwy 9; ◷ 8am-7pm May-Sep, 8am-6pm Apr & Oct, 8am-5pm Nov-Mar) Central source for information. Several rangers are on hand to answer questions and there's a huge bookstore. Schedules for nature walks and interpretive talks posted. The Backcountry Desk (☎ 435-772-0170) issues permits.

Zion Lodge (☎ 435-772-3213; Zion Canyon Scenic Dr) Free wi-fi and two free internet terminals in the lobby.

Zion Natural History Association (ZNHA; ☎ 435-772-3264, 800-635-3959; www.zionpark.org) Runs visitor center bookstore; great online selection.

Dangers & Annoyances

Flash floods occur year-round, particularly in July and August. Before hiking in river canyons, check weather and water conditions with rangers. If you hear thunder, if water rises suddenly or goes muddy, or if you feel sudden wind accompanied by a roar, immediately seek higher ground. Climbing a few feet can save your life; if you can't, get behind a rock fin. There's no outrunning a flash flood.

Sights & Activities

Cycling, rock climbing, canyoneering and driving tour outfitters operate from Springdale (p469). Under a mile east of the main visitor center is the air-conditioned **Human History Museum** (☎ 435-772-0168; admission free; ◷ 10am-6pm). Exhibits present the geological and human history of Zion; there's also a good 22-minute introductory film. The building is part of an original Mormon homestead.

SCENIC DRIVES

Zion Canyon Scenic Drive, which pierces the heart of Zion Canyon, is most visitors' primary destination. If you've time for only one activity, tour this 6-mile road (in the shuttle from April to October). It's 10 miles from Zion Canyon to the park's east exit.

Hwy 9, east of the park entrance, rises in a series of six switchbacks before the 1.1-mile Zion–Mount Carmel Tunnel (an engineering marvel constructed in the late 1920s; see p466). It then leads quickly into dramatically different terrain – a landscape of etched slickrock, culminating at the mountainous Checkerboard Mesa.

For a sunset perch, head to the **La Verkin Overlook**, 20 miles west of Zion on Hwy 9 between Virgin and La Verkin. Take the signed turnoff up the 1.5-mile-long gravel-and-dirt road for a 360-degree overlook. **Kolob Canyons Rd**, off I-15, lies 40 miles from the main visitor center. The 5-mile road, which penetrates the **Finger Canyons** area, sees one-tenth of the visitors that the south entrance does, though the scenery and hiking are stupendous. The red road pavement seems to add to the drive's color intensity.

HIKING

Distances for hikes listed are one way. Trails can be slippery; check weather conditions before you depart.

Zion Canyon

Spring to fall, the shuttle (see p468) stops at all major trailheads along the scenic drive, the park's centerpiece. In low season, you can park at these shuttle stops and several scenic pullouts.

Of the easy-to-moderate trails, the paved, mile-long **Riverside Walk** at the end of the road is a good place to start. When the trail ends, you can continue along (and into) the Virgin River for several miles, on the bottom portion

UTAH

I THINK I CAN, I THINK I CAN

As national parks grew in popularity in the 1920s, the pressure to link Zion and Bryce by road challenged engineers. The problem: how to bore through 2000ft-thick sandstone 225ft in the air? The solution? Three-and-a-half miles of switchbacks stacked over themselves in just a quarter mile, and the 9ft wide by 5600ft long **Zion–Mount Carmel Tunnel**. Engineers constructed an aerial tramway just to create a workers' base camp. During the three years of construction (1927–30), more than 146 tons of dynamite were used to move 72,000 cu yards of stone. Where'd all that rock go? Much of it was thrown out the galleries you see as you drive through; the rest was trucked out and used to fill in the roadway below. And you thought they'd engineered windows for your viewing pleasure. Well, that's nice, too.

---

of the Narrows (opposite) – a difficult back-packing trip. Day-trippers are allowed to hike 5 miles to Big Springs.

A steep, but paved, half-mile trail leads to the lower of the **Emerald Pools**. Here water tumbles from above a steep overhang, creating a desert varnish stain that resembles rock art. It's worth your while to hike the mile further up the gravel to the more secluded upper pool. Note: you will have to scramble up (and back down) some stairlike rocks. The quarter-mile-long **Weeping Rock Trail** climbs 100ft to hanging gardens.

Among harder trails, 2.5-mile **Angels Landing Trail** (1490ft ascent) is the one everyone's heard of, and fears. At times the trail is no more than 5ft wide, 1500ft above the canyon floor. Anyone with a fear of heights should stop at the wide saddle (aka Chicken-out Point) before you get to **Walters Wiggles**, the set of 21 stonework zigzags that takes you up a cleft in the rock. You'll emerge at **Scout Lookout**, which offers unbelievable vistas and a place to gather strength for the final scrabble to the landing.

Hidden Canyon Trail has sheer drop-offs and an 850ft elevation change in just over a mile before you reach the narrow, shady canyon. The most work (2150ft elevation change) is rewarded with great views from **Observation Point Trail** (4 miles).

The paved **Pa'rus Trail** parallels the scenic drive from Watchman Campground to the main park junction (about 2 miles). It's the only trail that allows bicycles and dogs.

The only marked trail along Hwy 9 is **Canyon Overlook Trail**, a moderately easy, half-mile walk, yielding thrilling views 1000ft down into Zion Canyon. But there are some interesting narrow canyon hikes that head off from Hwy 9 pullouts. Can you find the one to **petroglyphs**? (Hint: you start near a bridge. Buy a map, bring a compass.) There are also places where

locals park along a Hwy 9 turnout, climb down, cross under the road and follow a wash to the river for a dip. Happy searching.

Kolob Terrace Road

Fourteen miles west of Springdale, Kolob Terrace Rd takes off north weaving in and out of BLM and national park highlands. (The road is closed because of snow at least November through March.) **Wildcat Canyon Trailhead** lies about 28 miles north, after a hairpin turn. From here follow the Wildcat Canyon Trail till you get to the turnoff for **North Peaks Trail**. You'll traipse through meadows, filled with wildflowers in spring, and pine forests before you descend to the viewpoint overlooking the peaks. It's a whole different, and much less visited, side of Zion. It's 2.2 miles one way from Wildcat Canyon to North Peaks overlook. North of Wildcat Canyon, about 5 miles, is the gravel road to **Lava Point**, where there's a lookout.

Kolob Canyons Road

In the northwestern section of the park, the easiest trail is at the end of the road: **Timber Creek Overlook Trail** (0.5 miles). It follows a 100ft ascent to a small peak with great views. The main hike is the 2.7-mile-long **Taylor Creek Trail**, which crisscrosses the creek. The hike to **Kolob Arch** has a big payoff: this arch competes with Landscape Arch in Arches National Park in terms of being one of the biggest in the world. Fit hikers can do the 14.4-mile round-trip in a day.

Backcountry

Zion has 100 miles of backcountry hiking trails (permits required), wilderness camping and enough quiet to hear the whoosh of soaring ravens overhead. If you hike the entirety of Zion north to south, it's a four-day traverse of 50-plus miles. Check with the Backcountry Desk (p465) at the Zion Canyon Visitor Center for permits; roughly half the available passes for a route can be reserved online.

The **Narrows** is a 16-mile journey into narrow canyons along the Virgin River's north fork, best done June through October. The easiest and busiest of the backcountry hikes, it's unforgettable. Plan on getting wet: about 50% of the hike is in the river. The trip takes 12 hours; split it into two days, spending the night at one of the designated campsites you reserved or finish the hike in time to catch the last park shuttle. The trail ends among the throngs of day hikers on Riverside Walk at the north end of Zion Canyon.

Shuttle companies operate vans to backcountry trailheads. Typical fares run $25 to $35 per person, with a two-person minimum. Make reservations with **Zion Adventure Company** (☎ 435-772-0990; www.zionadventures.com), **Zion Rock & Mountain Guides** (☎ 435-772-3303; www.zionrockguides .com) or **Red Rock Shuttle & Tours** (☎ 435-635-9104; www.redrockshuttle.com).

CANYONEERING
If there's one sport that makes Zion special, it's canyoneering. Rappel over the lip of a sandstone bowl, swim icy pools, trace a slot canyon's curves – canyoneering is beautiful, dangerous and sublime all at once. Zion's slot canyons are the park's most sought-after backcountry experience; reserve far in advance.

Guided trips are prohibited in the park. Springdale outfitters (p469) hold courses outside Zion, after which students can try out their newfound skills in the park. One of the most popular routes is the **Subway** (9.5 miles, 1850ft elevation change), with four or five rappels of 20ft or less, and the namesake tube-looking slickrock formation. You start at the Wildcat Canyon trailhead off Kolob Terrace Rd.

Pine Creek Canyon and **Mystery Canyon** are gorgeous, popular routes with moderate challenges and rappels of 50ft to 100ft. Pine Creek has easy access. Mystery Canyon lets you be a rock star – the last rappel drops into the Virgin River before admiring crowds hiking the Narrows. Ask rangers for more info.

CYCLING & MOUNTAIN BIKING
No cars on Zion Canyon Scenic Dr in summer makes cycling there great. Bikes are only allowed there and on the 2-mile Pa'rus Trail. Mountain biking is prohibited in the park.

HORSEBACK RIDING
Zion's official horseback-riding concessionaire, **Canyon Trail Rides** (☎ 435-679-8665, 435-772-3810; www.canyonrides.com; ⊙ Mar-Nov), operates across from Zion Lodge. Take a one-hour ($35) or three-hour ($60) ride on the **Sand Bench Trail** along the Virgin River.

ROCK CLIMBING
Zion Canyon has some of the most famous big-wall climbs in America. However, there's not much for beginners or those who like bolted routes. Contact the Backcountry Desk (p465) at the Zion Canyon Visitor Center for permits. It also has route descriptions written by climbers.

Sleeping
You'll need a permit ($5) from the Backcountry Desk at the visitor center (see p465) for wilderness camping at designated areas along the West Rim, La Verkin Creek, Hop Valley and the Narrows. About half the permits can be reserved online. The remaining permits are distributed on a first-come, first-served basis a day ahead. Trying to get a walk-in permit on a busy weekend is like getting tickets to see Hannah Montana; lines form at the desk by 6am. Sites at the park's established campgrounds fill by mid-morning.

Lava Point Campground (Lava Point Rd; campsites free; ⊙ Jun-Sep) Drive 35 miles up Kolob Terrace Rd, one hour from the park's main visitor center, where the air's cooler at 7800ft. Six first-come, first-served sites are rarely full; no water.

South Campground (☎ 435-772-3256; Hwy 9; campsites $16; ⊙ mid-Mar–Oct) The 116 first-come, first-served tent sites just north of the visitor center are just as pretty as those at Watchman. Problem is, riverside spaces adjoin busy Pa'rus Trail.

Watchman Campground (☎ 800-365-2267; http:// reservations.nps.gov; Hwy 9; tent sites $16-20, electrical hookups $18) Reserve far ahead and request a riverside site at this cottonwood-shaded campground. (Allergy sufferers should avoid the May pollen season.) Toilets, no showers; south of the visitor center.

Zion Lodge (lodge 435-772-7700, reservations 888-297-2757; www.zionlodge.com; Zion Canyon Scenic Dr; r $150-170, cabins $165-180; ☐) The park lodge at Zion is admirably green: more than 85% of power consumed comes from solar and wind sources and lodge vehicles are all hybrids. Six ecofriendly suites ($165) have renewable bamboo flooring, recycled-material carpet and organic cotton sheets; chemical-free cleansers are used. Don't expect rustic bliss if you book one of the 81 motel rooms though; they're decorated in late-'90s American motel style. The cabins with rock fireplaces are a better choice. No TVs; wi-fi in lobby.

Eating

The lodge has the only in-park dining; otherwise head to Springdale (p470).

Castle Dome Café (☎ 435-772-7700; Zion Lodge, Zion Canyon Scenic Dr; dishes $4-8; ⊙ 11am-5pm Apr-Oct) Looking for something fast? The café serves sandwiches, pizza, salads, soups, Asian-ish rice bowls and ice cream.

Red Rock Grill (☎ 435-772-7760; Zion Lodge, Zion Canyon Scenic Dr; sandwiches $6-8, mains $14-19; ⊙ breakfast, lunch & dinner) Settle into your log-replica chair and peer out of the window-lined dining room or relax on the big deck with magnificent canyon views. Breakfast is a buffet ($9). At dinner, expect solidly good, but not great, prime rib, grilled trout etc. Make reservations.

Getting There & Around

Arriving from the east on Hwy 9, you have to pass through the free Zion–Mt Carmel Tunnel. If your vehicle is 7ft 10in wide or 11ft 4in high or larger, it must be escorted through, since vehicles this big need both lanes. Motorists requiring an escort pay $10 over the entrance fee, good for two trips. Between April and October, rangers are stationed at the tunnel from 8am to 8pm daily; at other times, ask at the entrance stations. Vehicles prohibited at all times include those more than 13ft 1in tall, single vehicles more than 40ft long and combined vehicles more than 50ft long.

From mid-March through October, the park operates two free, linked shuttle loops. The Zion Park Shuttle makes nine stops along the canyon, from the main visitor center to the Temple of Sinawava at the end of the Zion Canyon Scenic Dr (a 90-minute roundtrip). The Springdale Shuttle makes six regular stops and three flag stops along Hwy 9 between the park's south entrance and the Majestic View Lodge in Springdale, the hotel furthest from the park. Take the Springdale Shuttle to Zion Canyon Giant Screen Theatre and walk across a footbridge into the park where rangers collect fees at a kiosk. The visitor center and the first Zion shuttle stop lie just on the other side of the kiosk. It couldn't be easier.

The wheelchair-accessible shuttle buses accommodate large backpacks and carry up to two bicycles or one baby jogger. Pets aren't allowed. Schedules change, but shuttles operate from at least 6:45am to 10pm. Shuttles run every six minutes, from 9am to 8pm, and every 15 to 30 minutes early and late in the day.

SPRINGDALE

pop 551 / elevation 3800ft

Positioned at the entrance to Zion National Park, Springdale is the perfect little park town. Stunning red cliffs form the backdrop to eclectic cafés and restaurants that are big on local produce and healthy ingredients. Artist galleries and shops line the main drag, interspersed with indie motels and B&Bs. Many of the outdoorsy folk who live here moved from somewhere less beautiful, but you will occasionally run into a life-long local.

Information

There's no information office; go online to www.zionpark.com and www.zionnational park.com.

Pioneer Lodge Internet Café (☎ 435-772-3233; 838 Zion Park Blvd; per 25min $2.50; ⊙ 6:30am-9pm) Two internet terminals.

Washington County Police (☎ 800-624-9447)

Zion Canyon Medical Clinic (☎ 435-772-3226; 120 Lion Blvd; ⊙ 9am-5pm Tue-Sat) Walk-in urgent-care clinic.

Zion Rock & Mountain Guides (☎ 435-772-3303; www.zionrockguides.com; 1458 Zion Park Blvd; ⊙ 8am-7pm) Outfitter shop that stocks sport-specific guides.

Sights & Activities

In addition to hiking trails in Zion, outfitters lead **hikes**, **climbs** and **rappelling** trips on adjacent BLM lands. There are some awesome single-track, slickrock **mountain-bike** trails as good as Moab's. Ask local outfitters about **Gooseberry Mesa**, **Hurricane Cliffs** and **Rockville Bench**.

After a hard day's hike, the river-stone massage from **Deep Canyon Adventure Spa** (☎ 435-772-3244; www.deepcanyonspa.com; Flanigan's Inn, 428 Zion Park Blvd; 1hr treatments $89-150) will be your muscles' new best friend.

Kids love petting the elk, buffalo, Texas longhorns, horses and miniature donkeys at **Zion Canyon Elk Ranch** (☎ 435-619-2424; 792 Zion Park Blvd; admission $2; ⊙ sunrise to sunset; ♿).

TOURS & OUTFITTERS

What don't the two main outfitters in town do? They both sell and rent gear (tents, wet suits, climbing harnesses) and bikes (full day $38 to $50), run various sport tours (half-day $100 to $150), offer climbing and canyoneering lessons (four hours $100 to $120), provide a hiking trailhead shuttle service ($25 to $35) and can outfit you to hike to the Narrows. They operate on varying shorter schedules December through February.

The hard-core rock climbing and canyoneering experts at **Zion Rock & Mountain Guides** (☎ 435-772-3303; www.zionrockguides.com; 1458 Zion Park Blvd; ☿ 8am-7pm) are a great choice for experienced outdoors people. **Bike Zion** (☎ 435-772-3303; www.bikingzion.com) is its on-site cycle shop. Ask about multiday hike-bike-climb-canyoneer trips.

Beginners who want a little more hand-holding should contact **Zion Adventure Company @ Outdoor Center** (☎ 435-772-0990; www.zionadventures.com; 868 Zion Park Blvd; ☿ 8am-9pm); its guides are born teachers. Snowshoes and crampons available for winter. Its on-site bike shop is **Zion Cycles** (☎ 435-772-0400; www.zioncycles.com).

Explore Zion by moonlight, take a wildflower photography class, investigate Kolob Canyon's geology or help clean up the Narrows on an outing with **Zion Canyon Field Institute** (☎ 435-772-3264, 800-635-3959; www.zionpark.org). All include hiking; fees run $50 to $75 per day.

For a more motorized approach to exploring the land, take a **Zion Outback Safaris** (☎ 866-946-6494; www.zionjeeptours.com) 4WD tour in a 12-seat modified truck. Three-hour tours crossing Gooseberry Mesa cost $59. **ATV Wilderness Tours** (☎ 888-656-2887; www.atvadventures.com) leads similar group 4WD tours and does guided ATV trips (from $50).

November through March, **Red Rock Shuttle & Tours** (☎ 435-635-9104; www.redrockshuttle.com; tours $80) offers a five-hour scenic bus tour of the park with lunch and picture-taking opportunities included; reservations required.

TUBING

The Virgin River is swift, rocky and only about knee-deep: more of a bumpy adventure ride than a leisurely float. But tubing (outside the park only) is popular in the summer. (Note that from June to August, the water warms to only 55°F to 65°F.) Put in at the Zion Canyon Campground (right), where there are tube rentals ($10) but no shuttle. Both **Zion Tubing** (☎ 435-772-8823; www.ziontubing.com; Tsunami Juice & Java, 180 Zion Park Blvd; ☿ 8am-8pm) and the sister location of **Zion Adventure Company** (☎ 435-772-1001; www.zionadventures.com; 36 Lion Blvd; ☿ 8am-8pm), across from the campground, rent tubes and bus you back after two hours for $13 to $17.

Festivals & Events

On St Patrick's Day (March 17) is the hilarious **green Jell-O sculpture competition**. July 4 brings a parade and fireworks. The festivities continue with **Utah's Pioneer Day** (July 24), the **Zion Canyon Jazz & Arts Festival** (August) and in November the **Butch Cassidy 10km Marathon**. Contact the Zion Canyon Visitor Center (p465) for more.

Sleeping

Prices listed here are for April through November; rates plummet in winter. Look for slightly less expensive B&Bs a few miles away in Rockville (p471). Most local lodgings don't accept pets; board your pampered pooch at the **Doggy Dude Ranch** (☎ 435-772-3105; www.doggyduderanch.com; 800 Hwy 9), 3.7 miles west of the park boundary.

The lower the address number on Zion Park Blvd, the closer the park entrance; all lodgings are near shuttle stops.

BUDGET

Zion Canyon Campground (☎ 435-772-3237; www.zioncamp.com; 479 Zion Park Blvd; tent sites per day/week $25/150, RV sites per day/week $30/160; ⬚ wi-fi) A riverside campground in sight of the Watchman spire. Sites are dusty and close together, but shaded. Buy supplies at the camp store, or rent a tube for river floating.

El Rio Lodge (☎ 435-772-3205, 888-772-3205; www.elriolodge.com; 995 Zion Park Blvd; r $59-79; wi-fi) A great little bargain. The 10 plain and simple older rooms have TV and microwave but no phone. Pet rooms available.

Quality Inn (☎ 435-772-3237; www.zioncamp.com; 479 Zion Park Blvd; r $70-90; ⬚ wi-fi) Ask for a king room, for a patio with a mountain view. All have a microwave, mini-refrigerator and coffee maker.

Canyon Ranch Motel (☎ 435-772-3357; www.canyonranchmotel.com; 668 Zion Park Blvd; r $74-94; ⬚ wi-fi) Cottagey motel buildings surround a shaded lawn with redwood swings, picnic tables and a small pool at this 1930s motor-court motel. Inside, rooms are thoroughly modern; add $10 for a full kitchen.

MIDRANGE

Pioneer Lodge (☎ 435-772-3233, 888-772-3233; www
.pioneerlodge.com; 838 Zion Park Blvd; r $79-99, ste $119-169;
🅿 🖥 wi-fi) Pine beds and deep-red comfort-
ers lend rooms a rustic feel in keeping with
the name. The historic restaurant fronting
the place began life as the Allred Café in
the 1930s.

Under-the-Eaves Bed & Breakfast (☎ 435-772-
3457, 866-261-2655; www.under-the-eaves.com; 980 Zion Park
Blvd; r incl breakfast $80-$175; wi-fi) British wit Steve
Mansfield is a rushing river of information
about area hiking and eating. Co-owner and
wife Deb hangs her gorgeous mixed-media
art around the 1930s cottage. Rooms can
be a snug fit; for space choose the family
room, with a wood-burning fireplace nestled
under the eaves. Breakfast is a voucher for a
nearby café.

Cliffrose Lodge (☎ 435-772-3234, 800-243-8824;
www.cliffroselodge.com; 281 Zion Park Blvd; r $99-169; 🅿 wi-
fi) Kick back in a lounge chair or take a picnic
lunch to enjoy on the five gorgeous acres of
lawn and flower gardens leading down to the
river. High-thread-count bedding and pillow-
top mattresses seem at odds with occasional
cheap furnishings.

Red Rock Inn (☎ 435-772-3139; www.redrockinn.com;
998 Zion Park Blvd; r incl breakfast $112-117, ste $189; wi-fi)
Solid desert hues – mossy green, sky blue,
red-rock orange – paint the walls of these
country-contemporary cottages. A full hot
breakfast (egg dish and pastries) appears daily
at your door.

Zion Canyon Bed & Breakfast (☎ 435-772-9466;
www.zioncanyonbandb.com; 101 Kokopelli Circle; r $125-169;
wi-fi) Tucked back on a side street, this new-
construction B&B has great views and loads
of privacy. Details such as a king-size, rough-
hewn log canopy bed and a double-headed
steam shower could be called upscale casual.

Canyon Vista B&B (☎ 435-772-3801; www.canyon
vistabandb.com; 897 Zion Park Blvd; ste incl breakfast $130;
wi-fi) Four huge (300 to 600 sq ft), new-looking
rooms may seem spare on furniture, but each
one has a kitchenette, dining table, sitting area,
jetted tub, private entrance and front porch.

Also consider the following:

Harvest House (☎ 435-772-3880; www.harvesthouse
.net; 29 Canyon View Dr; r incl breakfast $105-140; wi-fi)
Homey B&B; looks like Aunt Mabel decorated.

Best Western Zion Park Inn (☎ 435-772-3200, 800-
934-7275; www.zionparkinn.com; 1215 Zion Park Blvd;
r $115-119; 🅿 🖥 wi-fi) Two pools, a restaurant and the
town's only liquor store.

TOP END

ourpick Desert Pearl Inn (☎ 435-772-8888, 888-828-
0898; www.desertpearl.com; 707 Zion Park Blvd; r $148-178, ste
$350; 🅿 wi-fi) Twig art on the walls, sculptural
metal headboards, full granite showers: Desert
Pearl Inn puts natural materials to stylish use.
The result is mod, yet grounded. All 61 earth-
tone rooms come with DVD players, game
tables, mini-refrigerators and wet bars with
microwave. Opt for a roomy riverside king
suite to get a waterfront patio.

Flanigan's Inn (☎ 435-772-3244, 800-765-7787; www
.flanigans.com; 428 Zion Park Blvd; r $120-160, ste $169-279;
🅿 wi-fi) Rejuvenate your spirit by indulging
in a seaweed and mineral mud wrap, walking
the hilltop meditation labyrinth and sinking
into your king-size bed in front of a crackling
fire. Rooms have vaulted ceilings, bold color
schemes, good art and Aveda bath products.

Eating

Restaurants serving dinner have beer and
wine only unless otherwise noted.

Mean Bean (☎ 435-772-0654; 932 Zion Park Blvd;
sandwiches $3-6; 🕑 6:30am-5pm; wi-fi) Local hikers
and bikers grab organic coffee and a breakfast
bagel here before heading off to the trails.
You'll want to linger on the rooftop patio.

Spotted Dog Café (☎ 435-772-3244; Flanigan's Inn,
428 Zion Park Blvd; breakfast $4-10, mains $19-28; 🕑 breakfast & dinner) Just ignore any affect coming from
the black-shirted waiters with slicked-back
hair; instead, coo over the anchiote-spiced
lamb shank. The menu changes seasonally,
but Spotted Dog always maintains a high regard for food. Appetizers and drinks (full bar)
are served on the patio starting at 4pm.

Springdale Market (☎ 435-772-3222; 2491 Zion
Park Blvd; sandwiches $6; 🕑 9am-5pm) The timber-
framed, healthy food market at the west end of
town has its own orchard. Order your focac-
cia and smoothie to go, or enjoy them in the
parklike picnic area.

Oscar's Café (☎ 435-772-3232; 948 Zion Park Blvd;
breakfast & lunch $6-10, dinner mains $10-18; 🕑 8am-
10pm) Join other travelers on the tiled patio for
heaping portions of Mexican standards with
a Southwestern twist. The slow-roasted pork
chile verde is very good; skip the ribs.

Whiptail Grill (☎ 435-772-0283; 445 Zion Park Blvd;
mains $9-20; 🕑 11am-7pm Apr-Oct) Organic beef is
brought in for dishes such as the Mexican
pizza and baked tortillas piled high with
steak, peppers and cheese. Grab one of the
few outdoor tables at this healthy hole-in-

the-wall, and don't forget to recycle your compostable tableware.

Thai Sapa (☎ 435-772-3009; 145 Zion Park Blvd; mains $12-17; ☿ dinner) All things Asian are on the menu at Thai Sapa. The tasty Indian, Thai, Chinese and Vietnamese selection is as eclectic as the service; you may be seated but not greeted until it's 'your turn.'

Bit & Spur Restaurant & Saloon (☎ 435-772-3498; 1212 Zion Park Blvd; mains $14-24; ☿ dinner Mar-Oct, dinner Thu-Sat Nov-Feb) Bit & Spur is a local institution and the liveliest place in town (full bar). All menu items have Southwest-Mexican flair; try the chile-rubbed rib-eye. Reserve ahead weekends.

Stock up on picnic supplies at **Sol Foods Market** (☎ 435-772-0277; 95 Zion Park Blvd; ☿ 8am-9pm), the town's only grocery store.

Also consider the following:

Café Soleil (☎ 435-772-0505; 205 Zion Park Blvd; breakfast & sandwiches $5-9; ☿ 8am-4pm) Fluffy frittatas for breakfast, turkey-and-cranberry panini for lunch.

Jessie's Bar & Grill (☎ 435-772-0105; 1515 Zion Park Blvd; sandwiches $6-10, mains $11-17; ☿ lunch & dinner) Back patio, beer and burgers.

Zion Pizza & Noodle Company (☎ 435-772-3815; www.zionpizzanoodle.com; 868 Zion Park Blvd; mains $11-16; ☿ dinner) Great local photography on walls.

Entertainment

Bit & Spur Restaurant & Saloon (☎ 435-772-3498; www.bitandspur.com; 1212 Zion Park Blvd) hosts live music some Saturdays, March through October. The other place to hear concerts is at the outdoor **OC Tanner Amphitheater** (☎ 435-652-7994; www.dixie.edu/tanner; 300 Lion Blvd; ☿ mid-May–Aug). Pack a picnic.

Catch the 40-minute *Zion Canyon: Treasure of the Gods* on a six-story screen at **Zion Canyon Giant Screen Theatre** (☎ 888-256-3456, 435-772-2400; www.zioncanyontheatre.com; 145 Zion Park Blvd); it's light on substance but long on beauty. The nostalgia-heavy variety show at **Bumbleberry**

Playhouse (☎ 866-478-4854, 435-772-3611; www.bumbleberry.com; 897 Zion Park Blvd) raises its curtain weekend nights April through October.

Shopping

Artist galleries and eclectic boutiques are scattered the length of Zion Park Blvd. Stunning photography is particularly well represented – not surprising given Zion's beauty. Check out the work of a Utah son at **David Petit Photography** (☎ 435-772-3206; 868 Zion Park Blvd; ☿ 5-10pm), in the old church. His stunning work is also on view in Zion Pizza & Noodle Company (see left), above the gallery.

The infamous Michael Fatali exhibits at the **Museum of Photography** (☎ 435-772-2422; 145 Zion Park Blvd; ☿ 1-7pm Tue-Sat). The colors in his photos are surreal, but before you plop down thousands of dollars, note that is the artist who started a fire under Delicate Arch to get a better shot (and a $10,900 fine).

Getting Around

From mid-March through October, the free Springdale Shuttle operates between stops in town and Zion National Park. For more information, see p468.

AROUND ZION NATIONAL PARK

Five miles west of Zion National Park, **Rockville** (no gas or food) seems like an extension of Springdale. The bicycle scene in *Butch Cassidy and the Sundance Kid* was filmed in the nearby Grafton ghost town. The restored 1886 meeting house, general store and pioneer log homes (on private property) stand empty and there's a pioneer cemetery. Getting to Grafton can be tricky. Turn south on Bridge Rd in Rockville, cross the bridge and turn right on Grafton Rd; bear left when the road becomes gravel. Bear right at the fork and follow signs two miles more to the ghost town.

LIKE A VIRGIN

Fourteen miles west of Springdale, you can't help but pass a Virgin. The town, named after the river (what else?), has an odd claim to fame – in 2000 the council passed a law requiring every resident to own a gun. Locals are fined $500 if they don't. Kolob Terrace Rd takes off north from here to Lava Point in Zion National Park. The huge store at the **Virgin Trading Post** (☎ 435-635-3455; 1000 W Hwy 9; ☿ 9am-7pm) sells homemade fudge, ice cream and every Western knickknack known to the free world. But it's the hard-to-miss **Old West Village** (admission $1; ☿) that's the real reason to stop. Have your picture taken inside the 'Virgin Jail' or 'Wild Ass Saloon' before you feed the deer, donkey and llama in the petting zoo. It's pure kitschy fun.

Rockville's four B&Bs can be a slightly cheaper alternative to those in Springdale. Full of frills, **Dream Catcher Inn** (☎ 435-772-3600, 800-953-7326; www.dreamcatcherinnzion.com; 225 E Main St; r incl breakfast $60-80) is run by a lovely older couple who welcome children. Renewable energy use, recycled flooring and organic breakfasts help the ranch-style **Bunk House at Zion** (☎ 435-772-3393; www.bunkhouseatzion.com; 149 E Main St; r incl breakfast $60-80) stay green.

Guest spaces are large, if Spartan, at the **Amber Inn** (☎ 435-772-0289, 866-370-1515; www.amber-inn.com; 244 W Main St; r $85-105; wi-fi); the effusive Eastern European owner takes a little getting used to. A big backyard pool makes the romantic, modern **Desert Thistle Bed & Breakfast** (☎ 435-772-0251; www.thedesertthistle.com; 37 W Main St; r incl breakfast $110-145; 🞋) a top choice on hot summer days.

KANAB

pop 3500 / elev 4925ft

Vast expanses of rugged desert extend in each direction from the remote outpost of Kanab. Don't be surprised if it all looks familiar: hundreds of Western movies were shot here. Founded by Mormon pioneers in 1874, John Wayne and other gun-slingin' celebs really put Kanab on the map in the 1940s and '50s. Just about every resident had something to do with the movies from the 1930s up till the '70s. You can still see several movie sets in the area and hear old-timers talk about their roles. Come August, the Western Legends Roundup celebrates 'Utah's little Hollywood' with tours, screenings and returning star appearances.

Kanab makes a good base for exploring the southern side of Grand Staircase-Escalante National Monument (GSENM) and Paria Canyon-Vermilion Cliffs Wilderness formations such as the Wave (p475). Coral Pink Sand Dunes State Park (p474) is a big rompin' playground to the northwest.

Orientation & Information

Kanab sits at a major crossroads: GSENM is 20 miles, Zion 40 miles, Bryce Canyon 80 miles, Grand Canyon's North Rim 81 miles and Lake Powell 74 miles. Most businesses lie along Hwy 89. Kanab has grocery stores, banks and ATMs. For family-friendly area activities, check out www.kane4kids.com.

BLM Kanab Field Office (☎ 435-644-4600; 318 N 100 East; 🕑 8am-4:30pm Mon-Fri) Provides information and,

November 16 through March 14, issues permits for hiking the Wave in Paria Canyon-Vermilion Cliffs Wilderness Area.

GSENM Visitor Center (☎ 435-644-4680; www.ut.blm.gov/monument; 745 E Hwy 89; 🕑 8am-4:30pm Apr-Oct, 8am-4:30pm Mon-Fri Nov-Mar) Provides road, trail and weather updates.

Kane County Hospital (☎ 435-644-5811; 355 N Main St)

Kane County Office of Tourism (☎ 435-644-5033, 800-733-5263; www.kaneutah.com; 78 S 100 East; 🕑 8am-8pm Mon-Fri, 9am-5pm Sat, 9am-1pm Sun Mar-Oct, 8:30am-5pm Mon-Sat, 1-5pm Sun Nov-Feb) The main source for area information; great old Western movie posters and artifacts are on display. The center's main volunteer was a stunt gal in the famous films.

Library (☎ 435-644-2394; 374 N Main St; 🕑 9am-5pm Mon & Fri, 9am-7pm Tue-Thu, 10am-2pm Sat) Free internet access.

Local police (☎ 435-644-5807; 140 E 100 South)

Post office (☎ 435-644-2760; 39 S Main St)

Sights

Many of the buildings on Kanab's main street have false fronts and Western store names such as Denny's Wig Wam. **Parry Lodge** (☎ 435-644-2601; www.parrylodge.com; 89 E Center St) became movie central when it was built in the 1930s. Stars stayed here and owner Whit Parry provided the horses, cattle and catering for the sets. Look for the nostalgic photos on lobby and dining room walls.

For a guide to the movies made around town, seek out Bonnie Riding, owner of **Bob-Bon Inn Motel** (☎ 435-644-3069; www.bobbon.com; 236 N 300 West). She's put together a great little booklet of area sites and stars ($10).

Frontier Movie Town & Trading Post (☎ 435-644-5337, 800-551-1714; 297 W Center St; 🕑 8am-10pm Apr-Oct, 10am-5pm Nov-Mar) stages gunfights in summer in a cluster of actual Western movie sets ($20 with buffet dinner). It's free to walk through the buildings at other times and the beer at the saloon is nice and cold.

A classic tourist trap, **Moqui Cave** (☎ 435-644-8525; www.moquicave.com; adult/child $4/2; 🕑 9am-7pm Mon-Sat Mar-Nov) holds an odd collection of fluorescent minerals, dinosaur tracks and cowboy and Indian artifacts inside a real cave. Head 5 miles north on Hwy 89.

Also off Hwy 89, 0.25 miles from Moqui Cave, is the nation's largest no-kill sanctuary on a 33,000-acre ranch: the donation-run **Best Friends Animal Sanctuary** (☎ 435-644-2001; www.bestfriends.org; tours free; 🕑 8:30am-5pm; 🞋). Best Friends gives facility tours (45 minutes); longer tours

---

UTAH, YOU OUGHTA BE IN PICTURES

The movie industry has known about the rugged wilds of southern Utah since the early days. In the 1920s, film adaptations of Zane Grey novels were shot here. All told, more than 700 films (and many TV shows) have been shot on location across the state. Iconic movies with Utah cameos include:

- *Thelma & Louise* – Remember where they drive off the cliff? That was outside Canyonlands National Park at Dead Horse Point (p426). Scenes were also filmed in Arches National Park (p436).

- *Forrest Gump* stopped his cross-country run in front of Monument Valley (p418), which straddles the Utah–Arizona line. *Easy Rider* also motorcycled through and *2001: A Space Odyssey* used the monoliths to represent outer space.

- *Con Air* and *Independence Day* both have landing scenes shot on the super smooth Bonneville Salt Flats (p492).

- In *High School Musical I & II*, Zac Efron danced his way through East High School in SLC (p480), just like Kevin Bacon had done at Payson High School, south of Provo (p510), in *Footloose*.

---

let you meet some of the 1500 horses, dogs, cats and birds. You can spend the night in one of eight one-bedroom cottages with kitchenettes ($125) or in a one-room cabin ($70) on the property. A clifftop above the sanctuary in Angel Canyon (Kanab Canyon to locals) is where the Lone Ranger reared up and shouted 'Hi Ho Silver!' every TV episode.

You can also take the popular drive through **Johnson Canyon**, where more films were made. Turn north off Hwy 89, 9 miles east of Kanab. Six miles along you'll pass the Western set where the long-time TV classic *Bonanza* was filmed. It's on private land, but the owner gives tours during the Western Legends Roundup. You can continue for 30 or 40 miles (roughly graded, but passable), emerging at either Glendale or Alton.

The **Paria movie set** (pa-*ree*-uh), where many Westerns were filmed, was burnt down during the 2007 Western Legends Roundup. The town is collecting money to rebuild and something may be up by the next shindig. In any case, the drive along Paria Valley Rd gives a glimpse of the GSENM, which it traverses. The signed turnoff for Paria Valley is 33 miles from Kanab on Hwy 89; a 5-mile dirt road (which is passable with a 2WD when dry) follows the Vermilion Cliffs to the movie set location. A mile further north, on the other side of the river, hike to look for the little that's left of **Pahreah ghost town**. Floods in the 1880s rang the death knell for the 130-strong farming community. Since then, time and fire have taken the buildings and all but the most rudimentary signs of settlement.

TOURS & OUTFITTERS

Canyon Country Outback Tours (☎ 435-644-3807, 888-783-3807; www.ccobtours.com; per person per hr $50) guides day trips to slot canyons in GSENM; it's also one of only two companies permitted into the Coyote Buttes section of the Paria Canyon-Vermilion Cliffs Wilderness Area, which includes the Wave (p475).

Dreamland Safari Tours (☎ 435-644-5506; www .dreamlandtours.net; per person per hr $48) runs 4WD tours in GSENM, Coral Pink Sand Dunes State Park and Kanab Canyon, among others. It also leads movie site tours.

Festivals & Events

The town lives for the annual **Western Legends Roundup** (☎ 800-733-5263; www.westernlegendsroundup .com) in late August. There are concerts, gunfights, cowboy poetry, dances, quilt shows, a film festival and more. Take a bus tour to all the film sites, or sign up for a Dutch oven cooking lesson.

Sleeping

Kanab has a surplus of indie budget motels and some house rentals. For a full list, see www.kaneutah.com.

Hitch'n Post Campground (☎ 435-644-2142, 800-458-3516; 196 E 300 South; tent sites/RV sites $16/24, camping cabins $22-26) This friendly, 17-site campground is near the town center, within walking distance of shops and restaurants. Loads of shade; pets OK.

Bob-Bon Inn Motel (☎ 435-644-3069, 800-644-5094; www.bobbon.com; 236 N 300 West; r $40-60; 🐾) The small-but-spotless 16 log cabin rooms here

UTAH

are Kanab's best deal. Every inch of every reception room wall is covered with old Western movie stars' autographed photos. Pet rooms available.

Parry Lodge (☎ 435-644-2601; www.parrylodge.com; 89 E Center St; r $60-80; ☒) This rambling motel has become a faded dowager compared with the leading lady she once was. Rooms are clean enough, but the only thing special is the aura of days gone by. May through October it shows Westerns on a big screen out back in the barn, free (8pm). The restaurant only serves a breakfast buffet.

Victorian Charm Inn (☎ 435-644-8660, 800-738-9643; www.victoriancharminn.com; 190 N Hwy 89; r incl breakfast $100-125; ☐) From the architecture to appointments, the inn is a modern-day interpretation of period Victoriana. Ethan Allen furnishings, gas fireplaces and jetted tubs grace every room.

At time of writing, there was a **Holiday Inn Express** (☎ 800-315-2621; www.hiexpress.com: cnr 100 East & 200 South Sts) under construction. More camping is to be had in nearby parks (see right). Also good choices:

Redrock Country Inn (☎ 435-644-2562, 800-222-2244; www.redrockcountryinn.com; 330 S 100 East; r $50-60; ☒ wi-fi) Three-bedded rooms sleep up to six ($89). Some pets OK.

Treasure Trail Motel (☎ 435-577-2645, 800-603-2687; www.treasuretrailmotel.com; 150 W Center St; r $60-75; ☒ wi-fi) Microwaves and mini-refrigerators standard.

Eating & Drinking

Willow Canyon Outdoor Gear, Books & Coffee (☎ 435-644-8884; 263 S 100 East; ☽ 7:30am-6:30pm) Sip organic espresso while you peruse the terrific selection of outdoor books.

Escobar's (☎ 435-644-3739; 373 E 300 South; dishes $5-11; ☽ lunch & dinner) The mom-and-pop Mexican food joint of choice is so authentic that the owners occasionally shut down for a week or so to go home and visit.

Nedra's Café (☎ 435-644-2030; 310 S 100 East; mains $6-10; ☽ breakfast, lunch & dinner) After a day on the trail, fill up on big plates of cheesy, greasy Mexican goodness and Navajo tacos on fry bread. The salsa is delicious – even if it is only Utah-hot (not).

Houston's Trail's End Restaurant (☎ 435-644-2488; 32 E Center St; mains $10-20; ☽ 6am-9:30pm Mar-Dec) 'Where women wear guns.' Fake six-shooters flash at the waiters' sides while they dish out down-home chicken-fried steaks, barbecued ribs and fried chicken. No beer or bar.

Rocking V Café (☎ 435-644-8001; 97 W Center St; dinner mains $15-20; ☽ 11:30am-9pm) The food and decor here blend rustic and modern Southwest style. Great seafood and pasta, made all the better by margaritas. The upstairs gallery is packed with work by talented local artists.

Entertainment

The **Crescent Moon Theater** (☎ 435-644-2350; www .crescentmoontheater.com; 150 S 100 East) hosts cowboy bands such as Bar G Chuckwagon, puts on theatrical productions and occasionally screens old Westerns. The main season is May through September.

Getting Around

Rent your own jeep for exploring at **Canyon Country Jeep Rental** (☎ 435-644-8250; 285 S 100 East; per day $150).

AROUND KANAB
Coral Pink Sand Dunes State Park

Restless winds shift giant Sahara-like sand dunes across half of this 3700-acre park. For lovers of the strange, it's worth the 24-mile, 90-minute round-trip off Hwy 89 to see the shocking coral-colored hills. The pinkish hue results from the eroding, red Navajo sandstone in the area. Note that 1200 acres of the park are devoted to ATVs, so it's not necessarily a quiet experience. The **visitor center** (☎ 435-648-2800; ☽ 9am-9pm Mar-Oct, 9am-4pm Nov-Feb) has displays and water. Day-use is $6. Follow the half-mile interpretive dune hike to the 265-acre conservation area that's closed to off-highway vehicles (OHV).

The same winds that shift the dunes can make tent camping unpleasant at the 22-site **campground** (☎ reservations 800-322-3770; www .reserveamerica.com; campsites $16), with toilets and hot showers. Reservations are essential on weekends when off-roaders come to play.

Paria Canyon-Vermilion Cliffs Wilderness Area

One of the state's most popular wilderness areas attracts serious day hikers, canyoneers and photographers. This remote and rugged spot near the Arizona state line has endless slot canyons and miles of sculptural slickrock. No wonder hiking permits here are so tough to get. For info in the high season, go directly to the **Paria Contact Station** (www.blm.gov; Mile 21, Hwy 89; ☽ 8:30am-4:15pm Mar 15-Nov 15), 44 miles east of Kanab. Year-round the rangers at the BLM

Kanab Field Office (p472) provide advice, but they're only in charge of permits from November 16 through March 14. Day-hike permits cost $5. Most trailheads and formations are part of the GSENM. Remember that summer is scorching; spring and fall are best. Beware of flash floods.

Day hikers fight like dogs to get a **North Coyote Buttes** permit. This trail-less expanse of slickrock includes one of the Southwest's most famous formations – the **Wave**. The nearly magical sight of the slickrock that appears to be seething and swirling in waves is well worth the 6-mile, four- to five-hour round-trip hike. Go online to www.blm.gov to request advance permits four months ahead. Otherwise you can hope for one of the few next-day walk-in permits available. Line up early.

The 3.4-mile round-trip hike starting at **Wire Pass** trailhead is the most popular slot canyon day hike. The pass dead-ends where Buckskin Gulch narrows into some thrillingly slight slots. Alternatively, you can start at the **Buckskin Gulch** trailhead and hike 3 miles one way to its narrow section. Both trailheads lie along House Rock Valley Rd (4.7 miles west of the contact station); it's a passable dirt road in dry weather.

Two miles south of the contact station along a dirt road, you come to primitive **White House Campground** (tent sites $5). The five walk-in sites have pit toilets, but no water and few trees. Overnight backcountry camping permits are easier to get than day-hike ones, and can be reserved online. Use of human-waste carry-out bags is encouraged; the contact station provides them for free.

Paria Outpost & Outfitters (☎ 928-691-1047; www .paria.com; r $65, campsites/tepees $16/20) has Spartan B&B rooms at its kicked-back lodge and campground. It even rents sleeping bags so you can bunk down in one of the tepees. Sign up for a half-day 4WD tour ($125 with lunch) to area slot canyons or hire a hiking guide to lead you to the Wave ($30 per person per hour). Set up a trailhead shuttle with them ($30 per hour), or with Canyon Country Outback Tours (p473) in Kanab.

ST GEORGE
pop 67,600 / elev 2880ft

Jagged red rock peaks tower over suburban subdivisions in the state's southernmost city. The climate once attracted Mormon pioneers who grew cotton here, but today

it's retirees and golfers who come. (Summers sizzle, with highs exceeding 100°F, but winter is rather mild, with average temps around 50°F.) Mansionlike getaways for wealthy Las Vegasites line the clifftops encircling town.

From here you can explore Zion National Park and several interesting state parks and public lands. While you're in town, don't forget to check out one of the best dinosaur trackways in the state. Mormon heritage is strong down here, and there are some well-preserved historic buildings. That said, there ain't much goin' on after dark.

Orientation
St George is on I-15 just north of the Arizona border, 120 miles from Las Vegas, and 305 miles from Salt Lake City. The town lies about 41 miles (50 minutes) from Zion National Park's south entrance, 30 miles (25 minutes) from the Kolob Canyons' entrance on I-15, and 57 miles (45 minutes) from Cedar City to the north.

St George's center is the intersection of Main and Tabernacle Sts. The city's main commercial streets are St George Blvd and Bluff St, which, with I-15, form a triangle that encompasses most of the town.

Information
Additional online information is available at www.utahsdixie.com and www.sgcity.org.

Book Cellar (☎ 435-652-0227; www.sgbookcellar.com; 130 N Main St) Fiercely independent bookstore in conservative country. Great selection of local interest books, including frank Mormon and Fundamentalist Church of Jesus Christ of Latter-day Saints (FLDS) histories.

Chamber of Commerce Visitor Center (☎ 435-628-1658; www.stgeorgechamber.com; 97 E St George Blvd; ☺ 9am-5pm Mon-Fri, 10am-2pm Sat) Mainly catering to relocating pensioners, the visitor center has loads of area info.

Dixie Regional Medical Center (☎ 435-251-1000; cnr 700 South & River Rd)

Library (☎ 435-634-5737; 50 S Main St; ☺ 9am-9pm Mon-Thu, 9am-6pm Fri & Sat) Internet access ($1 per hour).

Local police (☎ 435-634-5001; 175 E 200 North)

Post office (☎ 435-673-3312; 180 N Main St)

St George Field Office (☎ 435-688-3246; 345 E Riverside Dr; ☺ 7:45am-5pm Mon-Fri, 10am-3pm Sat) Provides interagency information on surrounding public lands: USFS, BLM and state parks. Maps and guides available.

Utah Welcome Center (☎ 435-673-4542; I-15; ☺ 8:30am-5:30pm) Statewide information, 2 miles south of St George.

Sights

St George's oldest residents aren't retirees from Idaho, but Jurassic-era dinosaurs. Entry to the **Dinosaur Discovery Site** (☎ 435-574-3766; www .dinotrax.com; 2200 E Riverside Dr; adult/child $3/2; ☺ 10am-6pm Mon-Sat) gets you an interpretive tour of the huge collection of tracks, beginning with a video. It's a bit of a slow-go for children, but fascinating scientifically. The casts were first unearthed in 2000 and rare paleontology discoveries, such as dinosaur swim tracks, continue to be made.

Pick up a full-color, historic building walking-tour brochure at the visitor center, or reserve ahead for a costumed docent-led tour by **Historic St George Live!** (☎ 435-634-5942; www .stgeorgelive.org; adult/child $2/1; ☺ 9:30am & 10am Tue-Sat Jun-Aug). The 1877 **Mormon Temple** (☎ 435-673-5181; 440 S 300 East; ☺ 9am-9pm), Utah's first, has a visitor center. Built at the same time, the red-brick **Mormon Tabernacle** (☎ 435-628-4072; cnr Tabernacle & Main Sts; ☺ 9am-5pm) hosts free music programs and tours. **Brigham Young Winter Home** (☎ 435-673-2517; 67 W 200 North; admission free; ☺ 9am-5pm) was once the Mormon leader's seasonal headquarters.

St George's **Daughters of Utah Pioneers Museum** (DUP; ☎ 435-628-7274; 145 N 100 East; admission free; ☺ 10am-5pm Mon-Sat) is filled with historic artifacts and exhibits; it's the best of its kind outside Salt Lake City. For a more evocative picture of the Mormon pioneer experience, head 5 miles north of town to Santa Clara and the 1863 **Jacob Hamblin Home** (☎ 435-673-2161; Santa Clara Dr; admission free; ☺ 9am-5pm), where orchards still grow.

Activities

Trails crisscross St George. Eventually they'll be connected and the trail along the Virgin River will extend to Zion; get a map at the visitor center. There's also first-rate mountain biking, particularly at **Gooseberry Mesa** and the **Green Valley Loop** (also called Bearclaw Poppie Trail).

Paragon Climbing (☎ 435-673-1709; www.para gonclimbing.com) runs excellent introductory rock-climbing courses ($120 for 2½ hours) and guided mountain-biking excursions ($35 to $50 per hour). If you just want to rent a bike (about $35 per day), contact **Red Rock Bicycle Company** (☎ 435-674-3185; www.redrockbicycle .com; 446 W 100 South; ☺ 9am-5pm Mon-Sat) or **Bicycles Unlimited** (☎ 435-673-4492, 888-673-4492; www.bicy clesunlimited.com; 90 S 100 East; ☺ 9am-6pm Mon-Sat).

The following golf courses are open to the public (many more are private). Eighteen holes costs about $70 with cart rental. Reserve up to two weeks in advance online; see www.sgcity.org/golf.

Dixie Red Hills (☎ 435-634-5852; 1250 N 645 West) Red-rock setting; nine holes, par 34.

St George Golf Club (☎ 435-634-5854; 2190 S 1400 East) Smooth greens. Eighteen holes, par 73.

Southgate (☎ 435-628-0000; 1975 S Tonaquint Dr) Eighteen holes along Santa Clara River; par 70.

Sunbrook (☎ 435-634-5866; 2366 Sunbrook Dr) Highly rated 27 holes, par 36 each nine.

Festivals & Events

Avoid St George around Easter, when it becomes Utah's spring-break capital. Mid-September ropes in the **Dixie Roundup** (☎ 435-628-8282), a rodeo, and the **St George Marathon** (www.stgeorgemarathon.com), which descends from the Pine Valley Mountains. October welcomes the **World Senior Games** (www.seniorgames.net).

Sleeping

Head to St George Blvd and Bluff St near I-15 for chain motels. Pretty much every lodging offers a golf package. Tent campers will do best on nearby public lands; see p478.

BUDGET

Dixie Palm Motel (☎ 435-673-3531; 185 E St George Blvd; r $40-50; ☒) It may not look like much outside, but regular maintenance and TLC put the Dixie Palm at the head of the low-budget pack. The 15 rooms have refrigerators and microwaves.

Ambassador Inn (☎ 435-673-7900, 877-373-7900; www.bestvalueinn.com; 1481 Sunland Dr; r $55-65, ste $65-90, all incl breakfast; ☒ wi-fi) Owners take pride in their 68 updated motel rooms. Microwaves and mini-refrigerators are standard; suites have jetted tubs and sitting areas.

More options:

Templeview RV Resort (☎ 435-673-6400, 800-776-6410; www.templeviewrv.com; 975 South Main St; tent sites $26-29, RV sites $35-39; ☒ ☐ wi-fi) Full-service resort; even has craft and computer rooms.

Sullivan's Rococo Inn (☎ 435-628-3671, 888-628-3671; www.rococo.net; 511 S Airport Rd; r $50-60; ☒) Semiscruffy motel with gorgeous blufftop views. Some pets OK.

MIDRANGE

Best Inn & Suites (☎ 435-652-3030; www.stgeorge innsuites.com; 245 N Red Cliffs Ave, exit 8 off I-15; r incl breakfast

$54-85; 🖳 wi-fi) Ten percent of the guest rooms are 'evergreen,' meaning they have air- and water-filtration systems installed. Right off I-15, this spick-and-span motel allows easy access to outlying sights.

Seven Wives Inn (☎ 435-628-3737, 800-600-3737; www.sevenwivesinn.com; 217 N 100 West; r incl breakfast $80-180; 🖳) An eclectic and historic B&B, Seven Wives has 13 rooms, all individually decorated. 'Sarah,' with its own private hot tub inside an actual Model T Ford, is worth a splurge.

Green Gate Village (☎ 435-628-6999, 800-350-6999; www.greengatevillageinn.com; 76 W Tabernacle St; r incl breakfast $99-139, houses $177-500; 🖳) Grassy lawns separate nine historic buildings brought together to make a B&B community. You can rent a room or a whole small house; all feature lovely antiques such as white iron beds and ornate carved vanities. Don't forget to have ice cream at Thomas Judd's General Store.

More options:

Best Western Coral Hills (☎ 435-673-4844; www .coralhills.com; 125 E St George Blvd; r incl breakfast $71-94; 🖳 ♿ wi-fi) Indoor, outdoor and kids' wading pools.

Ava Inn & Spa (☎ 435-673-7755; www.quicksandbnb .com; 346 N Main St; r incl breakfast $119-149) Restrained florals and light colors define the lovely rooms. Spa services available.

TOP END

Red Mountain Spa (☎ 435-673-4905, 800-407-3002; www.redmtn.com; 1275 E Red Mountain Circle; r per person $139-269; 🖳 🖳 wi-fi) Copper silk pillows offset the natural colors and a Zen-chic sensibility. Guided hikes, fitness classes and all meals are included in the packaged pampering.

Inn at Entrada (☎ 435-634-7100; www.innatentrada .com; 2588 W Sinagua Dr; r $199-439) Studios and one-bedroom condos with full kitchens allow you to pretend for a while that you live beneath the red cliffs.

Green Valley Spa (☎ 435-628-8060, 800-237-1068; www.greenvalleyspa.com; 1871 W Canyon View Dr; r $199-439; 🖳 🖳) Analyze your swing at the 4000-sq-ft golf center, take a tennis lesson on one of 14 courts or dive into your choice of six pools at this ultra cushy sports resort.

Eating & Drinking

St George's dining scene is mediocre. There are a number of family eateries on Ancestor Sq. Springdale, an hour away at Zion, has better choices.

Bean Scene (☎ 435-574-6434; 511 E St George Blvd; sandwiches $4.50; 🕙 6am-7pm Mon-Fri, 7am-4pm Sat, 8am-1pm Sun) Check out the avant-garde art upstairs at this bohemian coffee house.

Bear Paw Café (☎ 435-634-0126; 75 N Main St; dishes $5-9; 🕙 breakfast & lunch) Mmmm…the Belgian waffles here are the best, and the blueberry pancakes aren't bad either. Salads and sandwiches served at lunch.

Ernesto's Mexican Restaurant (☎ 435-656-0200; 939 E St George Blvd; mains $6-14; 🕙 lunch & dinner) Voted readers' choice for Mexican food in a *St George Magazine* poll. The fresh chips and salsa alone are reason enough to come.

Painted Pony (☎ 435-634-1700; 2 W St George Blvd, Ancestor Sq; sandwiches $8-10, mains $20-25; 🕙 lunch & dinner Mon-Sat) Subtlety characterizes the creative dishes at St George's top restaurant. Green onion enlivens sweet potato hash, lemongrass broth complements local salmon rolls. The decor – Navajo prints, tin sconces and colorful contemporary art – enhances the experience. Make reservations.

Scaldoni's Restaurant & Bar (☎ 435-674-1300; www.scaldonis.com; 929 W Sunset Blvd, Phoenix Plaza; mains $11-28; 🕙 lunch & dinner Mon-Fri, dinner Sat & Sun) Contemporary American-Italian classics are cooked to order. Care is taken with both presentation and service. Too bad it's in a strip mall.

Gun Barrel Steak & Game House (☎ 435-652-0550; 1091 N Bluff St; mains $18-31; 🕙 lunch & dinner Mon-Fri, dinner Sat) Slice into a big hunk of mesquite grilled red meat – cow, elk or buffalo – at this trophy-head-filled lodge restaurant.

Entertainment

The **St George Musical Theater** (☎ 435-628-8755; www.sgmt.org; 37 S 100 West) puts on musicals year-round. The outdoor **Tuacahn Amphitheater** (☎ 435-652-3300, 800-746-9882; www.tuacahn.org), 10 miles northwest in Ivins, hosts musicals in summer and other performances year-round.

Getting There & Around

St George Municipal Airport (☎ 435-673-3451; www .sgcity.org/airport; 444 S River Rd) sits west above downtown. **Skywest Airlines** (☎ 435-634-3000, 800-453-9417; www.delta.com) operates five daily flights for Delta Airlines to Salt Lake City. A $90 million new airport is in the works. **St George Shuttle** (☎ 435-628-8320, 800-933-8320; www .stgshuttle.com) runs regular bus services to Las Vegas Airport ($30). **Aztec Shuttle** (☎ 435-635-9040; www.aztecshuttle.com) also has van services to Salt Lake City ($65).

Greyhound (☎ 435-673-2933, 800-231-2222; www .greyhound.com) leaves from McDonald's at 1235 S Bluff St, with buses to Salt Lake City ($39 to $68, six hours) and Las Vegas ($27 to $34, two hours).

AROUND ST GEORGE

Follow Hwy 18 northwest out of St George and you'll come to a series of parks and attractions before reaching higher elevations and Dixie National Forest. Go northeast of town on I-15 for more parks and a small ghost town.

Snow Canyon State Park

Red and white swirls of sandstone flow like lava, and lava lies broken like sheets of smashed marble in this small, accessible park. **Snow Canyon** (☎ 435-628-2255; www.stateparks.utah.gov; Snow Canyon Pkwy, off Hwy 18; per car $6; � day-use 6am-10pm; ☉) is a 7400-acre sampler of southwest Utah's famous land features, 11 miles northwest of St George. Easy trails, perfect for kids, lead to tiny slot canyons, cinder cones, lava tubes and fields of undulating slickrock. Summers are blazing hot: visit in early morning or come in spring or fall. The park was named after prominent Utah pioneers, not precipitation, but for the record it does occasionally snow here.

Hiking trails loop off the main road. **Jenny's Canyon Trail** is an easy 1-mile round-trip to a short slot canyon. Wind through a cottonwood-filled field, past ancient lava flows to a 200ft arch on **Johnson Canyon Trail** (2-mile round-trip). There are some steep sections on **Petrified Sand Dunes Trail** (1-mile round-trip), as you cross sandstone dunes frozen in time.

Cycling is popular on the main road through the park, a 17-mile loop from St George, where you can rent bikes (see p476). There's also great **rock climbing** in-park, particularly for beginners, with over 150 bolted and sport routes, plus top roping.

Except during the unrelenting summer here, the 35-site **campground** (☎ reservations 800-322-3770; www.reserveamerica.com; tent sites/RV sites $14/20) is great, so scenic. Restrooms and showers available; campers can reserve 20 of its 33 sites ahead.

Veyo

The tiny village of Veyo lies 17 miles north of St George on Hwy 18. A warm spring-fed swimming pool (about 80°F) on the Santa Clara River is the main attraction at **Veyo Pool**

& Crawdad Canyon Climbing Park (☎ 435-574-2300; www.veyopool.com; Veyo Pool Resort Rd; adult/child swim $6/4; ☉ 11am-8pm May-Sep). But there's also a café, picnicking area and sun deck. Eighty-foot high basalt walls in Crawdad Canyon are perfect for rock climbing and have been equipped with more than 100 bolted routes ($5 per day).

Mountain Meadows Massacre Monument

About 10 miles north of Veyo on Hwy 18 is a somber monument to one of the darkest incidents in the Mormon settlement of Utah. In 1857, for reasons that remain unclear, Mormons and local Indians killed about 120 non-Mormon pioneers – including women and children – who were migrating through the area. You can visit the freely accessible graveyard and get a scenic panorama of the valley where the incident occurred.

Pine Valley Mountain Wilderness

Mountains rise sharply in the 70-sq-mile **Pine Valley Wilderness Area** (www.fs.fed.us/r4/dixie) in the Dixie National Forest, 32 miles northwest of St George off Hwy 18. The highest point, **Signal Peak** (10,365ft), remains snow-capped till July and rushing streams lace the mountainous area. The St George Field Office (p475) provides information and free backcountry permits.

When the desert heat blurs your vision, Pine Valley offers cool respite. Most hikes here begin as strenuous climbs. The 5-mile round-trip **Mill Canyon Trail** and the 6-mile **Whipple Trail** are most popular, each linking with the 35-mile **Summit Trail**. The best guide is *Loving the Laccolith*, by Bridget McColville.

Pine Valley Recreation Complex (☎ reservations 877-444-6777; www.recreation.gov; campsites $11, day-use $2; ☉ May-Sep), 3 miles east of Pine Valley, has three pine-shaded campgrounds at 6800ft – Blue Springs, Juniper Park and Pines. They all have water but no showers; bring mosquito repellent.

Silver Reef Ghost Town

A few of the old stone buildings are inhabited, others are crumbling at this 19th-century silver-mining ghost town. The restored **Wells Fargo building** (☎ 435-879-2254; admission free; ☉ 10am-4pm Mon-Sat) houses a museum and art gallery. Diagrams of the rough-and-tumble town and mine give a feel of what it was like back in the day. Take exit 23 off I-15, 13 miles northeast of St George (past Leeds).

Hildale-Colorado City

On the far southern edge of the state, straddling the Utah–Arizona border, sit the twin towns of Hildale-Colorado City. Only 42 miles southeast of St George on Hwy 9, the towns

are light years away in thinking from modern America. The majority of the approximately 7000 residents belongs to the polygamy-practicing Fundamentalist Church of Jesus Christ of Latter-day Saints (FLDS). Utah locals call

---

LOCAL VOICES: CAROLYN JESSOP'S ESCAPE FROM POLYGAMY

Best-selling author Carolyn Jessop has appeared on talk shows from Larry King to Oprah discussing her harrowing flight from the Fundamentalist Church of Jesus Christ of Latter-day Saints (FLDS), a cultlike polygamist community on the southern Utah border. In her book *Escape*, she describes her first 30-odd years of life as a sixth-generation polygamist, her multiple marriage at age 18 to a 50-year-old community leader, abuse in the family, and manipulative 'sister wives' and stepdaughters her own age. Ultimately she narrowly escaped in the middle of the night with her eight children – aged four to 15 – and was chased into hiding before winning custody.

You've likened the move to life outside the restrictive FLDS religion to landing on another planet... It wasn't just a religion. You [a woman] were never allowed to make any decisions. When you first leave you have no life skills. You've never been allowed to have your own money, to make decisions for yourself, for your family...

That's got to be a huge difference. Yes, and then you don't understand basic traditions when you've been isolated. For instance in the society I came from, to talk to a man who was not your husband was considered coming on to him. When I first started dating and we'd go out to dinner with other couples, I'd greet the woman but I wouldn't say anything to the man. My boyfriend had to teach me that what I was doing was rude. I was clueless. In the society where I come from, you're not a human being, you're a possession, you're owned – and don't try to become anything other than that. You have to watch every breath of air you take or else you're in trouble and someone's making accusations against you.

So is it easier to breathe now? It's interesting, because you have to learn how.

One of your first jobs in the outside world was sewing costumes for HBO's TV series *Big Love*? I really needed the money, needed the job, but I said if they're going to portray polygamy in Colorado City as anything that has any level of freedom, I can't participate. It's not a problem if it's set in a city where women have the chance to choose it; that just was not the case with what I was involved with.

In the FLDS community, private books and TV were banned; how did your children react after you left? It was totally overwhelming in every area. For the first time in their lives, somebody wasn't breathing down their throat, they weren't going to be in trouble if they ate something. They weren't just having to get up early and work. They went to school, for the first time they could be kids.

So they adjusted? All except Betty. But even when she went back [at age 18] I could tell it was really hard for her to give up the life she had out here. Hardly a day goes by now that they don't thank me for getting them out of that. But right in the beginning it was difficult for all of them. I had *no* money. I'd taken them from a 17,000-sq-ft home, one of the nicer ones in the community, and moved into a trailer. They just thought I'd completely lost my mind. They had no sense of a biological family and were closer to their same-age [half] siblings whom they'd spent all their time with. Now they have an identity that is totally about them.

What's become their favorite pastime in the wider world of Utah? The biggest novelty has been skiing and snowboarding. It'd be hard to move to another state. They're very athletic, into all sorts of activities now – football, karate, girl scouts.

And your favorite? This is going to sound crazy, but I really like being able to go to a gym and work out. It was taboo to take care of yourself. Anything you wanted to take and do for yourself was just taboo.

If you want to help women and children trapped in abusive polygamous relationships, Carolyn suggests checking out the not-for-profit **Hope Organization** (www.thehopeorg.org).

FUNDAMENTALIST FIRE

Whether the secretive nature of polygamist sects engenders monstrous behavior or just hides it, there's no denying that some shocking crimes have been associated with fundamentalist polygamist groups. In the 1980s, followers of Ervil LaBaron killed at least 25 people in Mexico and the US. The Lafferty brothers, whose murderous story is told in *Under the Banner of God*, sliced the throats of their youngest brother's wife and baby. Jeremy Kingston was prosecuted for the rape of a 15-year-old relative.

Then there's Warren Jeffs. In 2002 he assumed the role of prophet in the FLDS when his father died. Reports have it that the charismatic leader imposed stricter and stricter regulations – closing the schools, banning private books (TV had long been taboo) and putting 13-year-old boys to work in construction in ever-more isolated Hildale-Colorado City. For years after he was indicted on two counts of accomplice to rape for officiating at the marriage of two underage girls, he evaded arrest and continued joining girls as young as 13 in 'spiritual wifery' (aka plural marriage) to men as many as 60 years their senior. Given the generations of indoctrination, the threat of eternal damnation, harsh recriminations for dissent and the lack of education, these girls had little choice.

When Jeffs was convicted in 2007, he renounced his leadership role, but reports are that not much has changed. After allegations of rape and child abuse in 2008, Child Protective Services entered Jeffs' followers' compound in El Dorado, Texas, and removed more than 400 children. At the time of writing, a lengthy legal battle was underway. Of course, most of what we know comes from those who have left or 'escaped' the FLDS (for more, see the boxed text, p479). Stories of forced marriages, physical and sexual abuse, and deprivation have come out in numerous memoirs. Check out the documentary *Banking on Heaven*, by Dot Reidelback and Laurie Allen, for an introduction to the local FLDS.

the residents 'polygs' (*pawl-igs*). The spotlight focused on this remote community when leader Warren Jeffs was arrested (see boxed text, above). Since then, many of the FLDS faithful have moved to a fenced compound in Texas.

Other than a proliferation of really large houses (for multiple wives and even more multiple children) and women wearing pastel ankle-to-wrist dresses, the twin towns look pretty normal. This is an extremely insular community and we don't recommend driving around much; there's been no violence, but nonresidents have been followed. You can enter any Wal-Mart in St George and you're sure to notice the characteristic long dresses and upswept hairdos worn by FLDS 'sister wives' shopping together. Remember, they are human beings, so please be respectful.

You could stop in at the **Merry Wives Café** (☎ 435-874-9425; Hwy 59; dishes $5-10; ☯ 11am-7:30pm Mon-Sat), inside the Hildale gas station. Members of a separate polygamist sect opened the restaurant in 2007, and actually, the fried shrimp specials are pretty good. Note the pastoral mural of women romping through a garden and the family portraits on the wall.

SALT LAKE CITY & AROUND

The vast Salt Lake Valley is what Brigham Young referred to when he announced 'this is the place!' to his pioneering followers in 1847. Today almost 80% of the state's population, nearly 2 million people, live along the eastern edge of the Wasatch Mountains from Ogden to Provo. Salt Lake City (SLC) sits smack in the middle of this concentration, but you'd never know it from the small size of the city. To the north and west is the Great Salt Lake and 100 miles of salt flats stretching into Nevada.

SALT LAKE CITY
pop 181,700 / elev 4330ft

Utah's capital city, and the only one with an international airport, has a surprisingly small-town feel. Yes, it is the Mormon equivalent of Vatican City, and the LDS's Temple Square is the biggest thing in town, but beyond the church walls you can find good dining and a couple of interesting museums. People are extraordinarily friendly (go to Temple Square on a night when there are few visitors and you may feel in danger of being nice-d to death), but only about half the town's population are LDS members. A hint of liberal spirit, however slight, is evident in the coffee houses and bookshops. Downtown is easy to get around, and come evening it's downright quiet – boring even. When the trail beckons, you're only 45 minutes from the Wasatch Mountains' brilliant hiking and skiing. Residents and visitors alike take advantage of all the facilities built for the 2002 Winter Olympics.

Orientation

Salt Lake City is laid out in a spacious grid with street addresses radiating east–west from Main St or north–south from South Temple St. North Temple St, westbound, goes to the airport, 6 miles from downtown. Streets are so wide (132ft) because they were originally built so that four oxen pulling a wagon could turn around.

Two major interstates cross at SLC: I-15 runs north–south, I-80 east–west. I-215 loops the city. Springdale and Zion National Park are 308 miles to the south; Moab and Arches are 234 miles south and east.

Information
BOOKSTORES

Ken Sanders Rare Books (Map p483; ☎ 801-521-3819; www.kensandersbooks.com; 268 S 200 East) Specializes in Western authors; the epicenter of SLC's counterculture.

King's English (Map p481; ☎ 801-484-9100; http://kingsenglish.booksense.com; 1511 S 1500 East) First-rate indie bookseller, staffed by enthusiastic bookworms.

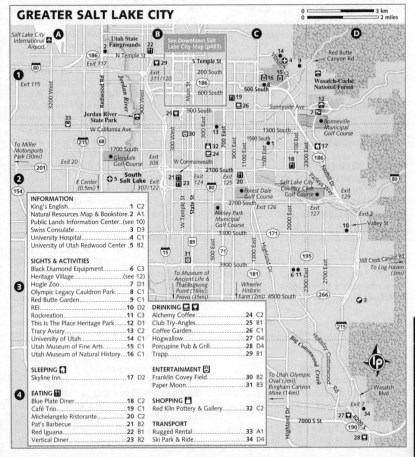

GREATER SALT LAKE CITY

UTAH

Sam Weller Books (Map p483; ☎ 801-328-2586; www.samwellers.com; 254 S Main St) The best selection of travel books, guides and maps at SLC's biggest independent bookstore.

EMERGENCY
Local police (Map p483; ☎ 801-799-3000; 315 E 200 South)

INTERNET ACCESS
Cup of Joe (Map p483; ☎ 801-363-8322; 353 W 200 South; ♥ 7am-midnight Mon-Sat, 9am-8pm Sun) Free wi-fi.
Salt Lake City Main Library (Map p483; ☎ 801-524-8200; www.slcpl.lib.ut.us; 210 E 400 South; ♥ 9am-9pm Mon-Thu, 9am-6pm Fri & Sat, 1-5pm Sun) Free internet access.

MEDIA
City Weekly (☎ 801-575-7003; www.slweekly.com) Free alternative weekly with good restaurant and entertainment listings; twice annually it publishes the free *City Guide*.
Deseret News (☎ 801-236-6000; www.desnews.com) Ultraconservative, church-owned paper.
Salt Lake Magazine (☎ 801-485-5100; www.saltlakemagazine.com) Lifestyle and food.
Salt Lake Metro (☎ 801-323-9500; www.slmetro.com) SLC's free, gay newspaper.
Salt Lake Tribune (☎ 801-257-8742; www.sltrib.com) Utah's largest-circulation paper.

MEDICAL SERVICES
University Hospital (Map p481; ☎ 801-581-2121/2291; 50 N Medical Dr) For emergencies, 24/7.
University of Utah Redwood Center (Map p481; ☎ 801-887-2499; 1525 W 2100 South; ♥ by appointment 8am-5pm, walk-in clinic 5-8pm Mon-Fri, 9am-8pm Sat & Sun) Non-emergency care.

MONEY
It's difficult to change currency outside SLC. On weekends visit the airport.
Wells Fargo (Map p483; ☎ 801-246-2677; 79 S Main St)

POST
Post office (Map p483; ☎ 800-275-8777; www.usps.com; 230 W 200 South)

TOURIST INFORMATION
Public Lands Information Center (Map p481; ☎ 801-466-6411; REI, 3285 E 3300 South; ♥ 10:30am-7pm Tue-Sat) Central source for all public land (state parks, BLM, USFS) information.
Salt Lake Ranger Station (☎ 801-733-2660; www.fs.fed.us/r4/wcnf/unit/slrd) Covers the Wasatch-Cache

National Forest. No walk-ins; telephone information provided.
Visitor Information Center (Map p483; ☎ 801-521-2822, 800-541-4955; www.visitsaltlake.com; 90 S West Temple St; ♥ 9am-5pm Jun-Aug, 8:30am-5pm Mon-Fri Sep-May) Inside the Salt Palace Convention Center. Publishes the free *Salt Lake Visitors Guide*. Good website.

Sights
Also see Salt Lake City for Children, p485.

TEMPLE SQUARE & AROUND
The city's most famous sight, **Temple Square** (Map p483; ☎ 801-240-2534, 800-537-9703; www.visittempleplesquare.com; admission free; ♥ 9am-9pm) occupies a 10-acre block surrounded by 15ft-high walls. LDS docents give free, 30-minute tours continually, leaving from the visitor centers at the two entrances, on South and North Temple Sts. Sisters, brothers and elders are stationed every 20ft or so to answer questions. (Don't worry, no one is going to try to convert you – unless you express interest.)

Lording over the square is the impressive, 210ft-tall **Salt Lake Temple**. Atop the tallest spire stands a statue of the angel Moroni who appeared to LDS founder Joseph Smith. Rumor has it that when the place was renovated, cleaners found old bullet marks in the gold-plated surface. The temple and ceremonies are private, open only to LDS in good standing.

Make sure you visit the 1867 **Tabernacle** (www.mormontabernaclechoir.org). The building acoustics are amazing, but to listen to the 360-member volunteer choir perform here, you'll have to visit off-season (see p489). In season, performances are held at the 21,000-seat **Conference Center** (free in-depth tours available). Ascend to the rooftop garden for killer views. **Assembly Hall** (☎ 801-240-3323; www.visittemplesquare.com) is a lovely 1877 Gothic building that also hosts concerts.

Adjoining Temple Square, the **Museum of Church History & Art** (Map p483; ☎ 801-240-3310; 45 N West Temple St; admission free; ♥ 9am-9pm Mon-Fri, 10am-7pm Sat & Sun) has impressive exhibits of pioneer history and fine art.

Thousands of people come to Salt Lake City every year to research their family history at the largest genealogical resource on Earth, the **Family History Library** (Map p483; ☎ 801-240-2331; www.familysearch.org; 35 N West Temple St; ♥ 7:30am-10pm Tue-Sat, 7:30am-5pm Mon). Because the LDS believes you must pray on your ancestors behalf to help them on their path, it has acquired a

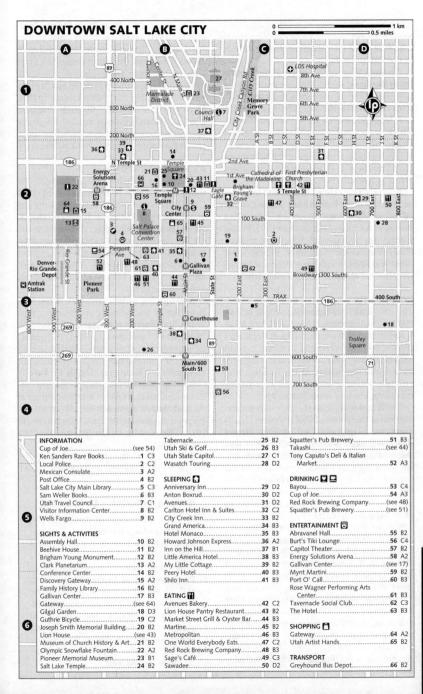

DOWNTOWN SALT LAKE CITY

UTAH

mind-boggling amount of genealogical information to help identify ancestors. Volunteers scour the globe microfilming church records in the tiniest of villages.

On Main St at South Temple St the **Brigham Young Monument** marks the zero point for the city. East of the monument is the **Joseph Smith Memorial Building** (Map p483; ☎ 801-240-1266; 15 E South Temple St; admission free; ☺ 9am-9pm Mon-Sat), which was, until 1987, the elegant Hotel Utah. Inside there's a large-screen theater with nine daily screenings of the 65-minute *Joseph Smith: The Prophet of the Restoration*, about Mormon beliefs.

Brigham Young lived with one of his wives and families in the **Beehive House** (Map p483; ☎ 801-240-2671; 67 E South Temple St; admission free; ☺ 9am-8:30pm Mon-Sat) at the time of his death in 1877. Period furnishings and artwork have been meticulously maintained. Next door, the 1855 **Lion House** (Map p483; 63 E South Temple St), now a restaurant, housed many of Young's other wives.

DOWNTOWN

The 1916 **Utah State Capitol** (Map p483; ☎ 801-538-1563; http://utahstatecapitol.utah.gov; cnr 300 North & State St; admission free; ☺ 8am-6pm), modeled after the US capitol, cost an amazing $2.7 million to build back in the day. After six years, and 500 cherry trees, a full renovation of the building and grounds was completed in 2007. Free guided tours begin hourly from 9am to 4pm.

You'll find relics from the early days gathering dust at Daughters of Utah Pioneers (DUP) museums throughout Utah, but the **Pioneer Memorial Museum** (Map p483; ☎ 801-532-6479; www.dupinternational.org; 300 N Main St; admission free; ☺ 9am-5pm Mon-Sat year-round, 1-5pm Sun Jun-Aug) is by far the biggest. The vast, four-story treasure trove is like Utah's attic, with a taxidermy two-headed lamb and human-hair artwork in addition to more expected artifacts.

See the stars at **Clark Planetarium** (Map p483; ☎ 801-456-7827; www.clarkplanetarium.org; 110 S 400 West; adult/child $8/6; ☺ 10:30am-8pm Mon-Thu, 10:30am-11pm Fri & Sat, 10:30am-6pm Sun), home to the latest and greatest 3-D sky shows and Utah's only Imax theater. Adjoining the planetarium, the **Gateway** (Map p483; ☎ 801-456-0000; www.shopthegateway.com; 400 W 100 South) is a combination indoor-outdoor shopping center and dynamic memorial to the thousands of local volunteers who worked at the 2002 Olympics. The centerpiece is the **Olympic Snowflake Fountain** – water you can play in!

The grand 1909 **Union Pacific Railroad Depot** and the 1910 **Denver-Rio Grande Depot** anchor the Gateway. South Temple St is lined with **historical buildings**; the visitor center has a free walking-tour map and guide.

One of the best things to do on Sunday is to visit the Salt Lake City Main Library (p482). Here you can meander through dramatic glass-walled architecture, stroll through the roof garden or stop by the ground-floor shops (from gardening to comic-book publishing).

AROUND DOWNTOWN

The **University of Utah** (Map p481; ☎ 801-581-7200; www.utah.edu), or 'U of U,' bounded by 1300 East, 2 miles east of downtown, was the site of the Olympic Village in 2002. The **Olympic Legacy Cauldron Park** (Map p481; ☎ 801-581-8849, 866-659-7275; Rice-Eccles Stadium, 451 S 1400 East; admission free, adult/child film $3/2; ☺ 10am-6pm Mon-Sat) has giant panels detailing the games. A heavy-handed but heartfelt film booms with artificial fog and sound effects.

Also on campus, you can watch technicians clean fossils and wonder at allosaurus eggs in the **Utah Museum of Natural History** (Map p481; ☎ 801-581-6927; www.umnh.utah.edu; 1390 E President's Circle; adult/child $6/3.50; ☺ 9:30am-5:30pm Mon-Sat, noon-5pm Sun). It's not the most high-tech place, but there are a few hands-on exhibits for kids.

Soaring galleries showcase permanent collections of tribal, Western and modern art at the **Utah Museum of Fine Arts** (Map p481; ☎ 801-581-7332; www.umfa.utah.edu; 410 Campus Center Dr; adult/child $4/2; ☺ 10am-5pm Tue, Thu & Fri, 10am-8pm Wed, 11am-5pm Sat & Sun).

Dedicated to the 1847 arrival of the Mormons, **This is the Place Heritage Park** (Map p481;

DETOUR: BINGHAM CANYON MINE

Fourteen miles south of downtown SLC, you'll find what's reputedly the only construction on earth beside the Great Wall of China that's visible from outer space. Six *billion* tons of rock have been removed from **Bingham Canyon Copper Mine** (off Map p481; ☎ 801-252-3234; per car $5; ☺ 8am-8pm Apr-Oct) since 1906. It's an environmental disaster – and whaddaya know, also a tourist attraction. The **visitor center** (☺ 8am-dusk Apr-Oct) includes a museum, film presentation and overlook. Take I-15 south to exit 301, then Hwy 48 west.

☎ 801-582-1847; www.thisistheplace.org; 2601 E Sunnyside Ave; park admission free, village adult/child $6/4; ⏰ 10am-5pm) covers 450 acres. The park's centerpiece is **Heritage Village**, a living-history museum where, June through August, costumed docents depict life in the mid-19th century. The rest of the year you can walk around the 41 buildings, some replicas, some originals, such as Brigham Young's farmhouse.

Nearby, in the Wasatch Foothills, the lovely **Red Butte Garden** (Map p481; ☎ 801-581-4747; www .redbuttegarden.org; Wakara Way; adult/child/senior $5/3/3; ⏰ 9am-9pm May-Aug, 10am-5pm Sep-Apr) has 150 acres with trails, 25 acres of gardens and gorgeous views. **Gilgal Garden** (Map p483; ☎ 801-519-0871; www .gilgalgarden.org; 749 E 500 South; admission free; ⏰ 8am-8pm Apr-Sep, 9am-5pm Oct-Mar) is a quirkier green space. The tiny sculpture garden is home to a giant stone sphinx wearing Joseph Smith's face.

Activities
OUTFITTERS
The best of SLC's outdoor activities are in the Wasatch Mountains (p492), but gear is available in town. Rent road and mountain bikes (about $35 per day) from **Guthrie Bicycle** (Map p483; ☎ 801-363-3727; www.guthriebicycle.com; 156 E 200 South). It'll provide information on in-town trails or you could head for the hills. **Wasatch Touring** (Map p483; ☎ 801-359-9361; www.wasatchtouring.com; 702 E 100 South) rents bikes, kayaks, climbing shoes and ski equipment. **REI** (Map p481; ☎ 801-486-2100, 800-426-4840; www.rei.com; 3285 E 3300 South) rents camping equipment, climbing shoes, kayaks and most winter-sports gear. It also stocks a great selection of maps and activity guides.

ROCK CLIMBING
If you're into rock climbing, check out **Rockreation** (Map p481; ☎ 801-278-7473; www.rockrea tion.com; 2074 E 3900 South; day pass $15; ⏰ 6am-10pm Mon-Thu, noon-6pm Fri, 9am-6pm Sat & Sun), which has 7000 sq ft of indoor climbing terrain with bouldering, top rope and lead rope. Next door is **Black Diamond Equipment** (Map p481; ☎ 801-278-5552; www.bdel.com), a leading manufacturer of climbing and ski gear; take the very cool tour to see how it's done (times vary). The retail store is like a candy store for gearheads.

ICE SKATING
The ice skating rink at **Gallivan Center** (Map p483; ☎ 801-535-6117; www.thegallivancenter.com; 200 South, btwn State & Main Sts; adult/child $5/4; ⏰ noon-7pm Sun-Thu, noon-11pm Fri & Sat Dec-Mar; ♿) is a children's

winter favorite. Skate rental available. You can learn to curl as well as skate at **Utah Olympic Oval** (off Map p481; ☎ 801-968-6825; www.olyparks.com; 5662 S 4800 West; adult/child $6/4), the site of speed skating events in the 2002 Winter Olympics. Check online for public hours.

MOTORSPORTS
Feel the need for speed? Head 30 miles west of town to **Miller Motorsports Park** (off Map p481; ☎ 435-277-7223; http://millermotorsportspark.com; 2901 N Sheep Lane, Tooele), where you can take a lesson and get behind the wheel of a 325 horsepower Mustang GT race model. Book ahead. Utah Jazz' own Larry Miller opened the raceway in 2006.

GOLF
SLC's municipal **golf courses** (☎ tee times 801-484-3333; www.slcgov.com/publicservices/golf; 18 holes $27-34) are easily accessible. Rent equipment from **Utah Ski & Golf** (Map p483; ☎ 801-355-9088; www.utah skigolf.com; 134 W 600 South).

Salt Lake City for Children
There's lots for tots in SLC. In addition to some of the sights already listed, the wonderful hands-on exhibits at the **Discovery Gateway** (Map p483; ☎ 801-328-3383; www.childmuseum.org; 444 W 100 South; admission $9.50; ⏰ 10am-6pm Mon-Thu & Sat, 10am-9pm Fri, noon-6pm Sun; ♿) stimulate imaginations and senses.

Kids can help farmhands milk cows, churn butter and feed animals at **Wheeler Historic Farm** (off Map p481; ☎ 801-264-2241; www.wheelerfarm.com; South Cottonwood Regional Park, 6351 S 900 East; admission free, hay ride $2; ⏰ 9:30am-5:30pm; ♿), which dates from 1886. There's also blacksmithing, quilting and hay rides in summer.

Asian Highlands, combining big cat habitats with architecture of the East, is the newest exhibit at **Hogle Zoo** (Map p481; ☎ 801-582-1631; 2600 E Sunnyside Ave; adult/child $8/6; ⏰ 9am-6:30pm Jun-Sep, 9am-5:30pm Oct-May; ♿). Kids still love the petting zoo and miniature-train rides ($1).

Feed the penguins ($2) at the **Tracy Aviary** (Map p481; ☎ 801-322-2473; www.tracyaviary.org; 589 E 1300 South; adult/child $5/3; ⏰ 9am-4:30pm Oct-Feb, 9am-6pm Mar-Sep; ♿). More than 400 winged creatures from around the world call this aviary home. You can also feed ducks, colorful lories and parrots.

Fifty-five acres of gardens, a petting farm, a golf course, a giant movie theater, dining and shopping: what doesn't the **Thanksgiving Point** (off Map p481; ☎ 801-768-2300, 3003 N Thanksgiving Way,

UTAH

Lehi; all-attraction pass adult/child $25/19; ⊗ 10am-8pm Mon-Sat; 🖐) infotainment complex have? The on-site **Museum of Ancient Life** (adult/child $10/8) is the highest-tech and kid-friendliest dinosaur museum in the state. Little ones can dig for their own bones, dress up a dinosaur, play in a watery Silurian reef… Interactive exhibits teach about fossils found all over the world. Take exit 287 off I-15; Lehi is 28 miles south of downtown SLC.

Tours

Grayline (☎ 801-534-1001; www.saltlakecitytours.org) Four-hour sightseeing tours cost $35.
Utah Heritage Foundation (☎ 801-533-8058; www.utahheritagefoundation.com) Terrific historic tours.

Festivals & Events

The **Utah Arts Festival** (www.uaf.org) happens in June. July's **Days of '47** (☎ 801-254-4656; www.daysof47.com), affectionately nicknamed 'Mormon Mardi Gras,' brings everything from a rodeo to an enormous parade.

Sleeping

Downtown chain properties cluster along S 200 West near 500 South and 600 South; there are more in Mid-Valley (off I-215) and near the airport. At high-end hotels, rates are lowest on weekends. Parking is freely available at all lodgings. Look for camping and alternative lodging in the Wasatch Mountains (p492).

BUDGET

Avenues (Map p483; ☎ 801-359-3855, 888-884-4752; www.hostelhandbook.com/slc; 107 F St; dm/s/d $15/37/47; 🖳 wi-fi) There are beat-up couches everywhere – with long-time guests entrenched on them – at this scruffy former apartment building. Sunday barbecues ($3) on the patio and weekly LDS talks give the place a strong community feel. Pay less with semiprivate rooms (shared bathroom single/double $27/42).

City Creek Inn (Map p483; ☎ 801-533-9100, 866-533-4898; www.citycreekinn.com; 230 W North Temple St; r $48-58; wi-fi) For a budget choice, City Creek is close to Temple Square (under two blocks away). The old-fashioned, family-owned motel has small bathrooms and the occasional paint chip.

Skyline Inn (Map p481; ☎ 801-582-5350; www.skylineinn.com; 2475 E 1700 South; r $55-69; 🖳 wi-fi) A good choice for bargain-hunting skiers and hikers. Skyline Inn is only 30 minutes from the slopes, and has a hot tub, too. Rooms could use some renovation.

Howard Johnson Express (Map p483; ☎ 801-521-3450; www.hojo.com; 121 N 300 West; r $59-79; 🖳 wi-fi) The decor's a bit blah, but what do you expect from a standard chain? At least there's a big pool, a fitness room, coffee makers in the clean-enough rooms and a downtown location. Slow wi-fi; some pets OK.

MIDRANGE

Anton Boxrud (Map p483; ☎ 801-363-8035, 800-524-5511; www.antonboxrud.com; 57 S 600 East; r incl breakfast $75-120; wi-fi) The warm and welcoming innkeeper, Jane, always has cookies, drinks and dining advice on hand. In the morning a cook comes in to whip up a multicourse meal (and irresistible banana bread). Stay in one of the restored 1901 Victorian's seven rooms and you're a healthy walk away from downtown.

Little America Hotel (Map p483; ☎ 801-363-6781, 800-453-9450; www.littleamerica.com/slc; 500 S Main St; r $109-149; 🖳 🖳) Order room service and enjoy it poolside in the walled garden or up in your 17th-story tower room overlooking the city. The demure sister to the opulent Grand America gets everything just right. High-speed internet.

Peery Hotel (Map p483; ☎ 801-521-4300, 800-331-0073; www.peeryhotel.com; 110 W 300 South; r $109-159; 🖳 wi-fi) Egyptian-cotton robes and sheets, carved dark-wood furnishings, individually decorated rooms – prepare to be charmed by the 1910 Peery Hotel. Small but impeccable bathrooms have pedestal sinks and aromatherapy jams and jellies.

Inn on the Hill (Map p483; ☎ 801-328-1466; www.inn-on-the-hill.com; 225 N State St; r incl breakfast $119-149; 🖳 wi-fi) Maxfield Parrish Tiffany glass adorns the entryway of this 1906 Renaissance Revival mansion overlooking Temple Square. Play billiards or read by the fire in one of three parlors. The two-story carriage house ($249) sleeps six and has a kitchenette.

Hotel Monaco (Map p483; ☎ 801-595-0000, 877-294-9710; www.monaco-saltlakecity.com; 15 W 200 South; r $149-199; 🖳 wi-fi) The Monaco is clearly SLC's least conservative hotel. You can tell by the raspberry stripes, Dr Seuss-ish armoires and leopard-print robes. The whimsical decor shows signs of age but free evening wine hours make up for it. Pampered pets (dogs, cats, birds) receive a toy and souvenir water bowl on check in.

Also try the following:
Carlton Hotel Inn & Suites (Map p483; ☎ 801-355-3418, 801-633-3500; www.carltonhotel-slc.com; 140 E

South Temple St; r $80-120; (wi-fi) Great location, ho-hum rooms, historic building (c 1920).

My Little Cottage (Map p483; ☎ 801-347-3155; www .mylittlecottage.com; 161 N 200 West; house $89-119) Full, but tiny, one-bedroom house rental.

Shilo Inn (Map p483; ☎ 801-521-9500, 800-222-2244; www.shiloinns.com; 206 S West Temple St; r incl breakfast $119-159; wi-fi) High-rise convention hotel. Microwaves and mini-refrigerators.

TOP END

Anniversary Inn (Map p483; ☎ 801-363-4953, 800-324-4152; www.anniversaryinn.com; 678 E South Temple St; ste incl breakfast $169-289) Fourteen over-the-top suites occupy an 1886 mansion in the Avenues neighborhood (good eats nearby). Stay in the Moroccan-inspired Sultan's Suite or the log-lined Mountain Hideaway.

Grand America (Map p483; ☎ 801-258-6000, 800-621-4505; www.grandamerica.com; 555 S Main St; r $299-329;) SLC's only true luxury hotel towers over the city like a 24-story wedding cake. Murano-glass chandeliers drip from the ornate lobby's ceiling. Rooms are decked out with Italian-marble bathrooms, English-wool carpeting, tasseled damask draperies and other cushy touches. If you like afternoon tea, complimentary shoe shines and a mint on your pillow, you've found your place.

Eating

Foodies will be surprised to learn how well you can eat in SLC. Make reservations at top-end places. A **Whole Foods** (www.wholefoods. com) grocery and take-out was in the works at the time of writing.

BUDGET

All the coffee houses (p488) offer sandwiches ($3 to $6) in addition to a good cuppa java.

our pick One World Everybody Eats (Map p483; ☎ 801-519-2002; 41 S 300 East; meals by donation; 11am-9pm) Let your conscience dictate how much or how little you pay for the organic, unprocessed, omnivorous and vegetarian meals at this boho 'community kitchen'. Sit down with your Italian spaghetti squash salad and always-free dhal and rice at a Formica table in the mismatched rooms or on the small patio. Volunteering for an hour in the serving line or garden will earn you a meal voucher, and lots of good karma.

Tony Caputo's Deli & Italian Market (Map p483; ☎ 801-531-8669; 308 W 300 South; sandwiches $4-5; 9am-6pm Mon-Fri, 9am-5pm Sat, 11am-3pm Sun) Crowds line up at this old-fashioned Italian

market for mouth-watering meatball sandwiches; save some room for the cannoli, too.

Blue Plate Diner (Map p481; ☎ 801-463-1151; 2041 S 2100 East; breakfast & sandwiches $4-8, mains $8-10; 7am-9pm Sun-Thu, 7am-10pm Fri & Sat) How cool is this place? A hip, retro diner with a full soda fountain, colorful patio and postcards from around the country as decoration. Specials include hometown faves such as meatloaf and spaghetti; best greasy fries around.

Avenues Bakery (Map p483; ☎ 801-746-5626; 481 E South Temple St; sandwiches $7-10; 7am-7pm Mon-Fri, 7am-3pm Sat & Sun) Enjoy a crusty loaf with soup and salad or the ultimate grilled cheese, with provolone and Asiago. The weekend brunch menu is huge.

Lion House Pantry Restaurant (Map p483; ☎ 801-363-5466; 63 E South Temple St; meals $7-10; 7am-10pm Mon-Sat) Down-home, carb-rich cookin' just like your Mormon grandmother used to make, only it's served cafeteria-style in a historic house. Twenty-seven of Brigham Young's wives used to live here.

MIDRANGE

Pat's Barbecue (Map p481; ☎ 801-463-6149; 2158 S 155 West Commonwealth; sandwiches $7-8, mains $8-13; lunch Mon-Wed, lunch & dinner Thu & Fri, noon-9pm Sun) Tuck into the city's best ribs in a rustic dining hall that hosts live bands Thursday through Saturday nights.

Sage's Café (Map p483; ☎ 801-322-3790; 473 E Broadway; breakfast & sandwiches $7-10, mains $12-15; lunch & dinner Mon-Fri, 9am-10pm Sat & Sun) Enjoy vegan, mostly organic, made-in-house meals (including the root beer) in a comfy former home. Tuesday is all-you-can-eat pizza ($10).

Red Rock Brewing Company (Map p483; ☎ 801-521-7446; 254 S 200 West; sandwiches $7-10, mains $14-18; lunch & dinner) Office workers crowd in for weekday lunches such as champagne and Dijon-glazed chicken, and who isn't here on weekends?

Sawadee (Map p483; ☎ 801-328-8424; 754 E South Temple St; mains $9-11; lunch & dinner Mon-Sat) A front wall of glass makes you feel like you're enjoying the upscale dark-wood-and-fountain decor whether you're sitting inside or out. This neighborhood favorite is a must-try for Thai food; expect a wait.

Red Iguana (Map p481; ☎ 801-322-1489; 736 W North Temple St; mains $9-15; lunch & dinner) M-olé! The savory chocolate-based mole sauce makes tongues take notice. The room isn't much, but with Mexican food this good, who cares?

UTAH

Café Trio (Map p481; ☎ 801-533-8746; 680 S 900 East; mains $10-22; 🕙 11am-10pm) The under-40 set gathers here for flatbreads and roasted meats fired in the wood-burning oven. You always get big portions of the California-influenced Italian meals.

Also eat at the following:

Vertical Diner (Map p481; ☎ 801-484-8378; 2280 S West Temple St; sandwiches & brunch $6-8, mains $14-18; 🕙 lunch & dinner Tue-Sat, brunch Sun) Yet another atmospheric foodie fave for local and organic.

Squatter's Pub Brewery (Map p483; ☎ 801-363-2739; 147 W 300 South; burgers $8-10, mains $10-14; 🕙 lunch & dinner) Eclectic brewpub menu.

Takashi (Map p483; ☎ 801-519-9595; 18 W Market St; lunch mains $9-12, dinner mains $13-19; 🕙 lunch & dinner Mon-Sat) Tops in town for sushi.

TOP END

Market Street Grill & Oyster Bar (Map p483; ☎ 801-322-4668, 801-331-0644; 48 W Market St; breakfast $5-10, lunch specials $13, mains $19-28; 🕙 breakfast, lunch & dinner) The always-bustling Market Street has both a formal restaurant and an eat-in 'bar' ($4 cover). SLC's favorite seafood is served at this cosmopolitan fish house.

Martine (Map p483; ☎ 801-363-9328; 22 E 100 South; tapas $8-10, mains $21-27; 🕙 lunch Mon, lunch & dinner Tue-Fri, dinner Sat) The chef at this soulful downtowner serves small plates of earthy cooking spiked with infused oils and flavor-packed reductions, such as sablefish with lavender-leek cream.

Metropolitan (Map p483; ☎ 801-364-3472; 173 W Broadway; mains $18-28; 🕙 dinner Mon-Sat) If Salt Lake had celebs, they'd hang out at Metropolitan. The sexy concrete-and-velvet dining room complements the chef's culinary artistry. Budget gourmets: order small plates from the bistro menu ($8 to $12) while swilling martinis at the bar.

More options:

Michelangelo Ristorante (Map p481; ☎ 801-466-0961; 2156 Highland Dr; mains $18-25; 🕙 dinner Tue-Sat) A bit of a drive, but the oh-so-Italian owner-chef makes all his pasta fresh.

Log Haven (off Map p481; ☎ 801-272-8255; Mill Creek Canyon Rd; mains $24-32; 🕙 dinner) Romantic restaurant in the hills.

Drinking

Bars and nightspots are 'private clubs' (brewpubs excepted) and require a couple of dollars cover charge for 'membership.'

Cup of Joe (Map p483; ☎ 801-363-8322; 353 W 200 South; 🕙 7am-midnight Mon-Sat, 9am-8pm Sun) A modern urban coffee house, Joe's serves some of the city's best beans. Take a book from the exchange shelf or come for Friday night acoustic music or Saturday evening poetry.

Alchemy Coffee (Map p481; ☎ 801-322-0735; www.alchemycoffee.com; 390 E 1700 South; 🕙 7am-9pm) Eclectic neighborhood café with overstuffed sofas and lots of noncaffeinated options. Saturday nights it brings in singer-songwriters.

Bayou (Map p483; ☎ 801-961-8400; 645 S State St) Choose from more than 150 kinds of beer before you head off to the pool table at the Bayou. Friday and Saturday nights there's live jazz. Cajun food served.

Hogwallow (Map p481; ☎ 801-733-5567; 3200 E Big Cottonwood Canyon Rd) A real bar's bar. Come here to mix with old-timers and outdoorsy folk alike. Some music Saturdays. Smoking allowed.

Microbreweries are big in Utah. Try the interesting rye and oat beers at **Red Rock Brewing Company** (Map p483; ☎ 801-521-7446; 254 S 200 West) or the organic amber at **Squatter's Pub Brewery** (Map p483; ☎ 801-363-2739; 147 W 300 South). **Porcupine Pub & Grill** (Map p481; ☎ 801-942-5555; 3698 E Fort Union Blvd) doesn't brew its own but it has the state's best on tap. Besides, cute skiers of both genders hang out here on their way back from mountain resorts.

Entertainment

Classical entertainment options, especially around Temple Square, are plentiful. We wouldn't say the nightlife is all that hot though; few clubs have music more than a couple of nights a week.

NIGHTCLUBS

Tavernacle Social Club (Map p483; ☎ 801-519-8900; 201 E Broadway) What visitor hasn't had a laugh at the punny name of the Tavernacle? From dueling pianos to karaoke and comedy, there's always something happening at this neighborhood club with good martinis.

Port O' Call (Map p483; ☎ 801-521-0589; 78 W 400 South) Watch sports downstairs, shake your groove thang upstairs on the giant dance floor. Nice patio, too.

Burt's Tiki Lounge (Map p483; ☎ 801-521-0572; http://burtstikilounge.com; 726 S State St) Show off your tattoos and piercings at this divey club. Music may be punk, funk, dance or hip-hop.

Major dance clubs change frequently; see the *City Weekly* (www.slweekly.com) for listings. The **Hotel** (Map p483; ☎ 801-478-4310; 155 W 200 South) attracts top DJs. At **Mynt Martini** (Map p483; ☎ 801-355-6968; 63 W 100 South) different

---

GAY & LESBIAN SLC

SLC has Utah's only gay scene, however limited. Pick up the free *Salt Lake Metro* for listings. The town's gay-ish neighborhood is 9th and 9th (900 South and 900 East); **Coffee Garden** (Map p481; ☎ 801-355-3425; 898 S 900 East; ✆ 6am-11pm) is the neighborhood café. Play pool and drink beer at **Club Try-Angles** (Map p481; ☎ 801-362-3203; 215 W 900 South) or at the **Trapp** (Map p481; ☎ 801-531-8727; 102 S 600 West). **Paper Moon** (Map p481; ☎ 801-713-0678; 3737 S State St) is a lesbian club.

---

days mean different music – top 40, house or indie-electric.

LIVE MUSIC & THEATER

September through November and January through May, the **Mormon Tabernacle Choir** (☎ tickets 435-570-0080; www.mormontabernaclechoir .org) rehearsals, open to the public, are held in Temple Square's Tabernacle (p482) from 8pm to 9pm Thursdays. You can attend organ recitals here daily (at noon Monday through Saturday, 2pm Sunday) and listen to the choir broadcast in person on Sunday (arrive by 9am). The other months of the year (June to August and December), performances are held at the 21,000-seat Conference Center (p482). Performance times stay the same, except that an extra Monday-to-Saturday organ recital begins at 2pm.

Also in Temple Square, Assembly Hall (p482) holds national and international concerts on Friday and Saturday evenings. The schedule's available online.

The **Salt Lake City Arts Council** (☎ 801-596-5000; www.slcgov.com/arts) has a complete cultural-events calendar, which lists theater, dance, opera, symphony and free outdoor concerts. Primary venues include the historic **Capitol Theater** (Map p483; ☎ 801-355-2787; 50 W 200 South), dramatic **Rose Wagner Performing Arts Center** (Map p483; 138 W 300 South) and acoustically rich **Abravanel Hall** (Map p483; ☎ 801-533-6683; 123 W South Temple St). For tickets call **ArtTix** (☎ 801-355-2787; 888-451-2787; www.arttix.org).

In summer, bring a picnic to the outdoor concert and movie series at the **Gallivan Center** (Map p483; ☎ 801-535-6110; www.thegallivancenter.com; 200 South, btwn State & Main Sts), an amphitheater in a garden.

SPORTS

Utah Jazz (☎ 801-325-2500; www.nba.com/jazz), the men's professional basketball team, plays at the **Energy Solutions Arena** (Map p483; ☎ 801-325-7328; www.energysolutionsarena.com; 301 W South Temple St), where concerts are also held. The International Hockey League's **Utah Grizzlies** (☎ 801-988-7825; www.utahgrizzlies.com) plays at the **E Center** (Map p481; ☎ 801-988-8888; www.theecenter.com; 3200 S Decker Lake Dr, West Valley City), which hosted most of the men's ice hockey competitions during the Olympics.

Franklin Covey Field (Map p481; ☎ 801-485-3800; 77 W 1300 South) hosts the **Salt Lake Bees** (☎ 801-325-2273; www.slbees.com) baseball team, the AAA minor-league affiliate of the Anaheim Angels.

Shopping

Look for artists' studios, indie boutiques and second hand stores in SLC's warehouse district (around Pierpont Ave, between 300 and 400 West).

Gateway (Map p483; ☎ 801-456-0000; www.shopthe gateway.com; 200 South to 50 North, 400 West to 500 West) Major-label shopping is right downtown at this diverse indoor-outdoor mall.

For local artists' work, head to **Utah Artist Hands** (Map p483; ☎ 801-355-0206; 61 W 100 South) or **Red Kiln Pottery & Gallery** (Map p481; ☎ 801-484-4016; 393 E 1700 South; ✆ noon-6pm Mon-Sat).

Getting There & Away

AIR

Salt Lake City International Airport (Map p481; ☎ 801-575-2400; www.slcairport.com) is 6 miles west of downtown.

BUS

Greyhound (Map p483; ☎ 801-355-9579; www.greyhound .com; 160 W South Temple St) has several daily buses south through St George ($50, five hours) to Las Vegas, NV ($59, 8½ hours). Destinations within Utah are limited.

UTA (☎ 801-743-3882, 888-743-3882; www.rideuta .com) buses go to Provo, Tooele, Ogden and other Wasatch Front–area cities and suburbs ($4); during the ski season it serves the four local resorts and Sundance, near Provo (all $8 round-trip).

TRAIN

The *California Zephyr* stops daily at the **Amtrak station** (Map p483; ☎ 801-322-3510, 800-872-7245; www.amtrak.com; 340 S 600 West) en route between Oakland, CA ($68, 18 hours) and Chicago

---

THE GREAT SALT LAKE

The Great Salt Lake is the largest body of water west of the Great Lakes. It's hard to say just how big it is. Since 1873 the lake has varied from 900 to 2500 sq miles. Maximum depths have ranged from 24ft to 45ft – it's wide and shallow, like a plate. Spring runoff raises levels; summer's sweltering heat lowers them. Evaporation is why the lake is so salty, but its salinity varies drastically, from 6% to 27% (compared with only 3.5% for seawater), depending on location and weather.

Prehistoric variations in lake levels were much greater. Sixteen thousand years ago this was part of Lake Bonneville, which was 900ft higher and covered almost 20,000 sq miles. Then it burst through Red Rock Pass and drained into the Snake River (in present-day Idaho), dropping 350ft. Today's lake, a puddle by comparison, receded to its present size 8000 years ago. Look at the mountains and you'll see terraces marking the ancient levels etched into the skirts of the Wasatch Front, about 900ft and 550ft above present lake levels.

The Great Salt Lake is a Unesco World Heritage Site for its importance to millions of migratory birds. The height of the fall and spring migrations are not-to-be-missed wildlife pageants. The best place to see the lake (and the birds) is at Antelope Island State Park (below).

($130, 35 hours). Green River ($31, 4½ hours) and Denver, CO ($119, 18 hours) are stops.

Getting Around
TO/FROM THE AIRPORT
Express Shuttle (☎ 800-397-0773; www.xpressshuttle .com) will take you from the airport to a downtown hotel for $7. **UTA** (☎ 801-743-3882, 888-743-3882; www.rideuta.com; one way $1.75) bus 550 travels downtown from the parking garage between Terminals 1 and 2.

CAR & MOTORCYCLE
National rental agencies have city and airport offices; see p537.

Rugged Rental (Map p481; ☎ 801-977-9111, 800-977-9111; www.ruggedrental.com; 2740 W California Ave) specializes in 4WDs and SUVs, but also has passenger cars. Rates are often better here than at the majors.

PUBLIC TRANSPORTATION
UTA (☎ 801-743-3882, 888-743-3882; www.rideuta .com; one way $1.75) buses serve Salt Lake City and the Wasatch Front area from 5am until about 11pm (limited service Saturday and Sunday). TRAX, UTA's light-rail system, runs east from the Delta Center to the university; a second suburban line runs south to Sandy. The center of downtown Salt Lake is a free-fare zone.

TAXI
Yellow Cab (☎ 801-521-2100) is a 24-hour taxi service.

ANTELOPE ISLAND STATE PARK
White-sand beaches, birds and buffalo are what attract people to the pretty, 15-mile-long **Antelope Island State Park** (☎ 801-773-2941; http://stateparks.utah.gov; per car $9; ◷ 7am-10pm May-Sep, 7am-7pm Oct-Apr). That's right, the largest island in the Great Salt Lake is home to a 600-strong herd of American bison, or buffalo. The **November roundup**, for veterinary examination, is a thrilling wildlife spectacle. And then there are the hundreds of thousands of migratory birds that descend on the park to feast on tiny brine shrimp along the Great Salt Lake's shore en route to distant lands during fall (September to November) and spring (March to May) migrations. The island is a year-round home to burrowing owls and raptors as well as namesake antelope, bighorn sheep and deer.

Nineteen miles of **hiking trails** provide many opportunities to view wildlife; however, some trails are closed during mating and birthing seasons. Rangers lead hikes and star parties from the **visitor center** (◷ 9am-5pm). At the end of an 11-mile paved road, several short nature trails lead off from **Fielding Garr Ranch**. There's also a small marina and a simple **restaurant** (☎ 801-776-6734; ◷ lunch & dinner May-Sep). There's also a small marina and simple restaurant on the island.

Bridger Bay Campground (☎ 800-322-3770; camp-sites $13) has water and pit toilets. The white, sandy **beach** nearby has showers and flushing toilets that both swimmers (more like floaters with all that salt) and campers use.

To get to the park (25 miles north of Salt Lake City, 10 miles south of Ogden), head west from I-15 exit 335 and follow the signs; a 7-mile causeway leads to the island.

BRIGHAM CITY & AROUND

pop 17,100 / elev 4315 ft

Drive north on I-15 from Salt Lake City, past Ogden (p506), a gateway to the Wasatch Mountains ski resorts, and after 50 miles you'll get to the turnoff for Brigham City. People come from all over Utah to eat steak here, but the area also has a few natural attractions. The stretch of Hwy 89 south of town is known as the 'Golden Spike Fruitway' – from July through September it is crowded with fruit stands vending the abundant local harvest. Contact **Box Elder County Tourism** (☎ 435-734-2634; www.boxelder.org) for area information. The old Mormon town is pretty small, but the 1896 **Tabernacle** (☎ 435-723-5376; 251 S Main St; admission free; 9am-9pm May-Oct), with 16 spires, is considered one of Utah's finest.

West of town, the **Bear River Migratory Bird Refuge** (☎ 435-723-5887; www.fws.gov/bearriver; W Forest St; admission free, dawn-dusk) engulfs almost 74,000 acres of marshes on the northeastern shores of the Great Salt Lake. The best time for bird-watchers is during fall (September to November) and spring (March to May) migrations. Birds banded here have been recovered as far away as Siberia and Colombia. Cruising along the 12-mile, barely elevated touring road feels like you're driving on water. You can hear the replicated migratory calls year round at the **Wildlife Education Center** (☎ 435-734-6426; 2155 W Forest St; admission free; 8am-5pm). The center is just after the I-15 intersection; the driving tour is 16 miles west.

Get into hot water year-round at **Crystal Hot Springs** (☎ 435-279-8104; www.crystalhotsprings.net; 8215 N Hwy 38; adult/child $6/5, slides $10; 10am-10pm Jun-Aug, noon-7pm Sep-May), 10 miles north in Honeyville. Adults float in different temperature soaking pools while kids zip down the water slides (open shorter hours than the pools November through February). Camping at RV/tent sites is $25/15.

Brigham city is an easy day trip from Salt Lake, but you could also stay over at the family-run **Howard Johnson Inn** (☎ 435-723-8511, 800-446-4656; www.hojo.com; 1167 S Main St; r $50-70; wi-fi). It's the closest lodging to *the* place to eat in town, **Maddox Ranch House** (☎ 435-723-8545, 800-544-5474; 1900 S Hwy 89; mains $18-30; 11am-9:30pm Tue-Sat). People travel for hours to get one of Maddox' thick beef or bison steaks cut from locally raised livestock since 1949. You can still see the ranch out back where they started in the cattle business. Pay extra to get shrimp on your complimentary seafood cocktail appetizer and be sure to try the raspberry butter on the homemade bread. Even if you go early, expect to wait.

LOGAN & AROUND

pop 42,700 / elev 4775ft

Logan is a quintessential old-fashioned American community with strong Mormon roots. It's situated 80 miles north of Salt Lake City in bucolic Cache Valley, which offers year-round outdoor activities. Get oriented at the **Cache Valley Tourist Council** (☎ 435-752-2161, 800-882-4433; www.tourcachevalley.com; 160 N Main St; 9am-5pm Mon-Fri). Pick up a free interpretive booklet there before you head off on the 40-mile drive through **Logan Canyon** (Hwy 89 to Garden City on Bear Lake); it's beautiful year

DETOUR: THE REMOTE NORTHWEST

On May 10, 1869, the westward Union Pacific Railroad and eastward Central Pacific Railroad met at Promontory Summit. With the completion of the transcontinental railroad, the face of the American West changed forever. **Golden Spike National Historic Site** (☎ 435-471-2209; www.nps.gov/gosp; per car $7; 9am-5pm), 32 miles northwest of Brigham City on Hwy 83, has an interesting museum and films, auto tours and several interpretive trails. Steam engine demonstrations take place June through August. Aside from Golden Spike National Historic Site, few people visit Utah's desolate northwest corner. But while you're here…

At the end of a dirt road (4WD recommended but not required), 15 miles west of the Golden Spike visitor center, there's a wonderfully unique outdoor art installation, the **Spiral Jetty** (www.spiraljetty.org). Created by Robert Smithson in 1970, it's a 1500ft coil of rock and earth spinning out into the water. It's a little hard to find; get directions from the visitor center.

round, but spring wildflowers (July) and fall foliage (October) are particularly brilliant.

Along the way through the mountains and up dugways, there are signposted **hiking** and **biking** trails, and campgrounds such as the 35-site **Tony Grove Lake** (☎ reservations 877-444-6777; www.recreation.gov; campsites $15), with its tight and winding roads (not good for long trailers), big trees and wildflower meadows.

A 19th-century frontier community comes to life with hands-on activities at the **American West Heritage Center** (☎ 435-245-6050; www.awhc.org; 4025 S Hwy 89; adult/child $7/5; ☺ 10am-5pm Tue-Sat Jun-Aug; ⓐ), south of town. The center hosts the popular weeklong **Festival of the American West** in July, a must for frontier buffs and great for families.

Chain motels are well represented on Hwy 89. Families are welcome at the comfy **Seasons at the Riter Mansion** (☎ 435-752-7727, 800-478-7459; http://theritermansion.com; 168 N 100 East; r incl breakfast $99-150; wi-fi) B&B, where whirlpool tubs and fireplaces come standard. **Beaver Creek Lodge** (☎ 435-946-3400, 800-946-4485; www.beavercreeklodge .com; Mile 487, Hwy 89; r $99-139) in Logan Canyon offers horseback riding and snowmobiling packages. No room phones.

For all-round American food, try **Angie's Restaurant** (☎ 435-752-9252; 690 N Main St; breakfast & sandwiches $4-8; mains $8-12; ☺ breakfast, lunch & dinner). **Caffe Ibis** (☎ 435-753-4777; 52 Federal Ave; sandwiches $3-6; ☺ 8am-4pm) serves gourmet coffees and sandwiches.

BONNEVILLE SALT FLATS

Millennia ago, ancient Lake Bonneville covered northern Utah and beyond. Today all that remains is the Great Salt Lake and 46 sq miles of shimmering white salt. The Bonneville Salt Flats are public lands managed by the **BLM** (☎ 801-977-4300; www.blm.gov/ut/st/en/ fo/salt_lake/recreation/bonneville_salt_flats.html). The surface you see is mostly made up of sodium chloride (common table salt) and is 12ft deep in spots (though officials are worried about shrinkage and have started salt reclamation efforts). Driving up to the flats, about 100 miles east of SLC, is a singular optical experience. The vast whiteness tricks the eye into believing it's snowed in August, and the inexpressible flatness allows many to see the Earth's curvature here.

You may recognize the flats from numerous movies, such as *Con Air* and *Independence Day*, that have been filmed in part here, but they're most well known for racing. On October 15, 1997, Englishman Andy Green caused a sonic boom on the salt flats by driving the jet-car *ThrustSSC* to 763.035mph, setting the first ever supersonic world land-speed record. The flat, hard salt makes this possible here like nowhere else. Several clubs hold racing events throughout the year; for a complete list, check the BLM website.

To get here, take exit 4, Bonneville Speedway, off I-80 and follow the paved road to the viewing area parking lot (no services). From here you can drive on the hard-packed salt during late summer and fall (it's too wet otherwise). Obey posted signs: parts of the flats are thin and can trap vehicles. Remember, salt is insanely corrosive. If you drive on the flats, wash your car – especially the undercarriage – afterward. If you're traveling west, there's an additional rest stop where you can walk on the sand (and wash off your shoes in the bathroom).

WENDOVER
pop 1500 / elev 4232 ft

Straddling the Utah–Nevada state line near Bonneville Salt Flats, Wendover is actually two sharply contrasting municipalities: on one side are the prosperous Nevada suburbs and casinos, while in upright Utah the run-down homes and businesses struggle to survive. Except to wash your car, or stop over if you must, there's little reason to spend long in town. For more about casinos (which all have several restaurants), contact the **Nevada Welcome Center** (☎ 775-664-3138, 866-299-2489; www .westwendovercity.com; 937 W Wendover Blvd; ☺ 9am-5pm Mon-Fri). The **Days Inn** (☎ 435-665-2215; www.daysinn .com; 685 E Wendover Blvd; ⓐ wi-fi), in Utah, is a nice, newish, interior-access chain motel. Go to Nevada to eat.

WASATCH MOUNTAINS

Giant saw-toothed peaks stand guard along the eastern edge of Utah's urban centers. When the crush of civilization gets too much, locals escape to the forested slopes. The Wasatch Mountain Front is nature's playground all year long, but in winter a fabulous low-density, low-moisture snow – 300in to 500in of it a year – blankets the terrain. Perfect snow and thousands of acres of high-altitude slopes helped earn Utah the honor of hosting the 2002 Winter Olympics. The skiing

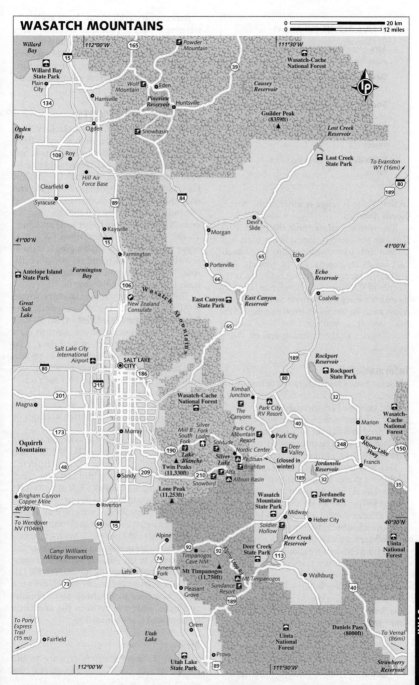

WASATCH MOUNTAINS

TOP FIVE ALPINE SKI AREAS

- **Alta** (right) The quintessential Utah ski experience.
- **Deer Valley** (p501) Impeccable grooming, incredible service.
- **Snowbird** (p496) Mind-blowing steeps and vast bowls.
- **Snowbasin** (p506) Utah's best-kept secret.
- **Solitude** (p497) Lives up to its name.

---

in the Wasatch range is some of the best in North America.

Resort towns cluster near the peaks; Park City, on the eastern slopes, is the most well known and quasi-cosmopolitan of the bunch. Salt Lake City resorts, on the western side, are easiest for townies to reach. Ogden is the sleeper of the bunch and Sundance is known as much for its film festival as its ski trails. Most areas lie within 45 to 60 minutes of the SLC airport, so you can leave New York or Los Angeles in the morning and be skiing by noon.

Information

Ski season runs mid-November to mid-April. Saturday is busiest; Sunday ticket sales drop by a third because LDS members are in church. Buses and shuttles are widely available, so you don't need to rent a car to reach most resorts. For Wasatch-wide ski information, contact **Ski Utah** (☎ 800-754-8724; www.skiutah.com).

Day lifts usually run from 9am to 4pm. Children's prices are good for ages six to 12; under sixes ski free. All resorts rent equipment (about $30 per day for ski or snowboard packages, $35 per day for a mountain bike). You may save a few bucks by renting off-mountain, but if there's a problem with the equipment, you're stuck. No pets are allowed at resorts and four-night minimum stays may be required December through March.

Advanced skiers looking for knock-your-socks-off adventure should definitely consider a backcountry **Ski Utah Interconnect Adventure Tour** (☎ 801-534-1907; www.skiutah.com/interconnect; ⏰ mid-Dec–mid-Apr). This guided, out-of-bounds tour allows you into six resorts in one day. The $195 price tag includes lunch, lift ticket and transportation.

Backcountry enthusiasts: heed avalanche warnings! Take a course at a resort, carry proper equipment and check conditions with the **Utah Avalanche Center** (☎ 801-524-4304; www .avalanche.org/~uac; ⏰ 4am–noon). For road conditions, dial ☎ 511. Drink plenty of fluids: dehydrated muscles injure easily.

SALT LAKE CITY RESORTS

The four resorts east of Salt Lake City sit at the end of two canyons, 30 to 45 miles from the downtown core. Because of Great Salt Lake–affected snow, SLC resorts receive almost twice as much snow as Park City. Follow Hwy 190 up to family-oriented Solitude and skier-dude fave Brighton in Big Cottonwood Canyon. In summer you can continue over the mountain from there to Heber and Park Cities. To the south, Little Cottonwood Canyon is home to the seriously challenging terrain at Snowbird and the all-round ski-purist special, Alta. Numerous summer hiking and biking trails lead off from both canyons.

The USFS offers ranger-led skiing programs at Alta, Brighton and Snowbird; contact the **Cottonwood Canyons Foundation** (☎ 801-947-8263; www.cottonwoodcanyons.org). If you want to ski a different SLC resort each of four days, a **Ski Salt Lake Super Pass** (www.visitsaltlake.com/ski_salt_lake; 4-day pass adult/child $208/120) may be worth your while. You get a day's lift pass for each resort and all your transportation on UTA ski buses and light rail in town. For lodging-skiing package deals, see www.visitsaltlake.com or contact resorts directly.

Reach the resorts for $6.50 round-trip via SLC's public transit system, **UTA** (☎ 801-743-3882; www.rideuta.com). Bus route 995 goes from the downtown core to Snowbird and Alta. Drop your car at the SLC **Ski Park & Ride** (Map p481; 6200 S Wasatch Blvd) lot and take bus 991 to Solitude and Brighton or bus 996 to Snowbird and Alta. Buses run between resorts in the same valley.

Alta Shuttle (☎ 435-274-0225, 866-274-0225; www .altashuttle.com; one way $30) will take you from the SLC airport to the Alta or Snowbird resorts. **Canyon Transportation** (☎ 801-255-1841, 800-255-1841; www.canyontransport.com; one way $34) does the same, also goes to Brighton and Solitude, and will shuttle you between Big and Little Cottonwood Canyons for $90.

Alta

Dyed-in-the-wool skiers pilgrimage to **Alta** (☎ 801-359-1078, 888-782-9258; www.alta.com; Little

Cottonwood Canyon; day lift pass adult/child $59/30). No snowboarders are allowed here, which keeps the snow cover from deteriorating, especially on groomers. Locals have grown up with Alta, a resort filled not with see-and-be-seen types, but rather the see-and-say-hello crowd. Wide-open powder fields, gullies, chutes and glades, such as **East Greeley**, **Devil's Castle** and **High Rustler**, have helped make Alta famous. Warning: you may never want to ski anywhere else.

The lowdown: 2020ft vertical drop, base elevation 8530ft; 2200 acres, 25% beginner, 40% intermediate, 35% advanced; three high-speed chairs, four fixed-grip chairs. You can ski from the Sunnyside lift for free after 3pm, which is great for families with little ones who tire easily (lifts close at 4:30pm). Get the $84 Alta-Snowbird pass, which permits access to both areas for a stunning 4700 acres of skiing. Expert powder hounds, ask about off-piste snow cat skiing.

No lifts run in the summer, but there are 10 miles of local trails. From July to August, **Albion Basin** is abloom with wildflowers. For help finding the peak blooms, call ☎ 888-258-2840.

The lodging options at Alta are like the ski area: simple and just as it's been for decades. Every place here has ski-in, ski-out access and a hot tub. Winter rates, as listed, include breakfast and dinner and require a four-night minimum stay. Lodge restaurants and snack bars are seasonal (December through March) and open to the public.

Sleep surrounded by July and August wildflowers at **Albion Basin Campground** (☎ reservations 877-444-6777; www.reserveamerica.gov; Little Cottonwood Canyon Rd; campsites $13; ☼ Jul-Sep). The 19 sites sit at 9500ft among meadows and pine trees, 11 miles up the canyon. Drinking water, no showers; no dogs allowed.

Granite-block-built **Snowpine Lodge** (☎ 801-742-2000; www.thesnowpine.com; dm $106, r per person with

---

LOCAL VOICES: SHANNON BAHRKE

Shortly after moving to Salt Lake City to attend college in 1998, Shannon Bahrke earned a spot on the US Freestyle Ski Team. She won an Olympic silver medal in moguls at the Salt Lake City Winter Olympics. Despite injuries, career to-date she's had seven World Cup wins and recently she cofounded Silver Bean Coffee Company (www.silverbeancoffee.com).

What did it feel like to win an Olympic medal? It's so funny, because every time I look at my medal, I'm like 'Oh my God, I won that!' To this day it still feels surreal. You know you have goals in life, and to accomplish anything great like that makes anything else seem OK. Any obstacle I have, or if I get scared, I think 'God, you won an Olympic medal, you can do anything.' It's been a really cool ride, and I've met a lot of amazing people. To have friends who are so passionate about what they do and have been really successful in their sport really means a lot.

How do you think where you live contributes? This is far and away the best place to live if you want to be a winter Olympian. One of the really cool things about the 2002 games is that they wanted to leave a legacy for athletes. So whether you are cross-country skiing or you are a speed skater, a freestyle aerialist or mogul skier, all those training facilities, the best in the world, are here. For the guys out at the Olympic Oval, it's the fastest ice on earth, and that's kind of a cool thing. We're surrounded by so many other athletes. I can watch the bobsledders and work out with those guys – nothing gets old. Days when you don't want to do it, you feed off their energy. Whenever you go to a party you never know who you're going to see. There are all these athletes in one room, just hanging out thinking nothing of each other. I don't think there's any place else like this in the US.

I've heard you're full of energy, on the go 24/7 year-round. What other kinds of non-winter sports do you enjoy? I enjoy living here so much because you can be in the city and then you can be up the side of the mountain hiking in not even 10 minutes. In the summertime we get up as early as possible to get everything in. But we hike and we bike, and we just got into car racing. Larry Miller built a new track. I'm really trying to get into that. We ride motorcycles...

It definitely sounds like you like adrenaline. I do! Pretty much everything I do is a little bit crazy.

Any advice your the young freestyle skiers coming up? In our sport we don't make very much money, so you've got to love what you do. That's really what it's all about. Kids need to understand that you've got to love it, you've got to have so much passion for it.

private bathroom $169-199, with shared bathroom $134-152), Alta's most basic, is the die-hard skier's first choice.

You'll likely see families with teenagers embarrassed by their parents at the sometimes-raucous, always-fun **Alta Peruvian** (☎ 801-742-3000, 800-453-8488; www.altaperuvian.com; dm $127, r per person with/without bathroom $179/138; 🐾 🖳 wi-fi). Spacious knotty-pine common areas (movies shown nightly) make up for the tiny rooms. The bar here has Alta's most happening après-ski scene.

Mid-century modernist **Alta Lodge** (☎ 801-742-3500, 800-707-2852; www.altalodge.com; dm $138, d $330-496, d without bathroom $301-332; 🐾 🖳 wi-fi) is frequented by Ivy Leaguers playing backgammon in the cozy attic bar (open to nonguests). Expect to make friends at family-style dinners in this simply comfortable Alta classic. None of the previous three lodges has TVs.

Enjoy all the creature comforts of a city hotel at **Rustler Lodge** (☎ 801-742-3333, 888-532-2582; www.rustlerlodge.com; dm $160, d $482-653, d without bathroom $315-410; 🐾 🖳 wi-fi). Take an early morning stretch class before you hit the slopes and refresh in the eucalyptus sauna afterwards.

Chef Curtis Kraus uses locally produced ingredients whenever possible on his seasonally changing menu at **Shallow Shaft Restaurant** (☎ 801-742-2177; 10199 E Hwy 210; mains $28-36; ⏰ dinner). In winter, pine nuts and quince flavor seafood and meats such as double-cut pork chops; in summer it may be fresh salsa. Midmountain try **Collin's Grill** (☎ 801-799-2297; Watson's Shelter, Angle Station; mains $8-15; ⏰ lunch) for homemade artisanal soups and breads (make reservations) and **Alf's** (☎ 801-799-2295; Cecret lift base; sandwiches $6-10; ⏰ 9:30am-4:30pm) for a burger and a look at the antique skis on the walls.

Snowbird

If you can see it, you can ski it at **Snowbird** (☎ 801-933-2222, 800-453-3000; www.snowbird.com; Little Cottonwood Canyon; day lift ticket adult/child $69/39), the industrial-strength resort with extreme steeps, long groomers, wide-open bowls (one of them an incredible 500 acres across) and a kick-ass terrain park. The challenging slopes are particularly popular with speed demons and testosterone-driven snowboarders. The 125-passenger aerial tram ascends 2900ft in only eight minutes; die-hards do 'tram laps,' racing back down the mountain to re-ascend in the same car they just rode up on. If you

like to ski like a teenager, you'll flip out when you see this mountain.

The lowdown: 3240ft vertical drop, base elevation 7760ft; 10 lifts, one tramway; 2500 acres, 27% beginner, 38% intermediate, 35% advanced. A conveyor-pull tunnel links the high-speed Peruvian Gulf quad lift and intermediate terrain in **Mineral Basin**. Wednesdays, Fridays and Saturdays, one lift remains open until 8:30pm for night skiing. Cliff Lodge has a slopeside ice skating rink. Skiers (not boarders) can get an $84 Alta-Snowbird pass, which permits access to both areas, for a total of 4700 skiable acres. Snowbird has the longest season of the four SLC resorts, with skiing usually possible mid-November to mid-May.

The resort is active year-round. In summer, the Peruvian lift and tunnel offer access to Mineral Basin hiking and wildflowers. You can take the tramway up to **Hidden Peak**, ride the luge-like **Alpine Slide**, **zipline** down 1000ft or mount a mechanical bull. An all-activities pass costs $36; horseback riding and ATV tours are available, too.

Good, though strenuous, hiking trails include the **White Pine Lake Trail** (10,000ft), which is just over 3 miles one way. Watch rocky slopes around the lake for the unique pika, a small, short-eared, tailless lagomorph (the order of mammals that includes rabbits). At the end of the canyon road is **Cecret Lake Trail**, an easy 1-mile loop with spectacular wildflowers (July and August).

Snowbird has four overnight accommodation lodges (and 15 eateries), all booked through the resort's central phone number and website; packages including lift tickets are available. In summer prices drop precipitously. The splashy black-glass-and-concrete 500-room **Cliff Lodge** (r $400-500; 🐾 🖳 wi-fi) is like a cruise ship in the mountains, with every possible destination-resort amenity, from flat-screen TVs to a full-service spa. (Choose 'spa level' rooms for unlimited access.) Check out the dramatic 10th-story glass-walled bar and the rooftop swimming pool. At the other end of the spectrum is **Inn at Snowbird** (r $199-400; 🐾 wi-fi), Snowbird's most homey and inviting property. Studio rooms have kitchens and wood-burning fireplaces. Bring groceries and save a bundle.

The 10th-floor **Aerie Restaurant** (☎ 801-933-2160; Cliff Lodge; mains $36-49; ⏰ breakfast & dinner Dec-Feb, dinner Mar-Nov) is worth a splurge. Look out through 15ft windows to spectacular mountain views while you're sampling pan-seared foie gras and prosciutto-wrapped veal. Reservations are a must. The adjacent lounge has a full bar and sushi menu. The 3000-sq-ft deck at **Creekside Café & Grill** (☎ 801-933-2477; Gadzoom lift base; breakfast & sandwiches $6-10; ☺ breakfast & lunch Dec-Apr) is a great place to grab a sandwich slopeside.

Solitude

True to its name, you'll feel you've got the mountain to yourself at **Solitude** (☎ 801-534-1400; www.skisolitude.com; Big Cottonwood Canyon Rd; day lift ticket adult/child $55/34). It's like a great local secret – room to learn plus lots of speedy, roller-coaster-like corduroy to look forward to once you've gotten your ski legs. If you're an expert, you'll dig the cliff bands, gullies, over-the-head powder drifts and super-steeps at **Honeycomb Canyon**. But it's the attitude-free vibe that makes Solitude so cool: there are no corporate tie-ins, hardly any show-offs and practically nobody's here.

The lowdown: 2047ft vertical drop, base elevation 7988ft; 1200 acres; 8 lifts; 20% beginner, 50% intermediate, 30% advanced. Ask about helicopter skiing with **Wasatch Powderbird Guides** (☎ 801-742-2800; www.powderbird.com; per day from $525). North of the resort's base, Solitude's **Nordic Center** (☎ 801-536-5774; day pass adult/child $15/free; ☺ 11am-5pm Dec-Mar & Jun-Aug) has 12 miles of groomed classic and skating lanes and 6 miles of snowshoeing tracks through enchanting forests of aspen and pine. In summer the Nordic Center becomes a visitor center and the boardwalk encircling **Silver Lake** becomes the easiest child and mobility-impaired nature trail around. Ask about guided **owl-watching walks**.

June through August, the Sunrise lift (day pass $15) opens for chair-assist **mountain biking** and **hiking** from Wednesday through Sunday. You can also rent mountain bikes and motorized mountain scooters, and play disc (Frisbee) golf at the resort.

Many hiking trails leave from various trailheads along Hwy 190. Look for trailhead signs. One of the most attractive hikes is the 2-mile round-trip **Lake Blanche Trail**, beginning at the Mill B South Fork trailhead, about 5 miles into the canyon.

Book Solitude's on-mountain rooms through **central reservations** (☎ 800-748-4754; www.skisolitude.com), which often has packages that cut room rates by as much as 50%. Summer rates

are significantly lower. Of the four full-kitchen condo-lodge properties, the wood-and-stone **Creekside Lodge** (1-/2-bedroom condos $404/531; wi-fi) is closest to the slopes; rooms have wood-burning fireplaces and balconies. The Alpinesque **Inn at Solitude** (r $269-299; ☎ ☐ wi-fi) is the only hotel-style lodging; there's an on-site spa and hot tub. All accommodations share Club Solitude's heated outdoor pool, sauna, fitness room, games room and movie theater.

Cross-country ski or snowshoe by lantern light a mile into the woods for a sumptuous, but unpretentious, five-course dinner in a bona fide canvas **Yurt** (☎ 801-536-5709; www.skisolitude.com/yurt.cfm; dinner $75; ☺ 5:30pm Tue-Sun Dec-Mar). Bring your own wine and reserve way ahead. (Note: there's another yurt dinner at the Canyons in Park City, but this is the original and the best.)

Cozy up fireside at **St Bernard's** (☎ 801-535-4120; Inn at Solitude; breakfast buffet $14, mains $28-32; ☺ breakfast & dinner Dec-Mar) for an unexpectedly good French dinner, with wine pairing. **Stone Haus Pizzeria & Creamery** (The Village; pizzas $6-14; ☺ 7am-10pm Dec-Mar, 9am-9pm Apr-Nov) serves snacks and Starbucks year round. You can sip suds at the **Thirsty Squirrel** (The Village; ☺ 2-9pm Dec-Mar), but the Big Cottonwood Canyon's best après-ski and bar scene is at Brighton.

A great alternative to resort eating and drinking is the classic mountain roadhouse, **Silver Fork Lodge** (☎ 801-533-9977, 888-649-9551; www.silverforklodge.com; 11332 E Big Cottonwood Canyon; breakfast & sandwiches $6-10, mains $13-25; ☺ breakfast, lunch & dinner), a mile west of Solitude. The rustic dining room feels like a cozy log cabin with a crackling fireplace. In summer sit outside and watch hummingbirds buzz across gorgeous alpine scenery. Western furnishings outfit the twin, queen and bunk-bed rooms ($90 to $145, including breakfast); floors creak a little. In winter, warm up in the hot tub. Consider staying here instead of Salt Lake City, 11 miles down the canyon.

Brighton

Slackers, truants and bad-ass boarders rule **Brighton** (☎ 801-532-4731, 800-873-5512; www.brightonresort.com; Big Cottonwood Canyon Rd; day lift ticket adult/child $41/25), the mountain where many Salt Lake residents first learned to ski. The low-key resort remains a good first-timers' spot, especially if you want to snowboard. Thick stands of pines line sweeping groomed trails and wide boulevards, and from the top, the views are gorgeous. The whole place is a throwback: come for the ski-shack appeal coupled with high-tech slope improvements.

The lowdown: 1745ft vertical drop, base elevation 8755ft; 1050 acres, 21% beginner, 40% intermediate, 39% advanced; four high-speed chairs, four fixed-grip chairs. There's a half-pipe and terrain park, a liberal open-boundary policy on non-avalanche-prone days, and good night skiing (200 acres, 22 runs) until 9pm, Monday to Saturday. New for 2008: a magic carpet beginner slope lift (just step on and go) and the Milly Express high-speed quad, which means 100% of Brighton's terrain is now lift accessible.

The 20 bare-bones-basic rooms at **Brighton Lodge** (☎ 801-532-4731, 800-873-5512; www.bright onresort.com; dm $99, r $125-175) go quick; they're a good deal within spitting distance of the lifts. No room TVs, but there are more than 200 movies you can watch in the common room, or just sit by the fireplace after you've hot-tubbed it.

For après-ski drinks and pub grub, you gotta go to the A-frame right on the hill. **Molly Green's** (Brighton Manor; mains $5-11; ☺ lunch & dinner Dec-Mar) has a roaring fire, a gregarious old-school vibe and great slopeside views. It's a private club, so you'll need to pay a $5 'membership charge.' There's also a funky red bus snack bar in the parking lot.

Camp near the top of Big Cottonwood Canyon, 13 miles in, at 44-site **Redman Campground** (☎ reservations 877-444-6777; www.re serveamerica.gov; Big Cottonwood Canyon Rd; campsites $15; ☺ late Jun-Sep). Trails lead off to lakes from this creekside ground at 8500ft. No swimming, no dogs allowed; this is SLC's watershed. Water is available, but no showers.

PARK CITY
pop 7400 / elev 6900ft
It's hard to imagine that this one-time silver boomtown ever went bust. Today condos and multimillion-dollar mansions are popping up left, right and center at Utah's glitziest ski village. OK, it's no Jackson Hole, but there are more bars and liberal attitudes here than in the whole rest of Utah. And the skiing is incomparable, truly world class.

Park City skyrocketed to international fame when it hosted the downhill, jumping and sledding events at the 2002 Winter Olympics. The permanent home base for the US Ski Team, at one time or another most US win-

ter Olympians train at the three ski resorts and Olympic Park here. Winter (December through March) is high season, but come June, the town gears up for hiking and mountain biking in the peaks towering over town.

Century-old buildings line the one main street; they look particularly charming at nightfall after a new dusting of snow, when the twinkling lights outlining the eaves have been turned on. Shops are mostly of the tourist-crap variety, but restaurant chefs here are doing some really great things with food. Salt Lake is close by, but all you need to eat, play, drink and stay is right here in Park City.

Though the eastern front gets fewer inches per year than the western front of the Wasatch Mountains, there's usually snow from late November through mid-April. June to August, temperatures average in the 70s (°F); nights are chilly. Spring and fall can be wet and boring; resort services, limited in summer compared with winter, shut down entirely between seasons. Even some restaurants take extended breaks.

Orientation
Downtown is 5 miles south of I-80 exit 145, 32 miles east of SLC and 40 miles from the airport. Hwy 190 (closed October through March) crosses over Guardsman Pass between Big Cottonwood Canyon and Park City. Traffic can slow you down, especially on weekends. Bypass Main St by driving on Park Ave. Better yet, take a shuttle from the airport and use the comprehensive Park City bus system.

Information
The local weekly newspaper is *Park Record*. KRCL 96.5FM is the indie radio station with the best programming.
Alpine Cybercafé (☎ 435-649-0051; 748 Main St; ☺ 7am-10pm) Comfy couches, coffee and internet for $9 per hour.
Dolly's Bookstore (☎ 435-649-8062; 510 Main St)
Library (☎ 435-615-5600; 1255 Park Ave; ☺ 10am-9pm Mon-Thu, 10am-6pm Fri & Sat, 1-5pm Sun) Free internet access.
Local police (☎ 435-615-5500; 445 Marsac Ave)
Park City Family Health & Emergency Center (☎ 435-649-7640; 1665 Bonanza Dr) Urgent care and 24-hour emergency room.
Post office (☎ 435-649-9191; 450 Main St)
Visitor Information Center (☎ 800-453-1360; www .parkcityinfo.com) Main St Mall (☎ 435-615-9559; 333 Main St; ☺ 11am-7pm Mon-Sat, noon-5pm Sun); Kimball

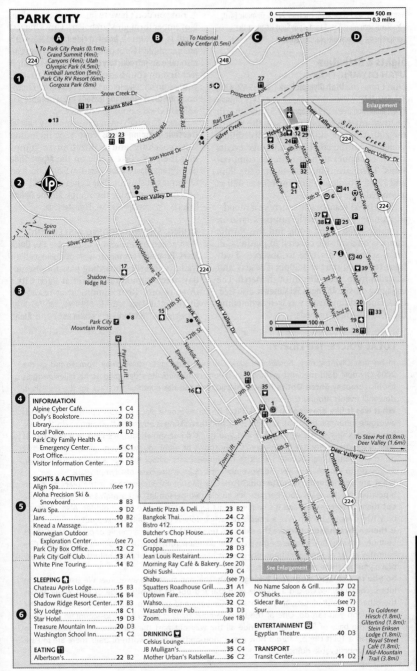

PARK CITY

Junction (☎ 435-658-9616; cnr Hwy 224 & Olympic Blvd; ☯ 9am-5pm Mon-Sat, 11am-4pm Sun) Request the comprehensive vacation-planner booklet.

Sights & Activities

UTAH OLYMPIC PARK

Don't miss the **Utah Olympic Park** (☎ 435-658-4200, 866-659-7275; www.utaholympicpark.com; 3419 Olympic Pkwy; admission free; ☯ 9am-6pm), 4.5 miles north of town off Hwy 224. This was the site of the 2002 Olympic ski jumping, bobsledding, skeleton, Nordic combined and luge events and it continues to host national competitions. There are 10m, 20m, 40m, 64m, 90m and 120m Nordic ski-jumping hills as well as a bobsled-luge run.

The US Ski Team practices here year round – in summer, the freestyle jumpers land in a bubble-filled jetted pool, and the Nordic jumpers on a hillside covered in plastic. Call for a schedule; it's free to observe. Two-hour **tours** ($25) start at 1:30pm Tuesday and Saturday from December through March. The engaging on-site **Alf Engen Ski Museum**, also free, traces local skiing history as well as detailing the 2002 Olympic records.

But you don't have to just watch the action: November through March, Park City's biggest thrill is an 80mph **bobsled ride** (adult $200) with an incredible 4Gs of centrifugal force. You can also take an **introductory class** and sail at 60mph feet first on your back (luge) or head first on your stomach (skeleton) for $150 each. Three-hour **Nordic ski-jumping lessons** are available for $85. BYO skis; book in advance.

June through August, one-day **aerial freestyle-jumping camps** cost $85, including skis, coaching and a dozen-or-so jumps into the pool. Take a ride on the **Alpine Slide** ($65; ☯ noon-4pm Tue-Sat, 11am-4pm Sun), a de-iced Olympic bobsled run. For a cheaper thrill, clip on a harness and ride the 50mph **Xtreme Zipline** (ride $25; ☯ noon-4pm Tue-Sat, 11am-4pm Sun).

SKIING, SNOWBOARDING & SLEDDING

Plan ahead online and you can use the **Quick Start Program** (www.parkcityinfo.com/quickstart) to trade your airline boarding pass for a same-day, free afternoon lift ticket at Park City's three resorts. Rent equipment at resorts or in town at **Jans** (☎ 435-649-4949, 800-745-1020; www.jans.com; 1600 Park Ave; ☯ 8am-9pm) and **Aloha**

LOCAL VOICES: TED LIGETY

In his first Olympic race, hometown Park City boy Ted Ligety came away from Torino as the 2006 Olympic gold medalist in downhill slalom combined. He's designed some killer goggles for his company **Shred Optics** (www.shredoptics.com) and has continued to rack up the medals in downhill events around the world.

What was it like growing up in Park City? It's an awesome place to grow up. There's so much awesome mountain biking all summer long, and then skiing is obviously the thing to do. If you're here in Park City in the winter time and you don't ski or snowboard, it's kind of a faux pas. It basically snows every day in January. It only snows at night too, with very sunny days. I didn't go to the normal high school; I went to the inner-sports school that has a reverse school year, so you go to school from April to November. It's right at the base of Olympic Park.

What are your specific favorite runs? Park City [Mountain] Jupiter chair is the place to be on a powder day. It's really cool because it's an old two-person lift, not a high-speed quad. You're out there powder skiing and it's so raw; it just feels right for it to be an old lift. Also, since it's only two people you can take a couple of runs before it gets totally tracked out.

Is there a local hangout where the ski team unwinds? There are a couple of places. The Celsius Lounge; actually one of the ex-guys on the ski team runs that. Also, O'Shucks is a Park City mainstay as far as the bar community goes. It has schooners that I'd say hold three beers. Every place you go, there are tons of skiers.

So you're also into mountain biking? Yeah, the trail system is awesome. We usually do big loops. This summer we did a 70-mile loop starting out on the other side of I-80, came across the other side of Park City, then across the Canyons and back out past the highway. That's the kind of loop you can do. One of the more famous trails is called the Mid-Mountain Trail. You start at the base of Silver Lake and ride all the way out past the Canyons; you're never doing more than a 100ft climb. I forget how many thousands of miles worth of trails there are in Park City. It's unbelievable riding.

Precision Ski & Snowboard (☎ 877-222-7600; www
.aloahskirentals.com; Lodge at Resort Center, Park City
Mountain; ☉ 7:30am-9pm).

Deer Valley

Want to be pampered? **Deer Valley** (☎ 435-649-
1000, 800-424-3337; www.deervalley.com; Deer Valley Dr;
day lift ticket adult/child $79/47, round-trip gondola ride
$15), a resort of superlatives, has thought of
everything, from tissue boxes at the base
of slopes to ski valets. Slalom, mogul and
freestyle-aerial competitions in the 2002
Olympics were held here, but the resort is
most famous for superb dining, white-glove
service and uncrowded slopes as meticulously
groomed as the gardens of Versailles. Every
trail follows the fall line perfectly, which
means you'll never skate a single cat-track.
Only a prescribed number of daily lift tickets
is sold, so powder hounds can find hundreds
of acres of untracked glades and steeps, days
after a storm.

The lowdown: 3000ft vertical drop, base elevation 6570ft; 2026 acres, 27% beginner, 41%
intermediate, 32% advanced; one high-speed
gondola, 11 high-speed quads, 10 fixed-grip
chairs. Two hundred acres of new terrain (65
acres of which is gladed), and a high-speed
quad lift to access it, opened for 2008. There's
no snowboarding allowed here.

Park City Mountain Resort

From boarder dudes to moms and dads, everyone skis **Park City Mountain Resort** (☎ 435-649-
8111, 800-222-7275; www.parkcitymountainresort.com; 1310
Lowell Ave; day lift ticket adult/child $79/50; ♿), host of
the Olympic snowboarding and giant slalom
events. The awesome terrain couldn't be more
accessible, rising right over downtown, or
more family-friendly. The resort will hook
teens up with area locals who provide the lay
of the land. Check out the online activity plan-
ner at www.mymountainplanner.com.

The lowdown: 3100ft vertical drop, base
elevation 6900ft; 3300 acres, 17% beginner,
50% intermediate, 33% advanced; six high-
speed lifts, nine fixed-grip chairs, one magic
carpet. To avoid crowds, stay up high. Night
skiing lasts till 7:30pm.

Park City's skiable area covers nine peaks,
ranging from groomers to wide-open bowls
(750 acres of them!) to cotton-mouth-
inducing super steeps. Experts: make a beeline
to **Mount Jupiter**; the best open trees are in the
Black Forest. For untracked powder, hike up

Pinecone Ridge. Test your aerial technique on
an Olympic-worthy boarding and freestyle
course at four amazing terrain parks; there's
also a huge superpipe.

Gorgoza Park

Lift-served snow tubing takes place at Park
City Mountain's **Gorgoza Park** (☎ 435-658-2648;
www.parkcitymountain.com; 3863 West Kilby Rd, at I-80; 4hr
adult/child 6 & under $27/14; ☉ 1-8pm Nov-Mar; ♿), 8
miles north of town, off I-80. Plunge down
three beginner or four advanced lanes; for
kids under 12 there's a **miniature snowmobile
track** (per ride $9), and for littler ones the **Fort Frost
play area** (admission $6) with carousel. The Park
City Mountain Resort–wide **shuttle** (☎ 435-645-
9388) will take you out there.

The Canyons

More than $10 million has been invested in
the **Canyons** (☎ 435-649-5400; www.thecanyons.com;
4000 Canyons Resort Dr; day lift ticket adult/child $79/46)
during the past few years. Consequently its
identity is evolving, too. The 152 runs include varied terrain for all levels, with wide
groomers for beginners and intermediates.
Experts: head to **Ninety-nine Ninety**. There's a
liberal open-boundary policy (heed avalanche
warnings) as well as six natural half-pipes,
one of them a whopping mile long, perfect
for boarding. The resort sprawls across eight
aspen-covered peaks, and has lots of freshies
on a powder day. A nasty skirmish with neighbors means you should avoid skiing through
the area marked on maps as 'the Colony,'
part of a residential community. **Dogsledding,
cross-country skiing** and **geo-caching treasure hunts**
are also available.

The lowdown: 3190ft vertical drop, base
elevation 6800ft; 3700 acres, 14% beginner,
44% intermediate, 42% advanced; one high-
speed gondola, five high-speed chairs, seven
fixed-grip chairs. The resort is 4 miles outside
of town, close to the freeway. On Saturday,
when Park City Mountain Resort is teeming
with people, you'll find more shoulder room
here. On weekends in summer and winter,
live-music concerts rock the base area. If you
want to set up a home base at the mountain,
the resort is booming with new development,
but it's more fun to stay in town.

CROSS-COUNTRY SKIING

White Pine Touring (☎ 435-649-8710; www.whitepine
touring.com; 1790 Bonanza Dr; day pass adult/child $18/8)

grooms a 12-mile cross-country course (rental available), with 2-, 3- and 6-mile loops of classic and skating lanes. The Canyons also has cross-country skiing opportunities.

SNOWMOBILING

Park City Snowmobile Adventures (☎ 435-645-7256, 800-303-7256; www.rockymtnrec.com) leads snowmobile tours from Park City Mountain, and **All Seasons Adventures** (☎ 435-649-9619; www .allseasonsadventures.com) starts at the Canyons. A one-hour ride will cost you about $85; book ahead.

SUMMER ACTIVITIES

You'll feel on top of the world in the peaks over Park City, where over 300 miles of trails crisscross the mountains. The visitor center has trail maps. One of the best for mountain biking is the 15-mile one-way **Mid-Mountain Trail**, which follows the topography at 8000ft, connecting Deer Valley to Olympic Park. You can also start at Park City Mountain, bike the steep **Spiro Trail** up to Mid-Mountain, then return on roads for a 22-mile loop. **Rail Trail** is an easy, near-town bike ride. Rent bikes at the resorts, or with **Jans** (☎ 435-649-4949, 800-745-1020; www.jans.com; 1600 Park Ave) or **White Pine Touring** (☎ 435-649-8710; www.whitepinetouring.com; 1790 Bonanza Dr). Both have guided rides (about $120 for three hours) as well.

Take a hike with **Norwegian Outdoor Exploration Center** (☎ 435-649-5322, 800-649-5322; www.outdoorcenter.org; 333 Main St Mall), a nonprofit educational guide service supporting at-risk youths. It leads terrific wildflower and backcountry tours for about $20 per person, as does White Pine Touring.

In summer, **Deer Valley** (☎ 435-649-1000; www .deervalley.com; Deer Valley Dr; per lift ride $8-15; ☺ 10am-5:30pm Jun-Aug) has 50 miles of hiking and biking trails served by its two operating lifts.

Park City Mountain Resort (☎ 435-649-8111; www .parkcitymountainresort.com; 1310 Lowell Ave; per lift ride $8; ☺ 10:30am-5pm Jun-Aug) has lift-served biking and hiking via the Town Lift. It also operates a 3000ft-long **alpine slide**, where a wheeled sled flies down 550ft in height along a cement track ($10). And it has a super-long **zipline ride** (2300ft long, 550ft vertical; $20). Not tired yet? Check out its **climbing wall, miniature golf course** and **kids' playground**.

The **Canyons** (☎ 435-649-5400; www.thecanyons .com; 4000 Canyons Resort Dr; gondola ride adult/child $12/6; ☺ 10am-4pm Jul & Aug) runs its gondola in summer for scenic rides, mountain biking and hiking.

HORSEBACK RIDING

Park City Stables (☎ 435-645-7256; www.rockymtn rec.com) leads trail rides into the mountains from Park City Mountain; **All Seasons Adventures** (☎ 435-649-9619; www.allseasonsadventures. com) starts at the Canyons. A one-hour ride costs about $50.

The nonprofit **National Ability Center** (NAC; ☎ 435-649-3991; www.nac1985.org; 1000 Ability Way) runs a year-round adapted sports program for people with disabilities and their families; the facilities, trails and lessons are also open to the nondisabled public. Horseback riding is the most popular program; call for details on others, including skiing, rafting, climbing and biking. NAC is the world leader in recreational therapy; its headquarters are in Park City.

HOT-AIR BALLOONING

Sunrise hot-air ballooning rides cost $200 per person; look for internet specials at **Park City Balloon Adventures** (☎ 435-645-8787, 800-396-8787; www.pcballoonadventures.com) and **Morning Star Balloons** (☎ 435-608-7433, 877-685-8555; www.morning starballoons.com).

GOLF

Because the ball flies so far in the thin air at 7000ft, they call it 'ego golfing' at **Park City Golf Club** (☎ 435-615-5800; www.parkcity.org; 1541 Park Ave).

SPAS & MASSAGE

When you've overdone it on the slopes, a spa treatment may be just what the doctor ordered (60-minute massage about $85). Stein Eriksen

---

DETOUR: MIRROR LAKE HWY

A breathtaking alpine route, Mirror Lake Hwy (Hwy 150) begins in Kamas, about 12 miles east of Park City, and covers 65 miles as it climbs to elevations of more than 10,000ft. Along the way into Wyoming, the road passes picture-perfect, beautiful vistas of the western Uinta Mountains and scores of lakes, campgrounds and trailheads. Contact the **Kamas Ranger Station** (☎ 435-783-4338; 50 E Center St, Kamas; ☺ 8am-4:30pm Mon-Fri) for information on the Wasatch-Cache National Forest.

GETTING INTO SUNDANCE FILM FESTIVAL

In late January, the two-week festival takes over both Park City and Sundance Resort completely. Films screen not just there but at venues in Salt Lake City and Ogden as well. Room rates soar across the Wasatch front, and all available space is snapped up months in advance. Tickets for film screenings ($15) are similarly difficult to get. You reserve a timeslot to purchase online at www.sundance.org/festival, starting in December (sign up for text message announcements). You then call during your appointed hour to reserve tickets, but there are no guarantees. Note that seats may be a little easier to secure during week two (week one is generally for the industry). Any remaining tickets are sold a few days ahead online and at the main **Park City Box Office** (Gateway Center, 136 Heber Ave; ✆ 8am-7pm mid-Jan–late Jan). If you don't succeed, do like the locals and go skiing. The slopes are remarkably empty during this two-week period.

Lodge (p504) has a swanky spa. Short on glitz but long on relaxation, **Align Spa** (☎ 435-647-9300; Shadow Ridge Resort Center, 50 Shadow Ridge Rd) has a down-to-earth Zen-like calm. Schedule energy-balancing chakra work after your rubdown at **Aura Spa** (☎ 435-658-2872; 405 Main St). **Knead a Massage** (☎ 435-615-8440; 875 Iron Horse Dr) has quiet, massage-only studios and reasonable prices.

Festivals & Events

Besides skiing, nothing has brought more attention to Park City than the **Sundance Film Festival** (☎ 801-328-3456; www.sundance.org/festival). In late January, the town becomes the premier showcase for independent film. For more, see the boxed text, above. In February, the 10-day-long **Winterfest** (☎ 435-649-6100) commemorates the 2002 Olympics, with concerts, competitions, ice-sculpture contests and other events. During ski season, major international competitions occur regularly at the resorts. See www.parkcityinfo.com.

Sleeping

Prices in this section are for ski season (mid-December through mid-April); Christmas and New Year's cost more, and off-season rates drop 50% or more. Packages that combine condo or hotel accommodations and lift tickets can be a good deal; check the ski resorts' websites. Unlike the other resorts, Park City Mountain has no directly associated hotel, but plenty are within walking distance.

Much of Park City lodging is in condominium complexes, where you at least get a kitchenette and space for extra people. Private Park City rentals are well represented at **Vacation Rental By Owner** (www.vrbo.com) and **Owner Direct** (www.ownerdirect.com). A full list of condo rentals is online at www.parkcityinfo.com; the following manage several properties:

Park City Travel & Lodging (☎ 801-487-1300, 800-421-9741; www.parkcitytravel.com)

ResortQuest (☎ 435-649-6606, 800-519-4764; www.parkcityski.com)

Resort Rentals of Utah (☎ 800-888-9875; www.resortrentalsofutah.com)

BUDGET

There's a dearth of budget lodging in Park City in winter. Consider staying down in Salt Lake.

Park City RV Resort (☎ 435-649-8935; www.parkcityrvresort.com; 2200 Rasmussen Rd; tent sites $20, RV sites $30-45; ☒ ☕ ☐ wi-fi) It's amenities galore (games room, playground, laundry, hot tub, fishing pond, kids' climbing wall…) at Park City's closest RV resort, 6 miles north of town at I-80.

Chateau Après Lodge (☎ 435-649-9372, 800-357-3556; www.chateauapres.com; 1299 Norfolk Ave; dm/d/tr $35/100/135; ☐ wi-fi) This old-fashioned alpine lodge, with cool common-area fire pit, is walking distance to Park City Mountain. Ragtag rooms here are the best deal going. Segregated dorms have 15 bunks each.

Star Hotel (☎ 435-649-8333; www.rixey.net/starhotel; 227 Main St; per person $95; wi-fi) The town's last remaining boarding house contains 11 small rooms with shared bathroom, sagging beds and creaky floors. Breakfast and dinner, whatever the 80-plus-year-old proprietor feels like fixing, is included. No parking on site.

MIDRANGE

Newpark Hotel (☎ 435-649-3600, 877-649-3600; www.newparkresort.com; r $145-225, 2br town homes $350-550; ☒ wi-fi) This new complex, adjacent to Swaner Nature Reserve near Kimball Junction, is open for business. Still to come (at the time of writing) is an attached retail and dining center.

Park City Peaks (☎ 435-649-5000, 800-333-3333; www.radisson.com/parkcityut; 2121 Park Ave; r $149-229;

wi-fi) Hobnob with junior bobsledders and other US team hopefuls who stay at this hotel between downtown and Olympic Park. December through April, breakfast is included with the cushy contemporary rooms.

our pick **Treasure Mountain Inn** (☎ 435-658-1417, 800-344-2460; www.treasuremountaininn.com; 255 Main St; studios $175, 1-/2-bedroom condos $225/350) Park City's first member of the Green Hotel Association, Treasure Mountain recycles, is committed to using wind energy, serves organic food in its breakfast restaurant and has replaced the old-fashioned, energy-sucking pool with a large efficient spa. Some of the studios and condos have fireplaces, all have kitchens and are decorated in earthy tones. Staying here at the top of Main St, where it's easy to use public transportation to get around, you can go green, too.

Old Town Guest House (☎ 435-649-2642, 800-290-6423; www.oldtownguesthouse.com; 1011 Empire Ave; r incl breakfast $189-229;) Grab the flannel robe, pick a paperback off the shelf and snuggle under a quilt on your lodgepole bed at this in-town B&B. Innkeeper Deb is a master skier who will give you the lowdown or guide tours (mountain biking, too).

Yet more options:

Shadow Ridge Resort Center (☎ 435-649-4300, 800-451-3031; www.shadowridgeresort.com; 50 Shadow Ridge Rd; r $152-257, condos $210-336;) A hundred yards from Park City Mountain lifts.

Best Western Landmark Inn (☎ 435-649-7300, 800-548-8824; www.bwlandmarkinn.com; 6560 N Landmark Dr, Kimball Junction; r $159-199; wi-fi) Save by staying near the freeway. Free skier shuttle.

Holiday Inn Express (☎ 435-658-1600, 888-465-4329; www.holidayinnexpress.com; 1501 W Ute Blvd, Kimball Junction; r incl breakfast $170-207; wi-fi) Multistory motel outside center.

TOP END

All three ski resorts have upscale condos; contact them directly. At this writing, a St Regis is underway at Deer Valley and a Waldorf-Astoria collection hotel at the Canyons. Rates bottom out off-season, putting the rarefied world within reach.

Goldener Hirsch (☎ 435-649-7770, 800-252-3373; www.goldenerhirschinn.com; 7570 Royal St; r incl breakfast $279-579;) You can tell the Goldener was fashioned after a lodge in Salzburg by the hand-painted Austrian furniture, feather-light duvets and European fireplaces. 'Stay & Ski Deer Valley' packages available.

Washington School Inn (☎ 435-649-3800, 800-824-1672; www.washingtonschoolinn.com; 543 Park Ave; r incl breakfast $285-495;) A large limestone schoolhouse (1889) retains its oversized windows and 16ft-high classroom ceilings, but the only lessons left to learn are how to dip your fork in the chocolate fondue during evening hors d'oeuvres or which aromatherapy bath product is best for you. For history and charm, you won't find better. Professional chef-cooked breakfast; hot tub and sauna on site.

Sky Lodge (☎ 435-658-2500, 888-876-2525; www.thesky lodge.com; 201 Heber Ave; r $285-495; wi-fi) An urban loft in a mountain setting, the boutique-bliss Sky Lodge opened in early '08 to some serious acclaim. Three preserved historic buildings (housing restaurants and spa) are surrounded by 22 luxury condos (at least 1200 sq ft each). Lodgings share a clubhouse floor with soaking grotto and sundeck. Environmental commitment runs deep here – from wood-free frame construction to ecofriendly laundry soap.

Also recommended:

Grand Summit (☎ 866-604-4171; www.thecanyons .com; 4000 Canyons Resort Dr; r $310-586; wi-fi) The Canyons four-diamond ski-in, ski-out lodge.

Stein Eriksen Lodge (☎ 435-649-3700, 800-453-1302; www.steinlodge.com; 7700 Stein Way, Deer Valley; r $735-1030; wi-fi) Deer Valley's signature slopeside luxury; your ski valet and spa appointments await.

Eating

Park City has dozens of good, and several great, restaurants – many more than we can list. Pick up a *Mountain Gazette Menu Guide* and a two-for-one **Best Deals Coupon Book** (☎ 435-640-8210) at your hotel or the visitor center; dining here ain't cheap. Dinner reservations are essential December through March; some places close for a varying few weeks in October and November and have abbreviated hours in summer.

BUDGET

Uptown Fare (☎ 435-615-1998; 227 Main St; sandwiches $5-9; lunch) Only mom could make a more comforting meal than the house-roasted turkey sandwiches and homemade soups at this hole-in-the-wall that is below a section of the Treasure Mountain Inn. Super chocolaty scratch brownies, too.

Morning Ray Café & Bakery (☎ 435-649-5686; Treasure Mountain Inn, 227 Main St; breakfast & sandwiches $7-10; 7am-2pm Wed-Sun) Locals call it the 'Morning Wait,' but it's worth it for the strong

UTAH

coffee, organic veggie scrambles, lox and bona fide New York bagels – flown in par-boiled and baked on site.

Stew Pot (☎ 435-645-7839; Deer Valley Plaza, 1375 Deer Valley Dr; mains $7-10; ☻ 11am-9pm) A local secret tucked into a condo complex. Come here for hearty warm-you-up dishes such as pot roast and chipotle chicken stew.

Albertson's (☎ 435-649-6134; 1760 Park Ave) is the best and busiest of the four in-town grocers.

MIDRANGE

Atlantic Pizza & Deli (☎ 435-940-1009; 1776 Park Ave; sandwiches $5-10, mains $10-15; ☻ lunch Tue, lunch & dinner Wed-Mon) You have to travel outside downtown to watch the line cooks whip up great pasta and pizza at this small eat-in deli. Delivery available.

Good Karma (☎ 435-658-0958; 1782 Prospector Ave; breakfast $6-10, mains $9-14; ☻ breakfast, lunch & dinner Mon-Fri, breakfast & dinner Sat & Sun) Tibetan prayer flags greet you at this fab little eclectic eatery with the top breakfast in town. Whenever possible, local and organic ingredients are used in the Indian-Japanese-Persian meals. Try the challah French toast with ginger or vanilla-cinnamon – yum.

Squatters Roadhouse Grill (☎ 435-649-9869; 1900 Park Ave; burgers $8-10, mains $12-17; ☻ breakfast, lunch & dinner) This is the better of the brewpubs for food and fun; great mac 'n' cheese.

Oishi Sushi (☎ 435-615-2255; Summit Watch, 710 Main St; mains $10-20; ☻ dinner) Fresh, fresh, fresh sushi and sashimi. The specialty roll list goes on forever at this contemporary sushi bar and restaurant (try one of the deep-fried tempura variety).

Royal Street Café (☎ 435-645-6724; Silver Lake Lodge, 4000 Deer Valley Dr; lunch mains $11-16, dinner mains $14-22; ☻ 11:30am-9pm Dec-Mar, 11:30am-2:30pm Apr-Nov) Foodies love Deer Valley's slopeside lodge, where you can ooh and aah over dishes such as duck-confit and butter-lettuce wraps, and wild-salmon napoleon. Weekend entertainment.

More good eats:

Butcher's Chop House (☎ 435-647-0040; 751 Main St; pizzas & mains $9-13, steaks $28-35; ☻ lunch & dinner) Clubby and casual; big beefy prime steaks and chops. Bar food served till 1am December through March.

Wasatch Brew Pub (☎ 435-649-0900; 250 Main St; mains $10-19; ☻ dinner Mon-Fri, lunch & dinner Sat & Sun) Pub grub on Main.

Bangkok Thai (☎ 435-649-8424; 605 Main St; mains $12-18; ☻ dinner) Good early bird specials (4pm to 6pm).

Bistro 412 (☎ 435-649-8211; 412 Main St; mains $18-22; ☻ lunch & dinner) Seasonal French fare.

TOP END

Zoom (☎ 435-649-9108; Sky Lodge, 660 Main St; sandwiches $11-13, mains $21-30; ☻ lunch & dinner) See if you can spot co-owner Robert Redford at this upscale American eatery. The sweet-and-tangy ribs and vanilla-bean cheesecake are excellent renditions of the classics. Inside of a rehabbed Union Pacific Railroad Depot, Zoom is also part of the super luxe Sundance Resort–owned Sky Lodge.

Jean Louis Restaurant (☎ 435-200-0602; 136 Heber Ave; mains $27-40; ☻ dinner) Renowned restaurateur, formerly of Sundance resort, chef Jean Louis has done it again. He's created an upscale, world-cuisine restaurant that still manages to feel warm and welcoming. Here it's all about the food.

Grappa (☎ 435-645-0636; 151 Main St; mains $35-40; ☻ dinner) The rambling old home at the top of the historic downtown hill is perfect for a romantic Italian meal. Dine under the soft patio lights in summer.

Shabu (☎ 435-645-7253; 333 Main St; mains $36-45; ☻ dinner) Park City's hipsters flock to this modern pan-Asian phenomenon for fiery-hot shrimp, sake-steamed bass and the namesake *shabu shabu*, a hotpot of flavorful broth with meat or veggies. There's often live music.

Also top-notch:

Glitretind (☎ 435-645-6455; Stein Eriksen Lodge, 7700 Stein Way, Deer Valley; breakfast & lunch $9-14, mains $22-38; ☻ breakfast, lunch & dinner) Best Sunday brunch (adult/child $35/20).

Goldener Hirsch (☎ 435-649-7770; 7570 Royal St, Deer Valley; mains $21-35; ☻ dinner) Alpine specialties such as fondue and Wiener schnitzel.

Wahso (☎ 435-615-0300; 577 Main St; mains $25-36; ☻ dinner) Stellar Indochine French-Asian cooking.

Drinking

Crowds go where the specials are, meaning the bar scene changes nightly. Outside of winter, only weekends really rock. Several restaurants, such as Bistro 412, Squatters and Butcher's, also have good bars.

Sidecar Bar (☎ 435-645-7468; 333 Main St, 2nd fl) One of the only places in town that's happening nightly. Local and regional bands (rock, funk, swing) play often.

Spur (☎ 435-615-1618; 350 Main St) What an upscale Western bar should be: rustic walls, leather couches, roaring fire. A single gal would feel plenty comfortable here. Good grub, too. Live music weekends.

No Name Saloon & Grill (☎ 435-649-6667; 447 Main St) Rugby players and mountain bikers get hammered on Jäger here. The joint is famous for its buffalo burgers. Smoking allowed.

O'Shucks (☎ 435-645-3999; 427 Main St) The floor crunches with peanut shells at this hard-drinkin' bar for snowboarder and skier dudes. Tuesdays see $3 schooners of beer.

Also guzzle at the following:

Celsius Lounge (☎ 435-615-7200; 625 Main St) Low and loungey, a sexy bar.

JB Mulligan's (☎ 435-658-0717; 804 Main St) Monday draft beers cost 50¢.

Entertainment

Symphony, chamber music, bluegrass, jazz and other musical events happen throughout summer and winter; pick up the free *This Week in Park City* (www.parkcityweek.com). The restored 1926 **Egyptian Theatre** (☎ 435-649-9371; www.egyptiantheatrecompany.org; 328 Main St) is a primary venue for Sundance; the rest of the year it hosts plays, musicals and concerts.

Shopping

Main St is chockablock with tourist junk and souvenir Ts. **Factory Stores at Park City** (☎ 435-645-7078; Kimball Junction, Hwy 224), at the junction with I-80 (exit 145), has dozens of outlets.

Getting There & Around

Several companies run vans from SLC's airport and hotels to Park City (about $35 one way). Make reservations with **Park City Transportation** (☎ 435-649-8567, 800-637-3803; www.parkcitytransport ation.com) or **All Resort Express** (☎ 435-649-3999, 800-457-9457; www.allresort.com). **Park City Cabs & Shuttles** (☎ 800-724-7767, 435-658-2227; www.parkcityshuttle.com) also operates charters to Alta and Snowbird ($30 per person) and arranges car rental.

The excellent **Park City Transit** (☎ 435-615-5350; www.parkcity.org) system covers most of Park City, including the three ski resorts, and makes it easy not to rent a car. Free buses run three to six times an hour from 8am to 11pm, with diminished service from 6am to 8am and 11pm to 2am. Pick up schedules and maps at the **Transit Center** (558 Swede Alley) or the Visitor Information Center.

Parking can be challenging. Meter regulations are strictly enforced; carry quarters. Free lots are available off Main St; follow signs. Hail taxis on Main St, or you can call

Ace Transportation (☎ 435-649-8294) or **Advanced Transportation Services** (☎ 435-647-3999).

OGDEN & AROUND

pop 77,200 / elev 4300ft

During its heyday, historic 25th St was lined with brothels and raucous saloons; today a modest selection of restaurants and bars fills the restored buildings. The main attraction is 20 miles east on the Wasatch Mountain slopes of Ogden Valley. Since skiing here is more than an hour's drive from Salt Lake City, most metro area residents head to Park City or the SLC resorts, leaving Snowbasin and Powder Mountain luxuriously empty. The villages of **Huntsville** and **Eden**, halfway between town and mountains, are nearest to the resorts.

For more information, check with the **Ogden Visitors Bureau** (☎ 866-867-8824; www .ogdencvb.org; 2501 Wall Ave; ☿ 9am-5pm Mon-Fri). The USFS **Outdoor Information Center** (☎ 801-625-5306; ☿ 9am-5pm Mon-Fri year-round, 9am-5pm Sat Jun-Sep) is in Union Station (below).

Sights & Activities

Prepare for your children to squeal as a couple of animatronic dinosaurs roar to life inside the museum at **Ogden Eccles Dinosaur Park** (☎ 801-393-3466; www.dinosaurpark.org; 1544 E Park Blvd; adult/child $6/4; ☿ 10am-6pm Mon-Sat, noon-6pm Sun; ☖). Outside, it's like a giant playground where you can run around, under and over life-size plaster-of-Paris dinosaurs. The kids will also love piling in the car to catch a flick at **Motor-Vu Drive-In** (☎ 801-394-1768; http://motorvu.com; 5368 S 1050 West; ☿ dusk Sat & Sun Mar-Nov). There's a swap meet here Saturdays at 8am.

Take off on an indoor skydiving adventure at **iFly** (☎ 801-528-5348; http://iflyutah.com; 2261 Kiesel Ave; per flight $44-69; ☿ 10am-10pm Mon-Sat).

Union Station (☎ 801-629-8535; 2501 Wall Ave; museums adult/child $6/4; ☿ 10am-5pm Mon-Sat) is an old train station worth a stop for the three museums it houses – dedicated to antique autos, natural history and firearms.

SKIING
Snowbasin

To attain high-end resort status, and attract the Olympic downhill races, **Snowbasin** (☎ 801-620-1000, 888-437-5488; www.snowbasin.com; 3925 E Snowbasin Rd, Huntsville; day lift ticket adult/child $62/39) developed everything from gentle slow-skiing zones to wide-open groomers and boulevards, jaw-dropping steeps to gulp-and-go chutes. Snowbasin also grooms 15 miles of **cross-country skiing**, both classic and skating, has four terrain parks and a dedicated **snow tubing** lift and hill.

In 20 years the resort will be the next Vail, but for now Snowbasin remains a hidden gem with fantastic skiing, top-flight service and nary a lift line. The exposed-timber-and-glass Summit **day lodge** (accessible to nonskiers) has a massive four-sided fireplace and a deck overlooking daredevil steeps.

The Snowbasin lowdown: 2950ft vertical drop, base elevation 6400ft; 2820 acres, 15% beginner, 50% intermediate, 35% expert; one high-speed tram, two gondolas, four high-speed chairs, four fixed-grip chairs.

Powder Mountain
If you're someone who likes to don a backpack and spend the day alone, you'll groove on the old-fashioned mom-and-pop **Powder Mountain** (☎ 801-745-3772; www.powdermountain.net; Rte 158, Eden; day lift ticket adult/child $53/30). There's no snowmaking, but Mother Nature provides 500in annually. With 5500 skiable acres, this is America's largest ski area, but only 2900 acres are lift-served by just four chairs (one high speed) and three rope tows. There's also snow cat skiing (per ride $10), two terrain parks and night skiing till 10pm. Best of all, two weeks after a storm, you'll still find powder. The rest of the lowdown: 3005ft vertical drop, base elevation 6895ft; 25% beginner, 40% intermediate, 35% advanced.

Wolf Mountain
At only 110 skiable acres and with a 1000ft vertical drop, who'd think **Wolf Mountain** (☎ 801-745-3511; www.wolfmountaineden.com; 3567 Nordic Valley Way, Eden; day lift ticket adult/child $26/17; ♿) would garner any superlatives? But since all four lifts are lit, Wolf Mountain has the largest **night skiing** terrain in Utah. The resort goes out of its way to attract families, with learning packages and a special kids website (http://boycottmonster.com).

Sleeping
Cradled by mountains, Ogden Valley is the preferred place to stay. If you choose to stay in town, you have a couple options.

OGDEN TOWN
Ben Lomond Historic Suite Hotel (☎ 801-627-1900, 877-627-1900; www.benlomondsuites.com; 2510 Washington Blvd; r $69-99; wi-fi) Traditional rooms in this 1927 hotel could use a fluff, but you can't beat the downtown location. Some pets OK.

Chain motels line up near Ogden's I-15 exits; **Best Western High Country Inn** (☎ 801-394-4974; 1355 W 12th St; s/d $33/40; ♿ 🐕 wi-fi) is the best of the bunch. The modern-mountain-lodge-look of the place is actually appealing, and rooms are as big as all outdoors.

OGDEN VALLEY
There are no accommodations at the ski resorts, so ask about ski packages at the places listed following. Eden is closest to Powder and Wolf Mountains; Huntsville is closest to Snowbasin.

Jackson Fork Inn (☎ 801-745-0051, 800-255-0672; www.jacksonforkinn.com; 7345 E 900 South, Huntsville; r incl breakfast $70-120) A big ol' white barn has been turned into a simple, seven-room B&B. Downstairs there's a homey restaurant (dinner and Sunday brunch).

Red Moose Lodge (☎ 801-745-6667, 866-996-6673; http://theredmooselodge.com; 2547 N Valley Junction Dr, Eden; r $89-139; ♿ ♿ wi-fi) The owners here have created a kid-friendly log lodge with games room, climbing fort, ball courts and heated pool. Take the free shuttle to ski resorts and downtown for dinner. Condos available ($179 to $199).

Wolf Creek Resorts (☎ 801-745-3787, 800-301-0817; www.wolfcreekresort.com; condos $90-175) The same management company that runs Wolf Mountain owns several condo buildings in Eden and Huntsville. All have full kitchens and ski lockers.

Atomic Chalet B&B (☎ 801-745-0538; www.atomicchalet.com; r incl breakfast $125; 🖵) During the Olympics, the men's US downhill team stayed here, 10 minutes from Snowbasin (call for directions). Super-comfy modern rooms have blond-wood furniture and extras such as bathrobes, in-room VCRs and continental breakfast.

Eating & Drinking
Restaurants and a few bars line historic 25th St between Union Station and Grant Ave.

Shooting Star Saloon (☎ 801-745-2002; 7350 E 200 South, Huntsville; burgers $5-8; 🕒 noon-8pm Wed-Sun) Hands down the best place to eat and drink. It's been open since 1879, making it Utah's oldest continuously operating saloon. Seek this place out: the cheeseburgers – and cheap beer – are justly famous.

Roosters 25th Street Brewing Co (☎ 801-627-6171; 253 25th St; sandwiches $7-9, mains $10-14; ☉ lunch & dinner) Once a house of ill repute, this old town building is now an upscale brewpub.

Bistro 258 (☎ 801-394-1595; 258 25th St; sandwiches $4-8, mains $10-17; ☉ lunch & dinner) For more formal dining, order steaks and seafood at Bistro 258; don't miss desserts such as the chocolate terrine.

Eats of Eden (☎ 801-745-8618; 2529 N Hwy 162, Eden; mains $10-16; ☉ 11am-9pm Tue-Sat) Munch on pizza or pasta surrounded by mountains on the great valley patio.

For a treat, pick up honey and peanut butter made by the Trappist monks at the **Abbey of Our Lady of the Holy Trinity** (☎ 801-745-3784; 1250 S 9500 East; ☉ 10am-noon & 1:15-5pm Mon-Sat), 3 miles east of Huntsville.

Getting There & Away
Greyhound (☎ 801-394-5573, 800-231-2222; www.greyhound.com; 2393 Wall Ave), north of Union Station, has daily buses to SLC ($11.50, 45 minutes). Express **UTA** (☎ 888-743-3882; www.rideuta.com) buses 472 and 473 have frequent services to 400 South and State St in SLC ($4).

HEBER CITY & MIDWAY
elev 5593ft

Twenty miles south of Park City, Heber City (population 9775) and its vast valley make an affordable base for exploring the surrounding mountains. A steam-powered railway runs from here. Nearby Midway (population 2121) is modeled after an Austrian alpine town, with hand-painted buildings set against the slopes. Here you'll find interesting places to stay and a hot spring crater you can swim in. Cross-country skiing and golf are close to both towns.

Orientation & Information
Main St (Hwy 40), Heber City's main commercial street, runs north–south; 100 South westbound goes through Heber the scant 3 miles to Midway. Hwy 190 continues over Guardsman Pass to Big Cottonwood Canyon and SLC (closed in winter).

Most of the services are in Heber City. Pick up information about both towns at the **Heber Valley Chamber of Commerce** (☎ 435-654-3666; www.hebervalleycc.org; 475 N Main St; ☉ 8am-5pm) or the **Uinta National Forest Heber Ranger Station** (☎ 435-654-0470; 2460 S Hwy 40). Log onto the internet (free with purchase) over coffee and sand-

wiches at **Sidetrack Café** (☎ 435-654-0563; 94 S Main St; ☉ 6:30am-5pm Mon-Fri, 7:30am-5pm Sat & Sun).

Sights & Activities
Fifteen miles southwest of Heber City along Hwy 189 is the beginning of beautiful and steep-walled Provo Canyon. The 1904 **Heber Valley Historic Railroad** (☎ 435-654-5601; www.hebervalleyrr.org; 450 S 600 West; adult/child $32/20; ☉ Jun-Oct) chugs along on scenic trips through the gorgeous canyon and goes on themed runs for Halloween and Christmas.

In Midway, swim in the grotto-like **Homestead Crater** (☎ 435-654-1102, 800-327-7220; www.homesteadresort.com; Homestead Resort, 700 N Homestead Dr; swim Mon-Fri $10, Sat & Sun $15; ☉ 10am-7pm) beneath the 50ft-high walls of a limestone cone open to the sky. Scuba divers often learn in the 65ft-deep geothermal pool that stays 90°F year round. Reservations required. This is way cool.

A must-ski for cross-country aficionados, **Soldier Hollow** (☎ 435-654-2002; www.soldierhollow.com; off Hwy 113; cross-country skiing adult/child $18/9; ☉ 9am-4:30pm), 2 miles south of Midway, was the Nordic course used in the Olympics. Its 19 miles of stride-skiing and skating lanes – tucked in a valley beneath 7000ft ridgelines – are groomed every night. You can also create your own biathlon – a combo of skiing and target shooting using the actual Olympic targets.

For nonskiers, there's a 1201ft-long **snowtubing hill** (adult/child 3-6 $18/8; ☉ noon-8pm Mon-Sat, noon-4pm Sun); book in advance on weekends, since ticket sales are capped. Snow season is December through March. In the summer, the resort's gorgeous 36-hole **golf course** (☎ 435-654-0532, 888-927-2824; 18 holes $38) is quite popular. Soldier Hollow's marked **mountain biking** trails are exposed May through October.

Sleeping
The standard chain motels are available in Heber City (winter rates $80 to $110).

Swiss Alps Inn (☎ 435-654-0722; www.swissalpsinn.com; 167 S Main St; r $65-80; ⬚ wi-fi) This independent Heber City Main St motel has huge rooms with hand-painted doors, and you get a free milkshake from the associated restaurant next door.

Homestead Resort (☎ 435-654-1102, 800-327-7220; www.homesteadresort.com; 700 N Homestead Dr, Midway; r $110-220, ste $190-250, condos from $280; ⬚ ⬚ ⬚ wi-fi) Most destination family resorts of this caliber

---

DETOUR: MT TIMPANOGOS

On the north side of Provo Canyon, take the paved, 16-mile **Alpine Loop Road** (Hwy 92), an incredibly scenic, twisting road past 11,750ft Mt Timpanogos. At 6800ft, stay overnight at the **Mount Timpanogos Campground** (☎ 877-444-6777; www.reserveamerica.gov; campsites $14; ☺ May-Oct); pit toilets, water. A trailhead leads from here into the surrounding wilderness area filled with fir trees.

Spectacular, star-like helictite formations are on view at three midmountain caverns in **Timpanogos Cave National Monument** (☎ 801-756-5239; www.nps.gov/tica; off Hwy 92; per car $3; ☺ mid-May–Oct). Book ahead or get there early for a 1½-hour ranger-led tour; they fill up. To get to the caves, you have to wait until an hour before your tour to make the uphill hike. Hwy 92 is closed December through March.

---

faded into obscurity a generation ago. A collection of homey buildings and cottages gathers around the resort's village green. Activities include golf, cycling, horseback riding, hot-spring swimming, spa-going, volleyball, shuffle board and croquet. The restaurants are terrific, too.

Midway has several other character-filled lodgings, including the following:

Inn on the Creek (☎ 435-654-0892; www.innoncreek .com; 375 Rainbow Ln; r $139-199; ☒ wi-fi) Luxury inn and spa.

Blue Boar Inn (☎ 435-654-1400, 800-650-1400; www .theblueboarinn.com; 1235 Warm Springs Rd; r incl breakfast $175-295; ☐) Elaborate European-country B&B.

Zermatt Resort & Spa (☎ 866-937-6288; http://zer matt.dolce.com; 784 West Resort Dr; r incl breakfast $175-295; ☒ ☐ wi-fi) Complimentary ski and golf shuttles.

Eating

Dairy Keen (☎ 435-654-5336; 199 S Main St, Heber City; burgers $3-6; ☺ lunch & dinner) Look for the miniature train that travels overhead at this local play on Dairy Queen. The ice-cream sundaes and shakes can't be beat (try bosenberry!).

Snake Creek Grill (☎ 435-654-2133; 650 W 100 South/Hwy 113; mains $16-20; ☺ dinner Thu-Sun) One of northern Utah's best restaurants looks like a saloon from an old Western. The all-American Southwest-style menu features blue-cornmeal-crusted trout and finger-lickin' ribs. Halfway between downtown Heber City and Midway.

In Midway, the European-inspired experience at the **Blue Boar Inn** (☎ 435-654-1400, 800-650-1400; www.theblueboarinn.com; 1235 Warm Springs Rd; breakfast & sandwiches $8-11, dinner mains $24-28; ☺ breakfast, lunch & dinner) dining room, open to nonguests, is worth the reservation you need to make. And there's the **Mountain House Grill** (☎ 435-654-5370; 79 E Main St, Midway; mains $9-19; ☺ breakfast & lunch) for casual all-American.

Getting There & Around

From Ogden, **Greyhound** (☎ 801-394-5573, 800-231-2222; www.greyhound.com; 2393 Wall Ave) has daily buses to SLC ($11.50, 55 minutes). **UTA** (☎ 801-743-3882, 888-743-3882; www.rideuta.com; cnr Wall & 23rd Sts) runs express bus service to SLC ($4, 50 minutes), with diminished frequency on weekends.

SUNDANCE RESORT
elev 6100ft

Art and nature blend seamlessly at **Sundance** (☎ 801-225-4107; www.sundanceresort.com; Hwy 92), a magical resort-cum-artists-colony founded by Robert Redford, where day-trippers and bedraggled urbanites connect with the land and rediscover their creative souls. Aside from winter sports, you can ride horseback, fly-fish, do yoga, indulge in spa treatments, write, climb or hike Mt Timpanogos, nosh at several wonderful eateries, and spend the night in rustic luxury.

Every building is a discrete, rough-hewn beauty, including the way-cool **art shack** (☎ 801-225-4107; ☺ 10am-5pm), where you can throw pottery and make jewelry. Sundance hosts numerous year-round **cultural events**, from its namesake film festival (p503) and screenwriting and directing labs, to writers' workshops and music seminars. In summer there are outdoor films and music series, one with the Utah Symphony. Day-guests should ask for trail maps and activity guides at the **general store** (☎ 801-225-4107; ☺ 9am-9pm), which shoppers love for the artisan handicrafts and home furnishings and jewelry (catalog available).

Mount Timpanogos, the second-highest peak in the Wasatch, lords over the **ski resort** (☎ reservations 801-223-4849; day lift ticket adult/child $45/20), which is family- and newbie-friendly. The hill is primarily an amenity for the resort;

UTAH

if you're an accomplished skier or rider, you'll groove on the super-steeps, but you'll see the whole place in two hours. From the top, the views over Utah Lake are mesmerizing.

The lowdown: 2150ft vertical drop, base elevation 6100ft; 500 acres, 20% beginner, 40% intermediate, 40% advanced; three fixed-grip chairs. May through September, there's lift-assist **hiking** and **mountain biking**. The **Cross Country Center** (☎ 801-223-4170; 9am-5pm) has 16 miles of groomed classic and skating lanes on all-natural snow. You can also snowshoe 6 miles of trails past frozen waterfalls (ask about nighttime owl-watching walks). The woods are a veritable fairyland.

Lucky enough to be staying over? The **lodging** (☎ 800-892-1600; r $294-659; wi-fi), in cottage rooms scattered across the grounds, makes the perfect place to honeymoon or write your next novel. Tucked among the trees, they've got pine walls and ever-so-comfy furnishings, plus quilts, paperback books and board games; some have kitchens. Three-bedroom houses ($1022) are also available.

The **Deli** (☎ 801-223-4211; sandwiches $7-10; 7am-9pm) carries tasty picnic supplies and makes to-go sandwiches such as hand-carved turkey with cranberry relish. **Foundry Grill** (☎ 801-223-4211; breakfast & sandwiches $8-16, dinner mains $16-31; breakfast, lunch & dinner) cooks up sizzling burgers and steaks, salads and a scrumptious Sunday brunch buffet (adult/child $28/15).

Sundance's top-flight restaurant, **Tree Room** (☎ 801-223-4200; mains $25-35; dinner) is a study in rustic-mountain chic (reservations essential). The sophisticated menu items are as artfully presented as the chichi clientele. Try the wild mushroom and goat cheese tart before you cut into a succulent buffalo chop. You'll be hard-pressed to find a better meal this side of San Francisco – and what's more, there's a big tree trunk in the middle of the room.

Built of cast-off barn wood, the centerpiece of the **Owl Bar** (☎ 801-223-4222; 5pm-midnight Mon-Fri, noon-midnight Sat & Sun) is a century-old bar where the real Butch Cassidy once drank. The place looks like a Wild West roadhouse, but it's full of art freaks, mountain hipsters and local cowboys imbibing by a roaring fireplace. On Fridays and Saturdays there's good live music.

PROVO
pop 105,400 / elev 4490ft

The reddest of the reds, Provo is truly a conservative town and the third-largest city in Utah. The most compelling reason to visit is to see Brigham Young University (BYU) on a day trip from SLC (45 miles north). The place shuts down on Sunday.

Orientation & Information

University Ave (Hwy 189), north off I-15, exit 266, is Provo's main drag. It intersects Center St in the old downtown core. Get information at the **Utah Valley Visitors Bureau** (☎ 801-370-8393, 800-222-8824; www.utahvalley.org/cvb; 111 S University Ave; 8:30am-5pm Mon-Fri, 9am-3pm Sat), inside the beautiful courthouse. For forest service information, contact the **Uinta National Forest Ranger Station** (☎ 801-377-5780; 88 W 100 North).

Sights & Activities

The **BYU campus** (☎ 801-378-4636; www.byu.edu) is enormous and known for its squeaky-clean

---

DONNY & MARIE

A good Mormon family, the Osmonds have long called Provo, Utah home. Seven of the nine children born to George and Olive Osmond participated in the family singing group that was a sensation in the '70s. Pop icons Donny and Marie branched out, singing and hosting a live variety show. Remember 'A Little Bit Country, A Little Bit Rock 'n' Roll'? Most of the Osmond offspring have spawned large families of their own (at last count, 55 children and 48 grandchildren). Marie's 2007 success on the TV hit *Dancing with the Stars* helped reignite interest in the entertaining family. That same year marked the 50th anniversary of their showbiz debut, and the PBS special, the *Osmond's 50th Anniversary Reunion*.

But singing is not all this creative family has done. During their lifetime, George and 'Mother' Osmond started the Osmond Foundation, which has become the **Children's Miracle Network** (www.childrensmiraclenetwork.org). Marie has been busy collecting and designing her own line of porcelain dolls; see them online at www.mariedolls.com or shop in person at **Saving Graces Doll Shoppe** (☎ 801-377-5948; 3549 N University Ave, Provo). Donny's latest album, *From Donny with Love* came out in 2008. There's talk of an extended run for he and Marie in Vegas…

student dress codes. Drive 450 East north toward the **Hinckley Alumni & Visitor Center** (☎ 801-422-4678; cnr W Campus & N Campus Drs; ☾ 8am-6pm Mon-Sat). Call ahead for tours. The university's what's-doing-here **Museum of Art** (☎ 801-378-2787; admission free; ☾ 10am-6pm Tue, Wed & Fri, 10am-9pm Mon & Thu, noon-5pm Sat) is one of the biggest in the Southwest, with a concentration on American art. BYU sporting events take place at **Lavell Edwards Stadium** (☎ 801-422-2981; www.byutickets.com; 1700 N Canyon Rd).

You can ice skate in town at **Peaks Ice Arena** (☎ 801-377-8777; www.peaksarena.com; 100 N Seven Peaks Blvd; adult/child $5/4; ☾ Mon-Sat), where the Olympic hockey teams faced off in 2002. Free-skate hours vary. In summer, cool off at **Seven Peaks Resort Water Park** (☎ 801-373-8777; www.sevenpeaks.com; 1330 E 300 North; adult/child $22/16; ☾ 11am-8pm Mon-Sat Jun-Aug).

Sleeping & Eating

Provo's close enough to SLC that you can easily make it in a day. The historic downtown has 20 little independent restaurants (and a couple of great used bookstores), around the intersection of Center St and University Ave.

Travelodge (☎ 801-373-1974; www.travelodge.com; 124 S University Ave; r incl breakfast $62-68; ☒ wi-fi) A modern motel close to downtown. The cereal, coffee and egg burritos are complimentary in the morning.

Hines Mansion B&B (☎ 801-374-8400, 800-428-5636; www.hinesmansion.com; 383 W 100 South; r incl breakfast $129-159; ☐ wi-fi) Antiques are used sparingly in this 1895 mansion-turned-B&B. The 'Library' guest room has a 'secret passage' door to the bathroom.

Guru's (☎ 801-377-6980; 45 E Center St; mains $6-11; ☾ 11am-9pm Mon-Sat) Tasty rice bowls, including vegetarian options, and big salads top the casual menu.

Of the many hole-in-the-wall ethnic eats in the old town, **Se Llama Peru** (☎ 801-377-4792; 368 W Center St; mains $8-14; ☾ lunch & dinner Tue-Sat) is good for Latin American spice, and **Four Season's Hot Pot & Dumplings** (☎ 801-375-6888; 236 N University Ave; mains $7-13; ☾ lunch & dinner Mon-Sat) for Asian noodle soups.

Getting There & Away

Greyhound (☎ 801-373-4211, 800-231-2222; www.greyhound.com; 124 N 300 West) serves SLC ($11.50, 55 minutes). **UTA** (☎ 801-743-3882, 888-743-3882; www.rideuta.com) runs frequent express services to

---

> **DETOUR: PONY EXPRESS TRAIL**
>
> Follow more than 130 miles of the original route horse-and-rider mail delivery followed along **Pony Express Trail Backcountry Byway** (www.byways.org) from Fairfield to Callao. The trail begins at one of the former stops, in **Camp Floyd/Stagecoach Inn State Park** (☎ 385-768-8932; http://stateparks.utah.gov; admission $2; ☾ 9am-5pm; closed Sun Oct-Mar), 25 miles southwest of I-15 along Hwy 73. Most of the road is maintained gravel or dirt and is passable to ordinary cars in good weather. In winter, snow may close the route; watch for flash floods in summer.

SLC ($4), with diminished service Sunday. **Amtrak** (☎ 800-872-7245; www.amtrak.com; cnr 300 West & 600 South) runs the *California Zephyr* once a day in both directions (Chicago and LA).

NORTHEASTERN UTAH

Rising oil prices have turned the shale fields of northeastern Utah into a gold mine. What was once too costly to extract is being actively exploited. The result for travelers? Convoys of tankers clog up scenic back roads, lodging prices have risen to insane levels and restaurants have shut down because they can't keep staff – minimum-wage workers make more in the oil fields. The primordial ooze that created all this hubbub was laid down in the time of the dinosaurs, and you can find several related digs and museums in the area. The high wilderness terrain (more than a mile above sea level) of the Uinta Mountains and Flaming Gorge attracts trout fishers and wildlife lovers alike.

VERNAL & AROUND
pop 7800 / elev 5331ft

As the closest town of any size to both Flaming Gorge (35 miles north) and Dinosaur National Monument (20 miles east), Vernal is unavoidable for food and fuel fill-up. An amazing in-town dinosaur museum makes the town worth a brief stop, but we don't recommend staying. The hotels are insanely overpriced and much of the food just isn't good. Either make your visit a long day trip from Salt Lake City (170 miles) or spend the night up in Flaming Gorge.

The local **Vernal Chamber of Commerce** (☎ 435-722-4598; www.dinoland.com; 138 E Main St; ⊗ 9am-5pm) has area-wide info, while the **Utah Welcome Center** (☎ 800-200-1160; Hwy 40, Jensen; ⊗ 9am-5pm), 13 miles east, covers the state. The **Vernal Ranger Station** (☎ 435-789-1181; 355 N Vernal Ave; ⊗ 8am-5pm Mon-Fri) has details on camping and hiking in Ashley National Forest, to the north.

The informative film at the **Utah Field House of Natural History** (☎ 496-789-3799; http://stateparks.utah .gov; 496 E Main St; ⊗ 8am-7pm May-Sep, 9am-5pm Oct-Apr; ♿) is the best all-round introduction to Utah's dinosaurs. Interactive exhibits, video clips and, of course, giant fossils are wonderfully relevant to the area. As soon as the growing institution fills up its new 22,000-sq-ft space, this museum will be tops in the state. Some kids we know think it is already. Ask about volunteering for museum curator-led digs.

Check out hundreds of fossilized dinosaur tracks at **Red Fleet State Park** (☎ 435-789-4432; http://stateparks.utah.gov; admission $7; ⊗ 6am-10pm Apr-Oct, 8am-5pm Nov & Dec), 10 miles northeast of Vernal on Hwy 191. Also worth the drive are the **McConkie Ranch Petroglyphs** (Dry Fork Canyon Rd; donation $2; ⊗ dawn-dusk), 10 miles northeast of town. The 800-year-old Fremont Indian petroglyphs require some rock scrambling to see. Generous ranch owners built a little self-serve info shack with posted messages and a map. Being on private land has really helped; these alien-looking anthropomorphs are in much better shape than the many that have been desecrated by vandals on public lands. Follow 3000 West to the north out of Vernal.

The Green and Yampa Rivers are the main waterways in the area; both have rapids and genteel floats. Trips run from $85 to $800 for one to five days. Check with **Hatch River Expeditions** (☎ 800-342-8243; www.donhatchriver trips.com) or **Adrift Adventures** (☎ 800-824-0150; www.adrift.com).

If you *have* to stay (and we warned you), the semi-seedy **Sage Motel** (☎ 435-789-1442, 800-760-1442; www.vernalmotels.com; 54 W Main St; r $89-149), surrounded by downtown buildings, is the cheapest. Anywhere else it would rate $30 tops. If you can get one, it's better to stay in one of the simple, homey rooms at **Landmark Inn B&B** (☎ 435-781-1800, 888-738-1800; www.landmark -inn.com; 288 E 100 South; r incl breakfast $79-179), in an old schoolhouse. There are several exorbitant Super 6–like chain motels, too.

If your destination is Dinosaur National Monument, book at the comfortable, modern-home **Jensen Inn B&B** (☎ 435-789-5909; Rte 149; r $95-105, ste $125-145, all incl breakfast; 🖳 wi-fi), three miles north of Jensen, off Hwy 40. Camp in a tepee ($88) or pitch your tent in the grassy field ($35) and you still get breakfast.

The all-American grub at **Naples Country Café** (☎ 435-789-9970; 1010 E Hwy 40; breakfast & sandwiches $4-8, mains $9-13; ⊗ breakfast, lunch & dinner) is OK, especially if you count the coconut cream pie. **Cobble Rock** (☎ 435-789-8578; 250 S Vernal Ave; sandwiches $5-9, mains 11-18; ⊗ lunch & dinner Mon-Sat) will do for a brew and a bite.

DINOSAUR NATIONAL MONUMENT

One of the largest dinosaur fossil beds in North America was discovered here in 1909.

ROADS THAT RULE: NORTHEASTERN UTAH

Sheer drop-offs and mountain scenery dominate many of the northeastern routes; the **Vernal Chamber of Commerce** (☎ 435-722-4598; www.dinoland.com; 138 E Main St; ⊗ 9am-5pm) publishes several backroad brochures (available online too).

■ **Red Cloud Loop** Twenty-one miles north of Vernal on Hwy 191, take off west on Red Cloud Loop. The road starts out tame, then rises sharply up to 10,000ft in twists and turns. The one-and-a-half lane road has steep drop-offs and dramatic pine scenery amid the eastern Uinta peaks. Allow three hours to return the full 72 miles back to Vernal via Dry Fork Canyon Rd.

■ **Sheep Creek Canyon** A dramatic 13-mile paved loop through the Sheep Creek Canyon Geological Area leaves Hwy 44 about 15 miles west of Greendale Junction in the Flaming Gorge area.

■ **Wedge Overlook/Buckhorn Wash** South of Price, take a 60-mile drive through San Rafael Swell (p514), stopping along the way to see dramatic canyon views at Wedge Overlook and ancient rock art near Buckhorn Wash.

DINOSAUR DIAMOND

Some darn clever marketing people have come up with a new national scenic byway, **Dinosaur Diamond** (www.dinosaurdiamond.org), which aims to give Dino his due by promoting and protecting paleontology and archaeology in Colorado and Utah. The not entirely logical 512-mile suggested route does link some fine ancient sites. Our Utah favorites include the following:

- **Dinosaur Discovery Site** (St George; p476) Some of the most amazing dinosaur trackways ever found.
- **Utah Field House of Natural History** (Vernal; opposite) Still growing, but an amazing, kid-friendly Utah dinosaur museum.
- **Museum of Ancient Life** (Lehi; p486) Interactive exhibits provide an overview of world dinosaurs.
- **Cleveland-Lloyd Dinosaur Quarry** (Price; p515) Watch 'em digging up new discoveries daily.
- **Red Fleet State Park** (Vernal; opposite) More 200-million-year-old footprints.

And just for fun:

- **Dinosaur Museum** (Blanding; p420) Dino movie memorabilia and models.
- **Ogden Eccles Dinosaur Park** (Ogden; p506) Jurassic era playground for kids.

The quarry was enclosed and hundreds of bones were left on view in the rock. Amazing, right? But the engineers misjudged, the clay soil moved and the wonderful viewing room had to be shut down indefinitely. You can still hike the 45 minutes uphill to see if you can find the three, count 'em, *three* bones that are exposed on the trail in the **Dinosaur Quarry Section** (☎ 435-789-2115; www.nps.gov/dino; per car $10; ☑ 8am-5:30pm May-Sep, 9am-4:30pm Oct-Apr), which is 20 miles east of Vernal, 7 miles north of Jensen. In summer, the makeshift Quarry visitor center shows slides; off-season you're pretty much outta luck as far as interpretive information goes.

The park headquarters are in the **Canyon Section** ☎ 970-374-3000; www.nps.gov/dino; per car $10; ☑ 8am-4:30pm May-Aug, 8am-4:30pm Wed-Sun Sep & Apr) across the state line in tiny Dinosaur, CO. There are no dinosaurs bones here, but the visitor center shows a good movie and there are pretty hikes. The fee is good for both. The best thing about the Colorado town is all the kitschy dinosaurs on business signs.

Pitch your tent at the first-come, first-served **Green River Campground** (Dinosaur Quarry; campsites $12; ☑ May-Sep). The 88 sites have access to running water (indoor plumbing and the river), but no showers.

FLAMING GORGE NATIONAL RECREATION AREA

Named for its fiery red sandstone canyon, Flaming Gorge provides 375 miles of shore-line around Flaming Gorge Reservoir, which straddles the Utah–Wyoming line. As with many artificial lakes, **fishing** and **boating** are prime attractions. Various records for giant lake trout and kokanee salmon have been set here. The area also provides plenty of **hiking** and **camping** in summer, **cross-country skiing** and **snowmobiling** in winter. Keep an eye out for common wildlife such as moose, elk, pronghorn antelope and mule deer; you may also see bighorn sheep, black bears and mountain lions. The lake's 6040ft elevation insures pleasantly warm but not desperately hot summers – daytime highs average about 80°F.

Information is available from the USFS **Flaming Gorge Headquarters** (☎ 435-784-3445; www .fs.fed.us/r4/ashley/recreation; 25 W Hwy 43; ☑ 8am-4:30pm May-Sep, 8am-4:30pm Mon-Fri Oct-Apr), the **Flaming Gorge Dam Visitor Center** (☎ 435-885-3135; Hwy 191; ☑ 9am-5pm May-Sep) and the **Red Canyon Visitor Center** (☎ 435-889-3713; ☑ 10am-5pm May-Sep), 4 miles west of Greendale Junction. Get general information online at www.flaminggorge country.com. Day use of some Flaming Gorge areas costs $2 at self-pay stations.

In Dutch John, rent a fishing ($110 per day) or ski boat ($260 per day) from **Cedar Springs Marina** (☎ 435-889-3795; www.cedarsprings marina.com; off Hwy 191; ☑ Apr-Oct), 2 miles east of Flaming Gorge Dam. The best fishing is found with a guide; ask at the marina or contact **Trout Creek Flies** (☎ 435-885-3355; www

---

DETOUR: STARVATION STATE PARK

No one is quite sure who did the stealing, but either trappers in the area stashed some winter stores in the mountains, or Native Americans did, and then the other group took the food. Advance planners starved when they found no tasty treats buried under the snow, or so the story goes. In all likelihood bears were to blame for the theft and the name of **Starvation State Park** (☎ 435-738-2326; Hwy 40, Duchesne; per car $5, ☺ 6am-10pm). Subsequent homesteaders tried to make a go of it here on the Strawberry River, but with a short growing season and frozen ground they had no better luck fending off hunger. Today the park contains a 3500-acre reservoir as well as plenty of picnickers. The 60-site **campground** (campsites $16; ☺ Jun-Sep) has showers and features a sandy beach. Primitive camping is also available here – don't forget to bring food.

.fishgreenriver.com; cnr Hwy 191 & Little Hole Rd). A guided full-day trip will cost you about $395. Aim to fly-fish late June to early July, before the river is flooded with fun floaters. Trout Creek also rents rafts ($60 to $80 per day) and runs a floater shuttle.

Ashley National Forest (www.fs.fed.us/r4/ashley) runs numerous May-to-September campgrounds in the area. The ponderosa pine forest, at 7000ft-plus elevation and with excellent clifftop views, makes **Canyon Rim** (☎ reservations 877-444-6777; www.reserveamerica.com; Red Canyon Rd; campsites $15) a top choice. Keep an eye out for bighorn sheep. **Red Canyon Lodge** (☎ 435-889-3759; www.redcanyonlodge.com; 790 Red Canyon Rd; cabins $95-125; ▣) provides rustic and luxury cabins without TVs; **Flaming Gorge Resort** (☎ 435-889-3773; www.flaminggorgeresort.com; 155 Greendale/Hwy 191; r/condos $83/123) rents motel rooms and modern condominiums. Both are open year-round and have decent restaurants. Convenience stores in Dutch John have deli counters.

HIGH UINTAS WILDERNESS AREA

The Uinta Mountains are unusual in that they run east–west, unlike all other major mountain ranges in the lower 48. Several peaks rise to more than 13,000ft, including Kings (13,528ft), which is the highest point in the Southwest. The central summits lie within the High Uintas Wilderness Area, which provides 800 sq miles of **hiking** and **horseback riding** opportunities. No roads, no mountain biking, no off-road driving permitted. The reward? An incredible, remote mountain experience, one without snack bars or lodges.

Ashley National Forest's **Roosevelt Ranger Station** (☎ 435-722-5018; www.fs.fed.us/r4/ashley/recreation; 244 W Hwy 40, Roosevelt; ☺ 8am-5pm Mon-Fri)

provides trail and free camping information. The shortest route to **Kings Peak** requires a 32-mile round-trip hike, with over 4000ft elevation gain, from Henry's Fork trailhead on the north side. About 20 trailheads provide access to all sides of the Uintas; July to August is hiking season on the highest peaks, but even then you should be prepared for possible snow.

Backcountry camping is free in the wilderness area. Several campgrounds in Ashley National Forest abut the High Uintas; **Moon Lake Campground** (☎ reservations 877-444-6777; www.recreation.gov; campsites $16; ☺ Jun-Sep), at 8150ft, is a good choice for the scenic body of water and the fish within it. Water; no showers.

On the way up to the wilderness area, on Hwy 35 in Hanna, **Defa's Dude Ranch** (☎ 435-848-5590; www.defasduderanch.com; cabins $50; ☺ May-Oct) has rustic cabins in a beautiful, remote setting; bring your own bedding (or request it). There's also a café, a saloon and horseback riding ($20 per hour).

PRICE & SAN RAFAEL SWELL
elev 5566ft

A big-enough (population 8500) and somewhat blah town, Price mostly serves as a base for exploring outlying dinosaur and ancient Native American sites. Stock up on supplies for exploring the colorful geological formations of nearby San Rafael Swell BLM lands.

The incredibly knowledgeable staff at the **Castle Country Travel Desk** (☎ 800-842-0789; www.castlecountry.com; 155 E Main St; ☺ 8am-5pm Apr-Sep, 9am-5pm Mon-Sat Oct-Mar) can tell you all the secret rock art sites. In the same building (same hours), you can see real fossils, not replicas, at the **College of Eastern Utah Prehistoric Museum** (☎ 435-613-5060; www.museum.ceu.edu; adult/child $5/2).

Look for the Utah raptor, first identified in this part of the world. All the bones on display were discovered within two hours of the museum and the university sponsors many active digs.

Thirty miles south of Price, you can visit an active dinosaur dig site. More than 12,000 bones have been taken from the ground at **Cleveland-Lloyd Dinosaur Quarry** (☎ 435-636-3600; adult/child $6/2; ☺ 10am-5pm Jun-Sep, 10am-5pm Fri-Sun mid-Mar–May & Oct). A dozen species of dinosaur were buried here 150 million years ago, but the large concentration of meat-eating allosaurs has helped scientists around the world draw new conclusions. Excavations are intermittent but ongoing; check out the visitor center's excellent exhibits. Take Rte 10 south to the Elmo/Cleveland turnoff and follow signs on the dirt road.

South between Hwys 10 and 6/24 lie the canyons, arches and cliffs of the **San Rafael Swell**. Look for the purples, grays and greens that indicate ancient seabeds, in addition to the oxygenated oranges and reds of this anticline. The area is all BLM land where camping and four-wheeling is allowed; **Price Field Office** (☎ 435-636-3600; 125 S 600 West; ☺ 9am-5pm Mon-Fri) has information. For the best drive, follow Wedge/Buckhorn signs east 2 miles north of Castle Dale (28 miles from Price). After 12½ undulating miles, a spur road leads 6 miles south to **Wedge Overlook** and spectacular canyon views of the San Rafael River, 1200ft below.

Backtrack and continue 8 miles to the **Buckhorn Wash Pictographs**, a 100ft-long panel of ghostly Barrier Canyon–style rock paintings. Four miles further, you reach a historic **suspension bridge** (foot traffic only) spanning the river. The first-come, first-served, free primitive campground here has toilets but no drinking water. Continue south for 19 miles to get to I-70 (allow two to three hours total from Price).

For more than six decades, the Wilcox Ranch protected the ancient archaeological sites in what is now **Range Creek Wildlife Management Area** (☎ 435-636-0260; www.wildlife .utah.gov/range_creek), east of East Carbon (25 miles southeast of Price). Since the family turned the property over to the government, the public has been allowed limited access. The best way to explore is with a full-day 4WD tour ($125 per person) run by **Tavaputs Ranch** (☎ 435-637-1236; www.tavaputsranch.com; ☺ mid-Jun–mid-Sep). In addition to various guided trips, the ranch offers lodging. Stay the night in the main house rooms or in cabins ($175 per person including meals) and you also have access to the backcountry hikes, drives and horseback rides on a 15,000-acre spread.

ON BUTCH CASSIDY'S TRAIL

Nearly every town in southern Utah claims a connection to Butch Cassidy (1866–?), the Old West's most famous bank and train robber. As part of the Wild Bunch, Cassidy (né Robert LeRoy Parker) pulled 19 heists from 1896 to 1901. Most accounts describe him with a breathless romanticism, comparing him to Robin Hood. All stories usually have one thing in common: a dilapidated shack or a canyon, just over yonder, that served as his hideout. The most credible claim for the location of the famous Robbers' Roost hideout is in the **Henry Mountains** (p441).

In the wee town of **Circleville**, located 28 miles south of Panguitch, stands the honest-to-goodness boyhood home of the gun-slingin' bandit. The cabin is partially renovated but uninhabited, and is situated 2 miles south of town on the west side of Hwy 89. When reporters arrived after the release of the film *Butch Cassidy and the Sundance Kid* (1969), they met the outlaw's youngest sister, who claimed that Butch did in fact not die in South America in 1908, but returned for a visit after that. Writers have been digging for the truth to no avail ever since. You can see where they filmed Robert Redford's famous bicycle scene at the **Grafton ghost town** (p471), outside Rockville.

The Wild Bunch's only heist in Utah took place in April 1897, when the gang stole more than $8000 from Pleasant Valley Coal Company in Castle Gate, 4 miles north of Helper on Hwy 191. The little **Western Mining & Railroad Museum** (☎ 435-472-3009; 296 S Main St, Helper; adult/child $2/1; ☺ 10am-5pm Mon-Sat), 8 miles north of Price, has exhibits on the outlaws, including photos, in the basement. For more, check out *The Outlaw Trail*, by Charles Kelly.

DETOUR: NINE MILE CANYON

Abundant rock art is the attraction on the **Nine Mile Canyon National Backcountry Byway** (www .byways.org), billed as the 'longest art gallery in the world.' You can also spot Fremont granaries and structures along the canyon walls (bring binoculars). Many of the petroglyphs are easy to miss; most are on private property. Pick up a free guide at area restaurants or at the Castle Country Travel Desk in Price (p514). Allow at least three to five hours for the rocky, 70-mile ride (4WD preferred) from **Wellington** (on Hwy 6) to **Myton** (on Hwy 40). Be warned that convoys of trucks use, and degrade, the road daily. Get gas before you go: there are no services. About 23 miles northeast along Nine Mile Canyon Byway from the Hwy 6/191 turnoff, you can stay at the simple **Nine Mile Ranch** (☎ 435-613-9794; campsites $10, cabins incl breakfast $55-70), which has spacious grounds and rustic pioneer accommodations run by a 'retired' ranching couple who are the nicest folks you'd ever want to meet.

As far as other sleeping arrangements go, free camping is allowed off established roads in San Rafael Swell. The motel chain gang is situated off Hwy 191. **Holiday Inn** (☎ 435-637-8880, 800-315-2621; www.holidayinns.com; 838 Westwood Blvd; r $89-129) is top of the heap in Price. **Budget Host Inn & RV Park** (☎ 435-637-2424, 800-283-4678; 145 N Carbonville Rd; RV sites $20, r $44-59; 🖳 wi-fi), the best cheap-sleep, has neat-and-clean lit-

tle rooms located within an old-fashioned one-story building.

Munch on casual food favorites and deli sandwiches at **KoKo Pelli's** (☎ 435-613-1991; 189 N Carbonville Rd; sandwiches $5-9, mains $9-14; 🕑 lunch & dinner), served under images of the feisty flute-playing Native American deity. Or get ready to twirl some pasta at the Italian-American **Farlaino's Café** (☎ 435-637-9217; 87 W Main St; mains $10-16; 🕑 dinner).

Directory

CONTENTS

ACCOMMODATIONS

The Southwest provides a vast array of accommodation options: from pitching a tent under a starlit sky and budget motels to midrange B&Bs, adobe inns and historical hotels to four-star lodgings, luxurious spas, dude ranches and over-the-top casinos. The most comfortable accommodations for the lowest price are usually found in that great American invention, the roadside motel.

For last-minute deals, check www.triporati .com, www.sidestep.com, www.expedia.com, www.travelocity.com, www.orbitz.com, www .priceline.com and www.hotels.com. For more on discounts, see p23 and p521.

Accommodation listings in this book are ordered by price. A double room in the budget category costs $80 or less; midrange doubles cost $80 to $175; top-end rooms start at $175 (except in Las Vegas, where they generally start at $300 a night).

Unless otherwise noted, breakfast is *not* included, bathrooms are private and all lodging is open year-round. Rates generally don't include taxes, which vary considerably between towns and states (see p529).

As for icons (see the inside front cover), a parking icon is only used in the biggest cities. The internet icon appears where a place has computers available for public use or where an innkeeper is OK with people using their personal computer for an hour or so. If you're carrying a laptop, look for the wi-fi icon. Child-friendly hotels now have their own icon, and the Our Pick icon indicates a place is the author's favorite.

High season varies depending on the region within the Southwest. In general, the peak travel season runs June through August, except in the hottest parts of Arizona, when some places slash their prices in half because it's just too darn hot. The peak travel season for southern Arizona and the ski areas of northern Utah (for different reasons) and other mountainous areas are mid-December to mid-April. Throughout the book, when it is not obvious, we define which months constitute high season. Generally, we only list high-season rates. For more seasonal discussions, see p23.

Holidays (p524) command premium prices. When demand peaks, and during special events no matter the time of year, book lodgings well in advance.

If you're traveling with children, be sure to inquire about child-related policies before making reservations (see p92).

> **BOOK YOUR STAY ONLINE**
>
> For more accommodation reviews and recommendations by Lonely Planet authors, check out the online booking service at www.lonelyplanet.com/hotels. You'll find the true, insider lowdown on the best places to stay. Reviews are thorough and independent. Best of all, you can book online.

PRACTICALITIES

■ Major newspapers are published in Salt Lake City *(Desert News* and *Salt Lake Tribune),* Albuquerque *(Albuquerque Journal),* Phoenix *(Arizona Republic),* Tucson *(Tucson Citizen)* and Las Vegas *(Las Vegas Sun* and *Las Vegas Review-Journal).*

■ National Public Radio (NPR) features a level-headed approach to news and talk radio and is found on the lower frequencies of your FM dial. In rural areas, country-and-western music, Christian programming and Spanish-language radio predominates.

■ All the major US TV and cable networks are represented and readily available.

■ Video systems use the NTSC color TV standard (not compatible with the PAL system).

■ Distances are measured in feet, yards and miles; weights are tallied in ounces, pounds and tons.

■ Voltage is 110/120V, 60 cycles.

■ Self-service, coin-operated laundry facilities are located in all but the tiniest towns, most campgrounds and many motels.

B&Bs & Inns

In the Southwest, you'll find everything from cozy B&Bs to rambling old hostels that have sheltered travelers for several centuries. In smaller towns, guesthouses with simple rooms may charge $75 to $125 a night for rooms with shared bathroom, breakfast included. Some have more charming features, such as kiva fireplaces, courtyards or lounge areas. These fancier B&Bs tend to charge $125 to $175 per night with private bathroom. Other places may be ensconced in historical buildings, exquisite haciendas or luxurious urban homes. These tend to be equipped with every conceivable modern amenity and easily cost $225 and up a night. Most inns require a minimum stay of two or three nights on weekends and advance reservations. Many don't accept children or pets. It's always best to call ahead.

Camping

Spending at least one night camping out under the stars – preferably many more – should be a mandatory part of your Southwest experience. This region is chock-full of fabulous places to pitch a tent – from the Grand Canyon and Arches National Park to national forest and Bureau of Land Management (BLM) land to lakes nestled in state parks. The more developed areas (especially national parks) usually require reservations in advance. To reserve a campsite on federal lands book through **Recreation.gov** (☎ 877-444-6777, 518-885-3639; www.recreation.gov).

Many state parks and federal lands allow camping, sometimes free, on a first-come,

first-served basis. Contact information for local ranger stations is interspersed throughout the book. Developed camping areas usually have toilets, water spouts, fire pits, picnic tables and even wireless internet. Some don't have access to drinking water. At any rate, it is always a good idea to have a few gallons of water in the vehicle when you're out on the road. Some camping areas are open year-round, while others are only open from May through to the first snowfall – check in advance if you're planning on slumbering outdoors in winter.

Basic tenting usually costs $8 to $25 a night and cabins and teepees are available too. More developed campgrounds may be geared to RV travel and cost $25 to $40 a night. For information on renting an RV, see p539. **Kampgrounds of America** (KOA; ☎ 406-248-7444; www.koa.com) is a national network of private campgrounds with sites averaging $24 per night plus taxes.

Hostels

Staying in a private double at a hostel can be a great way to save money and still have privacy (although you'll usually have to share a bathroom), while a dorm bed allows those in search of the ultimate bargain to sleep cheap under a roof. Dorms cost between $15 and $22, depending on the city and whether or not you are an HI member. A private room in a Southwestern hostel costs between $25 and $45.

US citizens and residents can join **Hostelling International USA** (HI; ☎ 301-495-1240; www.hihostels .com; 8401 Colesville Rd, Suite 600, Silver Spring, MD 20910) by calling and requesting a membership form or by downloading a form from the website. Membership can also be purchased at regional council offices and at many (but not all) youth hostels. Non–US residents should buy a HI membership in their home countries. If you don't, you can still stay in US hostels by purchasing 'Welcome Stamps' for each night you stay in a hostel. When you have six stamps, your stamp card becomes a one-year HI membership card valid throughout the world.

HI has its own toll- and surcharge-free **reservations service** (☎ 800-909-4776), but not all hostels participate in it. The HI card may also be used to get discounts at some local merchants and for local services, including some intercity bus companies.

There are many more independent hostels in the Southwest, which have comparable rates and conditions to HI hostels and may sometimes be better. They often have a few private single or double rooms available, sometimes with their own bathrooms. Kitchen, laundry, notice-board and TV facilities are available. **Hostels.com** (www.hostels.com) lists hostels throughout the world.

Hotels

Southwest hotels, mostly found in cities, are generally large and luxurious, except for a few boutique hotels, which are small and understatedly lavish. Prices generally start at $200 and shoot straight up; ask about discounts and special packages when making reservations. Las Vegas hotels, though, are an entirely different animal. Attractions in and of themselves, they are as flashy as a sequined dress. Since the hotels expect you to lose (er…spend) money in their casinos, many offer great room deals. Always check online first when booking a hotel – consolidators such as **Orbitz** (www.orbitz.com), **Travelocity** (www.travelocity.com) and **Priceline** (www.priceline.com) all offer discounted rooms. **Triporati** (www.triporati.com) is a clearing house for comparing the cheapest rooms in much of the Southwest.

Lodges

Normally situated within national parks, lodges are often rustic looking but are usually quite comfy inside. Rooms generally start at $100 but can easily be double that in high season. Since they represent the only option if you want to stay inside the park without camping, many are fully booked well in advance. Want a room today? Call anyway – you might be lucky and hit on a cancellation. In addition to on-site restaurants, they also offer touring services.

Motels

Budget chain motels ('If you've stayed in one, you've stayed in them all!') are quite prevalent throughout the Southwest. In smaller towns, they will often be your only option. Many motels have at-the-door parking, with exterior room doors. These are convenient, though some folks, especially single women, may prefer the more expensive places with safer interior corridors.

Advertised prices are referred to as 'rack rates' and are not written in stone. If you simply ask about any specials that might apply, you can often save quite a bit of money. Children are often allowed to stay free with their parents; call and inquire if traveling with a family.

The Motel 6 chain is usually the cheapest of the lot. Although we generally don't include details on chain motels throughout the book, here's a handy list with contact information:

Best Western (☎ 800-937-8376; www.bestwestern.com)
Budget Host (☎ 800-283-4678; www.budgethost.com)
Clarion Hotel (☎ 800-252-7466; www.clarionhotel.com)
Comfort Inn (☎ 800-228-5150; www.comfortinn.com)
Courtyard by Marriott (☎ 800-321-2211; www.courtyard.com)
Days Inn (☎ 800-329-7666; www.daysinn.com)
Econo Lodge (☎ 800-553-2666; www.econolodge.com)
Fairfield Inn by Marriott (☎ 800-228-2800; www.fairfieldinn.com)
Hampton Inn (☎ 800-426-7866; www.hampton-inn.com)
Holiday Inn (☎ 800-465-4329; www.holiday-inn.com)
Howard Johnson (☎ 800-446-4656; www.hojo.com)
La Quinta (☎ 800-531-5900; www.laquinta.com)
Motel 6 (☎ 800-466-8356; www.motel6.com)
Quality Inn (☎ 800-228-5151; www.qualityinn.com)
Ramada (☎ 800-272-6232; www.ramada.com)
Red Roof Inn (☎ 800-843-7663; www.redroof.com)
Sleep Inn (☎ 800-753-3746; www.sleepinn.com)
Super 8 Motel (☎ 800-800-8000; www.super8.com)
Travelodge (☎ 800-578-7878; www.travelodge.com)

Resorts & Guest Ranches

Luxury resorts and guest ranches (often called 'dude ranches') really require a stay of several days to be appreciated and are often destinations in themselves. Start the day with a round of golf or a tennis match, then luxuriate with a massage, swimming, sunbathing, hot-tubbing and drinking. You get the idea. Guest ranches are even more like 'whole vacations,' with active schedules of horseback riding and maybe cattle roundups, rodeo lessons, cookouts and other Western activities. Ranches in the desert lowlands may close in summer, while those in the mountains may close in winter or convert into skiing centers. Depending how close to the slopes you want to stay, hotels in ski resort towns range from $100 for a simple double to upwards of $250 for a luxe condo right by the lift. During the off-season, prices can drop by more than 50%. Not bad, especially since many resorts offer mountain biking down or hiking around their slopes come summer.

ACTIVITIES

For millions of visitors to the Southwest, especially first-time visitors, the sheer scale and grandeur of the place as seen from car windows and scenic overlooks is reward enough. Locals, however, know that the Southwest offers an enormous variety of world-class outdoor activities, some of which, such as skiing or boating, may not be the first things that come to mind when one thinks about desert states.

For a complete discussion of the wealth of ways to have fun in the Southwest, see p81.

BUSINESS HOURS

Generally speaking, business hours are from 9am to 6pm. In large cities, a few supermarkets and restaurants are open 24 hours a day. In Utah, many restaurants are closed on Sunday; if you find one open, snag a seat and be happy. Unless there are variances of more than half an hour in either direction, the following serve as 'normal' opening hours for places reviewed in this book:

Banks 9am or 10am-5pm or 6pm Mon-Fri, some open Sat

Bars 4pm-1am

Government offices 9am-5pm Mon-Fri

Post offices 8am-4pm or 5:30pm Mon-Fri, some open Sat

Restaurants Breakfast 7am-10am; lunch 11am-3pm; dinner 5-10pm. In larger cities and resort towns many restaurants serve at least a limited menu from open to close; in Vegas restaurants can stay open 24 hours.

Shops 10am-5pm or 7pm (until 9pm in shopping malls) Mon-Sat, noon-5pm Sun

CHILDREN

As parents will be all too aware, successful travel with young children requires a bit of planning and effort. To help you out, we've created a special chapter for traveling with the little ones; see p89.

CLIMATE CHARTS

Except for southern Arizona, which stays sunny and warm year-round, the Southwest USA experiences four distinct seasons. The coldest months are January through March, when temperatures in the Grand Canyon and Santa Fe routinely dip below freezing and it snows regularly. This is a good time to visit Phoenix, as winter temps average about 65°F in the daytime.

Spring and fall are our favorite seasons to visit the Southwest – it is neither too hot nor too cold. In summer, temperatures throughout the region vary based on topography. In places like Santa Fe and Salt Lake City you can expect July temperatures to be in the mid-80s. At the same time in Phoenix, temps are normally well above 100°F, with the thermometer often hovering around 115°F! Now that's hot! But as they love to tell you out here, it's a dry heat (not a lot of humidity in the desert).

For more on when to visit, see p23.

COURSES

Opportunities to educate and enhance yourself while on vacation aren't as endless as the Southwestern sky, but you'll have plenty of choices nonetheless. Take meditation and tai chi classes at Sedona's Center for the New Age (p186) or Albuquerque's T'ai Chi Chih Center (p293). With all that relentlessly perfect light, hone your image-making skills with photographic offerings from the Santa Fe Workshops (p318).

Practically every sport has an outfitter who wants to teach you how to enjoy it with confidence; these are listed throughout the guide. For cooking courses, the best of the bunch is the Santa Fe School of Cooking (p317).

DANGERS & ANNOYANCES

Southwestern cities generally have lower levels of violent crime than larger cities like New York, Los Angeles and Washington, DC. Nevertheless, violent crime is certainly present and you should take the usual precautions. For health matters pertaining to dehydration and the like, see p542.

Whether you're in rural or urban areas, follow these safety tips:

- Lock your car doors and don't leave any valuables visible.

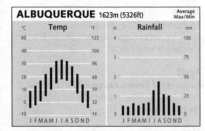

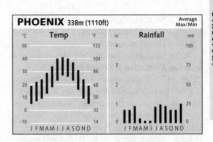

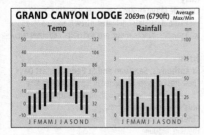

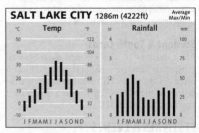

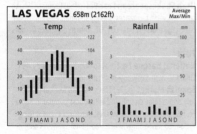

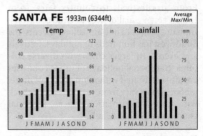

- Avoid walking alone on empty streets or in parks at night.
- Try to use ATMs only in well-trafficked areas.
- Avoid being in the open, especially on canyon rims or hilltops, during lightning storms.
- Avoid riverbeds and canyons when storm clouds gather in the distance; flash floods are deadly.
- When dust storms brew, pull off to the side of the road, turn off your lights and wait it out. They don't usually last long.
- Drivers should watch for livestock on highways and in Indian reservations and areas marked 'Open Rangelands.' Hitting an animal at 65mph can total your car and kill the creature.
- When camping where bears are present, place your food inside a food box (one is often provided by the campground).

- Watch where you step when you hike – particularly on hot summer afternoons and evenings, when rattlesnakes like to bask on the trail.
- Scorpions spend their days under rocks and woodpiles; use caution.

DISCOUNT CARDS

From internet coupons that you can print out before departure to coupons found in tourist magazines, there are price reductions aplenty. You just have to know where, when and whom to ask for them.

Senior Cards

Travelers aged 50 and older can receive rate cuts and benefits at many places. Inquire about discounts at hotels, museums and restaurants before you make your reservation. With the Golden Age Passport, US citizens aged 62 or over receive free admission to national parks and a 50% reduction on camping fees. For information call **Recreation.gov** (☎ 877-444-6777, 518-885-3639; www.recreation.gov).

Some national advocacy groups include:

American Association of Retired Persons (AARP; ☎ 888-687-2277; www.aarp.org; 601 E St NW, Washington, DC 20049) Advocacy group for Americans aged 50 years and older; a good resource for travel bargains. US residents can get one-/two-/three-year memberships for $12.50/21/29.50.

Elderhostel (☎ 877-426-8056; www.elderhostel.org; 11 Ave de Lafayette, Boston, MA 02111) Nonprofit organization offering seniors the opportunity to attend academic college courses throughout the US and Canada.

Student & Youth Cards

Most hostels in the US are members of Hostelling International (HI; see p518) and offer discounts to HI members. Often museums or theatres will give you a discount if you have a student ID.

FESTIVALS & EVENTS

From arts festivals to country fairs, from Indian ceremonial dances to chile cook-offs, from duck races to hot-air balloon ascents, the Southwest has hundreds of holidays, festivals and events. In larger cities with diverse cultures, traditional holidays of other countries are also celebrated with as much, if not more, fanfare. Dates vary from year to year, so check with tourist information offices. Regional chapters are full of details.

January

Cowboy Poetry Gathering (p142) Cowboys gather for folklore performances in January in Elko, NV.

Ouray Ice Festival (p405) Four days of climbing competitions, clinics, food and microbrew beer in Ouray, CO, in mid-January.

Sundance Film Festival (p503) Aspiring filmmakers, actors and industry buffs gather in Park City, UT, in late January for cutting-edge indie films.

February

Tucson Gem and Mineral Show (p240) This huge expo for jewelry and lapidary dealers is held early in the month in Tucson, AZ.

ART Feast (p318) Eat, drink and be merry gallery-hopping in Santa Fe, NM, during this weekend-long festival in late February that comes at just the right time – the fashion shows and wine tastings do a good deal to temper the late-winter cold weather.

Fiesta de los Vaqueros (p240) The world's largest non-motorized parade – followed by a rodeo and other cowboy events – takes place in Tucson, AZ, in late February.

March

Territorial Days (p251) Mining demonstrations, firemen's hose-cart competitions and a pet parade held mid-March in Tombstone, AZ.

April

Gathering of Nations Powwow (p297) Over 3000 Native American dancers and singers gather to compete in late April in Albuquerque, NM.

May

Cinco de Mayo Mexico's 1862 victory over the French in the Battle of Puebla is celebrated in New Mexico on May 5 with parades, dances, music, arts and crafts, and street fairs.

June

St Anthony's, San Juan and St Pedro's Feast Days These feast days are celebrated in New Mexico on June 13, 24 and 29 respectively, with an intermixing of Catholic rituals and traditional dances.

CineVegas (p118) Sin City's film festival lights up the Palms in mid-June.

Utah Shakespearean Festival (p460) Dramatic 'Shakespearience' performances, literary seminars and educational backstage tours in Cedar City, UT, from mid-June to October.

July

National Basque Festival (p142) Held over July 4 in Elko, NV, with a cowboy-style running of the bulls.

Spanish Market (p319) This weekend festival in late July draws huge crowds and is the most popular in Santa Fe, NM, after the Indian Market. The main event is the acclaimed juried show when traditional Spanish Colonial arts, from *retablos* and *bultos* to handcrafted furniture and metalwork, are shown.

August

Inter-Tribal Indian Ceremonial Gallup (p272) Extremely popular event drawing dozens of tribes with rodeos, dances, powwows, parades, races, food and arts and crafts to Gallup, NM, in mid-August.

San Lorenzo Day Food and craft booths, dances and races on August 9 and 10 at Laguna Pueblo (p284) and Picuris Pueblo (p287), NM.

Santa Fe Indian Market (p318) Only the best get approved to show their work at Santa Fe's most famous festival, held the third week of August, that includes a world-famous juried show where more than 1000 artists from 100 tribes and pueblos exhibit.

Bryce Canyon Rim Run (p455) A scenic 6-mile run along the canyon rim at Bryce Canyon National Park, UT.

September

Burning Man (p148) A city of artists rises in the Nevada desert before Labor Day weekend.

All American Futurity (p369) A quarter-horse race with a $2 million purse held on Labor Day (the first Monday of the month) at Ruidoso Downs, NM.

Navajo Nation Fair (p227) The country's largest Native American fair, with a rodeo, a parade, dances, songs, arts and crafts, and food, is held in early September in Window Rock, AZ.

Santa Fe Fiestas (p319) One of the oldest annual fiestas in the country, with concerts and a carnival in Santa Fe, NM, in early September.

International Camel Races (p146) Cheer on the hopeful dromedaries in Virginia City, NV, in mid-September.

New Mexico State Fair (p363) One of the largest state fairs in the country, with a rough 'n' tough rodeo, entertainment, carnival rides, livestock and culinary delicacies often served on a stick, every mid-September in Albuquerque, NM.

Whole Enchilada Fiesta (p363) A chile cook-off, entertainment, arts and crafts, races, and the world's largest enchilada at Las Cruces, NM, from late September to early October.

October

International Balloon Fiesta (p297) The world's biggest gathering of hot-air balloons, with daily mass ascensions in early October that invoke childlike awe in Albuquerque, NM.

Sedona Arts Festival (p185) A juried show overflowing with jewelry, ceramics, glass and sculptures in Sedona, AZ, in early October.

November

Day of the Dead A traditional Mexican celebration on November 2 honoring deceased relatives. Breads and sweets resembling skeletons are made and families visit graveyards.

Folk Music Festival (p433) A week of concerts powered 100% by wind-generated electricity in early November in Moab, UT.

San Diego Feast Day (p285) Traditional dancing on November 12 at Tesuque Pueblo, NM.

December

National Finals Rodeo (p119) Ten days of cowboy hoopla in Las Vegas, NV, every December.

Fiesta of Our Lady of Guadalupe (p363) A procession accompanying a statue of Mary from the church, with ceremonies and dancing, in Tortugas, NM, from December 10 to 12.

Christmas Month-long festivities, including Nativity pageants and festivals of lights, held in many Southwestern towns. Christmas Eve in Santa Fe, NM, is particularly special. The entire city is lit by candles and everyone walks down Canyon Rd after sunset for caroling by outdoor bonfires and steaming cups of hot cider served inside brightly lit gallery doors.

FOOD

Eating sections are broken down into three price categories: budget (with main dishes costing $10 or less), midrange (where most main dishes cost $10 to $20) and top end (where most dinner mains cost more than $20). These price estimates do not include taxes, tips or beverages.

Note that many Utah restaurants are closed on Sunday; when you find one open (even if it's not your first choice), consider yourself among the fortunate.

For details about Southwestern specialties and delicacies, see p63.

GAY & LESBIAN TRAVELERS

Per usual, the most visible gay communities are in major cities. Gay travelers should be careful in the predominantly rural areas – simply holding hands might get you bashed. Between the Mormons in Utah, right-wing Republicans in Arizona and conservative Hispanics in New Mexico, there's no mistaking the region for San Francisco.

The most active gay community in the Southwest is in Phoenix, not surprising considering that metro Phoenix has a larger population than either Utah or New Mexico. Although Santa Fe and Albuquerque have active gay communities – and boast pride parades (p318 and p297) – there are still three times more single-sex households in Arizona than in New Mexico. In Santa Fe, no one bothers much about wondering who's a lesbian and who isn't for two reasons: 'everyone' looks like a lesbian and folks are so groovy that no one cares. Perhaps some day there will be a saying, 'As Santa Fe goes, so goes the country.' In response to gay marriage becoming legal in Massachusetts in 2003, Sandoval Community, just north of Albuquerque, began issuing same-sex marriage licenses in early 2004. Las Vegas has an active gay scene, while conservative Utah has almost no visible gay life outside Salt Lake City.

According to www.epodunk.com, here's how the Southwest's big cities fare on a 'gay index,' a comparative score based on the percentage of same-sex households in a state: Las Vegas 123, Albuquerque 140, Phoenix 159, Salt Lake City 193 and Santa Fe 201. A score of 100 is the national norm; the higher the number, the more gays and lesbians there are.

Good national guidebooks include *Damron Women's Traveller*, providing listings for lesbians, *Damron Men's Travel Guide,* for men, and *Damron Accommodations,* with listings of gay-owned or gay-friendly accommodations nationwide. All three are published by the **Damron Company** (☎ 415-255-0404, 800-462-6654; www.damron.com).

Another good resource is the **Gay and Lesbian Yellow Pages** (☎ 800-697-2812; www.glyp.com), with 33 national and regional directories.

National resources include the **National AIDS/HIV Hotline** (☎ 800-232-4636), the **National Gay and Lesbian Task Force** (☎ 202-393-5177; www.thetaskforce.org) in Washington, DC, and the **Lambda Legal Defense Fund** (☎ in NYC 212-809-8585, in LA 213-382-7600; www.lambdalegal.org).

In the Southwest, there are few gay organizations compared to coastal cities.

HOLIDAYS
New Year's Day January 1
Martin Luther King Jr Day 3rd Monday of January
Presidents Day 3rd Monday of February
Easter March or April
Memorial Day Last Monday of May
Independence Day July 4
Labor Day 1st Monday of September
Columbus Day 2nd Monday of October
Veterans Day November 11
Thanksgiving 4th Thursday of November
Christmas Day December 25

INSURANCE
It's expensive to get sick, crash a car or have things stolen from you in the US. For rental-car insurance see p538 and for health insurance see p541. To insure yourself from theft from your car, consult your homeowner's (or renter's) insurance policy before leaving home.

Worldwide travel insurance is available at www.lonelyplanet.com/travel_services. You can buy, extend and claim online anytime – even if you're already on the road.

INTERNATIONAL VISITORS
US entry requirements continue to change as the country fine-tunes its national security guidelines. All travelers should double-check current visa and passport regulations *before* coming to the USA.

Entering the Country
Since the establishment of the Department of Homeland Security following the events of September 11, 2001, immigration now falls under the purview of the **Bureau of Citizenship & Immigration Service** (BCIS; www.uscis.gov).

Getting into the US can be a bureaucratic nightmare, depending on your country of origin. To make matters worse, the rules are rapidly changing. For up-to-date information about visas and immigration, check with the **US State Department** (☎ 202-663-1225; www.travel.state.gov).

Most foreign visitors to the US need a visa. However, there is a Visa Waiver Program in which citizens of certain countries may enter the US for stays of 90 days or less without first obtaining a US visa. This list is subject to continual reexamination and bureaucratic rejigging. At the time of writing these countries included Andorra, Australia, Austria, Belgium, Brunei, Canada, Denmark, Finland, France, Germany, Iceland, Ireland, Italy, Japan, Liechtenstein, Luxembourg, Monaco, the Netherlands, New Zealand, Norway, Portugal, San Marino, Singapore, Slovenia, Spain, Sweden, Switzerland and the UK.

Because the Department of Homeland Security is continually modifying its requirements, even travelers with visa waivers may be subject to enrolment in the US-Visit program. This program may require that visa recipients have a machine-readable passport and/or a digital scan of their fingerprints. Contact the **Department of Homeland Security** (www.dhs.gov) for current requirements.

Your passport should be valid for at least another six months after you are due to leave the US and you'll need to submit a recent photo (50.8mm x 50.8mm) with your visa application. Documents of financial stability and/or guarantees from a US resident are sometimes required, particularly for travelers from developing countries. Visa applicants may be required to 'demonstrate binding obligations' that will ensure their return home. Because of this requirement, those planning to travel through other countries before arriving in the US are generally better off applying for their US visa while they are still in their home country rather than while on the road.

The validity period for a US visitor visa depends on your home country. The actual length of time you'll be allowed to stay in the US is determined by BCIS at the port of entry.

Each visitor is allowed to bring 1L of liquor and 200 cigarettes duty-free into the US, but you must be at least 21 years old to possess the former and 18 to possess the latter. In addition, each traveler is permitted to bring up to $100 worth of gift merchandise into the US without incurring any duty.

Embassies & Consulates

US EMBASSIES & CONSULATES

Australia (☎ 02-6214-5600; http://canberra.usembassy.gov; 21 Moonah Pl, Yarralumla, Canberra, ACT, 2600)

Austria (☎ 31339-0; http://vienna.usembassy.gov/en; Boltzmanngasse 16, A-1090, Vienna)

Canada (☎ 613-238-5335; http://canada.usembassy.gov; 490 Sussex Dr, Ottawa, ON K1N 1G8)

Denmark (☎ 33-41-71-00; www.usembassy.dk; Dag Hammarskjölds Allé 24, 2100 Copenhagen)

Finland (☎ 9-616-250; www.usembassy.fi; Itäinen Puistotie 14 B, 00140 Helsinki)

France (☎ 1-43-12-22-22; http://france.usembassy.gov; 2 Av Gabriel, 75382 Paris)

Germany (☎ 030-8305-0; www.usembassy.de; Neustädtische Kirchstrasse 4-5, 10117 Berlin)

Greece (☎ 30-210-721-2951; http://athens.usembassy.gov; 91 Vasilissis Sophias Blvd, 10160 Athens)

Ireland (☎ 1-668-8777; http://dublin.usembassy.gov; 42 Elgin Rd, Ballsbridge, Dublin 4)

Israel (☎ 3-519-7575; www.usembassy-israel.org.il; 71 Hayarkon St, Tel Aviv 63903)

Italy (☎ 39-06-46741; www.usembassy.it; Via Vittorio Veneto 119/A, 00187 Rome)

Japan (☎ 03-3224-5000; http://tokyo.usembassy.gov; 1-10-5, Akasaka, Minato-ku, Tokyo)

Mexico (☎ 5-209-9100; www.usembassy-mexico.gov; Paseo de la Reforma 305, Colonia Cuauhtémoc, 06500 México, DF)

The Netherlands (☎ 070-310-9209; http://netherlands.usembassy.gov; Lange Voorhout 102, 2514 EJ The Hague)

New Zealand (☎ 04-462-6000; http://newzealand.usembassy.gov; 29 Fitzherbert Tce, Thorndon, Wellington)

Spain (☎ 91-587-2200; http://madrid.usembassy.gov; Calle Serrano 75, 28006 Madrid)

Sweden (☎ 08-783-5300; http://stockholm.usembassy.gov; Dag Hammarskjölds Väg 31, SE-115 89 Stockholm)

Switzerland (☎ 031-357-7011; http://bern.usembassy.gov; Jubiläumsstrasse 93, CH-3005 Bern)

UK (☎ 020-7499-9000; www.usembassy.org.uk; 24/31 Grosvenor Sq, London W1A 1AE)

EMBASSIES & CONSULATES IN SOUTHWEST USA

Most nations' main consulates or embassies are in Washington, DC. To find the telephone number of your embassy or consulate, call **Washington, DC, directory assistance** (☎ 202-555-1212).

There are few foreign consular offices in the Southwest. Even the skimpy list here changes regularly, so it's best to do an internet search before departing your country of origin.

Germany (Map p289; ☎ 505-872-0800; 8500 Louisiana Blvd NE, Albuquerque, NM)

Mexico (www.sre.gob.mx) Albuquerque, NM (Map p289; ☎ 505-247-4177; 1610 4th St NW); Nogales, AZ (☎ 520-287-2521; 571 Grand Ave); Phoenix, AZ (Map pp158-9; ☎ 602-242-7398; 1190 W Camelback Rd, Suite 110); Salt Lake City, UT (Map p483; ☎ 801-521-8502; 155 S 300 West); Tucson, AZ (Map p239; ☎ 520-882-5595; 553 S Stone Ave)

New Zealand (Map p493; ☎ 801-237-2664; 1379 N Brookhurst Circle, Centerville, Salt Lake City, UT)

Switzerland (Map p481; ☎ 801-272-7102; 4641 S Hunters Ridge Cr, Salt Lake City, UT)

Money

The dollar (commonly called a buck) is divided into 100 cents. Coins come in denominations of one cent (penny), five cents (nickel), 10 cents (dime), 25 cents (quarter) and the rare 50-cent piece (half dollar). Notes come in one-, five-, 10-, 20-, 50- and 100-dollar denominations.

See the inside front cover for exchange rates and p23 for information on costs in this region.

ATMS & CASH

ATMs are great for quick cash influxes and can negate the need for traveler's checks entirely, but watch out for ATM surcharges. Most banks in the Southwest charge around $1.50 per withdrawal. Beware of ATMs in Vegas that can charge as much as $10 for withdrawing cash – read before you click enter.

The Cirrus and Plus systems both have extensive ATM networks that will give cash advances on major credit cards and allow cash withdrawals with affiliated ATM cards. Look for ATMs outside banks and in large grocery stores, shopping centers, convenience stores and gas stations.

CREDIT CARDS

Major credit cards are widely accepted throughout the Southwest, including at car-rental agencies and most hotels, restaurants, gas stations, grocery stores and tour operators.

American Express (☎ 800-528-4800)

Diners Club (☎ 800-234-6377)

Discover (☎ 800-347-2683)

MasterCard (☎ 800-826-2181)

Visa (☎ 800-336-8472)

DIRECTORY

MONEYCHANGERS

Some banks exchange cash or traveler's checks in major foreign currencies, though banks in outlying areas do this infrequently and it may take some time. It's easier to exchange foreign currency in larger cities. You'll find Thomas Cook and American Express exchange windows in international airports, but you'll get a better rate at a bank or at home.

TIPPING

Taxi drivers expect a 15% tip. Waiters and bartenders rely on tips for their livelihoods: tip $1 per drink to bartenders and 15% to waiters unless the service is terrible (in which case a complaint to the manager is warranted) or about 20% if the service is great. Don't tip in fast-food, takeout or buffet-style restaurants where you serve yourself. Baggage carriers in airports and hotels should get $1 or $2 per bag. In hotels with daily housekeeping, leave a few dollars in the room for the staff for each day of your stay when you check out. In budget hotels, tips are not expected but are always appreciated.

TRAVELER'S CHECKS

Traveler's checks provide protection from theft and loss. For refunds on lost or stolen traveler's checks, call **American Express** (☎ 800-992-3404) or **Thomas Cook** (☎ 800-287-7362). Keeping a record of the check numbers and those you have used is vital for replacing lost checks, so keep this information separate from the checks themselves.

Foreign visitors carrying traveler's checks will find things infinitely easier if the checks are in US dollars. Most midrange and upscale restaurants, hotels and shops accept US dollar traveler's checks and treat them just like cash.

Post

No matter how much people like to complain, the **US Postal Service** (USPS; ☎ 800-275-8777; www.usps.gov) provides great service for the price. For 1st-class mail sent and delivered within the US, postage rates are 42¢ for letters up to 1oz (27¢ for each additional ounce) and 27¢ for standard-size postcards. If you have the correct postage, drop your mail into any blue mailbox. However, to send a package weighing 16oz or more, you

must bring it to a post office. See the individual Information listings in city and town sections for post office locations.

International airmail rates for letters up to 1oz are 72¢ to Canada or Mexico, 80¢ to other countries. Postcards cost 50¢ to Canada or Mexico, 94¢ to other countries.

You can have mail sent to you care of General Delivery at most big post offices in the Southwest. When you pick up your mail, bring some photo identification. General delivery mail is usually held for up to 30 days. Most hotels will also hold mail for incoming guests.

Call private shippers such as **United Parcel Service** (UPS; ☎ 800-742-5877; www.ups.com) and **Federal Express** (FedEx; ☎ 800-463-3339; www.fedex.com) to send more important or larger items.

Telephone

Always dial '1' before toll-free (800, 888 etc) and domestic long-distance numbers. Remember that some toll-free numbers may only work within the region or from the US mainland, for instance. But you'll only know if it works by making the call.

All phone numbers in the US consist of a three-digit area code followed by a seven-digit local number. All five Southwestern states require you to dial the full 10-digit number for all phone calls because each state has more than one area code. You will not be charged for long-distance fees when dialing locally. When calling a cell phone anywhere in the USA you need to always dial the 10-digit number; however, you do not need to dial the country code (☎ 1) when calling within the United States.

Pay phones aren't as readily found at shopping centers, gas stations and other public places now that cell phones are more prevalent. But keep your eyes peeled and you'll find them. Calls made within town are local and cost 25¢ or 50¢.

To make international calls direct, dial ☎ 011 + country code + area code + number. (An exception is to Canada, where you dial ☎ 1 + area code + number. International rates apply for Canada.)

For international operator assistance, dial ☎ 0. The operator can provide specific rate information and tell you which time periods are the cheapest for calling.

If you're calling the Southwest from abroad, the international country code for the US is ☎ 1. All calls to the Southwest are then followed by the area code and the seven-digit local number.

CELL PHONES

In the USA, cell phones use GSM 1900 or CDMA 800, operating on different frequencies than systems in other countries. The only foreign phones that will work in the US are triband models operating on GSM 10 as well as other frequencies. If you have a GSM tri band phone, check with your service provider about using it in the US. Make sure to ask if roaming charges apply; these will turn even local US calls into pricy international calls. If your phone is unlocked, however, you may be able to buy a prepaid SIM card and place it in your triband phone – you will then have a local number. Even though the US has an extensive cellular network, you'll still find a lot of coverage holes when you're driving in the middle of nowhere. Don't take undue risks thinking you'll be able to call for help from anywhere. Once you get up into the mountains, cell phone reception can be sketchy at best.

PHONECARDS

Private prepaid phonecards are available from convenience stores, supermarkets and pharmacies. Cards sold by major telecommunications companies such as AT&T may offer better deals than start-up companies.

INTERNET ACCESS

Most towns have at least one shop that offers a computer to get online, and in big cities like Phoenix, Las Vegas and Salt Lake City you'll find dozens. It generally costs between $10 and $20 an hour to log on, which isn't cheap – if you can bring your laptop do so, as most places that serve coffee also offer free wi-fi so

long as you order a drink. See the individual Information listings in city and town sections for internet café locations. When places reviewed in this book have computers available for public use, it's noted with an 🖳 icon. If you're traveling with a laptop, look for the wi-fi icon.

Besides coffee shops, airports, campgrounds, and in a few cases, entire cities have gone wireless, offering laptop owners the chance to get online for free or a small fee. You're most likely to be charged for wi-fi usage in hotels – some places charge up to $20 per day. Check the following websites for wi-fi hotspots:

- www-hotspot-locations.com
- www.wi-fi.com
- www.wififreespot.com
- www.wi-fihotspotlist.com

For a selection of useful websites about Southwest USA, see p27.

LEGAL MATTERS

If you are arrested for a serious offence in the US, you are allowed to remain silent, entitled to have an attorney present during any interrogation and presumed innocent until proven guilty. You have the right to an attorney from the very first moment you are arrested. If you can't afford one, the state must provide one for free. All persons who are arrested have the right to make one phone call. If you don't have a lawyer or family member to help you, call your embassy or consulate.

The minimum age for drinking alcoholic beverages in the US is 21; you'll need a government-issued photo ID to prove it (such as a passport or a US driver's license). Stiff fines, jail time and penalties can be incurred if you are caught driving under the influence of alcohol or providing alcohol to minors.

The legal ages for certain activities around the Southwest vary by state. For information about speed limits and other road rules, see p539.

MAPS

The most detailed state highway maps are those distributed free by state governments. Order them from state tourism offices (p529) in advance or pick them up at highway tourism information offices when you enter a state on a major highway.

TOP FIVE PHOTOGRAPHY TIPS

For a very complete short course on photographic ins and outs and dos and don'ts, consult Lonely Planet's *Travel Photography*. In the meantime, try these tips:

- Shoot at dusk and dawn. Sure, it's hard to wake up and be in the right place at the right time, but the light is more angular and dramatic.

- Include people for perspective. When you get home, your friends won't ask 'How big was that?'

- Shoot street life. Shots of one building after another will test your friends' patience.

- Change perspective. Get low and shoot up; get high and look down.

- Move in closer. Whether it's people or places, there's almost no such thing as too close (and when there, it's called an abstraction!).

The **Delorme Mapping Company** (☎ 207-846-7100; www.delorme.com) publishes great atlas-style state maps that cost about $20. Nothing compares to these maps for delving into backcountry roads.

Hiking trail maps are available from outdoor equipment stores, local outfitters, outdoors organizations, National Park Service (NPS) visitor centers and US Forest Service (USFS) ranger stations.

The **American Automobile Association** (AAA; ☎ 800-564-6222; www.aaa.com) publishes the *Indian Country Map,* which is sold in gas stations around the Southwest and comes in useful for exploring these areas.

PHOTOGRAPHY

You'll find dozens of shops offering services for transferring digital photos onto CDs in cities and towns throughout the Southwest. If you're travelling on the highways, look for exits with Target or Walgreens stores – both of these offer this service and are found even in smaller towns.

For the traditionalists out there, both print and slide film are readily available in the Southwest. Furthermore, every town of any size has a photo shop that stocks cameras and accessories. With little effort you should be able to find a shop to develop your color print film in one hour, or at least on the same day. Expect to pay about $7 to process a roll of 24 color prints.

With the implementation of high-powered X-ray at many airports, don't pack film into checked luggage or carry-on bags. Instead, carry your film in a clear plastic bag to show separately to airport security officials (ask for a hand check). Remember to finish off the roll

in your camera and take it out, too, or those photos may end up foggy. Don't leave your film and camera in your car on a hot summer's day, and don't place your camera on your dashboard while you are driving.

For information on photographing reservations and pueblos, see p61.

SHOPPING

Local arts and crafts top most shopping lists. The dividing line between traditional tribal or Hispanic crafts and Southwestern art can be a hazy one, with the latter often heavily influenced by the former. Buying Native American crafts on reservations, directly from the makers, is often substantially cheaper than buying it in off-reservation gift shops. However, the latter afford the buyer a much greater selection and, in the best stores, knowledgeable sales staff who have chosen only the finest quality work and can tell you about it. Buying from roadside stands in reservations can be fun, and you know that you are avoiding the middleman, but it's definitely a case of 'buyer beware' – the quality will vary tremendously.

Just about all the tribes make beautiful jewelry. Most New Mexico pueblos produce distinctive ceramics and pots, which vary from tribe to tribe. Taos Pueblo (p287) is always a good bet. In Arizona, look for Navajo items at the Hubbell Trading Post (p226) and Hopi crafts at the Hopi Cultural Center (p228). Gift shops at major museums are quite reliable outlets for authentic goods, too. Don't miss the Heard Museum (p156) in Phoenix, the Millicent Rogers Museum (p336) in Taos and the Museum of Northern Arizona (p190) in Flagstaff. Many visitors build entire vacations around shopping at the Santa Fe Indian Market (p318) each August.

For information on Navajo rugs and Hopi kachinas, see p60 and p56 respectively.

SOLO TRAVELERS

Travel, including solo travel, is usually safe and easy. In general, women need to exercise more vigilance in large cities than in rural areas. Everyone, though, should avoid hiking, cycling long distances or camping alone, especially in unfamiliar places. For more safety advice see p530 and p520.

TAXES

Meal and lodging taxes vary from county to county, but here is a guide:

State	Meal (%)	Lodging (%)	Sales (%)
Arizona	2-4.5	8-10	5.6
Colorado	2.5-7.4	8.9-9.25	2.9
Nevada	7.25	9	6.5
New Mexico	6.75-7.3	9-14.5	5
Utah	7.25-8	9-10	4.75

TIME

Most of the Southwest is on Mountain Time, which is seven hours behind Greenwich Mean Time. Nevada is an hour behind, on Pacific Time.

Daylight-saving time begins on the first Sunday in April, when clocks are put forward one hour, and ends on the last Sunday in October, when the clocks are turned back one hour.

Arizona does not use daylight-saving time, so during that period it's one hour behind the other Southwestern states. The Navajo Reservation, most of which lies in Arizona, uses daylight-saving time, but the small Hopi Reservation, which is surrounded by the Navajo Reservation, doesn't. Confused?

For a rundown of world times, see the World Time Zone map (pp566-7).

TOURIST INFORMATION

State and regional tourist offices include the following:

Arizona Office of Tourism (Map pp158-9; ☎ 866-275-5816; www.arizonaguide.com; 1110 W Washington, Suite 155, Phoenix, AZ 85007)

Colorado Travel & Tourism Authority (☎ 800-265-6723; www.colorado.com; PO Box 3524, Englewood, CO 80155)

Las Vegas Convention & Visitors Authority Visitor Information Center (Map pp104-5; ☎ 702-892-0711, 877-847-4858; www.vegasfreedom.com; 3150 Paradise Rd, Las Vegas, NV 89109)

New Mexico Tourism Bureau (Map pp312-13; ☎ 800-545-2040; www.newmexico.org; 491 Old Santa Fe Trail, Santa Fe, NM 87503)

Utah Travel Council (Map p483; ☎ 801-538-1030, 800-200-1160; www.utah.com; Council Hall, Capitol Hill, Salt Lake City, UT 84114)

TOURS

For travelers with a limited amount of time or specialized interests, tours may be the best option. Always read the fine print; tour prices may or may not include airfare, meals, taxes and tips. **Backroads, Inc** (☎ 800-462-2848; www.backroads.com; 801 Cedar St, Berkeley, CA, 94710) offers hiking and cycling trips for all ages across Arizona, New Mexico and southern Utah.

The sophisticated Washington, DC, **Smithsonian Journeys** (☎ 887-338-8687; www.smithsonianjourneys.org) organizes academically inclined, upscale tours such as Santa Fe Opera, National Parks of the West, Las Vegas Art and Architecture, and the Atomic Age in New Mexico.

Elderhostel (☎ 877-426-8056; www.elderhostel.org) also offers a whole host of educational programs (see p521).

For an alternative to pure tourism, look into **Global Citizens Network** (GCN; ☎ 651-644-0960, 800-644-9292; www.globalcitizens.org; 130 N Howell St, St Paul, MN 55104), where socially conscious visitors can work with the Navajo Nation in both Arizona and New Mexico. Smaller site- or town-specific tour companies are sprinkled throughout the individual chapters of this guidebook.

TRAVELERS WITH DISABILITIES

Travel within the Southwest is getting easier for people with disabilities, but it's still not easy. Public buildings are required to be wheelchair accessible and to have appropriate restroom facilities. Public transportation services must be made accessible to all, and telephone companies have to provide relay operators for the hearing impaired. Many banks provide ATM instructions in braille, curb ramps are common, many busy intersections have audible crossing signals, and most chain hotels have suites for guests with disabilities. Still, it's best to call ahead to check.

A number of organizations specialize in the needs of travelers with disabilities:

Mobility International USA (☎ 541-343-1284; www .miusa.org; PO Box 10767, Eugene, OR 97440) Advises on mobility issues but primarily runs an educational exchange program.

Society for the Advancement of Travel for the Handicapped (SATH; ☎ 212-447-7284; www.sath.org; 347 Fifth Ave, Suite 610, New York, NY 10016) Publishes a quarterly magazine; has various information sheets.

Twin Peaks Press (☎ 360-694-2462, 800-637-2256; http://home.pacifier.com/~twinpeak; PO Box 129, Vancouver, WA 98666) Publishes a quarterly newsletter, directories and access guides.

Disabled travelers seeking outdoor adventures should check out Splore (p428) and the National Ability Center (p502) in Utah.

WOMEN TRAVELERS

Women travelers everywhere face challenges particular to their gender. Avoiding vulnerable situations and conducting yourself in a commonsense manner will help you to avoid most problems. You're more vulnerable if you've been drinking or using drugs than if you're sober, and you're more vulnerable alone than if you're with company. If you don't want company, most men will respect a firm but polite 'no, thank you.'

If you are assaulted, you do not need to call the police directly in order to get help. The best course of action is often to call a rape-crisis hotline; contact numbers for these are normally listed in the telephone directory. Rape-crisis center staff act as a link between medical, legal and social service systems, advocating on behalf of survivors to ensure their rights are respected and their needs addressed. They often provide free translation services as well. Outside of urban areas, usually you can go directly to the nearest hospital for help first, then decide later whether or not to call the police. For the telephone number of the nearest center, call directory information (☎ 411 or ☎ 1 + area code + 555-1212).

The **National Organization for Women** (NOW; ☎ 202-331-0066; www.now.org; 1100 H St NW, 3rd fl, Washington, DC 20005) is a good resource for a variety of information and can refer you to state and local chapters. **Planned Parenthood** (☎ 212-541-7800; www.plannedparenthood.org; 26 Bleecker St, New York, NY 10012) can refer you to clinics throughout the country and offer advice on medical issues.

WORK

Seasonal work is possible in national parks and other tourist sites, especially ski areas; for information, contact park concessions or local chambers of commerce. These are usually low-paying service jobs filled by young people (often college students) who are happy to work part of the day so they can play the rest. You can't depend on finding a job just by arriving in May or June and looking around.

If you are not a US citizen, you must apply for a work visa from the US embassy in your home country before you leave. The type of visa varies, depending on how long you're staying and the kind of work you plan to do. Generally, you need either a J-1 visa, which you can obtain by joining a visitor-exchange program (issued mostly to students for work in summer camps), or an H-2B visa, when you are sponsored by a US employer.

The latter can be difficult to procure unless you can show that you already have a job offer from an employer who considers your qualifications to be unique and not readily available in the US. There are, of course, many foreigners working illegally in the country. Controversial laws prescribe punishments for employers employing 'aliens' (foreigners) who do not have the proper visas. BCIS officers can be persistent and insistent in their enforcement of the laws.

Transportation

GETTING THERE & AWAY

Most travelers to the Southwest arrive by air and car, with bus running a distant third place. The train service is little used but available. Major regional hubs include Las Vegas (p130), Phoenix (p170), Albuquerque (p301) and Salt Lake City (p489).

Flights, tours and rail tickets can be booked online at www.lonelyplanet.com/travel_services.

AIR

Unless you live in or near the Southwest, flying in and renting a car is the most time-efficient option. If time is not of the essence, drive. Most domestic visitors fly into Phoenix, Las Vegas or Albuquerque. International visitors, however, usually first touch down in Los Angeles, New York, Miami, Denver or Dallas/Fort Worth before catching an onward flight to any number of Southwest cities.

Airports & Airlines

There are many good options for flying into this region from elsewhere in the country, and around the world, for that matter. In addition to the major airports listed here, international visitors might consider flying into San Francisco or Los Angeles and driving. **Los Angeles Airport** (LAX; ☎ 310-646-5252; www.los-angeles-lax.com), busier than any of the airports listed here, is an easy day's drive from

western Arizona or southwestern Utah, via Las Vegas.

Albuquerque International Sunport (ABQ; ☎ 505-244-7700; www.cabq.gov/airport; wi-fi) Serving Albuquerque and all of New Mexico. A small and friendly airport (p301) that's easy to navigate – our favorite in the Southwest for this reason alone; a hub for low-cost carriers Southwest Airlines and America West and offers free wi-fi.

Denver International Airport (DEN; ☎ 303-342-2000; www.flydenver.com) Serving southern Colorado. If you rent a car in Denver, you can be in northeastern New Mexico in four hours; a United and (low-cost) Frontier hub.

El Paso International Airport (ELP; ☎ 915-780-4749; www.elpaso-elp.com) On the border with southern New Mexico; a possible minor gateway. For a teaser and primer on El Paso and West Texas, see p281.

McCarran International Airport (LAS; ☎ 702-261-5211; www.mccarran.com) Serving Las Vegas, NV, and southern Utah. The region's other busiest airport (p130), handling over 30 million passengers annually; a hub for America West, Continental and Southwest.

Salt Lake City International Airport (SLC; p489; ☎ 801-575-2400; www.slcairport.com) Serving Salt Lake City, UT, and northern Utah. Receives about half as many flights as Phoenix; a hub for Delta.

Sky Harbor International Airport (PHX; p170; ☎ 602-273-3300; www.phxskyharbor.com; wi-fi) Serving Phoenix, AZ, and the Grand Canyon. It's one of the region's two busiest airports, handling over 30 million passengers annually; a hub for America West and Southwest Air. It offers free wi-fi.

Tucson International Airport (TUS; p244; ☎ 520-573-8000; www.tucsonairport.org) Serving Tucson, AZ, and southern Arizona. A small airport that's easy to find your way around; a hub for low-cost carriers Southwest Airlines and America West.

THINGS CHANGE...

The information in this chapter is particularly vulnerable to change. Check directly with the airline or a travel agent to make sure you understand how a fare (and ticket you may buy) works and be aware of the security requirements for international travel. Shop carefully. The details given in this chapter should be regarded as pointers and are not a substitute for your own careful, up-to-date research.

CLIMATE CHANGE & TRAVEL

Climate change is a serious threat to the ecosystems that humans rely upon, and air travel is the fastest-growing contributor to the problem. Lonely Planet regards travel, overall, as a global benefit, but believes we all have a responsibility to limit our personal impact on global warming.

Flying & Climate Change

Pretty much every form of motor travel generates CO_2 (the main cause of human-induced climate change) but planes are far and away the worst offenders, not just because of the sheer distances they allow us to travel, but because they release greenhouse gases high into the atmosphere. The statistics are frightening: two people taking a return flight between Europe and the US will contribute as much to climate change as an average household's gas and electricity consumption over a whole year.

Carbon Offset Schemes

Climatecare.org and other websites use 'carbon calculators' that allow jetsetters to offset the greenhouse gases they are responsible for with contributions to energy-saving projects and other climate-friendly initiatives in the developing world – including projects in India, Honduras, Kazakhstan and Uganda.

Lonely Planet, together with Rough Guides and other concerned partners in the travel industry, supports the carbon offset scheme run by climatecare.org. Lonely Planet offsets all of its staff and author travel.

Airlines flying to and from the Southwest include:

Aer Lingus (EI; ☎ 800-223-6537; www.aerlingus.com)
AeroMexico (AM; ☎ 800-237-6639; www.aeromexico.com.mx)
Air Canada (AC; ☎ 888-247-2262; www.aircanada.ca)
Air France (AF; ☎ 800-237-2747; www.airfrance.com)
Air New Zealand (NZ; ☎ 800-262-1234; www.airnz.co.nz)
Alaska Airlines (AS; ☎ 800-252-7522; www.alaskaair.com)
America West Airlines (HP; ☎ 800-235-9292; www.americawest.com)
American Airlines (AA; ☎ 800-223-5436; www.aa.com)
ATA (TZ; ☎ 800-225-2995; www.ata.com)
British Airways (BA; ☎ 800-247-9297; www.britishairways.com)
China Airlines (CI; ☎ 800-227-5118; www.china-airlines.com)
Continental Airlines (CO; ☎ 800-523-3273; www.continental.com)
Delta (DL; ☎ 800-221-1212; www.delta.com)
Frontier (F9; ☎ 800-432-1359; www.flyfrontier.com)
Japan Airlines (NQ; ☎ 800-525-3663; www.jal.co.jp)
JetBlue (JB; ☎ 800-538-2583; www.jetblue.com)
Lufthansa (LH; ☎ 800-645-3880; www.lufthansa.de)
Mesa Air (YV; ☎ 800-637-2247; www.mesa-air.com)
Midwest Express (YX; ☎ 800-452-2022; www.midwestairlines.com)

Northwest-KLM (NW; ☎ 800-225-2525; www.nwa.com)
Qantas (QF; ☎ 800-227-4500; www.qantas.com.au)
Southwest Airlines (SW; ☎ 800-435-9792; www.southwest.com)
Song (SQ; ☎ 800-359-7664; www.flysong.com)
Spirit Airlines (NK; ☎ 800-772-7117; www.spiritair.com)
United (UA; ☎ 800-241-6522; www.united.com)
US Airways (US; ☎ 800-428-4322; www.usairways.com)
Virgin Atlantic (VS; ☎ 800-862-8621; www.virginatlantic.com)

Tickets

Airfares to the US and Southwest range from incredibly low to obscenely high, although if gas prices continue to climb in the manner they have been, expect air travel to become increasingly more expensive. The best deals are almost always found on the internet (see p534) these days. **STA Travel** (☎ 800-777-0112; www.statravel.com), which offers on-line booking, also has offices (with real, live people!) in major cities nation- and worldwide.

For one-way flights, low-cost airlines such as Southwest, America West, Frontier and JetBlue are the best places to look.

Many domestic carriers offer special fares to visitors who are not US citizens. Typically, you must purchase a booklet of coupons in conjunction with a flight into the US from a foreign country other than Canada or Mexico.

In addition to other restrictions, these coupons typically must be used within a limited period of time.

Round-the-world (RTW) tickets can be a great deal if you want to visit other regions on your way to or from the Southwest. Often they are the same price – or just a tad more expensive – than a simple round-trip ticket to the US, which means you get to visit other places for nothing. RTW itineraries that include stops in South America or Africa, though, can be substantially more expensive. **British Airways** (☎ 800-247-9297; www.britishairways.com) and **Qantas** (☎ 800-227-4500; www.qantas.com.au) offer the best plans through tickets called Oneworld Explorer and Global Explorer, respectively.

Count on ticket prices to be highest from mid-June through August, which is the height of the US tourist season. You can often get much cheaper fares should you choose to visit in off months, like October, November, April or May. Fares into Salt Lake City, Denver and Albuquerque can be higher during the December to March ski season, when thousands flock to the slopes in these states.

Asia

Hong Kong is the discount plane ticket capital of the region, but its bucket shops can be unreliable. Ask the advice of other travelers before buying a ticket. China Airlines flies to San Francisco and Los Angeles from Hong Kong. Summertime round-trip fares are around $1100 to $1700.

There are nonstop flights to the West Coast from several Japanese cities with various airlines. Japan Airlines flies to San Francisco and Los Angeles from Tokyo. Summertime round-trip fares are generally around $1300 in July and $2200 in August.

Connector flights are usually available from the West Coast to the Southwest for about $100 (one-way) on Southwest Airlines and America West.

STA Travel proliferates in Asia, with branches in **Bangkok** (☎ 02-236-0262; www.statravel.co.th), **Singapore** (☎ 6737-7188; www.statravel.com.sg), **Hong Kong** (☎ 2736-1618; www.statravel.com.hk) and **Japan** (☎ 03-5391-2922; www.statravel.co.jp). Another resource in Japan is **No 1 Travel** (☎ 03-3205-6073; www.no1-travel.com); in Hong Kong try **Four Seas Tours** (☎ 2200-7760; www.fourseastravel.com/english).

Australia

Qantas flies to Los Angeles from Sydney, Melbourne and Brisbane. United flies from Sydney to San Francisco and Los Angeles. Summertime round-trip fares are generally around $2500 from Melbourne or Sydney to the West Coast. Connector flights are available to the Southwest from the West Coast for about $100 (one-way) on Southwest Airlines and America West.

For the location of STA Travel branches call ☎ 1300-733-035 or visit www.statravel.com.au. **Flight Centre** (☎ 133-133; www.flightcentre.com.au) has offices throughout Australia. For online bookings, try www.travel.com.au.

Canada

The Canadian Federation of Students' **Travel CUTS** (www.travelcuts.com) travel agency offers low fares and has offices in major cities throughout Canada. It has good prices for students and deal with the general public as well. The Toronto *Globe and Mail* and *Vancouver Sun* carry travel agents' ads. For online bookings try www.expedia.ca and www.travelocity.ca.

Many connections between Canada and the Southwest are through Vancouver, BC. Air Canada flies from Toronto to Vancouver for a round-trip fare of about C$725 ($600). From Vancouver, there are relatively frequent flights to Phoenix and Salt Lake City. You can expect round-trip summertime airfares from Vancouver to Phoenix for $400 to $600 and to Salt Lake City for around $550.

Continental Europe

There are no direct flights to the Southwest from Europe. Flying straight to the West Coast is quicker than transferring in a city such as New York or Chicago. Nonstop summertime flights to Los Angeles are available from Amsterdam with Northwest-KLM (costing about $1600); from Frankfurt with Delta, United and Lufthansa (costing about $1400); and from Paris with Air France (costing about $1500). Nonstop flights from Europe to San Francisco are priced comparably.

It usually costs about $200 less to fly round-trip to the West Coast from London than it does from the Continent.

Recommended travel agencies:
Airfair (☎ 020-620-5121; www.airfair.nl) In the Netherlands.
Anyway (☎ 0892-893-892; www.anyway.fr) In France.

Barcelo Viajes (☎ 902-116-226; www.barceloviajes .com) In Spain.

CTS Viaggi (☎ 06-462-0431; www.ctsviaggi.it) In Italy.

Just Travel (☎ 089-747-3330; www.justtravel.de) In Germany.

Lastminute France (☎ 0892-705-000; www .lastminute.fr); Germany (☎ 01805-284-366; www .lastminute.de)

Nouvelles Frontières France (☎ 0825-000-747; www .nouvelles-frontieres.fr); Spain (☎ 90-217-09-79)

STA (☎ 01-44-41-89-80; www.sta.com) In Paris.

Voyageurs du Monde (☎ 01-40-15-11-15; www.vdm .com) In France.

New Zealand

United and Air New Zealand both fly to San Francisco and Los Angeles from Auckland (via Sydney) for about $2000 round-trip during the summer. Connecting flights are readily available to the Southwest for about $100 (one-way) aboard Southwest Airlines and America West.

Both **Flight Centre** (☎ 0800-243-544; www .flightcentre.co.nz) and **STA Travel** (☎ 0508-782-872; www.statravel.co.nz) have branches throughout the country. For online bookings, try www.travel.co.nz.

South & Central America

Most flights from Central and South America to the Southwest via Miami, New Orleans, Houston, Dallas/Fort Worth or Los Angeles. Most countries' international flag carriers, as well as US airlines like United Airlines, American Airlines and Continental Airlines, serve these destinations from Latin America, with onward connections to cities in the Southwest. There are infinite permutations of airfares that we could quote here, but we suggest that our South American readers plug their own specifics into an internet site or consult a local travel agency.

America West, United Airlines, Continental Airlines and AeroMexico have flights from Phoenix and Tucson to numerous Mexican cities. From Mexico City expect to pay $450 to Phoenix and $600 to Tucson.

Recommended agencies:

ASATEJ (☎ 54-011-4114-7595; www.asatej.com) In Argentina.

IVI Tours (☎ 0212-993-6082; www.ividiomas.com) In Venezuela.

Student Travel Bureau (☎ 3038-1555; www.stb.com .br) In Brazil.

UK & Ireland

London is arguably the world's headquarters for bucket shops specializing in discount tickets, and they are well advertised. Two good, reliable agents for cheap tickets in the UK are **Trailfinders** (☎ 020-7628-7628; www.trail finders.co.uk; 1 Threadneedle St, London) and **STA Travel** (☎ 020-240-9821; www.statravel.co.uk; 33 Bedford St, Covent Garden, London).

A flight in the summer from London to Phoenix (with one stop) is available on British Airways for about $1500. Several carriers fly nonstop to Los Angeles for about $1000, but then you'll have to add the cost (and time) of getting where you want to go in the Southwest.

Aer Lingus has direct flights from Shannon (one stop) and Dublin (nonstop) to Las Vegas for about $1300 in summer, from where you can catch a connecting flight to the Southwest.

USA

Competition is high among airlines flying to the Southwest from major US cities. With a little advance planning and some savvy internet browsing, you can usually get a nonstop summertime flight on a major carrier from Los Angeles to Las Vegas for about $150 round-trip, and from San Francisco for $200. From Washington, DC, fares to these same cities are in the $250 round-trip range. From Chicago, expect to spend about $225 round-trip.

You have a choice: talk to a live agent or tap the computer keys. Frankly, your odds are better doing it yourself if you have the time.

Atevo (www.atevo.com)

Best Fares (www.bestfares.com)

Cheap Tickets (www.cheaptickets.com)

Expedia (www.expedia.com)

Orbitz (www.orbitz.com)

STA Travel (☎ 800-777-0112; www.statravel.com)

Travelocity (www.travelocity.com)

LAND
Border Crossings

From Yuma, AZ (p233), you can cross into Baja California and Mexico. Nogales, AZ (p248), is also a prime border town. For more information about traveling south of the Southwest, pick up Lonely Planet's *Baja & Los Cabos* and *Mexico* guides. The biggest gateway if you're traveling in New Mexico is

> **INSPECTION STATIONS**
>
> Agricultural inspection stations at the Arizona–California border may ask you to surrender fruit when entering California, in an attempt to halt the spread of pests associated with produce.

actually El Paso, TX (p281), to reach bustling Ciudad Juarez.

Don't forget your passport if you are crossing the border; see p250.

For information on visas, see p524.

Bus

If you wish to or must travel by bus, long-distance buses can get you to major points within the region, but then you will need to rent a car (see p537), as public transportation to any of the national parks, including the Grand Canyon, is nonexistent. Bus lines also don't serve many of the smaller towns and even important tourist stops like Moab, making a car pretty much essential. Additionally, bus terminals are often in more dangerous areas of town. Having said that, **Greyhound** (☎ 800-231-2222; www.greyhound.com) is the main US bus system. Parts of New Mexico and southern Colorado, though, are served by the TNM&O (Texas, New Mexico & Oklahoma) bus line in conjunction with Greyhound.

To save money on bus travel, plan seven days in advance, travel on weekdays, travel with a companion and avoid holiday travel. Search the internet for special deals. Students, military personnel and seniors receive discounts.

From	To	Fare*	Duration
Los Angeles, CA	Las Vegas, NV	$65-85	6hr
Chicago, IL	Las Vegas, NV	$170-259	4-18hr
Portland, OR	Salt Lake City, UT	$125-150	18hr
Dallas, TX	Albuquerque, NM	$110-175	13-15hr

*Round-trip prices

When you've graduated from **Green Tortoise** (☎ 800-867-8647; www.greentortoise.com), a rolling mosh pit of youthful sightseers, but you still want to sleep on a bus and hang with like-minded adventurers, look into **Adventure Bus** (☎ 888-737-5263; www.adventurebus.com). It specializes in travel to the national parks of

southern Utah, the Grand Canyon and the Moab area.

Car & Motorcycle

Although the quickest way to get to the Southwest is by plane, the best way to get around is by car. If you have time, it's less expensive to drive to the Southwest than fly and rent a car – although this could change with increasing fuel costs. Regardless, getting around the Southwest is a heck of a lot easier if you've got a vehicle. Many places can only be reached by car, and it's nearly impossible to explore the national parks by bus… And then there's the little matter of driving. If you love driving, you'll be in heaven driving to and around the Southwest. Simply put, mile-for-mile, of the 160,000 miles (or so) in the national highway system, the Southwest has more stunning ones than any other part of the country – there are more than 100 designated scenic byways in the region, and that doesn't even include off-the-grid routes to get lost on.

Although little compares to the feeling of wind in your hair and the freedom of the open road, long-distance motorcycle driving is dangerous because of the fatigue factor that settles in. Please use caution during long hauls.

From	To	Via	Duration
San Diego, CA	Phoenix, AZ	I-8	7hr
Los Angeles, CA	Las Vegas, NV	I-15	5hr
San Francisco, CA	Santa Fe, NM	I-5 & I-40	19hr
Denver, CO	Santa Fe, NM	I-25	6½hr
Dallas, TX	Albuquerque, NM	I-35 & I-40	11½hr

For more detail on getting around the region by car or motorcycle, including road rules, see p539.

Train

Three **Amtrak** (☎ 800-872-7245; www.amtrak.com) trains cut a swath through the Southwest, but are unconnected with one another. Use them to reach the region but not for touring around. The *Southwest Chief* offers a daily service between Chicago and Los Angeles, via Kansas City. Significant stations include Albuquerque, NM, and Flagstaff and Williams, AZ. As an added value, on-board guides provide commentary through

Native American regions and national parks. The *California Zephyr* offers a daily service between Chicago and San Francisco (Emeryville) via Denver, with a stop in Salt Lake City, UT. The *Sunset Limited* runs thrice weekly from Los Angeles to Orlando and stops in Tucson, AZ.

Book tickets in advance and look for plenty of available deals. Children, seniors and military personnel receive good discounts. Amtrak offers various rail passes to non–US citizens (that must be purchased outside the US; check with a travel agent) as well as to Americans and Canadians.

From	To	Fare*	Duration
Los Angeles, CA	Flagstaff, AZ	$125	11hr
Chicago, IL	Albuquerque, NM	$350	26hr
Chicago, IL	Salt Lake City, UT	$185	35hr
San Francisco, CA	Salt Lake City, UT	$150	20hr
Los Angeles, CA	Tucson, AZ	$90	10hr

*Round-trip prices

GETTING AROUND

Once you reach the Southwest, traveling by car is the best way of getting around and allows you to reach rural areas not otherwise served by public transportation. If you do not relish long drives, you can always take buses and trains between select (read: a limited number of) major destinations and then rent a car. But that's both time consuming and more expensive than driving yourself and stopping everywhere along the way. Besides, isn't that why you bought this book?

AIR

Because distances between places in the Southwest are so great, regional airports are located in a number of smaller towns such as Yuma and Flagstaff (both in Arizona), and Carlsbad and Taos (both in New Mexico). But since these places primarily serve residents and business people, and because it is quite expensive and impractical to consider flying between these places, we have emphasized the major air gateways (see p531). Still, you can find information about these smaller airports scattered throughout the regional chapters. If you're flying your own plane, consult **Flyguides** (www.flyguides.com).

Airlines in the Southwest

America West Airlines (HP; ☎ 800-235-9292; www .americawest.com) Major regional and budget carrier with hubs in Las Vegas and Phoenix. Flies to Albuquerque and Farmington (both in NM), El Paso (TX), Durango and Telluride (both in CO), Salt Lake City (UT), and Tucson, Yuma, Prescott, Lake Havasu, Kingman and Flagstaff (all in AZ).

Mesa Air (YV; ☎ 800-637-2247; www.mesa-air.com) Flies to Farmington, Albuquerque, Roswell and Carlsbad (all in NM), and to Kingman, Prescott, Lake Havasu and Phoenix (all in AZ). Also flies to Denver (CO).

Southwest Airlines (SW; ☎ 800-435-9792; www .southwest.com) Major regional and budget carrier; flies to Albuquerque (NM), Tucson and Phoenix (both in AZ), and to Las Vegas (NV), Salt Lake City (UT) and El Paso (TX).

BICYCLE

Cycling is a cheap, convenient, healthy, environmentally sound and, above all, fun way of traveling. In the Southwest – because of altitude, distance and heat – it's also a good workout. Cyclists should carry at least a gallon of water and refill bottles at every opportunity since dehydration (p542) is a major problem in the arid Southwest.

Airlines accept bicycles as checked luggage. But since each airline has specific requirements, it's best to contact them for details. Bicycle rentals are listed throughout this guide when we've found a desirable place to cycle that also offers rentals. Expect to spend $15 to $25 a day for rental. For more on cycling, see p84. Moab (p430) is generally considered the mountain-biking capital of the Southwest. The countryside around Sedona (p183) is great for biking.

Bicycles are generally prohibited on interstate highways if there is a frontage road. However, where a suitable frontage road or other alternative is lacking, cyclists are permitted on some interstates. On the road, cyclists are generally treated courteously by motorists. In most states helmets are required by law (in Arizona, New Mexico and Utah under-18s have to wear a helmet, all riders must wear them in Las Vegas, and there are no requirements in Colorado); in any case, they should be worn to reduce the risk of head injury.

Cycling has increased in popularity so much in recent years that concerns have risen over damage to the environment, especially from unchecked mountain biking. Know your environment and regulations before you ride. Bikes are restricted from entering wilderness areas and some designated trails but may be used in National Park Service (NPS) sites, state parks, national and state forests and Bureau of Land Management (BLM) single-track trails.

BUS

Greyhound (☎ 800-231-2222; www.greyhound.com) is the main carrier to and within the Southwest, operating buses several times a day along major highways between large towns. Greyhound only stops at smaller towns that happen to be along the way, in which case, the 'bus terminal' is likely to be a grocery-store parking lot or something similar. Under this scenario, boarding passengers usually pay the driver with exact change. If Greyhound serves a town, look for the blue and red Greyhound symbol. The best schedules often involve overnight routes; the best fares often require seven days' advance notice.

In New Mexico, the TNM&O (Texas, New Mexico and Oklahoma) bus line supplements Greyhound routes. Local phone numbers are given throughout the regional chapters.

From	To	Fare*	Duration
Las Vegas, NV	Phoenix, AZ	$45-60	8-11hr
Phoenix, AZ	Tucson, AZ	$25	2hr
Tucson, AZ	Albuquerque, NM	$60-100	13hr
Albuquerque, NM	Santa Fe, NM	$15	1¼hr
Santa Fe, NM	Durango, CO	$45	7hr
Santa Fe, NM	Salt Lake City, UT	$60-120	19hr

*One-way prices

CAR & MOTORCYCLE

You've heard it a few times already: distances are great in this mighty region and car travel is easily the best mode of transport. Betting against that is akin to Las Vegas bookies taking money from children.

The interstate system is thriving in the Southwest, but smaller state roads and fine scenic byways (see the regional chapters for these beauties) offer unparalleled opportunities for exploration. As for the former, you should know that I-10 runs east–west through southern Arizona; I-40 runs east–west through Arizona and central New Mexico; I-70 runs east–west through central Utah; and I-80 runs east–west through northern Utah. As for the north–south interstates, I-15 runs

from Las Vegas to Salt Lake City; I-25 runs through central New Mexico to Denver, CO. The oh-so-classic Route 66 more or less parallels the modern day I-40 through Arizona and New Mexico; see p255 and p270 for detailed information.

Automobile Associations

The **American Automobile Association** (AAA; ☎ 800-564-6222; www.aaa.com) provides members with maps and other information. Members also get discounts on car rentals, air tickets, some hotels, some sightseeing attractions, as well as emergency road service and towing (☎ 800-222-4357). AAA has reciprocal agreements with automobile associations in other countries. Be sure to bring your membership card from your country of origin.

Main offices in the Southwest are located in **Phoenix** (☎ 602-274-1116), **Salt Lake City** (☎ 801-364-5615), **Las Vegas** (☎ 702-870-9171) and **Albuquerque** (☎ 505-291-6611). Many other smaller cities like Tucson, Santa Fe and Ogden also have offices; consult the *Yellow Pages*.

Emergency breakdown services are available 24 hours a day.

Driver's License

An international driver's license, obtained before you leave home, is only necessary if your country of origin is a non-English-speaking one.

Fuel

Gas stations are ubiquitous and many are open 24 hours a day. Small-town stations may be open only from 7am to 8pm or 9pm. Plan on spending $2.00 to $2.50 per US gallon.

At some stations, you must pay before you pump; at others, you may pump before you pay. The more modern pumps have credit/debit card terminals built into them, so you can pay with plastic right at the pump. At more expensive, 'full service' stations, an attendant will pump your gas for you; no tip is expected.

Rental

Rental cars are readily available at all airports and many downtown city locations. With advance reservations for a small car, the daily rate with unlimited mileage is about $30 to $40, while typical weekly rates are $150 to $200. Rates for midsize cars are often only a

APPROXIMATE ROAD DISTANCES (miles)

	Bryce Canyon NP, UT	Cortez (Mesa Verde NP), CO	Grand Canyon (North Rim), AZ	Grand Canyon (South Rim), AZ	Las Cruces, NM	Las Vegas, NV	Phoenix, AZ	Salt Lake City, UT	Santa Fe, NM
Bryce Canyon NP, UT	620								
Cortez (Mesa Verde NP), CO	280	390							
Grand Canyon (North Rim), AZ	470	130	340						
Grand Canyon (South Rim), AZ	410	290	370	210					
Las Cruces, NM	230	820	500	710	530				
Las Vegas, NV	580	250	570	270	280	670			
Phoenix, AZ	420	430	400	340	220	390	290		
Salt Lake City, UT	620	260	350	390	520	1030	420	710	
Santa Fe, NM	60	660	280	530	470	280	640	520	630
Tucson, AZ	500	540	470	470	350	280	410	120	820	560

Column headers: Albuquerque, NM | Bryce Canyon NP, UT | Cortez (Mesa Verde NP), CO | Grand Canyon (North Rim), AZ | Grand Canyon (South Rim), AZ | Las Cruces, NM | Las Vegas, NV | Phoenix, AZ | Salt Lake City, UT | Santa Fe, NM

tad higher. Since deals abound and the business is competitive, it pays to shop around between rental companies. You can often snag great last-minute deals via the internet; rental reservations made in conjunction with an airplane ticket often yield better rates too. In planning, if you decide to fly into one city and out another (quite likely given the distances and sights), drop-off charges for a rental car may not matter much. Nonetheless, don't forget to ask. Bidding for cars on **Priceline** (www.priceline.com) is the cheapest way to hire a vehicle – you can pick the city, just not the rental company. We've gotten deals on vehicles out of major cities in this region for as low as $12 per day. Priceline even allows you to pick up cars in one city and drop them off in another for the same price – very handy if, for example, you're flying into Phoenix and out of Santa Fe.

Having a major credit card greatly simplifies the car-rental process. Without one, some companies simply will not rent vehicles, while others require things such as prepayment, a deposit of $200 per week, pay stubs, proof of round-trip airfare and more.

The following companies operate in the Southwest:

Alamo (☎ 800-327-9633; www.alamo.com)
Avis (☎ 800-831-2847; www.avis.com)
Budget (☎ 800-527-0700; www.budget.com)
Dollar (☎ 800-800-4000; www.dollar.com)
Enterprise (☎ 800-325-8007; www.enterprise.com)
Hertz (☎ 800-654-3131; www.hertz.com)
National (☎ 800-227-7368; www.nationalcar.com)
Rent-A-Wreck (☎ 800-944-7501; www.rent-a-wreck.com)
Thrifty (☎ 800-847-4389; www.thrifty.com)

Insurance

Liability insurance covers people and property that you might hit. For damage to the actual rental vehicle, a collision damage waiver (CDW) is available for about $15 a day. If you have collision coverage on your vehicle at home, it might cover damages to rental cars; inquire before departing. Additionally, some credit cards offer reimbursement coverage for collision damages if you rent the car with that credit card; again, check before departing. Most credit card coverage isn't valid for rentals of more than 15 days or for exotic models, jeeps, vans and 4WD vehicles.

Note that many rental agencies stipulate that damage a car suffers while being driven on unpaved roads is not covered by the insurance they offer. Check with the agent when you make your reservation.

Road Conditions & Hazards

Be extra defensive while driving in the Southwestern states, especially in New Mexico. In fact, New Mexico has one of the highest ratios of fatal car accidents to miles driven in the whole country. Hwy 666 heading north to Shiprock has an especially high accident rate, and Gallup has an unfortunate reputation for careless and drunken drivers.

Distances are great in the Southwest, and there are long stretches of road without gas stations. Running out of gas on a hot and desolate stretch of highway is no fun, so pay close attention to signs that caution 'Next Gas 98 Miles.'

For updates on wintertime road conditions, contact:

Arizona (☎ 888-411-7623)
New Mexico (☎ 800-432-4269)
Southern Colorado (☎ in Colorado 877-315-7623)
Utah (☎ in Utah 511)

Road Rules

Driving laws are slightly different in each of the Southwest states, but each requires the use of safety belts. In every state, children under five years of age must be placed in a child safety seat secured by a seat belt. In New Mexico, children under one year old must be properly restrained in a rear-facing seat.

The maximum speed limit on all rural interstates is 75mph, but that drops to 65mph in urban areas in Colorado, Nevada and Utah. New Mexico allows urban interstate drivers to barrel through at 75mph, but Arizona makes drivers crawl through high-density areas at 55mph. On undivided highways, the speed limit will vary from 30mph in populated areas to 65mph on stretches where tumbleweeds keep pace with wily coyotes. Police enforce speed limits by patrolling in marked and unmarked cars; fines can be upwards of $300.

Consult p520 for general safety rules regarding driving in the Southwest, and p527 for matters concerning drinking and driving.

HITCHHIKING

Hitching is never entirely safe in any country in the world, and we don't recommend it. Travelers who decide to hitch should understand that they are taking a small but serious risk. You may not be able to identify the local rapist/murderer before you get into the vehicle. People who do choose to hitch will be safer if they travel in pairs and let someone know where they are planning to go. Ask the driver where he or she is going rather than telling the person where you want to go.

LOCAL TRANSPORTATION

Salt Lake City, UT, is the region's only city that has a light-rail system (p490). Most cities and some larger towns have local bus systems that will get you around (albeit slowly), but these buses generally run on very limited schedules on Sunday and at night. For more information on local transport, see the individual Getting Around sections throughout the regional chapters.

MOTOR HOME (RV)

Touring remote canyonlands, sparse deserts and Native American reservations by recreational vehicle can be as low-key or as over-the-top as you are. Rentals range from ultra-efficient VW campers to plush land yachts that resemble suites at the Bellagio in Las Vegas. Whatever mode you choose, what you've bought (or rented) represents freedom (except when you venture into big cities, when freedom's just another word for a parking nightmare).

After the size of the vehicle, consider the impact of gas prices, gas mileage, additional mileage costs, insurance and refundable deposits; these can add up quickly. It pays to shop around and read the fine print. Given the myriad permutations in rental choices, it's incredibly hard to generalize, but to get you started, you might expect a four-person vehicle with 1000 'free' miles to run $1100 to $1400 weekly in the summer, plus 32¢ for each additional mile. Get out a good map and a calculator to determine if that's too steep a price for freedom. Perhaps tent camping in a rental car doesn't sound so bad after all?

Before heading out, consult www.rvtravel .com for tips galore, including wi-fi locations. Then purchase a campground guide from **Woodall's** (www.woodalls.com), which also has a great all-round website, or **Kampgrounds of America** (KOA; ☎ 406-248-7444; www.koa.com), and hit the road.

For RV rentals contact:

Adventure Touring RV Rentals (☎ 866-672-3572; www.adventuretouring.com) Serving Las Vegas.

American RV Rentals (☎ 909-613-0562; www .americanrvrentals.com) Out of Los Angeles, with deliveries to Las Vegas.

Canyondlands RV Rentals (☎ 800-597-3370; www .rentrvutah.com) Serving Utah and Las Vegas.

Cruise America (☎ 800-327-7799; www.cruiseamerica .com)

Vacation RV Rentals (☎ 866-837-4502; www .vacation-rv-rentals.com) Serving Albuquerque.

TRAIN

Several train lines provide services using historic steam trains and are mainly for sightseeing, although the Williams to Grand Canyon (p261) run is a destination in itself. More scenic train rides are detailed in Chama, NM (p351), Santa Fe, NM (p318) and Durango, CO (p387).

For info on Amtrak trains, see p535.

Health David Goldberg MD

The Southwest encompasses a wide range of climates and temperatures, from the blistering heat of the desert summer to several 12,000ft-plus peaks where snow lingers almost year-round. Because of the high level of hygiene here, as in the rest of the USA, infectious diseases are rarely a significant concern for most travelers.

BEFORE YOU GO

INSURANCE

The US offers possibly the finest health care in the world. The problem is that unless you have good insurance, it can be prohibitively expensive. If you're coming from abroad, you're advised to buy supplemental travel health insurance if your regular policy doesn't cover you for overseas trips. If you are covered, find out in advance if your insurance plan will make payments directly to providers or reimburse you later.

Domestic travelers who have insurance coverage should check with their insurance company for affiliated hospitals and doctors. US citizens who don't have regular health coverage can purchase domestic travel insurance, but be aware that most plans only cover emergencies.

Bring any medications you may need in their original containers, clearly labeled. A signed, dated letter from your physician describing your conditions and medications, including generic names, is a good idea.

INTERNET RESOURCES

There is a wealth of travel health advice on the internet. The World Health Organization (WHO) publishes the superb *International Travel and Health,* which is revised annually and is available free online at www.who.int/ith. Another website of general interest is MD Travel Health at www.mdtravelhealth.com, which provides complete travel health recommendations for every country, updated daily, also at no cost.

IN SOUTHWEST USA

AVAILABILITY & COST OF HEALTH CARE

In general, if you have a medical emergency, the best bet is to find the nearest public hospital and go to its emergency room; these hospitals are committed to providing emergency care to anyone who walks in the door, regardless of ability to pay.

If the problem isn't urgent, you can call a nearby hospital and ask for a referral to a local physician, which is usually cheaper than a trip to the emergency room if you have insurance. You should avoid stand-alone, for-profit urgent care centers, which tend to perform large numbers of expensive tests, even for minor illnesses.

Pharmacies are found in abundance, but international travelers may find that some medications which are available over-the-counter at home require a prescription in the US, and, as always, if you don't have insurance to cover the cost of prescriptions, they can be shockingly expensive.

INFECTIOUS DISEASES
Rabies

Rabies is a viral infection of the brain and spinal cord that is almost always fatal. The rabies virus is carried in the saliva of infected animals and is typically transmitted through an animal bite, though contamination of any break in the skin with infected saliva may result in rabies. In the US, most cases of human rabies are related to exposure to bats. Rabies may also be contracted from raccoons, skunks, foxes and unvaccinated cats and dogs.

If there is any possibility, however small, that you have been exposed to rabies, you should seek preventative treatment, which consists of rabies immune globulin and rabies vaccine and is quite safe. In particular, any contact with a bat should be discussed with health authorities, because bats have small teeth and may not leave obvious bite marks. If you wake up to find a bat in your room, or discover a bat in a room with small children, rabies prophylaxis may be necessary.

Giardiasis

This parasitic infection of the small intestine occurs throughout North America and the world. Symptoms may include nausea, bloating, cramps and diarrhea, and may last for weeks. To protect yourself from giardia, you should avoid drinking directly from lakes, ponds, streams and rivers, which may be contaminated by animal or human feces. The infection can also be transmitted from person to person if proper hand washing is not performed. Giardiasis is easily diagnosed by a stool test and readily treated with antibiotics.

HIV/AIDS

As with most parts of the world, HIV infection occurs throughout the Southwest. You should never assume, on the basis of someone's background or appearance, that they're free of this or any other sexually transmitted disease. Be sure to use a condom for all sexual encounters.

Plague

While rare, plague (aka Black Death, the little flea-borne bacterium that killed some 25 million Europeans in the 1350s) still infects about a dozen people in northern New Mexico each year, usually between April and November. Medical technology has improved a bit since the Middle Ages, and prompt diagnosis and treatment almost always means a full recovery.

Plague has an incubation period of two to seven days and rather nonspecific symptoms: headache, chills, high fever and painful, swollen lymph nodes in the groin, armpit and/or neck. If you display these symptoms shortly after your vacation, tell your doctor that you've been in a plague area and ask to be tested for the disease.

Plague is usually contracted by hikers and campers bitten by fleas shared with infected rodents and small animals, in particular rock squirrels and gophers. Stay on trails, avoid stirring up the undergrowth in piñon forests and give wide berth to sick, slow-moving or disoriented animals. It cannot be transmitted directly from person to person in the bubonic form.

ENVIRONMENTAL HAZARDS
Altitude Sickness

Visitors from lower elevations undergo rather dramatic physiological changes as they adapt to high altitudes, and while the side effects are usually mild, they can be dangerous if ignored. Some people – age and fitness level are not predictors of who these will be – will feel the effects of altitude strongly, while others won't even notice.

Symptoms, which tend to manifest during the first day after reaching altitude, may include headache, fatigue, loss of appetite, nausea, sleeplessness, increased urination and hyperventilation due to overexertion. Symptoms normally resolve within 24 to 48 hours. The rule of thumb is, don't ascend until the symptoms descend. More severe cases may display extreme disorientation, ataxia (loss of coordination and balance), breathing problems (especially a persistent cough) and vomiting. These folks should descend immediately and get to a hospital.

To avoid the discomfort characterizing the milder symptoms, drink plenty of water (dehydration exacerbates the symptoms) and take it easy – at 7000ft, a pleasant walk around Santa Fe can wear you out faster than a steep hike at sea level. Schedule a nap if you have a sleepless night and put off serious hiking and biking for a few days, if possible. A mild painkiller like aspirin should take care of the headache.

Dehydration

Visitors to the desert may not realize how much water they're losing, as sweat evaporates almost immediately and increased urination (to help the blood process oxygen more efficiently) can go unnoticed. The prudent tourist will make sure to drink more water than usual – think a gallon a day if you're active. Parents can carry fruit and fruit juices to help keep kids hydrated.

Severe dehydration can easily cause disorientation and confusion, and even day hikers have gotten lost and died because they ignored their thirst. So bring plenty of water, even on short hikes, and drink it!

Heat Exhaustion & Heatstroke

Dehydration or salt deficiency can cause heat exhaustion. Take time to acclimatize to high temperatures and make sure you get enough liquids. Salt deficiency is characterized by fatigue, lethargy, headaches, giddiness and muscle cramps. Salt tablets may help. Vomiting or diarrhea can also deplete your liquid and salt levels. Anhydrotic heat exhaustion, caused by the inability to sweat, is quite rare. Unlike other forms of heat exhaustion, it may strike people who have been in a hot climate for some time, rather than newcomers. Always use water bottles on long trips. One gallon of water per person per day is recommended if hiking.

Long, continuous exposure to high temperatures can lead to the sometimes-fatal condition of heatstroke, which occurs when the body's heat-regulating mechanism breaks down and the body temperature rises to dangerous levels. Hospitalization is essential for extreme cases, but meanwhile get out of the sun, remove clothing, cover the body with a wet sheet or towel and fan continually.

Hypothermia
Skiers and winter hikers will find that temperatures in the mountains or desert can quickly drop below freezing. A sudden soaking or even high winds can lower your body temperature rapidly. Travel with a partner whenever possible.

Seek shelter when bad weather is unavoidable. Woolen clothing and synthetics, which retain warmth even when wet, are superior to cottons. Carry a good-quality sleeping bag and high-energy, easily digestible snacks such as chocolate or dried fruit.

The symptoms of hypothermia are exhaustion, numbness, shivering, slurred speech, irrational or violent behavior, lethargy, stumbling, dizzy spells, muscle cramps and violent bursts of energy. Get hypothermia victims out of bad weather and into dry, warm clothing. Give hot liquids (not alcohol) and high-calorie, easily digestible food. In advanced stages, place victims in warm sleeping bags and get in with them. Do not rub victims.

Animal Bites
Do not attempt to pet, handle or feed any wild animal, no matter how cuddly it may look; most injuries from animals are directly related to people trying to do just that.

Any bite or scratch by a mammal, including bats, should be promptly and thoroughly cleansed with large amounts of soap and water, followed by application of an antiseptic such as iodine or alcohol. The local health authorities should be contacted immediately for possible rabies treatment, whether or not you've been immunized against rabies. It may also be advisable to start an antibiotic, since wounds caused by animal bites and scratches frequently become infected.

Mosquito Bites
When mosquitoes are present, keep yourself covered (wear long sleeves, long pants, hats and shoes rather than sandals) and apply a good insect repellent, preferably one containing DEET, to exposed skin and clothing. Don't overuse the stuff, though, because neurologic toxicity – though uncommon – has been reported from DEET, especially in children. DEET-containing compounds should not be used at all on kids under the age of two.

Insect repellents containing certain botanical products, including oil of eucalyptus and soybean oil, are effective but last only 1½ to two hours. Products based on citronella are not effective.

Tick Bites
Ticks are parasitic arachnids that may be present in brush, forest and grasslands, where hikers often get them on their legs or in their boots. Adult ticks suck blood from hosts by burrowing into the skin and can carry infections such as Lyme disease (rare in the Southwest).

Always check your body for ticks after walking through high grass or thickly forested area. If ticks are found unattached, they can simply be brushed off. If a tick is found attached, press down around the tick's head with tweezers, grab the head and gently pull upwards – do not twist it. (If no tweezers are available, use your fingers, but protect them from contamination with a piece of tissue or paper.) Do not rub oil, alcohol or petroleum jelly on it. If you get sick in the next couple of weeks, consult a doctor (diagnosis will be easier if you kept the tick).

Snake Bites
There are several varieties of venomous snakes in the USA, but unlike those in other countries they do not cause instantaneous death, and antivenins are available. Rattlesnake bites are fairly common. First aid is to place a light constricting bandage over the bite, keep the

wounded part below the level of the heart and move it as little as possible. Stay calm and get to a medical facility as soon as possible. Bring the dead snake for identification if you can, but don't risk being bitten again. Do not use the mythic 'cut an X and suck out the venom' trick, as this causes more damage to snake-bite victims than the bites themselves.

The Arizona Poison Control System reports that half of reported snake bites result from people picking up the snake, either out of bravado or mistakenly assuming that the animal is dead. Keep a healthy distance away from snakes and watch where you step.

Spider & Scorpion Bites

Although there are many species of spiders in the Southwest, the main two that cause significant human illness are the black widow and brown recluse. The black widow is black or brown in color, measuring about 15mm in body length, with a shiny top, a fat body and a distinctive red or orange hourglass figure on its underside. It's usually found in barns, woodpiles, sheds, harvested crops and bowls of outdoor toilets. The brown recluse spider is brown, usually 10mm in body length, with

a dark violin-shaped mark on the top of the upper section of the body. It's active mostly at night and lives in dark sheltered areas, such as under porches and in woodpiles, and typically bites when trapped.

If bitten by a black widow, you should apply ice or cold packs and immediately go to the nearest emergency room. Complications of a black widow bite may include muscle spasms, breathing difficulties and high blood pressure. The bite of a brown recluse typically causes a large, inflamed wound, sometimes associated with fever and chills. If bitten, apply ice and see a physician.

If stung by a scorpion, you should immediately apply ice or a cold pack, immobilize the affected body part and go to the nearest emergency room. To prevent scorpion stings, be sure to inspect and shake out clothing, shoes and sleeping bags before use, and wear gloves and protective clothing when working around piles of wood or leaves.

Poison Control Centers are staffed 24 hours a day and advise about bites, stings and ingested poisons of all kinds. Call ☎ 800-222-1222 anywhere in the Southwest for the one nearest you.

The Authors

BECCA BLOND
Coordinating Author, New Mexico, Southwestern Colorado

This was Becca's first time coordinating *Southwest USA*, although she wrote the Arizona, Las Vegas and Southwestern Colorado chapters for the previous edition. For this book, Becca had the pleasure of researching her beloved Colorado, again, and also tackled her adopted home state of New Mexico. Becca fell in love with Santa Fe after her parents moved there a few years ago, and plans to marry her best friend and Lonely Planet writing partner Aaron Anderson in an October 18, 2008, ceremony at the Loretto Chapel. Becca has authored more than 25 books for Lonely Planet over the last five years and has been the sole author of all Colorado content during that time.

SARA BENSON
Las Vegas & Nevada

First awestruck by the Strip's neon lights during a cross-country trek to California, Sara had a serendipitous one-night stand with Las Vegas that became a torrid love affair. Now she travels down to the Nevada desert every chance she gets, and has racked up more hours gambling and carousing around Sin City than she'll readily admit to her grandmother. Sara is also an avid outdoor enthusiast. Her travel writing has featured on popular websites and in magazines and newspapers from coast to coast, including the *Las Vegas Review-Journal*. The author of 30 travel and nonfiction books, Sara has also written Lonely Planet's *Las Vegas* and *Las Vegas Encounter* guides.

LISA DUNFORD
Utah

Perhaps it was inevitable that Lisa would be fascinated by Utah, since her great-great-great-grandfather Brigham Young helped found the state. She's likely related to a third of the local population, but it's the red rock that keeps her coming back. Hiking through slot canyons and over slickrock, seeking out little-known petroglyphs, Lisa can't help but think about buying a jeep and a piece of the southern Utah wilderness. For now, she, her husband and their dog call a river in southeast Texas home.

THE AUTHORS

LONELY PLANET AUTHORS

Why is our travel information the best in the world? It's simple: our authors are passionate, dedicated travelers. They don't take freebies in exchange for positive coverage so you can be sure the advice you're given is impartial. They travel widely to all the popular spots, and off the beaten track. They don't research using just the internet or phone. They discover new places not included in any other guidebook. They personally visit thousands of hotels, restaurants, palaces, trails, galleries, temples and more. They speak with dozens of locals every day to make sure you get the kind of insider knowledge only a local could tell you. They take pride in getting all the details right, and in telling it how it is. Think you can do it? Find out how at **lonelyplanet.com**.

ANDREA SCHULTE-PEEVERS   Arizona

Andrea grew up in Germany watching movies and day-dreaming about the American Wild West with its cowboys and Indians, tall cacti and rugged mountains – a land of startling expanse canopied by infinite blue skies. She eventually made it out West, settling in Los Angeles, picking up a degree from UCLA and launching her career as a travel writer. Although she thinks of herself as a 'big-city person,' her fascination with the Southwest never waned, which is why she was giddy with delight when asked to return to Arizona, one of her favorite stomping grounds, for this book.

CONTRIBUTING AUTHORS

Jeff Campbell has been the coordinating author of *Southwest USA 3, Zion & Bryce Canyon National Parks 1*, and the last three editions of *USA*, among other Lonely Planet titles. He wishes that he called the Southwest home, but next best is meeting and writing about those who do. He wrote the Native American Southwest chapter.

Jennifer Denniston caught the travel bug at age nine, when her parents took the family on a 10-week trip through Europe. After college, she lived in New Mexico, earned a Masters degree in American Studies with a focus on the American West, and taught writing at the University of Iowa. Now mother to Anna (7) and Harper (5), Jennifer is committed to making travel a cornerstone of her children's lives. Jennifer has contributed to Lonely Planet's *USA, Arizona* and *Grand Canyon National Park* guides. She wrote the Southwest with Kids chapter.

David Goldberg MD completed his training in internal medicine and infectious diseases at Columbia-Presbyterian Medical Center in New York City, where he has also served as voluntary faculty. At present, he is an infectious diseases specialist in Scarsdale, NY, and the editor-in-chief of the website MDtravel-health.com. The Health chapter was adapted from his text.

David Lukas is a professional naturalist whose travels and writing take him around the American West and further afield. He has contributed environment and wildlife chapters to about 20 Lonely Planet guides. David's favorite Southwest moment was getting up to watch the sunrise on the magnificent hoodoos at Bryce Canyon (don't miss it!). He wrote the Environment chapter.

Behind the Scenes

THIS BOOK

This 5th edition of *Southwest USA* was researched and written by Becca Blond (coordinating author), Sara 'Sam' Benson, Lisa Dunford and Andrea Schulte-Peevers, with contributions from Jeff Campbell, Jennifer Denniston and David Lukas. The Health chapter was adapted from text by Dr David Goldberg. The 'Burning Man' box was based on text from Mark Morford, and some content in the book was based on text from *Grand Canyon National Park* 2, by Wendy Yanagihara and Jennifer Denniston.

The 4th edition was written by Kim Grant, Becca Blond and John A Vlahides.

This guidebook was commissioned in Lonely Planet's Oakland office, and produced by the following:

Commissioning Editor Suki Gear
Coordinating Editors Gabrielle Stefanos, Trent Holden
Coordinating Cartographer Andy Rojas
Coordinating Layout Designer Carol Jackson
Managing Editor Geoff Howard
Senior Editor Helen Christinis
Managing Cartographer Alison Lyall
Managing Layout Designer Celia Wood
Assisting Editors Sarah Bailey, Michelle Bennett, Peter Cruttenden, Carly Hall, Kate James

Assisting Cartographers Ross Butler, Owen Eszeki, Jacqueline Nguyen, Sophie Reed, Andrew Smith, Sam Sayer
Cover Designer Pepi Bluck
Project Manager Rachel Imeson

Thanks to Mark Germanchis, Penelope Goodes, Lisa Knights, Chris Lee Ack, John Mazzocchi, Raphael Richards, Wibowo Rusli, Jacqui Saunders, Glenn van der Knijff

THANKS
BECCA BLOND

I want to dedicate this book to my Grandma Jennie, who died in November 2007 at the age of 95. She has always been my inspiration and personal hero, and always encouraged me to write and pursue my dreams. Her attitude and spunk will live on forever in my heart. I miss you, Grandma... Big thanks also go to my parents, David and Patricia, for hosting me in Santa Fe and putting up with all my drama and loving me overall. Also to Teddy Flicker for allowing me to interview him even when he wasn't feeling well. On the home front, I want to thank Aaron for helping me research and also for being my rock. I love you babe and can't wait to marry you! To my favorite bulldog in the world, Duke, thanks for all the help.

THE LONELY PLANET STORY

Fresh from an epic journey across Europe, Asia and Australia in 1972, Tony and Maureen Wheeler sat at their kitchen table stapling together notes. The first Lonely Planet guidebook, *Across Asia on the Cheap*, was born.

Travelers snapped up the guides. Inspired by their success, the Wheelers began publishing books to Southeast Asia, India and beyond. Demand was prodigious, and the Wheelers expanded the business rapidly to keep up. Over the years, Lonely Planet extended its coverage to every country and into the virtual world via lonelyplanet.com and the Thorn Tree message board.

As Lonely Planet became a globally loved brand, Tony and Maureen received several offers for the company. But it wasn't until 2007 that they found a partner whom they trusted to remain true to the company's principles of traveling widely, treading lightly and giving sustainably. In October of that year, BBC Worldwide acquired a 75% share in the company, pledging to uphold Lonely Planet's commitment to independent travel, trustworthy advice and editorial independence.

Today, Lonely Planet has offices in Melbourne, London and Oakland, with over 500 staff members and 300 authors. Tony and Maureen are still actively involved with Lonely Planet. They're travelling more often than ever, and they're devoting their spare time to charitable projects. And the company is still driven by the philosophy of *Across Asia on the Cheap*: 'All you've got to do is decide to go and the hardest part is over. So go!'

SARA 'SAM' BENSON

Researching and writing this book would not have been nearly as much fun without commissioning editor Suki Gear, whose enthusiasm for Sin City never needs a Red Bull boost, and my partner Mike Connolly, acting as my chauffeur, research assistant, photographer and poker coach ('if you just keep playing, you'll win'). Many thanks to all of the Nevadans who have aided my research around the Silver State, especially those who kindly agreed to be interviewed.

LISA DUNFORD

Thanks to all the lovely people I met along the way, including: Carolyn Jessop; Gary and Sheri Catmull; Jane Reiss; Harvey Hammack; John Davis; Kathy and Jason Rabb; Shari Zollinger; Jessica Kunzer, Stephanie Nitsch, Juliann Fritz, Doug Haney, Shannon Bahrke, Ted Ligety; officer J Tatangelo in Bull Frog; the professional Santa in Panguitch; the bartender who knew a camel in Torrey… Aunt Tracy and Uncle Tom, your experiences were so helpful. Andrea, your friendship helped me push my boundaries. And Billy, just because. Suki, Becca, Andrea, Sam, Jeff and Jennifer – you were a great crew to work with!

ANDREA SCHULTE-PEEVERS

Suki Gear – thanks for the gig and for being such a big part of my professional life all these years. David – thanks for being my life, period. And then there are all those wonderful people I met on the road and who fed me tips, advice and insights. Standouts include (in no particular order): Stephanie Heckathorne, Mike Finney, Susan Schepman, Kathy Curley, Allison Raskansky, Robert Bravo Jr, Mona Mesereau, Tony Battiste, Erika Breckel, Meg Daniel, Dwayne Cassidy, Jessica Stephens and Stephanie. Finally, big thanks to my awesome coauthors Becca, Lisa, Sam and Jeff. You guys rock!

OUR READERS

Many thanks to the travelers who used the last edition and wrote to us with helpful hints, useful advice and interesting anecdotes:

Erik Aaboe, Lyn Angene, Peter Birkert, Andrew Boni, Patricia Brouwer, Catherine Cross, Anna Dunkerley, Sarah Eastabrook, Jim Feist, Heidi Fuchs, Renee Gibb, Matthew Kennedy, Gareth

SEND US YOUR FEEDBACK

We love to hear from travelers – your comments keep us on our toes and help make our books better. Our well-traveled team reads every word on what you loved or loathed about this book. Although we cannot reply individually to postal submissions, we always guarantee that your feedback goes straight to the appropriate authors, in time for the next edition. Each person who sends us information is thanked in the next edition – and the most useful submissions are rewarded with a free book.

To send us your updates – and find out about Lonely Planet events, newsletters and travel news – visit our award-winning website: **www.lonelyplanet.com/contact**.

Note: we may edit, reproduce and incorporate your comments in Lonely Planet products such as guidebooks, websites and digital products, so let us know if you don't want your comments reproduced or your name acknowledged. For a copy of our privacy policy visit www.lonelyplanet.com/privacy.

Key, Stephan Kindgen, Rick Laborde, Allison Manley, Norman Moore, Miranda Ring, Teri Rowan, Scott Russell, Emilio Salami, Lawrence Siddall, Lynette Stewart, Eric Su, Polly Tucker, E van White, Susan West

ACKNOWLEDGMENTS

Many thanks to the following for the use of their content:

Globe on title page ©Mountain High Maps 1993 Digital Wisdom, Inc.

Internal photographs: p4, p11 (#5) Sara Benson; p4 Becca Blond; p4 Lisa Dunford; p4 Andrea Schulte-Peevers; p10 (#4) ©Douglas Peebles Photography/Alamy; p16 (#1) ©Tony Roberts/ CORBIS. All other photographs by Lonely Planet Images, and by Carol Polich p5, p9 (#7); Witold Skrypczak p6 (#6), p7 (#2); Richard Cummins p6 (#5), p7 (#1), p14 (#4); Ralph Hopkins p8 (#3); Neil Setchfield p8 (#5); Izzet Keribar p9 (#6); Kraig Lieb p10 (#1); Lou Jones p11 (#2); Cheyenne Rouse p12 (#3, #4); Philip & Karen Smith p13 (#1); Andrew Peacock p13 (#5); Woods Wheatcroft p14 (#5); Judy Bellah p15 (#2).

Index

000 Map pages
000 Photograph pages

000 Map pages
000 Photograph pages

GreenDex

GOING GREEN

It seems like everyone's going 'green' in Southwest USA these days, but how can you know which businesses are actually ecofriendly and which are simply jumping on the bandwagon? The following attractions, services, activities and accommodations choices have been selected by our authors because they demonstrate an active sustainable-tourism policy. Some are involved in conservation or environmental education, and many are owned and operated by local and indigenous operators, thereby maintaining and preserving local identity and culture. We want to keep developing our sustainable-tourism content. If you think we've omitted someone who should be listed here, or if you disagree with our choices, email us at talk2us@lonelyplanet.com.au and set us straight for next time. For more information about sustainable tourism and Lonely Planet, see www.lonelyplanet .com/responsibletravel.

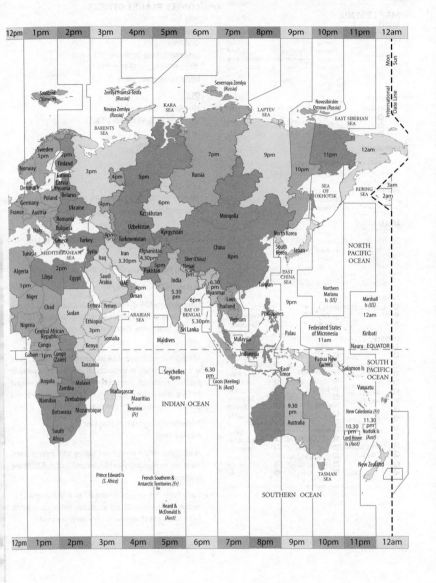

MAP LEGEND

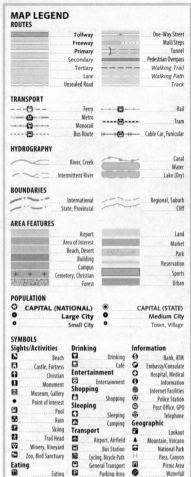

ROUTES

Tollway	One-Way Street
Freeway	Mall/Steps
Primary	Tunnel
Secondary	Pedestrian Overpass
Tertiary	Walking Trail
Lane	Walking Path
Unsealed Road	Track

TRANSPORT

Ferry	Rail
Metro	Tram
Monorail	
Bus Route	Cable Car, Funicular

HYDROGRAPHY

River, Creek	Canal
Intermittent River	Water
	Lake (Dry)

BOUNDARIES

International	Regional, Suburb
State, Provincial	Cliff

AREA FEATURES

Airport	Land
Area of Interest	Market
Beach, Desert	Park
Building	Reservation
Campus	Sports
Cemetery, Christian	Urban
Forest	

POPULATION

◎ CAPITAL (NATIONAL)	◉ CAPITAL (STATE)
● Large City	● Medium City
● Small City	● Town, Village

SYMBOLS

Sights/Activities
- Beach
- Castle, Fortress
- Christian
- Monument
- Museum, Gallery
- Point of Interest
- Pool
- Ruin
- Skiing
- Trail Head
- Winery, Vineyard
- Zoo, Bird Sanctuary

Eating
- Eating

Drinking
- Drinking
- Café

Entertainment
- Entertainment

Shopping
- Shopping

Sleeping
- Sleeping
- Camping

Transport
- Airport, Airfield
- Bus Station
- Cycling, Bicycle Path
- General Transport
- Parking Area

Information
- Bank, ATM
- Embassy/Consulate
- Hospital, Medical
- Information
- Internet Facilities
- Police Station
- Post Office, GPO
- Telephone

Geographic
- Lookout
- Mountain, Volcano
- National Park
- Pass, Canyon
- Picnic Area
- Waterfall

LONELY PLANET OFFICES

Australia
Head Office
Locked Bag 1, Footscray, Victoria 3011
☎ 03 8379 8000, fax 03 8379 8111
talk2us@lonelyplanet.com.au

USA
150 Linden St, Oakland, CA 94607
☎ 510 250 6400, toll free 800 275 8555
fax 510 893 8572
info@lonelyplanet.com

UK
2nd fl, 186 City Rd,
London EC1V 2NT
☎ 020 7106 2100, fax 020 7106 2101
go@lonelyplanet.co.uk

Published by Lonely Planet Publications Pty Ltd
ABN 36 005 607 983

© Lonely Planet Publications Pty Ltd 2008

© photographers as indicated 2008

Cover photograph: Red Rock Crossing, Arizona, Ann Cecil/Lonely Planet Images. Many of the images in this guide are available for licensing from Lonely Planet Images: www.lonelyplanetimages.com.

Printed through Colorcraft Ltd, Hong Kong.
Printed in China.